SIXTIES SURREAL

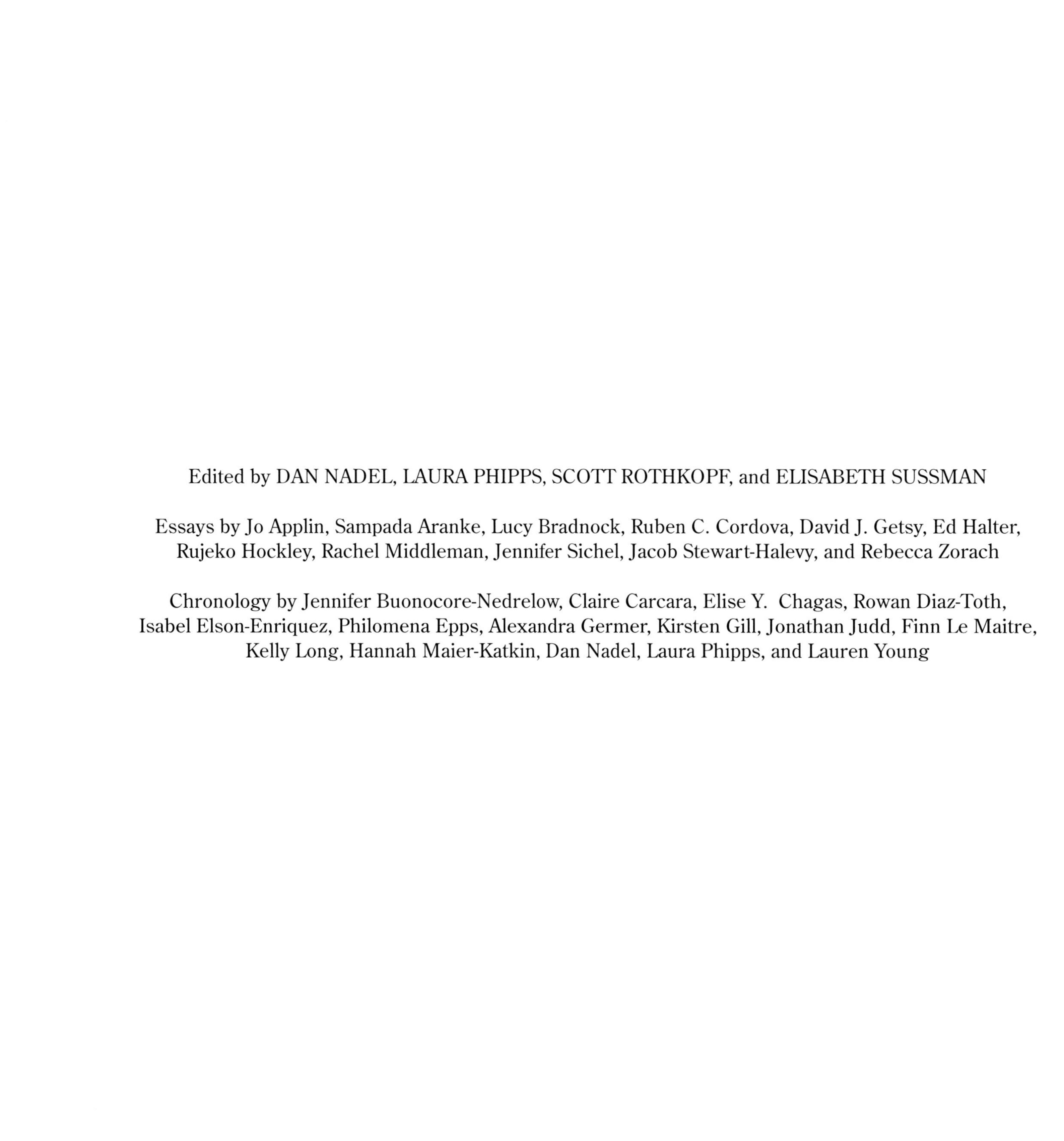

Edited by DAN NADEL, LAURA PHIPPS, SCOTT ROTHKOPF, and ELISABETH SUSSMAN

Essays by Jo Applin, Sampada Aranke, Lucy Bradnock, Ruben C. Cordova, David J. Getsy, Ed Halter, Rujeko Hockley, Rachel Middleman, Jennifer Sichel, Jacob Stewart-Halevy, and Rebecca Zorach

Chronology by Jennifer Buonocore-Nedrelow, Claire Carcara, Elise Y. Chagas, Rowan Diaz-Toth, Isabel Elson-Enriquez, Philomena Epps, Alexandra Germer, Kirsten Gill, Jonathan Judd, Finn Le Maitre, Kelly Long, Hannah Maier-Katkin, Dan Nadel, Laura Phipps, and Lauren Young

Distributed by Yale University Press, New Haven and London

SIXTIES SURREAL

Whitney Museum of American Art, New York

CONTENTS

FOREWORD

Exhibitions often need five or even ten years to develop from the germ of an idea to an opening, but this one took closer to thirty. *Sixties Surreal* began, improbably, during the summer of 1998 when I was an intern at the Whitney Museum of American Art working with Elisabeth Sussman, now one of the project's co-curators. At the time, she was an eminent figure researching what would become a landmark retrospective devoted to Eva Hesse, and I was an eager college senior studying art history at Harvard. Together we spent that summer in the Whitney's old Marcel Breuer building scouring Lucy Lippard's 1976 critical biography of Hesse for clues about her social and artistic milieu in the mid-1960s. Digging further in the months that followed, I became increasingly fascinated by Hesse's association with then little-known characters, such as the artists Paul Thek and Joseph Raffaele and the critic Gene Swenson, on whom I developed something of an intellectual crush. These connections, along with Lippard herself, seemed to offer a mysterious portal onto a facet of Hesse's oeuvre quite different from her iconic Post-Minimal sculpture of the later 1960s—and even an alternative view of that whole turbulent decade.

My initial curiosity ultimately grew into a 1999 undergraduate thesis, "The Other Sixties: The Return of Surrealism in American Art and Criticism," advised by Yve-Alain Bois. In it I argued that a group of young artists and critics in the United States, mostly born after 1930, turned to Surrealism as a touchstone and license for exploring psychosexual concerns that were anathema to the formalist critical orthodoxy of the day. If European Surrealism had been a generative wellspring for American artists including Mark Rothko and Jackson Pollock, its "literary" bent had subsequently been suppressed in favor of a homegrown brand of abstraction. Yet for a younger generation in the mid-1960s Surrealism offered a radical escape hatch through which to journey deeper into aspects of human experience and imagination, particularly for queer and women artists. This was a risky proposition for those making their way in the mostly male, mostly straight New York art world, and the figures I chronicled knew better than to advance an uncritical return of the repressed. Instead, they carefully "negotiated," in my formulation, a new approach to Surrealism through the lens of Pop and Minimalism. On the former side, Swenson promoted a group of figurative artists who transformed everyday objects in the vein of Salvador Dalí and René Magritte. On the latter, Lippard advocated a biomorphic abstraction closer in spirit to André Masson and Max Ernst. Both, however, agreed on the importance of a sexual charge in art but also on tempering the overt narcissism and frequent histrionics of European Surrealism to suit the art world's prevailing cool intellectualism.

The final section of my study mapped how these contemporary activities unfolded within the context of a surging scholarly and curatorial reappraisal of historic Surrealism. In New York, Dalí himself prowled the St. Regis Hotel, and whether thanks to serious tomes or the high camp confections of Huntington Hartford's Gallery of Modern Art, Surrealism was more accessible to younger artists than it had been in a generation. All this transpired against the apt backdrop of a roiling social and political landscape that made the world itself seem surreal as never before. Sexual liberations, drug culture, and psychedelia; struggles for racial equality; political assassinations; and the war in Vietnam were only the most conspicuous signposts on which to hang art that variously reflected, challenged, or sought refuge from its time.

Writing this thesis was both an intellectual and emotional adventure for a still-closeted gay man from Texas. Many of the period's actors were alive, and I was lucky and plucky enough to gain access to them. Quite a few felt that their contributions to the era had never been properly acknowledged, whether due to aesthetic bias, market neglect, sexism, homophobia, or some combination thereof. I reached Lippard in New Mexico by phone from my dorm room, and tracked down one of the veterans of her landmark show *Eccentric Abstraction* (1966) only to learn his sculptures were rotting in a barn in New Jersey. I met the impish former critic Robert Pincus-Witten in an uptown gallery ostensibly to interview him about Thek and Swenson whom he knew in their early days. Seated across from him in a formal parlor, I must have come off as nerdy, embarrassed, and possibly corruptible. At one point in the conversation, he reached over the table and stopped my cassette recorder only to insist that the queer-surreal content I hesitantly circled was directly related to an artist's taste in S&M gatherings so hardcore they required an on-call physician. AIDS-related complications claimed some of these people, mental illness others, and obscurity still more. Not long after graduation, I signed a contract with Yale University Press to publish my thesis as a book, but I abandoned the project with some regret after spinning off a few related essays and setting my sights more squarely on finding myself and the artists of my age.

With hindsight, I can see this missed opportunity as both a failure of nerve and a stroke of good fortune. For although my youthful research shed light on many underestimated figures, it overlooked far more. My initial framework focused almost exclusively on white artists and critics living in New York. Yet the story of Surrealism's American aftershocks is richer, weirder, and wider than I could have originally known. Over the intervening quarter century, scholars and curators across the country have done pioneering work on widespread locales and a range of racially diverse artists and thinkers. It is now abundantly clear that although historical Surrealism reified sexist and often racist world views, it also suggested radical modes of formal, social, and political resistance that took on even greater transgressive power in the hands of those it once excluded and objectified. Today we must recognize the Hairy Who and AFRICOBRA artists in Chicago or those of the Bay Area and Texas who cared little for East Coast aesthetic dogma. There have been pioneering shows like Kellie Jones's *Now Dig This!: Art and Black Los Angeles, 1960–1980* (2011), which recontextualized the otherworldliness of David Hammons and Suzanne Jackson, or Connie Butler's *WACK!: Art and the Feminist Revolution* (2007), which spotlit women artists who used distorted and dreamy figuration to trouble patriarchal and heteronormative mores.

Now that scholars have done the indispensable work of chronicling these specific communities and critical frameworks, one aim of this exhibition is to knit them loosely together to form a broader if still heterogenous whole. While I once viewed my chosen subjects as actors in an eccentric sideshow to a grand march of movements, including Minimal and Conceptual Art, today we might see those lauded "-isms" as manifestations of an almost perversely delimited discursive practice. *Sixties Surreal*, by contrast, posits the *surreal* as the most fulsome animating impulse of American art in the 1960s and the most perspicacious mirror of its era. While the project includes more than a hundred artists, it could easily have featured two or three times more.

Few museums could be better poised than the Whitney to advance this revisionist argument. For one, the Whitney's founding mandate as a museum of art of the United States lends special resonance to our project's national focus. This scholarly purview was not based on jingoistic pride but on the notion that Surrealism's afterlives in Europe and elsewhere, including Latin America, had developed with greater continuity and fewer challenges when compared to the ruptures, negative critical biases, and local efflorescences that characterized its return and proliferation in the 1960s across the United States. Furthermore, the Whitney has throughout its history showcased artists who in one way or another train their sights on the nation's rawest nerves and social preoccupations. Most specifically, the Museum has for more than sixty years played a pivotal role in advancing the work of many artists in this show through its exhibition program and collection. Indeed, the Whitney—with its sometimes quirky and always catholic taste—has had a special place in its heart and holdings for the likes of Edward Kienholz and Yayoi Kusama, H. C. Westermann and Jay DeFeo. The Whitney should always be a home to extraordinary, venturesome artists and to exhibitions that honor their work with scholarly rigor and poetic sensitivity.

Although this project germinated from the initial kernel of a college thesis, what has grown, blossomed, and ultimately overshadowed that study owes to the generous collaboration and brilliant scholarly insights of co-curators Dan Nadel, Laura Phipps, and Elisabeth Sussman. I returned to the Whitney in 2009 with an idea in mind to finally make "this" show, but whatever that exhibition might have been is certainly not what it became. Dan, Laura, and Elisabeth did the lion's share of the hard thinking and harder work to broaden then synthesize such a wide range of voices past and present, while never losing hold of each individual's specific circumstances or point of view. I am enormously grateful to them as their increasingly intermittent curatorial partner and even more so as the Whitney's director. I am also indebted to the many catalogue authors and collaborators over the years whom my co-curators acknowledge in the pages that follow. A show of this scope and ambition, as they note, could truly only have been possible with tremendous tenacity and teamwork, including that of the Whitney's entire staff, for which I add my deepest thanks.

I am extremely grateful to the following foundations, funds, and individuals for recognizing the importance of this reappraisal of American art: the Barbara Haskell American Fellows Legacy Fund; Kevin, Rosemary, and Hannah Rose McNeely of the KHR McNeely Family Foundation; the Whitney's National Committee; the Keith Haring Foundation Exhibition Fund; the Robert Lehman Foundation; and George Freeman. In addition, I extend my gratitude to the Wyeth Foundation for American Art for its generous support of this ambitious catalogue.

Finally, I would like to recognize all the artists whose work we present. Many of them toiled tirelessly and courageously—with limited critical attention or financial reward—to challenge prevailing notions of what an artwork, a life, and a world can be. This exhibition is a testament to their inquisitive, incisive, and transgressive spirit, which remains both enduring and all too urgent.

— Scott Rothkopf
Alice Pratt Brown Director

ACKNOWLEDGMENTS

A project of the scope of *Sixties Surreal* is only possible through years of work with a staggeringly diverse cast possessed of myriad talents. It has been our good fortune to collaborate with and learn from so many wonderful artists, writers, and colleagues across the artworld to bring to fruition this exhibition and catalogue.

The latter here is an attempt to surface and cohere the years of research that formed the ground of the exhibition and to tell a new story of the Long Sixties. We hope this book will function as both a good read and an inspiration for future scholars. We, in turn, are deeply grateful for the inspiration we received from many current scholars, in particular those who transformed their ideas into the insightful thematic essays published here: Jo Applin, Sampada Aranke, Lucy Bradnock, Ruben C. Cordova, David J. Getsy, Ed Halter, Rujeko Hockley, Rachel Middleman, Jennifer Sichel, Jacob Stewart-Halevy, and Rebecca Zorach. We thank them for their willingness to dive into a big river. We likewise extend our gratitude to the group of scholars who contributed writing to the expansive chronology: Jennifer Buonocore-Nedrelow, Claire Carcara, Elise Y. Chagas, Isabel Elson-Enriquez, Philomena Epps, Alexandra Germer, Kirsten Gill, Jonathan Judd, Finn Le Maitre, and Hannah Maier-Katkin.

This catalogue would not have been possible without the support and expertise of Beth Huseman, director of publications at the Whitney Museum of American Art. Project manager Elizabeth Levy impressively steered our team, approaching every conversation with an open mind and every word with great care. Audrey Warne, editorial coordinator, deftly initiated the process of researching and acquiring the book's images. Editor Jason Best brought great attention, care, and style to all of the texts in the book. Designer Joseph Logan lent his passion and impeccable eye in order to produce this beautiful and incisive volume. Nerissa Dominguez Vales and Sue Medlicott at the Production Department refined the images and expertly coordinated the book's printing.

At the outset of this process we convened conversations with scholars and curators, the outcomes of which greatly informed the project. We thank: Michael Auping, LeRonn Brooks, Huey Copeland, Alexander Dumbadze, David J. Getsy, Joshua Guild, Ed Halter, Chrissie Iles, Robin D. G. Kelley, Michelle Kuo, Ann Reynolds, Paul Chaat Smith, Jacob Stewart-Halevy, Sandra Zalman, and Rebecca Zorach.

At the Whitney, we were lucky to work with Kelly Long, senior curatorial assistant, who contributed more than we can ever thank her for, adding ideas and artists with care, keeping us on track, and offering invaluable encouragement and support. Lauren Young, senior curatorial assistant, broadened the scope, lent her expert eye, and helped corral everyone. Rowan Diaz-Toth, curatorial project assistant, shepherded our unusual catalogue project from idea to reality, acting tirelessly as supporter, sleuth, and comrade. For their hard work over the years, we are also grateful to: Jessica Man, curatorial assistant; Amelia Russo, curatorial project assistant; Maya Harakawa, Mellon curatorial fellow; Elizabeth Keto, curatorial intern and research assistant; Jamin An, research assistant; and Micah Musheno, curatorial project assistant. We thank the following curatorial interns on this project: Kat Chavez, Canada Choate, Wendy Cohen, Alexandra Dean, Ebru Eltemur, Bryn Evans, Brianna Golub, Sally Eaves Hughes, Charlotte Kinberger, June Kitahara, Esther Knuth, Corey Loftus, Brian Orozco, Selena Parnon, Francisco Rocha Salazar, Caroline Hunter Wallis, and Lisa Zhang.

For his recognition of the importance of this exhibition and for his unwavering support, we are profoundly grateful to Adam D. Weinberg, former Alice Pratt Brown Director of the Whitney Museum. Kim Conaty, Nancy and Steve Crown Family Chief Curator, and Adrienne Edwards, Engell Speyer Family Senior Curator and Associate Director of Curatorial Programs, not only encouraged our work but also created space for the deeper process of learning. Our gratitude extends to those in their offices who keep it all afloat seemingly with ease: Alex Tonetta, chief of staff; Gemma Curnin, interim executive coordinator to the director; Laura Busby, former director's office coordinator; Samantha Franklin, former executive coordinator to the director; Joanna Epstein, curatorial department manager; and Ophelia Deng, executive assistant to the chief curator.

For their work in realizing the exhibition itself, we are grateful to a core group of Whitney colleagues: Melanie Taylor, director of exhibition design, and Aseeli Coleman, associate exhibition designer, expertly interpreted the conceptual underpinnings of the show as they planned its graceful layout. Senior exhibitions coordinator Noam Parness provided key oversight of the show and its budget, kindly keeping us all on track and building on the work of former senior exhibitions manager and registrar Seth Fogelman. Brenna Cothran, registrar, exhibitions; Elisa Flynn, registrar, exhibitions; and Reagan Duplisea Kelley, former associate registrar, exhibitions, managed the transportation of the artworks with steadfast sensitivity and coordinated with the Museum's exceptional conservators—Clara Rojas-Sebesta, Ellsworth Kelly Conservator of Works on Paper; Matthew Skopek, Cy Twombly Conservator of Paintings; and Margo Delidow, assistant conservator—to thoughtfully care for the works in a wide range of mediums. Caitlin Bermingham, head preparator for exhibitions, brought her signature attention and leadership to the installation. Our thanks extend to those in the Museum's library for their early and dedicated research assistance: Ivy Blackman, managing librarian, and Tara Hart, managing archivist.

We thank other members of the Whitney's curatorial department past and present, in particular Chrissie Iles, Anne and Joel Ehrenkranz Curator; Jane Panetta, former Nancy and Fred Poses Curator and Director of the Collection; Marcela Guerrero, DeMartini Family Curator; Jennie Goldstein, Jennifer Rubio Associate Curator; and Elisabeth Sherman, former assistant curator. We are grateful as well to Cris Scorza, Helena Rubinstein Chair of Education, who leads an incredible team that includes Anne Byrd, director of interpretation and educational content; Emma Quaytman, associate manager of interpretation and educational content; Dyeemah Simmons, director of learning and social impact; Bojana Coklyat, associate manager of access programs and initiatives; and Viridiana García Choy, associate manager. Education department colleagues Megan Heuer, director of academic engagement and public programs, and Andrew Hawkes, coordinator of public programs and public engagement, were key interlocutors and partners in planning public discourse surrounding the exhibition, and we are so appreciative of their efforts.

Sixties Surreal benefited from the expertise of many others at the Museum, to whom we want to extend our gratitude: I. D. Aruede, deputy director; Amy Roth, chief operating officer; Jacqueline Woo, chief financial officer; Nicholas S. Holmes, general counsel; Andrew Cone, chief strategy officer; Maura Heffner, chief exhibitions and collection officer; Joshua Rosenblatt, director of exhibition and collection preparation; and Matthew Larson, paper preparator. Neither the exhibition nor the catalogue would have been possible without crucial fundraising leadership by Karaugh Brown, chief advancement officer; Marilou Aquino, chief philanthropy officer; Morgan Arenson, director of foundation, government, and planned giving; Giulia Nicita, manager of foundation and government relations; Eunice Lee, director of strategic partnerships and events; and Sunny Wang, major gifts officer. Marketing and communications efforts were led by Brianna O'Brien Lowndes, chief marketing officer, and Angela Montefinise, chief communications and content officer, and admirably executed with their colleagues: Ashley Reese, director of communications; Nora Gomez-Strauss, assistant director of digital content; Emily Stoller-Patterson, digital content manager; Meghan Ferrucci, publicist; and Casey Betts, senior social media manager. We thank Micah Musheno, licensing manager, and Dzifah Danso, temporary licensing assistant, for their assistance with imagery of works in the Museum's collection and for coordinating installation photography of the exhibition. Thanks to Hilary Greenbaum, director of graphic design and brand creative, and Erika Wentworth, project manager, for the visually compelling graphic treatment of texts in the galleries and promotional materials. We gratefully acknowledge all of the incredible staff in the Museum's department of visitor and member experience, including Wendy Barbee-Lowell, assistant director; Kimie Page, senior manager, sales and service; and managers Melinda Freudenberger, Luccas Israel, and Natasha Pereira. Our appreciation goes as well to Peter Scott, chief facilities officer, who led the facilities and securities teams; to Larry DeBlasio, director of security; and to all of the guards providing critical support to keep our visitors safe and the art secure.

Above all, we owe countless debts of gratitude to the artists whose works make up this show and catalogue, and we extend further thanks to those who were able to share their time so generously with us and to provide invaluable insight and guidance, among them: Ed Bereal, Jean Conner, Robert Crumb, Dale Brockman Davis, Martha Edelheit, Melvin Edwards, Nancy Grossman, Mike Henderson, Lynn Hershman Leeson, Suzanne Jackson, Linda Lomahaftewa and Tatiana Lomahaftewa-Singer, Senga Nengudi, Joseph Raffaele, Lucas Samaras, Peter Saul, Joan Semmel, Michael Todd, Timothy Washington, William T. Wiley, Franklin Williams, and Karl Wirsum. Many artist estates and galleries have provided immeasurable research support, and we are grateful for their time and for their commitment to the artists and their work, including the Diane Arbus estate, Estate of Jordan Belson, Estate of Wallace Berman, the Mel Casas Family Trust, the Ching Ho Cheng Estate, the Conner Family Trust, the Jay DeFeo Foundation, the Nancy Graves Foundation, Estate of Barbara Hammer, Wanda Hansen, Nancy Hoffman Gallery, the Kiki Kogelnik Foundation, John Maloof, Betty Moody, the Noah Purifoy Foundation, Robin Ragan, Roberts Projects, Michael Rosenfeld Gallery, Erin Stennis and Jaime Washington, Estate of Jack Whitten, and the William T. Wiley Family Trust.

We wish to thank the institutional and private lenders acknowledged on page 367 who graciously allowed their works to be included in the exhibition. And a special acknowledgment goes to those collections that opened their doors for our additional research, in particular: Tina and Larry Jones; KAWS; the Menil Collection; the Mills College Art Museum; the National Museum of the American Indian; the Roger Brown Study Collection, School of the Art Institute of Chicago; and the San Francisco Museum of Modern Art.

Dan Nadel wishes to thank: Elisa and Henry, Beverly and Mark Nadel, Andrew Lampert, Zachary Leener, Gary Panter, Sam Parker, Marian Parmenter, Jenelle Porter, and Jordan Stein.

Laura Phipps wishes to thank: Alex, June, and Cyrus Abdo, Sascha Crasnow, Christina de Gersdorff, and Jeffrey Fraiman.

Elisabeth Sussman wishes to thank: Herb, Charlotte, and Lucas Sussman, Michele Gerber Klein, the late Ted Bonin, Jeffrey Fraenkel, and Glenn Phillips.

— Dan Nadel, Laura Phipps, and Elisabeth Sussman

JEREMY ANDERSON

BENNY ANDREWS

KENNETH ANGER

DIANE ARBUS

ROBERT ARNESON

RALPH ARNOLD

ROMARE BEARDEN

JORDAN BELSON

ED BEREAL

WALLACE BERMAN

JUDITH BERNSTEIN

LEE BONTECOU

LOUISE BOURGEOIS

JOAN BROWN

KAY BROWN

ROGER BROWN

T. C. CANNON

EDUARDO CARRILLO

MEL CASAS

VIJA CELMINS

BARBARA CHASE-RIBOUD

CHING HO CHENG

JUDY CHICAGO

ROBERT COLESCOTT

BRUCE CONNER

JEAN CONNER

ADGER COWANS

ROBERT CRUMB

DALE BROCKMAN DAVIS

JAY DeFEO

ROY DE FOREST

NIKI de SAINT PHALLE

JEFF DONALDSON

MARTHA EDELHEIT

MELVIN EDWARDS

ED EMSHWILLER

ROY FRIDGE

LEE FRIEDLANDER

RUPERT GARCIA

NANCY GRAVES

NANCY GROSSMAN

BARBARA HAMMER

DAVID HAMMONS

ALEX HAY

WALLY HEDRICK

MIKE HENDERSON

LYNN HERSHMAN LEESON

EVA HESSE

OSCAR HOWE

LUCHITA HURTADO

MIYOKO ITO

SUZANNE JACKSON

KEN JACOBS

JAE JARRELL

JESS

LUIS JIMENEZ

DANIEL LaRUE JOHNSON

BARBARA JONES-HOGU

EDWARD KIENHOLZ

KIKI KOGELNIK

SHIGEKO KUBOTA

YAYOI KUSAMA

LINDA LOMAHAFTEWA

LEE LOZANO

MARISOL

DAVID McMANAWAY

ANA MENDIETA

RON MIYASHIRO

BRUCE NAUMAN

GUNVOR NELSON

SENGA NENGUDI

JIM NUTT

CLAES OLDENBURG

JOHN OUTTERBRIDGE

EDWARD OWENS

DON POTTS

KENNETH PRICE

NOAH PURIFOY

JOSEPH RAFFAELE

CHRISTINA RAMBERG

DEBORAH REMINGTON

FAITH RINGGOLD

SUELLEN ROCCA

JAMES ROSENQUIST

MARTHA ROSLER

BARBARA ROSSI

ED RUSCHA

BETYE SAAR

LUCAS SAMARAS

PETER SAUL

RAYMOND SAUNDERS

CAROLEE SCHNEEMANN

FRITZ SCHOLDER

KAY SEKIMACHI

JOAN SEMMEL

JACK SMITH

MING SMITH

ROBERT SMITHSON

NANCY SPERO

ANITA STECKEL

HAROLD STEVENSON

STURTEVANT

DOROTHEA TANNING

PAUL THEK

MICHAEL TODD

CARLOS VILLA

SHAWN WALKER

TIMOTHY WASHINGTON

H. C. WESTERMANN

JACK WHITTEN

DOROTHY WILEY

WILLIAM T. WILEY

HANNAH WILKE

FRANKLIN WILLIAMS

KARL WIRSUM

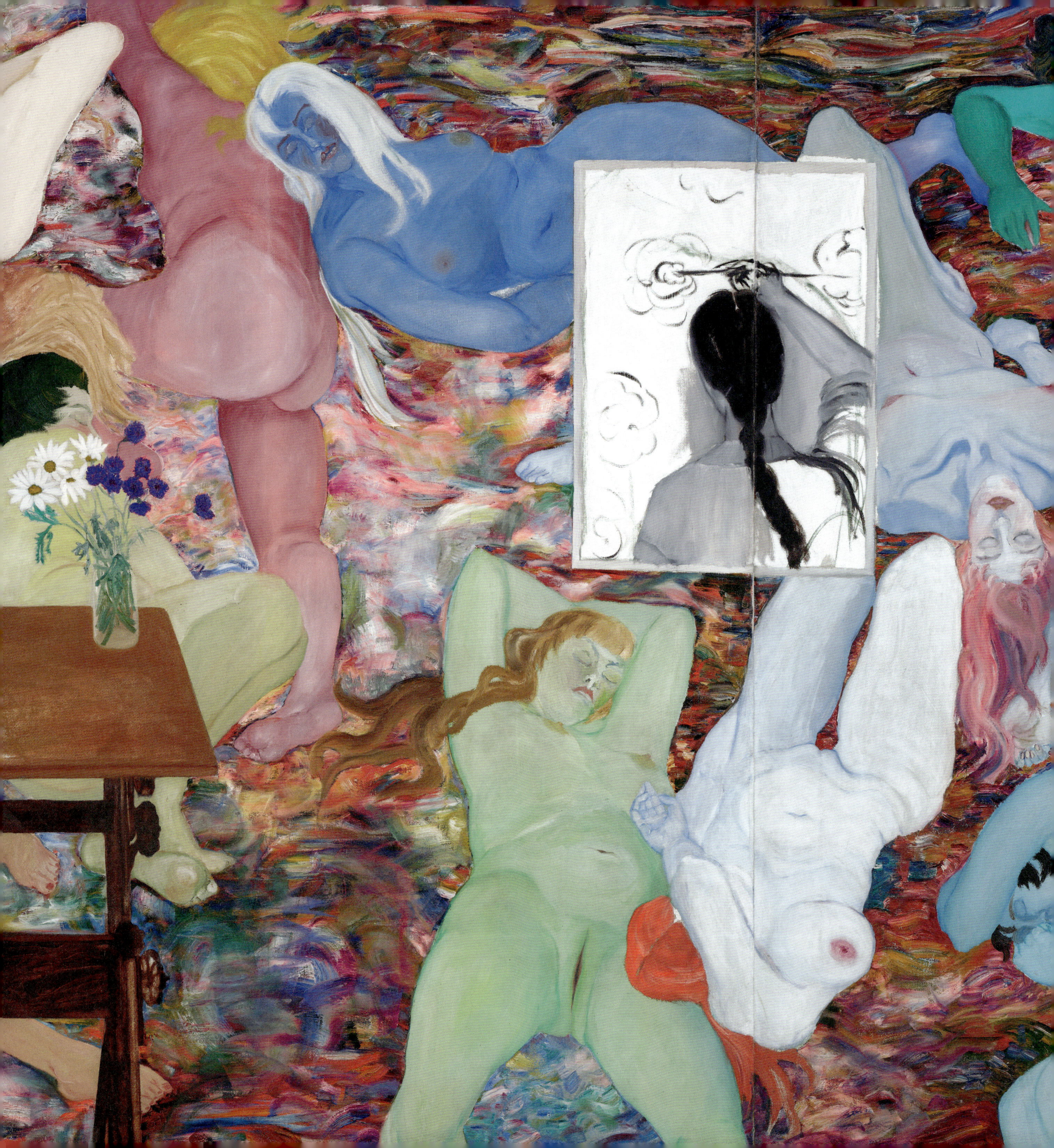

FEELINGS ARE THINGS: A SIXTIES SURREAL

Dan Nadel, Laura Phipps, and Elisabeth Sussman

This project began with a counterfactual: What if Surrealism, not Cubism, had emerged as the dominant force to shape the course of postwar art in America? Proposed in 1966 by critic and curator Gene Swenson, in his formulation this meant: What if it were subject matter, not form, that had been primary to artists in those crucial Atomic years in the United States?[1] For Swenson, who was just in his early thirties at the time, the critical veneration of European abstraction and fetishization of form had all but eclipsed the work of artists who were taking up other ideas—psychological, emotional, queer—that could be traced to an entirely distinct artistic precedent. In charting an alternative nonformal lineage for this kind of contemporary art of the 1960s, Swenson was intentionally opening the way for a plurality of voices, among them his friends Paul Thek and Joseph Raffaele, whose largely figurative mode merged the psychosexual concerns of Surrealism with the cool, impersonal imagery and facture of Pop art. His exhibition *The* Other *Tradition* (1966), at Philadelphia's Institute of Contemporary Art, which brought together historic Surrealist and then-contemporary artists, demonstrated this idea.

Swenson was onto something. His tragic death three years later cut short his championing of other 1960s artists whom he might have brought into his surrealist fold, a project that is enthusiastically taken up here. With Swenson's provocation as a guide, *Sixties Surreal* offers a reappraisal of American art during one of the country's most socially and politically turbulent eras. Whether well known today or less so, the artists in this exhibition have often been considered marginal, eccentric, or provincial actors in relation to the period's heroic "-isms," such as Pop and Minimalism, which functioned at an emotional remove from the audience. Yet this panoply of artists from diverse backgrounds and geographies were protagonists in what may be the era's most fundamental, if underrecognized, aesthetic current—an efflorescence of psychosexual, fantastical, spiritual, and revolutionary tendencies. The revisionist—and additive—survey here focuses on the heady tensions that took hold of the American psyche in the 1960s: between cohesion and rupture, repression and freedom, sex and death. These artists, largely born after 1930, in the wake of the "Greatest Generation," mirrored these conditions through processes that included found-object assemblage, dismantling and reimagining bodies, and picturing altered consciousnesses through surreal forms.

Drawing on ideas embedded in the period's curatorial and theoretical networks that run counter to what would become the prevailing modernist narrative, *Sixties Surreal* proposes a new art-historical framework that recontextualizes the decade. The era begins in 1958, at the moment when the artistic, social, and political currents that manifested the "Sixties" began to coalesce, and it ends with 1972, when the aesthetic pluralism that had been on view in museums and in print began to give way to the idea of a single formalist mainstream centered in New York (which, not coincidentally, was also the center of the art market), with the unfortunate consequence that most other places were cast as "regional," including major centers of activity like San Francisco and Chicago.

The so-called Long Sixties are also what Native American scholar and philosopher Vine Deloria Jr. has called "the rugged 1960s," a time "when any type of change was considered beneficial, and the institutions of society were considered not only obsolete but malignant."[2] For artists, this anti-institutional, anti-establishment ethos extended far beyond academia and the art market as they confronted the structures of politics, religion, gender, sex, family, education, and housing through their art in ways both subtle and combative. This was the decade of the escalation of the Vietnam War; the burgeoning civil rights movement for Black people as well as Native Americans and Chicanos; the dawn of second-wave feminism and the push for reproductive freedom; the early days of queer liberation; the youthquake, drug experimentation, rock and roll, and so much more. As the 1960s progressed it was infused with darker currents, with hope yielding to righteous anger at the fierce suppression of the civil rights and antiwar movements by reactionary forces. The brutality they unleashed was splashed across the mass media in horrifying images from Vietnam and from protests at home, creating a disorientating and polarizing era of change.

Indeed, mass media became both a record and a tool. As the tidal wave of young Americans who came of age during this time of both incredible social upheaval and economic prosperity set out to determine their own identities and fates—whether through political action, artistic activity, or upending the conventions of everyday life—they had those activities reflected back at them through television, magazines, and newspapers. Artists, in turn, pulled from this profusion of language and imagery and made it their own, whether in underground newspapers and video art or through traditional studio practices, often expanded and redefined. Suddenly the contemporary situation was broadcasting from within galleries and museums, which themselves were changing. Artist-run spaces and commercial galleries launched by people of color, community art projects, and other exhibition venues proliferated throughout the decade, challenging the artworld's historic gatekeepers and providing bases—and an expanded public—for the era's dizzying proliferation of expression.

*

Sixties Surreal is imprinted by the many meanings and geographical touchpoints of Surrealism as it permeated the zeitgeist of the Long Sixties, as well as its origins as a literary movement in interwar Paris. In his foundational 1924 manifesto, André Breton described Surrealism as "psychic automatism in its pure state, by which one proposes to express—verbally, by means of the written word, or in any other manner—the actual functioning of thought. Dictated by the thought, in the absence of any control exercised by reason, exempt from any aesthetic or moral concern . . . Surrealism is based on the belief in the superior reality of certain forms of previously neglected associations, in the omnipotence of dream, in the disinterested play of thought. It tends to ruin once and for all other psychic mechanisms and to substitute itself for them in solving all the principal problems of life."[3] Soon adding a liberatory political dimension, Surrealism became a calling card for those revolting against a supposedly rational world that oppressed the working class and stifled free expression, even as its championing of individual revelation via the subconscious made for an uneasy and fitful synthesis with, alternately, anarchism (a revolt against all bourgeois values) and communism (taking back control for the proletariat).

Surrealism as a movement was broadly disseminated in the United States through exhibitions and publications, including New York's *View,* along with the wartime immigration of many of its key European practitioners to the city and their crucial teachings in automatic drawing. Yet by the early 1950s, formalist critics and curators had largely reduced Surrealism to a wellspring of automatism and abstraction with nods to pictography or Jungian archetypes, casting it primarily as a pathway from figures such as Max Ernst and André Masson to the early Abstract Expressionism of artists such as Jackson Pollock and Mark Rothko. This narrative dismissed the "literary content" of Surrealism's dream-based and erotic imagery, as well as the academic rendering in paintings by artists such as Salvador Dalí or René Magritte, and it entirely ignored the ongoing influence of Surrealism not only in contemporary visual art but in film, fashion, ballet, set decoration, and graphic design, as well as its broader political implications. In this New York–centric formulation, with critic Clement Greenberg as its leading advocate, so-called advanced art needed to concern itself solely with the conditions of its own making. In this conception, art didn't require anything outside of itself—it was to eschew referents, focus on the flatness of the picture plane, and solve internal, formal problems. Figuration, pictorial depth, and narrative were to be consigned to the dustbin of history.

But even as formalist critics discredited Surrealism, by the late 1950s most of its visual and philosophical aspects had become baked into American culture at large through film, advertising, commercial art, and literature, while Abstract Expressionism itself had become doctrinaire and Pop was beginning to percolate. Soon, with the emergence of psychedelia, Surrealism's influence on popular culture would only become more pronounced. Its pervasiveness proved double-edged. The more it proliferated, the more easily dismissible it was by artists and curators who believed in a notion of modernist progress as a march toward newer, ever more pure ideas. But that also meant that Surrealism had escaped being put through the mill of academic theorization in the United States that Cubism had. For a generation of younger artists who either actively rejected or were blithely unconcerned with formal orthodoxies, Surrealism and its broader and more generic dissemination, the "surreal," became exciting and potent touchstones, a permissive and permission-granting set of ideas that could be cherry-picked and opened to an individual artist's interpretation.

Meanwhile, the social and political energy of the country was growing increasingly tumultuous. The jubilation over the end of what had been a horrible, all-encompassing world war had given way to anxieties surrounding the Cold War and nuclear era, coupled with mounting tension between those who sought to address the country's deeply rooted racial and gender inequalities and their reactionary opponents. Such seismic sociopolitical forces had roiled Europe in the wake of World War I, and artists there had turned to Surrealism. Writing twenty years later during the throes of World War II, Suzanne Césaire remarked that Surrealism "remains what it has always been, an activity which assigns itself the goal of systematically exploring and expressing the forbidden zones of the human mind in order to neutralize them."[4] Césaire had studied in Paris in the 1930s and, after developing a close relationship with André Breton, founded the cultural review *Tropiques* in Martinique with her husband, Aime Césaire, and a likeminded circle. She credited Breton's efforts in 1924 with attempting to free the mind of the absurd logic of Western thinking while at the same time advancing her own notion that Surrealism could collapse binary thinking, and thus collapse the space between colonist and colonized, allowing for a transformation into coexistence. The ideas disseminated by the Césaires and their Caribbean cohort fueled anti-colonialist activism and encouraged a reappraisal of the influence of European artistic references that would accelerate in the coming decades. In the late 1960s, the doctrinaire Chicago Surrealist Group, formed by Franklin and Penelope Rosemont with the blessing of Breton, continued the Surrealist tradition of dissident politics by throwing weight behind the labor movement and Students for a Democratic Society and disseminating Black Panther newspapers. Indeed, the political dimensions of the organizing done by cultural workers during this period exemplified the diaspora of Surrealist thinking and the ways in which Breton's ideas were finding expression beyond the making of art, from the South Side Community Art Center, Art & Soul, and DuSable Museum in Chicago to the Watts Towers Arts Center, Gallery 32, and Brockman Gallery in Los Angeles.

The social and political convulsions of the 1960s were for many "surreal," something reflected in mass culture. The jarring juxtapositions and woozy aesthetics of European Surrealism were deployed and manipulated by the new youth culture in music, light shows, comics, psychedelic posters, and underground newspapers. The source material appeared on posters in dorm rooms and apartments across the country featuring the works of Dalí and Magritte, which perhaps inevitably led to the popular interpretation of "surreal" as a synonym for "weird" or "dream-like."

Commenting on the ubiquity of the term "Surrealistic" throughout popular media as well as in art criticism, curator and writer Lucy Lippard in 1966 noted, "To most people it means anything odd, suspicious, impolite, unfamiliar, threatening, obscene, or just plain unconventional."[5] Lippard posited this after identifying the recent conundrum of critics and art historians who, on the one hand, were decrying the classification of art and artists by their peers yet, on the other, seemed unable to leave the practice behind. Lippard had written her dissertation on Max Ernst and edited an anthology of Surrealist writings in translation; she knew that the movement itself was more capacious and generative than suggested by the status to which it had been relegated by contemporary art historians. Still, she remained doubtful whether it functioned as a useful descriptor any longer. "Perhaps the layman's use of the term is correct," she writes, a use that nevertheless obfuscates not only the art-historical significance of the surreal but also the broader political and intellectual aims of those who took up Surrealism's legacy in the 1960s.

It was precisely those terms that Lippard enumerated as synonymous in the popular lexicon with "surreal"—odd, unfamiliar, obscene, etc.—that were often applied to the artists across the United States who were chafing against a proscribed definition of "Art" that privileged formal considerations over content. Surrealism, it seems, was in the air. The same year that Gene Swenson made his case for the *other* tradition, *Artforum* published an entire issue (with a cover by Ed Ruscha) devoted to Surrealism. Within its pages, curator William Rubin worked out the premise for his sprawling exhibition *Dada, Surrealism and Their Heritage*, which opened in March 1968 at New York's Museum of Modern Art and traveled to the Los Angeles County Museum of Art and the Art Institute of Chicago later that year. An enormous undertaking at over three hundred artworks, it brought together historic figures such as Dalí, Magritte, and Breton with those whom Rubin deemed their heirs, including Robert Arneson, Niki de Saint Phalle, Jasper Johns, and H. C. Westermann. Reviewing the exhibition in *ARTnews*, John Ashbery wrote, "We all 'grew up Surrealist' without even being aware of it."[6]

This sense of the surreal operating on an almost osmotic level perhaps explains why it manifested itself in the work of so many artists and the organic nature of their connection-building. They coalesced in loose geographical networks—especially in California, Texas, and Chicago—that functioned as a de facto opposition to the demands of New York–centric formalism, and they were linked through group exhibitions, magazine articles, and their own publications. In Chicago, Surrealism in its most historic and classic sense had a broad influence on the education in the city's arts institutions. Artists such as Ernst and Magritte were visible in local collections, and a pluralist ethos reigned in particular at the School of the Art Institute (SAIC), where instructors such as Whitney Halstead and Kathleen Blackshear encouraged their students to look as closely at insects in the natural history museum as at Piero della Francesca, at pinball machines as much as reliquaries.[7] From SAIC's studios came artists who took up the challenge, including Westermann, Roger Brown, Jeff Donaldson, Jae Jarrell, Jim Nutt, Claes Oldenburg, Christina Ramberg, and Karl Wirsum.

The influence of Douglas MacAgy, who during the 1940s served as curator at the San Francisco Museum of Art, then as an instructor at the California School of Fine Arts, helped pave the way in Northern California for artists' embrace of Surrealism during the 1950s. Now they were joined by a younger generation, including Joan Brown, Jay DeFeo, and William T. Wiley, who were far more interested in free self-expression than in any notion of artistic "progress." Curators such as James Monte and Phil Linhares both evangelized for their home team and looked across the country to bring in artists whose work rhymed with the Bay Area. For its part, Los Angeles could lay claim to bona fide Surrealist transplants in Man Ray, who lived and worked in the city from 1940 to 1951, and Dalí, who collaborated with Alfred Hitchcock and Walt Disney, as well as to deep private collections of Surrealist art, such as that of Louise and Walter Arensberg, that were open to artists and enthusiasts. The relatively new city built both on manufacturing and Hollywood filmmaking fostered a dual sense of wonder and suspicion. Underneath the glossy movie magic, artists such as Ed Bereal, Wallace Berman, Edward Kienholz, and Noah Purifoy detected roiling tensions, both social and psychological. Curator and Ferus Gallery cofounder Walter Hopps encouraged the talent around him and kept an eye out for artists who were particularly disinterested in orthodoxies or lineages, among them Berman and Purifoy. Hopps later took this approach to his work in Washington, DC, and Houston.

In Texas, where the deep Surrealist holdings within the private collection of Dominique and John de Menil, guided, in part, by Jermayne MacAgy, who had spent more than a decade at the California Palace of the Legion of Honor before coming to the Contemporary Arts Museum Houston, became a beacon of Surrealist art both for local artists and for those from around the state, such as Roy Fridge and David McManaway. McManaway, who pulled as much from the detritus of the Dallas streets as he did from the sculptural traditions of Marcel Duchamp, was among the Texas artists who caught the attention of Douglas MacAgy. MacAgy moved to the state to direct the Dallas Museum for Contemporary Arts, where he organized the first U.S. exhibition of Magritte, in 1960. In Austin, curator and writer Dave Hickey's gallery A Clean, Well-Lighted Place and his work at St. Edward's University mixed the Texans with their poetic soulmates in California.

From the contemporary vantage point, it now looks rather like a caravan of art, often related to the material poetics of Westermann and Kienholz, the playful autobiography of Joan Brown, and the mysticism of Wallace Berman, touring from one coast to another. In their embrace of Surrealism in its most expansive mode—i.e., freedom—these curators, writers, and artists opened the way for an even broader plurality of voices: those who were exploring the possibilities of an art history beyond European antecedents, those uninterested in art history, and those invisible to it.

*

How, then, to go about wrangling the freewheeling, multivalent art that made the sixties surreal into a reasonably cohesive survey, without rehashing history or redoubling categorizations? The work started by identifying six historic exhibitions that took place in 1966–67 and were organized by artists and curators for whom the surreal provided an alternative means to understand art making in the contemporary moment: *The* Other *Tradition*, *Hairy Who*, *New Documents*, *Eccentric Abstraction*, *Funk*, and *66 Signs of Neon*. As the 1960s progressed, Minimalism and Pop art became recognized in the modernist canon as the acceptable reactions against Abstract Expression, each in its own way a turn from the painterly, expressionist, or personal yet still possessed of a formalist vocabulary. (Even as Pop could be said to link to Surrealism through its sense of incongruity, it refused psychological or emotional readings, focusing instead on the layers of commercial imagery swamping the imaginations of the postwar public.) Examining the material or formal tendencies of the artists who appeared in these exhibitions and tracing their networks revealed modes of art making that sit outside this modernist canon. Using the key exhibitions as a starting point, the thematic galleries of *Sixties Surreal* pose critical arguments that both complement and expand upon the organizing principles of the historic shows. Objects are organized by their positions within histories and themes that have been expanded and reimagined based, in part, upon the work of building the chronology that follows here, a voluminous account of our Long Sixties punctuated with informative and inventive essays and the artworks from the exhibition. If the exhibition argues for imagining a new visualization of the decade, this book as a whole, we hope, offers innumerable pathways to further expand that imagination—geographically, thematically, and aesthetically.

Of the titular concept of his groundbreaking exhibition, Gene Swenson wrote, "The paintings of the *other* tradition are not . . . mirrors of society. They are mirrors of what happens to us without our knowing it or realizing it. In a way they might be said to objectify experience, to turn feelings into things so that we can deal with them."[8] Suzanne Césaire had already identified Surrealism as a means by which one might access the "forbidden zones of the human mind in order to neutralize them," a sentiment that Swenson seemed to intuit. For him, this centered specifically on no longer repressing one's sexuality but instead living with it as an integrated consciousness. Yet an expanded notion of this process can be seen in a number of artists of the era who, in making artwork from an experience of extreme sociopolitical change, were attempting to create a new reality for themselves as visual thinkers, and in some cases to build opposition and advocate for radical change. Artists who took a hard look at the world around them (specifically the material media landscape) and whose work indicated a similar desire for new or altered realities include Alex Hay (*Paper Bag*; p. 231), Vija Celmins (*Untitled [Comb]*; p. 287), and Harold Stevenson (*The New Adam*; pp. 76–77). These objects seem to have grown and morphed while we briefly looked away, while others have become embodied and sexualized, such as Lee Lozano's *No Title* (p. 68). The strategy of shifting the scale of recognizable objects (or bodies) has a Pop-like quality to it, though the perversity and even humor of destabilizing these non-commercial *things* reeks of a Surrealist relationship to reality.[9] Other works reflect how the process of visioning oneself in the commercial era can turn back on itself, presenting humans as amalgamations of commodified fetishes, as in the works of Jean Conner, Kiki Kogelnik, Joseph Raffaele, and Martha Rosler. Paul Thek's sculpture illustrates the extreme of how feelings might be objectified: impossibly smooth exteriors forever cloaking squishy flesh within.

Halfway across the country and almost simultaneous to Swenson's exhibition, other examples of such tendencies could be found in the psychosexual figural painting by the likes of Karl Wirsum and Jim Nutt, whose six-artist exhibition group, the Hairy Who, held its first show in 1966. For the next three years, in their hometown of Chicago as well as in shows in Washington, DC, San Francisco, and New York, the Hairy Who opened up a path for an explicit attention to charged psychological or physical states and reinvigorated painting with humor, sex, narrative, and material experimentation.

If Swenson's interest was in art that externalized what lurked within, John Szarkowski's 1967 Museum of Modern Art exhibition, *New Documents*, flipped the script, showing the work of three photographers who looked outside the self and into an everyday America that was off-kilter, "weird," and yes, "surreal" around every corner. In correspondence with Szarkowski, artist Stan VanDerBeek called what unified these photographers' output "social surrealism," and indeed, the works in the show by Diane Arbus, Lee Friedlander, and Garry Winogrand have the feeling of the strangeness of ordinary interactions suddenly revealed.[10] *Sixties Surreal* expands the conceit of this small photography show to include artists working in other mediums in addition to contemporaneous photographers such as Shawn Walker and Adger Cowans. The two, both involved in the Kamoinge Workshop, captured moments of sudden, unexpected juxtapositions on the streets of New York that point to a heightened reality. This sense of surrealism's immediate proximity to everyday reality was pointed out by other Black artists: to paraphrase Romare Bearden, he didn't need to look for the surreal, it was happening outside his window in Harlem.[11] Similarly, the impulse to capture the surreality of everyday experience was taken up by Robert Crumb, whose drawings imagine the new states of mind within the "man on the street." As in Luis Jimenez's *Blonde TV Image* (p. 215), mediated entertainment added another dimension to the sense of ordinary surrealism, one in which the television is not just an object but a presence in the room, another body and mind to contend with at the foot of your bed.

Also working in New York, Lucy Lippard watched closely *The* Other *Tradition*, but she found the direct line that Swenson drew from Surrealism and Dada to contemporary art suspect. Nevertheless, the allusive ideas within Surrealism no doubt informed her thinking as she sought to theorize the tendencies she was noticing in Minimal sculpture that moved toward an embodied abstraction. In 1966 she gave a series of talks and organized an exhibition called *Eccentric Abstraction*, which gathered works that sought to evoke but not picture the sensual figure. In Lippard's formulation, this was not so much a "tradition" as another "stream" of art, a way of handling materials and processes that might allow for a more bodily feel and reading. What Lippard was seeing primarily in New York (with the notable West Coast exceptions of Don Potts and Bruce Nauman in *Eccentric Abstraction*) was materially related to what was happening in California and would be brought together the following

year in the exhibition *Funk* at the University Art Museum at the University of California, Berkeley, which showcased the handmade, abject approach to sculpture in the Bay Area and Los Angeles and a return to subject matter. As Joan Brown explained: "Uppermost in the minds of people like [Bruce] Conner, myself, and others around us was the idea of shocking ourselves with the objects we made. We made things that were a kind of revelation to each of us because of the baseness, cheapness, and crudity of the materials and techniques each of us employed in making the paintings, drawings, or sculptures. It should be emphasized that being drawn to the ephemeral materials, as we all were, was important also because the final art object defied accepted tastes in an outrageous manner. The best funky things were those containing humorous elements that poked fun at sex, religion, pets, patriotism, art, and politics."[12]

While eccentric abstraction was weighted to the unnamable and inscrutable, the artists gathered in *Funk*, among them Potts, Jeremy Anderson, Ken Price, and Franklin Williams, were far more willing to make one-to-one references to bodies, landscapes, and icons, albeit on their own terms in often rough-hewn forms.[13] Gathering as it did from currents in Northern California, *Funk* was also adjacent and overlapping with the Slant Step project initiated in 1965 by Nauman and William T. Wiley, in which, through object-making and performance, the artists sought to give biographical life to a thrift-store footstool. What began as a Duchampian readymade became a subject about which numerous artists made work, focusing on this once-neglected found object. In many of the works related both to *Funk* and Slant Step, it was the sometimes loud showing, not the telling, that was most important.

The material impetus to make sculpture that veers toward the grotesque while loudly stating what it is and what it's made of can be traced to assemblage art, which had a particularly vital resurgence in California. In 1962–63, the then San Francisco–based *Artforum* published several articles about the distinctive qualities of California assemblage, and later essays cemented the art form as an important outgrowth of the California avant-garde. Assemblage-related work by the likes of Berman, Kienholz, and Bruce Conner served as critiques of consumer culture and commentaries on the neglect of cities and the suburbanization of the country. As this practice of collage-pastiche-assembling became "the first home-grown California modern art," as identified by artist and critic Peter Plagens, its emergence at the time was initially understood as the domain of these white artists picking up the mantle of Dada and Surrealism.[14] MoMA's 1961 exhibition *The Art of Assemblage* traced the lineage of contemporary assemblage tactics straight back to Europe in the early twentieth century, specifically to Cubism. But for Black artists in Los Angeles who were also working in assemblage and collage, these strategies often had antecedents that were entirely unrelated and ran much deeper.[15] Black families migrating from the American South had brought the traditions and strategies of West African and Caribbean communities to many Los Angeles neighborhoods. John Outterbridge, who grew up in North Carolina and whose father had made a living as a "junkster," had a strong connection with the material of making do and of using items for purposes outside their origins: "Assemblage, for me, means more than the manipulation of objects. It has a great deal to do with the piecing together of possibilities."[16] And Noah Purifoy spelled out what this means for art: "Assuming that the assemblage puts together two or more unrelated inanimate objects, transpose the concept thus: two or more seemingly unrelated inanimate objects assembled constitutes the possibility of communication."[17]

Purifoy had served as the founding director of the Watts Towers Arts Center, connected to the spiraling towers encrusted in shell, ceramic, and glass that Italian immigrant Simon Rodia had constructed in the Watts neighborhood of Los Angeles over the course of three decades starting in the 1920s. The landmarks exerted a tremendous influence on the artistic mindset of the city. Not only were the towers themselves emblematic of a method of accumulation and assemblage, but their site became an important marker for race relations in response to the Watts Rebellion in 1965, which dramatically shaped artistic production and circulation in the region. One year after the uprising, Purifoy and fellow artist and community organizer Judson Powell organized *66 Signs of Neon*, a key exhibition in Los Angeles art history. The show comprised works made from melted neon shop signs and other wreckage scavenged in the wake of the violence, illustrating the importance of an assemblage aesthetic as a means to honor and reconstitute an oppressed urban community. The approach to assemblage that was highlighted in *66 Signs* is exemplified by Outterbridge when he says, "What is available to you is not merely material but the material and essence of the political climate, the material in the debris of social issues."[18]

*

Indeed, throughout the 1960s, there seems to have been a pervasive sense that the country was on the brink of blowing apart. The combustible sociopolitical climate generated scenes of protest and violence that were broadcast nightly into living rooms nationwide, interspersed with ads that depicted a surreally idealized America. These disparate messages yielded a complicated amalgamation of artistic responses that itself reflects the capaciousness of surrealism. Black artists in particular turned to surrealism, both as a possible agent of radical change and as a means to approach difficult subjects from a position of revolutionary imagination. The Black Arts Movement, which burgeoned in the mid-1960s, was "the aesthetic and spiritual sister of the Black Power concept," as poet Larry Neal described it, one that proposed "a radical reordering of the western cultural aesthetic."[19] The movement encompassed visual arts, music (particularly new jazz), literature, and poetry, and it attracted artists from across the country who saw this cultural work as an extension of the civil rights movement. For artists like Melvin Edwards, making work that directly addressed racist violence, both past and present, felt imperative. Taking lynching as his subject, he said, "[called] into question the whole society. The whole of art, the whole of everything."[20] Halfway across the country, and in a dramatically different medium, *Unfinished Collage* (p. 245) relays Ralph Arnold's own volumetric reaction to the violence of this period, to the spectacle of its media coverage, and to the specter of further horrors to come. John F. Kennedy, Robert F. Kennedy, and Martin Luther King Jr. each occupy a rectangle that wraps around the sculpture, but a fourth rectangle is left blank, an ominous suggestion of a story still unfolding.

As the second wave of feminism began to crest in the 1960s and challenge conventional ideas surrounding a woman's place and women's work, other artists experimented in a surrealist vein as a means to explore the tension between traditional expectations and liberatory aspirations. Anita Steckel and Suellen Rocca did this by composing self-portraits as collage-like amalgamations of iconography and historical figures that point to identities in flux. Some, like Hannah Wilke, made explicit their bodies in order to show that censoring the image of, say, a vagina, was a form of misogynist suppression. Using genitalia as a subject matter normalizes it, removing the stigma of the forbidden. Other artists, like Niki de Saint Phalle, imagined powerful female bodies moving through and dominating the world. Joan Semmel's *Untitled* (p. 323) is an example of a new and radical attention to the emotional and political implications of representing the nude female body—vulnerable, sexual, imperfect, aging, and autonomous, sometimes all together at once. More than subverting art history, Semmel's paintings destabilize both the eye that looks upon them and their own comprehensibility, suggesting a subject who is active in shaping her own image. "Rather than simply self-representation," Semmel writes, "I am interested in the possibility of a female self-articulation."[21] That this kind of articulation has the capacity to reach beyond ideas of sexual or individual empowerment is illustrated by Jae Jarrell: her leadership role within the Chicago-based Black artists' collective AFRICOBRA and her use of textiles and fashion (with all of their attendant associations of softness, femininity, and frivolity) situate her in feminist conversations but also in broader discussions revolving around collective action and representation. Gesturing to self-fashioning and bodily autonomy, Jarrell's work, such as *Ebony Family* (p. 249), importantly also celebrates the strength of Black family life, a crucial consideration for AFRICOBRA artists in their aim to propel social and political change in their communities through art.

From its emphasis on cultivating artistic personae to the Freudian calculation of making the unconscious conscious, central to historic Surrealist thinking was the concept of individual self-empowerment, which manifested as well through religious iconoclasm and a turn to more personal investigations of spirituality that often involved the occult, magic, and mysticism. The religion most critiqued by Surrealist artists, from Luis Buñuel to Leonora Carrington, was Catholicism, which by the early 1960s was undergoing its own internal convulsions in the form of the Second Vatican Council.[22] The religion's association with the devastating impacts of colonialism, as well as its dogmatic rituals and the conflicted associations of its visual iconography and splendor, meant it lived in the histories and imaginations of a number of artists working in the 1960s. Artists such as Eduardo Carrillo and Barbara Rossi (a former Catholic nun) drew upon their own experiences of the art and rituals of Catholicism and distorted the imagery of their memories to tell new stories through their otherwise unrelated practices. The widespread questioning of mainstream institutions and authority that was a hallmark of the 1960s led other artists, like many of their counterculture peers, to turn to ancestral knowledge, alternative forms of spirituality, or ideas of the occult. For Oscar Howe, the balancing of two belief systems—Christianity and Očhéthi Šakówiŋ—in his paintings could be considered a sacred ritual that carried forward both the spiritual and artistic traditions of his ancestors. Betye Saar and Carlos Villa were interested in uncovering and recovering histories of mysticism and spirituality—from palmistry and astrology to North African and Oceanic religious traditions—and employed found things that they could imbue with their own meaning, thereby creating new objects of, if not worship, then spiritual contemplation.

Making a world anew, even in the palm of your hand, is at the core of both Surrealism and *Sixties Surreal*. Transmuting a feeling into a thing, and then examining and learning from it, allowing it to occupy space with oneself, moving past repression and into recognition: this was Gene Swenson's psychoanalytic–artistic mission. But this doesn't mean that *Sixties Surreal* advocates for one-to-one meanings. In our expanded read of art in the Long Sixties, the permission-giving ethos of Surrealism that permeated artistic cultures from coast to coast allowed for and encouraged subject matter that was in some way "cloaked," as Karl Wirsum once said.[23] *Sixties Surreal* surfaces art that embraced content, that trafficked in ideas surrounding sexuality, religion, gender, class, liberation, and the often disorienting conditions of everyday modern life, and yet refused literal readings; this is art that courted ambiguity.

The ambiguity in which this project is steeped is what makes *Sixties Surreal* so unyieldingly contemporary. As we are all too aware in our current moment, both repression and freedom thrive in ambiguity. But whereas the politician might use ambiguity to obfuscate intent, the artist might seize upon it as a way to encompass contradictory feelings—to make something that is generous enough to speak to people in the language they bring to it. And while we cannot argue collective intent across such a diverse array of talent, it could be true that the artists in this exhibition wanted to knock themselves and their viewers slightly off-kilter so as to make all involved reconsider their own attitudes. This could mean the act of gently squeezing one's own arm to check its elasticity, or it could mean contemplating just what was lost or gained in the Watts Rebellion—art making that is not embarrassed by its own earnestness or emphasis on subject matter. The specific qualities of societal distrust that rendered the 1960s destabilizing pushed

artists to imagine new futures; surrealism gave explosive, kaleidoscopic dimension to those imaginings. From our current vantage point, we envision *Sixties Surreal* as a reassessment of history that allows for continued imagining—of futures and future histories.

NOTES

1   Gene R. Swenson, *The Other Tradition* (Philadelphia: Institute of Contemporary Art, University of Pennsylvania, 1966), 12–16.

2   Vine Deloria Jr., *God Is Red: A Native View of Religion*, 3rd ed. (Wheat Ridge, CO: Fulcrum Publishing, 2003), 45. Deloria's characterization comes as he reflects on the American Indian Movement's 1972 occupation of the Bureau of Indian Affairs headquarters in Washington, DC, and its occupation the following year of Wounded Knee, South Dakota. That he describes these protest events as the "final spasm" or "last hurrah" of the sixties makes his characterization no less true, but it does introduce a poignant sense of finality to this revolutionary era.

3   André Breton, "Manifesto of Surrealism" [1924], reprinted in Breton, *Manifestoes of Surrealism*, trans. Richard Seaver and Helen R. Lane (Ann Arbor: University of Michigan Press, 1972), 26.

4   Suzanne Césaire, "Surrealism and Us" [1943], reprinted in Césaire, *The Great Camouflage: Writings of Dissent (1941–1945)*, ed. Daniel Maximin, trans. Keith L. Walker (Middletown, CT: Wesleyan University Press, 2012), xi.

5   Lucy Lippard, "An Impure Situation (New York and Philadelphia Letter)," *Art International* 10, no. 5 (May 1966): 63.

6   John Ashbery, "Growing Up Surreal," *ARTnews* 67, no. 3 (May 1968): 41.

7   Private collections of particular note in Chicago that were also accessible to students included those of Lindy and Edward Bergman and Ruth and Leonard J. Horwich.

8   Swenson, *The Other Tradition*, 28.

9   Apt here are the words of Surrealist poet Pierre Reverdy: "Characteristic of strong image is that it derives from the spontaneous association of two very distant realities, whose relationship is grasped solely by the mind." As quoted in Breton, "Manifesto of Surrealism," 20.

10   Stan VanDerBeek to John Szarkowski, May 17, 1966. Museum of Modern Art Archives, Museum of Modern Art, New York.

11   As Bearden told *Time* magazine in 1964: "As a Negro, I do not need to go looking for 'happenings,' the absurd, or the surreal, because I have seen things out of my studio window on 125th Street that neither Dalí nor Beckett nor Ionesco could have thought possible." Romare Bearden, quoted in "Art: Uptown," *Time*, Oct. 23, 1964.

12   Joan Brown, quoted in James Monte, "'Making It' with Funk," *Artforum* 5, no. 10 (Summer 1967): 56.

13   None of the participants in the exhibition, however, thought of themselves as part of a specific movement, and many of the artists involved rejected the labels "funk" or "funky" to describe their work. Nevertheless, this exhibition and the verbiage related to it has remained an important touchstone in understanding the art of Northern California in the 1960s.

14   Peter Plagens, *Sunshine Muse: Contemporary Art on the West Coast* (Westport, CT: Praeger, 1974), 74.

15   For an in-depth reconsideration of assemblage in Southern California, see Kellie Jones, "Claim: Assemblage and Self-Possession," chap. 2 in *South of Pico: African American Artists in Los Angeles in the 1960s and 1970s* (Durham, NC: Duke University Press, 2017).

16   John Outterbridge, quoted in Jorge Daniel Veneciano, "A Conversation with John Outterbridge," *Artweek* 24, no. 21 (November 4, 1993): 20.

17   Noah Purifoy, "One to One: Quarterly Report on Aspects of Creativity (January–March 1967)": 1–2. Noah Purifoy Papers 1935–1998, Archives of American Art, Smithsonian Institution, Washington, DC; as quoted in Jones, *South of Pico*, 71. Purifoy's thinking here recalls the importance in historical Surrealism of associations between multiple distinct realities.

18   John Outterbridge, interview by Karen Anne Mason, 1993, African American Artists of Los Angeles Oral History Transcript, UCLA Oral History Program, 362; as quoted in Jones, *South of Pico*, 95.

19   Larry Neal, "The Black Arts Movement," *Drama Review* 12 (Summer 1968): 29.

20   Melvin Edwards, "Lynch Fragments," in Franklin Rosemont and Robin D. G. Kelley, eds., *Black, Brown, and Beige: Surrealist Writings from Africa and the Diaspora* (Austin: University of Texas Press, 2009), 264.

21   Joan Semmel, "Feminist Artist Statement" [2006], Brooklyn Museum Feminist Art Base: https://www.brooklynmuseum.org/eascfa/about/feminist_art_base/joan-semmel.

22   The first ecumenical council of the Catholic Church in nearly a century, it was convened by Pope John XXIII in 1962 and met in regular sessions during the next three years with the aim of modernizing the church and making it more inclusive. Among the reforms, Vatican II allowed priests to celebrate Mass in the local language, not solely in Latin.

23   Karl Wirsum, quoted in Dan Nadel, "A Hairy Who's History of the Hairy Who," *The Ganzfeld* 3 (2003): 144.

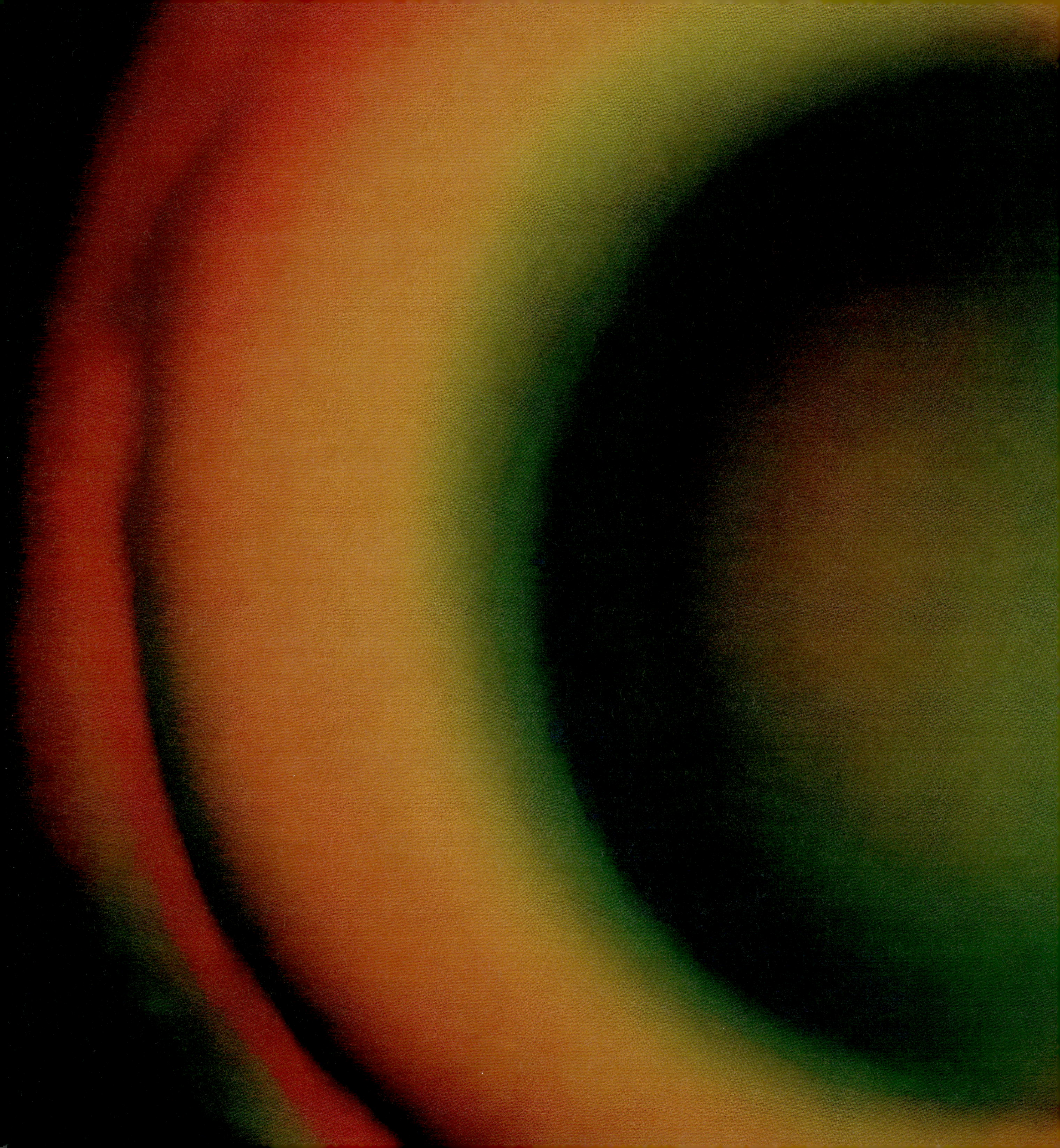

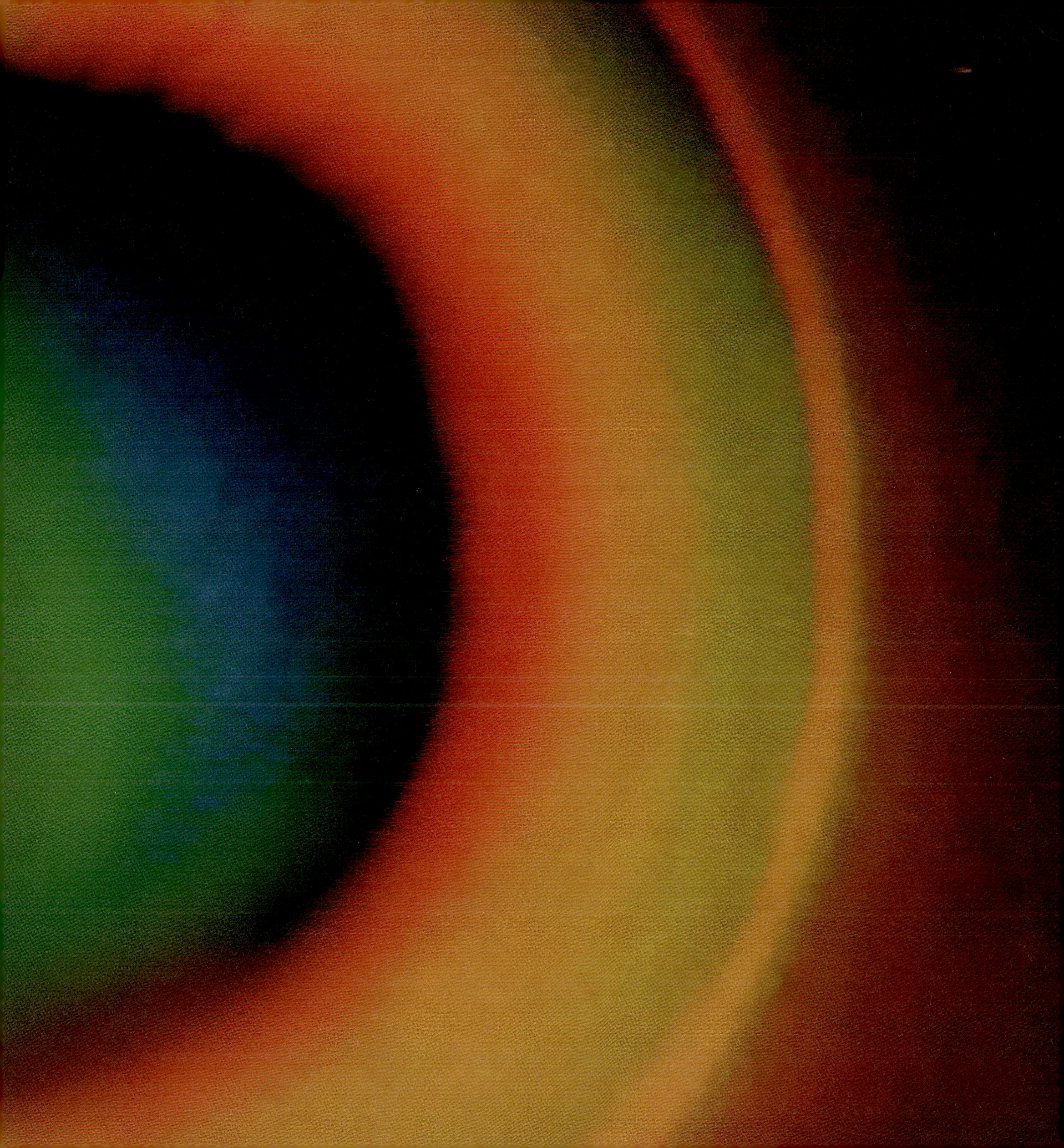

1958–1972

Often described as "the Long Sixties," this turbulent era sparked a plurality of artistic ideas influenced by Surrealism or its popular cousin, surrealism, which by 1958 had infiltrated the public imagination beyond art, literature, and politics to describe the fantastical writ large. Yet many of the stories surrounding the profusion of surreal art during this time have not been mapped, much less widely disseminated. The process of building the chronology that follows began by focusing on the biographies of the artists whose work comprises *Sixties Surreal*, with an emphasis on salient moments in their lives and artistic careers that tended to revolve around education, exhibitions, and personal encounters with one another. In the process, important relationships among artists, places, curators, and institutions emerged, which were often represented by key group exhibitions and thematic projects, such as *66 Signs of Neon* (1966) and *Funk* (1967). Whether through popularity or notoriety, these became historical markers of certain modes of art making at the time. The lesser-known group exhibitions charted here also exemplify how artistic networks flourished through overlapping interests across regional divides and trace various conceptual and aesthetic currents. Of particular note is how this chronology maps the racial divides in the art worlds of the period and the strategies Black and Latinx artists employed to grow artistic communities when the white market and institutions kept their backs turned, as in Los Angeles, where Black artists and collectors created their own galleries, or in Chicago, where Black organizers sustained neighborhood arts centers and institutions.

Keyed to relevant years throughout the chronology are essays that pick up on or underscore themes and ideas that the artists here explored with particular vibrance. The topics range from Gene Swenson's critical articulation of the Surrealist tendencies at work in the era's art in *The Other Tradition* (1966), as discussed by Jennifer Sichel (p. 159); Jo Applin on ideas that informed and surrounded Lucy Lippard's concept of "eccentric abstraction" (p. 189); and Lucy Bradnock's look at esotericism and, particularly, the notion of Kabbalah surrealism (p. 50). Other essays are rooted in specific geographies: Jacob Stewart-Halevy inquires into the changing meanings of assemblage in California (p. 139), and Ruben Cordova relates the emergence of Latinx and Chicano perspectives in Texas, through the careers of Mel Casas and Luis Jimenez (p. 266). A cluster of essays, including Sampada Aranke's (p. 121), point to the activation—and reassessment—of Surrealism's politics through Black radical traditions and the ways music, poetry, and art interacted and engaged with the surreality of the "the real." Rebecca Zorach offers a deeper exploration of this phenomenon in Chicago (p. 233), while Rujeko Hockley highlights this reassessment of Surrealism through the radical experiences of Black women artists (p. 328). Ed Halter explores how filmmaker Edward Owens is linked to networks of historic Surrealism (p. 220). Rachel Middleman and David Getsy each look at the politics of gender and sexuality: Middleman to uncover the proto-feminist works often grouped under the term *erotic art* (p. 22); Getsy to explore the absence of explicitly queer artworks in what is often understood as a particularly permissive era (p. 276).

In tandem with the chronology and images of exhibition artworks, the essays offer ways of thinking and interpreting how Surrealism and the surreal operated in the lives of artists and their art across the Long Sixties. Yet this survey, extensive as it is, is by no means exhaustive. What follows, then, seeks to fill, in some measure, what has been a lacuna in the history of twentieth-century American art, and to encourage further exploration and scholarship.

1958

January 6–31, 1958 • Ferus Gallery, Los Angeles, hosts a three-person show of works by John Altoon, Jay DeFeo, and Edward Kienholz. A review by Jules Langsner in *ARTnews* refers to the exhibition as a "three-man" show—indicating that DeFeo's adopted nickname obscures her gender—and calls the art, including paintings by Altoon and wood reliefs by Kienholz, "honest, though somewhat uneven."

DeFeo (1929–1989) had been born Mary Joan DeFeo in New Hampshire and raised mostly in Northern California. In 1951 she graduated from the University of California, Berkeley, having studied art under Margaret Peterson, the sole female art faculty member whose daring paintings at the time incorporate both embodied forms and an interest in the symbology of Indigenous peoples. Across the bay in San Francisco, spiritual abstraction is in bloom, and DeFeo grows curious about the style even as she seeks her own language, befriending artists Sam Francis and Fred Martin; the latter would champion her work and one day employ her at the San Francisco Art Institute.

From 1951 to 1953, DeFeo travels throughout Europe, before settling back in Berkeley, making jewelry to make ends meet. In 1954 she mounts her first one-person exhibition at the bar called The Place. Poet Michael McClure, a recent transplant to the area, describes the experience as "a sudden esthetic illumination," and contemporary art curator Walter Hopps sees the show, taking note of the artist for the future. DeFeo also begins exhibiting her work, and occasionally acting as a gallery attendant, at San Francisco's Six Gallery, founded by her husband, Wally Hedrick, artist Deborah Remington, and others. Famously, the Six Gallery hosts Allen Ginsberg's first public reading of "Howl," in October 1955. As Remington will later recall, "Nobody would have us . . . so we had to have a place of our own. It never occurred to us that we couldn't do it. We just did it. Then we sat around for hours and tried to decide what to call it."

In 1955 DeFeo and Hedrick move to the rambling Victorian home at 2322 Fillmore Street that would become known to some as Painterland, which in addition to its artist residents becomes a gathering place for other artists and poets in the neighborhood, such as Wallace and Shirley Berman, Robert Duncan, George Herms, and Jess. Embedded in the center of the San Francisco avant-garde now, DeFeo makes work that is marked by her love of William Blake, Renaissance art, and an ongoing interest in the poetic occult; crosses and celestial bodies appear in works that have a gestural verve and are already coalescing into a grayscale vision of her inner world. She completes two pieces that illustrate her diverse sensibilities: the monumental *Doctor Jazz* (1958), an enormous emblem in tribute to Count Basie, whose music is a constant at Painterland; and *The Eyes* (1958), a large, finely rendered imagining of her own eyes in metaphysical space crossed by vertical lines, as if signaling the apprehension of knowledge in real time. The original title, *Tell Him I Have Eyes Only for Heaven,* derives from a poem by the poet Philip Lamantia, who read alongside Allen Ginsberg in 1955.

April 12, 1958 • Roy De Forest (1930–2007) exhibits his work alongside Wallace Berman, Joan Brown, Jay DeFeo, Wally Hedrick, and others at Dilexi Gallery's inaugural group show. Founded by Jim Newman and Bob Alexander in San Francisco, Dilexi will be the site of five important exhibitions by De Forest over the next decade. Together with its brief 1962–63 outpost in Los Angeles, the gallery is a vital space for California art through 1969. Dilexi itself is a product of both cities, Newman having been a silent partner in Ferus Gallery in Los Angeles and very close friends with one of its founders, Walter Hopps.

De Forest had grown up in the Yakima Valley of southern Washington State. A lifelong obsessive reader with omnivorous tastes and interests—from Jack London to John Neumann—he began drawing at an early age. He is obsessed with adventure stories, dogs, mathematics, and the metaphysical underpinnings of the life-forms

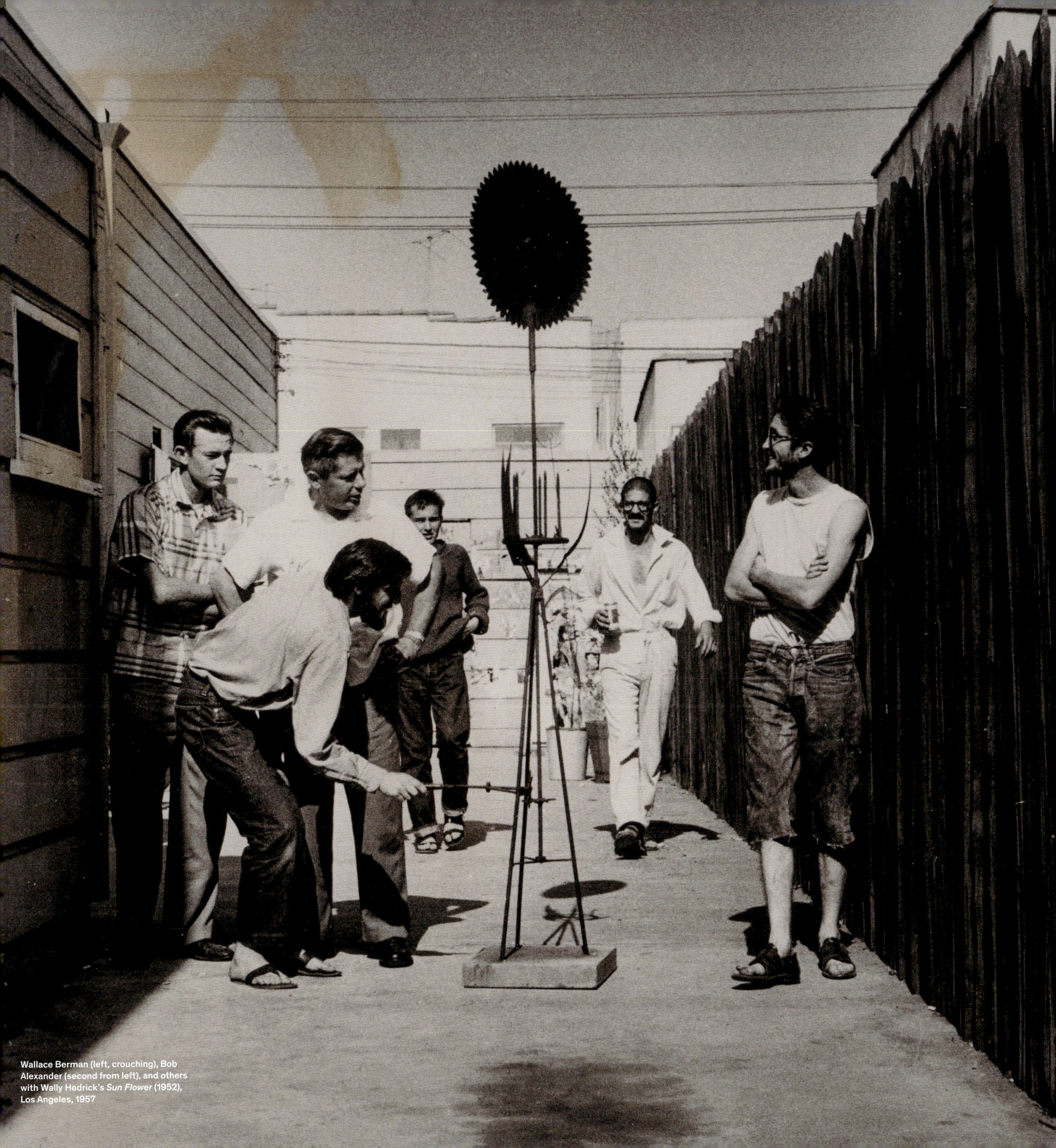

Wallace Berman (left, crouching), Bob Alexander (second from left), and others with Wally Hedrick's *Sun Flower* (1952), Los Angeles, 1957

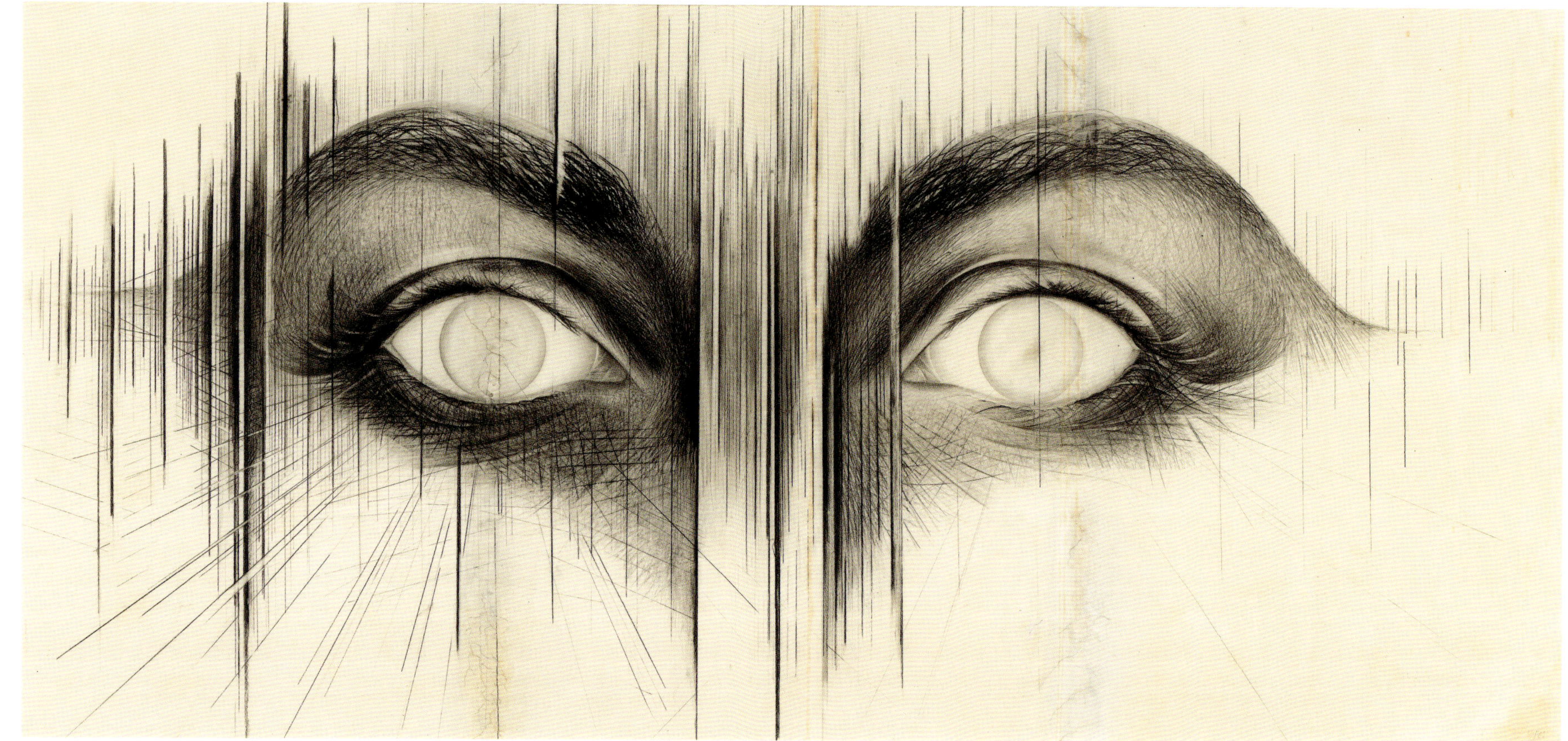

Jay DeFeo, *The Eyes*, 1958. Graphite pencil on paper, 42 × 84 ¾ in. (106.7 × 215.3 cm). Whitney Museum of American Art, New York; gift of the Lannan Foundation 96.242.3

all around him on his family's small farm. In 1950 De Forest enrolls at the California School of Fine Arts, where his instructors include Elmer Bischoff, Richard Diebenkorn, David Park, Mark Rothko, and Hassel Smith. He is fellow students with Deborah Remington and, importantly, Jess, with whom he shares a fascination with adventure stories and personal mythologies. After graduating in the summer of 1953, De Forest exhibits at King Ubu Gallery, the short-lived gallery on Fillmore Street opened by Jess, painter Harry Jacobus, and poet Robert Duncan. The military draft forces De Forest to take a brief break from his art career, and he serves in the Army for two years, mostly as a sign painter. Upon his return, in 1955 he joins his former classmates and the art-and-poetry cohort around Painterland. Exhibiting regularly, he is included in the 1955 São Paulo Biennial with Diebenkorn and Park.

In the late 1950s, De Forest develops his wall constructions, covering signpost-like forms with dollops of acrylic paint, squiggles, hatchings, curlicues, and impasto dot patterns. His found objects and carved forms are country cousins to the urban sculptures of Bruce Conner. Whereas Conner uses the cast-off junk of contemporary life to meditate on consumer culture and spiritual emptiness, De Forest repurposes discarded items to joyously track and celebrate the movement of objects and psyches in the world. If Conner is pointing to the void, De Forest is mapping a spirit world.

Mapping is not uncommon among mid-century Northern California artists. As with Jeremy Anderson, Fred Martin, Lee Mullican, and, later, William T. Wiley, De Forest deploys a set group of symbols, often in cartographic formations, to communicate a sense of personal inner space. Having earned a master's degree at San Francisco State College in 1956, he returns to the Yakima Valley to develop the symbolic and material language that will infuse his work for the rest of his life: signpost fingers, bundles of lines, contoured animals, patches of color, and aerial maps of the terrain. In 1965 De Forest joins the faculty at the University of California, Davis, living in nearby Port Costa.

1958 • Joan Brown (1938–1990) moves with her first husband, Bill Brown, to the home in San Francisco's Fillmore neighborhood dubbed Painterland that is a hub for the city's avant-garde. There, the Browns live next door to artists Wally Hedrick and Jay DeFeo and one floor below poets Michael and Joanna McClure. During this time, Brown becomes part of Bruce Conner's Rat Bastard Protective Association, a group of idiosyncratic artists brought together by a shared interest in creating anti-art, inflammatory work that challenges commercial tendencies.

Brown had grown up in San Francisco as an only child raised in a small apartment by her father, who worked for Bank of America and drank heavily, her depressive mother, who lived with epilepsy, and her elderly grandmother. Brown initially planned to attend Catholic Lone Mountain College for Women to pursue her interest in Egyptology but impulsively enrolls at the California School of Fine Arts in 1955 after seeing a newspaper advertisement, although she has only minimal knowledge of art and has never taken an art class. She later explains, "The only artist I'd ever heard of was Rembrandt when I went to art school. I'd never heard of Picasso, or any of the Impressionists." In the spring of 1956, she meets fellow student Bill Brown, a talented figurative painter and Korean War veteran eight years her senior; she marries him in August. This same summer, she enrolls in her first class with the instructor Elmer Bischoff, who helps her develop her signature intuitive style of figuration: "Elmer, although I'd never heard that kind of language, talked my language. It connected."

A year after moving to Painterland, Brown moves to North Beach with sculptor Manuel Neri, who in 1962 will become her second husband. Brown and Neri carry out an intimate artistic dialogue through a series of bird assemblages that each constructs for the other.

April 18, 1958 • Yanktonai Dakota artist Oscar Howe (1915–1983) pens a letter to the Philbrook Museum of Art in Tulsa, Oklahoma, decrying the museum's exclusion of his painting *Umine Wacipe* from consideration as part of its 1958 Annual National Indian Painting Competition. The jury's reasoning for the work's rejection is that it deviates from the "traditional" style of Native American painting, defined rather narrowly as the illustrative approach established in the early 1930s with origins in the Studio School of the Santa Fe Indian School; these paintings are known for their stylized depiction of scenes of Native American life and culture through flat areas of color and the repetition of decorative or symbolic figures. Howe has been educated in this method, having attended the Studio School in 1934 under its founder, Dorothy Dunn, before

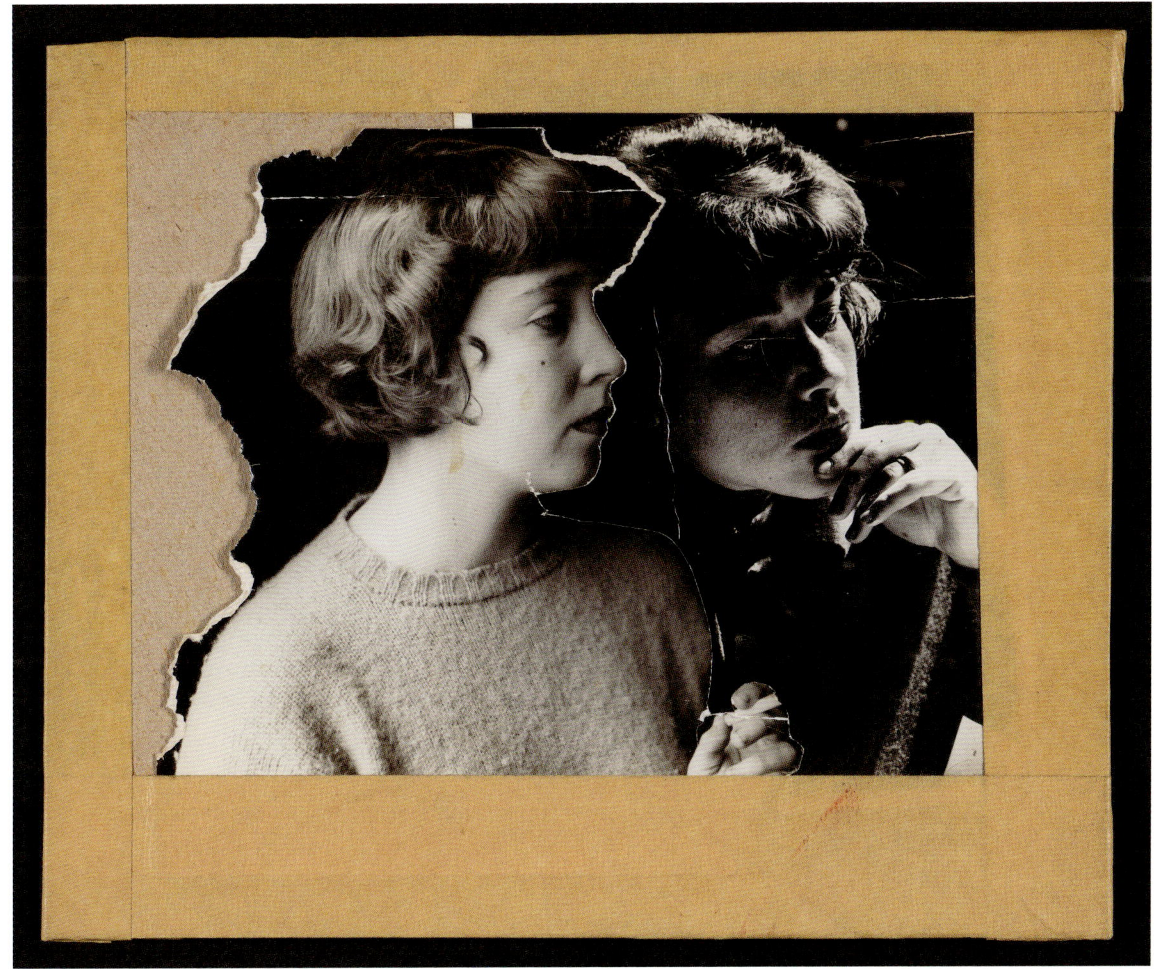

Collage of Joan Brown and Jay DeFeo, c. 1958

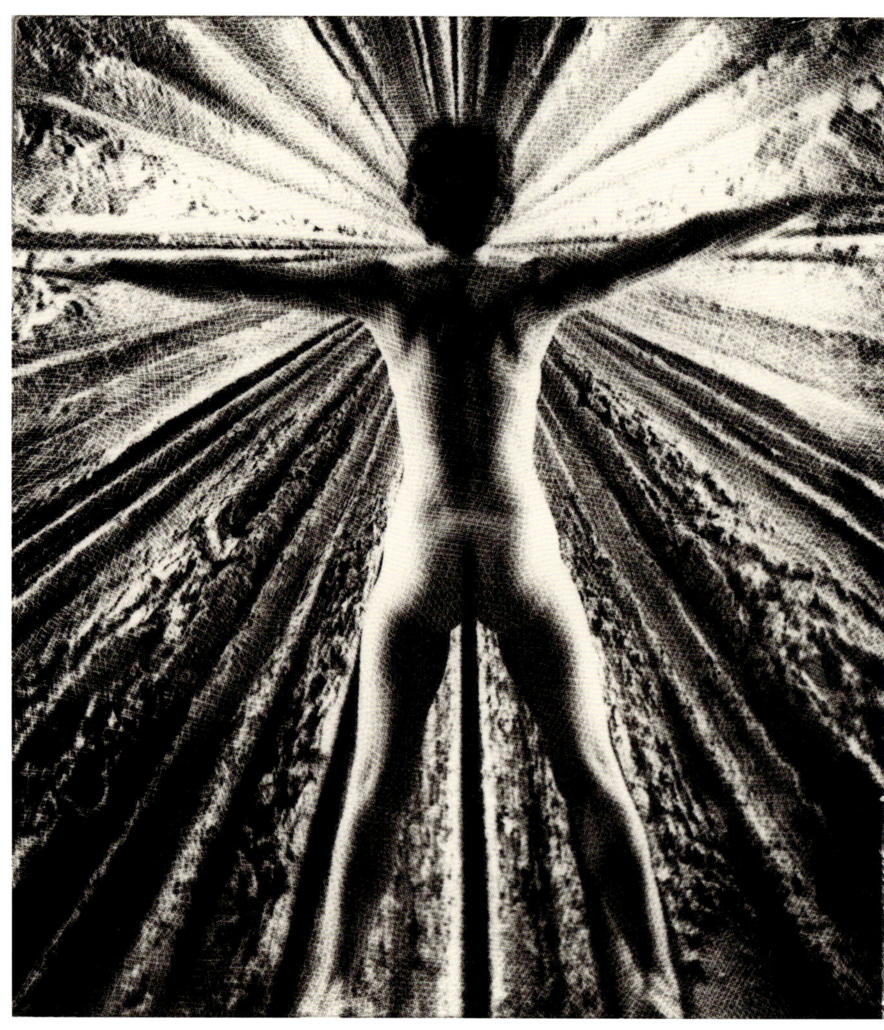

Wallace Berman and Jay DeFeo, *Untitled*, 1958. Gelatin silver print mounted on board, 5 ⅛ × 4 ½ in. (13 × 11.4 cm). Whitney Museum of American Art, New York; gift of the Lannan Foundation 96.243.8

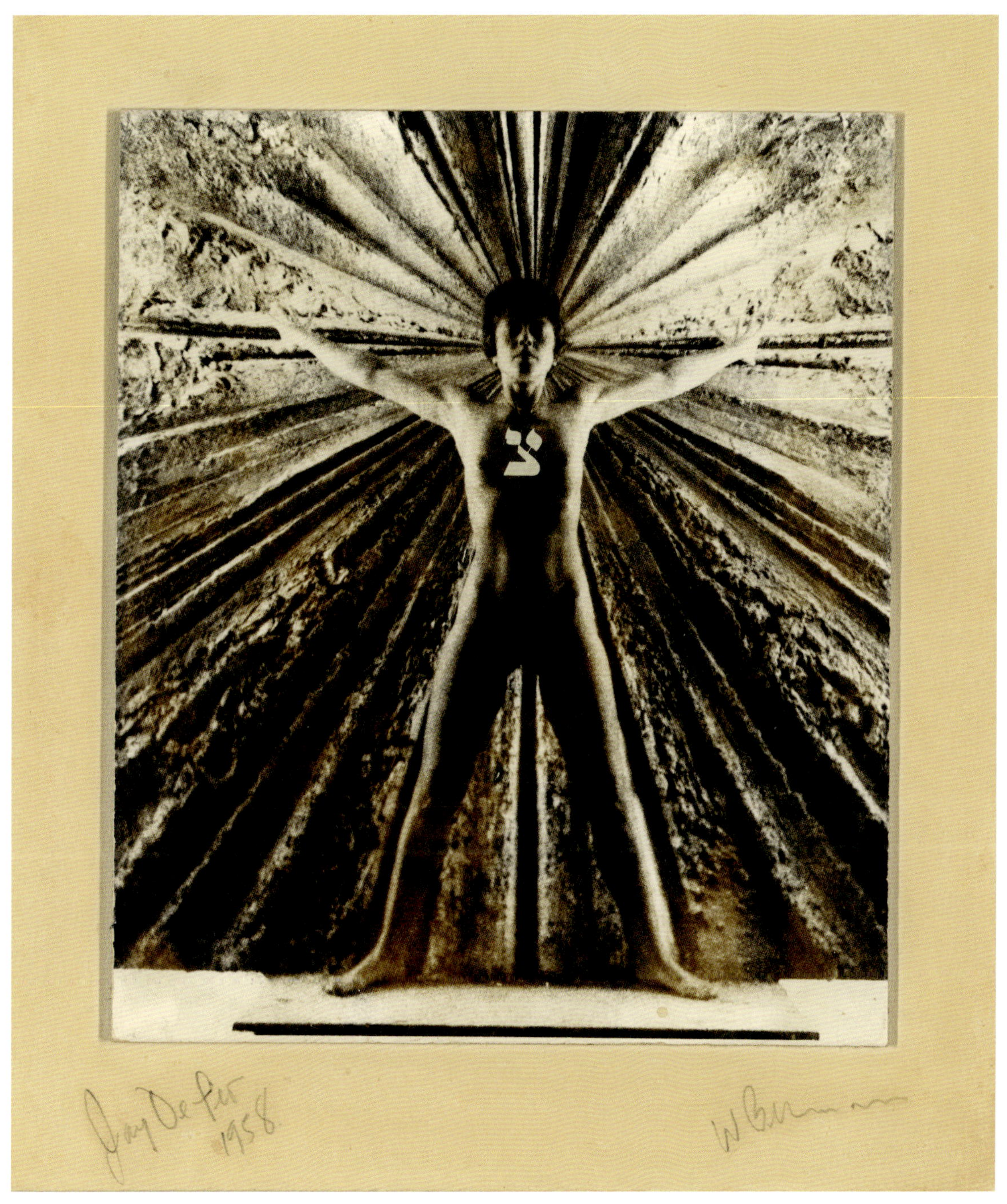

Wallace Berman and Jay DeFeo, *Untitled*, 1958. Gelatin silver print with transfer type mounted on board, 7 ⅛ × 5 ⅞ in. (18.1 × 14.9 cm). Whitney Museum of American Art, New York; gift of the Lannan Foundation 96.243.9

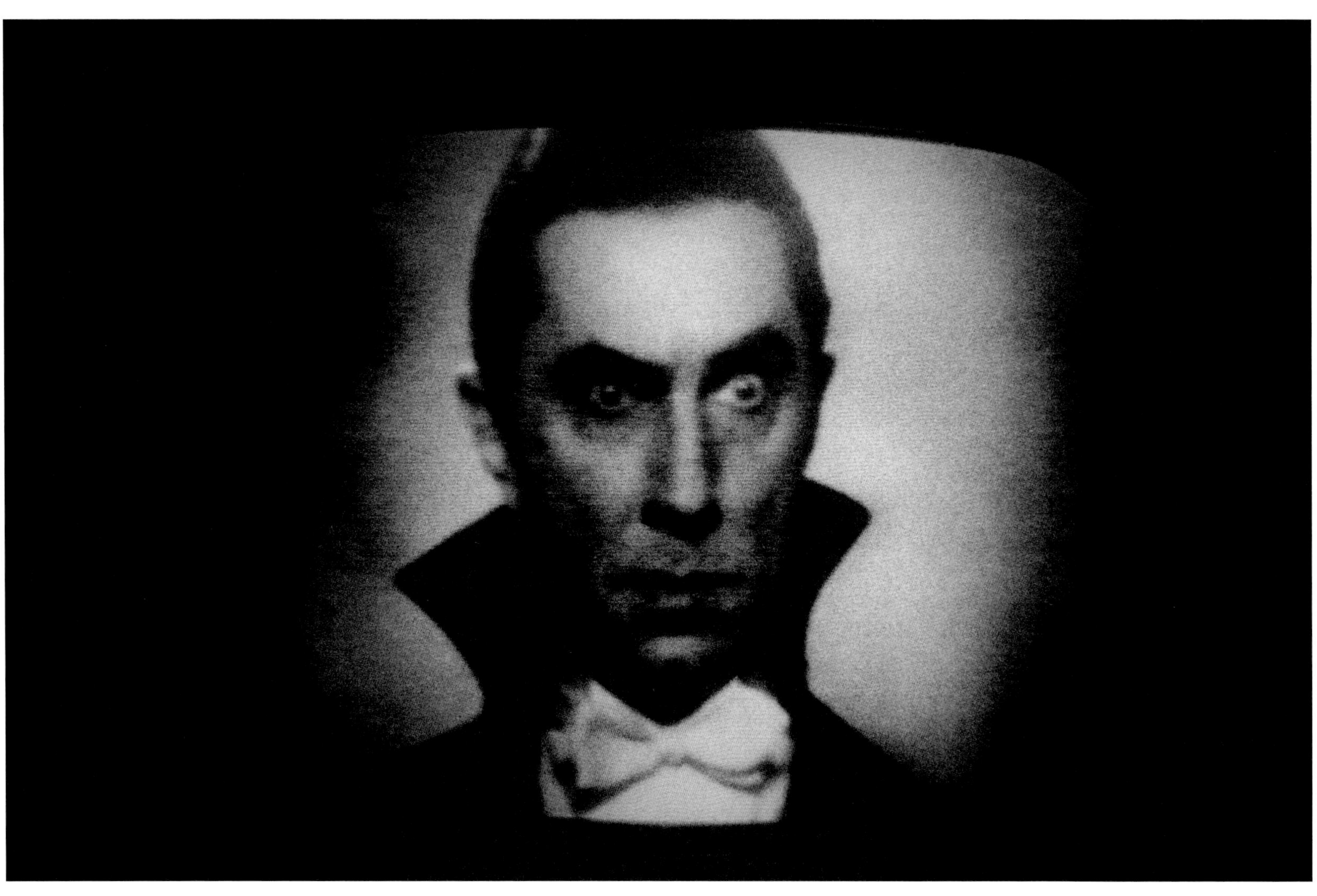

Diane Arbus, *Bela Lugosi as Dracula on television 1958*, 1958. Gelatin silver print: sheet, 11 × 14 in. (27.9 × 35.6 cm); image, 6 ½ × 9 ¾ in. (16.5 × 24.8 cm). Fraenkel Gallery, San Francisco

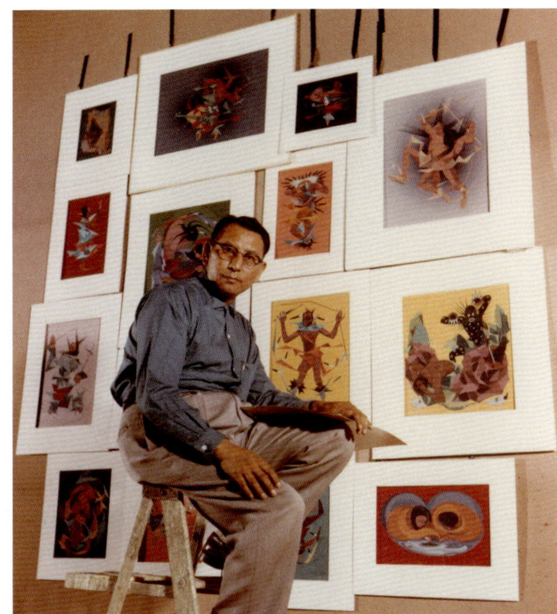

Oscar Howe in his studio, State University of South Dakota, Vermilion, SD, 1958

continuing his education at the University of Oklahoma in 1952 and expanding his increasingly abstract visual vocabulary. Questioning anyone's right to determine the authenticity of "Indian art," he closes his letter by saying, "One could easily turn to become a social protest painter. I only hope, the Art World will not be one more contributor to holding us in chains."

Born on the Crow Creek Reservation in South Dakota, Howe began attending the Pierre Indian School about forty miles away from his home at seven years old. As in most residential boarding schools for Native Americans at the time, students are not allowed to speak their native language, and they must conform to military-like regimes. While Howe is away at school, his mother dies and, suffering from an eye and skin affliction, he returns home to recover both physically and emotionally. He lives with his grandmother Shell Face, and in the stories she relates about their ancestors, she passes on her knowledge of Očhéthi Šakówiŋ—known by some as the Sioux Nation, the linguistically related peoples who speak Lakota, Dakota, and Nakota dialects—and its cultural traditions, instilling in Howe the urge to keep that knowledge alive. He takes this interest and his talent to the Studio School, where he learns to paint, studies European art history, and establishes himself as one of the program's most accomplished artists. Although his style changes as he discovers more about the art of other cultures, his work is embedded in traditional Očhéthi Šakówiŋ customs and aesthetics, and he does not see a contradiction between the Studio School approach and the experimental forms of his paintings.

Vermillion, So. Dak.
April 18th, 1958

Miss Jeanne Snodgrass
Curator: American Indian Art
Philbrook Art Center
Tulsa, Oklahoma

Dear Miss Snodgrass:

Who ever said, that my paintings are not in the traditional Indian style, has poor knowledge of Indian Art indeed. There is much more to Indian Art, than pretty, stylized pictures. There was also power and strength and individualism (emotional and intellectual insight) in the old Indian paintings. Every bit in my paintings is a true studied fact of Indian paintings. Are we to be held back forever with one phase of Indian painting, that is the most common way? We are to be herded like a bunch of sheep, with no right for individualism, dictated as the Indian has always been, put on reservations and treated like a child, and only the White Man knows what is best for him. Now, even in Art, "You little child do what we think is best for you, nothing different." Well, I am not going to stand for it. Indian Art can compete with any Art in the world, but not as a suppressed Art. I see so much of the mismanagement and treatment of my people. It makes me cry inside to look at these poor people. My father died there about three years ago in a little shack, my two brothers still living there in shacks, never enough to eat, never enough clothing, treated as second class citizens. This is one of the reasons I have tried to keep the fine ways and culture of my forefathers alive. But one could easily turn to become a social protest painter. I only hope, the Art World will not be one more contributor to holding us in chains.

Oscar Howe

Letter from Oscar Howe to Jeanne Snodgrass, April 18, 1958

June 1958 • After serving in the Army, Carlos Villa (1936–2013) enrolls at the California School of Fine Arts (CSFA) on the G.I. Bill. Born in San Francisco's Tenderloin district to Filipino immigrants from the Ilocos region, Villa had first experienced art through lessons with his cousin, artist Leo Valledor, who introduces him to Manuel Neri, a Mexican American sculptor and professor at CSFA. Villa, as well as his fellow students Robert Hudson and Joan Brown, is encouraged by the generative exchange with Neri's wide network of artists. In Neri's summer class, Villa makes a coffin-like sculpture out of a used wooden box, lining it with a garbage bag, placing a wooden figure wrapped in an American flag inside of it, and covering its exterior with red, white, and blue bunting. The sculpture catches the attention of artist Bruce Conner, and he includes it as a key component of that summer's "Rat Bastard Parade" that he and other artists, writers, and poets lead through

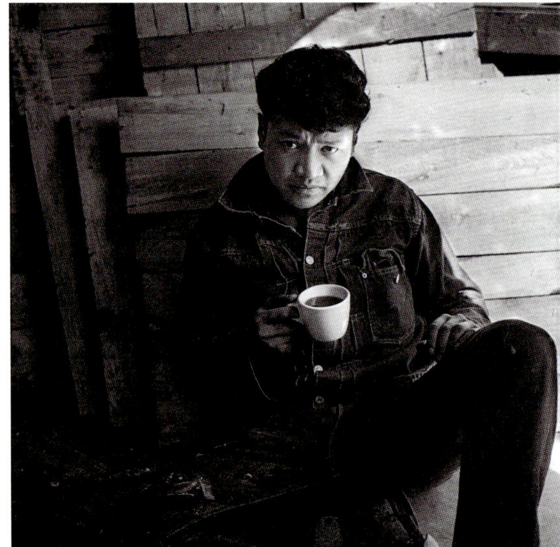

Carlos Villa, San Francisco, c. 1958

North Beach on their way to the opening of *Ratbastard*, the collective exhibition Conner has co-organized at Spatsa Gallery, a converted garage/storefront down the street from the recently closed Six Gallery.

June 1958 • Yayoi Kusama (b. 1929) moves from Japan to New York, after having exhibited twenty-six watercolor and pastel works at Seattle's Zoë Dusanne Gallery the previous December. Born into an affluent feudal family in Matsumoto City, Nagano Prefecture, Kusama had grown up during the Pacific War. She began showing her works on paper in group exhibitions as a teenager, submitting them to open competitions. Although a young woman pursuing an artistic career in conservative postwar Japanese society is fraught with prejudice and viewed as unconventional, as evidenced by her parents' objections, Kusama persists. In 1948 she studies the modern Japanese *nihonga* style of painting at Kyoto's arts high school. Disillusioned by the teaching methods and strict hierarchies, she instead starts to experiment with a range of artistic techniques and materials, staging solo exhibitions in Tokyo and Matsumoto and becoming interested in Surrealism and psychology. According to scholar Midori Yamamura, Kusama benefitted from a close relationship with the Japanese surrealist poet and critic Shūzō Takiguchi: "Surrealism provided fertile ground for Kusama to explore the depths of the human psyche as a way to critique polite society."

In 1955 Kusama initiates a written correspondence with Georgia O'Keeffe, asking for advice about moving to the United States. The same year, three of Kusama's works appear in the *International Watercolor Exhibition, 18th Biennial* at the Brooklyn Museum in New York. These paintings receive particularly high praise from artist Kenneth Callahan, who introduces the work to Zoë Dusanne.

June 8, 1958 • Lucy Lippard (b. 1937) graduates from Smith College and immediately moves to New York City—having spent much of her childhood there—where she works at the library of the Museum of Modern Art (MoMA) between 1959 and 1960. Beyond her specific assignments at the library, she is tasked with various research projects for curators such as William Seitz and Peter Selz, which help expand her understanding of art history and curating before she begins a master's degree program at the Institute of Fine Arts at New York University. As Lippard later recalls regarding her experience at MoMA: "Dada and Surrealism were sort of my art historical fondness and [Bernard] Karpel, the librarian of the Modern, was also interested in Dada and Surrealism. He got me pushed in that direction. And then I met Sol [LeWitt] who was at the desk downstairs at the Modern . . . so he was responsible for another part of my education."

June 10, 1958 • Bruce Conner (1933–2008) premieres *A MOVIE* (1958) at East & West Gallery, San Francisco, and forms the Rat Bastard Protective Association (RBPA), a loose confederation of artists united by an unabashed (and financially necessary) love of discarded junk, storefront signage, and the dark grotesque, and deeply involved with assemblage art.

In 1956 Conner had enrolled as a graduate student at the University of Colorado, Boulder, joining his future wife, artist Jean Sandstedt. Together, they founded the Experimental Cinema Group and organized screenings of avant-garde films, including those of Stan Brakhage, who advised the group and encouraged Conner to continue in his art. Motivated by high school friend and poet Michael McClure's description of San Francisco, Conner and his wife move to the city in 1957 to experience its mix of art, poetry, and life, staying with McClure at Painterland. The city is alive with avant-garde activity, but it attracts little public, let alone financial, interest. According to Conner:

> The only gallery that might show [art] would be a co-op gallery like the [Six] Gallery, or

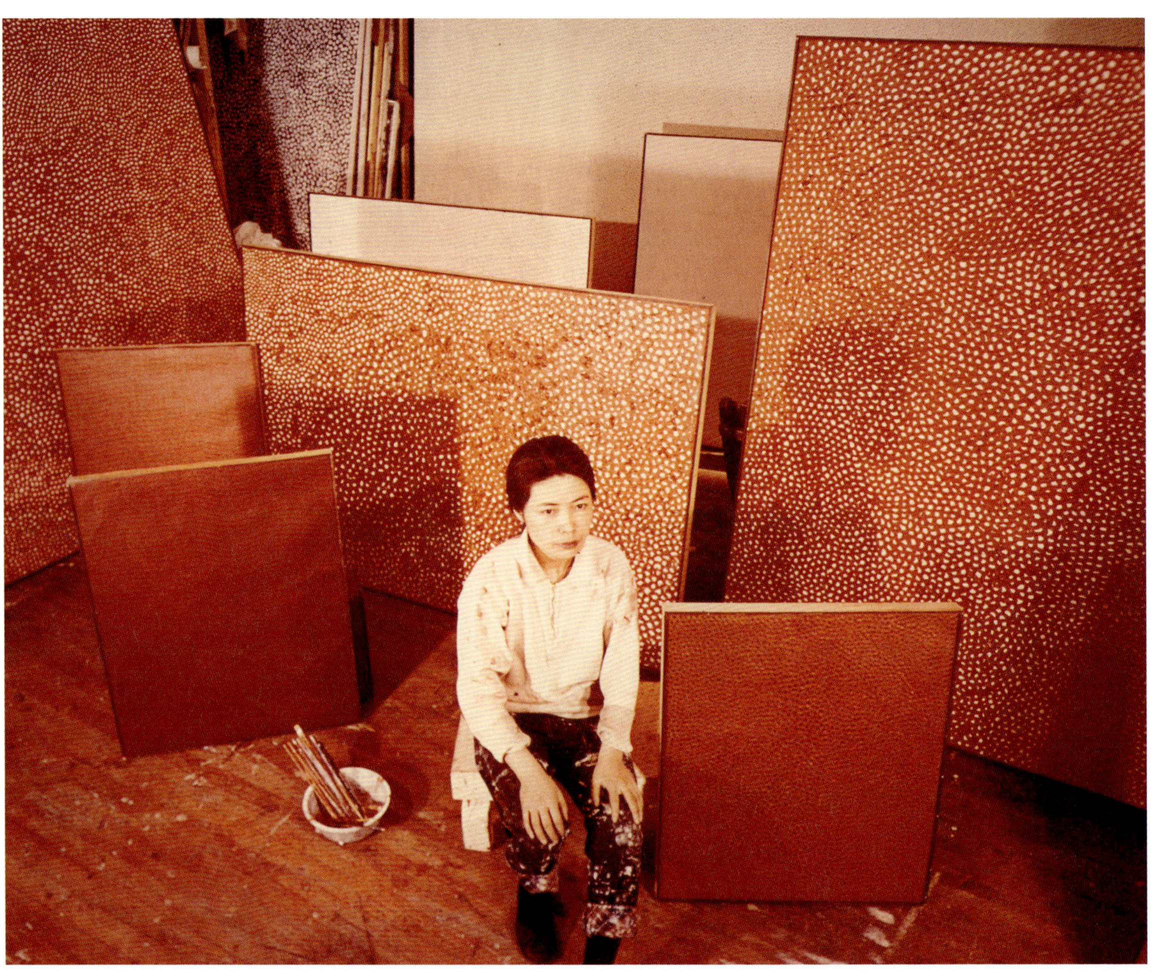

Yayoi Kusama in her studio, New York, 1961

some other gallery run by artists. And invariably what would happen is that at the opening everybody would come and have a party, Wally [Hedrick]'s band would play, everybody would get drunk, and after the opening the guy who ran the gallery would get tired of coming in. You'd never get into the place unless he'd open the door for you. . . . The idea of having shows was silly. Most of the other people that I knew that were artists just figured it was absurd. Why have a show? Just have a party. If you are going to have a show, why bother to take on all the trimmings and expectations of what art should be as a permanent work of art? Why spend your money on that if nobody is going to buy it? You really are doing it for yourself.

As both an acknowledgment of the ridiculousness of his situation and an attempt to form an ad hoc community, Conner creates the RBPA, with Joan Brown, Jay DeFeo, Wally Hedrick, and Carlos Villa among its founding members, combining the name of the municipal garbage collectors—Scavengers Protective Association (SPA)—with the fittingly abject phrase "rat bastard." Indeed, Conner's early, sometimes wearable assemblages are inspired by the sight of pendulous bags of trash hanging from passing SPA trucks, and *A MOVIE* emerges from reels of unclaimed film he scavenges from a local photography store. For Conner, art is in the finding and making, not the owning or theorizing.

———

Summer 1958 • After graduating from Ohio University with a bachelor of fine arts in photography, Adger Cowans (b. 1936) begins working with photographer Gordon Parks at *Life* magazine in New York City. Initially, Cowans lives with the Parks family in White Plains, New York, before renting an apartment on West 82nd Street with Gordon Parks Jr. After serving two years in the Navy, Cowans returns to New York in 1960 and moves into a building with newlyweds Parks Jr. and Barbara Chavous on West 87th Street.

Cowans had grown up in Columbus, Ohio, in a large, tight-knit family. His mother and uncle Wilbur are amateur photographers, and his mother supports his decision to pursue what his father dismisses as an impractical trade. At Ohio University he studies under Clarence H. White Jr., the son of Photo-Secessionist Clarence H. White, and takes classes with Minor White. He recalls asking a professor after graduation if he knew of any Black photographers working professionally; the professor replied that he believed he had heard of someone at *Life* magazine, though he could not remember the name. Nevertheless,

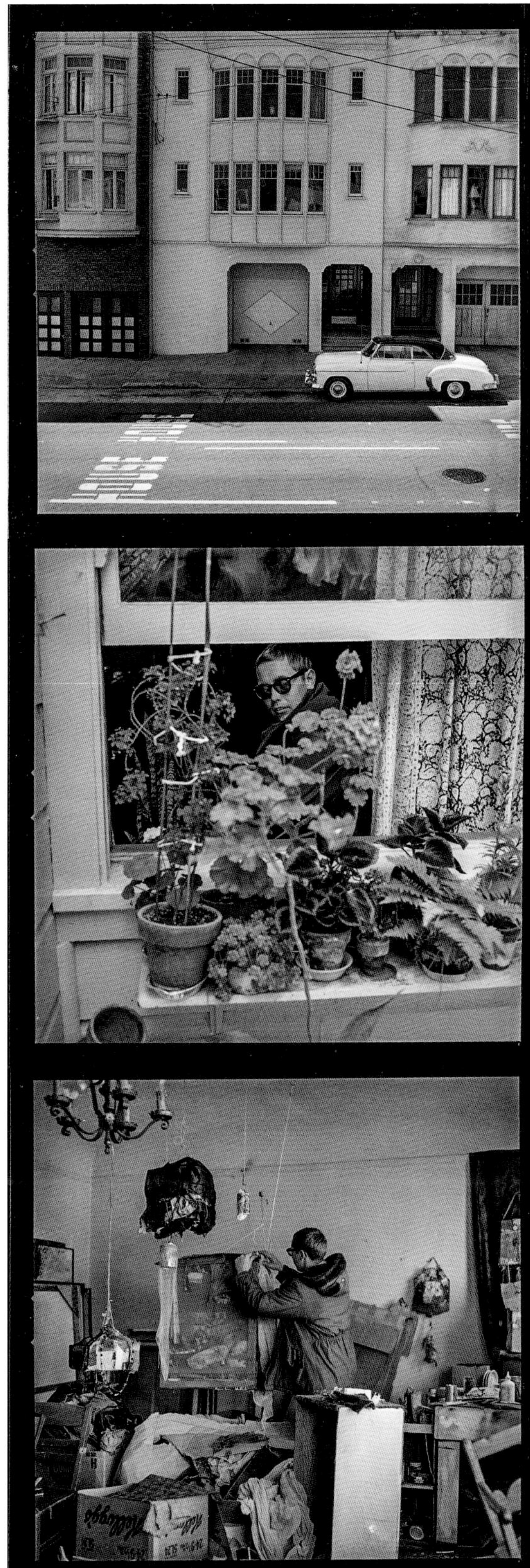

Contact sheet of Bruce Conner's studio, San Francisco, c. 1958–59

Cowans finds Parks's information, writes him a letter, and is invited to come to New York and work as his assistant.

Cowans's work is a departure from both Parks's and the photojournalistic style associated with *Life*. His poetic approach to photography

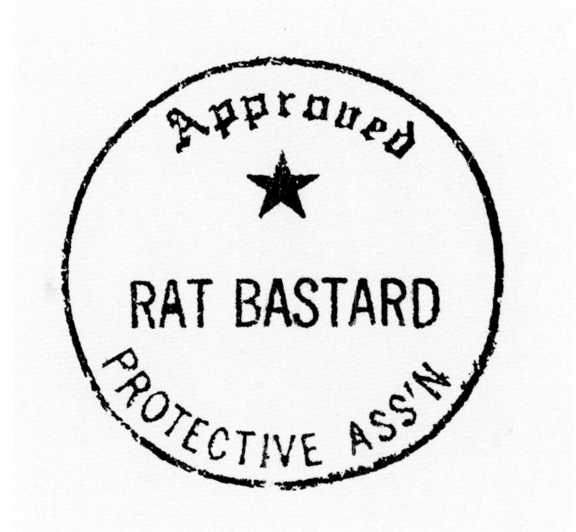

Bruce Conner's logo for the Rat Bastard Protective Association, c. 1957–58

encompasses a range of subject matter—from documentary shots capturing the strange beauty of the everyday through unusual angles and an eye for the uncanny, to delicate abstractions produced by patterns of light and reflections on water in motion. Although he will document some of the most important political events of the 1960s, including the activities of the Student Nonviolent Coordinating Committee in Mississippi as well as stunning views of a Malcolm X rally in Harlem, he remains staunch in his commitment to the practice of photography as an art.

———

July 1958 • Having just completed his bachelor of fine arts in painting at the School of the Art Institute of Chicago (SAIC), Benny Andrews (1930–2006) moves to New York City, settling in an apartment on the Lower East Side and immersing himself in the downtown arts scene.

Born into a sharecropping family in Plainview, Georgia, Andrews began working in the cotton fields under a thinly veiled plantation system at the age of five. His mother arranged for him to attend high school, if only for part of the year, outside of the planting and harvesting seasons. After receiving a scholarship that allows him to attend Fort Valley State College for two years, Andrews enlists in the Air Force and serves for the duration of the Korean War. The G.I. Bill enables him to pursue his dream of going to art school, and he moves to Chicago to study at SAIC in 1954.

There Andrews hones his style of expressive figurative painting, defending his adherence to the figure against the doctrine of Abstract Expressionism then dominant at the school while simultaneously metabolizing the movement's loose, gestural brushwork into a representational approach. He studies closely with Paul Wieghardt, a German artist who works in a figurative style that blends German Expressionism and Bauhaus design, and who also taught Claes Oldenburg and H. C. Westermann. Instructor Herman Graff, visiting professor Boris Margo, and visiting artist Roberto Matta all have a surrealist impact on Andrews's art. Near the end of his time at SAIC, Andrews starts incorporating collaged material into his canvases, frequently giving the collaged materials volume so that aspects of his figures project three-dimensionally toward the viewer.

Referencing conversations with his brother, Raymond, a writer who had also moved to New York, Andrews would later reflect:

> We always felt that we lived in a very surreal world. It was full of such great contrasts between what we would have liked it to be, what we imagined we could be and what we were. And, so, in a sense, we lived in a stark reality. And, whenever we could, we let our imaginations take us into the surreal. . . . I still sometimes am amused by how unreal this is, that from my earlier position in life I am now able to do this. So it stays surreal. I still exist between the two, between the real and the surreal. . . . Somehow, it has never been resolved, whether I am a conceptual surrealist or this down and out realist. It is the attempt to balance between the two that keeps me going.

In his work, Andrews develops a means of exploiting these real contrasts, using an uncanny approach to figuration to amplify and explode a dissonant and contradictory reality.

Fall 1958 • H. C. Westermann (1922–1981) makes his solo debut at Allan Frumkin Gallery, Chicago, exhibiting works that will ultimately come to define his art, including *Memorial to the Idea of Man If He Was an Idea* (1958). Combining his thematic, craft, and imagistic languages, the work is a summation of his art and ideas up to that point. The sculpture depicts a cyclops, its mouth agape, its body a highly polished wood cabinet, its arms taking an authoritative posture. Painted on the inside of the mouth, a tiny humanoid appears trapped. Bottle caps and a few sculptural vignettes cover the interior of the cabinet, attesting to madness, helplessness, and entrapment—all feelings well earned by the artist.

Born and raised in Los Angeles, Westermann had been a prodigious artist growing up. Like many others of his generation, he longed to work for Disney, and at the age of sixteen, he submits drawings to the studio, which in turn offers him a job but subsequently rescinds the proposal when

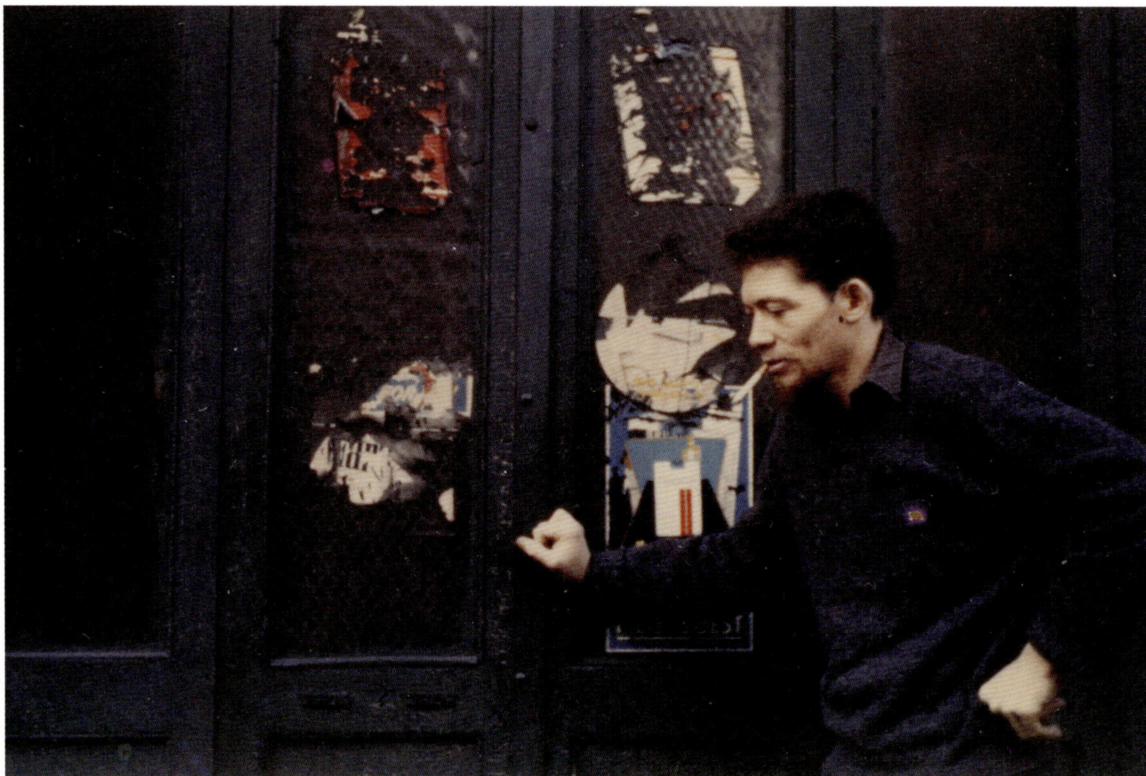

Benny Andrews, New York, 1958

they discover his age. Following his beloved mother's death, Westermann joins the US Marine Corps at age nineteen and is eventually stationed in the Pacific theater as an antiaircraft machine gunner aboard the USS *Enterprise*. In 1945 an attack on the *Enterprise* by a kamikaze kills fourteen men, and this scene of surprise, dedication (by fellow Navy men and the enemy alike), and devastation has a lifelong effect on the artist.

In 1947, thanks to the G.I. Bill, Westermann enters the School of the Art Institute of Chicago (SAIC), where he studies until the summer of 1950, when he reenlists in the Marine Corps, arriving in the Korean combat zone in April 1951. After another period of horrific battles, he returns to Chicago and reenrolls at SAIC in the fall of 1952 to study painting. He gets by doing carpentry and other odd jobs, making art the center of his life. He participates in the student exhibition series *Momentum* along with his SAIC peers—Leon Golub, Miyoko Ito, June Leaf, Evelyn Statsinger, among others—many of whom are, like him, experimenting with a hybrid figuration and expressionism that is aware of itself but is necessarily dark, urban, and directly political in a way shunned elsewhere in a postwar artworld dominated by formalism. Even in this environment, Westermann is an outlier, preferring tightly crafted and nicely finished objects over raw surfaces. He is also forever conscious of being a working-class "ordinary guy" who loves craftsmanship and physical fitness and has no interest in theory or doctrine.

Westermann's achievement in these early years makes searing indictments of the American war machine from the inside, and in the vernacular idiom practiced by the working-class "folks" to whom the politicians preach blind patriotism and who are imagined to blindly support the same. Westermann leans into the language of the people to tell us something profound about art, death, and the dangers of ideology. He leaves Chicago to settle in Connecticut in 1961, remaining there until his death.

1958 • A year after moving to Los Angeles from Honolulu, Hawaii, Ron Miyashiro (b. 1937) begins attending the Chouinard Art Institute, where he becomes friends with fellow students Larry Bell, Ed Bereal, Joe Goode, Daniel LaRue Johnson, and Ed Ruscha. Like many in his cohort, he studies under Robert Irwin. As a Japanese American raised in Hawaii, Miyashiro speaks pidgin and struggles with language barriers in class, but he understands Irwin's assignments through the professor's energy. Although he has much experience in charcoal figure drawing, he eventually quits his drawing courses and pursues the broad ideas of painting he learns in Irwin's class. Miyashiro begins to combine materials like cardboard, metal, and wood with found objects, such as cans, photographs, crosses, and crucifixes, painting them with acrylic or house paint and giving his assemblage works often smooth surfaces.

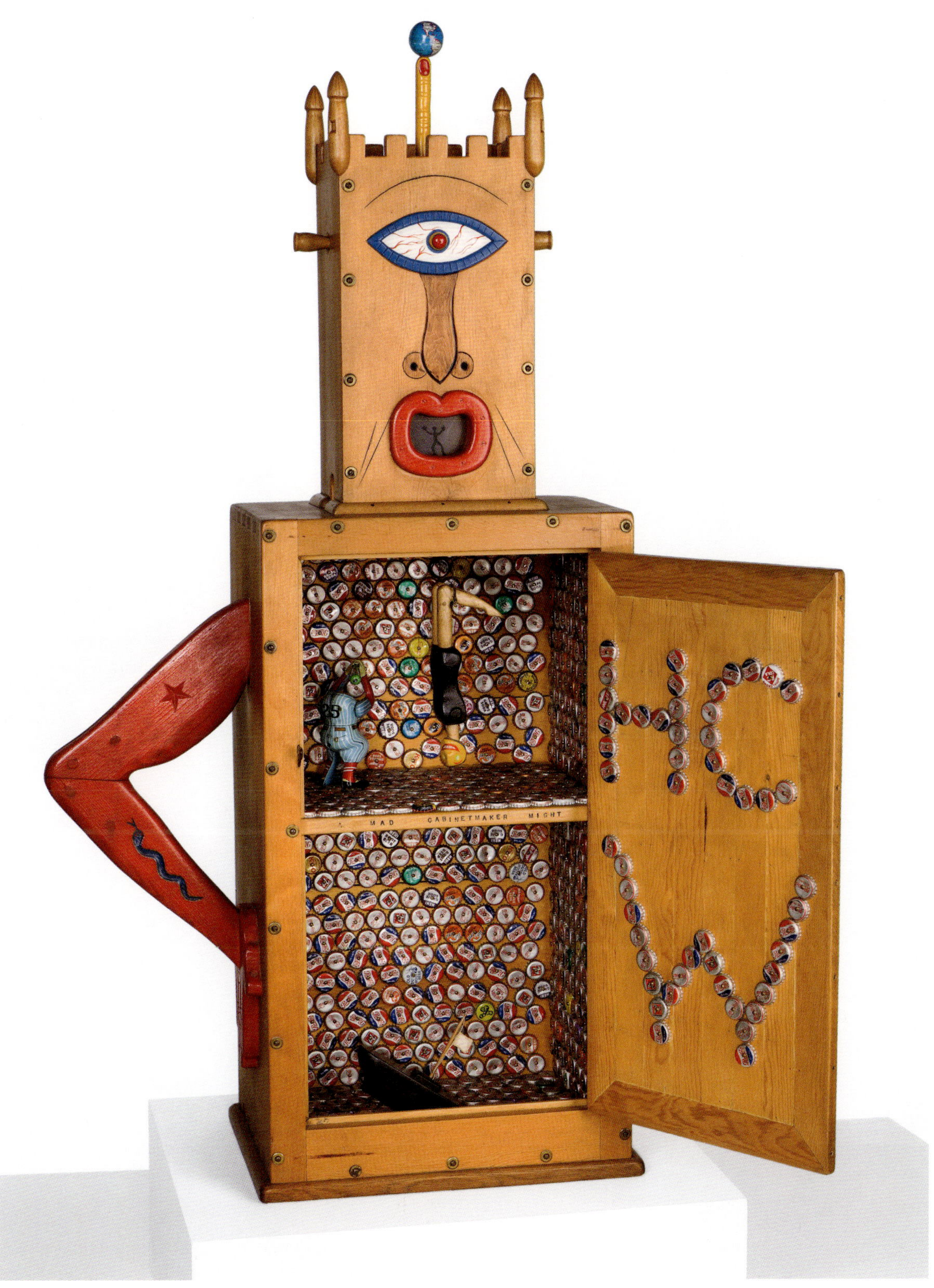

H. C. Westermann, *Memorial to the Idea of Man If He Was an Idea*, 1958. Pine, bottle caps, cast-tin toys, glass, metal, brass, ebony, and enamel, 56 ½ × 38 × 14 ¼ in. (143.5 × 96.5 × 36.2 cm). Museum of Contemporary Art Chicago; Susan and Lewis Manilow Collection of Chicago Artists 1993.34

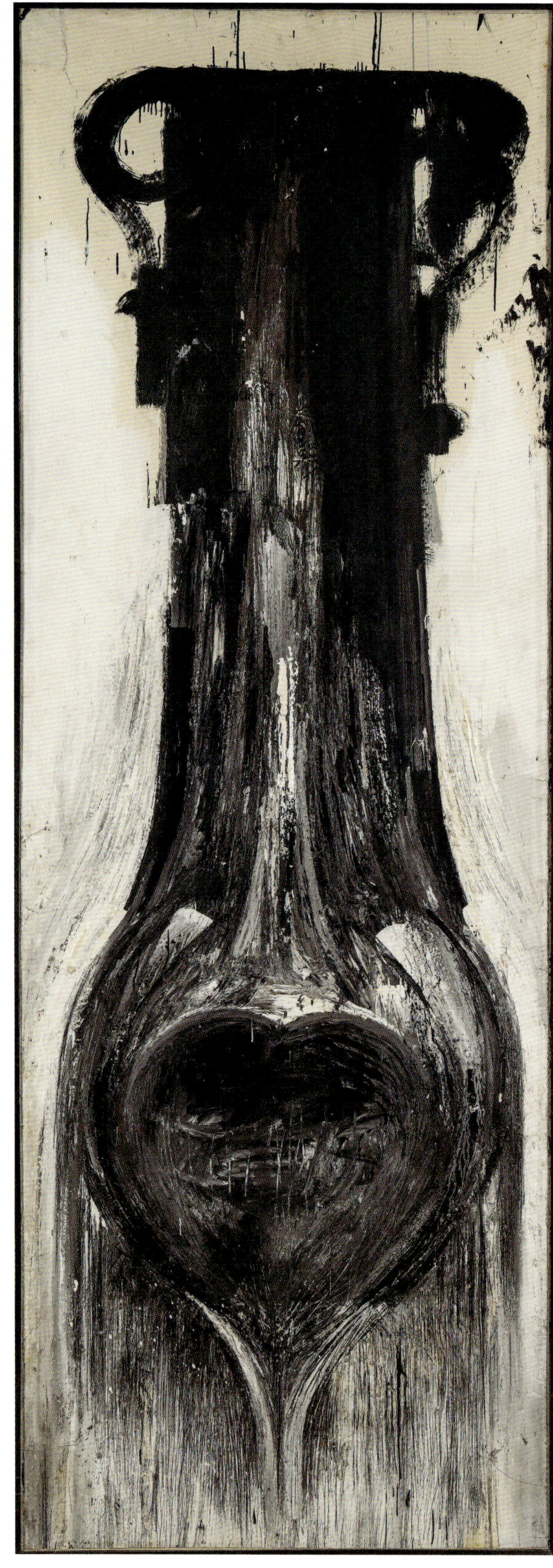

Jay DeFeo, *Doctor Jazz*, 1958. Ink, acrylic, graphite, synthetic polymer, and tinsel on paper, 125 ½ × 42 ½ × 3 ½ in. (318.8 × 108 × 8.9 cm). Nora Eccles Harrison Museum of Art, Logan, UT; gift of the Marie Eccles Caine Foundation 2001.11

This combination of approaches teases at many of the artistic sensibilities of the moment—not only assemblage but also Finish Fetish, in particular, which blends painting and sculpture. Despite the sometimes slick surfaces of his works from the 1960s, Miyashiro makes all of his pieces by hand, without the help of machines, so the importance of the artist's hand and labor seen in his earlier drawings never entirely disappears. Through his use of found materials, the question of decipherability reoccurs throughout Miyashiro's oeuvre, as his Okinawan identity and a commentary on war, sex, and religion often linger just below the surfaces of his assemblages.

1958 • Ed Bereal (b. 1937) begins his studies at the Chouinard Art Institute, after not being accepted into the renowned illustration program at the ArtCenter School in Los Angeles. Ultimately, Bereal's experience at Chouinard is similar to that of fellow graduate Ed Ruscha, who describes the program as "freer and more bohemian." At Chouinard, Bereal gravitates toward the classes of Robert Irwin, a new and first-time professor who sees art making as inquiry, challenging students to embrace their own individuality. Bereal, along with artists like Ruscha, Larry Bell, and Ron Miyashiro, takes Irwin's teaching to heart and abandons plans to pursue advertising or illustration, instead adopting new modes of art. Bereal begins to experiment with incorporating into his painted surfaces materials from his

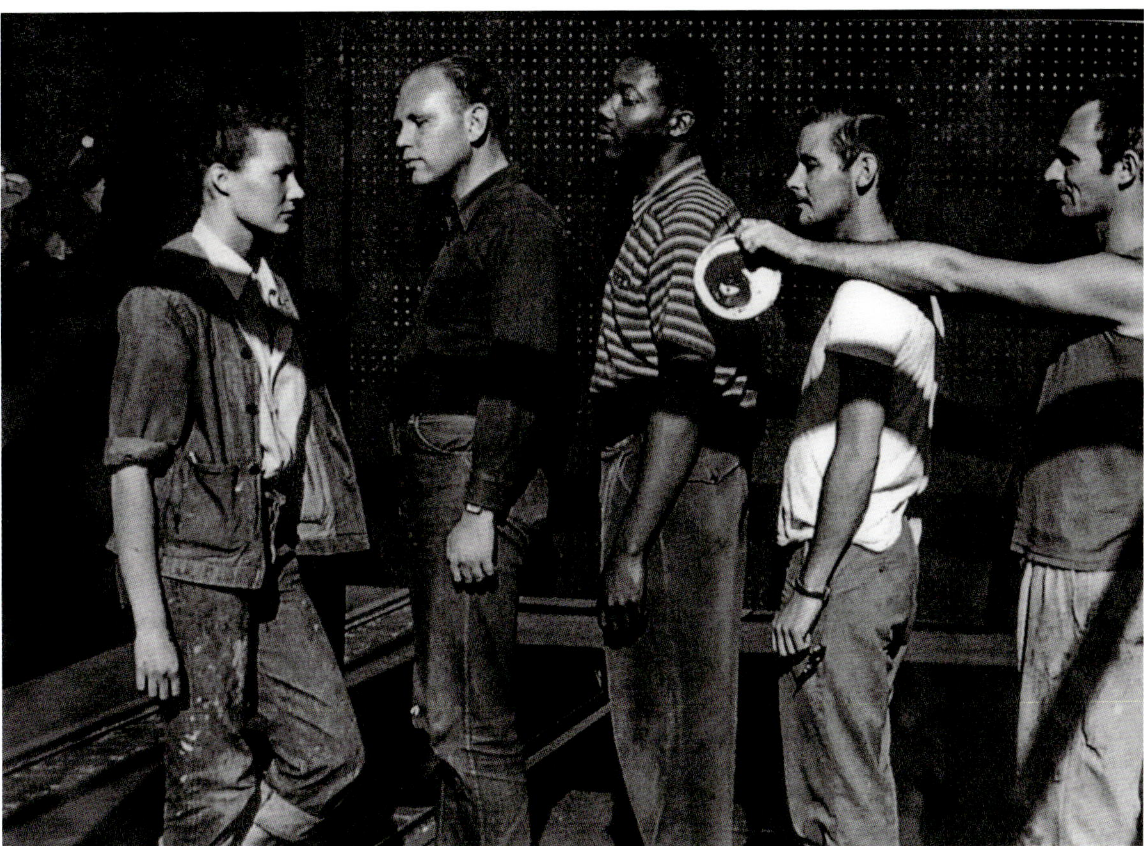

Deborah Remington, Jack Spicer, Hayward King, John Allen Ryan, and Wally Hedrick, Six Gallery, San Francisco, 1955

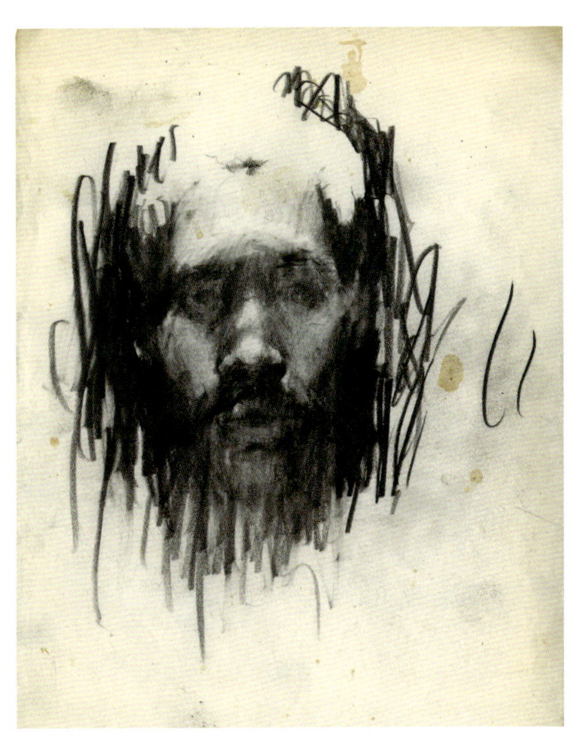

Ed Bereal, *Untitled (Self Portrait)*, 1958–65. Graphite on paper, 11 × 8 ½ in. (27.9 × 21.6 cm)

summer job as a mechanic in his hometown of Riverside, California. This approach introduces him to a community of artists outside of school at a time when the practice of assemblage was gaining attention in Los Angeles through the works of Edward Kienholz and George Herms and through the interest of Ferus Gallery cofounder Walter Hopps. Through these connections, Bereal's pieces begin to garner notice, but as a Black man in America, he feels some discomfort with his work being considered in the tradition of these white artists or within a European lineage of collage and assemblage. He believes his method aligns more closely with that of blues and jazz musicians, explaining, "There was always for me a continuous resonance and dialogue with the art of Muddy Waters, James Brown, Screamin' Jay Hawkins, and assemblage as a cultural phenomenon with intimate ties to my community."

Fall 1958 • After nearly two years living in Asia, Deborah Remington (1930–2010) returns to San Francisco, where she is hired by the California School of Fine Arts (CSFA) to teach Japanese calligraphy and begins to expand the processes that will culminate in her "mirror" paintings of the mid-1960s onward. Remington had spent her earliest years in New Jersey before moving to Pasadena as a teenager, where she met and befriended Wally

Hedrick, among other young artists. She attends CSFA from 1949 to 1955, studying under Elmer Bischoff, Edward Corbett, David Park, Hassel Smith, and Clyfford Still, and developing a gestural, landscape-based mode of abstraction. Finding few receptive outlets for exhibiting her work locally, in 1954 she cofounds Six Gallery with Hedrick and others. She leaves San Francisco in 1957 and travels for two years throughout Southeast Asia and India, spending ten months in Japan, where she studies Japanese and Chinese calligraphy. Back in San Francisco, she sets out to combine her training in calligraphy with an image-based approach to abstraction, as she will recall:

I became very interested in drawing from nature but not representationally. In San Francisco near the ocean, the trees are all bent in a certain direction and the grasses and things from the wind and the constant of the battering of the wind against the coast. You have this—all of these elements in nature . . . that lent themselves to linear interpretation, let's say. Now, I built up forms during this time with pen and ink, but the forms were always made up of many, many, many pen-and-ink strokes. In other words, these things were built, and I was working only in black and white.

1959

1959 • David McManaway (1927–2010) moves to Dallas, Texas, after attending the University of Arkansas in Fayetteville, where he had been introduced to historical Surrealism in his art classes and exposed to the art of Marcel Duchamp, which proves epiphanic: McManaway is enamored with the idea of creating a new context for ordinary objects. In Texas he returns to what was one of his favorite pastimes in his native Chicago and walks the streets of the older, less pristine neighborhoods of East Dallas, filling his pockets with things like flattened run-over cans, discarded toys, buttons, and pins. He combines his found objects and transforms them into constructions on boards or arrangements made from boxes, display cases, or doors. As McManaway will later explain, "People are always trying to take my work too literally, to list the things that are nothing more than ingredients of my pieces. . . . It's like gestalt: the whole is always more than the sum of its parts. Most people never go beyond that list of objects to deal with the content, the meaning those objects assume in their new context."

McManaway's work is recognized shortly after his move to Dallas, and his art is included in two exhibitions at the Dallas Museum of Fine Arts in 1959. As a part-time preparator at the newly formed Dallas Museum for Contemporary Arts, he meets the dynamic curator Douglas MacAgy, who will organize the first major museum exhibition of René Magritte's work, in 1960, and an early major survey of American Pop art in 1961. Through the 1960s, MacAgy also plans exhibitions of Texas artists, putting them in broader contexts, and employs a number of them at the museum, making the ultimately short-lived institution an artist gathering place. McManaway's work is included in the museum's presentation of *The Art of Assemblage*, the 1961 Museum of Modern Art exhibition that also travels to the San Francisco Museum of Art, situating his work in dialogue with national and international artists.

January 6, 1959 • Ed Emshwiller (1925–1990) wins the Creative Film Foundation's annual Award of Exceptional Merit for *Dance Chromatic* (1959), in which the filmmaker combines abstract animation with live-action footage of a young ballet dancer. In its fusion of "external" reality and nonobjective phenomena, the film establishes a pattern for Emshwiller. As he later puts it, "I like to deal in my work with various states of consciousness, often involving external 'reality' and subjective feelings, and it is in the various ways in which images meet one another, as in poetry, that provide many of the 'truths' that I find most interesting." Winning the award helps propel Emshwiller's shift from abstract painting to film.

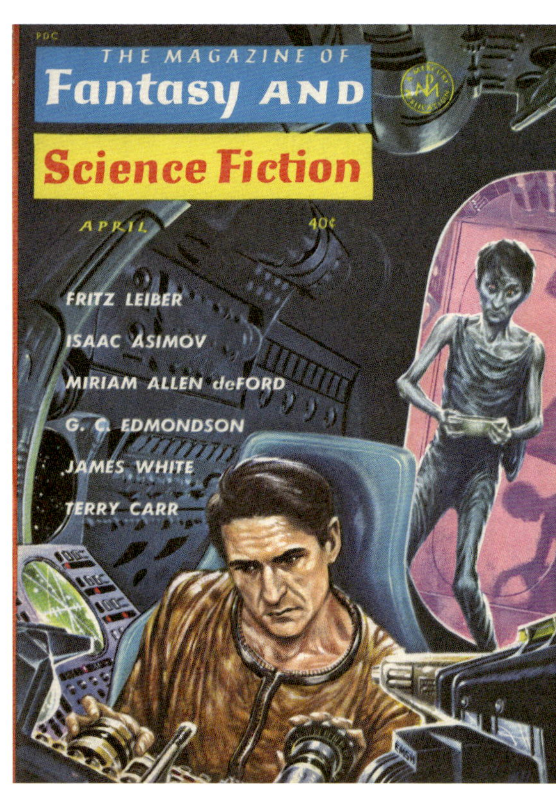

Cover of *The Magazine of Fantasy and Science Fiction*, April 1963, with Ed Emshwiller's drawing of figures modeled on Jonas and Adolfas Mekas

After returning from combat in World War II, Emshwiller had studied painting at the University of Michigan and the École des Beaux-Arts in Paris.

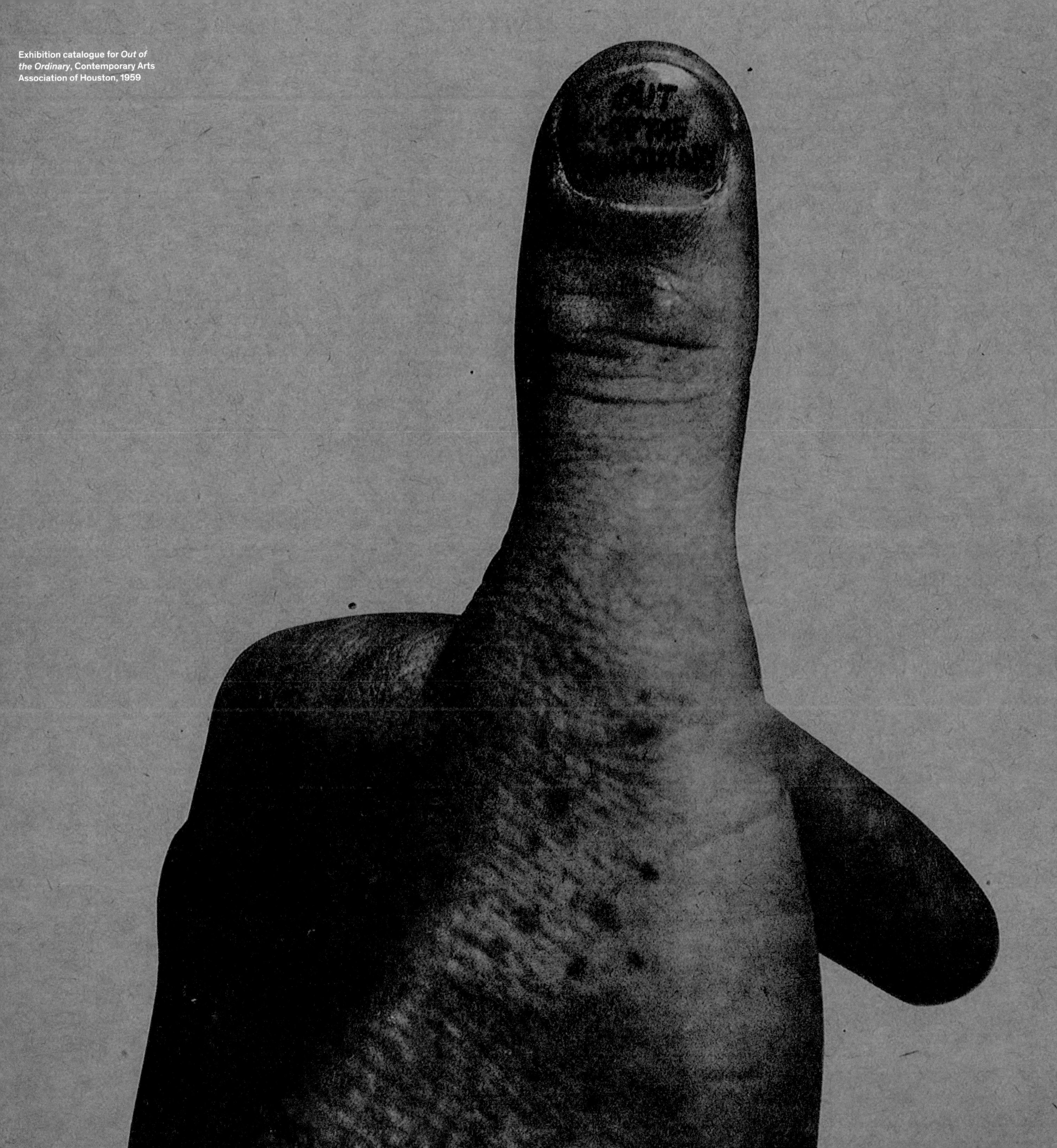

Exhibition catalogue for *Out of the Ordinary*, Contemporary Arts Association of Houston, 1959

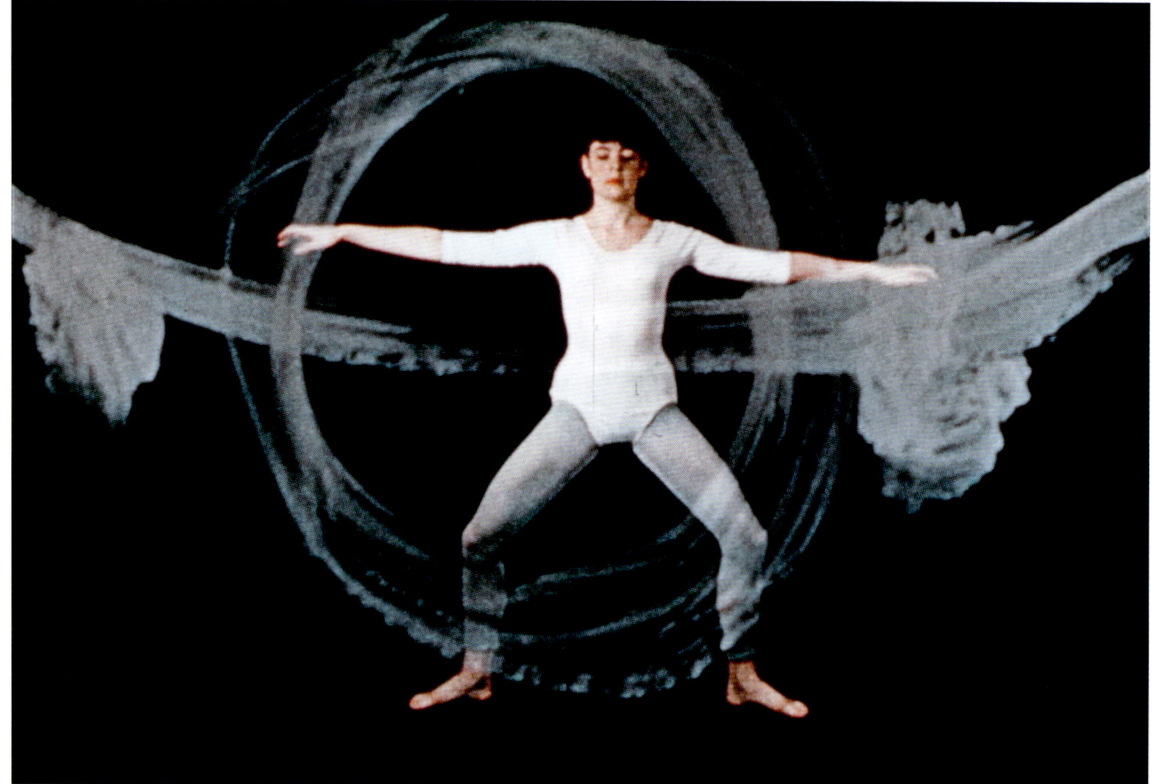

Ed Emshwiller, *Dance Chromatic*, 1959. 16mm film, color, sound; 7 min.

In the early 1950s, he and his wife, Carol, moved to New York, where he works in commercial illustration, specializing in covers for science-fiction magazines including *Galaxy* and *Fantasy and Science Fiction*. Emshwiller soon gains a reputation as a talented and prolific illustrator, winning the highest prize in science fiction, a Hugo, in 1953. He will later be inducted into the Science Fiction Hall of Fame. The income from his illustrations allows him to pursue a modestly successful career as an abstract painter and, later, filmmaker. During this time, Emshwiller joins Cinema 16, a film society run by Amos Vogel, who has built a large and loyal audience for avant-garde shorts and documentaries. With the Emshwillers' 1952 move to the suburban planned community of Levittown, New York, the screenings at Cinema 16 provide the artist with an ongoing connection to the downtown arts scene. He is especially drawn to several documentaries depicting the work processes of Abstract Expressionist painters. Through his initial forays making films of his own illustration process, he comes to recognize a link between the "action" of making abstract paintings and the motion of abstract animations.

January 8–February 8, 1959 • In her first public showing, Jean Conner (b. 1933) exhibits her work alongside her husband, Bruce Conner, in an untitled group exhibition at Spatsa Gallery.

The daughter of a University of Nebraska professor and raised in Lincoln, Jean had been an avid artist from a young age, and she enrolls at the university to study art, where she meets Bruce. The couple move to Boulder—first Jean, followed later by Bruce—where they found the Experimental Cinema Group and, in 1957, Jean completes her master of fine arts. Back in Lincoln, the couple wed on September 1, then fly to San Francisco the same day, beckoned by the diverse and accepting art scene and by Bruce's high school friend Michael McClure. The newlyweds initially stay with McClure and his wife, Joanna, at Painterland.

Although Jean Conner's art had included lush paintings in a Symbolist mode, her work would soon be dominated by her prolific activity in collage. Northern California in the 1950s and '60s was steeped in assemblage art; materially it sprang from the wealth of discarded materials on the street, the relative poverty of the artists, and the lack of any formal network of commercial galleries. These circumstances were enhanced by a genuine love of vernacular objects, as well as by an interest in the absurd, Dada, and the esoteric. The artists made work for each other using the stuff at hand. Jean Conner's work with magazine-sourced collage began almost upon her arrival in San Francisco, and she approached it as assemblage made two-dimensional, with meaning achieved through an accumulation of associations among magazine pages, found photos, and advertisements. As she will recall:

Bruce and I were both making collages then, but it's hard to remember exactly what they were. I do remember that we were using the wrong kind of glue at the beginning. Not rubber cement, because we knew that wasn't good, but I think we used Duco Cement, which might have been worse! Eventually we started using YES! Glue, which was something that I think Jess Collins recommended. My collages were made mostly from the ladies' magazines that they had during that time, *Ladies Home Journal*, *McCall's*, *Good Housekeeping*. Sometimes I got a *LIFE* magazine from somebody, although I'm not sure *LIFE* had many color pictures at that time. But the ladies' magazines did. I subscribed to them. My mother always had all the magazines, so I just kept on going with the subscriptions.

In her collages Conner addresses male/female relations, representations of the body, gender expectations, the perilous state of the environment, and psychic phenomena, with equal parts dry wit and a Surrealist sense of imagery and space.

January 27, 1959 • Jordan Belson (1926–2011) collaborates with electronic composer Henry Jacobs on the last documented date of the Vortex Concerts. Vortex, which began in 1957, was described by Belson as "a series of electronic music concerts illuminated by various visual effects." The collaborators stage the performances using the high-tech audiovisual equipment and concave screen at San Francisco's Morrison Planetarium, and the concerts will later be recognized as precursors to the light shows and expanded cinema of the 1960s.

Born in Chicago, Belson had studied fine arts at the California School of Fine Art and the University of California, Berkeley, where his friend circle included the artist, filmmaker, and musicologist Harry Smith. Belson's first exposure to experimental films came in 1947, when he attended the San Francisco Museum of Art's influential Art in Cinema film series. The series, run by Frank Stauffacher, cultivates audiences for prewar and contemporary avant-garde film. An abstract painter in the nonobjective mode, Belson is impressed by the animated films of Oskar Fischinger, Norman McLaren, and Hans Richter. Art in Cinema screens Belson's first abstract film, *Transmutations*, in October 1947, after which he develops an animation method that involves painting and photographing scrolls. His intellectual development during this period reflects larger cultural currents; he lives in North Beach, ground

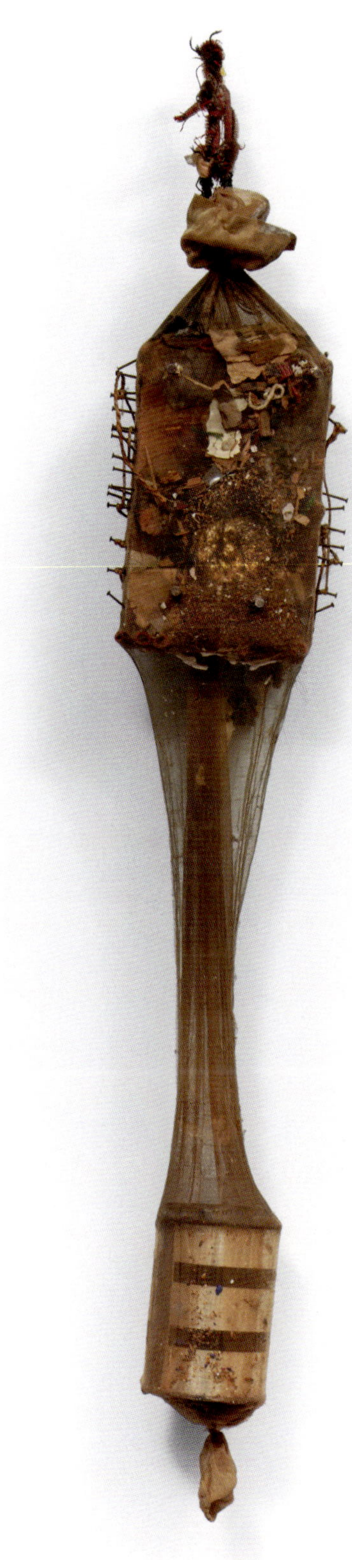

Bruce Conner, *RAT PURSE*, 1959. Nylon, wax, gold leaf, tin can, fur, sequins, string, and cardboard box, 37 × 6 × 7 in. (94 × 15.2 × 17.8 cm). Los Angeles County Museum of Art; purchase, with funds provided by the Modern and Contemporary Art Council and the Modern and Contemporary Art Council Acquisitions Endowment and Gift of the Tomeo Family and Michael Kohn Gallery

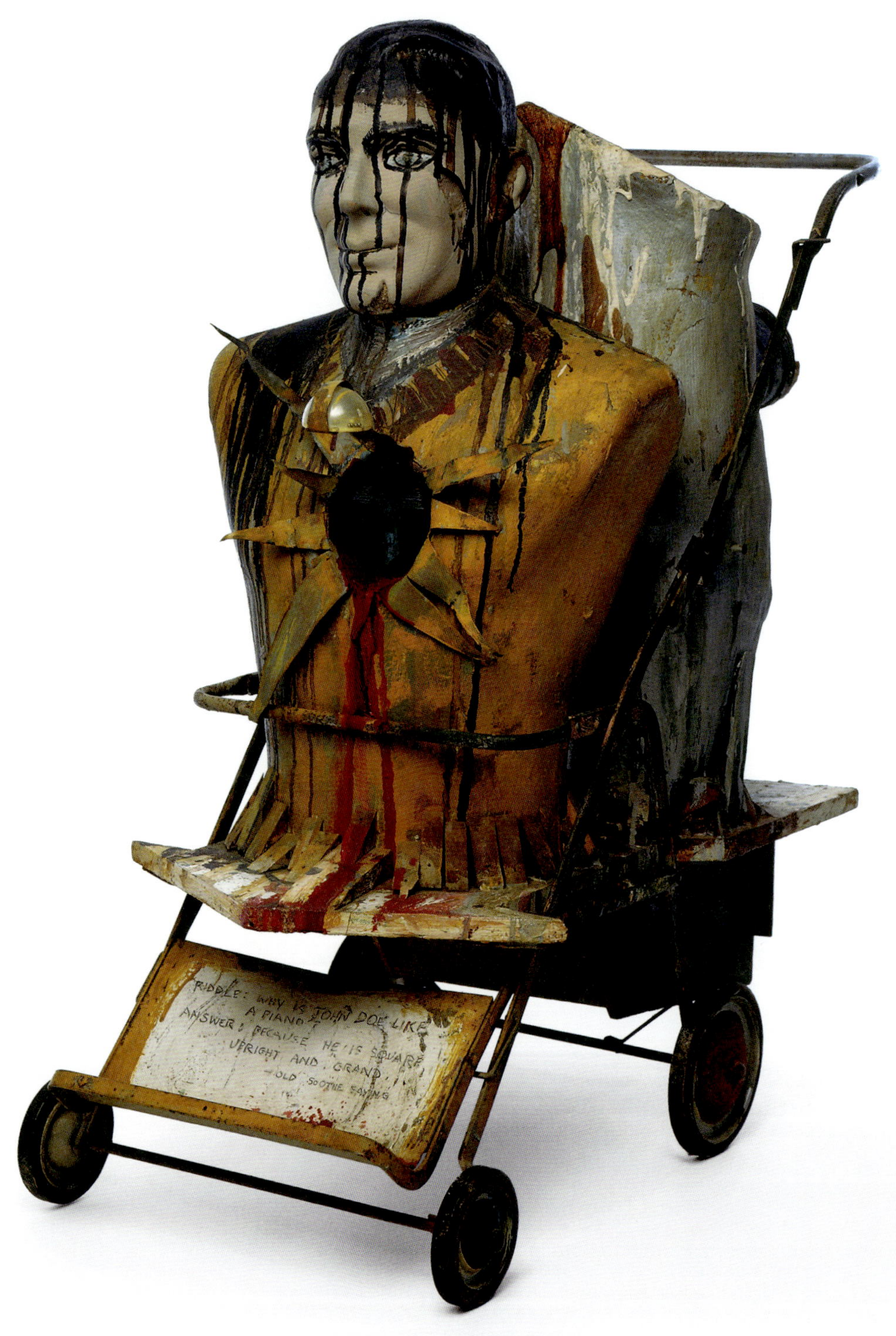

Edward Kienholz, *John Doe*, 1959. Oil, metallic paint, resin, plaster, and graphite on mannequin parts with wood, metal, plastic, paper, rubber, and stroller, 39 ½ × 19 × 31 ¼ in. (100.3 × 48.3 × 79.4 cm). The Menil Collection, Houston

Poster for Vortex Concerts, Series 5, Morrison Planetarium, San Francisco, 1959

zero for the emergent Beat counterculture. The moody transcendentalism of the Beats finds expression in films such as Christopher MacLaine's *The End* (1953), for which Belson serves as cameraman, and the parodic *Odds & Ends* (1959) by Belson's then partner, Jane (later Jane Conger Belson Shimané). More important to Belson's development is the countercultural embrace of Mahayana and Vajrayana Buddhism, and a burgeoning sense that films can represent and induce the egoless transcendental states of mysticism.

Belson will incorporate interference pattern imagery similar to that used in the Vortex Concerts, as well as a soundtrack made with Jacobs, into his 1961 film, *Allure*, in which multicolored light patterns radiate, twist, flicker, and explode against a black field.

***

March 1959 • The library at the Cooper Union School of Art hosts *Figure Drawings*, the first New York solo exhibition of artwork by Claes Oldenburg (1929–2022). He had previously shown his work in Chicago, displaying a group of drawings that portray artist-model Patty Mucha, his future wife.

Born in Stockholm, Sweden, Oldenburg had relocated to Chicago in 1936, when his diplomat father began serving as consul general of Sweden. Demonstrating a predilection for fantasy, as a child Oldenburg imagines life in elaborate detail in a place he calls Neubern, a fictional island nation between Africa and South America. Later, scholar Barbara Rose will note that Oldenburg emulates the style of newspapers and advertisements in the pages of his Neubern notebooks. He will continue this practice into the 1960s, creating collages from found images and texts that he then uses as the basis for erotic drawings—a technique familiar to Surrealists like Joan Miró.

In 1950 Oldenburg earns a bachelor of arts from Yale University, having focused on literature and art, and returns to Chicago to work at City News Bureau, a cooperative news agency. He enrolls in classes at the School of the Art Institute of Chicago (SAIC) from 1952 to 1954 and is one of the youngest artists to display work in *Exhibition Momentum*. Inaugurated in 1948, the show is a response to SAIC's refusal to include undergraduate artwork in its annual exhibition *Artists of Chicago and Vicinity*. Miyoko Ito, Nancy Spero, and H. C. Westermann participate alongside Oldenburg, whose work captures "both Chicago imagery and Surrealism in his ability to fuse fantasy and irony into large monuments of incongruity," according to curator Peter Selz.

Invitation by Claes Oldenburg for *Claes Oldenburg: Drawings, Sculptures, Poems*, Judson Gallery, New York, 1959

Shortly after moving from Chicago to New York in 1956, Oldenburg begins shelving books at the Cooper Union School of Art library, immersing himself in art of the past and developing an interest in fetishism and psychoanalytic writing, which he thinks of as poetry for artists. He also meets Allan Kaprow, who the year prior had coined the term *happening* to describe a new participatory art form in his iconic essay "The Legacy of Jackson Pollock." Through Kaprow, Oldenburg meets Lucas Samaras, with whom he will soon collaborate. Although New York remains dominated by the legacy of Abstract Expressionism, Oldenburg continues to work figuratively, and his solo exhibition at the Cooper Union leads to a more public New York debut: *Drawings, Sculptures, Poems* runs from May 22 to June 10 at Judson Gallery, housed in a basement room of Judson Church at 239 Thompson Street, Greenwich Village.

***

1959 • After spending several years in Miami, Paul Thek (1933–1988) returns to settle in New York and changes his name from George to Paul. Thek had previously attended classes at the Art Students League of New York and Pratt Institute before enrolling at the Cooper Union School of Art and graduating in 1954. Living in Manhattan, he eventually becomes friends with other young artists, including Eva Hesse, Joseph Raffaele, and Peter Hujar, who will become his lover. Thek also befriends writers Gene Swenson and Susan Sontag, the latter of whom with which Thek has a particularly fruitful back-and-forth; the writer will dedicate her influential 1966 book *Against Interpretation* to him.

Born into what he will later describe as an unhappy family in Brooklyn, New York, Thek had been raised Catholic and attended Catholic school, developing a complicated relationship with the religion. The *Technological Reliquaries* series (1964–67) as well as *The Tomb* (1967) and other installations he describes as "Processions" are rife with Catholic references, revealing an ambivalence toward the religion that he will later characterize as "agnostic," yet he returns to Catholicism throughout his life. In his final years, he tries to join the order of the Carthusians in Vermont, but they are unable to care for him following his HIV diagnosis.

———

April 1959 • Jay DeFeo and Wallace Berman collaborate on a group of photographs in her studio in which DeFeo presents herself as her own creation, both the source of the images she makes and part of them (p. 23, fig. 1). These images—with crosshatch overlays and other embellishments by Berman—are nearly Symbolist in their expression of a creative spirit embodied in human form.

———

May 1, 1959 • Kay Sekimachi (b. 1926) is profiled in *Craft Horizons* magazine for her mastery of double weaving. Sekimachi had taken two summer courses with the German American weaver Trude Guermonprez at the California College of Arts and Crafts (CCAC) in 1954–55, later teaching as a substitute for her instructor at the Haystack Mountain School of Crafts in Deer Isle, Maine. Sekimachi learns to approach weaving as an experimental enterprise in the tradition of the Bauhaus, paying special attention to the particular textural and structural qualities of fibers. "I use traditional tapestry techniques modified for my own personal needs," she tells *Craft Horizons*. "In each tapestry I try to achieve a harmonious integration of design, material, and technique." Sekimachi will recognize certain resonances of Japanese aesthetics in her practice much later; she will make her first visit to Japan in 1972 with a grant from the National Endowment for the Arts.

Born to Japanese immigrants in San Francisco's Japantown, Sekimachi had been a teenager when her family was forcibly relocated by the US government following the outbreak of World War II, first to the incarceration camp at Tanforan Assembly Center in San Bruno, California, and then to Topaz, Utah. In the camps, Sekimachi takes art classes with the painter Chiura Obata and befriends Miné Obata, another Bay Area *nikkei* artist. After graduating from high school in Topaz, Sekimachi works for a year before enrolling part-time at CCAC in Oakland in 1946 to study printmaking. In 1949 she Continued on page 26

"WHAT HAPPENS IN PUBLIC": FEMINIST CONCEPTIONS OF THE EROTIC BODY IN 1960S ART

RACHEL MIDDLEMAN

In her widely read book *The Second Sex*, first published in the United States in 1953, Simone de Beauvoir wrote: "What peculiarly signalizes the situation of woman is that she—a free and autonomous being like all human creatures—nevertheless finds herself living in a world where men compel her to assume the status of the Other. They propose to stabilize her as object."[1] Perhaps nowhere was Beauvoir's point more evident, quite literally, than in the fine arts, where sexual discrimination hindered women from becoming professional artists while the vaunted tradition of the female nude objectified them. As the fight for women's equality during the 1960s ignited questions about the construction, reinforcement, and policing of gender roles within American society, women artists began to explore self-representation and the body to visualize female subjectivity and sexuality on their own terms. A number of these artists engaged with surrealist sensibilities to represent sexuality and desire as modes of female autonomy beyond restrictive binary definitions, in resistance to sexism and despite systemic obstacles and threats to their careers. The elasticity of the word *surreal* during this period encompassed a broad set of aesthetic characteristics whose oppositional approaches could be adapted by these artists in rebellion against both social and artistic conventions.[2]

In the late 1950s, Jay DeFeo was in the midst of creating abstract paintings, photocollages, drawings, and *The Rose* (1958–66), a work that itself defies categorization. In two surviving collages from 1958, *Blossom* and *Applaud the Black Fact*, she incorporated cutouts of nude women from magazines into phantasmagorical compositions. In 1959, she collaborated with Wallace Berman on a series of photographs of herself posing in her San Francisco studio.[3] In one sequence, she playfully adorns her nude body with objects such as a hat, beaded necklace, and Christmas tinsel. Other photographs create a visual dialogue between her body and her artwork. In one (fig. 1), she stands in front of *The Eyes* (1958; p. 4), a precise graphite drawing of two symmetrical eyes cut through with vertical and radiating lines.[4] Even when depicting recognizable things in works such as *The Eyes*, DeFeo did not consider her imagery to be representational and often heightened the abstract and mysterious qualities of everyday things.[5] Likewise, the photograph in which the drawing becomes a winged extension of her figure evokes symbolic meaning, suggesting her artistic vision is situated in an erotic body and yet not limited by it. Shortly after their session, Berman showed the photographs at his home in a one-day exhibition for invited guests. The pair's early and relatively private engagement with eroticism anticipated the more public dismantling of sexual taboos in the coming decade.[6]

In New York, a number of women artists gained visibility in the 1960s for their "erotic art," as any

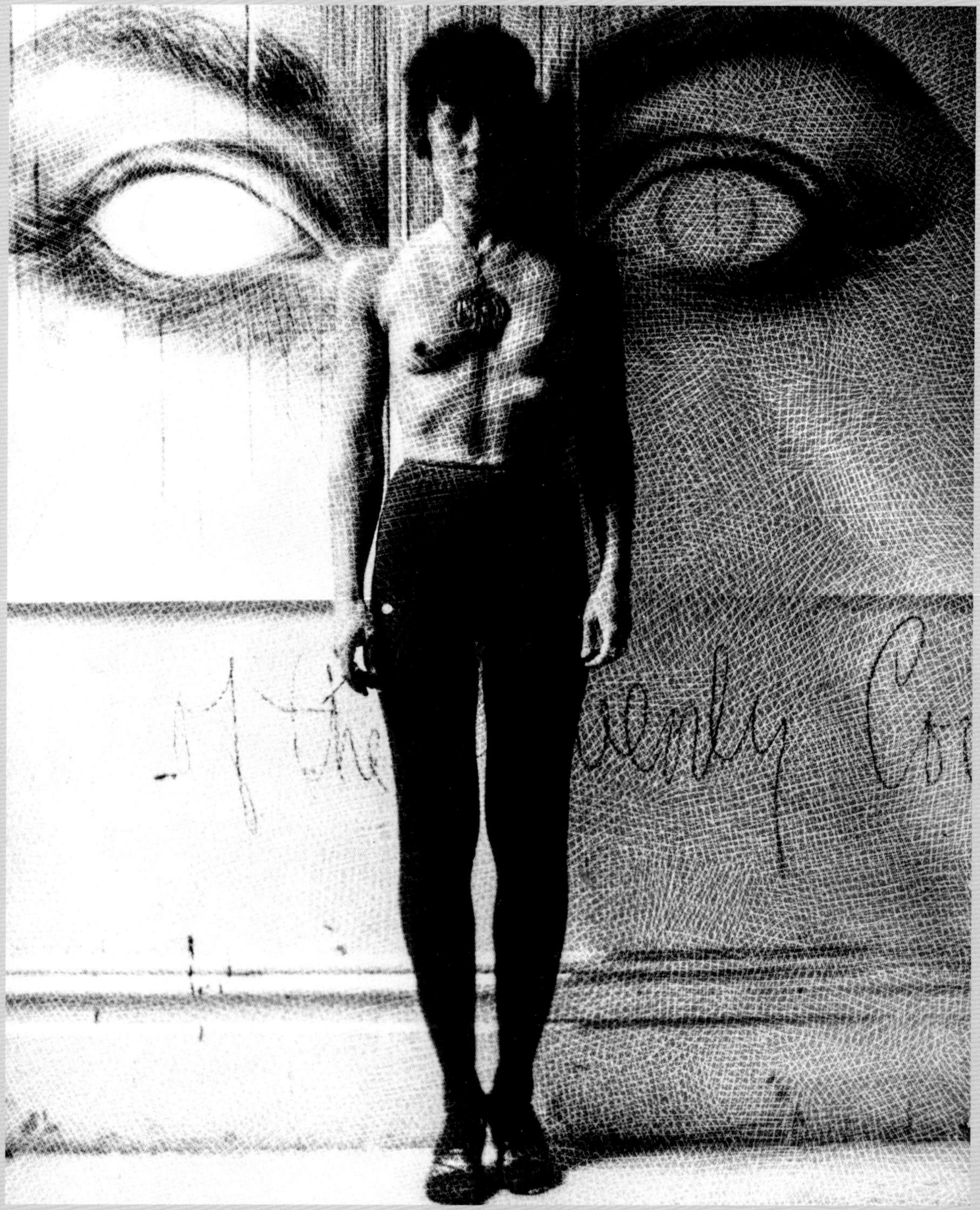

Esquire: "This self-portrait is not true any longer for before the paint is dry the very act of having made the picture has already altered me."[8] She reflects this constant state of change through the turmoil of bodies crowding her image. In later interviews, Steckel revealed that *The Big Rip-Up* was about the separation from her child and the dissolution of her romantic relationship, qualifying the work as a profound statement on eroticism, motherhood, and grief.

In February 1965, Steckel participated in *Contemporary Erotica*, a show of artists with diverse stylistic approaches to the figure, including Salvador Dalí, Marisol, Tom Wesselmann, Martha Edelheit, and many others.[9] While such erotic-art exhibitions attracted publicity and visitors, critics were generally skeptical. In *Artforum*'s May 1965 issue, Barbara Rose criticized the explicit and "unappealing" treatment of the nude in recent art, writing that there was "something about the new erotic art, which, for all its frankness, strikes one as . . . essentially perverse, either because of the odd ways bodies are coupled or the unpleasant quality flesh takes on."[10] She saw this approach as a reflection of the broader social "confusions about the nature of eroticism, sexuality, perversion, pornography and obscenity."[11] Her disapproval exposes a deep anxiety about the growing instabilities of these categories while also indicating the inadequacy of formalist approaches to account for work that directly addressed the subjectivity of desire.

Martha Edelheit's explicit nude paintings confronted social taboos that discouraged women

Fig. 1. Wallace Berman and Jay DeFeo, *Untitled*, 1959. Gelatin silver print mounted on board, 5 × 3 ⅞ in. (12.7 × 9.8 cm)

artwork containing sexual content was termed at the time. This work took many forms, across media, that would soon come to be regarded as feminist: reimagining the Western tradition of the nude, subverting images of women in pop culture, representing bodies with explicit figuration or through biomorphic abstraction, and incorporating self-images to create new visual forms of sexual expression.[7] Anita Steckel, an artist known for her satirical use of the politically charged medium of photomontage, enlarged a photograph of herself as a young woman for the basis of *The Big Rip-Up* (1964; p. 124). Steckel's drawings on the reproduction's surface complicate the notion of a self-portrait as a mimetic representation of outward appearance and address sexuality as central to her identity. The colorful tendrils painted down the right side of her face and below her nose suggest both the inner psyche and visceral tears, splitting the grainy photographic surface of her skin. Layered nudes and faces weave through and surround her, intertwining like ambiguous memories. When the piece was exhibited in a group exhibition of self-portraits in January 1965, she told

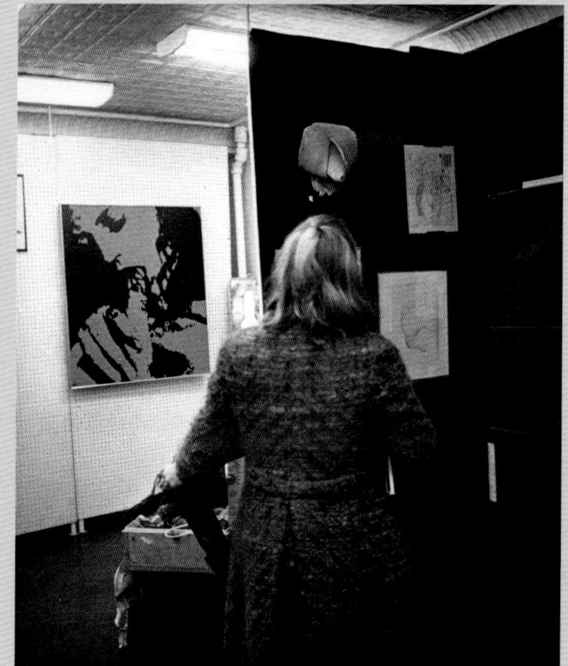

Fig.2. *Hetero Is*, New York City Arts Theater Association Gallery, New York, 1967, with Bob Stanley's *Going Down* (1966) and Hannah Wilke's *Untitled* (1966)

from dealing with sexual themes. Her erotic figuration developed alongside her abstract painting constructions and her participation in happenings, in the milieu of artists like Carolee Schneemann, who fearlessly explored the erotic and creative possibilities of incorporating her own body into performances and film. Edelheit's solo exhibition at New York's Byron Gallery in April 1966 featured erotic watercolors, large-scale oil paintings of multiple nudes, and assemblages made from the limbs of mannequins (p. 174).[12] In the *East Village Other*, feminist critic and avant-garde artist Lil Picard described the show: "Small sculptures with a personal touch, glittering with metallic paper-coverings, masks, feet, legs, hands are painted and studded with bric-a-brac, in surrealistic, poetic manner . . . studies for the large works and watercolors show sadomaso details and disclose a sex-dream-world fantasy in which this young and very talented artist seems to be involved."[13] In *Flesh Wall—Female* (1965; pp. 152–53), the artist's table in the foreground denotes the studio space and emphasizes the flatness of the "wallpaper" of nudes. Against this field of colorful naked bodies hangs a mirror reflecting the artist herself in the act of painting. This portrait of the artist at work shattered conventions about appropriate subject matter for a woman artist. While Picard praised the exhibition in the underground press, decades later Edelheit would recall how *New York Times* critic John Canaday spent hours at her show only to declare, "I cannot review this obscene woman!"[14] This slippage between the artist and her work meant the loss of wider recognition.

While "erotic art" was often defined in terms of figuration and narrative, Lucy Lippard advocated for the "abstractly sensuous object" in her writings on what she termed "eccentric abstraction."[15] This was also title of the group exhibition she organized of works with "indirect affinities with the incongruity and often sexual content of Surrealism," which opened in September 1966.[16] Arguing that "the best erotica being made today is abstract to a greater or lesser degree, concentrating on a purity of sensation which in turn engenders a stronger response," she noted that "the erotic is always particular" and those particularities are subjective.[17] In one article,

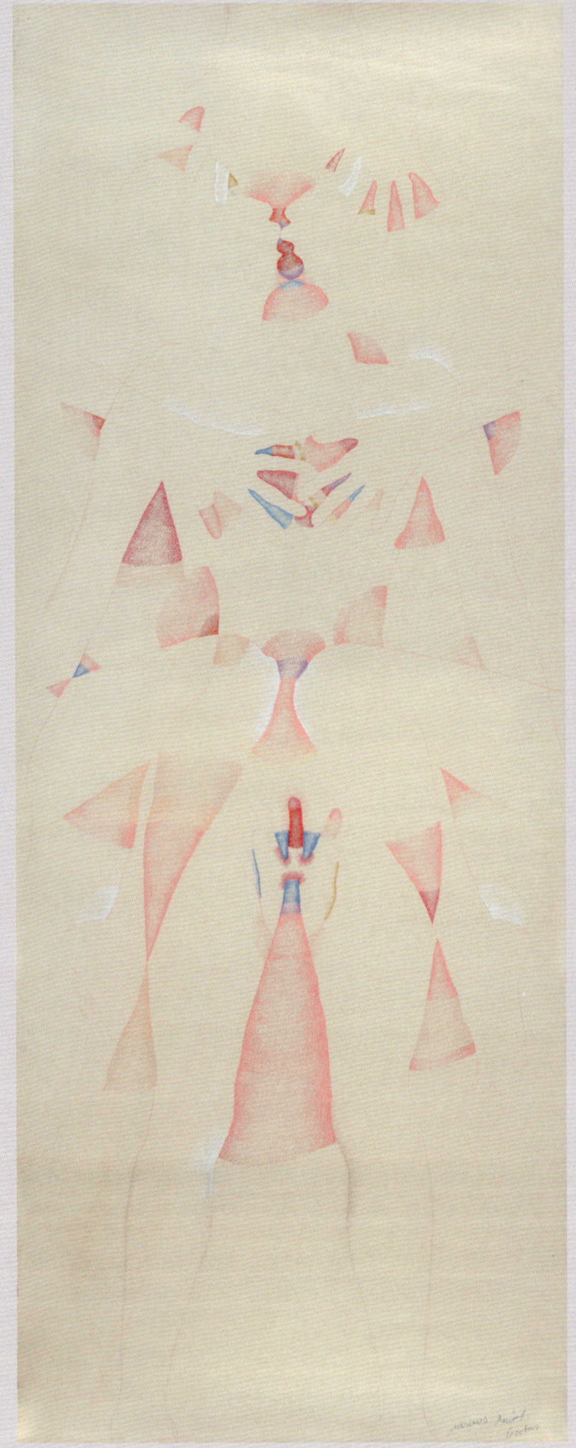

Fig. 4. Marisol, *Love*, 1966. Colored pencil on paper, 73 ⅞ × 27 ¾ in. (187.6 × 70.5 cm)

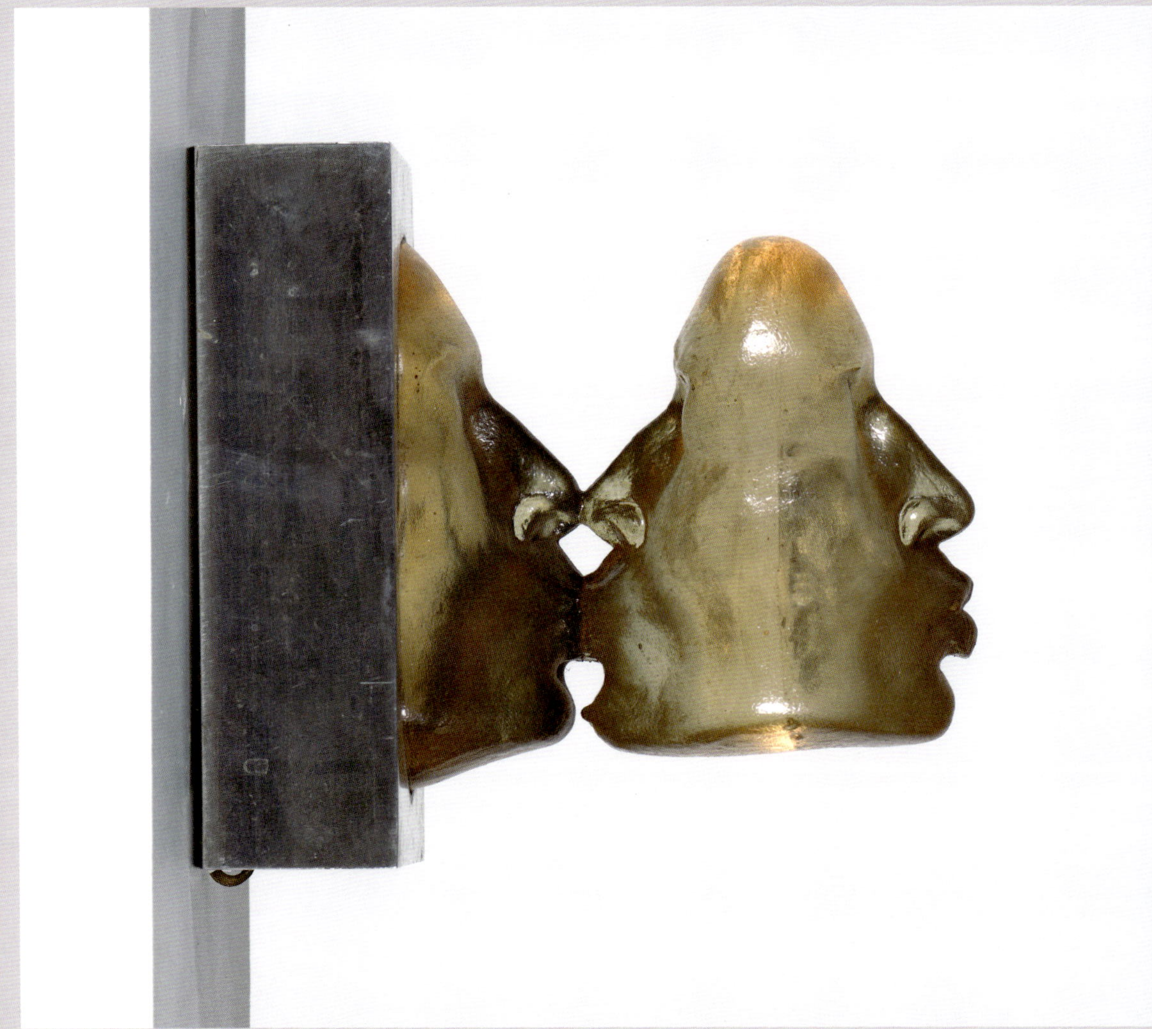

Fig. 3. Marisol, *Kiss*, 1964. Cast polyester, metal, and lighting, 9 ¼ × 6 ⅛ × 10 in. (23.5 × 15.4 × 25.4 cm)

she referenced a hand-built ceramic sculpture by Hannah Wilke that had been exhibited alongside more figurative work in the erotic-art exhibition *Hetero Is* (1967; fig. 2). Wilke explored the erotic potential of biomorphic abstraction in works like this and *Teasel Cushion* (1967; p. 213), in which a pink terra-cotta sculpture suggestive of labial and floral folds rests on a bed of wiry plastic material reminiscent of pubic hair. The process of making the work can be seen in the layers of clay, this evidence of the material's mutability operating as a

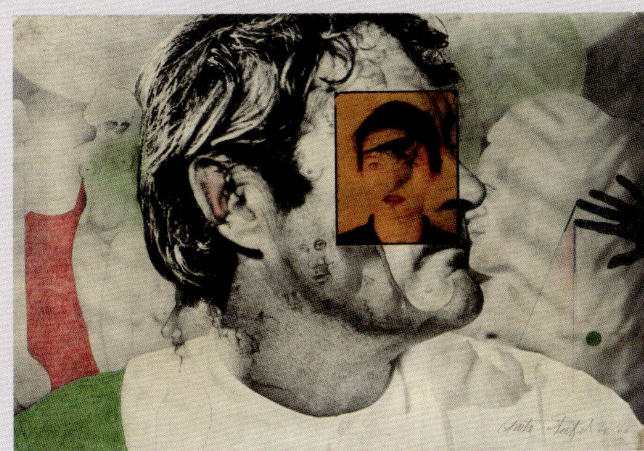

Fig. 5. Anita Steckel, *Timothy Leary*, 1964–68, from the series *Multiple Image* (1964–68). Pencil and paint on print, 28 ¼ × 40 ½ in. (71.8 × 102.9 cm)

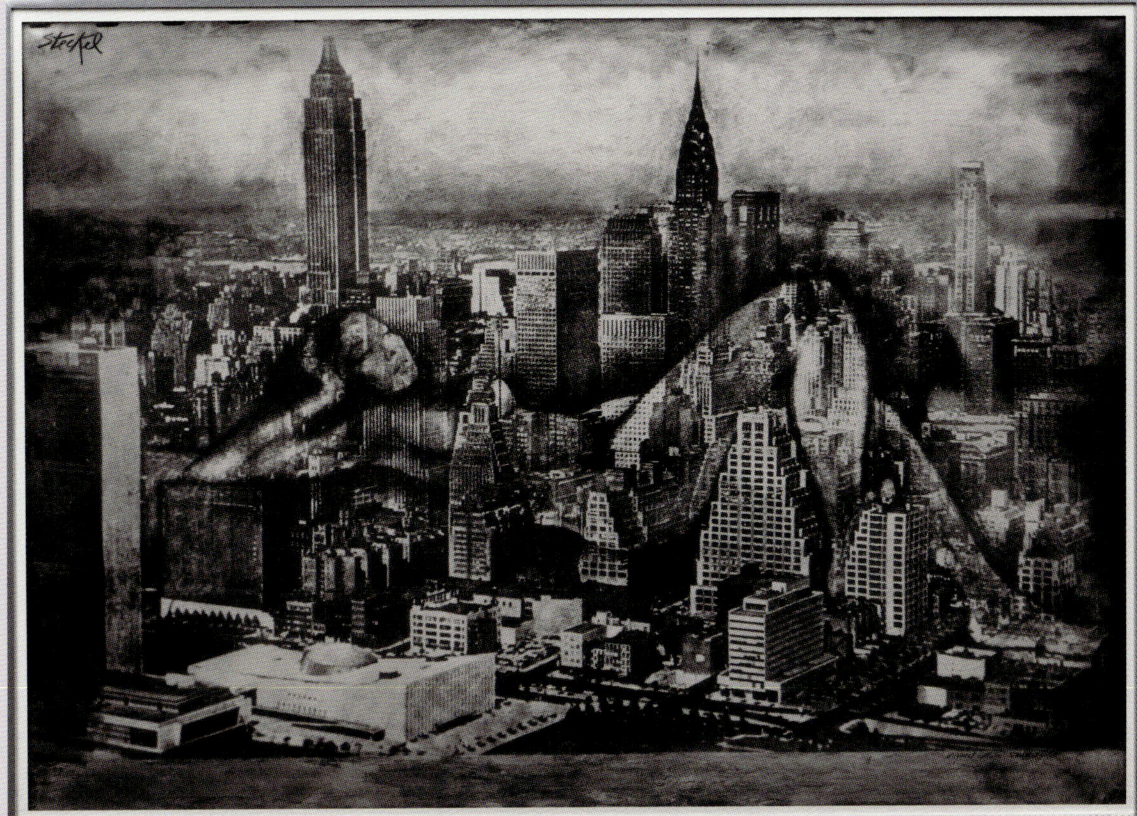

Fig. 6. Anita Steckel, *My Town*, c. 1969–74, from the series *Giant Women on New York* (c. 1969–74). Gelatin silver print, 37 × 49 in. (94 × 124.5 cm)

visual metaphor for the unfixity of sexuality.[18] In a 1966 interview, Wilke discussed her similar ceramic boxes as the physical representation of the "whole female experience of fulfillment," and relayed her concerns about keeping her teaching job if she "got the wrong sort of publicity."[19]

The trend of erotic-art exhibitions arguably reached its peak in October 1966 with Sidney Janis's *Erotic Art '66*.[20] Marisol, the only woman included in the show, often used multiple copies of her own image in her artwork, denaturalizing the facade of appearance and, by extension, social norms of femininity and its display.[21] Her contributions to *Erotic Art '66* included the illuminated sculpture *Kiss* (fig. 3). *Newsweek*'s review of the show is notable both for Marisol's articulation of the redemptive potential of the eroticism in her art as well as the reviewer's focus on her physical appearance and perceived femininity, typical for the era: "'I have always done erotic art,' says the dark-haired, wide-eyed, whisper-voiced Marisol, who is exhibiting 'Kiss,' a plastic sculpture in which both kissers are Marisol. 'Erotic art is a way out from war and bombing,' adds the Venezuelan artist. 'It's a good moral idea to distract people from destroying themselves.'"[22] Marisol's drawing *Love* (fig. 4), also in the exhibition, works against binary notions of gender and sexuality with its multiplicity of overlapping traced outlines of limbs and fingers. The simultaneous indexing and abstraction of her body registers a deep ambiguity in the realm of figurative representation and exemplifies the thread of "surrealist and dream imagery" that Grace Glueck had noted in Marisol's work.[23]

In 1969, Steckel again exhibited her self-portrait *The Big Rip-Up* in a solo exhibition.[24] Reviews of her show noted her "surrealistic" collages and how she "pencils erotic fantasies into and against the chemical greys of found-object photographs."[25] Among other works on view were early versions from her series *Giant Women on New York* (c. 1969–74), outsize nudes painted into the cityscape, and *Multiple Image* (1964–69), in which she added figures to mass-market posters, some of which, like *Timothy Leary* (fig. 5), incorporated photographs of herself among the sexual imagery. The general amusement in the reception of Steckel's surreal erotic work in the New York artworld, however, was not enough to assuage conservative attitudes and threats of censorship. When preparing for her next exhibition, at Rockland Community College in Suffern, New York, Steckel received a call from a faculty member warning not to bring any sexual art if she wanted to be considered for a teaching position, something she desperately needed to support herself. Instead of conforming, Steckel defended her artistic freedom and publicly declared her work as feminist. In response to explicit nudes and phallic symbolism in the exhibition, *The Feminist Art of Sexual Politics* (1972), a local politician accused her of obscenity and attempted, unsuccessfully, to close the show.[26] This experience was pivotal for Steckel in two significant ways. First, she transformed her *Giant Women* images into self-portraits (fig. 6). In doing so, she, like many women creating erotic art, used her own image to establish her position and her right to exist as both the artist and the subject of her work. Second, in 1973, she founded the group Fight Censorship, which included Edelheit and Wilke as well as artists Judith Bernstein, Louise Bourgeois, Eunice Golden, Joan Glueckman, Juanita McNeely, Barbara Nessim, Joan Semmel, and Anne Sharp to advocate for sexual art made by women artists, whether it included un-idealized nudity, abstract sexual forms, explicit imagery, or everyday materials. At their first meeting, Bourgeois related to the group: "I have found many times men are very complimentary in private. They will come and say, 'It was wonderful.' But in public—nothing. In other words, this is where the prejudice comes in: They appreciate your work, and they have nothing against you personally, but they will not come out and say it. And when you become a professional, this is what counts. What happens in public."[27]

NOTES
1   Simone de Beauvoir, *The Second Sex*, trans. and ed. H. M. Parshley (New York: Vintage Books, 1989; reprint of the 1953 ed. published by Knopf, New York; originally published Paris: Librairie Gallimard, 1949), xxxv.
2   On the reception of Surrealism in the United States in the 1960s, see Sandra Zalman, *Consuming Surrealism in American Culture: Dissident Modernism* (Farnham, UK: Ashgate, 2015). For an introduction to the feminist literature on women and Surrealism, see Anna Watz, "Feminist Encounters with Surrealism: Revisiting the Formative Critiques," in *The Routledge Companion to Surrealism*, ed. Kirsten Storm (New York: Routledge, 2023), 339–47.
3   Marla Prather, "Forward: Beside *The Rose*: DeFeo's Work at the Whitney Museum," in Jane Green and Leah Levy, *Jay DeFeo and* The Rose (Berkeley: University of California Press; New York: Whitney Museum of American Art, 2003), xvii; xxi, n23. For an extended analysis of Berman and DeFeo's collaboration, see Elizabeth Ferrell, "Model Artist," *About* The Rose*: Creation and Community in Jay DeFeo's Circle* (New Haven, CT: Yale University Press, 2022), 31–75.
4   On the wall below the drawing is the partial inscription of a poem that inspired DeFeo by Philip Lamantia, a figure in the San Francisco counterculture who had worked among Surrealists in New York. In the 1940s, as a teenager, Lamantia was published in the

Surrealist magazine *View* and briefly worked at the publication. See Michael Duncan and Kristine McKenna, *Semina Culture: Wallace Berman and His Circle* (New York: D.A.P.; Santa Monica, CA: Santa Monica Museum of Art, 2005), 206–7. DeFeo wrote a stanza from the untitled poem on the back of the drawing: "Tell Him I have eyes only for Heaven / as I look to you / Queen mirror / of the heavenly court."

5   Jay DeFeo, oral history interview, June 3, 1975 and January 23, 1976. Archives of American Art, Smithsonian Institution, Washington, DC.

6   On the gendered dynamics of the public circulation and reception of the photographs, see Jason Goldman, "Concealed Exposures: Jay DeFeo, *The Rose*, and the Photographic Image," in "Open Secrets: Publicity, Privacy, and U.S. Artistic Practice in the Sixties" (PhD diss., University of Southern California, 2011), 49–123.

7   See Rachel Middleman, *Radical Eroticism: Women, Art, and Sex in the 1960s* (Oakland: University of California Press, 2018).

8   Anita Steckel, quoted in "How to Crystallize Basic Plastic Organic Unity: Seventeen Contemporary Artists Experiment with Self-Portraits and Explanations," *Esquire*, May 1965: 75. The article featured artists in the exhibition *65 Self-Portraits* at the Visual Arts Gallery, New York, January 8–29, 1965.

9   *Contemporary Erotica*, Van Bovenkamp Gallerie, New York, February 16–March 20, 1965.

10   Barbara Rose, "Filthy Pictures: Some Chapters in the History of Taste," *Artforum* 3, no. 8 (May 1965): 24, 22.

11   Ibid., 25.

12   *Martha Edelheit*, Byron Gallery, New York, April 12–May 7, 1966.

13   Lil Picard, "Voyeurama," *East Village Other*, May 1–15, 1966: 11.

14   Martha Edelheit, interview with the author, August 2, 2012.

15   Lucy R. Lippard, "Eros Presumptive," *The Hudson Review* 20, no. 1 (Spring 1967): 91.

16   Lucy R. Lippard, exh. pamphlet for *Eccentric Abstraction*, Fischbach Gallery, New York, September 20–October 8, 1966.

17   Lippard, "Eros Presumptive," 91.

18   This interpretation draws on David Getsy's argument for the "transgender capacity" of 1960s abstract sculpture in *Abstract Bodies: Sixties Sculpture in the Expanded Field of Gender* (New Haven, CT: Yale University Press, 2015).

19   Lillian Roxen, "Hannah Wilke: Ceramic Erotica," *Comment* [Sidney], August 1966: 9.

20   *Erotic Art '66*, Sidney Janis Gallery, New York, October 3–29, 1966.

21   Revisionist histories of Pop art have considered Marisol's uncanny casts of her own face as protofeminist parodies of feminine display and works of subversive feminine narcissism. Cécile Whiting, *A Taste for Pop: Pop Art, Gender, and Consumer Culture* (Cambridge, UK: Cambridge University Press, 1997), 189–93; and Kalliopi Minioudaki, "Pop Proto-Feminisms: Beyond the Paradox of the Woman Pop Artist," in *Seductive Subversion: Women Pop Artists, 1958–1968*, ed. Sid Sachs and Minioudaki (Philadelphia: University of the Arts; New York: Abbeville Press, 2010), 90–141.

22   "Eros in Polyester," *Newsweek*, October 10, 1966: 103.

23   Grace Glueck, "It's Not Pop, It's Not Op—It's Marisol," *New York Times*, March 7, 1965: SM34. It is very likely that Marisol traced herself for this drawing, which resembles the untitled series of drawings from 1960–65 that she exhibited at Sidney Janis Gallery in 1966 and are referenced in Roberta Bernstein, "Marisol's Self-Portraits: The Dream and the Dreamer," *Arts Magazine* 59 (March 1985): 88. Cathleen Chaffee cites a notebook in which Marisol wrote that she began tracing her body in Paris, on a trip that dates to 1960, in "Hereafter, Marisol," *Marisol: A Retrospective*, ed. Chaffee (Buffalo, NY: Buffalo AKG Art Museum and DelMonico Books, 2023), 39.

24   *Anita Steckel*, Kozmopolitan Gallery, New York, March 1–29, 1969.

25   "Scenes [Anita Steckel]," *Village Voice*, February 27, 1969: 12; Al Brunelle, "Exhibition at Kozmopolitan Gallery," *ARTnews* 68, no. 1 (March 1969): 69.

26   *Anita Steckel: The Feminist Art of Sexual Politics*, Rockland Community College, Suffern, New York, February 2–25, 1972. On the male body in feminist art, see Richard Meyer, "Hard Targets: Male Bodies, Feminist Art, and the Force of Censorship in the 1970s," in Cornelia Butler et al., *WACK!: Art and the Feminist Revolution* (Los Angeles: Museum of Contemporary Art, 2007), 362–83.

27   Louise Bourgeois, recording of Fight Censorship meeting, New York, March 1973. Estate of Anita Steckel and Anita Steckel Papers, Archives of Women Artists, Betty Boyd Dettre Library & Research Center, National Museum of Women in the Arts, Washington, DC.

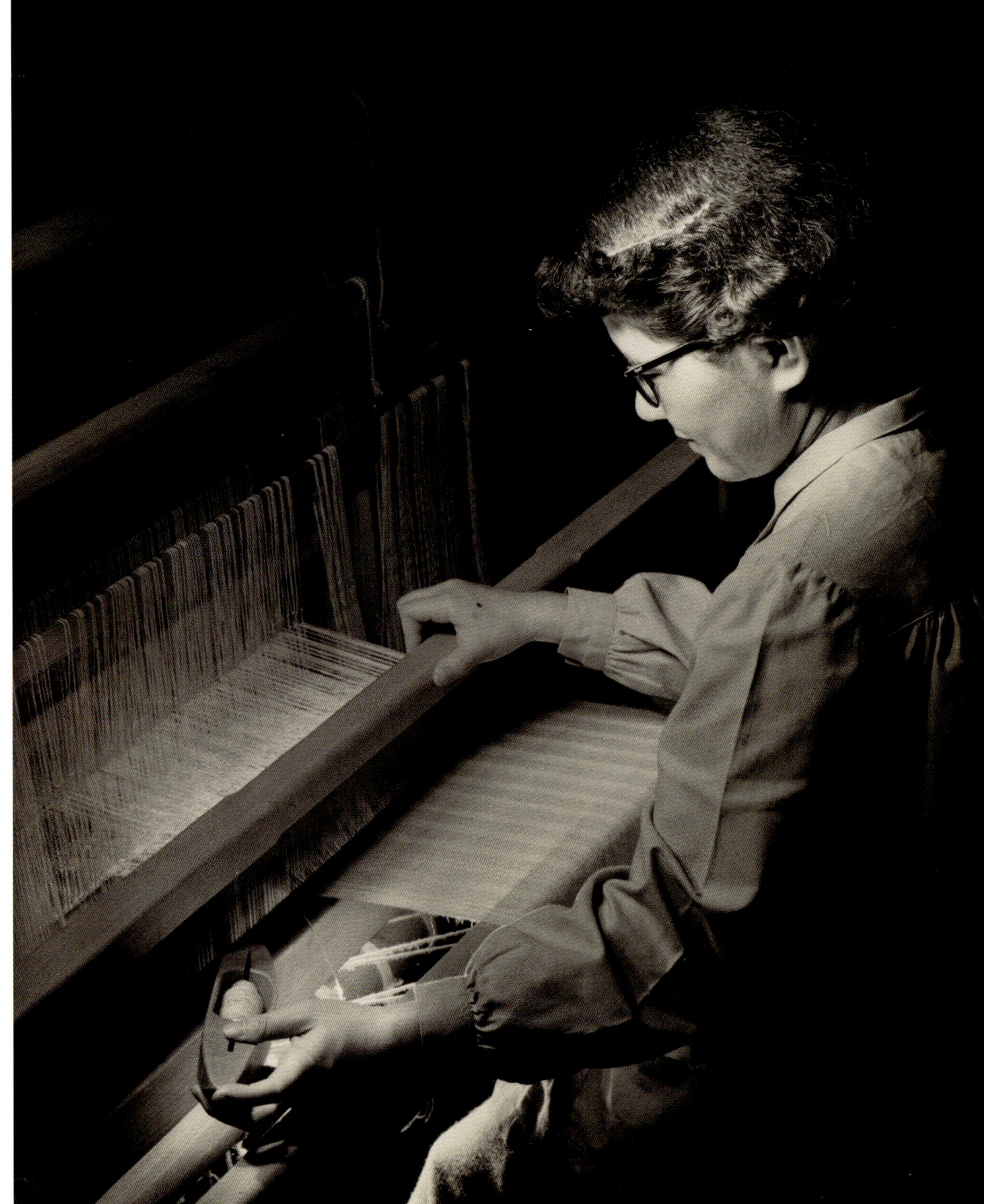

Kay Sekimachi at the loom, 1950

decides to purchase a loom on a whim after observing weaving students, but the price of the loom leaves her with no money for classes, and she initially learns to weave through free classes at the Berkeley Adult School and local guilds.

***

Spring/Summer 1959 • Nancy Spero (1926–2009) moves from Chicago to Paris with her husband and fellow artist, Leon Golub. While living in Paris, the couple witness increasingly violent protests against the Algerian War that will influence their own antiwar activism upon their return to the United States in 1964.

Born in Cleveland, Ohio, and raised in Chicago, Spero studied at the School of the Art Institute of Chicago (SAIC), receiving her bachelor of fine arts in 1949, before spending a year at the École des Beaux-Arts and Academy André L'Hote in Paris. At SAIC she meets Golub, a fellow student, whom she marries in 1951. In school, both Spero and Golub look to European "outsider art" for influence: "I was in a loosely knit group then," Spero will recall, "and we were

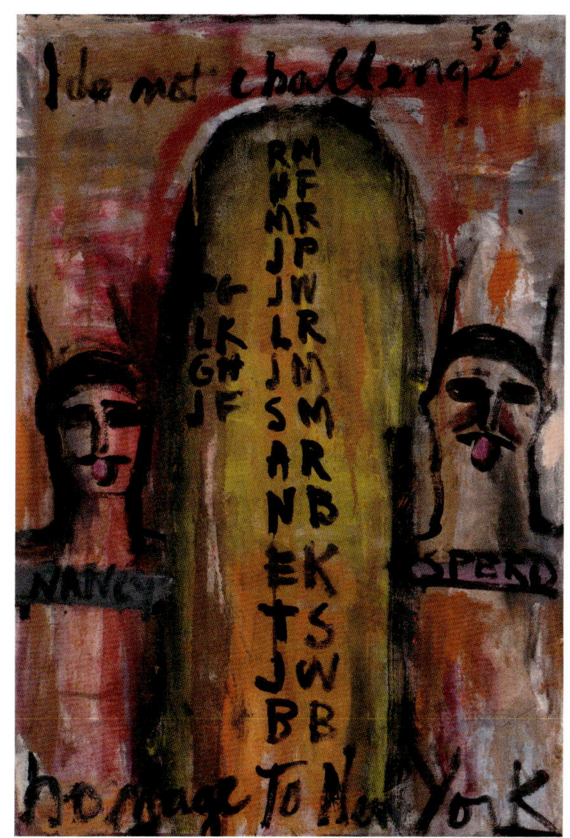

Nancy Spero, *Homage to New York (I Do Not Challenge)*, 1958. Oil on canvas, 47 ⅛ × 31 ¼ in. (119.7 × 79.4 cm)

interested in German Expressionism, Insane Art, so-called Primitive Art." While living in Chicago after graduation, and parenting two young sons, Spero struggles to gain recognition, lamenting the city's location on the periphery of the artworld—at the time centered in New York with the Abstract Expressionists—as well as her difficulty in being taken seriously as a woman artist. In Paris, the artist explains, "the art world opened for me as it hadn't in Chicago. Perhaps because I wasn't characterized as 'wife' or 'mother.'"

Fall 1959 • A native of Topeka, Kansas, Gene Swenson (1934–1969) earns a bachelor of fine arts from Yale University before meeting fellow student Lucy Lippard at New York University's Institute of Fine Arts. Lippard will describe him as "a nice-looking, tweed-jacketed, bespectacled boy from Kansas, very earnest." She goes on:

At that point, hardly a man likely to become a pioneer supporter of Pop Art, one of the most articulate critics of art and most vociferous enemies of the art-world establishment in the coming decade. We both worked in modern art, he on Picasso, I on Ernst, which separated us from the "real scholars" at the Institute of Fine

Arts by their own definition. What I liked best about Gene then was his unashamed intensity and tremendous earnestness, combined, of course, with an acute and restless intellect. I ran into him on a subway after I'd left the Institute and he said he was working full-time for Lefkowitz in the mayoral elections. Another time, on a bus, we talked about Picasso, but Gene's mind was already wandering far beyond a thesis format and it didn't look like it would be enough for him. I was interested but not surprised by the change in the clothes and the attitudes with which he had arrived in New York. He became somewhat unkempt but never lost that American boyishness.

Swenson soon drops out of the Institute to dive headlong into New York's vibrant cultural milieu. He is an editorial associate at *ARTnews* from 1961 to 1965, covering the emergent Pop art while developing ideas about an emotive, subject-based approach to art that might act as a bulwark against what he perceives as the onrush of formalism.

———

1959 • Jack Smith (1932–1989) makes two short 16mm films, *Scotch Tape* and *Overstimulated*, and collaborates with underground filmmakers Ken Jacobs and Bob Fleischner on *Blonde Cobra*. Smith has to borrow Jacobs's camera to film his two shorts.

Smith had grown up between Ohio, Texas, and Wisconsin, and left home shortly after graduating from high school. Following brief stints in Chicago, where he worked at the Orpheum Theatre, and Los Angeles, where he made the early film *Buzzards Over Baghdad* (1952), he moves to New York City sometime in 1953. In 1956 he meets Jacobs and Fleischner while taking film classes at the City College of New

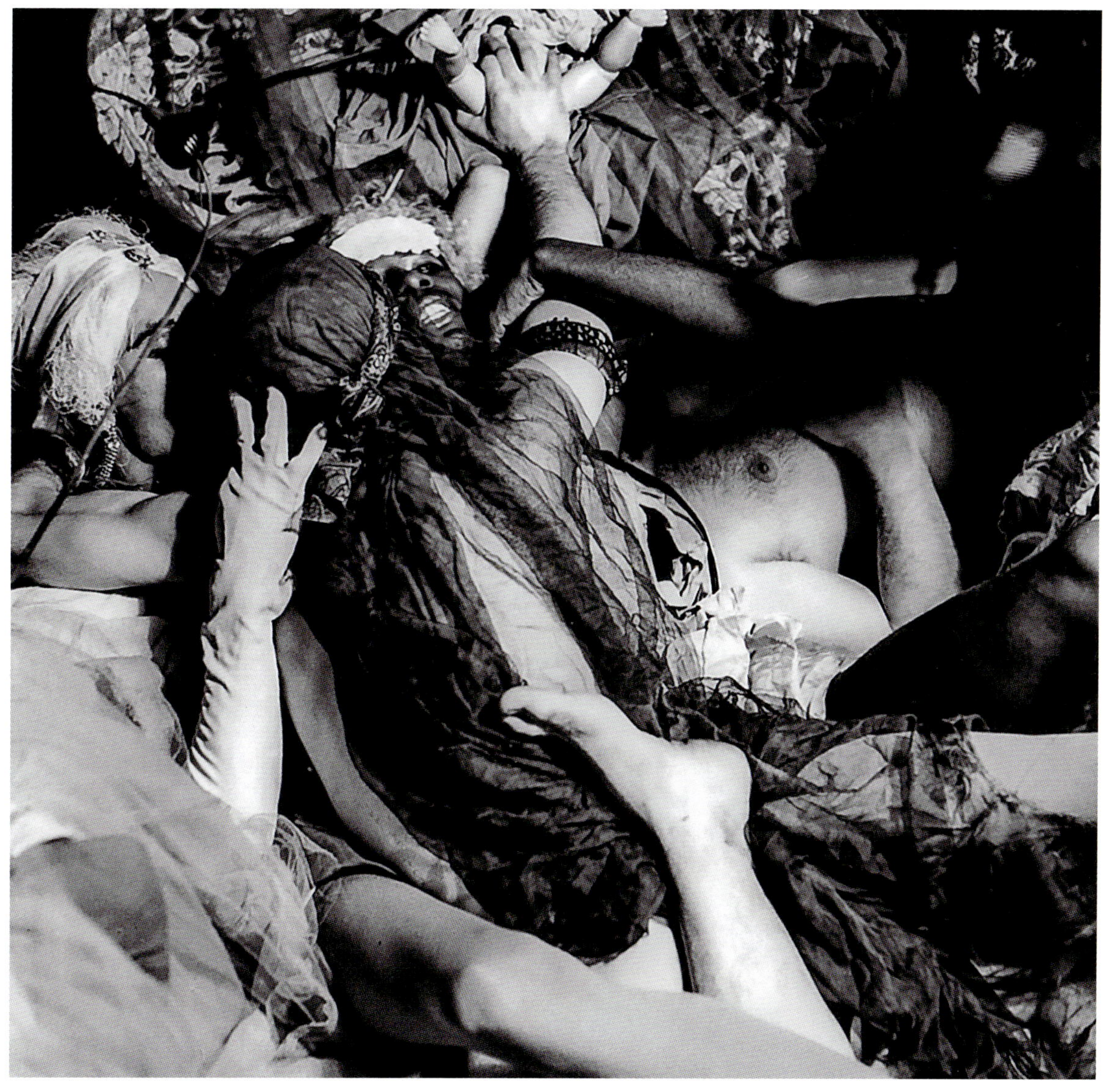

Jack Smith, *Untitled*, c. 1958–62 (printed 2011). Gelatin silver print, 10 × 8 in. (25.4 × 20.3 cm)

York and starts performing in the movies of other aspiring filmmakers: *Saturday Afternoon*, *Blood Sacrifice*, and *Little Cobra Dance* in 1957, then *Star-Spangled to Death* and *Little Stabs at Happiness* in 1958, followed by *Blonde Cobra*. Bereft of his own movie camera, Smith opens Hyperbole Photography Studio, where he focuses on still photography of staged, elaborately costumed tableaux.

Jacobs, who assisted Joseph Cornell in the mid- to late 1950s, borrows a 1936 collage movie made by Cornell, *Rose Hobart*. Titled after its leading lady, it is twenty-four minutes of repeating and re-montaged scenes of the Hollywood star Cornell made from a cast-off print of her 1931 film *East of Borneo* and overlaid with a loop from the album *Holiday in Brazil* by Brazilian composer Nestor Amaral. Jacobs and Smith watch the movie obsessively. As Jacobs will recall, "We looked at it in every possible way: on the ceiling, in mirrors, bouncing it all over the room, in focus, out of focus, with a blue filter that Cornell had given me, without it, backwards, it was just like an eruption of energy." Cornell's appropriation and fragmentation of the film, so characteristic of Surrealist and Dadaist collage practices, liberated gesture and mood from narrative structure. This, and the obsession with stardom, likely resonate with Smith,

influencing both his approach to filmmaking and his own fascination with film star Maria Montez. As Smith's muse, the deceased Hollywood star will be a constant reference in his work, her oeuvre a trash heap through which he sifts endlessly for the motifs and themes in his film and performance work.

October 1959 • Yayoi Kusama opens her first solo exhibition at the Brata Gallery, a radically diverse artist's co-op in the East Village. The show features five of her *Infinity Net* paintings, in which she hones her strategies of serial repetition. "My desire was to predict and measure the infinity of the unbounded universe, from my own position in it, with dots," she later recalls. "Did infinite infinities exist beyond our own universe? In exploring these questions I wanted to examine the single dot that was my own life."

October 17–November 5, 1959 • Robert Smithson (1938–1973) has his first solo gallery exhibition. He shows sixteen paintings exploring mythical, fantastic, and literary themes. He later calls this his "archetypal imagistic period," during which he merges gestural and geometric abstraction with "latent imagery."

A ravenous reader and autodidact, Smithson has nourished an interest in natural history and the earth sciences since childhood, when he frequently visited the American Museum of Natural History, where his paternal grandfather had designed the ornamental plasterwork. His father constructs a museum for him in the basement of their New Jersey home, allowing Smithson to maintain a collection of artifacts—reptiles, insects, fossils, and shells. During high school, Smithson enrolls in the Art Students League of New York, studying illustration and painting from 1954 to 1956. Around this time, he meets Alan Brilliant, an undergraduate at Columbia University who shares Smithson's interest in the work of poet-artists such as William Blake, and together they begin attending student discussions on art and making trips to see local exhibitions, often at Sidney Janis Gallery. From 1957 to 1959, Smithson illustrates four issues of Brilliant's literary magazine, *Pan*.

Smithson's canvases feature dinosaurs and recall his childhood fascinations. Critic Irving Sandler in the October 1959 *ARTnews* describes the work on view as "monsters, whelped by Surrealism and primitive art, are reared by frenzied Action Painting. *Walls of Dis*, a three-part panel, with its crude totemic creatures would have looked well in the temple of some savage cult." Drawing inspiration from Dante's *Inferno*, Smithson writes a corresponding poem, also titled "From the Walls of Dis," with lines that read, "Eye staring without a face. / Ear hearing without a face. / Mouth shouting without a face."

November 6, 1959 • Lucas Samaras (1936–2024) opens his first solo exhibition at Reuben Gallery in New York, having joined the gallery earlier that year and participated in happenings as part of the group show *18 Happenings in 6 Parts*, organized by Allan Kaprow. Samaras becomes close with other members, including Jim Dine, Martha Edelheit, Red Grooms, and Claes Oldenburg. During its brief, two-year existence, the gallery brings together artists who share an interest in the materiality of urban life and a stylistic ruggedness. Samaras's early assemblages and figurative sculptures from this period reflect the style of the gallery in their gritty accumulation of plaster, nails, razor blades, and feathers. Critic Lawrence Alloway later writes that this "rough handling was partly expression, an exploration of the textures of urban waste, and partly improvisatory, using what materials were available."

For the first eleven years of his life, Samaras had lived in his native Kastoria, Macedonia. His early experiences in the Greek Orthodox church would go on to inform his later art, particularly his *Box* works, in which he enshrines often mundane

Robert Smithson, *Wall of Dis*, 1959. Oil on canvas, 50 × 64 in. (127 × 162.6 cm)

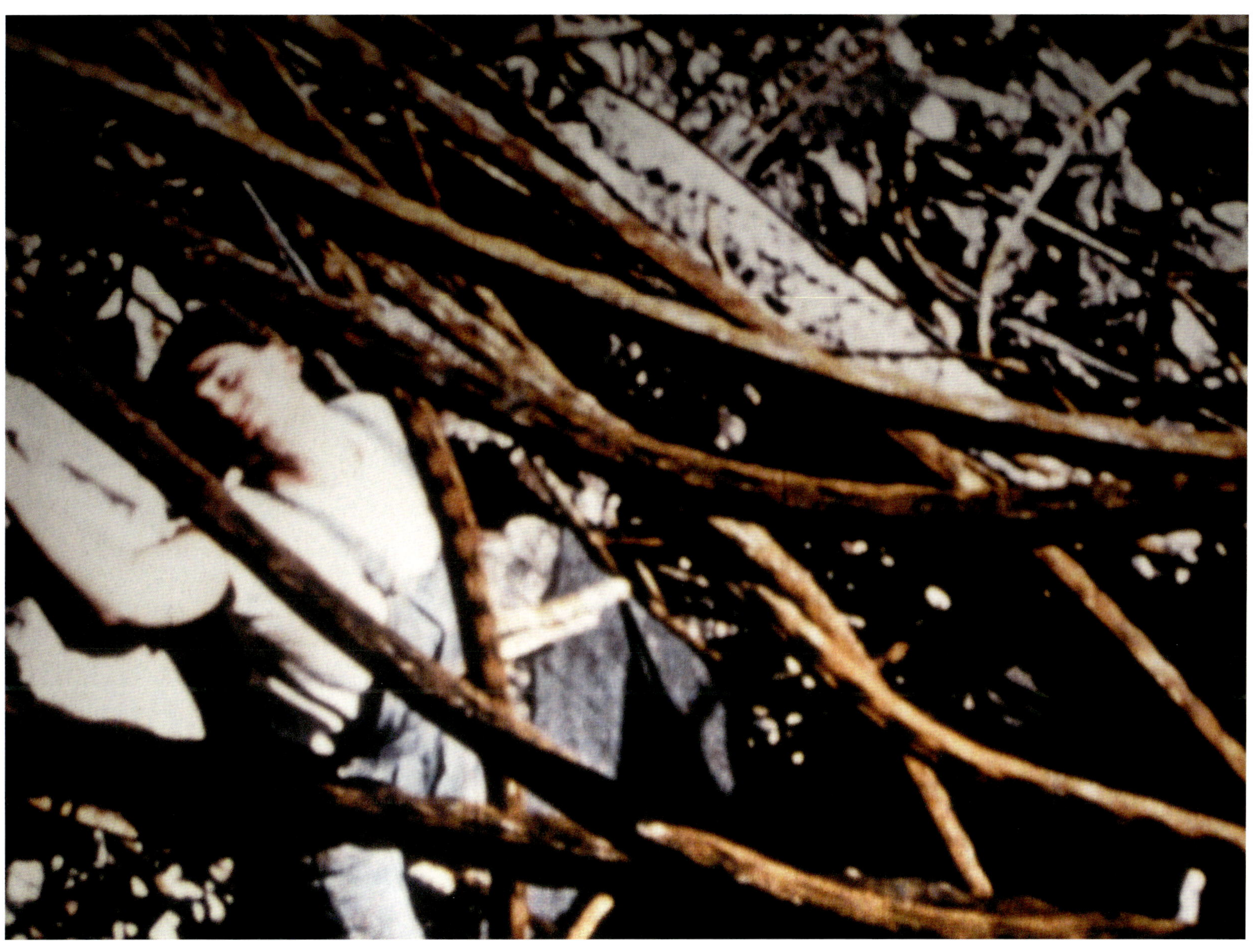

Jack Smith, *Scotch Tape*, 1959–62. 16mm film, color, sound; 3 min. Whitney Museum of American Art, New York; gift of Gladstone Gallery, New York 2010.207

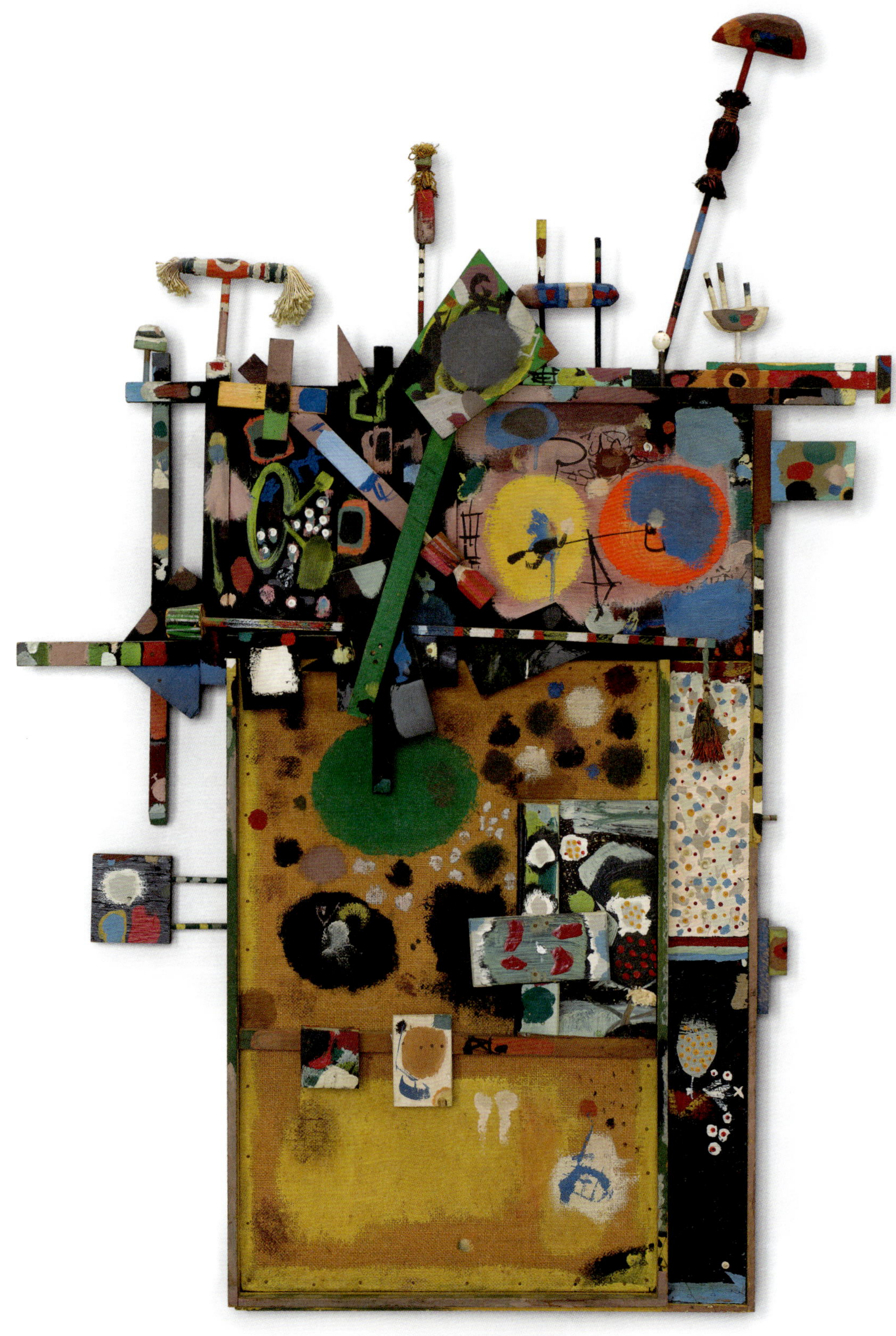

Roy De Forest, *Drifting Down the Mississippi*, 1959. Acrylic, enamel, string, and wood on wood, 55 ½ × 37 ½ × 5 in. (141 × 95.3 × 12.7 cm). San Francisco Museum of Modern Art; gift of Kathan Brown 84.1465

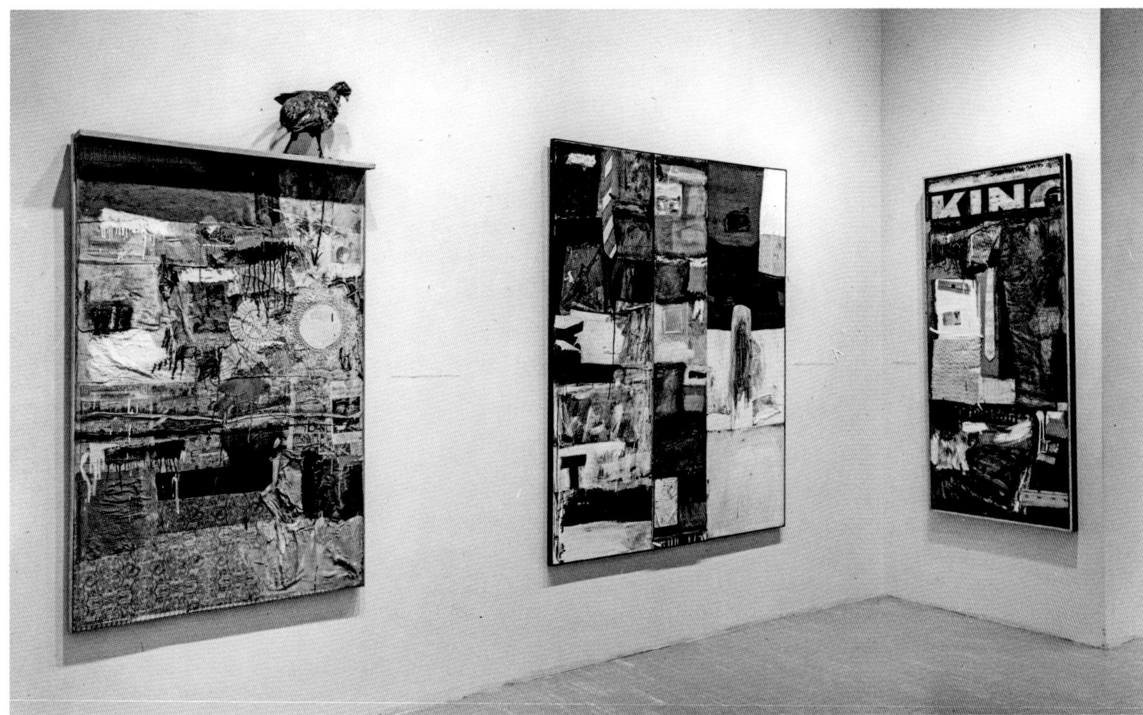

Sixteen Americans, The Museum of Modern Art, New York, 1959

objects of personal significance as devotional relics. In 1948 Samaras and his family immigrated to the United States, settling in New Jersey, where he attends Rutgers University, taking classes with Kaprow and George Segal, before studying art history with Meyer Schapiro at Columbia University.

November 26–December 27, 1959 • Contemporary Arts Association of Houston hosts *Out of the Ordinary*. Positing a form of American Neo-Dada, the exhibition highlights contemporary artists who, through their art, hold up "crooked mirrors" to their audience. Organized by curators Robert C. Morris and John Hackney, the show includes American artists based in New York, Chicago, and Texas, namely, Joseph Cornell, Jasper Johns, Ray Johnson, Allan Kaprow, Jim Love, Robert Rauschenberg, and H. C. Westermann, along with more historical work by European artists presented as progenitors of "neo-Dada," such as George Grosz, Joan Miró, Francis Picabia, and Yves Tanguy.

Critic Harold Rosenberg's introduction to the catalogue attempts to encapsulate the various strains of American art emerging in the late 1950s, grouping them under his short-lived term *Neo-Dada*, which he summarizes as such:

Would one of Shakespeare's clowns or half-wits ever admit that anyone could be crazy? The madman, or the simulated madman, is, above all, logical and factual; Objectivity is his obsession. American neo-Dada is neither a movement nor a tendency. It does not supersede any other kind of art: it is not the answer to abstraction; it is not "a revolt of youth." Revival of a perennial motive in art, it is full of pep in having found out how to make materials talk back in unexpected ways to the civilization that is producing them.

December 16, 1959–February 17, 1960 • Curated by Dorothy Miller at the Museum of Modern Art, New York, *Sixteen Americans* includes works by Jasper Johns, Ellsworth Kelly, Alfred Leslie, Robert Mallary, Louise Nevelson, Robert Rauschenberg, and Frank Stella, among others, and is the New York debut of Jay DeFeo and Wally Hedrick (1928–2003). Married in 1954, the couple cannot afford to travel from San Francisco for the opening of the exhibition, which in any case Hedrick views as an "arrogant" professionalization of art. Art, he vehemently contends, is neither a sales game nor a romantic reverie:

I'm a used car salesman. I don't believe in this European notion, "the materials got me—I went to bed and I woke up and the painting was there." Jackson Pollock is a perfect example of somebody who gets loaded and paints, and that's fine. I understand how that could happen, but for me that's an alien idea. I think the mind is more important than the heart. I like control; I like using one's mind to make decisions. I'm a politician. I'm trying to make these paintings do what politicians should be doing.

Hedrick had grown up in Pasadena, California, and began making art inspired by the nascent custom-car culture and, especially, the pinstriper Kenny Howard, aka "Von Dutch." As a teenager, Hedrick befriends several artists and poets, including Hayward King, Deborah Remington, John Allen Ryan, and David Simpson, who form the Progressive Art Workers and attend Pasadena City College together. In 1946 the group visits the California School of Fine Arts (CSFA), then under the sway of Elmer Bischoff, David Park, Clyfford Still, and the bohemian swing of traditional jazz. Hedrick cannot afford the tuition and returns to Pasadena, enrolling in the Army National Guard. At the beginning of the Korean War, his unit is the first to be deployed overseas, and he spends a year stationed in Japan and another year in combat as an infantryman in Korea itself. In 1952 he reunites with some of his Pasadena friends, including Remington, with whom he would later cofound the Six Gallery in San Francisco.

Hedrick's paintings of the 1950s and early 1960s are heavily brushed riffs on the objects around him, as well as meditations on war, incorporating everything from American flags to televisions to the alchemical books then au courant at Painterland, the Fillmore Street artists' community where he and DeFeo live. Fred Martin, who hires Hedrick as an instructor while a dean at San Francisco Art Institute, writes of Hedrick in 1967: "He was not a precursor [to Pop], because the works were not participants in some large and objective cultural involvement: They were only Hedrick making what he could make out of the stuff of his life."

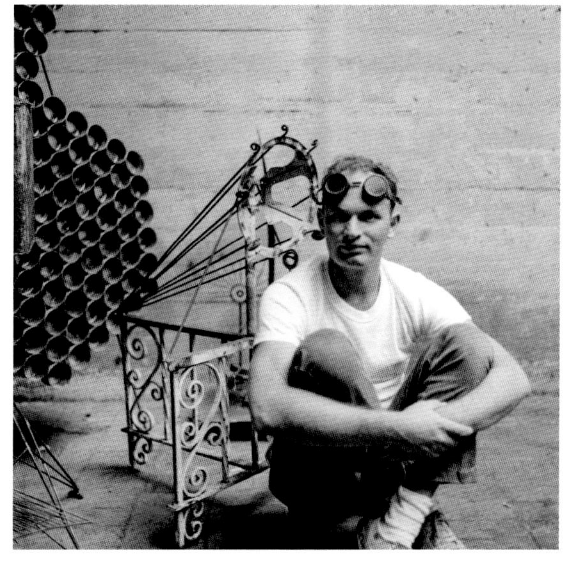

Wally Hedrick with *His Master's Voice* (1957), c. 1958–60

1960

Februrary 29–March 2, 1960 • Claes Oldenburg performs *Snapshots of the City* at Judson Gallery, Judson Memorial Church, New York, with his first wife, artist-model Patty Mucha, and Lucas Samaras. Samaras, occasionally joined by Carolee Schneemann, participates in nearly every performance through 1962. The happening takes place within *The Street* (1960), an installation of accumulated newspaper, cardboard, burlap, and found debris that is part of a program of performances Oldenburg calls *Ray Gun Spex*.

In *Snapshots of the City*, Oldenburg appears partially nude and wrapped in detritus, while Samaras, offstage, switches the lights on and off to simulate a camera's flash. Stan VanDerBeek later completes a film using footage of the event, which he describes as "a black statement about the City in which two people represent the populace after a bomb raid." Critics are quick to acknowledge the work's social content: "The theme of his show was *The Street*, but the gallery … might be a museum of the future for the charred relics of the atomic age. A series of battered 'ray-guns' are mounted like objets d'art. . . . Oldenburg is a social artist with a fresh way of putting across his message," writes Irving Sandler. In his review of Oldenburg's happening *Injun* (1962), commissioned by the short-lived Dallas Museum for Contemporary Arts,

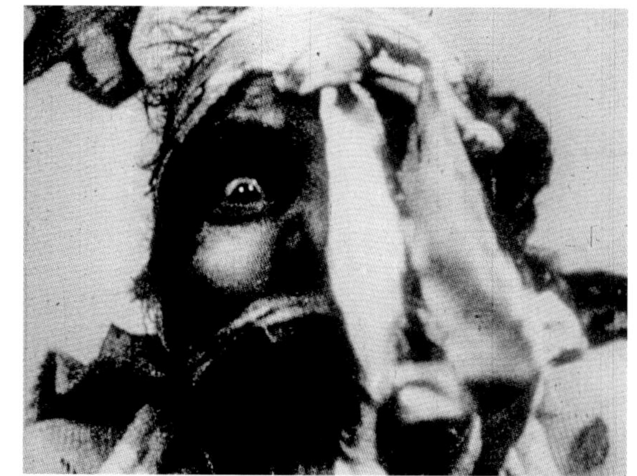

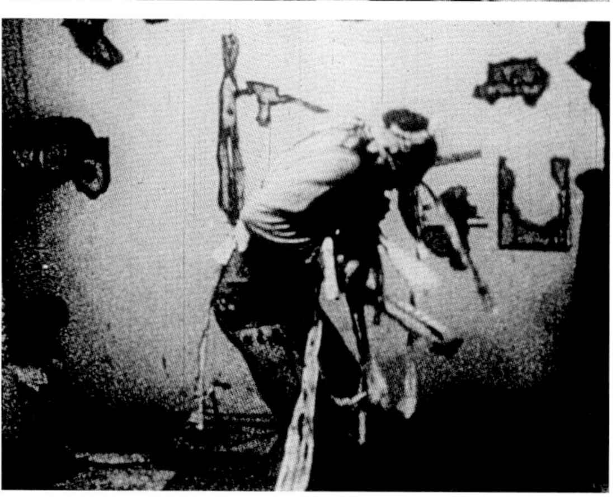

Stan VanDerBeek, *Snapshots of the City*, 1960, with performance by Claes Oldenburg. 16mm film transferred to video, black-and-white, sound; 3:41 min.

David Irwin argues that happenings are surreal, insisting that certain performances "can justly be regarded as pure Surrealism, with firm roots in the common source of [Alfred] Jarry," the turn-of-the-century French Symbolist writer. In the same article, Irwin goes on to discuss Surrealism as it manifests in the work of James Rosenquist and Edward Kienholz. Peter Selz will later compare Oldenburg to Kienholz and the artists associated with the California Funk art movement.

April 25–May 21, 1960 • Jeremy Anderson (1921–1982) opens his first solo exhibition of work in different media, at San Francisco's Dilexi Gallery. In the coming decade, the gallery will go on to host another four shows by the artist. This first exhibition comes on the heels of a brief flurry of interest in New York that will include a 1953 two-person show with Louise Bourgeois at Allan Frumkin Gallery and a 1954 solo show at Stable Gallery.

Born and raised in Northern California, Anderson had served in the Navy from 1941 until the end of World War II. In 1946 he enrolled in the California School of Fine Arts (CFSA), studying with Robert Howard, David Park, Mark Rothko, Clay Spohn, and Clyfford Still. At the time, Rothko and Still are advancing both the formal and spiritual agendas of abstraction, while Howard and

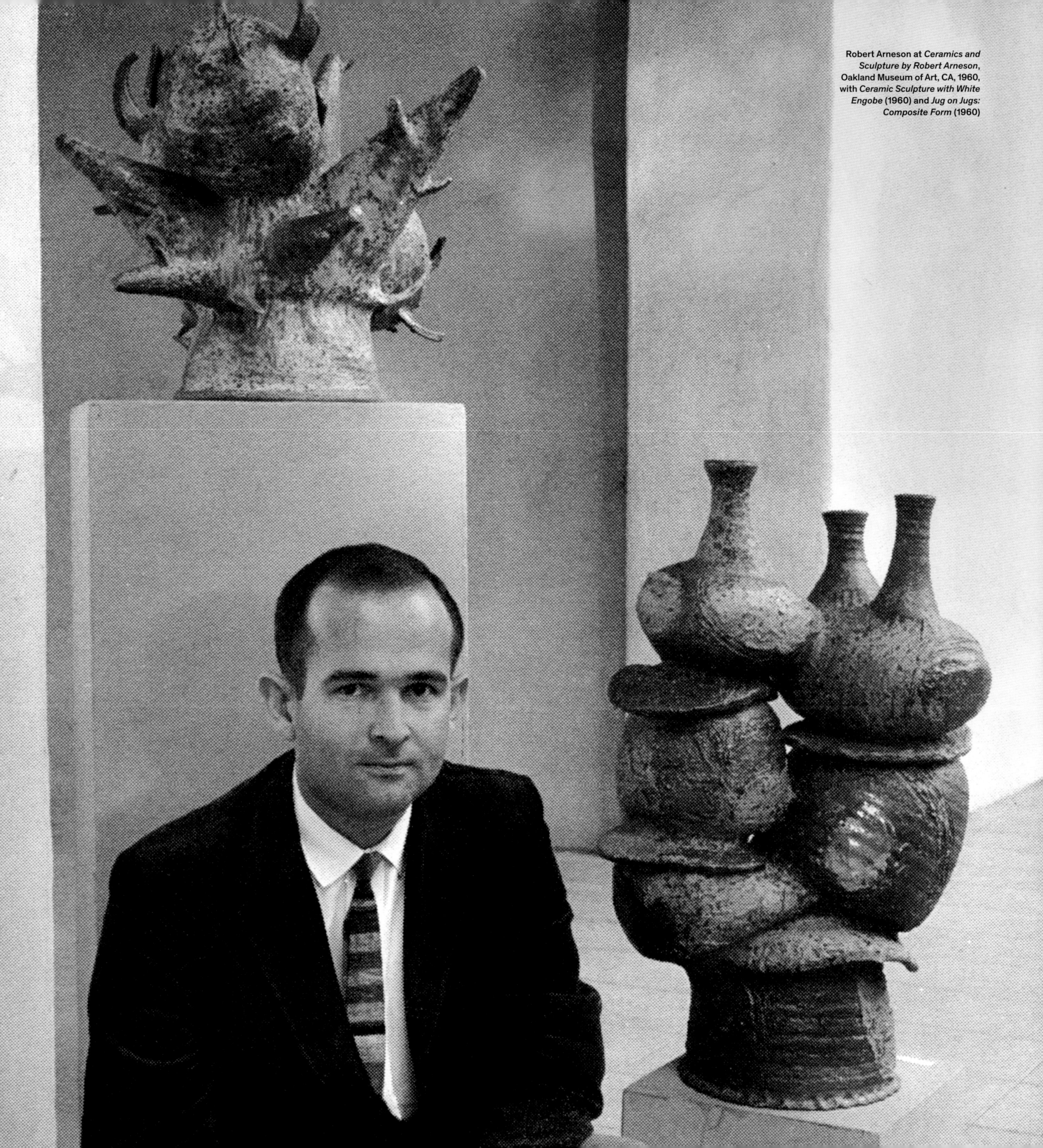

Robert Arneson at *Ceramics and Sculpture by Robert Arneson*, Oakland Museum of Art, CA, 1960, with *Ceramic Sculpture with White Engobe* (1960) and *Jug on Jugs: Composite Form* (1960)

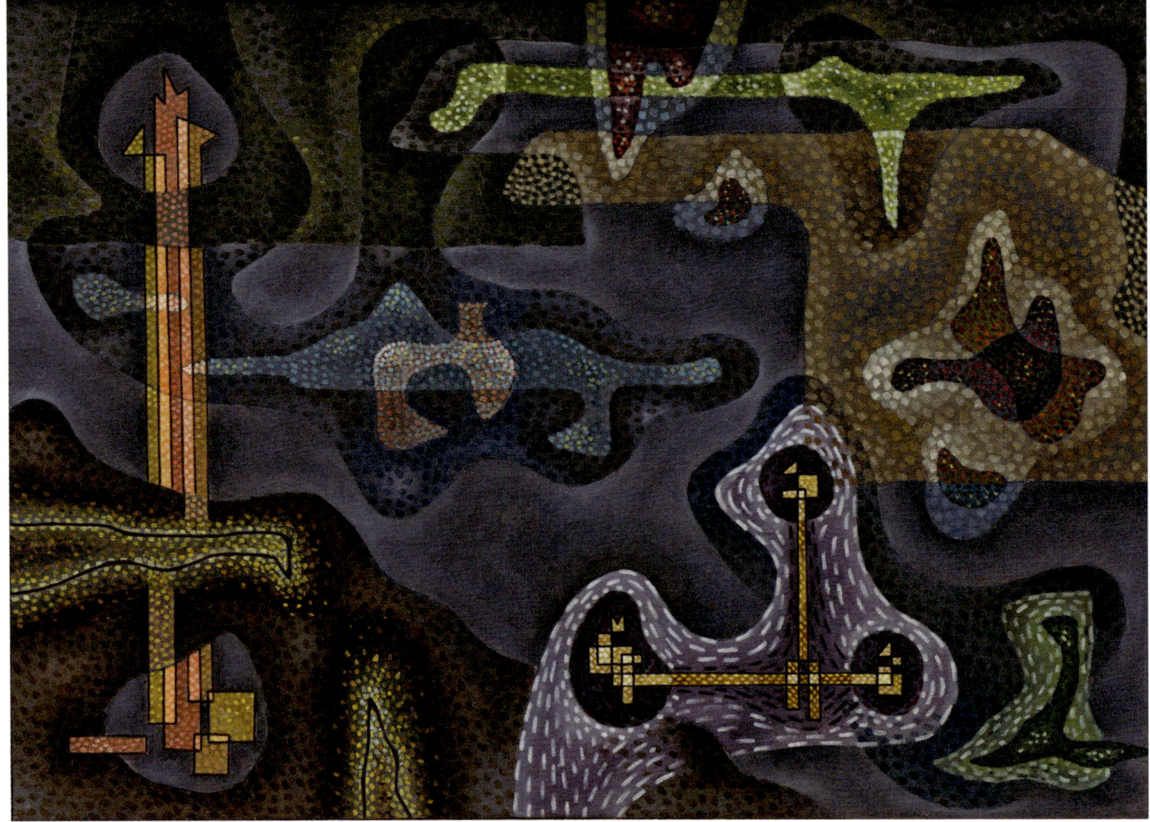

Gordon Onslow Ford, *Seductions of the Day*, 1943. Oil on canvas, 31 ¾ × 43 ½ in. (80.6 × 110.5 cm)

Spohn are experimenting with assemblage, unorthodox materials, and fantastical forms. While CSFA is a bastion of modernism in those years, San Francisco—importantly for Anderson—is also highly receptive to Surrealism: copies of the surrealist magazines *View* and *VVV* are available from earlier in the decade, and Gordon Onslow Ford's Surrealist painting collection is frequently on view at the San Francisco Museum of Modern Art. Moreover, the de Young Museum is a favorite haunt for Anderson, who is fascinated by its ancient weapons collection as well its holdings of Oceanic and African statuary—an interest shared by many Surrealist painters. Anderson will focus on the psychological crossings of Surrealism, eroticism, death, and craftsmanship for most of his life.

By the early 1950s, Anderson had settled on the medium of redwood, the most readily available material around his studio and one with a deep, ruddy coloration that becomes a hallmark of his work until he shifts to polychrome in the mid-1960s. Much of his early work moves in two directions: horizontal planes, à la Alberto Giacometti and Isamu Noguchi, with nods to chess games, boats, and topographical maps of landscapes, which become the artist's primary mode of drawing in the 1960s; and complex vertical totems that twist, feature protruding bulbous masses, and house other boxes. The latter come very close to the worship objects Anderson loves.

In 1958, when he begins teaching at CSFA, he finds his students eager for his blend of craft and spirituality.

May 1960 • Martha Edelheit (b. 1931) opens her first solo exhibition, at Reuben Gallery, New York, exhibiting assemblages that employ a circle symbol to indicate her female subject and that include clippings from the Yiddish papers of her youth.

Born and raised in New York, Edelheit had enrolled at the University of Chicago, where she became friends with fellow student Susan Sontag, before returning east to study at Columbia University. There she studies early childhood education, but on the side she works with art historian Meyer Schapiro. Soon after her solo debut at Reuben Gallery, she begins making art that is more straightforwardly personal and connected to her life and sexuality, imagining her subject matter through tattoo and BDSM imagery. Her vivid ink drawings of sexual fantasies are unusual for any artist at the time. Edelheit, who maintains a dialogue with Lucas Samaras and is well versed in Simone de Beauvoir's *Second Sex*, wants to engage the subject of female sexuality and permissiveness directly, but she is leery of labels and movements. She continues working into the mid-1960s, showing at New York's Judson Gallery and OK Harris Works of Art.

May 16–June 11, 1960 • Kenneth Price (1935–2012) mounts his inaugural solo exhibition at Ferus Gallery, Los Angeles, the first in a series that will track the development of his ceramics from mounts to cups to eggs. Joining John Altoon, Billy Al Bengston, Ed Ruscha, and other artists centered at the gallery, Price refines his visual language: his palette and biomorphic forms see the influence of Joan Miró and his display the impact of Joseph Cornell, whose 1962 exhibition at Ferus Gallery inspires much of Los Angeles art in those years.

Price had been born and raised in Los Angeles, enamored with cars, surfing, music, and art. He attended Santa Monica City College in 1954 before taking classes around the city, which, like the rest of the state, is experiencing a boom in ceramic studies, led in part by Peter Voulkos at Otis Art Institute in Los Angeles. Price finishes his master of fine arts in one year at New York's Alfred University, returning to Los Angeles in 1959 to use ceramics not for craft but for abstraction and painting. He is well trained and eager to blend his passions into object making, taking a serious approach to irreverence.

Two years after his Ferus debut, Price will describe the appeal of his eggs:

My work has evolved into these naturally erotic forms. Using my current vocabulary of form means always making references to sex, whether intended or not. People find images in my work that I don't even see. And the colors I use are sensual too. So viewers think my work is sexy, which I like. But I call it sensual and erotic, because "sexy" implies being turned on by sex appeal or sexual content. It's weird to think that one of my pieces could actually arouse someone's sexual desire. If that were to happen, it would be the viewer's doing, not mine. I've always seen those pieces to be more about nature than about sex. My work is layered

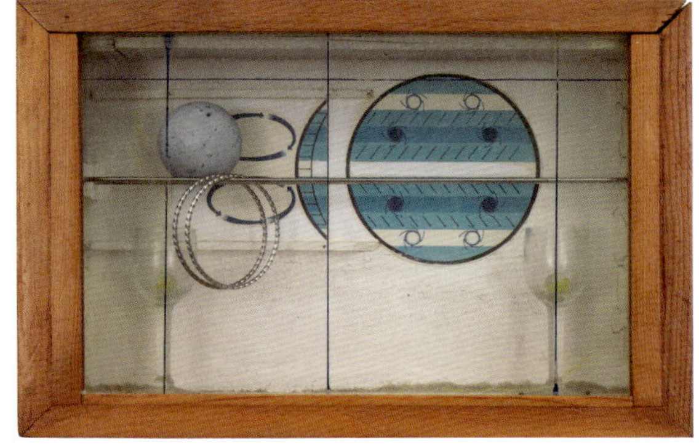

Joseph Cornell, *Sun Box*, 1960. Assemblage, 10 ⅛ × 15 ¼ × 3 ½ in. (25.7 × 38.7 × 8.9 cm)

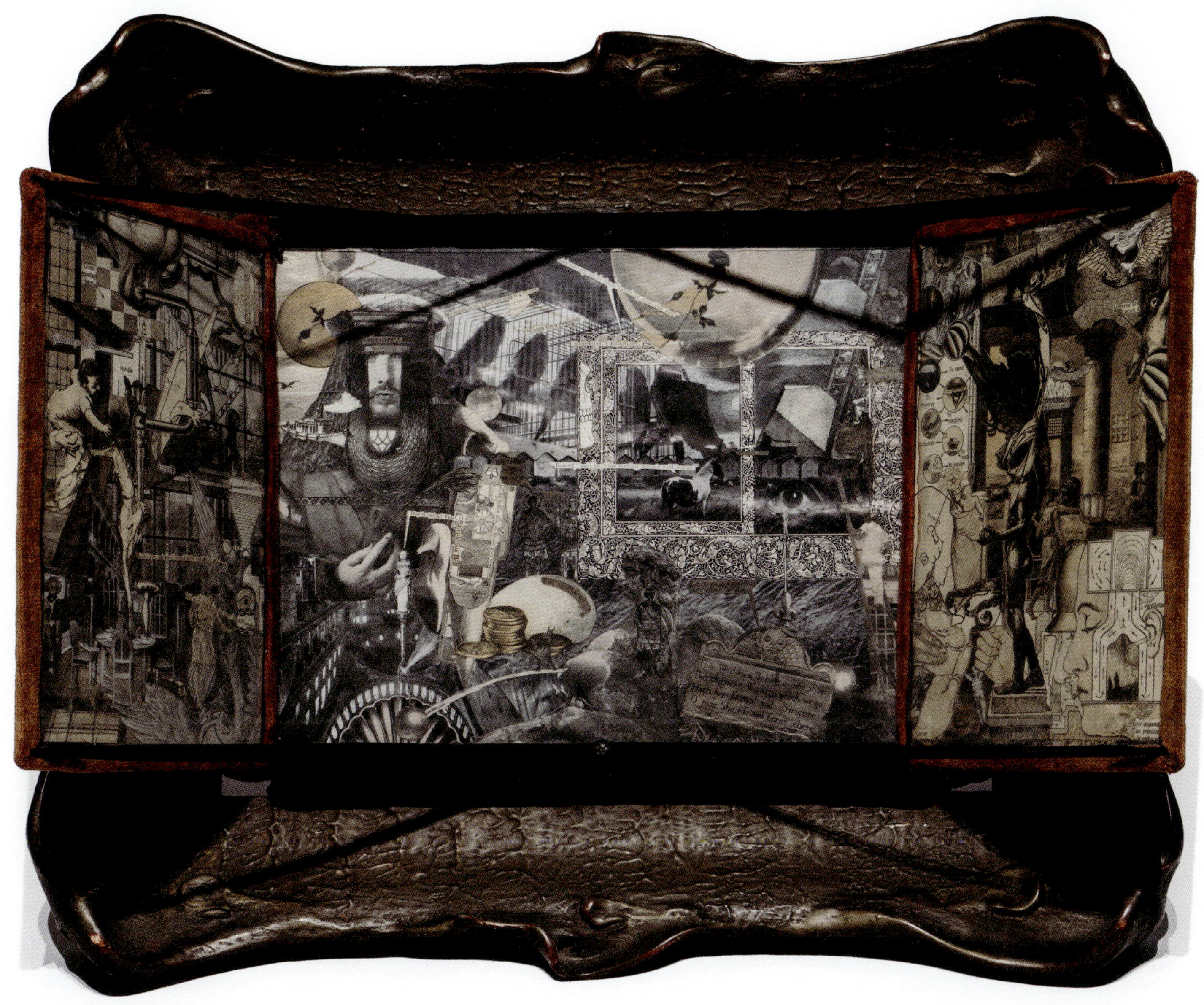

Jess, *Variations on Dürer's Melancholia I*, 1960. Collage on paper, Art Nouveau frame, and mixed media, 38 × 24 × 20 in. (96.5 × 61 × 50.8 cm). Collection of Jim Newman

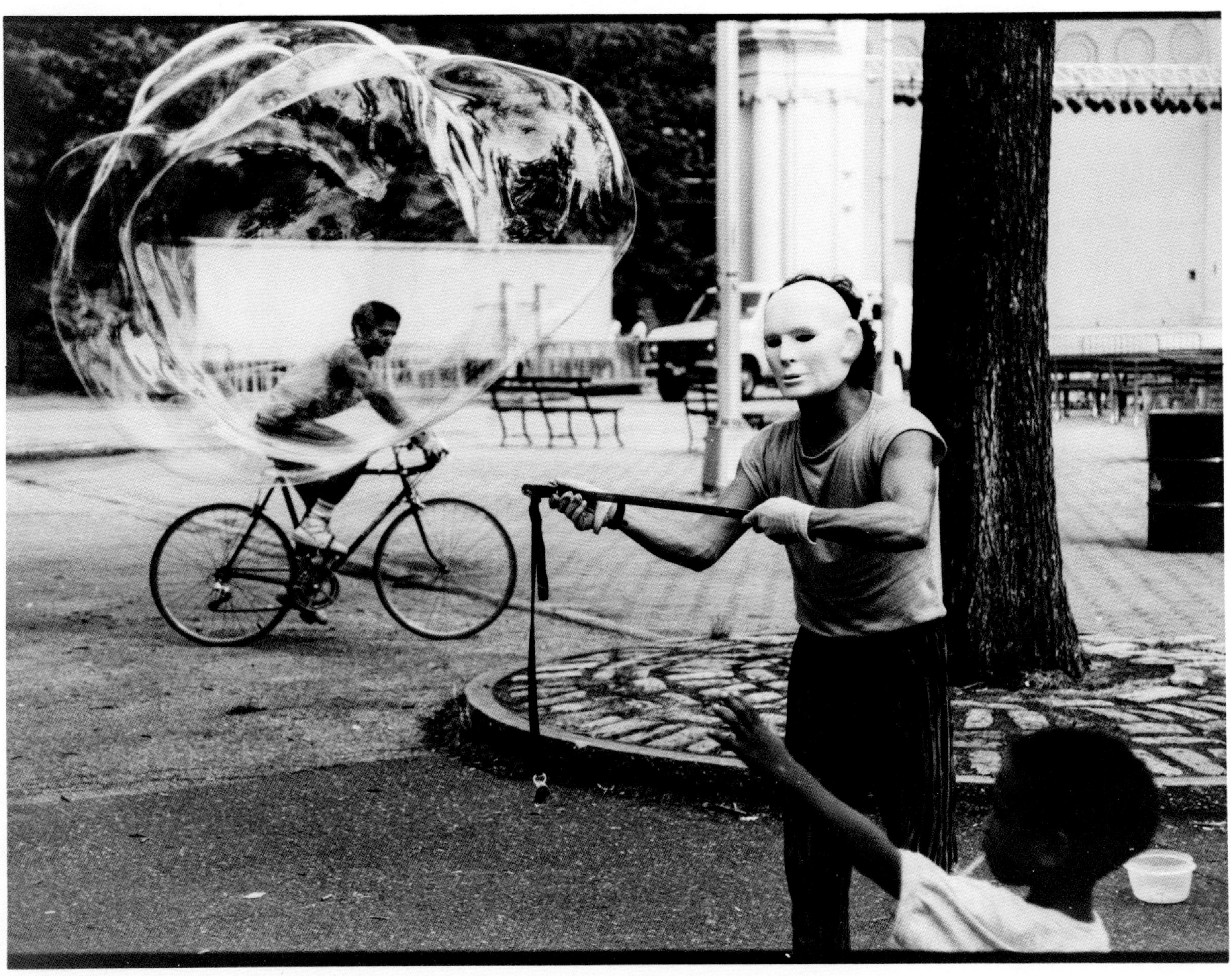

Shawn Walker, *Man with Bubble, Central Park (Near Bandshell)*, c. 1960–79, printed 1989. Gelatin silver print: sheet, 8 × 10 in. (20.3 × 25.4 cm); image, 7 ⅜ × 9 ⅜ in. (18.7 × 23.9 cm).
Whitney Museum of American Art, New York; purchase, with funds from the Photography Committee 2020.62

with references, many of which are unintentional. I wanted to leave their meanings open to personal interpretation.

———

June 1960 • Barbara Chase-Riboud (b. 1939) is the first Black woman to graduate with a master of fine arts in architecture and design from Yale University, having been encouraged to apply by the graphic artist Jane Doggett, whom she had met in 1957 as a John Hay Whitney Fellow at the American Academy in Rome. Although Chase-Riboud had entered Yale as an architecture student, she quickly transitioned to design while retaining an eye for the monumental. Doggett commissions her to create a fountain for the Wheaton Plaza Shopping Center in Maryland, a project she hands in as her master's thesis.

A native of Philadelphia, Chase-Riboud had taken classes at the Philadelphia Museum of Art as a child. She received her bachelor of fine arts from the Tyler School of Art and Architecture at Temple University in 1956, a year after selling her first work, the woodcut *Reba* (1955), to the Museum of Modern Art, New York. Her year in Rome as a Whitney Fellow is productive, as she travels extensively. She meets writer Ralph Ellison, poet Ezra Pound, and artist Cy Twombly, among others, and participates in the international art and culture event Festival of the Two Worlds in Spoleto. She also learns the direct lost-wax method for creating unique bronze castings from wax originals—a technique to which she will return a decade later in her abstract sculptures.

When Chase-Riboud returns to the United States in the fall to begin her graduate studies, she faces culture shock, "homesick for adults, sophistication, and continental-style intellectualism." During her first year at Yale, she frequently escapes to New York on weekends, renting a room in the maids' quarters of the Plaza Hotel, visiting exhibitions, and exploring Greenwich Village. While at Yale, she works with Herbert Matter and Paul Rand and takes classes with Josef Albers, Alvin Eisenman, Philip Johnson, Louis Kahn, and Vincent Scully. She also meets fellow graduate student Sheila Hicks, who becomes a lifelong friend.

———

1960 • Lee Lozano (1930–1999) moves to New York City, leaving her husband of four years, Mexican American architect Adrian Lozano, in Europe, where they had been traveling; they subsequently divorce. She quickly embraces the arts scene in her new city, befriending many artists, including Carl Andre, Donald Judd, Sol LeWitt, and Robert Morris, as well as the dealer Richard Bellamy, whose Green Gallery champions avant-garde American art. Lozano begins painting and

drawing highly eccentric and personal figurative works—surreal genre scenes and raunchy cartoons. Phalluses proliferate, penetrating or emerging from voids, openings, and depressions; a hyper, flexible airplane reels around; and a crescent grin flashes without a face. In paint or in pencil, her strokes are strong, dark, and aggressive. Although there is an affinity with Pop—with mass-produced everyday objects and with humor—her work veers into the absurd, inappropriate, and profane. The rude sexual nature of her art is explicit in a cartoon, which blurts "cocks! cunts! tits! balls!"

Born Lenore Knaster in Newark, New Jersey, Lozano had changed her name to Lee at age fourteen, foreshadowing a future of name changes and phases. She earns a bachelor of arts in 1951 from the University of Chicago, studying natural science and philosophy, before receiving a master of arts from the School of the Art Institute of Chicago in 1960. In between obtaining her degrees, Lozano works in the design department of the Container Corporation of America, where she meets her future husband, marrying him in 1956.

———

June 5, 1960 • After moving from Oklahoma City to Los Angeles in 1956 to pursue an art career, Ed Ruscha (b. 1937) graduates from the Chouinard Art Institute with fellow Oklahomans Joe Goode and Jerry McMillan, as well as artist Larry Bell. Artists Ed Bereal and Ron Miyashiro had also been among his fellow classmates. Ruscha describes Chouinard as having a bohemian environment,

despite the influence of Walt Disney. Ruscha sees the art school and California itself as places that enable him to unlearn so much from his upbringing, primarily the strict Catholicism and expectations of decorum and propriety.

He works as a commercial artist in book design and graphic design throughout school and after graduation, but as he will later explain, he "just gradually began to lean over to the hot side of life, the stuff that really was happening, like the fine arts and the painters, being aware of galleries and the sort of things that were happening in galleries. That art could be made out of sort of flimsy fun, and that there was a lot of style involved in it, so it was very appealing." The scene that Ruscha comes to understand and be a part of includes painters and sculptors such as John Altoon, Billy Al Bengston, Dan Graham, Robert Irwin, and Edward Kienholz—artists with incredibly diverse practices yet who share a commitment to making art that does not shy away from things like humor, the absurd, polished finishes, or premeditation, which Ruscha feels and embraces.

———

July 1960 • Diane Arbus (1923–1971) publishes her first photographic essay, "The Vertical Journey: Six Movements of a Moment within the Heart of the City," in *Esquire* magazine. The first spread juxtaposes an anonymous, elegantly dressed couple attending a Grand Opera ball with Hezekiah Trambles, a performer known professionally as Congo the Jungle Creep from Hubert's

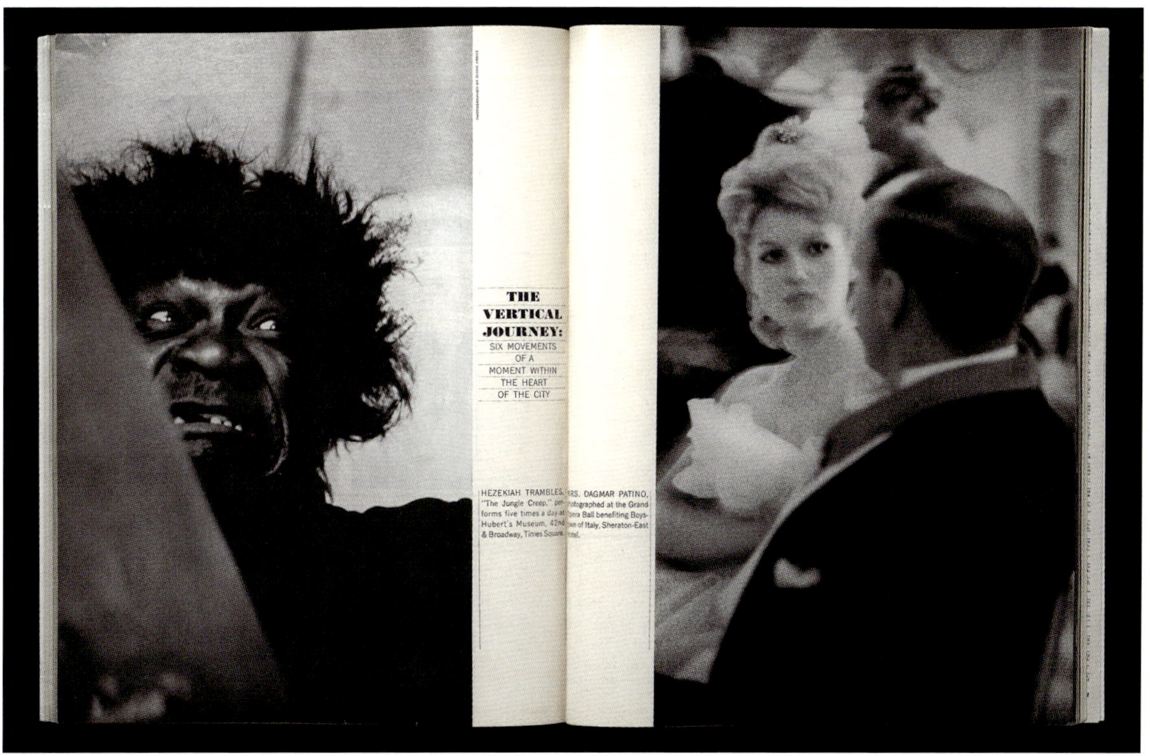

Spread from *Esquire*, July 1960, with photographs by Diane Arbus

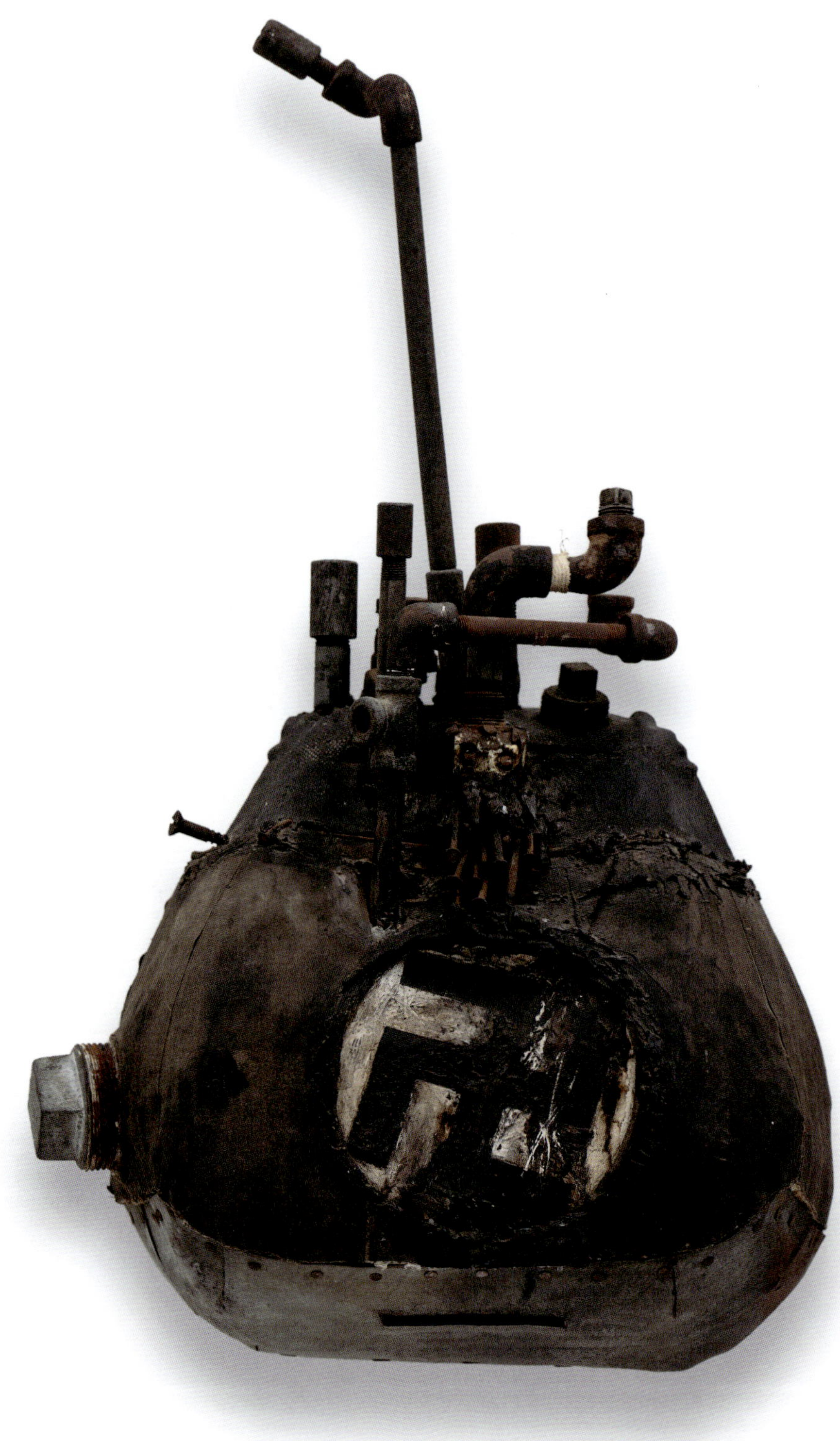

Ed Bereal, *Focke-Wulf FW 190*, 1960. Mixed-media assemblage, 21 ¼ × 12 × 6 in. (54 × 30.5 × 15.2 cm). The Buck Collection at the UC Irvine Jack and Shanaz Langson Institute and Museum of California Art

Dime Museum and Flea Circus, a Times Square sideshow. Arbus will continue to shoot at Hubert's until it closes in 1966, when, in an unpublished essay, she memorializes the museum as the keeper of "a thousand souvenirs of human aberrations, as if the world had quite literally stashed away down there everything it didn't need."

Born Diane Nemerov, Arbus at eighteen had married Allan Arbus, who shortly thereafter gifted her a Graflex camera. She studies darkroom principles and techniques with Berenice Abbott. Immersing themselves in historical and contemporary photography, the Arbuses visit An American Place, Alfred Stieglitz's last gallery, and from time to time show him their work. Beginning around 1946 the couple establish a commercial fashion photography business together, in which Allan takes the pictures and Diane acts as art director and stylist. A decade later, Edward Steichen includes one of their photographs, originally shot for *Vogue*, in his ambitious exhibition *The Family of Man* (1955) at the Museum of Modern Art.

In 1956, around the time Arbus quits the photographic partnership with her husband, she takes a class with Lisette Model, the impact of which she will later recount: "A photograph has to be specific. I remember a long time ago when I first began to photograph I thought, there are an awful lot of people in the world and it's going to be terribly hard to photograph all of them, so if I photograph some kind of generalized human being, everybody'll recognize it. It'll be like what they used to call the common man or something. It was my teacher, Lisette Model, who finally made it clear to me that the more specific you are, the more general it'll be." In the spring of 1959, Arbus meets with Robert Benton, the art director for *Esquire*, because the magazine is planning its issue dedicated to New York City. Six Arbus photographs will ultimately appear in the issue, and Arbus will publish editorial projects throughout her career.

July 21–August 17, 1960 • Having just finished his undergraduate degree at the California School of Fine Arts (CSFA), William T. Wiley (1937–2021) is included with Seymour Locks in the two-person exhibition *The Image Makers* at the San Francisco Museum of Art. The show features Wiley's large-scale paintings that incorporate his emerging vocabulary of pyramids, lightning bolts, and cartographic marks.

Wiley had grown up mostly in transit, moving from Indiana through Wyoming and across the Southwest, touching down for a year in a small, forgotten town fifty miles south of Dallas—where his parents purchased a gas station and the Red Top Café—before finally settling in Richland, Washington. There Wiley's father secures a job

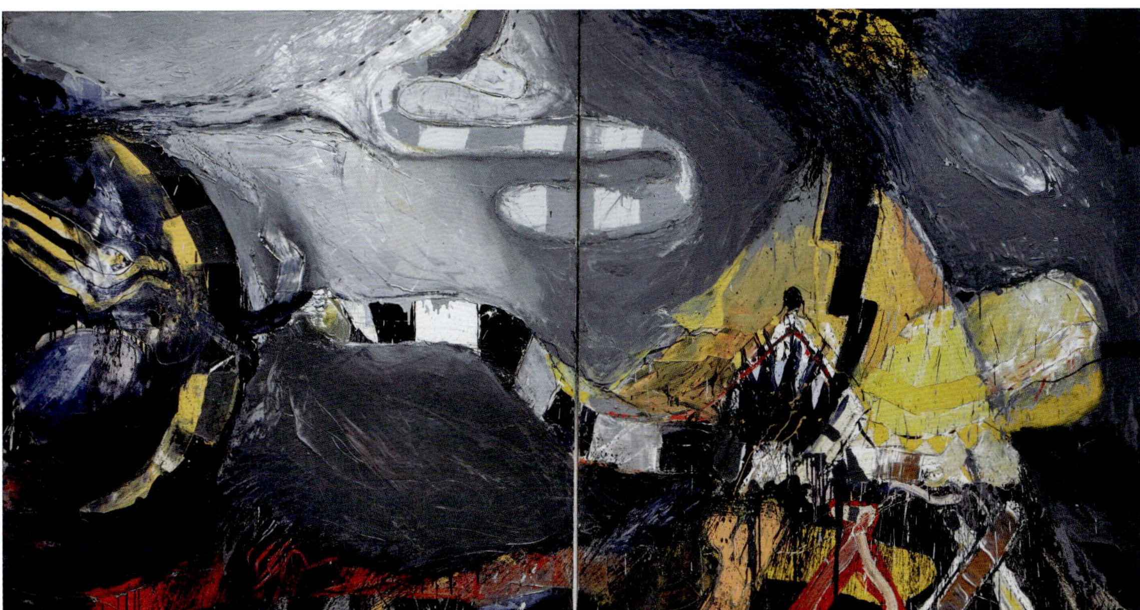

William T. Wiley, *Columbus Re-Routed*, 1961. Oil on canvas, 59 × 75 in. (149.9 × 190.5 cm)

pouring concrete for Hanford Engineer Works, the site of plutonium production facilities, and the family lives in Chubbs Trailer Court, in one of the hundreds of prefabricated homes that had sprung up to accommodate the Manhattan Project. The politics of human and environmental destruction are ever present: parents bring home radioactive wrenches from the jobsite to show their children; adventures in the desert end with stern warnings from military police; and the high school teams are named the Bombers, their logo a mushroom cloud. At Columbia High School, Wiley meets William Allan and Robert Hudson, all of whom share the same transformative high school teacher, Jim McGrath, who encourages their art. In 1956 Wiley enrolls at CSFA, where Allan is already a student and Hudson soon will be.

When Wiley first sees Jasper Johns's *Target with Four Faces* (1958) on the cover of the January 1958 issue of *ARTnews*, and Johns's painting *Flag* (1954–55) shortly after, he recognizes the older artist's understanding of absurdity and contradiction and grasps the works' relationship to Marcel Duchamp and Dada. Most crucially, he takes it as a sign that he can focus his art on the idea of the United States as embodied in the sights of his childhood—America as both subject and terrain, ideology and physical entity. Through his itinerant childhood, Wiley had picked up a taste for maps, local slang, and the great American visual vernacular: oddball mascots, folk signage, and comic books, especially Fred Harman's *Red Ryder*, with its law-and-order cowboy adventures, and Walt Kelly's *Pogo*, with its environmentalist messages and cutting wordplay rendered in virtuosic calligraphy.

September 1960 • Eduardo Carrillo (1937–1997) travels to Madrid with fellow University of California, Los Angeles (UCLA) student John Fox to study the painting techniques of the old masters and absorb the language and culture of Spain. While at Madrid's Círculo de Bellas Artes and at the Prado Museum, he analyzes works by Hieronymus Bosch, Giorgio de Chirico, El Greco, and other European painters, and he practices replicating these artists' glazing techniques in order to understand their manipulation of light and luminescence. At one point he even creates a copy of

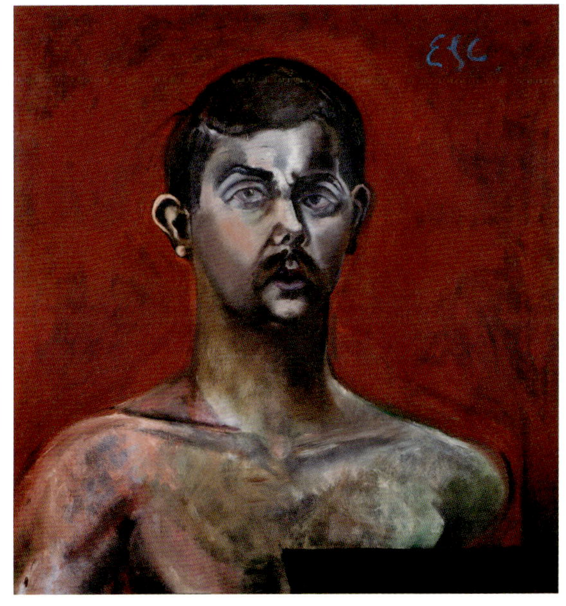

Eduardo Carrillo, *Self Portrait*, 1960. Oil on canvas, 29 ½ × 27 ¾ in. (74.9 × 70.5 cm)

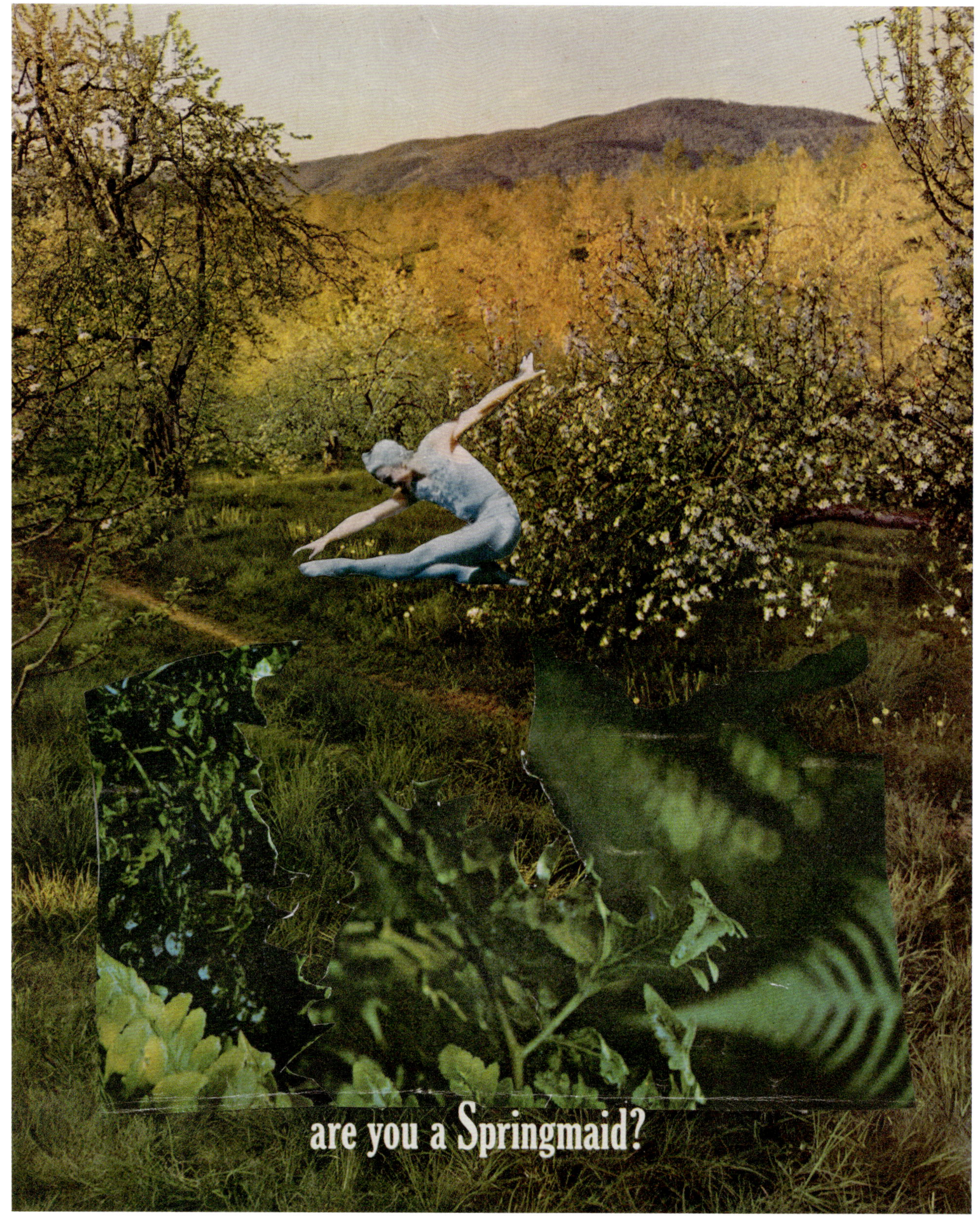

Jean Conner, *Are You a Springmaid?*, 1960. Collage, 10 ⅛ × 8 ⅛ in. (25.7 × 20.6 cm). Whitney Museum of American Art, New York; purchase, with funds from Sheree and Jerry Friedman 2018.203

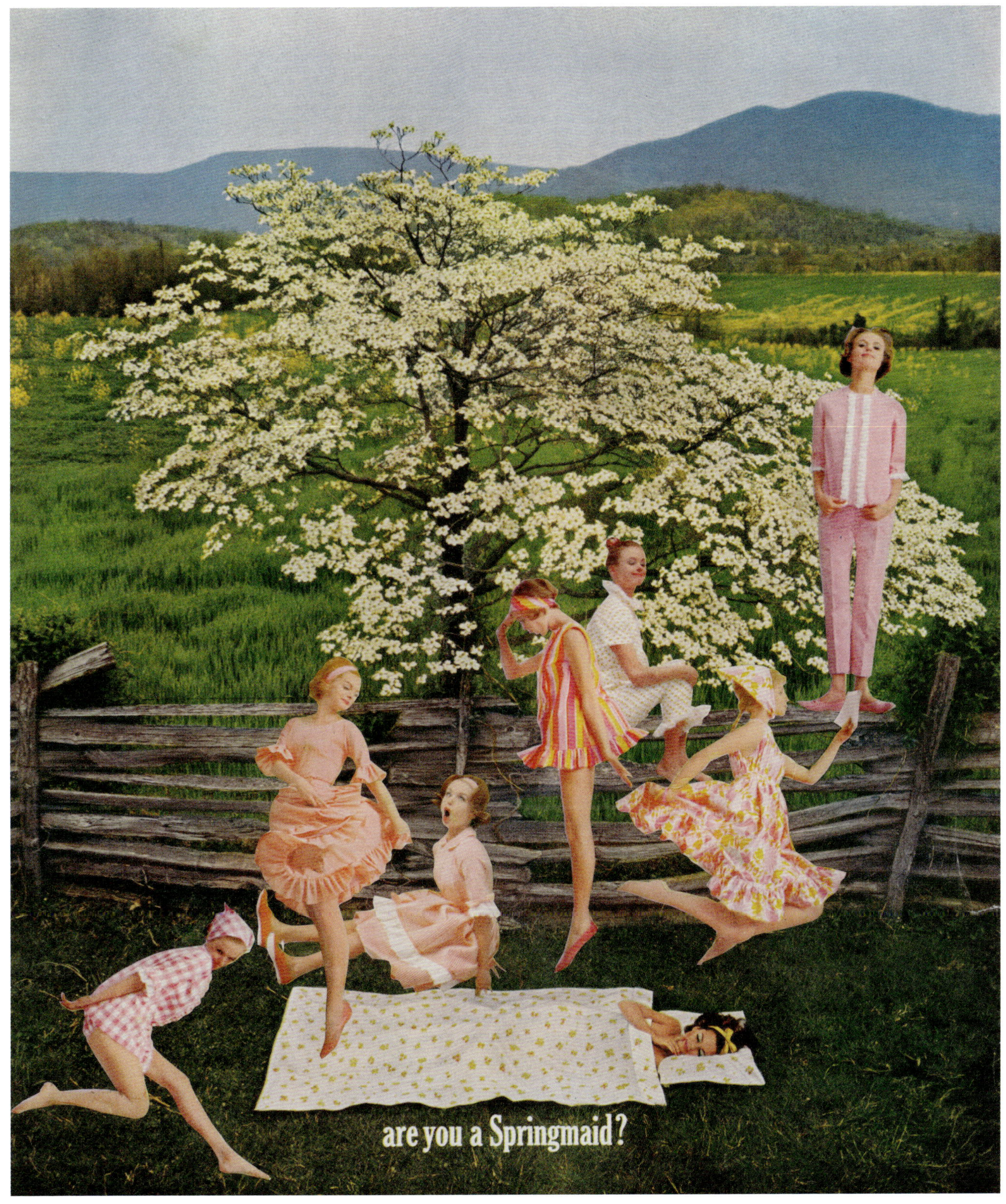

Jean Conner, *Are You a Springmaid? II*, 1960. Collage, 11 ⅞ × 9 ¾ in. (30.2 × 24.8 cm). Whitney Museum of American Art, New York; purchase, with funds from Sheree and Jerry Friedman 2018.204

Bosch's *Temptation of Saint Anthony* (1500–25). Returning from Spain in 1961 to complete his bachelor of fine arts at UCLA, Carrillo merges his study of the Mannerists such as El Greco with his interest in Surrealist spatial constructions, drawing on the metaphysical paintings of De Chirico. The Magical Realist style he develops in his mature work, after receiving his master of fine arts from UCLA in 1964, fuses old-master techniques with the uncanny charge of surreal juxtapositions and the expressive power of the Chicano art movement.

Carrillo had been born in Santa Monica, California, and raised in a household steeped in art and Catholic faith. Both his father and older brother are artists—though his father dies when he is young—and some of Carrillo's earliest memories are of the paintings, stained glass, and figurative sculpture in the churches of Los Angeles. He spends many of his boyhood summers in his mother's hometown of San Ignacio, Baja California, Mexico, a place that will hold his imagination as he develops in his artistic practice.

September 1960 • Jack Whitten (1939–2018) enrolls in the bachelor of fine arts program at the Cooper Union, beginning a nearly lifelong relationship with the institution: he and his future wife, Mary Staikos, are night students who work during the day, both finishing their degrees in 1964, and Whitten will return to teach from 1971 to 1995. While a student, he meets Willem de Kooning and is introduced to Norman Lewis by Romare Bearden. Living on the Lower East Side, he spends his free time in jazz clubs such as the Five Spot Café at Cooper Square and at the Cedar Tavern, which is frequented by de Kooning and Mark Rothko. (He later writes, "If Cooper Union offered me the Bauhaus, the Cedar Bar offered me Abstract Expressionism. Balance is an important word in my vocabulary.") Alongside his studies, he paints window displays for Marvin Sylvor, famed window and merry-go-round designer; many of the techniques he learns at this job will filter into his early paintings.

Whitten had been born in Bessemer, Alabama. His father died in 1944, leaving his mother to raise seven children. Although he had excelled in shop class in middle school, he enrolls at Tuskegee Institute in 1957 as a premed student and ROTC Air Force cadet, spending at least two summers in New York, working construction jobs and waiting tables while living with an uncle. Then, in 1959, he transfers to Southern University in Baton Rouge to study art. At this time, the civil rights movement is in full swing, and Whitten is an active participant, helping to organize a march in Baton Rouge. The violence he both sees and experiences motivates his move to the North, as he will later explain: "I knew I had to leave the South because I would be killed

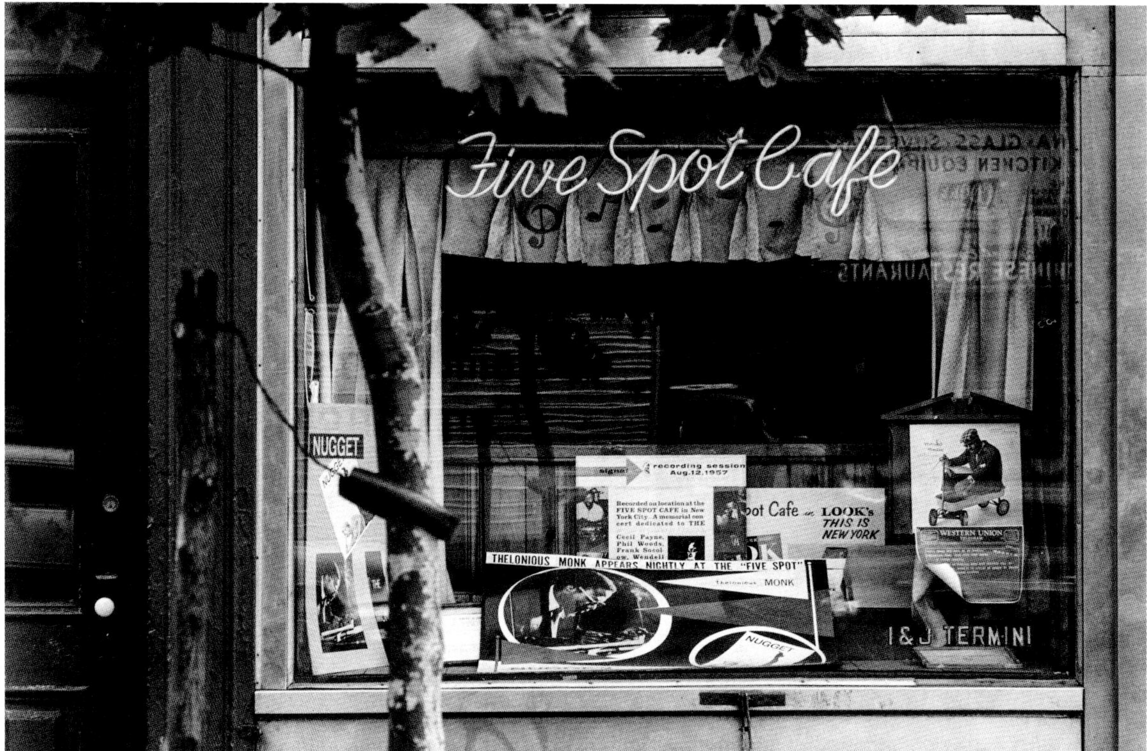

Five Spot Café, New York, c. 1957

or I would end up killing somebody." Whitten's career is inflected by both his deep engagement with philosophers—from Friedrich Nietzsche to André Malraux—and his view of art's capacity to be an "antidote" to the "poison of racism."

September 10–October 12, 1960 • Robert Arneson (1930–1992) holds his inaugural solo exhibition at the Oakland Art Museum and shows forms that reference organic shapes, signaling his move away from ceramics as either craft or abstraction. By 1960 he is sure that clay can embody ideas as well as any other medium, and this show is the first manifestation of this rethinking of ceramic art.

A native of Benicia, California, Arneson received a bachelor of arts from the California College of Arts and Crafts in 1954 and spent several years teaching high school just south of San Francisco, all the while honing his skills as a ceramicist. The medium's association with the domain of craft results in a limited number of exhibition venues willing to show such work. Nevertheless, in 1957 Arneson sees a Peter Voulkos ceramic sculpture at a state fair and embraces the idea that ceramics can be transformed into non-object art. He enrolls at Mills College, earning a master of fine arts, and in 1958 he begins making the gnarled, expressionist forms pioneered by Voulkos.

September 14–October 30, 1960 • The Whitney Museum of American Art's exhibition

Young America 1960: Thirty American Painters under Thirty-Six includes twenty-two-year-old Joan Brown on its roster, the youngest artist ever to exhibit at the museum and, according to critic Philip Lieder, "everybody's darling." She has just received a master of fine arts from the California School of Fine Arts, having completed her bachelor of fine arts only the previous year. The show tours for two years. Brown enters this new decade on an upward trajectory as a fixture of the Bay Area Figurative School and, at the time, arguably the most successful member of the Rat Bastard Protective Association, the group of artists joined in their interest in creating anti-art. The Whitney Museum, the Museum of Modern Art, Los Angeles County Museum of Art, and the Albright-Knox Art Gallery all acquire her works for their permanent collections. Having first encountered Brown in the spring of 1959 at the artist enclave Painterland in San Francisco, George Staempfli supports her through his New York gallery. Staempfli initially gives Brown $300 for two of her paintings and then offers her that amount as a monthly stipend, signaling his commitment to selling her work. Soon, however, the commercial success that Brown receives will come to feel increasingly limiting and coercive to the young artist.

October 1960 • Having read that painter Roberto Matta had given Jackson Pollock a big break, Peter Saul (b. 1934), a twenty-six-year-old expatriate living in Paris, seeks out Matta to discuss his own work. Matta, in turn, nominates Saul for a William and Noma Copley Foundation grant, which he receives in 1962; the Copleys will amass one of the largest collections of Surrealist works in the United States and had established their foundation to foster the creative arts. Matta also recommends Saul to gallery owner Allan Frumkin, who soon exhibits his work in Chicago and New York.

As a boy growing up in San Francisco, Saul had believed his father's curved spine—a complication of having contracted measles as a child—to be as grotesque as the deformed villains in his beloved *Dick Tracy* comic strips, drawn with cruel precision by Chester Gould. Out of fear that Saul might catch the disease and suffer his father's fate, his parents had sequestered him inside their home until sending him at the age of ten to Shawnigan Lake School, a boarding school deemed the strictest in North America by *Time* magazine in 1945. There, Saul learns violence, bigotry, and the absurdity of systemic thinking. He is routinely beaten with a stick for not shining his shoes, for missing multiplication problems, and even for stepping on the grass. He excels in Latin, history, and English, and is so obviously brilliant—and terrified—that he graduates from high school at the age of fifteen.

Galled by the hypocrisy of regulated, "normal" life, Saul is fascinated by artists such as Thomas Hart Benton, Paul Cadmus, and George Tooker, as well as by the artwork in the comic book *Crime Does Not Pay*. Inspired, he studies painting at Washington University in St. Louis and, upon graduating in 1956, moves first to England and then to Holland, before staying in Paris from 1958 to 1962 and finally settling in Rome until the end of 1964. Over the course of those years, he develops a unique approach to painting and drawing that draws on the vernacular language of the United States, the freedom of exquisite corpses, and the violent attack of Willem de Kooning's abstraction to offer up images that are as funny as they are horrific. Saul's insistence on showing viewers the worst of themselves is a potent, savage critique of capitalism and conformity.

November 8, 1960 • In a narrow upset victory, Democrat John F. Kennedy is elected president, capturing just two-tenths of a percent more of the popular vote than his opponent, Republican vice president Richard Nixon, and ushering in what he calls "a new generation of leadership."

November 9–December 4, 1960 • Lee Bontecou (1931–2022) holds her first solo exhibition, at Castelli Gallery, New York. The only woman on the gallery's roster, Bontecou shows variations on an idiosyncratic motif: sculptural reliefs with cavernous orifices nested in a network of concentric fabric-and-soot-covered frames. The swelling and receding structures are sinister, evoking malignant growth and industrial, scientific, and technological equipment in equal measure. Writing in *Arts Magazine*, Donald Judd praises Bontecou's work, as he will continue to do throughout the 1960s.

Coming of age on the East Coast during World War II, Bontecou had attended Bradford Junior College in Massachusetts in the early 1950s before continuing her studies at the Art Students League of New York, where she began making sculpture. In Maine in 1954, she learns welding, a skill that, along with her anger over the war, will later influence her artistic practice. While living in Rome after being awarded a Fulbright fellowship in the late 1950s, she begins to draw with soot, using a welding blowtorch with the oxygen to it turned off, later remarking, "I finally got that dark that I wanted, and a black that I wanted. And a kind of landscape or a worldscape. It just opened up kind of a new thought." She returns to New York in 1959 and starts stretching coarse cloth over welded armatures, constructing increasingly large structures from industrial and scavenged materials: automobile and airplane parts, industrial saw teeth, gears, helmets, and shrapnel.

When Bontecou has her second of five solo exhibitions at Castelli Gallery, Judd pronounces her "one of the best artists working anywhere." He describes works such as *Untitled* (1961) as consisting of "numerous and varied holes and much bellicose detail—orifical washers, mouths with saw-blades inside, barred ones, muzzles and straps" that extend "from something as social as war to something as private as sex, making one an aspect of the other."

December 7, 1960–January 22, 1961 • The Whitney Museum of American Art's *Annual Exhibition 1960: Contemporary Sculpture and Drawings* includes work from both Lee Bontecou and Louise Bourgeois. At this time and throughout the 1960s, the museum's annual survey of trends in contemporary American art switches focus every other year between painting and sculpture, with drawings or prints sometimes included with the latter. Although the shows' attempts to identify prevailing currents often garner as much criticism as praise, they nevertheless serve as indicators of the attention paid to particular artists, certain regions, and modes of making. While Annuals certainly reinforced biases in the artworld, because of their frequency and oft-changing curatorial leadership they also serve as an opportunity for lesser-known artists and less easily categorized art from across the country to be seen.

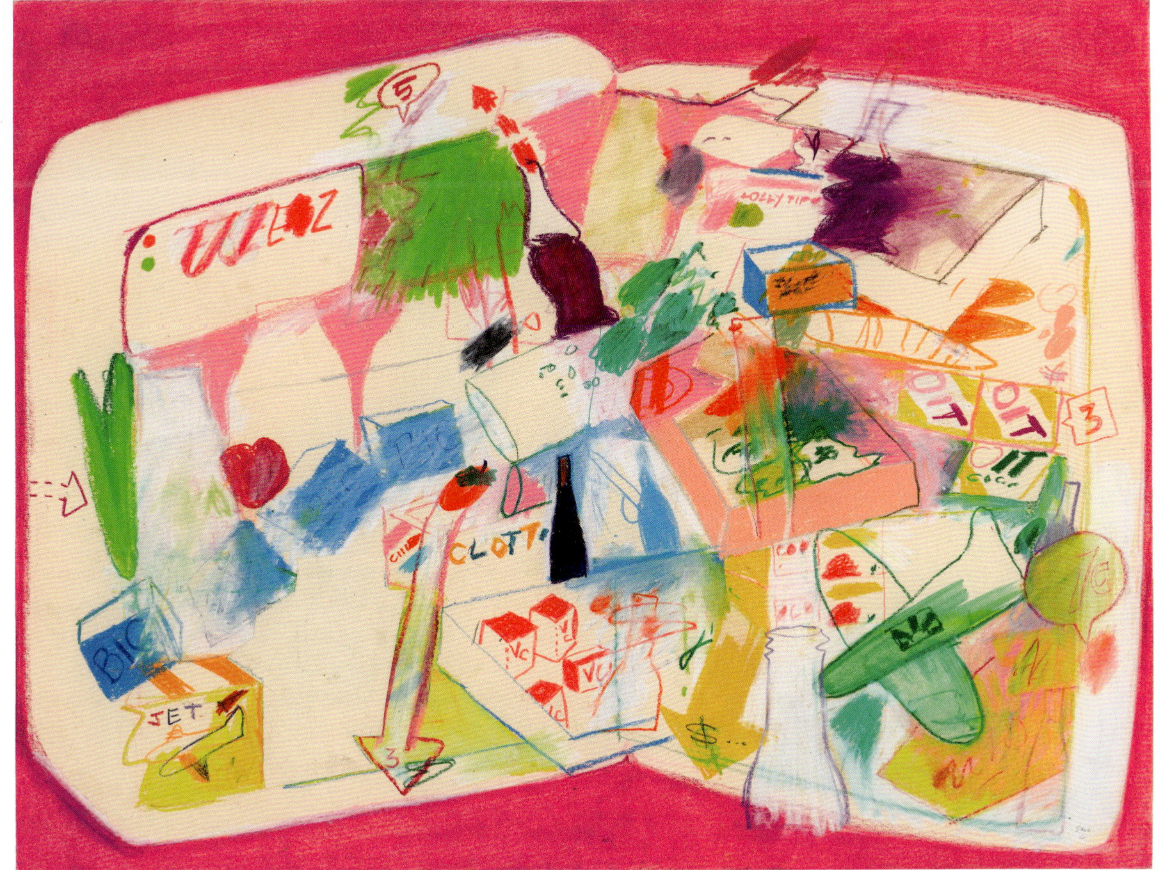

Peter Saul, *Ice Box*, 1960. Oil pastel on paper, 20 × 25 ⅞ in. (50.8 × 65.7 cm)

1961

April 1961 • Kiki Kogelnik (1935–1997) visits New York for the first time at the encouragement of Sam Francis, the American artist whom she had met in Paris the prior June. The influence of New York on her work will be remarked upon come October, when she has her first solo show, at Galerie St. Stephan in Vienna. Kogelnik had been born in Graz, Austria, and grew up in the small town of Bleiburg before studying in Vienna, first at the Academy of Applied Arts and then, in 1955, at the Academy of Fine Arts. Informed by her training at the latter, the artist's work to this point had consisted of gestural and spontaneous abstract paintings stylistically related to Art Informel and Tachisme. The economic and political climate of New York—vastly different from the austerity of the European countries still recovering from World War II—influences Kogelnik's interest in representation and new materials, and as she returns to settle in the city in September 1962, she soon meets a number of artists who share these ideas. She befriends Roy Lichtenstein, Patty Mucha and Claes Oldenburg, Tom Wesselmann, and Larry Rivers, among others, and she quickly adopts new mediums and ways of making work. "The new ideas are here, the materials are here," she says. "Why not use them?"

Spring 1961 • Raymond Saunders (b. 1934) receives his master of fine arts from the California College of Arts and Crafts before moving to New York.

Saunders had been born and raised in Pittsburgh, Pennsylvania, a city that had helped define him: he participated in the city's outstanding children's art programming; became familiar with European modernism through the Carnegie Internationals; and, as a student in the Carnegie Museum of Natural History's classes for talented children, will recall traversing the galleries every Saturday, learning about dinosaurs, birds, and history. For Saunders, this formation was a direct and total "art experience," as he will characterize it: "No one had to say, this is Picasso, this is Matisse, this is the French school, the Italian school. . . . I saw all that, and took it in, as a kind of vicarious experience." In elementary school and high school, he studies art under Joseph C. Fitzpatrick, whose other students include Mel Bochner, Philip Pearlstein, and Andy Warhol, and who helps Saunders secure a fellowship to attend the Pennsylvania Academy of Fine Arts in Philadelphia.

While in Philadelphia in the mid-1950s, Saunders also studies at the University of Pennsylvania as well as the Barnes Foundation, whose eclectic collection of European modernism and art from Africa and the precolonial Americas—all displayed in jam-packed, heterogeneous wall ensembles—encourages his affection for montage. After moving to Oakland following a two-year stint in the military, he feeds this sensibility and starts incorporating found objects into his paintings through a process of affinity and chance encounter that echoes André Breton's anecdote of discovering his first *objet trouvé* (*La grande cuiller*) during a trip to the flea market with Alberto Giacometti in 1935. Saunders will describe how the found object "finds you; you find it. You become visually receptive, attuned. You take something off the street not knowing if you'll use it, or how." The found object plays a central role in the improvisation that guides Saunders's process. Known to revise works while they are being exhibited, he understands paintings to be in a constant state of metamorphosis.

1961 • Luchita Hurtado (1920–2020) gains access to private studio space for the first time in her life. Her husband, Lee Mullican, takes a teaching position at the University of California, Los Angeles, and the stability after years of travel enables Hurtado to rent a studio space with a door that closes. In this "room of her own," she makes figurative ink drawings on paper and begins to paint self-portraits, which she will not show to anyone for another decade.

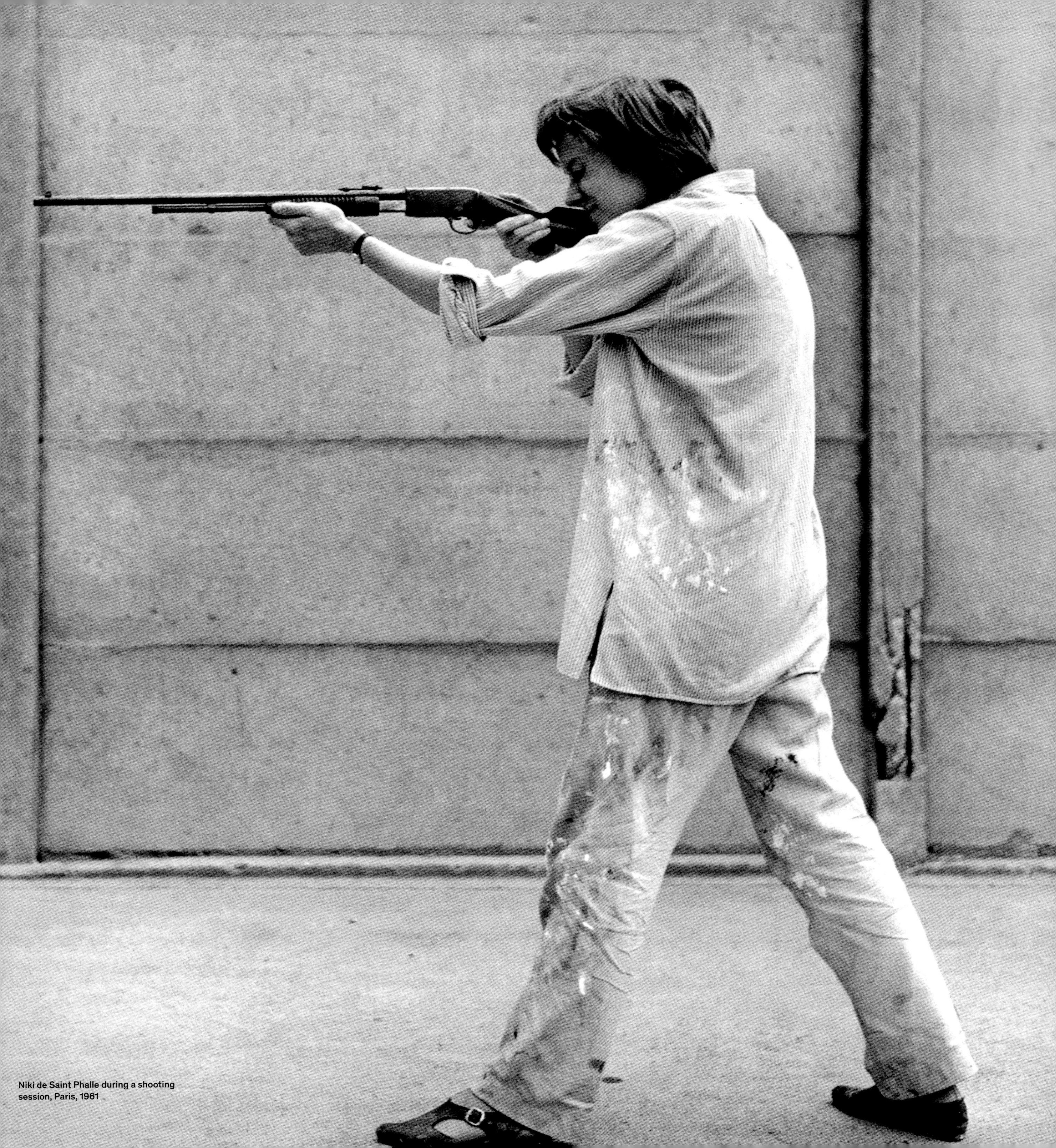

Niki de Saint Phalle during a shooting
session, Paris, 1961

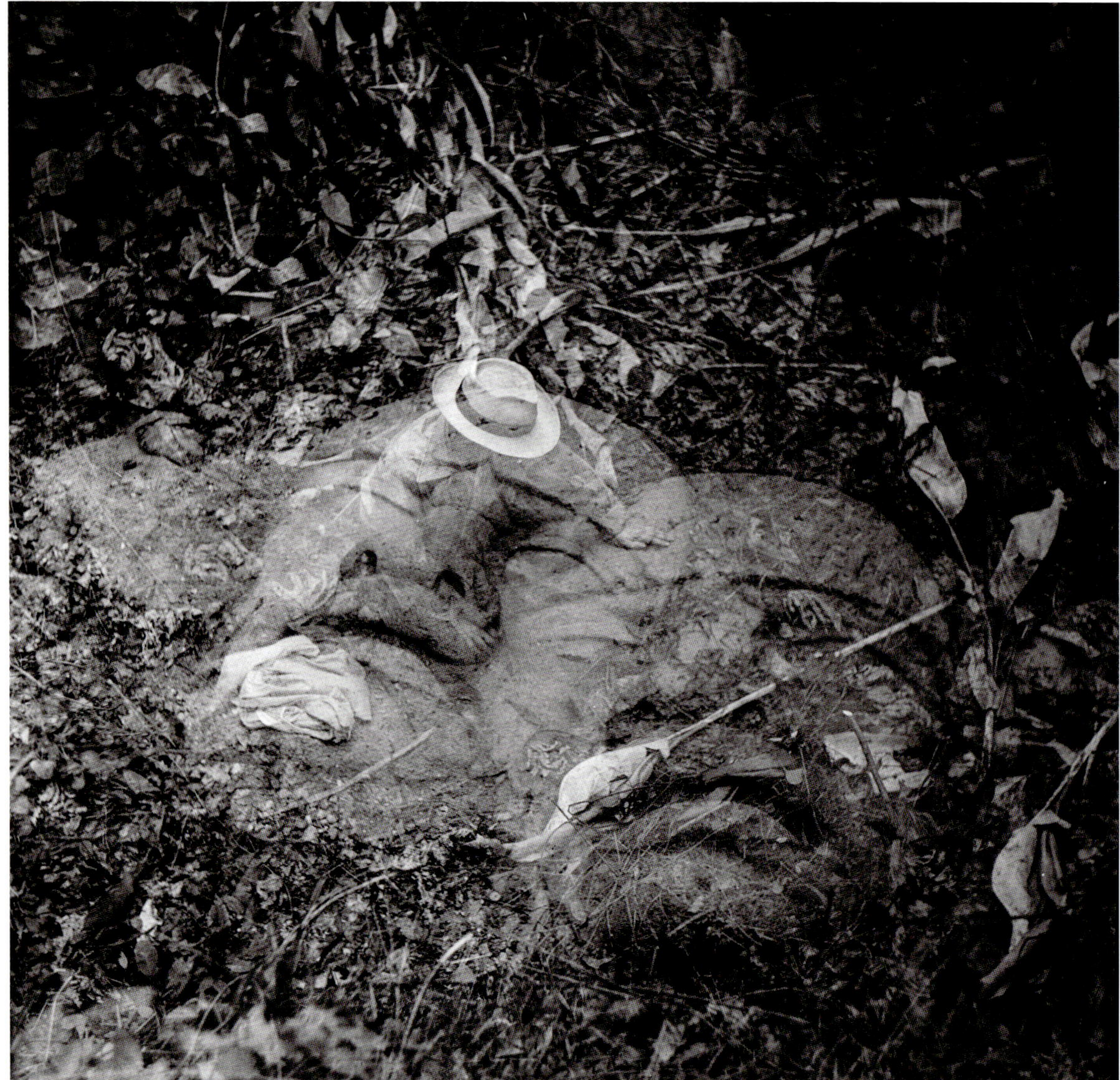

Photograph by Luchita Hurtado of Wolfgang Paalen with an Olmec colossal head, San Lorenzo, Mexico, 1946

Born in Maiquetía, Venezuela, Hurtado immigrated to the United States at age eight. While living with extended family in New York, she studies art at Washington Irving High School and, briefly, at the Art Students League. However, after 1938, the year Hurtado married the Chilean journalist Daniel Del Solar, her artistic practice became a private pursuit. She paints and draws at night, after her family has gone to sleep. Despite her secrecy surrounding her own work, Hurtado spends her life around art and artists, forging intimate friendships with modern artists in every city in which she lives. She meets Isamu Noguchi and his social circle—including Surrealists Maya Deren, Roberto Matta, and Rufino Tamayo—while living in New York in the 1940s.

Her marriage to Del Solar ends in 1946, and she moves with her two young sons to Mexico City to be with the Austrian Surrealist and amateur anthropologist Wolfgang Paalen, her second husband. In Mexico, Hurtado begins to seriously collect ancient Indigenous art of the Americas, joining Paalen on expeditions to view monumental ruins; her photographs of their trip to see the Olmec heads in Veracruz illustrate an article Paalen publishes in 1952. In 1948 Hurtado's son Pablo dies of polio, and in her grief, she insists on leaving Mexico. The family moves to Mill Valley, California, in 1949, and their home becomes the headquarters of Dynaton, a new group of painters who bring Surrealism to the West Coast and exhibit together at the San Francisco Museum of Art in 1951. Hurtado and Paalen's marriage dissolves, and she begins a relationship with the American abstract painter Lee Mullican, who is part of Dynaton. Mullican's career takes the family to Europe, where Hurtado sees cave paintings in the South of France, and to Chile, where she paints in a closet that she has transformed into a makeshift studio.

———

Spring 1961 • Karl Wirsum (1939–2021) graduates from the School of the Art Institute of Chicago (SAIC). Born and raised in the city, he is the only child of German immigrants, both of whom are skilled at art and making crafts at home. For a young Wirsum, the hyperbole of Riverview, Chicago's amusement park, had a profound impact: "The major draw for me . . . was the sideshow tent. The exterior banners were painted by artists such as Snap Wyatt and Fred Johnson, who had a Chicago studio in the back of an awning factory a couple blocks north of Wrigley Field on Clark Street. The banners pictured exaggerated scenes that featured the various sideshow attractions such as the 'Alligator Lady.'" He then finds music to be stimulating for his art: "In my teens and twenties, two venues for musical inspiration of the blues and gospel variety were Maxwell Street and, later, the blues clubs on the South and West Sides. . . . One might ask how audio would aid the visual. A main regard here was the premise of me secretly wanting to be a blues singer. Having no musical skills and not seeing the possibility for expression in that way, I reacted by painting images that would be the blues equivalent to it."

The education Wirsum receives at SAIC will inform the rest of his artistic life:

Kathleen Blackshear . . . presented the art of Asia, China and Japan, the Mideast, Persia and India, ancient art of the Americas and Africa, and showed how this art influenced artists from the Impressionists to Picasso. Whitney Halstead . . . focused on some of the different movements of the twentieth century along with similar material to what Blackshear covered. Both of them had a lot of slide material that they would show for

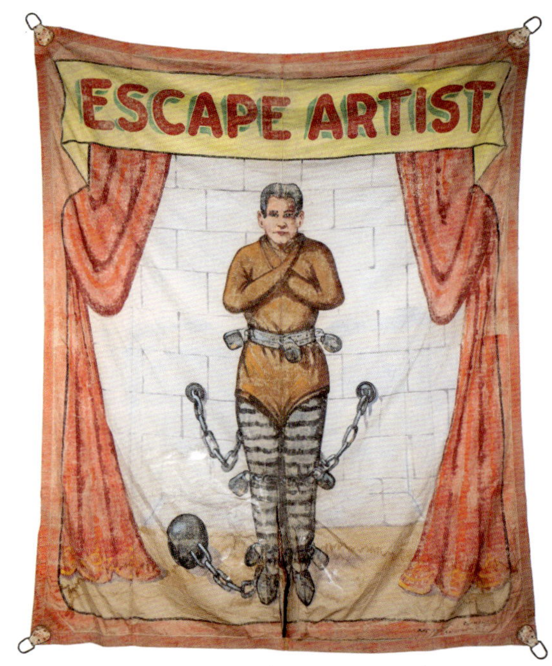

Banner by Fred Johnson for "Escape Artist" sideshow, Chicago, c. 1950s

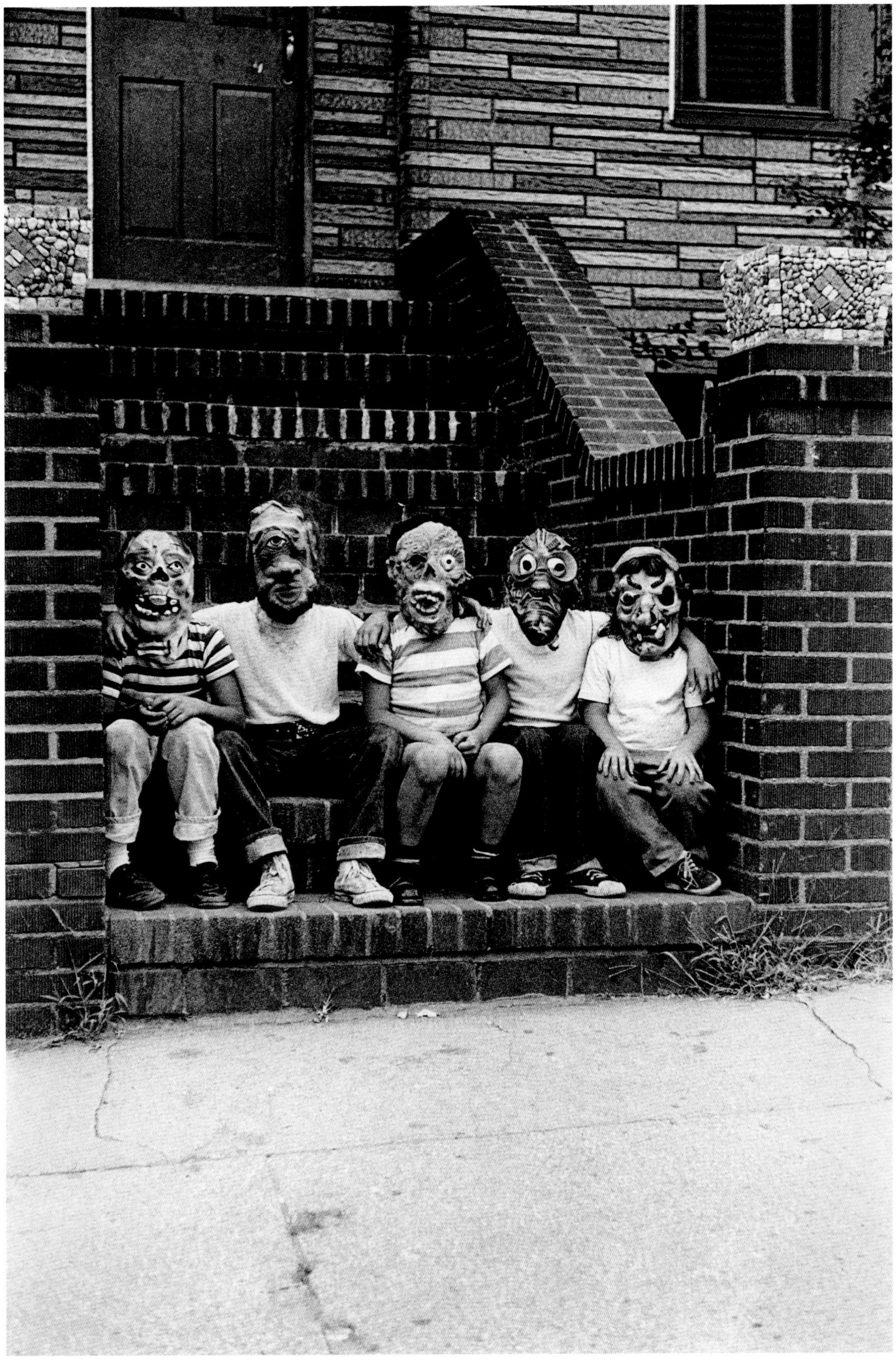

Diane Arbus, *Five members of The Monster Fan Club, N.Y.C. 1961*, 1961. Gelatin silver print, 10 ⅜ × 6 ½ in. (26.4 × 16.5 cm). Collection of Steve Lockshin and Allison Schaengold Lockshin

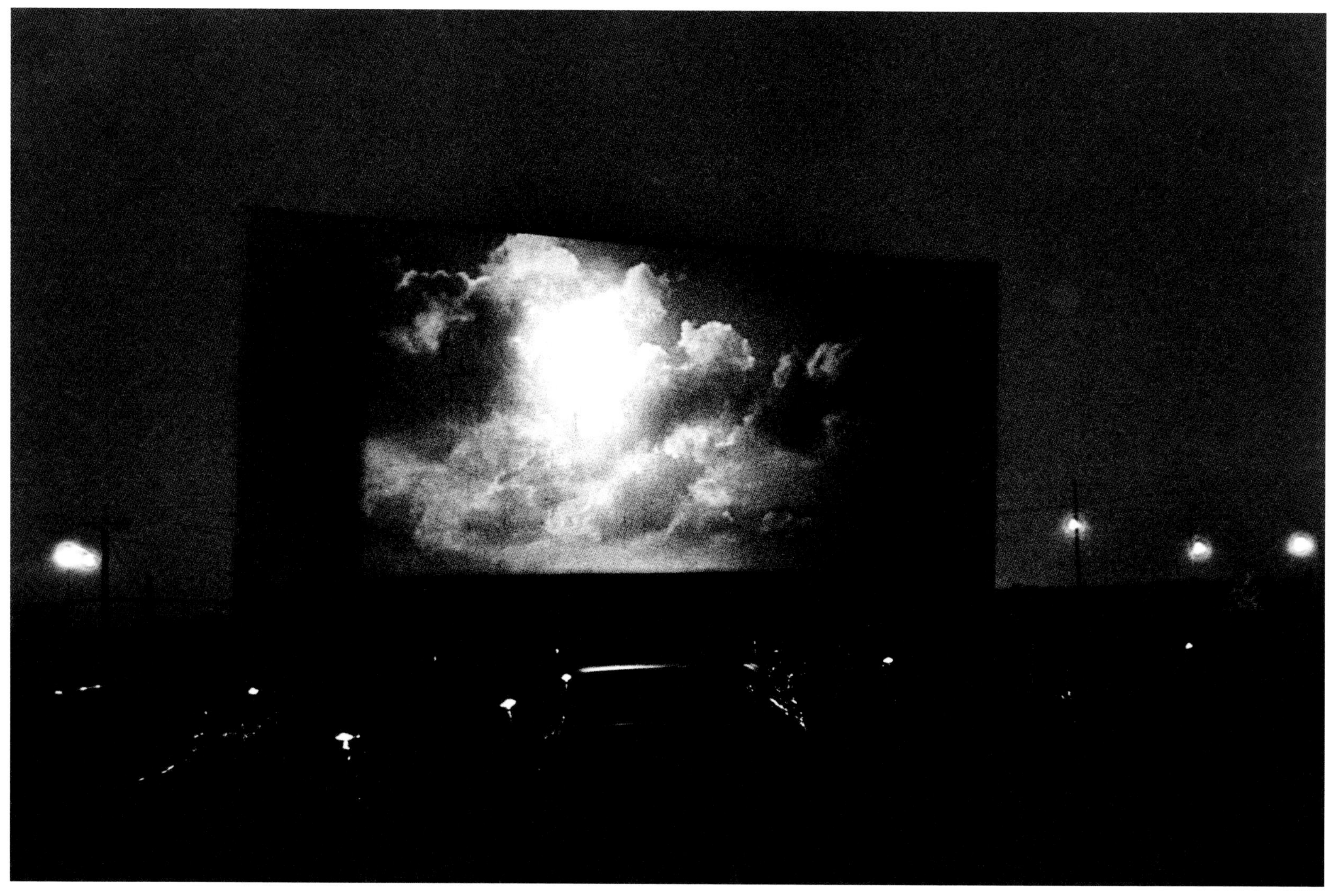

48   Diane Arbus, *Clouds on-screen at a drive-in movie, N.J. 1961*, 1961. Gelatin silver print: sheet, 16 × 20 in. (40.6 × 50.8 cm); image, 12 ¼ × 18 ¼ in. (31.1 × 46.4 cm). The Metropolitan Museum of Art, New York; gift of Neil Selkirk, 2012 2012.552.60

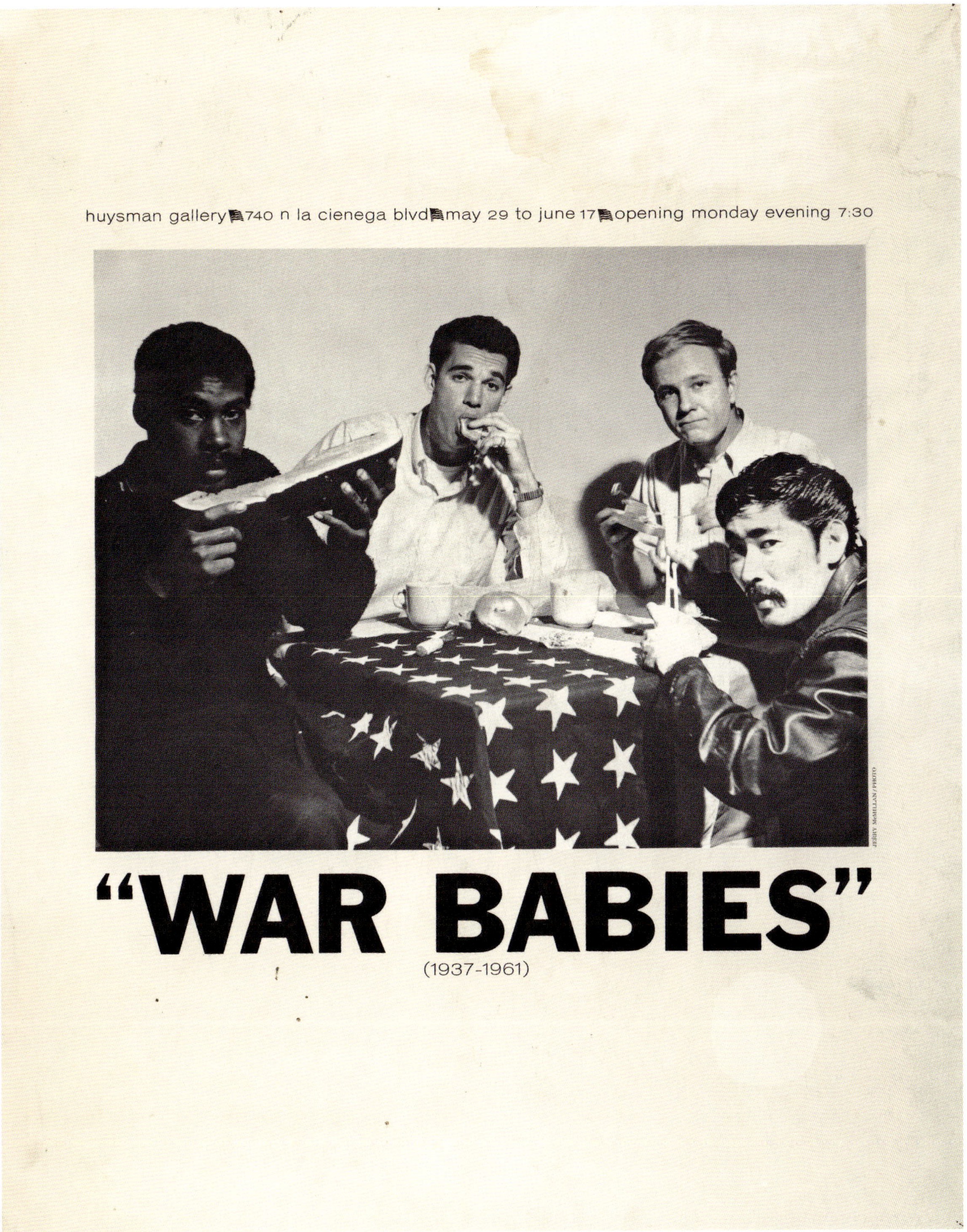

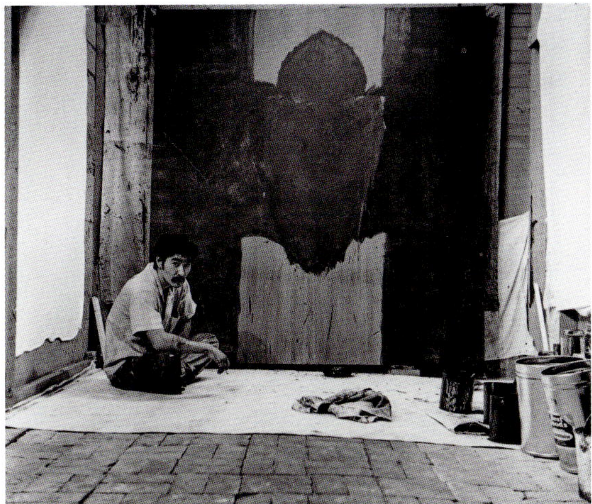

Ron Miyashiro in his studio, Los Angeles, 1961

his peers to adopt a flat, acrylic-on-Plexiglas technique, uniting the sights and sounds around him with an exacting contour line.

May 4, 1961 • The first Freedom Ride departs from Washington, DC, en route to New Orleans. Organized by student activists from the Congress of Racial Equality (CORE), the rides are intended to challenge segregation on interstate buses and at bus terminals. Violence erupts in Rock Hill, South Carolina, when a few riders are beaten, and others are arrested. The attacks intensify in Anniston and Birmingham, Alabama, where violent mobs that include members of the Ku Klux Klan assault riders. Local authorities condone the violence and do not intercede. Nevertheless, the Freedom Rides persist until, and to some extent after, President John F. Kennedy's administration directs the Interstate Commerce Commission to ban segregation in all facilities under its jurisdiction, an order that goes into effect on November 1, 1961.

May 29–June 17, 1961 • The exhibition *War Babies* is on view at Huysman Gallery and includes works by Larry Bell, Ed Bereal, Joe Goode, and Ron Miyashiro. This show is unique in the Los Angeles scene at the time, as it features a racially and ethnically diverse list of artists. The impact of the show, however, lay mostly in its iconic poster. Conceived by Goode, the exhibition's organizer, and executed by photographer Jerry McMillan, the poster depicts Bell, Bereal, Goode, and Miyashiro sitting around a table covered by an American flag and consuming foods stereotypically associated with their individual identities— Bereal holds a watermelon, for example. The staunchly conservative John Birch Society takes offense to the use of the flag—and, likely, also to

Poster by Jerry McMillan and Joe Goode for *War Babies*, Huysman Gallery, Los Angeles, 1961

most of the class, and their focus was less on the scholarly aspects of art history and more on the visual components of what we were looking at. An example to illustrate their approach: when we were studying the Egyptian period, the assignment would be to do a modern-day tableau in the manner of Egyptian art. This allowed the instructor to assess each student's understanding of the visual approach to art in this culture in a way that a scholarly-paper product might not.

Alert to the surrealist currents in Chicago— namely, the work of Richard Lindner and H. C. Westermann—Wirsum is also fascinated with Mesoamerican art, Peruvian pottery, and the schematic, grotesque comic-strip art of George Wunder (*Terry and the Pirates*) and Chester Gould (*Dick Tracy*), all of which combine with his engagement with the city itself—an urban stew of hand-painted signage, eccentric characters, and gritty music—to form the artist's unique sensibility. By 1965 Wirsum has become the first among

the implication of racial social mixing, given the group's position against the civil rights movement. The subsequent controversy leads the gallery's financial backers to withdraw their support, and Huysman Gallery closes that summer.

June 1961 • Wallace Berman (1926–1976) and his family return to Los Angeles after four years in Northern California, where Berman had met Bruce and Jean Conner and collaborated with Jay DeFeo and other avatars of the San Francisco scene.

Berman had been born on Staten Island but from the age of ten had lived in Los Angeles, where he eventually finds the jazz scene, gets busted for marijuana and, when offered a choice between the military and jail, enters the Navy for a disastrous stint. Back in Los Angeles, Berman collects issues of the New York–based surrealist journal *View*; visits William Copley's short-lived gallery, which also exhibits European Surrealism; and meets Walter Hopps, poet Bob Alexander, Dean Stockwell, and Dennis Hopper. Alexander, Hopps, and artist Ed Kienholz open Ferus Gallery in 1957, and a few months later, Berman opens his first one-person show there, in which he exhibits an explicitly sexual drawing by the artist Cameron. Someone calls the LAPD, which closes the exhibition and fines Berman $150 for obscenity. After the show, Berman decamps to Northern California and makes art mostly for himself and his friends, including issues of *Semina*, the ever-changing publication which he Continued on page 53

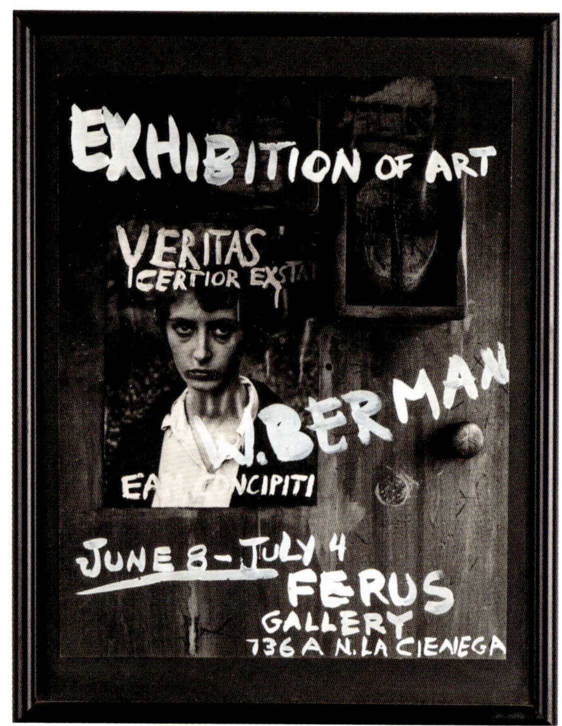

Poster by Wallace Berman for *Wallace Berman*, Ferus Gallery, Los Angeles, 1957

KABBALAH SURREALISM

LUCY BRADNOCK

Kabbalist Surrealism is nothing if not the mythic confirmation of art-as-life-as-purest-friendship, the poem itself.

– Jack Hirschman[1]

On July 19, 1972, at the Evergreen Stage in Hollywood, poet Jack Hirschman inaugurated an exhibition of his glyphic-graphic works by reading at length from his translations of the dissident Surrealist writer Antonin Artaud, then performing a speech on what Hirschman termed "Kabala Surrealism."[2] The phenomenon he described, a countercultural fusion of esoteric Judaism and literary surrealism, he discerned in the practice of a group of poets and artists active predominantly on the West Coast in the 1960s and early 1970s, among them the poets Robert Duncan, David Meltzer, and Jerome Rothenberg, and the artist Wallace Berman, whom Hirschman hailed as "one of K.S.'s leading fotographic exponents."[3]

Hirschman's praise of Berman was perhaps unsurprising, given the latter's sustained interest in Dada and Surrealist artists and poets (Artaud in particular), his repeated use of Hebrew letters in his work, and his status as a crucial member of Beat circles. Hirschman's speech, like Berman's art, was dense with literary and artistic allusions. In it, he identified California as the cultural crucible in which Kabbalah surrealism had been forged in the postwar decades, via an encounter between the automatic techniques of the French Surrealists and those practiced by early modern Kabbalists, the two belief systems merging with Beat poetics and the counterculture's enthusiasm for diverse strains of spiritualism. An incongruous hybrid, Kabbalah surrealism was epitomized for Hirschman, as it was for Meltzer and Berman, in the unlikely coincidence of Artaud and thirteenth-century Kabbalist poet Abraham ben Samuel Abulafia, on the grounds of their shared alchemical approach to language and mutual outsider status that disrupted social and cultural norms. For the community of American postwar poets and artists that coalesced around Hirschman, Meltzer, and Berman, Kabbalah surrealism held, too, the promise of a world shaped according to poetic essence rather than commercial imperatives, operating as a form of resistance to the superficialities of American postwar culture, including the mainstream co-option of Surrealism.

While the interest in esoteric Judaism of the group Hirschman termed Kabbalah surrealists undoubtedly connects to the broader Beat and countercultural interest in non-Western spiritualism, in many cases it was also informed by close study and the practice of translation.[4] For Duncan, access to Kabbalah came via his parents' theosophical meetings, which included group readings of important Kabbalistic texts; Duncan, in turn, shared with his friends sources such as Gershom Scholem's seminal tome *Major Trends in Jewish Mysticism*, published in the United States in 1941, with a full chapter on Kabbalah.[5] Meltzer drove the dissemination of several of these texts via his Kabbalah imprint Tree Books, which between 1970 and 1975 published both medieval and twentieth-century Kabbalistic writing, sources which, Meltzer explained, "I have found to have supreme relevance to my work & quest."[6] Hirschman's translation work included both Kabbalistic texts and Surrealist ones, as well as those that touched on both categories, such as his work on the 1965 *Artaud Anthology*, which included Artaud's own Kabbalah-inspired writings.[7]

As the role played by translations of Artaud's work suggests, Americans also encountered the Kabbalah indirectly via the work of European Surrealists, either by means of their presence in exile in the United States or by the publication and circulation of their work in English translation. As such, Beat esotericism was to a large degree Surrealist in both origin and tenor. As Stephen Fredman has noted, several of the Surrealists, including writer and poet René Daumal and painter Kurt Seligmann, turned to Kabbalah and other hermetic systems of thought, such as tarot, astrology, and alchemy, for their potential to serve as "an assault on the reign of rationality."[8] Seligmann's

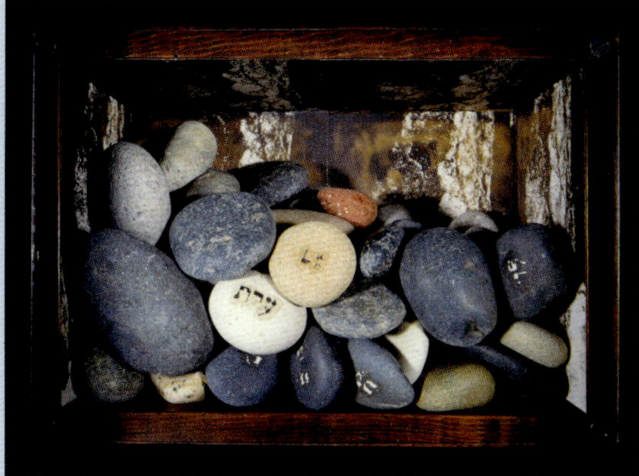

Fig. 1. Wallace Berman, *Untitled*, 1972. Stone, wood, paint, Plexiglas, and screws, 9 ¾ × 13 ½ × 6 ½ in. (24.8 × 34.3 × 16.5 cm)

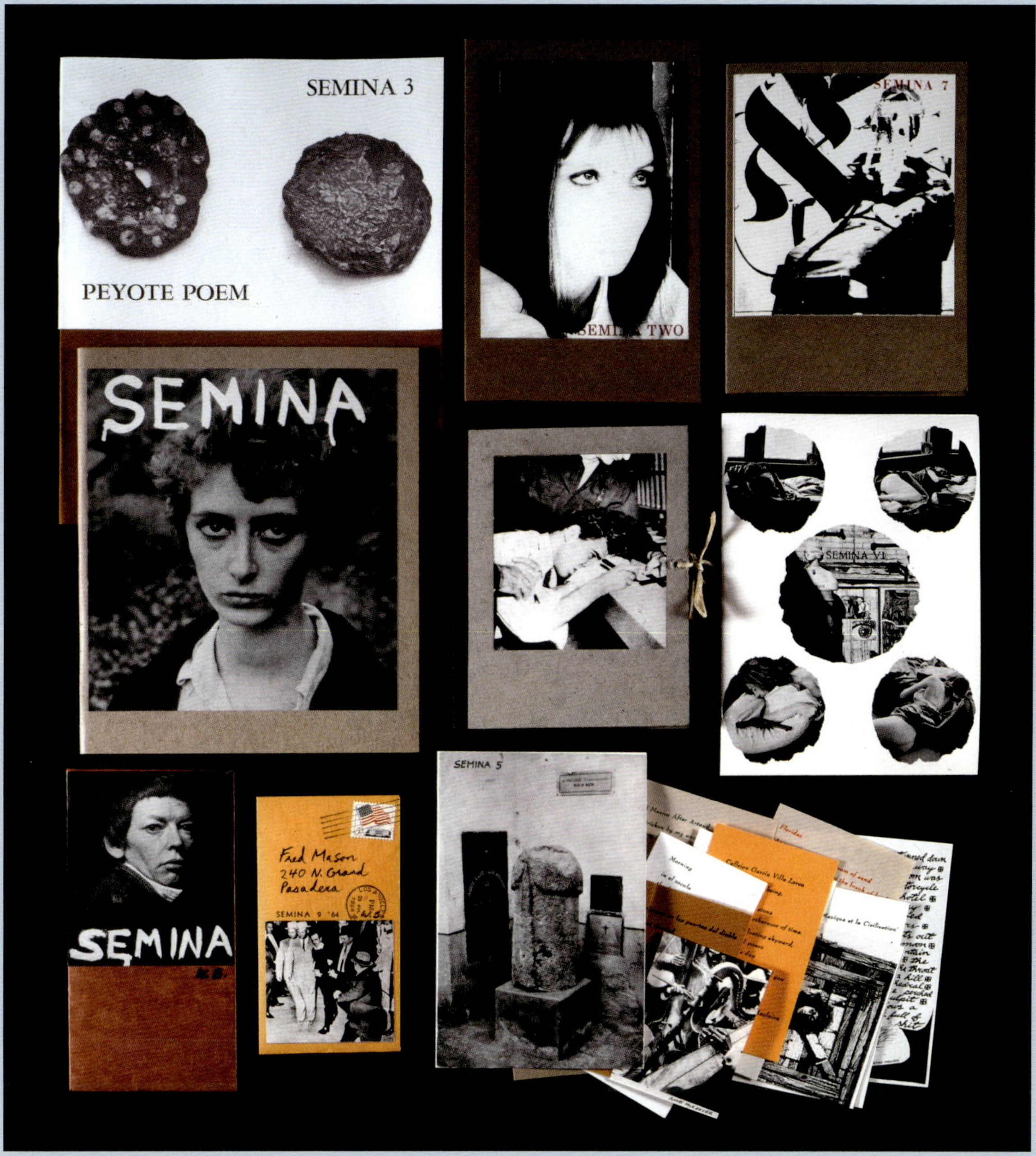

History of Magic, published in the United States in 1948 and richly illustrated from the artist's personal collection of esoterica, offered American poets and artists an important primer on hermetic belief systems and practices, including a chapter on Kabbalah that explicated what Seligmann termed the "magic of letters."[9]

Inspired by the investigations of such Surrealist forebears, West Coast artists in the postwar decades similarly turned to a panoply of hermetic sources to create works that invoked partially forgotten ritual languages and forms. Such esoteric Beat cosmologies might be discerned, for example, in Wally Hedrick's 1961 painting *HERMETIC IMAGE* (p. 59); in the work of the poet Diane di Prima, whose collages combined cut-and-pasted images of ancient, non-Western cultures; or in the arcane visual references that nestle among Victoriana and popular visual culture in the densely allusive "Paste-Ups" of the Bay Area artist known as Jess. Hirschman's art that he exhibited at Evergreen Stage and described as "glyphic-graphic works, grimoires [spell-books], kameas [magic mathematical squares], collages, etc" embodied this fascination with the potent fusion of magic, alchemy, and art. These talismanic formats are evident, too, in collaged missives that Berman sent to friends and family, wooden boxes he filled with pebbles inscribed with Hebrew letters (fig. 1), and the loose-leaf, letterpress journal *Semina*, which he produced sporadically between 1955 and 1964 (fig. 2). In all of these, Hebrew letters structure an encounter with the world, appearing painted, printed, and transferred onto images, objects, even film. In Berman's eclectic visual lexicon, references to the Kabbalah mingle with European and American poetry and art, contemporary sporting figures, pop and jazz music, and the people and objects in his immediate California environs (p. 115).

Berman's understanding of Kabbalah was informed, like Hirschman's, by his friendship with

Fig. 2. Wallace Berman, *Semina 1–9*, 1956–64. Letterpress and collage on cardstock, various sizes

Meltzer and other Jewish poets, his collection and study of books on Judaism, and his reading of Surrealist poets and writers, many of whom he included in *Semina*. Among those he most revered was Artaud, whose work first appeared in translation in the United States at the turn of the 1950s, and whose evocation in Kabbalistic terms of the numerological-alchemical landscape of Mexico Berman published in excerpted form in *Semina*'s fifth issue.[10] That text figures what Hirschman would recognize as Kabbalah surrealism in the form of signs and symbols that both structure and animate the twisted natural forms that Artaud describes. As Colin Gardner has noted, in the Kabbalistic worldview, "the truth or meaning of language is not to be found in or 'behind' the words

themselves, but *between* the lines, *between* the letters as visual signs."[11] The Hebrew characters that Berman incorporated into his work function not to convey some hidden narrative but as elements in their own right, the building blocks of the world itself, and as sparks that galvanize meaning amid an assemblage of other cultural references. His engagement with the Kabbalah, mediated through surrealism, was practice as much as subject matter, to the extent that Berman identified with the *aleph* as his personal symbol.

The Kabbalistic notion of signs as matter and energy combines in Berman's work with ideas gleaned from Surrealism, of the strange or incongruous, of magic, and of inert matter brought to life. As Hirschman recalled it, "The word *Kabbalah* means 'reception' and receiving was important to Wallace—he kept channels open at all times."[12] The notion of art as a receiver of poetic vibrations is most clearly epitomized in Berman's *Radio/Aether* series, works which combine a found advertisement for a handheld Sony transistor radio with an eclectic range of imagery overlaid with Hebrew letters, then run through a Verifax copier machine (fig. 3). In burnished tones that are redolent of alchemical processes—indeed, the Verifax necessitated a complex mixing of photoreproductive chemicals—the images were presented singly or combined to form cascading grids. Transcending straightforward Pop representation of mass culture, the Verifax works embed the artist and viewer alike in an expansive and undifferentiated field of images and letters in a manner shaped by Kabbalah surrealism.

If Kabbalah surrealism represented a poetic and artistic credo of receptiveness or expansiveness for American poets and artists, it was one that carried with it a distinct countercultural politics. And if Hirschman observed it as an insistently localized phenomenon, specific to the California coast, it also had wider potential in the context of the postwar United States. The fusion of Kabbalah and surrealism represented a form of expression at the limits of visibility, one that undercut the superficial mainstream quotation of Surrealism that Hirschman aligned with the neutralizing impetus of academia, the forces of corporate America, or the world of commercial entertainment. Instead, Kabbalah surrealism offered American poets and artists "a space *under* the electric-line of corporate fascism" or "cinematic fascism."[13] It sidestepped what many in the American counterculture saw as the empty co-option of Surrealism evident in the shopwindows of Fifth Avenue or the movies of Hollywood, symptomatic of a superficial tendency to "merely *use* them [Surrealists] rather than discover *through* them."[14] In contrast, breathing in Surrealism in its visionary manifestation chimed with Kabbalah in that it grounded the self in the world across time.

This collapsing of time that is at the heart of Kabbalah surrealism is evident in the mélange of historical and contemporary sources out of which collagists such as Hedrick, di Prima, Berman, Jess, and others assembled their works. In his account, Hirschman singles out an early Berman photomontage that combines the *aleph* with an image of jazz saxophonist Charlie Parker and visual references to the Old Testament as paradigmatic of the Kabbalah surrealist tendency, evidence both of the transhistorical sources of Kabbalah surrealism and of its contemporary poetic and political relevance beyond white Jewish American culture. Kabbalah surrealism's roots in the combined condition of diaspora and linguistic fragmentation, he proposed, made it relevant for postwar Black poetics and protest, and for a repoliticized reception of Surrealism in the Cold War period. Though explicit deployment of this countercultural Kabbalah surrealism would remain relatively contained, its ethos of cultural eclecticism—reception as aspiration in the sense of breath—held radical potential for postwar artistic practices more widely as an approach to cultural exchange, in a manner that nuances the pervasive narrative of Surrealism "in exile."

NOTES
1   Jack Hirschman, "K.S." (Venice, CA: Beyond Baroque Foundation Publications, 1972), 10.
2   The text of Hirschman's speech was published, with extensive footnoted exegesis, as "K.S.," first in the fall 1972 issue of Beyond Baroque's house journal *Newletters* and then as an autonomous chapbook, volume 4, no. 2 of Beyond Baroque Foundation Publications.
3   Hirschman, "K.S.," 8.
4   See Christine A. Meilicke, "Abulafianism Among the Counterculture Kabbalists," *Jewish Studies Quarterly* 9, no. 1 (2002): 71–101.
5   The book remains in Berman's archive, along with several other texts on Judaism and Jewish mysticism.
6   Meltzer to Jerome Rothenberg, September 18, 1970; cited in Christine A. Meilicke, "The Forgotten History of David Meltzer's Journal 'Tree,'" *Studies in American Jewish Literature* 22 (2003): 55.
7   *Artaud Anthology*, ed. Jack Hirschman (San Francisco: City Lights, 1965). The volume includes, for example, Artaud's "Concerning a Journey to the Land of the Tarahumaras" (pp. 69–83) and "Letter Against the Kabbala" (pp. 113–23).
8   Stephen Fredman, "Surrealism Meets Kabbalah: Wallace Berman and the Semina Poets," in *Semina Culture: Wallace Berman and His Circle*, ed. Michael Duncan and Kristine McKenna (New York: D.A.P.; Santa Monica, CA: Santa Monica Museum of Art, 2005), 45. See also *Surrealism and Magic: Enchanted Modernity* (Munich: Prestel, 2022); and Will Atkin, *Surrealist Sorcery: Objects, Theories, and Practices of Magic in the Surrealist Movement* (London: Bloomsbury, 2023).
9   Kurt Seligmann, *The History of Magic* (New York: Pantheon, 1948), 338–58.
10   Antonin Artaud, excerpt from "Le Mexique et la Civilization" (1935–36), translation uncredited, *Semina* 5 (1959).
11   Colin Gardner, "The Influence of Wallace Berman on the Visual Arts," in *Wallace Berman: Support the Revolution*, ed. Eduardo Lipschutz-Villa (Amsterdam: Institute of Contemporary Arts, 1992), 87.
12   Jack Hirschman, in conversation with Kristine McKenna, February 25, 2000, cited in "Chronology: 1926–1976," in Duncan and McKenna, eds., *Semina Culture*, 345.
13   Hirschman, "K.S.," 8, 13.
14   Ibid., 7.

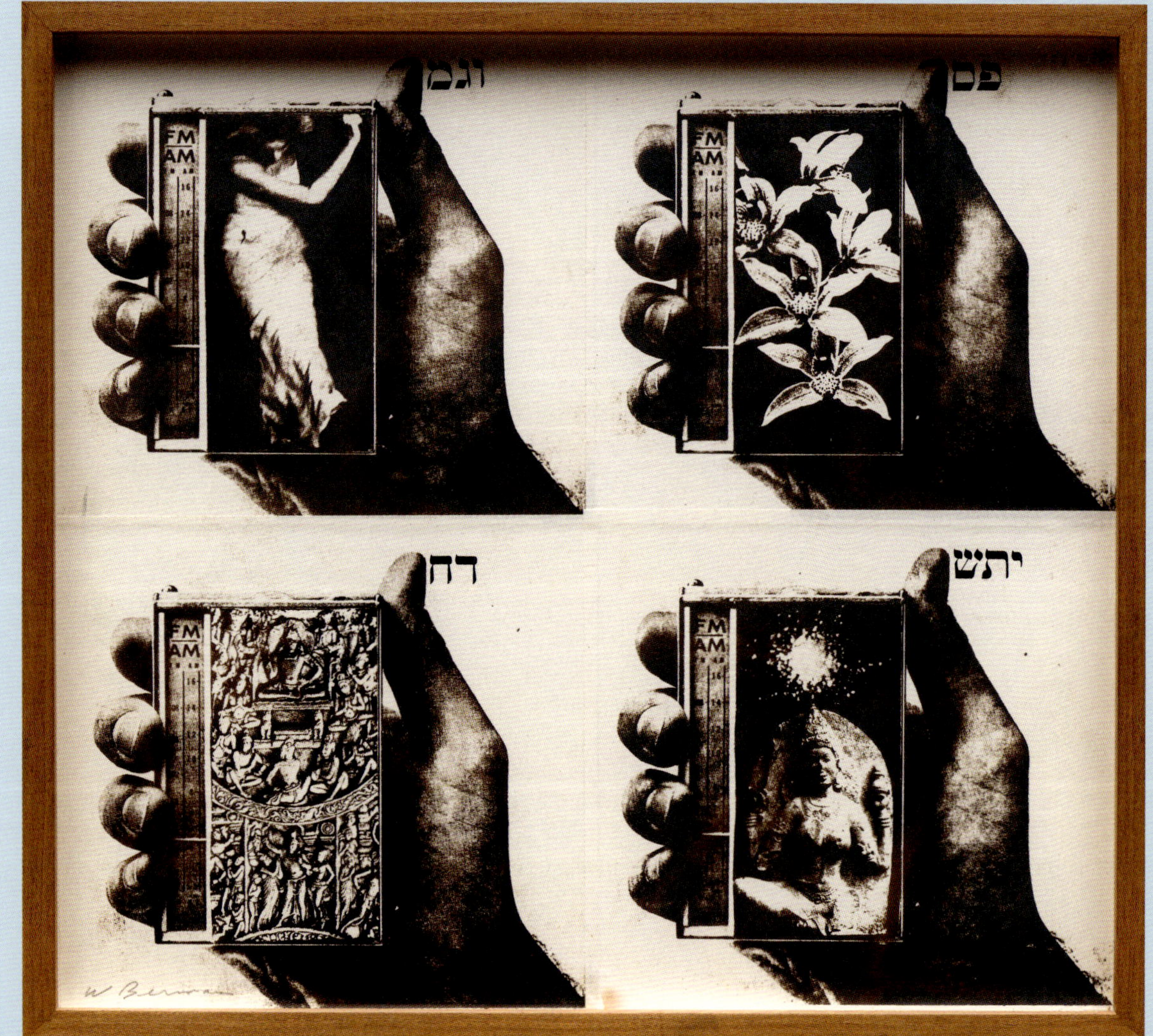

Fig. 3. Wallace Berman, *Untitled*, 1966. Verifax collage, 11 ⅝ × 12 ⅜ in. (29.5 × 31.4 cm)

begins in 1955 and will produce nine issues until 1964. It is Berman's way of disseminating his and his friends' artwork to a small group of like-minded souls.

June 30–July 12, 1961 • Critic Pierre Restany organizes Niki de Saint Phalle's (1930–2002) first solo exhibition, *Fire at Will*, at Galerie J in Paris. The show debuts her series *Shooting Paintings*, which Saint Phalle creates by firing a .22-caliber rifle at primed canvases; the rifle's bullets pierce bags of pigment, paint cans, and other materials to generate the final images. In an undated letter, Saint Phalle describes her reaction to producing the series: "It was an amazing feeling shooting at a painting and watching it transform itself into a new being. It was not only EXCITING and SEXY but TRAGIC—as though we were witnessing a birth and death at the same moment." Through 1963 she will orchestrate a number of shooting sessions (*tires séances*), which she conceives as performances. The sessions begin as casual gatherings among friends and fellow artists but evolve into large-scale public events carried out in a gallery or museum setting. In regard to her work at the time, Saint Phalle will remark that "through painting, I could explore the magical and the mystical which kept the chaos from possessing me. Painting put my soul-stirring chaos at ease."

Saint Phalle had been born in France, the daughter of a French father and an American mother. She is raised in New York, spending summers in France, until she elopes with family friend Harry Mathews at the age of eighteen. Throughout the 1950s, she travels with her husband and two young children around Europe, drawing inspiration from artists she sees at the Musée d'Art Moderne in Paris—where she discovers Jasper Johns, Willem de Kooning, Jackson Pollock, and Robert Rauschenberg—as well as sites such as Antoni Gaudí's Park Güell in Barcelona. In 1960 she and Mathews separate, and she sets up a studio, devoting herself to her work. She begins living and working with sculptor Jean Tinguely, whom she will later marry, and in the early 1960s, she becomes part of Nouveau Réalisme, a group that includes Christo, Yves Klein, and Tinguely.

Throughout her body of work, Saint Phalle focuses on generating "real" images of women—"artworks for and about women and their real, mostly painful experiences." Her found-object sculpture *Tu est moi* (1960) is included in the 1961 Museum of Modern Art exhibition *The Art of Assemblage*.

1961 • While building their house in Muir Beach, California, Gunvor Nelson (b. 1931) and

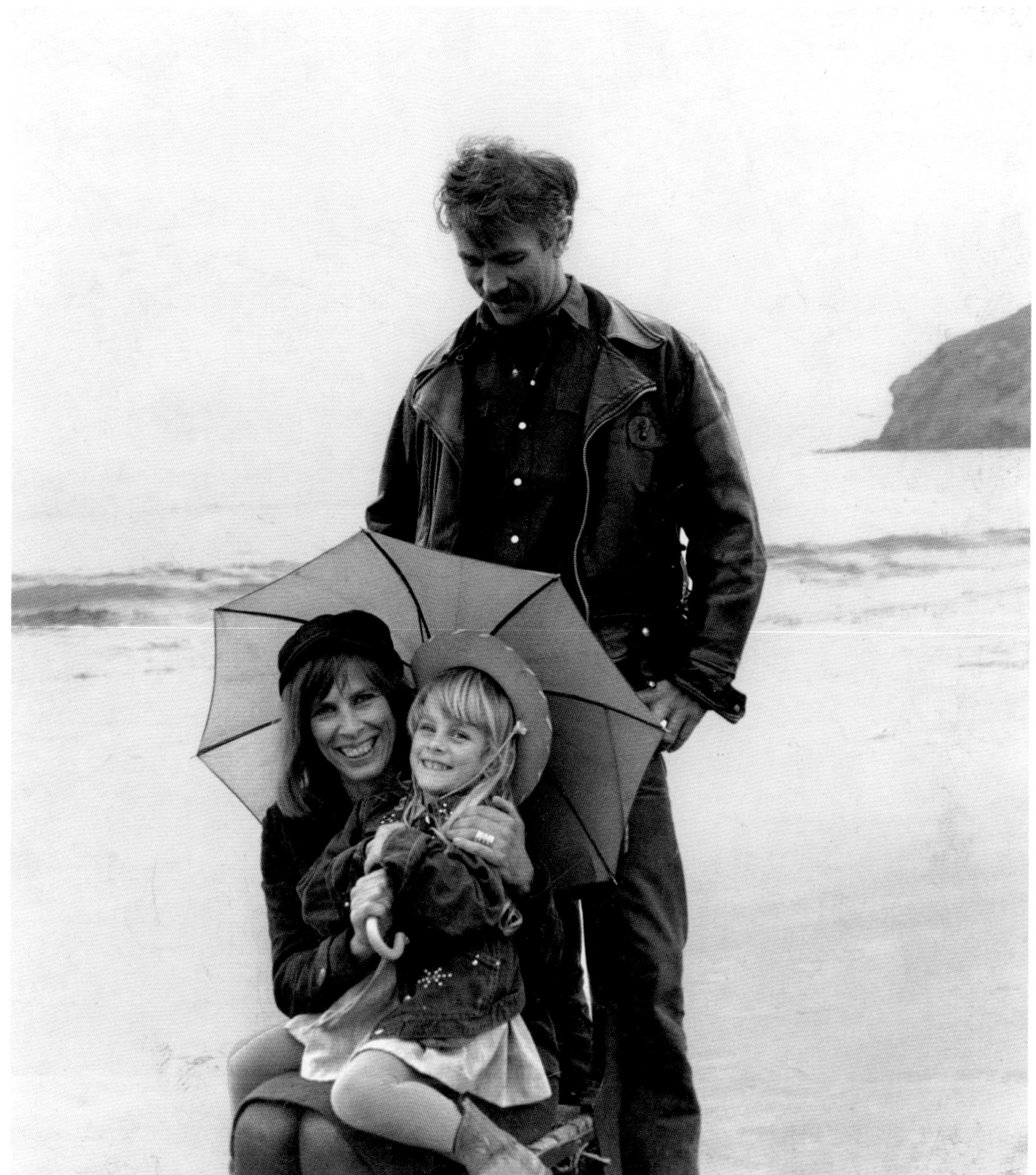

Gunvor, Oona, and Robert Nelson, Muir Beach, CA, 1967

her husband, Robert, document the construction in their early film *Building Muir Beach House* (1961). Robert shoots and Gunvor edits. The following year they send the film—as well as *Last Week at Oona's Bath* (1962), which records them caring for Oona, their newborn daughter—to Gunvor's parents in Sweden. While Gunvor won't include these early films in later filmographies, the movies suggest an emergent approach to film as a fundamentally "personal" medium.

Born in Kristinehamn, Sweden, Nelson had come to California in 1953. Intending to make her career as a painter, she studies at Humboldt State University, Mills College, and the California School of Fine Arts, where she meets experimental filmmaker Robert Nelson, whom she marries in 1958. The Nelsons attend early screenings at Canyon Cinema, then an improvised theater and community hub for experimental filmmakers. She sees work by established avant-garde filmmakers such as Stan Brakhage, Maya Deren, and Lawrence Jordan projected in the backyard of filmmaker Chick Strand. Upon their move to Muir Beach in Marin County, the Nelsons' neighbors include William T. and Dorothy Wiley, another artist couple with whom they soon become friends and artistic collaborators: William with Robert, Dorothy with Gunvor.

Gunvor Nelson's embrace of "personal film" connects her to a constellation of postwar avant-

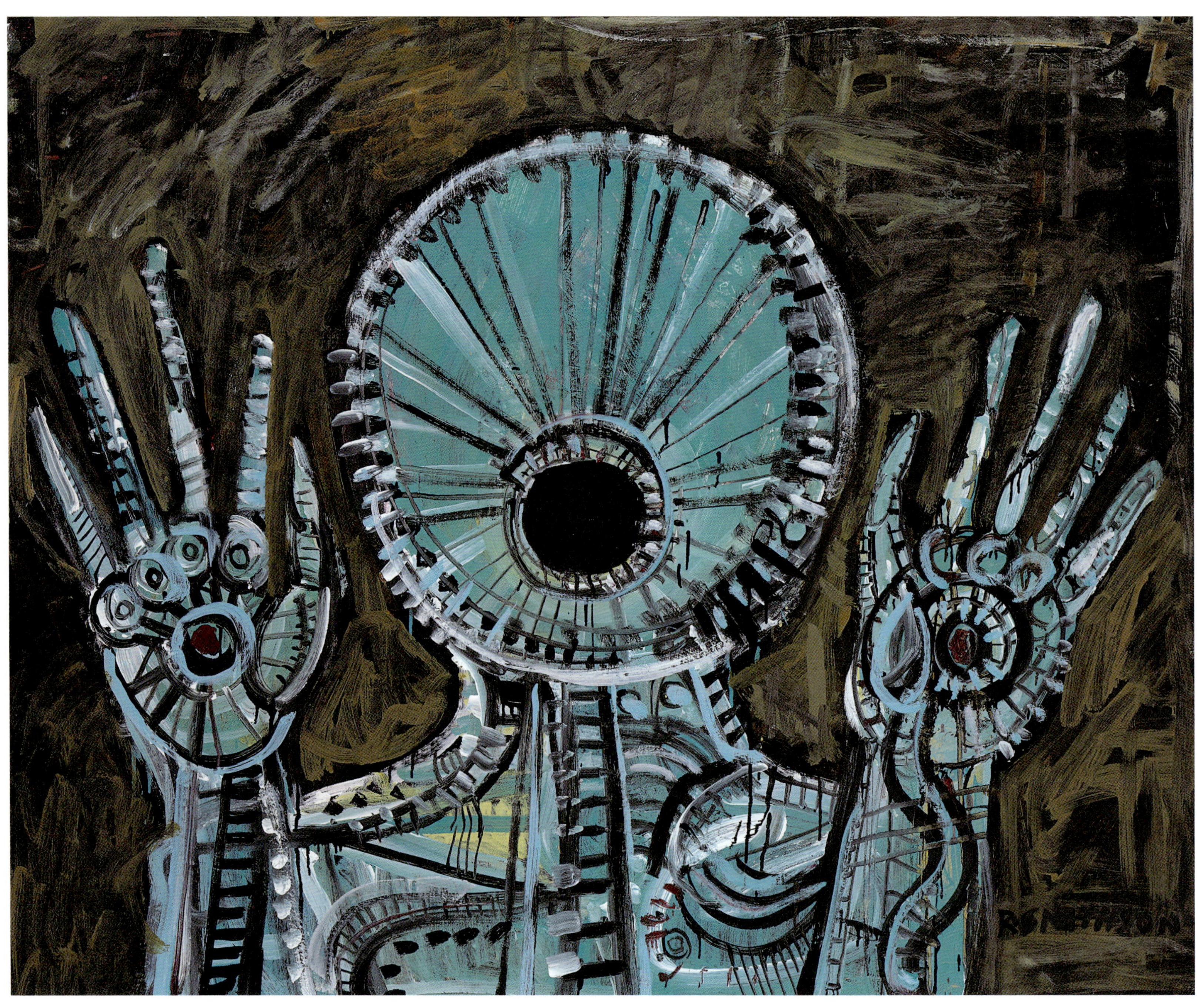

Robert Smithson, *Green Chimera with Stigmata*, 1961. Oil on canvas, 47 ¾ × 57 in. (121.2 × 144.7 cm). Collection of Joe Bradley

garde filmmakers who use the term to characterize their opposition to the ostensibly impersonal processes and products of commercial cinema. For filmmakers such as Brakhage, Deren, and Jonas Mekas, the "personal" connotes the autonomy of amateur home moviemakers from the values of the film industry. But the term also implies the filmmakers' unique access to certain subject matter: repressed images and affects ordinarily buried in the private realms of the individual subconscious and family life. Insofar as the discourse of personal film allies familial life with the subconscious, expressing or externalizing these contents in film entails practices analogous to Surrealist automatic writing.

———

Summer 1961 • Fritz Scholder (1937–2005) attends the Southwest Indian Art Program (SWIAP), an experimental summer series for Native American artists sponsored by the Rockefeller Foundation at the University of Arizona, Tucson, to which he will return the next summer as well. An enrolled member of the Luiseño tribe, Scholder feels ambivalent about this identification at various points throughout his career, though it comes to shape his art and his relationship with the artworld. Scholder's father is an administrator for the Bureau of Indian Affairs, and the family had moved often throughout the Dakotas and Wisconsin. While attending high school in Pierre, North Dakota, Scholder is taught by the artist Oscar Howe and creates some of his first figurative work, before attending art camp at the University of Kansas in 1955 and graduating high school in Wisconsin in 1956. A year later, he follows his family to Sacramento and begins studying at Sacramento State College with Wayne Thiebaud, whose approach to handling paint has a lifelong influence on Scholder.

SWIAP's objective is to support and emphasize the development of a modern context for Native American artists and craftspeople, shifting away from the market for ethnographic objects. It helps form the basis of the Institute of American Indian Arts (IAIA), which will be founded in Santa Fe, New Mexico, in 1962. Scholder will later recall of his experience with SWIAP: "At the project we were bombarded with Indian art and European art. It was a tremendous cultural shock. In fact, some of the Indians couldn't really take it and I think it messed some of them up. But what the project opened up was freedom in Indian painting. When people went off to work they were permitted to do whatever they wanted to do. The result was quite amazing. Out of this came a merging of rich Indian heritage with contemporary art." For Scholder this experience grants him permission to think outside the relatively narrow limits of what was considered "Indian Art," and he synthesizes the lessons he learns from both contemporary art teachers such as Thiebaud and historical European art. His paintings from this time—years before he begins depicting Native Americans—are expressionist explorations of color and pattern that often conjure the desert landscape.

Scholder will complete his master of fine arts at the University of Arizona and begin teaching at IAIA in 1964, bringing his opinions and understanding of Native American art to his teaching.

———

July 15–August 4, 1961 • Robert Smithson's solo show is on view at the Galleria George Lester in Rome. Continuing to explore "mythological religious archetypes," Smithson begins including Catholic iconography in a series of "ikons." In variations on the crucifixion and stigmatization of Christ, including *Christ Series: Christ Carrying the Cross* (1960), *Untitled (INRI—Christ on Crucifix)* (1961), and *Green Chimera with Stigmata* (1961), he draws inspiration from Byzantine art and poets T. E. Hulme and T. S. Eliot. George Lester offers Smithson the show after seeing the artist's *Quicksand* (1959) alongside work by Claes Oldenburg in the exhibition *New Work by New Artists* at the Allan Stone Gallery, New York, in March. In advance of his solo show, Smithson writes to Lester, explaining, "The paintings I am sending you reveal my spiritual crisis. A crisis born out of an inner pain; a pain that has overwhelmed my entire nervous system."

While in Rome, Smithson reads William S. Burroughs and begins to employ a collage technique similar to the "cut-up" method of composition the poet uses in his art and writing. That fall, Smithson sees *The Art of Assemblage* at the Museum of Modern Art, New York.

———

August 1961 • Carolee Schneemann (1939–2019) moves to New York City after finishing her master of fine arts in painting at the University

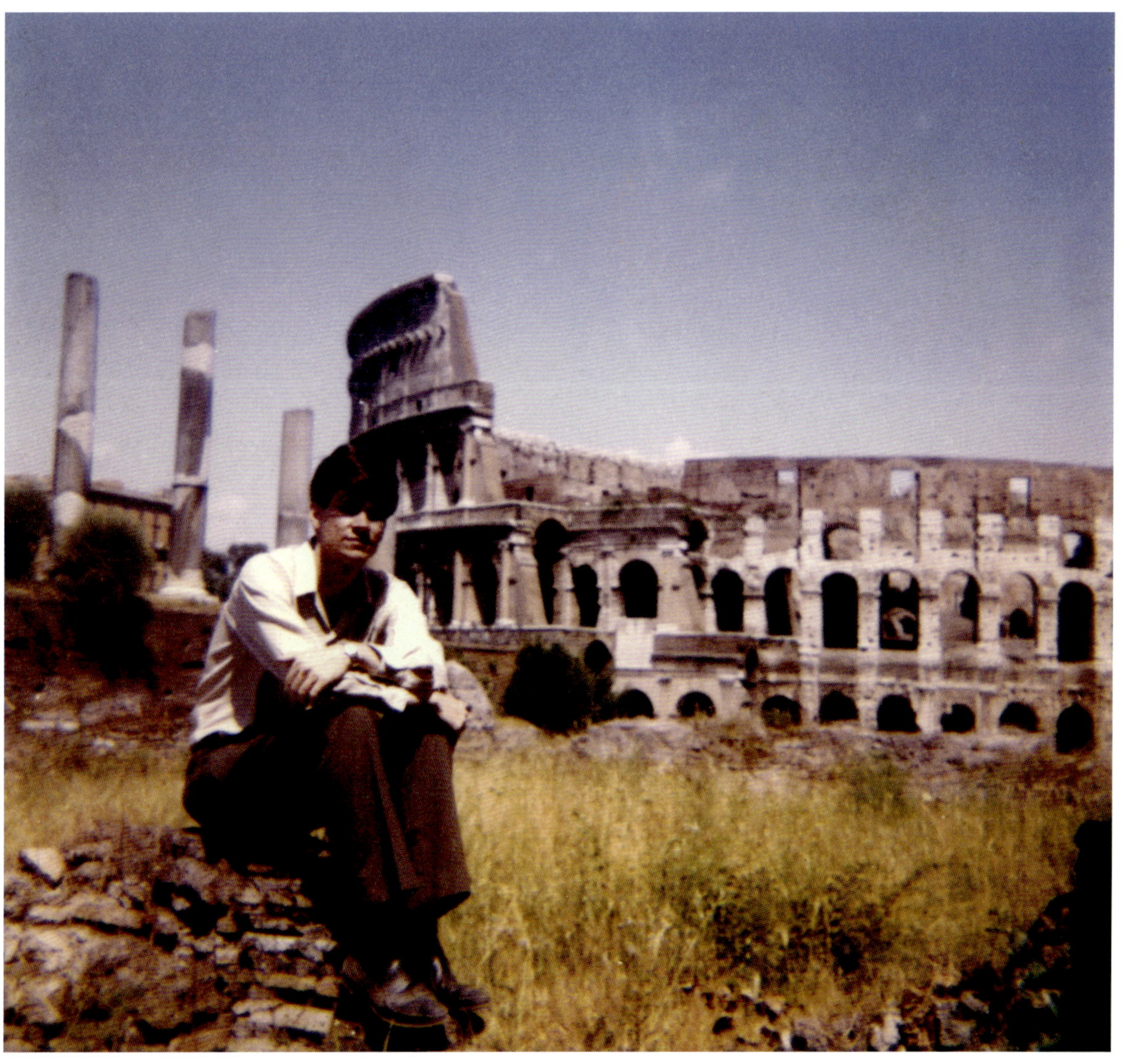

Robert Smithson in Rome, 1961

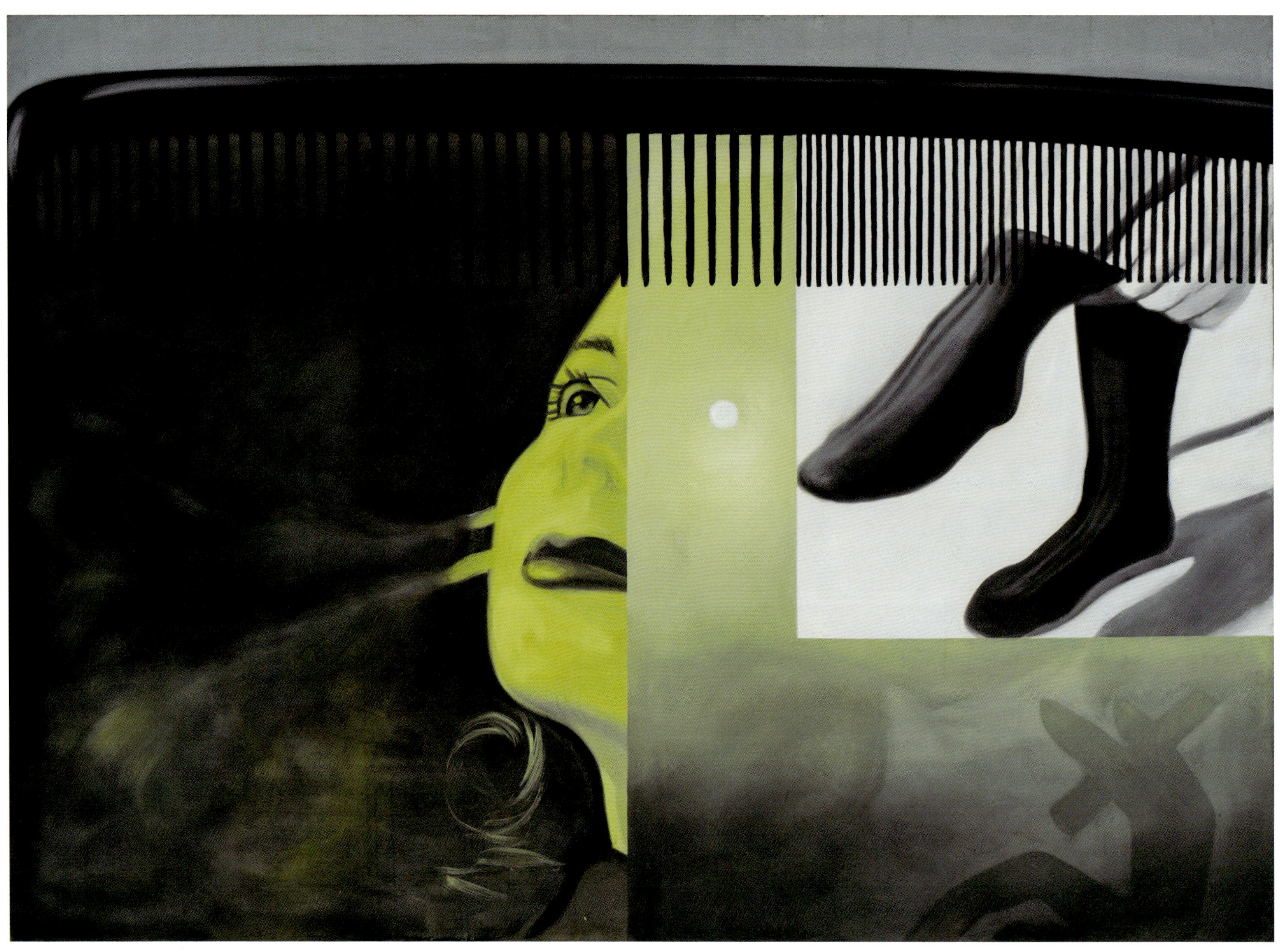

James Rosenquist, *The Light That Won't Fail I*, 1961. Oil on canvas, 71 ¾ × 96 ¼ in. (182.1 × 244.3 cm). Hirshhorn Museum and Sculpture Garden, Smithsonian Institution, Washington, DC; gift of the Joseph H. Hirshhorn Foundation, 1966 66.4402

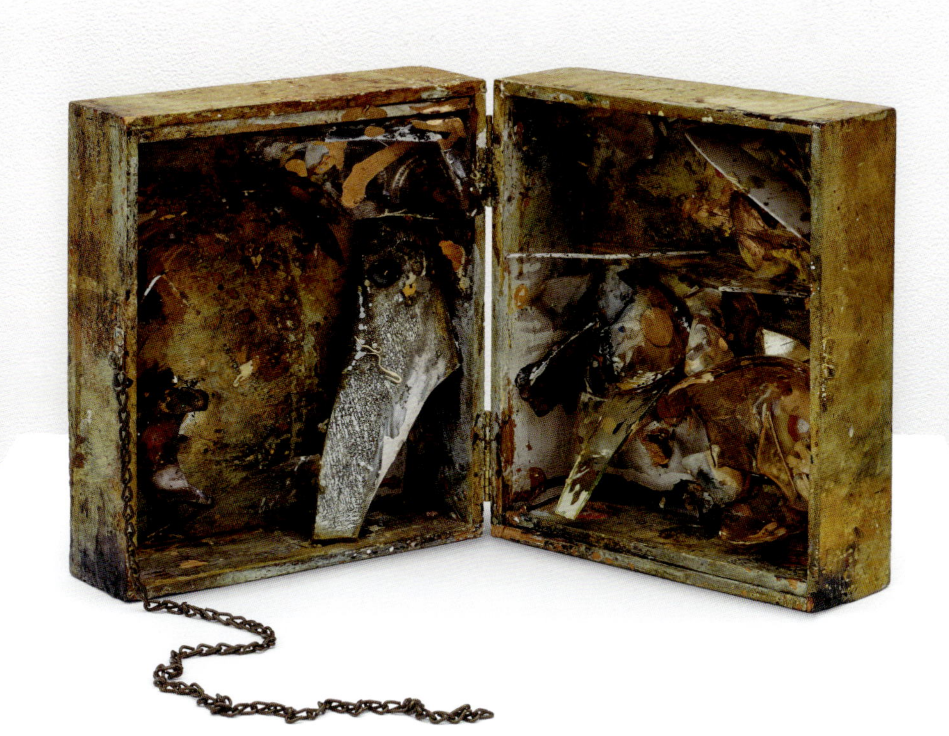

Carolee Schneemann, *For Yvonne Rainer's Ordinary Dance*, 1962. Wood box, glass, mirrors, and oil paint, 15 ¾ × 9 ¼ × 2 ½ in. (40 × 23.5 × 6.4 cm)

September 11, 1961 • Just before Ana Mendieta (1948–1985) turns thirteen, she and her older sister immigrate to the United States to escape the increasing political persecution in Cuba under Fidel Castro, two of the more than fourteen thousand unaccompanied minors who migrate as part of Operation Peter Pan, an initiative sponsored by the US State Department and the Catholic Church to relocate Cuban children to America. After a month in Miami, the Mendieta girls are placed at St. Mary's Home in Dubuque, Iowa, a group home for disturbed and neglected children. They grow up in multiple foster homes, some of which, as Mendieta intimates, were difficult and abusive. The sisters remain separated from their family until their mother and brother join them in the United States in 1966. Their father is imprisoned in Cuba and will not reunite with the family until 1979.

Mendieta graduates from Regis High School in 1965 and first attends Briar Cliff College in Sioux City, Iowa, before transferring to the University of Iowa in Iowa City, where she studies French and art. She earns her bachelor of arts in 1969 before continuing her graduate studies in painting at the university. Mendieta will begin showing in New York in 1976, moving to the city in 1978.

October 1961 • Pop art enthusiast Robert Scull purchases *The Light That Won't Fail II* (1961), marking the first sale for artist James Rosenquist (1933–2017). Scull, a taxi tycoon, and

of Illinois, Urbana-Champaign. Her first "painting constructions" date to her move to the East Coast and her friendship with the Surrealist Joseph Cornell.

Born and raised near Philadelphia in Fox Creek, Pennsylvania, Schneemann had enrolled at Bard College in 1955 but was temporarily expelled for "moral turpitude" later that year—possibly because she was painting nude self-portraits. During her leave of absence, she takes classes at Columbia University's School of Painting and Sculpture and at the New School. During this interlude, she meets the composer James Tenney, who becomes her partner and artistic collaborator for the next thirteen years.

While in school, Schneemann works through the influences of Paul Cézanne and the Abstract Expressionists, exploring the figure in the landscape in increasingly gestural and abstract canvases. She will insist that she has always been a painter, though her oeuvre expands to encompass assemblage, performance, experimental film, and installation, pushing the limits of painting further than any of her contemporaries. Yet her methods in every medium remain consistent in an expanded sense of painting, a collage methodology of incongruous and irrational juxtaposition, and an interest in "the fractured plane as an event," a lesson that she takes from Cézanne.

Schneemann's assemblages—sometimes referred to as "Boxes" in the lineage of Cornell—incorporate the detritus of everyday life, motorized

elements, and materials found in her studio, a former fur-cutter's loft on West 29th Street. She develops a friendship with the elderly Cornell over the course of her visits to his studio, helping him with work, though she attests that she was more his "muse" than his assistant.

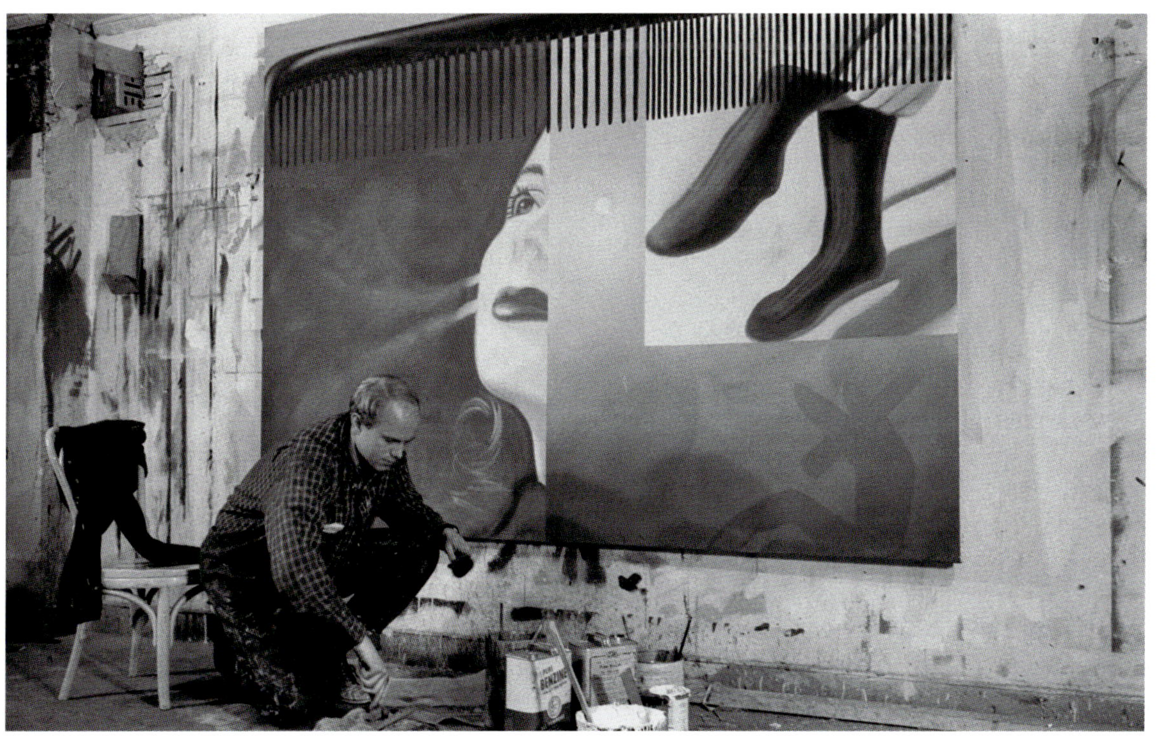

James Rosenquist working on *The Light That Won't Fail I* (1961) in his studio, New York, 1961

his wife, Ethel, world-famous collectors of Pop and Minimal art, will purchase works throughout the 1960s and 1970s at the urging of gallerists Richard Bellamy and Leo Castelli. Scull also offers financial support to Bellamy's Green Gallery, which will represent Rosenquist beginning in 1962. Between 1961 and 1964, Rosenquist paints a number of grisaille pictures, explaining that he always "started on black and white," a process informed by the grayscale storyboards used as a reference point for sign painting. These early works—which include *Flower Garden* (1961), *Zone* (1960–61), and *1947–1948–1950* (1960)— are described by the artist as a first attempt to "duplicate the sensation I had when painting billboards: of being so close to the image while painting it that I was no longer thinking about what it was. These shapes fascinated me. They were provocative, enigmatic, unresolved."

Rosenquist had been born in Grand Forks, North Dakota, and his family had moved across various Midwestern farming communities throughout his childhood, shaping his self-referenced identity as a "farm-boy who just happens to be an artist." He attended the University of Minnesota between 1952 and 1954, graduating with an associate's degree in studio art, before enrolling at the Art Students League of New York. Rosenquist leaves the school in 1956 but stays in New York, painting billboards in Brooklyn and Manhattan, including in Times Square; his billboard work is recognized as "some of the world's biggest pictures in one of the world's most populous art galleries." In his spare

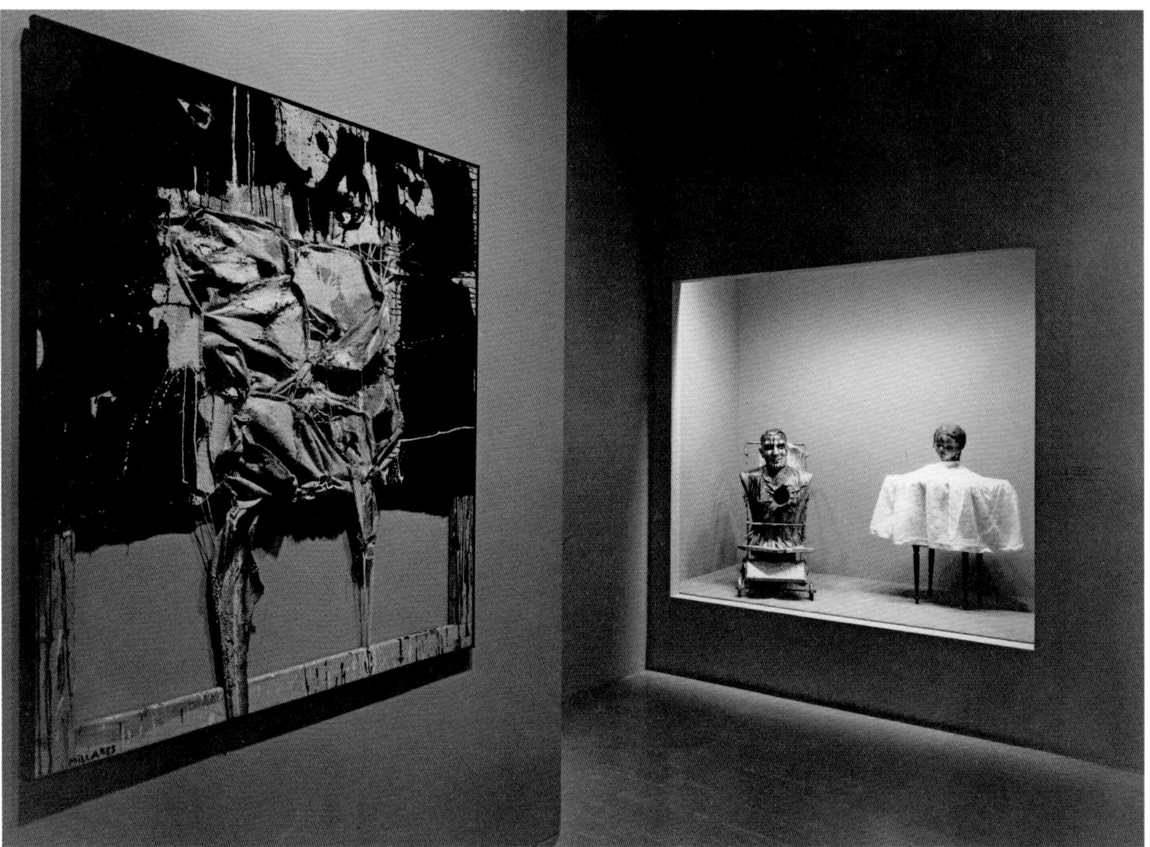

The Art of Assemblage, Museum of Modern Art, New York, 1961

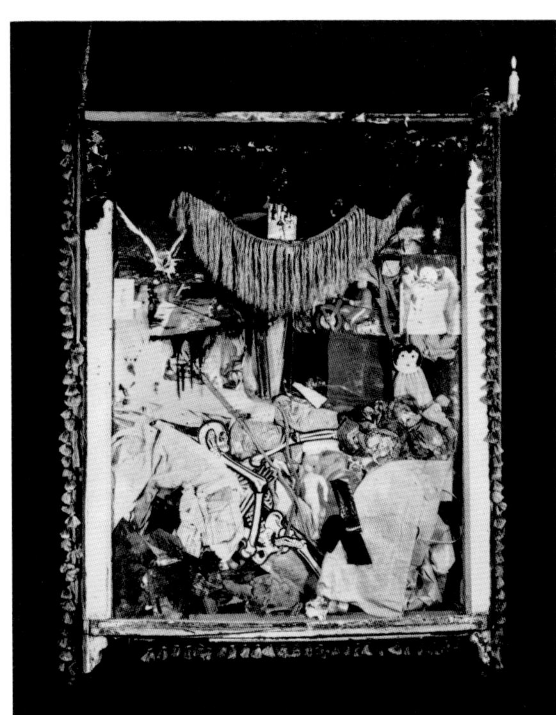

Bruce Conner, *SUPERHUMAN DEVOTION*, c. 1959. Assemblage, dimensions unknown

time, he attends drawing classes organized by Robert Indiana and Jack Youngerman, while simultaneously creating abstract works, including a 9 × 17–foot drawing that foreshadows the monumental scale of his mature style.

October 4–November 12, 1961 • *The Art of Assemblage* is on view at the Museum of Modern Art, New York (MoMA). Featured artists include Lee Bontecou, Bruce Conner, Jess, Jasper Johns, Edward Kienholz, Marisol, Niki de Saint Phalle, Lucas Samaras, and H. C. Westermann. The exhibition traces the current wave of assemblage art back to early twentieth-century Cubist collage, with curator William C. Seitz explaining:

> Every work of art is an incarnation: an investment of matter with spirit. The term "assemblage" has been singled out, with this duality in mind, to denote not only a specific technical procedure and form used in the literary and musical, as well as the plastic arts, but also a complex of attitudes and ideas. Just as the introduction of oil painting in fifteenth-century Flanders and Italy paralleled a new desire to reproduce the appearance of the visible world, collage and related modes of construction manifest a predisposition that is characteristically modern.

As MoMA curator William S. Rubin would later comment, Seitz uses the steady march of art movements—Dada, Futurism, Surrealism—to diagnose the situation at the dawn of a new decade: "Assemblage has become, temporarily at least, the language for impatient, hypercritical, and anarchistic young artists. With it, or admixtures of it with painting and sculpture, they have given form to content drawn from popular culture: more recent equivalents, as the English critic Reyner Banham argues, of Boccioni's love of 'all anti-art manifestations of our epoch—cafe-chantant, gramophone, cinema, electric advertising, mechanistic architecture, skyscrapers . . . nightlife . . . speed, automobiles, airplanes and so forth.'" For Seitz, assemblage is the art most reflective of personal, cultural, and technological anxiety, and the show's tough grittiness is ill-timed for what was about to become the Pop era.

Despite the refusal of MoMA's board of trustees to purchase his work *CHILD* (1959–60) at this time, Bruce Conner acts as Seitz's guide in San Francisco, unsuccessfully trying to persuade the curator that assemblage is not a language or a movement but, rather, a part of everyday life and not something to be historicized. He embodies this point of view on opening night. Two of his works, including *SUPERHUMAN DEVOTION*, arrive damaged, and because the owner has collected on an insurance claim, Conner is not permitted to repair them. Instead, he remarks:

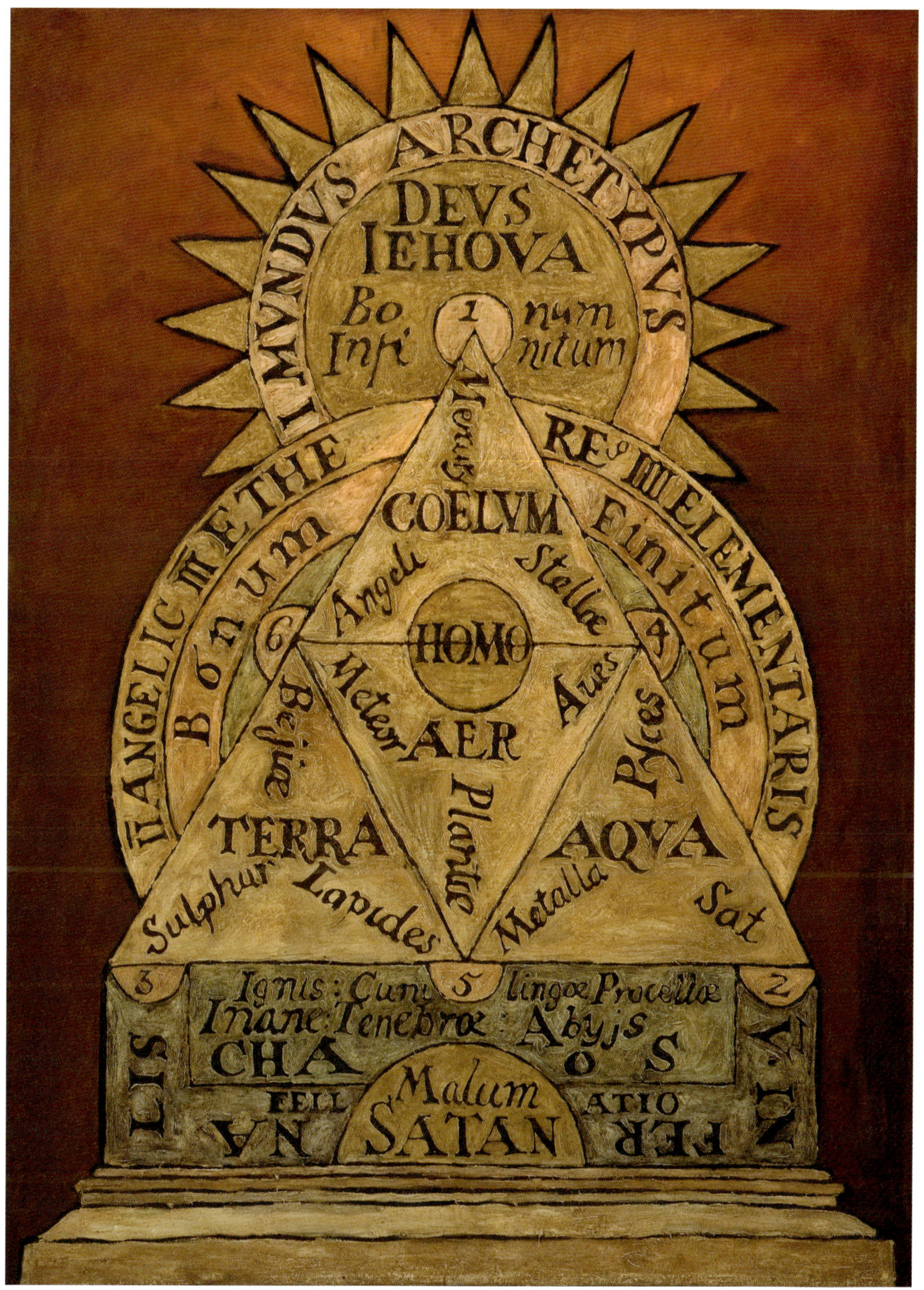

Wally Hedrick, *HERMETIC IMAGE*, 1961. Oil on canvas, 84 × 60 in. (213.3 × 152.4 cm). Mills College Art Museum, Northeastern University, Oakland, CA; Museum Purchase 1984.21

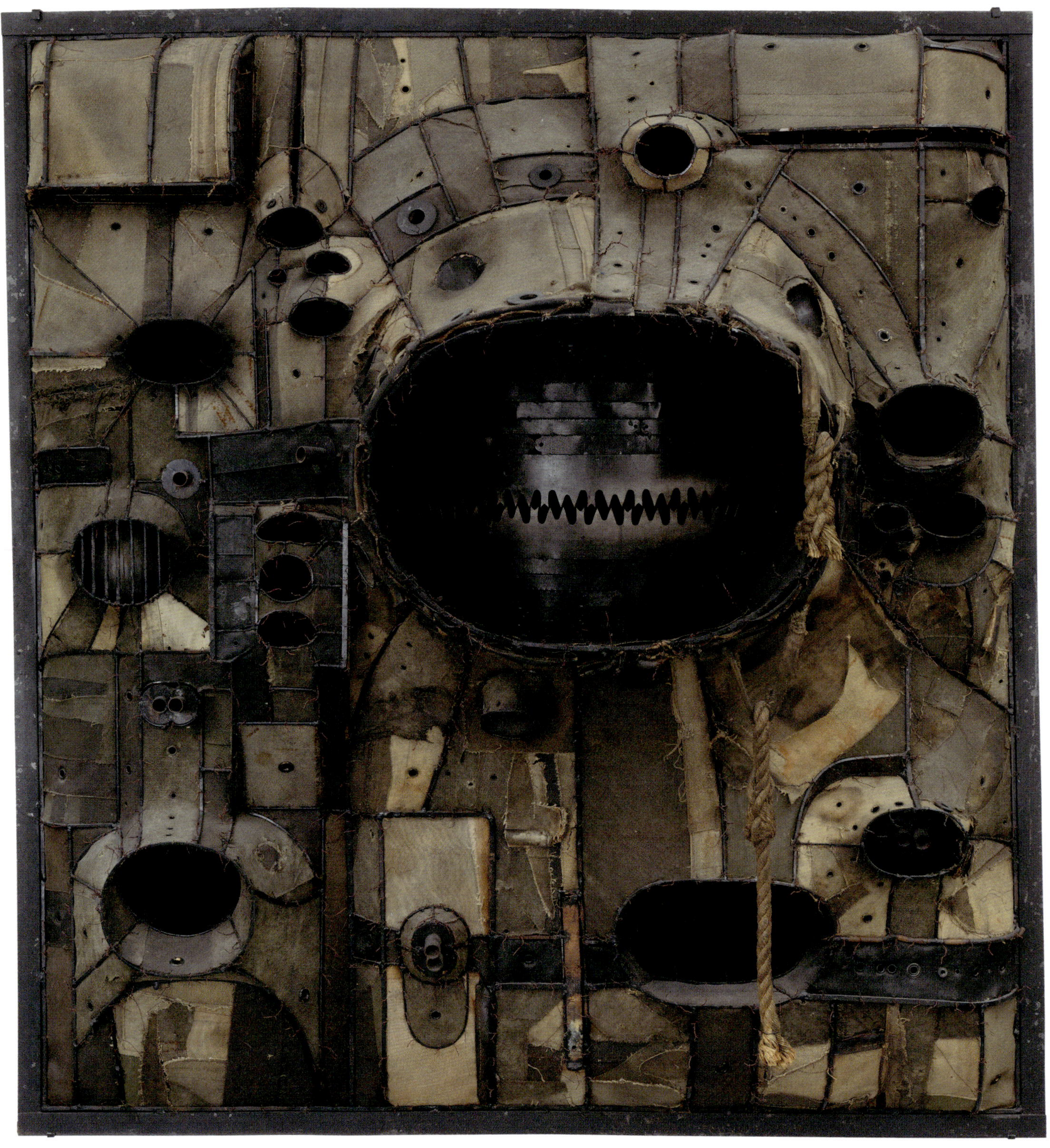

Lee Bontecou, *Untitled*, 1961. Steel, canvas, wire, and rope, 72 ½ × 66 × 24 ¾ in. (184.2 × 167.6 × 62.9 cm). Whitney Museum of American Art, New York; purchase 61.41

A moment of superhuman devotion is not repeatable. I took all of its innards out, as if it was being prepared for embalming. The next day was the opening of the "Assemblage Art" show. I forgot to bring my invitation for the black tie reception. I put a rope handle on *SUPERHUMAN DEVOTION* and told [the artist] Ray Johnson to meet me at the museum. . . . When the General Members opening started I went to check the box in the museum checkroom. They refused to accept it. . . . I was carrying my canopic box in the exhibition entrance and the guards stopped me. . . . "Only authorized works of art are allowed here." I walked out the revolving door. . . . I stood with it on the pavement while people walked around me to go into the Assemblage show. I took it back through the revolving door and put it down in a direct line from the door to the guarded entrance. Set it down and walked in.

Later, together with Johnson, Conner takes *SUPERHUMAN DEVOTION* for a ride on the Staten Island ferry: "When we were closest to the Statue of Liberty I asked Ray to come with me to the end of the ferry. He held one side of the box and I held the other," Conner recalls. "We swung it back and forth three times and then tossed it into the ocean."

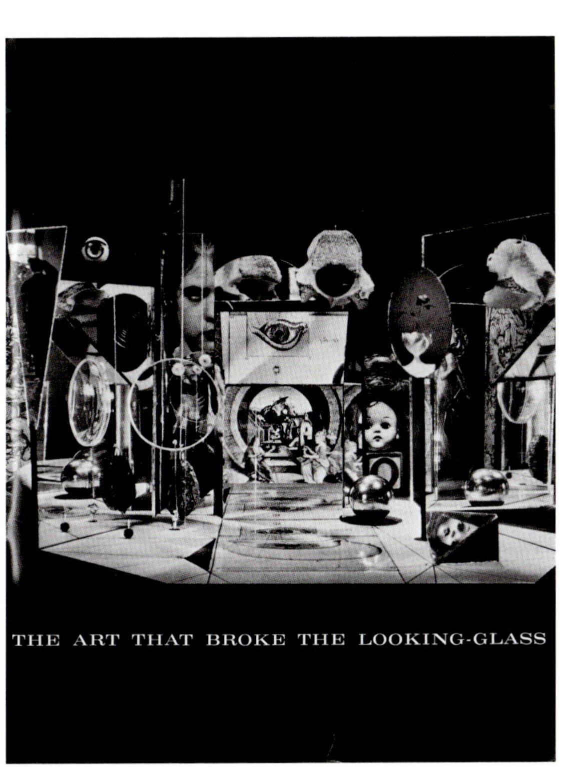

Exhibition catalogue for *The Art That Broke the Looking Glass*, Dallas Museum for Contemporary Arts, 1961

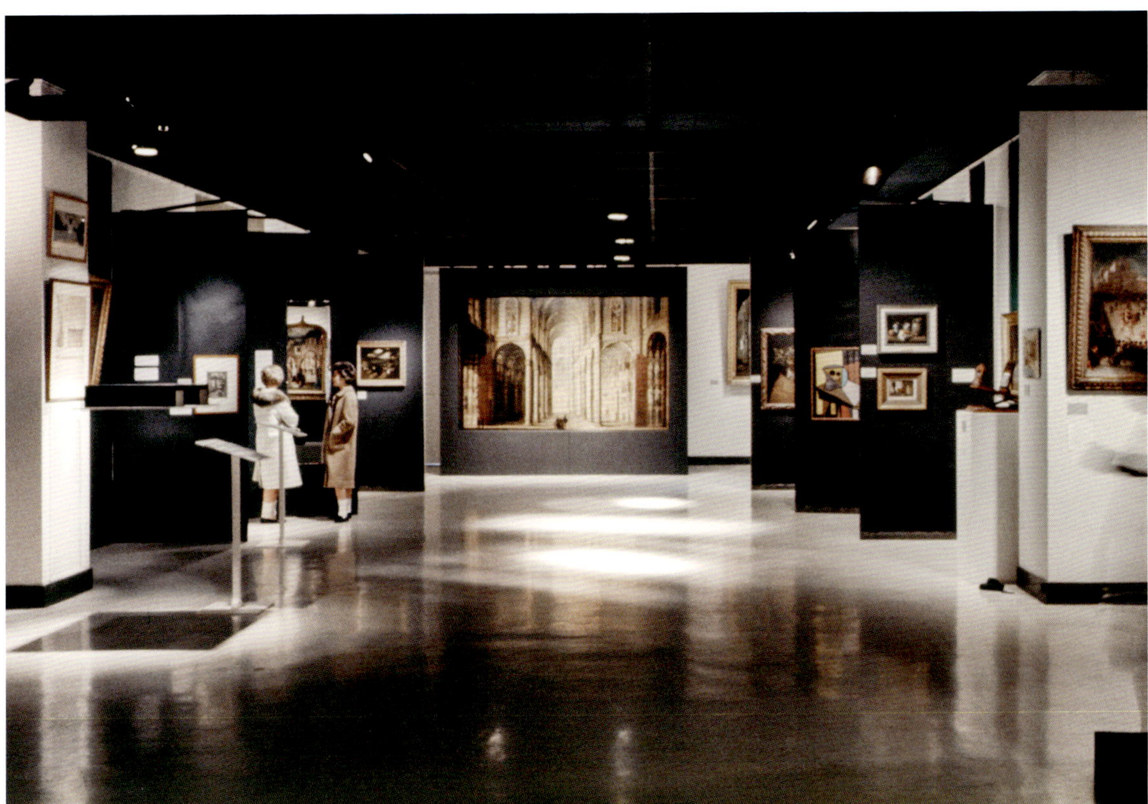

The Art That Broke the Looking Glass, Dallas Museum for Contemporary Arts, 1961

November 1961 • Diane Arbus publishes her second photo-essay, "The Full Circle," in *Harper's Bazaar*, which features her photographs and texts about five "eccentrics," including Jack Dracula, a sideshow performer at Hubert's Dime Museum and Flea Circus who earned his nickname by reading Bram Stoker's novel *Dracula* nine times. Her photograph *Five members of The Monster Fan Club, N.Y.C. 1961* (1961) is published in *Famous Monsters of Filmland*, the monthly magazine that upon its debut in 1958 for the first time offered the filmgoing public easy access to movie stills from horror and fantasy film, the seemingly impossible images of cinematic wonders. These pictures will have a profound impact on the imaginations of the baby boomers growing up and looking for permission to free themselves from the antiseptic Atomic Age.

November 15–December 31, 1961 • Douglas MacAgy organizes the exhibition *The Art That Broke the Looking Glass* at the Dallas Museum for Contemporary Arts. The show is the first in a series called *The Past in Review* and is meant to "align certain aspects of art from the past with creative concerns of the present." Here, this goal takes the form of a survey exhibition that includes art made in the fourteenth through the twentieth centuries in Europe, the United States, and South America, including works from such widely diverse practices as Albrecht Dürer, Juan Gris, Canaletto, Sari Dienes, and Joseph Cornell. MacAgy also includes the work of Dallas-based artist David McManaway, who is known for his assemblage works called "Jomo Boards," compositions of objects collected from across the city and in collaboration with other artists. One of McManaway's closest friends is fellow artist Roy Fridge (1927–2007), who also has work in the show and designs the catalogue for it.

Fridge had been born in Beeville, Texas, and studied film at Baylor University in Waco, graduating in 1950. Throughout the 1950s he operates a commercial film studio in Dallas, and by mid-decade he has become involved in set design and is screening his experimental films at the Dallas Little Theater. His sculpture practice evolves out of his experience making set-design models, which he first begins displaying in the lobby of the Dallas Little Theater in 1956. The pieces develop more structurally into artworks, and he exhibits them at the solo exhibition *Sculptural Constructions* at the Baylor Theater in 1958. Although he begins making sculpture in 1957—mostly carved wood structures that incorporate elements of movement and that he refers to as "wooden machines"—his practice expands when he moves to Houston and eventually to Port Aransas, Texas, in 1965.

1962

Early 1962 • Kenneth Anger (1927–2023) relocates to Brooklyn, New York, and moves in with experimental filmmakers Marie Menken and Willard Maas as well as Gerard Malanga, who will later become an assistant to Andy Warhol. Obsessed with the new biker subculture he observes around the Coney Island boardwalk, Anger befriends a group of bikers and starts shooting for his new film project, *Scorpio Rising* (1963).

Having grown up near Hollywood, Anger got his start in movies as a child, playing the Changeling Prince in the 1935 adaptation of *A Midsummer Night's Dream*. When he is ten years old, he begins making his own movies on 8mm film, though he later destroys most of his adolescent work. *Fireworks*, his earliest mature work and thought to be the first openly queer film, is made over the course of a weekend in 1947. Anger will later reflect on making it: "I had my razor blade in my eyeball and I was able to do something spectacularly existential"—an homage to Luis Buñuel and Salvador Dalí's Surrealist classic *Un Chien Andalou* (1929). Anger submits a copy of *Fireworks* to the 1949 Festival du Film Maudit organized by Jean Cocteau and André Bazin and is awarded the Poetic Film Prize. Cocteau even writes Anger a personal letter praising the film. The receipt of such enthusiastic recognition from

a poet and a critic whom he idolizes compels Anger to move to Paris in 1950, where he will live on and off for the next decade. Although only two short works—*Rabbit's Moon* (1950) and *Eaux d'Artifice* (1953)—date to his Paris years, numerous projects demonstrate Anger's influences and interests: he collaborates with Cocteau and gets a job with the archivist Henri Langlois at the Cinémathèque Française, where he is able to re-cut a print of Sergei Eisenstein's unfinished *¡Que viva México!*, and he begins work on *Maldoror*, a new film he describes as an adaptation of the proto-Surrealist *Chants de Maldoror* (1868–69), which sadly he never completes. To support himself financially, he publishes the infamous gossip book *Hollywood Babylon* (1959), which is full of apocryphal tales of the scandalous sex lives and gruesome deaths of the stars of Hollywood's Golden Age.

January 5, 1962 • Rapidly immersed in the New York City arts scene, Carolee Schneemann debuts her own first "kinetic event," *Glass Environment for Sound and Motion*, at Living Theatre. She also starts participating in avant-garde film and dance productions as well as happenings, performing in Claes Oldenburg's *Store Days* the following month.

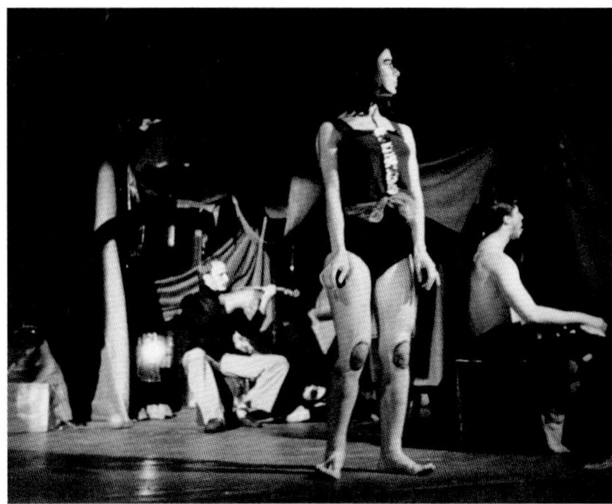

Carolee Schneemann, *Glass Environment for Sound and Motion*, Living Theatre, New York, 1962

January 27–February 10, 1962 • Benny Andrews's first New York solo exhibition opens at Forum Gallery, founded by Bella Fishko the year before, and features the artist's textural collage paintings, which one reviewer describes as "awkward and harsh, but forceful."

January 30–February 17, 1962 • James Rosenquist's first solo exhibition is on view at Green Gallery, New York. Critic Gene Swenson

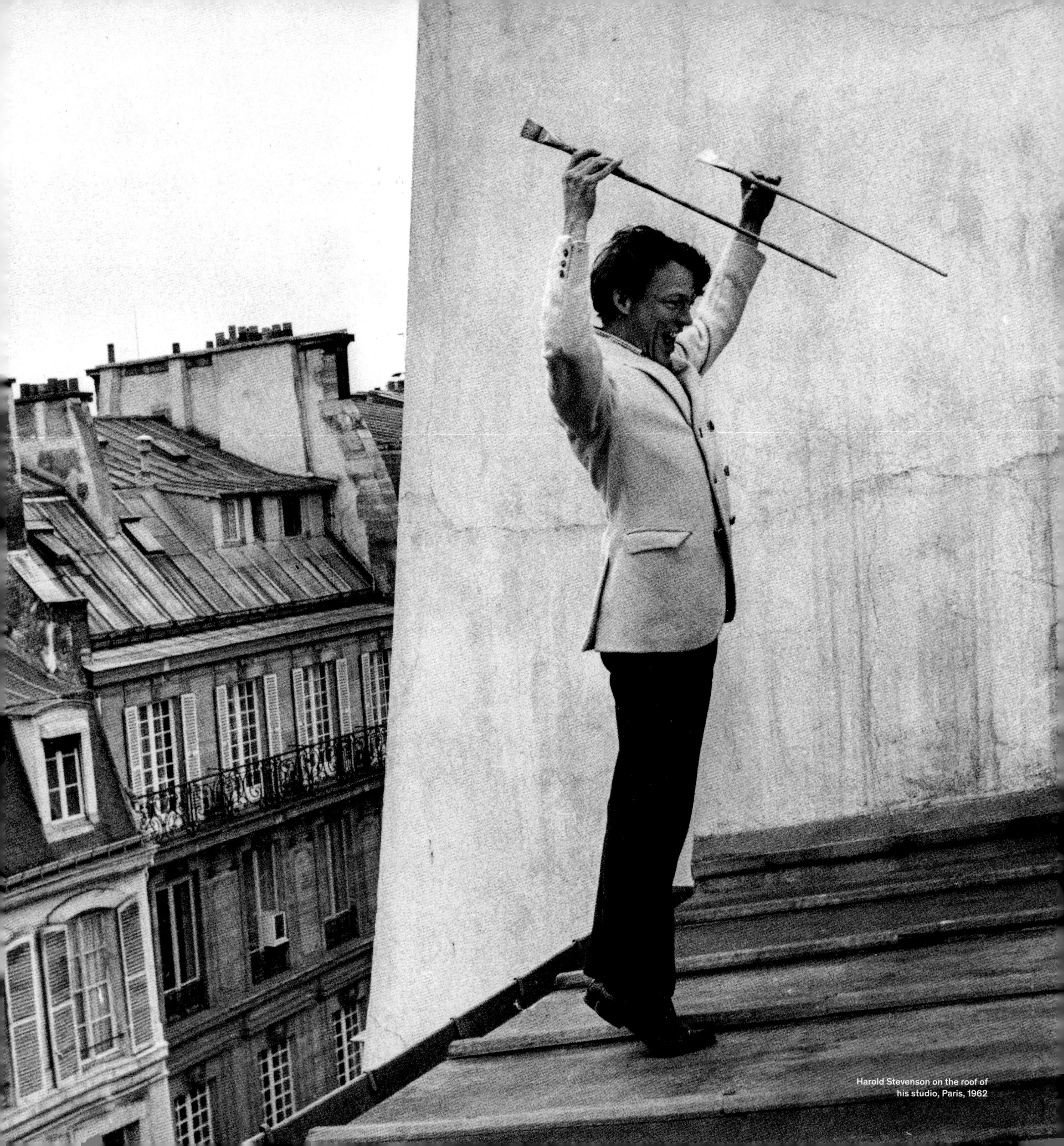

Harold Stevenson on the roof of
his studio, Paris, 1962

writes a review of the show, recalling his life-changing collision with the artist's paintings at his Coenties Slip studio the year prior: "They temporarily had defeated me, my training and my esthetic philosophy." Swenson channels this paradigm shift in his review, writing that "the viewer's experience is . . . a sense of violence at seeing fragments of a billboard environment in actual, full-size proportions; we are not permitted distance with its numbing illusion of escape. . . . The elements of this impersonal Brobdingnagian world are pieced together with a ruthless clarity." The "soft, close-up imagery" of these early Pop paintings tie Rosenquist's work as a commercial painter to all his future work, recreating the sensation the artist had while working on his commercial jobs—that is, "of being suspended in the middle of an image, in effect immersed in it."

Swenson's essay "Sign Painters," published in the September issue of *ARTnews*, will group Rosenquist with Jim Dine, Robert Indiana, Roy Lichtenstein, and Andy Warhol, noting a movement that is cohesive in its direct content and reference to commonplace objects. An ardent supporter of Pop, Swenson notes the way in which these painters, "like all artists who are unwilling to imitate . . . force a re-examination of the nature of painting and its changing relation to the world."

1962 • James Mannas tells his friend Shawn Walker (b. 1940) about an upcoming meeting of photographers and encourages him to attend. Mannas and Walker join Lou Draper, Al Fennar, Ray Francis, Calvin Mercer, Herbert Randall, Herb Robinson, Larry Stewart, and Calvin Wilson to discuss the development of a Black photographic workshop, laying the foundations for what will coalesce as the Kamoinge Workshop in 1963.

Born and raised in Harlem on 117th Street, Walker had started photographing after receiving a Brownie camera for his thirteenth birthday. He will recall being hooked by the "magic" of photography from the moment he saw his uncle develop film, and he passes on his passion to Mannas, who lives on the same block. Walker studies photography at his high school, which has a photography program and a darkroom, but by the time he reconnects with Mannas in the summer of 1961, he has given up the hobby. For Walker, the Kamoinge Workshop provides a way back to the pursuit and becomes, in his words, his "Sorbonne." The workshop supplies not only the network and infrastructures that the segregated art world still so often withholds but also training and mentorship from the more established members of the workshop, rigorous group critiques, and professional opportunities.

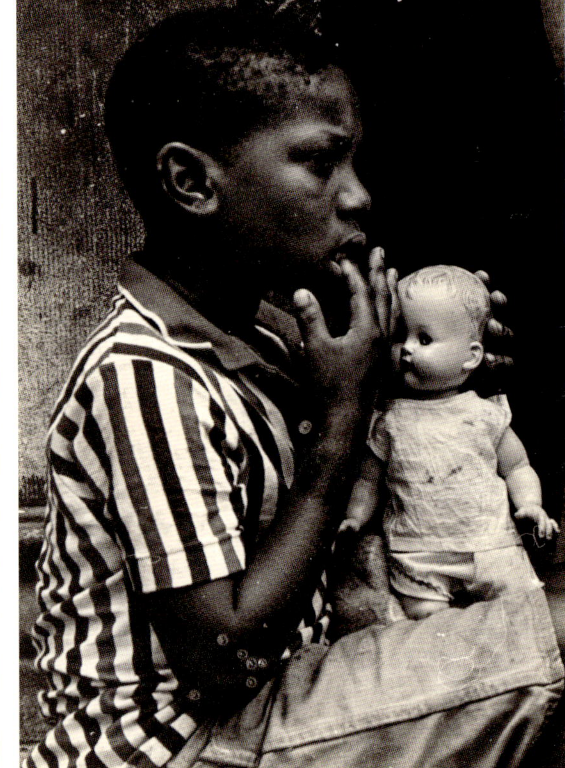

Shawn Walker, *W. 117th St. (Lenox–7th Ave.)*, 1960s. Gelatin silver print mounted to board, 6 ½ × 4 ½ in. (16.5 × 11.4 cm)

As Walker later recollects, "We decided that we were tired of what had been going on in the Black community and in the white world. We wanted to make a statement, to effect a change."

The pursuit of a Black aesthetic, conceived in the most expansive sense, is a central artistic concern for Kamoinge members. Walker, who had always "been taken by Surrealism," explores photographic luminosity and blackness, often reworking the purely formal definition of contrast so that it becomes, additionally, a social relationship. Working in the shadows is the photographer's poetic methodology for negotiating the entangled conditions of social and photographic (in)visibility. In an unpublished artist statement, he elucidates this idea: "I lived in the darkness into which I was chased, but now I see. . . . I've illuminated the blackness of my invisibility and vice versa; and so I play the invisible music of my isolation."

May 8–25, 1962 • Marisol Escobar (1930–2016) has a solo exhibition on view at the Stable Gallery, New York, solidifying her status as a significant contemporary artist. She exhibits *Love* (1962), a plaster cast of disembodied mouth appearing to swallow an entire Coca-Cola bottle, along with the painted mixed-media assemblage *Ruth* (1962), a five-headed, nine-legged portrait of artist-friend Ruth Kligman. "Rarely has the Surrealist method of the 'poetic dislocation,' to

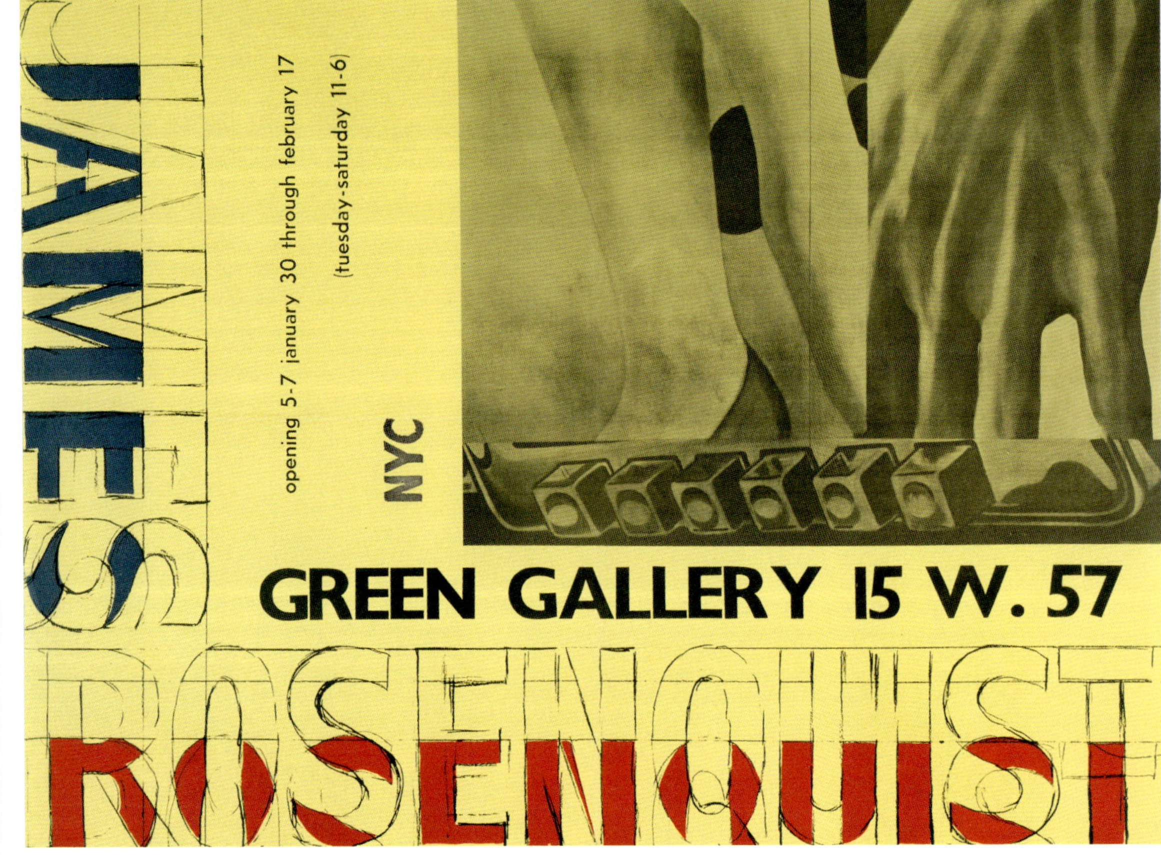

Poster by James Rosenquist with *Pushbutton* (1961) for *James Rosenquist*, Green Gallery, New York, 1962

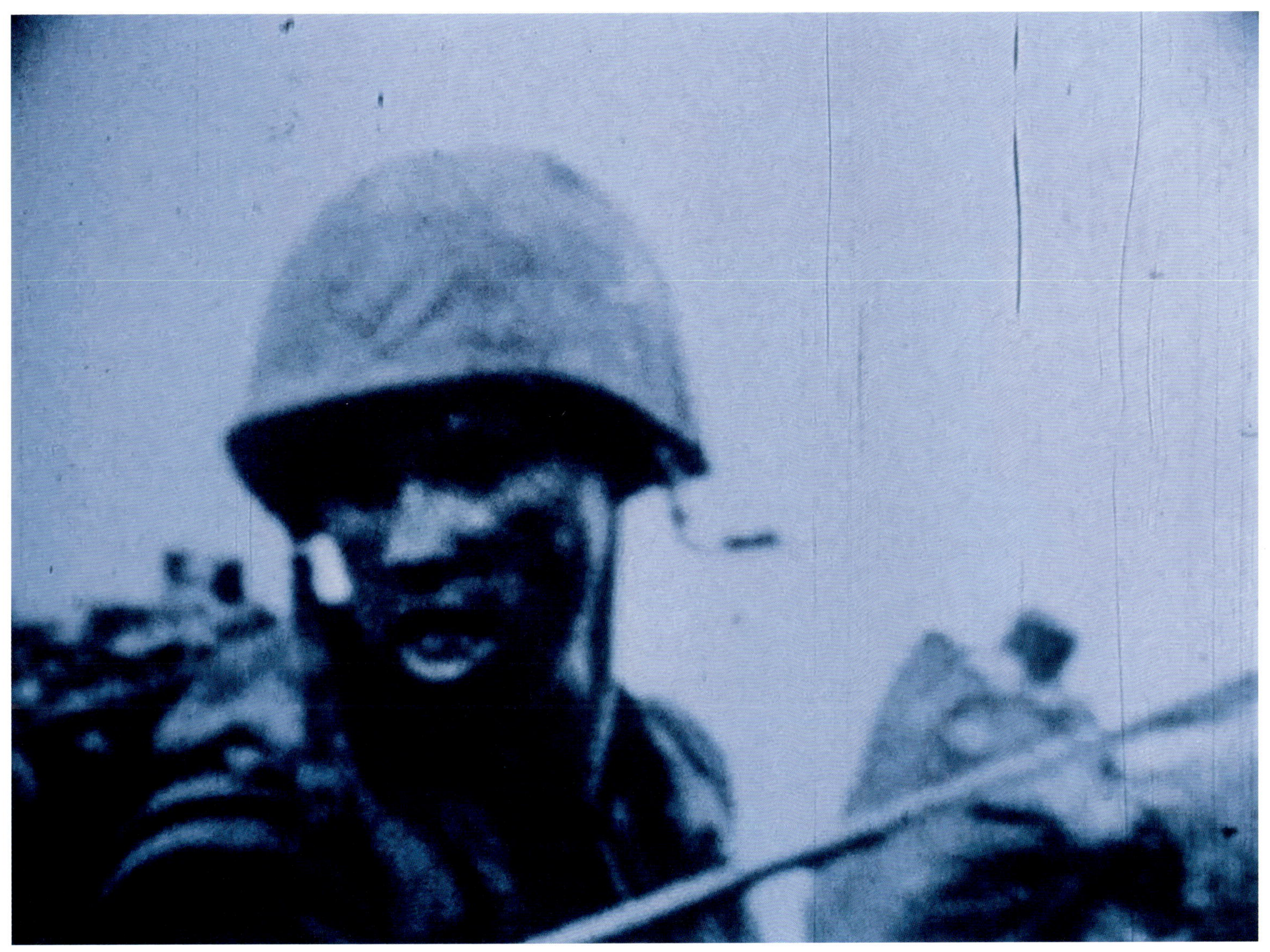

Carolee Schneemann, *Viet-Flakes*, 1962–67. 16mm film transferred to HD video, black-and-white, sound; 8:31 min. Electronic Arts Intermix, New York

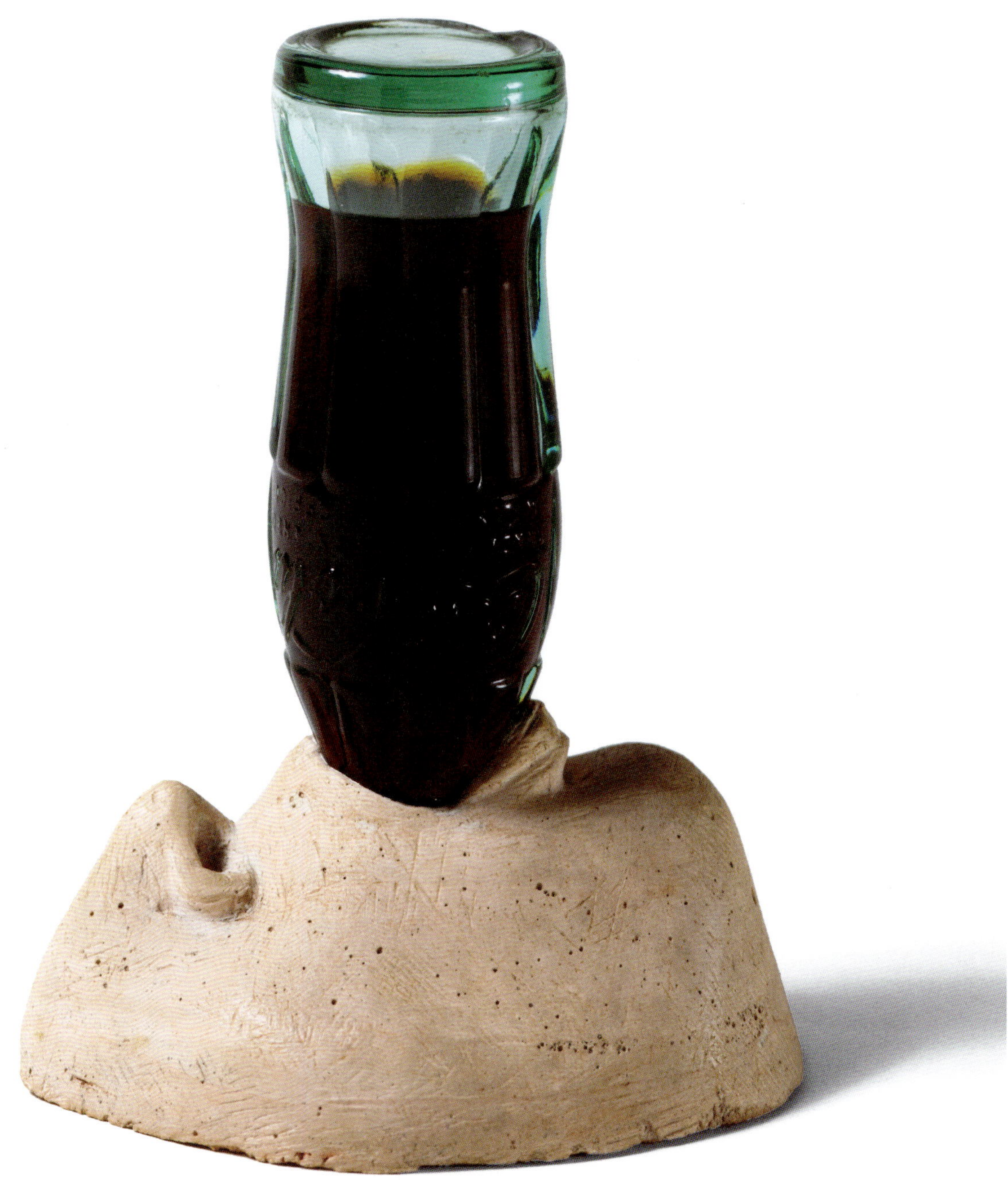

Marisol, *Love*, 1962. Plaster and Coca-Cola bottle, 6 ¼ × 4 ⅛ × 8 ⅛ in. (15.8 × 10.5 × 20.6 cm). The Museum of Modern Art, New York; gift of Claire and Tom Wesselmann 1405.1974

I LiKe To MAKe combiNATioNs that seem INCONGRUOUS _ wood with plAsTeR _ peNciL drawiNG oN wood but FiNALLY I put things where They beloNG _ A hANd aT the eNd of AN ARM _ A Nose oN the middle of the FACE _ A HAT oN ToP of the head _ A SHoe oN A FooT _ A FooT oN A leg _ A bReAsT oN a WoMAN's ToRSO _ A mouth A liTTle below The Nose ANd A NoSTRiL iNSide The Nose.

SoMeTiMeS I also MAKe horses aNd dogs aNd cATS.

Artist's statement by Marisol, c. 1962

Marisol takes a course with the Swiss American Surrealist painter Kurt Seligmann that includes two sessions on "the surrealist method." Her early paintings briefly emulate Kuniyoshi's faux-naive style. But in her mature assemblages of found, manufactured, and hand-carved objects, Marisol achieves an analogous, though entirely distinctive, synthesis of Surrealism and folk art. Like Lee Bontecou, Marisol is one of the few female artists to impress Leo Castelli, the dealer who gives the artist her first solo exhibition, in 1958. In the early 1960s, she begins casting molds of her own body, a technique she will use throughout her career.

Like sculptor Jeremy Anderson, Marisol begins showing with Stable Gallery in 1954. Through the gallery, she meets Andy Warhol, who shortly thereafter includes footage of her kissing painter Harold Stevenson in his silent film *Kiss* (1963).

June 25, 1962 • The Ceeje Gallery, Los Angeles, recently opened by Cecil Hedrick and Jerry Jerome, premieres its first major group exhibition, *Four Artists: Charles Garabedian, Roberto Chavez, Edward* [Eduardo] *Carrillo, Louis L. Lunetta*, featuring work by a group of young, ambitious graduate students from the University of California, Los Angeles. This exhibition and subsequent shows at the gallery defy the dominance of cool 1960s Minimalist abstraction and Conceptualism in favor of the romantic and figurative surrealism and Magical Realism of its artists. Writing for the *Los Angeles Times*, Henry Seldis will remark that the work of Ceeje Gallery artists "ranges from the lightly satirical to the nearly blasphemous,"

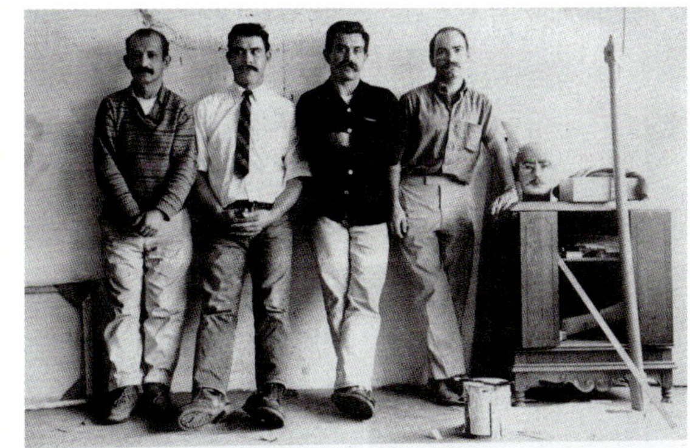

Flyer for *Four Artists: Charles Garabedian, Roberto Chavez, Edward Carrillo, Louis L. Lunetta*, Ceeje Gallery, Los Angeles, 1962

use James Thrall Soby's phrase, been employed more daringly and effectively," writes critic Irving Sandler in the *New York Post* of Marisol's amalgamation of disparate techniques and aesthetic motifs. Sandler also notes the artist's tendency to parody the work of others, including Marcel Duchamp, René Magritte, and H. C. Westermann, all while making art that is wholly her own.

Born in Paris to Venezuelan parents, the artist, who goes simply by Marisol, has led a transient life, moving between Venezuela, Europe, and the United States. Training all over the world, she acquires many similarly transitory mentors, including Hans Hofmann, William King, and Yasuo Kuniyoshi. While living in Los Angeles in the 1940s, she takes classes at the Otis Art Institute and Jepson Art Institute, and for a year she studies at the École des Beaux-Arts in Paris, before relocating in 1950 to New York, where she enrolls at a number of art schools: the Art Students League, Hans Hofmann School, the New School, and Brooklyn Museum Art School. In the early 1950s,

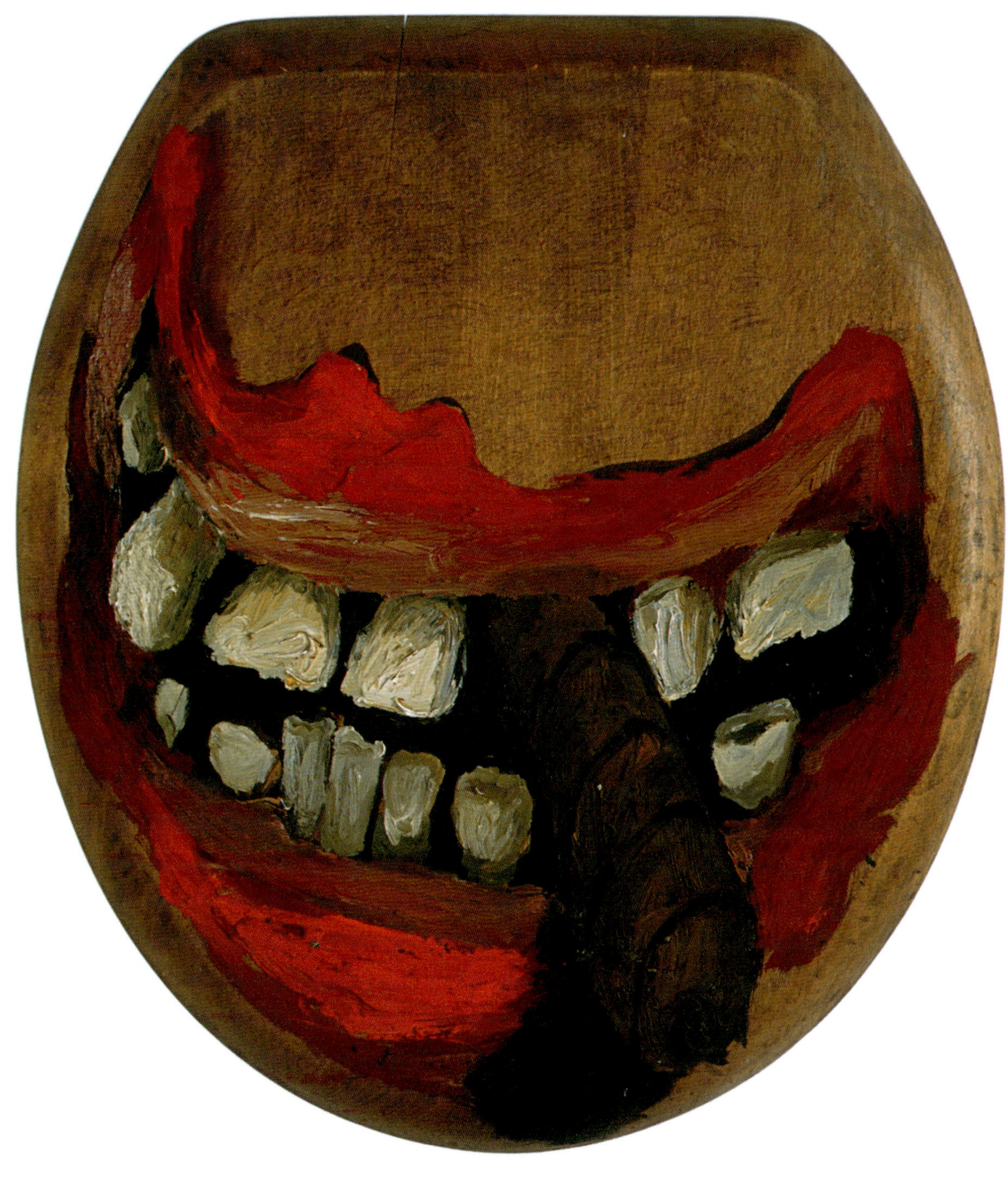

Lee Lozano, *No Title*, c. 1962–63. Oil on wood, 14 ¾ × 13 ⅛ × ¾ in. (37.5 × 33.5 × 2 cm). Pinault Collection, Paris

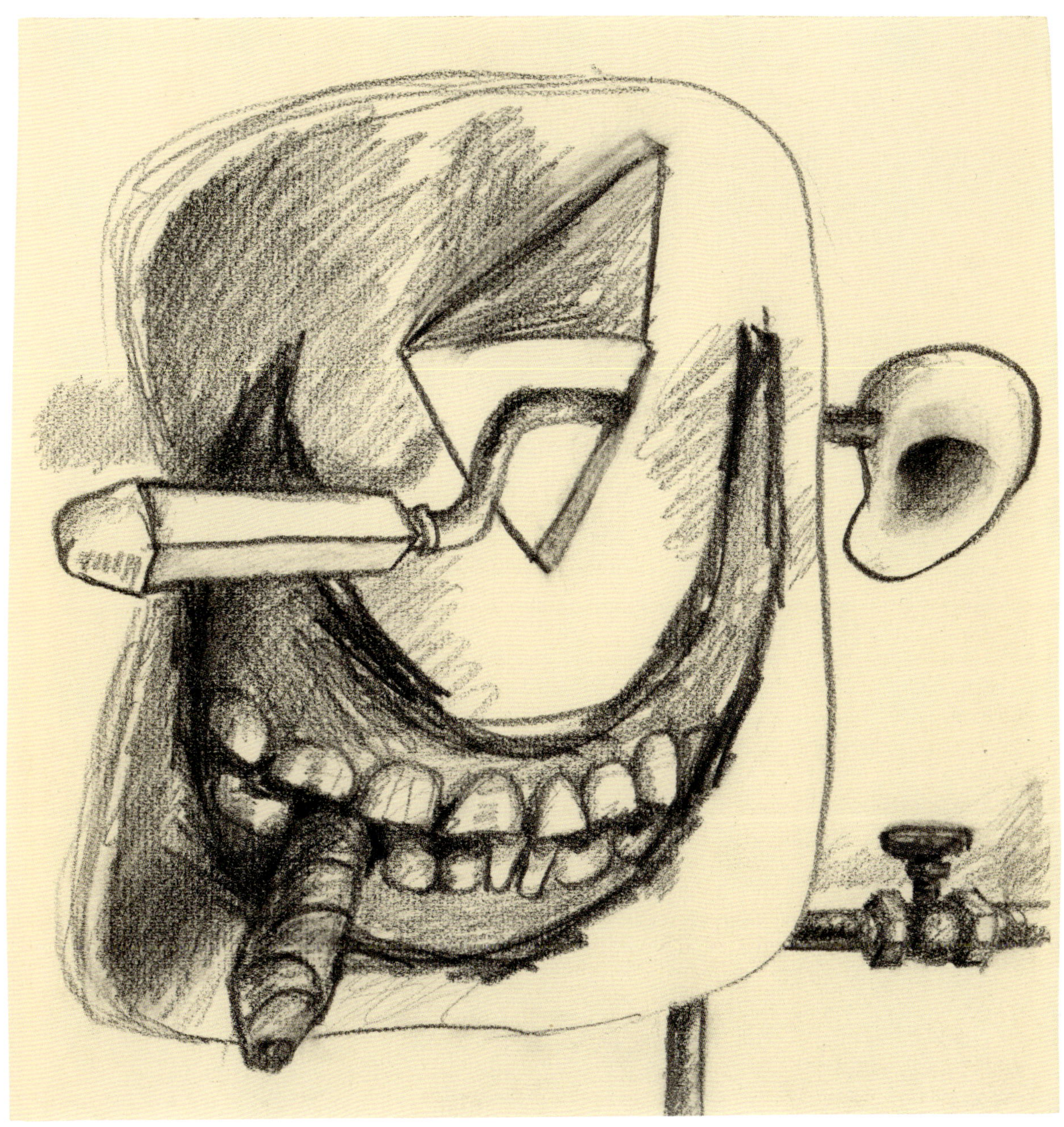

Lee Lozano, *No title (Grinning Face with Ear/Crank)*, 1962. Graphite pencil on paper: sheet, 9 ¼ × 8 ⅝ in. (23.5 × 21.9 cm). Whitney Museum of American Art, New York; gift of Susan Lorence 2008.247

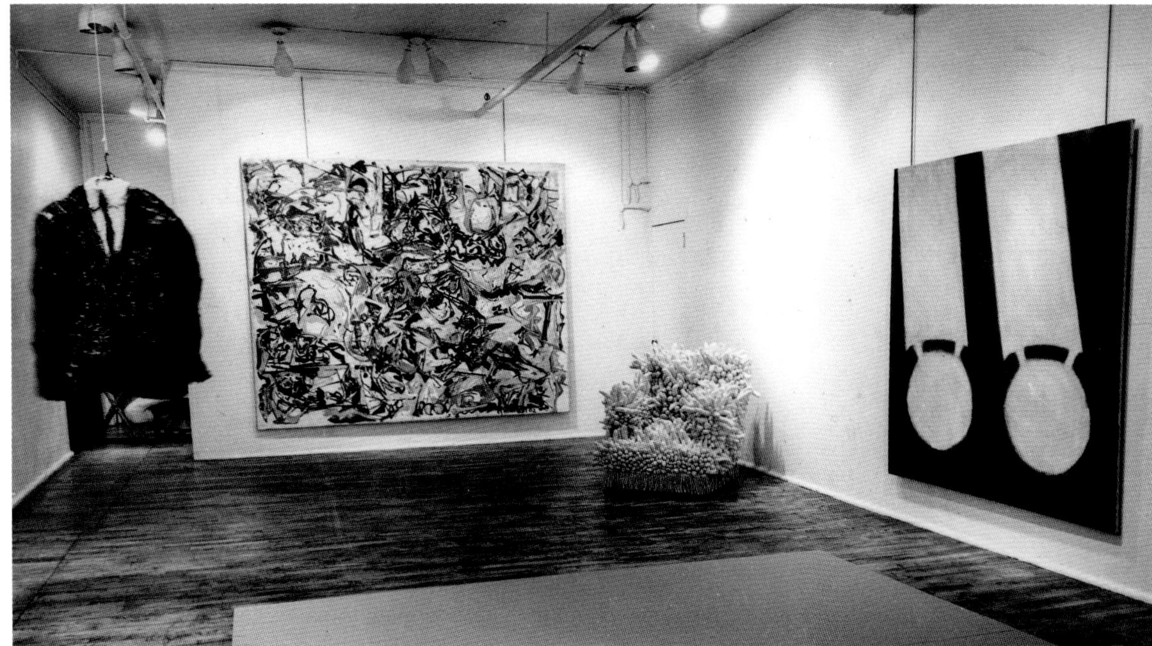

Group exhibition, Green Gallery, New York, 1962, with Yayoi Kusama's *Accumulation 1* (1962)

representative of the group's diversity of gender, race, and sexuality as well as the variety of subject matter, approaches, materials, and scale of their art. Yet Susan B. Larsen will identify a "carefully wrought, homegrown Surrealism" as the most salient style practiced by the core group of Ceeje artists, one clearly embodied by Carrillo's *Evolution* (1962) as well by other paintings, such as *Cabin in the Sky* (1965) and *Pearly Gates* (1966), shown in subsequent Ceeje exhibitions. In *Evolution*, an acrobat balances the skeletal figure of death on his upturned feet in a surreal jungle landscape accompanied by shadowy figures and wild vegetation. Considered iconoclastic and producing an outsider art that is at times full of self-parody, satire, wild self-expression, and eroticism, the Ceeje artists fight for relevance and representation in bold ways.

June 1962 • Yayoi Kusama exhibits in a group show alongside Robert Morris, Claes Oldenburg, James Rosenquist, George Segal, Richard Smith, and Andy Warhol at New York's Green Gallery, which is at the center of the flourishing Pop art movement. Kusama shows for the first time two of her *Accumulation* soft sculptures, in which her strategies of repetition, replication, and compulsion become exaggerated to the point of parodic absurdity, initiating an extensive body of work categorized as her "compulsion furniture" that writer Judith F. Rodenbeck will suggest had possibly been prompted by the Museum of Modern Art's landmark historical survey *The Art of Assemblage* the previous fall. Kusama's *Accumulation 1* (1962), an oversize old armchair, and *Accumulation 2* (1962), an eight-legged sofa, are both painted white and covered in large phallic protuberances that have been stuffed with cotton batting and sewn onto the furniture pieces.

Having moved to a new studio at 53 East 19th Street the previous year, Kusama now resides in a building next door to Sidney Janis Gallery, living on the floor below Donald Judd. The artists had become friends after Judd saw Kusama's show at the artist-run Brata Gallery in 1959, reviewing the exhibition for *ARTnews* and even buying one of the paintings.

————

July 6, 1962 • Alex Hay (b. 1930) helps found the Judson Dance Theater by participating in the three-hour inaugural event A Concert of Dance at Judson Memorial Church, subsequently becoming an important presence in the theater's diverse group of players. The core group is composed of Merce Cunningham's Dance Company; however, a host of visual artists, musicians, actors, and composers also enliven the multidisciplinary atmosphere of the performances. Hay meets Robert Rauschenberg during this period, and both are inspired by the energy and excitement of experimentation at Judson Church, guiding each in part to direct their "fine art" practices outside the discrete disciplinary confines of painting and sculpture. Toward the late 1960s and early 1970s, Hay will draw on his experiences at Judson Church, using elements of spontaneity and chance to create a series of proto-Conceptual "process" pieces on his increasingly frequent trips to California.

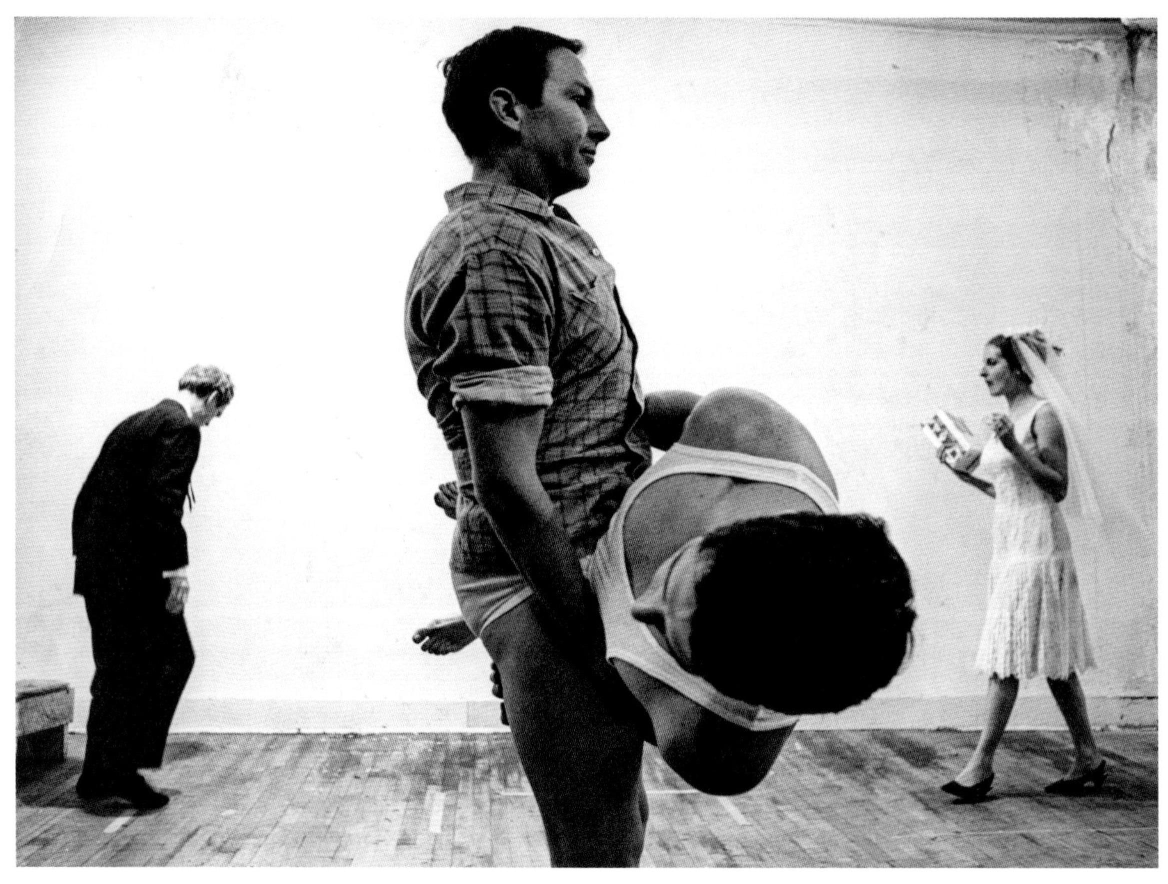

Alex Hay, Robert Rauschenberg, Steve Paxton, and Trisha Brown rehearsing *Spring Training* (1965) in Rauschenberg's studio, New York, 1965

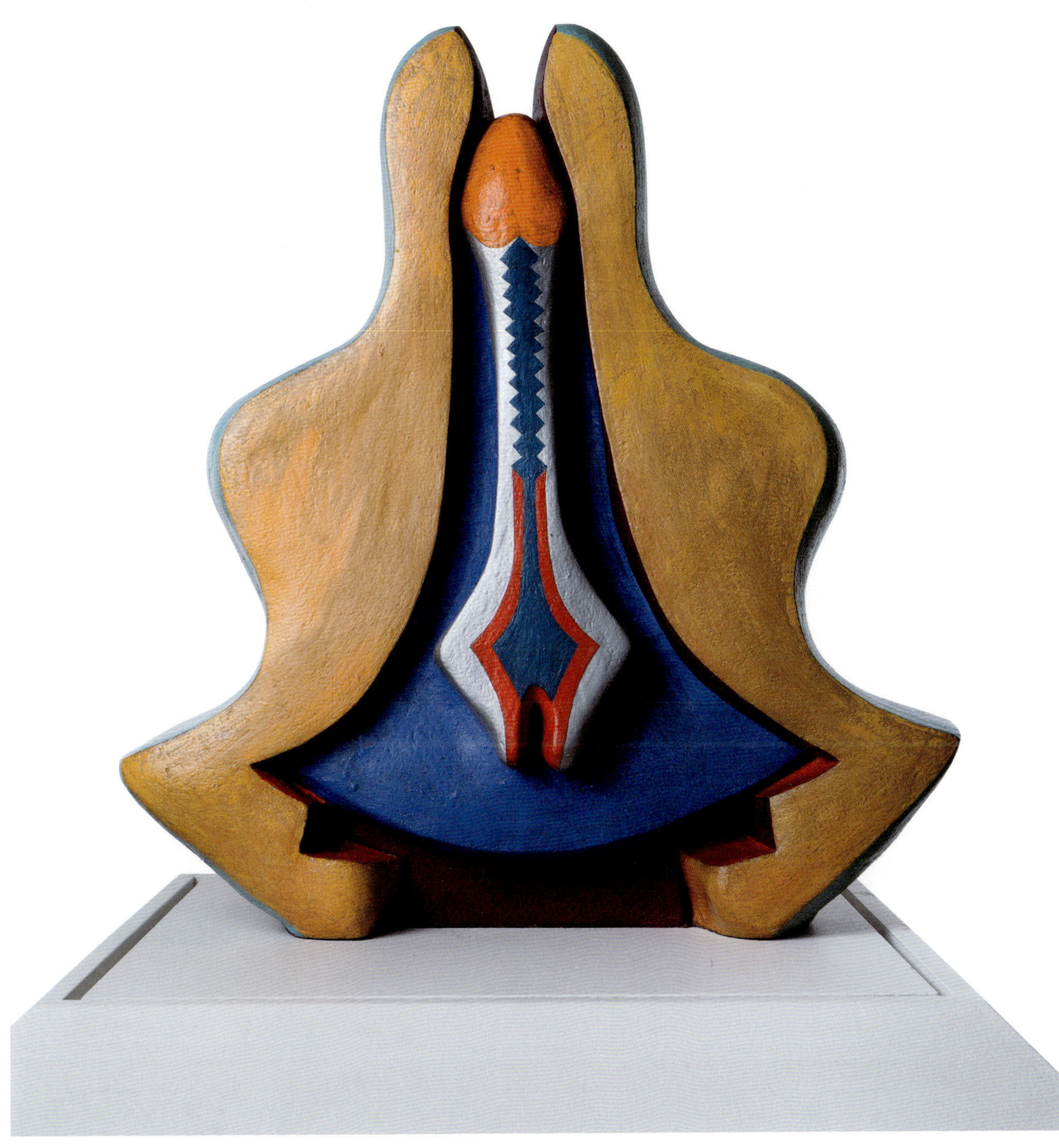

Judy Chicago, *In My Mother's House*, c. 1962–64. Acrylic on stoneware, 24 × 18 × 6 in. (61 × 45.8 × 15.2 cm). Monterey Museum of Art, CA; purchase by exchange: Gift of Mr. and Mrs. Gerald Bates, Mrs. J. B. Heywood, Elizabeth George Lawlor in memory of Dorothy George Meakin, William and Renee Peterson, Mr. and Mrs. John Shephard, Mr. and Mrs. E. V. Stuade, Carolyn Lewis Nielson, Albert Denney, Nancy Stillwell Easterbrook, Margaret Wentworth Owings, Naedra B. Robinson, Elizabeth Tompkins, and an anonymous donor 2019.002

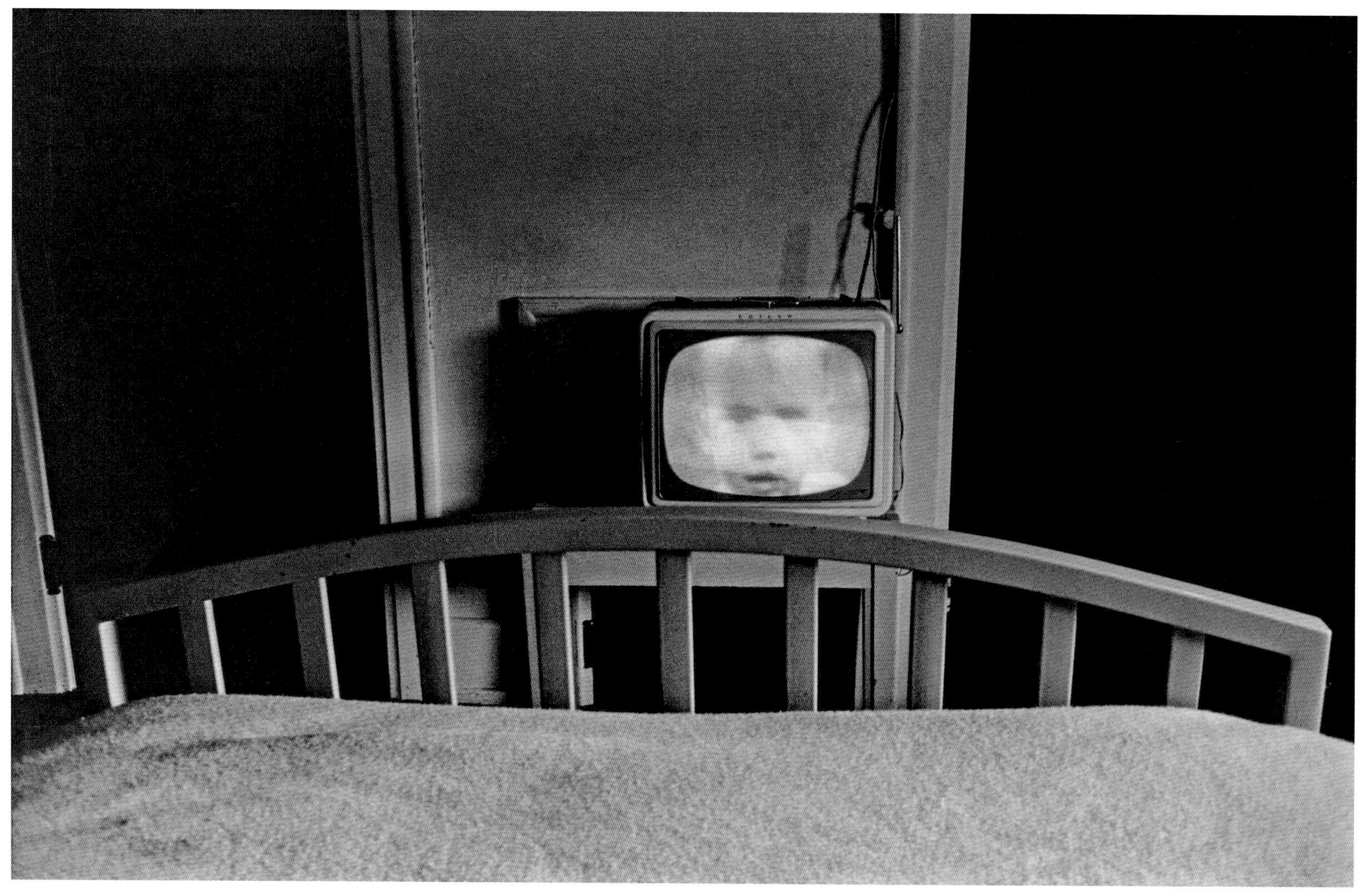

Lee Friedlander, *Galax, Virginia*, 1962. Gelatin silver print, 5 ⅞ × 8 ⅞ in. (14.9 × 22.5 cm). The Museum of Modern Art, New York; acquired through the generosity of Celeste Bartos 56.1975

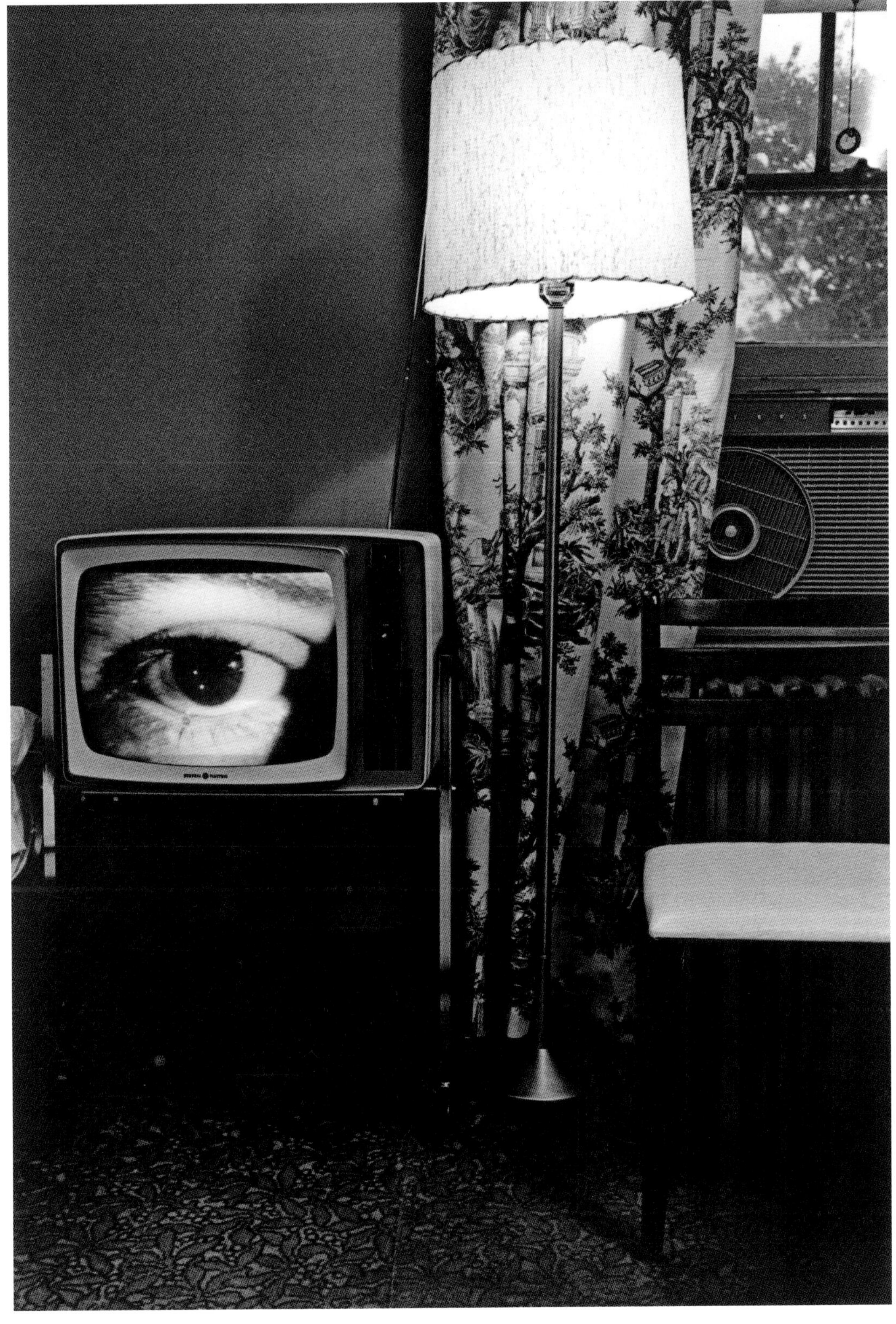

Lee Friedlander, *Washington, D.C.*, 1962. Gelatin silver print, 8 ⅛ × 5 ½ in. (20.6 × 13.8 cm). The Museum of Modern Art, New York; purchase 8.2006

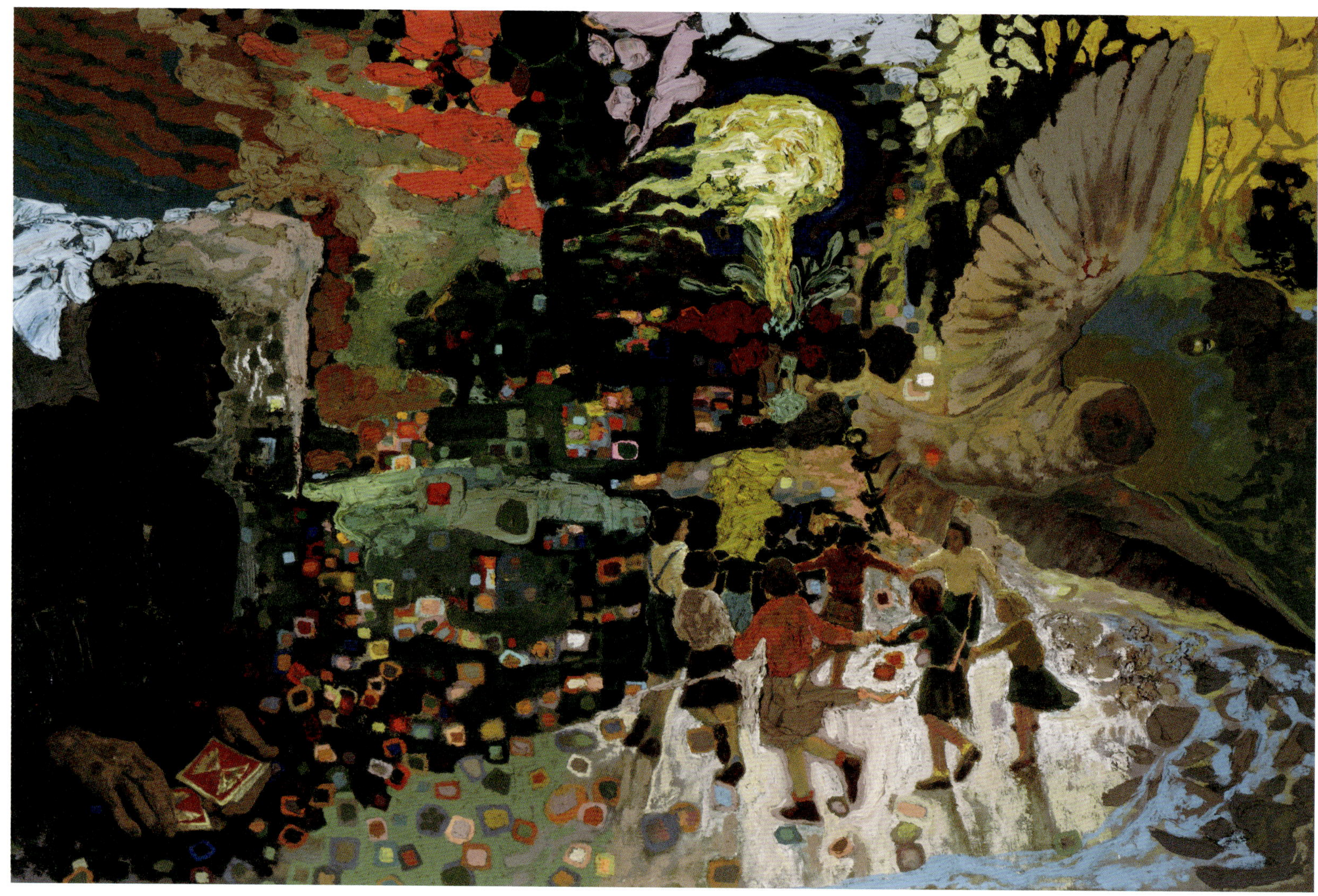

Jess, *If All the World Were Paper and All the Water Sink*, 1962. Oil on canvas, 38 × 56 in. (96.5 × 142.2 cm). Fine Arts Museums of San Francisco; Museum purchase, Roscoe and Margaret Oakes Income Fund, Museum Society Auxiliary, Mr. and Mrs. John N. Rosekrans Jr., Walter H. and Phyllis J. Shorenstein Foundation Fund, Mrs. Paul L. Wattis Fund, Bobbie and Michael Wilsey, Mr. and Mrs. Steven McGregor Read, Mr. and Mrs. Gorham B. Knowles, Mrs. Edward T. Harrison, Mrs. Nan Tucker McEvoy, Harry and Ellen Parker in honor of Steven Nash, Katherine Doyle Spann, Mr. and Mrs. William E. Steen, Mr. and Mrs. Leonard E. Kingsley, George Hopper Fitch, Princess Rainieri di San Faustino, Mr. and Mrs. Richard Madden 1994.31

Born at the outset of the Great Depression, Hay had spent his childhood on a family farm in rural Florida before his family relocated to Tampa, where he attended high school in a predominantly Cuban American neighborhood before serving in an Army National Guard reserve unit at the outset of the Korean War. He earns his bachelor of fine arts and master of fine arts at Florida State University in Tallahassee, then promptly moves to New York City in 1959. Lloyd Wise, writing for *Artforum*, will later succinctly summarize Hay's time in the city: "He hung out at Max's Kansas City, sipped whiskey at Robert Rauschenberg's dining table, married dancer Deborah Hay (née Goldensohn), and appeared in '9 Evenings,' 1966. Then, roughly a decade later, he left and has remained largely absent from received accounts of New York's storied 1960s art world." In somewhat typical enigmatic fashion, Hay will spend the next fifty years after his New York departure in obscurity, working odd jobs in the trades, restoring a defunct hotel in Bisbee, Arizona, and, since 2002, periodically returning to New York to exhibit new artwork.

Fall 1962 • Vija Celmins (b. 1938) begins graduate school at the University of California, Los Angeles. Focused on painting, the Latvia-born artist who had spent the last years of World War II as a refugee in various German towns before immigrating to the United States struggles to escape the expectations of Expressionism: "I tried to bypass my active little brain, which of course was very active, and is still quite active. But by trying to find something that was not of the brain with, of course, a nod to Duchamp, although I didn't know too much about Duchamp. But going back to, not a stupid eye, but somehow like engaging

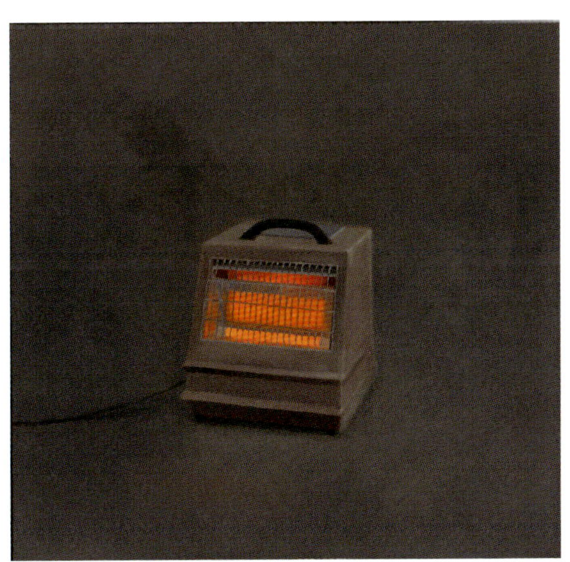

Vija Celmins, *Heater*, 1964. Oil on canvas, 47 9/16 × 48 in. (120.8 × 121.9 cm)

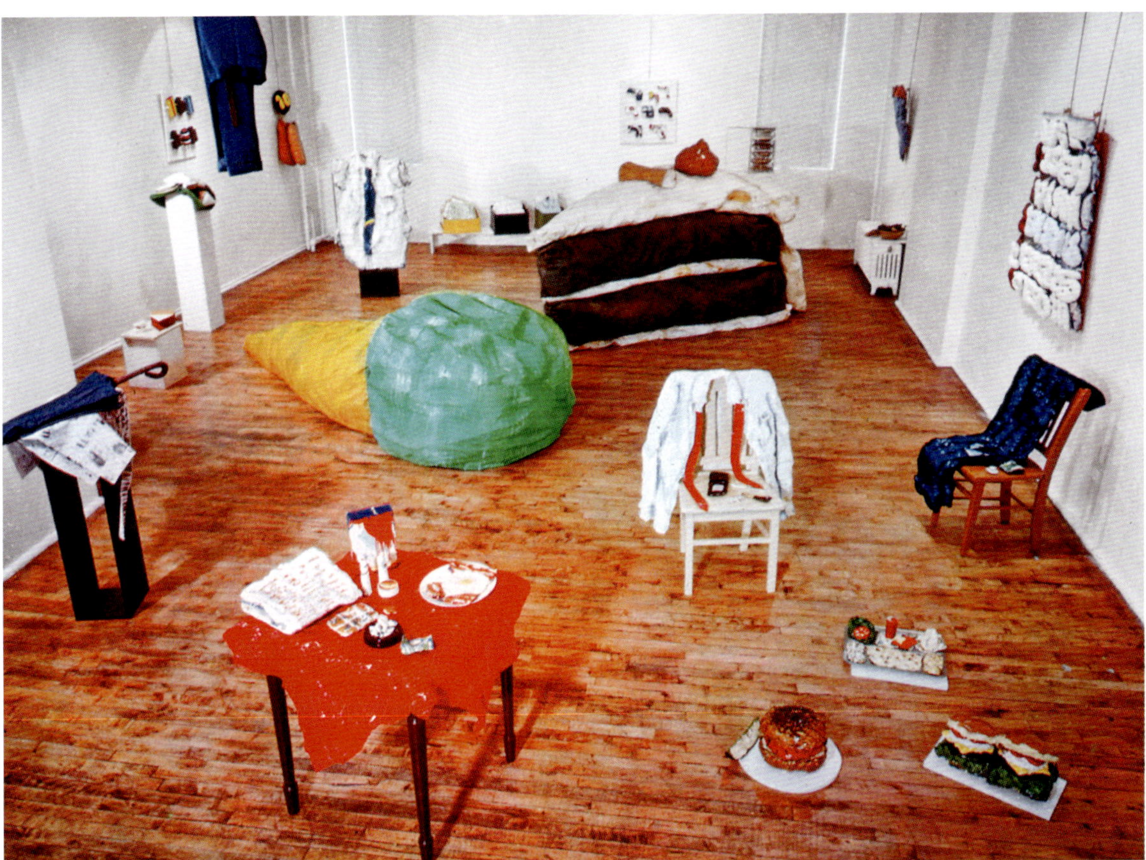

Claes Oldenburg, Green Gallery, New York, 1962

a more intuitive part like my whole body, like a touch." In the early and mid-1960s, Celmins paints objects in her studio—like a space heater on its own, isolated from further context—and attempts to void them of expression to simplify the object to its physical qualities alone.

September 1962 • Robert Arneson and William T. Wiley join the University of California, Davis faculty alongside Manuel Neri and Wayne Thiebaud. All of the artists are lured to what is then an agriculture university on the condition that they will be able to devote as much time as possible to their studio work.

September 24–October 20, 1962 • Claes Oldenburg shows quasi-soft and soft sculptures in his first solo exhibition at Green Gallery, New York. In realizing *The Store* in downtown Manhattan the previous December with funding from Green Gallery owner Richard Bellamy, Oldenburg had created a series of everyday commodities from chicken wire, muslin soaked in plaster, and layers of enamel paint, his ragged dress shirts, ice skates, cigarettes, and whatnot at times barely recognizable. These efforts had produced modest, emphatically imperfect sculptural things—caked in vibrant drips—that recall reality through their sloppy materiality but defy realism in shape, texture, and scale. With the Green Gallery show, Oldenburg now moves his ambiguous objects uptown to the 57th Street gallery district. To fill the large gallery space, Oldenburg also makes his first large-scale soft sculptures, sewn by his wife, Patty Mucha. Critics immediately take notice of the disconcerting aspects of this body of work, describing it as "vulgarized," "unnecessarily gross," and "debauched." Writing for *Art International*, Sonya Rudikoff remarks, "Oldenburg's food is intriguing, but repulsive; it juggles and vulgarizes the illusion." David Irwin remarks that the large-scale sculptures, "influenced by shop signs in streets," become "surreal" when moved indoors. Lucy Lippard will later recognize Oldenburg's work as a "major prototype for soft sculpture" and, more broadly, for the unconventional materials employed by artists such as Eva Hesse and Bruce Nauman.

September 25–October 19, 1962 • One of the earliest shows of Pop art, *New Paintings of Common Objects* is organized by Walter Hopps and is on view at the Pasadena Art Museum. The show includes work by Jim Dine, Robert Dowd, Joe Goode, Phillip Hefferton, Roy Lichtenstein, Ed Ruscha, Wayne Thiebaud, and Andy Warhol. In the November issue of *Artforum* John Coplans writes of the show:

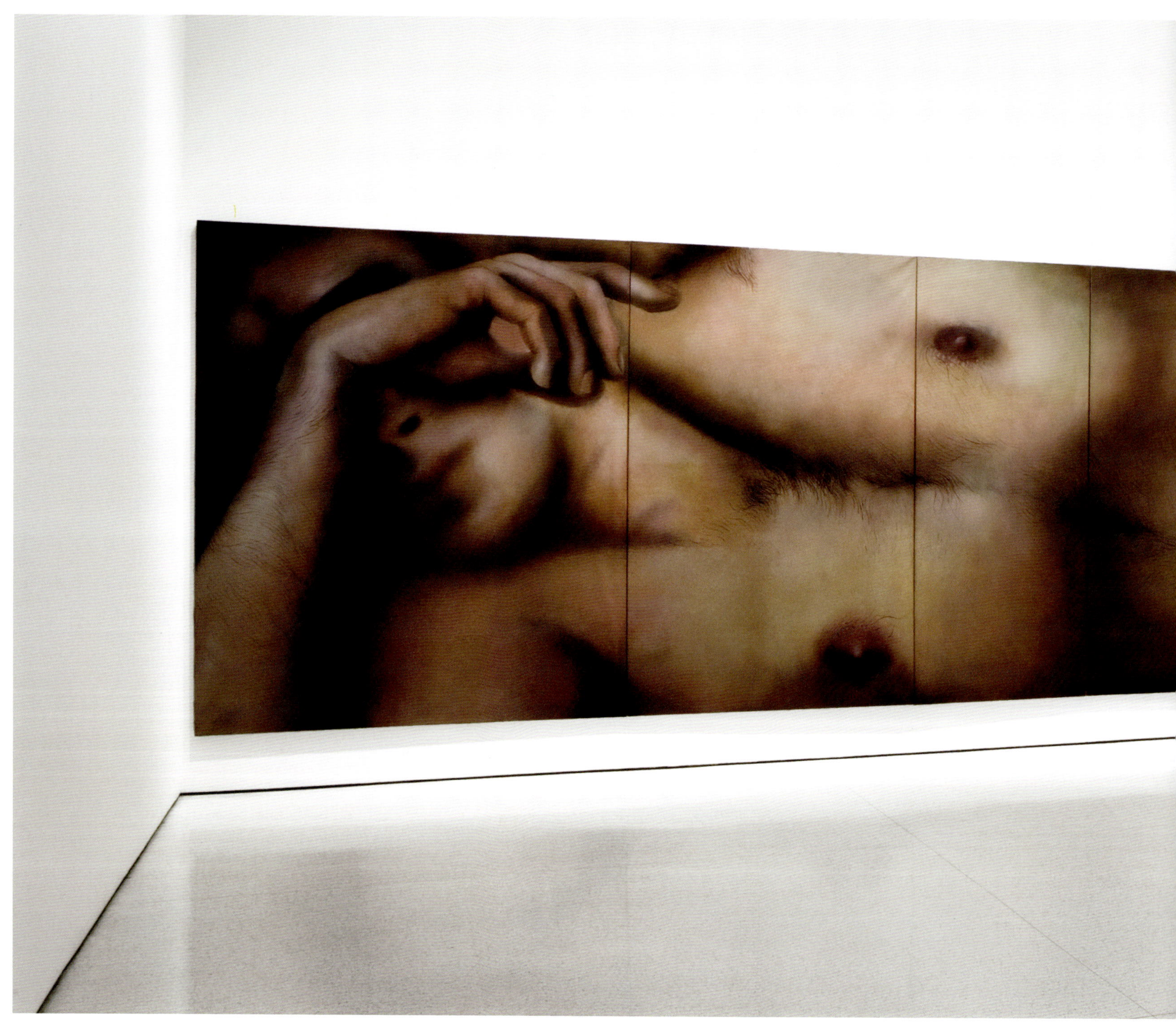

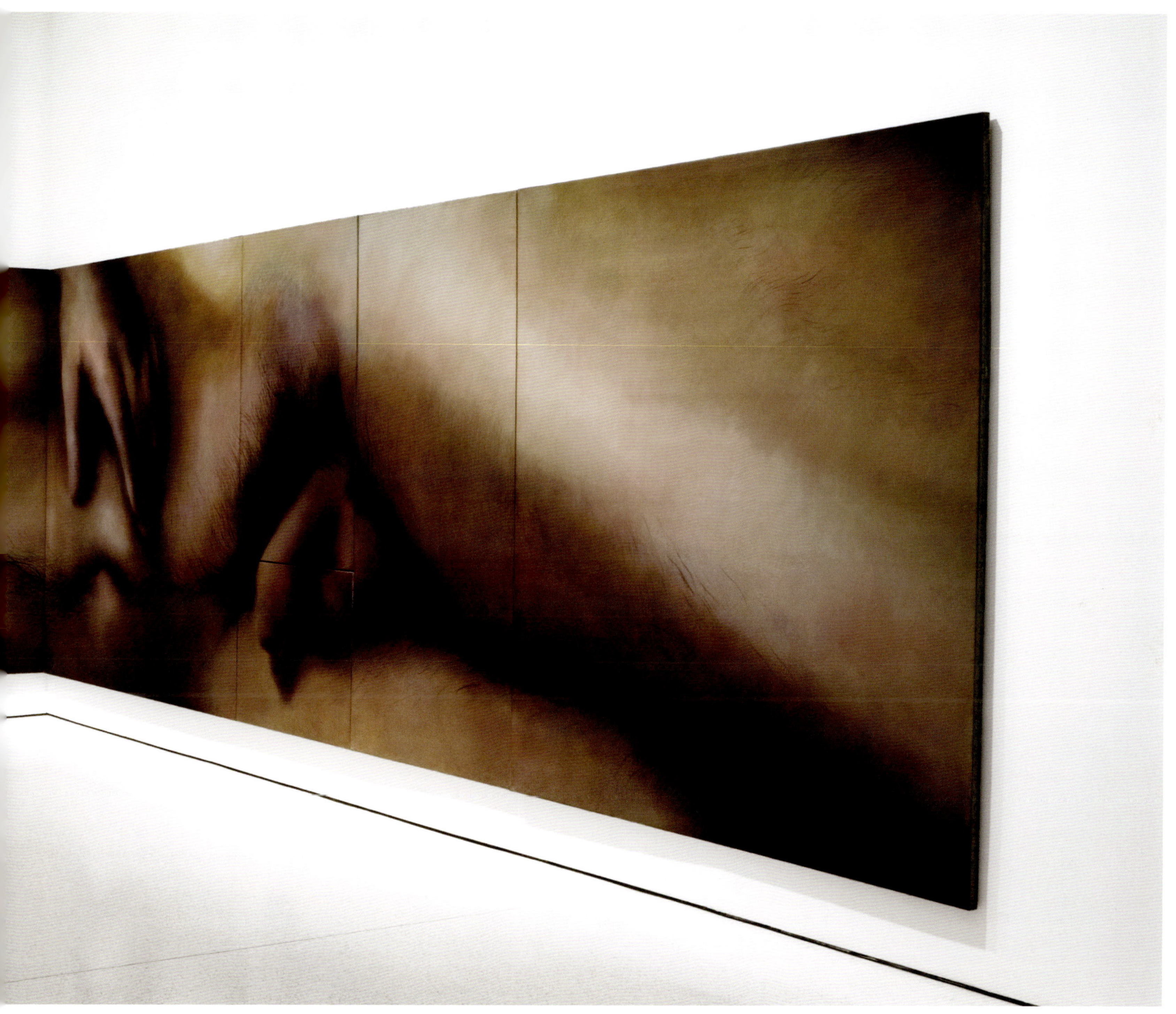

Harold Stevenson, *The New Adam*, 1962. Oil on linen: nine panels, 96 × 468 in. (243.8 × 1188.7 cm) overall. Solomon R. Guggenheim Museum, New York; anonymous gift 2005 2005.35

Neither philosophical newness nor modernism of metaphysics has ever necessarily led to the deepest art. The intuitive understanding of this position differentiates to a great degree the American artist from his European counterpart and the result has been an art of direct response to life rather than to "problems." The proverbial dumbness of most younger artists on the West Coast, for example, is a reflection not only of their deep understanding of the lie of the evolution of progress, but also an affirmation of the basis of both Jazz and Beat poetry, that art springs directly from life, with all its anguish.

Of Ruscha's work in particular, Coplans says, "Ruscha's art reminds us of the visual humor of Mondrian's *Broadway Boogie Woogie*, but he is impressive for his creation of a totally new visual landscape. [He] combines a beautiful use of typography with an exquisite sense of placing and extraordinary color to upset our whole aesthetic balance." Ruscha will also show at Hopps's Ferus Gallery the following May after having met the curator through their mutual friend and fellow artist Ed Bereal earlier in the year.

October 12–November 3, 1962 • Nancy Spero has her first solo exhibition at Galerie Breteau, Paris, where she shows the *Paris Black Paintings*, in which coupled figures emerge as entangled shadows from a dark fog of blacks, purples, and browns. Several works feature the expletives "*merde*" and "fuck you" floating alongside disembodied heads screaming or

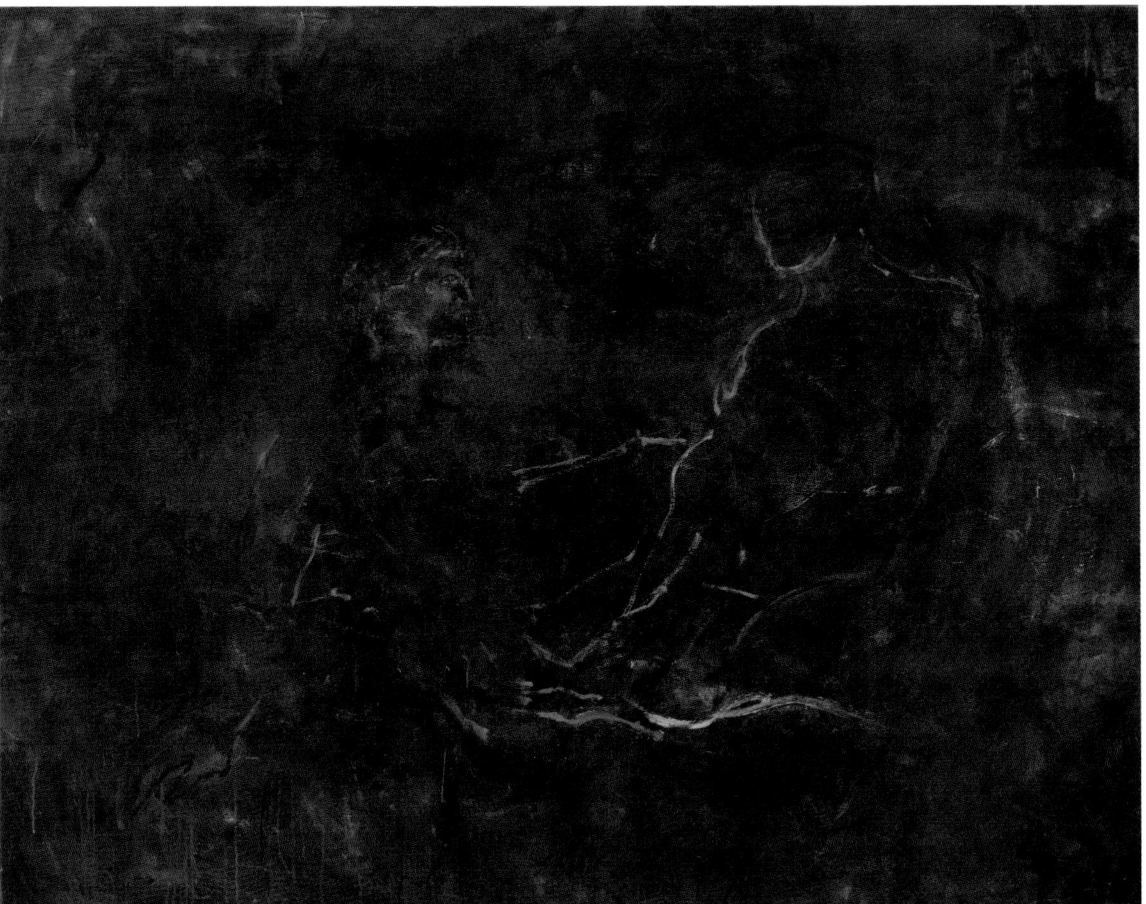

Nancy Spero, *Lovers*, 1962. Oil on canvas, 64 ⅜ × 80 ⅜ in. (163.5 × 204.2 cm)

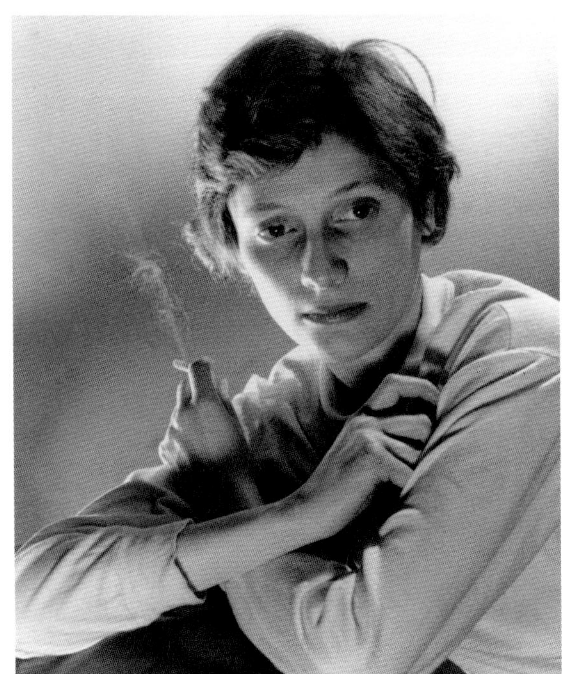

Nancy Spero, c. 1952

vomiting—wormlike precursors to the heads in her later *War Series*. Much like the painting process of the Surrealists before her, Spero's approach relies on instinct more than on a predetermined image, in a process she will later explain: "As I work and re-work my canvases, eventually the image appears (sometimes only to elude me, then to re-assert itself much later). The composition and figures are never reconceived yet my themes are recurrent. For many years I have returned to a double image which has assumed diverse forms—in a series of 'le couple' or 'the lover'—existentially expressed through the inspiration of Tarot cards. . . . I would like to believe I am creating images of poetic ritual."

October 31–December 1, 1962 • Heralding a shift from Abstract Expressionism to Pop art, *New Realists* at Sidney Janis Gallery, New York, includes work by Christo, Robert Indiana, Yves Klein, Roy Lichtenstein, Marisol, Claes Oldenburg, James Rosenquist, Jean Tinguely, and Andy Warhol, as well as Harold Stevenson (1929–2018). *New York Times* critic Brian O'Doherty remarks that the artists on display harness imagery of commonplace objects, often from advertisements that are then "isolated, surrounded, manipulated in attempts to divert them from their everyday function to esthetic ends." The show features Stevenson's *The Eye of Lightning Billy* (1962), a painting that combines the artist's stylistic particularities—notably, his preference for working with carefully selected live models as well as his experimentation with portraying isolated fragments of human anatomy.

Stevenson had been born in Idabel, Oklahoma, and briefly attended the University of Oklahoma to study art before winning a scholarship in June 1949 to the Art Students League of New York, where he works with Yasuo Kuniyoshi. Although Stevenson soon drops out—finding Kuniyoshi's class uninteresting—his cohort includes the then unknown Robert Rauschenberg. In 1949 Stevenson meets a young Andy Warhol, and the two become lifelong friends. He moves to Europe in 1959 and settles primarily in Paris, returning to the United States periodically for major exhibitions, including *New Realists*.

December 12, 1962–February 3, 1963 • The Whitney Museum of American Art's *Annual Exhibition 1962: Contemporary Sculpture and Drawings* continues the trend of showing largely New York–based artists and features artists Lee Bontecou, Louise Bourgeois, and Marisol.

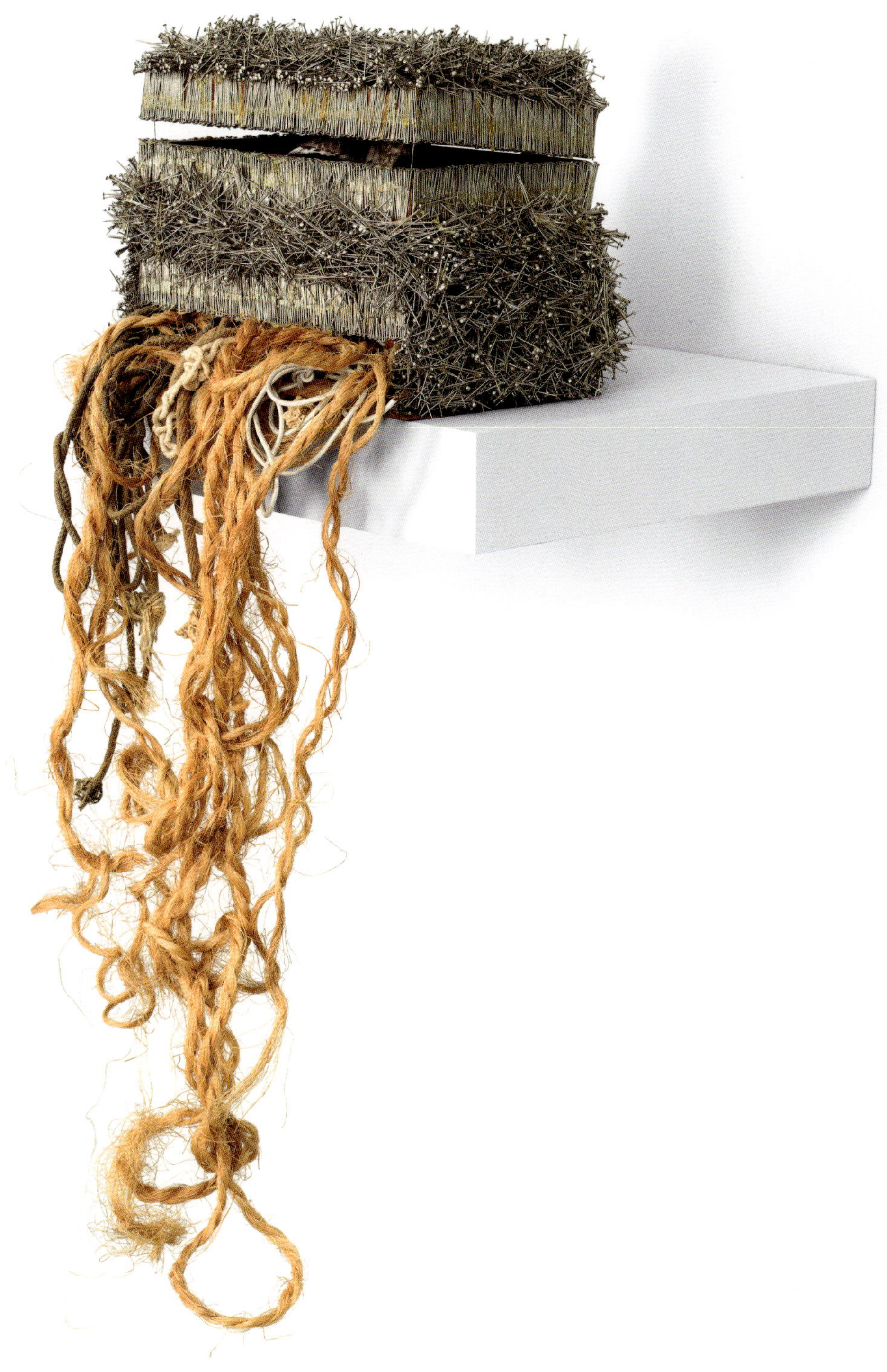

Lucas Samaras, *Box #3*, 1962–63. Wood box with straight pins, rope, wire, taxidermy bird, and metal hardware, approximately 28 ¾ × 10 ⅝ × 10 in. (73 × 27 × 25.4 cm) overall. Whitney Museum of American Art, New York; gift of the Howard and Jean Lipman Foundation, Inc. 66.36

1963

1963 • Lee Lozano smooths her style to depict anthropomorphized and sexualized tools such as hammers, clamps, and screws. She will present these works in group shows in New York: first in an exhibition titled *New Work (Contemporary American Group Show)* at Green Gallery in fall 1964, where she shows her work alongside that of Dan Flavin, Donald Judd, Richard Smith, and Mark di Suvero, among others, and early the following year in *Contemporary Erotica* at Van Bovenkamp Gallerie, where she joins artists such as Jean Cocteau, Salvador Dalí, Marisol, Lucas Samaras, and Tom Wesselmann. Her solo show at Green Gallery, which is supposed to open in September 1965, never happens, because the gallery suddenly closes due to financial hardship.

In 1965 Lozano's paintings become fully abstract, minimally illustrating the verbs of their titles, such as *Lean*, *Verge*, and *Peel*. In just a few years, her work has evolved from Expressionism and Pop to process and Minimal painting. Soon she will turn to language-based works, participating in the "dematerialization" of art in the late 1960s.

January 8–February 2, 1963 • The group show *New Work: Part I* is on view at Green Gallery, New York, and debuts Lucas Samaras's pin-covered books and boxes alongside works by Yayoi Kusama, Robert Morris, George Segal, H. C. Westermann, and others. Samaras had begun making boxes in late 1960. At first small, crude wooden containers stuffed with plastered rags, the boxes over time had become increasingly complex and filled with accumulated found objects. "I was using things that were partly ruined or about to be thrown away," the artist will later explain. "I think I was interested in the idea that when something became useless I could rescue it and give it a dignity it never had." In this way, Samaras's containers are comparable to those of Joseph Cornell, who in combining found material in his open-faced boxes reveals an enchantment hidden in the everyday. However, Samaras's boxes, temptingly ajar yet covered in pins that threaten to harm those who dare handle them, evoke the transgressive crossing of boundaries. Often containing personal items ranging from kitchen knives to jewelry to false teeth, Samaras's "intimate but quite lethal things" fall within a Surrealist legacy of corrupted domestic objects, such as Meret Oppenheim's fur-clad tea cup (*Object*; 1936) or Man Ray's thumb-tack-studded iron (*The Gift*; 1921).

1963 • Kay Sekimachi makes her first hanging sculptural textile. "I got very fascinated with the idea of see-through objects," Sekimachi will recall about the inspiration for her sculptural

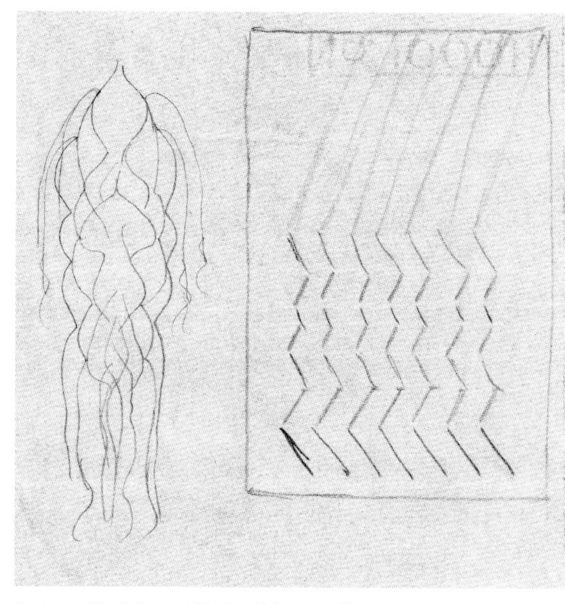

Sketch by Kay Sekimachi for her Mylar monofilm experiments, undated

weaves. "I wanted to weave a tapestry that was in three layers, and one that you could look through the top layer to the second layer, to the third layer. And so, as I was just fooling around making samples for it, when I took a piece off the loom, I realized that it would open up and stay opened out if I chose the right materials." A friend at the Haystack Mountain School of Crafts gives her a sample of Vylor, an extremely strong

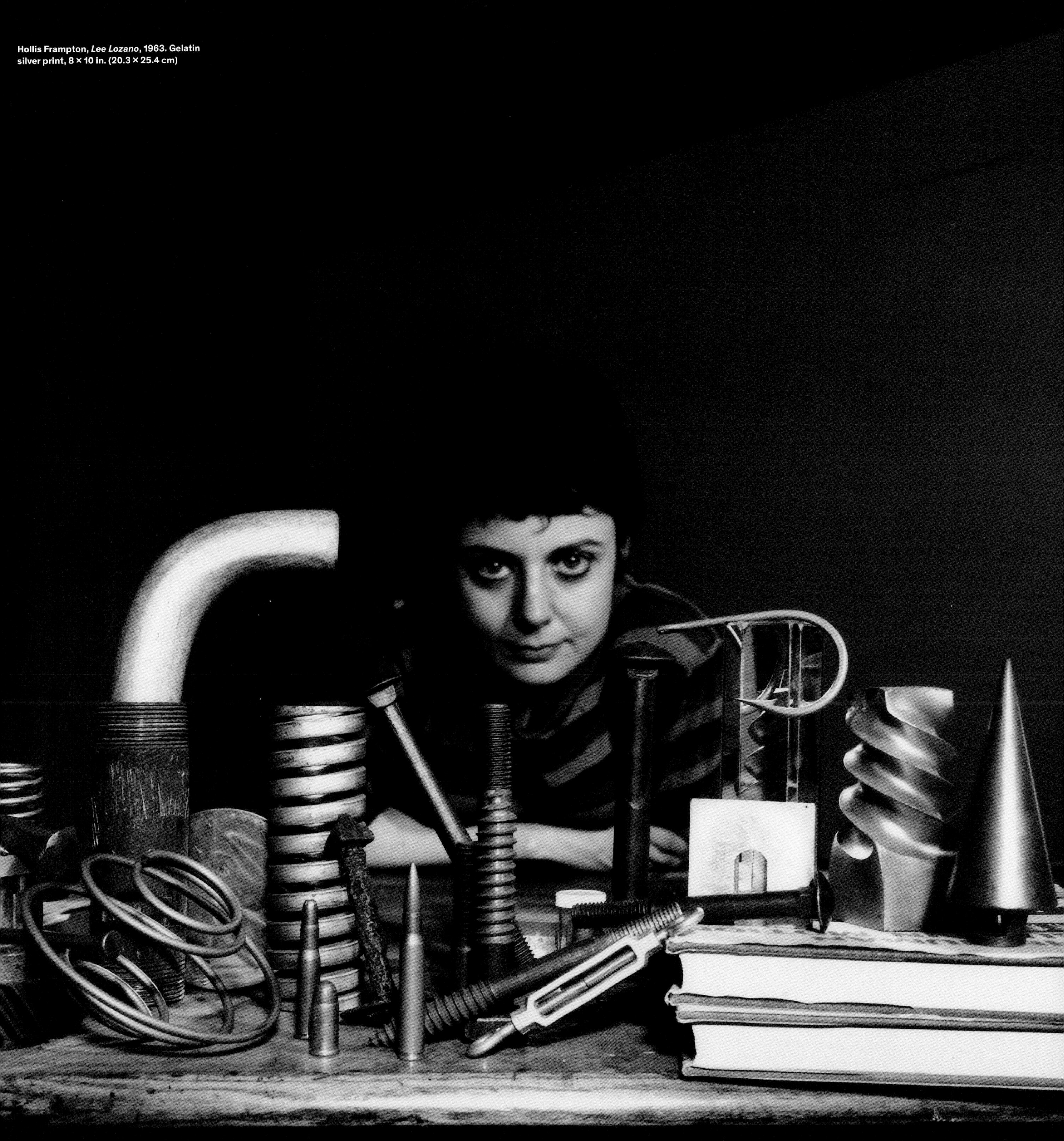

Hollis Frampton, *Lee Lozano*, 1963. Gelatin
silver print, 8 × 10 in. (20.3 × 25.4 cm)

nylon monofilament developed by DuPont Chemical, and Sekimachi finds that the material is perfect for the triple- and quadruple-woven hangings she envisions. The works made of the durable, synthetic material are deceptively diaphanous, elegant, and organic. Where previously Sekimachi had given her tapestries generic titles—as in *White Study* and *Square Variations* (both c. 1959)—she gives some of these sculptural works Japanese names, choosing words for the natural forms each sculpture calls to mind. Examples include *Nagare* (Flow) (1967) and *Kurogawa* (Black River) (1975).

———

February 1963 • Harold Stevenson shows his colossal 40-foot-long painting *The New Adam* (1962) at an exhibition at Galerie Iris Clert, where "everybody in the art world who passed through Paris came to see it," as Stevenson will recall. An homage to his previous model and partner, Lord Timothy Willoughby, the work approaches Stevenson's plateau of ideal in its execution. Primarily modeled on Academy Award–nominated actor Sal Mineo—a "very well-proportioned person," according to Stevenson—*The New Adam* self-consciously channels art-historical language. At once Stevenson complicates the odalisque genre by focusing on the queer gaze and alters Michelangelo's iconic image of Adam extending his figure toward the hand of God into a seemingly self-referential gesture directed inward.

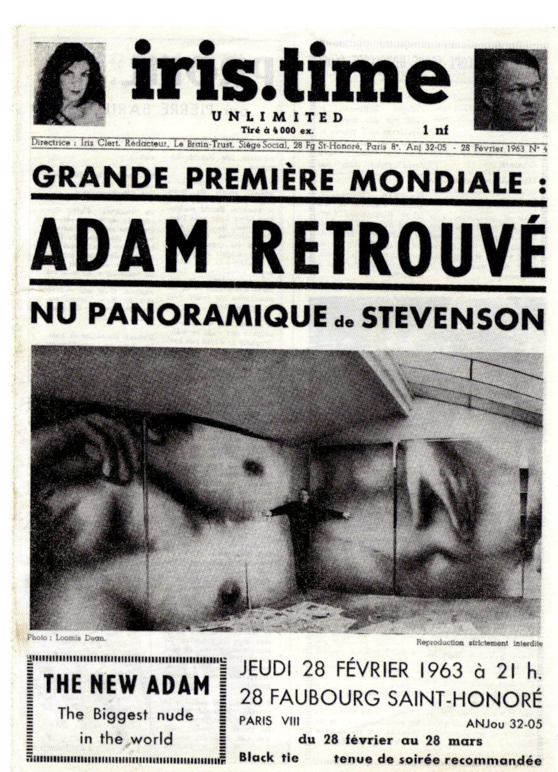

Pamphlet for the exhibition of Harold Stevenson's *The New Adam* (1962), Galerie Iris Clert, Paris, 1963

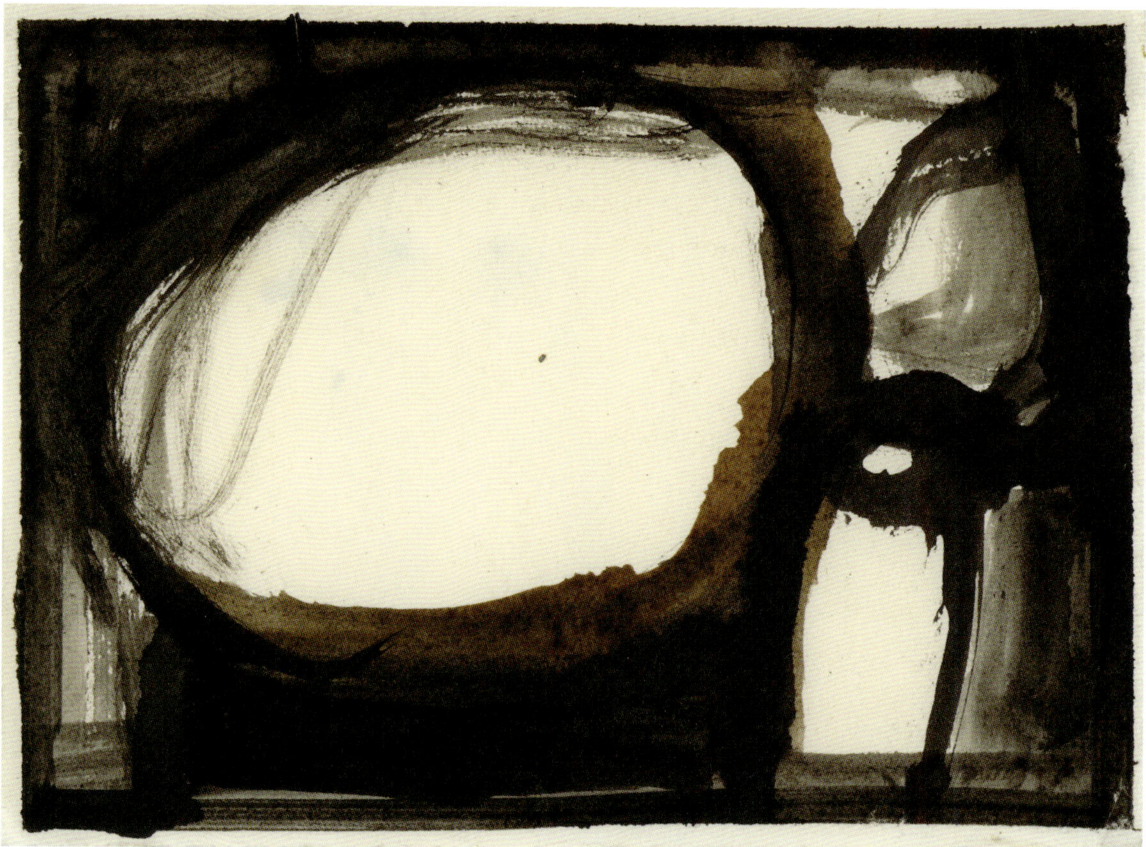

Eva Hesse, *No title*, 1961. Ink and watercolor on paper, 4 ½ × 6 in. (11.5 × 15.2 cm)

Stevenson sees "the message of art . . . [as] a glimpse at the ecstasy for the human experience." Even more explicitly, he will note that "the only thing I find significant to glorify is the human body which houses the human spirit," a not-so-subtle rebuke to the popular aesthetic currents of the 1960s. His paintings arguably operate both as antidotes to the increasingly modernized—and mechanized—world through a turn to the soft, sensual quality of flesh and as monumental homages to the human body as a site of desire. Stevenson's preference for painting at an incredible scale was, according to the artist, inherently strategic: "Since people had stopped looking at the human figure except in terms of fashion or some function with machines, et cetera, I wanted to make sure that—and this was rather naive—everyone could see the image. So I knew that if the image was very small, like life-size or a tiny bit more, I was afraid that people couldn't see it. So I thought the bigger the figure, the better."

———

March–April 1963 • Eva Hesse (1936–1970) has her first solo exhibition, *Eva Hesse: Recent Drawings*, at New York's Allan Stone Gallery, where she shows varied and energetic collages, geometric abstractions endowed with the irreverence and brashness of Pop art.

Born in Hamburg, Germany, Hesse with her Jewish family had fled the Nazi regime in 1938, eventually settling in the Washington Heights neighborhood of New York City. She studies drawing and painting at the Art Students League, Pratt, and at the Cooper Union School of Art before continuing her education at the Yale School of Art, where Josef Albers is one of her instructors and where she earns a bachelor of arts in 1959. By 1962 Hesse is working as an artist in Lower Manhattan, having recently met and married the sculptor Tom Doyle; the couple will move into an apartment at 134 Bowery at the end of 1963. Lucy Lippard, whom Hesse will soon befriend, lives one block away with her husband, Robert Ryman. With the exception of a fifteen-month period spent in Kettwig, Germany, Hesse will work out of this building until her life is tragically cut short following the diagnosis of a brain tumor.

Hesse "could always draw, even if she was having trouble with painting," as Lippard, who was also the artist's first biographer, would later recall. In 1960 Hesse had attended Lee Bontecou's first exhibition at Castelli Gallery, one of the few art-related events she would note in her diary. The drawings she makes in the months that follow are, in Lippard's words, "among the most beautiful in Hesse's oeuvre" and could have "led her directly into the mature sculpture which they so often

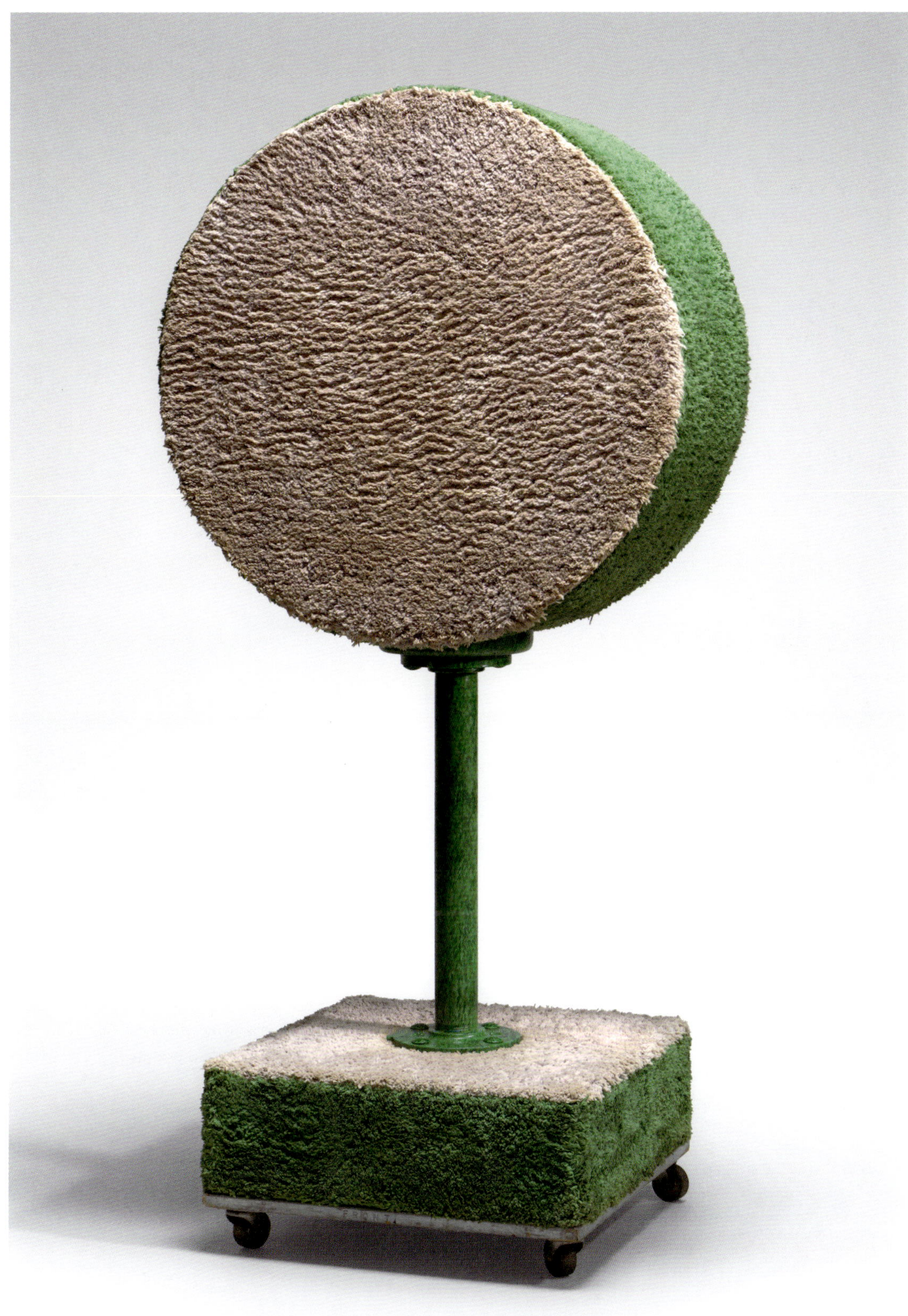

H. C. Westermann, *The Plush*, 1963–64. Cotton-pile shag carpet with latex backing, cast iron, paint, wood, and metal casters, 59 × 29 × 21 in. (149.8 × 73.7 × 53.3 cm). National Gallery of Art, Washington, DC; Corcoran Collection (gift of Samuel J. Wagstaff Jr.) 2014.136.287

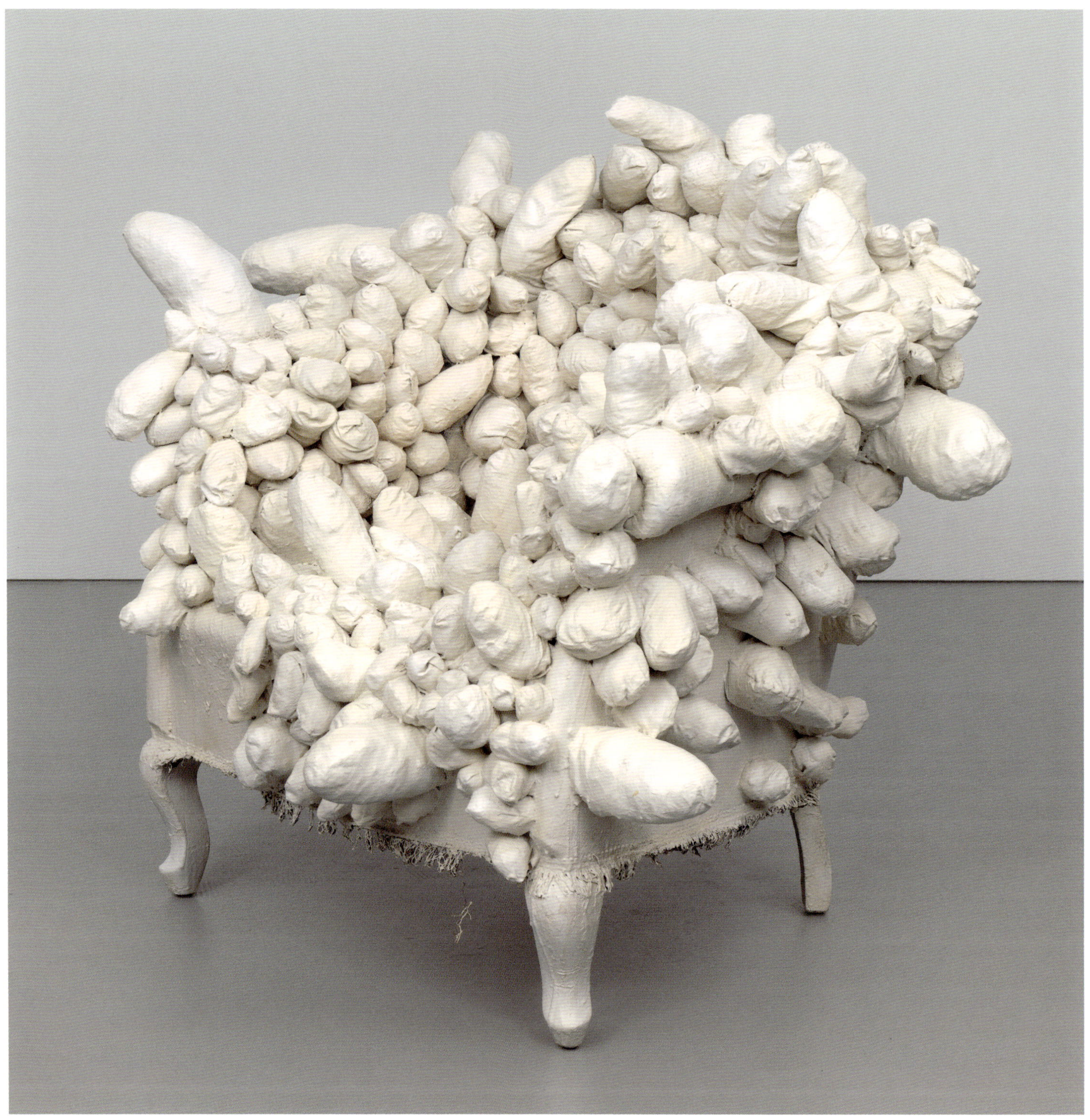

Yayoi Kusama, *Accumulation*, c. 1963. Sewn and stuffed fabric, wood chair frame, and paint, 34 ⅜ × 38 ⅜ × 36 ⅜ in. (87.2 × 98.9 × 92.2 cm). Whitney Museum of American Art, New York; purchase 2001.342

resemble." At the same time, Hesse draws inspiration from the work of Claes Oldenburg, as she herself remarked in a notebook: "Oldenburg: As eroticism his work is abstract / the stimuli arise from pure sensation rather than direct association with objects depicted." Later in her career she will admire Marisol for her inventiveness. After visiting the artist's studio in May 1966, she praises her unconventional use of materials: "Marisol . . . will try anything. Experiment with any media, incorporating all things."

Spring 1963 • After being invited by the Harlem photography club Group 35—so called for its use of 35mm cameras—to give lessons to its members, Adger Cowans helps found the Kamoinge Workshop, which forms when Group 35 merges with a loose circle of photographers that includes Louis Draper, Al Fennar, James Mannas, Herbert Randall, and Shawn Walker. In the language of the Kikiuyu people of Kenya, *kamoinge* means "a group of people acting together." "It was just a group of guys that met on Sundays up at Ray [Francis]'s house . . . and we'd just talk about photography," Cowan will later recall of the origins of what would become the longest-running nonprofit photography organization in history. "We felt we could do a better job in showing the truth of our people, rather than someone else coming in and photographing us, because that was always in a sort of 'native' vein or from somebody else's point of view." This sentiment echoes the mission statement the workshop will include in its two collective portfolios from 1964 and 1965, announcing itself as "a group of black photographers whose creative objectives reflect a concern for truth about the world, about the society and about themselves."

But it would be a mistake to interpret this "truth" as purely a matter of documentary veracity. The concern for a more hidden truth can be seen in Cowans's and Walker's explorations of that which lies at the limits of social and photographic visibility. In *Shadows* (1966), Cowans captures three foreshortened figures from above, their shadows dramatically elongated onto the sidewalk ahead of them by the low, late-day sun as they perhaps return home from work. Cowans's shadows brim with gestural liveness but remain opaque. The uncanniness and inscrutability of the shadows undercut the presumption of realism and cultural insight often brought to street photography, particularly in the sociological interest of outsider photographers in Harlem, a tendency that the Kamoinge Workshop criticizes. In Walker's *Tiffany's Window on 57th St., NYC* (1968–72), the silhouetted shadow of a boy is thrown against the facade of the flagship Tiffany & Co. store and appears next to a mannequin—ghostly, waifish, and glaringly white—that is elevated and secure in the display window. Photographic luminosity and blackness, traditionally called contrast, are here cast together in a social relationship. The photograph's comfort with the darkness that surrounds the overexposed mannequin shows that as much can be seen in a shadow as in a spot of light.

1963 • Kenneth Anger moves to San Francisco, where he rents an apartment above The Movie, an underground theater in North Beach that hosts dedicated screenings of his films. A hotbed for experimental and avant-garde film, San Francisco is also home to Bruce Baillie, Jordan Belson, Bruce Conner, Lawrence Jordan, and, briefly, Anger's friend Stan Brakhage. Conner and Jordan's short-lived Camera Obscura Film Society, founded in 1957, also shows Anger's films. Jordan will recall that Bill and Joanne Rainey, who run The Movie, "were very loyal to Kenneth Anger, and he lived in one of the apartments for a while, the place where

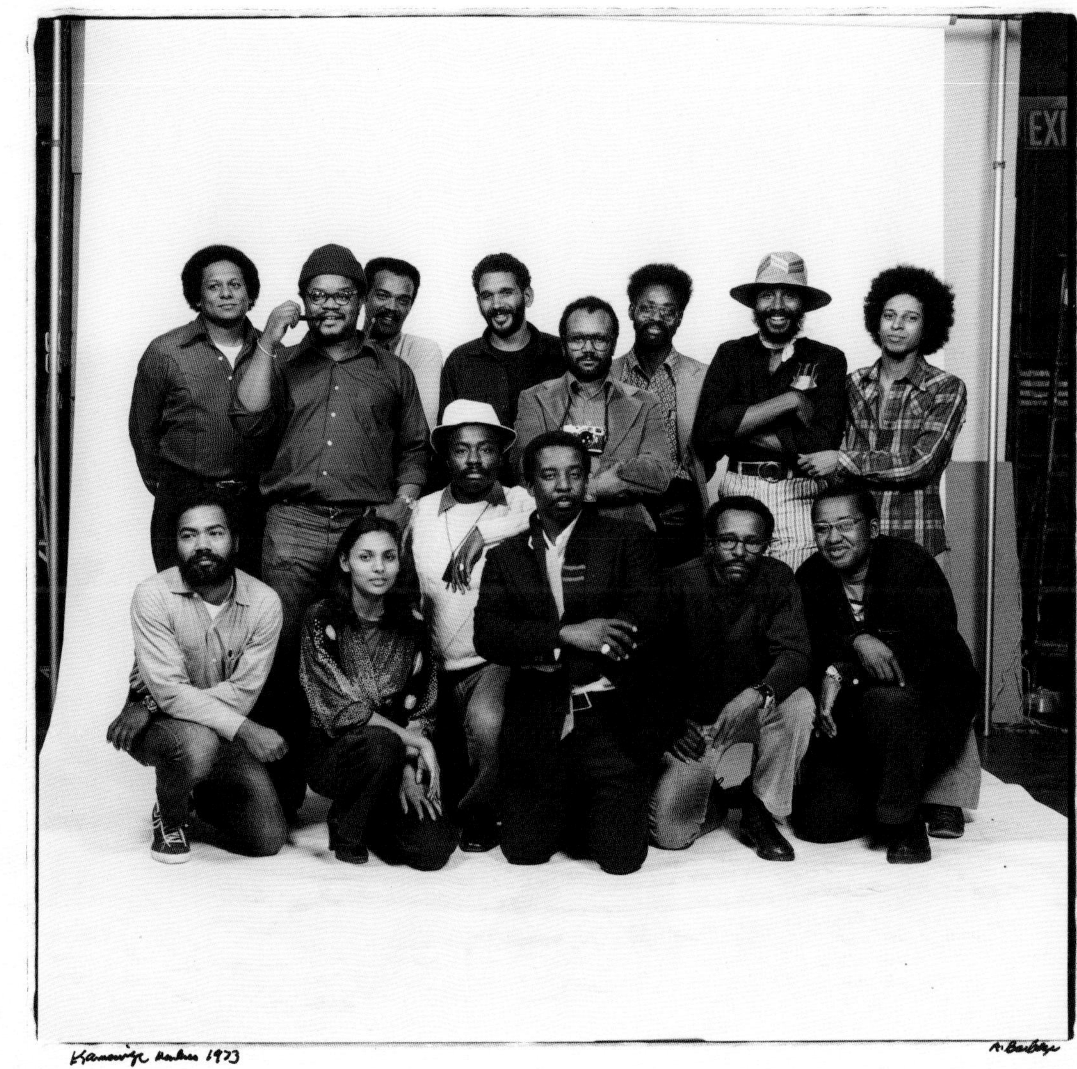

Anthony Barboza, *Kamoinge Members*, 1973. Gelatin silver print, 9 13/16 × 10 in. (24.9 × 25.4 cm). Front row, from left: Herman Klean Howard Jr., Ming Smith, James Mannas, Louis Draper, Calvin Wilson, and Shawn Walker; back row: Al Fennar, Ray Francis, Herbert Randall, C. Daniel Dawson, Beuford Smith, Herb Robinson, Adger Cowans, and Anthony Barboza

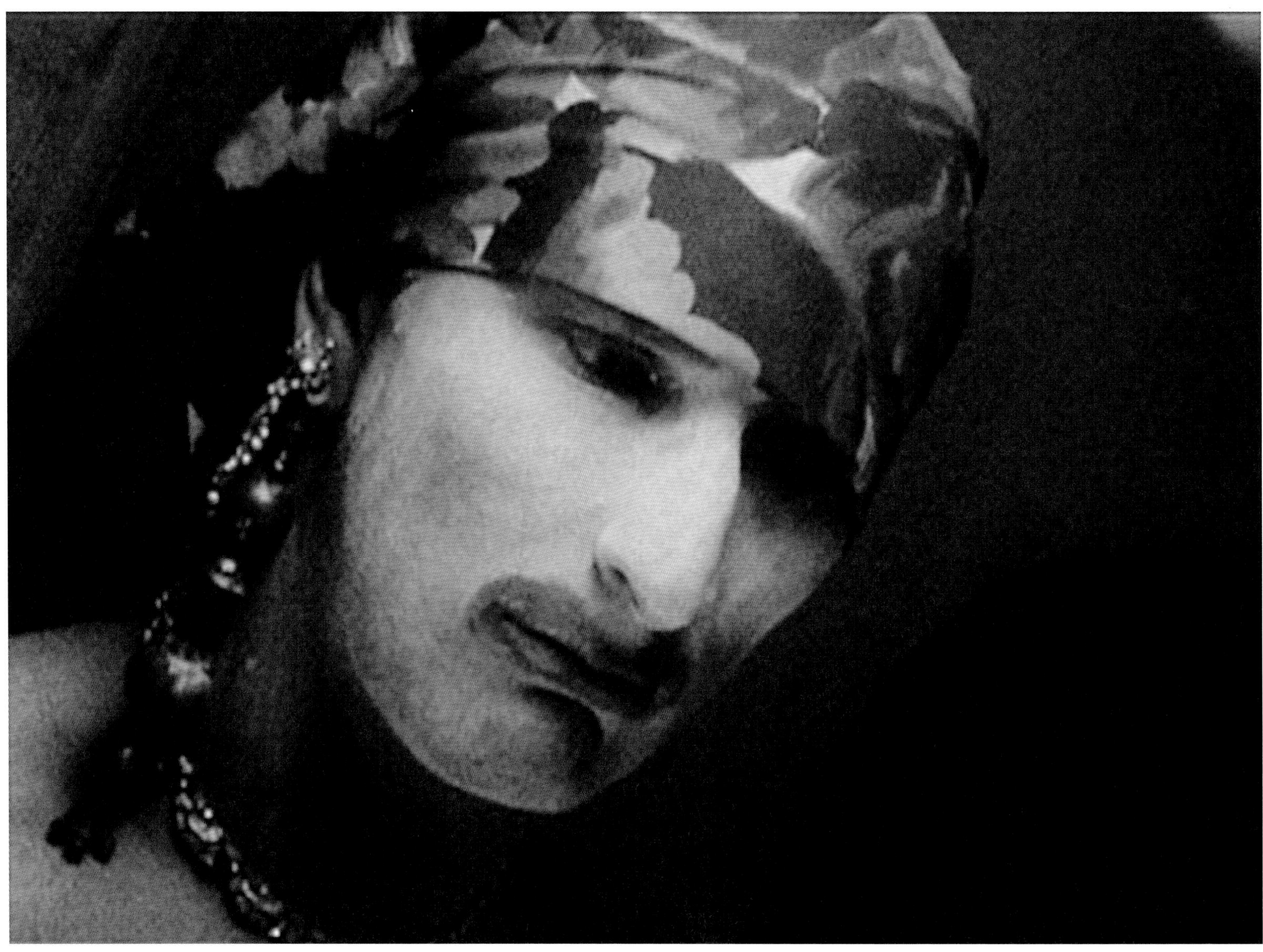

Ken Jacobs, *Blonde Cobra*, 1963. 16mm film transferred to video, color and black-and-white, sound; 33 min. Electronic Arts Intermix, New York

I had lived while I was making the theater. I'd go and visit him there, and he'd be painting the fan on a print of *Eaux d'artifice* [1953] in emerald green." During this time, Anger also works on *Kustom Kar Kommandos*, for which he has been awarded a grant by the Ford Foundation. In his grant proposal, he describes the film as "an oneiric vision of a contemporary American (and specifically Californian) phenomenon, the world of the hot-rod and customized car . . . a dream-like probe into the psyche of the teenager for whom the *unique* aspect of the power-potentialized customized car represents a poetic extension of personality." Ultimately, he only shoots one scene. Prone to constantly revising his films—as Jordan's anecdote suggests—Anger instead uses the grant money to rework *Scorpio Rising* (1963) and other films.

April 1963 • Diane Arbus is awarded the first of two Guggenheim Fellowships for her project "American rites, manners, and customs." In notes preparing for her application, Arbus lists "the stuff of dreams, ritual, aristocracy, imposters, fame, anonymity, figments, real visions, American dreams, daily dreams, walking dreams, American hallucinations, real mirage." Throughout her career, in addition to other subject matter alluding to issues of identity, she pursues a fascination with multiples, as seen in her 1963 photograph *Triplets in their bedroom, N.J. 1963*. Having submitted a portfolio of her photographs to the Museum of Modern Art, she meets with John Szarkowski, the new head of the photography department. At first, Szarkowski is impressed by only one image among the many 35mm pictures, a square image made with a twin-lens reflex camera, *The Junior Interstate Ballroom Dance Champions, Yonkers, N.Y. 1962*. The curator, on behalf of the museum, will eventually acquire, show, and champion her work, most notably with that of Lee Friedlander and Garry Winogrand in the landmark MoMA exhibition *New Documents* in 1967.

April 29, 1963 • The films *Flaming Creatures* by Jack Smith and *Blonde Cobra* by Ken Jacobs (b. 1933) premiere on a double bill at midnight as part of fellow filmmaker Jonas Mekas's screening series at the Bleecker Street Cinema in New York. The screening is a milestone in both the development of avant-garde cinema in the United States and activist struggles around issues of censorship and artistic freedom during the 1960s.

Shot over late summer into early fall of the previous year on the roof of the Windsor Theatre in New York, *Flaming Creatures* has already circulated in various stages of completion in private screenings for friends in the early months of 1963. The film is a riotous camp orgy performed by a group of friends and Lower East Side bohemians, artists, and drag queens, all flamboyantly costumed in Hollywood glamour drag. While receiving an overwhelmingly enthusiastic response among those in the underground, *Flaming Creatures* will arouse outrage in more mainstream sectors for its supposed obscenity: apathetic hands jerking on flaccid penises; relentlessly jiggling breasts; and a dramatic, comedically drawn-out cunnilingus rape scene. Perhaps most troubling to its detractors, however, are the indeterminate genders and indiscriminate sexualities of the cast; here, a queer aesthetic is inaugurated and given form through fantasy, uninhibited play, and the metamorphosis of junk into exotic treasure. According to Smith, the film set is "a place where it is possible to clown, to pose, to act out fantasies, to not be seen . . . (movie sets are sheltered, exclusive places where nobody who doesn't belong can go)."

Mekas becomes a staunch defender of the movie and praises it frequently in his *Village Voice* column in the spring of 1963. On May 2, he

FILM-MAKERS' COOPERATIVE
175 Lexington Avenue
New York, NY   10016

Area code: 212, 889-3820

FILM-MAKERS' COOPERATIVE

<u>BLONDE COBRA SCREENING INSTRUCTIONS:</u>

A loud and clear A.M. radio planted in or near the audience is used twice — 1.) in the beginning, right after the first black and white sequence ending with the sung words: "Let's call the whole thing off," and followed by scribbled-on leader. After five seconds of silent leader, pick up radio volume and dial in scratches of mostly talk, any kind. A <u>color</u> image of three men will come on. Keep the radio going but lower volume as central character begins sliding down into a bathtub; he'll be heard singing a brief song on the soundtrack...

— At its conclusion ("...and the whole world is drowning too!") again pick up radio volume, cutting it off sharply when image returns to black and white.

2.) Towards film end. Blonde Cobra is seen in bed, dressed as a baby. Baby music is heard. He begins to play "peek-a-boo" with audience; radio comes on, interrupting music...which will soon go off for the duration of a shot of Cobra poising, aiming a hammer over radio tubes seen in the close foreground.

— He'll strike a tube twice, the third time it'll break; immediately cut radio sound. (Radio can be tuned to only one stream of chatter for this second use.) Thank you.

----(Ken Jacobs)

Screening instructions for a presentation of *Blonde Cobra* (1963), Film-Makers' Cooperative, New York

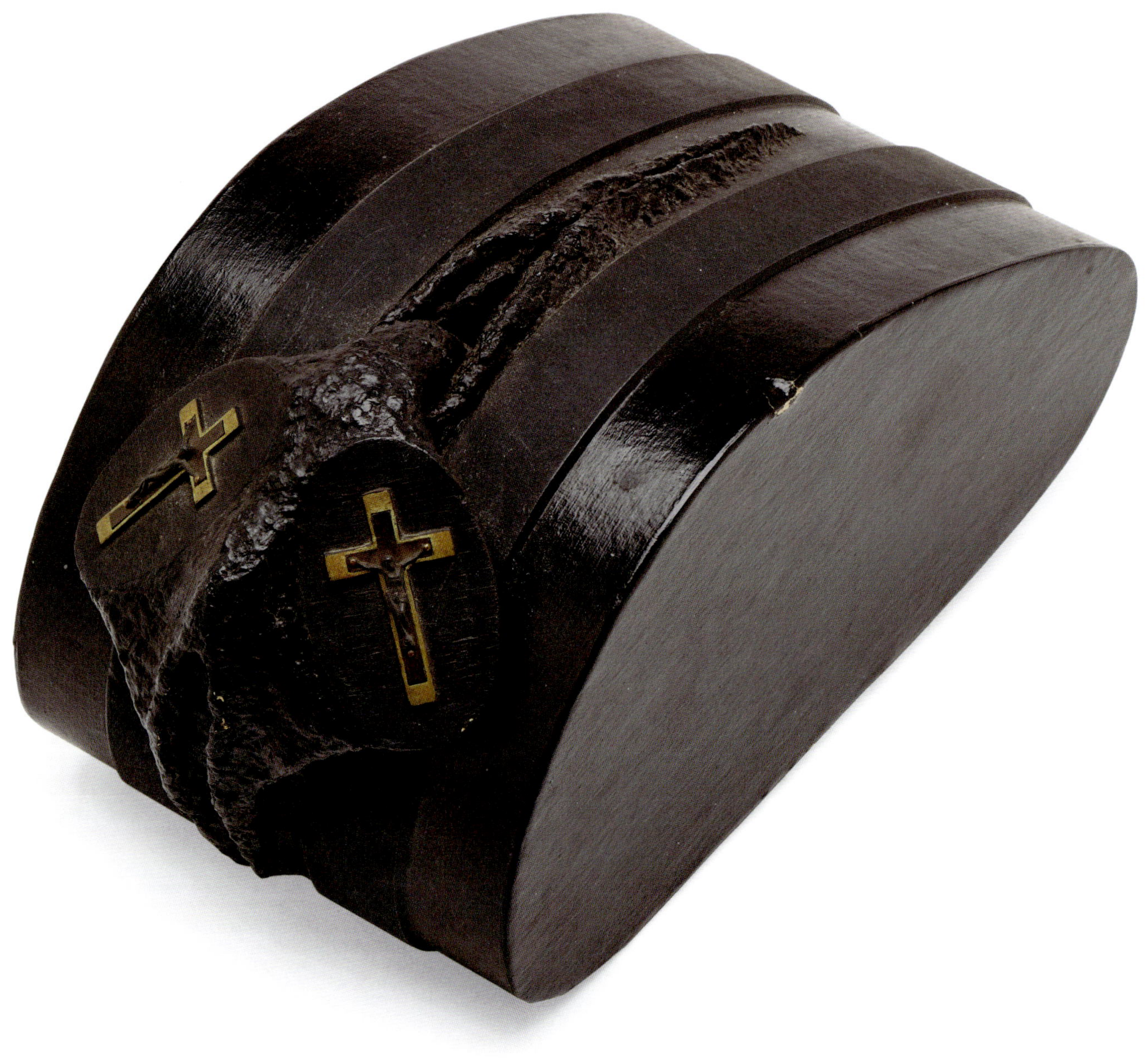

Ron Miyashiro, *Concord No. 8*, 1963. Enamel on wood and papier-mâché with metal assemblage. 6 × 11 × 6 in. (15.2 × 27.9 × 15.2 cm). Collection of Larry and Tina Jones

includes *Flaming Creatures* in his essay "On the Baudelairean Cinema," which features three other films that all happen to star Smith: *Blonde Cobra, Little Stabs at Happiness* (also by Ken Jacobs), and Ron Rice's *The Queen of Sheba Meets the Atom Man*. The selection drives home the extent to which Smith's sensibility is at the heart of Mekas's "Baudelairian" cinema. Explicitly linking the "New American Cinema" of the 1960s to the "symbolist-surrealist" avant-garde of the 1940s and 1950s and to the oft-referenced forefathers of Surrealism, Mekas writes: "These movies are illuminating and opening up sensibilities and experiences never before recorded in the American arts; a content which Baudelaire, the Marquis de Sade, and Rimbaud gave to world literature a century ago and which Burroughs gave to American literature three years ago. It is a world of flowers of evil, of illuminations, of torn and tortured flesh; a poetry which is at once beautiful and terrible, good and evil, delicate and dirty." Mekas goes so far as to praise the films' "perversity," demonstrating his change of heart since his 1955 declamation against the "conspiracy of homosexuality" in underground film.

In the same year Jacobs releases *Blonde Cobra*, shot by Bob Fleischner, he releases two other short experimental films that feature Smith, his creative compatriot in the New York underground film scene: *Little Stabs at Happiness* and *Baud'larian Capers*. Part of Jacobs's ongoing attempt to blur the lines between exhibition and production, *Blonde Cobra* comes with instructions to play live radio broadcasts during specific sequences. The film is an uncanny combination of horror and film noir references, with nods to Robert Siodmak's 1944 film *Cobra Woman*, starring Maria Montez; the work of Josef von Sternberg; and Bela Lugosi's *Dracula* (1931). Jacobs himself describes the film as "an erratic narrative—no, not really a narrative, it's only stretched out in time for convenience of delivery. It's a look in on an exploding life, on a man of imagination suffering pre-fashionable Lower East Side deprivation and consumed with American 1950s, 40s, 30s disgust. . . . He carries on, states his presence for what it is. Does all he can to draw out our condemnation, testing our love for limits . . . enticing us into an absurd moral posture the better to dismiss us with a regal 'screw-off.'"

Jacobs had been born in the Williamsburg neighborhood of Brooklyn, where he grew up on Berry Street living with his mother and extended family. Exposed early on to the arts by watching his mother create watercolor paintings at home and by making regular trips to the Museum of Modern Art as a teenager, he becomes enamored with Abstract Expressionism and the art films he views at Amos Vogel's film society, Cinema 16. After an obligatory stint in the Coast Guard Reserve at the outset of the Korean War, he studies painting directly with Hans Hofmann at the artist's eponymous private art school, which he had opened in 1934 at 137 East 57th Street. Because it is a nonaccredited institution and not recognized as an official art school, Jacobs cannot pay for his classes with the G.I. Bill. Luckily, Hofmann gives him a "scholarship," so he attends for free.

Jacobs eventually begins to focus more exclusively on film, putting together his first movie, *Orchard Street*, in 1955 and studying the medium at the City University of New York, where he meets Fleischner and Smith. As a pivotal figure in the underground film scene of the 1960s, Jacobs pushes the boundaries of cinematic experience with his experimental "paracinema," Nervous Magic Lantern, and Nervous System screening performances. Ultimately, he will inspire scores of young filmmakers as the head of the free film school Millennium Film Workshop in the East Village, and then as cofounder of the cinema department at Binghamton University, where he and his students will establish the Collective for Living Cinema in 1973.

———

May 21–June 29, 1963 • Anita Steckel (1930–2012) exhibits her *Mom Art* series at New York's Hacker Gallery. Born and raised in Brooklyn, she had attended the High School of Music & Art in Manhattan, like so many talented native New York artists of her generation. *Mom Art* is but her second exhibition, a punning response to the noticeably male-dominated Pop art movement. Far from just a gag, Steckel paints and draws over images of canonical artworks, teasing out sexual and racial tensions from their white and male histories. She is influenced as much by Marcel Duchamp's alterations as by her own status, presumed to be a woman first and an artist second. These works earn her some notice, and she continues the practice with her *Multiple Image* series, in which she sketches over Personality Posters, a mid-1960s publishing company that brings to American walls enormous mass-produced sheets depicting celebrities and famous twentieth-century figures, from Sigmund Freud to Billie Holiday to James Dean. The ubiquity of the posters, similar to that of the reproductions of the "masterpieces" she alters, makes them prime surfaces on which Steckel can inscribe a critique. She spares no one, not even herself; these works resemble the dredged dream lives of their subjects, rendered with freehand ebullience. She later explains the efficacy of her technique: "No matter how upsetting is the subject matter of a painting, we feel relatively safe. We know it isn't real. But paint an image into a photograph, we are conditioned to believe is an unquestioned reality—then there sets up an uneasiness of another sort. A little more disquieting, a little harder to disbelieve."

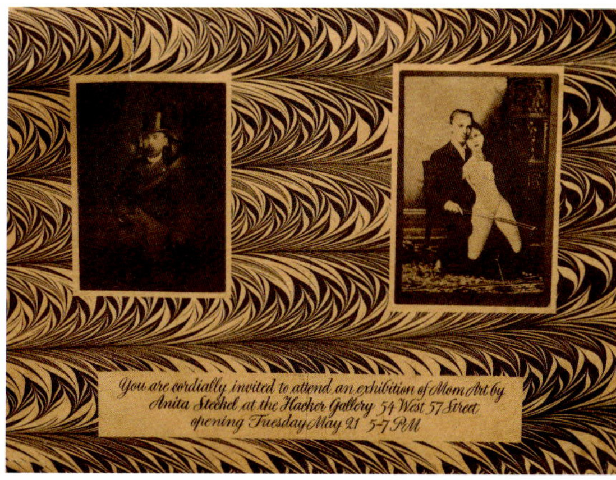

Invitation for *Mom Art*, Hacker Gallery, New York, 1963

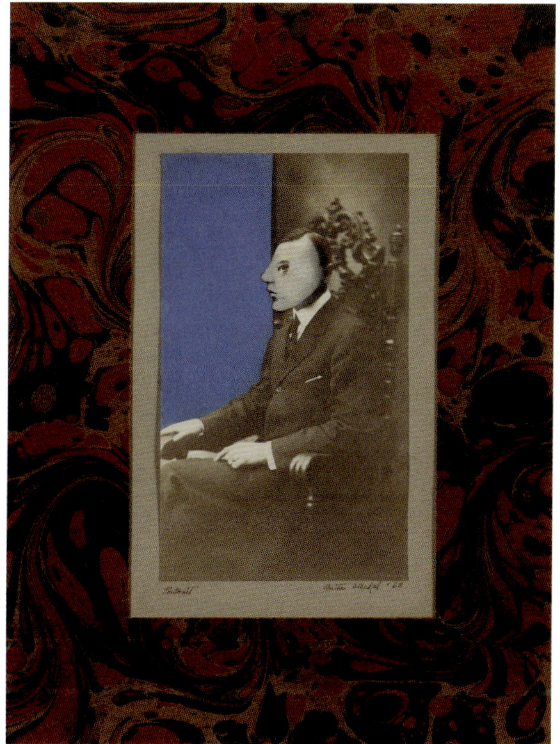

Anita Steckel, *Portrait*, 1963, from the series *Mom Art* (1963). Acrylic on vintage gelatin silver print mounted in a marbled paper mat, 7 ⅝ × 4 ⅜ in. (19.4 cm × 11.1 cm)

———

May 22–August 18, 1963 • *Americans, 1963*, an attempt to showcase a range of contemporary practices, is on view at the Museum of Modern Art and features more than one hundred works by fifteen artists, including sculptural objects and reliefs by Lee Bontecou and Marisol as well as Claes Oldenburg's uncanny *Dual Hamburgers* (1962).

———

June 1963 • David Hammons (b. 1943) moves to Los Angeles from his hometown of Springfield, Illinois. He works a variety of odd jobs and cobbles together a roving, and often unofficial, art education in the city, studying at several schools including Los Angeles City College, Los Angeles

Trade-Technical College, Chouinard Art Institute, and Otis Art Institute. At Otis he takes night and weekend classes with master printer and draftsman Charles White, whose work places an emphasis on the lives of Black Americans and their struggles for equality. White's art makes an indelible impression on Hammons and helps him understand the artworld from the perspective of Black artists who need to negotiate their paths and create community despite the centrality of whiteness and often exclusionary thinking. Throughout his decade in Los Angeles, and before his move to New York in 1974, Hammons is involved with a community of experimentally and politically minded Black artists, namely Suzanne Jackson, Senga Nengudi, John Outterbridge, and Noah Purifoy, and he shows primarily at galleries such as Jackson's Gallery 32 and Brockman Gallery, founded by muralist Alonzo Davis and his brother, Dale.

Summer 1963 • Michael Todd (b. 1935) returns to New York after a two-year fellowship in Paris. Living in downtown Manhattan, he continues what will become known as his *Fetish* series, assemblages of shoehorns, wheels, and other found miscellany painted white and taking the form of an ovoid shape, such as *Fetish 3*. "I was doing them subconsciously, and feeling an anxiety located in my stomach, and attracted to Ken Price's egg forms; I was trying to get into the egg, trying to get back in," Todd will later remember. He will debut his *Fetish* sculptures and other assemblages at a solo exhibition at Pace Gallery in 1964.

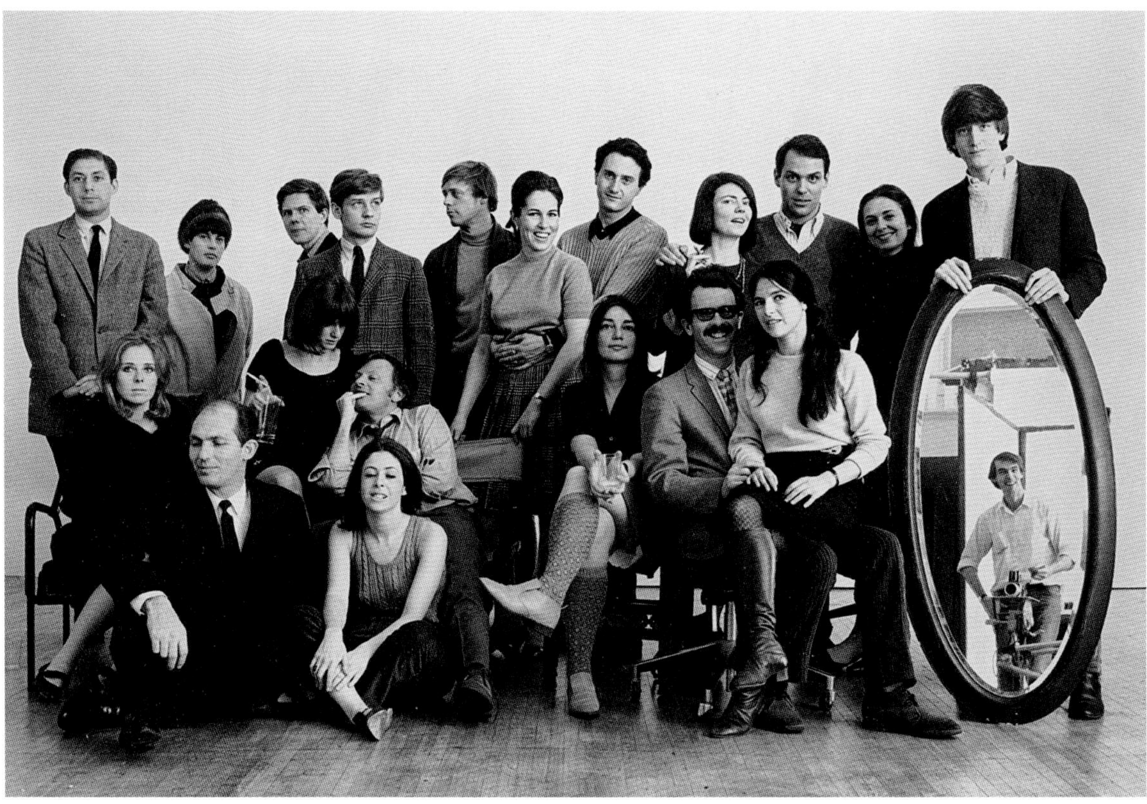

Peter Hujar, *Paul Thek's Group Portrait (III)*, 1966–67. Gelatin silver print, 13 ½ × 16 in. (34.3 × 40.6 cm). Standing, from left: Allen Rosenbaum, Susi Bloch, Gene Swenson, Kes Zapkus, Paul Thek, Simona Morini, Frederic Tuten, Diane Kelder, Joseph Raffaele, Marion Greenstone, and Steve Lawrence; seated: Barbara Pallenberg, Larry Sapir, Nancy Worthington Fish, Harold Krieger, Linda Rosenkranz [Finch], Marisol, Mike Todd, and Eva Hesse; Peter Hujar is reflected in the mirror

Born in Omaha, Nebraska, Todd had grown up in Chicago. He earned a bachelor of fine arts from the University of Notre Dame, and at the University of California, Los Angeles, he receives a master's degree with a focus in printmaking in 1961. Having begun making some assemblages by then, he moves to Paris for two years to continue exploring Freudian combinations of objects. In New York, Todd falls into the same social circle as Eva Hesse, Paul Thek, and other downtown sculptors and artists captured in Peter Hujar's group portrait.

June 21–August 17, 1963 • Lee Friedlander (b. 1934) has his first solo show, at George Eastman House in Rochester, New York. Born and raised in Aberdeen, Washington, he is still a teenager when he takes his first photograph and builds himself a darkroom. In 1952 he briefly studies photography at the ArtCenter School in Pasadena, California, but he moves to New York in 1955 and begins photographing jazz musicians for album covers and taking freelance jobs for publications such as *Sports Illustrated* and *Seventeen*. This freelance work introduces him to other artists working in photography, such as Robert Frank and Walker Evans, whose belief in the medium's capacious artistic possibilities greatly encourages him.

Friedlander's approach to photography is not dissimilar to Frank's and Evans's in their search for a visual language of what Friedlander will call "the American social landscape," but he injects— or at least does not shy away from—playful aspects of life in his images. Many of his photographs

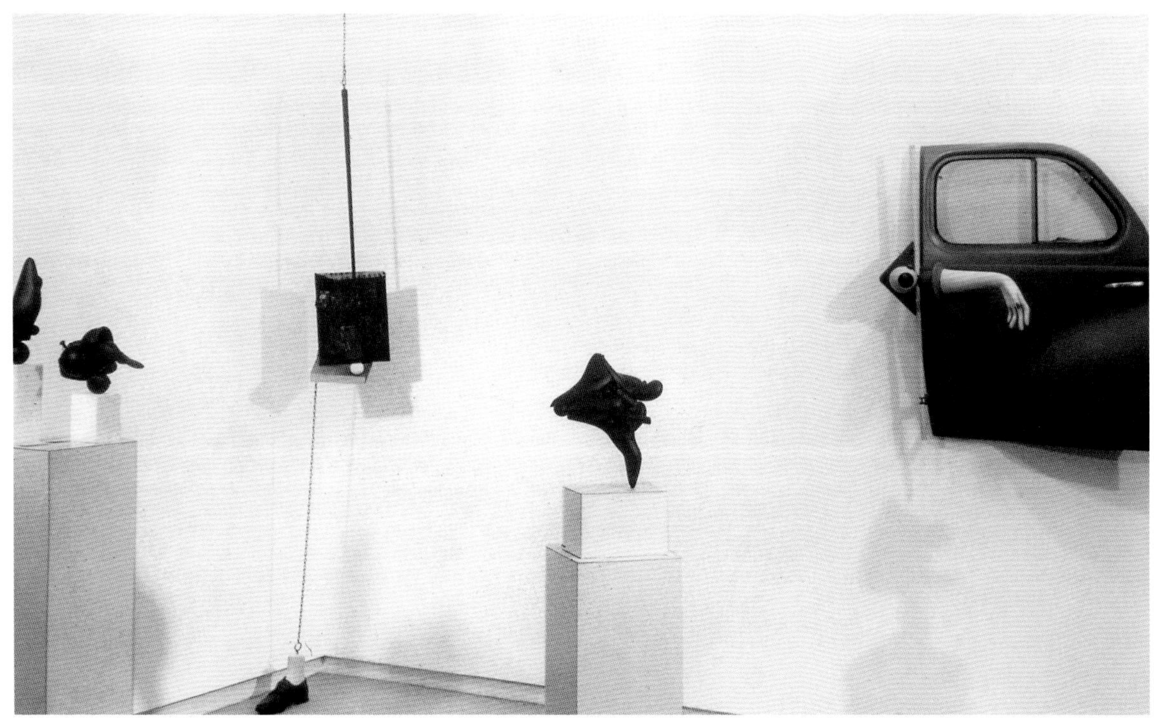

Michael Todd: Sculpture, Pace Gallery, New York, 1964

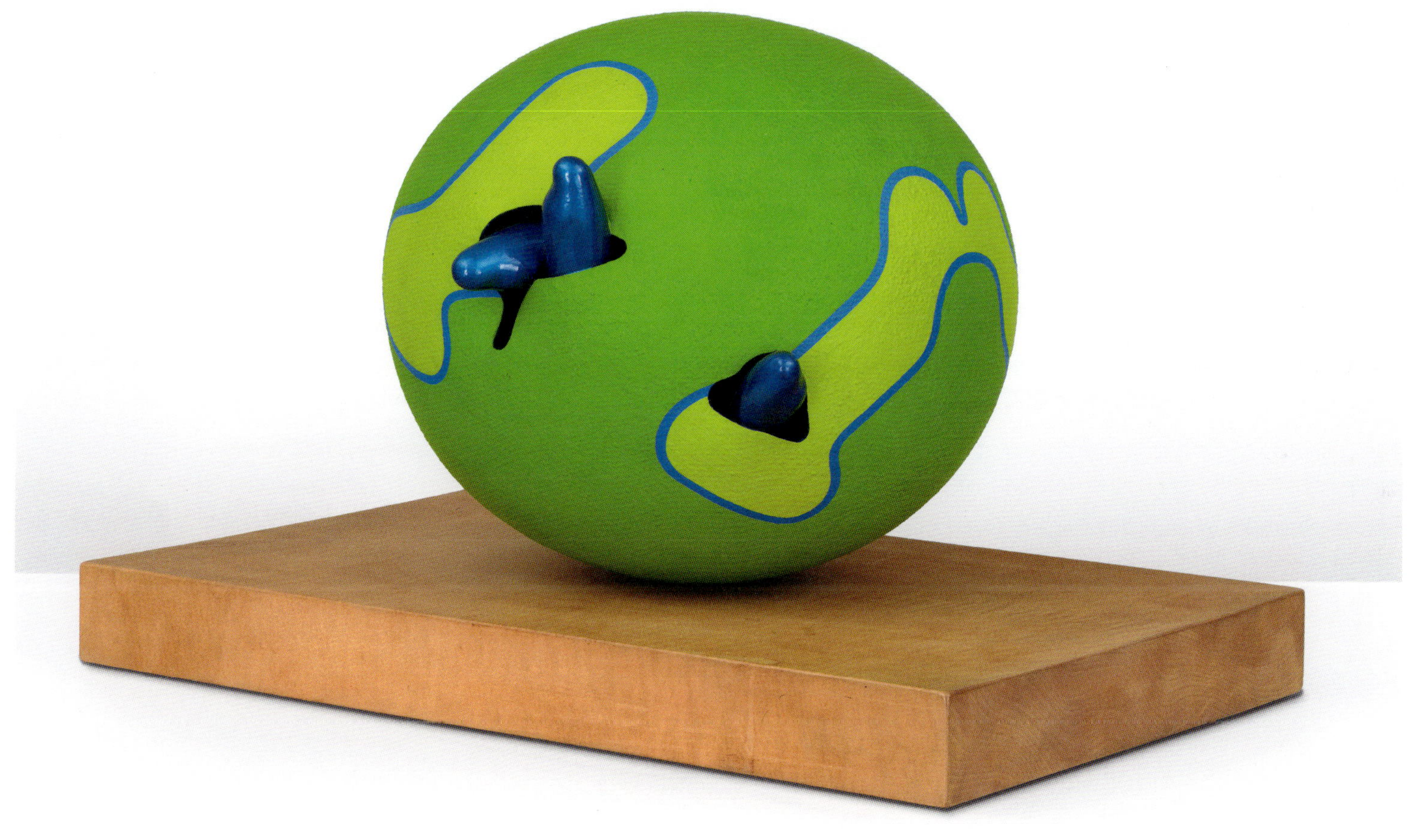

Kenneth Price, *S. L. Green*, 1963. Painted ceramic and wooden base, 11 ⅜ × 17 ⅞ × 10 ⅞ in. (28.9 × 45.4 × 27.6 cm). Whitney Museum of American Art, New York; gift of the Howard and Jean Lipman Foundation, Inc. 66.35a–b

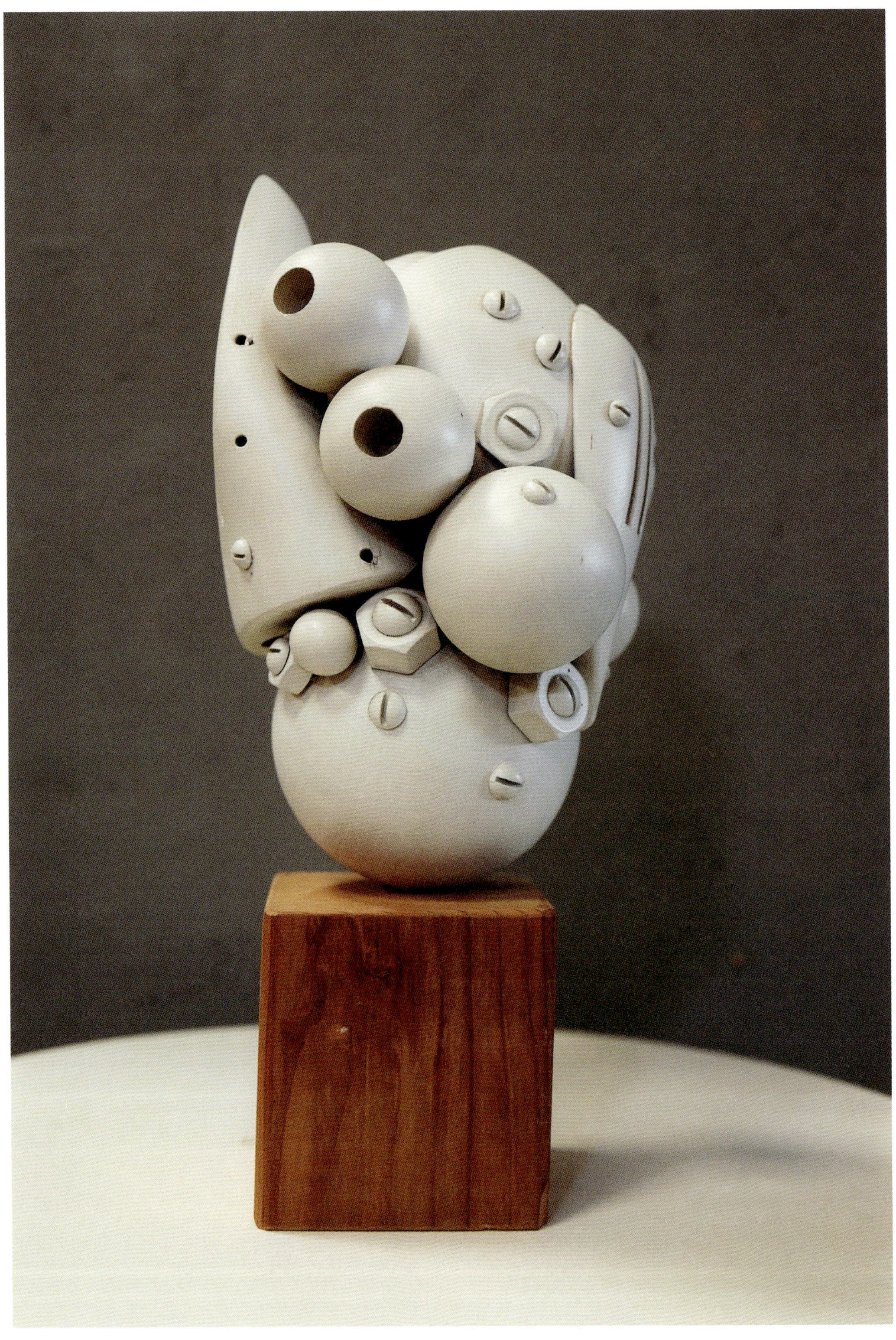

Michael Todd, *Fetish 2*, 1963. Wood and metal, 12 ½ × 7 × 6 in. (31.7 × 17.8 × 15.2 cm). Collection of Mia Doi Todd

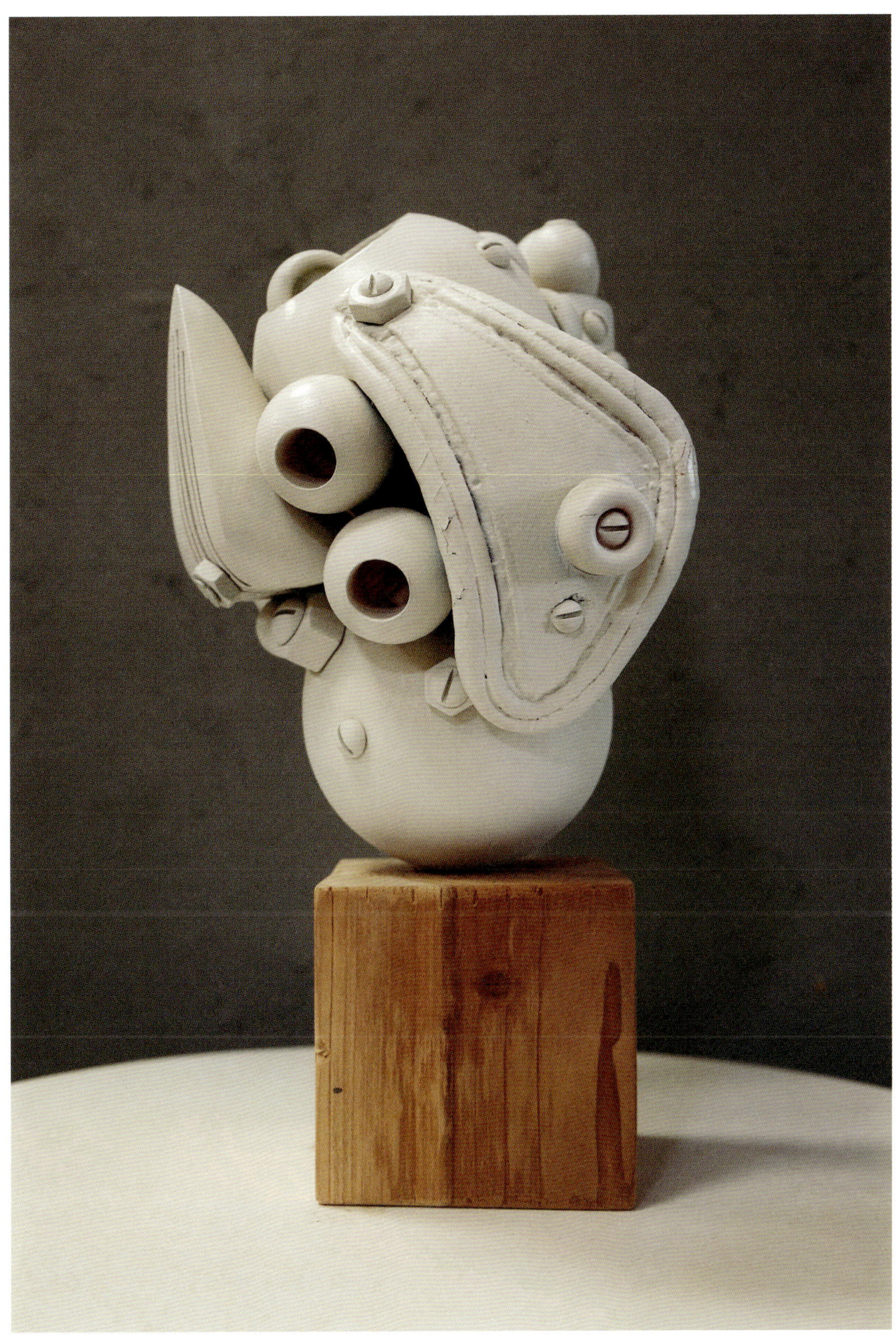

Michael Todd, *Fetish 3*, 1963. Wood and metal, 12 ½ × 6 ½ × 7 in. (31.7 × 16.5 × 17.8 cm). Collection of Mia Doi Todd

from the 1960s include presumed compositional "mistakes," such as fragments of storefront reflections, structures interrupted by fences and poles, and his own reflection or shadow. This awareness of the artifice inherent in the medium of photography is a unique aspect of Friedlander's seemingly documentary approach.

———

Summer 1963 • Paul Thek and Peter Hujar visit Capuchin catacombs in Palermo, Sicily, an experience that inspires Thek's series *Technological Reliquaries*. The artist describes the catacombs as holding "8,000 corpses—not skeletons, corpses—decorating the walls, and the corridors are filled with windowed coffins. I opened one and picked up what I thought was a piece of paper; it was a piece of dried thigh. I felt strangely relieved and free." Soon Thek creates *La Corazza di Michelangelo*, the first work in which he paints wax to simulate human viscera. Upon his return

to New York later that year, he begins work on *Technological Reliquaries*: wax painted to mimic slabs of bloody meat and enclosed in vitrines made of Plexiglas and often fluorescently colored.

The following year, Thek meets Carolee Schneemann, who at the time is working on her own meat-related work, the film *Meat Joy* (1964). "You could say there was a veritable 'meat energy' happening between us," Schneemann will later recall.

Our works were volatile—they really started to flow into and fluster even the radical traditions in art and theater surrounding us. We were about visceral kinetics, getting to the innards, getting the inside out. And Ann Wilson, who performed in *Meat Joy* distributing—or dumping—the chicken, raw mackerel, and sausages, then went on to work with Paul. . . . We both had a lonely, isolated sense of what I called visceral plasticity. We wanted sensuousness in

materials. Things that others considered to be obscene were sacred to us; we talked of the "religiosity" of our sources.

———

July 5, 1963 • Charles Alston, Norman Lewis, Hale Woodruff, and Romare Bearden (1911–1988) initiate the formation of the Spiral Group, which will grow to include fifteen Black artists whose ages and artistic styles and approaches vary greatly, inspiring the group's name, a symbol of many differences united by a central core. While the following month's historic march on Washington is in the planning stages, the Spiral Group holds weekly meetings at its space in Greenwich Village to discuss its members' roles as artists in the civil rights movement and in the fight for social justice. In May 1965, the artists will organize their only group exhibition, *First Group Showing: Works in Black and White*, at their space before disbanding later that year, in part because the cost of rent doubles. The catalogue for the show includes the following artists' statement:

We, as Negroes, could not fail to be touched by the outrage of segregation, or fail to relate to the self-reliance, hope, and courage of those persons who were marching in the interest of man's dignity. . . . If possible, in these times, we hoped with our art to justify life . . . to use the black and white and eschew other coloration. . . . This consideration, or limitation, was conceived from technical concerns, although deeper motivations may have been involved. . . . What is most important now, and what has great portent for the future, is that Negro artists, of divergent backgrounds and interests, have come together on terms of mutual respect. It is to their credit that they were able to fashion art works lit by beauty, and of such diversity.

The importance of community and collaboration comes naturally to Bearden. Born in North Carolina, he had grown up in Harlem, where his home was often a gathering place for cultural icons such as Countee Cullen, W. E. B. Du Bois, and Paul Robeson, artists Charles Alston and Aaron Douglas, and jazz musicians Duke Ellington, Andy Razaf, and Fats Waller. While living in Pittsburgh for a brief stint, Bearden spends time with steelworkers there. As an undergraduate at New York University, he works as a cartoonist for the school's humor magazine. He later gets to know modernist icons such as artists Constantin Brancusi and Georges Braque while studying philosophy in Paris on the G.I. Bill after serving in World War II. The stylistic shifts in his career— from political cartoons to representational

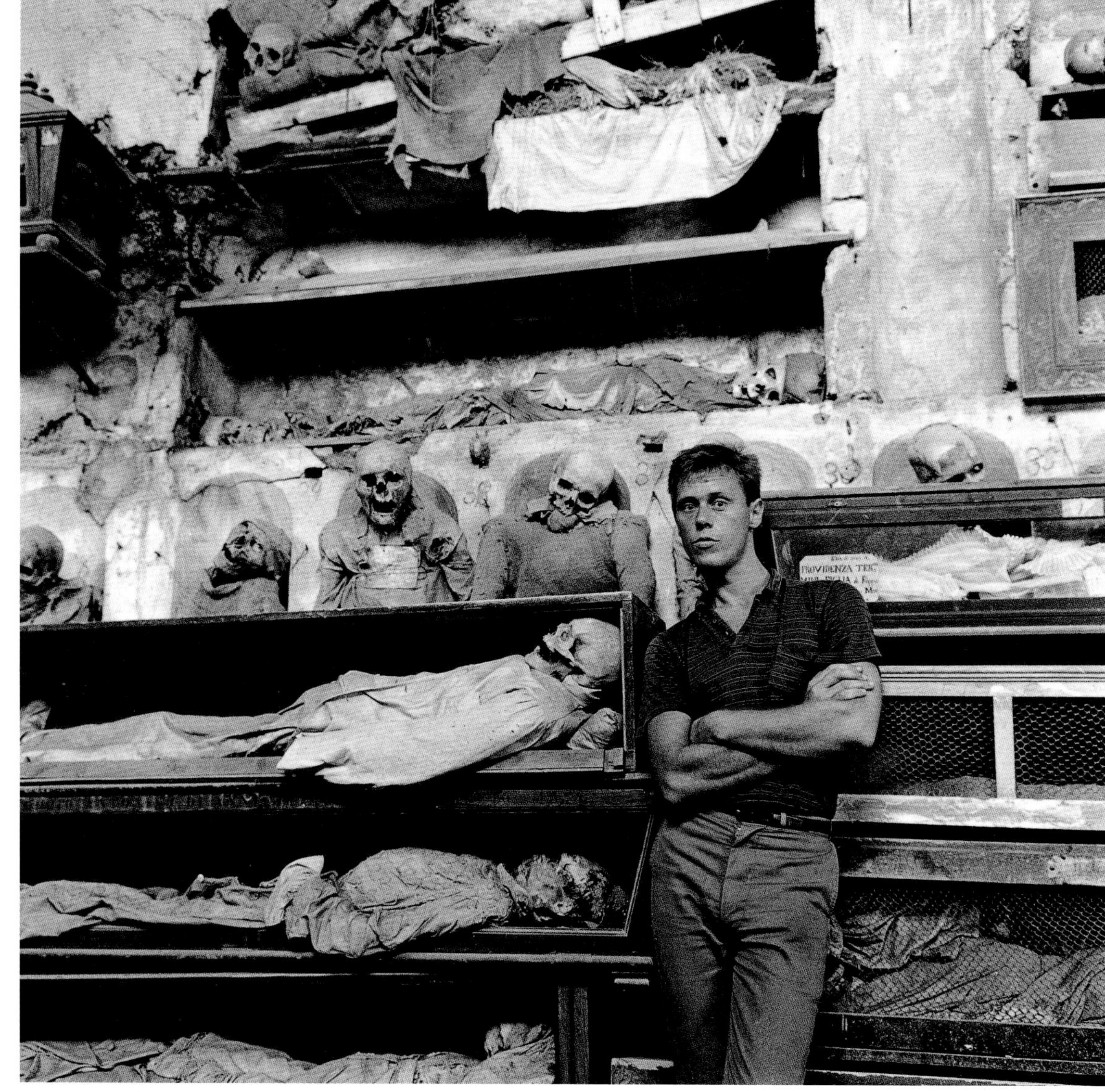

Paul Thek in the Capuchin catacombs, Palermo, Italy, 1963

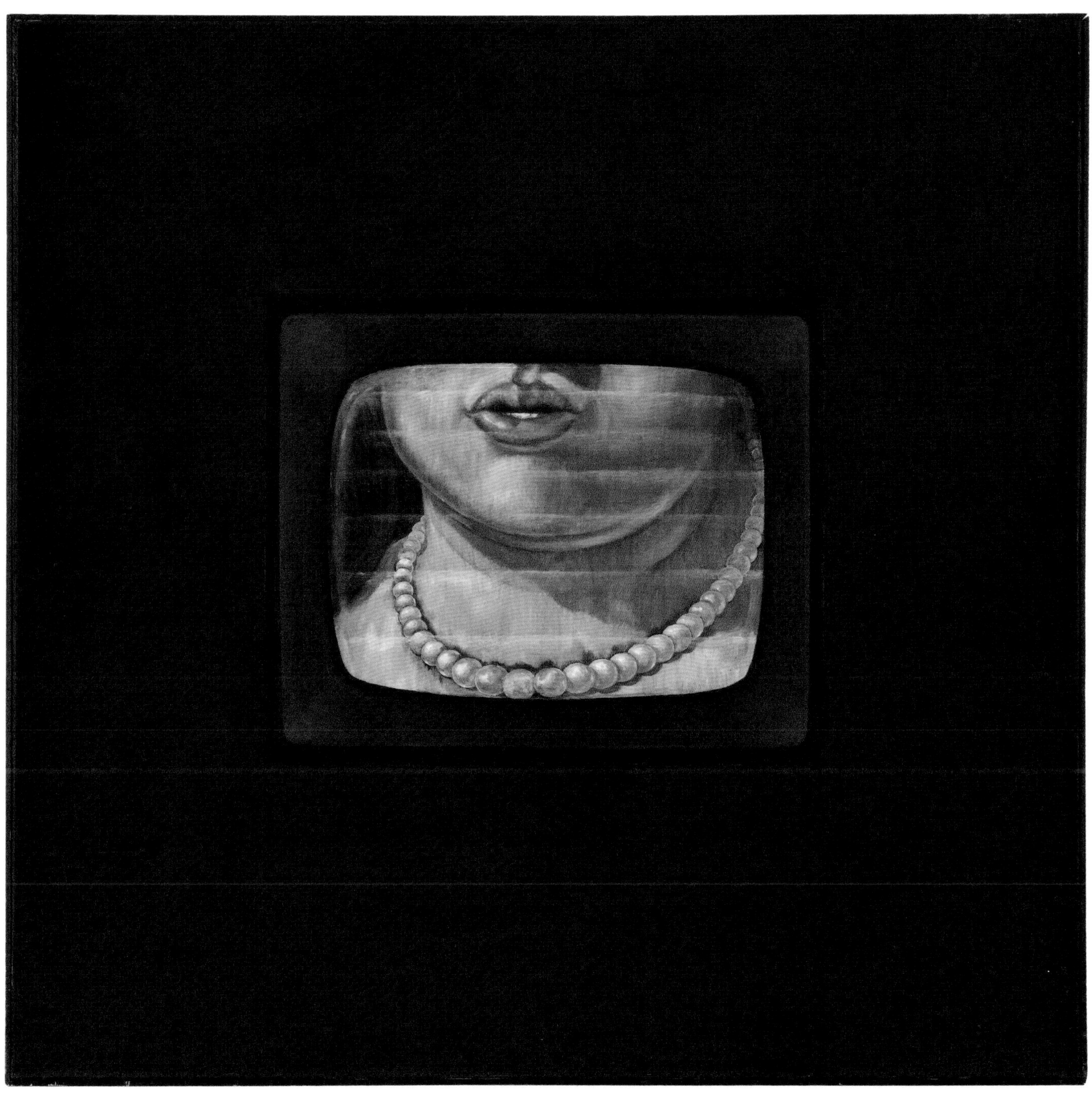

Paul Thek, *Untitled*, 1963, from the series *Television Analyzations*. Oil on canvas, 39 ½ × 39 ¾ in. (100.3 × 101 cm). Collection of Beth Rudin DeWoody

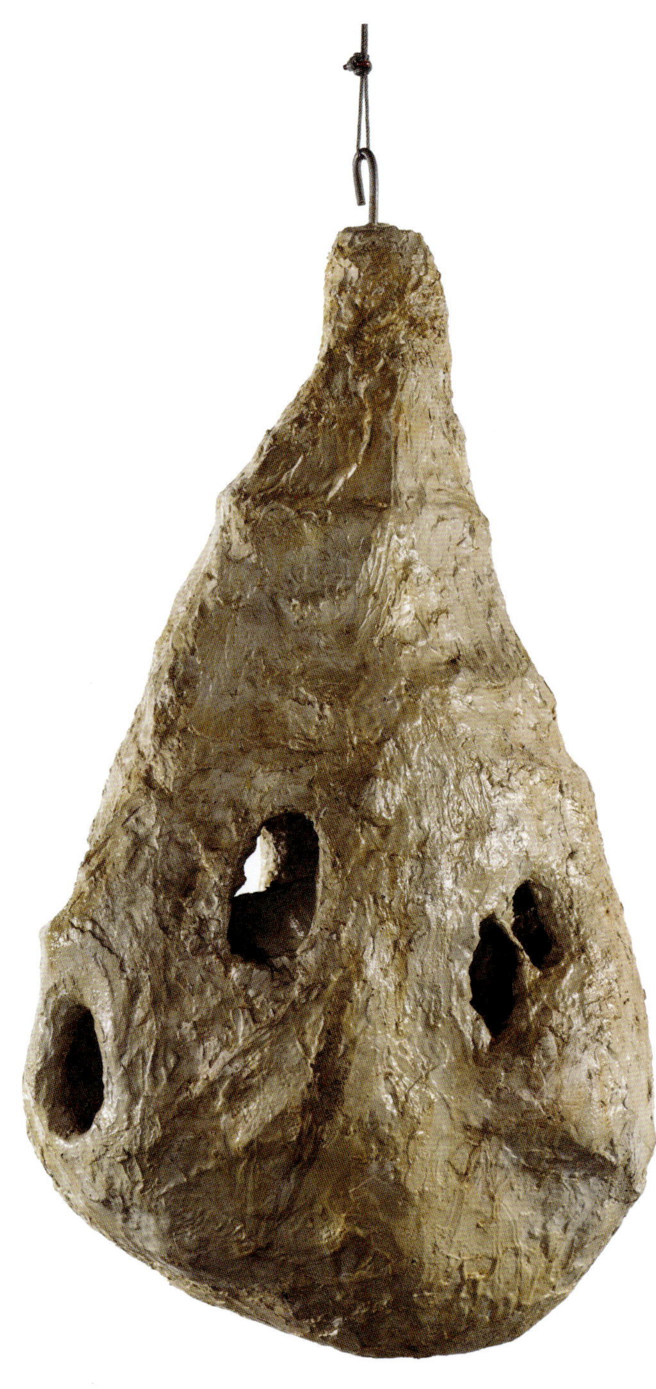

Louise Bourgeois, *Fée Couturière*, 1963. Plaster, 39 ½ × 22 ½ × 22 ½ in. (100.3 × 57.2 × 57.2 cm). Collection of the Easton Foundation

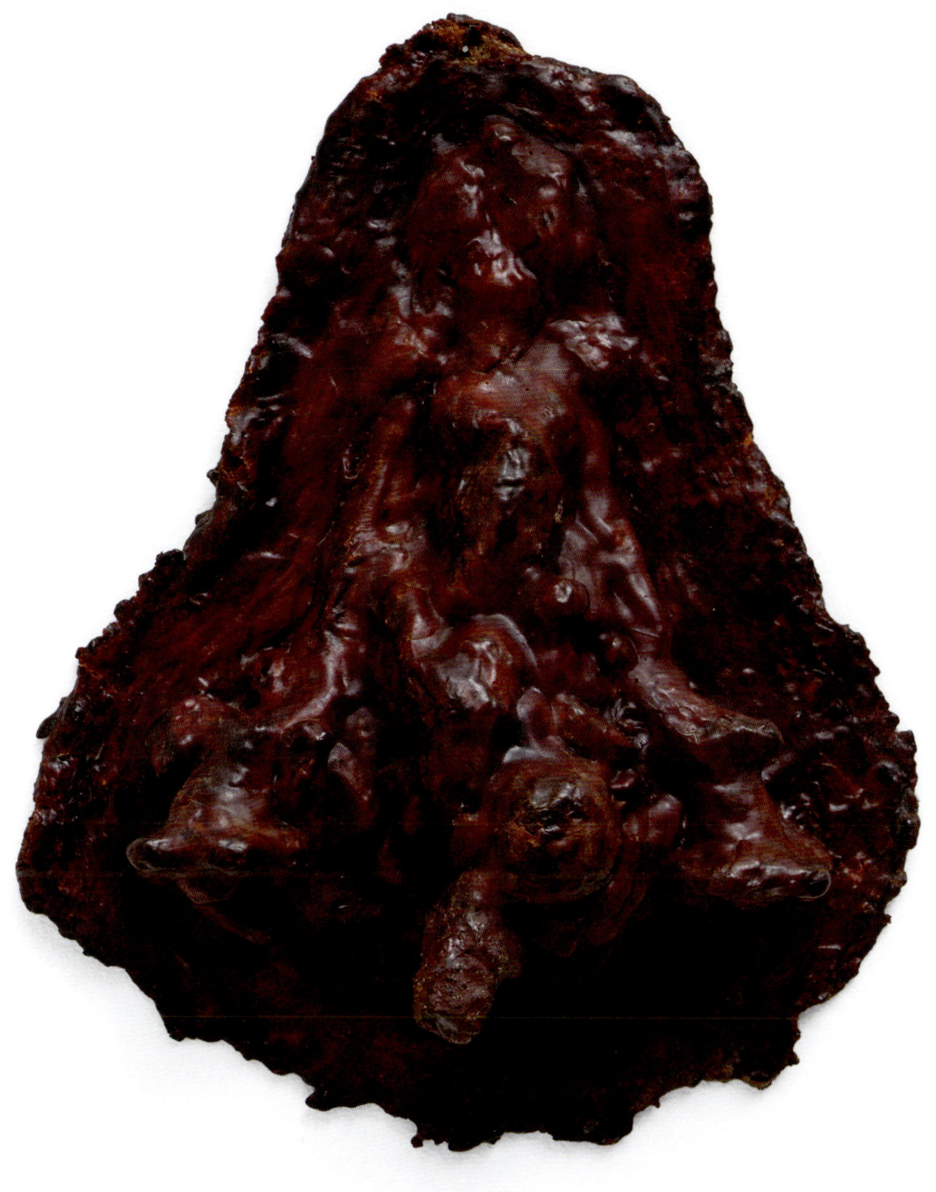

Louise Bourgeois, *Portrait*, 1963. Latex over plaster, 15 ⅜ × 12 ⅜ × 4 ⅛ in. (39 × 31.5 × 10.5 cm). The Museum of Modern Art, New York; gift of Arthur Drexler 385.1986

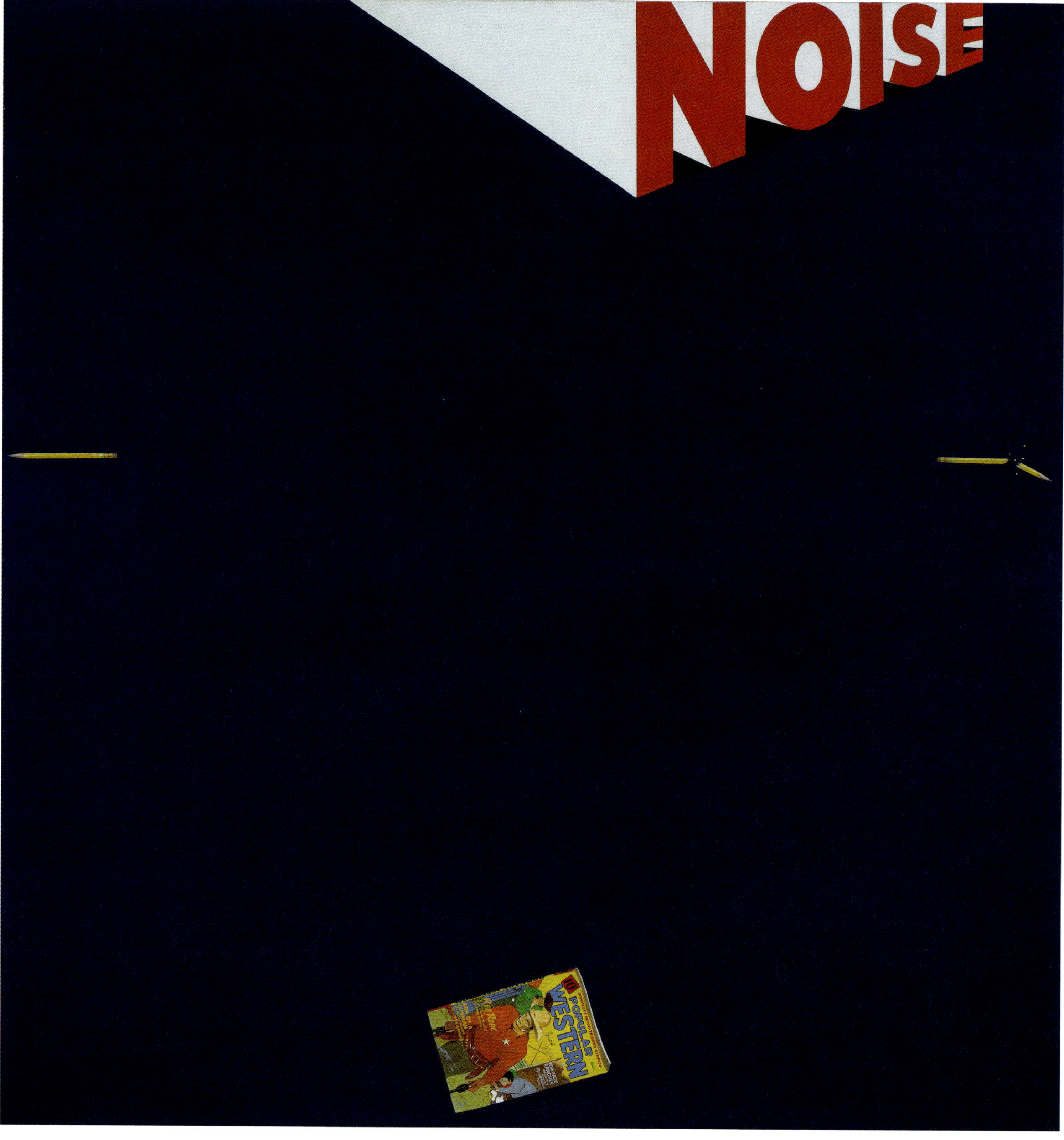

Ed Ruscha, *Noise, Pencil, Broken Pencil, Cheap Western*, 1963. Oil and wax on canvas, 71 ¼ × 67 in. (181 × 170.2 cm). Virginia Museum of Fine Arts, Richmond; gift of Sydney and Frances Lewis 85.439

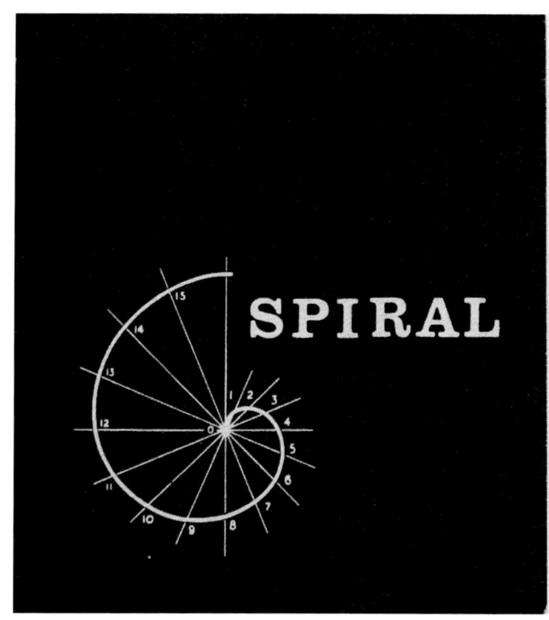

Exhibition flyer for *First Group Showing: Works in Black and White*, 147 Christopher Street, New York, 1965

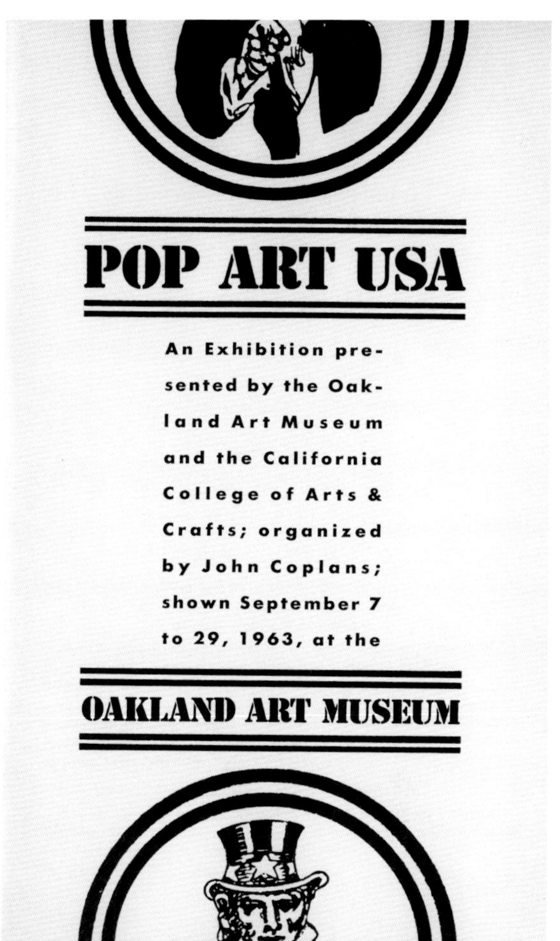

Brochure for *Pop Art USA*, Oakland Art Museum and the California College of Arts and Crafts, 1963

painting to Abstract Expressionism—reflect the diverse environments and influences he encounters throughout his life and in some ways foreshadow his collage approach, in which the artist employs abstraction and representation to invoke destabilizing scenes, as seen in works such as *Conjur Woman* (1964).

August 28, 1963 • More than two hundred thousand demonstrators participate in the March on Washington for Jobs and Freedom in the nation's capital, demanding political and economic justice for Black Americans, who are facing dire unemployment and racist hiring practices. The stated goals of the protest include "a comprehensive civil rights bill" that will outlaw segregated public accommodations; "protection of the right to vote"; options for seeking redress of violations of constitutional rights; immediate "desegregation of all public schools"; a federal works program "to train and place unemployed workers"; and "a Federal Fair Employment Practices Act barring discrimination in all employment." The march ends at the Lincoln Memorial on the National Mall, where Martin Luther King Jr. delivers his historic "I Have a Dream" speech.

September 7–23, 1963 • Curated by John Coplans, *Pop Art USA* at the Oakland Art Museum and the California College of Arts and Crafts is the broadest survey yet at the titular phenomenon. The exhibition includes Wally Hedrick, Jess, Claes Oldenburg, James Rosenquist, Ed Ruscha, Peter Saul, and H. C. Westermann.

Late 1963 • Deborah Remington's paintings coalesce into shield-like images at this point. She lets go of expressive paint handling and focuses on hard-edged subjects somewhere between mirrors, portals, and heralds. In 1965 the artist will move to New York, feeling that there is no way forward as a full-time painter in the Bay Area.

Late 1963 • John Outterbridge (1933–2020) and his wife, Beverly Marie McKissick, move from Chicago to Los Angeles, where Outterbridge pursues a job related more to his art making than the bus driving and jazz singing he was doing to get by in Chicago. After working briefly for the ceramicist Tony Hill, Outterbridge finds a job at Contemporary Crafts, a commercial production studio serving designers. While there, he recognizes that the artists are being underpaid, and he organizes his fellow workers to walk out and, successfully, negotiate for better pay. This action foretells Outterbridge's future as an organizer in the city: he will assume the position of artistic director of the Communicative Arts Academy, founded by Judson Powell in Compton, and, later, as the director of the Watts Towers Arts Center.

Outterbridge had grown up in Greenville, North Carolina, where his prodigious hobby of making model airplanes led to an expanded interest in creating art. He is encouraged to continue his arts education, and although he is officially enrolled in the engineering department at North Carolina Agricultural and Technical State University, a historically Black institution, his talent is recognized by the head of the art department. However, he leaves school to enter the Army during the Korean War and is stationed in Germany. Nonetheless, his artistic talents are noted by an officer who finds the drawings and paintings Outterbridge makes in his free time, and the officer offers him a studio space and commissions for paintings. Beginning in 1956, Outterbridge uses the G.I. Bill to attend the American Academy of Art College in Chicago, where he experiments with a mixed-media approach to painting, often out of necessity. "I think that I painted on wood because wood at times was much more available to me than canvas in terms of—somebody had a wood shop, and sometimes there were pieces of plywood nicely squared and laying around that would take paint, gesso," he will later recall. "I did use a lot of materials at the time that I used simply because they were within reach without any cost. Saturated cardboard."

1963 • By now, elements of sixteenth-century European Mannerism and Pop art comingle in Robert Smithson's work. *Untitled (Christ in Limbo)* (1963) recalls the serpentine form of the

Hellenistic *Laocoön* as well as Plato's gesture in Raphael's *School of Athens* (1509–11); Smithson's Christ pumps gas with one hand and points skyward with the other. In the contemporaneous essay "Iconography of Desolation" (c. 1962), he describes Clement Greenberg, a leading proponent of formalism, as a "middle-classic sycophant" sniffing "out the droppings of 'manners.'" Around the same time, he watches Kenneth Anger's underground film *Scorpio Rising* (1963), which exudes a sensualized Pop sensibility similar to that of *Untitled (Christ in Limbo)*.

October 1963 • *Arts Magazine* publishes Donald Judd's appraisal of H. C. Westermann's work: "With less knowledge than I should have, I would guess that Westermann is one of the best artists around. . . . It is obvious that Surrealist sources could be found for many of Westermann's ideas. It is just as obvious that the objects are something new. I think the fact that they are objects has a lot to do with that. They are very much objects in their own right, direct though their meaning is recondite."

October 8–November 3, 1963 • *Marcel Duchamp* is on view at the Pasadena Art Museum. The retrospective is organized by Walter Hopps, who remembers his visits as a teenager to the art-filled Hollywood home of Walter and Louise Arensberg to look in wonder at their collection

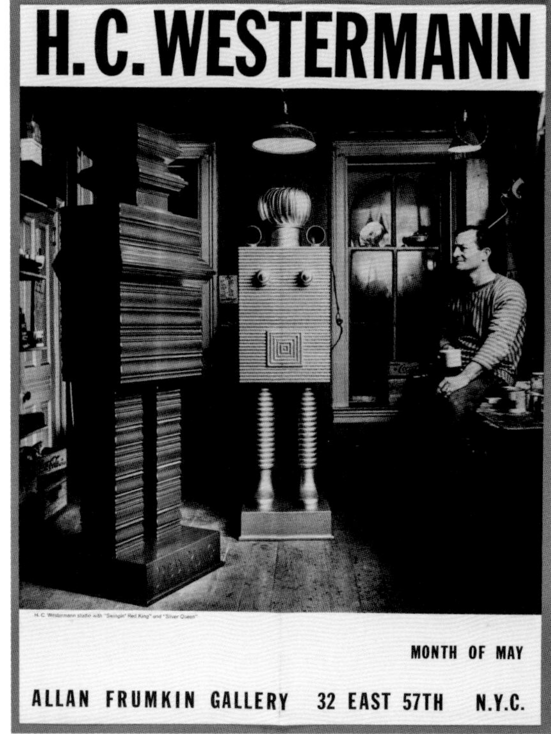

Poster for *H. C. Westermann*, Allan Frumkin Gallery, New York, 1961

of Duchamps and Surrealist artworks. The Arensbergs hold salons in support of Duchamp for all interested viewers, which also inspires artist, collector, and patron William Copley, who will ultimately connect Hopps with Duchamp. The exhibition is an event in Los Angeles and is attended

by Edward Kienholz, Noah Purifoy, Ed Ruscha, Andy Warhol, and many others.

October 28, 1963 • Kenneth Anger's *Scorpio Rising* premieres at midnight at the Gramercy Arts Theatre in New York. Among the audience are filmmaker Gregory Markopoulos, artist Carolee Schneemann, and critic Ken Kelman, each of whom reviews the film. (Whether Jonas Mekas attends the premiere is unclear; he publishes a review slightly later.) *Scorpio Rising* is an explosive combination of intercut footage of bikers attending a bacchanalian Halloween party and desecrating a church, Nazi imagery, and segments appropriated from a copy of the Sunday school feature *Last Journey to Jerusalem* that had arrived at Anger's doorstep entirely by accident while he was editing. Anger's radically disjunctive approach to montage leads Kelman to declare that the filmmaker "is no editor." Dismissing his technique as "formal masochism," Kelman writes, "In *Scorpio* he intercuts wildly, from place to place. . . . The tortuous uncertainties of editing in *Scorpio Rising* are just the cruelest cuts which Anger wished to self-inflict"—unwitting but apt praise, as Anger's montage technique is entirely deliberate.

Markopoulos's review is more sympathetic, calling the film a "very American motion picture," while Schneemann's poetic review the following spring in *Film Culture* will praise Anger's integration of the camera eye: "These images subsume a camera eye; where is Anger? *Scorpio Rising,* so complete to the eye it is impossible to establish the physical actions of 'making the film,' rather some sense of it sprung complete, in its complex rays and subtle ironies of terror and love, from a lucid dream moving more deeply into consciousness than any intention could provide."

While *Scorpio Rising* will not arouse the same level of controversy as Jack Smith's *Flaming*

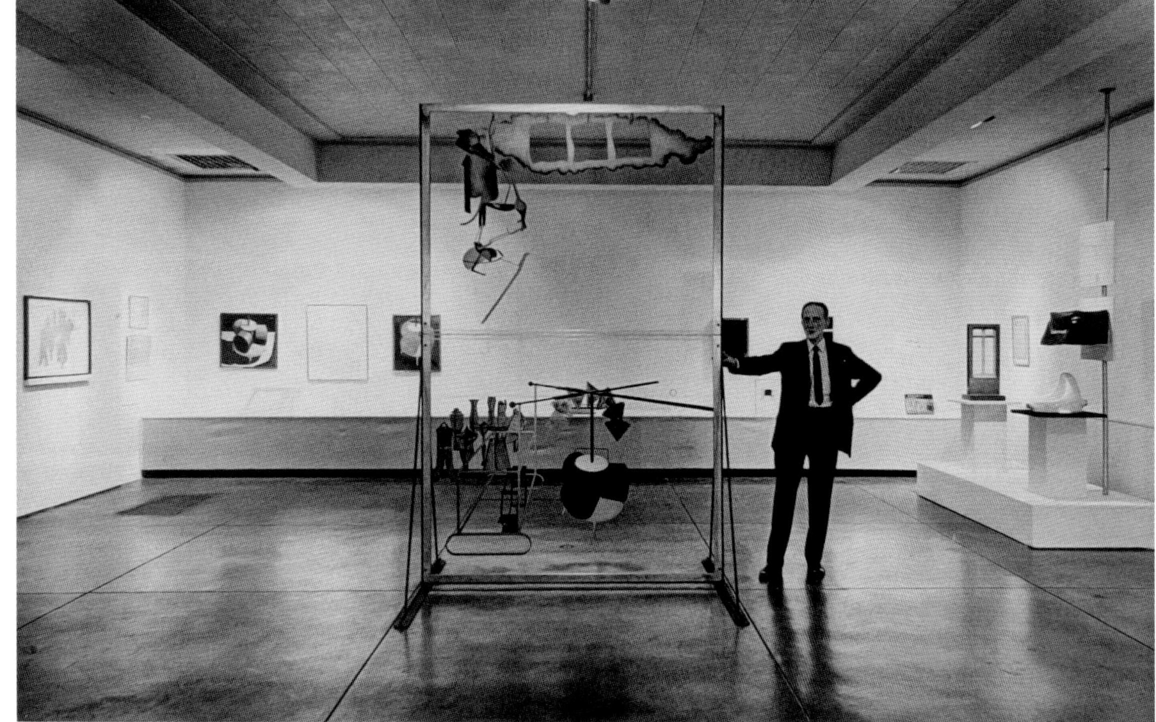

Marcel Duchamp standing with *The Bride Stripped Bare by Her Bachelors, Even (The Large Glass)* (1915–23), Pasadena Art Museum, CA, 1963

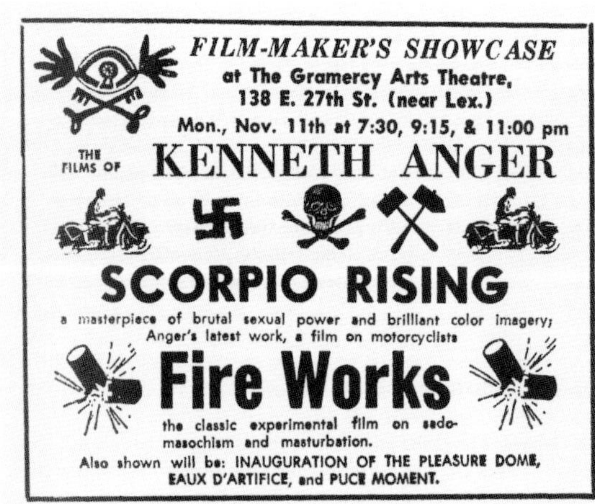

Advertisement for a presentation of Kenneth Anger's films, Film-Makers' Cooperative, New York, 1963

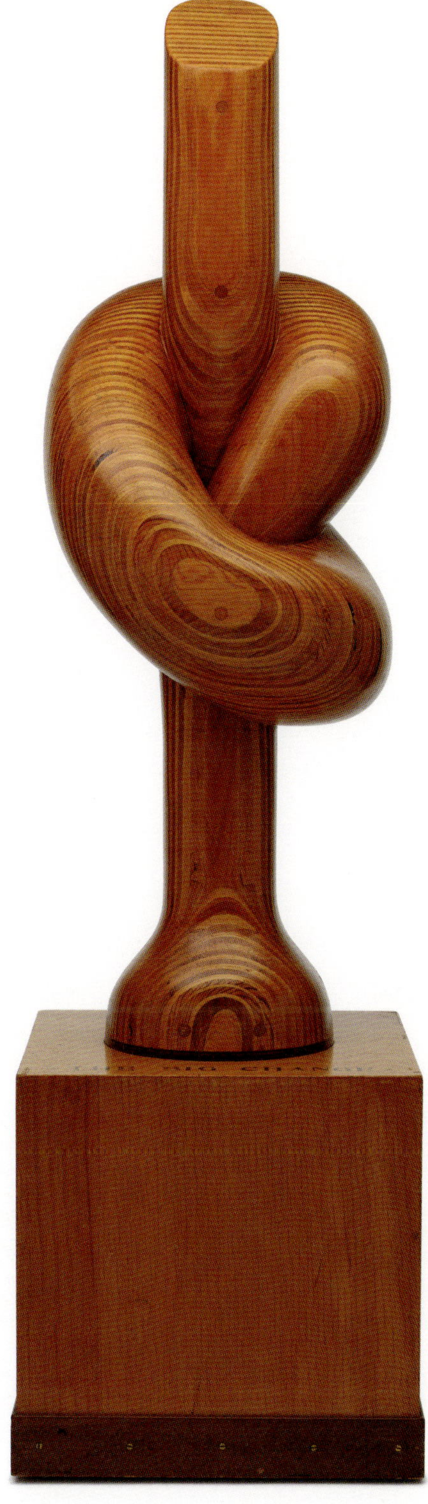

H. C. Westermann, *The Big Change*, 1963. Douglas-fir marine plywood, Masonite, and ink, 75 ⅜ × 20 ¼ × 20 ¼ in. (191.5 × 51.4 × 51.4 cm).
The Art Institute of Chicago; gift of the Estate of Alan and Dorothy Press in acknowledgment of their family 2023.2906

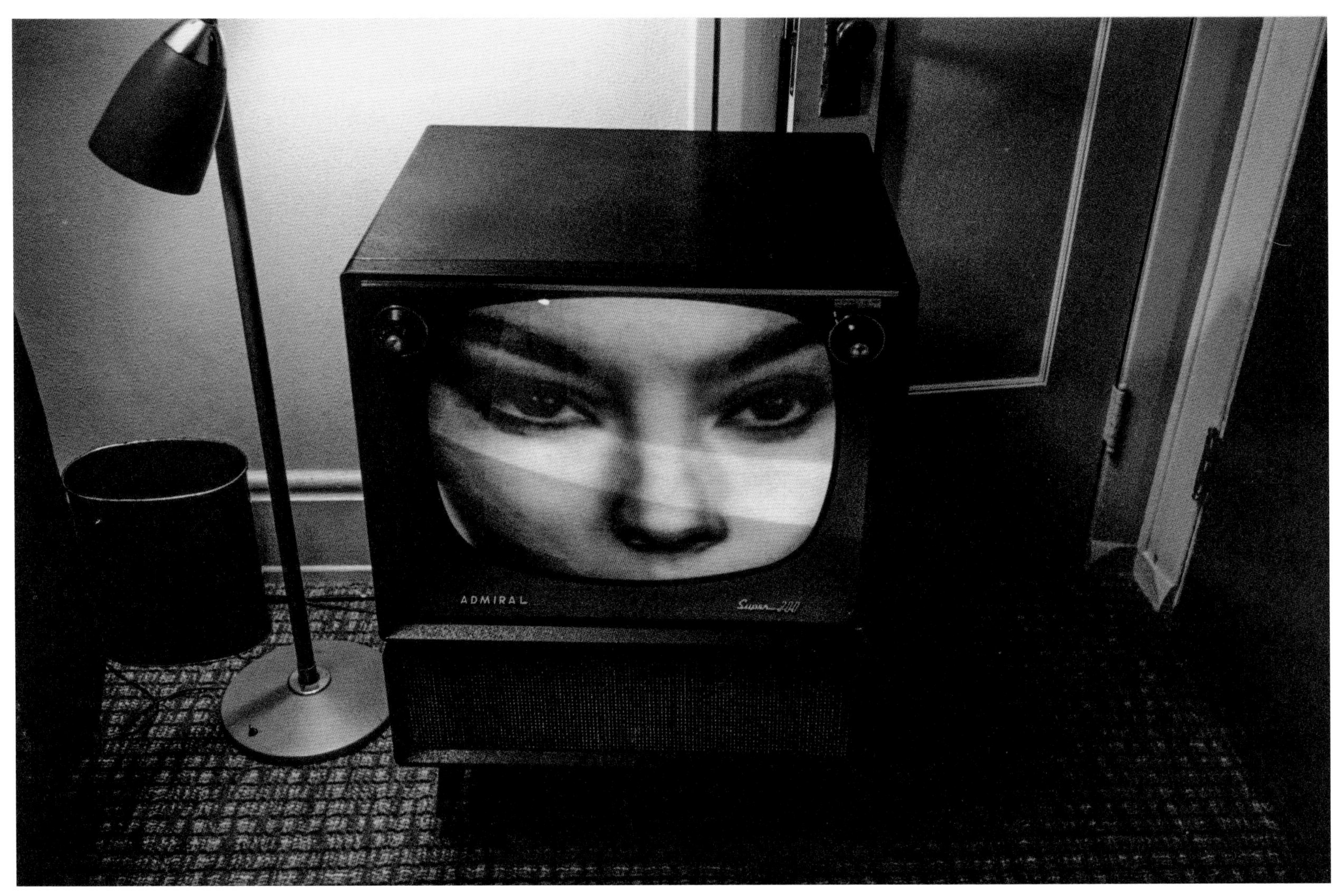

Lee Friedlander, *Florida*, 1963. Gelatin silver print, 8 ¾ × 13 ⅛ in. (22 × 33.1 cm). The Museum of Modern Art, New York; purchase 695.2000

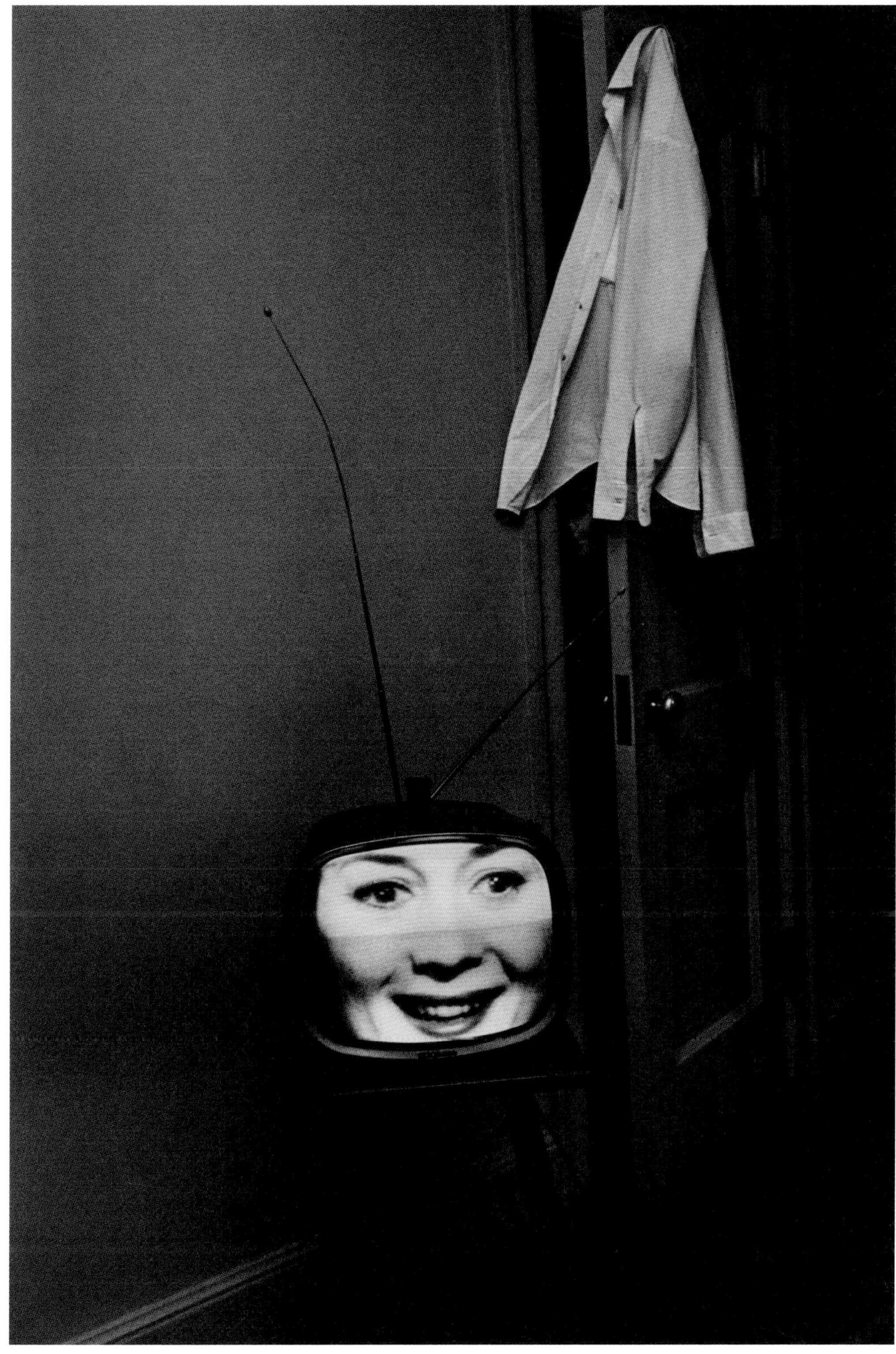

Lee Friedlander, *Nashville*, 1963. Gelatin silver print, 9 ¼ × 6 ⅛ in. (23.5 × 15.5 cm). The Metropolitan Museum of Art, New York; purchase, The Horace W. Goldsmith Foundation Gift, through Joyce and Robert Menschel, 1995 1995.168.2

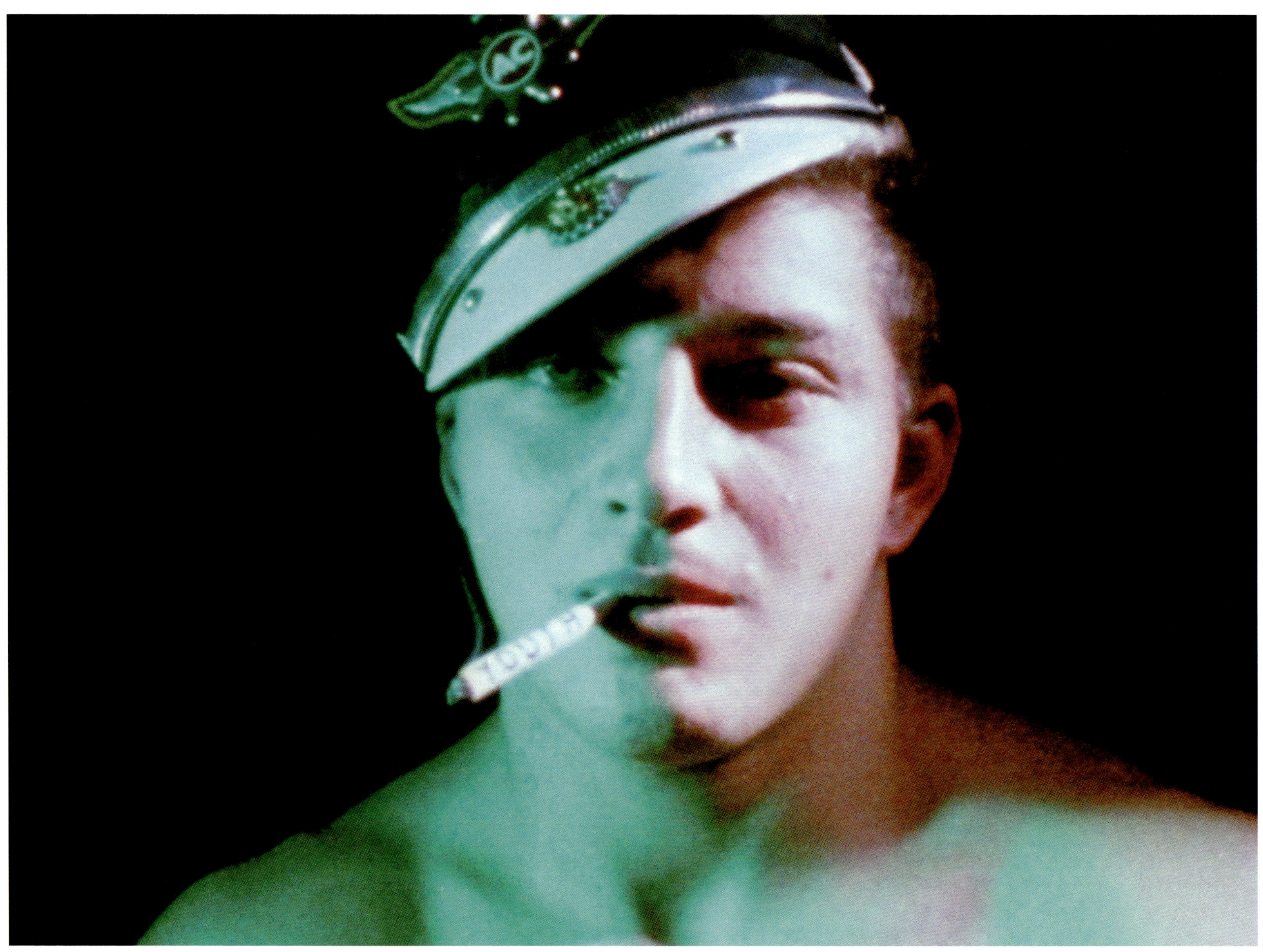

Kenneth Anger, *Scorpio Rising*, 1963. 16mm film, color, sound; 28 min. UCLA Film & Television Archive

Creatures, the police will confiscate the film at a screening in Los Angeles, only five days after Smith's film meets the same fate in New York, and both films will become the subjects of parallel censorship cases on opposite sides of the country.

———

November 1963 • *ARTnews* publishes the first of a two-part series, "What is Pop Art? Answers from 8 Painters" by Gene Swenson. This first installment includes the Pop enthusiast's interviews with Jim Dine, Robert Indiana, Roy Lichtenstein, and Andy Warhol. The second, published in February 1964, will feature Stephen Durkee, Jasper Johns, James Rosenquist, and Tom Wesselmann. More than a half century later, scholar Jennifer Sichel will uncover the original unedited interview recordings in Swenson's archive, and his interview with Warhol will become notorious for opening with the question, "What do you say about homosexuals?," a query rooted in Swenson's own queer identity and his understanding of a strong but unspoken current then running beneath so much modern and contemporary art.

———

November 22, 1963 • President John F. Kennedy Jr. is assassinated in Dallas, Texas. Later that day, the assassin, Lee Harvey Oswald, a former Marine, is arrested. Vice President Lyndon B. Johnson is sworn in as the new president at 2:38 p.m. on Air Force One, which then returns to Washington, DC, with Kennedy's body. On November 24, the same day as the former president's funeral, Oswald is shot and killed by Dallas nightclub owner Jack Ruby as the assassin is being transferred to the county jail; the murder is captured on live television. Although the Kennedy "Camelot" years will be subject to much hagiography, the assassination of the young, telegenic president deeply impacts the mood of the country and will be seen as a harbinger of an era of political violence.

———

December 1963 • Carolee Schneemann creates the series *Eye Body: 36 Transformative Actions for Camera*, in which the artist uses her body as maker *and* material, posing nude in an expanded painterly environment while her friend Erró photographs. As Schneemann will later recall:

> In 1962 I began a loft environment built of large panels interlocked by rhythmic color units, broken mirrors and glass, lights, moving umbrellas and motorized parts. I worked with my whole body—the scale of the panels incorporating my own physical scale. I then decided I wanted my actual body to be combined with the work as an integral material—a further dimension of the construction. . . . In December of '63 I was encouraged by my friend Erró (the Icelandic, Paris-based painter) when I told him I wanted to do a series of physical transformations of my body in my work—the constructions and wall environment. I thought the ritual aspect of the process could put me in a trance-like state.

Developing out of Schneemann's earlier fascination with portraying the body in the landscape as well as her interest in expanding the definition of painting, *Eye Body* brings the performing body into the painterly surface, already shattered by the artist's "constructions." In Erró's eighteen gelatin silver prints, Schneemann poses with props—sheets of plastic, broken mirrors, the spokes of a shredded umbrella—further breaking up the surface of the painterly assemblage. She later hand-colors and scratches a series of stark, high-contrast prints, adding an additional layer of mediation.

———

December 11, 1963–February 2, 1964 • The Whitney Museum of American Art's *Annual Exhibition 1963: Contemporary American Painting* identifies James Rosenquist and Harold Stevenson as prototypical of the growing movement of Pop art.

———

December 17, 1963–January 11, 1964 • Yayoi Kusama opens her first room-size installation, *Aggregation: One Thousand Boats Show*, at Gallery Gertrude Stein, New York. The installation consists of a rowboat filled with phallic protrusions sitting in the center of the darkened space, whose walls are papered with 999 black-and-white reproductions of the boat sculpture. *New York Times* critic Brian O'Doherty calls it a "genuine, obscurely poetic event" that "should not be dismissed as a surrealist caper."

To create the work, Kusama receives Donald Judd's help not only in stuffing the fabric phalli but also in retrieving the salvaged vessel during their nocturnal excursions, as Kusama will later recall: "We were both living in abject poverty. Judd had no money to buy art materials, so he would go to a nearby construction site, collect wood that was lying about, and carry it home. We called it collecting materials, but in fact it was stealing. . . . But everyone lived like that in New York in those days."

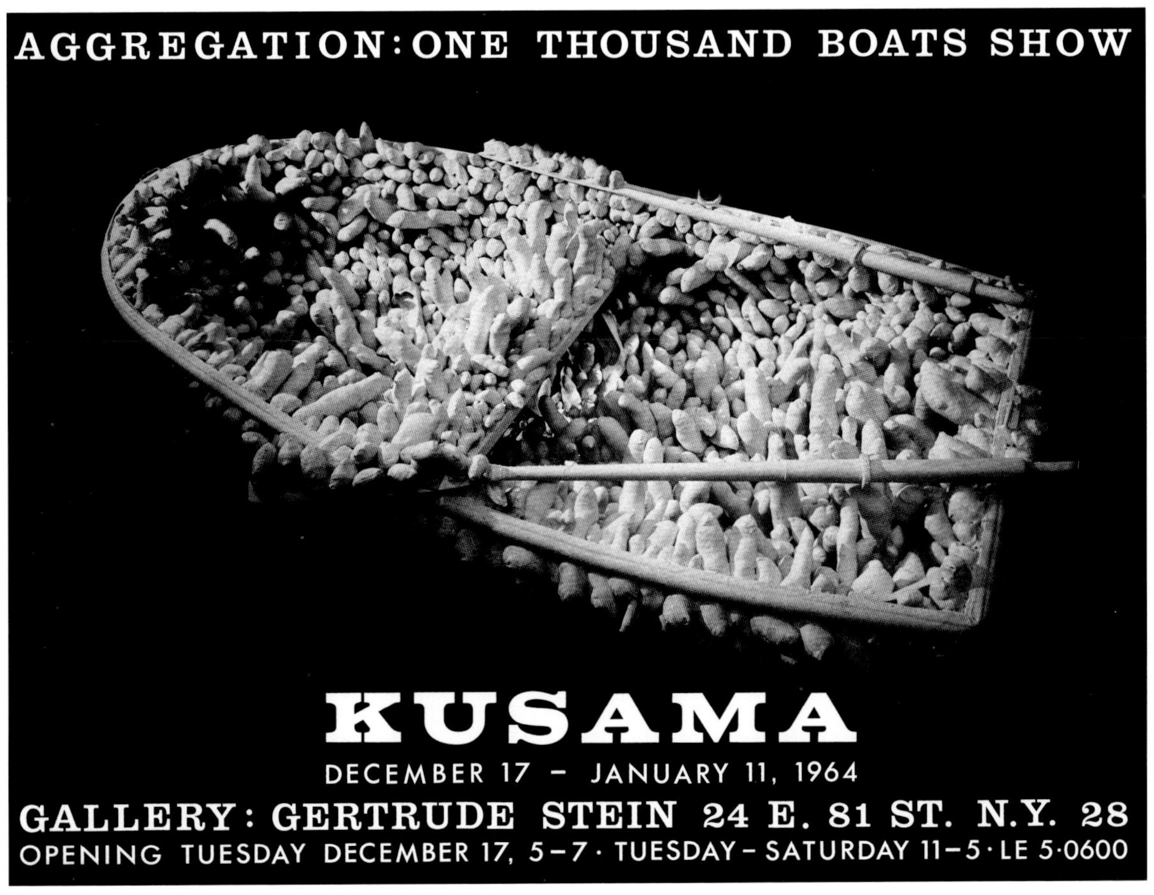

Poster for *Aggregation: One Thousand Boats Show*, Gallery: Gertrude Stein, New York, 1963

1964

1964 • Carolee Schneemann begins filming *Fuses* (1964–67), a representation of the lovemaking between herself and her partner, James Tenney. Schneemann's impassioned reaction to Kenneth Anger's treatment of the "psychosexual" in *Scorpio Rising*, as expressed in her recent *Film Culture* review, is matched by her frustration with the representations of sexuality in the films of their mutual friend Stan Brakhage, such as *Window Water Baby Moving* (1959)—about the birth of Brakhage's son—and *Loving* (1957), in which Schneemann and Tenney appear making love outdoors. While *Window Water Baby Moving* does not acknowledge Jane Brakhage's role as cocreator in the birth act, *Loving*, Schneemann recollects, "failed to capture our central eroticism, and I wanted to set that right." *Fuses*, the beginning of Schneemann's engagement with filmmaking, emerges from a desire to mediate the erotic body differently, starting from "the sense of the camera and me as an enmeshed system," which she also articulates as the idea of the "eye/body" in her earlier work of the same name.

Taking a painterly approach to the film, Schneemann paints directly onto the stock and subjects it to a variety of other manipulations: baking, scratching, burning, and leaving it outdoors exposed to the elements. Rapid montages and the embrace of contingency in flares of light, over- and underexposure, and other accidents of the unattended camera disrupt the narrative and, frequently, recognizable imagery. Her approach to the film also emphasizes collaboration: with Tenney, in lovemaking and in handling the camera; with friends, including Stan VanDerBeek, who films a sequence; with her cat, Kitch, a subject and a surrogate eye watching the couple; and with the natural elements.

January 7–30, 1964 • Louise Bourgeois (1911–2010) has her first solo exhibition in New York in eleven years. *Louise Bourgeois: Recent Sculpture* at Stable Gallery features poured and heaped nests, cocoons, caves, and beehives. *Lair* (c. 1962–63), *Portrait* (1963), and *Fée Couturière* (1963), a suspended pendant sculpture punctuated by irregular hollows, are highlights of the exhibition. Daniel Robbins observes in *Art International* that "they all share the same quality of a lair"—that is, "the viewer puts his open eye against a small opening and vast perceptions are realized." Obliquely erotic, Bourgeois's intimate objects evoke bodily cavities: "Like living flesh, the rubber quivers and flaps," and they have a "viscous sheen like the inside of a mouth."

Born in Paris two years before the outbreak of World War I, Bourgeois had spent her childhood visiting her father at military encampments and eventually at a hospital for injured combatants. Her mother, whom she will later describe as "a socialist and feminist," dies when the artist is in her early twenties. After studying mathematics at the Sorbonne, Bourgeois turns to art during a period dominated by Surrealism, briefly entering the École des Beaux-Arts before moving through a succession of ateliers. In the late 1930s, she opens a gallery, where she meets the art historian Robert Goldwater. Before the start of World War II, Bourgeois marries Goldwater and moves to New York, where she enrolls at the Art Students League and encounters European Surrealists living in exile, including André Breton, Max Ernst, Alberto Giacometti, Joan Miró, and Yves Tanguy. She has her first solo exhibition in 1945, showing a dozen paintings, a medium she soon abandons for sculpture's "fantastic reality." In the early 1950s, Bourgeois undergoes psychoanalysis and, like the Surrealists of the 1920s and 1930s, begins investigating unconscious fears and desires in her work. In the early 1960s, she starts experimenting with unorthodox techniques and materials, including rubber latex, plaster, and cement.

Her 1964 show at Stable Gallery brings the artist to the attention of the next generation. Lucy Lippard, a student of Goldwater while at New York University's Institute of Fine Arts, will include

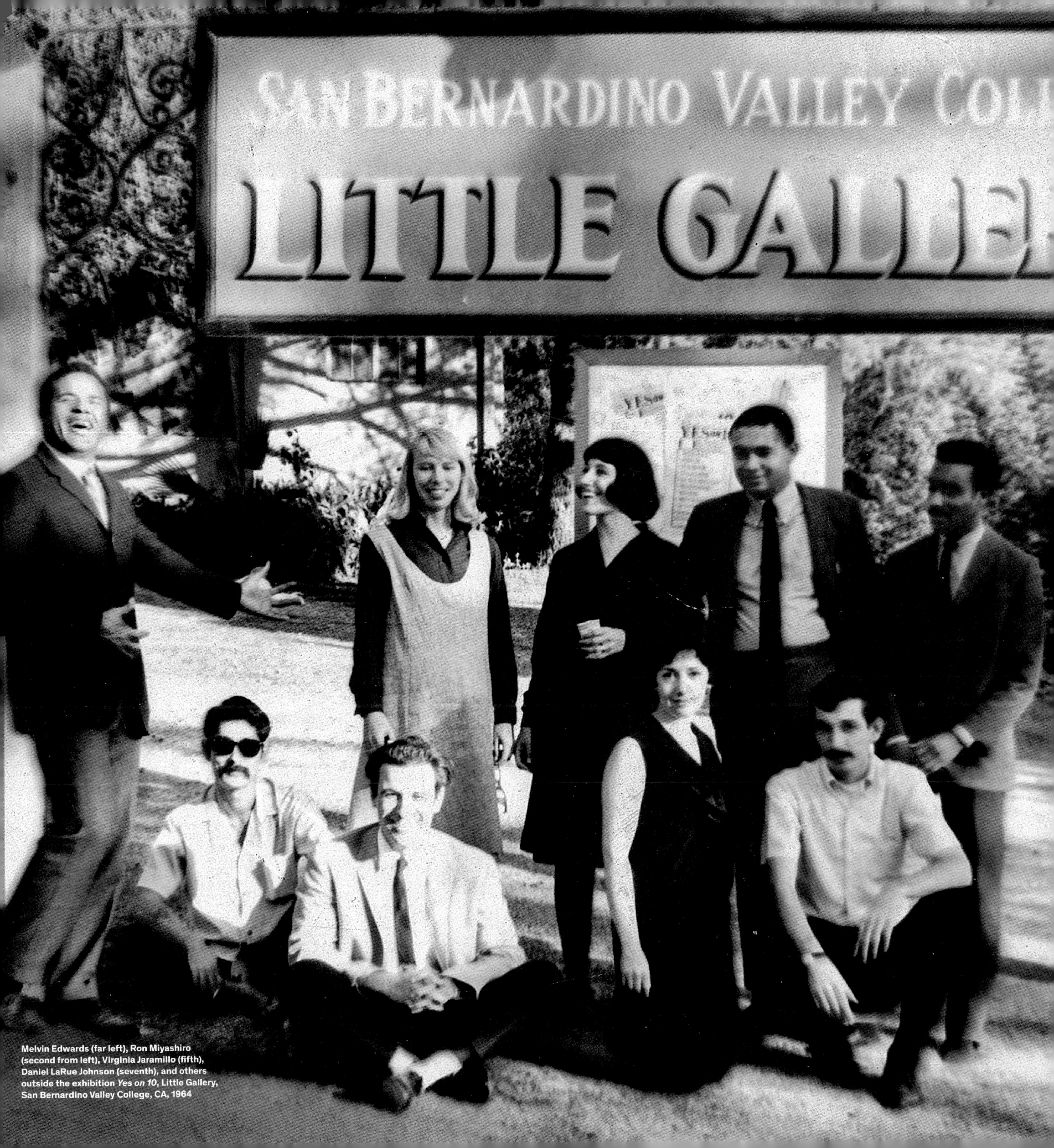

Melvin Edwards (far left), Ron Miyashiro (second from left), Virginia Jaramillo (fifth), Daniel LaRue Johnson (seventh), and others outside the exhibition *Yes on 10*, Little Gallery, San Bernardino Valley College, CA, 1964

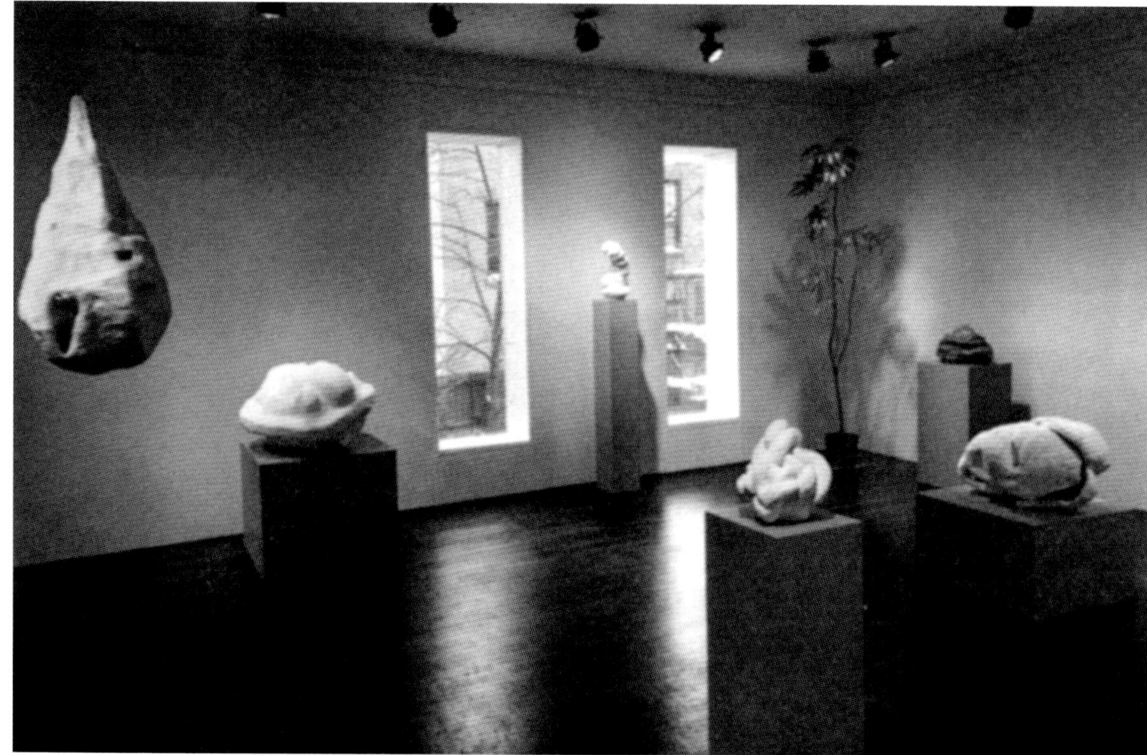

Louise Bourgeois: Recent Sculpture, Stable Gallery, New York, 1964

Bourgeois's *Portrait* in the exhibition *Eccentric Abstraction* at Fischbach Gallery in fall 1966, installing it alongside works by the younger Eva Hesse and Bruce Nauman, among others. "Louise Bourgeois' flexible, latex molds imply the location of metamorphosis rather than the act. Her work is less aggressively detached and more poetically mature than that of the younger artists, but like them, she does not ignore the uneasy, near repellant side of art," Lippard writes in an announcement for the show.

1964 • Barbara Chase-Riboud purchases La Chenillère, an eighteenth-century farmhouse, to use as an atelier for large sculptures. The house is in Pontlevoy, in the Loire Valley, two hours from the Paris apartment she shares with her husband, Marc Riboud. The following year, at the Bonvicini Brothers Foundry in Verona, she perfects the technique of direct cut and folded wax models from sheet wax. Using wax casting, she stretches bronze into thin sheets that can then be folded and undercut into monumental structures, learning the method from local foundry workers.

The levity of these thin-sheet sculptures is further emphasized by the loops and knots of wool that gather to obscure their bronze bases. Chase-Riboud credits Sheila Hicks with first showing her how to escape from the "tyranny" of the base, as seen in *Confessions for Myself* (1972). Her work during the 1960s also includes *Le Couple* (1963) and *Tiberius's Leap* (1965), examples of her large, spindly bronze figures cast from animal bones acquired from a Paris taxidermy shop.

February 2–29, 1964 • Dwan Gallery, Los Angeles, mounts the group exhibition *Boxes*, which explores the format and recurrence of the box in contemporary art. Walter Hopps writes the accompanying catalogue, and the show includes more than thirty artists—from Joseph Cornell, Louise Nevelson, and Andy Warhol to Ron Miyashiro, James Rosenquist, Lucas Samaras, and Daniel LaRue Johnson (1938–2017).

Johnson is still a student at the Chouinard Art Institute and has been making assemblage work, incorporating found objects into diorama-like structures or onto painterly surfaces, and then generally painting the entire construction black in these pieces from his "black box" period. While doing research in ten Southern states, Johnson collects objects such as saws, doll parts, and mousetraps, and covers them with black paint and resin, or pitch. The objects point to violence and fear, and their obscurement addresses racial issues and the fraught civil rights movement at the time. Johnson shows his work not only at Dwan Gallery in 1964 but also at a solo show at Rolf Nelson Gallery that year.

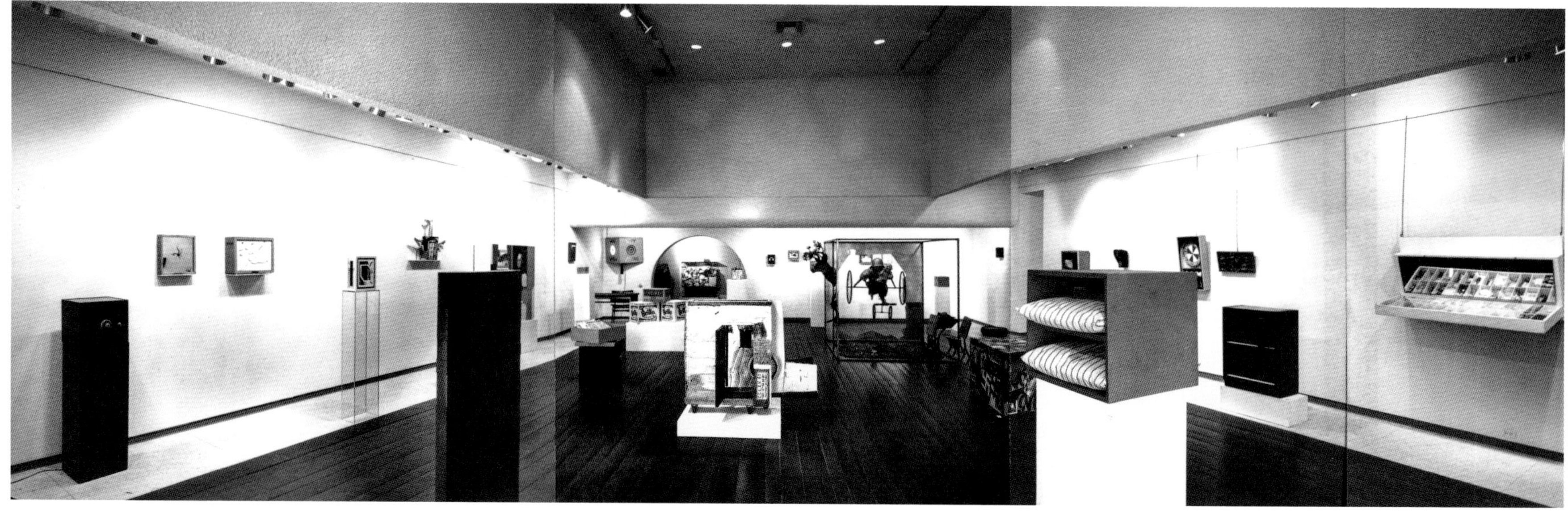

Boxes, Dwan Gallery, Los Angeles, 1964

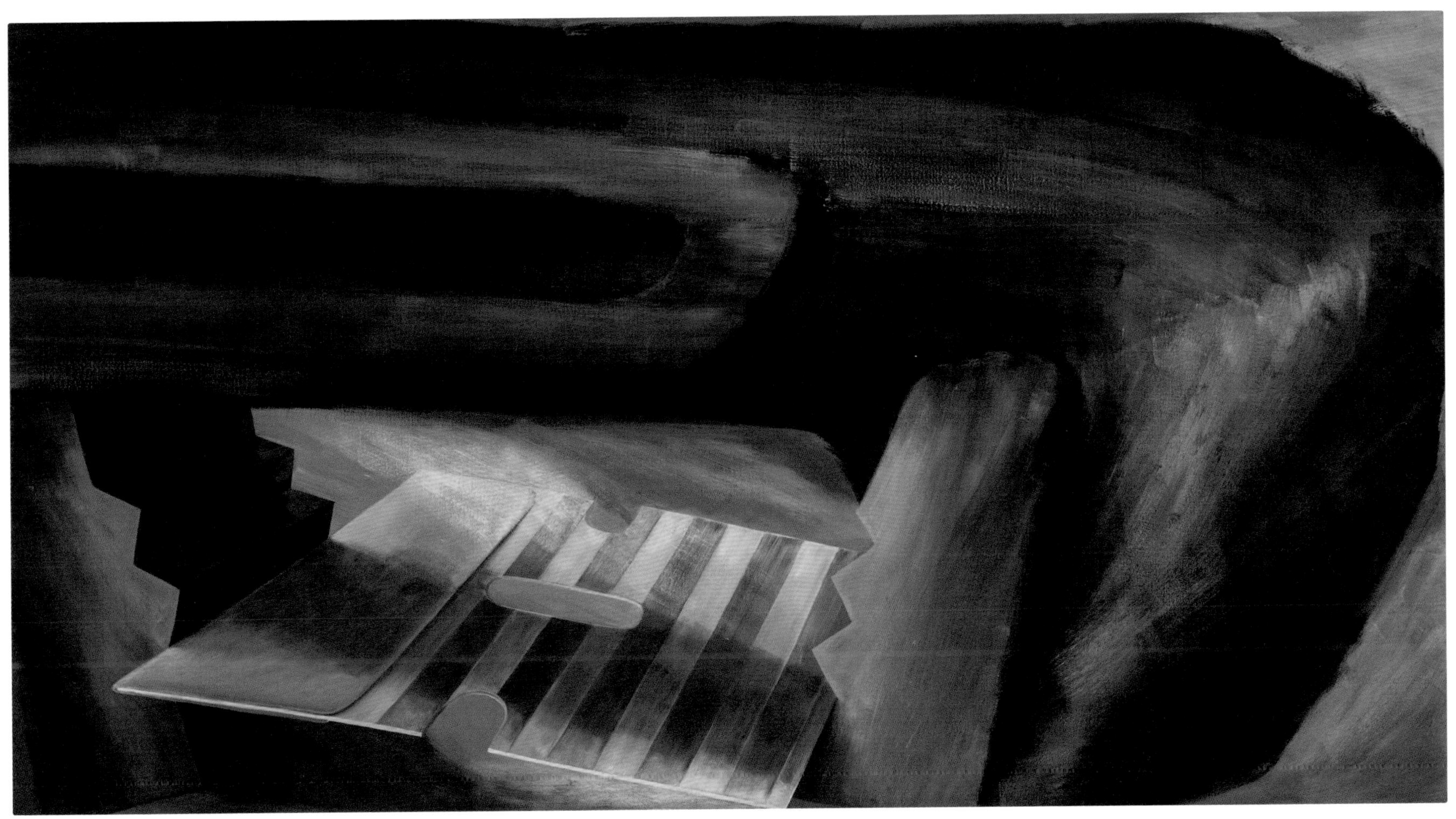

Lee Lozano, *No Title*, 1964. Oil on canvas, 65 ¾ × 118 ¾ in. (167 × 301.5 cm). The Estate of Lee Lozano

Daniel LaRue Johnson, *Freedom Now, Number 1*, August 13, 1963–January 14, 1964. Pitch on canvas with "Freedom Now" button, broken doll, hacksaw, mousetrap, flexible tube, and wood, 53 ⅞ × 55 ⅜ × 7 ½ in. (136.6 × 140.5 × 18.9 cm). The Museum of Modern Art, New York; given anonymously 4.1965

After graduating from Chouinard in 1965, Johnson and his wife, artist Virginia Jaramillo, travel, spending an extended time in Paris before eventually settling in New York. Johnson's work moves away from assemblage and direct representations of politics, but he remains engaged in issues of racial discrimination, especially in the artworld.

March 3, 1964 • Police raid a screening of Jack Smith's *Flaming Creatures* on the Lower East Side and seize the print, even though the film has been shown in New York and elsewhere for a year. Filmmakers Ken Jacobs and Jonas Mekas are arrested, along with a few others, which launches a legal battle over censorship and obscenity.

March 18, 1964 • Jordan Belson wins a Ford Foundation grant to make the film that will become *Re-Entry* (1964); other winners this year include Bruce Conner and Ed Emshwiller. Having withdrawn his films from circulation and dedicated the last three years to the study of hatha yoga, Belson initially refuses the $10,000 award before changing his mind and returning to his artistic practice. Beginning with *Re-Entry*, he connects the nonobjective phenomena in his films with personal experiences of the altered states achieved through sustained meditation. In their focus on subjective reality, Belson's films challenge the popular premise that the filmic medium is essentially tied to objective reality. Besides hinting at Belson's return to art making, the title *Re-Entry* invites identification of the film's abstract imagery with two allegorical narratives: reincarnation as described in *The Tibetan Book of the Dead* and astronaut John Glenn's 1962 reentry into Earth's atmosphere; Belson samples Glenn's radio communication in the film's soundtrack.

Spring 1964 • A prodigy raised into art by her supportive Jewish family on the North Side of Chicago, Suellen Rocca (1943–2020) graduates from the School of the Art Institute of Chicago (SAIC). In 1960, at just sixteen years old, she had entered the school, recalling that she "grew up in the Art Institute. It was like a second home." There, Rocca had encountered a formative influence in Ray Yoshida, her first-year drawing teacher, at the time a thirty-two-year-old artist just finding his own footing. Yoshida becomes a mentor to Rocca, encouraging her and her fellow students to follow their instincts rather than subscribe to any rigid ideology. By the time she graduates, Rocca is well versed in a variety of visual cultures and comfortable with painting on an unusually large scale. Many of her works

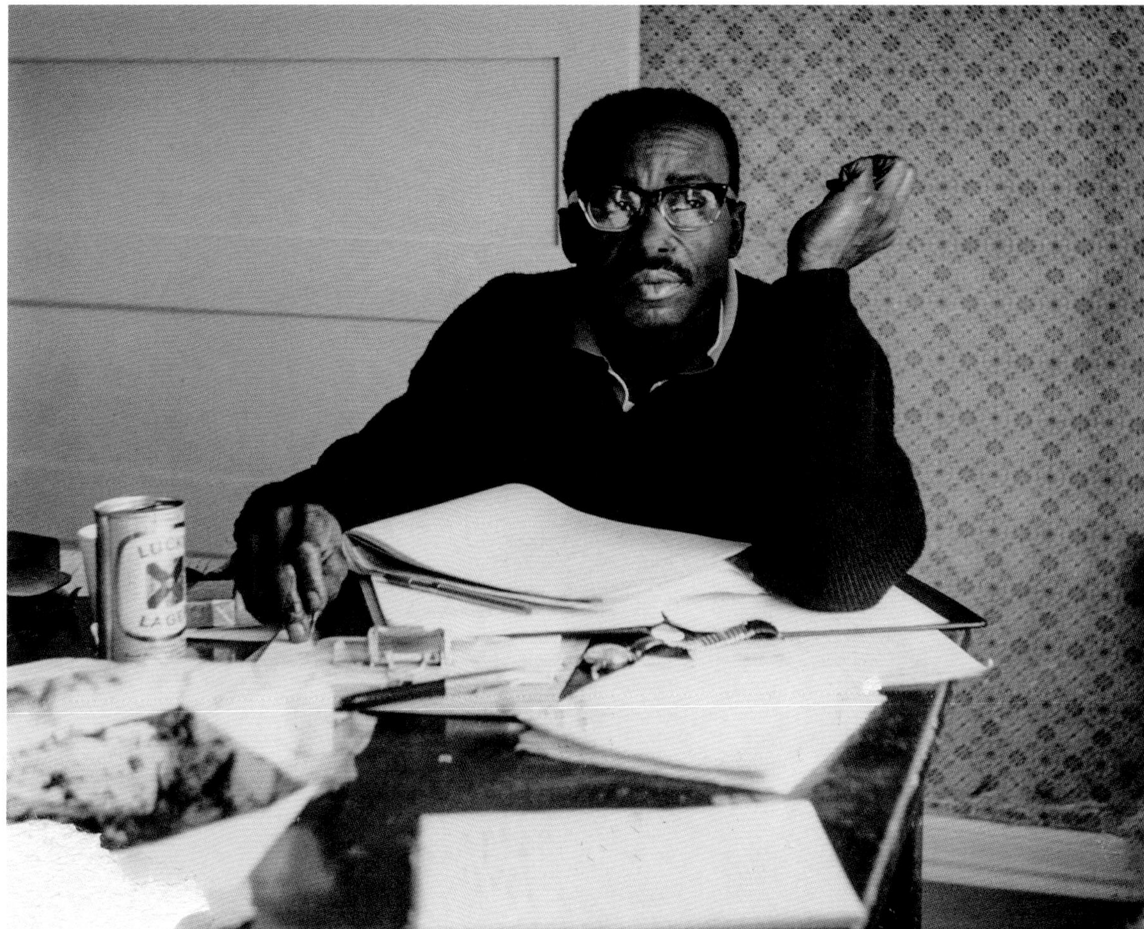

Noah Purifoy at the Watts Towers Arts Center, Los Angeles, 1965

depict objects that embody post-adolescent longing, incipient sexuality, and the transition into early adulthood.

Early 1964 • Noah Purifoy (1917–2004) cofounds the Watts Towers Arts Center (WTAC) together with Judson Powell and Sue Welsh, and he serves as its first director. The trio of artist/educators have spent the previous two years in the South Central Los Angeles neighborhood engaging with residents and the youth in particular to better understand the needs of the predominantly Black community. The center offers free art classes of all kinds, from art making to music, poetry, and theater, to a community that by the 1960s is underserved and under-resourced after years of racist housing and hiring practices in the city.

Purifoy is uniquely qualified to create such a program because of his experience in education, social service, and art. Born in Snow Hill, Alabama, Purifoy had received his first college degree in 1939, from Alabama State Teachers College in Montgomery, and he taught for a few years before enlisting in the Navy. After being discharged from the military in 1946, he earns his master's degree in social work at Atlanta

University and moves to Los Angeles to serve as a social worker. But after just two years, he returns to school, and in 1950 Purifoy is the first full-time Black art student at the Chouinard Art Institute, finishing his master of fine arts in 1954. But Purifoy will contend: "I wasn't an artist until Watts. That made me an artist."

Spring 1964 • Luis Jimenez (1940–2006) graduates from the University of Texas at Austin, where he has (unenthusiastically and at the behest of his father) studied architecture. This same year, Jimenez receives a scholarship to attend Ciudad Universitaria in Mexico City, and there works with painter and sculptor Francisco Zúñiga, who is best known for his figurative work and, particularly, depictions of women. The broader educational experience in Mexico City, however, proves disappointing; even Zúñiga tells his student, "For what you're doing, you have no business staying in Mexico." Jimenez leaves the country within the year. He does, however, absorb two important lessons: first, he finds examples of art and imagery unrelated to Abstract Expressionism that free him to break from that prevailing artistic approach, which doesn't interest him; and second, as he

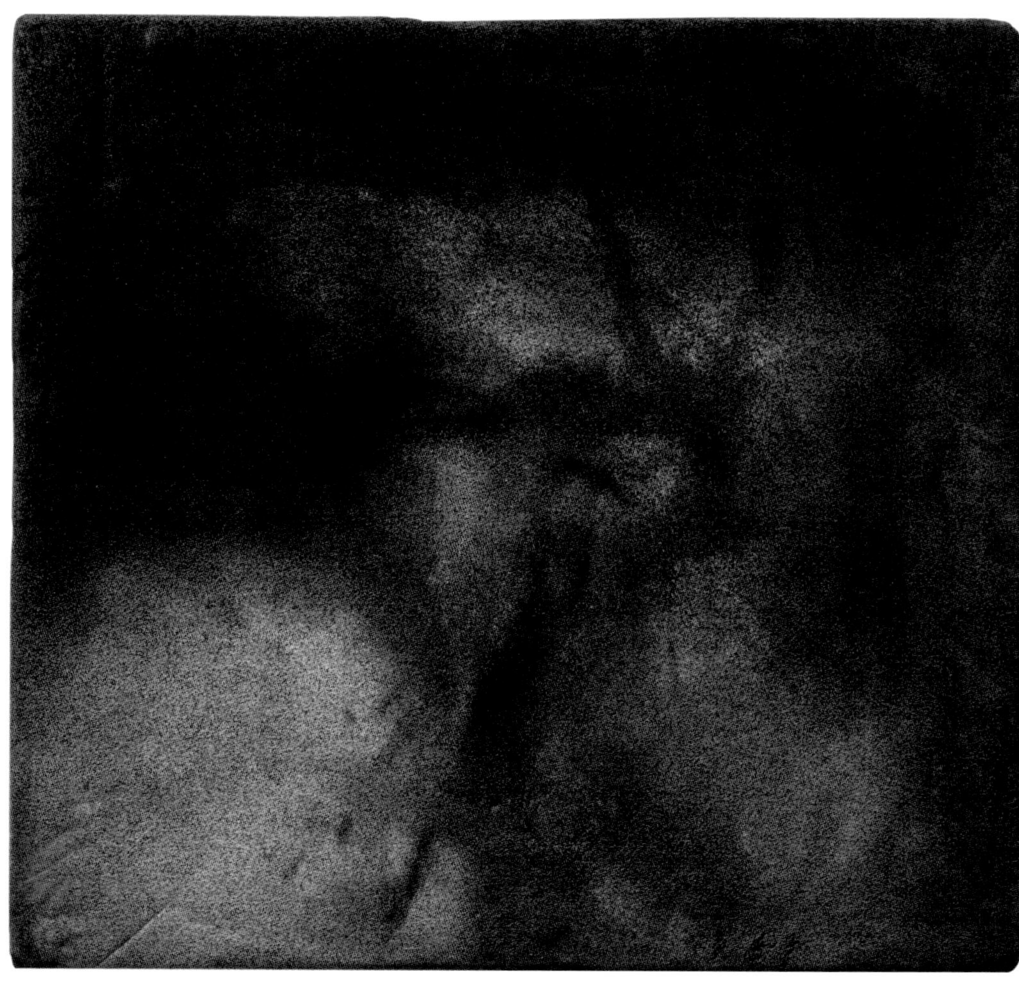

Jack Whitten, *Christ*, 1964. Acrylic on canvas, 15 × 16 in. (38.1 × 40.6 cm). The Jack Whitten Estate

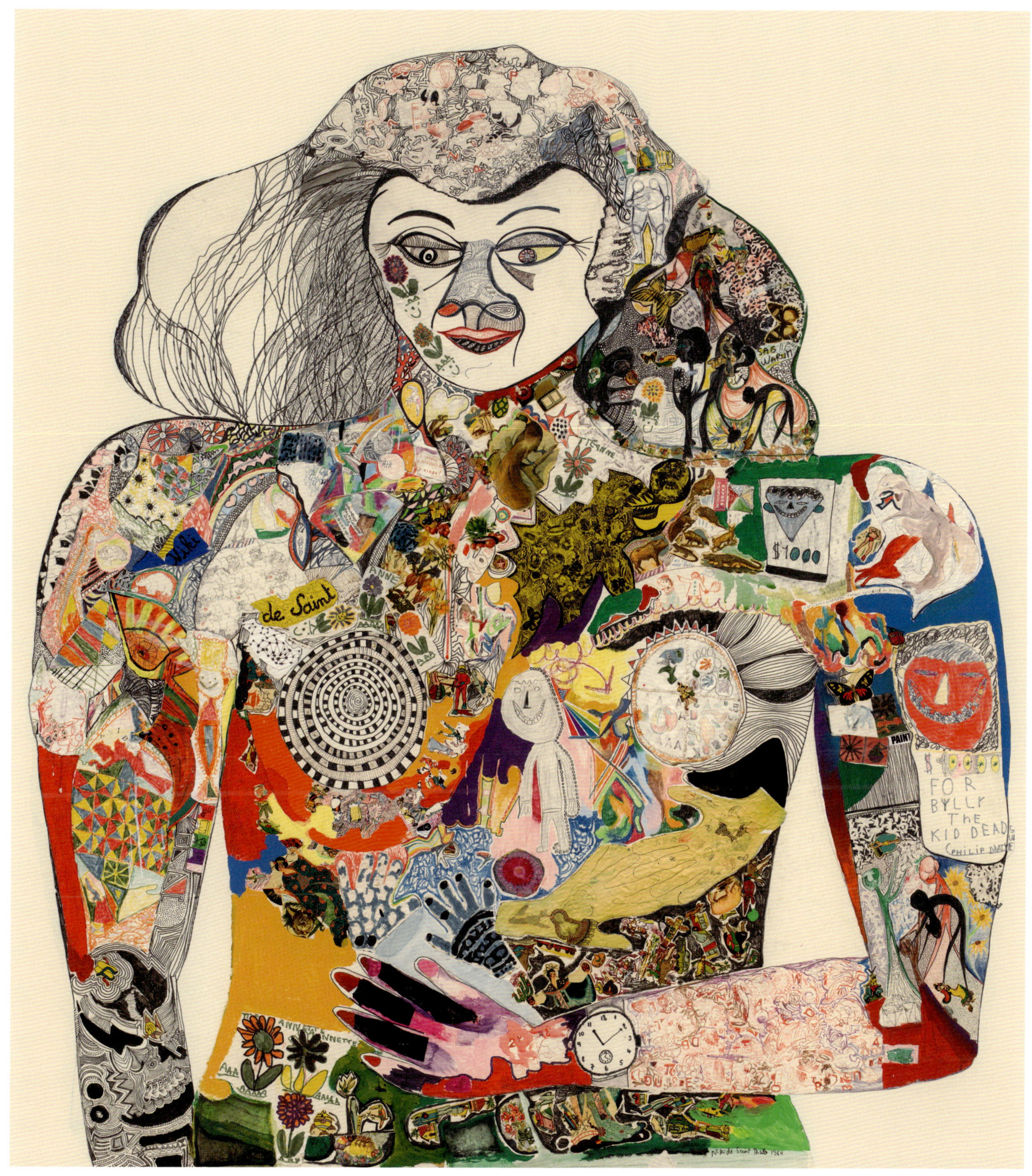

Niki de Saint Phalle, *Annette*, 1964. Paper, fabric, pencil, colored pencil, ink, ink stamp, photomechanical reproduction, gouache, watercolor, pastel, and enamel on canvas, 67 ¾ × 59 ⅛ in. (172.1 × 150 cm). Hirshhorn Museum and Sculpture Garden, Smithsonian Institution, Washington, DC; gift of Joseph H. Hirshhorn, 1966 66.4436

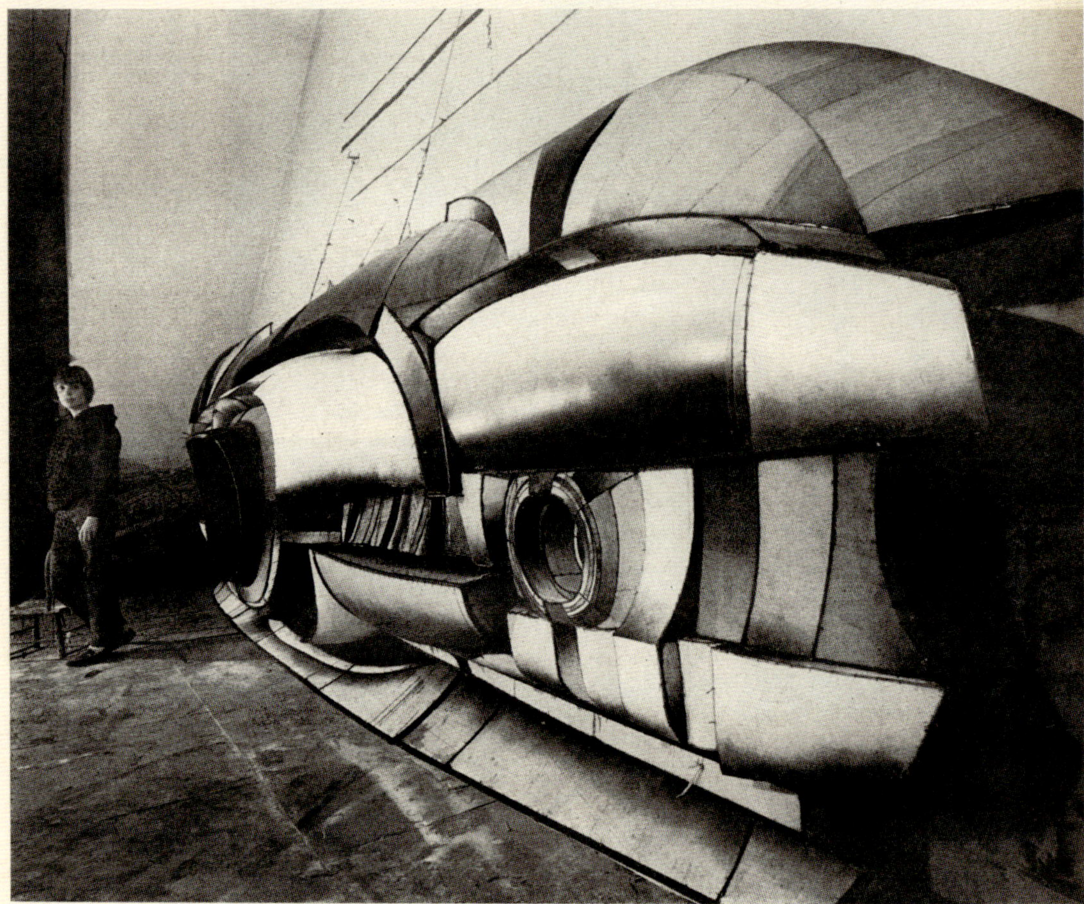

It's Art—But Will It Fly?

If it must be called something, *1964* is as good a title as any. This massive, three-dimensional structure of curving semigeometric shapes is to be installed this month on a wall near the entrance of Lincoln Center's New York State Theater. Its creator, Sculptor Lee Bontecou (*in background*), usually avoids titles for her elaborate, sometimes macabre works. "I get one reaction," she explains, "and other people get different reactions." But she accepts *1964* as a nice ambiguous title. "It could mean that I did it in 1964 or that it connotes 1964—either one would be right."

1964 is a 7x20-ft. assemblage of welded metal rods, pieces of canvas, epoxy resin and the plexiglass turret of an old World War II bomber. It suggests a complex flying machine that might actually be able to get up off the ground and soar. The artist herself has soared spectacularly up through the art world. At 33, she is looked on as one of the country's most original artists—and has also proved to be one of the most successful. Most of the sculpture she has completed over the past five years has been snapped up by collectors and museums. She works hard at her art and, when she isn't stitching or welding away at one of her huge jet-age assemblages, she makes tiny model airplanes in her studio.

CONTINUED

Page from *Life*, April 10, 1964, with Lee Bontecou's *1964* (1964)

will later recall: "When I got down to Mexico, I realized that I was an American. My whole way of thinking, my framework, etc., is American."

Jimenez had grown up in El Paso, Texas, which borders Mexico on the Rio Grande River and shares a close cultural connection with the country to the south. Both of his parents are natives of Mexico who came to the United States as children, and they raise Jimenez in a very strict Mexican Protestant household. His father owns a commercial sign fabrication business called Electric Neon, and Jimenez begins working in the shop when he is six years old. Between his time at Electric Neon and a trip to see the murals of *los tres grandes*—José Clemente Orozco, David Alfaro Siqueiros, and Diego Rivera—at the Museo Nacional de Bellas Artes as a child, Jimenez develops a strong sense of the possibilities of the melding of Chicano style with broader popular or commercial culture.

April 23, 1964 • The New York State Theater opens at Lincoln Center and features in its lobby Lee Bontecou's *1964*, a 21-foot relief commissioned by Philip Johnson, the building's architect. Following President Kennedy's assassination on November 22, 1963, Bontecou had spent five months erecting the work from molded fiberglass, cut and split fire hose, leather, canvas, and the canopy of a World War II bomber. She blows soot onto the relief's undulating surfaces with her welding blowtorch. Bontecou, who usually avoids titling her sculptures, likes the equivocation inherent in *1964*: "It could mean that I did it in 1964 or that it connotes 1964—either one would be right." In a contemporaneous statement, she says her abstract work attempts "to glimpse some of the fear, hope, ugliness, beauty and mystery that exists in us all and which hangs over all the young people today." The same month, Donald Judd praises Bontecou's work, writing "The bellicose detail and the formidable holes are experienced as one would experience a minatory object. The quality of the reliefs is exceptionally explicit or specific or single and obsessive," in a year-end appraisal of New York artists, "Local History," which comments on Yayoi Kusama, Claes Oldenburg, and H. C. Westermann as well. Privately, Eva Hesse remarks of Bontecou's work, "The complexity of her structures, what is involved, absolutely floored me."

June 1964 • Jack Whitten is awarded the John Hay Whitney Opportunity Fellowship, a one-time grant given to young American students (including Barbara Chase-Riboud) for travel or further study in the humanities. Romare Bearden, Lawrence Calcagno, Jacob Lawrence, and Wayne Thiebaud write his recommendation letters. The prize comes at a moment of financial difficulty for the artist. Struggling to support his daughter after the end of his first marriage, he will credit the award with preventing him "from going over the edge." He spends the $4,500 prize on art supplies and begins working in his New York studio on the series he refers to interchangeably as *Ghost*, or *Heads*, or *Gray*—which includes *Christ* (1964) and *Head IV Lynching* (1964)—preparing pieces that will be shown the following year in a group exhibition, his first, at Allan Stone Gallery. On his studio wall Whitten writes, "The image is photographic. Therefore, I must photograph my thoughts," an idea that reflects the thinking he has been doing about the relationship between perception and painting. He begins his process by applying black and white acrylic paint to a canvas, then stretches mesh netting across the pools of paint and wipes away the excess to blur the form into a hazy, ghostlike image.

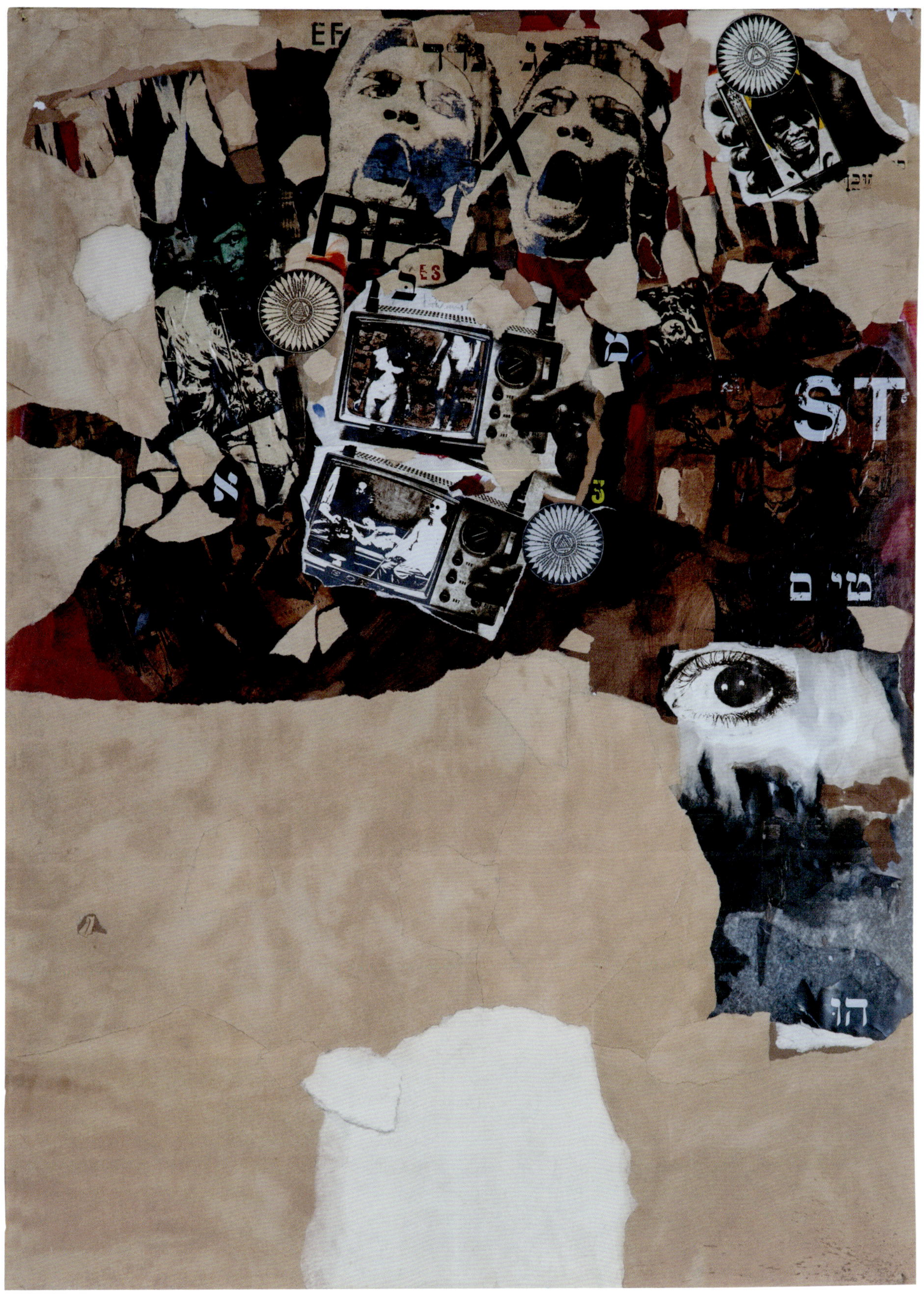

Wallace Berman, *Papa's got a brand new bag*, 1964. Mixed-media collage, 44 ½ × 32 ¼ in. (113 × 81.9 cm). Collection of David Yorkin and Alix Madigan

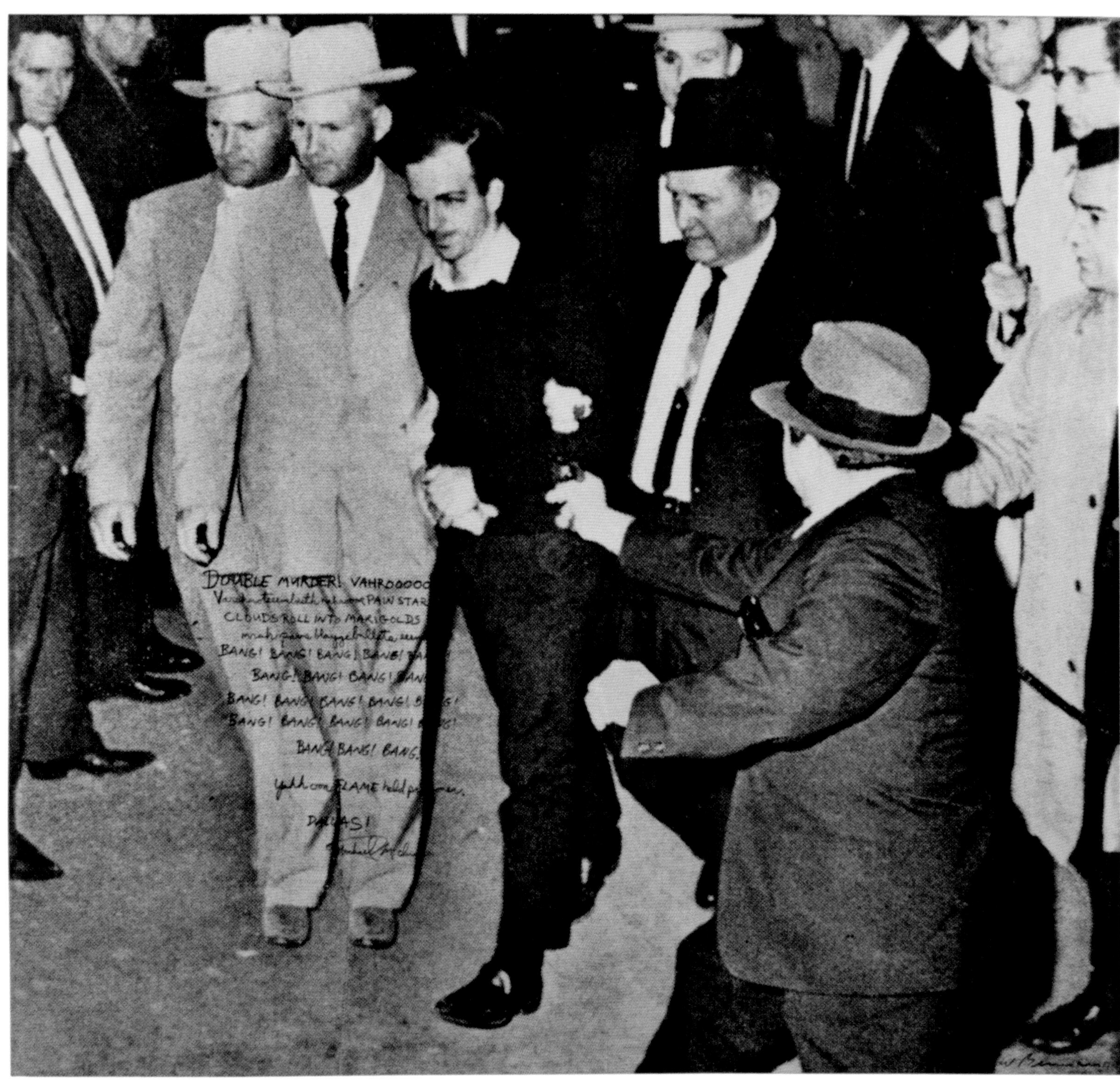

Wallace Berman, *Untitled (Jack Ruby)*, 1964. Positive Verifax with poem, 28 ½ × 29 in. (72.4 × 73.7 cm). Estate of Wallace Berman

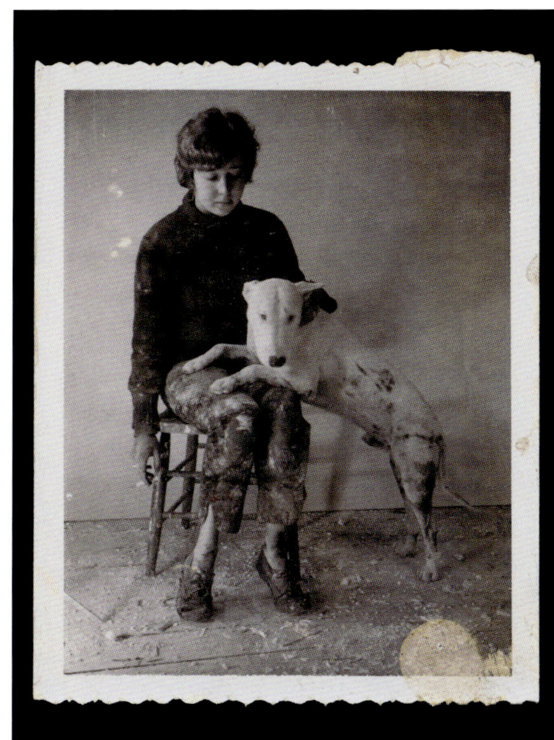

Joan Brown and her dog Bob, 1961

Summer 1964 • Joan Brown decides to stop exhibiting her work commercially. She will later recall, "I was doing very well. But inside I started getting restless. I wanted something quieter." George Staempfli, Brown's New York gallerist and an early supporter of her work, visits her in Colorado, where she is teaching, to convince her to make smaller paintings that he can sell more easily, which has the opposite effect on the artist. "I did a lot of study . . . became my own teacher and student of myself. The gallery flipped out of course. . . . I said to hell with it and I just went underground for three years," she says, echoing Marcel Duchamp's dictum that "the great artist of tomorrow will go underground." Brown turns her back on those Expressionist depictions of scenes of everyday life rendered in thick applications of paint upon which she built her reputation and begins painting self-portraits based on facts and fantasies as well as scenes of San Francisco—a decidedly rash maneuver that she never regrets. The following year, Brown formally ends her relationship with Staempfli Gallery and finalizes her divorce from Manuel Neri.

1964 • Carlos Villa moves from the Bay Area to New York and lives with his cousin and fellow artist Leo Valledor. He soon joins Valledor's group of artist-friends, including Mark di Suvero and Robert Grosvenor, and begins experimenting with some of the same new materials they are using, namely fiberglass, aluminum, and steel. Ultimately, these materials feel too removed from a physical experience, so Villa transitions back to painting. Instead of using brushes, however, he decides to employ spray guns and airbrushes, and in the process discovers a signature motif that will become prevalent in his paintings. "I would watch these colored coils come out of it [the compressor gun] and be mesmerized," the artist later recalls. "I would do yards and yards of these patterns and lose myself for hours."

Summer 1964 • Soon after returning to Los Angeles, Wallace Berman begins experimenting with a Verifax machine, which makes a wet photo negative that can be used to create a positive image. He exploits this primitive copy machine to express the shamanic ideas of transmission, seeing himself as a transmitter of images and ideas, cleverly illustrated through the photograph of a pocket transistor radio from a Sony magazine advertisement. Berman starts running the image in rows and columns, as in a comic strip—namely, Alex Raymond's science-fiction space opera *Flash Gordon*.

This year Berman also publishes the final issue of *Semina*: a simple manila envelope that includes an altered image of Jack Ruby assassinating Lee Harvey Oswald and features a poem by Michael McClure inside. Of the *Semina* project, Jess says, it "doesn't have to come of Europe/New York dialectics; it comes naturally, from youngsters' making of pictures/poem books for the pleasure of friends."

July 1964 • Through her friend Yoko Ono, Shigeko Kubota (1937–2015) connects with the experimental art movement Fluxus, which promotes de-skilling, contingency, and collaboration, and accepts founder George Maciunas's invitation to help her move from Japan to New York. Deciding that their opportunities as women artists in Japan are limited, she and her friend the artist and composer Mieko Shiomi leave their native country, settling in New York. At Maciunas's loft at 159 Canal Street, Kubota meets other Fluxus artists, namely George Brecht, Dick Higgins, Alison Knowles, and Nam June Paik, whom she will marry in 1977.

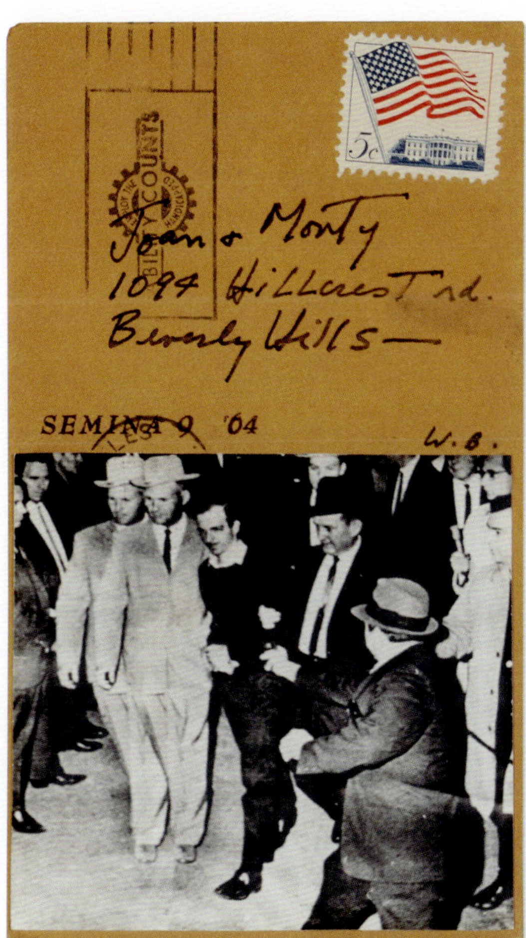

Wallace Berman, *Semina 9*, 1964. Letterpress and collage on cardstock, 5 ⅝ × 3 ⅛ in. (14.3 × 7.9 cm)

My dear Mr. George Maciunas

Thank you very much for your letter to me again and again.

In every day I was very worry which is better to be in Tokyo or to be in New York in order to live as an only artist.

But Now I made up my mind to go to New York. I'm very sorry to put you to a trouble by my act which is to go to New York.

It's my only hope to go to New York in order to live as a artist, but for you, It's no mean without the biggest trouble to you.

But I'd like to touch, to see and to feel something by touching a grop of Filmsing and living by myself in New York.

It's my biggest happening to go to New York "Now", I will not be able to forget to be you in a space of my eternal life.

I will arrive at International (J.E. Kennedy airport) in New York via NW #6 (North west) (orient airlines) At 10:30 pm on 20th (saturday) June.

May I meet you at airport?

be able to

I'm very sorry to eat your time for me but I'd like to blieve to meet you at airport, availing myself of your kindness.

So, as my mark, I will put on a dress and coat of green color.

1st my mark. Now I do believe to be able to meet you at airport. but if It's impossible .... oh. what shall I do!

Best regards to you
See you after few days.
good-bye

Shigeko Kubota.

Shigeko Kubota, *Letter to George Maciunas*, 1964. Ink on paper with collage addition, 38 ¾ × 11 ¹⁄₁₆ in. (98.4 × 28.1 cm)

Over the course of a fifty-year career, Kubota participates in the international expansion of experimental and new media art, pioneering the artistic use of video art as both an innovative practitioner and energetic curator and programmer.

Born in Niigata, Japan, in 1937, Kubota graduated with a degree in teaching from Tokyo University of Education in 1960 while being involved in the city's lively experimental and highly collaborative arts scene, partaking in the performances, concerts, and installations presented by Group Ongaku, a noise-and-sound-art collective that challenges conservative postwar Japanese society. Nearly a decade later, after visiting a pivotal 1969 exhibition of television art at Howard Wise Gallery, New York, Kubota recognizes the artistic possibilities of video. Once she acquires her own equipment in 1970, she sets to work manipulating the technology, producing sculptural works that exploit the malleability, fluidity, and presence of the video medium.

July 2, 1964 • President Lyndon B. Johnson signs the Civil Rights Act of 1964 into law with Martin Luther King Jr. and other civil rights leaders present, fulfilling the call made by former president John F. Kennedy the year before, five months prior to his assassination, for Congress to pass a comprehensive civil rights bill. Among other things, the law creates the Equal Employment Opportunity Commission to address race and sex discrimination in the workplace; authorizes federal intervention to ensure the desegregation of schools and other public facilities; and restricts the use of literacy tests as a requirement for voter registration.

September 16–October 10, 1964 • Lucas Samaras opens his first solo exhibition at New York's Green Gallery, for which he moves the entire contents of his bedroom into the gallery space. Blurring the boundary between private and public or, in Samaras's own words, producing "intolerable invasions of my privacy," the artist transforms the gallery space into a de facto large box displaying the intimacies of his life. The self-exposure of *Room #1* sets the stage for "the drama of the self" that Samaras will explore in his Polaroid auto-portraits at the end of the 1960s.

Fall 1964 • An artist of Kiowa and Caddo heritage raised in rural Oklahoma, T. C. Cannon (1946–1978) attends the Institute of American Indian Arts (IAIA), which had first been established two years prior as an experimental arts-based high school for Native American and Alaskan Native students before becoming a university. Responding to years of assimilationist-

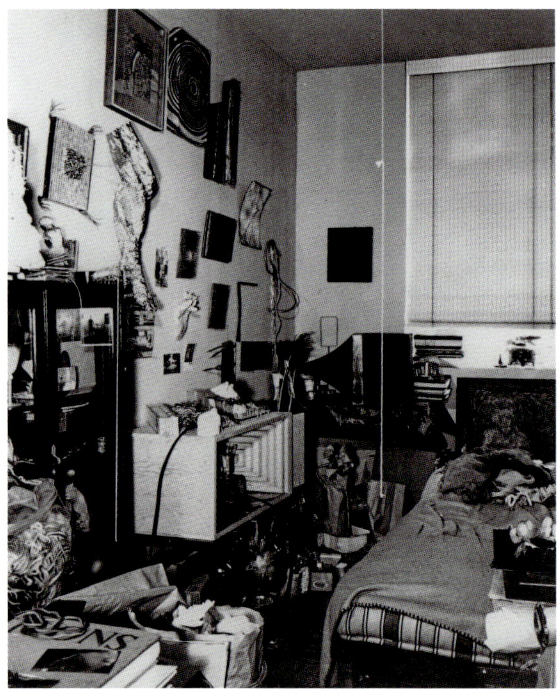

Lucas Samaras, Green Gallery, New York, 1964, with Samaras's *Room #1* (1964)

focused, government-run boarding schools for Native American children, IAIA's teaching philosophy is revolutionary at the time, emphasizing artistic freedom and encouraging students to embrace their own cultural identities while at the same time engage with the political and artistic currents of the moment. Many teachers use an apprentice-style approach and work alongside their students, including Fritz Scholder, who also teaches through a process of exchange between instructor and student that involves social commentary—something Cannon embraces in his own work from this early point. Scholder believes that "the Indian had . . . become caught in a tourist pleasing cliché of a flat style of painting." Before the early 1960s, the romanticization of Native American craftsmanship and the establishment of an ethnographic market by white collectors

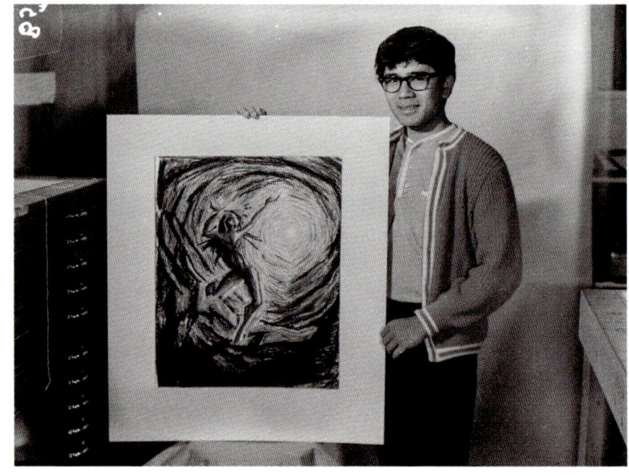

T. C. Cannon with student work, c. 1964

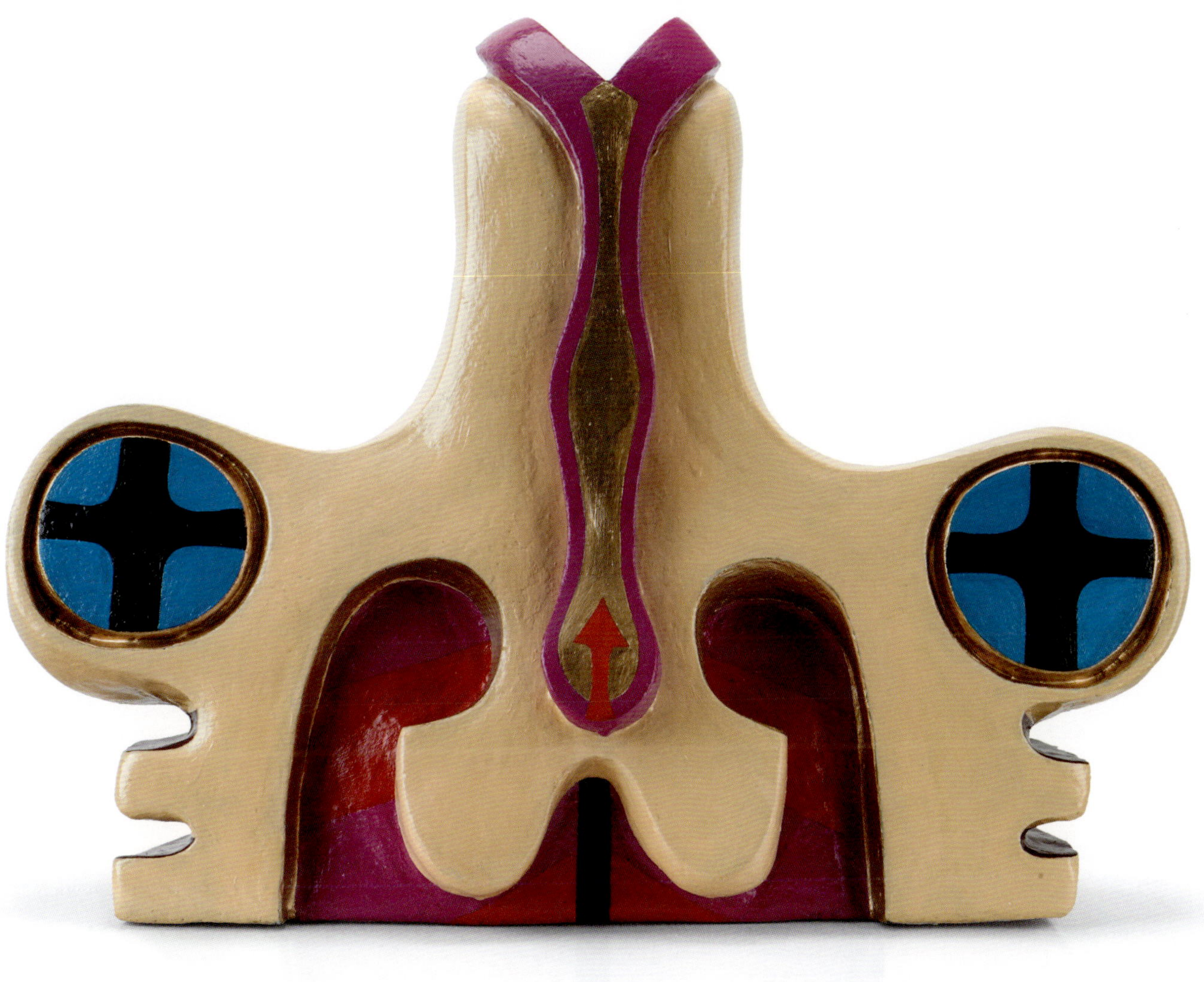

Judy Chicago, *Bigamy*, 1964. Acrylic on stoneware, 24 × 18 × 6 in. (61 × 45.7 × 15.2 cm). Private collection

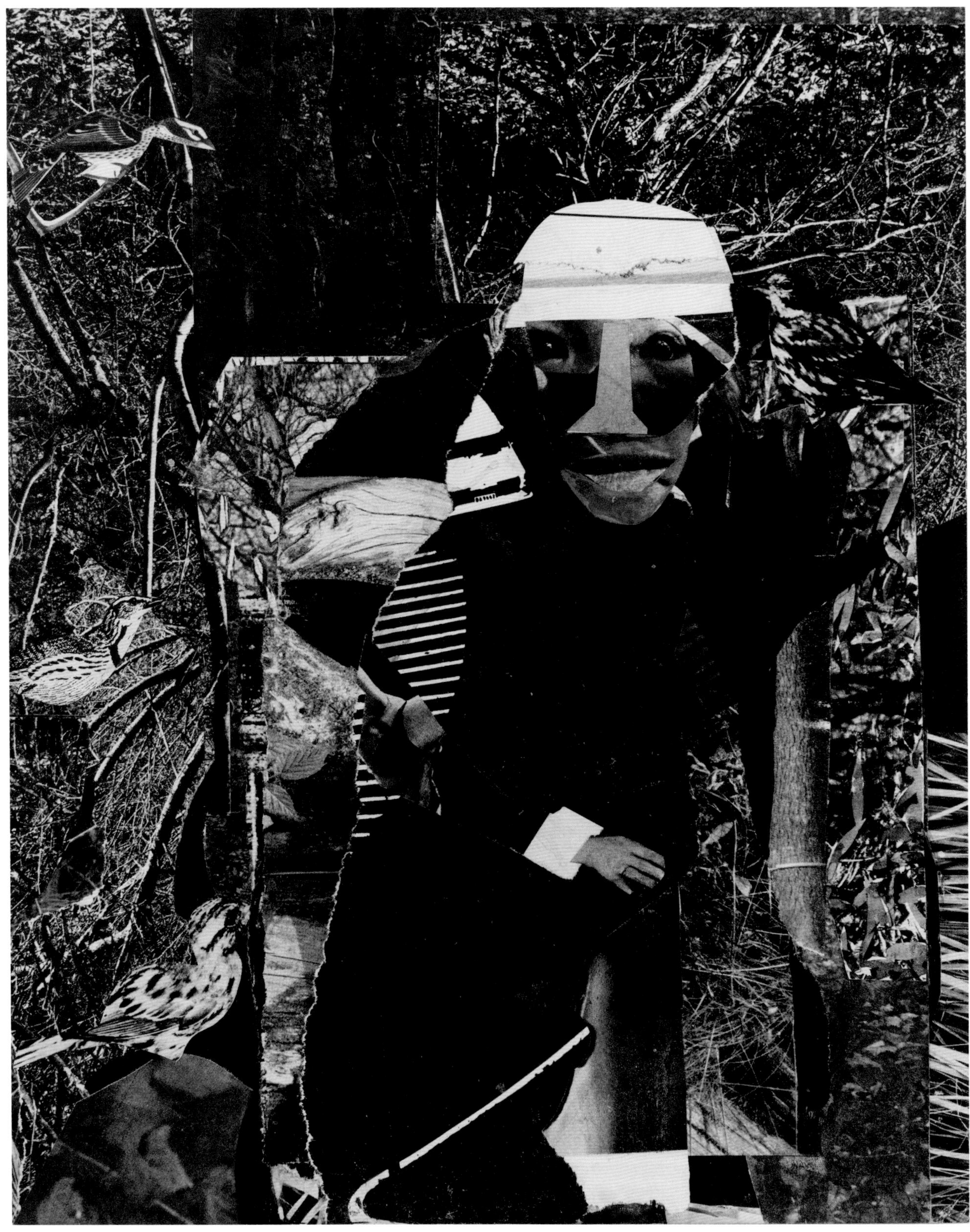

Romare Bearden, *Conjur Woman*, 1964. Photo projection on paper, 64 × 50 in. (162.6 × 127 cm). The Studio Museum in Harlem, New York; gift of the artist 1972.5

conspired to severely restrict the freedom of Native American artists to explore their own artistic paths. Scholder encourages his students at IAIA to break free from these constraints.

Within a few years at IAIA, Cannon has found his own approach to painting, one that focuses on representing the unique qualities of individual personalities, often as an antidote to the harmful Native American stereotypes and the co-option of "Indianness" or "Indian mystique" that is pervasive, particularly in the counterculture of the time.

October 6–24, 1964 • Romare Bearden's exhibition *Projections* is on view at Cordier & Ekstrom Gallery, New York. The show includes twenty-one black-and-white photomontages and photostats—such as *Conjur Woman* (1964)—that feature scenes of Black life in North Carolina, Harlem, and Pittsburgh. At the gallery, each image is displayed as a small-scale montage and as an enlarged photostat reproduction. Using existing photographs that depict quotidian joys and struggles gives Bearden the chance to physically deconstruct, improvise, and reconstruct the richness of everyday Black experience in the United States through an approach similar to that of improvisational jazz. Although jazz had influenced his earlier paintings as well, Bearden had first begun working on collage in this way at gatherings of the Spiral Group, bringing magazine and newspaper clippings to the group's meetings perhaps with the hope of creating collective works. In a *Time* magazine article published during the show, the artist remarks, "As a Negro, I do not need to go looking for 'happenings,' the absurd, or the surreal, because I have seen things out of my studio window on 125th Street that neither Dalí nor Beckett nor Ionesco could have thought possible." *Projections* is subsequently presented in Washington, DC, at the Corcoran Gallery, Bearden's first solo museum show. The success of these works allows him to create art full-time, and he leaves behind his career as a social worker.

October 6–31, 1964 • After eight years in Europe, Peter Saul returns to New York to visit his exhibition *Recent Paintings* at Allan Frumkin Gallery. Whereas artists such as Saul who made images with a gestural verve were initially included in what has become known as "Pop art," by now such work is an outlier among the airtight images and clean surfaces of New York Pop. It is a development that confounds Saul, and even though he isn't interested in the cool remove of irony, he resolves to leave his Expressionist leanings behind in favor of seamless surfaces. Continued on page 123

PRESSING UPON THE EDGES OF THE REAL: SURREALISM AS BLACK RADICAL AESTHETIC METHOD

SAMPADA ARANKE

As I was taught it, Surrealism as it emerged from a modernist arts scene in 1920s France was attached to a generalized practice of prioritizing the automatic aspects of unthought, those elements of the life of the mind that are just out of reach, obscured by the calcified behaviors and practices that acculturate us into the normative conditions of everyday life. These automatic aspects might be called *drives*—the pesky desires, fears, attachments, and repulsions that lie dormant deep in our psyches. A lesser theorized aspect of white, Western Surrealist

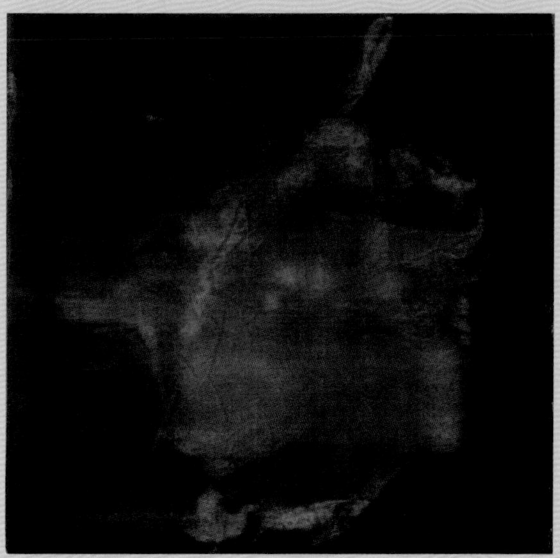

Fig. 1. Jack Whitten, *Head IV Lynching*, 1964. Acrylic on canvas, 11 × 11 in. (27.9 × 27.9 cm)

investments includes the very real fact that those automatic aspects might also be representative of what Frantz Fanon called the "weight of melanin" that internalizes a hierarchy along racial lines.[1]

The unconscious that Surrealism aimed to access was indeed a *racial* unconscious, one that appeared in the more palatable paintings of artists for whom the nonwhite body was at once delectable and deplorable, desirable and disposable. Much like the colonial practices that made Europe and the systemic racisms that made the United States, these historical artistic practices created images and imaginaries that forever condition the way we see or don't see nonwhite subjects. While Surrealists were indeed the rebellious younger siblings of these prior artists, their tendency to fall into the trappings of romanticizing nonwhite cultures and their histories shapes what I hold on to as a more complex engagement with a history of modern art, one that was indeed messier and more dislodged, fractured, sensual, and psychosocial than anything before it. Indeed, Surrealism was not the property of that small European cohort nor of the US artists who were exposed to its architects via early exhibitions encouraged by Julien Levy in the 1930s and '40s.[2] As such, Surrealism's promise as a method that could dislodge the normative conceits of modernism was activated in Black radical traditions in ways that deformed, critiqued, or even undid a commitment to modernism itself.[3] Black surrealist practices tended to work from the position of a live critique

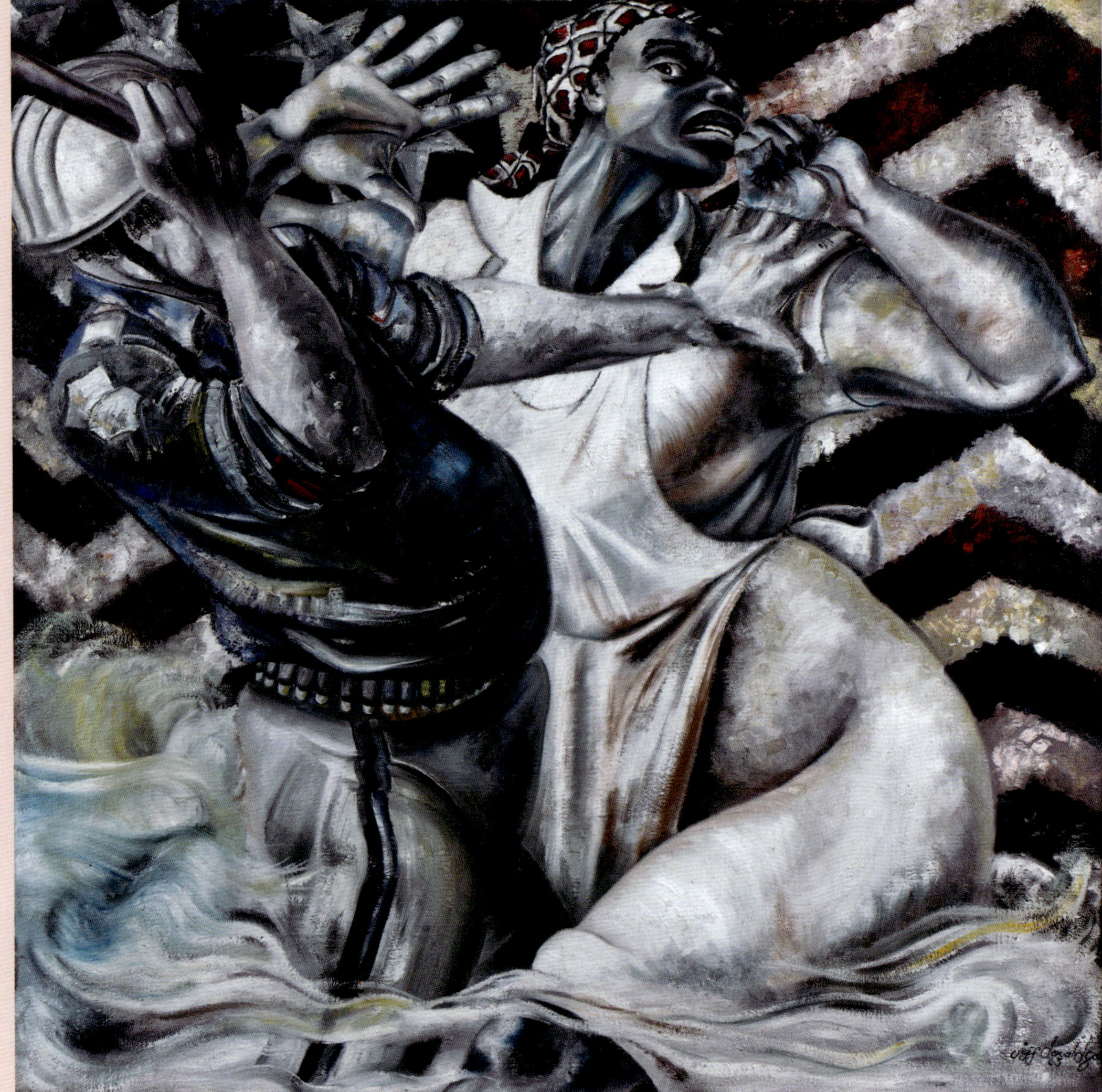

Fig. 2. Jeff Donaldson, *Aunt Jemima and the Pillsbury Doughboy*, 1963. Oil on linen, 48 × 48 in. (121.9 × 121.9 cm)

of violence that continued on into the 1960s and '70s and took a range of forms, from political organizing to art making and beyond (figs. 1 and 2).

Departing from that worldview, part of what constitutes "the real" is the violent terror of the Middle Passage where Black people were trafficked and transformed into enslaved subjects. The very *real* condition of that originary violence that made the modern remains well into the contemporary. Indeed, the apocalyptic anti-Black practices that surround Black life press upon the edges of "the real." So much so that I want to follow Black Arts Movement architect Amiri Baraka's lead in insisting that Black life is itself *over and above, extra* real, indeed *sur-*real.[4] Turning to poet Henry Dumas's writings as an exemplary illustration of what Baraka calls the *Afrosurreal*:

It is as though the whole world we inhabit rests on the bottom of the ocean, harnessed by memory, language, image to that "railroad of human bones" at the bottom of the Atlantic Ocean.

But in this genre the most violently antagonistic of contradictions, colors, shapes animates the personalities, settings, language of the work.[5]

Baraka firmly locates the violent antagonisms that structure Black life as at once historical (a whole world unaccounted for at the bottom of the ocean) and aesthetic (colors, shapes, settings, language). In other words, the aesthetic is always already political for Baraka because any and all forms of Black life are wedded to imagining and inhabiting the impossible, maybe even the unimaginable. What Dumas brought to poetry, Romare Bearden brought to the visual arts, according to Baraka.[6] Bearden's collage works do offer the possibility of what theorist Fred Moten calls "the cut"—the inhabited space that both fractures and adheres.[7] In a work such as *Jazz (Chicago) Grand Terrace Ballroom* (fig. 3), Bearden's use of collage embodies the artist's singular use of the form. His composition features an ensemble of jazz musicians playing in what feels like an intimate venue, horns and drums and hands and suits fill the surface, overlapping and sharing space. In this scene, space is compressed, giving the sensation of a raucous sound, a cacophonous visual and sonic collectivity. We are asked to consider the role of this collective at every level—from how it makes the individual subject to how it yields the singular musical note. *Jazz* is indeed a prime example of how Bearden deploys surrealism as a Black radical aesthetic method.

Take the artist's transformation of photography into photomontage and then photostat. Rather than reproduce a photographic scene, Bearden cuts it up. Each figure and object is composed of many, as original photographic source materials are cut, pasted, and arranged to form a new collective. These original sources come from a range of materials—popular magazines, scientific journals, newspapers, and commercial catalogs. As Bearden himself once reflected on his process:

In most instances in creating a picture, I use many disparate elements to form either a figure, or part of a background. I build my faces, for example, from parts of African masks, animal eyes, marbles, mossy vegetation, [and corn]. . . . I then have my small original works enlarged so the mosaiclike joinings will not be so apparent, after which I finish the larger painting. I have found when some detail, such as a hand or eye, is taken out of its original context and is fractured and integrated into a different space and form configuration it acquires a plastic quality it did not have in the photograph.[8]

Bearden's particular use of "the cut" is surrealist in practice, as the artist is interested in the potential of juxtaposition in opening up new associations, sensations, and meanings. In order to achieve these "mosaiclike joinings," Bearden emphasizes when the seam—the place where two (or more) source materials are joined together—is more visible (as is the case in the photomontage) or when it recedes (as is the case in the photostat reproductions, e.g., p. 120). As such, the seam is representative of where multiple sources come together yet stay separate; it is the space that at once preserves the autonomy of the subject and creates dependence between subjects. We can abstract this procedural quality out to be more representative of an aesthetic politic in Bearden's project more broadly. In

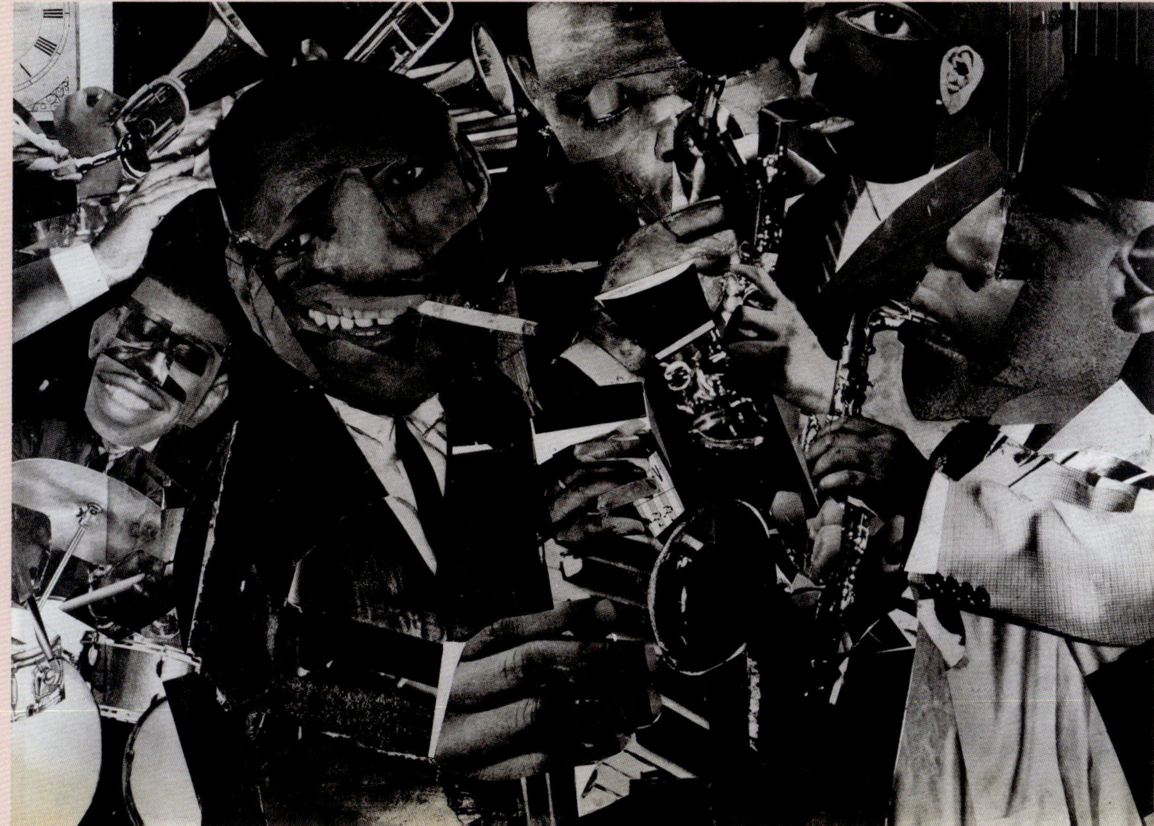

Fig. 3. Romare Bearden, *Jazz (Chicago) Grand Terrace Ballroom*, 1964. Photostat mounted on board, 49 ¾ × 68 ¼ in. (126.4 × 173.4 cm)

works such as *Jazz,* Bearden invites us to consider Blackness as multiple, as violently cut and carefully joined together, as richly made up of contexts and histories that remain unseen and yet spill over in their perceptual abundance in front of us.

Bearden's work gives us a sense of *a composition of a people*, that subjectivity is made and remade in ways that deform the violences of realism towards surrealist ends. What we're asked to hold is violence as destructive and constructive, an understanding of Black life that exceeds, overwhelms, and creates in the face of the real. This kind of surrealism is at once immediate and lasting; it is Baraka's description of a "very broken quality, almost to abstraction" and is indeed that extra-real world that Dumas wrote in the form of a poem he sent to Baraka in 1966 called "Mosaic Harlem."[9] In it, the poet lingers on the form of a question, a refrain he returns to as a form of collective inquiry embodied in the "I" and the "we":

what news from the bottle?
rats shedding hair in ice
nodding veins filled with snow
blackeyed peas, grits, red rice

through the broken glass I hear a breaking age
what song do we gurgle?

NOTES
1   Frantz Fanon, *Black Skin, White Masks* (New York: Grove Press, 2008), 128.
2   Julien Levy Gallery was a premiere institution for the collection and dissemination of Surrealist art in the United States from 1931 through 1949. For more, see Julien Levy, *Surrealism* [1936] (New York: Da Capo Press, 1995); Martica Sawin, "Surrealism in America," *Grove Art Online*, February 24, 2010: https://www.oxfordartonline.com /groveart/view/10.1093/gao/9781884446054.001.0001/oao -9781884446054-e-7002086108; and Kristine Somerville, "Julien Levy: Making It Surreal," *The Missouri Review* 39, no. 1 (2016): 75–84.
3   For more, see Houston A. Baker, *Modernism and the Harlem Renaissance* (Chicago: University of Chicago Press, 1987); Lori Cole, "*Légitime défense*: From Communism and Surrealism to Caribbean Self-Definition," *Journal of Surrealism and the Americas* 4, no. 1 (2010): 15–30; Terri Francis, "Introduction: The No-Theory Chant of Afrosurrealism," *Black Camera* 5, no. 1 (Fall 2013): 95–112; Brent Hayes Edwards, "The Ethnics of Surrealism," *Transition* 78 (1998): 84–135; D. Scot Miller, "Afrosurreal Manifesto: Black Is the New Black—a 21st-Century Manifesto," *Black Camera* 5, no. 1 (Fall 2013): 113–17; Franklin Rosemont and Robin D. G. Kelley, eds., *Black, Brown, & Beige: Surrealist Writings from Africa and the Diaspora* (Austin: University of Texas Press, 2009); and Rochelle Spencer, *AfroSurrealism: The African Diaspora's Surrealist Fiction* (New York: Routledge, 2020).
4   Amiri Baraka, "Henry Dumas: Afro-Surreal Expressionist," *Black American Literature Forum* 22, no. 2 (1988): 164.
5   Ibid., 166.
6   Ibid., 164.
7   Fred Moten, *In the Break: The Aesthetics of the Black Radical Tradition* (Minneapolis: University of Minnesota Press, 2023).
8   Romare Bearden to Michael Gibson, June 15, 1975. Romare Bearden papers, Archives of American Art, Smithsonian Institution, Washington, DC. Cited in Myron Schwartzman, "Romare Bearden Sees in a Memory," *Artforum* 22, no. 9 (May 1984): 64–70.
9   Henry Dumas to LeRoi Jones (Amiri Baraka), c. 1966. Henry Dumas papers, Sc MG 310, Schomburg Center for Research in Black Culture, Manuscripts, Archives and Rare Books Division, New York Public Library.

October 13–31, 1964 • Paul Thek first exhibits his *Technological Reliquaries* in a solo exhibition at Stable Gallery, New York, just a few months after joining the gallery. "Reality plus," is what critic Lil Picard in *Das Kunstwerk* calls Thek's visceral "crucified meat" encased within their minimalist, hygienic Plexiglas specimen boxes. "Perfectly done, insanely perverted and contrived. One wonders why this very young and able craftsman and graphic artist is obsessed with a scientific hell of reality."

November 10–28, 1964 • Robert Arneson's first New York exhibition is held at the Allan Stone Gallery and features toilets, urinals, and ceramic vessels. In the last couple of years, he has been working with common objects like soda bottles and trophies as a way to create opportunities for allusions and interventions with a touch that defies both Expressionism and tightly finished craft. The toilets, which he calls "the ultimate ceramic," deliberately push the bounds of taste. They are perhaps the rudest and most aggressive means of breaking away from the ceramic establishment while having fun not only with the art-historical potential—think Marcel Duchamp's 1917 *Fountain*—but also with ways to imbue many surfaces and forms with double and triple meanings that include and go beyond "bathroom humor." During the next two years,

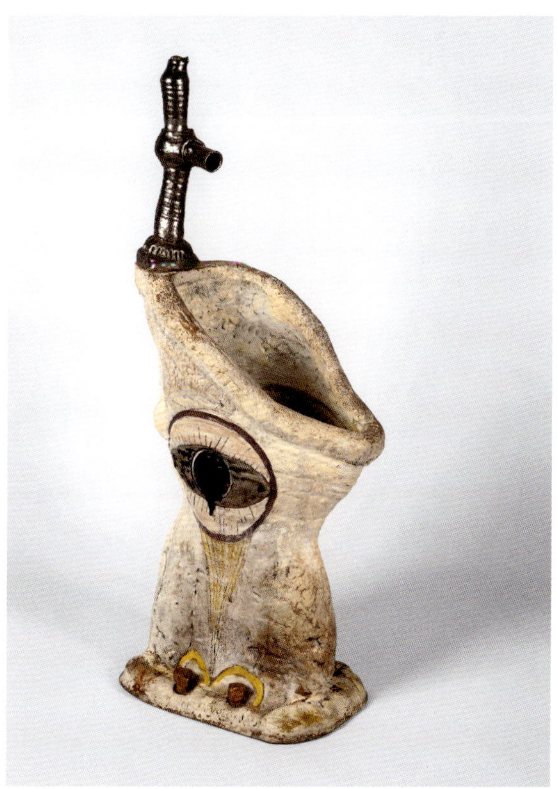

Robert Arneson, *Untitled (Urinal)*, c. 1963. Glazed ceramic, 46 ¾ × 23 × 13 ½ in. (118.7 × 58.4 × 34.3 cm)

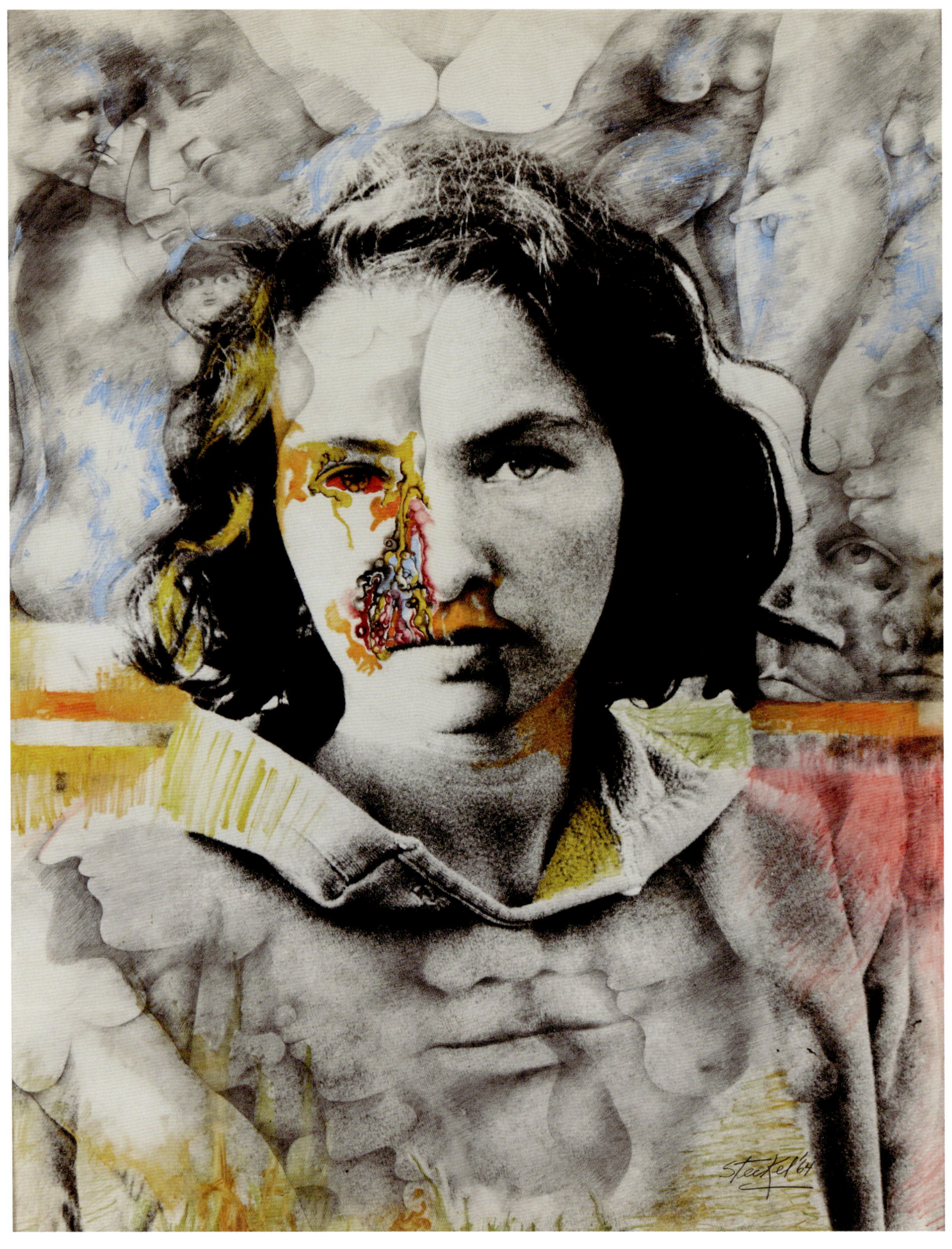

Anita Steckel, *The Big Rip-Up*, 1964. Paint and colored pencil on photograph, 30 × 23 in. (76.2 × 58.4 cm). Collection of Beth Rudin DeWoody

Poster for *Yes on 10*, curated by Melvin Edwards, Little Gallery, San Bernardino Valley College, CA, 1964

Arneson will move on to employ Surrealist techniques to defamiliarize everyday items pulled from a Montgomery Ward catalog, including a toaster and a typewriter. The shimmering surfaces of these works are achieved by applying china paints and metallic lusters to white, low-fire clay.

November 19, 1964 • Eva Hesse is reading *The Second Sex* (1949) and notes in her diary: "Simone De B[eauvoir] writes woman is object—has been made to feel this from first experiences of awareness." Hesse is living with her husband, Tom Doyle, in Kettwig, Germany, on a yearlong artist's residency. Not long after reading *The Second Sex*, Hesse abandons her practice of drawing and painting and begins to make reliefs that mix painted papier-mâché surfaces with materials such as wire sourced from her studio in a former textile factory. *Ringaround Arosie* is her first relief, made in March 1965. Although abstract, it references the body. In a letter to Sol LeWitt, Hesse describes this piece as being like a "breast and penis." Hesse's proto-feminist awareness, heightened by reading and experience, propels her to make a series of sculptures over the next six years that are at once abstract and

yet which vaguely suggest the body, anticipating her subsequent sculptural practice.

November 22–December 10, 1964 • *Yes on 10* is on view at the Little Gallery at San Bernardino Valley College, organized by Melvin Edwards (b. 1937). The exhibition includes work by Ed Bereal, Daniel LaRue Johnson, and Ron Miyashiro, friends of Edwards since 1962. While still in school at the University of Southern California (USC), Edwards organizes the show, featuring works by these and seven other Los Angeles–based artists. The title refers to Proposition 10, a measure on the November ballot that proposed repealing a provision requiring proceeds from the sale of state-owned land be kept in a perpetual fund to be used solely to support state schools. A "yes" vote advocated for the release of these funds for additional public uses, and the proposition passed with a small majority. During the early 1960s, Edwards participates in protests, particularly regarding housing issues, and develops a sense of how art can be employed in the fight for civil rights.

Edwards was born in Houston and grew up between Texas and Dayton, Ohio. He moved to Los Angeles after graduating from high school and enrolled at Los Angeles City College before transferring to USC, where he majors in art and plays football. He focuses primarily on painting, gaining some public recognition in this medium, yet he craves a more physical engagement with art. In early 1960, he is inspired to explore sculpture after seeing the work of John Chamberlain and David Smith in the exhibition *Recent Sculpture U.S.A.* at the Los Angeles County Museum of Art. He approaches fellow USC student George Baker to teach him the basics of welding, a process that is attractive to Edwards for its industrial utility as well as its ability to transform discarded metals into new sculptural forms.

December 9, 1964–January 31, 1965: The Whitney Museum of American Art's *1964 Annual Exhibition of Contemporary American Sculpture* features a number of California-based artists, such as Jeremy Anderson, Bruce Conner, and Edward Kienholz, as well as continuing to present the work of many New York artists, such as Marisol, Claes Oldenburg, Lucas Samaras, Mike Todd, and H. C. Westermann.

December 1964 • After a cross-country drive following his New York exhibition, Peter Saul settles near his recently widowed mother in Mill Valley, California. Unaware of the artistic ferment in the Bay Area and Central Valley, he begins

making his series of Vietnam paintings, the origins of which he will later recall:

> The idea of Vietnam pictures occurred to me on a train, reading *Newsweek* (or *Time*), Nov. 1964 [in Ohio]. My first efforts were later that month (our car having finally arrived from Rome, we returned to NY to get it + started driving to SF, where we intended to live)—in Joplin, Missouri, where my son got sick + we were laid up a few days. I discovered "dayglo" colors at the drugstore there (kids' crayons) + made a few drawings of "yellow" (commie Chinese perhaps) superwomen beating up GIs + brandishing hammer + sickle. In spring 1965, when [Allan] Frumkin visited me in Mill Valley, Calif., I showed him some more impressive crayon, ink + color pencil pictures of "pro-commie" or "anti-Vietnam" subjects on 40-by-60-inch cardboard + he said "Now that's really interesting!" So I made a whole series, which were shown in both his NY + Chicago galleries (around '66).

Saul's arrival in Mill Valley does not go unnoticed, as William T. Wiley also lives there and knows Saul's work from reproductions and from the 1963 group exhibition *New Directions* at the San Francisco Museum of Modern Art. Wiley is the center of an active arts scene in Northern California in those years and introduces Saul to peers and friends in the area and in nearby Davis, California. This community of artists, which includes William Allan, Robert Arneson, William Geis, Robert Hudson, and Bruce Nauman, does not share an aesthetic so much as a common set of values emphasizing wit, invention, private languages, and craft.

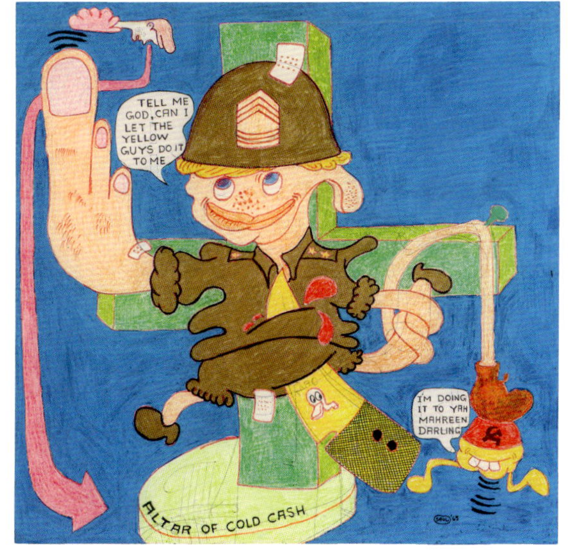

Peter Saul, *Altar of Cold Cash*, 1965. Watercolor and gouache on board, 30 × 30 in. (76.2 × 76.2 cm)

1965

February 16–March 25, 1965 • Anita Steckel's work appears in the exhibition *Contemporary Erotica* at New York's Van Bovenkamp Gallerie alongside that of artists such as Martha Edelheit and Lee Lozano. The same year, in addition to publishing collages in the underground newspaper *East Village Other*, she participates in *Hetero Is* at the New York City Arts Theater Association Gallery in December, earning herself a reputation as an "erotic artist." Her deft blend of handwork and mechanical reproductions brings a sense of danger to her art, as though the "reality" she ascribes to photography is also capable of arousing more than just aesthetic interest, which in the mid-1960s can result in an obscenity bust for a gallery.

1965 • Luchita Hurtado develops her *I Am* series of self-portraits while living in Los Angeles in the 1960s. Experimenting in her studio in Santa Monica Canyon, Hurtado employs an unlikely perspective in a self-portrait: looking down. She represents her body as it appears extremely foreshortened, a practice she will continue for the next several decades. She adds the textures and patterns of rugs, tables, and objects, subtly distorting scale to produce confounding compositions. These paintings defamiliarize the female body: from above, her breasts, knees, and feet appear monumental, even mountainous. The

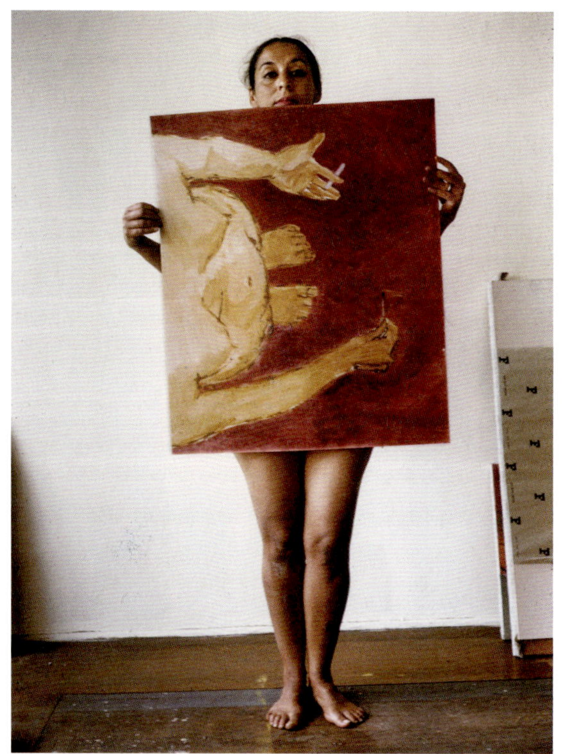

Luchita Hurtado in her studio with an unfinished version of *Untitled* (1971), Santa Monica, CA, c. 1968

artist explains, "This is a landscape, this is the world, this is all you have . . . you live there, this is where you live." The vertiginous perspective radically eliminates the pictorial space between artist and muse, a historically gendered and sexually charged field that offers particularly rich territory for Surrealists such as André Breton and Man Ray to explore across media. Hurtado herself acknowledges a "surrealist undercurrent" to her work but disavows any strict affiliation with the movement or a programmatic approach to her painting.

February 21, 1965 • Celebrated Black nationalist and former Nation of Islam minister and national spokesperson Malcolm X is assassinated at the age of thirty-nine during a speech for the Organization of Afro-American Unity at the Audubon Ballroom in Manhattan. Three men shoot him more than twenty times as he appears on stage. The week before, his house in Queens is firebombed, forcing him, his pregnant wife, and four daughters to flee in the middle of the night.

March 30–May 2, 1965 • A few months before graduating from the University of Southern California and joining the faculty at the Chouinard

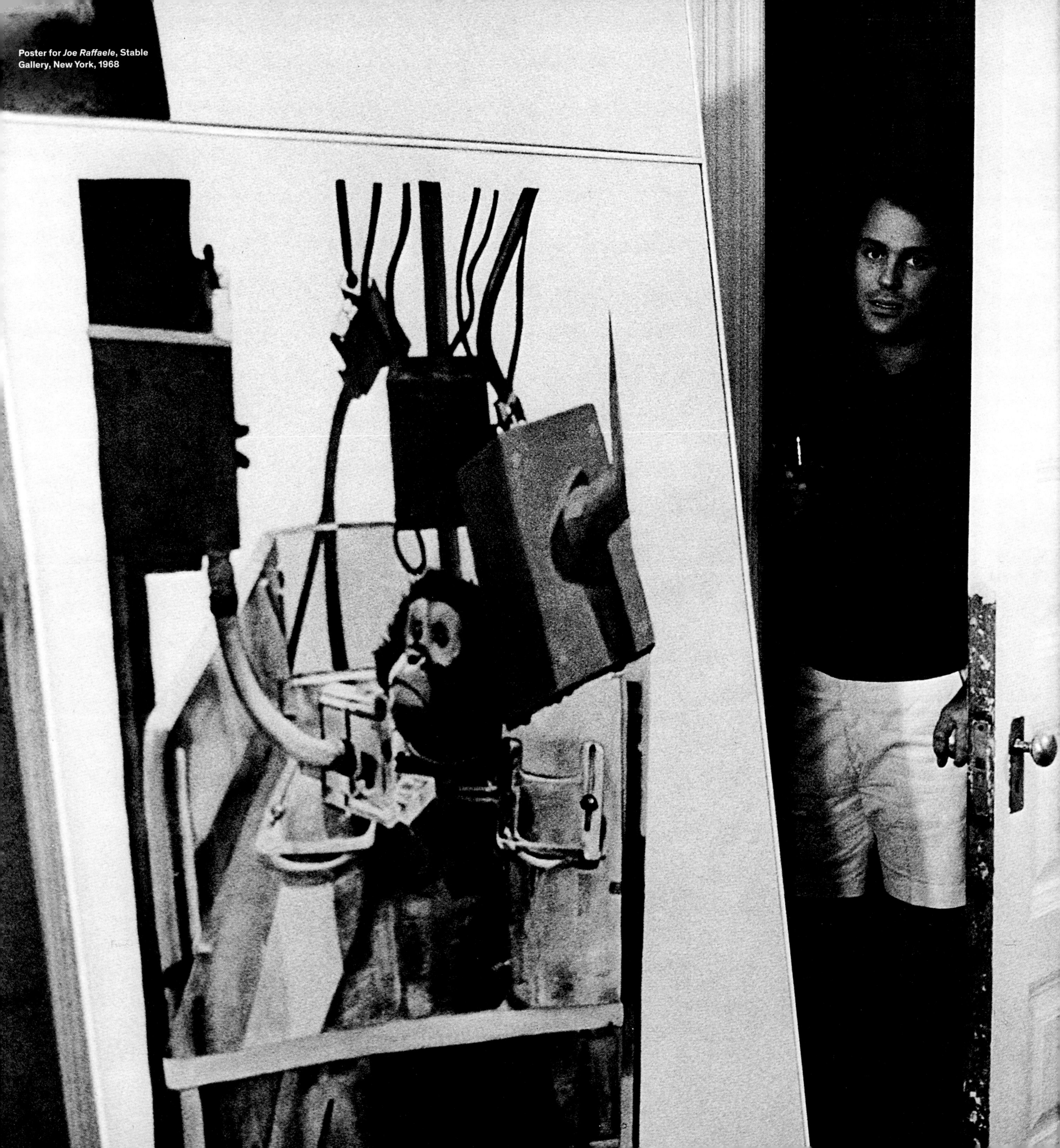

Poster for *Joe Raffaele*, Stable
Gallery, New York, 1968

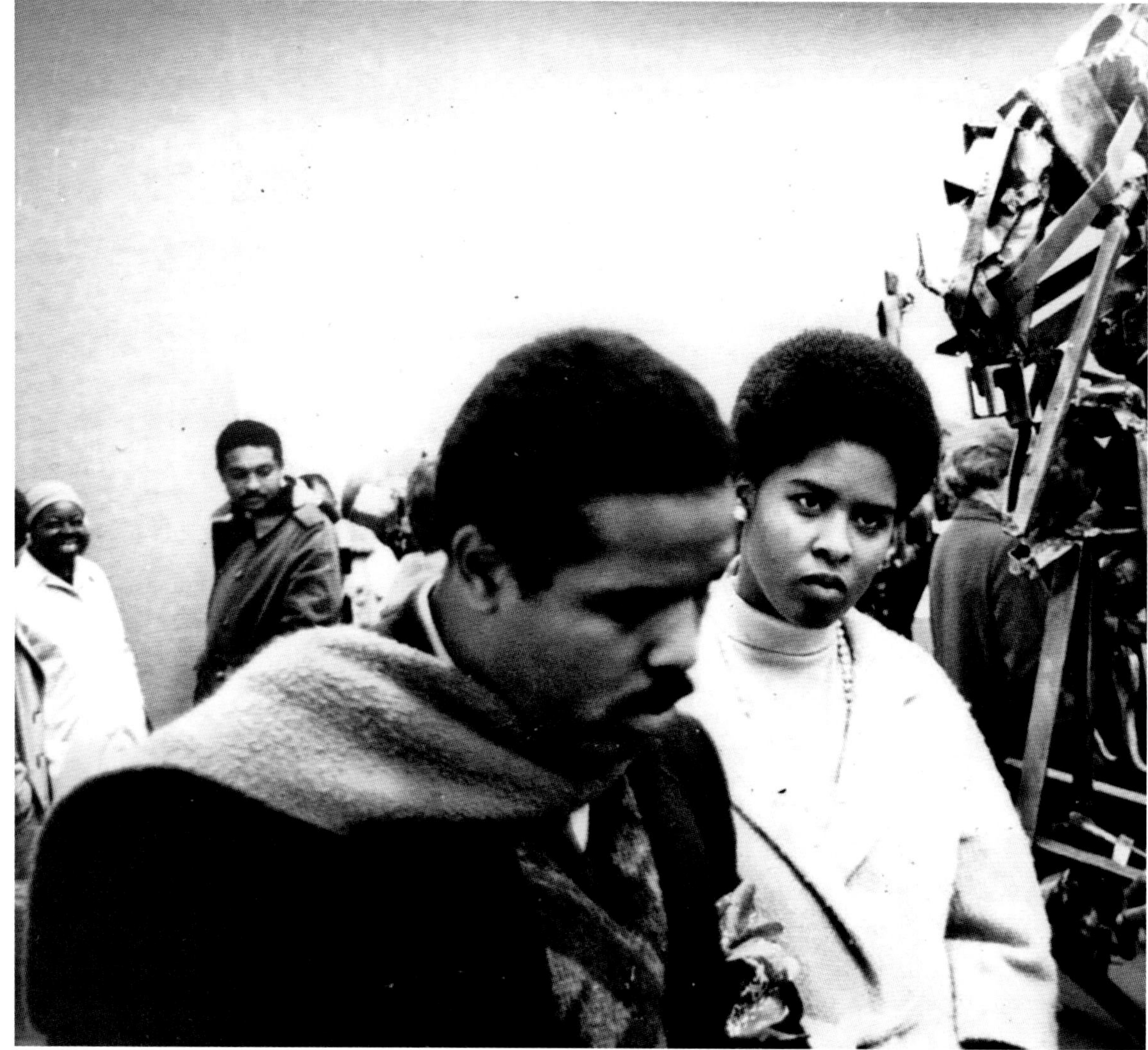

Ruth Waddy, Daniel LaRue Johnson, Melvin Edwards, and Anne Talltree at the opening of *Melvin Edwards*, Santa Barbara Museum of Art, 1965, with Edwards's *The Lifted X* (1965)

Art Institute, Melvin Edwards opens his first solo exhibition, at the Santa Barbara Museum of Art, and shows his *Lynch Fragments* for the first time. A series of welded relief sculptures that he works on from 1963 until 1967, the *Lynch Fragments* are Edwards's response to the 1962 killing of Nation of Islam member Ronald Stokes by the Los Angeles Police Department. Edwards places the killing in the context of Ralph Ginzburg's *100 Years of Lynchings* (1962), a compilation of newspaper accounts of lynchings across the United States, and the resulting *Lynch Fragments*—resolutely abstract despite the directness of their title—allude to this violent history rather than explicitly depicting it.

The *Lynch Fragments* are formed from metal objects such as hammers, chains, and gears, or what Edwards describes as "familiar-form" objects. As Catherine Craft suggests, these items "can also be used to *make* a sculpture—or build a house, or be taken up as weapons by intended victims as readily as aggressors." Edwards breaks down the symbolism of the chain in particular:

"[A chain is a] steel rope, a metal flexible line. You can move it, and it loops and hangs and suspends. Sometimes it's a connector. On one level, it's just a material that can be used a lot of ways. Sometimes I use it so much you can't see it. It's just steel, that melted steel. . . . [T]he word chain is the device for connecting. If you refine chains, they become love. Chain of love, chain of fools, chain, chain, chain. There are several songs about that. It's also symbolically chains of kinship linkage. The problem is not the chain; it's how people use it."

Spring 1965 • After moving into a vast new studio on East 14th Street, Claes Oldenburg begins working on a series of "proposed colossal monuments." In his notes, he initially defines such a monument as an object from *The Street* or *Store* that is "magnified and set into appropriate locations in the New York landscape." He proposes several "obstacle monuments," including a "war monument" that completely blocks the intersection of Canal and Broadway with "a square slab of butter in the slit (in the shape of a cross)" constructed from a "concrete block (weighing about 500 million pounds), inscribed with names of war heroes." Oldenburg starts exhibiting his proposed monuments right away; the first drawings are on view in May, in the group show *Recent Work by Arman, Dine, Fahstrom, Marisol, Oldenburg, Segal* at Sidney Janis Gallery. A few months later, in early summer, Oldenburg makes the political horror-comedy film *Birth of the Flag* (1965) with Lucas Samaras, Carolee Schneemann, and Stan VanDerBeek.

1965 • Driving at night, Mel Casas (1929–2014) is surprised by the sight of a drive-in movie screen in the distance, and it inspires him to begin his series of *Humanscape* paintings, each a rectangular screen-like image contrasted with a counter-drama in the foreground. The series, which will come to total 153 paintings made between 1965 and 1989, addresses sex, race, class, art, and every topic the artist can think of. In a statement for his 1976 exhibition at the Contemporary Arts Museum Houston, Casas will explain: "HUMAN SCAPES: Visual Conundrums, images are manipulated to create contradictory visual questions. A riddle whose answer depends [on] or refers to a pun and has only a conjectural answer. Contradictory visual perceptions are visualized more readily simultaneously. Interpretation of the imagery takes place at different levels but only one can be verified at a given moment. The conundrum plays with our cultural concepts, with our cultural vision."

Casas had been born and raised in El Paso, Texas. He is awarded a Purple Heart for his service in the Korean War, and after returning to the United States, he attends Texas Western College and the University of the Americas in

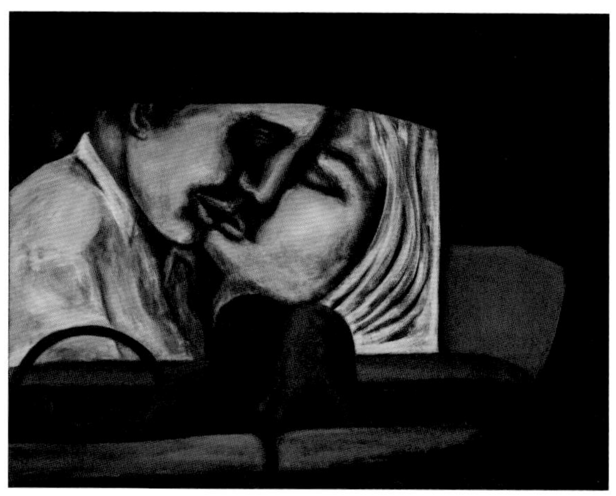

Mel Casas, *Humanscape 2*, 1965. Acrylic on canvas, 48 × 60 in. (121.9 × 152.4 cm)

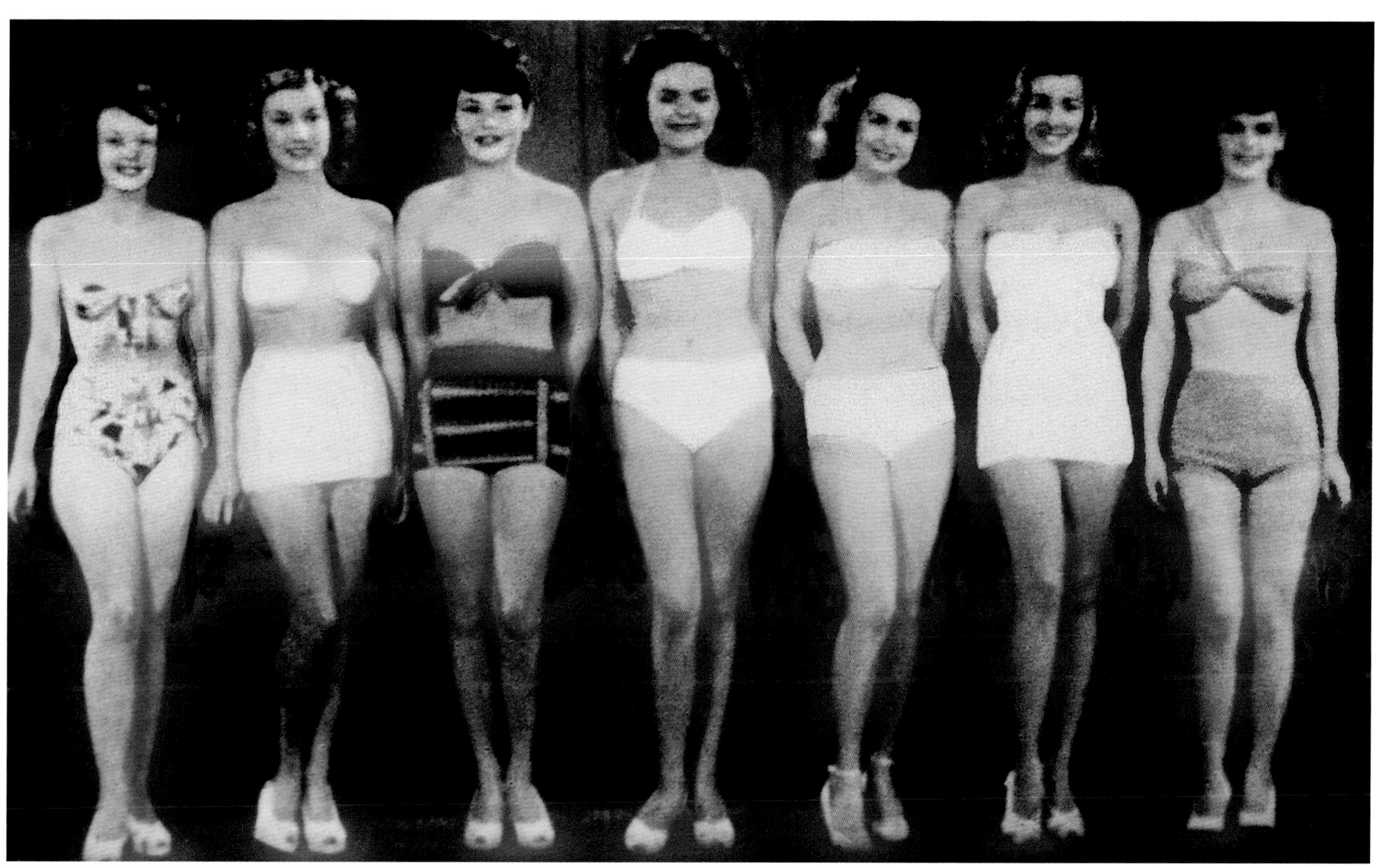

Gunvor Nelson and Dorothy Wiley, *Schmeerguntz*, 1965. 16mm film, black-and-white, sound; 15 min. Filmform, Stockholm

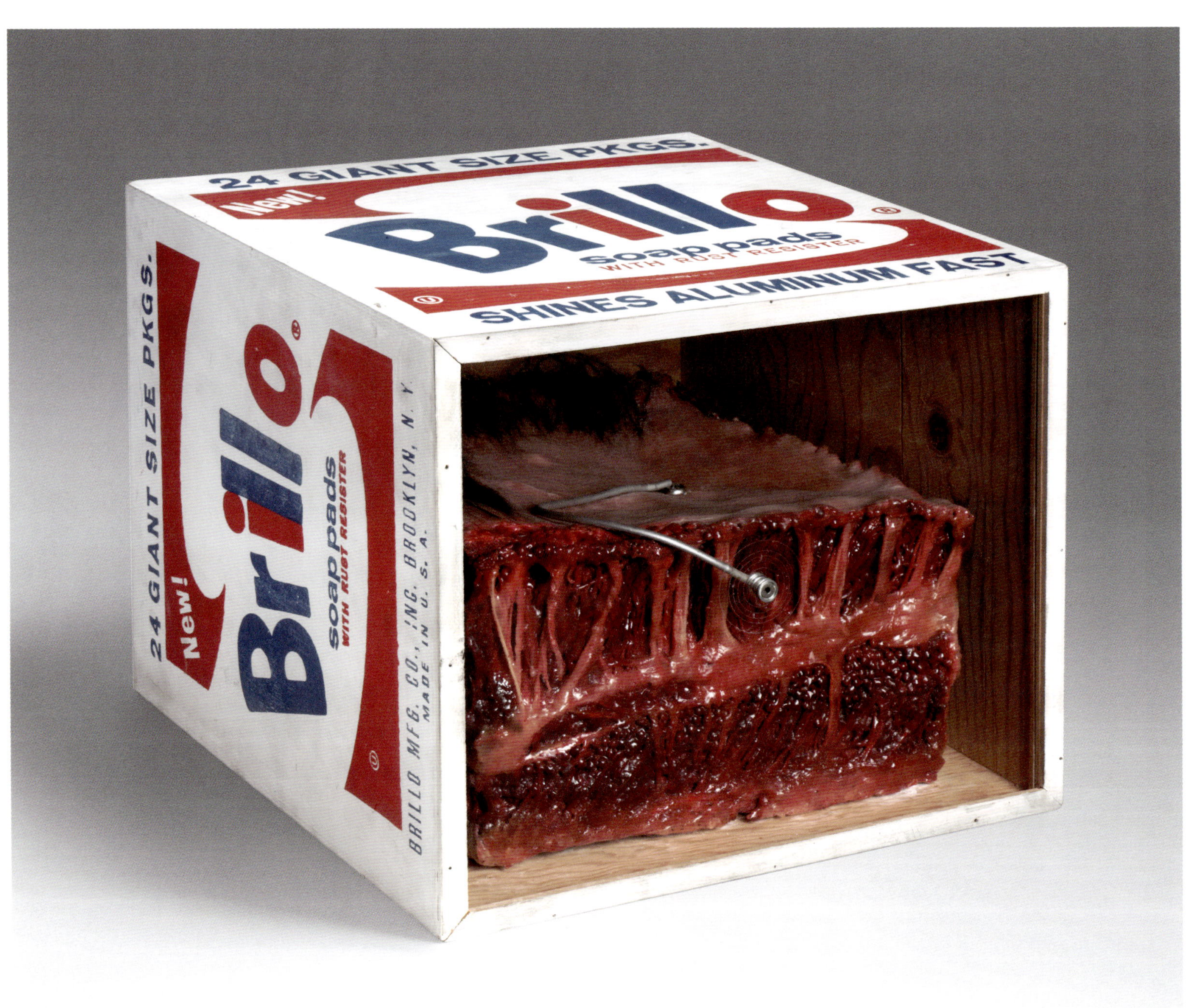

Paul Thek, *Meat Piece with Warhol Brillo Box*, 1965. Beeswax, painted wood, and Plexiglas, 14 × 17 × 17 in. (35.6 × 43.2 × 43.2 cm). Philadelphia Museum of Art; purchased with funds contributed by the Daniel W. Dietrich Foundation, 1990 1990-111-1

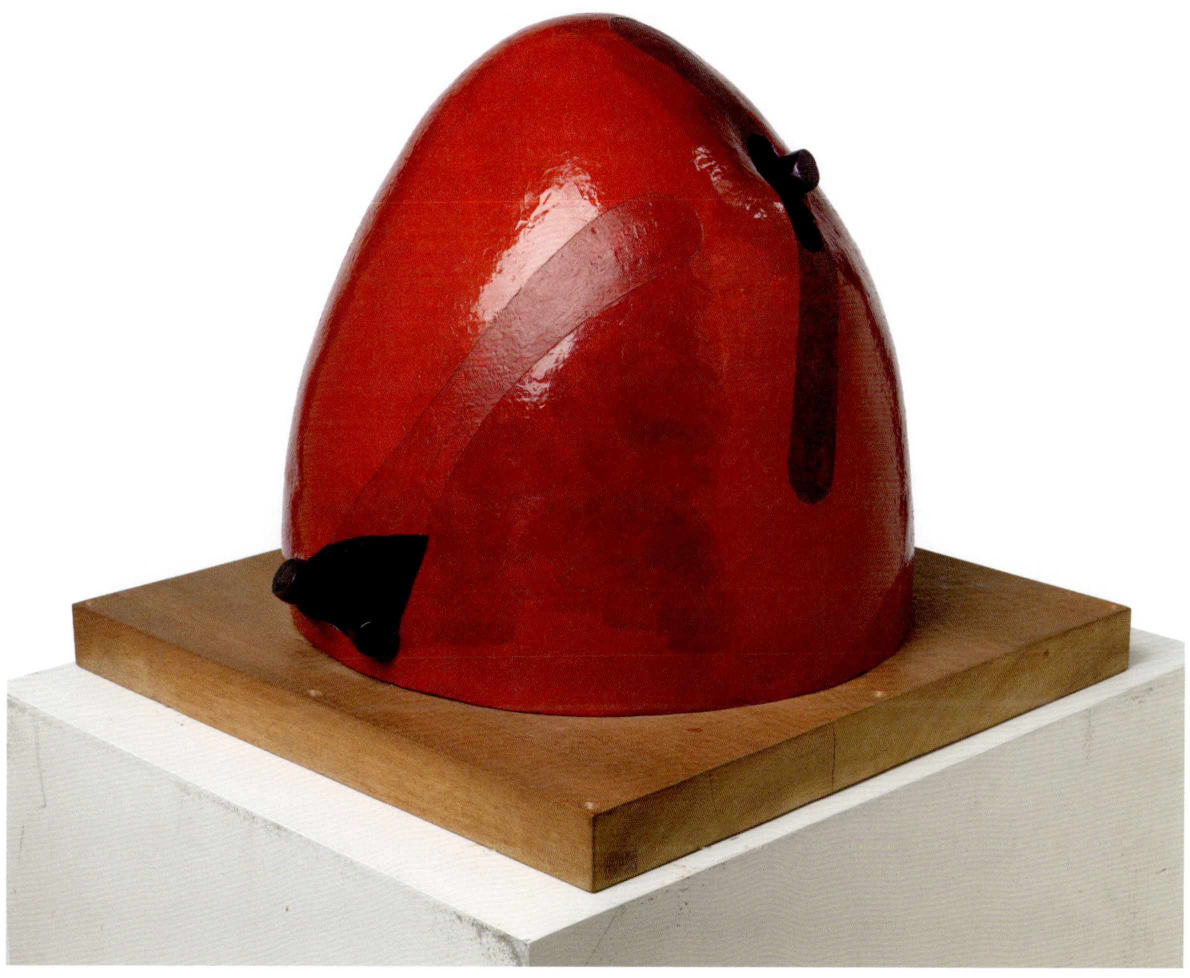

Kenneth Price, *Red*, 1965. Ceramic, paint, and wood, 14 ⅞ × 17 × 16 ¼ in. (37.8 × 43.2 × 41.3 cm). Rhode Island School of Design Art Museum, Providence; Museum purchase with the aid of the National Endowment for the Arts 71.062

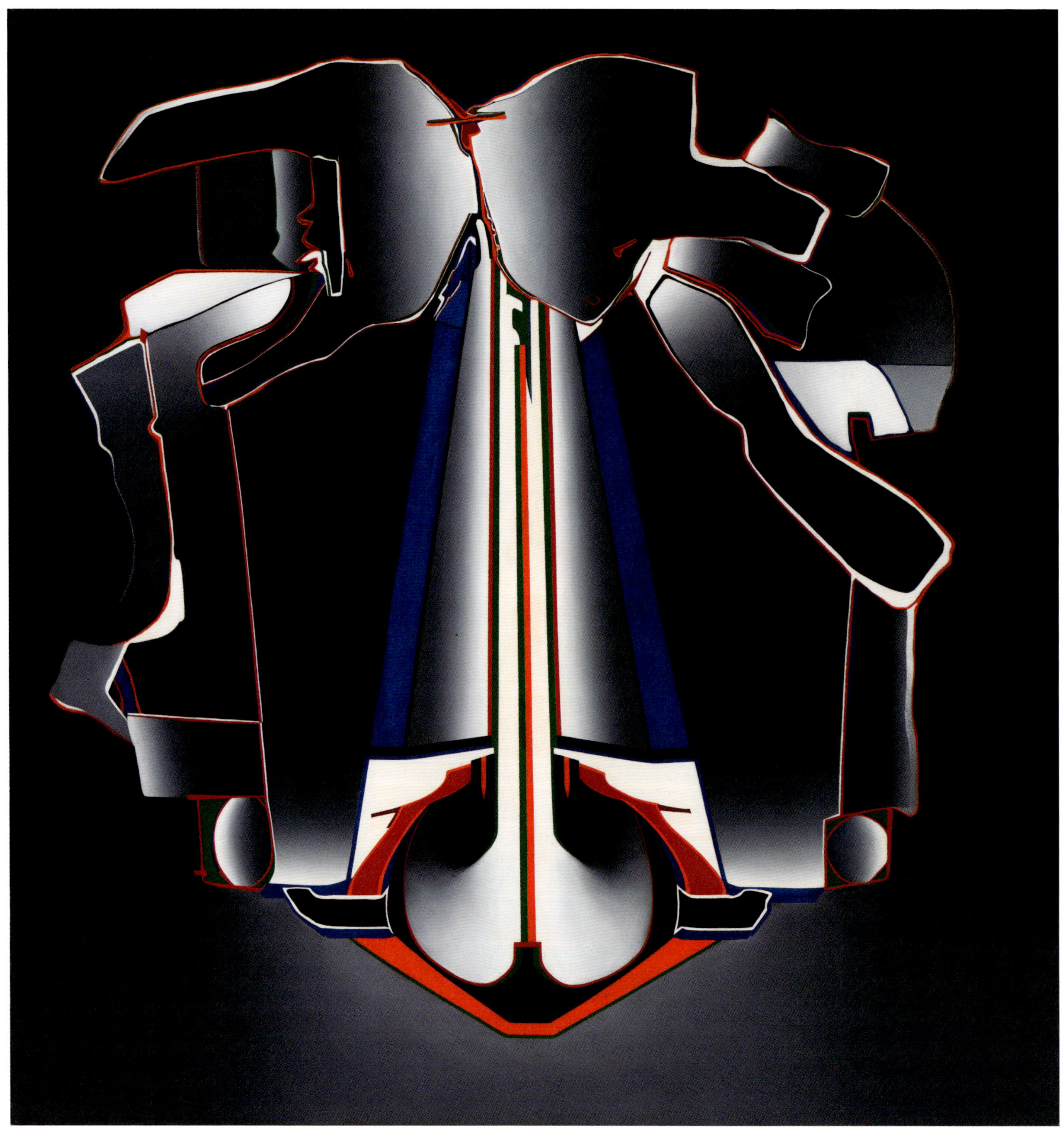

Deborah Remington, *Haddonfield*, 1965. Oil on canvas, 74 ⅛ × 69 in. (188.3 × 175.3 cm). Whitney Museum of American Art, New York; purchase, with funds from the Friends of the Whitney Museum of American Art 66.81

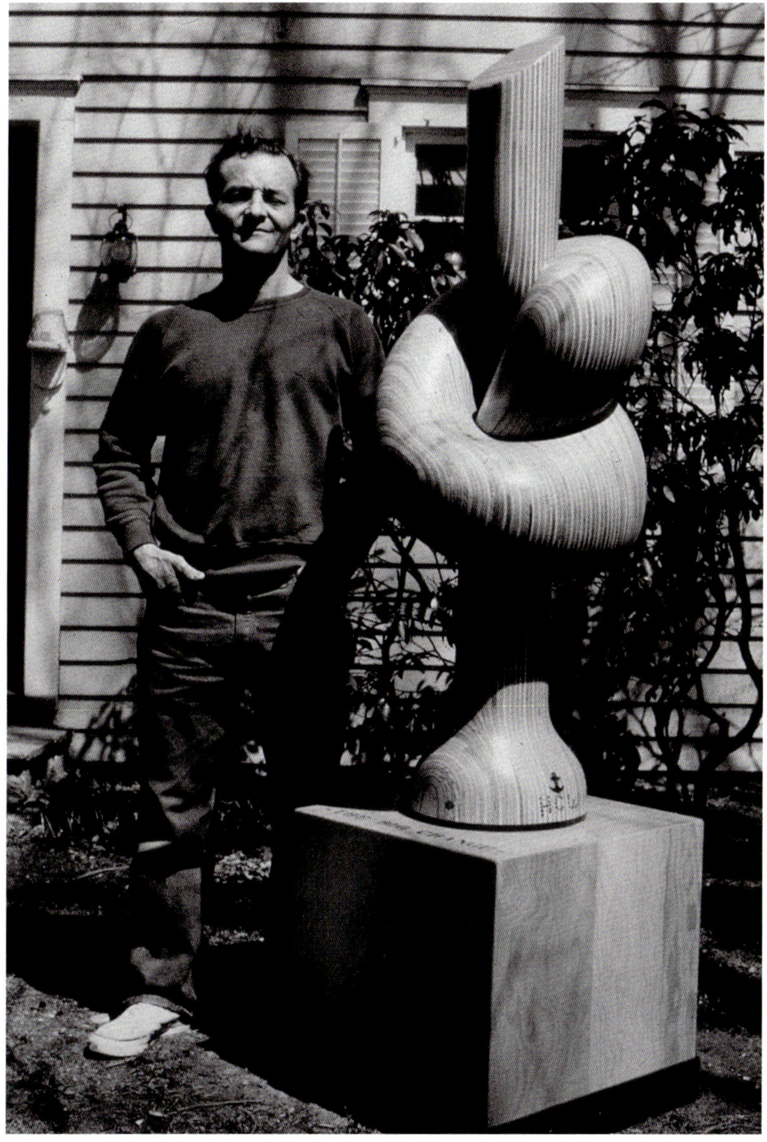

H. C. Westermann with *The Big Change* (1963), 1963

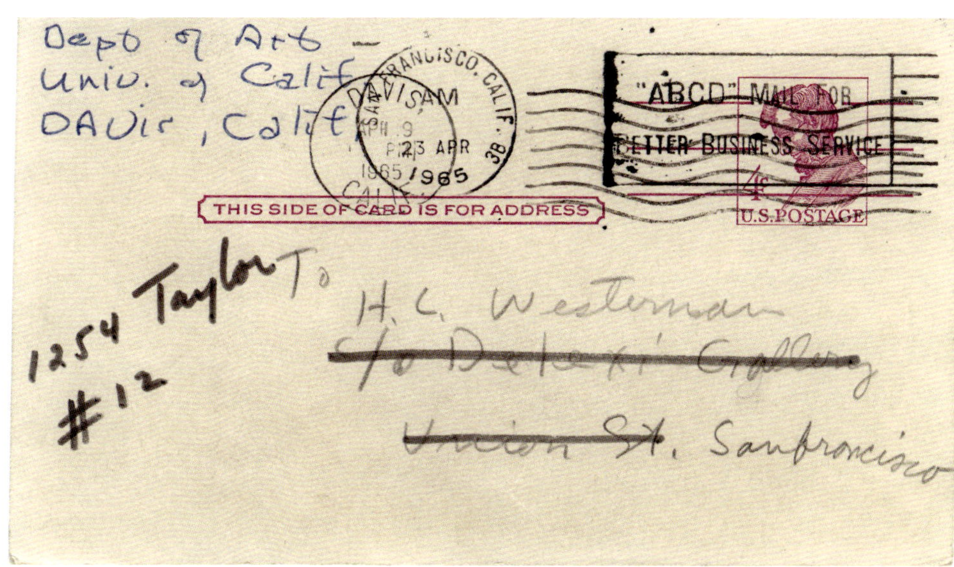

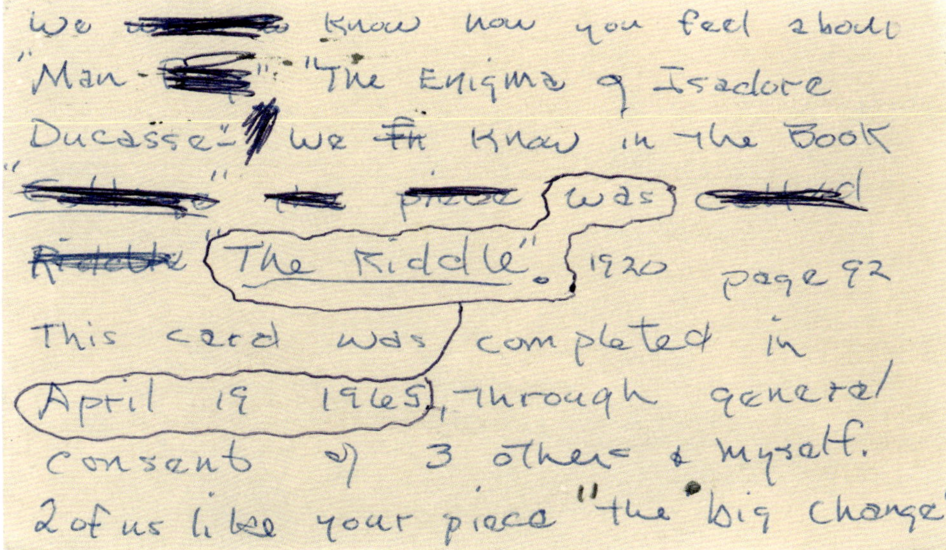

Postcard from William T. Wiley and Bruce Nauman to H. C. Westermann, 1965

Mexico City, from which he receives a master of fine arts in 1958. Casas works in San Antonio his entire career, teaching for three decades at San Antonio College, broaching topics of specific interest to the Chicano community, which he defines:

> We are truly outsiders. To me being an outsider is the next thing to being an artist. I think we are lucky to be born outsiders. The other thing, you think because you eat tortillas or you think in Spanish or in the Mexican tradition that this identifies you. I don't think it's quite true. You find us using certain materials in our work, Liquitex, canvas, stretcher boards, no *usamos bastidores* or *manta*. So we are a mixture. So there is no sense in trying to say that we are a pure this or that. We are entirely different. We're neither Mexicans nor Anglos. We are in between.

Spring 1965 • Jim Nutt (b. 1938) graduates from the School of the Art Institute of Chicago and begins looking for a way to distinguish his and his friends' work. Nutt, famously loath to explain the meaning of his art, will set up the contexts for it in a 1985 interview with fellow artist Roger Brown, where he will enumerate the origins of his sensibility:

> I had virtually no involvement with drawing or painting as a kid, and I wasn't one of the people who wanted to be an artist when I grew up. As a kid probably the most important visual imagery for me was the movies. I'd see two double bills every week, ranging from Roy Rogers and Gene Autry films to potboilers like *The Two Mrs. Carrolls* and *Thirty Seconds over Tokyo* and Hitchcock films, especially *Notorious*. I can remember being terrorized by *Rebecca* when I was a kid. I liked Donald Duck. I remember *Fantasia* because my parents were both involved with classical music. I was dragged to concerts but not museums.

April 19, 1965 • Bruce Nauman and William T. Wiley jointly write an admiring card to H. C. Westermann and prankishly ask what the artist, whom they haven't met, thinks of the fact that Man Ray's work *The Enigma of Isadore Ducasse* (1920) is mysteriously referred to as *The Riddle* in a contemporaneous catalogue. They praise Westermann's 1963 sculpture *The Big Change* and also include drawings of their own and some oblong strips of carbon paper so the correspondence will contain a record of its own movement. Westermann responds with a Valentine's Day card decorated on one side with a drawing and his own cryptic note: "Dear Sir, I am not familiar with Man Ray's 'RIDDLE.' Sincerely, H. C. W. S. F. '65." The

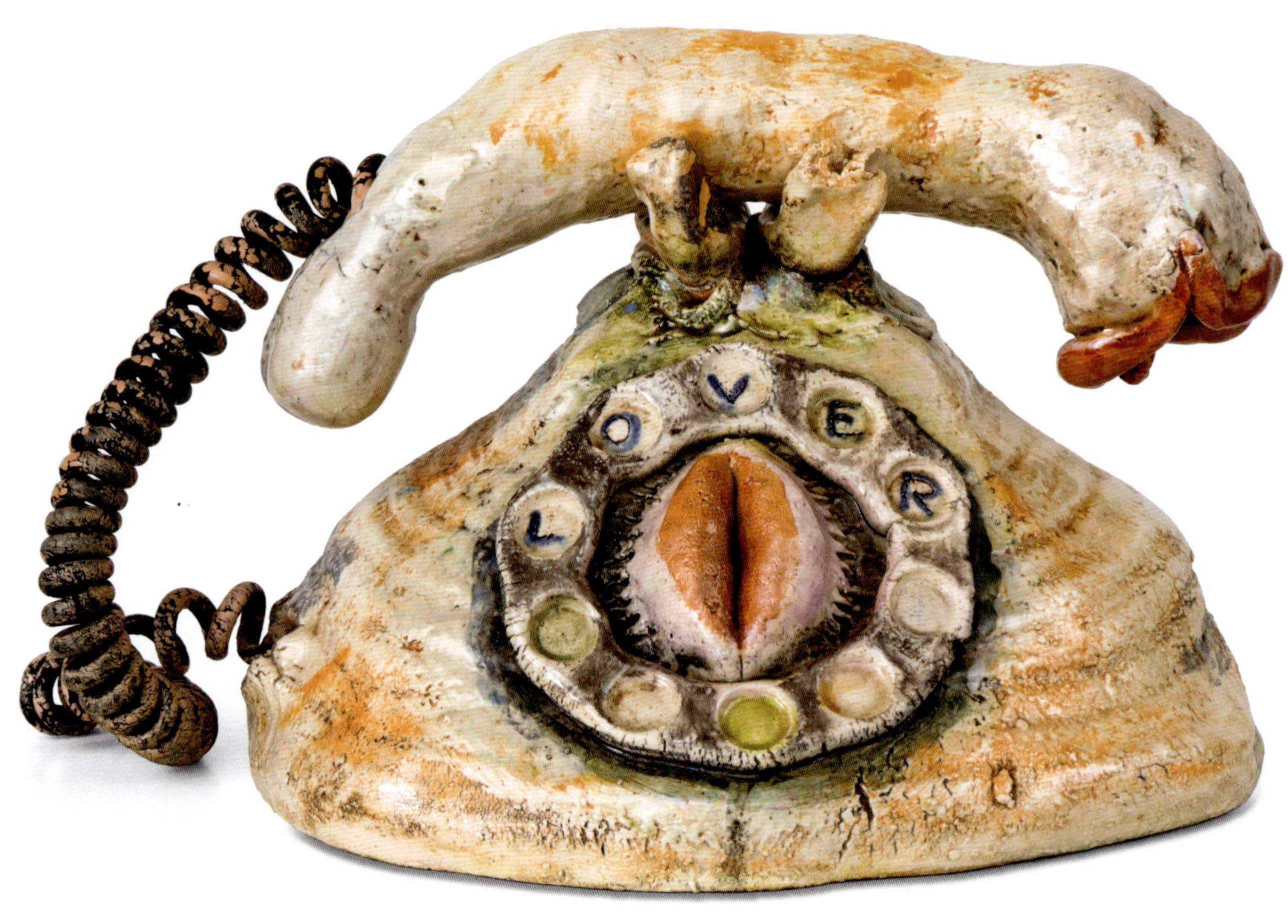

Robert Arneson, *Call Me Lover*, 1965. Glazed ceramic and mixed media, 8 × 11 × 9 in. (20.3 × 27.9 × 22.9 cm). Private collection

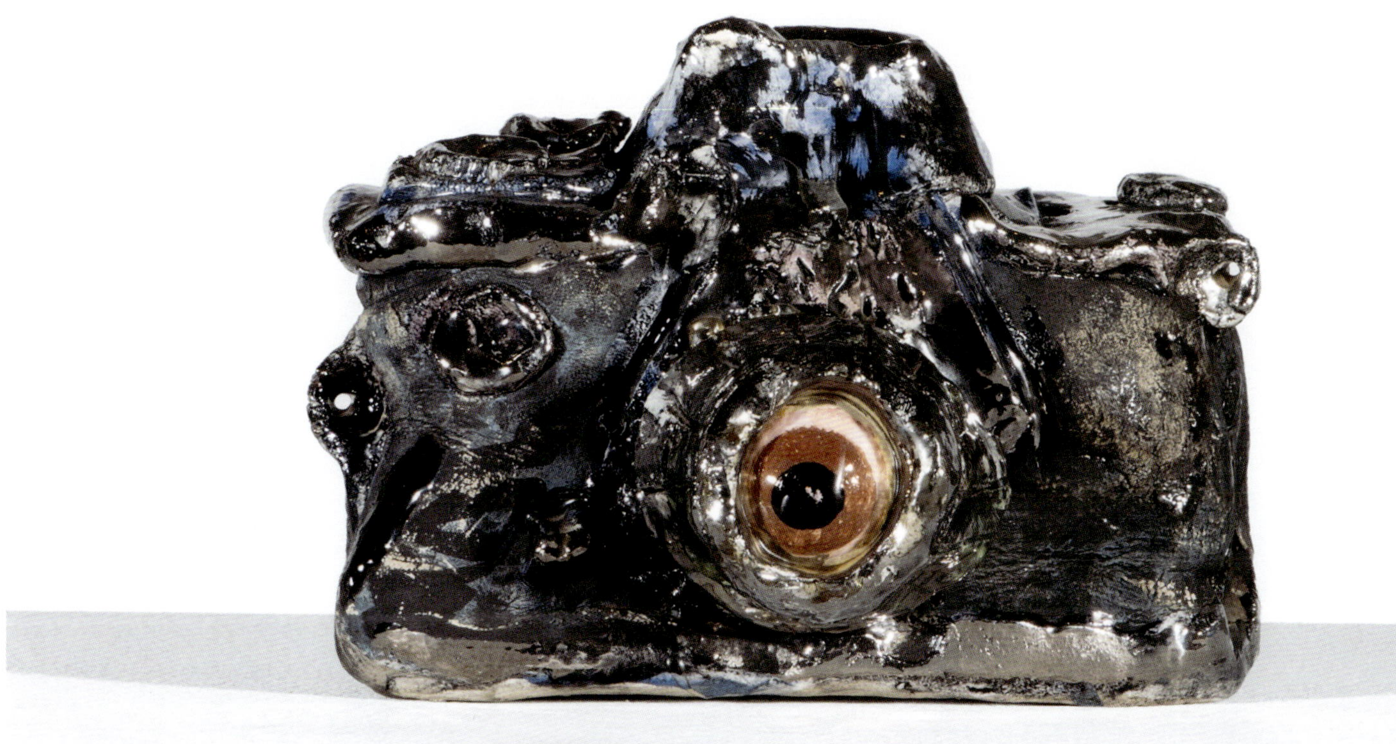

Robert Arneson, *Klick*, 1965. Glazed ceramic, 5 ¼ × 5 ½ × 7 ¼ in. (13.3 × 14 × 18.4 cm). Collection of Beth Rudin DeWoody

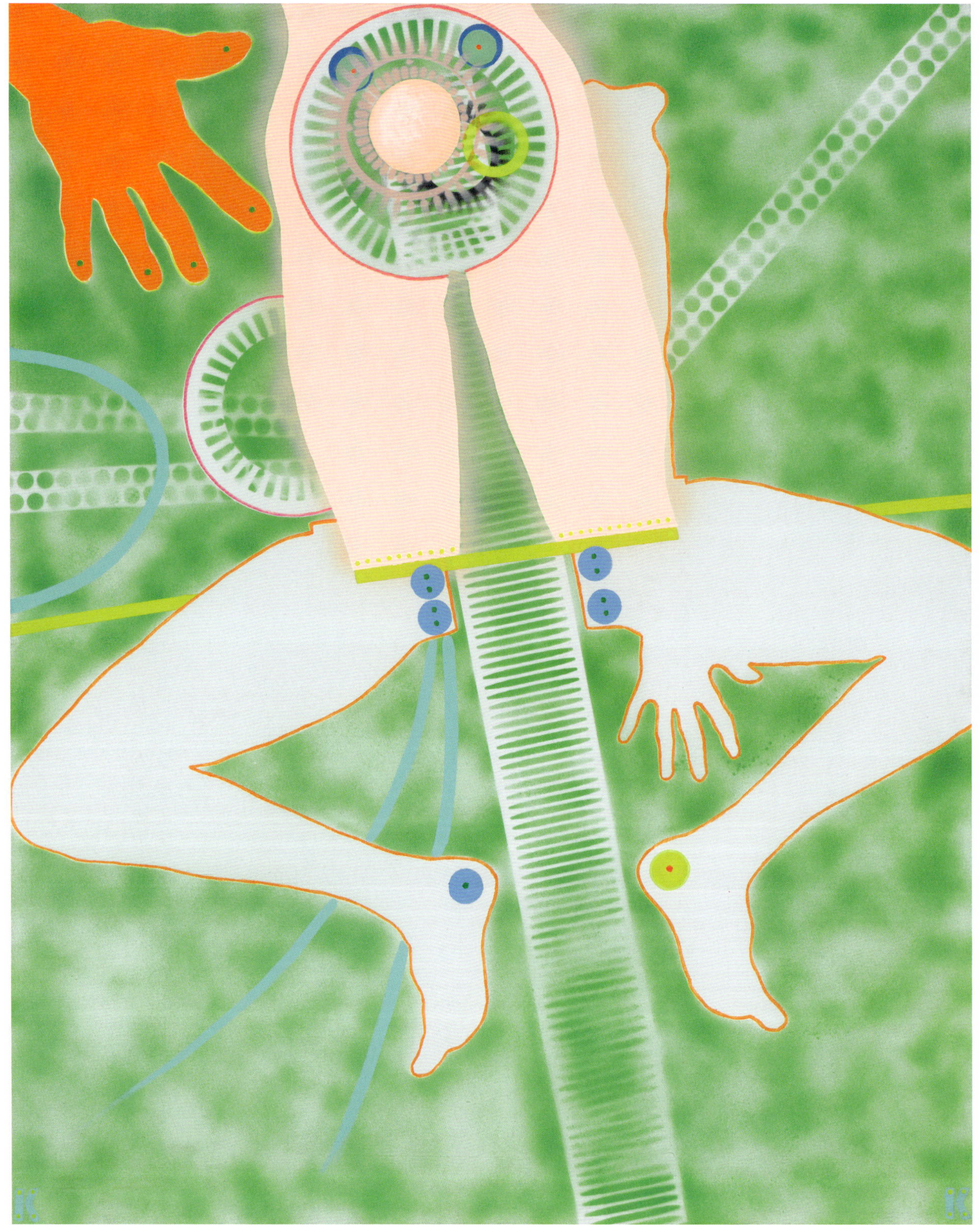

Kiki Kogelnik, *Gee Baby – I'm Sorry*, 1965. Oil and acrylic on canvas, 50 ⅛ × 39 ⅞ in. (127.4 × 101.4 cm). Kiki Kogelnik Foundation, New York

other side of the card reads: "TO WHOM IT MAY CONCERN I don't like to beat you down, but your card was almost an 'enigma'— In that I don't quite understand it, & for the fact that you just 'dashed' it off— Oh come on now, you couldn't possibly be in this big a HURRY— TAKE IT EASY MAN!! Sincerely, H. C. W. P.S. Yeh I know I'm a nasty ole thing—but don't be too hurt. But don't you like to get neat, personal things through the mail?" Wiley will meet Westermann later that spring at Peter Saul's Mill Valley studio, and the two men begin a warm friendship marked by exchanges of artwork and encouragement.

July 1965 • Nancy Graves (1939–1995) moves to Florence, Italy, for a year and encounters the work of Clemente Susini, an eighteenth-century anatomist, inspiring the first of her *Camel* works. She spends much of her time at La Specola, the city's museum of zoology and natural history, where she discovers Susini's hyperrealistic wax sculptures of dissected bodies and is drawn to their uncanniness and the marvelous surrealistic sense they elicit. Intrigued by these models that simultaneously present both the outside and the inside of the body, Graves spends the next decade grappling with the anatomy of the camel, an animal she likely encounters for the first time on a trip to North Africa with her husband, Richard Serra, during their European residencies. Graves constructs her first two life-size camel sculptures while in Florence but destroys both before returning to the United States in August 1966.

Graves had been born and raised in Pittsfield, Massachusetts, and spent much of her childhood visiting the Berkshire Museum, where her father works. The Berkshire is a museum of both natural history and art, and Graves's early experiences there will be ones she returns to when conceiving her *Camel* works years later. She attends Vassar College and then goes on to receive her master of fine arts in painting at the Yale School of Art, graduating alongside artists Chuck Close, Brice Marden, and Serra, to whom she is married from 1964 to 1970. After graduating, Graves receives a Fulbright-Hayes fellowship and studies painting in Paris before she joins Serra in Florence, where he is also completing a fellowship.

July 4, 1965 • A year after her arrival in New York, Shigeko Kubota stages *Vagina Painting*, an infamous work in performance history and in feminist art. In this performance, at Perpetual Fluxfest, the artist attaches a paintbrush to her underwear, squats to dip it in red paint, and drags it on a sheet of paper set beneath her. The resulting irregular marks evoke comparisons to menstrual blood and

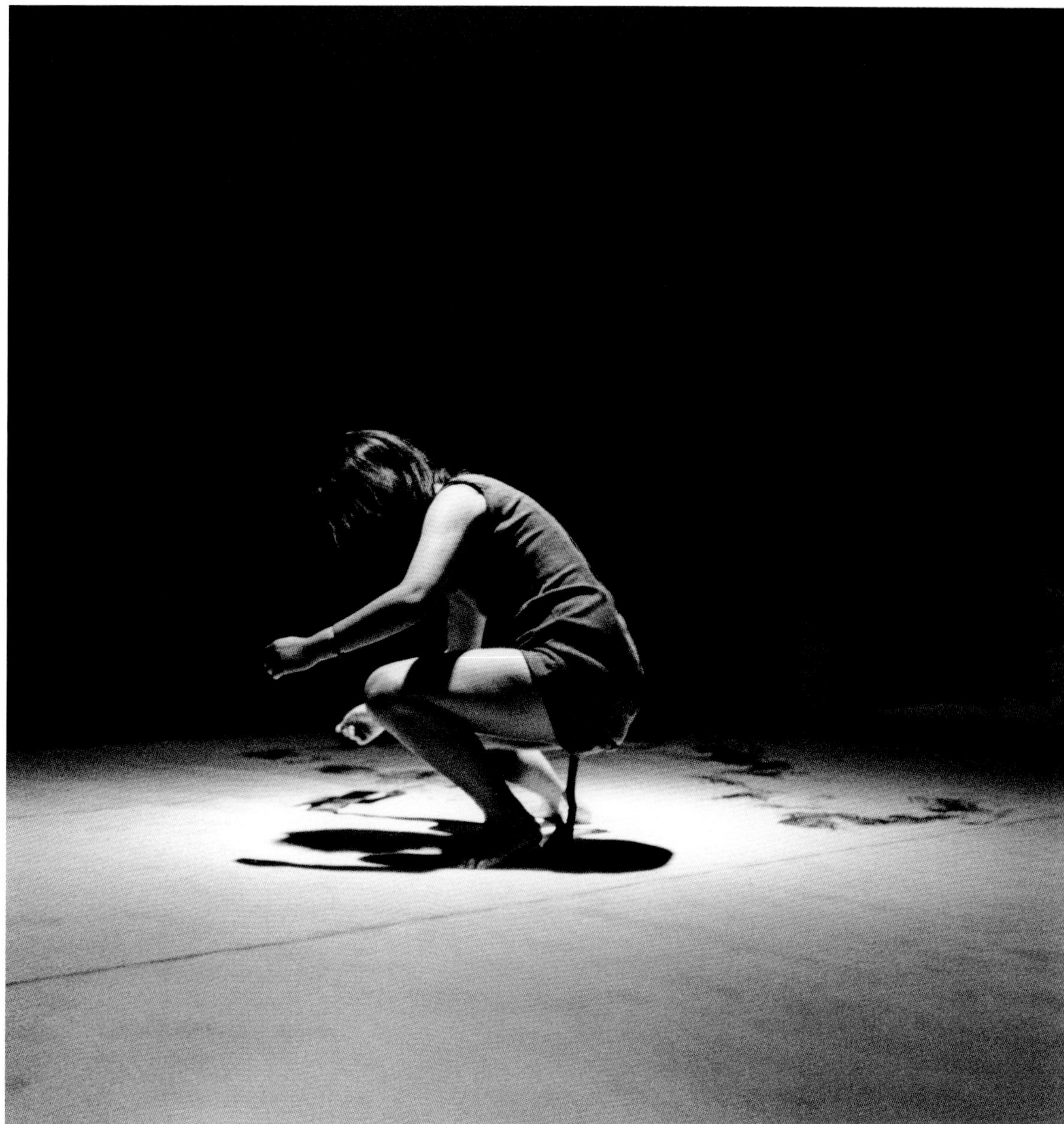

Shigeko Kubota performing *Vagina Painting* during Perpetual Fluxfest, Cinematheque, New York, July 4, 1965

to Abstract Expressionism, burlesquing the heroic virility of the so-called action painters. Despite abandoning performance thereafter, Kubota will continue to produce work in which she develops her interest in duration, gender, and the organic in new media, above all in video.

August 11–16, 1965 • The largest urban rebellion of the civil rights era breaks out in the Watts neighborhood in South Central Los Angeles. The event is precipitated by the violent arrest of Marquette Fry, a young Black man, for drunk driving by Lee W. Minikus, a white California Highway Patrol officer, and ignites residents' latent tensions and frustrations surrounding the systemic racism they face. Participants raze and wreck the area, burning cars and damaging businesses and other property. Over fourteen thousand California National Guard troops are mobilized to quell the uprising.

Artists who live, go to school, or have studios in Watts find themselves profoundly affected. Ed Bereal soon recalls that up until this point he had enjoyed the sense of safety and belonging that being embraced by the white Los Angeles art world has afforded him, yet his experience during the rebellion destabilized all that:

I opened my front door on Venice Boulevard, and parked across the road so cars had to slow down—and it was like a checkpoint. It just so happened this Jeep was pointed at my house. And on that Jeep was mounted a 50-caliber machine gun. And as I came through the door, that gun was pointing right at my chest. It was, you know, fifty feet away. And there was what I call a Neanderthal, a

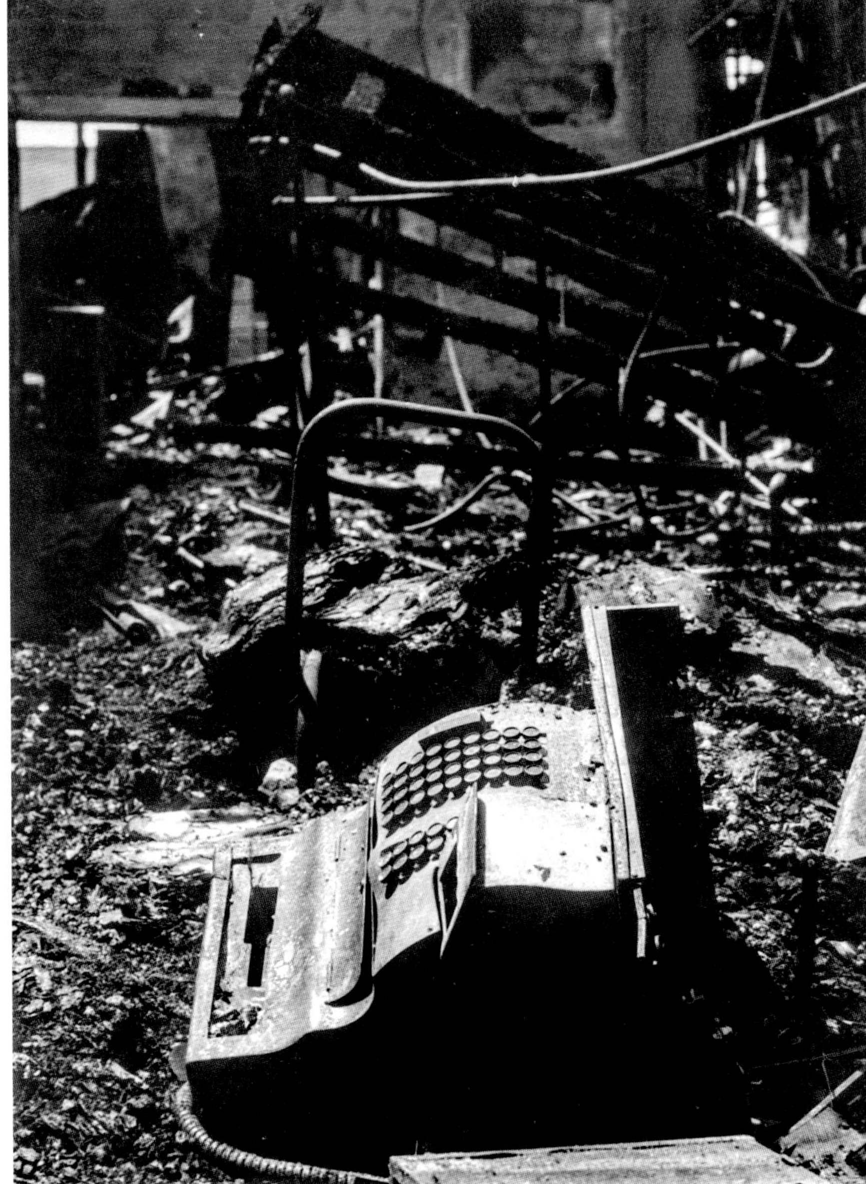

Melvin Edwards, *The Watts Rebellion, Los Angeles*, 1965. Gelatin silver print, 10 × 8 in. (25.4 × 20.3 cm)

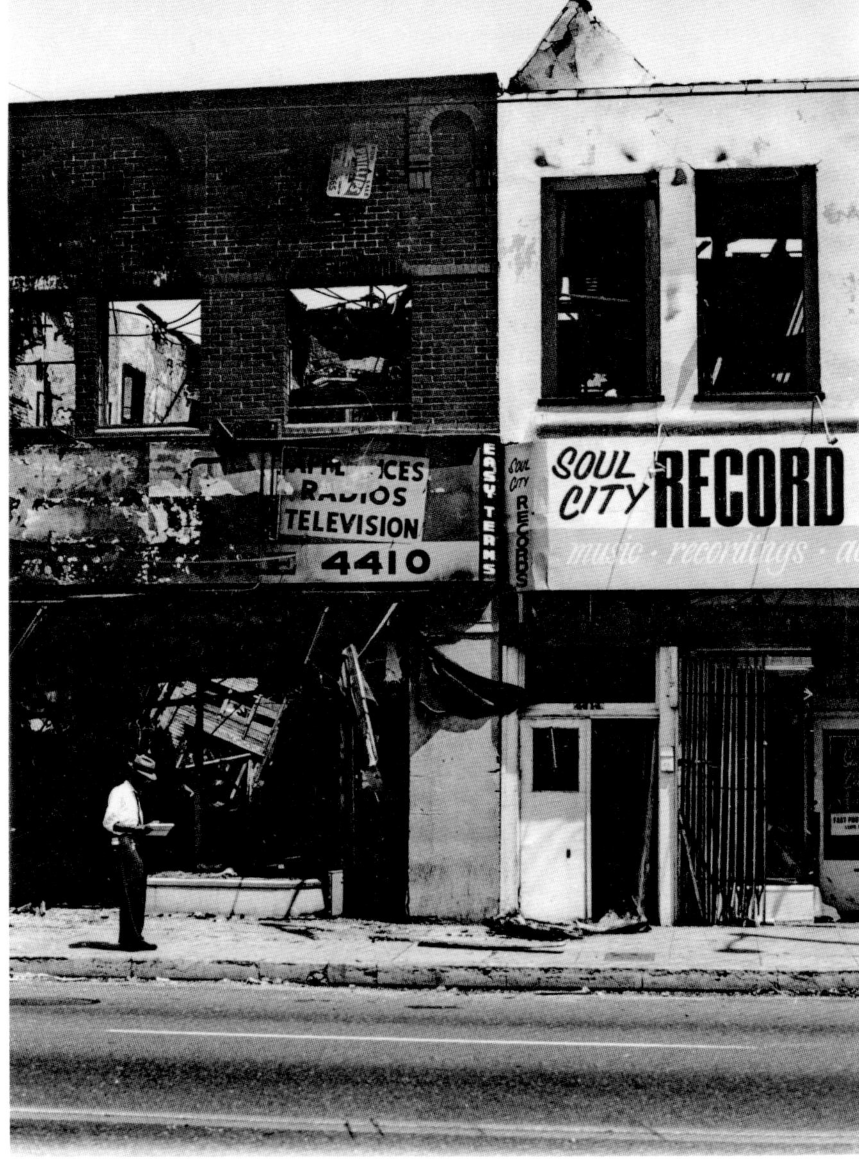

Melvin Edwards, *The Watts Rebellion, Los Angeles*, 1965. Gelatin silver print, 10 × 8 in. (25.4 × 20.3 cm)

National Guardsman, sitting behind it, so when I opened the door, he kind of went like that, and I'm going "Oh, shit. This is not cool." Because he could blow me away with immunity, man. "Black guy tried to jump me. All I could do was shoot him." And in that moment I realized that all the articles that had been written about me, all the PR and what's-his-name from *Los Angeles Times* who used to love my shit—William Wilson. And I said, "If William was standing in front of me trying to block that bullet. If Irving Blum was standing in front of it. If Walter [Hopps] was there—good, old, beautiful Walter, all that shit between me and that gun, I'd still be dead."

Artists such as Judson Powell and Noah Purifoy will come to use the wreckage of the neighborhood to create their work and engage in community and curatorial projects related to the Watts Rebellion.

———

September 1965 • Niki de Saint Phalle exhibits for the first time the *Nanas*, here a series of eleven archetypal female figures posed in differing postures—some stand, some sit, some are in motion—at Galerie Alexandre Iolas in Paris. Saint Phalle had created the first of her *Nanas*—an older French slang term for "girls" or "girlfriends"—in 1964. Art historian Jill Dawsey will describe the series as "a vehicle for exploring women's freedom and mobility," as the *Nanas* themselves are "athletic, acrobatic figures resembling fertility goddesses." As Saint Phalle sees them, the *Nanas* are "the symbol of a happy liberated woman."

Saint Phalle had stayed with Clarice Price and her husband, artist Larry Rivers, in September 1964, and Clarice's pregnancy purportedly inspires the *Nanas*. Her *Portrait de Clarice* (1964) is completed during this stay. Art historian Catherine Dossin will situate the *Nanas* in relation to French feminism, where, she says, the question "was not whether there is a female essence but, rather, what should be the new definition of 'woman.'" For Dossin, the *Nanas* mark a shift in Saint Phalle's work away from the deconstruction of womanhood to the construction of a new woman, reflected in "Saint Phalle's personal journey from breakdown to breakthrough." Although the *Nanas* often appear to deconstruct traditional images of women (mother, daughter, bride, etc.), similar in approach to Simone de Beauvoir's *Second Sex* (1949), Saint Phalle's presentation and attitude will Continued on page 144

ICONS OF IMPOVERISHMENT, RHETORICS OF REVITALIZATION: WEST COAST ASSEMBLAGE CIRCA 1965

JACOB STEWART-HALEVY

Assemblage means reassembly, to take things someone else threw away and make something new with them.[1] Unlike the rich transcultural resonances of premodern spolia, the materials of modern assemblage typically hold little value, leaving artists to animate their worth by displacing them from their original contexts of use.

Consider some canonical examples that stand at the origins of assemblage. Pablo Picasso used cardboard, sheet metal, and wire to put together his *Guitars* (1912–14), which were partially based on the construction methods of Krou masks from French-occupied Gabon, a colony used for rubber extraction. By the end of the decade and into the 1920s, Kurt Schwitters was combing the streets of Hanover for wooden and metallic debris, which he inserted into his early *Merzbild*. Picasso's Cubist *Guitars* and Schwitters's Dadaist *Merzbild* borrow from the techniques of the colonized mask-maker and the lumpen-proletariat ragpicker and, in the process, reveal them as integral to capitalist expropriation.

Assemblage is the genre most suited to deal with expropriation because it is also a recuperative process. In expropriation, people, labor, goods, and territory are profitably discarded and then reabsorbed at a lower cost into the economy. Capital excludes some forces of production from wage labor, zones of industrial production, and representative politics by hiding those forces away in the informal spheres of social reproduction, residual phases of accumulation (junking), and beyond legal governance (Gabon). Competing in the global marketplace, the modern state depends on the surplus value created from these forms of expropriation. It needs someone to pick up the trash and provide rubber, and it needs to compensate them as little as possible. Meanwhile, the state casts the classes it has dispossessed as dependent on its welfare, often typifying their plight in Franciscan tones of impoverishment and redemption. In turn, the historical avant-gardes reassembled these people, practices, and goods into assemblages in order to fashion their own sacred community of artists into cast-offs, seceding from the economic and social values of the dominant culture.

In the postwar period, assemblage experienced a second apotheosis under slightly different conditions. New institutional arrangements extended the use of the genre from the avant-gardes to the very dispossessed subjects whose techniques and materials they had traditionally borrowed. The broadening of the genre to new constituents and representational projects led, in turn, to its submission to market forces and to state regulation that incorporated contemporary art into its management of social welfare. Assemblage no longer symbolically represented expropriation but participated in it directly.

Well aware of historical avant-garde precedents, Beat artists expanded the media of assemblage by the 1950s, particularly in Los Angeles and the San Francisco Bay Area. Inspired by the Surrealists, Wallace Berman frequented jazz clubs in South Central Los Angeles. He illustrated the album covers of bebop musicians who performed there and imitated their style of dress and recreation, donning zoot suits and consuming heroin while drawing attention to the shared recourse of assemblage and jazz to spontaneity.[2] He leveraged these aesthetic affinities in order to establish a mostly white bohemian scene of artists, writers, and musicians in Venice Beach, which became subject to a milder version of the moral panic in mainstream news outlets and police repression that was often more violently directed at the city's impoverished and segregated Black and Brown communities.

In 1957, after Berman's arrest by the Los Angeles vice squad on charges of obscenity and the censorship of his Ferus Gallery exhibition, he moved north to a remote section of Marin County, in Larkspur, where he founded the exhibition space Semina in an abandoned houseboat with George Herms. Berman, Herms, and their fellow Beat artists sourced material for their assemblages from the dump, alongside highways, or in thrift stores, sometimes even using their own hair. Their iconography came from their dreams and under the influence of hallucinogens (p. 115). If their finds were not sufficiently damaged or opaque, the artists tore and burned them and then bandaged them up, concealing them inside lumpy sacks and melted wax, subjecting them to artificial distress and natural decay.

Having arrived from Wichita, Kansas, to the Bay Area in 1957, Bruce Conner quickly joined the Semina circle. His esophageal *RAT PURSE* (1959; p. 19) hangs from a scrap of fur on a hook, tied to a distended nylon stocking that covers a beaten-up cardboard box bound with twine and pierced with nails. Sequins, the barrel of a syringe, and other talismans are caught haphazardly in the weave, ultimately weighted down by a striped can, contents unknown. These careful calibrations between the heavy and flimsy, opaque and translucent, wear and sheen hint at repressed meanings that threaten to permeate their surfaces.

Seeking spiritual self-preservation in their fetish objects and fragile assemblages, material impoverishment and social deviance, the Beats fashioned a sacred community in Larkspur, at the artist-run spaces of the Rat Bastard Protective Association in San Francisco, and in their racialized "funky" performances in the culturally vibrant, predominantly African American Fillmore district.[3]

By the mid-1960s, however, assemblage had gained currency through the art market and museum exhibitions. The Beats, finding employment in the era's proliferating art schools, taught the genre to students who would go on to ironize it, deflating their mentors' claims to spiritual transcendence, notably through the *Funk* and Slant Step exhibitions of the later 1960s. Public radicals pushing against the Vietnam War, segregation, the sanctity of private property, and much else supplanted Beat-era assemblage with more convincing icons of community self-determination and dissent.

Meanwhile, images of Beat culture circulated widely on film and television, and in print. Readers of the August 1965 issue of *Vogue* encountered the assemblages of Berman and Conner nestled among Art Nouveau stained glass, Mexican oil cloth, and papier-mâché clowns in an article about Dennis Hopper and Brooke Hayward's house in the Hollywood Hills (fig. 1): "A house of such gaiety and wit that it seems the result of some marvelous scavenger hunt, full of improvised treasures, the bizarre and the beautiful and the banal in wild juxtaposition."[4] In an adjacent photo, the couple's children peer out through a hole in the open work of Simon Rodia's Watts Towers, "those romantic and extravagant constructions which—encrusted with shells and broken bottles and old dishes, fantastic and enchanting—suggest very well the Hoppers' approach to their own house."[5] But many of these potsherds had been gleaned off the street and donated to Rodia not by the Hopper-Hayward kids but by the children of Watts, who contributed to the towers as they reached their improbable heights.[6]

By then, the towers had become a tourist destination, a totem of neighborhood pride, and the paradigm of a new genre of naïve assemblage known as "outsider art."[7] In 1961, a committee devoted to the preservation of the towers beat back a demolition order from the city of Los Angeles and established the Watts Towers Arts Center (WTAC), a community arts program, nearby.[8] By 1964, local teachers and artists had successfully petitioned for federal funding to make WTAC a "Teen Post" and appointed the artist Noah Purifoy as the center's director.[9] An Alabama native, Purifoy had served in the Navy as a carpenter and worked briefly as a Douglas Aircraft machinist, but he also held a master's degree in social service administration and had been a social worker before relocating to Los Angeles, where he eventually became the first Black student to enroll full-time at the Disney-funded Chouinard Art Institute. He learned about historical avant-garde assemblage through his art history courses and contemporary assemblage through encounters with the work of the Kienholz circle.[10] Throughout the 1950s, he placed junk backgrounds behind shiny new commodities in his decorations for the Broadway department store downtown. When he arrived at WTAC, he recounted, "we utilized found objects to teach with. Oftentimes we'd take the children on trips to pick out objects—junk, et cetera—and bring it back to the towers, to the art center to do assemblages and collages and so forth."[11] The streets were full of junk.

Racist hiring practices, spotty transportation, police brutality, absentee landlords, environmental pollution, illegal dumping, and underfunded schools and healthcare systems all led to the increasing segregation of Watts residents, culminating in the Watts Rebellion in August 1965. Although President Lyndon Johnson had just announced a "war on poverty" as part of his Great Society reforms, the municipal government siphoned off and misdirected federal funds. During the uprising, WTAC students looted the stores that had been selling rancid meat and price-gouging them for years, and stored their spoils at the center. In the following days, Purifoy collected charred

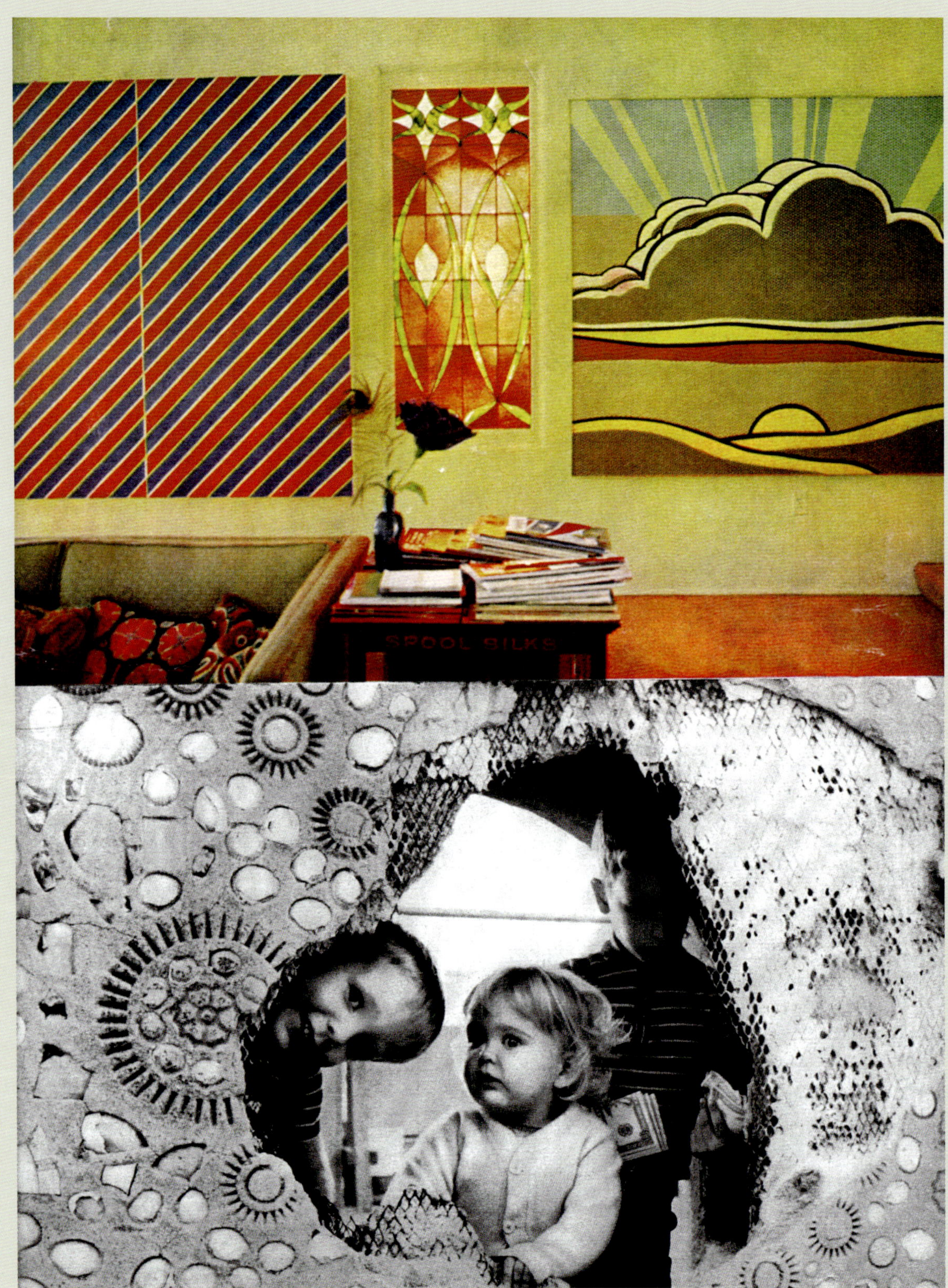

Fig. 1. Page from *Vogue*, August 1965, with photographs by Dennis Hopper

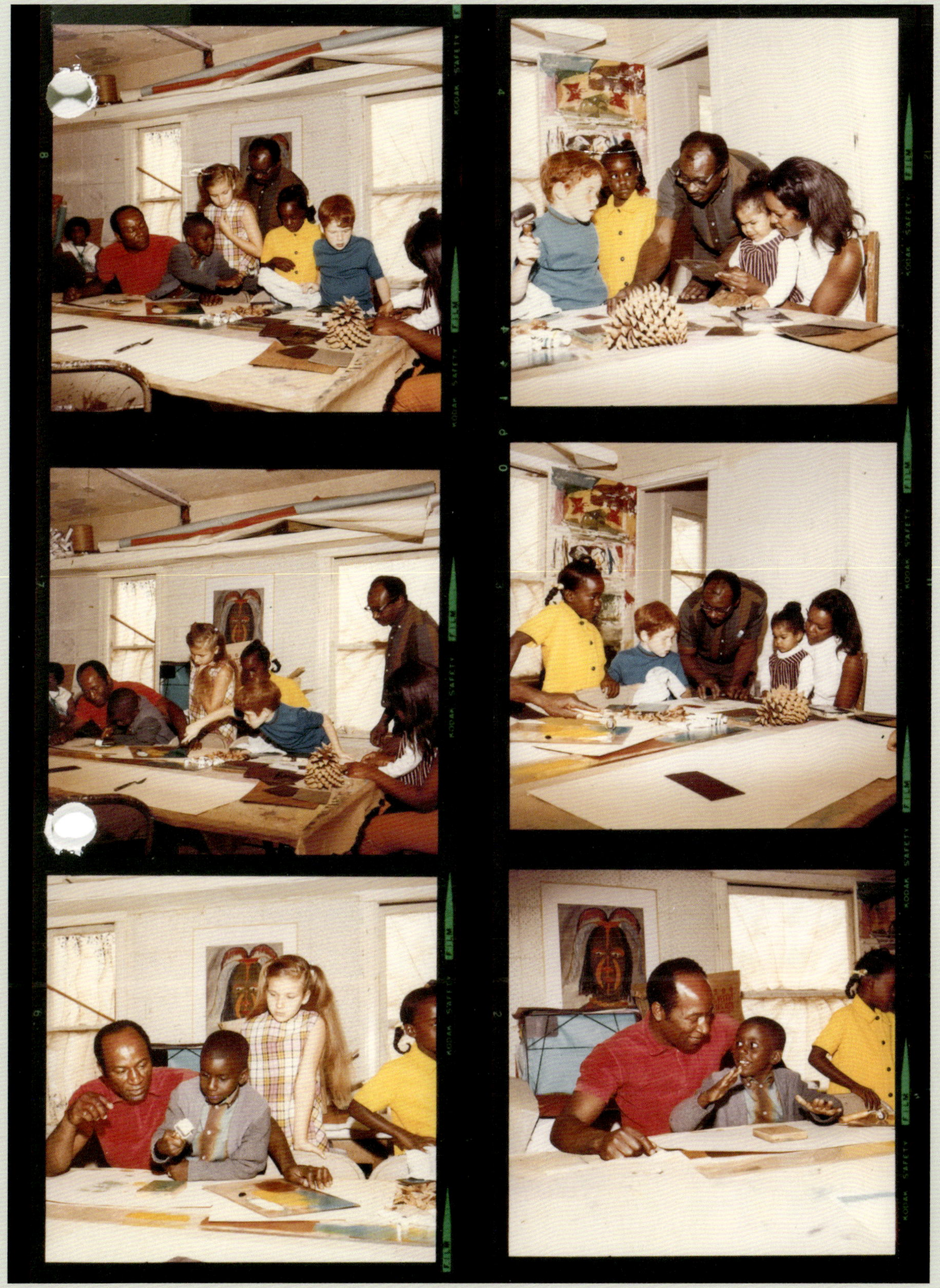

High School to the student unions of the University of California system, and then to Washington, DC, only to be co-opted by a US Information Agency show in Berin about "recycling art" (fig. 4).[14]

Hoping to suppress further uprisings, state and local officials tried to incorporate Watts residents into the regional economy through make-work programs; change their "attitudes" and "behaviors," as local press reports put it at the time, by stifling separatists; and displace the burden of civic infrastructure onto voluntary "community-based" projects, often piggybacking on grassroots arts initiatives such as Purifoy's. "Bootstraps on a shoestring," these post-Keynesian social-welfare reforms centered around cultural empowerment and spectacles of compassion carried out by fly-by-night enterprises. They were judged and funded according to their "creativity" and ability to "uplift" the psyche of the individual and the aesthetics of the neighborhood. The "scars" of the rebellion would be "healed" through corporate and Hollywood P.R. stunts, pocket parks in abandoned lots, incentives for real-estate developers and insurers, cleanup events, cultural heritage festivals featuring beauty queen contests and the LAPD Junior Band, and entrepreneurial skills centers.[15] The legacy of Simon Rodia became a simonized Rhodesia.

Given Purifoy's background in social services, technical know-how, and his organic grasp of community needs, local junking practices, and recent trends in contemporary art, he was uniquely situated to preserve the sacral traces of assemblage while shifting its orientation from hermetic secessionism toward such public displays of participatory

Fig. 2. Noah Purifoy and Judson Powell teaching students at the Watts Towers Arts Center, c. 1960s

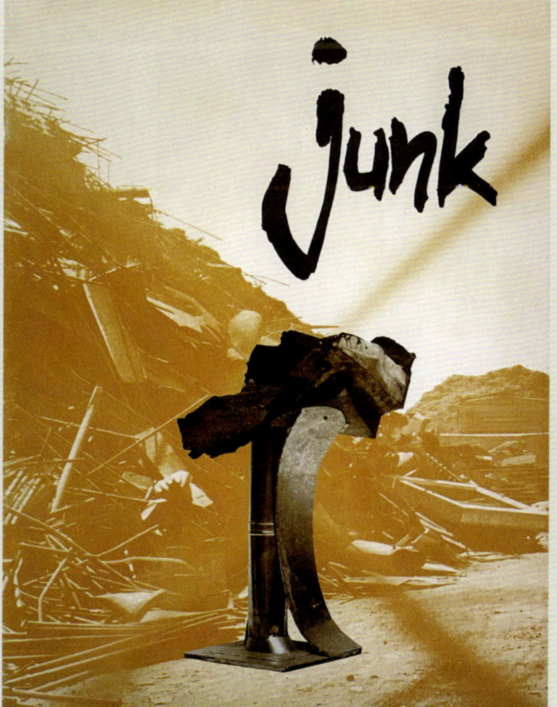

Fig. 3. Exhibition catalogue for *66 Signs of Neon*, Simon Rodia Renaissance of the Arts Festival, Los Angeles, 1966

debris with fellow artist and WTAC instructor Judson Powell (fig. 2), which they converted into assemblage art for their exhibition *66 Signs of Neon* (fig. 3), named after the "twisted, grotesque" drippings of melted neon liquor-store signs that had crystallized into "jewels."[12] Formed in the fires, glinting through the sand and dirt, the crystals provided an emblem of community resilience that countered prevailing narratives of violence and despair; so too works such as *Phoenix*—"a piece of bent-up metal mounted on a twelve foot pole"—literally arisen from the ashes.[13] Signaling a "Watts Renaissance," the show commemorated the first anniversary of the rebellion and traveled from nearby Markham Junior

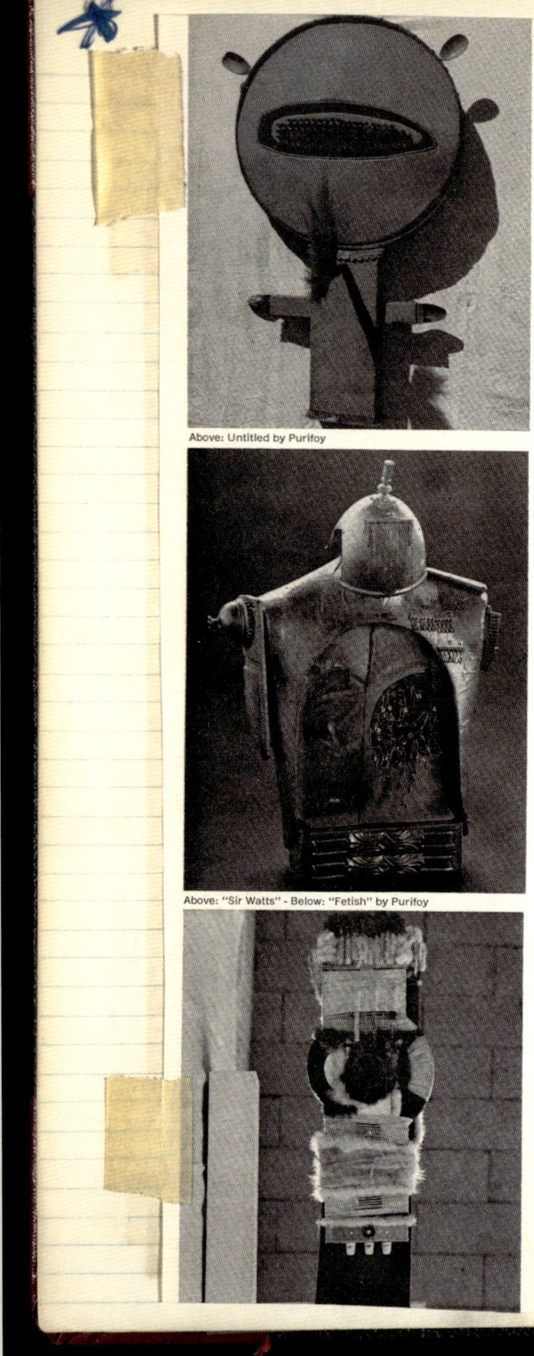

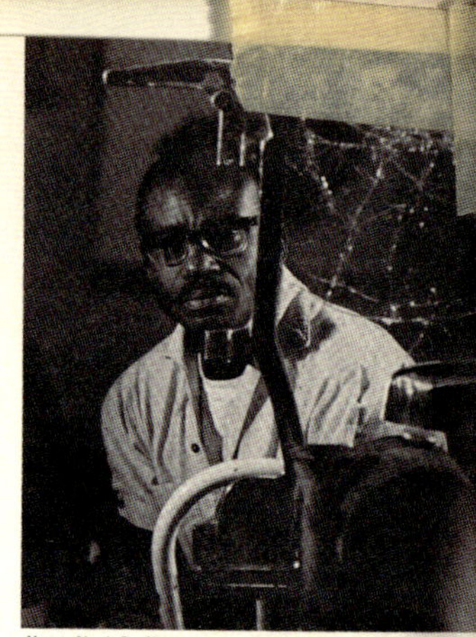

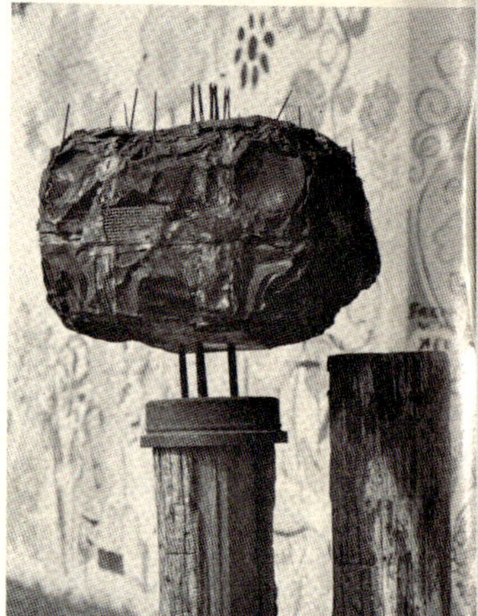

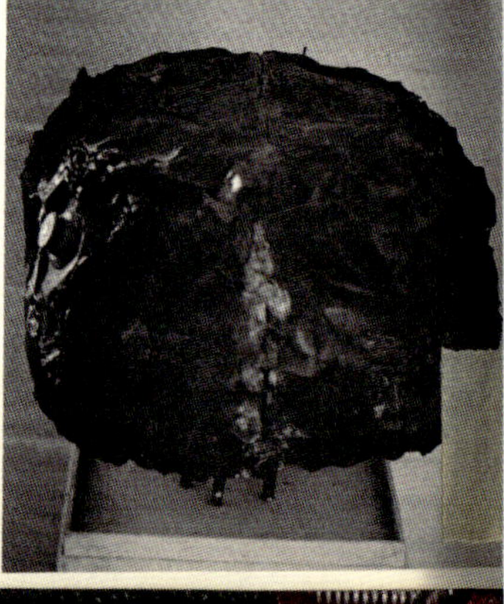

"Garbage — the Need to Recycle" was the theme of the United States Exhibition at the German Industries Fair Berlin 1972 held September 15-24. A press preview to which the media and other members of the Berlin art world were invited resulted in rave notices from the local press, whose unanimous opinion was that the Americans had drawn attention to a shocking problem (two billion tons of waste per year) with humor and creativity.

From the Los Angeles area, two artists were represented with sculptures utilizing "found" objects — Edward Kienholz and Noah Purifoy. Kienholz' contributions were "Good Ole Charlie Delegate," on loan from the Onnasch Gallery, Cologne; "The Marriage," from the collection of Daniel Varenne, Paris; and "Night of Nights," from the collection of Peter Ludwig at the Wallraf-Richartz museum in An der Rechtschule, Germany. Purifoy's four works in the show were "Fetish;" No. 14 untitled, assembly with brush and wooden spoons; No. 19 metal sculpture; and "Sir Watts." The latter originated with the 1966 "Signs of Neon" art show that grew out of the 1965 Watts upheaval.

The American display included illustrations of government, business and individual participation in alleviating the litter problem, particularly relative to recycling of waste materials. Practical applications of recycling in furnishings, household items and other products were shown, and artisans gave live demonstrations of how obsolete material could be transformed into useful objects. A major section was devoted to "art from junk," exhibiting artistic objects created from trash. A huge heap of junk in the center of the show was a part of the artistic creation.

Southland furniture manufacturers at the show with their designs demonstrating the use of recycled materials included Frank Gehry, Santa Monica; Easy Edges Furniture, L A; Environmental Concepts, Beverly Hills; and Huddle Environments, L A. An L A interior designer, Gere Kavanaugh, was represented with one of her art works.

Fig. 4. Press coverage of the United States Exhibition at the German Industries Fair, Berlin, 1972, featuring Noah Purifoy

redemption.[16] In the wake of the rebellion, he reported on the benefits of teaching junk art at the "Arts and the Poor" conference for the National Endowment for the Arts, where he pressed upon his colleagues: "The point of this conference ought to be the salvation of the world, not just the world of the poor, through self-affirmation."[17] In the following decades, while serving on the California Arts Council, he introduced assemblage to remedial public schools for the purposes of therapeutic introspection and visual literacy.[18]

The mid-1960s therefore mark a pivotal moment in the institutionalization of assemblage. As it lost its collective charge among the neo-avant-gardes, its indexical linkages to dispossession were refashioned for competing value projects: as decorative nostalgia, recycling propaganda, student irony, community junking, creative "uplift" and "resilience," neoliberal education reform, and many other tendencies that point to the contested significance of waste in urban political ecology.[19]

NOTES

1   The curator William Seitz defined assemblage as constructing with "preformed natural or manufactured materials" that were "assembled rather than drawn, modeled, or carved." William C. Seitz, *The Art of Assemblage* (New York: Museum of Modern Art, 1961), 6.

2   Rebecca Solnit, *Secret Exhibition: Six California Artists of the Cold War Era* (San Francisco: City Lights Books, 1990); and John Coplans, "Art is Love is God," *Artforum* 2, no. 8 (March 1964): 26–27.

3   Alexandra Aukeman, *Welcome to Painterland: Bruce Conner and the Rat Bastard Protective Association* (Berkeley: University of California Press, 2016). For Funk art's complex speculations on racialized identities, see Jacob Stewart-Halevy, *Slant Steps: On the Art World's Semi-Periphery* (Oakland: University of California Press, 2020), 84–99.

4   Terry Southern, "Fashions in Living: The Loved House of the Dennis Hoppers," *Vogue*, August 1965: 138.

5   Ibid.

6   Sarah Schrank, *Art and the City: Civic Imagination and Cultural Authority* (Philadelphia: University of Pennsylvania Press, 2009), 135–64.

7   Committee for Simon Rodia's Towers in Watts, *The Watts Towers*, 1961, p. 5. Committee for Simon Rodia's Towers in Watts Records, 1954–1997, Department of Special Collections, UCLA Library.

8   Jeanne S. Morgan, "Fifty Years of Guardianship: CSRTW," in *Sabato Rodia's Towers in Watts: Art Migrations, Development*, ed. Luisa Del Giudice (New York: Fordham, 2014), 225–26.

9   Noah Purifoy, interview by Karen Anne Mason, September 1990, African American Artists of Los Angeles Oral History Transcript, UCLA Oral History Program, 58; and Kellie Jones, *South of Pico: African American Artists in Los Angeles in the 1960s and 1970s* (Durham, NC: Duke University Press, 2017), 74–78.

10   For Purifoy's account of studying at Chouinard and learning about found objects, see: Purifoy, interview by Mason, 29–34, 77; see also Yael Lipschutz, "Noah Purifoy: Through the Fire" (PhD diss., University of Southern California, 2013), 39–44. For comparisons with Beat assemblage and especially Ed Kienholz, see Cecile Whiting, *Pop L.A.: Art and the City in the 1960s* (Berkeley: University of California Press, 2006), 158–64; and Noah Purifoy's ambivalent relationship toward Kienholz: Purifoy, interview by Mason, 45–49.

11   Purifoy, interview by Mason, 60.

12   Less than a year after the rebellion, Purifoy was quoted as saying, "We uncovered them and we thought they were little jewels. Nobody had ever seen shapes and forms quite like this," in Art Berman, "Junk from First Watts Riot Turned into Works of Art," *Los Angeles Times*, Mar. 28, 1966: 3.

13   Among the most prominent purveyors of the narrative was the commission convened by California governor Pat Brown to examine the events in Watts, headed by former CIA director John McCone: Governor's Commission on the Los Angeles Riots, "Violence in the City—An End or a Beginning?" Dec. 2, 1965. For subsequent criticism, see, for example, Bayard Rustin, "The Watts 'Manifesto' and the McCone Report," *Commentary* 41, no. 3 (Mar. 1, 1966): 29–35; and Paul Bullock, ed., *Watts: The Aftermath* (New York: Grove, 1969).

14   *Müll Macht's Möglich* (Garbage Makes It Possible; 1972) included Purifoy, Kienholz, Frank Gehry, John Chamberlain, Ruth Asawa, and many others. It was held at the Berlin Industries Fair and put on by the US Information Agency, and eventually traveled to Poland. For a detailed history, see Lipschutz, "Purifoy: Through the Fire," 120–25.

15   "Calming the Angry Voices," *Los Angeles Times*, Aug. 14, 1966: A6; Harry Bernstein, "Poverty Areas: 'Vest Pocket' Parks to Get Federal Funds," *Los Angeles Times*, Dec. 14, 1966: 11A; William James Williams, "Attacking Poverty in the Watts Area: Small Business Development under the Economic Opportunity Act of 1964" (PhD diss., University of Southern California, 1966); Art Berman, "Watts Scars Heal Slowly, Businessman's New Store Looted," *Los Angeles Times*, Dec. 6, 1965: A1; W. Stewart Oinkerton, "Watts a Year Later: Disparate Remedies," *Wall Street Journal*, Aug. 12, 1966: 8; "Watts Selects a Beauty Queen," *Baltimore Sun*, Aug. 15, 1966: A4; and "Watts Marks Anniversary of Riots with a Festival," *New York Times*, Aug. 13, 1966: 8.

16   Art and cultural historians would go on to read these aesthetics for their "hidden transcripts of resistance" and capacity for world-building and sense-making, among other things; see Jones, *South of Pico*; and Roderick Ferguson, "Purifoy: The Shit, the World, and Their Remaking," *The South Atlantic Quarterly* 119, no. 3 (July 2020): 447–60.

17   Noah Purifoy, cited in Judith Murphy and Ronald Gross, *The Arts and the Poor: New Challenge for Educators* (Washington, DC: Office of Education, 1968), 6.

18   Purifoy, interview by Mason, 72–75.

19   Brian Bartell, "Noah Purifoy's Aesthetic for the Racial Capitalocene: Reading *66 Signs of Neon*," *Cultural Critique* 112 (Summer 2021): 24–58; Rosalind Fredericks, *Garbage Citizenship: Vital Infrastructures of Labor in Dakar, Senegal* (Durham, NC: Duke University Press, 2018).

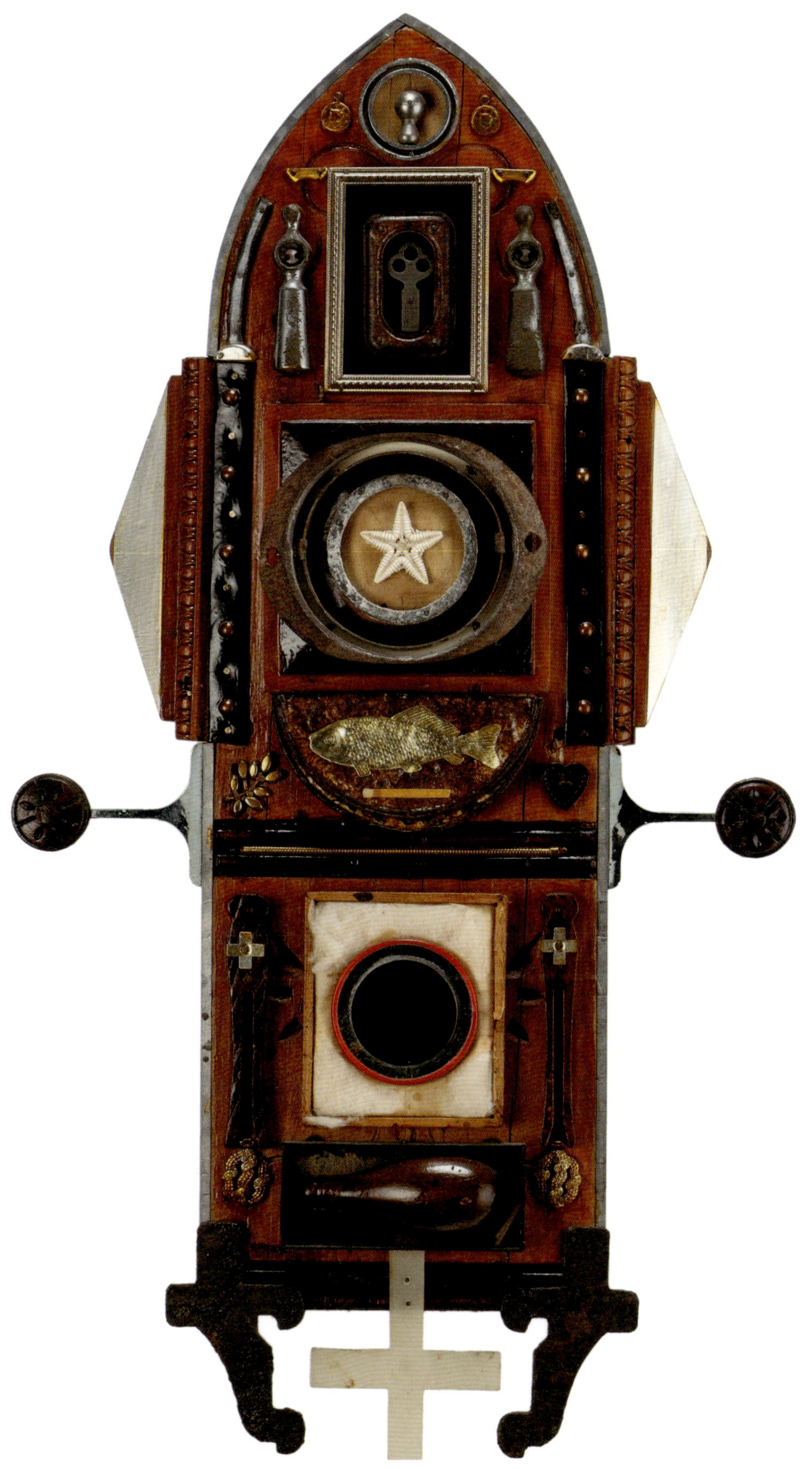

David McManaway, *Poseidon's Icon*, 1965. Mixed media on wood, 23 × 12 ½ × 2 ¾ in. (58.4 × 31.8 × 7cm). Collection of Peter and Carol York

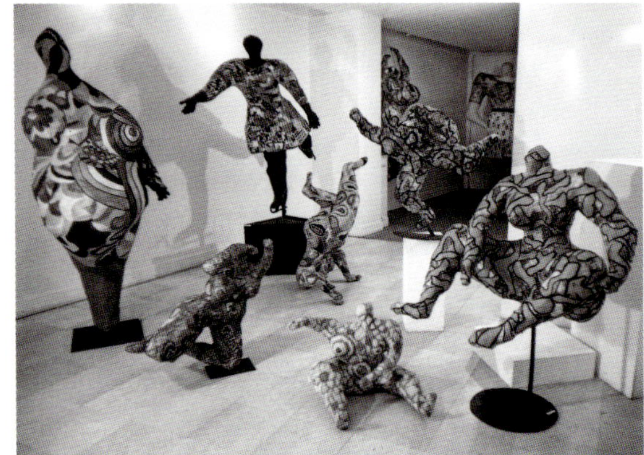

Niki de Saint Phalle, Galerie Alexandre Iolas, Paris, 1965, with *Nanas* (1965–2002)

often cause unease in the feminist community—an unease bolstered by the artist's ambivalent relationship with feminism. Still, as art historian Amelia Jones will assert, the *Nanas* "made future feminist art and culture possible." Their eventual monumental scale will make visible the notion of women taking up more space in the world, in a way that is, as the artist will describe, "neither intimidated nor repressed by their lives or by men."

———

September 25–October 23, 1965 • Deborah Remington's solo exhibition at San Francisco's Dilexi Gallery is the first focused on her hard-edge *Adelphi Series* paintings, which Alfred Frankenstein, writing in the *San Francisco Chronicle*, describes as "trembling on the edge

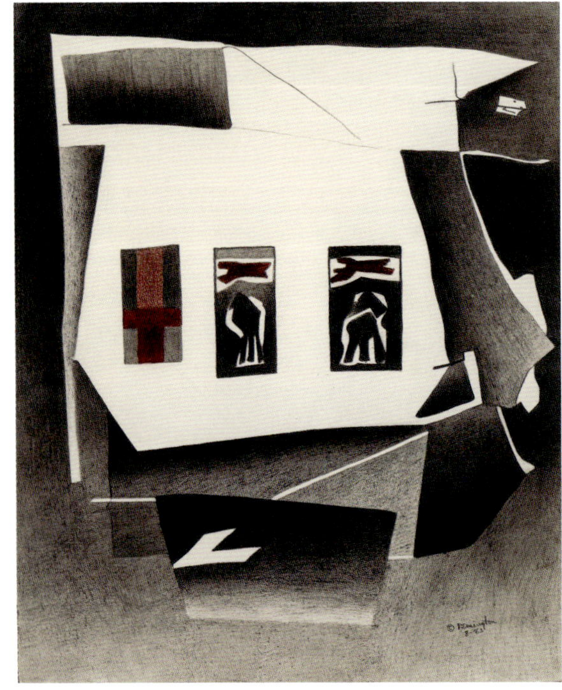

Deborah Remington, *Adelphi Series #3*, 1963. Pencil and crayon on paper, 14 ¾ × 11 ½ in. (37.5 × 29.2 cm)

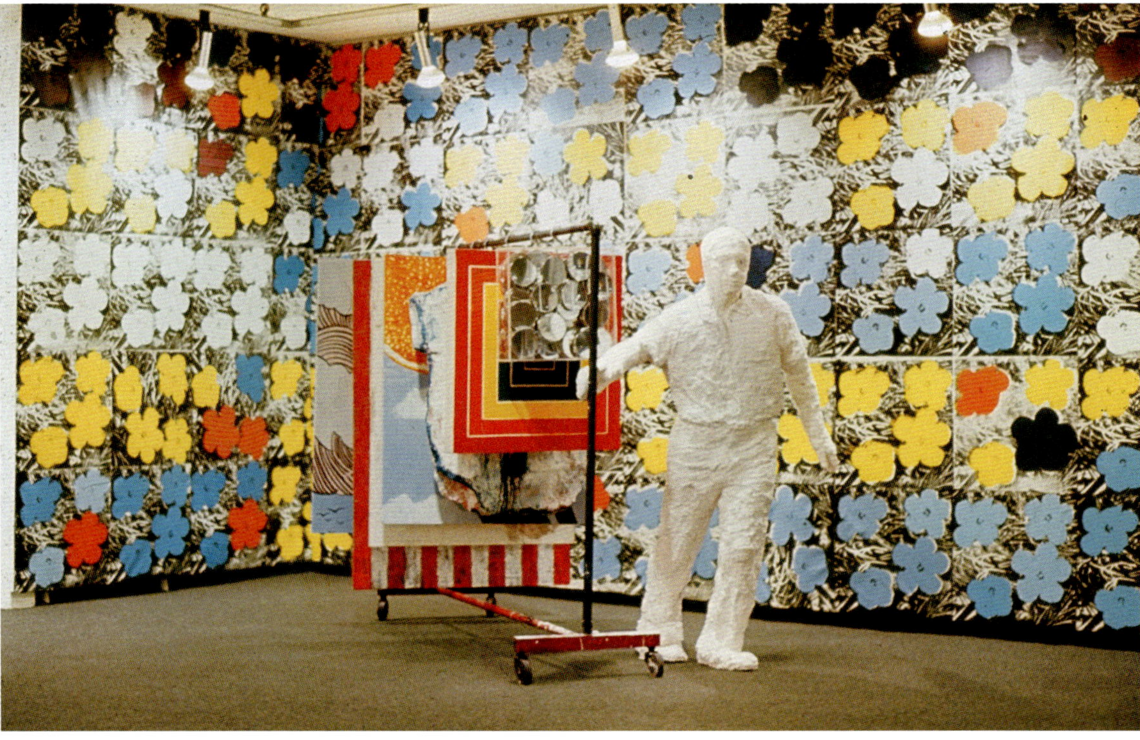

Elaine Sturtevant, Bianchini Gallery, New York, 1965, with *7th Avenue Garment Rack with Warhol Flowers* (1965)

between machine-like and organic." Remington moves to New York this same year and eventually joins Brice Marden, David Novros, and Dorothea Rockburne at Klaus Kertess's Bykert Gallery. Remington will live and paint in New York for the rest of her life.

———

October 2, 1965 • Bianchini Gallery, New York, presents what at first glance appears to be a survey of some of Pop art's finest but in fact is the first solo show for Sturtevant (1924–2014), featuring her perfected pastiche "simulations" of Andy Warhol's flower prints, Jasper Johns's flags, George Segal's plaster figures, and more. John Canaday jokes in his review in the *New York Times* that Sturtevant "must be the first artist in history to have held a one-man show that included everybody but herself." Canaday goes on to discuss the ramifications of an exhibition that seems like a "gag" but actually challenges the viewer to think about the implications of artworks (by Pop practitioners) that are "so perfectly imitable" they become a series of "trademarks." "Does Miss Sturtevant make the ultimate confession that art today is so superficial ('Way down deep, it's shallow,' somebody said) that it is only a series of copyrighted gags?," the critic asks. "But there is nothing stale about this show: Its very presumption gives it a fillip. But it makes you wonder. What about those fancy prices for big names, if a little name can give you the same thing just as good?" Presenting a critical restatement of

the very premises of "pop a la pop," the show underlines the idiom's self-reflexive critique of the art object as commodity through a strategic use of such commercial instruments as the clothing rack and the vitrine. Hanging together on a rack pulled by a haunting, paste-white Segal-esque figure or trapped behind the vitrine's glass walls, the juxtapositions at work in each grouping of "repeats" creates an uncanny simulacrum that is much more than the sum of its parts.

Born Elaine Francis Sturtevant in Lakewood, Ohio, the artist would come to be known exclusively as Sturtevant during her long career as an artworld provocateur and postmodern ironist. She received a bachelor's degree from the University of Iowa and a master's degree from the Teachers College of Columbia University, both in the study of psychology, an apt background for an enigmatic artist who rarely liked to share biographic details or discuss her work directly. She spent time at the School of the Art Institute of Chicago and at the Art Students League of New York, befriending Jasper Johns and Robert Rauschenberg in the late 1950s and exhibiting some of her early "paintings" at Betty Parsons Gallery. In 1964, Sturtevant started making her "repeats," thus adopting, as Peter Eleey has noted, "style as her medium in order to investigate aspects of art's making, circulation, consumption, and canonization." In 1960s New York the artist participates in such large-scale, experimental performance pieces as Claes Oldenburg's *Washes*, one of a series of dance concerts and happenings that made up the program of the 1965 First New

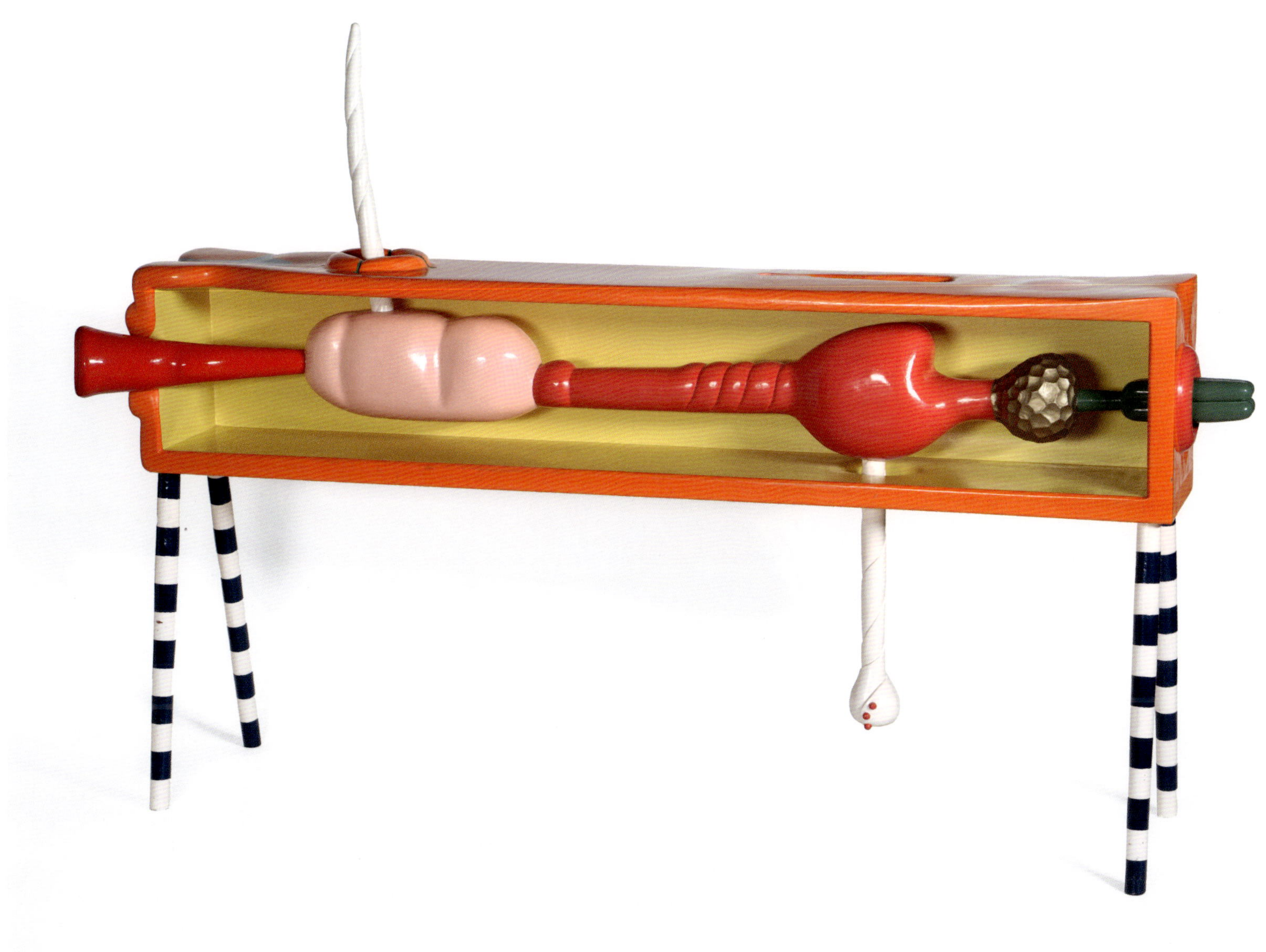

Jeremy Anderson, *Riverrun*, 1965. Redwood, pine, and enamel, 57 × 81 ⅜ × 16 ½ in. (144.8 × 206.7 × 41.9 cm). University of California, Berkeley Art Museum and Pacific Film Archive; gift of the University Art Museum Council

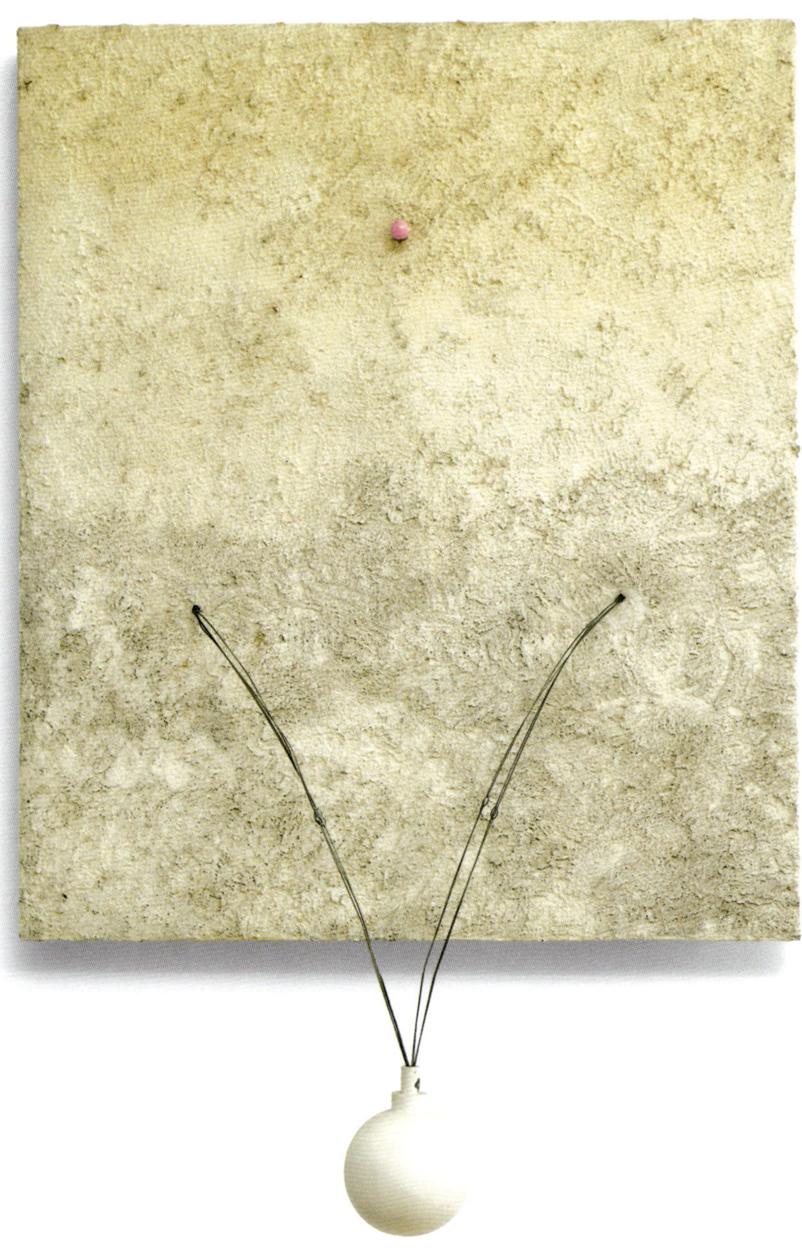

Eva Hesse, *C-Clamp Blues*, 1965. Paint, metal, found objects, unknown modeling compound, particleboard, and wood, 25 ⅝ × 21 ⅝ × 1 ½ in. (65.1 × 54.9 × 3.8 cm). Collection of Tony and Gail Ganz

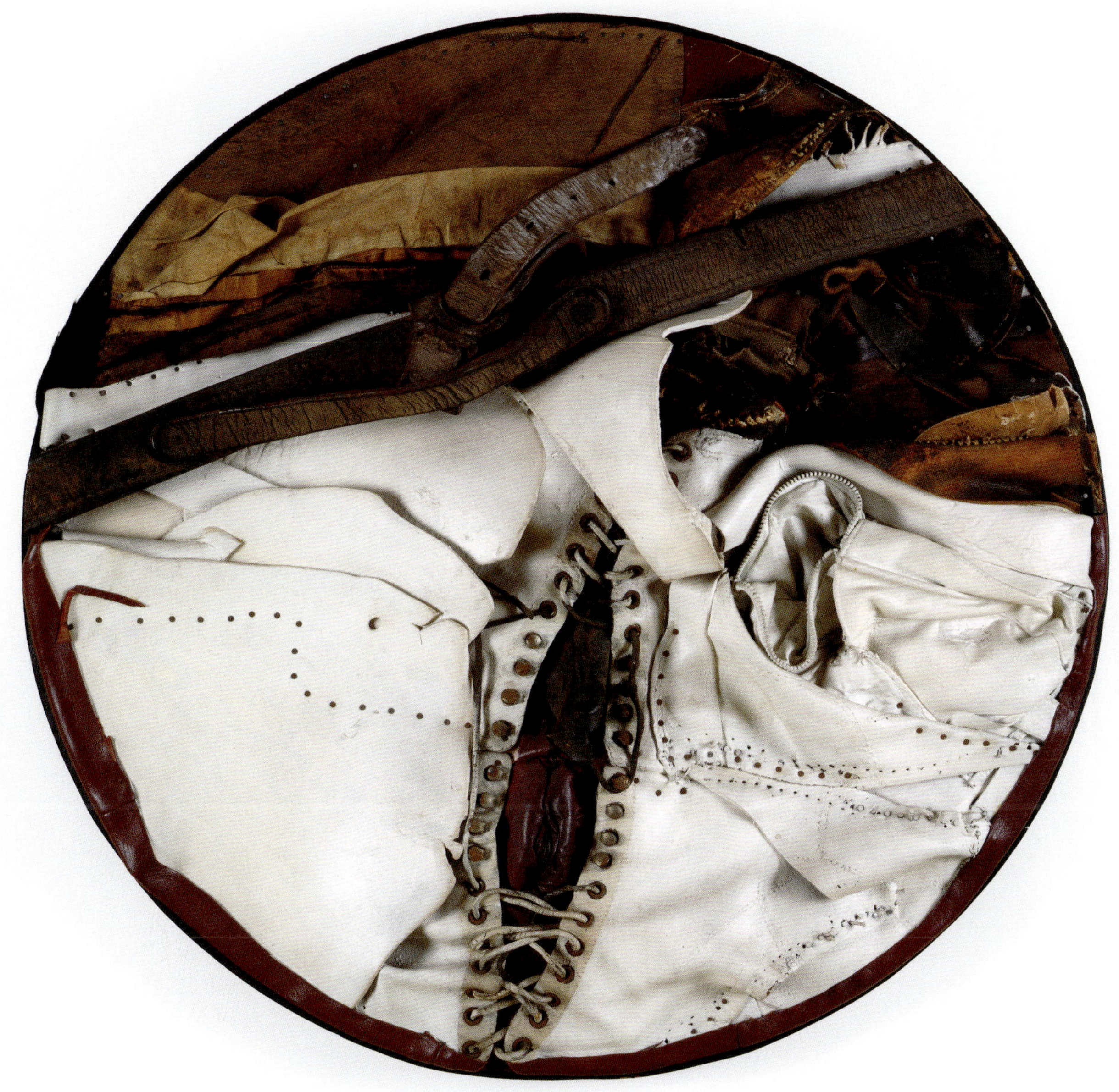

Nancy Grossman, *The Bride*, 1965. Leather, metal, fur, and fabric on canvas mounted on wood, 22 ⅝ × 22 ¾ × 5 ⅛ in. (57.5 × 57.8 × 13 cm). Collection of halley k harrisburg and Michael Rosenfeld

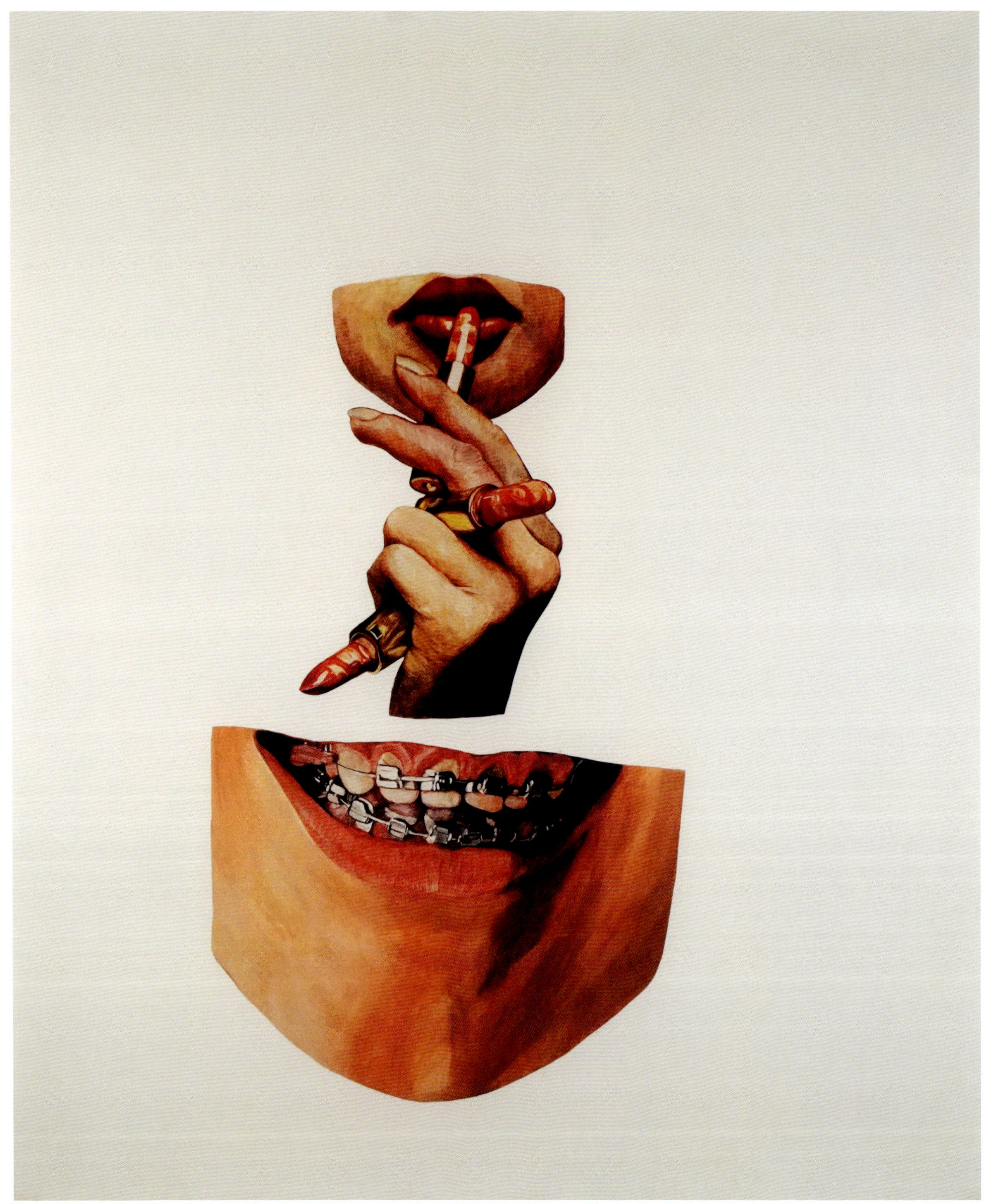

Joseph Raffaele, *Lipsticks, Braces*, 1965. Oil on canvas, 55 ¾ × 45 ¾ in. (141.6 × 116.2 cm). The Estate of Joseph Raffael and Nancy Hoffman Gallery, New York

York Theater Rally. Sturtevant's simulacral practice will reach a subversive peak in 1967, when the artist opens *The Store of Claes Oldenburg*, an exhibition that wholly reproduces Oldenburg's famous *Store* installation of 1961. The ensuing backlash, in which Sturtevant is criticized for having gone too far in "repeating" such an iconic milestone in the development of Pop art, causes the artist to partially retreat from the artworld during the 1970s, although such work would align her presciently with the coming Postmodernist turn of the 1980s.

1965 • A decade into his career, Joseph Raffaele (1933–2021) debuts his white-ground collage paintings at Stable Gallery, New York. Each of these paintings results from an intense period of psychoanalysis and functions like a nonspecific rebus, juxtaposing photorealistic images of body parts, machinery, and consumer products on a white ground, with a particular emphasis on iconography of male beauty and machismo. The show is a break from the artist's earlier graceful abstractions and, according to critic Gene Swenson, brings Raffaele in line with the work of Paul Thek and Michael Todd, known for their cool, inert kind of psychosexual surrealism.

Born and raised in Brooklyn, Raffaele had attended the Cooper Union School of Art alongside Thek, and soon meets Peter Hujar. The three will remain friends for over a decade, spending time together in Florida—where Thek lives with the set designer Peter Harvey from 1954 to 1959—as well as Long Island and Manhattan. In 1958 Raffaele is awarded a Fulbright fellowship to live and work in Rome. Upon his return to New York, he embarks on a series of floral abstractions and, alongside Thek and Hujar, socializes with a group of artists, poets, and writers that includes Todd as well as Eva Hesse and Ann Wilson. In 1966 and 1968, Raffaele will exhibit more works from the floral series at Stable Gallery before turning to collage and, finally, to watercolor.

November 1965 • In what would be a crossroads for her career, Jay DeFeo's longtime project *The Rose* is removed from her studio at Painterland, the Fillmore Street artist residences in San Francisco. A painting that recesses to a point of light as though rendering a mystical revelation in physical form, *The Rose* has been in progress for eight years, accumulating some 2,000 pounds of paint, as DeFeo has built it out from the center, moving from light to dark. At over 8 × 10 feet, the work can only be relocated by removing a part of a wall from the building itself. Bruce Conner records the event, later releasing the film *THE WHITE ROSE*.

November 3, 1965 • Yayoi Kusama's ambitious solo exhibition *Floor Show* opens at Castellane

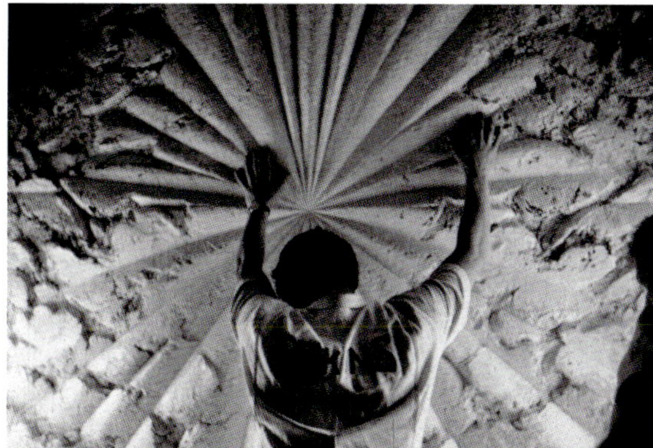

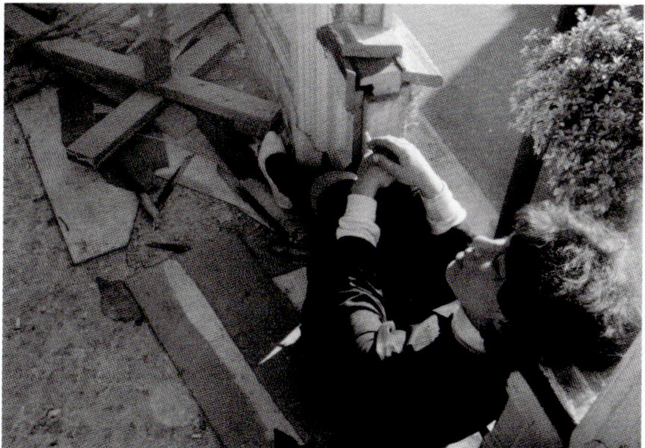

Bruce Conner, *THE WHITE ROSE*, 1967 (digitally restored 2022). 16mm to 35mm blow-up, black-and-white, sound; 7 min.

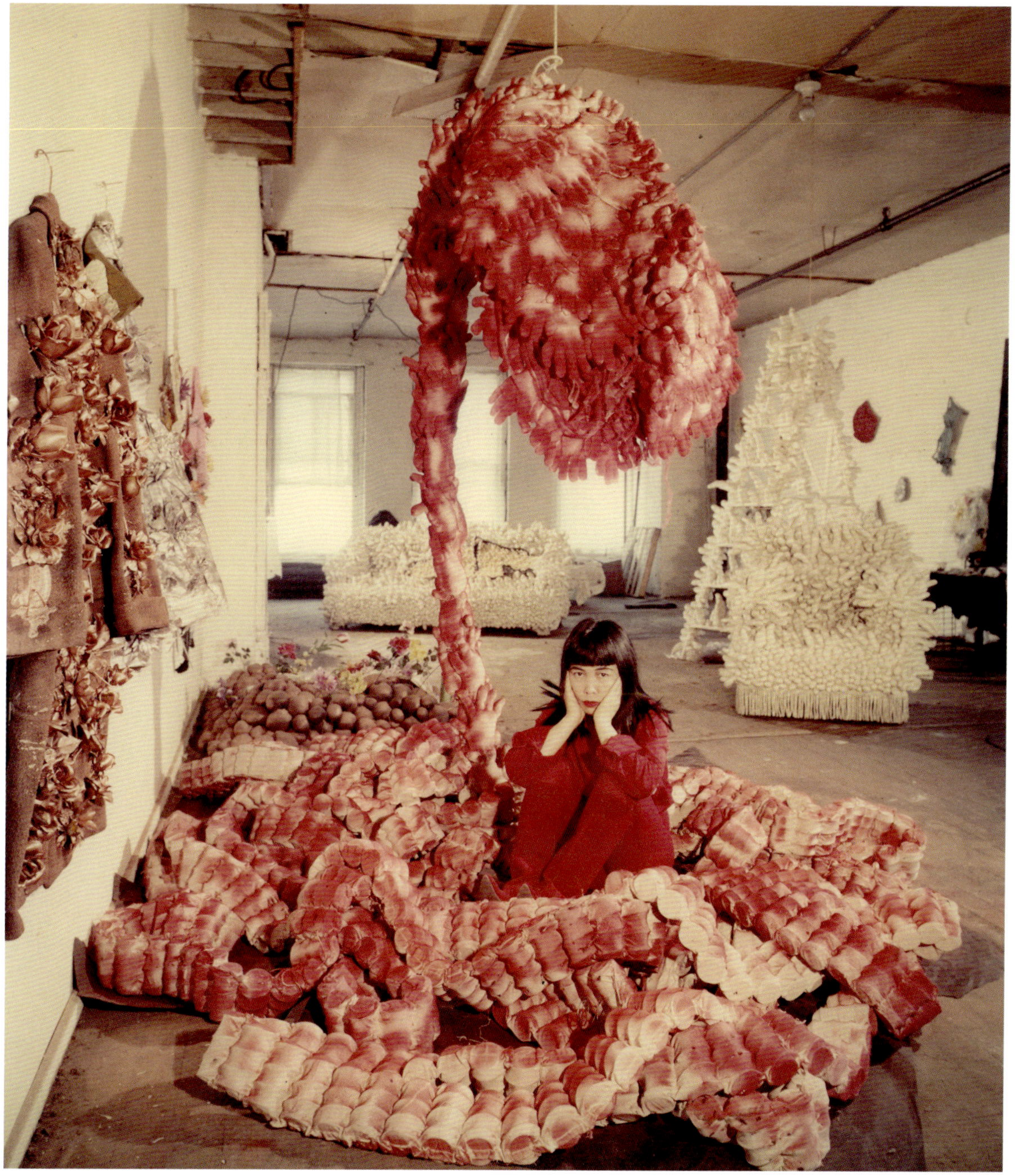

Yayoi Kusama sitting on *My Flower Bed* (1962), New York, c. 1965

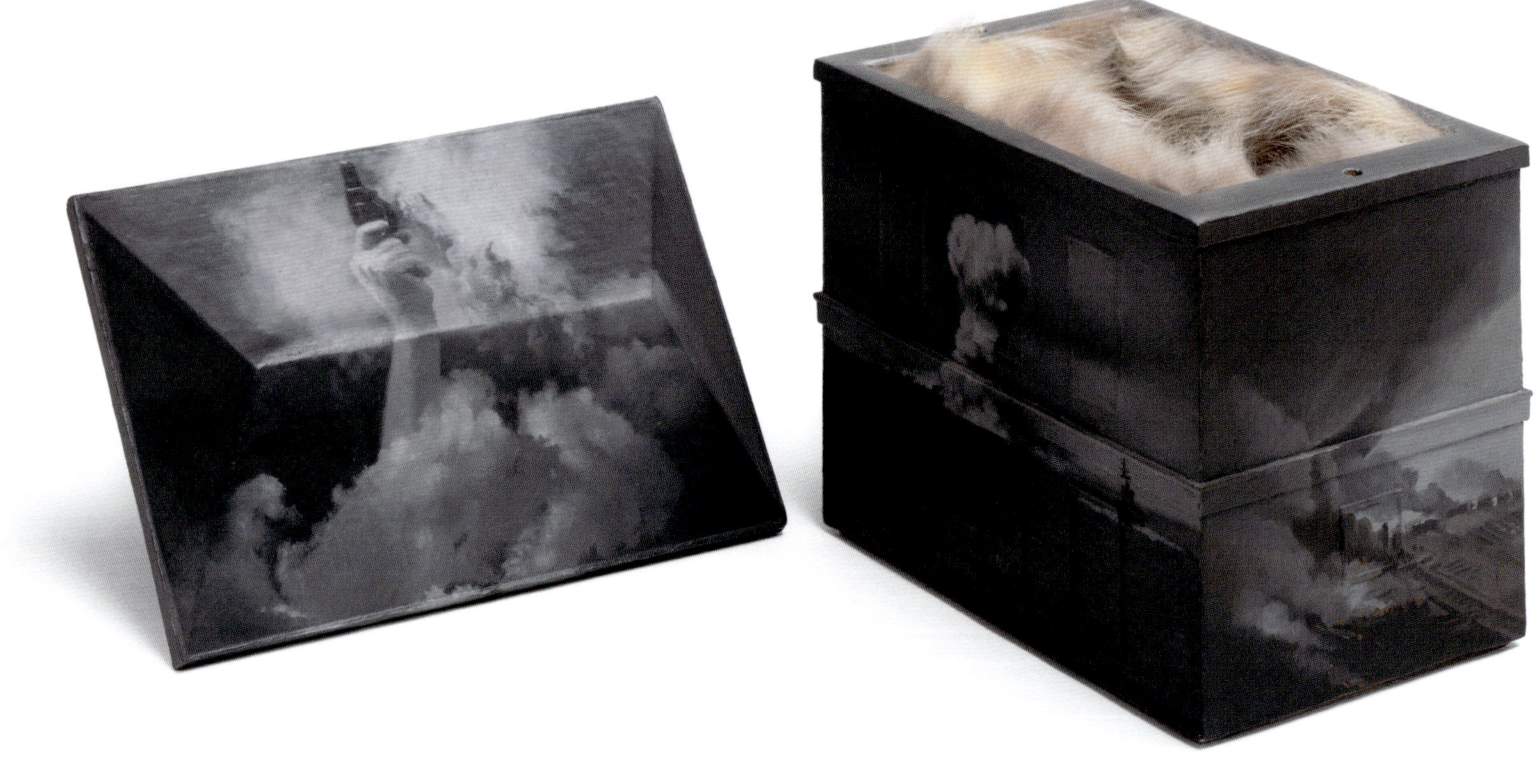

Vija Celmins, *House #1*, 1965. Oil on wood, metal, fur, and plastic: house, 7 ½ × 6 ½ × 10 in. (19.1 × 16.5 × 25.4 cm); roof, 2 ¼ × 7 ⅜ × 10 ½ in. (5.7 × 18.7 × 26.7 cm).
The Museum of Modern Art, New York; Gift of Edward R. Broida 670.2005.a–b

Gallery, New York, and includes *My Flower Bed* (1962), in which a flower stalk constructed from hundreds of stuffed-and-dyed cotton gloves rises from a base comprised of bedsprings; *Kitchen Utensils* (1963); a number of stuffed shoes (1964); the phallus-covered *Baby Carriage* (c. 1964–66); as well as Kusama's spatial installation *Infinity Mirror Room—Phalli's Field* (1965). The latter demonstrates her recent interest in creating three-dimensional environments. Mirrors encase the walls of the gallery, and the floor is littered with thousands of stuffed, white-fabric phallic forms covered with red polka dots in varying sizes, reflected infinitely in the mirrors. Kusama will recall, "Wandering into this infinite wonderland, where a grandiose aggregation of human sexual symbols had been transformed into a humorous, polka-dotted field, viewers found themselves spellbound by the imagination as it exorcized sexual sickness in the naked light of day." Writing in *Arts*, Jay Jacobs picks up on Kusama's obsessive and fetishizing strategies, in which her art is used to channel her neurosis and disgust surrounding issues of sex and consumption, commenting: "Stylistically, Miss Kusama may indeed be an original. Spiritually, however, she is one with the ingenious fanatic who constructs an Eiffel Tower of toothpicks, engraves the Lord's Prayer on a pinhead, or meticulously paints a full page of legible newsprint." Jo Applin will argue that Kusama's environmental works have much in common with the happenings and body festivals she organizes between 1967 and 1969, as they all share her desire to bring together diverse onlookers and participants.

November 7–8, 1965 • Jack Smith presents *Rehearsals for the Destruction of Atlantis* at the New Cinema Festival I (often referred to as the Expanded Cinema Festival), organized by Jonas Mekas at the Film-Makers' Cinematheque in New York. A landmark event in the expanded cinema movement, the festival's programs explore "the uses of multiple screens, multiple projectors, multiple images, inter-related screen forms and images, film-dance, multiple exposures, hand-held projectors, balloon screens, video tape and video projections, and light and sound improvisations." Stan VanDerBeek and Claes Oldenburg also participate. Fittingly, Smith's contribution furthers his idea of the "live film"—a shift away from film as a finished product and a push toward process and the durational experience of the filmic event. Described as a "Dream Weapon Ritual by Jack Smith Dedicated to Irving Rosenthal," the performance castigates the police, narcotics agents, and US aggression in Vietnam.

November 28 and December 4–5, 1965 • Roy Fridge begins "digging into psychological analysis"

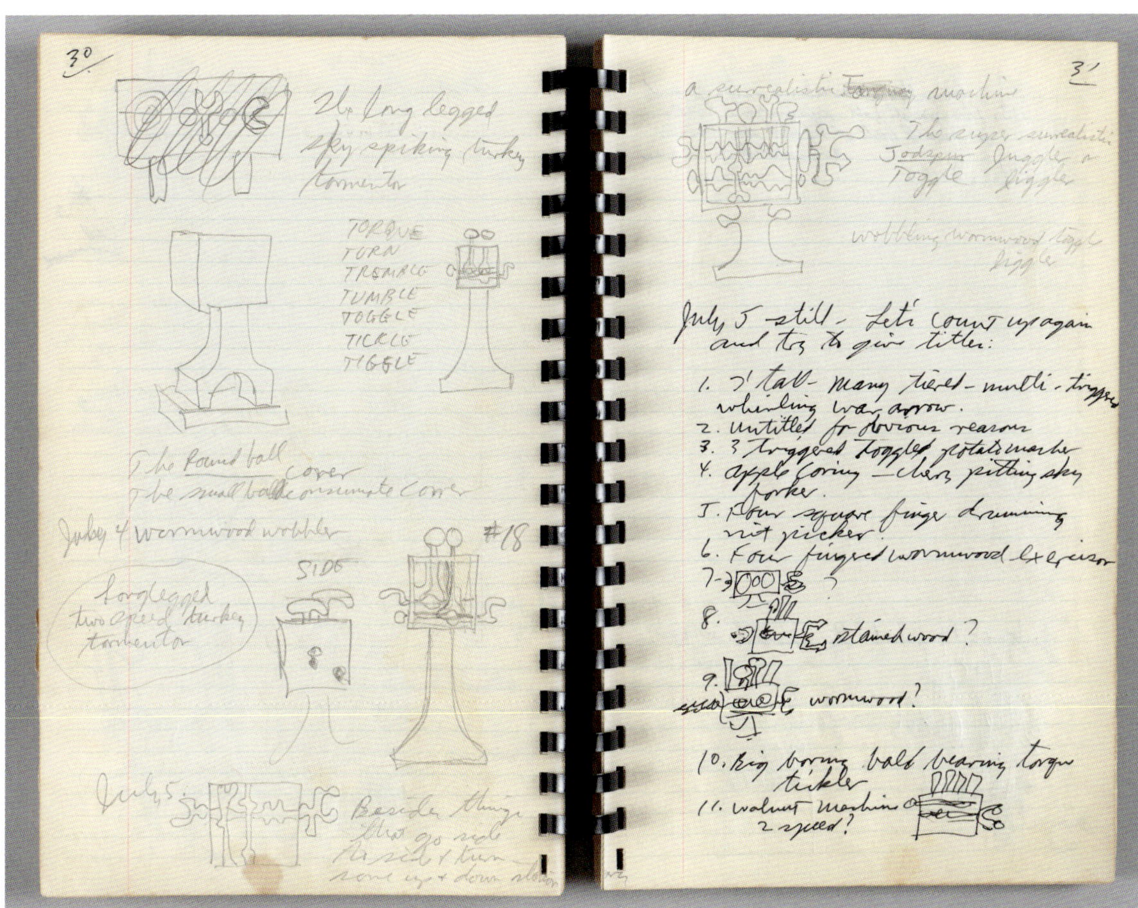

Pages from Roy Fridge's journal, July 4–5, 1966

and making wooden sculptures, often with moving parts. According to his extensive journals, he now creates "these little boxes with 'wormy' things inside," giving the works tongue-twisting titles such as *The Wobbling Wormwood Toggle Jiggler*, a piece he describes as a "surrealist machine" drawing. Fridge is living between Houston and his handmade A-frame in Port Aransas, having escaped his more traditional life in Dallas working in film and animation two years prior.

December 8, 1965 • Three thousand people pack Berlin's Congress Hall to see Experiments from New York, a program organized by Amos Vogel featuring the work of American underground filmmakers Stan Brakhage, Shirley Clarke, Bruce Conner, Ed Emshwiller, and Stan VanDerBeek.

Emshwiller previews *Relativity* (1966), a film he made with a 1964 grant from the Ford Foundation, which also awarded grants to Jordan Belson and Bruce Conner that year. The plotless 38-minute film is structured by the slow, roving attention of Emshwiller's camera, which passes through countless environments that are abstracted from the contexts that give them their ordinary meaning. Accompanied by the sounds of heavy breathing, the movement of the camera suggests a first-person stance characterized by a groping innocence, a blind approach to the future that enables a heightened sensitivity to the aural, visual, and tactile phenomena of the evolving present. While the technique invites comparison to collage, it also calls to mind the films and writings of Maya Deren, whose protagonists reach blindly across impossible spaces that are jointly constructed by their movements and by editing that allows the camera to elide stark spatiotemporal discontinuities. Emshwiller observes in his own work a recurrent interest in using "unrelated material" to build "a new sense of relationship." As one might expect from an artist steeped in the world-building ethos of Golden Age science fiction, his work in *Relativity* trades on the premise that the film medium looks out onto "another world," as Deren says, yet here that other world looks into our own, estranging us from our commonsense experience of distance, duration, and scale, as the title suggests.

December 8, 1965–January 30, 1966 • The Whitney Museum of American Art's *1965 Annual Exhibition of Contemporary American Painting* includes artist Deborah Remington, the same year she moves to New York from San Francisco.

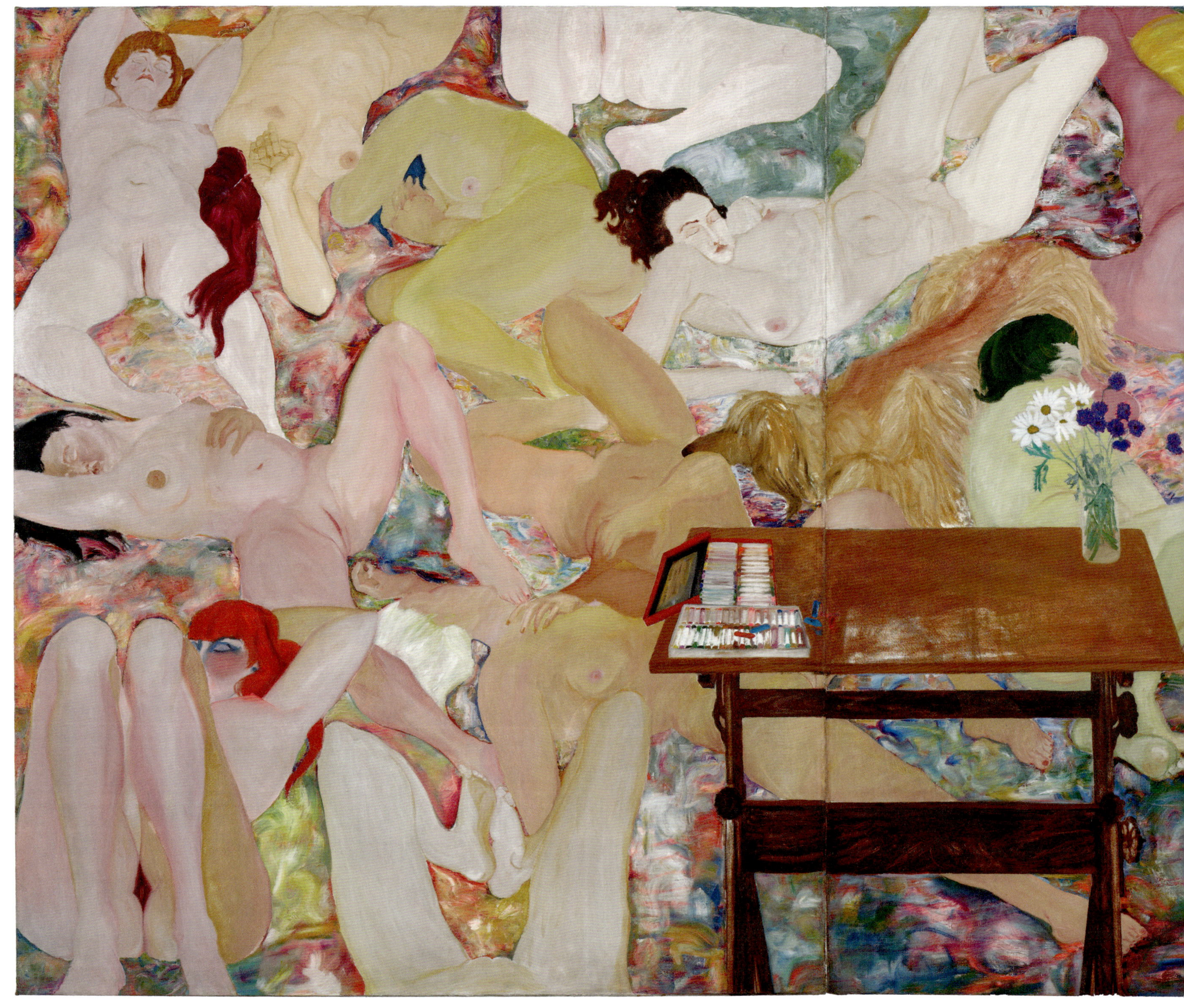

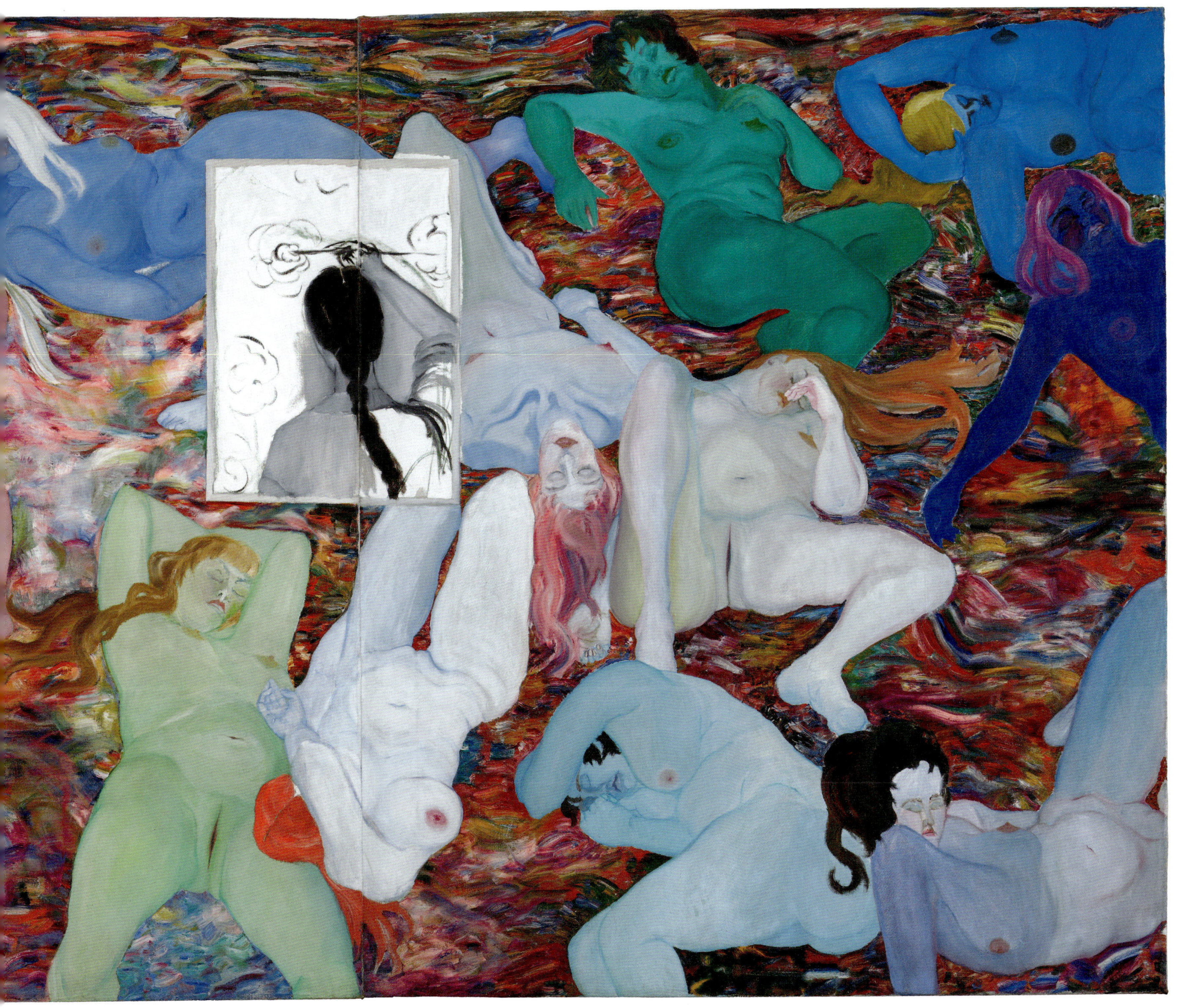

Martha Edelheit, *Flesh Wall–Female*, 1965. Oil on canvas: three panels, 80 × 195 in. (203.2 × 495.3 cm) overall. Minneapolis Institute of Art; The Mary Ingebrand-Pohlad Endowment for Twentieth-Century Paintings and the William Hood Dunwoody Fund 2019.24a–c

1966

1966 • Luis Jimenez moves to New York. The artist's mentor, the painter and sculptor Francisco Zúñiga, had encouraged the move two years before, but the birth of Jimenez's daughter, the need to save money, and a debilitating injury from a car accident led him to postpone it. By 1966 Jimenez is working with fiberglass and already exploring many of the symbols of American and Chicano masculinity—car culture and pinup girls—as well as consumer culture. Unlike the cool detachment of much Pop art at the time, however, Jimenez's approach is best understood as *rasquachismo*, an outsider viewpoint described by writer Tomás Ybarra-Frausto as a "funky, irreverent stance that debunks convention and spoofs protocol."

In New York, Jimenez finds employment that allows him time to make art during the day. The city Youth Board hires him despite his lack of social work experience in part because he speaks Spanish and lives on the Lower East Side, one of the so-called high hazard areas served by the Youth Board. Until 1968, he organizes youth programs such as afterschool dances, during what is a period of great tumult for many Hispanic and Puerto Rican neighborhoods, later recalling: "An area couldn't get a dance unless they'd had a riot. That's how the Federal funds were earmarked. Sometimes we had 2,000 kids at a street dance. . . . I liked being part of the real world. So the question was, how could I relate that world to my work?"

January 27–March 7, 1966 • *The* Other *Tradition* is on view at the Institute of Contemporary Art on the campus of the University of Pennsylvania, Philadelphia, organized by critic Gene Swenson. Having developed his ideas through his series of artist interviews exploring the question "what is Pop art?," Swenson now proposes to counter the imposing critical—and scholarly—bias in favor of abstraction, advocating for a shift away from the methodological constraints of formalism by encouraging critics to examine not only a style's visuality but also its content and subject matter. To make this case, *The* Other *Tradition* offers an alternative history of modern art, following a "nonformal" tradition that Swenson describes as "intellectual," an approach that includes styles typically "neglected" by the modernist canon, namely Dada and Surrealism, here represented with work from artists such as Jean Arp, André Breton, Salvador Dalí, Marcel Duchamp, Max Ernst, René Magritte, Joan Miró, Pablo Picasso, and Ernst Schwitters. To these Swenson traces the origins of Pop art, which together constitute what he calls the *other* tradition.

"The paintings of the other tradition are not, however, mirrors of society," Swenson writes. "They are mirrors of what happens to us without our knowing or realizing it. In a way they might be said to objectify experience, to turn feelings into things so that we can deal with them." Such art's emotive materialization is key: "It is as if

the art object which is hanging on the wall is the generalized feeling state I am experiencing." Among contemporary artists working in this vein, Swenson includes Jasper Johns, Claes Oldenburg, Joseph Raffaele, Robert Rauschenberg, James Rosenquist, Paul Thek, Michael Todd, Andy Warhol, and Ann Wilson (of the show's fifty-four artists, the only woman). He calls out sexuality as a major theme of *The* Other *Tradition*, though he deems the artists "post-Freudian" for having integrated into their lives, rather than repressed, their sexual impulses.

Critic and curator Lucy Lippard, in her review of the show in *Art International*, dismisses the work of Thek and Raffaele, saying it "leaves me cold"; enthuses over the work of Oldenburg

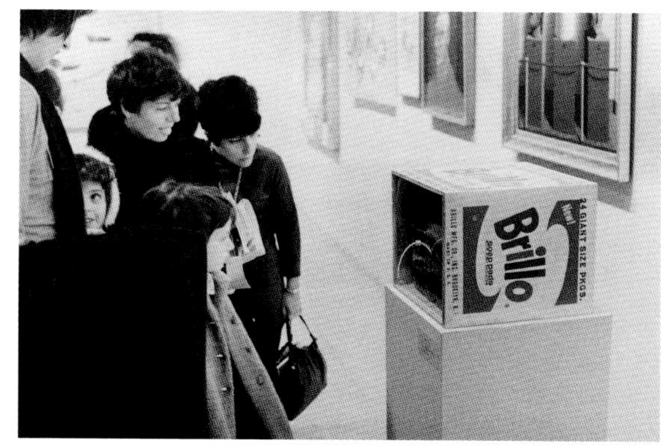

The Other *Tradition*, Institute of Contemporary Art, Philadelphia, 1966, with Paul Thek's *Meat Piece with Warhol Brillo Box* (1965)

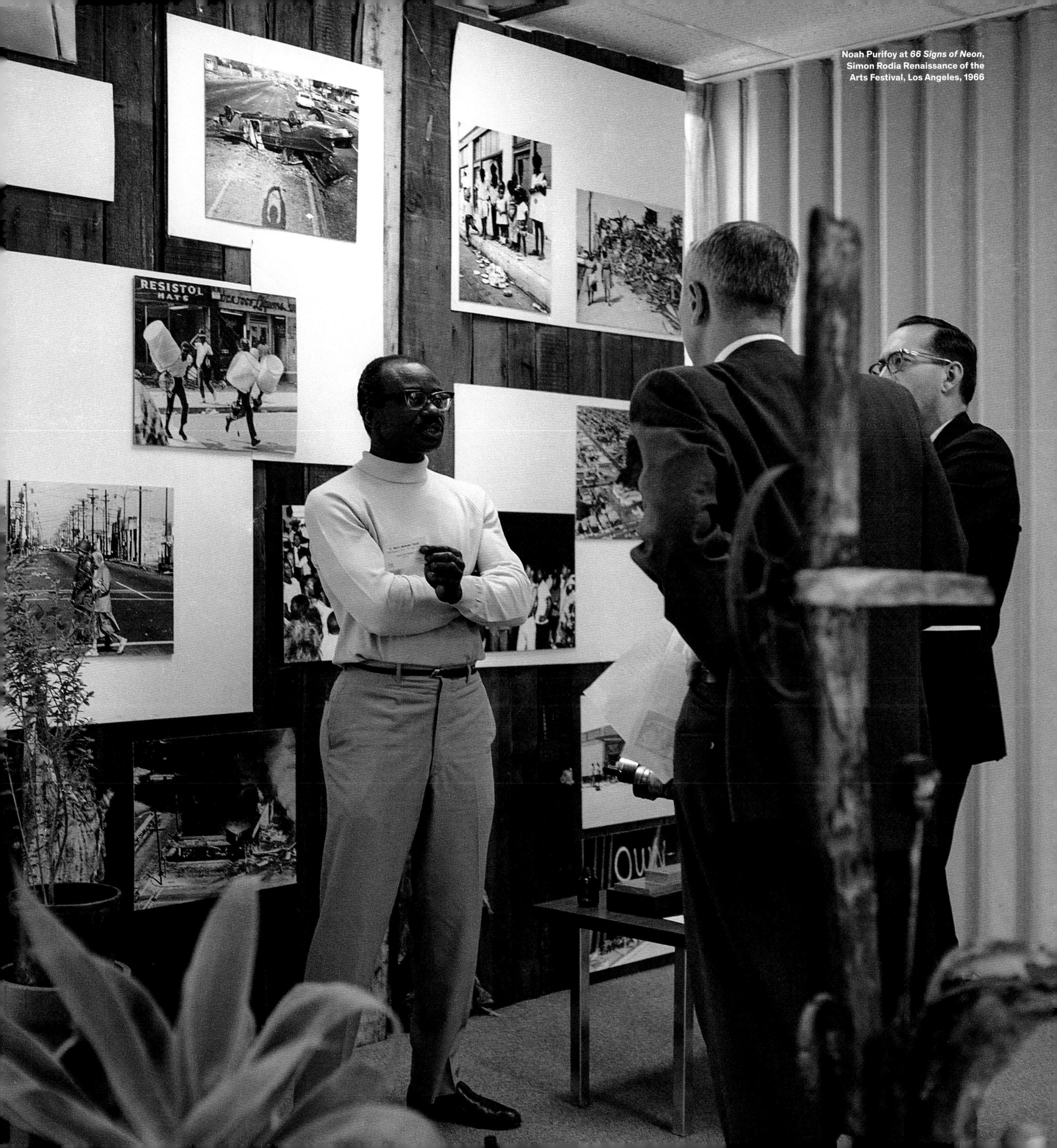

Noah Purifoy at *66 Signs of Neon*, Simon Rodia Renaissance of the Arts Festival, Los Angeles, 1966

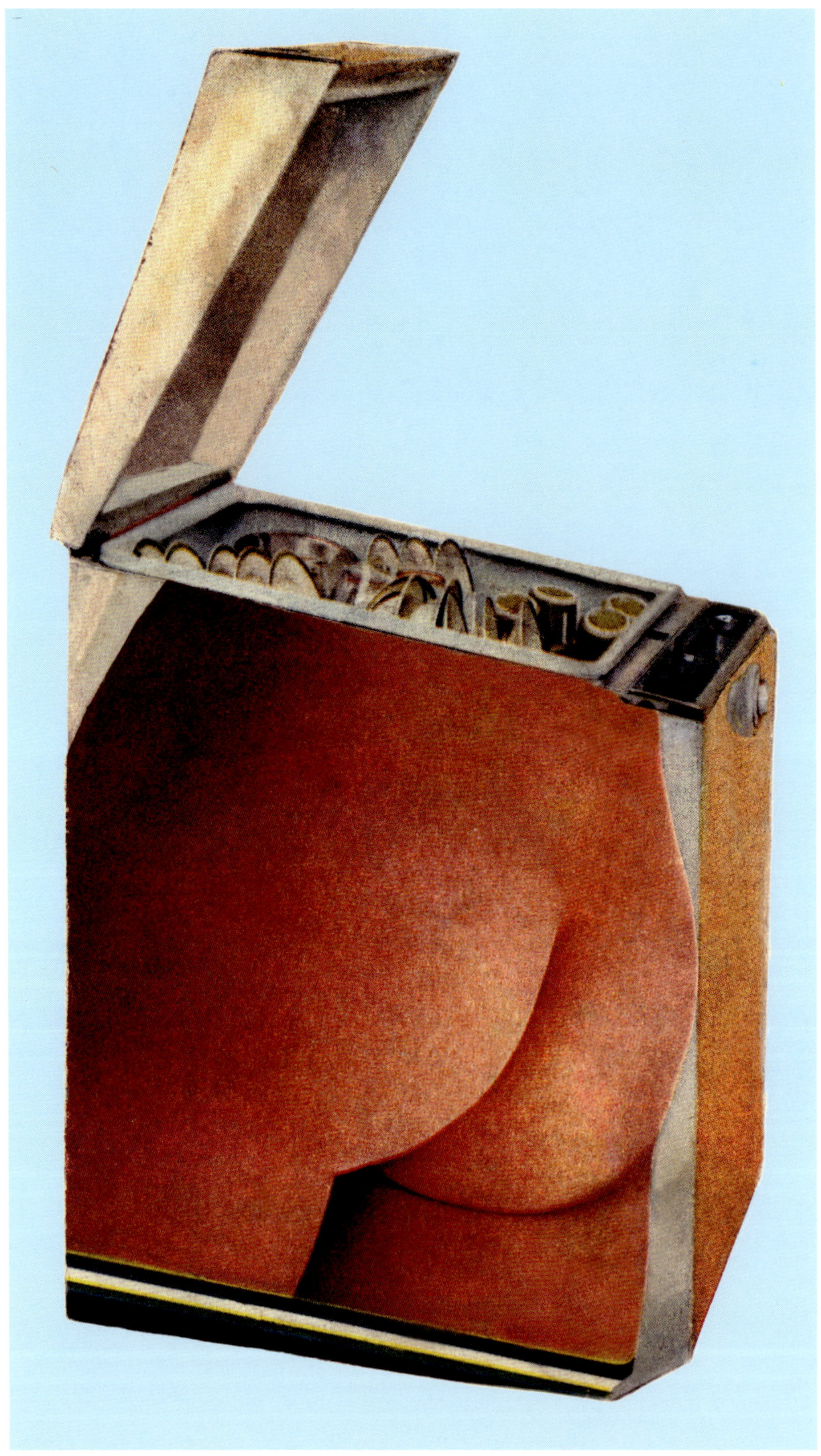

Martha Rosler, *Damp Meat*, c. 1966–72, from the series *Body Beautiful, or Beauty Knows No Pain*. Photomontage, 20 × 16 in. (50.8 × 40.6 cm). Collection of the artist

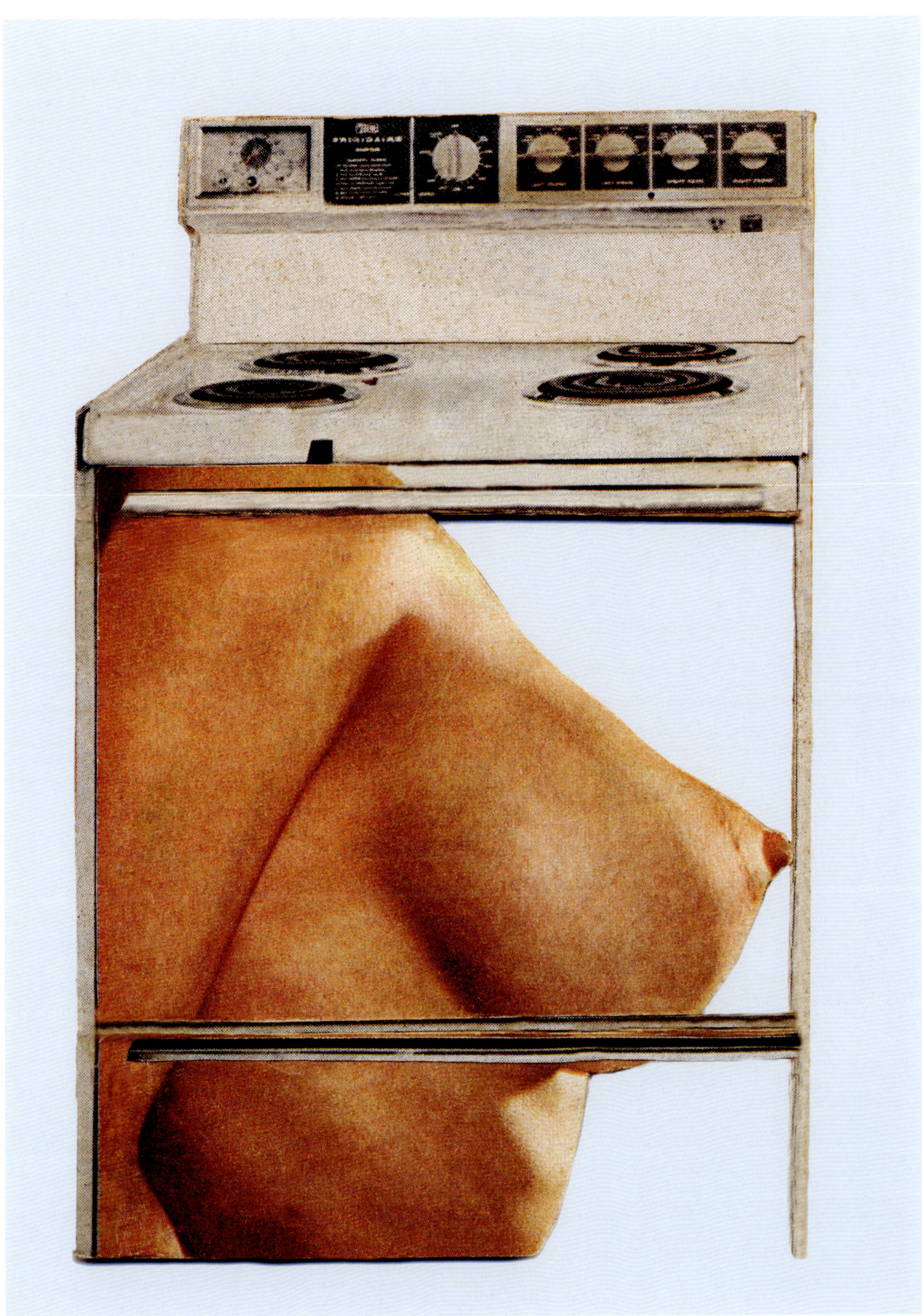

Martha Rosler, *Kitchen I, or Hot Meat*, c. 1966–72, from the series *Body Beautiful, or Beauty Knows No Pain*. Photomontage, 14 × 11 in. (35.6 × 27.9 cm). Collection of the artist

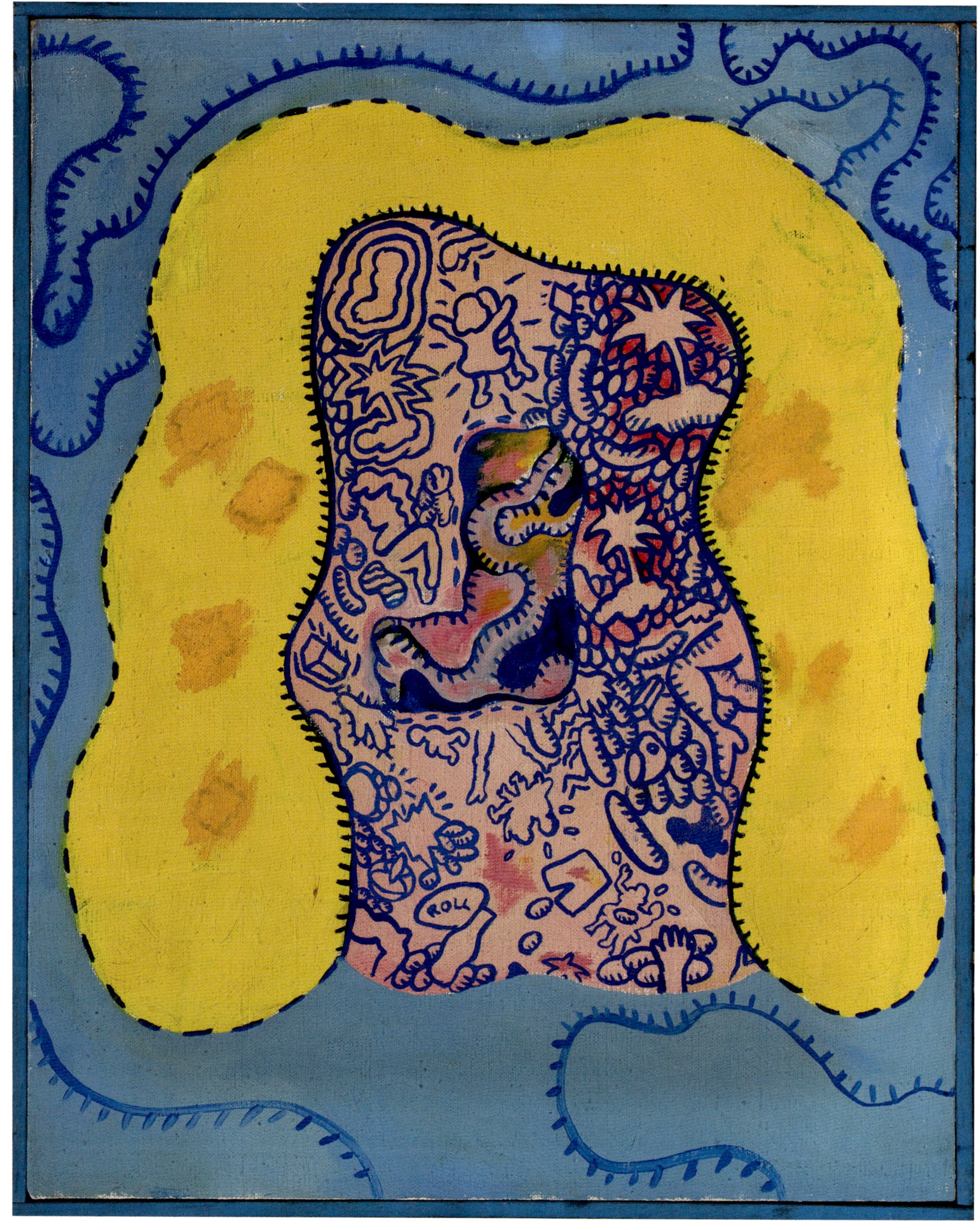

Suellen Rocca, *Foot Smells*, c. 1966. Oil on canvas, in artist's painted frame, 19 ⅝ × 15 ½ in. (49.9 × 39.4 cm). Madison Museum of Contemporary Art, WI; gift of the Raymond K. Yoshida Living Trust and Kohler Foundation, Inc.

(*American Trinity*, 1966); and proposes the inclusion of Eva Hesse to better illustrate Swenson's aims. In this same review, Lippard coins the term *eccentric abstraction*, which will become the titular focus of her own landmark show in September.

1966 • Martha Rosler (b. 1943) starts working on what will become the series *Body Beautiful, or Beauty Knows No Pain* (c. 1966–72). In these works, her earliest manipulations of mass-produced images, Rosler demonstrates what will be a lifelong commitment to integrating artistic activity and social activism. In works from the series such as *Damp Meat* and *Kitchen I, or Hot Meat*, Rosler relocates fragments of the female body from popular men's magazines to the surfaces of everyday kitchen appliances, signifiers of female domesticity, thereby critiquing the common cultural objectification of women through a Surrealist strategy of juxtaposition.

Born and raised in Brooklyn, Rosler comes of age during the civil rights movement and the Vietnam War, participating in social justice and antiwar protests. During her formative years in New York, she is exposed to happenings, Pop art, and various "radical theater/antitheater traditions," including places like the Living Theatre and La MaMa. Initially an abstract painter, by the mid-1960s Rosler is making ironic appropriations of imagery from the mass media and producing work in the Pop and Surrealist vein that is "fueled by a largely anti-war, antiracist, and feminist energy," counting among her influences Jess, Max Ernst, and the Futurists.

February 25–April 9, 1966 • *Hairy Who* opens at Hyde Park Art Center (HPAC) in Chicago, the first of a series of exhibitions featuring work by recent School of the Art Institute of Chicago (SAIC) graduates Jim Falconer, Art Green, Gladys Nilsson, Jim Nutt, Suellen Rocca, and Karl Wirsum. "There were very few galleries in Chicago at that time and very few spaces for new artists to show," as Nutt would later recall. He and Falconer approached artist and curator Don Baum, who had been organizing large group shows at HPAC, where, "it was hard to get noticed with all the established people with large bodies of work behind them," Nutt says. "Jim Falconer and I finally figured out that if we took these large shows and broke them down into groups of five or six people, each person could exhibit five to ten works. We went to Don with our idea for a small show and he liked it and suggested Karl. None of us knew him personally but all of us liked his work."

The group's moniker, which will become the show's title, is born at their first Continued on page 163

POST-FREUDIAN: ON GENE SWENSON'S *THE* OTHER *TRADITION*

JENNIFER SICHEL

On January 27, 1966, Gene Swenson's exhibition *The* Other *Tradition* opened at the Institute of Contemporary Art in Philadelphia, a fledgling institution housed in the University of Pennsylvania art library—"hardly the Museum of Modern Art," as critic Robert Pincus-Witten would later quip.[1] To accompany the show, Swenson published a black paperback catalogue containing a forty-page essay that circulated among artists and critics like "radioactive material," in the words of critic Peter Schjeldahl (fig. 1).[2] "It was *so* alternative," Pincus-Witten recalled, "it was *so samizdat* that it didn't even merit the nobility of glossy paper and real type."[3] Meandering, fragmentary, and padded with strange disclaimers, Swenson's text nonetheless became a "flying wedge into the heart of the matter," according to Lucy Lippard, who positioned her own 1966 exhibition, *Eccentric Abstraction*, in dialogue with Swenson's intervention.[4] Why did Swenson's scrappy, offbeat provocation land in New York's artworld with such a toxic blow? That it did is a testament both to the brazenness of Swenson's attacks and to the incredible novelty of his ideas.

With *The* Other *Tradition*, Swenson not only rewrote the history of modernism but also proposed bold new ways to understand subjectivity and sexuality in the contemporaneous moment of the mid-1960s. He offered a new theoretical account of what it means to be a person living and working in an increasingly automated and media-saturated world, and of how contemporary artists can and should respond. However, Swenson's account is also provisional and piecemeal, never congealing into a coherent theory. "This is an essay—a try," Swenson confesses in the introduction to his text. "Only the uniformity of contradictory opinions has emboldened me to make public these views at this time, without waiting to develop them more completely."[5]

Pulling no punches, Swenson argues that formalist critical standards had infected everyone's vision, engendering such widespread myopia that it was hardly possible for critics and curators to see certain works of art at all. The result: an entire

Fig. 1. Exhibition catalogue for *The* Other *Tradition*, Institute of Contemporary Art, Philadelphia, 1966

tradition of art that had emerged from Dada and Surrealism was occluded from view, completely "overlooked or neglected by art historians" who focused only on the "abstract-formal-Cubist tradition in modern art" to the exclusion of everything else.[6] Swenson expresses a kind of snarky boredom with this situation. "Why bother with 'modernist' originality if it is so easily defined?" he snaps.[7] With his exhibition, Swenson assembled the contours of an *other* tradition spanning early twentieth-century Dada and Surrealism to contemporary innovations in Pop and "post-Freudian" art—a term he proposes for new artistic experiments that took up the legacy of Surrealism. "The images of the *other* tradition possess artistic qualities beyond those which formalist critics have found in them—percipient and psychical qualities," Swenson proclaims, emphasizing the importance of content and subject matter over purely formal concerns.[8] These artworks force us "to reactivate our sense of the world around us," he writes.[9]

In terms of the historical roots of the *other* tradition, Swenson focuses on Dada explorations of "man as machine" and on Surrealist attempts "to make dreams 'concrete' so that it would be possible to deal with them," as he explained in the exhibition's press release. In both cases, he is interested in how artists of the early twentieth century engaged the world around them by imagining the conflation of subjective and objective reality. According to Swenson, by picturing man as "a partially receptive receiver of light, sound, heat, and other kinds of mass-energy wave lengths," Dada artists were among the first to expose the objective, material basis of our supposedly subjective, inner psychic life. Likewise (though in some ways reversed), Surrealist artists were among the first "to galvanize men against the unconscious," as Swenson argues, by hardening dreams and emotions into concrete things—a counterintuitive take on the legacy of Surrealism.[10] But the real thrust of Swenson's argument consists in his account of how contemporary artists of the 1960s took up these concerns—how they drew from historical examples of Dada and Surrealism "to objectify experience," as Swenson puts it, "to turn feelings into things so we can deal with them" in response to a rapidly changing world.[11]

Proposing revolutionary new ideas about what it meant to be a person in the 1960s (and presaging much postmodern theory), Swenson argues that desires and drives are no longer repressed in the subconscious but rather are explicit and conscious. As a result, "traditional Freudian psychological motivations" are just simply not "very interesting or applicable in telling stories of *later* twentieth century people."[12] We are dealing instead with a "post-Freudian" situation, as Swenson calls

it, or with the end of a Freudian model of repression. This gives way to a new model of subjectivity in which feelings are things that are already public and shared. Moreover, it engenders a whole new model of sexuality premised on the explicit embrace of Freudian "perversions," including fetishism, sadomasochism, and homosexuality, without moralism or shame. "We still psychoanalyze ourselves in a Freudian manner although we may not be the least bit suppressed with Victorian 'secrets,'" Swenson quips, accusing other critics and scholars of harboring "a cold and Victorian prissiness hidden beneath assurances of jaundiced boredom."[13]

With *The Other Tradition*, Swenson put forth three young artists—Joseph Raffaele, Michael Todd, and Paul Thek—as key exponents of the new "post-Freudian" sensibility. These artists embraced fetishism and sadomasochism as the explicit content of their work. As Lippard noted in her review: "Swenson's comments on the new objectivity of a post-Freudian sexuality are thought-provoking. Since sexuality, Freudian sexuality, is the prime mover of all Surrealist art, this provides both a connection to and a breakaway from the earlier movement."[14] When Swenson prods Raffaele in an interview to answer the question "Are your paintings a Surrealistic investigation of the subconscious?" Raffaele responds, "No, not really." He explains, "Everybody knows that fingers can be penises, mouths and ears are vaginas, nostrils are assholes."[15] Raffaele's hyperrealistic paintings

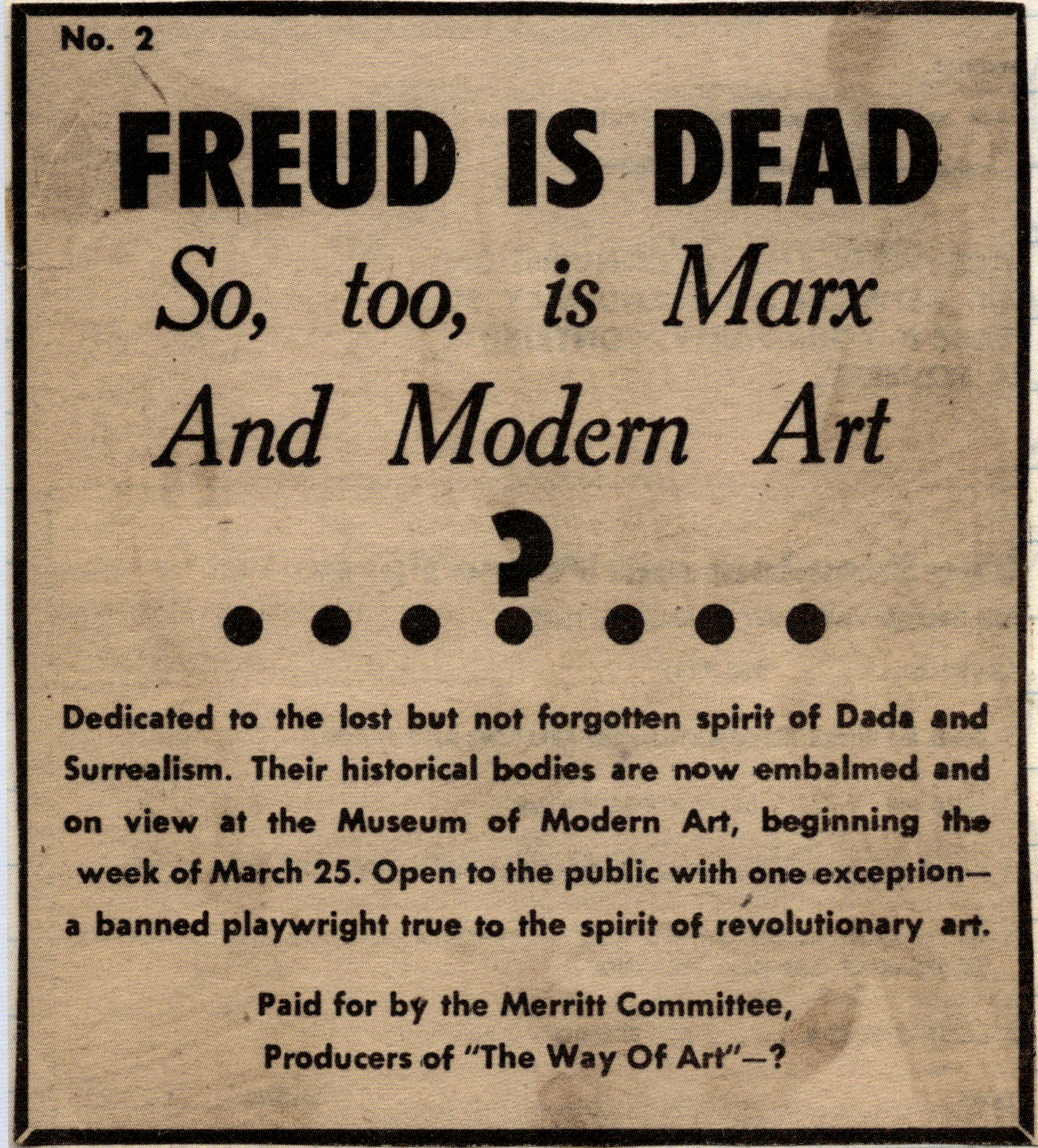

Fig. 2. Advertisement by Gene Swenson published in the *Village Voice*, March 21, 1968

of cut-up pictures of things like lipstick protruding from its tube, glossy fingernails, plump lips, and sharp metal braces present fetishistic attachment as fact—as something conscious on the surface, and not at all repressed (p. 148). Likewise, Todd draws from Surrealism while subverting its emphasis. According to Swenson, Todd's biomorphic sculptures make "some of the disturbing but abstract qualities of fetishism and sexuality in Yves Tanguy's work explicit" (pp. 92, 93).[16] Thek places hunks of butchered flesh, realistically rendered in wax, inside sleek plexiglass boxes, revealing the sadomasochism that undergirds the pleasures of space-age consumerism as a matter of fact. Thek's explorations connect to those of Andy Warhol, whose *Death in America* silkscreen paintings of 1962–64 held a mirror up to Americans' seemingly insatiable appetite for gruesome cruel images alongside cars, Cokes, and other commodities—a connection Thek makes explicit by placing a cube of bloody meat inside an upturned Warhol Brillo Box (p. 130). In an interview, Swenson asks Thek, "Are your works sado-masochistic?" To which he replies, "Yes. It's one—*one*—of the components." Thek forces the viewer to linger up close: "The dare of simply being able to look at it with a solid stomach," as he explains.[17]

All three artists picture sex and desire untethered from norms of heterosexual reproduction, spinning away from the so-called proper object-choice and congealing instead in body parts, strange things, bulbous forms, and sharp implements. But while Swenson alludes to how this explicit embrace of Freudian "perversions" might engender a better, more ethical, queerer world, he does not assert it directly. He does not even print the words *homosexual* or *queer* at all. With *The Other Tradition*, Swenson tempers his ideas to fit the institution—a tense balancing act that he would not sustain for very long.

In the end, *The Other Tradition* endures as a bold curatorial gambit and a tragically unfinished project. Swenson's roster of artists—all white men, with the lone exception of Ann Wilson—never quite caught up to the radical potential of his ideas. Swenson did not turn his critical attention to the many women artists and Black artists who were also drawing on legacies of Dada and Surrealism in the 1960s. He did not collaborate with others to explore how the pursuit of a "post-Freudian" world might also subvert norms that undergird so much sexism and racism. In an unpublished essay from 1968, Swenson proclaims, "One of the great contributions which the artists of our time can make is in the understanding of black history"—but he died just one year later in a car crash, at age thirty-four, without embarking on new projects.[18]

During the final two years of his life, Swenson was locked out of the establishment, as he took

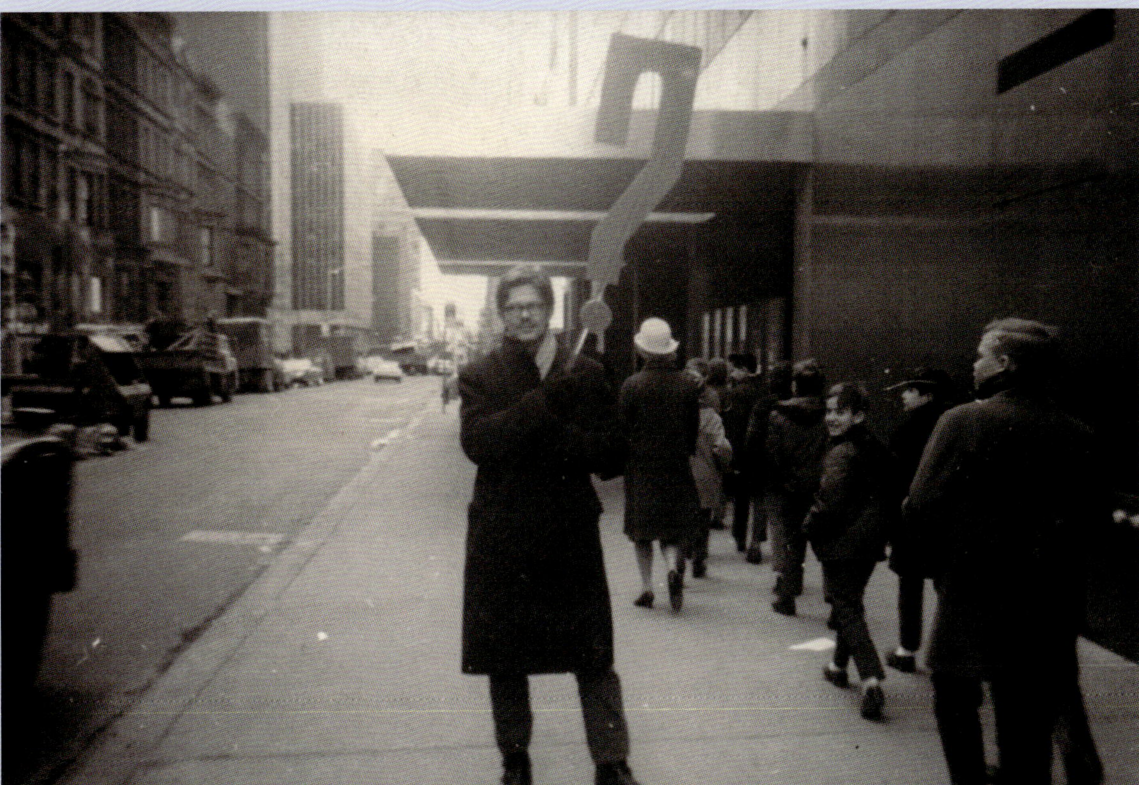

Fig. 3. Gene Swenson pickets outside the Museum of Modern Art, New York, 1968

up ranting and protesting outside artworld institutions. As Lippard would lament, "He wasn't listened to because what he said was said too strongly and it was too true."[19] On the opening night of the exhibition *Dada, Surrealism, and Their Heritage* at the Museum of Modern Art in March 1968, Swenson organized a large protest "dedicated to the lost but not forgotten spirit of Dada and Surrealism" whose "historical bodies are now embalmed at the Museum of Modern Art," as he put it in a *Village Voice* advertisement, proclaiming: "Freud is Dead. So, too, is Marx. And Modern Art . . . ? . . ." (fig. 2). In the month leading up to that, he picketed alone outside MoMA every weekday wielding only a giant blue question mark as a sign (fig. 3). With his lonely question mark, Swenson withheld the comforts of slogans and solidarity, of simple demands shouted in unison. He suspended the popular protest chant at "What do we want?" Only in his protest, the "we" never materialized. No rallying cry rose up in response. Instead, Swenson demanded a more difficult, disquieting kind of vigilance: to show up alert, uneasy, perhaps scared, and deeply committed. "We and our works are and must be involved with the time and the world we live in," he intones in *The Other Tradition* near the end of the text. "Our world is too dangerous and violent for us to be anything else."[20]

NOTES

1   Robert Pincus-Witten, quoted in Amy Newman, *Challenging Art: Artforum, 1962–1974* (New York: Soho Press, 2000), 192.

2   Peter Schjeldahl, quoted in Scott Rothkopf, "Banned and Determined," *Artforum* 40, no. 10 (June 2002): 143.

3   Pincus-Witten, quoted in Newman, *Challenging Art*, 192. Emphasis original.

4   In her review of Swenson's exhibition, Lippard coined the term "eccentric abstraction" to describe the work of artists including Eva Hesse, Frank Lincoln Viner, and Robert Breer who "share certain attitudes with the more conceptual branches of current art as well as with the Other Tradition." Lucy Lippard, "An Impure Situation (New York and Philadelphia Letter)," *Art International* 10, no. 5 (May 1966): 60–65.

5   Gene R. Swenson, *The Other Tradition* (Philadelphia: Institute of Contemporary Art, University of Pennsylvania, 1966), ix.

6   Ibid., viii.

7   Ibid., 12.

8   Ibid., 11.

9   Ibid., 17.

10   Ibid., 20–22.

11   Ibid., 28.

12   Ibid., 32. Emphasis original.

13   Ibid., 35.

14   Lippard, "Impure Situation," 63.

15   Joseph Raffaele, quoted in G. R. Swenson, "Paint, Flesh, Vesuvius: Joe Raffaele discusses the eruptive nature of his Post-Freudian art with writer G. R. Swenson," *Arts Magazine* 41, no. 1 (November 1966): 33–34.

16   Swenson, *The Other Tradition*, 35.

17   G. R. Swenson and Paul Thek, "Beneath the Skin," *ARTnews* 65, no. 2 (April 1966): 65. Emphasis original.

18   Gene Swenson, "We are all Nationalists—in our Art." Unpublished essay dated April–May 1968, Gene Swenson papers, 1950–1969, Archives of American Art, Smithsonian Institution, Washington, DC.

19   Lucy Lippard, contribution to "Gene Swenson: A Composite Portrait," *The Register of the Museum of Art, University of Kansas* 4, nos. 6–7 (1971): 16.

20   Swenson, *The Other Tradition*, 39.

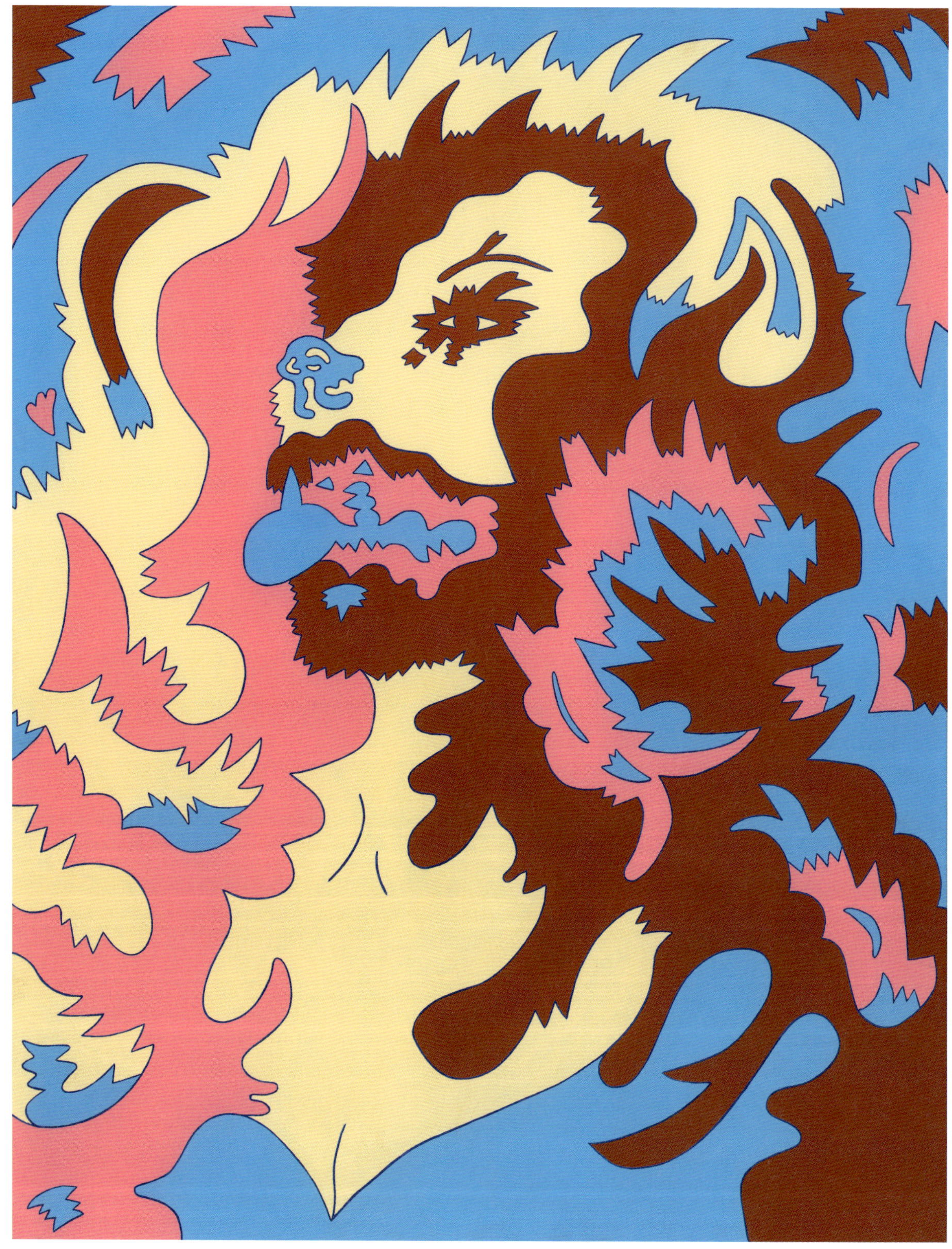

Karl Wirsum, *Doggerel II*, 1966. Acrylic on linen, 33 × 25 in. (83.8 × 63.5 cm). Whitney Museum of American Art, New York; purchase with funds from the Larry Aldrich Foundation Fund 67.38

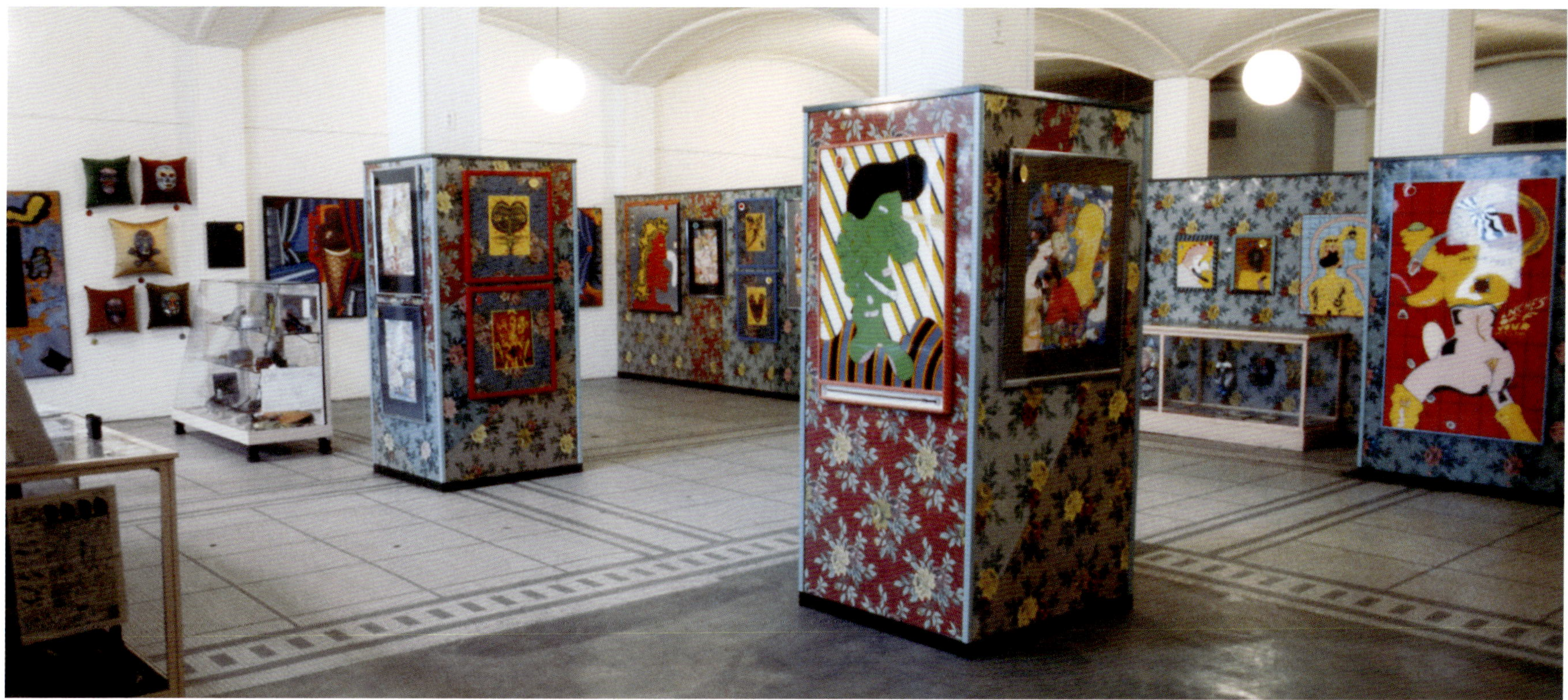

Now! Hairy Who Makes You Smell Good, Hyde Park Art Center, Chicago, 1968

meeting. Wirsum, who doesn't know the other artists very well, is listening as the five friends discuss Harry Bouras, an older artist who presented rather pompous art reviews on the Chicago classical music station WFMT. "Harry who?" Wirsum asks, which the others find hysterical. They quickly pun the change to "Hairy," and the name sticks.

The exhibition is a success, garnering a positive review in *Artforum* by Whitney Halstead, the artists' former teacher at SAIC. Subsequent Hairy Who exhibitions quickly follow at HPAC: one in 1967 and another in 1968. The group also exhibits in San Francisco in 1968, and in 1969 there are two shows: one at the School of Visual Arts in New York that consists of drawings and another at the Corcoran Gallery in Washington, DC, by invitation of curator Walter Hopps. The artworks exhibited in these shows are meant to be viewed as individual objects, not as parts of a collective or an installation. But a shared aesthetic is expressed through the execution of the exhibitions, particularly in Chicago in 1968 and Washington, DC, in 1969, that involves hand-drawn posters, laminated buttons, and installations with linoleum sheets mounted on walls, gallery labels affixed with chewing gum, displays of the artists' personal objects, and, most enduringly, four artists' books they call comic books: offset-printed, staple-bound publications that contain work made only for print, some of it riffing on exhibited paintings, some of it entirely original.

Most of the Hairy Who artists had grown up in Chicago and attended SAIC in the 1950s and 1960s. Instructors with unusually diverse tastes—Halstead and Kathleen Blackshear foremost among them—give equal weight to the Art Institute's collection of fine art and to the material on exhibit at the Field Museum of natural history. The artists receive an encyclopedic, nonhierarchical education: late medieval Italian and Northern Renaissance painting; nature drawings; Senufo tribal masks; Native American artifacts; Joan Miró and Jean Dubuffet; pinball machines and comic books and Sears catalogues; Nazca and Oceanic objects; hand-painted signs. Nothing is off the table. This education mixes with an appreciation for Surrealism and for older peers such as Peter

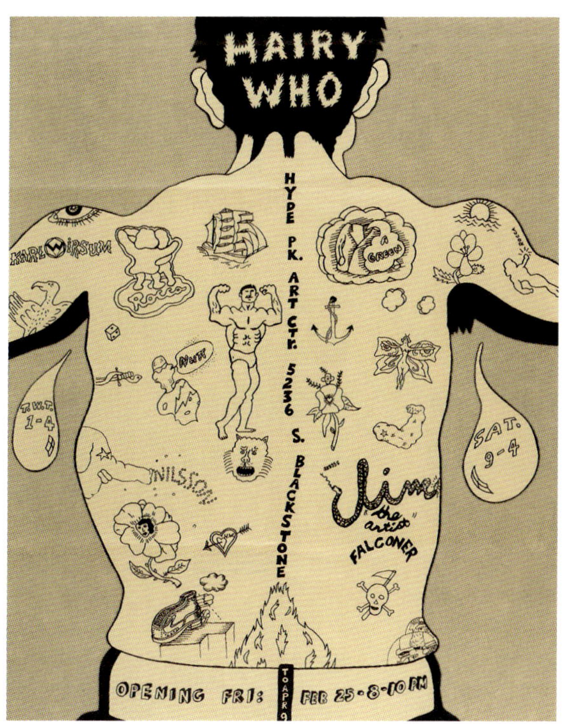

Poster for *Hairy Who*, Hyde Park Art Center, Chicago, 1966

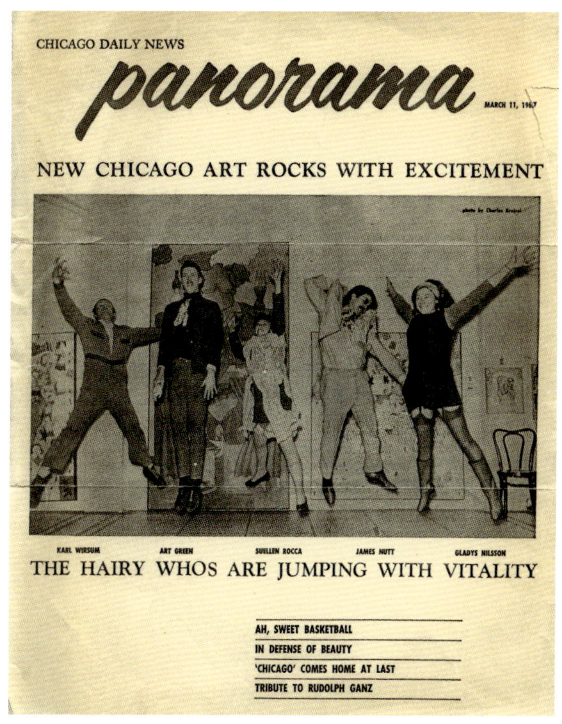

Cover of *Panorama*, March 11, 1967

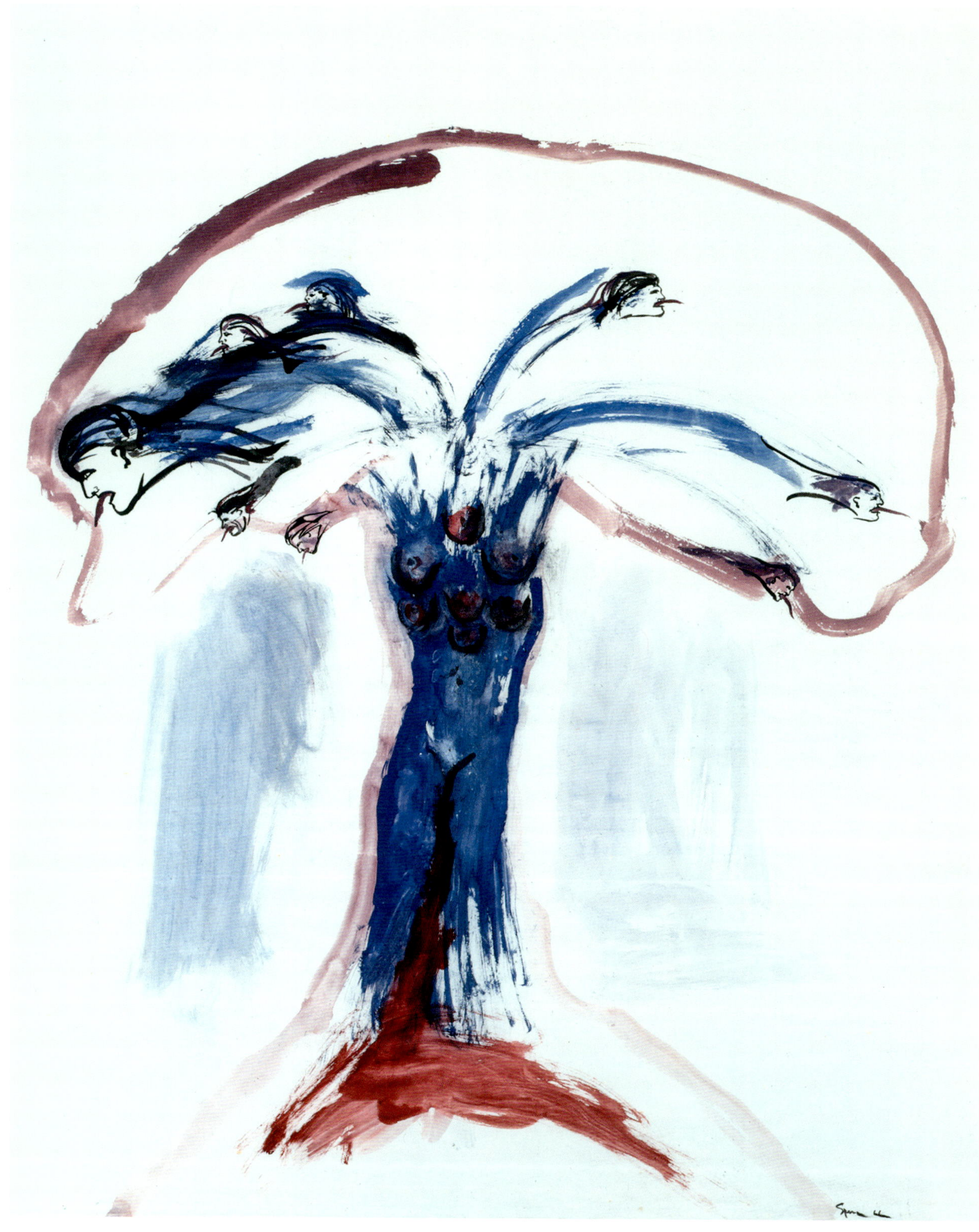

Nancy Spero, *Female Bomb*, 1966. Gouache and ink on paper, 34 × 27 in. (86.4 × 68.6 cm). The New School University Art Collection, New York

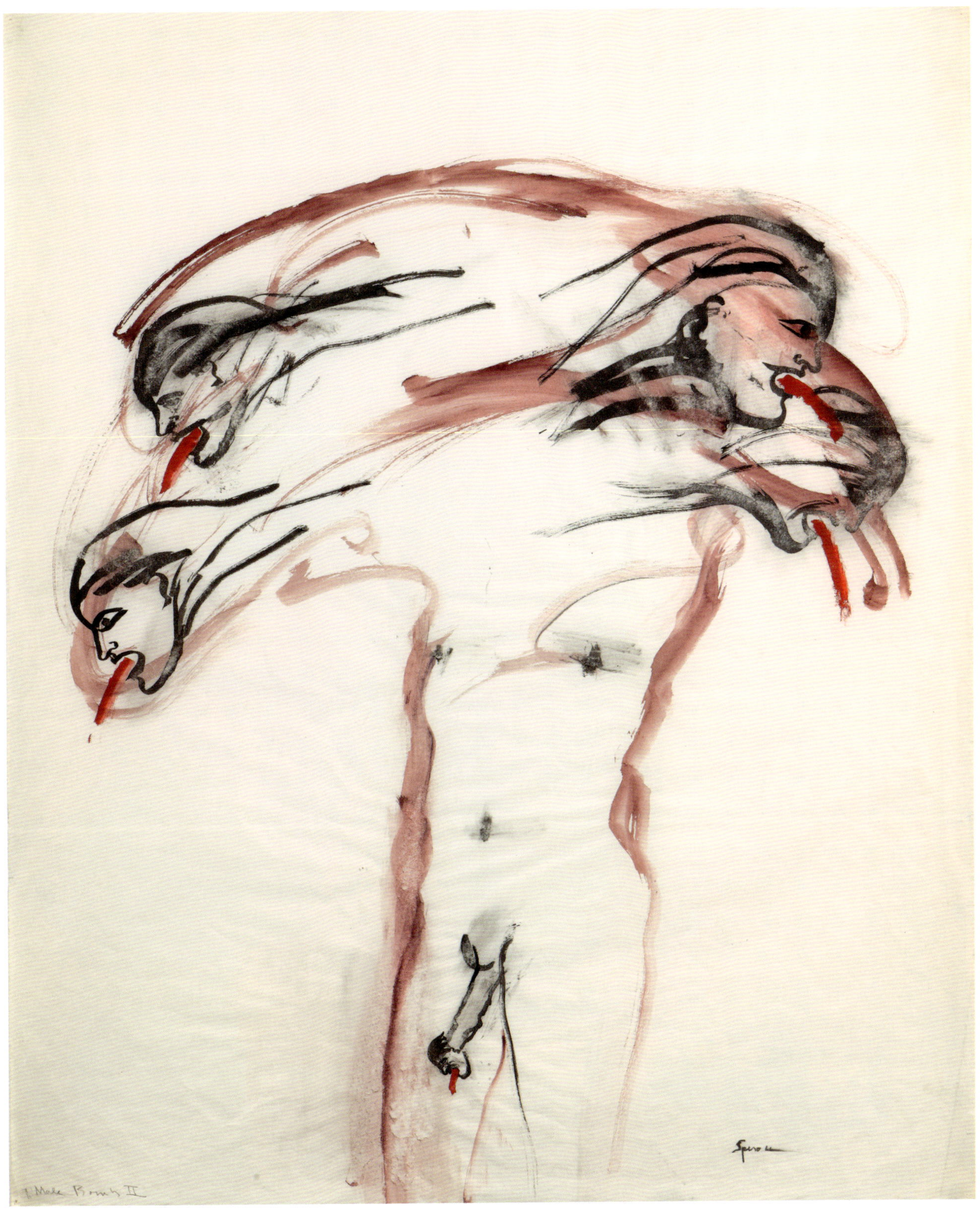

Nancy Spero, *Male Bomb II*, 1966. Gouache and ink on paper, 34 × 27 ¼ in. (86.4 × 69.2 cm). The Morgan Library and Museum, New York; Gift of the Modern and Contemporary Collectors' Committee 2014.22

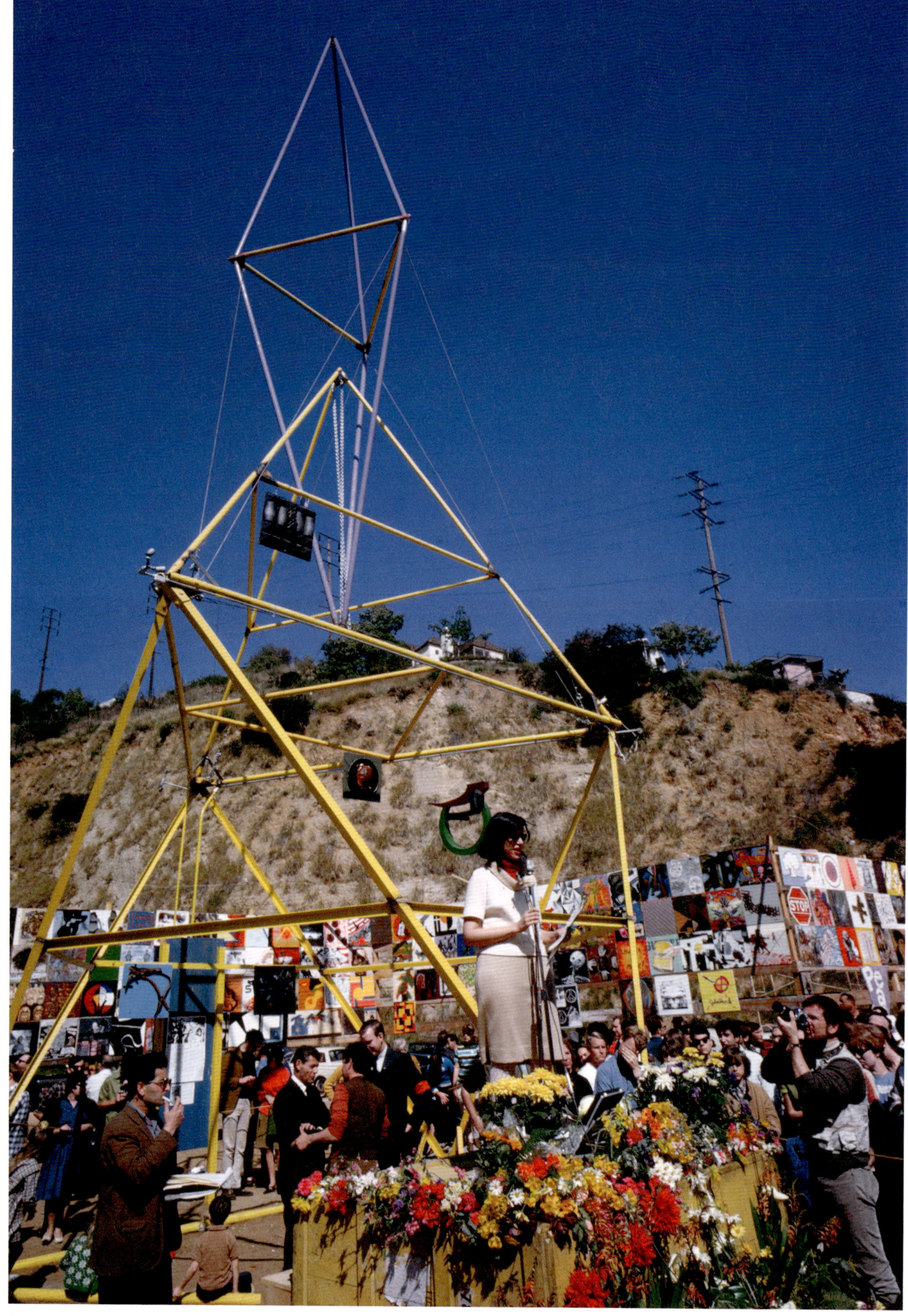

Susan Sontag speaks at the dedication of the LA Peace Tower, 1966

try to understand them too much, and we didn't have a manifesto. It could only happen in Chicago, and it did only happen in Chicago in that way. . . . [M]any ambitious artists moved to New York. It left behind a distillation of people who didn't really fit in with the mainstream."

February 26–May 1966 • LA Peace Tower is the first large-scale artist-led protest against the Vietnam War. Constructed in an empty lot on Sunset Boulevard, the six-story tower is designed by artists Irving Petlin and Mark di Suvero with construction help from Melvin Edwards. Around the tower's facade appears a collaborative antiwar collage of artworks by over four hundred artists, including Wallace Berman, Vija Celmins, Judy Chicago, Eva Hesse, James Rosenquist, Betye Saar, and Nancy Spero. Installed near Los Angeles's gallery row, the tower becomes an alternative space for artistic activity for the three months it is in place before it is dismantled and the panels auctioned off.

Spero's contribution, an anthropomorphic green helicopter simultaneously consuming and expelling bleeding, screaming people, spawns her subsequent *War Series*, which she will work on until 1970. Painted rapidly and exclusively on paper, the series consists of furious antiwar manifestos or "a personal attempt at exorcism." Each gouache painting features an American military weapon, from helicopters to bombers, grotesquely disfigured to resemble parasitic insects, reptiles, or male genitalia. "The *Bombs* are phallic and nasty," Spero writes, "exaggerated sexual representations of the penis: heads with tongues sticking out, violent depictions of the human (mostly male) body."

February 28–March 26, 1966 • Vija Celmins's eponymous exhibition is on view at David Stuart Galleries, Los Angeles, and includes *House #1* (1965), a sculpture made just months prior that, in Celmins's signature deadpan approach, conjures memories of buildings aflame from aerial bombings, the artist's experience of World War II inflecting her response to the war in Vietnam and the precarity of modern life. The artist speaks of how "in the studio, I think I relived all these things, the burning houses, the aeroplanes, the Latvian school in Germany, my eraser, my little pencils."

February 1966 • Roy Fridge rents studio space in Houston from his friend Jim Love. Their building becomes a gathering place for other artists, including James Boynton and David McManaway. Around this time, Fridge serves as a guest lecturer for Bob Camblin's and Earl Staley's drawing classes at Rice

Saul and H. C. Westermann. Summarizing the approaches of the Hairy Who artists, Rocca will note, "The only thing I can say in a general way is that [all of these images] were part of our personal history, I wasn't in any way making a comment."

Green takes Rocca's observation one step further: "We never talked about concepts. It never came up! . . . But it was more that we often looked at things that were not considered art. . . . As a group we didn't try to make activities explicable, we didn't

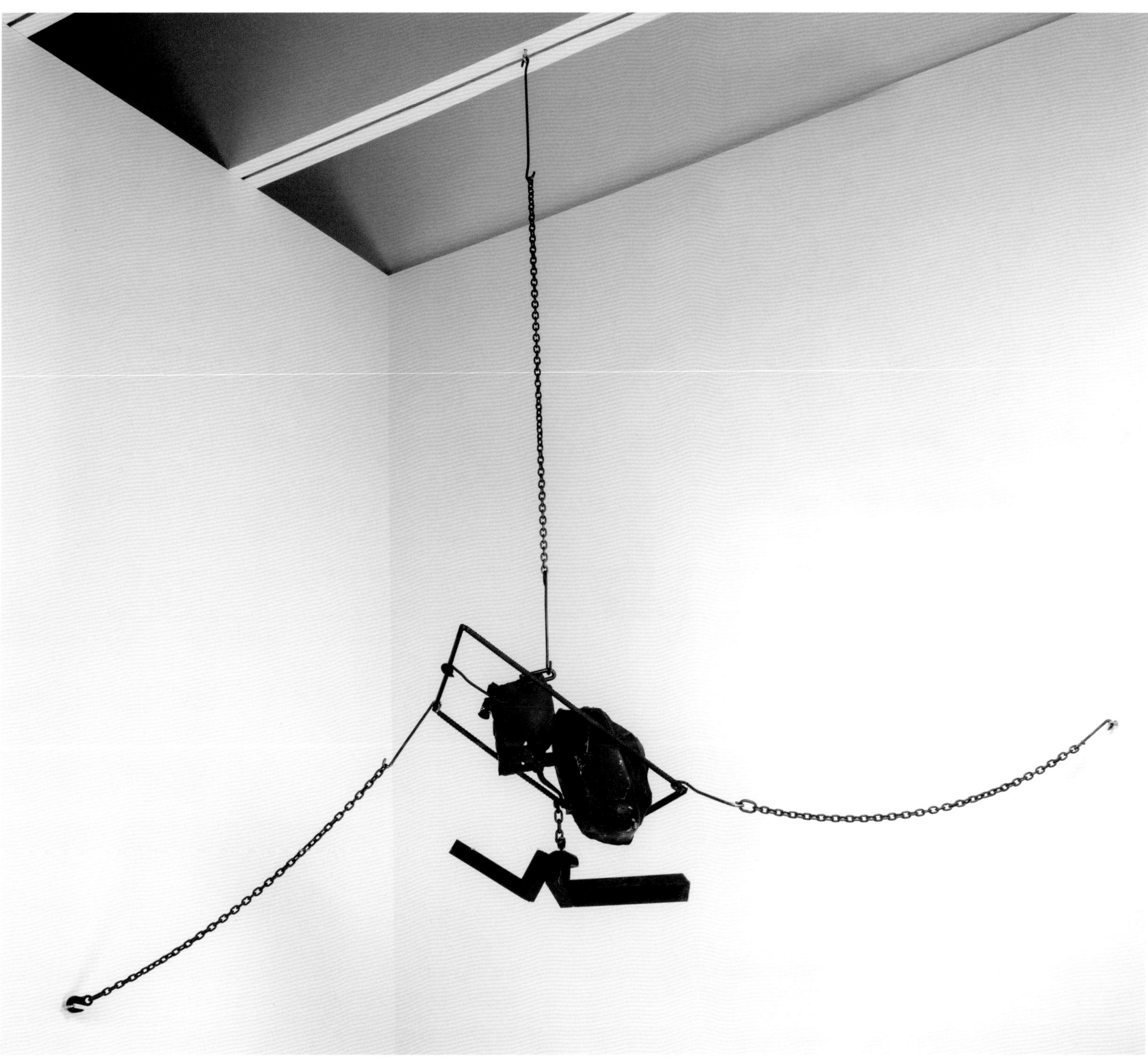

Melvin Edwards, *Cotton Hangup*, 1966. Steel, 32 × 30 × 30 in. (81.3 × 76.2 × 76.2 cm). Studio Museum in Harlem; gift of Mr. and Mrs. Hans Burkhardt 1991.21

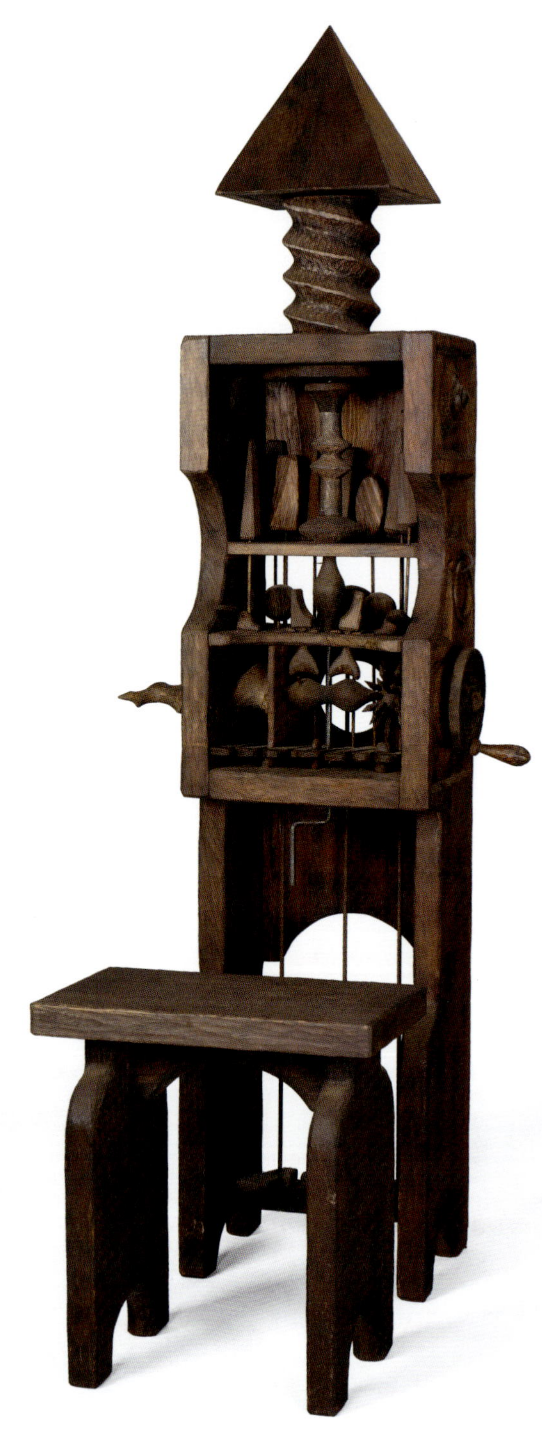

Roy Fridge, *The Great Spinning Arrow Consolating Console*, c. 1966. Wood and metal, 72 × 24 ½ × 14 ¼ in. (182.9 × 62.2 × 36.2 cm); stool, 17 ⅞ × 18 ⅛ × 11 ⅜ in. (45.4 × 46 × 28.9 cm). The Menil Collection, Houston

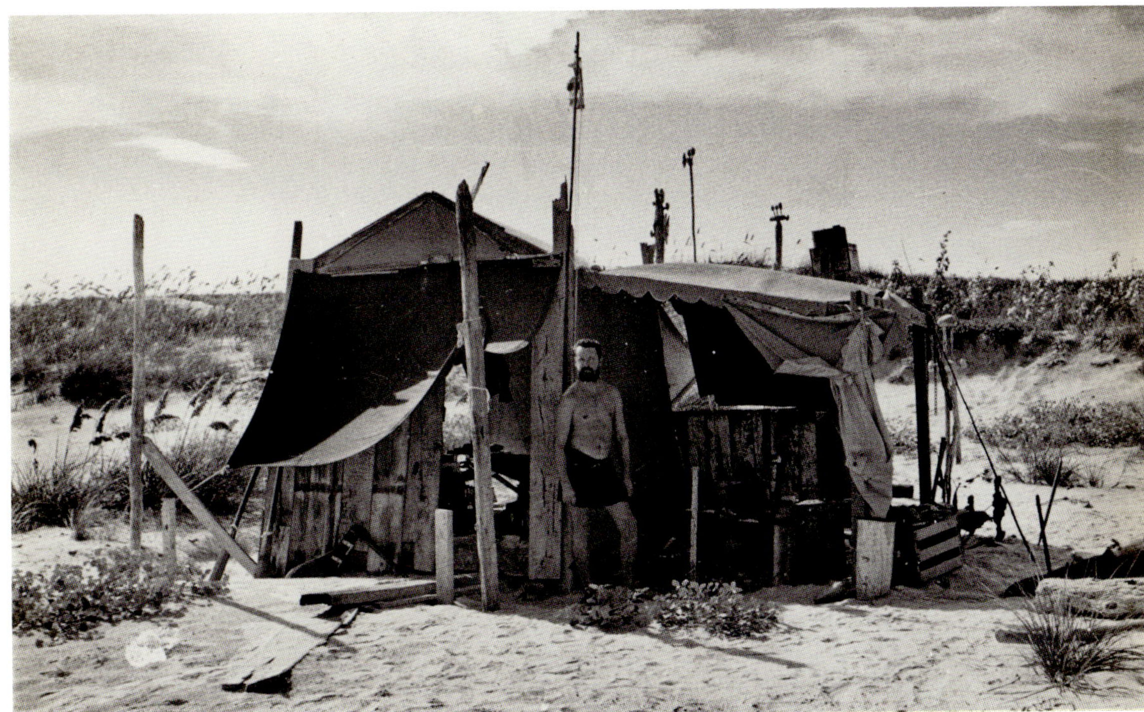

Roy Fridge in front of his summer beach house, Port Aransas, TX, c. 1962

University and collaborates with Gerald O'Grady on the development of the Rice Media Center, which focuses on photography and filmmaking.

Fridge splits his time between Houston and his home in Port Aransas on the Gulf Coast, where he lives a hermetic life infused by nature, journaling, reading, and making works with found natural materials, including artistic and functional boats, wood assemblages, and shamanistic shrines in the nearby woods.

March 1966 • Judy Chicago (then Gerowitz; b. 1939) opens her first solo show, *Judith Gerowitz*, at Rolf Nelson Gallery, Los Angeles. Referred to as "this young artist's first one-man show," it earns positive reviews in both *Artforum* and *ARTnews*. Chicago has only recently received her master of fine arts from the University of California, Los Angeles (UCLA), and her work mostly demonstrates an affinity for Minimalism, particularly the sculpture *Rainbow Pickett*, which will travel to New York's Jewish Museum for the exhibition *Primary Structures* that will open at the end of April. While Chicago's earlier work is less explicitly feminist in its imagery, her experimentation with simple forms, colors, and spatial patterning documents her self-directed, passionate, and emphatically personal approach to making art.

Born Judy Cohen, she is raised in the city she will claim for her nom de plume. In an early and formative tragedy, her father, a communist labor organizer, dies in 1953, when she is only thirteen. Chicago leaves the city in 1957 to attend UCLA but maintains the Midwestern accent that will earn her the nickname "Judy Chicago" from Nelson. Emerging professionally in the midst of an emphatically macho arts scene, Chicago develops a visual language throughout the 1960s that enables her to intertwine her identity as a woman with her identity as an artist and to express them together instead of holding them in discrete suspension.

March 1–27, 1966 • Eva Hesse, Jean Linder, Marc Morrel, Philip Orenstein, and Frank Lincoln Viner comprise the exhibition *Abstraction Inflationism and Stuffed Expressionism* at Graham Gallery, New York. "Surrealism may have been a formal influence in the forties, but now it is 'more important in opening intellectual possibilities for younger artists,'" writes Lucy Lippard, quoting Gene Swenson. "To most people it means anything odd, suspicious, impolite, unfamiliar, threatening, obscene, or just plain unconventional. Claes Oldenburg's recent exhibition at Sidney Janis, and the satirically titled 'Abstract Inflationism and Stuffed Expressionism' show at the Graham Gallery are both 'Surrealistic' in that sense." In response to *Hang Up* (1966), Hesse's piece in the exhibition, Lippard writes, "There is a yearning quality of suppression and release as well as pathos and humor to this strange relief. . . . It takes little imagination to perceive the 'body ego' that went into this work, but it adds the curiously withdrawn, objectified subjectivity of 'Swenson's new sexuality' in which matter-of-fact understatement of ideas usually overstated is paramount."

March 9–31, 1966 • Art collector Audrey Sabol, with advice from artists Ed Ruscha and William T. Wiley, opens *How the West Has Done! A Wild Wild West Show* at Philadelphia's Young Men and Young Women's Hebrew Association. In addition to Ruscha and Wiley, the exhibition

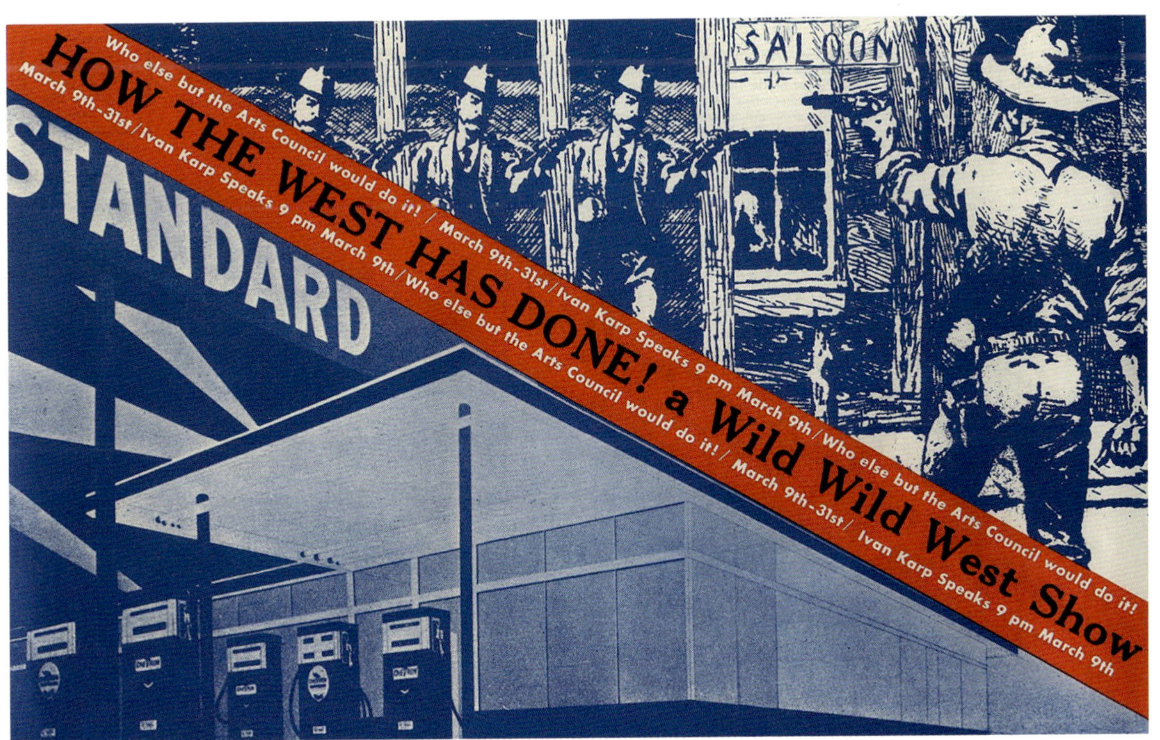

Announcement for *How the West Has Done! A Wild Wild West Show*, Young Men and Young Women's Hebrew Association, Philadelphia, 1966

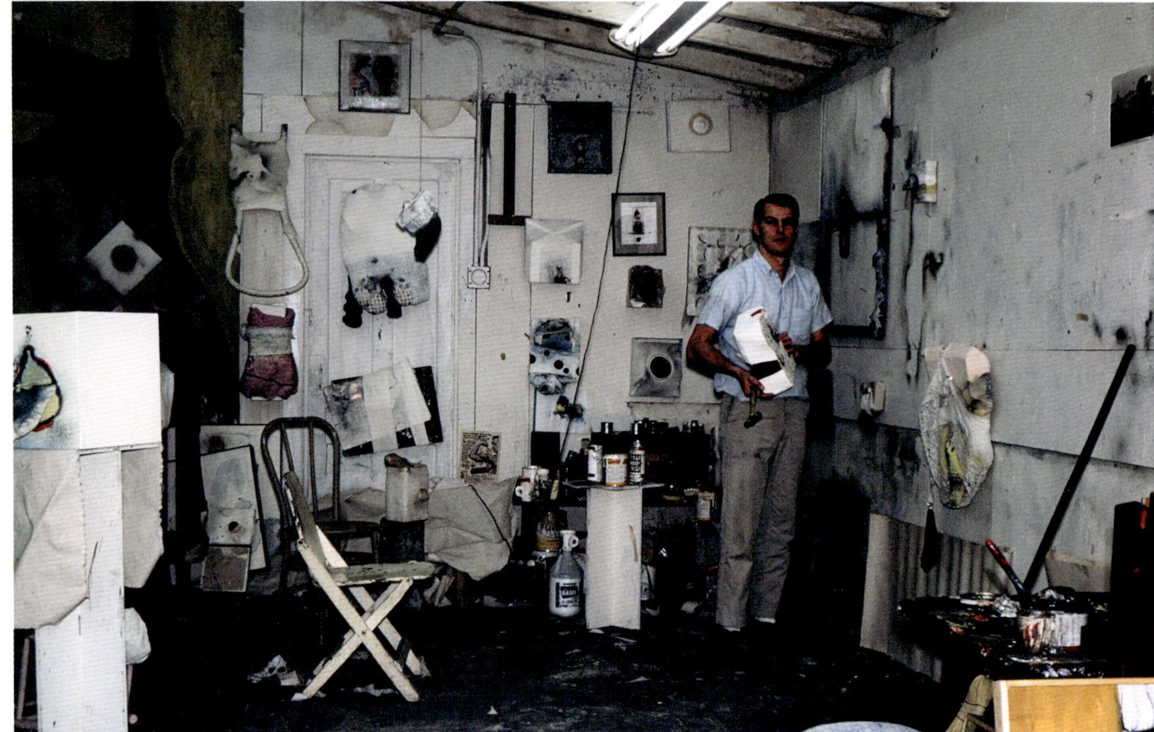

Franklin Williams in his studio, California College of Arts and Crafts, Oakland, c. 1964

includes Robert Arneson, Vija Celmins, and Jim Melchert, among other artists, and it is the first East Coast presentation of the new art of the West Coast, or, as Sabol exclaims, "Imagine a California show without Still, Tobey, Graves, Diebenkorn, Park, Bischoff, etc. etc.!!!"

March 9–April 2, 1966 • *New Work by Oldenburg* is on view at New York's Sidney Janis Gallery and includes soft sculptures of common bathroom fixtures, works from the artist's new *Airflow* series, and more drawings for proposed colossal monuments. Evidently moved by the Marcel Duchamp retrospective at the Pasadena Art Museum in 1963, Oldenburg creates *Soft Toilet* (1966), which appears on the cover of the modest exhibition catalogue and again, in rear view, on the back. Diane Arbus takes portraits of Oldenburg, his wife, artist-model Patty Mucha, and *Soft Washstand* (1965) for a feature titled "Not to Be Missed: The American Art Scene" that will appear in the July issue of *Harper's Bazaar*.

March 11, 1966 • Franklin Williams (b. 1940) debuts his wildly colorful, heavily worked sculptures and wall reliefs that merge verdant flora and fauna with bodily forms in a solo exhibition at the Richmond Arts Center in Richmond, California, followed a month later by another solo show, at Motion Gallery in San Jose. Williams's sui generis work is firmly rooted in his youth in Ogden,

Utah. The Ogden River is just blocks away from his childhood home, apple and cherry orchards extend just beyond the backyard, and mountains surround the high desert plain. He will describe his family as "dreamy, mystical people" of Welsh and English origin, the women prolific crafters, especially in knitting, crocheting, and quilting— all of which Williams himself is proficient in by the time he is eight years old. As he later remembers it, nearly everything in his home is hand-made, including the wallpaper, which the young artist assists his mother in stenciling.

Williams is given a studio in the basement of the home, and his mother keeps him well stocked in supplies. He enrolls at the California College of Arts and Crafts (CCAC) in Oakland, receiving his bachelor of fine arts in 1964 and his master of fine arts in 1966. While at CCAC, Williams develops his work in an unwitting conversation with the assemblage activities happening just across the bay, taking cast-off materials—including toilet bowls and sanitary napkins—from his job as a janitor and wrapping them in fabric to make sculptures that allude to bodily forms and excretions. Although Williams forswears any influence, there are resonances here with William T. Wiley (in the use of tendril-like lines and surreal space), Bruce Conner (in the grotesque protrusions and junk aesthetic), and Eva Hesse (in the bodily associations). When Williams begins making flat wall works later in the decade, he draws upon his interest in James Joyce to make associations between his childhood memories and his present

life: valleys, gardens, and plants of all kinds seem to emerge and then merge with the adult consciousness of intestinal and genital imagery.

Later in 1966, San Francisco Art Institute director Fred Martin offers Williams a teaching position, which he will hold until 1999.

March 12–26, 1966 • Benny Andrews exhibits his *Autobiographical Series* at Forum Gallery, New York. The solo exhibition marks a shift in Andrews's work, as he increasingly blends social commentary with dreamlike pastoral landscapes. The series comes about with the support of a John Hay Whitney Fellowship, which allows Andrews to travel to Georgia in 1965 to visit family and create work based on the rural Southern society of his childhood. Rural Georgia is in the midst of dramatic change, as encroaching urbanization, the mechanization of cotton farming, and the gradual inroads made by the civil rights movement in desegregating Southern institutions converge to phase out the sharecropper system and the ways of life familiar to Andrews. The paintings the artist had done in the early 1960s while attending the School of the Art Institute of Chicago and then living in New York rely on gestural brushwork and strong contour drawings to give form to figures that are often ambiguously sited or totally adrift in an undetermined space. Yet in the *Autobiographical Series*, figures populate pictorially coherent but otherworldly Southern landscapes, engaged in the everyday life and labor of cotton sharecropping. In *Processional* (1965), for example, two men carrying a statue of the Virgin Mary on a dais are flanked by an audience of ghostly gray bodies hanging from nooses.

Forum Gallery director Bella Fishko resists showing the series due to the subject matter, but Andrews fights to keep the work in the show and then withdraws from the gallery in protest afterward.

March 13, 1966 • Gunvor Nelson and her collaborator, Dorothy Wiley, win top prize for *Schmeerguntz* (1966) at the fourth Ann Arbor Film Festival. As Gunvor will explain in regard to the impetus for the film, "One day I was looking at all the gunk in the sink and thought of the contrast between what we do, and what we see that we 'should' be—in ads and things—and that was the idea right there, from the sink." *Schmeerguntz* is a short black-and-white film collage that feeds viewers a continuous flow of magazine photographs, found footage, and clips from television and home movies. The title is nonsense German for *sandwich* and alludes to the images that are sandwiched together by juxtaposition and superimposition: pregnant women between slim beauty

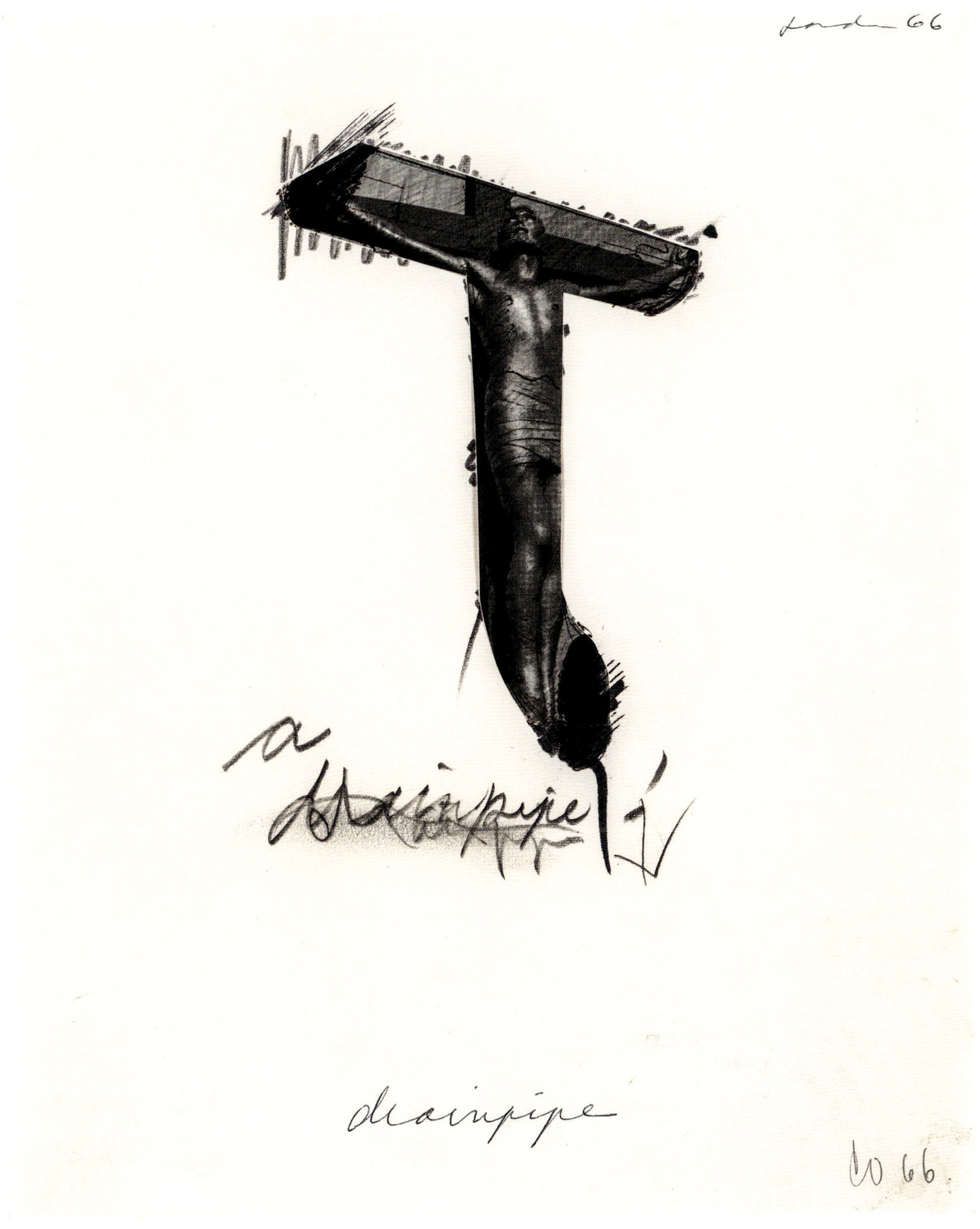

Claes Oldenburg, *Drainpipe*, 1966. Collage with graphite and pen on paper, 9 ¾ × 8 in. (24.8 × 20.3 cm). Collection of Robert Gober

queens; a vomiting head between smiling models. *Schmeerguntz* plays on the incoherence of the cultural expectations that operate upon the private lives of women, roiling beneath the surface of the ideal public face they are conditioned to maintain. Grounded in the artists' direct experience, rather than feminist theory, the film's overall effect is a visceral rather than intellectual irony. It hits in the gut.

Nelson and Wiley are surprised by their win at the prestigious Ann Arbor Film Festival. The award brings them sudden recognition in their male-dominated Bay Area artist circles and leads to their next film, the deliberately surrealistic *Fog Pumas* (1967).

———

March 15–April 9, 1966 • In *Three-Dimensional Art* at Castagno Gallery, New York, Hannah Wilke (1940–1993) debuts her ceramic vaginal "box" sculptures in the first of two group shows; the second, *Hetero Is*, will open in December at NYCATA, the New York City Arts Theater Association gallery. Wilke makes the evocative, abstracted vulva-like sculptures with clay, individually shaping each one with her hands. The works have a tactile quality, with rough edges and textured surfaces imprinted by the artist's fingers and by fabric. Some she paints—often using soft, chalky pinks and flesh tones—and some she leaves bare. Later, Wilke will explain her concept in an artist's statement:

> Since 1960 I have been concerned with the creation of a formal imagery that is specifically female, a new language that fuses mind and body into erotic objects that are nameable and at the same time quite abstract. Its content has always related to my own body and feelings, reflecting pleasure as well as pain, the ambiguity and complexity of emotions. . . . My interest in developing a specifically female iconography for both sexes in the early 60's was in direct conflict with a society that prohibited its citizens from and sometimes arrested them for using the words fuck, cock, and prick. . . . My concern is with the word translated into form, with creating a positive image to wipe out the prejudices, aggression, and fear associated with the negative connotations of pussy, cunt, box.

Wilke had taken up the motif of female genitalia in the late 1950s, well before her 1962 graduation from Temple University with a bachelor of science in education and a bachelor of fine arts in sculpture. There, she had worked with ceramics and fiberglass, and would begin to use early forms of latex in the 1970s. While maintaining a relatively private studio practice focused on vaginal forms, she teaches high school art from 1962 to 1970, first in Pennsylvania and then in White Plains, New York. She and her husband, Barry Wilke, an industrial designer, divorce in 1965, and Wilke moves to Manhattan, where she furthers her studies at the Institute of Fine Arts at New York University while teaching.

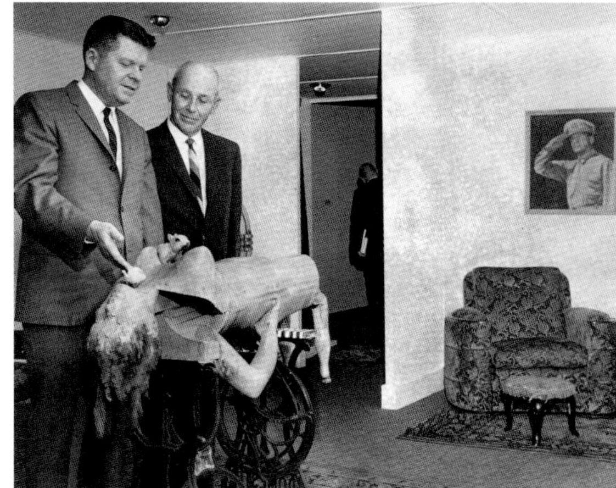

Los Angeles County supervisors view Edward Kienholz's *Five Dollar Billy* from the installation *Roxy's* (1960–61), Los Angeles County Museum of Art, 1966

———

March 30–May 15, 1966 • Having worked in Los Angeles since the 1950s, and known for having cofounded Ferus Gallery with Walter and Shirley Hopps, Edward Kienholz (1927–1994) is featured in the retrospective *Edward Kienholz: An Exhibition*, curated by Maurice Tuchman, at the Los Angeles County Museum of Art (LACMA). The Los Angeles County Board of Supervisors unsuccessfully attempts to close down the show because it views the sculpture *Back Seat Dodge '38* (1964) as pornographic.

Growing up on a farm in Washington State, Kienholz had received no formal art training, but he had learned carpentry, auto repair, and other mechanical skills. These he will put to use after arriving in Los Angeles in 1952, where he makes sculptures and large-scale installations with materials scoured from across the city. Soon Kienholz becomes involved in the development of an arts community in Los Angeles, opening a gallery at the Coronet Theatre in 1955 before meeting the Hoppses and cofounding Ferus Gallery in 1957.

———

1966 • Susan Sontag publishes *Against Interpretation*, dedicating it to her friend Paul Thek. The book includes the important 1964 essay "Notes on Camp," which popularizes the aesthetic that is the exaggerated, theatrical attraction to the retrograde and marginal known as "camp."

———

April 2–28, 1966 • Paul Thek's exhibition *Technological Reliquaries* is on view at Pace Gallery, New York. This same month, critic Gene Swenson publishes an interview with the artist in *ARTnews*.

> GS: How would you describe your work?
> PT: I hope the work has the innocence of those Baroque crypts in Sicily. . . . We

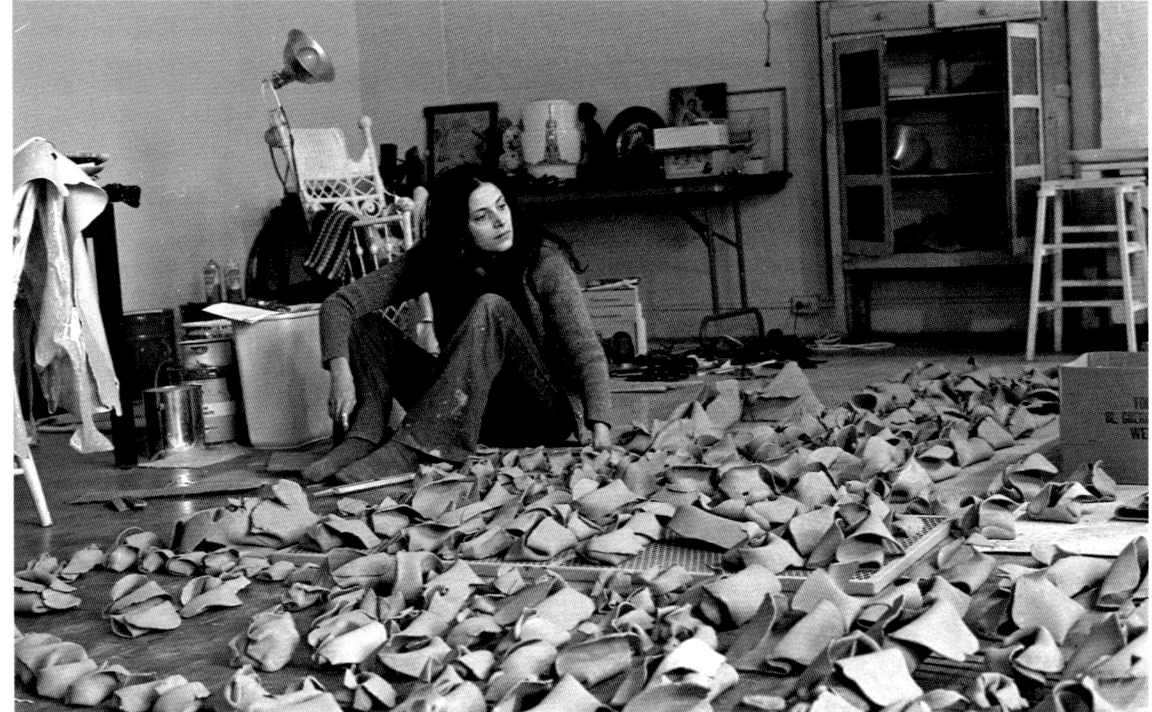

Hannah Wilke in her Westbeth Artists Housing studio, New York, 1973

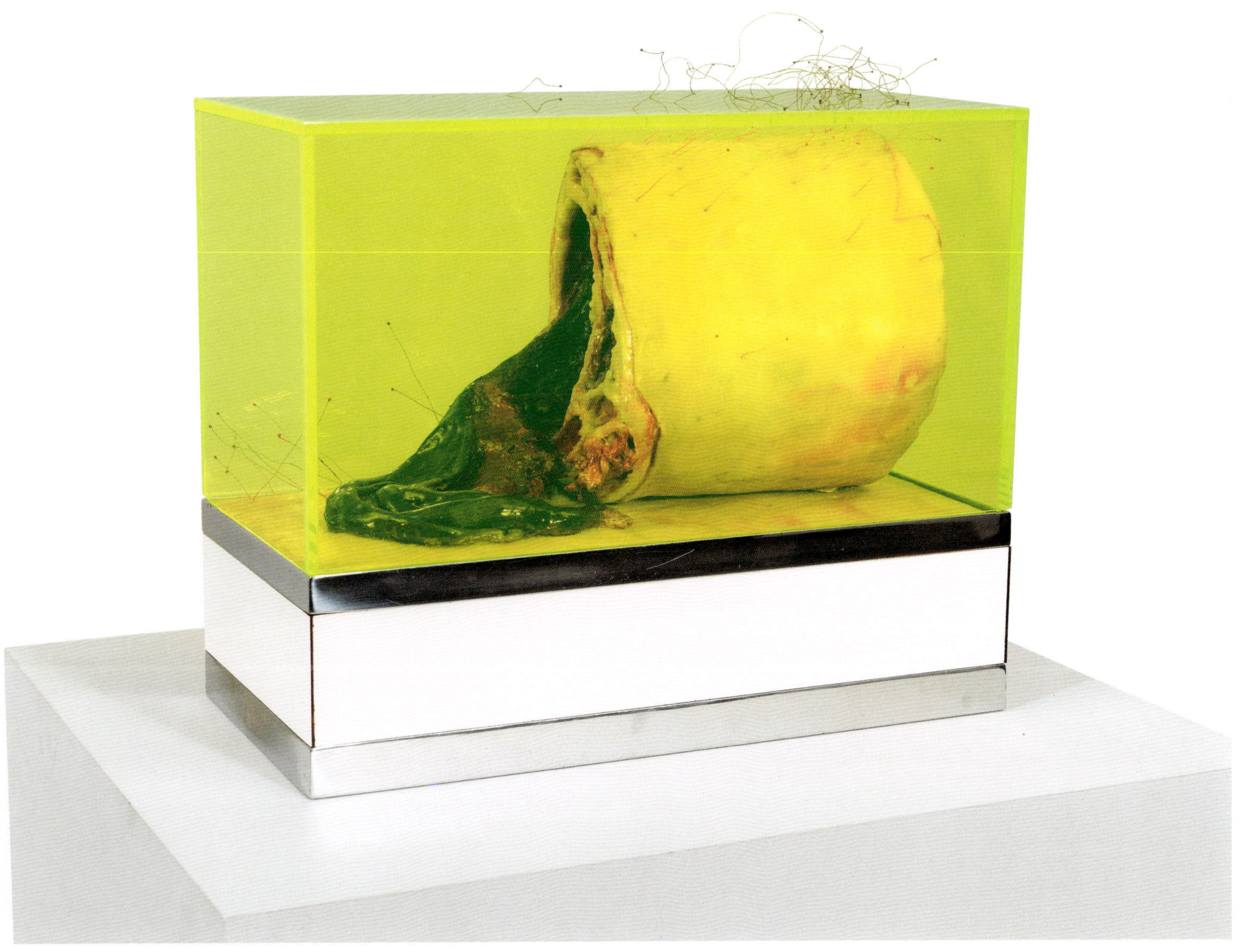

Paul Thek, *Untitled*, 1966, from the series *Technological Reliquaries*. Wax, paint, polymer resin, nylon monofilament, wire, plaster, plywood, melamine laminate, rhodium-plated bronze, and acrylic, 14 × 15 1/16 × 7 1/2 in. (35.6 × 38.3 × 19.1 cm). Whitney Museum of American Art, New York; purchase, with funds from the Painting and Sculpture Committee 93.14

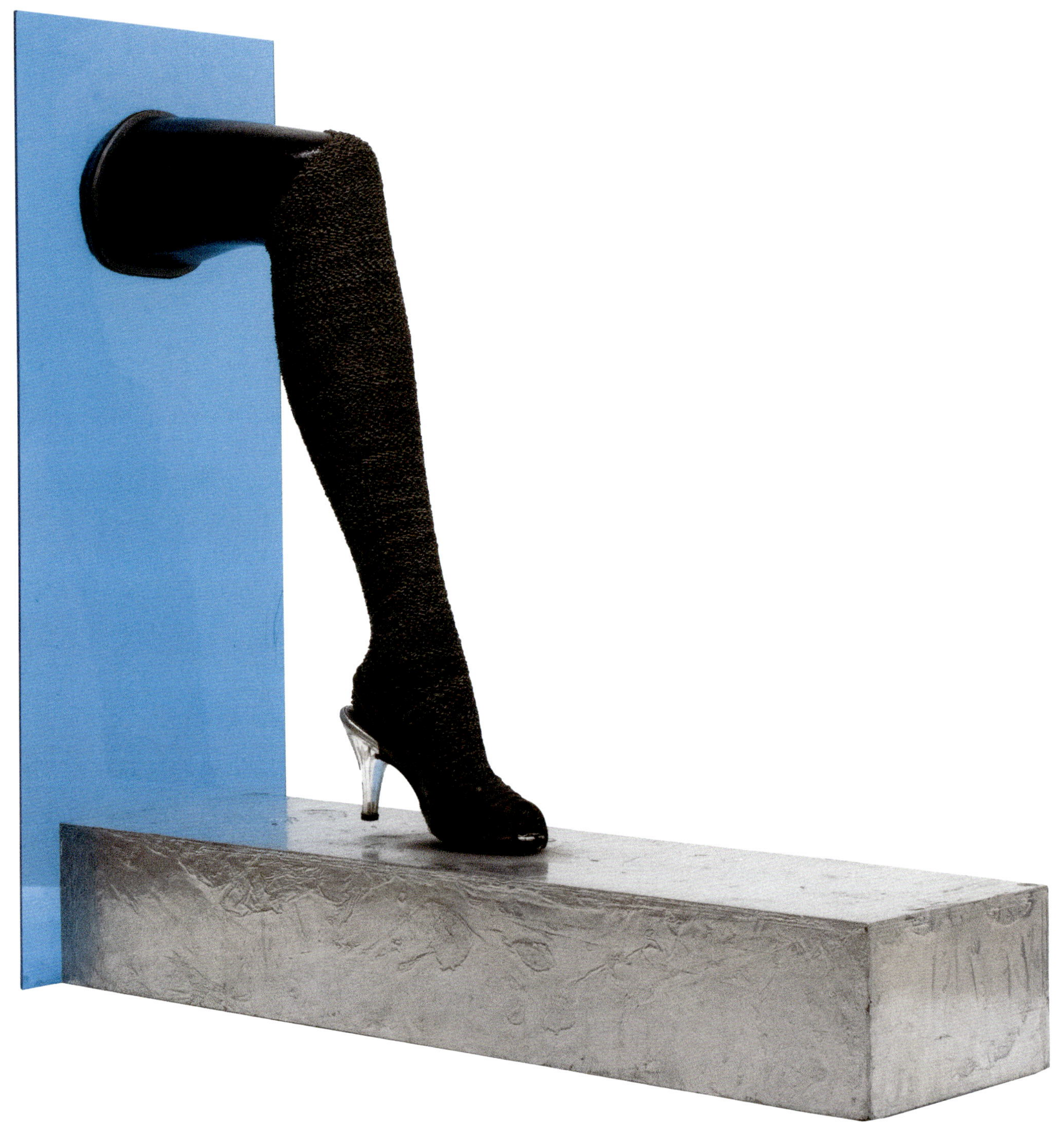

Martha Edelheit, *Leg*, c. 1966. Mixed media, 33 ¼ × 33 × 12 ¾ in. (84.5 × 83.8 × 32.4 cm). Collection of the artist

accept our thingness intellectually, but the emotional acceptance of it can be a joy.

GS: Isn't sex used in these works almost as a color?

PT: What do you mean by "sex"? Blue movie sex? There's nothing of that. Blood of the lamb sex? Maybe a little. I don't work in this way because it's "sexy" nor for shock, although I know it's weird to see a piece of flesh hanging on a wall. I choose this subject matter because it violates my sensibilities, but that's not the same thing as shock. I work with it to detach myself from it, like learning to control a heartbeat.

GS: Is your work Surrealistic?

PT: I suppose so, basically, but my work has nothing of that classic Surreal placing of illogical objects in illogical space; no concern for dream worlds. However, I've never heard a really good definition of Surrealism. I used to believe I had a terrible Surrealist bent. I felt I had to get it out of my system. I fought any departure from abstraction. But today there's a new kind of Surrealism around, a new facet at least, less theatrical. For one thing Surrealism seems to have seeped into the artist's hand, his manner of making, his materials. Maybe it has to do with the individual gone underground.

April 12–May 7, 1966 • Martha Edelheit exhibits her enormous wall paintings of bodies and flesh at Byron Gallery, New York. The gallery's press release notes, "Martha Edelheit's interest in the figure is expressed in another form in the objects in which she isolates parts of the body. The mixture of human references with materials like aluminum foil, plexiglass and polyester explores another possible relationship of the body and the formal and material properties of art."

April 13–May 7, 1966 • Following an enormously successful second show at Stable Gallery, New York, Marisol presents her first solo exhibition at Sidney Janis Gallery. Continuing to integrate casts of her own body into intricate assemblages, the artist experiments with new materials and fabrication techniques for this exhibition, making *Kiss* (1966), which consists of two layered, polyester-resin casts of her face with puckered lips, inset in an aluminum frame and lit from behind like a sconce.

Even though the show attracts large crowds each day, the critical response is mixed. Initially fascinated by her self-portraiture, some critics now call her art narcissistic and cynical: "The gaiety and wit of earlier work is vanishing, its place taken by a vein of bitter commentary," writes Lawrence Campbell of *The Party* (1965–66), a monumental installation of fifteen life-size figures, each directly or subtly resembling Marisol. In general, the mainstream press tends to focus on the artist's appearance at the expense of attention to the artwork itself. But in 1973, Cindy Nemser will recognize Marisol's art as a precursor to "the women's movement," in the sense that she is "trying to explore different aspects of woman's identity." Marisol agrees: "Yes. There comes a point where you start asking, 'Who am I?' I was trying to find out through

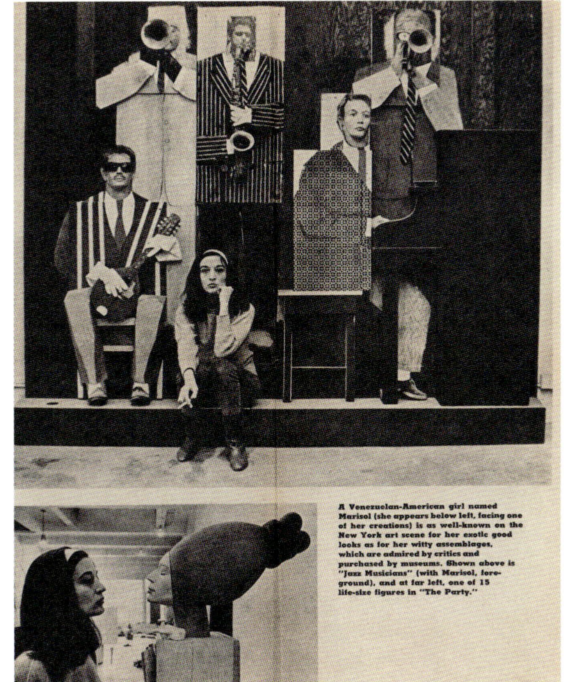

Clipping from *The New York Times*, March 7, 1965, with Marisol facing a figure from *The Party* (1965–66)

my sculpture. That's why I made all those masks and each one of them is different. Every time I would take a cast of my face it came out different. You have a million faces."

May 3–June 5, 1966 • Lynn Hershman Leeson (b. 1941) exhibits her cyborg drawings in the show *Adventure of a Line: Drawing Experiences by Lynn Lester Hershman* at Santa Barbara Museum of Art. Hershman Leeson had grown up in Cleveland, Ohio, with an avid interest in art and science, attending Case Western Reserve University in the early 1960s before moving to Berkeley, California, in 1963. Two years later, while pregnant, she had experienced cardiomyopathy, which led to five weeks in intensive care under an oxygen tent and several more months in and out of the hospital. The experience precipitated her swift move from a brushy Bay Area figuration to drawings of female cyborg figures, inspired by painter Richard Lindner, sculptor Jean Tinguely, and Fritz Lang's 1927 film *Metropolis*. In the film, Hershman Leeson will remember that "the master of the city of Metropolis orders a scientist/inventor to create an evil robotic version of a young woman named Maria by using electricity that would go through her body to affect the transformation," which jibes with Hershman Leeson's experience with a chronic heart condition. Her drawings replace organs with machine parts and feature stamped words and other artifacts that indicate that these are less portraits and more proposals for a new kind of body. As Hershman Leeson will later explain:

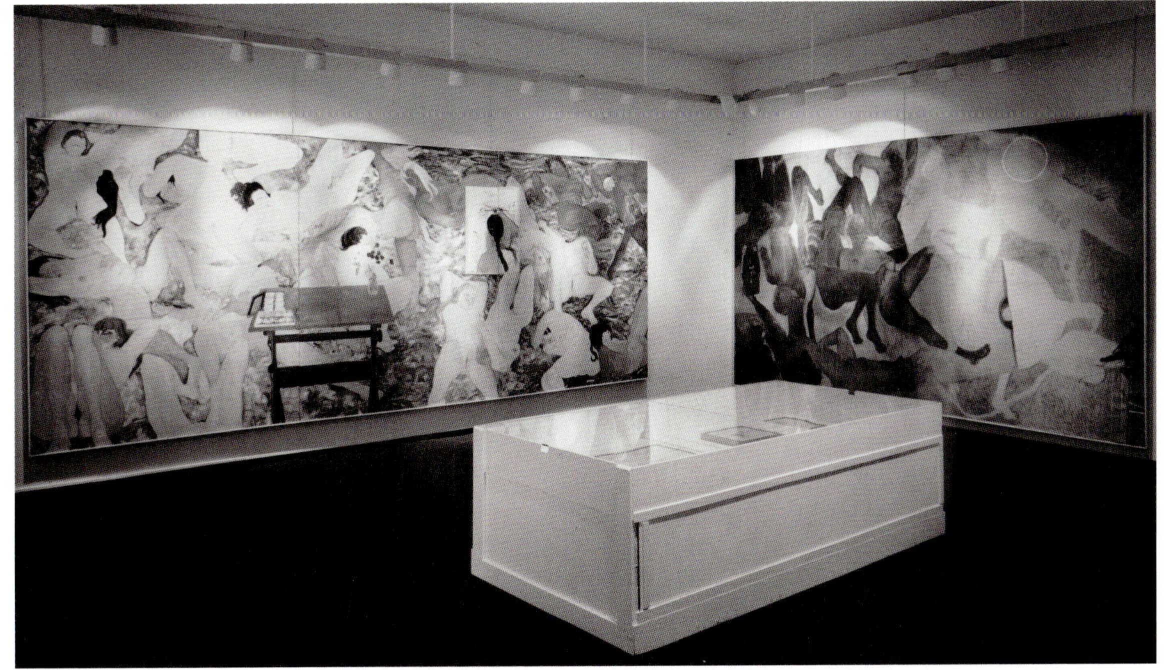

Martha Edelheit, Byron Gallery, New York, 1966, with *Flesh Wall–Female* (1966)

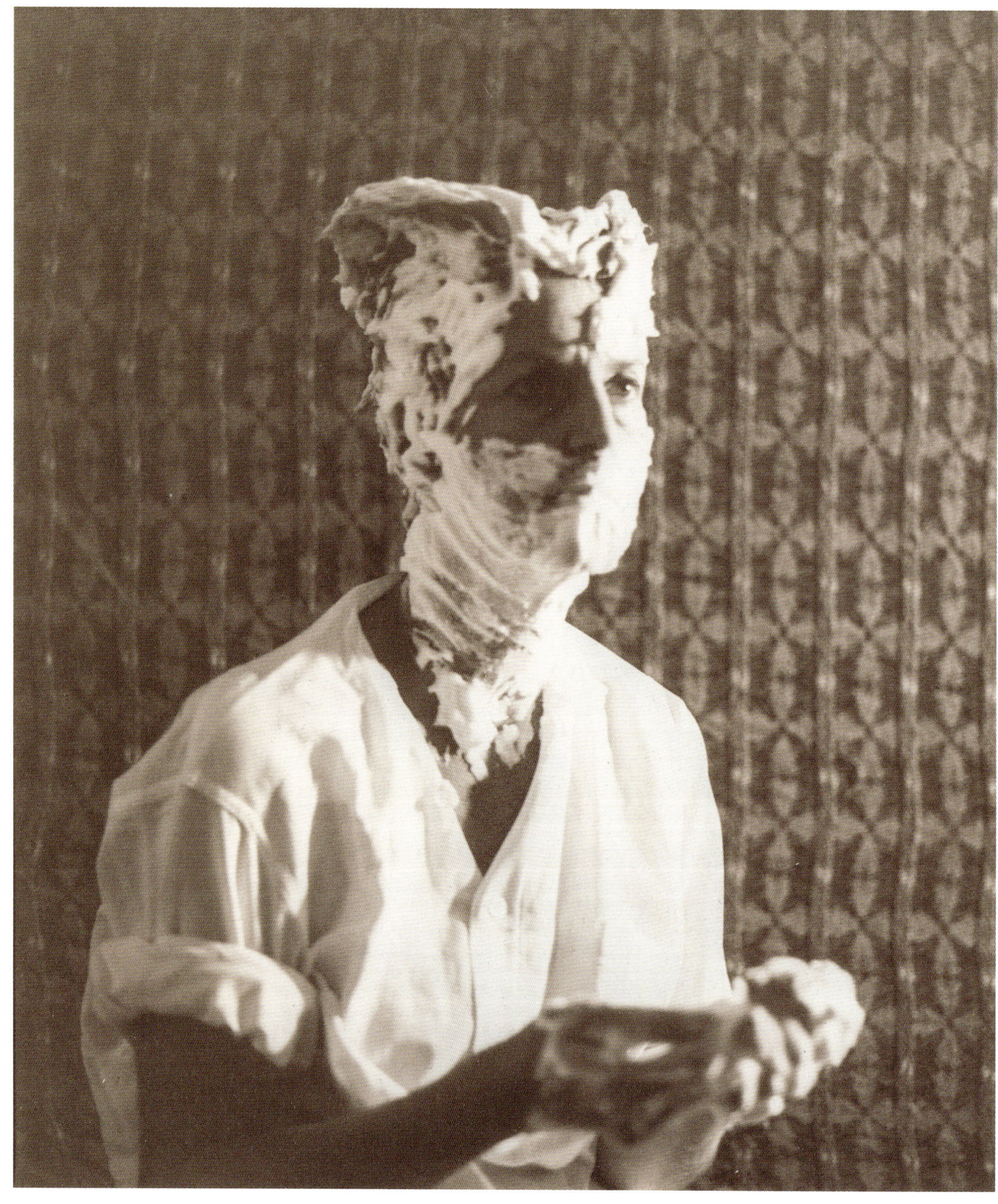

Sturtevant, *Duchamp Man Ray Portrait*, 1966. Gelatin silver print, 8 ⅝ × 7 ¼ in. (21.9 × 18.4 cm). Whitney Museum of American Art, New York; gift of Sascha S. Bauer and Kristen Dickey 2013.102

The cyborg drawings I was making in 1965 were made at exactly the same time as the word "cyborg" was coined by Manfred Clynes and Nathan S. Kline when they found something moving under a microscope. Maybe because my mother was a biologist and I got to look through a microscope, I have been interested in the idea that you could see things that weren't there to the naked eye. . . . After they started to look inside with catheters and MRIs, I started to think of the body as a surface where all the intrinsic parts and mechanics couldn't be seen.

The medical ordeal also inspires Hershman Leeson to begin work on her "breathing machines," mechanical visages molded from her own face that inflate with the illusion of life and sometimes speak through recorded sound. She seeks a way to combine her personal experience, her previous explorations of the cyborg, and her increasing awareness of the sociopolitical turmoil all around her, and the result is a series of sculptures that present self-evidently Frankensteinian machine-humans that depend on technology to both breathe and speak.

———

May 10–June 2, 1966 • Bruce Nauman (b. 1941) receives his master of fine arts from the University of California, Davis (UC Davis) and opens his inaugural solo exhibition—called simply

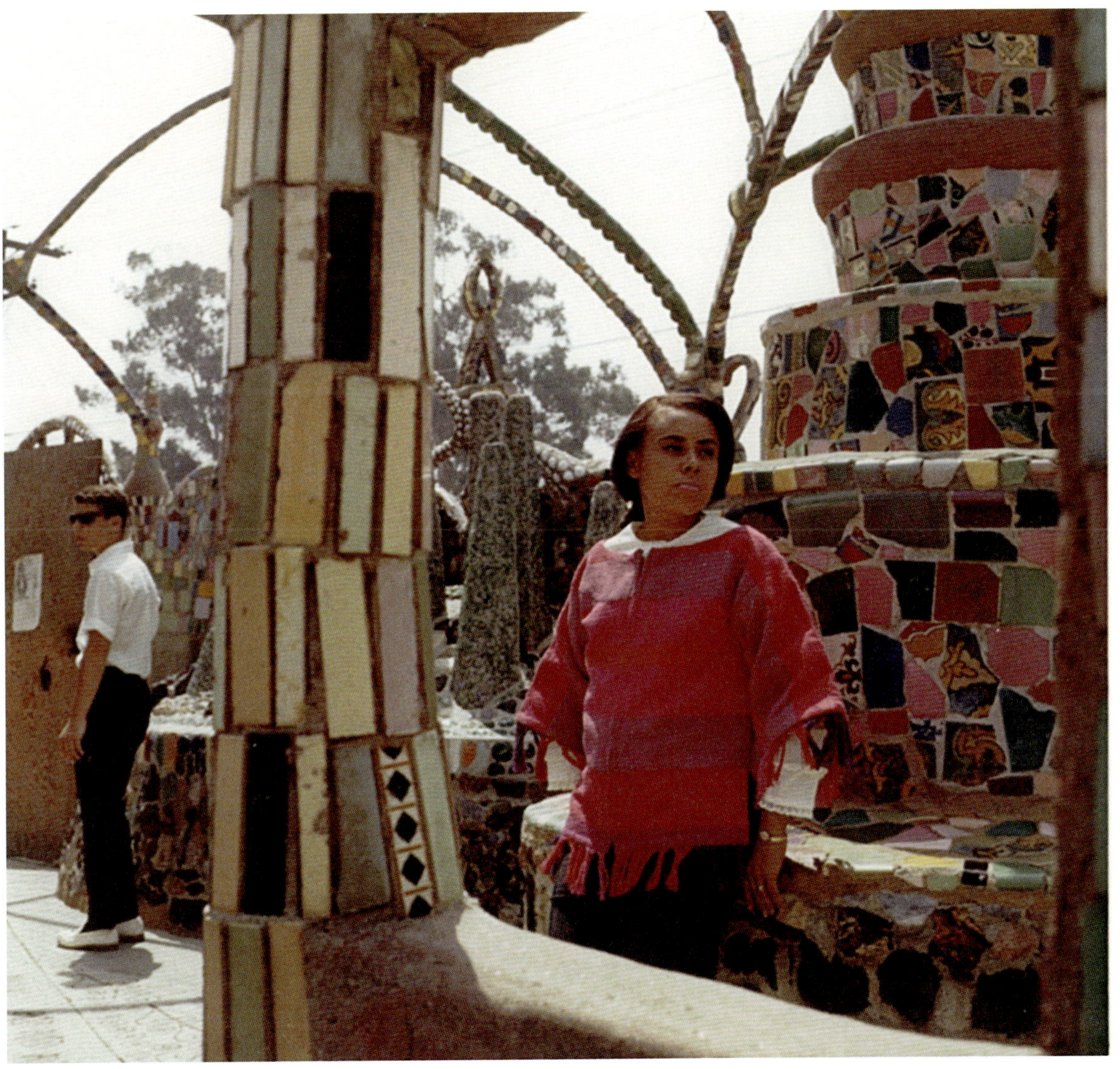

Photograph from the *Seattle Post-Intelligencer*, July 24, 1966, with William T. Wiley flying a question-mark kite

Bruce Nauman—at Nicholas Wilder Gallery, Los Angeles. He shows the body-surrogate fiberglass works he has been developing in his Mill Valley studio, including *Mold for a Modernized Slant Step* (1966), in which he manifests his Slant Step concept in exhibition form for the first time.

Born in Fort Wayne, Indiana, Nauman had grown up in suburban Milwaukee and studied art at the University of Wisconsin, Madison, where most of the professors are still working in a Works Progress Administration mode that leaves Nauman feeling somewhat alienated. He takes trips to nearby Chicago to see works by Pablo Picasso and paintings such as Willem de Kooning's *Excavation* (1950). He enters UC Davis in 1964 to study painting but, after a year, moves the two-dimensional bodily abstractions he is making from the canvas out into a sculptural three-dimensional space. The art department at the time, which includes Robert Arneson, Tio Giambruni, Ruth Horsting, Manuel Neri, and Wayne Thiebaud, encourages experimental approaches to materials—from fiberglass

to acrylic to plastics to clay. Nauman will recall William T. Wiley as his "strongest influence." "It was in being rigorous, being honest with yourself—trying to be clear—taking a moral position. . . . Wiley had great personal involvement with students. He might say it was terrible work but he would first get at why they made work. Bill was one of the first that gave me an idea of moral commitment, the worth of being an artist . . . that art is an ethic." By 1965 Nauman is making the movements of his body and the space around it the subject of his art, creating the lean, liminal fiberglass-and-rubber sculptures for which he will soon become known.

———

June 6, 1966 • *Betye Saar: Prints and Drawings* opens at the new Ankrum Gallery in Los Angeles. Born in Los Angeles and raised in Pasadena, Betye Saar (b. 1926) had grown up in an environment that nurtured her early interest in the arts and in craft. Some of this encouragement comes by way of her Depression-era mother, as Saar later explains: "I

Betye Saar at the Watts Towers, Los Angeles, 1965

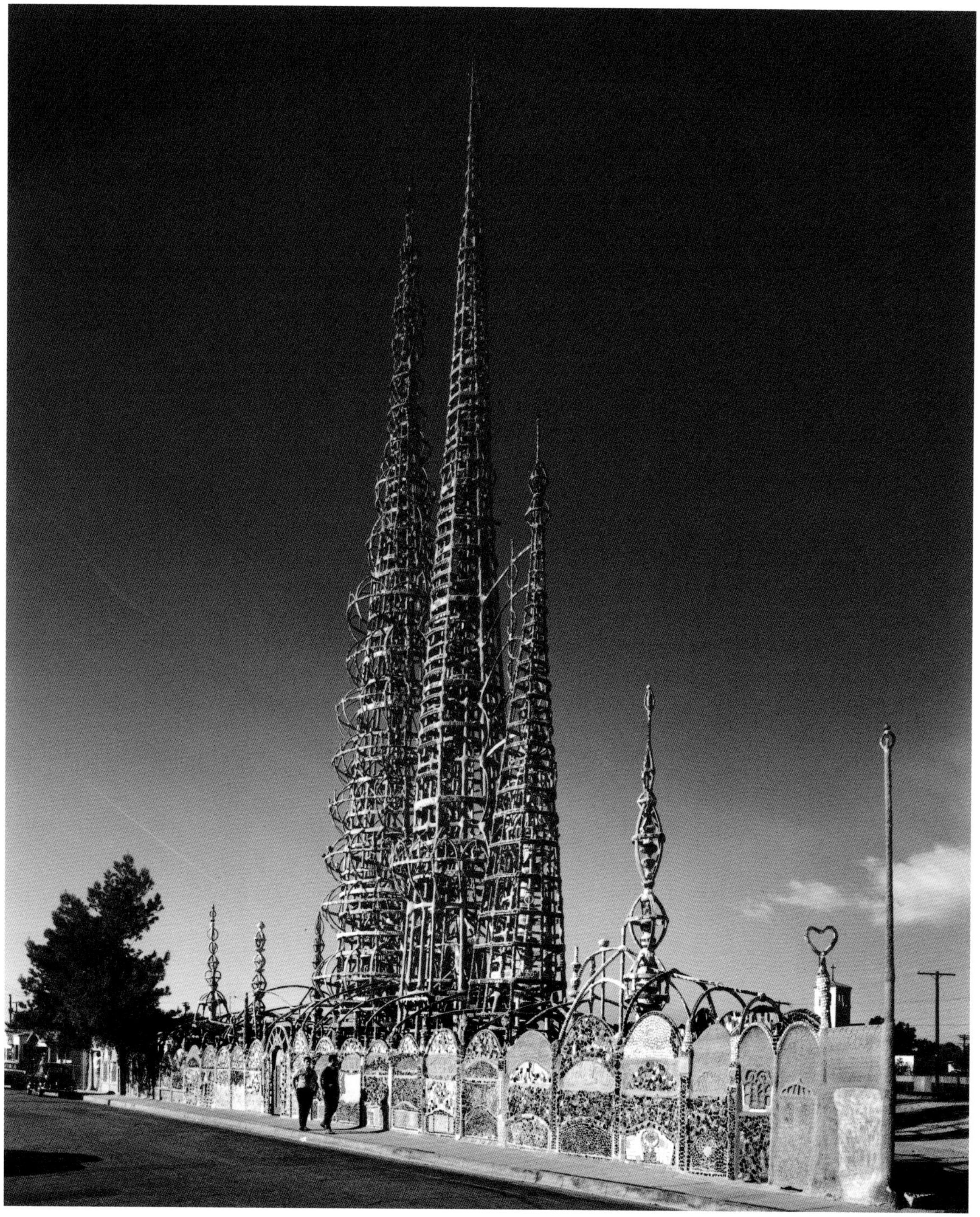

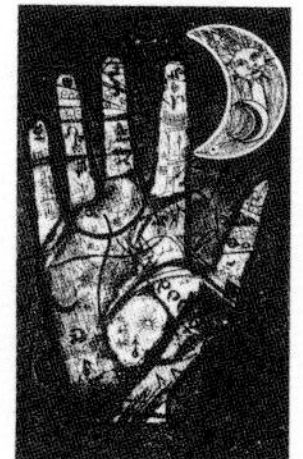

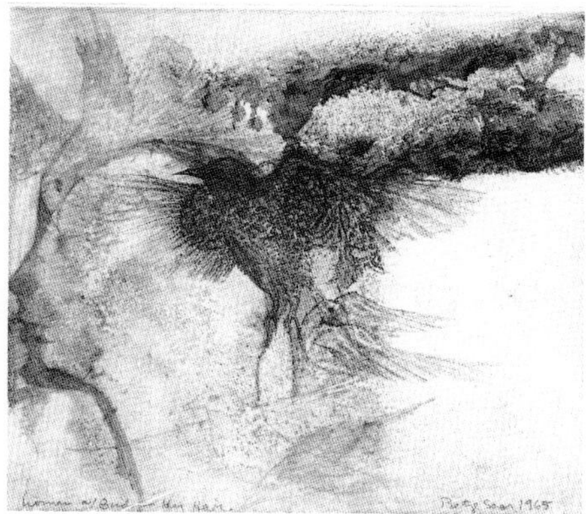

Invitation for *Betye Saar: Prints and Drawings*, Ankrum Gallery, Los Angeles, 1966

Simon Rodia, Watts Towers, 1921–54. Steel, concrete, wire mesh, and found objects, dimensions variable

was always doing something with my hands. My sisters, brothers and I were project-oriented because my mother was always making things—a gift, or an object that we liked." Saar also spends summers with her paternal grandmother in the Watts neighborhood of South Central Los Angeles in the shadow of the sculptural towers of iron, steel, cement, pottery shards, and pieces of broken glass that Italian immigrant Simon Rodia built between 1921 and about 1954, commonly known as the Watts Towers. Saar studies interior design at the University of California, Los Angeles and graduates in 1949. She initially makes jewelry and illustrates greeting cards before embracing printmaking in her shift to a career in fine arts. Introductions to artist and designer Curtis Tam, ceramicist Tony Hill, and, later, Charles White broaden Saar's artistic community and her understanding of the opportunities for Black artists in Los Angeles.

Saar's exhibition at Ankrum Gallery, one of the few galleries in Los Angeles that present and support the work of Black artists, includes her early prints depicting symbols associated with palmistry, tarot, and astrology. She traces her interest in not only the use of found materials but also mysticism and what she calls "mysteries" to her earlier experiences of the Watts Towers: "As a child, I was always really, really interested in mysteries. You know, I read mysteries. I was also interested in fairy tales and fantasy. I was intrigued by certain things that I saw, like the Watts Towers, because that was like a mysterious house. You know, 'What is this thing going up that this man is building?'"

———

June 30, 1966 • The National Organization for Women (NOW) is founded by a group of more than two dozen frustrated delegates to the federal government's Third National Conference of the Commissions on the Status of Women, after they realize the conference is but a bureaucratic exercise that will result in no real progress toward ending sex discrimination. NOW's purpose, formally adopted in October, "is to take action to bring women into full participation in the mainstream of American society now, exercising all the privileges and responsibilities thereof in truly equal partnership with men." Betty Friedan, best known for her 1963 book *The Feminine Mystique*, is chosen as the group's first president. It becomes one of the first national organizations for women's rights, modeled after civil rights groups.

———

1966 • Eduardo Carrillo is awarded a grant by the William and Noma Copley Foundation to establish El Centro de Arte Regional, a center for

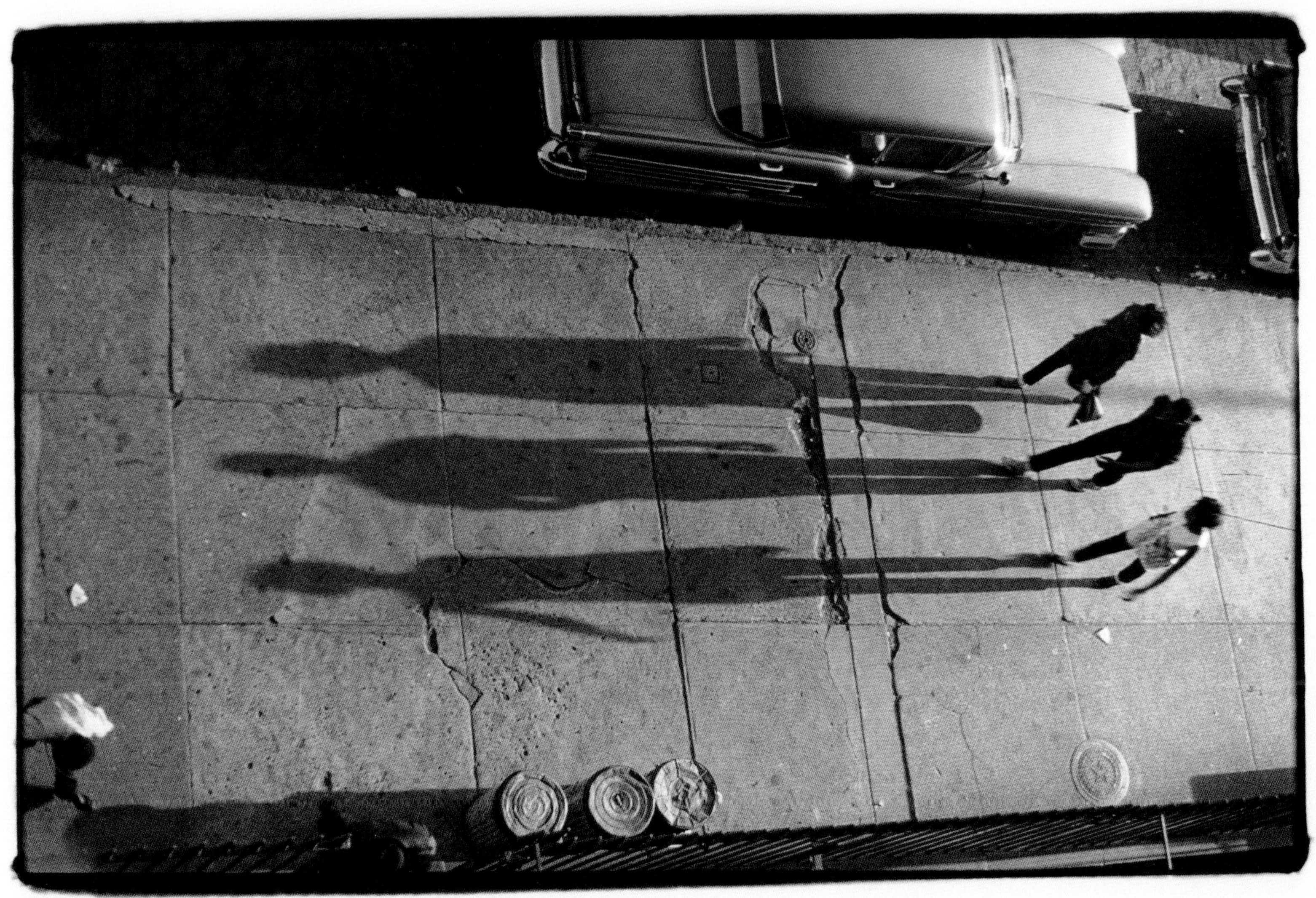

Adger Cowans, *Shadows*, 1966. Gelatin silver print: sheet, 11 × 14 in. (27.8 × 35.6 cm); image, 7 ⅝ × 11 ¼ in. (19.2 × 28.6 cm). Virginia Museum of Fine Arts, Richmond; Aldine S. Hartman Endowment Fund 2018.315

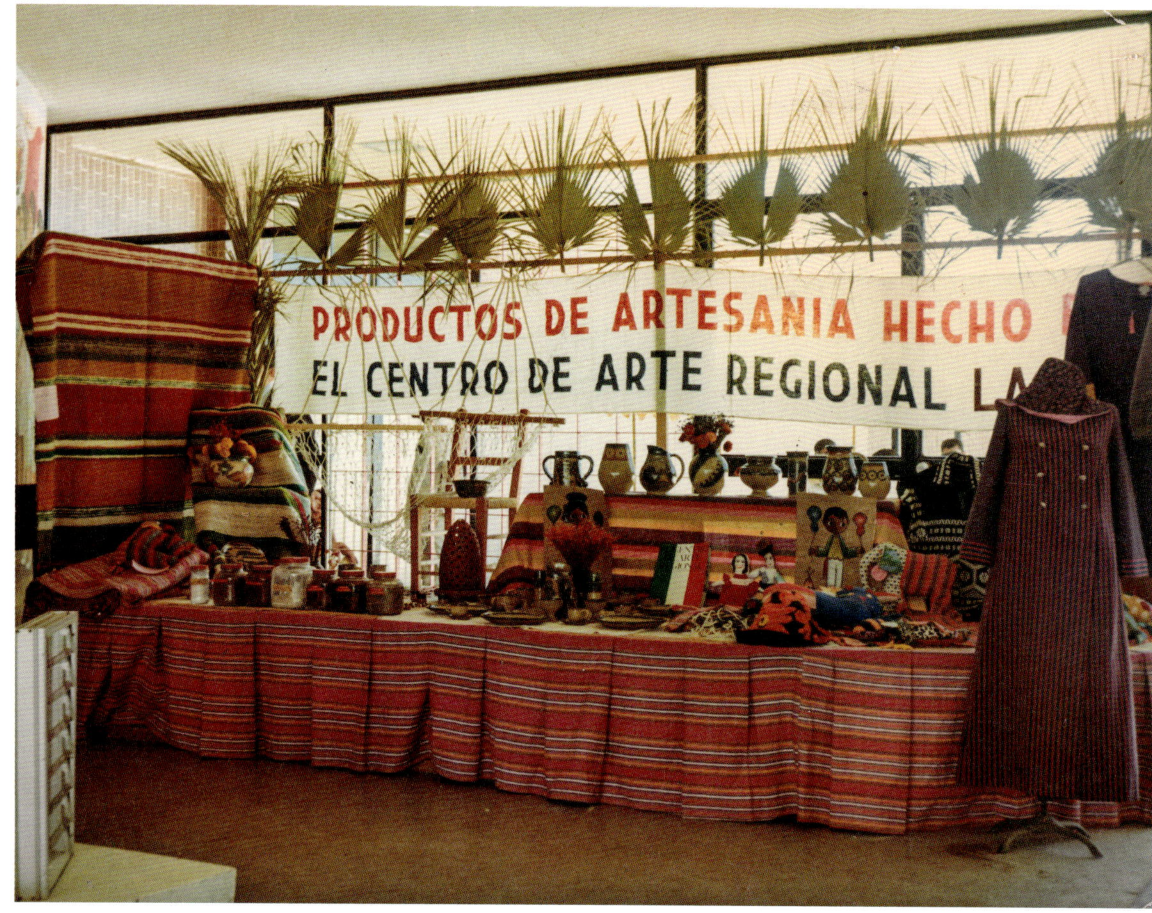

A display of items produced by artisans from El Centro de Arte Regional, La Paz, Mexico, c. 1960s

art in the pueblo of San Ignacio in Baja California, Mexico. In constructing the facility, Carrillo hires domestic craftsmen, and he and his staff use local materials and traditional methods, seeking to revive the artistic legacy of the area. Describing Carillo's efforts as "an all too isolated instance of the triumph of a 60s spirit of communal activity," art critic and Carillo's close friend John Fitz Gibbon will later recall:

> Value began to flourish in a dirt barren a chicken wouldn't bother to scrabble in. They fenced the perimeter, they put up adobe workshops and made benches and worktables. They built kilns and constructed looms. . . . The emphasis was on taking a craft item from the very beginning, from the fleece on the sheep's back, to the shearing, to the carding, spinning, weaving, dyeing and finally the marketing at a store the Carrillos [Eduardo and his wife, Sheila] set up on the airport road.

This experience influences Carrillo's deepening connection to his Indigenous Mexican roots, shaping his approach to Chicano art and to the movement that he and his fellow Ceeje Gallery alumnus Roberto Chavez help to inspire. Time

spent with Indigenous Zapotec potter Daniel Zenteno from 1966 to 1969 allows Carrillo to visit pre-Columbian sites and learn about the Zapotec and Miztec cultures.

Summer 1966 • Lucy Lippard commissions a new large sculpture from Eva Hesse, who begins to make drawings for what will become *Metronomic Irregularity II* (1966), a geometric relief consisting of three equidistant monochrome panels connected by a network of thin metal wires. It will soon be exhibited as part of Lippard's exhibition *Eccentric Abstraction* in September. Over the summer, Hesse makes drawings and constructs a two-panel model. She creates the larger version on site, threading wire through a series of gridded holes. Hesse will take this process to the extreme when executing five variations of *Accession*, perforated cubes interwoven with rubber tubing. Initially, Lippard is disappointed and later confesses:

> *Metronomic Irregularity* [*II*] wholly overshadowed *Several* (1965), which was a radical piece in its own right, and *Ingeminate* (1965), which were also in the show. I was not trying to "create a movement," but

rather to indicate that there were emotive or "eccentric" or erotic alternatives to a solemn and deadset Minimalism which still retained the clarity of that notion. I had traveled on both coasts to look at work, with Hesse's image at the back of my mind. . . . *Metronomic Irregularity*'s delicacy and assurance, its understatement and focus on structure, put me in the frustrating position of a critic whose generalizations have been proved untenable.

In a trade, Hesse eventually gives the model for *Metronomic Irregularity* to Robert Smithson, who is part of a circle of friends that includes Mel Bochner, Dan Graham, Nancy Holt, and Sol LeWitt. Hesse has also spent time with Joseph Raffaele, Gene Swenson, and Paul Thek, friends who, according to Lippard, encourage the "fetishistic aspects" of Hesse's work.

———

July 1966 • *Harper's Bazaar* publishes a six-page survey of "the American art scene." Among the artists whom Diane Arbus is assigned to photograph for the feature are Lee Bontecou and Lucas Samaras, as well as Claes Oldenburg and Patty Mucha. Oldenburg "sculpts the mediocrities of lower-middle-class life with his painted plaster arrays of hot dogs, cakes and ice cream cones," writer Geri Trotta notes. "He also designs supersized everyday objects that his wife Patty . . . runs up on her sewing machine in vinyl or natural duck to produce exhausted ghosts of our commercial culture."

———

July 7–September 4, 1966 • *Robert Irwin/ Kenneth Price* is on view at the Los Angeles County Museum of Art. Lucy Lippard reviews the two-person exhibition, which includes Price's

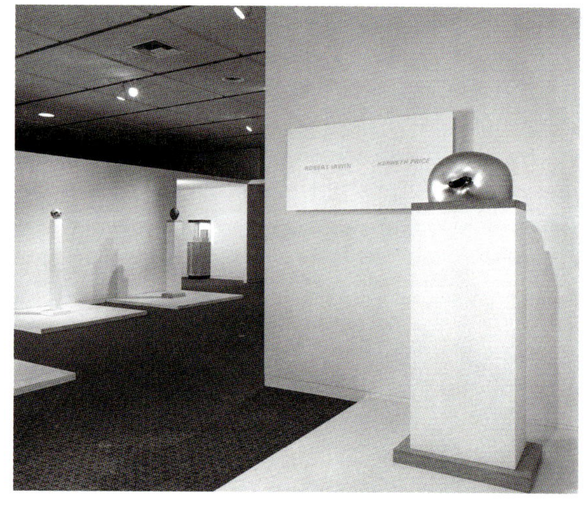

Robert Irwin / Kenneth Price, Los Angeles County Museum of Art, 1966

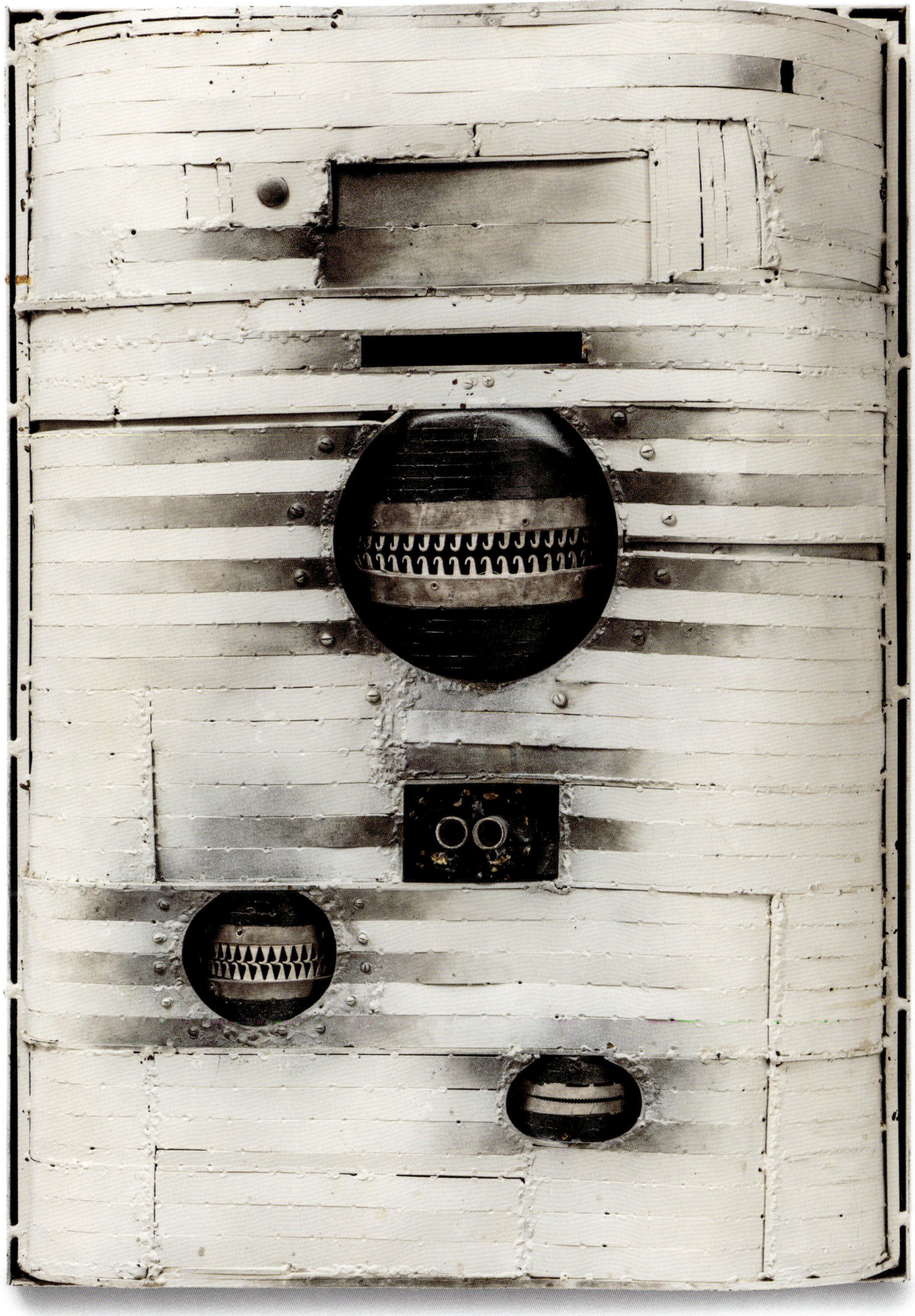

Lee Bontecou, *Untitled*, 1966. Painted iron, fiberglass, and fabric, 41 × 29 × 8 in. (104.1 × 73.7 × 20.3 cm). Akron Art Museum; gift of Leo Castelli, Castelli Galleries 1974.122

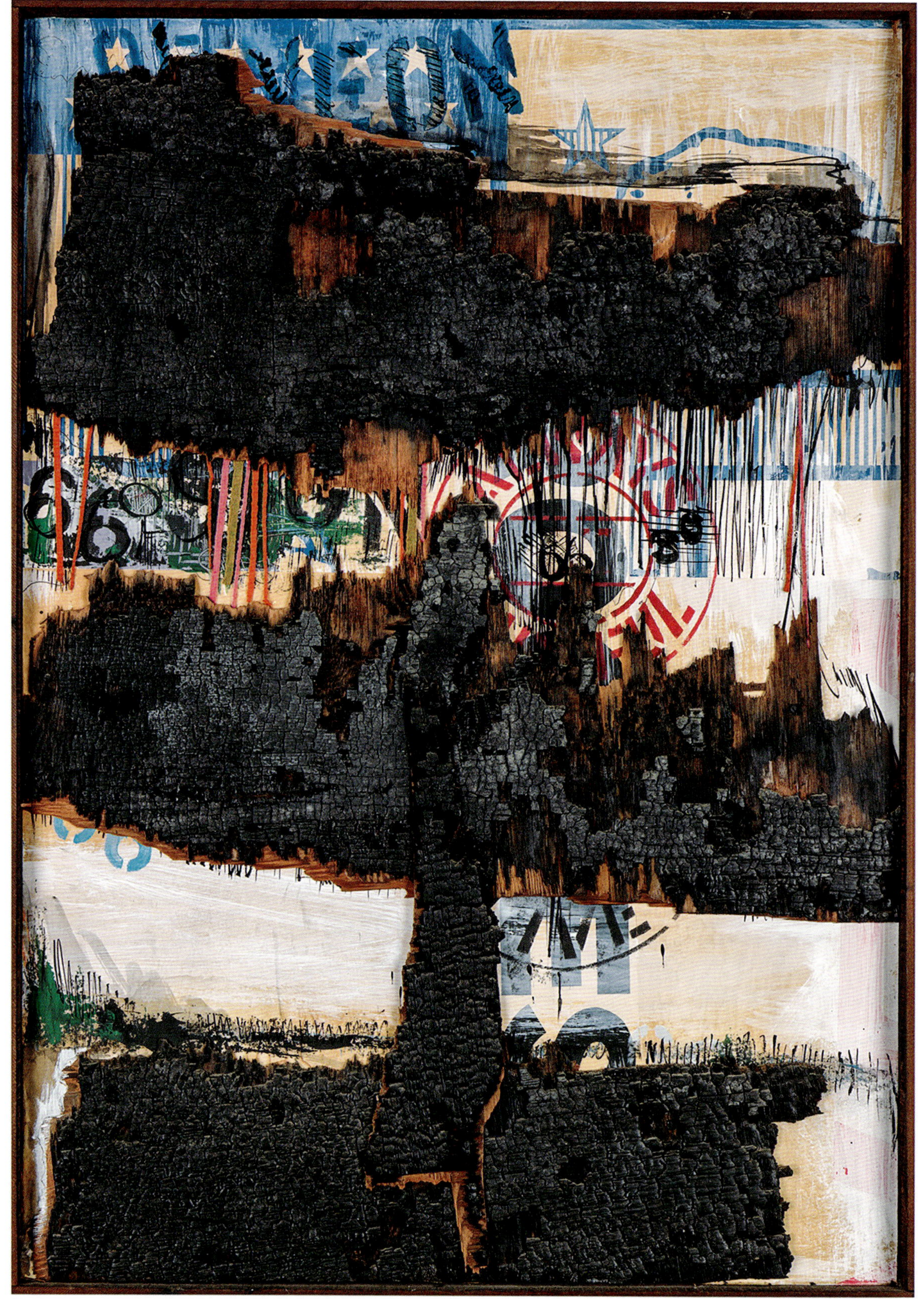

Noah Purifoy, *Untitled (66 Signs of Neon)*, 1966. Mixed-media assemblage, including burnt wood, acrylic, stencil, and color felt, on plywood board, 56 × 36 in. (142.2 × 91.4 cm). Collection of John Baker and Christine Ogata

egg-form ceramic sculptures, and observes that in addition to assemblage and unitary objects, recently "a third kind of 'object' is occurring independently to younger artists. . . . They share with the Structurists a painter's eye, a concern with unitary form rather than the multiple, additive premise of assemblage and mainstream sculpture, and because the form is single, the scale of such compact works often seems larger than normal. Like Price, these artists refuse to forego the sensuous effects of form first explored by the Surrealists, but reject direct Freudian or figurative allusion in favor of an anti-expressionist aloofness."

August 1966 • *66 Signs of Neon*, a group exhibition spearheaded by Judson Powell and Noah Purifoy, opens at the Simon Rodia Renaissance of the Arts Festival at Markham Junior High in Watts, California. The artists on view include Frank Anthony, Debby Brewer, Harry Drinkwater, Ted Michel, Max Neufeldt, Leon Saulter, Arthur Secunda, and Gordon Wagner, as well as Powell and Purifoy. In the exhibition catalogue, Purifoy explains the inspiration for the concept of the show:

> Judson and I, while teaching at the Watts Tower Arts Center, watched aghast the rioting, looting and burning during the August [1965] happening. And while the debris was still smoldering, we ventured into the rubble like other junkers of the community, digging and searching, but unlike others, obsessed without quite knowing why. By September, working during lunch time and after teaching hours, we had collected three tons of charred wood and fire-moulded debris. Despite the involvement of running an art school, we gave much thought to the oddity of our found things. Often the smell of the debris, as our work brought us into the vicinity of the storage area, turned our thoughts to what were and were not tragic times in Watts: and to what to do with the junk we had collected, which had begun to haunt our dreams.

The result is an exhibition that "exists on several levels: as an art education dominated by assemblages of artifacts of the Watts riots; as a one-to-one format of communication between individuals who otherwise would not or could not communicate; as an evolving system of philosophy."

Between 1966 and 1971, iterations of this original exhibition subsequently travel to a number of venues, including the Watts Summer

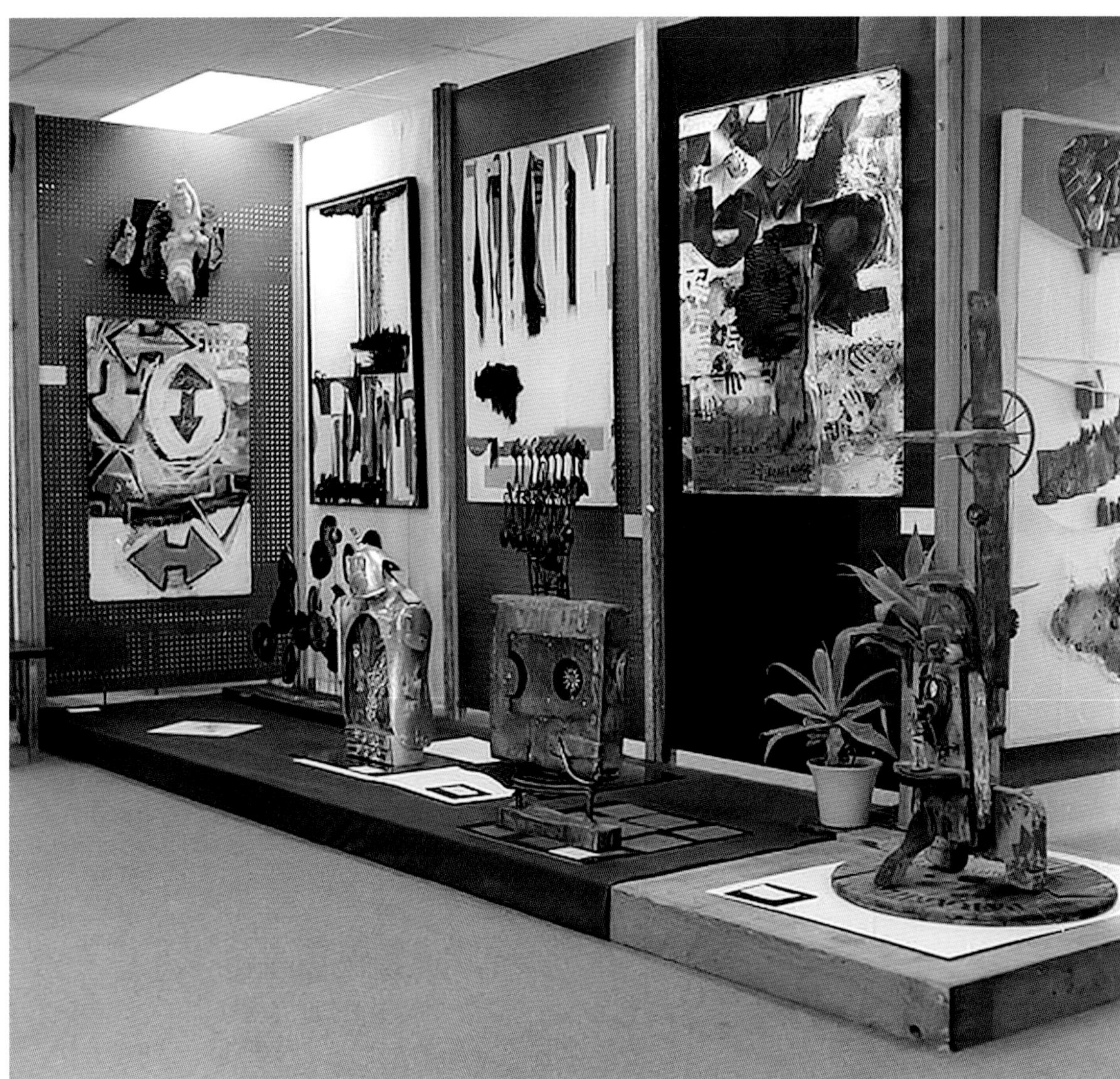

66 Signs of Neon, Simon Rodia Renaissance of the Arts Festival, Los Angeles, 1966

Art Festival; University of Southern California Christian Science Center, Los Angeles; University of California, Berkeley, Berkeley Art Galleries; Washington Gallery of Modern Art, Washington, DC; Hunter Art Gallery, Chattanooga, Tennessee; Huntington Galleries, Knoxville, Tennessee; and Orlando Galleries, Encino, California.

August 22, 1966 • In the midst of what would stretch on as a historic five-year strike against grape growers in California, the Agricultural Workers Organizing Committee and the National Farm Workers Association merge to form what will ultimately become the United Farm Workers (UFW). Through marches, national consumer boycotts, and fasts, the union successfully improves labor contracts, wages, and working conditions, and galvanizes the Chicano movement. UFW partners with religious organizations, student and civil rights activists, and politicians, including Martin Luther King Jr. and Robert F. Kennedy.

1966 • Having recently graduated from California State University, Los Angeles with a bachelor of fine arts, Senga Nengudi (then Sue Irons; b. 1943) moves to Tokyo to begin a yearlong course of cultural study at Waseda University. A fan of the avant-garde artist group Gutai Art Association—known for their experimental efforts combining performance, painting, and site-specific, interactive installation—Nengudi arrives in Japan hoping to see the artists in action, but it is local culture above all else that proves most influential. She finds particular interest in Noh and Kabuki theater, classical *gagaku* court music and dance, and the vestiges of ritual and tradition that she perceives as woven through everyday life in Japan. She returns to Southern California in 1967, working in the social services sector for a year before enrolling in a master's program in sculpture at Cal State LA.

Born Sue Ellen Irons in Chicago, Nengudi was three years old when her father died; several years later, she and her mother move to Southern

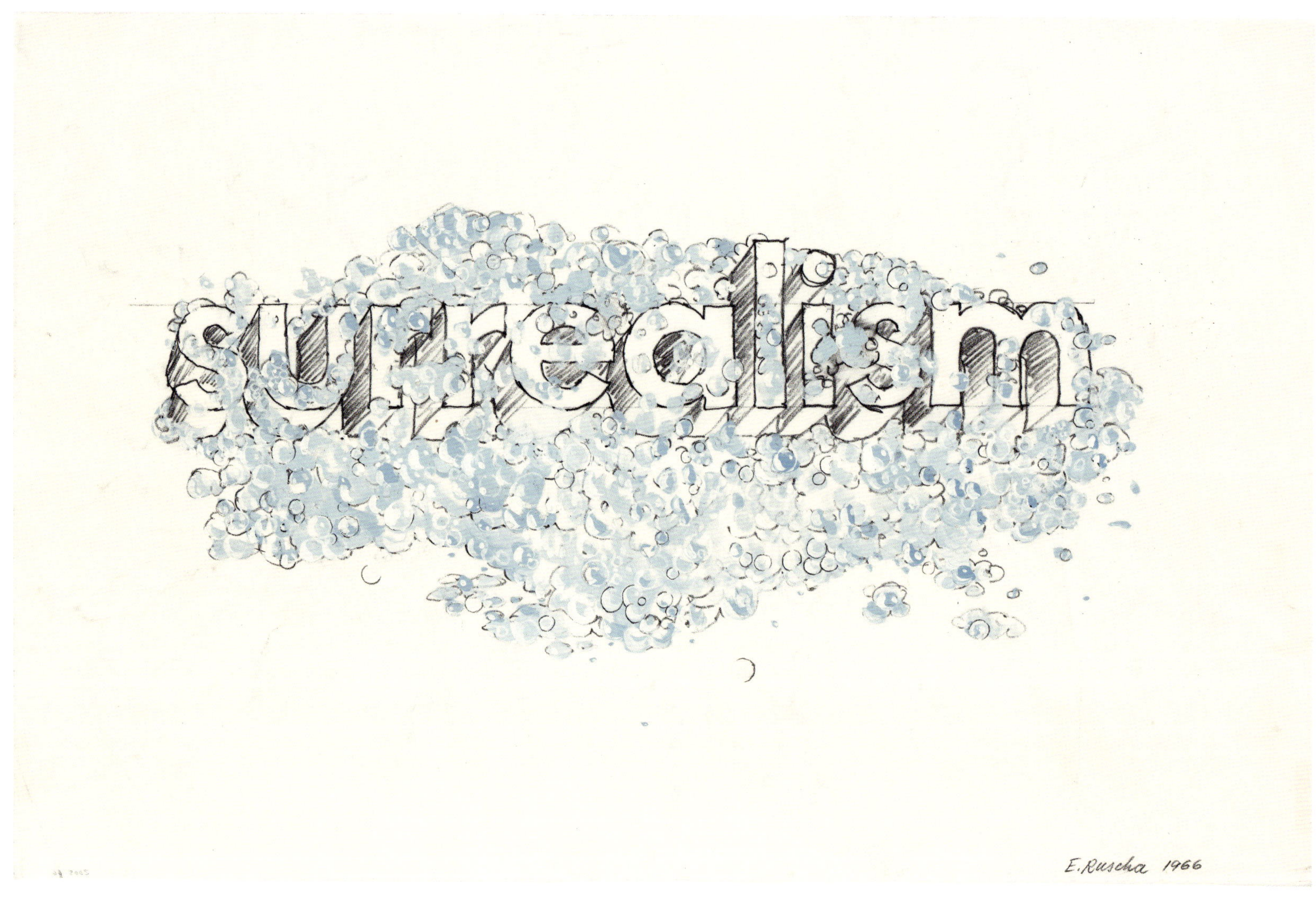

Ed Ruscha, *Surrealism*, 1966. Graphite pencil and tempera on paper, 12 × 18 in. (30.5 × 45.7 cm). Whitney Museum of American Art, New York; gift of The American Contemporary Art Foundation, Inc., Leonard A. Lauder, President 2005.66

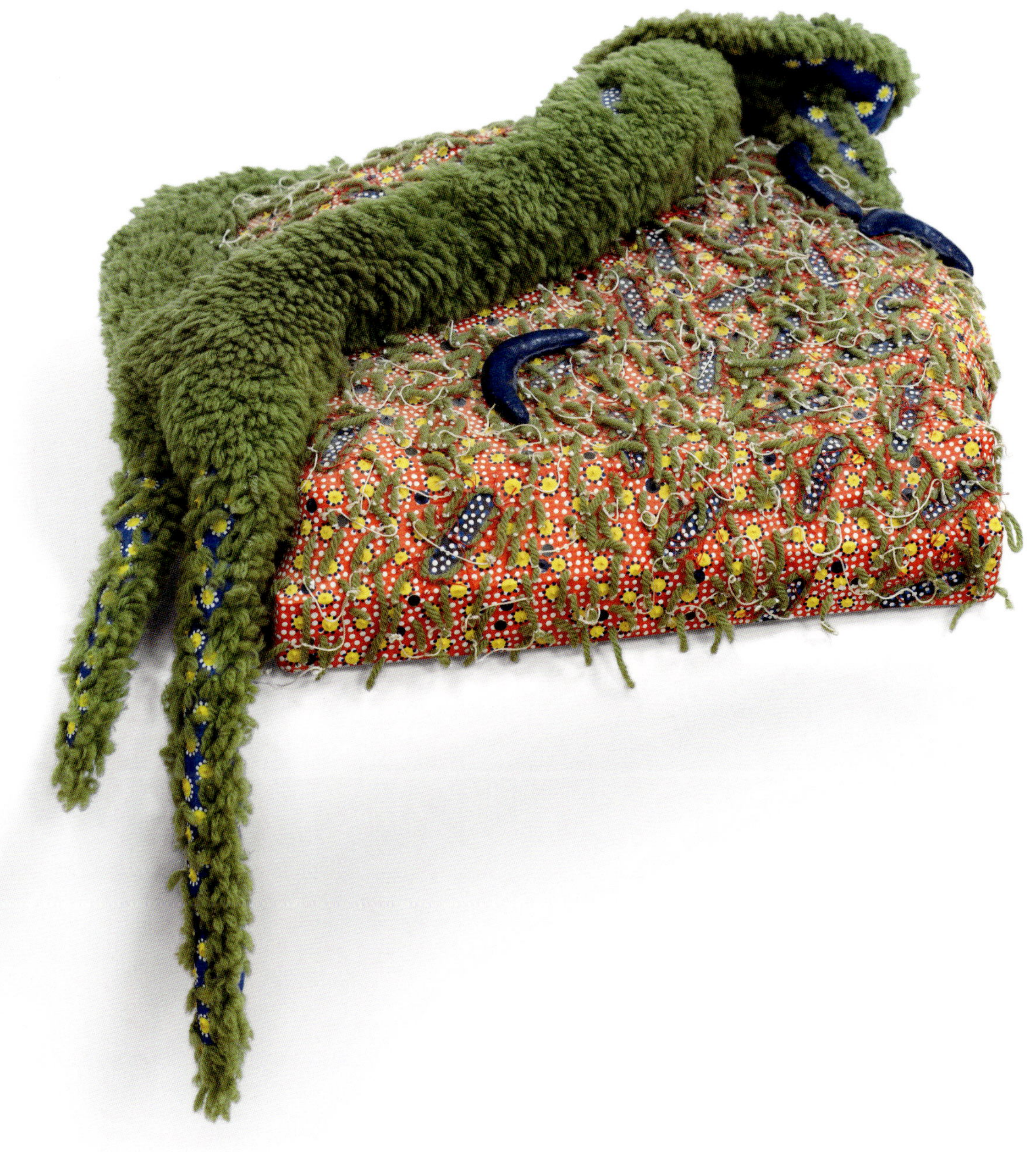

Franklin Williams, *Untitled*, 1966. Acrylic, crochet thread, and yarn on canvas stuffed with cotton batting, over wooden support, 20 × 20 × 9 in. (50.8 × 50.8 × 22.9 cm). Collection of the artist

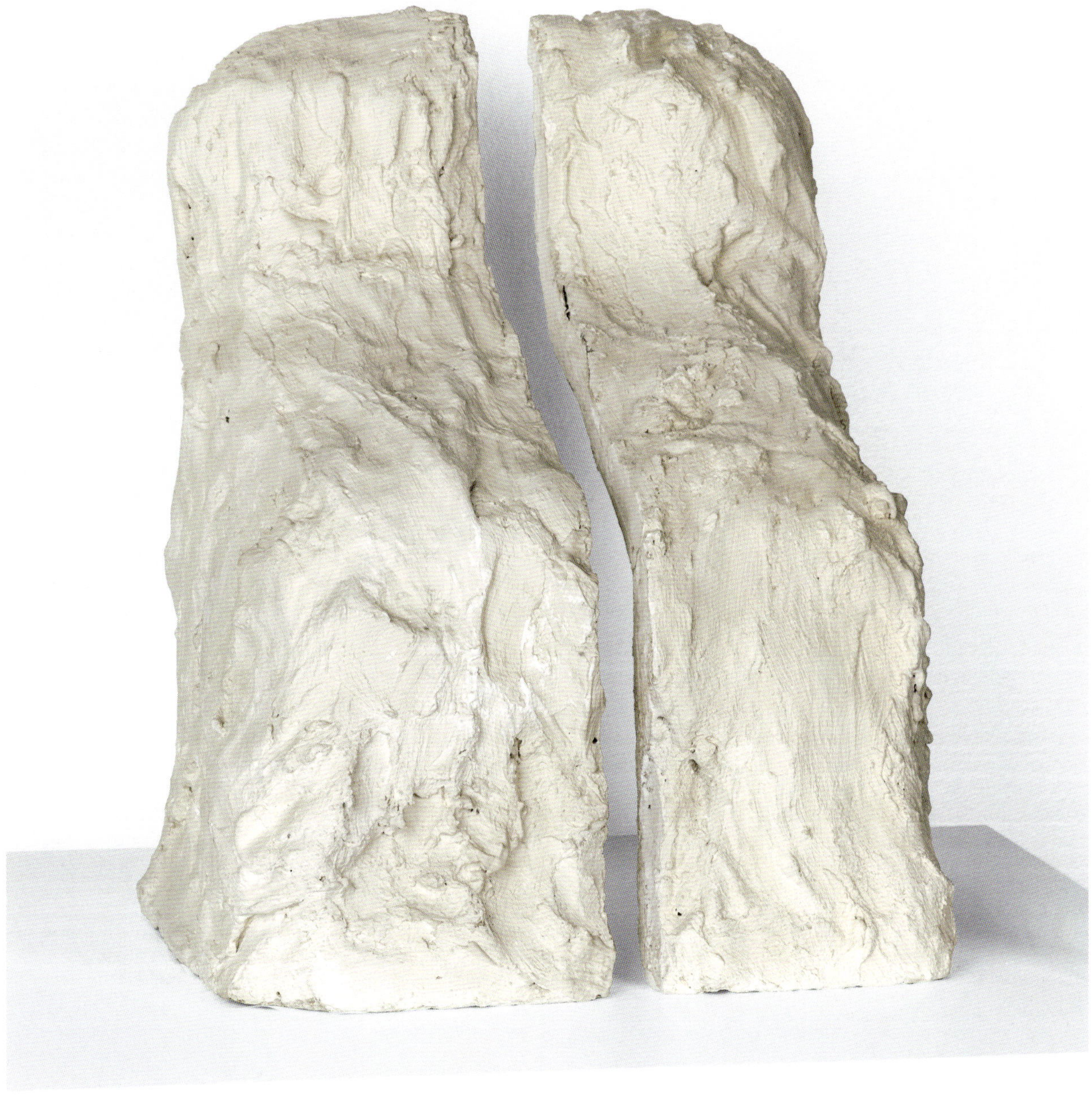

Bruce Nauman, *Mold for a Modernized Slant Step*, 1966. Plaster: installed, 18 ¼ × 14 ½ × 13 ⅜ in. (46.4 × 36.8 × 34 cm). Museum of Contemporary Art Chicago; Gerald S. Elliott Collection 1995.70.a–b

California, first to Pasadena before settling in Los Angeles. As a child, religious sculpture sparks a fascination with the interactivity and sensuousness of objects, as well as the possibility of being "embraced by something that's three-dimensional," a concept she explores further by taking art classes in high school. She begins her undergraduate studies in 1961 at Pasadena City College and shortly thereafter transfers to Cal State LA—where she will be the only Black female student in the art department—majoring in fine arts with a concentration in sculpture and a minor in dance. In 1965 Nengudi starts working as both a teaching assistant at the Pasadena Art Museum and a volunteer educator at the Watts Towers Arts Center (WTAC). In Pasadena she encounters Edward Kienholz's installations and Allan Kaprow's happenings; at WTAC she is exposed to the assemblage and junk art of sculptors Noah Purifoy and John Outterbridge, and further nourished by the broader community of Black artists who are working at the arts center and in the surrounding area. Though she is keenly aware of the racial and class divide between Pasadena and Watts, each remains a critical point of reference for Nengudi in her evolving early practice: "There was this rigorous experimentation going on in both parts of the city. One, of course, was recognized; the other was not. I just thought I was positioned in the best place possible to experience all of this and to be a part of it, and it all kind of fit into my energies and my aesthetic leanings, and so on. . . . I guess it . . . just kind of opened doors—doors I had actually started knocking on anyway."

September 1966 • This month's issue of *Artforum* focuses on Surrealism and includes over a dozen essays approaching the art movement from historical, architectural, filmic, and individual perspectives. Authors include Whitney Halstead, Lucy Lippard, and William Rubin. The cover features a photograph of Ed Ruscha's mixed-media piece *Surrealism Soaped and Scrubbed* (1966). Using the pseudonym "Eddie Russia," Ruscha works as a production designer and art director at the magazine under editor Philip Leider from 1965 to 1969. The issue sells out three weeks after publication, though later Leider will say, "I don't think I chose Surrealism for any deep reason. I don't think there was a new Surrealism about to happen or that anybody was particularly interested in Surrealism." In fact, as Sandra Zalman will note, Leider will ultimately dismiss the issue as "terrible," saying "I didn't see anything new in it. . . . The idea was mine, and everybody I respected laughed at it. Michael [Fried] didn't want any part of it. . . .

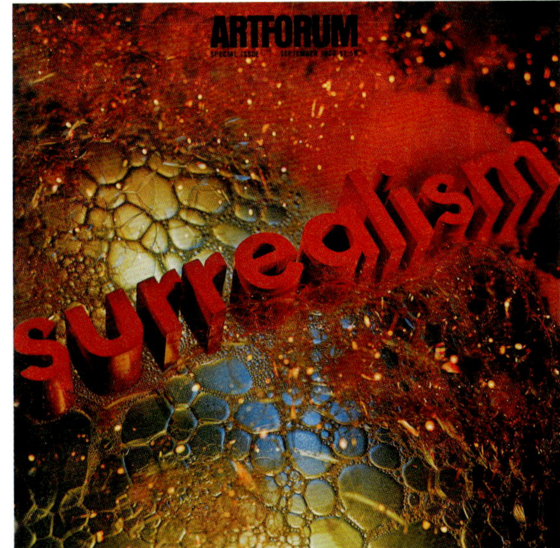

Cover of *Artforum*, September 1966, with Ed Ruscha's *Surrealism Soaped and Scrubbed* (1966)

Frank [Stella] hated it. Because nobody had any use for Surrealism.'"

September 1966 • After serving in the Air Force, Rupert Garcia (b. 1941) enrolls at San Francisco State College to study art on the G.I. Bill. A third-generation Mexican American, Garcia had been born and raised in California's Central Valley where he had grown up in a racially diverse working-class community. Without the means to pursue his dream of becoming a painter, he had

THE SLANT STEP
SHOW

including	excluding
William T. Wiley	Rene Magritte
William Witherup	Allen Ginsberg
James Melchert	. . . .
James Balyeat	. . . .
Bob Anderson	John Silverson
William Allan	Matrix Table
Charles Wiley	Gilbert Roland
Gary Groves	. . . .
Jerry Ballaine	. . . .
Jeanette Wiley	Roy L.
Bruce Nauman	Henry Aaron
Bob Nelson	Audrey Sabol
Dorothy Wiley	. . . .
Earl Eder	. . . .
Bob Hudson	. . . .
Dick Pervier	James White
William Geis	Dr. Linus Pauling
Paul Heald	Phil Specter
Jack Fulton	. . . .
Dan Welch	. . . .
Louise Pryor	. . . .

alternates

Ron Davis, Mighty Ursus,
Timothy Leary, Senior Eater,
Marshal Macluan, Alexander King,
Monique Benoit, Father Ted Fuchman,
Ted Mack's Original, Attila the Pun

films, drawings,
constructions, tapes, discussion,
poetry, painting, clothing, recipes

BERKELEY GALLERY   SEPTEMBER 9 through 17

PREVIEW   SEPTEMBER 9   8:00 PM

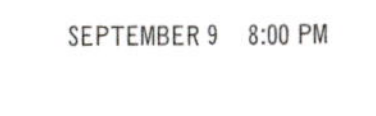

Poster for *The Slant Step Show*, Berkeley Gallery, San Francisco, 1966

enlisted in the Air Force in 1963. Two years later, he is deployed to northern Thailand on a special mission supporting the war in Vietnam. The anti-war movement is in full swing when he returns to San Francisco to study painting. A minor in sociology furnishes Garcia with new critical perspectives on the war, on American imperialism, and on racial and economic inequality, while the student strike of 1968 leads him to take up silkscreen—a medium more expedient for protest.

Garcia's printed and painted art is characterized by bold graphic images that repurpose the formal strategies of Pop art for popular causes. "My art is committed to the paradox that in using mass-media I am using a source with which I am at war," he will write in 1970 in his unpublished master's thesis. "In using images of mass-media I am taking an art form which is debased, exploitative, and indifferent to human welfare, and setting it into a totally new moral context. I am, so to speak, reversing the process by which mass-media betrays the masses, and betraying the images of mass-media to moral purposes for which they were not designed: the art of social protest."

September 9–17, 1966 • Bruce Nauman and William T. Wiley's Slant Step project comes to fruition as a group exhibition at Berkeley Gallery, San Francisco. *The Slant Step Show* features a peculiar wooden "step" covered in worn green linoleum that, despite its resemblance to an ordinary footstool, is set at a slant that seems absurdly to defy

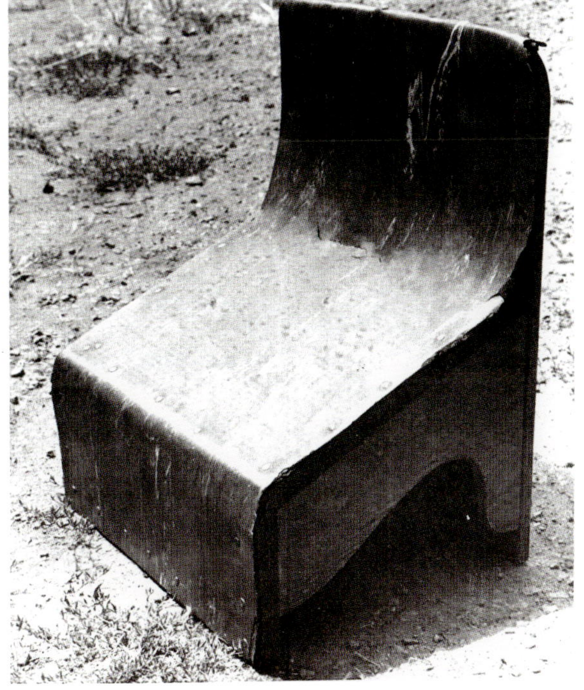

its purpose. Artist-friends including William Allan, William Geis, Robert Hudson, James Melchert, and Dorothy Wiley, among others, make work inspired by the step and show it in the exhibition.

The year prior, encouraged by Nauman, Wiley had purchased the step for 50 cents from the Mount Carmel Salvage Shop in Mill Valley, California. Nauman keeps it in his studio, and the two artists begin making drawings and sculptures about the item, investing it with a life and narrative all its own. For them, it becomes an enigmatic object in keeping with their fascination with Marcel Duchamp, Man Ray, and H. C. Westermann. Nauman and Wiley's friends begin to share their enthusiasm for this homely oddity, and when gallery owner Marian Parmenter asks local poet William Witherup to do a project at her Berkeley Gallery, he proposes a show about the Slant Step.

After installing the exhibition and leaving to have a few drinks, a handful of artists return to the scene, at which time they piled all the artworks into a corner, according to Wiley, leaving only the original Slant Step on display. "When the slant-steppers came the next day and saw their work in a heap they were kind of uptight. But we kept it that way for the show's duration. It was kind of fun watching people poke around the pile." During the run of the exhibition, a young local artist named Richard Serra stops by and, finding the storefront empty of people, absconds with the Slant Step, taking it first to New York, where it models for some Slant Steps of his own.

———

September 20–October 8, 1966 • Curated by Lucy Lippard, *Eccentric Abstraction* is on view at Fischbach Gallery, New York, and features eight artists: Alice Adams, Louise Bourgeois, Eva Hesse, Gary Kuehn, Bruce Nauman, Don Potts, Keith Sonnier, and Frank Lincoln Viner, all of whom are linked by what Lippard identifies as a "wholly sensuous, life giving element" inherent in their abstract sculptural forms. Using plaster, rubber tubing, wire, and vinyl sheets, the sculptures don't represent the body but, rather, evoke it, effecting a physical response that Lippard describes as "body ego," a term she borrows from the contemporary psychoanalyst Gilbert Rose and related to Sigmund Freud's ideas about bodily ego. In Lippard's use, it characterizes the simultaneous desire of the viewer "to caress, to be caught up in the feel and rhythms of a work" and repulsion against "certain forms and surfaces," the latter of which "takes longer to comprehend." In an article published in the November issue of *Art International*, she links Northern Californian artists with work she is experiencing in New York. "Funky art or West Coast eccentric abstraction deals with a raunchy, cynical eroticism

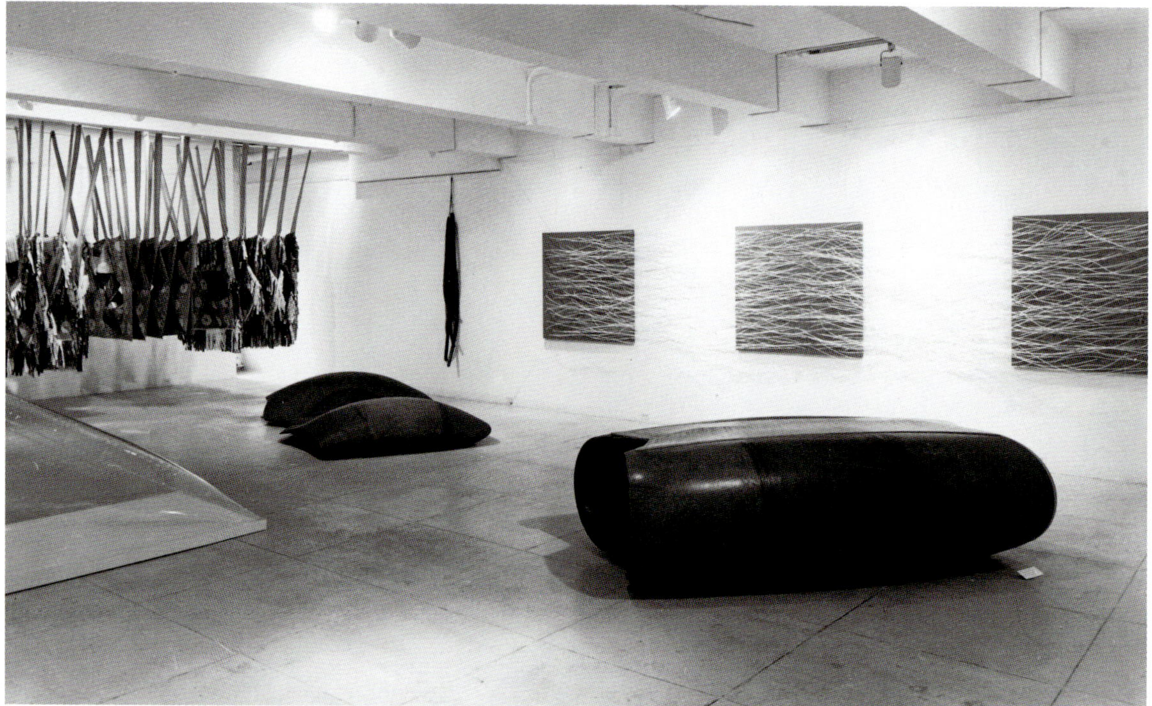

Eccentric Abstraction, Fischbach Gallery, New York, 1966

that parallels that of the New York artists," she comments, but the West Coast artists are more involved with assemblage, Bruce Nauman being "typical of a much cooler kind of Funk." Lippard recognizes historical Surrealism as a common antecedent for artists on both coasts, but she points to important differences between earlier modes and the surrealist tendencies of the 1960s: "The distinction made by the Surrealists between conscious and unconscious is irrelevant, for the current younger generation favors the presentation of specific facts—*what* we feel, *what* we see rather than *why* we do so." For her show at Fischbach Gallery, "Bay Area Funk . . . wasn't quite what I was thinking about, because I was so into Minimalism. . . . The idea was that I wanted Minimal kinds of forms but with a sensuous, sort of sexual aspect to them. And that was why it was called Eccentric Abstraction."

Writing about this and related exhibitions for the *Village Voice*, Lil Picard summarizes the moment: "The works are normal, gay, playful and quite inventive. No new geniuses, by any means, but rather a fresh clear view of things, experiments in plastic materials, wires, tubes, white plastic items, like milk spilled over on the floor, hammocks, ribbons, colors, all kinds of novelties to wade through, which roll around on the floor, hang from the ceiling."

———

September 28–October 17, 1966 • Before leaving New York for a three-month teaching stint at the University of California, Davis, Joseph Raffaele opens a solo exhibition at Stable Gallery. His

paintings offer enigmatic juxtapositions of objects on a white ground and are met with some consternation by the viewing public. Interviewed by Gene Swenson, Raffaele defends the Continued on page 191

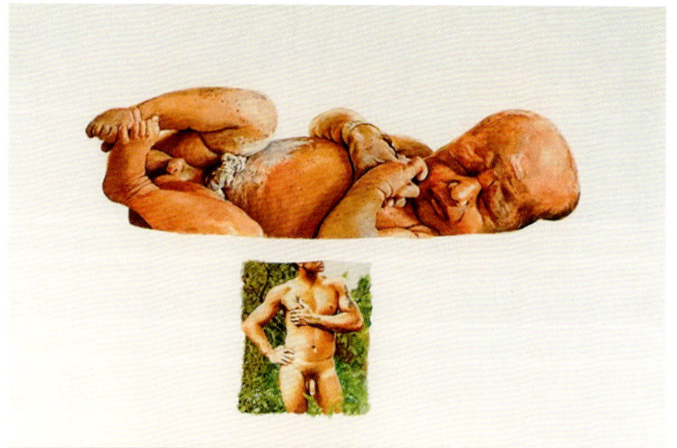

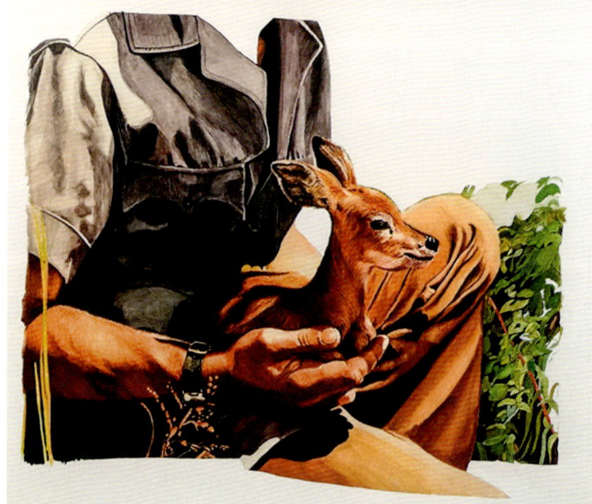

Joseph Raffaele, *Baby Man Doe*, c. 1967. Oil on canvas, 55 ¾ × 45 ¾ in. (141.6 × 116.2 cm)

ECCENTRIC ABSTRACTION

JO APPLIN

In the early to mid-1960s, a body of idiosyncratic objects began to appear on the New York art scene that defied easy categorization. They combined erotic bodily suggestion with Minimalist form and spare geometric shape. These abstract, often humorous forms employed surprising and unconventional materials that included latex, plaster, fiberglass, rubber, rope, cloth, leather, and plastic. "Eccentric abstraction" was the term critic and curator Lucy R. Lippard coined for the new work that was, she said, "devoted to opening up new areas of materials, shape, color, and sensuous experience."[1] With "eccentric abstraction," Lippard's aim was not to name a movement so much as to gesture towards a broader shift she saw taking place among a younger generation of sculptors whose work combined aspects of the nonobjective geometric and Minimal with an intimate and unexpected entanglement with the body. Lippard first tested out her ideas regarding eccentric abstraction in a series of lectures she delivered at the University of California, Berkeley's art museum and the Los Angeles County Museum of Art just a few months prior to the opening of her small exhibition of the same name in September 1966 at the Fischbach Gallery in New York (fig. 1).

Eccentric Abstraction showcased work by eight artists. Six were from New York and included Louise Bourgeois, Eva Hesse, Alice Adams, Frank Lincoln Viner, Keith Sonnier (fig. 2), and Gary Kuehn. Two were West Coast artists: Bruce Nauman, whose phallic "rubbery streamers" were propped against the wall as though an afterthought, and Don Potts, whose curvaceous leather-and-wood constructions combined, Lippard said, a "solid formal basis" with the sensuous tactility of their "almost maliciously perfect" surfaces.[2] Lippard had encountered the work of both artists for the first time during her lecture tour, when she visited a number of artists' studios and saw a lot of what she described as "Bay Area Funk," which despite some similarities to her notion of eccentric abstraction wasn't "quite what I was thinking about, because I was so into Minimalism," she later recalled.[3]

Potts and Nauman adopted a "cooler" approach than the rather more "raunchy cynicism" of their West Coast peers who were, Lippard said, more involved with assemblage than the kind of "structural frameworks" she was interested in, although notable exceptions included Jeremy Anderson, whose painted wooden sculptures were singled out by Lippard for their spare, less raucous approach to form.[4] Unlike their Californian counterparts, who a year later would be grouped together under the rubric "Funk" in an exhibition held at the University of California, Berkeley, the East Coast iteration of eccentric abstraction combined what Lippard described as a proclivity for "Pop art's perversity and irreverence" with a deep-rooted commitment to modernist abstraction and the development of "a visceral reciprocity" between artwork and viewer.[5] While eccentric abstraction "might be said to border on titillation," any overtly sexual reference was ultimately reined in by the work's formal "understatement."[6]

In an essay published in *Art International* to accompany the exhibition, Lippard discussed the work of other artists not included in *Eccentric Abstraction* but who nonetheless demonstrated a shared sensibility. She singled out Mike Todd and his totemic, breast-like, bulbous, wood-and-metal *Fetish* sculptures from 1963 for their mix of precisely the irreverence and perversion she identified as lying at the core of eccentric abstraction (pp. 92, 93). The potentially "titillating" aspect of the work was carefully thwarted both by the absurdity of its reliance on formal repetition and its monochrome, Minimalist

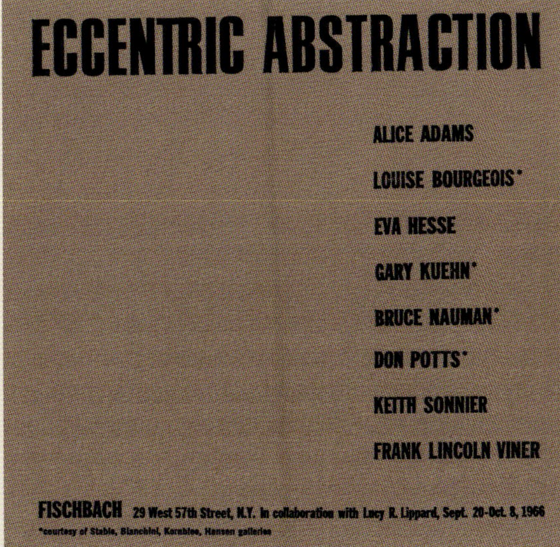

Fig. 1. Flyer for *Eccentric Abstraction*, Fischbach Gallery, New York, 1966

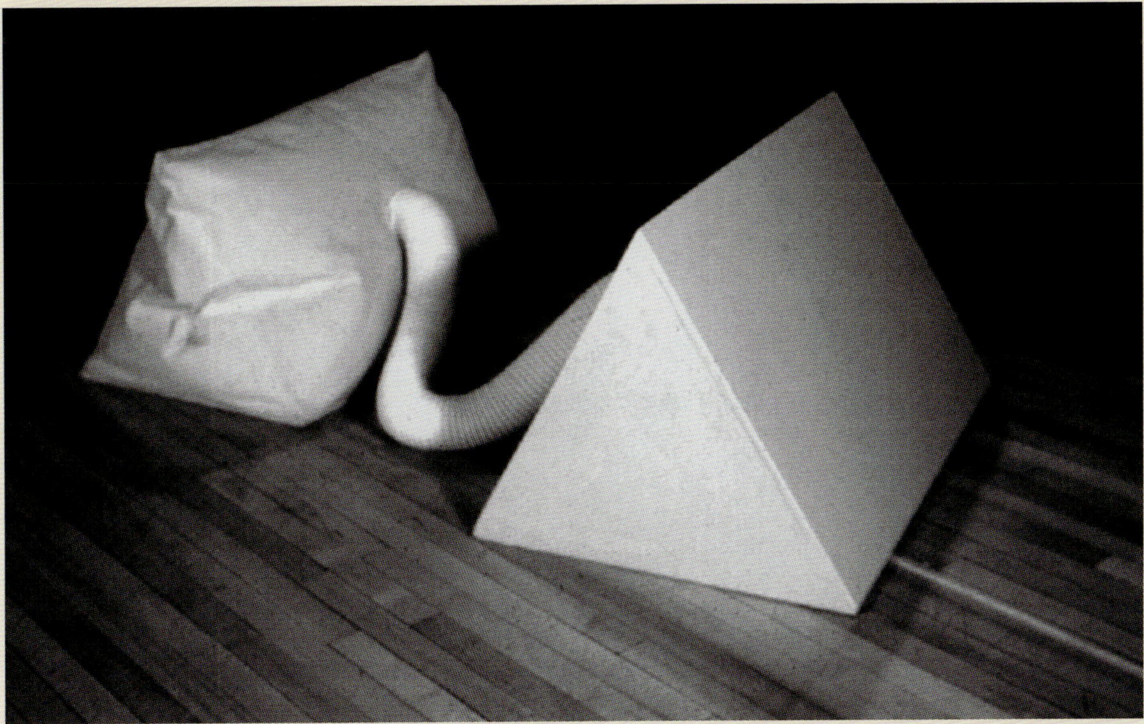

Fig. 2. Keith Sonnier, *Untitled*, 1966. Plywood, stitched canvas, polyurethane duct pipe, blower, motor, and timer, two pieces, 36 × 48 × 36 in. (91.4 × 121.9 × 91.4 cm) each

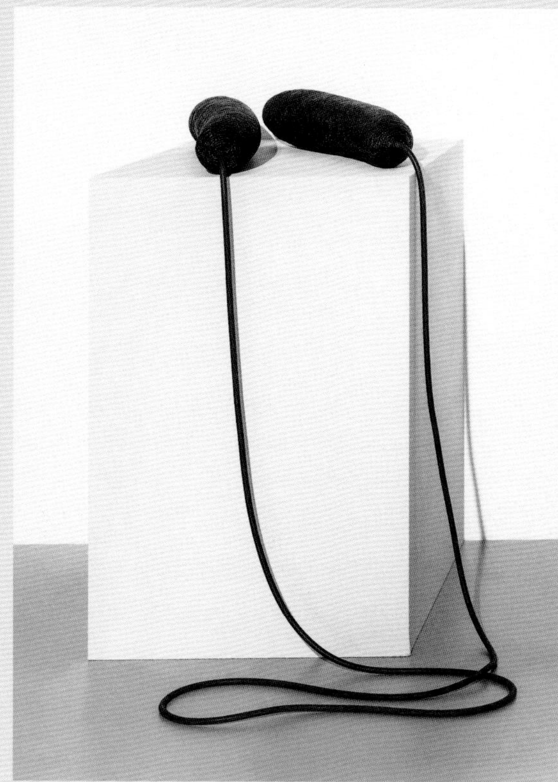

Fig. 3. Eva Hesse, *Ingeminate*, 1965. Enamel, cord, papier-caché, latex, and rubber, 188 × 4 ½ in. (478 × 11.5 cm)

surfaces. Hesse, also an admirer of Todd's work, was another important eccentric abstraction artist for Lippard, due to her use of serial repetition and unconventional tactile materials such as cord, papier-mâché, and latex. Hesse was one of three women Lippard included in *Eccentric Abstraction*, and a group of her sausage-like bound forms (fig. 3) were exhibited alongside latex pieces by Bourgeois and Adams's tubular wire tangles suspended from the ceiling and coiled in fat, squat puddles on the floor (fig. 4).

Lippard later recalled how she was "sick of 'beauty'" and that she relished the sculptural turn towards the "uglier" side of things.[7] One of her chief examples was Bourgeois's *Portrait* (1963; p. 97), an abstract pool of soft, set, blood-red latex, its dimpled surface puckered into rubbery phallic knots produced by pulling the latex from the plaster mold while still soft. More than one writer has compared the sculpture's appearance to a bloody blister.[8] Paul Thek's beeswax, wood, and plexiglass *Meat Pieces*, or *Technological Reliquaries*, modeled into disembodied hunks of bloodied flesh, trod a similar line between the ugly and unfamiliar to serve up an eccentric image of the body reconfigured in radical piecemeal ways. For Lippard, though, Thek's work was less successful than that of Bourgeois, due to its reliance on representation over abstraction. Lippard described it disparagingly as "warmed over and updated Surrealism" in her review of Gene Swenson's group exhibition *The Other Tradition*

that opened just a few months before *Eccentric Abstraction*.[9] Despite some significant conceptual overlap between Swenson's and Lippard's approaches to the new work, formally they had very different takes on what they were seeing, with Swenson far happier than Lippard with the label "surrealism." It was not surrealism per se, but Swenson's attempt to root modern art in Surrealism and Dada that was anathema to Lippard, as well as to many others trained in a modernist lineage of abstraction.[10] Lippard was particularly scathing regarding the lack of "intellectual stringency" among the younger generation of artists Swenson included, whose work signaled a certain "preciosity" compared to the formal rigor she sought.[11]

For Lippard there was also an important distinction to be made between earlier European Surrealist precedents and what she described as "Surrealism's eccentric progeny" in the 1960s, as seen in the work of Lee Bontecou, Claes Oldenburg, Lucas Samaras, and H. C. Westermann, whom Lippard described as "precursors" to eccentric abstraction. She characterized Westermann's *The Plush* (1963–64; p. 83), an awkward five-foot-tall upright form mounted on a wheeled base and covered in thick shagpile carpet, as an early example of eccentric abstraction due to the way it "humorously fused the sensuous element with deadpan

abstract form."[12] Westermann's achievement was to have successfully united the headier "pictorial associations" and "emotional interference" of Surrealism with the burgeoning austerity of the Minimalist object.

"Specific objects" was the term Minimalist critic and sculptor Donald Judd coined in 1965 to describe the new work emerging on the art scene. While his formal emphasis was different from Lippard's, they claimed several of the same artists in their respective roll call. Judd, like Lippard, was wary of the creeping surrealist aspect of the new work. He was also, like Lippard, at pains to emphasize where the new work differed from earlier surrealist precedents. Somewhat surprisingly, given his figurative, surrealist leanings, Westermann was an artist both Lippard and Judd agreed on: his wooden marbled question-mark sculpture was chosen as the lead image to accompany Judd's essay "Local History" (1964), in which he outlined many of the same arguments he would develop in his essay "Specific Objects" one year later.[13] The choice of Westermann's question mark was a suitably circumspect one for an essay describing the open-ended nature of the current art scene in which "a lot of things just can't be connected."[14]

Although Lippard appreciated artists' use of soft, phallic, sexy, sometimes funny-seeming forms, she

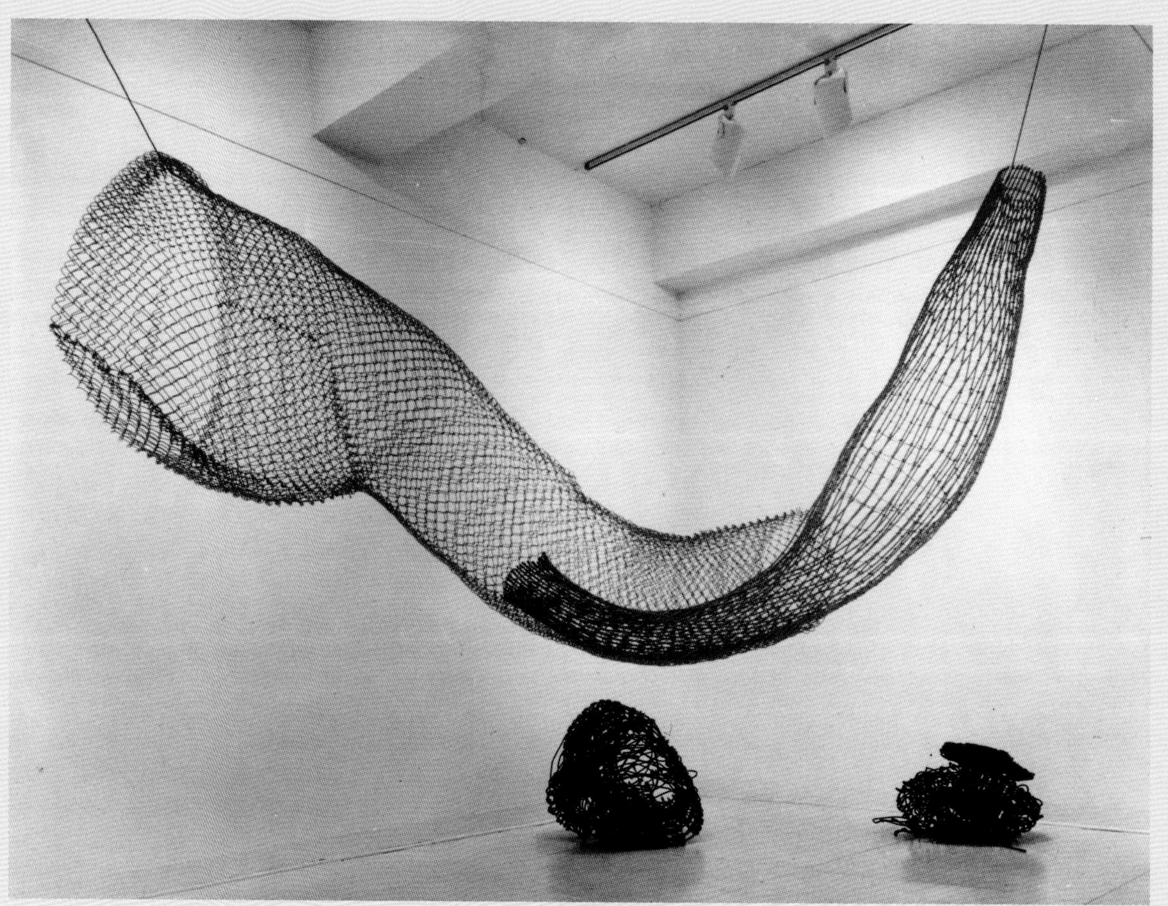

Fig. 4. *Eccentric Abstraction*, Fischbach Gallery, New York, 1966, with Alice Adams's *Big Aluminum 1* (1966)

recognized the very real risk they took in introducing humor into the "structural idiom," worrying the avant-garde threatened to lose some of its seriousness by trespassing into the realm of comedy, where, she noted, "angels feared to tread."[15] One artist with no such fear was Lee Lozano who, prior to her move into large-scale geometric abstraction around 1965, made eccentric, outrageous, funny, and polymorphously perverse crayon and graphite drawings of bodies, body parts, and inanimate tools (hammers, screwdrivers, and so on) muddled into strange erotic couplings. *No title* (1962; p. 69) fuses body and machine in a mechano-morphic muddle. A hand-turned crank substitutes for an ear, while Lozano's trademark image of a wide grinning mouth, with a fat, fecal, and unmistakably phallic cigar clamped between its teeth, adds an anarchic sense of humor. Lozano is better known today for what Lippard later described as her "equally eccentric decision never to associate with women," heralded by Lozano's 1969 announcement of her "boycott of women" that marked the beginning of the end for her career: She followed her boycott one year later with a decision to stop making art and to drop out of the artworld completely, eccentricity giving way, in the end, to abstraction as Lozano disappeared entirely from the scene after completing her final series of abstract *Wave* paintings.[16]

Lippard's feminist politics meant that by the 1970s she was rethinking the work she had previously grouped under the moniker of eccentric abstraction from an explicitly feminist, embodied point of view. In 1976 she published her important monograph on Hesse and began to question her prior insistence on the primacy of abstraction, which had led to the exclusion of artists working in a more figurative or bodily—including explicitly feminist—mode.[17] "The time has come," Lippard proposed, "to call a semisphere a breast if we know damn well that's what it suggests."[18] Hannah Wilke's *Teasel Cushion* (1967; p. 213), a petaled, pink terra-cotta object snugly nestled on a bed of dark plastic curls, is a work that knew damn well what it suggested. And yet Wilke's playful evocation of a vagina and patch of pubic hair is quickly, and deliberately, undone by the work's title and the abstract nature of the object.[19] Bontecou also rejected direct sexual interpretations of the blank black orifices protruding from the surfaces of her metal-and-fabric wall-relief sculptures such as *Untitled* (1961; p. 60) by insisting such erotic readings were moot, as her work was "neither male nor female."[20]

From the outset, eccentric abstraction encompassed work by a far wider pool of artists than those accommodated within Lippard's original exhibition. The theme of abstract eroticism dominated the article she published the following year, "Eros Presumptive" (1967), in which she probed further the recent erotic turn in several art exhibitions in New York. Lippard drew a clear line between the flat-out provocative, even pornographic works in shows such as Sidney Janis's *Erotic Art '66* and those such as *Eccentric Abstraction*, which pushed the parameters of the object in formally exciting, not sexually titillating, directions. The new work permitted a more flexible, open framework for thinking about the permeable boundaries of the object and the body, and the possibilities and politics of that body's eccentric, even surreal, expression in all its erotic, abstract, and gendered formulations.

NOTES

1   Lucy R. Lippard, "Eccentric Abstraction," *Art International* 10, no. 9 (Nov. 20, 1966): 28, 34–40; reprinted in Lucy R. Lippard, *Changing: Essays in Art Criticism* (New York: E. P. Dutton, 1971), 98–111, 99.
2   Lippard, "Eccentric Abstraction," 100.
3   Lucy R. Lippard, oral history interview, March 15, 2011. Archives of American Art, Smithsonian Institution, Washington, DC.
4   Lippard, "Eccentric Abstraction," 100, 108.
5   Ibid., 99. On this, see Jacob Stewart-Halevy, *Slant Steps: On the Art World's Semi-Periphery* (Berkeley: University of California Press, 2020), 115–124, 120.
6   Lippard, "Eccentric Abstraction," 105.
7   Lucy Lippard, "Eccentric Abstraction," in *Louise Bourgeois*, ed. Frances Morris (London: Tate Publishing, 2007), 113–14.
8   See, for instance, Mignon Nixon, *Fantastic Reality: Louise Bourgeois and a Story of Modern Art* (Cambridge, MA: MIT Press, 2005), 188; and Briony Fer, "Objects Beyond Objecthood," *Oxford Art Journal* 22, no. 2 (1999): 32. Deborah Wye described it as "almost offensive" as well as "exhilarating and amusing"; see *Louise Bourgeois*, ed. Deborah Wye (New York: Museum of Modern Art, 1984), 25.
9   Lucy Lippard, "An Impure Situation (New York and Philadelphia Letter)," *Art International* 10, no. 5 (May 1966): 62–63.
10   On Swenson's art criticism, see Jennifer Sichel, *Criticism Without Authority: Gene Swenson and Jill Johnston's Queer Practices* (Chicago: University of Chicago Press, forthcoming). See also Lucy R. Lippard, *Surrealists on Art* (New York: Prentice Hall, 1970), an edited compendium of writing by artists, poets, and writers associated with Surrealism; as well as Scott Rothkopf, "Banned and Determined," *Artforum* 40, no. 10 (June 2002): 144.
11   Lippard, "An Impure Situation," 63.
12   Lippard, "Eccentric Abstraction," 101n2. Here Lippard cites artists including Lucas Samaras and Lindsey Decker for their Surrealist-inflected sculpture.
13   See Jo Applin, *Eccentric Objects: Rethinking Sculpture in 1960s America* (New Haven, CT: Yale University Press, 2012).
14   Donald Judd, "Local History," *Arts Yearbook 7, New York: The Art World*, ed. James R. Mellow (New York: Arts Digest, 1964), 22–36; reprinted in *Donald Judd: The Complete Writings 1959–1975* (Halifax: Press of the Nova Scotia College of Art and Design; New York: New York University Press, 2005), 149–56, 149, 150.
15   Lippard, "Eccentric Abstraction," 100.
16   Lucy R. Lippard, "Escape Attempts," *Six Years: The Dematerialization of the Art Object from 1966 to 1972*, ed. Lucy R. Lippard (Berkeley: University of California Press, 1973), vii–xxii, xii. See also Jo Applin, *Lee Lozano: Not Working* (New Haven, CT: Yale University Press, 2018).
17   Lucy R. Lippard, *Eva Hesse* (New York: Da Capo Press, 1976).
18   Lucy R. Lippard, "The Women Artist's Movement—What Next?" [1975], reprinted in Lucy R. Lippard, *From the Center: Feminist Essays on Women's Art* (New York: E. P. Dutton, 1976), 139–48, 140. For a discussion of this, see Fer, "Objects Beyond Objecthood," 28.
19   See Rachel Middleman, *Radical Eroticism: Women, Art, and Sex in the 1960s* (Berkeley: University of California Press, 2018).
20   Lee Bontecou, personal correspondence with the author, June 2002.

work, "I'm exploring the conscious, my consciousness. Our time is Post-Freudian; there is an accumulation of everything we know about sex already. Today, ideas about sex have been integrated into our life and feelings and what we say."

———

Fall 1966 • After graduating from the Institute of American Indian Arts, T. C. Cannon moves to California with a scholarship to attend the San Francisco Art Institute (SFAI). He has an interest in expanding his understanding of color and of the possibilities of abstraction and has been looking forward to studying under artists whose work he admires, namely, Nathan Oliveira and Wayne Thiebaud. Although not much has been written of his time at SFAI, he seems disappointed that the professors are not engaged and that he does not experience the comradery with fellow students that other artists have spoken of.

Additionally, despite the political decisiveness of his work and his embrace of the music and poetry of the counterculture, Cannon feels disconnected from the Bay Area scene. He drops out of SFAI after two months and enlists in the Army. His voluntary enlistment surprises many of his family and friends, but the uncertainty of the draft and his commitment to the "Kiowa way"—his people's embrace of the protection and leadership of warriors—may have been powerful influences. Cannon joins the 101st Airborne Division and will earn two Bronze Stars for his service as a paratrooper in the Tet Offensive in 1968. However, he will remain deeply conflicted over this experience and continue to return to his memories of war and violence throughout his artistic career.

———

Fall 1966 • At the University of California, Davis, William T. Wiley and his friend and fellow artist William Allan meet Joseph Raffaele. While perusing the studios of his new acquaintances and other area artists, Raffaele observes that their fascination with "surreal" juxtapositions, assemblage, playfully allusive forms, and pictorial illusions shares ground with the current explorations of Paul Thek, Eva Hesse and other New Yorkers. He is also struck by their attitude, as he will later recall: "I was impressed by [Allan and Wiley]. They were married, fathers, family men, had a family life. It 'blew my mind' to use a term of that period to witness the casualness with which they approached art and how their lifestyle was expressed, there was a certain Westness about it, cowboy jeans, a casualness. It was like fresh air to me."

While in California, Raffaele describes in a playful note to Eva Hesse a fictional work she has supposedly been gifted by William T. Wiley:

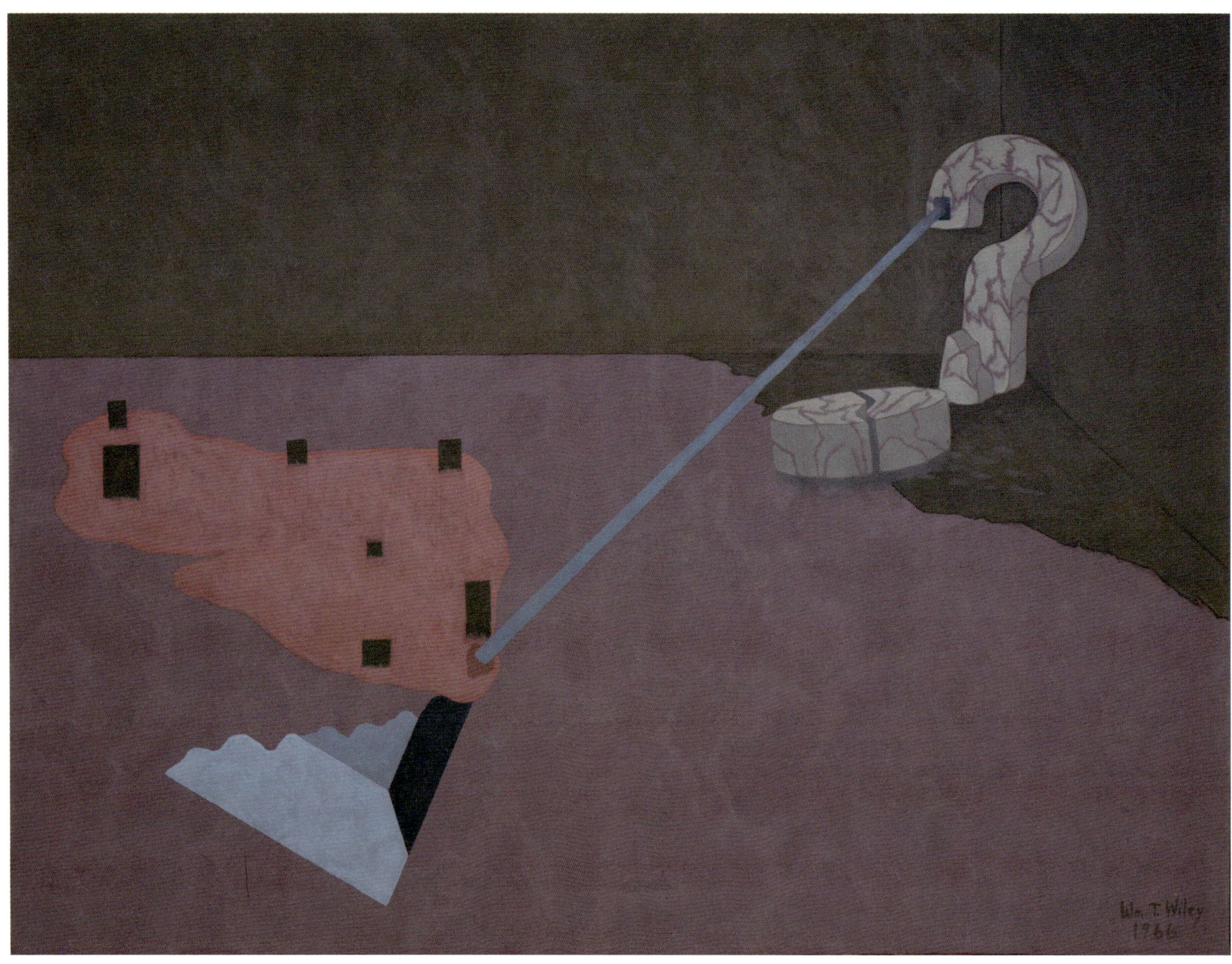

William T. Wiley, *Modern Art Teacher*, 1966. Acrylic on canvas, 66 × 86 in. (167.6 × 218.4 cm). Wiley Family Collection

Brown rubbered circle with cunty-bull-dogged head, mouth open and white, heavier than but like, bakery box string coming through hole moving on towards scotched [*sic*] tape center crossing which has hairs four and I don't know if they're Wiley's or Raffaele's and then the string moves on toward a tampaxian puff again scotch taped and then string on and on with 1st a blocky Romaned A, then a V, and then an E. With Cathalicolian Consciousness I assumed it was a religious beginning but then with inscriptions read realized that it was a western wireless to Eva Hesse, who once for the shortest time in Paul Thek's shadow was my wife. It was a Saturday and several people were surprised. The brown rubber is a bit darker but not too much to make one think it is the same brown as brown licorice. Could it be that this piece will be in Lucy Lippard's new show at the Goatgroin Gallery called "Concentric Extraction"?

Raffaele also undertakes a series of artist interviews in collaboration with critic Elizabeth Baker that will be published the following summer in *ARTnews*. They describe new trends in California that reflect an understanding of the New York arts scene:

Distant attachments to Dada and Surrealism exist, though the specifically antiart polemic of Dada is absent, as is traditional Surrealist imagery. Rather, there is a kind of Surrealism of everyday life—a nostalgia for the most insignificant things and events, a haphazard documentation, an automatist access to ideas, referential titles. In their commitment to art as inseparable from life, they are of course aware of [Robert] Rauschenberg's and [John] Cage's attitudes; but they are less intellectual about it. There is also a debt to [Jasper] Johns, [Claes] Oldenburg, and of course to [Edward] Kienholz. As with the last there is a hint of social protest, though lower keyed, much less definite. In their transformed reassertion of New York–originated ideas of the late '50s, the offshoot has really become a new plant. By taking such an isolated stance, there is an element of deliberate perversity. Of course all are obsessively well informed about New York. In fact, much of what they do is about not going along with New York, about not being overwhelmed by it. The work itself seems to suggest a crotchety, standoffish individualism.

Two years later, Raffaele will decide to start a new life far away from his New York coterie and

embrace the heterosexual family-man models he saw in Davis, California, settling in Marin County.

———

Fall 1966 • Gregory Markopolous leaves the School of the Art Institute of Chicago (SAIC) to return to New York, and Edward Owens (1949–2009) goes with him. Markopolous had come to establish a film program at SAIC, but had quickly become dissatisfied and now abandons the position. Owens is eighteen years old and living on the South Side of Chicago, where he had grown up. He had studied painting and sculpture at SAIC and participated in theater, both as a director and an actor, before he began working with 8mm film and, in 1966, is awarded a scholarship to pursue advanced studies with Markopolous. Impressed after seeing some of Owens's short Super-8 films, Markopolous encourages him to move to New York.

There, Markopoulos introduces Owens to the small scene of gay experimental filmmakers and poets. He meets Gregory Battcock, Willard Maas, Marie Menken, and Andy Warhol, spending evenings at the Stonewall Inn, where an uprising in 1969 will launch the gay rights movement. In 1967 Owens gets a job designing window displays at Brentano's Fifth Avenue bookstore and develops a relationship with his coworker, the poet and filmmaker Charles Boultenhouse. He also forms an enduring friendship with Boultenhouse's life partner, Parker Tyler, for whom Owens has a deep admiration: Tyler is a prominent film critic and, in the 1940s, had been coeditor of *View*, the avant-garde art and literary magazine that introduced European Surrealism to an American audience.

Owens shoots all of his best-known films between 1966 and 1968, adapting his collage aesthetics to a time-based medium. His film work makes frequent use of superimposition, sometimes of several images at a time. Montages of still pictures—paintings, photographs—interrupt moving sequences and are often intercut so rapidly as to create a flicker effect. Owens takes an associative, nonlinear approach to narrative and filmic structure, and his use of dramatic lighting, his embrace of heavy chiaroscuro, and his application of black leader as a formal device further undermine clarity. In *Remembrance: A Portrait Study* (1967), darkness frequently either swallows the image whole or allows only a face to emerge from its depths; in this case, the subject of the portrait study is the artist's mother, whom he returns to Chicago to shoot in 1967.

———

Fall 1966 • Robert Colescott (1925–2009) and his family move to Cairo for a two-year appointment at American University. His time in Egypt alters not only his self-perspective as a Black man but also his view of the history of the art with which he

engages. As he will later put it: "Two years in Cairo, Egypt, and three thousand years of non-white art history later, the pink pneumatic nudes of Europe faded. Then American society hit me like a ton of bricks." His ethereal figures of this era are redolent of the imagery on the tombs and statuary he sees in Egypt, and he finds himself embracing race and color as one and the same—that is, in Egypt, this Black man, whose parents passed as white and who himself has sometimes passed as white, finds a history for his and others' bodies.

Colescott had grown up in Oakland, California, and studied art at San Francisco State College and then the University of California, Berkeley. In 1949 he moved to Paris to work with Fernand Léger, who encouraged the young artist to adopt the figure as well as large-scale compositions and to allow emotional and social content into his art. Upon his return to the United States, and after his graduation from Berkeley in 1951, Colescott settled in the Pacific Northwest, making thickly painted, light-inflected compositions reminiscent of the Bay Area representational works of Elmer Bischoff and James Weeks. In the fall of 1964, Colescott is an artist-in-residence at the American Research Center in Cairo and happily returns to the city for his 1966 appointment to American University. Unfortunately, his time is cut short by the outbreak of the 1967 Arab-Israeli War, and Colescott leaves Cairo, moving to Paris before returning to the United States in 1969. Riven by unrest and assassinations, the nation he comes backs to is vastly

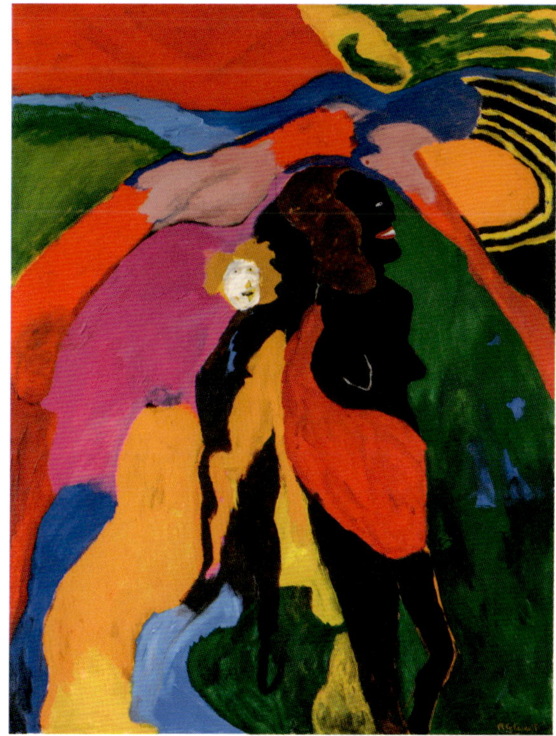

Robert Colescott, *Nubian Queen*, 1966. Acrylic on canvas, 78 × 59 in. (198.1 × 149.9 cm)

different from the one he left. His work continues following the figural and allegorical shift he initiated in Egypt, but now his satiric eye focuses on the United States.

October 3–29, 1966 • Marisol is the only woman represented in the exhibition *Erotic Art* at New York's Sidney Janis Gallery, where the other artists include Öyvind Fahlström, Richard Lindner, James Rosenquist, and Harold Stevenson. The show is not well received. "Mr. Janis, I am afraid, did not assemble an art show," one critic scoffs, "but a freak show that fails to deliver."

October 15, 1966 • Activists Bobby Seale and Huey Newton form the Black Panther Party for Self-Defense in Oakland, California. Related to the Black Power movement, the group advocates for justice for Black communities, as well as other oppressed citizens, through revolutionary theory, education, and community programs. It is a radical organization with an ideology grounded in Black nationalism, socialism, and armed self-defense, particularly against police brutality.

October 22, 1966 • Alex Hay stages *Grass Field* on the final evening of 9 Evenings: Theatre & Engineering, organized by Experiments in Art and Technology at the 69th Regiment Armory in Manhattan. In Hay's piece, he appears in a tradesman's jumpsuit with various electrical apparatuses strapped to his back, chest, and head, a cacophony of static and feedback noises enveloping the space. Moving about the stage to lay out in carefully ordered rows enormous numbered sheets that resemble calendar pages, Hay attempts to amplify and project his body's internal rhythms—heartbeat, breath, muscle contractions, and brain waves—and he does so with varying degrees of success. At one point in the piece, the artist sits down in the middle of the performance space, knees to his chest and eyes closed, while two technicians make adjustments to his gear. A close-up camera projection of his face stands as an eerie, outsize backdrop to the whole scene.

November 1966 • Gene Swenson's interview with Michael Todd appears in *Art and Artists*.

GS: Your work is strongly tactile . . .

MT: So much of the sexual experience is the caressing, gripping fiercely, or touching so delicately that the sensation is almost invisible. The tongue in the ear, the finger in the mouth or over the eyeball . . . The parts in the clusters I make are screwed together, sometimes barely touching one another and in a sense "kissing." One doesn't always know how they're held together other than by mutual attraction.

Touch is one of the primal experiences, I can almost feel inside of me. I have the same acute sense of touch within that my fingertips have on the surface. In my work I try for the externalization of pain and the interior sense of touch. I feel things tuning, the screw being turned . . . If I ask myself what do shoes mean to me, or even some of these clusters, I tell myself they are like an externalized womb brought from within the body and placed outside on a pedestal. All the pain the fetus is going to experience in later life is out there, impressed upon it by each individual screw or ball, by each "kiss."

November 30–December 31, 1966 • Jeremy Anderson's retrospective is on view at the San Francisco Museum of Modern Art, after which it will travel to the Pasadena Art Museum in January. In an unfinished manuscript of 1963–66, Anderson writes about the slippage of meaning inherent in the allusive artworks he and others are making at the time.

Often a slight shift of viewpoint can immediately change one "reality" to a completely different "reality." To go to a flower show thinking of it as a display of sexual organs has a quite different effect on the experience than the thought that they are merely flowers. What could be considered a garish display of bad taste, e.g., Geary Boulevard, with all the neon lights and signs and banners and an anarchistic display of architecture, can be quite fascinating if viewed as a landscape on Mars, or a festival day in an ancient kingdom. It also helps to recognize the fact that good taste is an attribute that no artist should have.

December 16, 1966–February 5, 1967 • The Whitney Museum of American Art's *Annual Exhibition 1966: Contemporary Sculpture and Prints* features artists Lee Bontecou, Edward Kienholz, Claes Oldenburg, Kenneth Price, Lucas Samaras, Robert Smithson, Michael Todd, and William T. Wiley. The first Annual to open in the museum's new Marcel Breuer–designed building on the Upper East Side, the show reflects curator William Agee's introduction to Funk art on his trip to Los Angeles earlier in 1966.

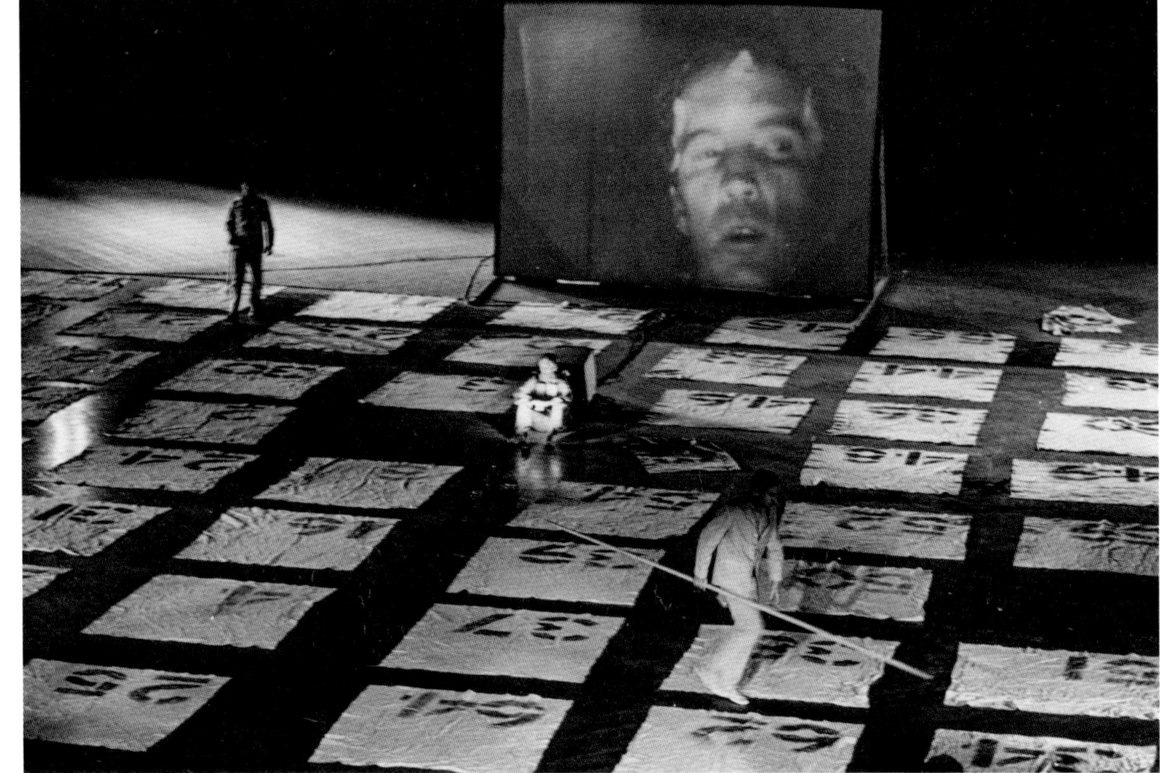

Steve Paxton, Alex Hay, and Robert Rauschenberg in Hay's *Grass Field* (1966), presented as part of 9 Evenings: Theatre & Engineering, New York, 1969

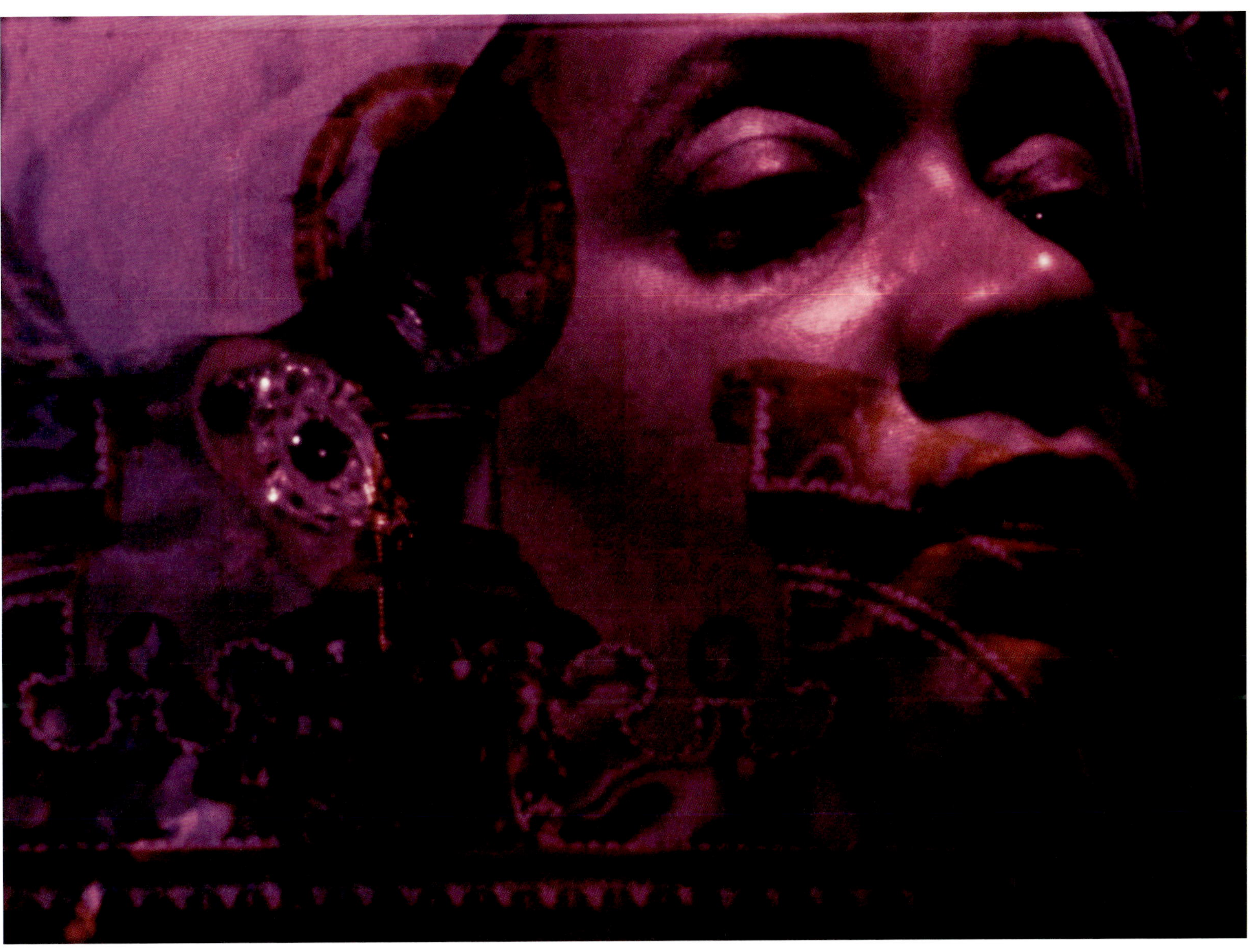

Edward Owens, *Private Imaginings and Narrative Facts*, 1966. 16mm film transferred to video, color, silent; 5:51 min. Whitney Museum of American Art, New York; purchase, with funds from the Film and Video Committee 2021.85

1967

1967 • Developing out of the *Body Beautiful* series, *House Beautiful: Bringing the War Home* is a group of photomontages that Martha Rosler constructs using images culled from popular magazines. Rosler borrows the subtitle from the anti-war slogan "Bring the war home," as the series protests the Vietnam War. (She will reprise it some thirty-seven years later in objection to the wars in Iraq and Afghanistan.) With works such as *Balloons*, Rosler places news photographs of the horror and devastation of Vietnam in the mundane living spaces of middle- and upper-class homes, sourced primarily from the magazine *House Beautiful*, creating what she calls "tableaus in stasis," juxtapositions that invite viewers to consider their moral proximity to warfare "in a more contemplative way."

A prolific writer, Rosler produces critical essays that often examine the history and practices of social documentary photography, including the work of Diane Arbus, Lee Friedlander, and Garry Winogrand. As Rosler will argue, when curators such as John Szarkowski began exhibiting social photography in mainstream institutions, assimilating the medium into high art, they also promoted an attitude of aestheticized complacency rather than activism. Countering this approach, Rosler distributes the *House Beautiful: Bringing*

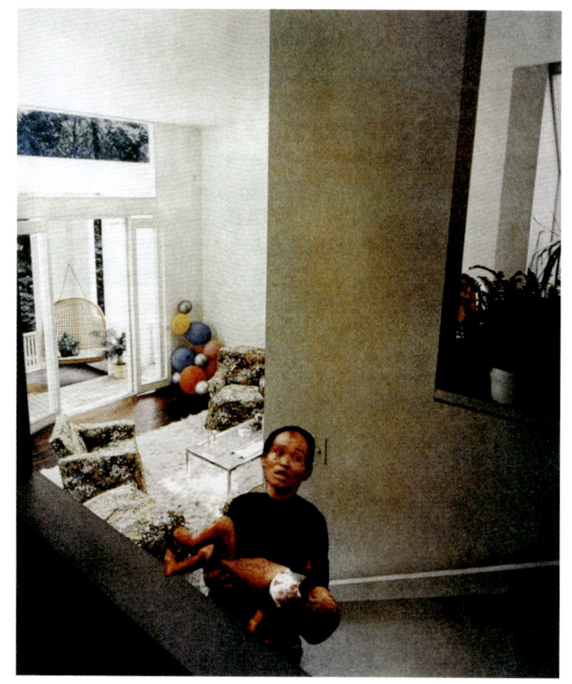

Martha Rosler, *Balloons*, c. 1967–72 (printed 2011), from the series *House Beautiful: Bringing the War Home* (1967–72). Inkjet print, 23 ¹¹⁄₁₆ × 18 ⅞ in. (60.2 × 47.9 cm)

the War Home series in the streets, eschewing art-world circulation and aspiring to operate outside dominant economic and cultural systems viewed as repressive, exploitive, and unethical:

I saw the *House Beautiful Series* not as art—I wanted it to be agitational. I distributed it to the anti-war community as flyers, Xerox copies, and this is very much in the context of the sixties. If I were pressed by people saying that's not art, that's propaganda, I would have to say okay. The difference for me was that there were no slogans. I did not want to say, "Stop the war." I did not want to say anything . . . just have the images convey the message, which I hoped would provoke enough of a shock and a recognition in people to recognize this as an anti-war offering.

January 8–29, 1967 • Karl's Wirsum's first solo exhibition, *C. A. Doctor*, is on view at Dell Gallery, Chicago.

January 9–February 11, 1967 • Joseph Cornell's first major retrospective is on view at the Pasadena Art Museum, the last exhibition Walter Hopps organizes there. Many contemporary artists will recall seeing the show, and Betye Saar, in particular, is taken by the complexity of Cornell's constructions and the mysteries they hold. Saar has opened up her print practice to experimentation

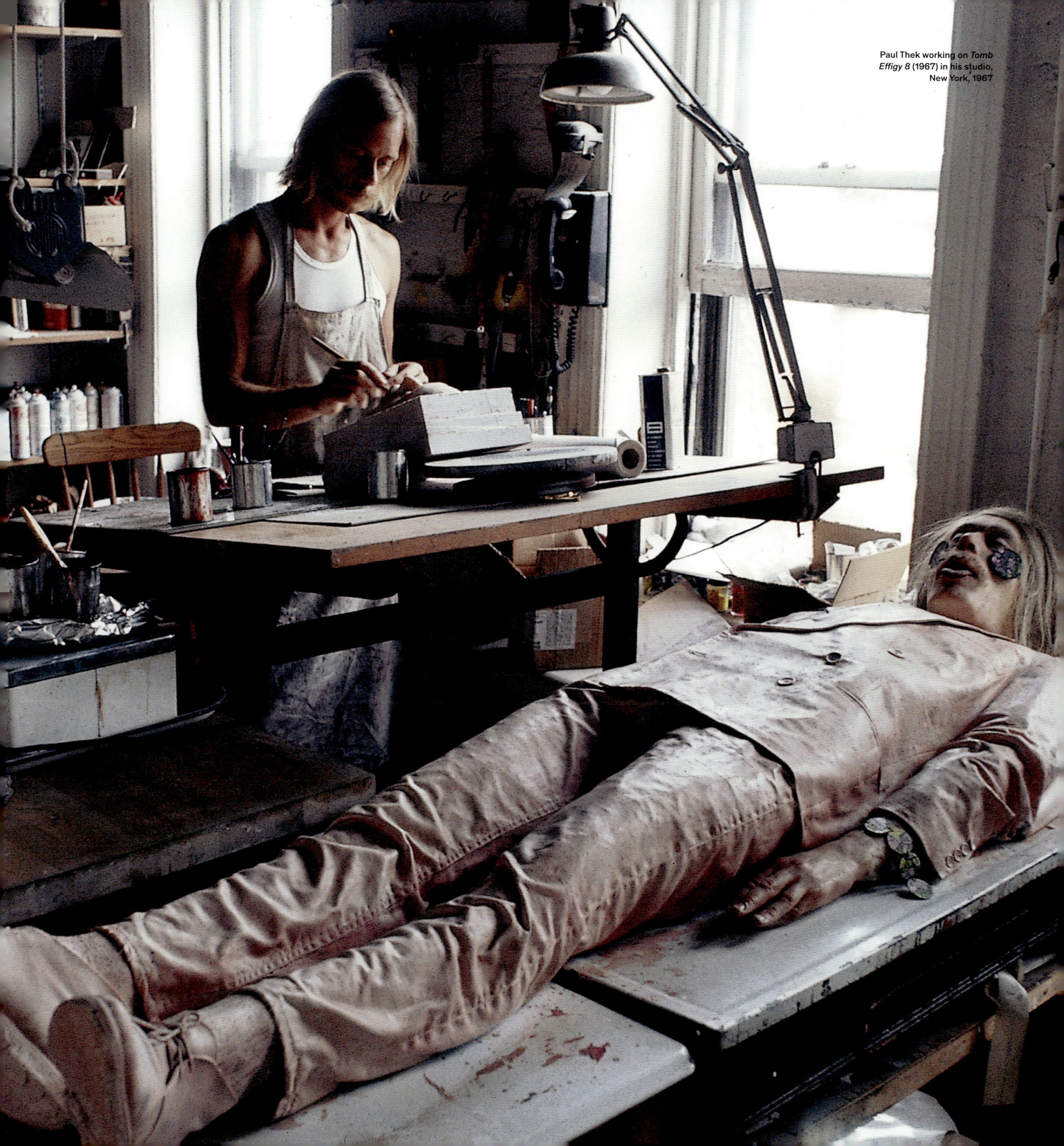

Paul Thek working on *Tomb Effigy 8* (1967) in his studio, New York, 1967

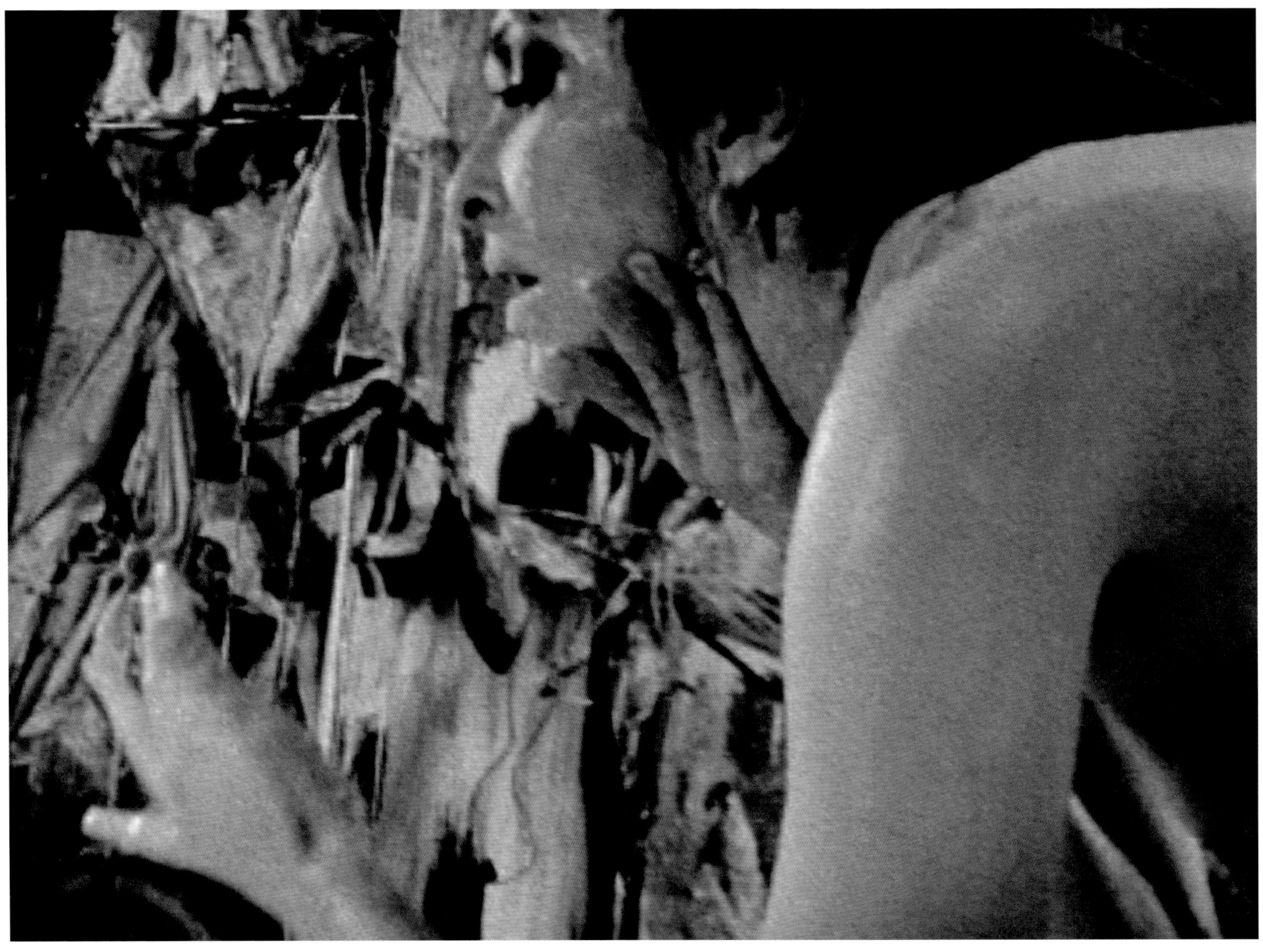

Carolee Schneemann, *Body Collage*, 1967. 16mm film transferred to video, black-and-white, silent; 3:30 min. Whitney Museum of American Art, New York; purchase, with funds from Randy Sifka 2009.127

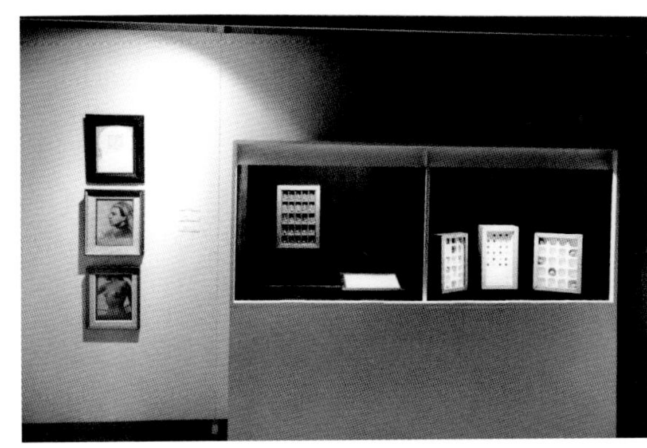

Joseph Cornell, Pasadena Art Museum, CA, 1967

with assemblage and a variety of materials by this time, and seeing Cornell's work encourages her to also consider encasing in boxes and containers the objects and materials she has been using—a way to both obscure and demarcate their symbolisms.

January 21–22, 27–29 and February 3–5, 1967 • Carolee Schneemann's "kinetic theater" event *Snows* debuts at the Martinique Theater in New York. The work is performed over eight nights overlapping with Angry Arts Week, which protests the Vietnam War. Schneemann announces the performance with a vehement indictment of the war: "SNOWS: to concretize and elucidate the genocidal compulsions of a vicious disjunctive technocracy gone berserk against an integral, essentially rural culture. The grotesque fulfillment of the Western split between matter and spirit, mind and body, individualized 'man' against cosmic natural unities. Destruction so vast as to become randomized, constant as weather. Snowing . . . purification, clarification, homogenization."

Snows involves a choreographed performance in conjunction with a screening of five movies that includes the centerpiece, *Viet-Flakes* (1962–67), a 16mm color-toned film that animates photographs depicting the atrocities happening in Vietnam set to a contrapuntal sound collage of pop songs made by Schneemann's partner, James Tenney. The kinetic event is orchestrated through a feedback system, with all electronics wired to seats and thus controlled by audience reactions. Meant to radically juxtapose the "winter environment" that surrounds its snug viewers with horrific images of war, *Snows* demonstrates Schneemann's theory of a collage methodology that slams together not only irreconcilable images and materials but also real worlds—namely, the world of the New Yorkers present at the performance with the world of the Vietnamese who are forced to endure the catastrophic violence of US aggression.

Schneemann writes that she "wanted to use film as integral to performance" and "as a textural and structural element extending the visual densities of the Kinetic Theater works." The increasing centrality of film to her practice of expanded painting and kinetic theater will inform *Body Collage*, which she will perform and film later this year in preparation for the kinetic theater event *Illinois Central*, at the Museum of Contemporary Art Chicago in late January 1968.

January 26–February 5, 1967 • Like the LA Peace Tower, New York's Angry Arts Week originates with a call for artist participation and includes many of those who had exhibited as part of the Los Angeles project. The organizers Dore Ashton and Max Kozloff request "happenings, poetry readings, films, music and theater, panoramic size canvases, upon which you the artists of New York, are asked to paint, draw, or attach whatever images or objects that will express or stand for your anger against the war. . . . We are also interested in whatever manner of visual invective, political caricature, or related savage materials you would care to contribute. Join in the spirit of cooperation with other artistic communities of the city in a desperate plea for sanity."

The *Collage of Indignation*, the central focus of Angry Arts Week, is a 10 × 120–foot installation of artworks at New York University. After being viewed by nearly ten thousand people there, the project travels uptown to Columbia University for exhibition, before the entire collage is burned to prevent its institutionalization, sale, or cooptation. The artworks incorporate a range of media, and contributions vary from painted signatures to antiwar slogans and poems to painted posters and collages. Artists who participate include Nancy Graves, Faith Ringgold, James Rosenquist, and Richard Serra. For her submission, Nancy Spero publicly shows for the first time several works from her *War Series*.

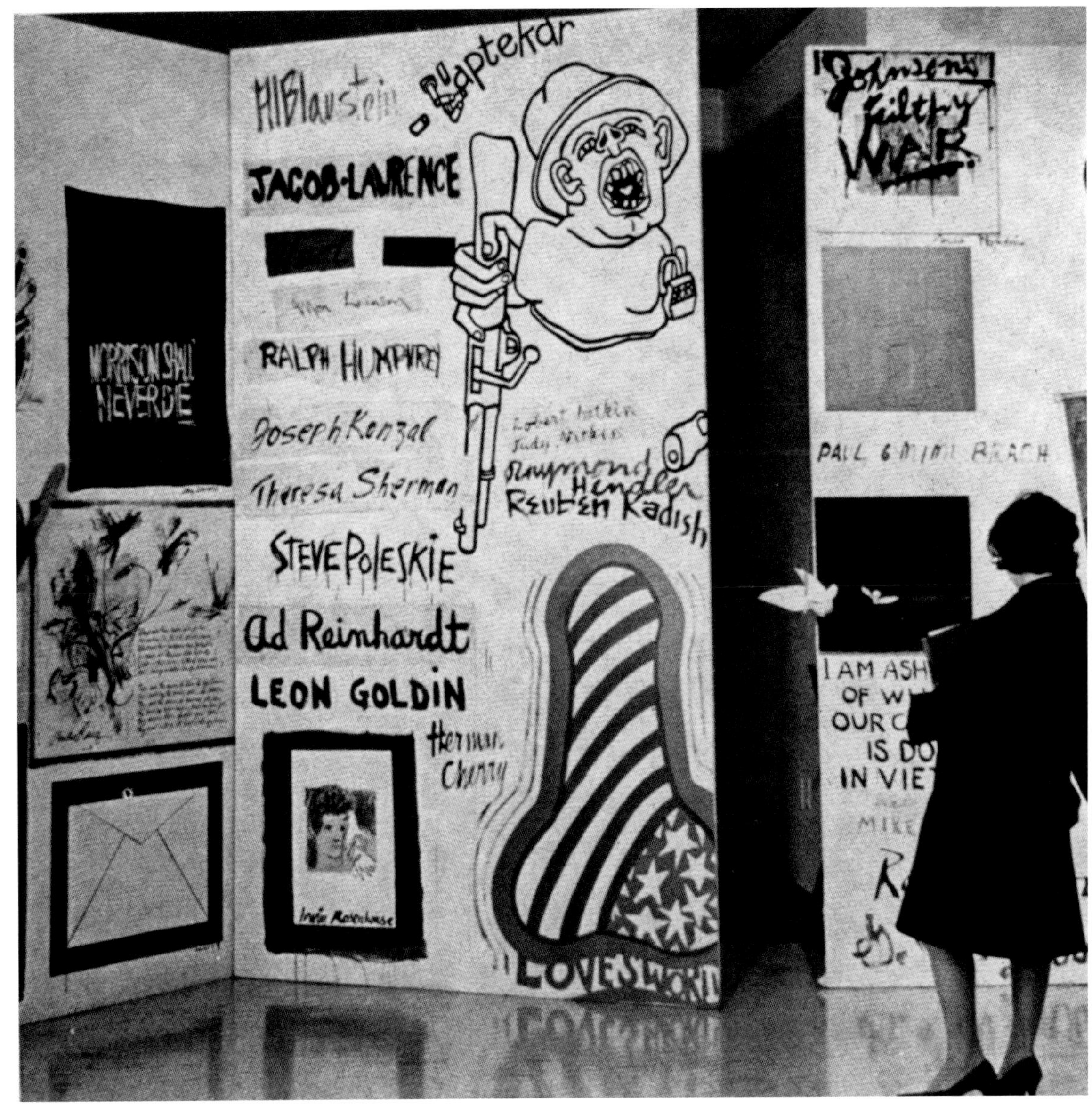

Collage of Indignation exhibited at New York University as part of Angry Arts Week, New York, 1967

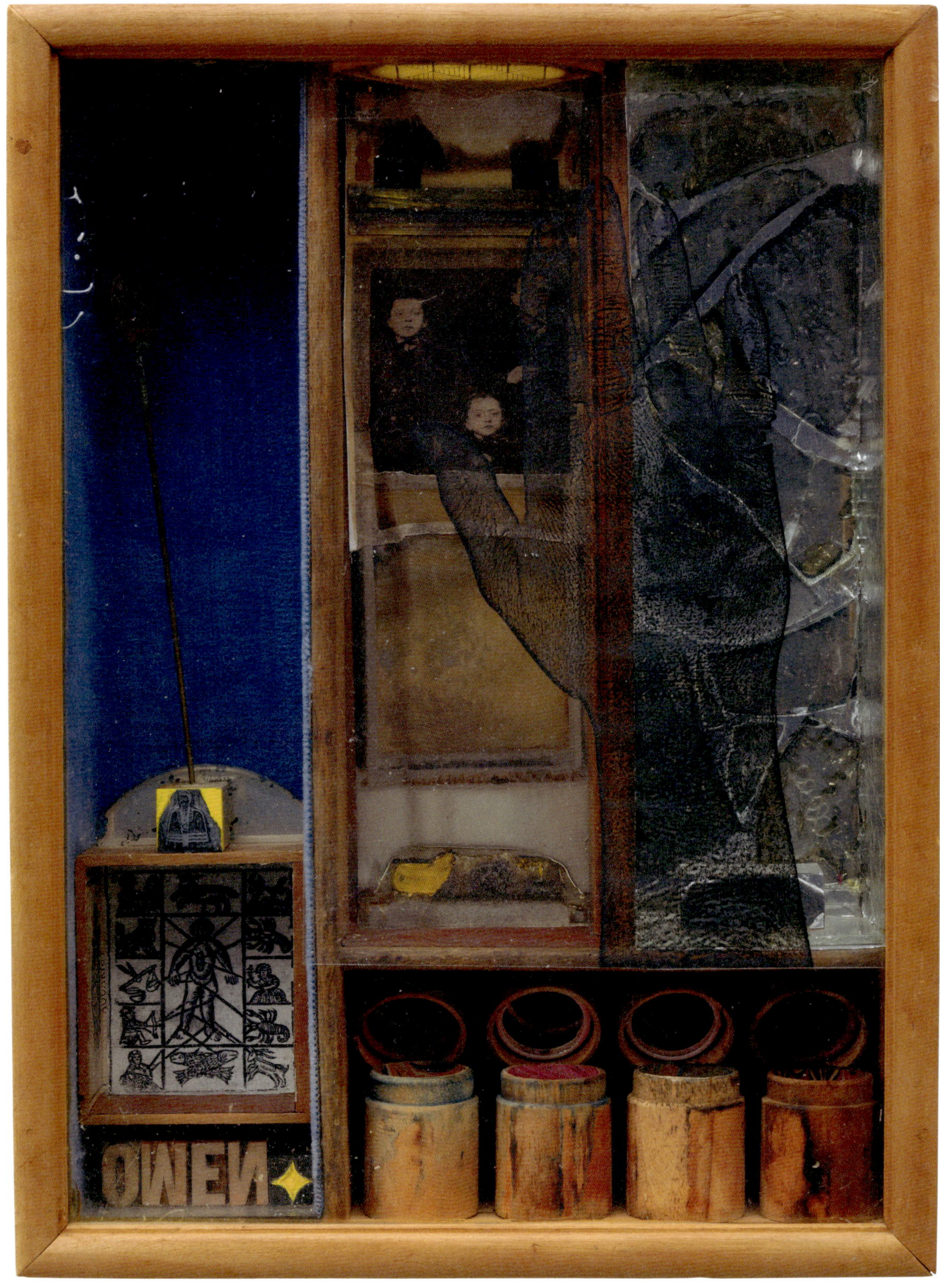

Betye Saar, *Omen*, 1967. Mixed-media assemblage, 12 ¾ × 9 ¼ × 3 ⅛ in. (32.5 × 23.5 × 8 cm). Collection of Candace Weir

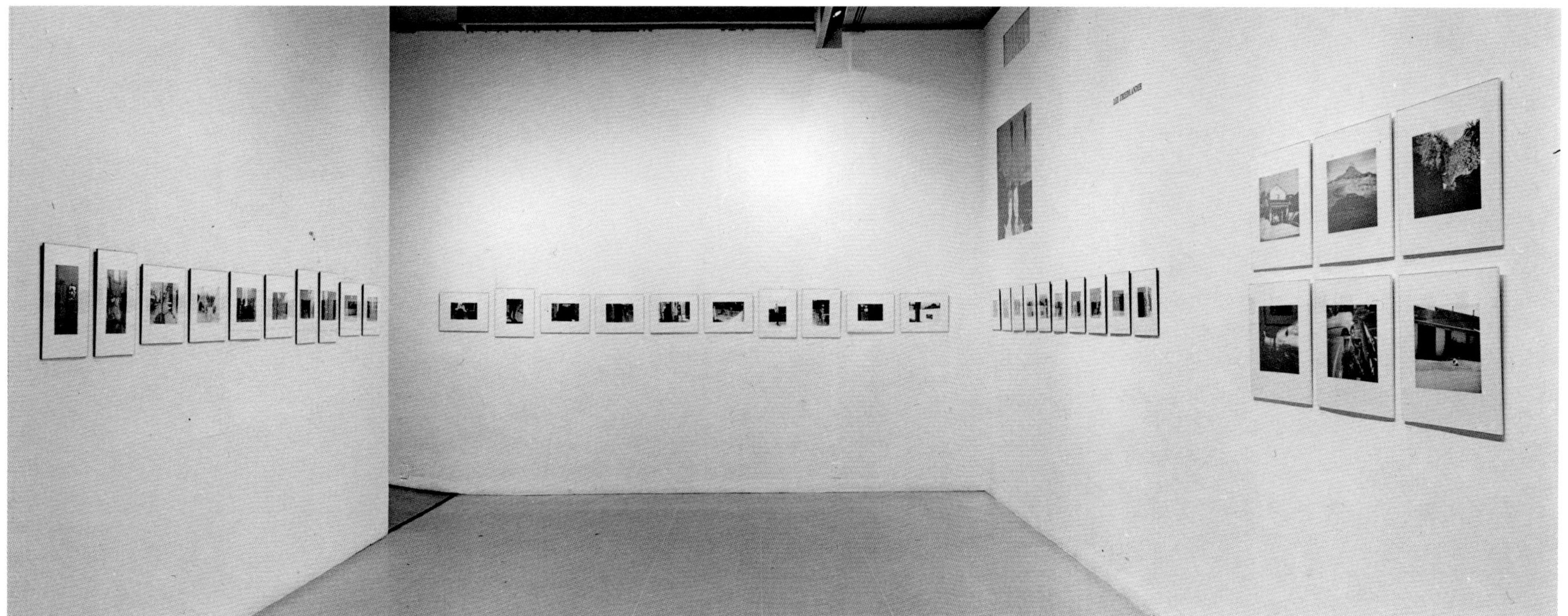

New Documents, The Museum of Modern Art, New York, 1967

January 1967 • Melvin Edwards grows dissatisfied with life in Los Angeles and decides to move his family to New York, where he had visited with Daniel LaRue Johnson in 1963. He becomes immersed in the Harlem art world, joining William T. Williams's collective, Smokehouse, which makes abstract murals across the storied neighborhood, and meeting artists, who include Romare Bearden, Norman Lewis, Al Loving, and Jack Whitten.

Early 1967 • "One winter evening in early 1967 I decided to paint an Indian"—this moment marks an important point in Fritz Scholder's career. He has been teaching at the Institute of American Indian Arts (IAIA) for three years and is determined to not paint Native American subjects because he feels to do so is "not only a visual cliché but a psychological cliché," the same

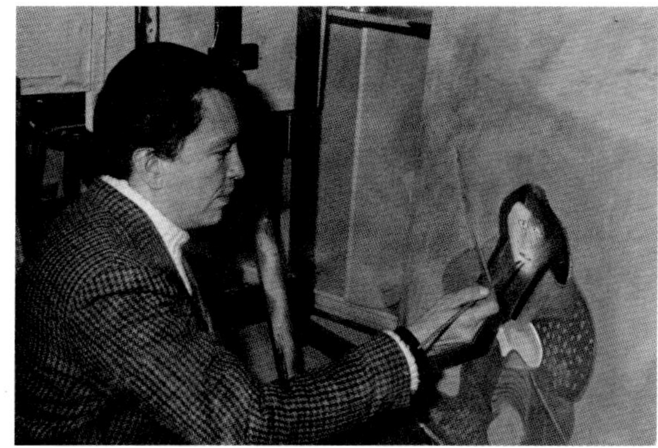

Fritz Scholder at the Institute of American Indian Arts, Santa Fe, NM, c. 1967

historical bind that T. C. Cannon and Oscar Howe are working against. But the influence of Pop art on Scholder's students at IAIA brings popular culture stereotypes of Native American life and history to the fore, and Scholder sets out to paint "the Indian the way he is today." The artist's expressionistic and often grotesque approach to painting portraits and figures does not shy away from illustrating issues such as poverty and alcoholism, and it proves controversial to many, especially art collectors in the Southwest who prefer the historicized views of Native Americans as the classical "noble savage."

February 28–May 7, 1967 • *New Documents* is on view at the Museum of Modern Art, New York. Curated by John Szarkowski, director of the museum's photography department, the show includes the works of only three photographers: Diane Arbus, Lee Friedlander, and Garry Winogrand. Szarkowski had been searching for a title to describe the work of these artists, which is not quite documentary or focused on social reform. A year prior, filmmaker Stan VanDerBeek had proposed the term *social surrealism* in a letter to Szarkowski, for the works' "mixture of the social body . . . and the artistic landscape," to which Szarkowski replied: "Thanks very much for your idea. Your point is relevant, and your title is very close to right. It is certainly much better than anything I have thought of. If we use it, we will credit you in a footnote."

Szarkowski never publishes a catalogue, and his wall text explains that the photographers "like the real world, in spite of its terrors, as the source of all wonder and fascination and value—no less precious for being irrational."

March 15–April 15, 1967 • *The Grotesque Image* is on view at the San Francisco Art Institute (SFAI) and includes Roy De Forest and Wally Hedrick among the six artists featured. The exhibition is curated by James Monte, a Bay Area native who began his career as an artist in Mill Valley, became an early contributor to *Artforum*, and has gradually moved into curatorial work at SFAI; he will go on to the Los Angeles County Museum of Art and, ultimately, the Whitney Museum of American Art, New York. Unlike the *Funk* exhibition that will open three days after this show closes, *The Grotesque Image* takes a historical rather than social or regional approach. Monte's concept grounds the contemporary artistic tendencies he's observed in a pre-twentieth-century tradition:

[I]n the San Francisco Bay Area in recent years there has been a revival of a fanciful or distorted figurative imagery which has its antecedents as far back in the history of Western art as the Gothic period. The tradition continued in the work of Flemish still life painters who thought the inclusion of a human skull amongst their rich table fare added a certain piquancy to the renditions of assembled objects. The artistic achievements of the expressionist precursors of the 19th century such as Odilon Redon, Gustave Moreau and James Ensor formed a link with the Gothic tradition and the later expressionist developments in the first decades of the twentieth century.

Spring 1967 • Alonzo and Dale Davis, both artists and educators, open Brockman Gallery in Los Angeles. The brothers had grown up in Tuskegee, Alabama, as their parents were working at the Tuskegee Institute—their father a professor, their mother a librarian. In 1956 the brothers had moved with their mother to Los Angeles, where Alonzo and Dale both studied art and education at Pepperdine University and USC, respectively. The summer prior to opening the Brockman Gallery, the brothers traveled across the country in their green Volkswagen Beetle, stopping at Historically Black Colleges and Universities and in Black communities, visiting artists such as Eugene Grisby in Arizona and John Biggers in Texas as well as screenwriter Topper Carew in Washington, DC. In Jackson, Mississippi, on June 6, they participated in the Meredith March, or March Against Fear. In Chicago they spent time at the South Side Community Art Center, which was founded by artist Margaret Taylor-Burroughs. Finally arriving in New York, they are introduced to Jacob Lawrence, and they meet Romare Bearden, Norman Lewis, and a number of other artists associated with the Spiral Group. Alonzo will recall that on their long

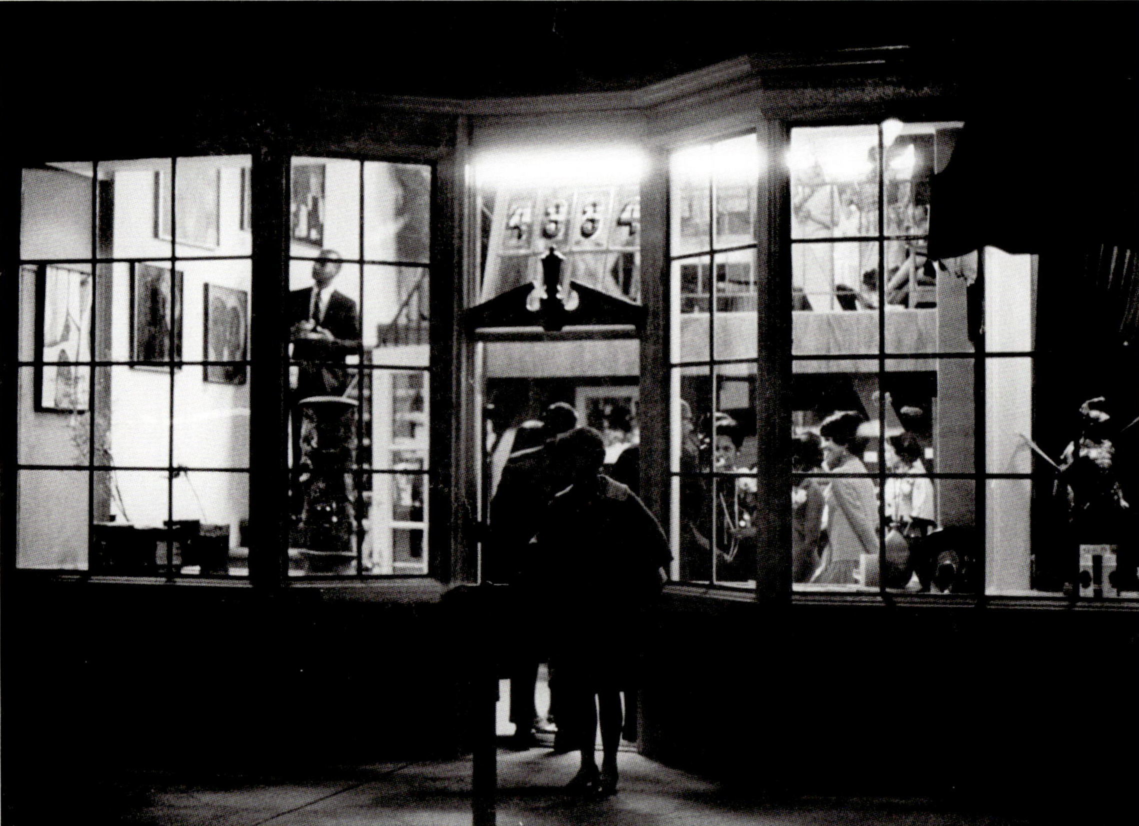
Opening night at Brockman Gallery, Los Angeles, 1967

drive back to Los Angeles, they think, "Wouldn't it be great if we could open an art gallery?"

Less than a year later, the brothers open Brockman Gallery on Deegnan Avenue in the Leimert Park neighborhood of Los Angeles, although neither brother has any experience owning a business—or an art gallery, for that matter. Named after the brothers' maternal grandparents, the gallery is part of the informal network of local Black arts and community organizations, namely, the Watts Towers Arts Center as well as Suzanne Jackson's Gallery 32 and Ruth Waddy's Art West Associated. In July 1967, a few months after Brockman Gallery opens, it sponsors the Leimert Park Festival of the Arts and outlines the gallery's goals in its brochure for the two-day arts celebration, explaining that the "gallery displays, which are changed every four weeks, include the work of local artists and have provided a much needed artistic stimulus to the Leimert Park Community."

Spring 1967 • Peter Saul completes work on *Saigon* (1967). Later, he will explain his approach to the painting:

> After a couple years, my Vietnam series had been relatively small works on 40-by-60-inch cardboard and a few medium-sized canvases, so I decided on a major effort on the subject, 12 feet wide, *Saigon*, 1967, which took me 5–6 months to paint. For that picture I decided to draw out the image completely before putting the paint on. I had been previously sketching on the canvas with markers, but not "exact," just to sort of get the idea in the right place. In *Saigon* I wanted an "exactly right" kind of drawing so I would have room for all the imagery to be there (various symbolic figures getting killed in symbolic ways). That took over 3 months! Also, I wanted to show the influence of psychedelic posters (dayglo surrounding some parts) and used "dots" for the first time to blend (the few people who saw my work then kept recommending a spray gun + I was too lazy or indifferent to buy one + learn to use, so just did it by hand for more or less the same appearance). The main thing was to get the subject clear + up front, and head off boring aesthetic criticism.

April 18–May 30, 1967 • *Funk* is on view at the University Art Museum at the University of California, Berkeley. Curated by gallery director Peter Selz, a veteran of the Museum of Modern Art, New York, the exhibition surveys trends of bodily inflected, sometimes grotesque sculpture and assemblage by mostly Northern Californian

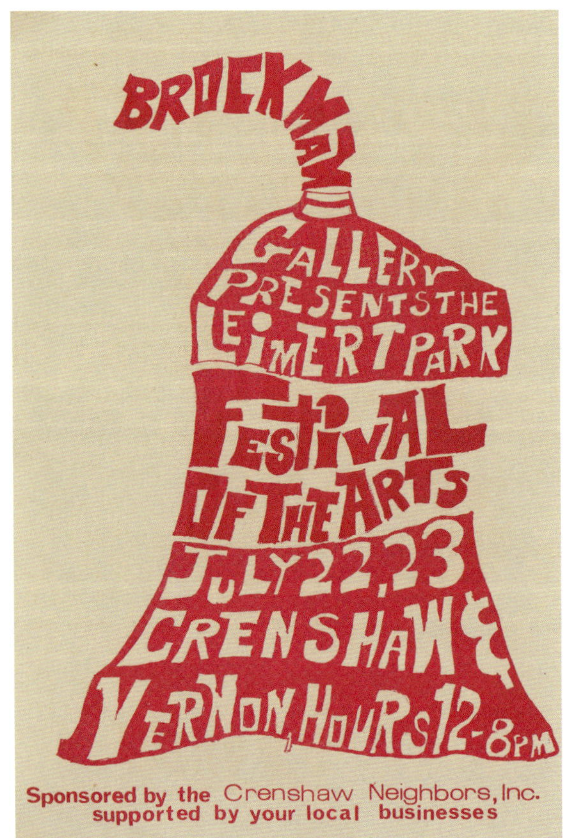

Brochure for the Leimert Park Festival of the Arts, Los Angeles, 1967

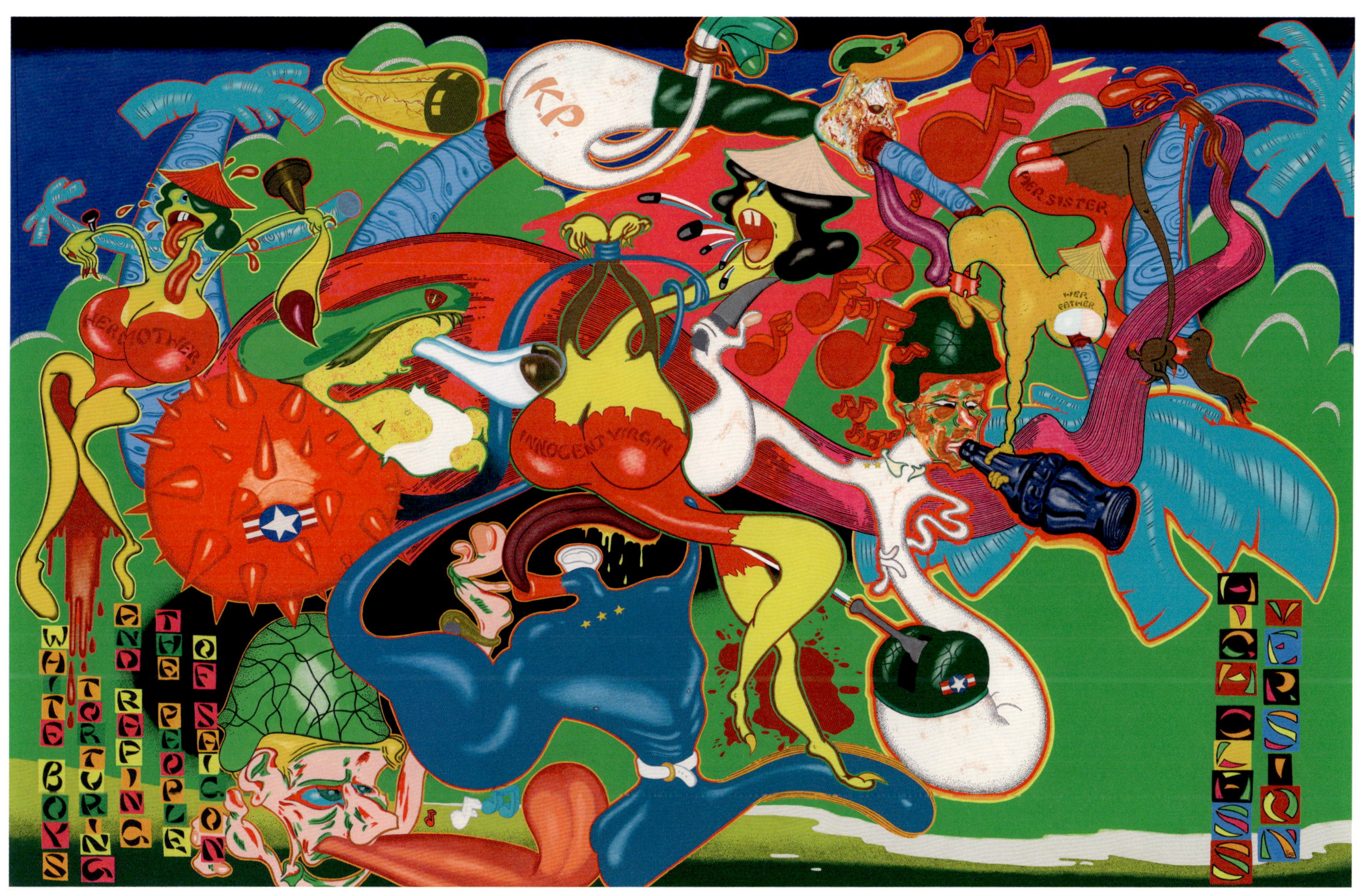

Peter Saul, *Saigon*, 1967. Acrylic, oil, enamel, and fiber-tipped pen on canvas, 93 ¼ × 142 ¼ in. (236.9 × 361.3 cm). Whitney Museum of American Art, New York; purchase, with funds from the Friends of the Whitney Museum of American Art 69.103

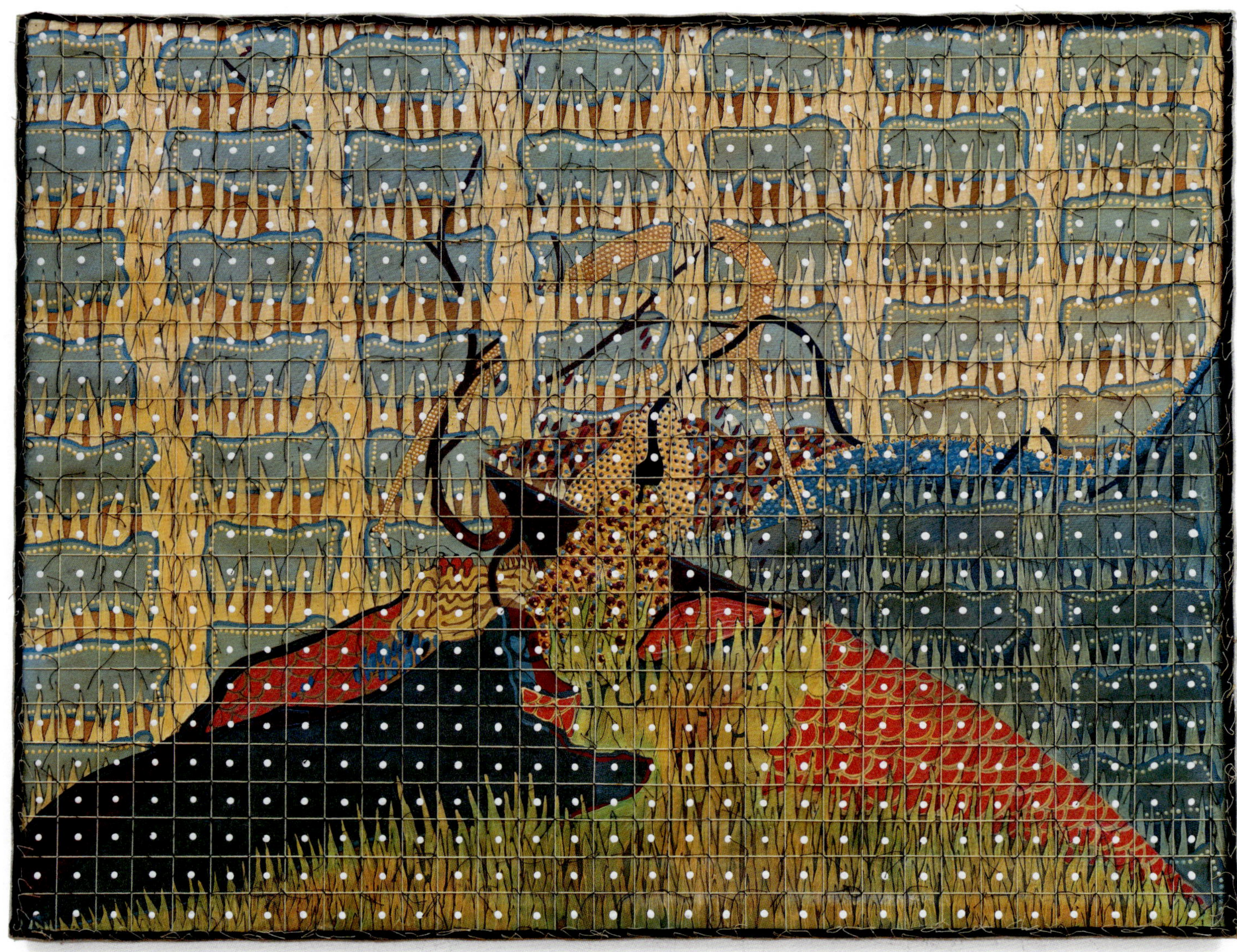

Franklin Williams, *Untitled*, 1967. Acrylic, crochet thread, and cotton on canvas, 24 × 31 ¾ in. (61 × 80.6 cm). Collection of the artist

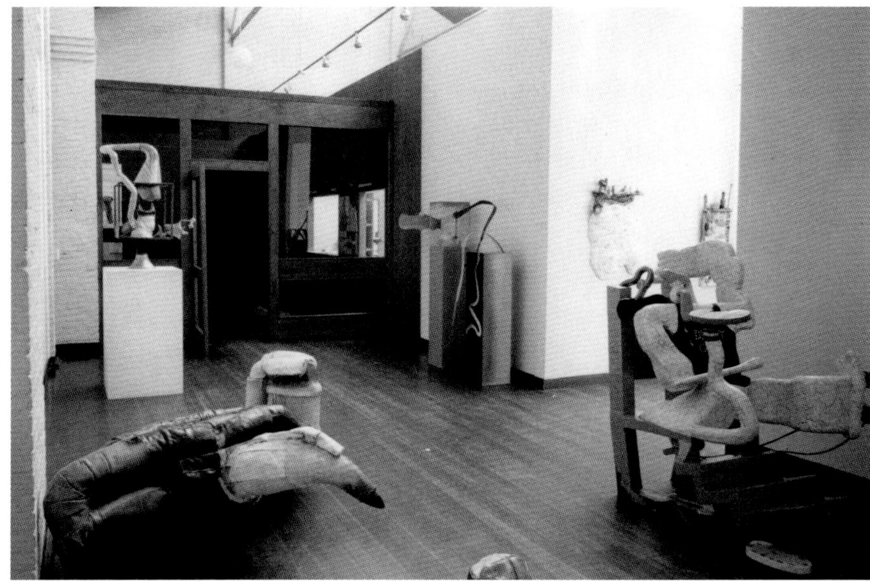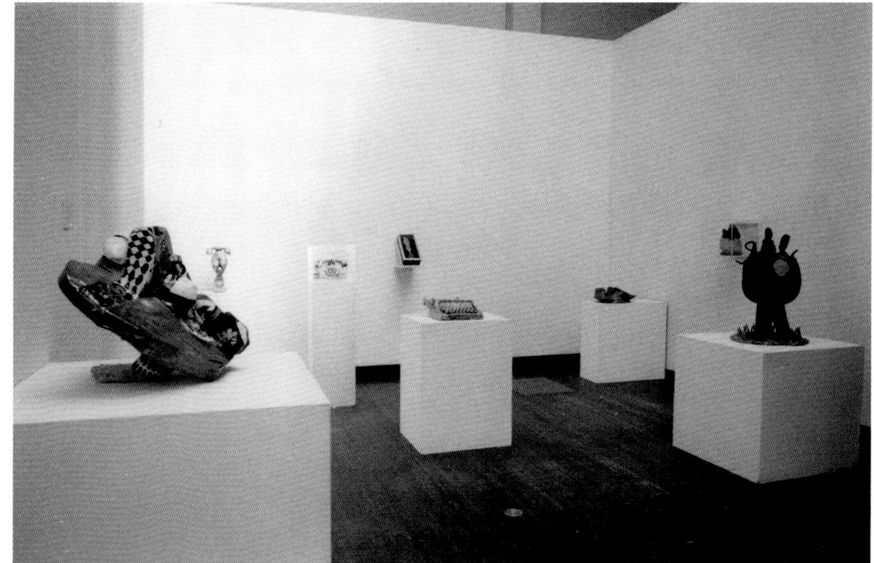

Funk, University Art Museum, University of California, Berkeley, 1967

artists. In an essay in the March 1967 issue of *Art in America*, with a forward by Selz, artist Harold Paris had described an attitude he perceived in California art and called it *funk*: "The casual, irreverent, insincere California atmosphere, with its absurd elements—weather, clothes, 'skinny-dipping,' hobby craft, sun-drenched mentality, Doggie Diner, perfumed toilet tissue, do-it-yourself—all this drives the artist's vision inward. This is the Land of Funk." With this countercultural ethos as a guide, Selz further delineates a regional manifestation of assemblage, which he describes in his catalogue essay:

> In the current spectrum of art, Funk is at the opposite extreme of such manifestations as New York "primary structures" or the "Fetish Finish" sculpture which prevails in Southern California. Funk art is hot rather than cool; it is committed rather than disengaged; it is bizarre rather than formal; it is sensuous; and frequently it is quite ugly and ungainly.

What Selz feels is a grouping of like objects, however, inadvertently becomes known as a movement, much to the chagrin of the exhibiting artists, who include Jeremy Anderson, Robert Arneson, Joan Brown, Bruce Conner, Roy De Forest, William Geis, Robert Hudson, Jean Linder, James Melchert, Don Potts, Kenneth Price, Peter Saul, William T. Wiley, and Franklin Williams. To them, *funk* indicates an attitude, not an aesthetic, in line with the word's use by North Beach's jazz musicians as a term of endearment to essentially mean go-for-broke soul and appropriated by Conner's anti-art group Rat Bastard Protective Association.

On April 18, the gallery hosts a symposium, where three artists in the show—Brown, Conner, and Melchert—are openly dismayed by the exhibition and publicly dispute its premise. Brown and Conner feel that funky art is long over by the late 1960s and is a meaningless idea co-opted by Selz. The panel, which also includes Mowry Baden, Manuel Neri, and Peter Voulkos, quickly descends into squabbling. Later, Brown argues, "The older artists in the show who were active in the fifties, instead of griping among themselves about the show after the fact, should have told Selz in no uncertain terms that he include genuinely funky work."

A rebuke to the show comes from the then local writer and curator James Monte in the summer issue of *Artforum*. Monte takes Selz to task for excluding an artist the critic feels to be central to funk, namely, Wally Hedrick, whose retrospective, not coincidentally, will happen at San Francisco Art Institute later this year. Monte goes on to note:

> [A] great deal of the work in the funk show merges indistinguishably with what Lucy Lippard has called "eccentric abstraction" [in her 1966 Fischbach Gallery exhibition], and which happens to be flourishing in, of all places, that sinful den of sales and status symbols, New York. . . . Dr. Selz's show—and, more important, the artists in the show—would have profited considerably from a similar fraternal invitation to artists like Gary Kuehn, Eva Hesse, Frank Viner, etc., but so sensible a move has several drawbacks. First, it would acknowledge Miss Lippard's prior activity; second, it would draw the artists in the exhibition into a broader movement, thus exposing the

funk label and the mystique that goes with it as the silly and meaningless things they are.

In July, the exhibition will travel to the Institute of Contemporary Art, Boston, its sole additional venue.

April 27–October 29, 1967 • Claes Oldenburg's massive black vinyl sculpture *Giant Soft Fan* (1967) is suspended inside the Buckminster Fuller–designed US pavilion at Expo 67, the World's Fair in Montreal. James Rosenquist is also selected to represent the United States. Later in the year, Oldenburg will reflect on his sculpture's evocative, crumpled, bodily form as he imagines it as a potential replacement for the Statue of Liberty in another drawing for a colossal monument. His new sculptures from this year *Giant Fagends*, *Soft Fan—Ghost Version*, and *Soft Drainpipe—Red (Hot) Version* are on view in a concurrent exhibition of new work at Sidney Janis Gallery, New York.

April 28–June 25 and September 15–October 9, 1967 • The Los Angeles County Museum of Art's survey *American Sculpture of the Sixties* attempts a sprawling overview of work that will soon be divided into -isms but for now resists labels. Artists include Jeremy Anderson, Bruce Conner, Bruce Nauman, Claes Oldenburg, Ken Price, Lucas Samaras, and H. C. Westermann. The accompanying catalogue, edited by curator Maurice Tuchman, offers ten essays by a cross-section of ideologically and generationally diverse authors, most notably, Clement Greenberg, Lucy Lippard, James Monte, and Barbara Rose.

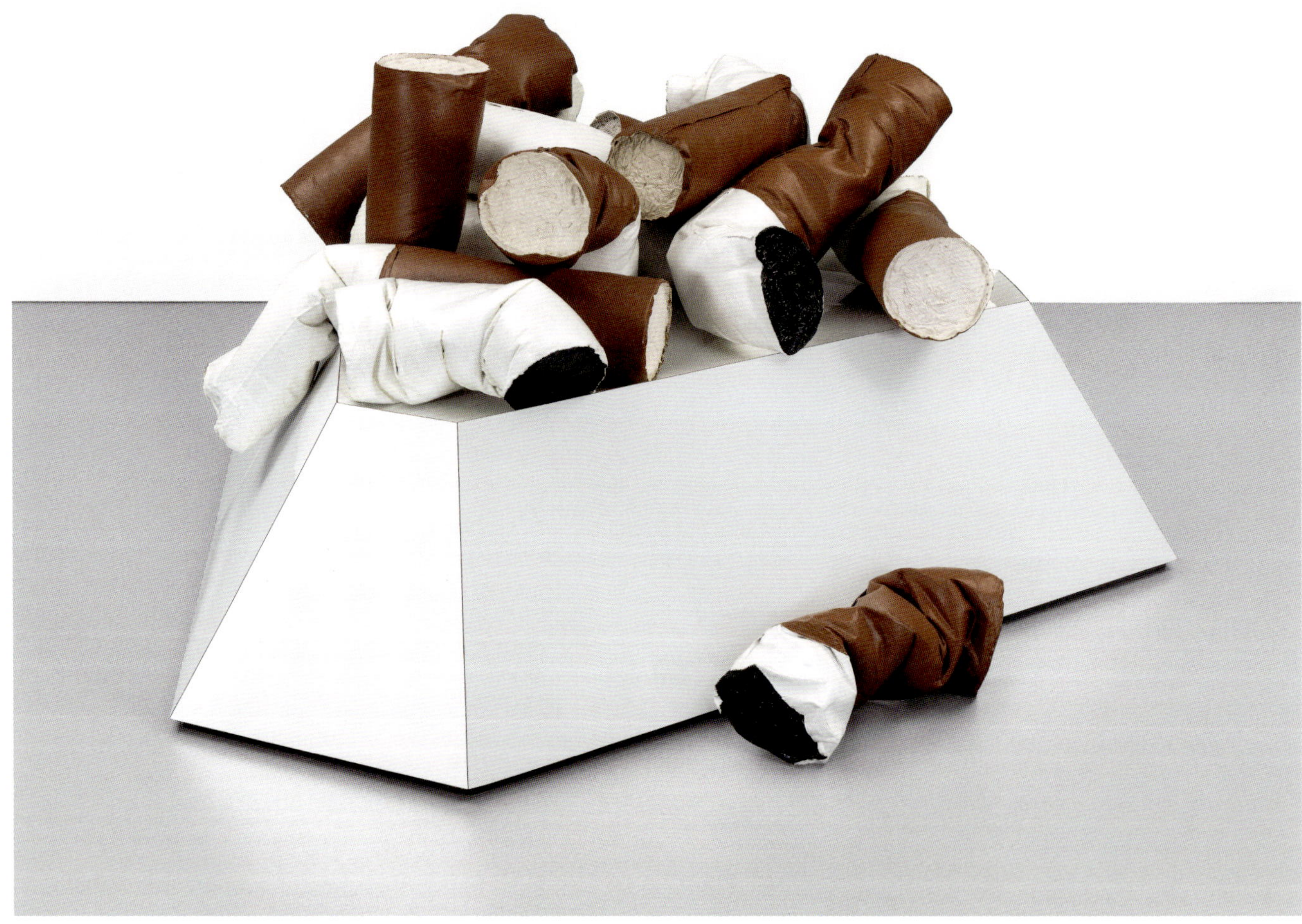

Claes Oldenburg, *Giant Fagends*, 1967. Canvas, urethane foam, wire, wood, latex, and melamine laminate, 52 × 96 × 96 in. (132.1 × 243.8 × 243.8 cm) overall (with base, irregular). Whitney Museum of American Art, New York; purchase, with funds from the Friends of the Whitney Museum of American Art 70.44a–o

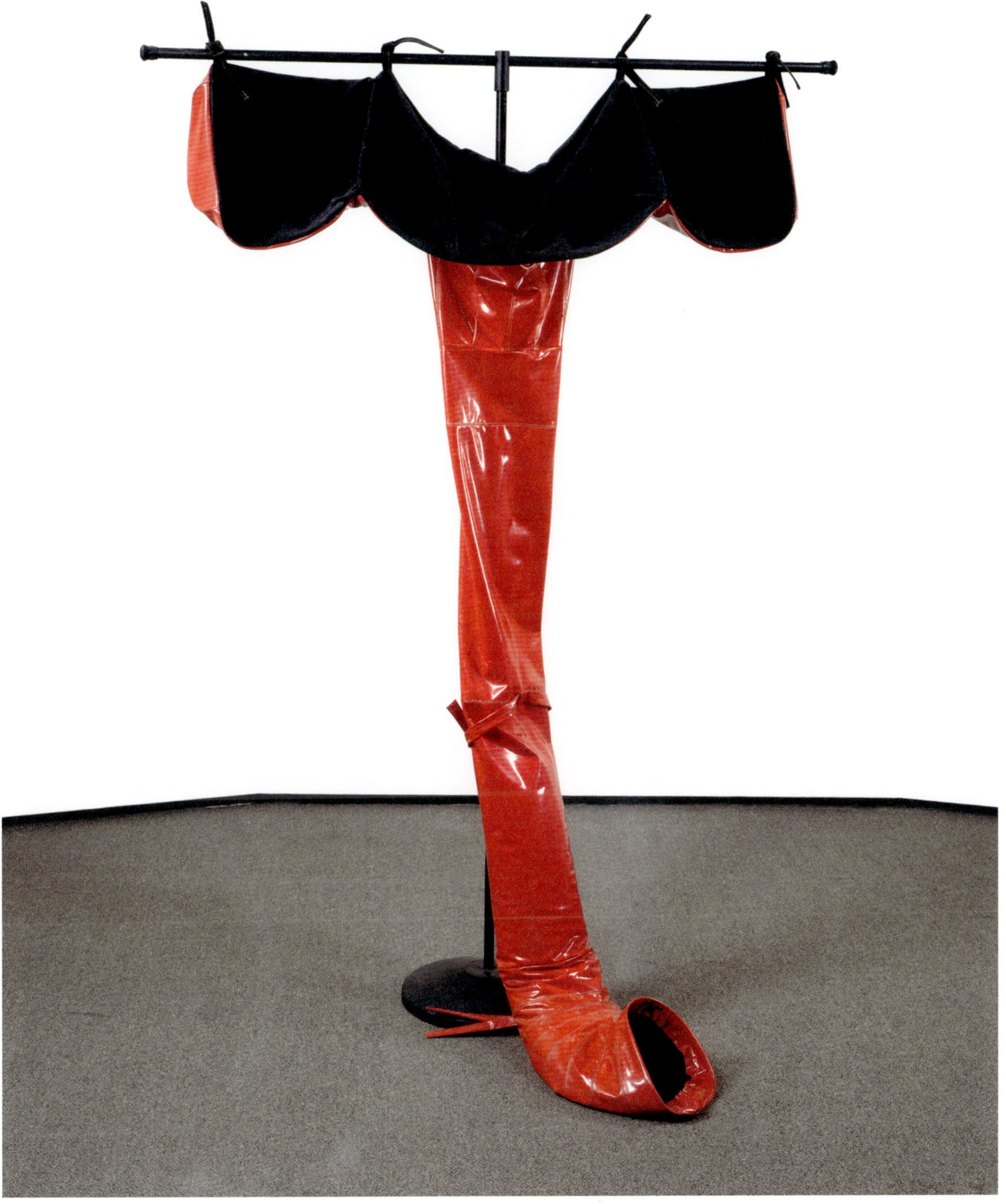

Claes Oldenburg, *Soft Drainpipe—Red (Hot) Version*, 1967. Vinyl filled with expanded polystyrene chips, on painted metal: drainpipe, 120 × 60 × 45 in. (304.8 × 152.4 × 114.3 cm); stand, 96 in. (243.9 cm) high.
National Gallery of Art, Washington, DC; Robert and Jane Meyerhoff Collection, gift in honor of the 50th anniversary of the National Gallery of Art 1990.75.1

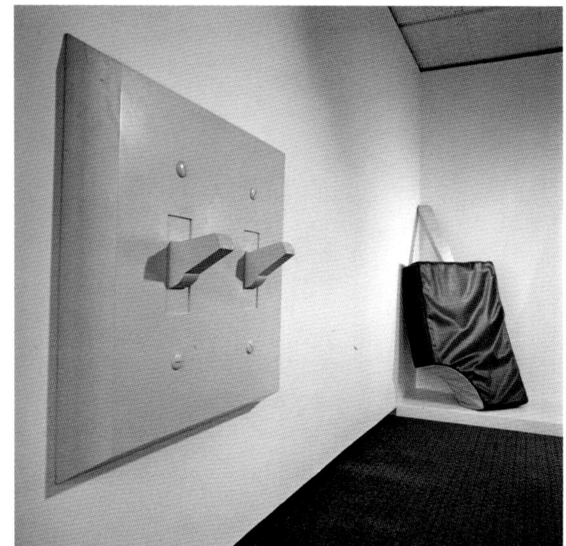

American Sculpture of the Sixties, Los Angeles County Museum of Art, 1967, with Claes Oldenburg's *Light Switch* (1964) and *Giant Good Humor* (1965)

Monte's essay, in particular, identifies a strain of American art that he feels stems from access to common materialism, an aversion to ideology, and a ground-level response to the American pavement. He identifies Westermann as the wellspring of this art, which he defines as distinct from Pop:

Westermann's multi-directional body of work presents younger artists with a multitude of clues about what is possible in sculpture today. Essentially Westermann's pieces are three-dimensional repositories of ideas [for example, *Memorial to the Idea of Man If He Was an Idea* (1958)]. To explain further one must begin by noting that sculptural form as an end product in his work is not what he wants or achieves. Westermann . . . refuses any high art tradition, but rather draws heavily from the parallel artifact cultures which throughout recorded history have been present if not always accounted for. Westermann has made art out of the clumsy aspects of twentieth century American culture. His bent cylindrical pieces with an all-over marbling of their painted surfaces pre-figure Pop art and draw more subtly on banal sources. Westermann's poker-faced exploitation of the cheapest vinyl tile design is altogether in keeping with Lichtenstein's comic book iconography. And yet if a hierarchy of subject matter were set up, Lichtenstein's contemptible sources seem heroic next to Westermann's tile designs, which are beneath contempt and therefore virtually invisible. So, in a sense, Westermann renders visible what everyone knows is around yet refuses to acknowledge because it is simply too distressing.

May 1967 • Judith Bernstein (b. 1942) graduates with a master of fine arts from the Yale School of Art, one of only three women enrolled in the graduate school at that time. Raised in a middle-class Jewish household in Bradley Beach, New Jersey, she had received both a bachelor's and a master's degree from Pennsylvania State University, studying art education with the intention of becoming a high school teacher, and had applied to Yale on a whim at the recommendation of a friend. While her graduate school classmates "concentrated on formal issues of color, line, material, shape, and scale," discussing Abstract Expressionism, Pop art, and the recent turn to Minimalism, Bernstein was "running reconnaissance missions in the men's bathroom," as Thomas Micchelli will later recount, entering into the male psyche by examining the sexual and scatological graffiti she found there. Playwrights John Guare and Ron Whyte as well as the actor Ron Leibman are among her friends in the drama program who guard the restroom doors.

Bernstein initiates her *Fuck Vietnam* (1966–68) protest paintings while at Yale, utilizing the same crude iconography and vulgar slang she finds in the men's room as a means to channel her outrage over American imperialism and sexual politics, offering a feminist critique of the patriarchy. *Vietnam Garden* (1967) is an overt antiwar image: erect phalluses are metaphors for tombstones, a reference to the college-age draft. In *L.B.J.* (1967), she uses Brillo pads to approximate pubic hair, with the profanities etched into the collage transmitting a raw and aggressive energy. Bernstein uses obscenity and humor as sublimation, laughter providing a psychic release. Throughout the series, the artist plays up the isolated and exaggerated phallus as the supreme corporeal symbol of brutal violence, capitalism, and misogyny. Her works thematically overlap with the art of Louise Bourgeois and Nancy Spero, who also address the psychoanalytic and social constructs associated with phallic symbolism. Spero, notably, produces the *War Series* (1966–70), representing exploding bombs through phallic and sexual imagery, as in her 1966 work *Sperm Bomb*.

May 20–June 6, 1967 • Alex Hay has his first solo exhibition, at Kornblee Gallery on New York's Upper East Side. He begins to show his large facsimile-style blowups of everyday objects—a receipt from a local hardware store, a breakfast plate with a fried egg accompanied by silverware, a manila dry-cleaning tag. The show

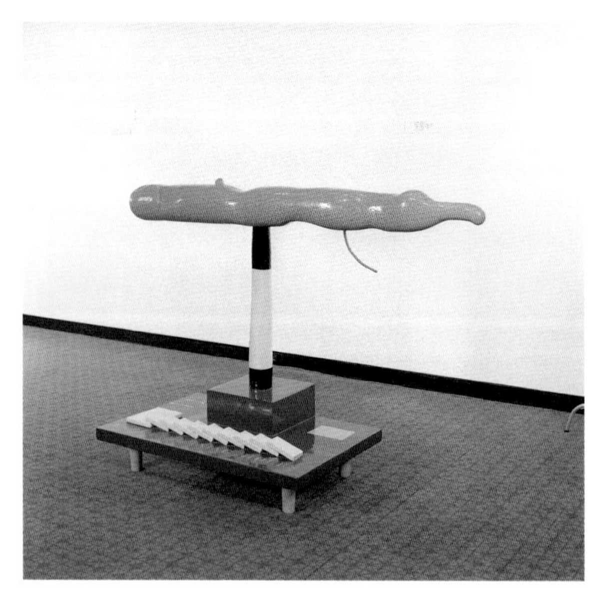

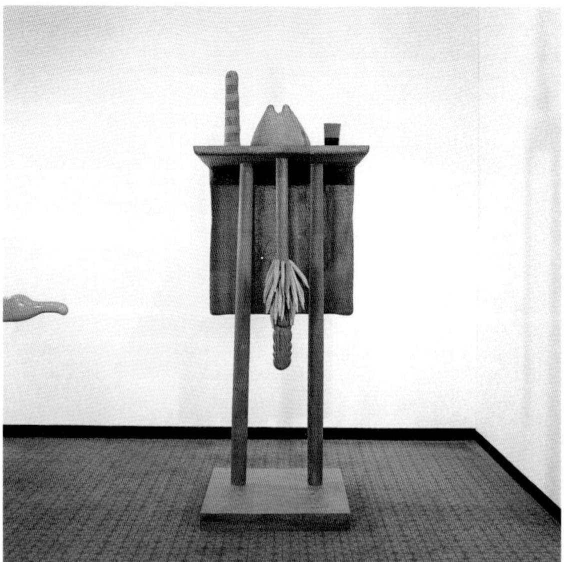

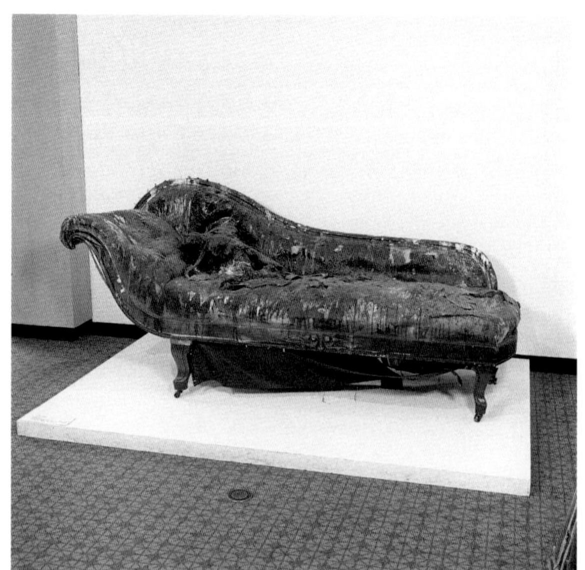

American Sculpture of the Sixties, Los Angeles County Museum of Art, 1967, with Jeremy Anderson's *Early Morning Hours* (1966) and *Altar* (1963), and Bruce Conner's *Couch* (1963)

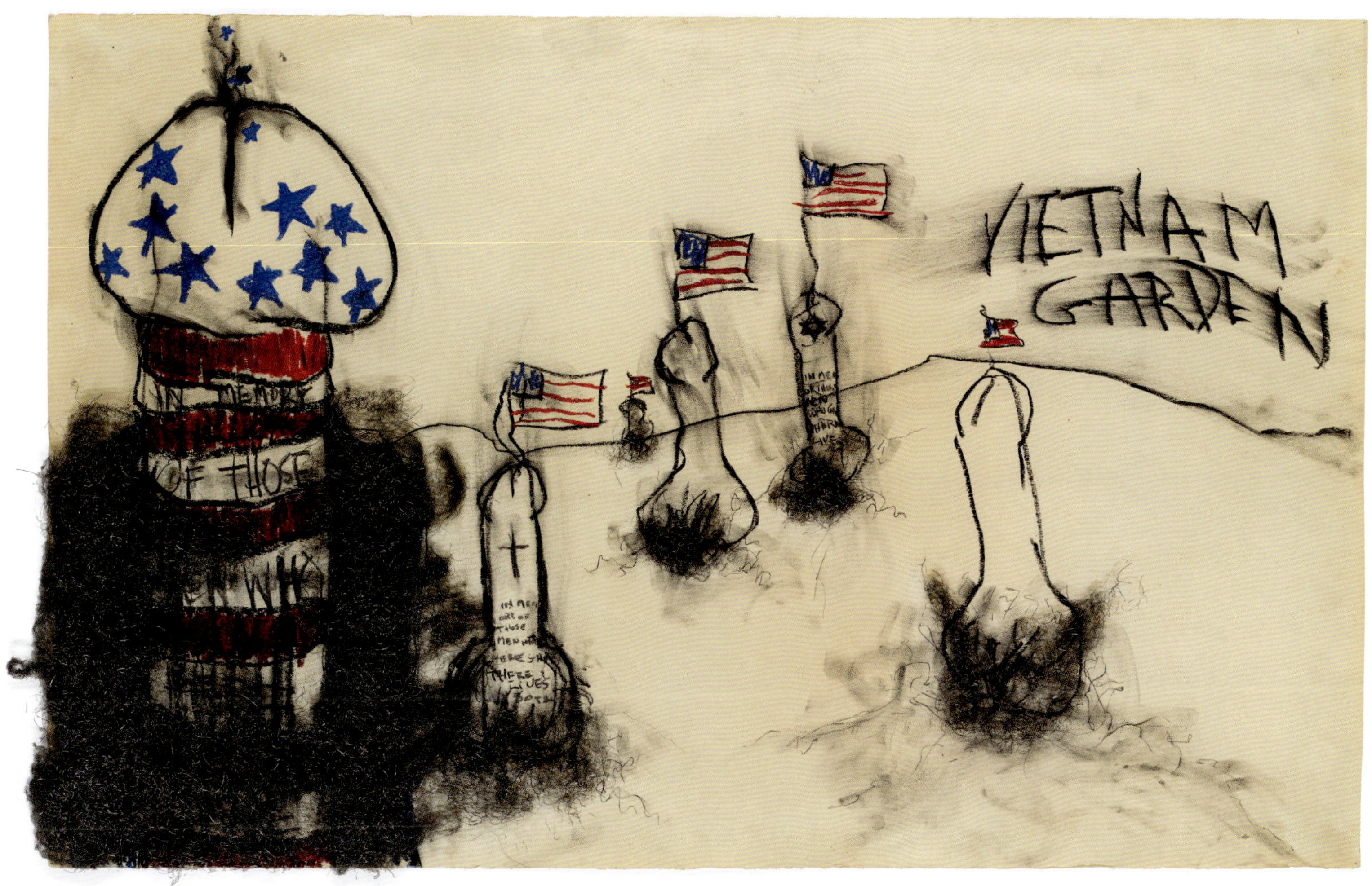

Judith Bernstein, *Vietnam Garden*, 1967. Charcoal, oil stick, and steel wool on paper: sheet, 26 × 40 in. (66 × 101.6 cm); image (irregular), 26 ⅜ × 41 ¼ in. (67 × 104.8 cm).
Whitney Museum of American Art, New York; purchase with funds from the Drawing Committee 2010.80

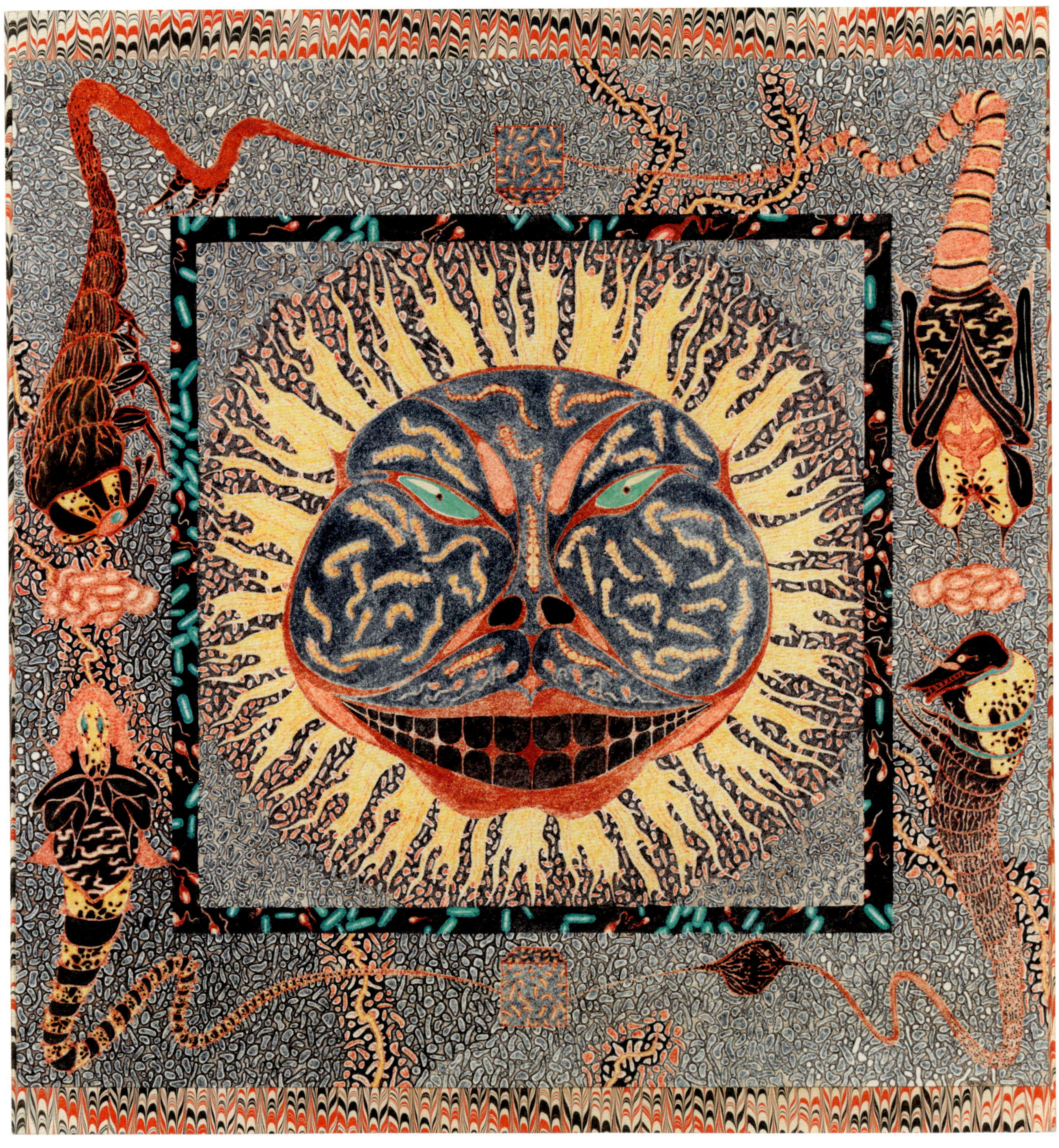

Ching Ho Cheng, *Sun Drawing*, 1967. Fiber-tipped pen on paper mounted on found paper on board: sheet, 20 × 20 in. (50.8 × 50.8 cm); mount (board), 21 ¹⁵⁄₁₆ × 20 ¼ × ⅛ in. (55.7 × 51.4 × 0.3 cm). Whitney Museum of American Art, New York; gift of the Ching Ho Cheng Estate 2010.46

is subsequently followed by one in 1968 and another in 1969. At this time, Hay begins to break away from the Judson Memorial Church scene, drifting apart from his wife, Deborah, and from Robert Rauschenberg.

1967 • Shawn Walker attends an underground screening of films by Jonas Mekas, D. A. Pennebaker, and Andy Warhol, finding the movies "frivolous." Nevertheless, this encounter with New York's avant-garde film world inspires Walker to join Allan Siegel's filmmaking workshop at the Free University of New York, a short-lived experiment in open education that is a haven for radical faculty dismissed from local accredited universities. Ken Jacobs and Mekas have recently screened Siegel's work at the Millennium Film Workshop and the New York Theater, and Jacobs subsequently encourages Siegel to start the film class at the university. Walker and other workshop members travel to Washington, DC, to document the March on the Pentagon in protest of the Vietnam War on October 21. The result is the film *No Game* (1968), an exposé of the excessive violence deployed by police against protestors' peaceful occupation of the Pentagon grounds. The film and Siegel's workshop become the seed for the formation of Newsreel, a disparate collective of activist filmmakers of which Walker is a founding member—indeed, in his account, "the only Black cameraman that they have."

August 20, 1967 • On weekends throughout 1967, Yayoi Kusama organizes several nude public art performances as part of her *Body Festival* series held at various New York City parks, including on this date in Washington Square. For these events, Kusama paints polka dots onto the nude or bathing-suit-clad of attendees in order to transcend individuality and promote an egoless state,

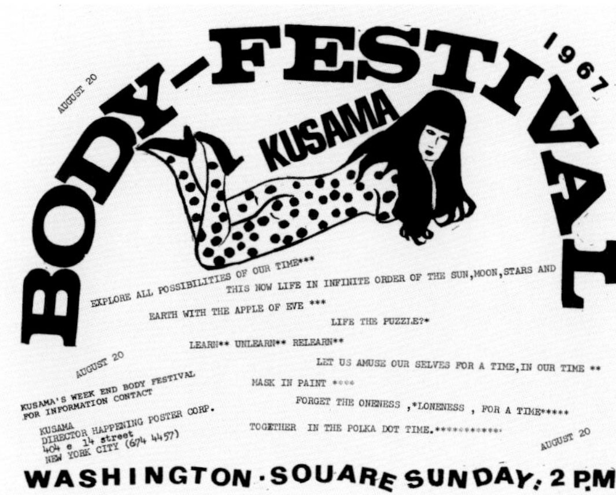

Flyer for Yayoi Kusama's *Body Festival* in Washington Square, New York, 1967

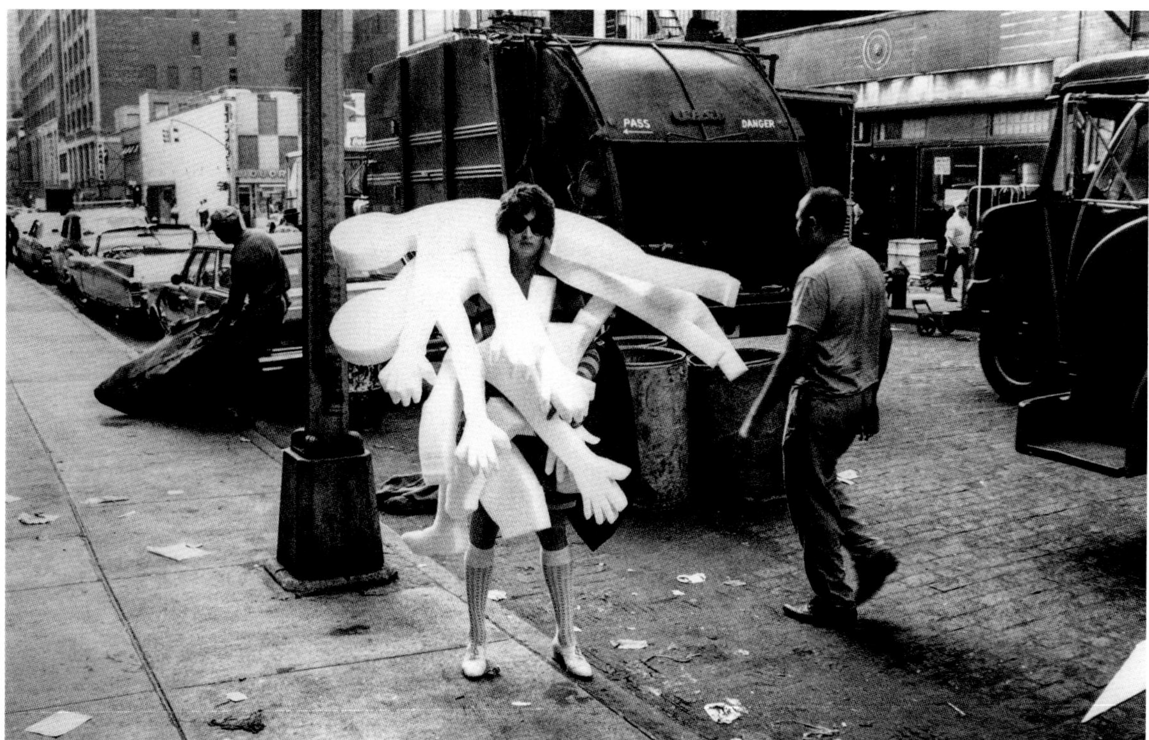

Kiki Kogelnik performing *Untitled (New York Street Performance)*, New York, 1967

after which everyone dances and blisses out. The following year, Kusama will rename these performances and happenings *Anatomic Explosions* and go on to stage them at high-profile locations such as the New York Stock Exchange, the Statue of Liberty, and the bronze Alice in Wonderland sculpture in Central Park. For each, Kusama will issue a press release featuring ecstatic language such as: "Burn Wall Street. Wall Street men must become farmers and fishermen. Wall Street men must stop all of this fake 'business.' OBLITERATE WALL STREET MEN WITH POLKA DOTS. OBLITERATE WALL STREET MEN WITH POLKA DOTS ON THEIR NAKED BODIES. BE IN . . . BE NAKED, NAKED, NAKED." Along the way, Kusama positions herself as the "High Priestess" of hippies, advertising in the *East Village Other*, producing her own newspaper, making clothes, and becoming involved with bohemian pornography. She establishes businesses such as Kusama Polka Dot Church and Kusama Fashion Institute. Her fashion designs feature unisex garments with holes cut to expose the wearer's genitals or breasts, as well as "Orgy Dresses" designed to fit between two and twenty-five people.

August 1967 • Kiki Kogelnik stages a performance in New York during which she attempts to carry a handful of large foam cutouts of the human body through the street, as evident in images of the event, in which the artist appears comically overwhelmed by these floppy, unwieldy forms. In one photograph, workmen nearby seem unfazed by the sight of a fashionably dressed woman with what appear to be life-size paper dolls piled atop her shoulders. Kogelnik stages a similar performance in Vienna the following month, in the Belvedere gardens, which culminates in her floating the thick foam forms in one of the grand ornamental fountains. A second performance involves her carrying a clothesline through the streets festooned with thin foam cutouts of the human body, much to the astonishment of the Viennese public. Kogelnik installs this work (*Menschen zum Trocknen*, 1967) across the span of the main space of Galerie nächst St. Stephan as part of her solo exhibition there.

In what can be seen as a Pop response to the visceral cathartic performances being staged by the Vienna Actionists at the time, Kogelnik's performances also mark a shift in the way that she has been approaching the human body in her work. Since her arrival in the United States, she had made paintings using literal translations of the human form based on her own body or the bodies of fellow artists and friends, which would act as templates, to which she would add stenciled mechanical elements to create works that explored the potential for the human body to exist in space.

August 1967 • Barbara Jones-Hogu (1938–2017) contributes to the mural *Wall of Respect* in Chicago as a member of the Organization of Black American

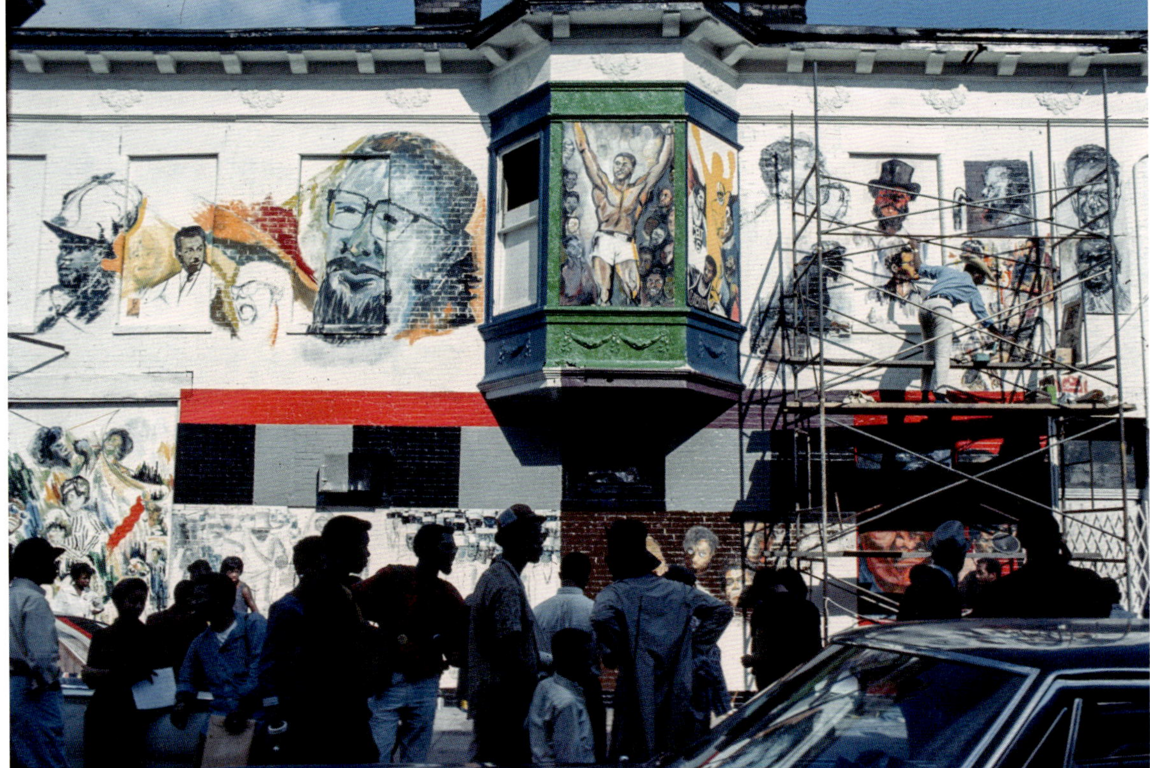

Residents and artists gather during the creation of *The Wall of Respect*, Chicago, 1967

Culture (OBAC). Initiated by the group's cofounder, veteran muralist William Walker, the mural measures 20 × 60 feet and appears on the side of a tavern on the city's South Side. Following a layout proposed by activist and artist Laini Abernathy, *Wall of Respect* depicts a variety of Black heroes and scenes from the civil rights movement as it unfolds. Jones-Hogu completes the mural's section on actors. The wall starts the mural movement in Chicago and becomes an important place for political gatherings as well as events featuring music, dance, and poetry.

Having studied art at Howard University, the School of the Art Institute of Chicago, and the Institute of Design at Illinois Tech, Jones-Hogu is originally a painter, but she embraces printmaking while at the Institute of Design in part because the head of the program, acclaimed printmaker Misch Kohn, is encouraging and accommodating. As she will later explain, "he gave me a key to the room so I could go and work in the studio and go to class periodically, because I was working during the day." Focusing on screenprinting, Jones-Hogu becomes known for her acerbic prints and for peppering her images with words and other images that often pointedly condemn war and racist policies, such as the skeletal figure in front of the American flag in *Mother of Man* (1968).

___

1967 • Barbara Hammer (1939–2019) has a transformative experience on her first day in William Morehouse's painting class at Sonoma State University, where the life model is a woman on a motorcycle. She "blew my mind," Hammer will later recall. "I stretched a canvas as large as life, and I put myself as close to her as possible. I was so excited to be standing right next to a woman on a motorcycle that I painted her with six arms and six legs. I had never heard of Duchamp." This episode leads Hammer to experiment with "expanded painting," using a stroboscopic black light and film coated in fluorescent colors to "paint" on a blank canvas using a 16mm projector. The technique will inform a series of erotic and joyous photographs of Hammer's friends, lovers, and collaborators, and of the artist herself, in the early to mid-1970s, as well as films concerned with the simultaneous expression of multiple moments—that is, Gertrude Stein's "simultaneity"—intimately depicting women's lives and bodies.

Born in Los Angeles, Hammer had earned a bachelor's degree in psychology from the University of California, Los Angeles, and master's degrees in English literature and film from San Francisco State College. There, she encounters Maya Deren's dream-like, fragmentary short film *Meshes of the Afternoon* (1943). The film's emphasis on the unconscious and on subjective experience will inspire Hammer's turn toward more unguarded depictions of her own personal life on film in the 1970s.

___

September 15–October 5, 1967 • Wally Hedrick's painting retrospective *Here's Art For'em*, Curated by Phil Linhares, is on view at the San Francisco Art Institute.

___

1967 • Raymond Saunders self-publishes the essay-manifesto "Black Is a Color," a biting response to a piece written by Ishmael Reed for the May issue of *Arts Journal*, "The Black Artist: Calling a Spade a Spade." In the latter, Reed, a poet, writer, and Black cultural nationalist, argues that the experience of being Black in America imprints on anything the Black artist makes, thereby distinguishing it specifically as "Black art."

Saunders, in contrast, defines *black* as nothing more than pigmentation, whether in a palette or of an artist's skin, and asserts that *blackness* as a term is fundamentally meaningless. Such an understanding allows each artist to chart their own negotiation between personal vision and broader social implications:

> black is bound to black not so much by color or racial characteristics as by shared experience, social or cultural. this is the same in any rarefied social (or racial) enclave, but "no man is an island, entire of itself." the artist deals with the human condition. He is "involved in mankind." this is as valid for the black artist as for any other. he uses his heart, his eyes, his mind as interpreters of his own deep vision of himself, and the world as it is reflected in those depths. . . . the creative imagination is his channel.

The exchange reflects a wider debate about the responsibilities of the Black artist during the 1960s. In his own work, Saunders does not shy away from subject matter pertaining to Blackness but neither does he wish to be defined by race. Thus, the artist's polemic stands as a defense of a deeply personal vision that comments on social realities *and* allows for the transcendence of "the cramped boundaries of stereotype"—a mode of art making that cannot be reduced to, but also cannot be divorced from, the artist's race.

___

September 19, 1967 • After a few years showing at Pace Gallery, Paul Thek returns to Stable Gallery, New York, to exhibit *The Tomb*, an installation that becomes his most celebrated and cited work. The piece is composed of a life-size, pale pink ziggurat tomb that on first glance appears to be a nod to then prevalent Minimalist sculpture. A sign at the entrance to the installation listing all materials and their measurements hints at the tongue-in-cheek nature of this reference, parodying Minimalism's self-reflexive emphasis on fabrication: "Welcome: You are in a replica of the

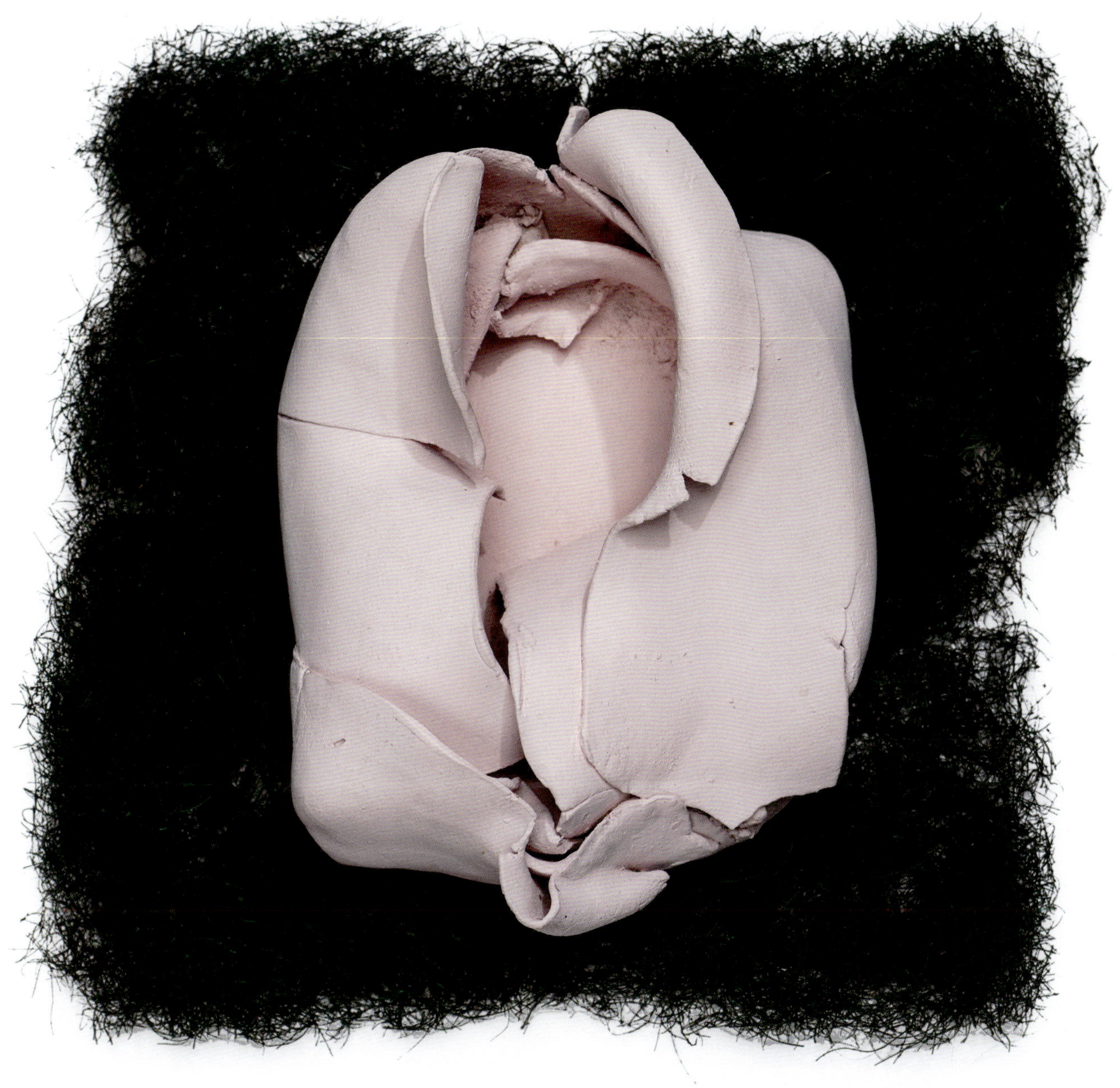

Hannah Wilke, *Teasel Cushion*, 1967. Terra-cotta, acrylic, and plastic, 12 × 12 × 4 in. (30.5 × 30.5 × 10.2 cm). Walker Art Center, Minneapolis; T. B. Walker Acquisition Fund 2002.69.1–.2

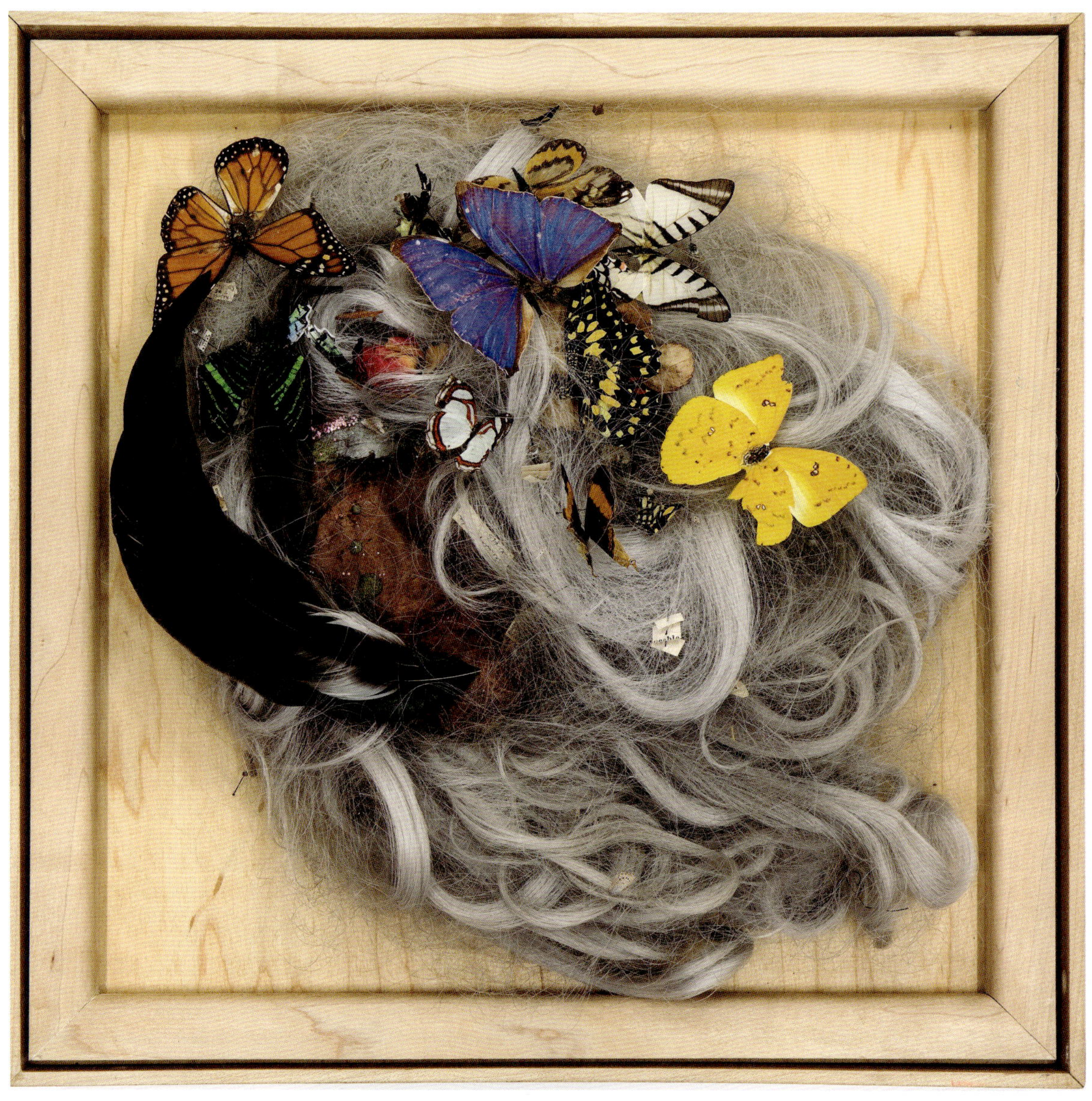

Lynn Hershman Leeson, *Butterfly Woman Sleeping*, 1967, from the series *Breathing Machines*. Wax, wig, paint, butterflies, feathers, sensors, sound, wood base, and acrylic, 16 ½ × 16 ½ × 13 in. (41.9 × 41.9 × 33 cm). Collection of Marguerite Steed Hoffman

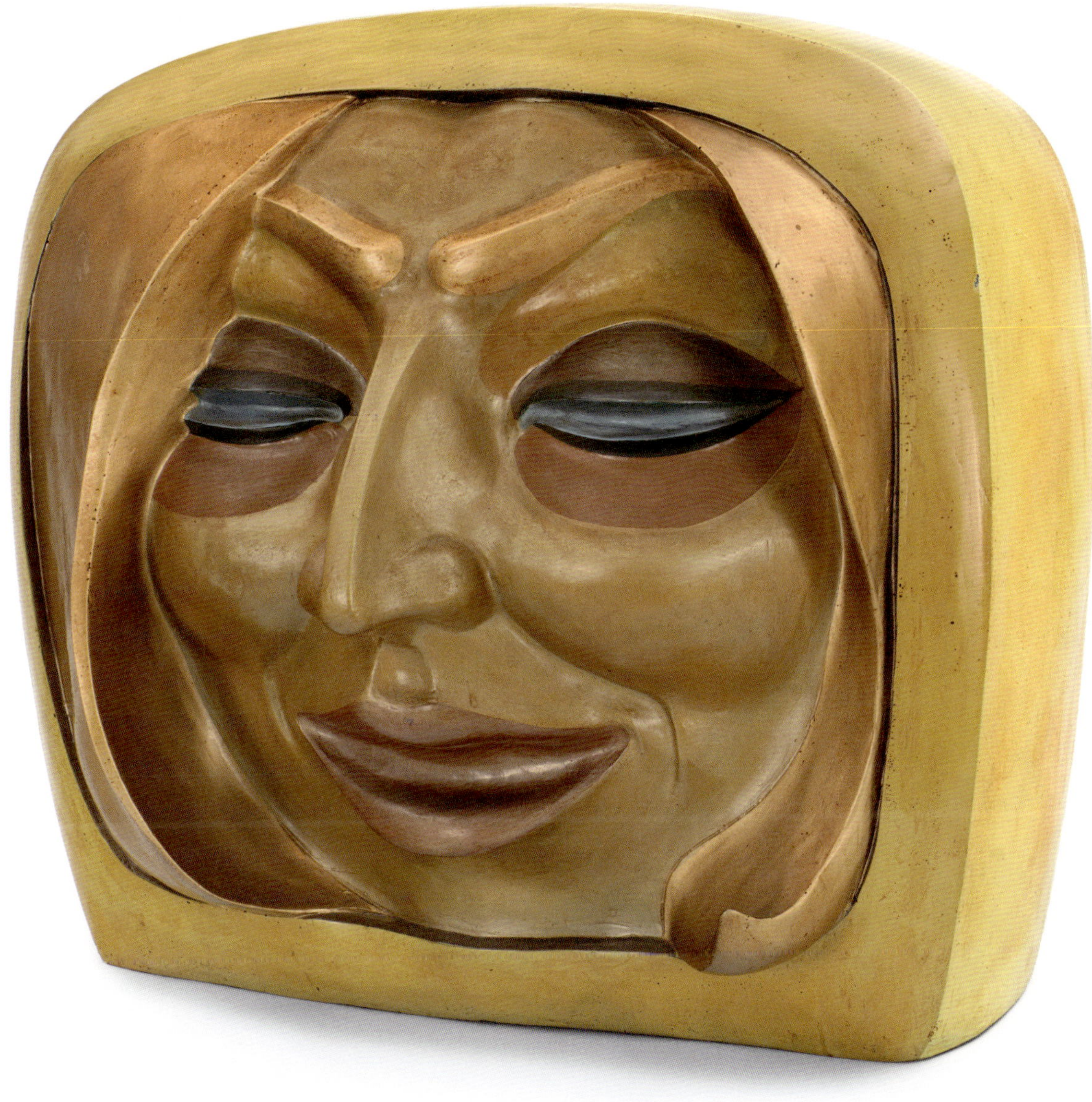

Luis Jimenez, *Blonde TV Image*, 1967. Fiberglass with polychrome, 27 × 19 × 30 in. (68.6 × 48.3 × 76.2 cm). Whitney Museum of American Art, New York; Josephine N. Hopper Bequest, by exchange 2024.352

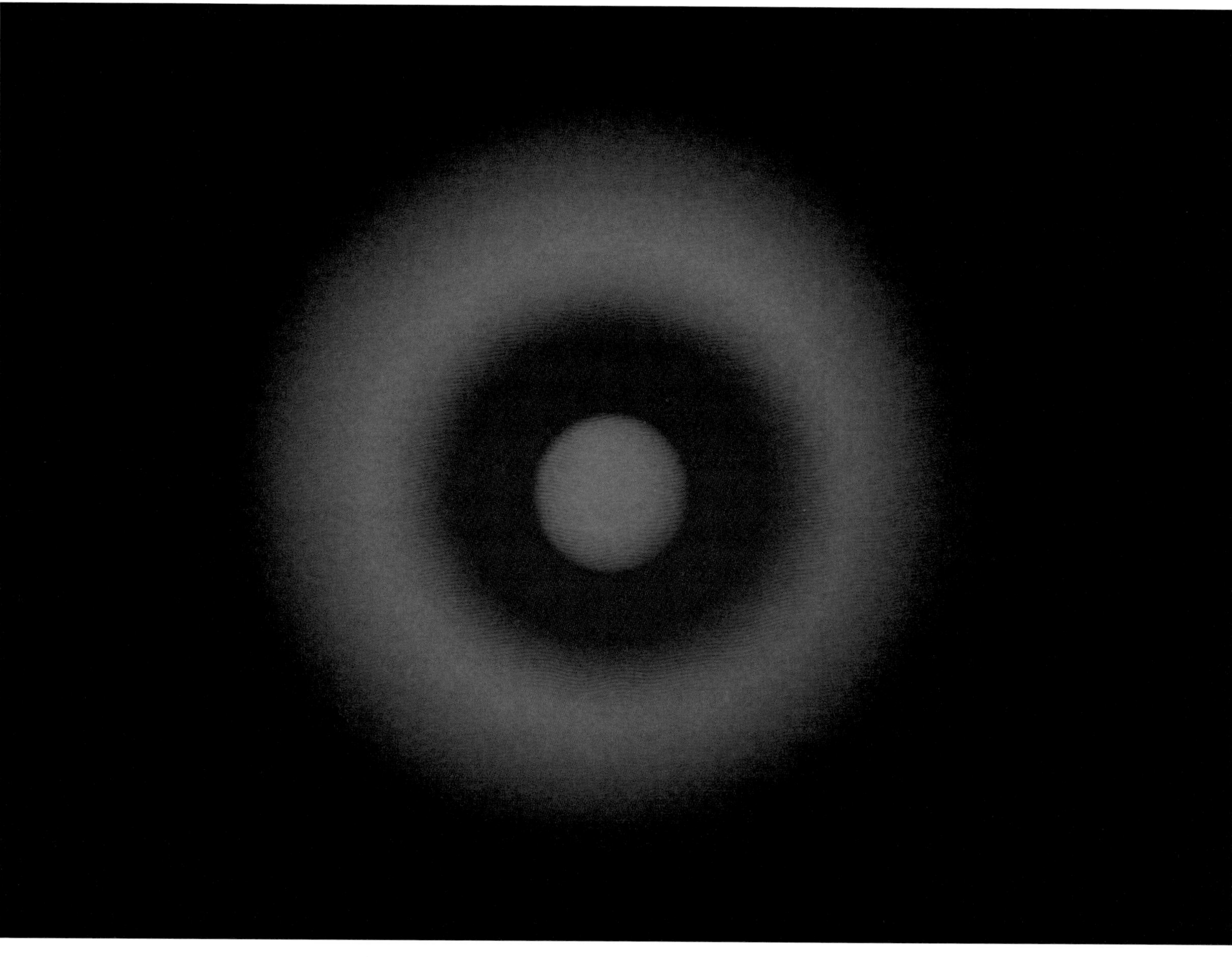

Jordan Belson, *Samadhi*, 1967. 16mm film transferred to video, color, sound; 6 min. The Estate of Jordan Belson and Matthew Marks Gallery, New York

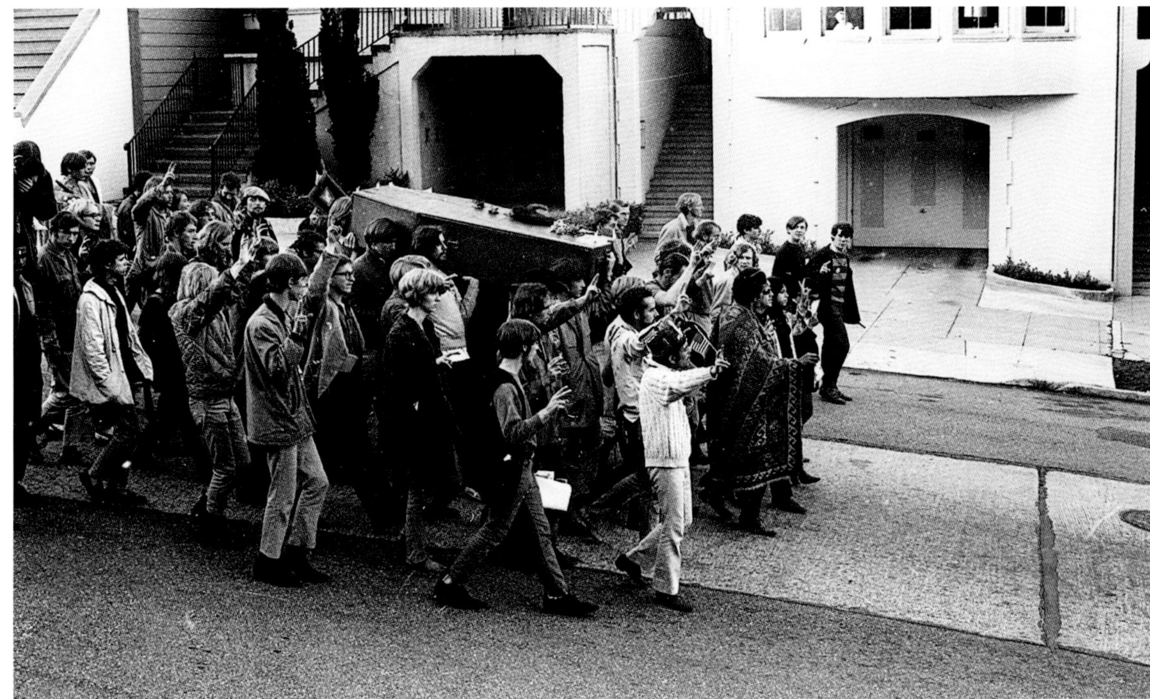

"Death of the Hippie" procession, San Francisco, 1967

tomb. It has been fabricated at a cost of $950.00. . . . Following an 85 degree angle, it rises in three tiers to its 8 ½' height . . ." Upon entering *The Tomb*, viewers are confronted with a life-size wax effigy of the artist's body, lying corpse-like in a pink suit, surrounded by funerary objects, which subverts the Minimalist commitment to both pure abstraction and "presentness" by invoking the art-historical trope of memento mori. With the help of fellow artist Neil Jenny, Thek has fabricated the full cast of his own body, as well as several cast body parts that lie scattered on the floor of the gallery around *The Tomb*. He will go on to make several works featuring parts of his own body, evincing a fascination with the at once alien and familiar qualities of mannequins resonant with the Surrealist notion of the "marvelous," which André Breton explained in his 1924 manifesto, "The marvelous is not the same in every period of history: it partakes in some obscure way of a sort of general revelation only the fragments of which come down to us: they are the romantic *ruins*, the modern *mannequin*."

The Tomb comes to be more popularly known as *Death of a Hippie*, a title that Thek often adamantly rejects, though one he himself sometimes uses. This retroactively assigned name alludes to the "Death of the Hippie" parades taking place concurrently in both San Francisco and New York as thousands travel to San Francisco, casting off conservative social values and experimenting with sex and drugs in search of a hopeful utopia. Disaffected young people protesting the Vietnam War stage their own collective funeral, carrying a symbolic coffin through the streets.

Despite the recognition he is receiving in New York, Thek returns to Italy, leaving the same week that *The Tomb* opens.

September 19–October 11, 1967 • Dilexi Gallery in San Francisco hosts a solo exhibition of Franklin Williams's work.

1967 • Barbara Rossi (1940–2023) begins taking graduate classes at the School of the Art Institute of Chicago (SAIC) while she is still a Catholic nun, having received the blessing of the Catholic Church to pursue her interest in art. At SAIC, she is influenced by professors Whitney Halstead and Ray Yoshida, who encourage a capacious approach to visual study and, famously, urge students to visit collections outside the fine art galleries. A 1964 graduate of St. Xavier College in Chicago, Rossi will earn her master of fine arts in 1970. Despite leaving her religious order to pursue art full-time, she often uses religious iconography in her work, as in her series of prints *Male of Sorrows* (1970–71), which are based on a fifteenth-century German color woodcut in the Art Institute of Chicago's collection that depicts the crucified Christ.

Rossi's time at SAIC—which includes her years teaching there after she graduates—puts her in contact with many artists associated with the Hairy Who exhibitions and the larger Chicago Imagists group. Rossi's work shares the Imagists' interest in non-Western and popular imagery as well as their pursuit of vivid and distorted figurative work. Her disorienting compositions, such as the contorted and cartoony Christ of *Male of Sorrows #5* (1970), however, remain idiosyncratic even among an eclectic set of peers.

October 26, 1967 • Kenneth Anger announces his death in a full-page advertisement in the *Village Voice*: "In Memoriam, Kenneth Anger, Film Maker (1947–1967)." Simultaneously, he sends telegrams to friends and acquaintances with a death notice. The prank, with its ring of Surrealist dark humor, is intended to protest the lack of financial support for avant-garde and underground filmmaking. Anger has waged an uphill battle against insufficient funding his entire career, consequently leaving many of his projects undone.

December 13, 1967–February 4, 1968 • The Whitney Museum of American Art's *1967 Annual Exhibition of Contemporary Painting* features artists Deborah Remington, James Rosenquist, Edward Ruscha, William T. Wiley, and Franklin Williams. For the first time, a Whitney Annual also includes two Chicago-based artists associated with the Hairy Who, Gladys Nilsson and Karl Wirsum.

December 19, 1967 • Faith Ringgold (1930–2024) opens her first one-person exhibition, *American People*, at Spectrum Gallery, New York. The poet and critic Robert Newman had invited Ringgold to join his cooperative gallery with the promise of a solo show. She is one of five women artists and the only Black artist among the co-op's twenty members. Ringgold has been working on her *American People* series since 1963, and Newman encourages her to continue confronting social issues in her work. He "wanted me to depict everything that was happening in America—the '60s and the decade's tumultuous thrusts for freedom," Ringgold will later recall. Newman gives her access to the gallery in the summer of 1967 to complete her paintings for the exhibition. This timing proves particularly important to the artist, as the summer of 1967 sees violent upheavals in cities across the United States that are mostly precipitated by brutality toward frustrated Black citizens and further escalated by police response. Cities such as Detroit, Milwaukee, Buffalo, Tampa, Cincinnati, and (closest to Ringgold) Newark experience protests that turn deadly and destructive with violent and outsize police and military reactions. President Lyndon B. Johnson forms the Kerner Commission to investigate. Even as the commission will bury its findings regarding police brutality when it publishes its report in 1968, it nevertheless concludes,

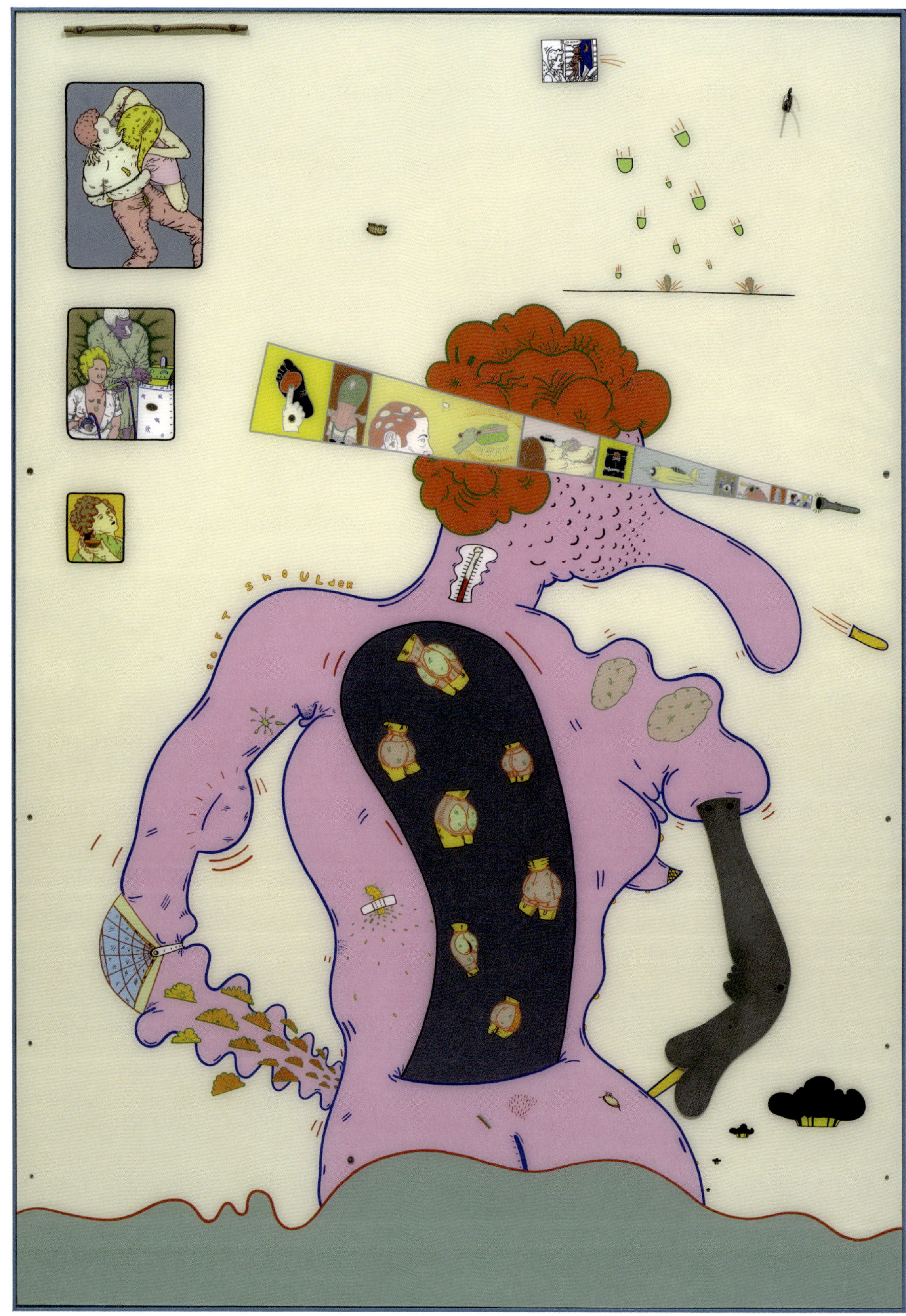

Jim Nutt, *Miss E. Knows*, 1967. Acrylic on Plexiglas with aluminum and rubber in artist's painted frame, 75 ⅝ × 51 ⅝ in. (192.1 × 131.1 cm). The Art Institute of Chicago; Twentieth-Century Purchase Fund 1970.1014

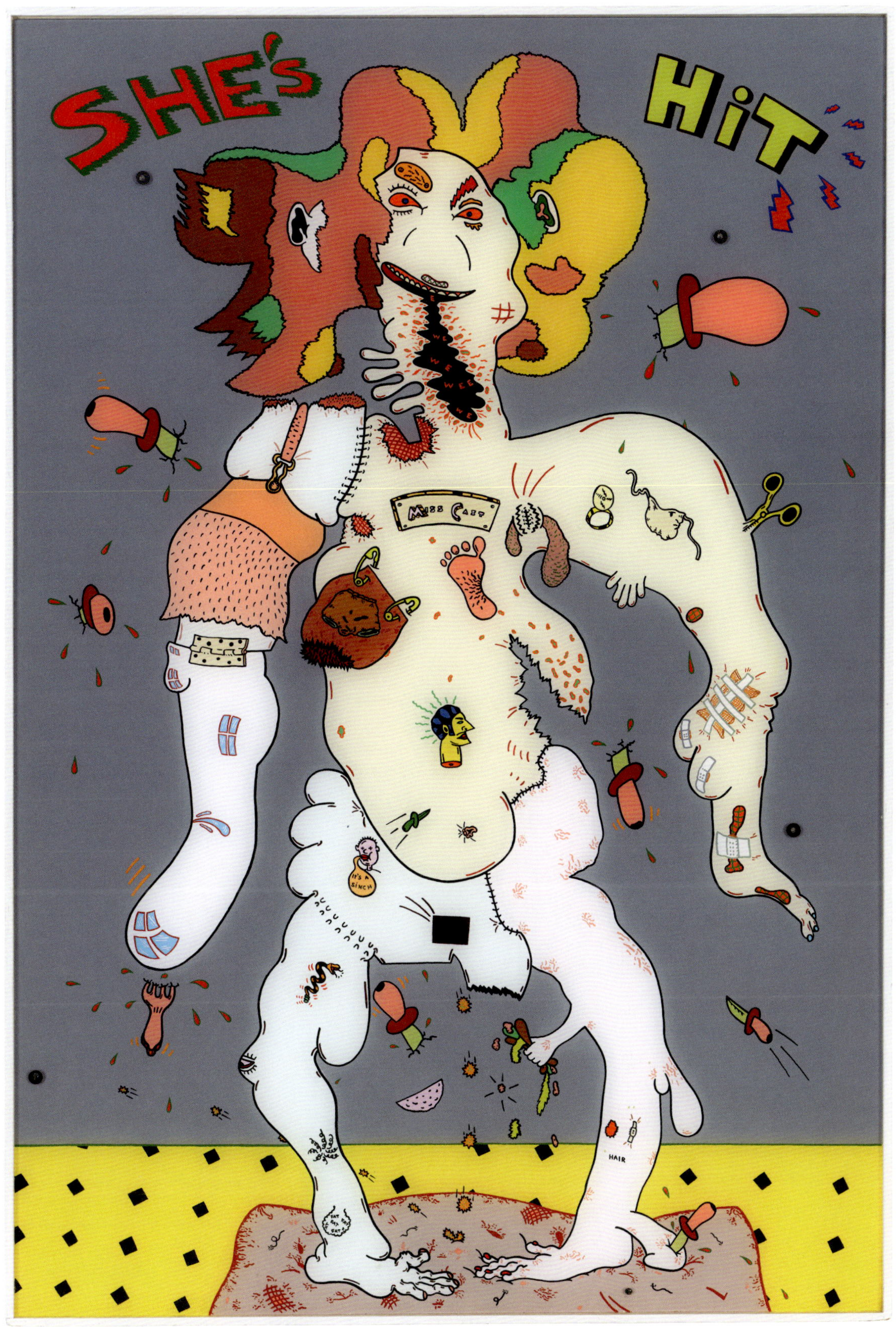

Jim Nutt, *She's Hit*, 1967. Acrylic on Plexiglas, with wood frame, 36 × 24 in. (91.4 × 61 cm). Whitney Museum of American Art, New York; purchase with funds from the Larry Aldrich Foundation Fund 69.101

"Race prejudice has shaped our history decisively; it now threatens to affect our future. White racism is essentially responsible for the explosive mixture which has been accumulating in our cities since the end of World War II."

Ringgold had been born in Harlem and, through her parents' interests and encouragement, had experienced much of the music, literature, and art prevalent in the neighborhood throughout her childhood—jazz musician Sonny Rollins frequently plays saxophone in her home. Ringgold learns to sew and craft from her mother, a fashion designer, and becomes serious about art as a high schooler. She graduates from City College of New York in 1955 with a degree in fine art and teaches art in public schools while pursuing a master's degree in art from her alma mater. Ringgold's work at this time is influenced not only by the paintings and tapestries she saw in the Louvre Museum on a trip to Europe in 1959 but also by the writings of LeRoi Jones (later Amiri Baraka) and James Baldwin, as well as jazz musicians in Harlem.

December 26, 1967 • Edward Owens's film *Tomorrow's Promise* screens in the opening program of the fourth edition of the International Experimental Film Competition (EXPRMNTL 4) at Knokke-le-Zoute in Belgium. Held intermittently, only five editions will occur between 1947 and 1974. EXPRMNTL 4 takes place between Christmas 1967 and early January of the new year, new tendencies in expanded cinema and structural film having a strong presence. Stan VanDerBeek shows his two-screen film *A Dam Rib Bed* (1967), and the jury's main prize is awarded to Michael Snow's *Wavelength* (1967).

In his description of *Tomorrow's Promise*, Owens suggests that the characters are allegories for his "personal life," hinting at a play on gender and a sense of the film as reflective of an interior state. He calls it "a film about vacantness. . . . There are several inter-cuts which serve . . . as relative links into the final section: which is actually the 'story.' . . . My film could have been edited with precise tensions and a lucid straight narrative, but it was my aim to 're-create' the protagonist of my personal life."

The film garners strong praise from critics Gregory Battcock and Parker Tyler. Tyler, coyly alluding to his mentorship of the young artist, comments that *Tomorrow's Promise* has "a style so pictorially exciting that the next thing [Owens] must do is listen to my advice." He will name Owens's *Remembrance: A Portrait Study* (1967) one of the most important underground films of 1968 in his seminal survey *Underground Film: A Critical History* (1969), which consistently links the 1960s underground with Surrealism.

EDWARD OWENS AND PARKER TYLER

ED HALTER

Private Imaginings and Narrative Facts (p. 195), a fluttering, adumbral portrait of the filmmaker's mother, was Edward Owens's fourth 16mm film, completed in 1970 when he was a mere twenty-one years old. By that age, Owens had already screened around the United States and internationally, at with-it venues for avant-garde film such as Jonas Mekas's Film-Makers' Cinematheque in New York, Standish Lawder's Yale Film Festival, and at the Fourth International Experimental Film Competition in Knokke-le-Zoute, Belgium, and was beginning to create a name for himself in the burgeoning world of New American Cinema. His work to this point included the impressionistic featurettes *Autrefois J'ai Aime Une Femme* (1966; Once I Loved a Woman) and *Tomorrow's Promise* (1967), each an abstracted psychodrama dwelling on desire, told through found photographs and posed studies of male and female figures, often superimposed and strobing, structured by long stretches of silent, imageless darkness. In contrast, his subsequent two films, *Private Imaginings* and a short, lyrical profile of his mother and aunt, *Remembrance: A Portrait Study* (1967), are more tightly focused on individual subjects, using documentary footage alongside dramatically staged tableaux, creating oneiric fusions of regal fantasy and homey realities. Owens shot each film in his native Chicago, using his family and friends as actors and subjects, and together they evince a level of gravitas and precision surprising for an artist in his teens and early twenties. A relatively minor figure in a wildly active moment for American cinema, Owens stands out historically not only for his youthful talents but also for being one of a small handful of independent Black filmmakers of the time—and the only Black artist of the 1960s who worked self-consciously within the visionary traditions explored by major experimental filmmakers such as Maya Deren, Stan Brakhage, and, most deeply, his teacher Gregory Markopoulos. Despite the promises that tomorrow seemed to hold for Owens, however, *Private Imaginings* would also be the last film he would ever complete.

Growing up on the Chicago's South Side, Owens had been artistically precocious, studying painting and sculpture from around age fourteen at the School of the Art Institute of Chicago, showing in a number of local exhibitions, and receiving a scholarship to study at the Art Institute's new film program. His filmmaking instructor would be Markopoulos, then one of the major figures of American avant-garde cinema, renowned for homoerotic, dreamlike near-narratives such as *Twice a Man* (1963) and *The Illiac Passion*

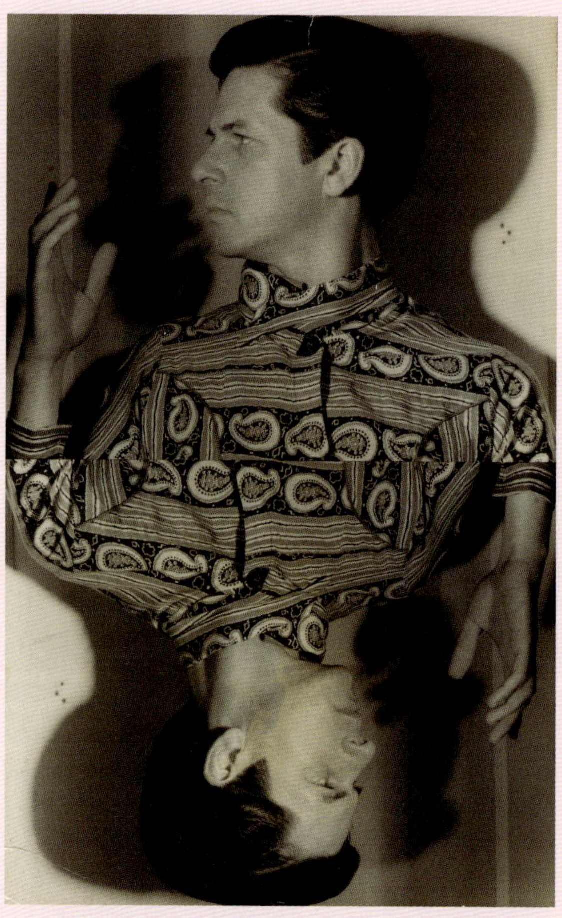

Maya Deren, *Parker Tyler*, c. 1944. Gelatin silver print, 13 3/16 × 8 1/8 in. (33.5 × 20.6 cm)

(1964–67) that drew on Classical aesthetics, and on a distinctive, pulsingly rhythmic practice of editing. The strong influence of Markopoulos's style and technique is evident throughout Owens's films; *Autrefois J'ai Aime Une Femme* even includes a title card thanking his teacher. On Markopoulos's encouragement, Owens moved to New York with him, where the older man introduced Owens to the social world of the arts in Manhattan at one of its most dynamic periods.

Among the important connections Markopoulos made for Owens was getting him a job at Brentano's Bookstore on Fifth Avenue, where Owens worked alongside poet and filmmaker Charles Boultenhouse, in 1967. Owens was eighteen; Boultenhouse was around forty-one and had for many years lived with his partner, the renowned critic Parker Tyler, then sixty-three. With Tyler's apparent consent, Owens and Boultenhouse began a romantic affair, and for years Owens would be a regular visitor to the Tyler-Boultenhouse apartment on Charles Street, one of the social centers of the queer avant-garde in Greenwich Village. Through Boultenhouse, Owens met important figures from the dance world such as Arthur Mitchell and Erick Hawkins; with Tyler, he attended the New York Film Festival. "Charles offered me the world," Owens would later state. "He introduced me to so much."[1] Thus, three gay men representing as many generations came to form an unabashedly untraditional triangle of friendships, linked through both erotic attachment and artistic admiration.

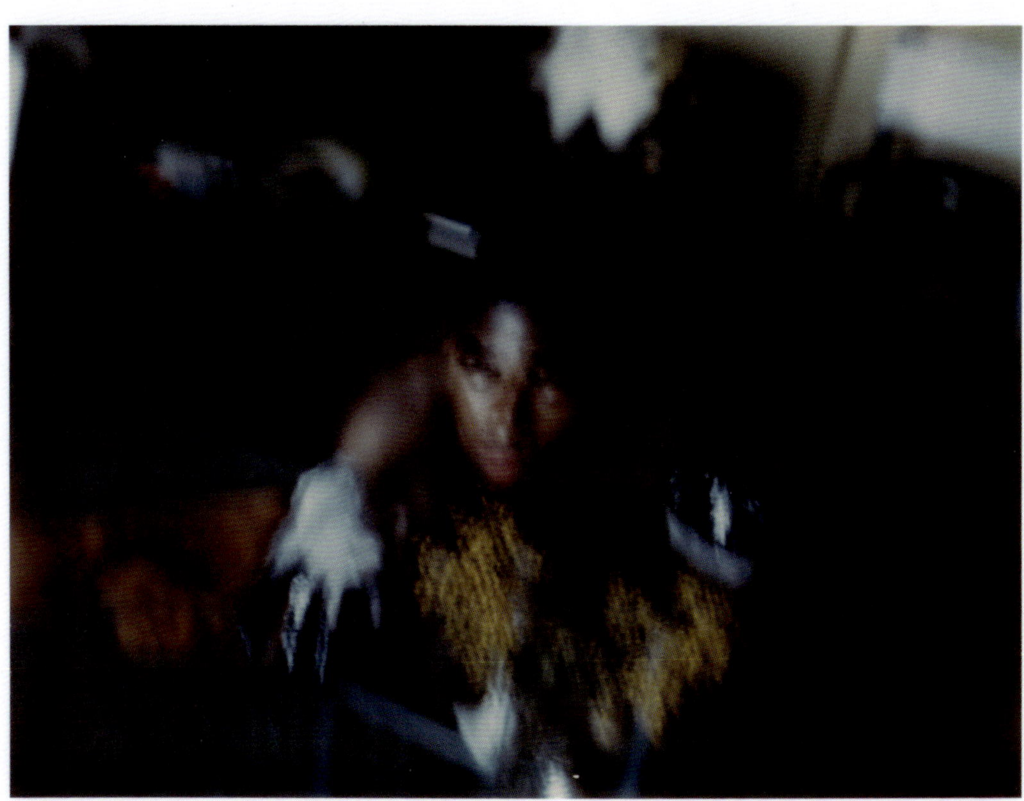

Polaroid of Edward Owens, c. 1966–70

By this time, Tyler was an éminence grise of the avant-garde, with a long reputation as a critic of unusual insight and provocative intellect. Born in 1904 to a New Orleans family who traced their roots back to Thomas Jefferson, Tyler had grown up in Louisiana and Birmingham, Alabama, before spending his teenage years in Chicago and moving with his family to New York City by the late 1920s. A few years later, he penned the candidly homosexual novel *The Young and Evil* with his lifelong friend Charles Henri Ford. Tyler served as an editor for Ford's magazine *View*, one of the primary postwar outlets for Surrealism in the United States; appeared in Deren's film *At Land* (1944); and published a series of influential books on cinema that included *The Hollywood Hallucination* (1944), *Magic and Myth of the Movies* (1947), and *The Three Faces of the Film: The Art, the Dream, the Cult* (1960). He continuously found himself at the forefront of new waves: in the 1950s and '60s, he wrote program notes for Amos Vogel's film society Cinema 16 and contributed theoretical essays to Mekas's journal *Film Culture*; toward the end of the '60s, his writing appeared regularly in *Evergreen Review*, the national magazine of the youth counterculture.

Like Markopoulos, Tyler was impressed by Owens's filmmaking. Both men, along with Boultenhouse and Gregory Battcock, provided positive endorsements for a promotional one-sheet for

Owens's films that was printed in late 1968 or perhaps early 1969. Tyler's cheeky statement reads: "Edward Owens shows in *Tomorrow's Promise* a style pictorially so exciting that the next thing he must do is listen to my advice."[2] This amusingly paternalistic pose is one that Tyler often struck in his criticism, increasingly so as he became a grande dame of the experimental film scene; as far back as 1958, he was already prodding avant-gardists of an earlier generation to produce films that serve as "more than a talented exercise [or] a stimulating blackboard lesson."[3]

In archived letters sent by Owens to Boultenhouse and Tyler, as well as in statements Owens made later in life, Owens expressed a deep emotional investment in Tyler as a mentor figure. In a letter to Boultenhouse postmarked January 1969, written during a trip back to Chicago—perhaps when he filmed footage for *Private Imaginings*—Owens describes his infatuation with film criticism via erotic exaggeration:

Reading articles on cinema—I all but dance in Space—at moments of. . . . Well I'm reading an article of Toby Mussman's & I lay here imagining myself strapped to the bed being gloriously whipped, lashed! by film criticism–ah life! Of course My dear–I read Parker's articles (in that old favorite '58 Film Culture & Battcock's book)[4] Damn dear–I'm about to become distracted—

In a postscript, Owens adds, "Give my heart <u>only</u> bliss to Parker, my . . . Ah! Parker."[5]

Later in 1969, Tyler published *Underground Film: A Critical History,* his longest consideration of experimental cinema, and one of his most controversial books, strongly peppered with admonitions of a new generation's aesthetic excesses and misdirections. Boultenhouse later reported that the book "was sometimes painful for him to write" since, despite Tyler's often withering assessments, "his sympathies were with the young, with the artist, and with the avant-garde."[6] One way of Tyler signaling such sympathies was the inclusion of a filmography, listed chronologically from 1915 to 1969, that included "virtually all key works stressed by the present writer as indicative, and often important, in the passage from avant-garde to Underground film."[7] Owens's *Remembrance* is listed as one of Tyler's five important films of 1968, alongside Storm De Hirsch's *Third Eye Butterfly*, Andy Warhol and Paul Morrissey's *Flesh*, Norman Mailer's *Beyond the Law*, and Frank Simon's *The Queen*. Tyler says nothing more about Owens in *Underground Film*, though perhaps this silence was a blessing, considering the harsh words the author wields against the work of close friends such as Brakhage and Markopoulos.

Owens wrote Tyler from Chicago in February 1970, mentioning that he had pinned the cover of

Underground Film to his wall, and discussed a new film that seems to be *Private Imaginings*:

> I <u>wanted</u> a story, a rather clear, lucid story from the film—but also since most of my footage is "beautiful"—searching, and even "pretty" at times, it was terribly rough and difficult to refrain from senseless (and un-<u>meaningful</u>) caprice and self indulgence—Soon I ran out of footage, seeming "narrative" as opposed to poetic footage, and there was no alternative, it was either stop editing or compromise as little as possible with the richness of my film's nature.[8]

Perhaps notably, "self indulgence" is one of the negative tendencies Tyler calls out in *Underground Film*, referring to the trait as "childish" and "infantile."[9] Owens continues, commenting on his mother's image:

> I must admit that she looks fabulous, gloriously beautiful in this film—maybe near other perfection [. . .] if you could see the quality <u>in</u> the eyes the emotion—the realism on her face—oh! in the small way of seeing it one detects inner sadness.—yet when projected one will see the inner questioning and other things which you can tell me for although I know—I <u>don't</u> know, I'm afraid and unsure but no one will see that side of me unless you do—I want to believe I can't fool you—when you view my work I like to think that you <u>know</u> what I'm after.

"What you think is important to me," Owens concludes. "I appreciate any concerns you show for my work. I need to know someone cares."

After returning to New York later that year, Owens moved back to Chicago for good in 1971. Three years later, a few months before Tyler passed away, Owens wrote him what would be a final letter, addressing him as a "literary giant" and mentioning how excited he was to see a copy of Tyler's newest (and last) study, *The Shadow of an Airplane Climbs the Empire State Building: A World Theory of Film*, displayed at a public library in Chicago.

> I hope someday to justify, through my own film work, the tremendous honor you bestowed upon me by putting my name in published print. I'm proud like a schoolboy touching your book. I pray I can understand you. [. . .] You are Parker Tyler and maybe someday I'll be
> [signed] Edward Owens[10]

But in Chicago, Owens never found the same kind of filmmaking community he has enjoyed in New York, nor anything like the gay white artistic demimonde that had encouraged and inspired him, and he was never able to complete another film. He continued to correspond with Boultenhouse,

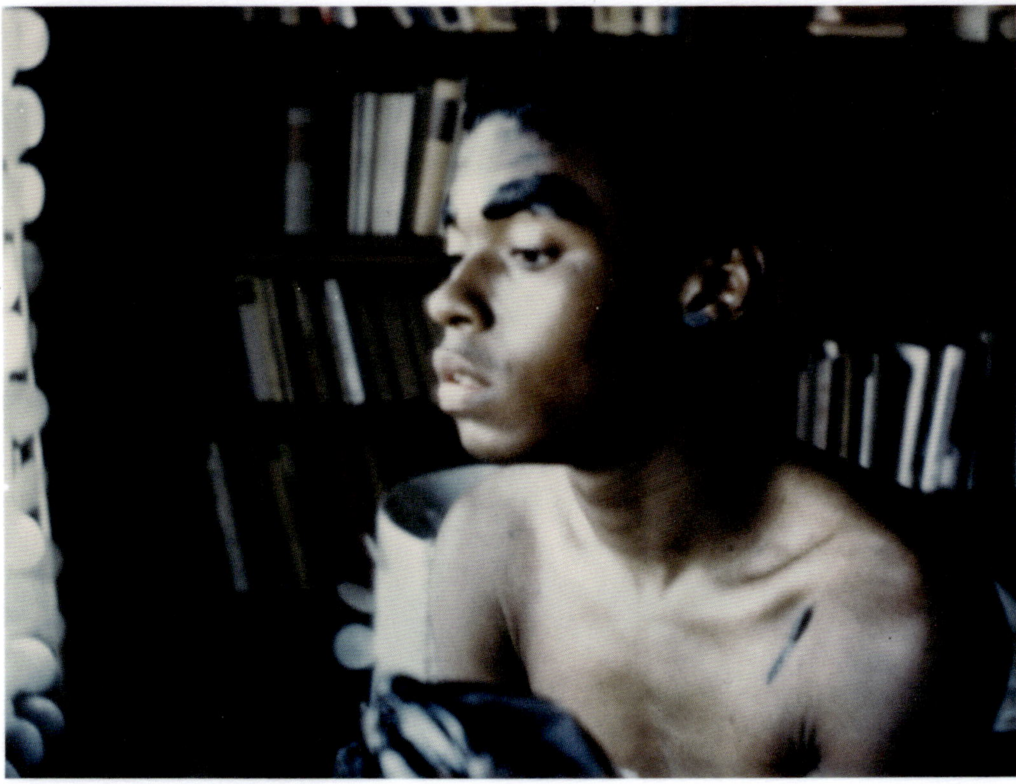

Polaroid of Edward Owens, c. 1966–70

often reminiscing about Tyler, expressing grief for the loss of an admired mentor as well as insecurity about whether Tyler fully reciprocated his friendship. In a typewritten letter to Boultenhouse from 1977, Owens lays out some of the nuances and complexities of a triangulated relationship among men from three generations:

> As thoughtless as it might sound I kept hoping Parker would disappear so that I might have you. However I could, and would never have wished him harm, I also loved him even though I felt a bit of a racial strain in him. I could be wrong. You know [and] I don't. Please never tell me. I cherish him. I do have memories of he and I meeting while you were at work. No matter how desperate I was if Parker cared I could live on one bread stuff for the day of our meeting. [. . .] I loved him too. I even loved the two of you together as much as I prized you for me, alone.[11]

Their correspondence continued until Boultenhouse passed away, in 1994. Owens died at age sixty, in 2009, just as a new generation had begun to rediscover the brilliance of his youth.

NOTES
1   Ed Halter, "In his Own Words: Edward Owens," *Little Joe* 6 (2022): 64–65.
2   "Films by Edw. Owens," Charles Boultenhouse and Parker Tyler Papers, Manuscripts and Archives Division, New York Public Library, Astor, Lenox, and Tilden Foundations; also in the collection of the Film-Makers' Cooperative, New York.
3   Parker Tyler, "A Preface to the Problems of the Experimental Film," original published in *Film Culture* 17 (1958); republished in *Film Culture Reader*, ed. P. Adams Sitney (New York: Praeger, 1970), 51.
4   In 1958, Tyler published two articles in *Film Culture*, "A Preface to the Problems of the Experimental Film" in issue 17 and a piece on Stan Brakhage in issue 18. In 1967, Gregory Battcock's edited collection *The New American Cinema* included Tyler's essay "Is Film Criticism Only Propaganda?," originally published in *Film Culture* 42 (1966). Which article by Mussman may be impossible to know; *New American Cinema* includes two pieces by him, one on Duchamp's *Anemic Cinema* and the other on artist Robert Whitman.
5   Edward Owens to Charles Boultenhouse, January 25, 1969. Boultenhouse and Tyler Papers, New York Public Library.
6   Charles Boultenhouse, "Afterword," in *Underground Film: A Critical History* by Parker Tyler (New York: Da Capo, 1994), 253.
7   Tyler, *Underground Film*, 241.
8   Edward Owens to Parker Tyler, February 24, 1970. Parker Tyler Collection (Manuscript Collection MS-04300), Harry Ransom Center, The University of Texas at Austin.
9   Tyler, *Underground Film*, 24 and 131.
10   Edward Owens to Parker Tyler, January 31, 1974. Boultenhouse and Tyler Papers, New York Public Library.
11   Edward Owens to Charles Boultenhouse, December 3, 1977. Boultenhouse and Tyler Papers, New York Public Library. Later in life, Owens reiterated a sentiment similar to one in his 1977 letter: "Parker was very firm and—well, he was Southern. I don't think he ever forgot the Dixie flag flew once, you know what I mean? That there was a racial divide." See Halter, *Little Joe*, 66. Owens's perceptions might not be surprising given Tyler's Southern heritage and the large generation gap between them. But in Tyler's writing, at least, any such attitude is harder to locate: though race is not a frequent topic for Tyler, he takes a liberal stance when he does mention it, criticizing the Jim Crow color line as "arbitrary," for example, and describing African Americans as an "oppressed minority." See, respectively, Tyler, *The Three Faces of Film* (New York: Thomas Yoseloff, 1960), 112–13; and Tyler, *The Divine Comedy of Pavel Tchelitchew* (New York: Fleet, 1967), 382.

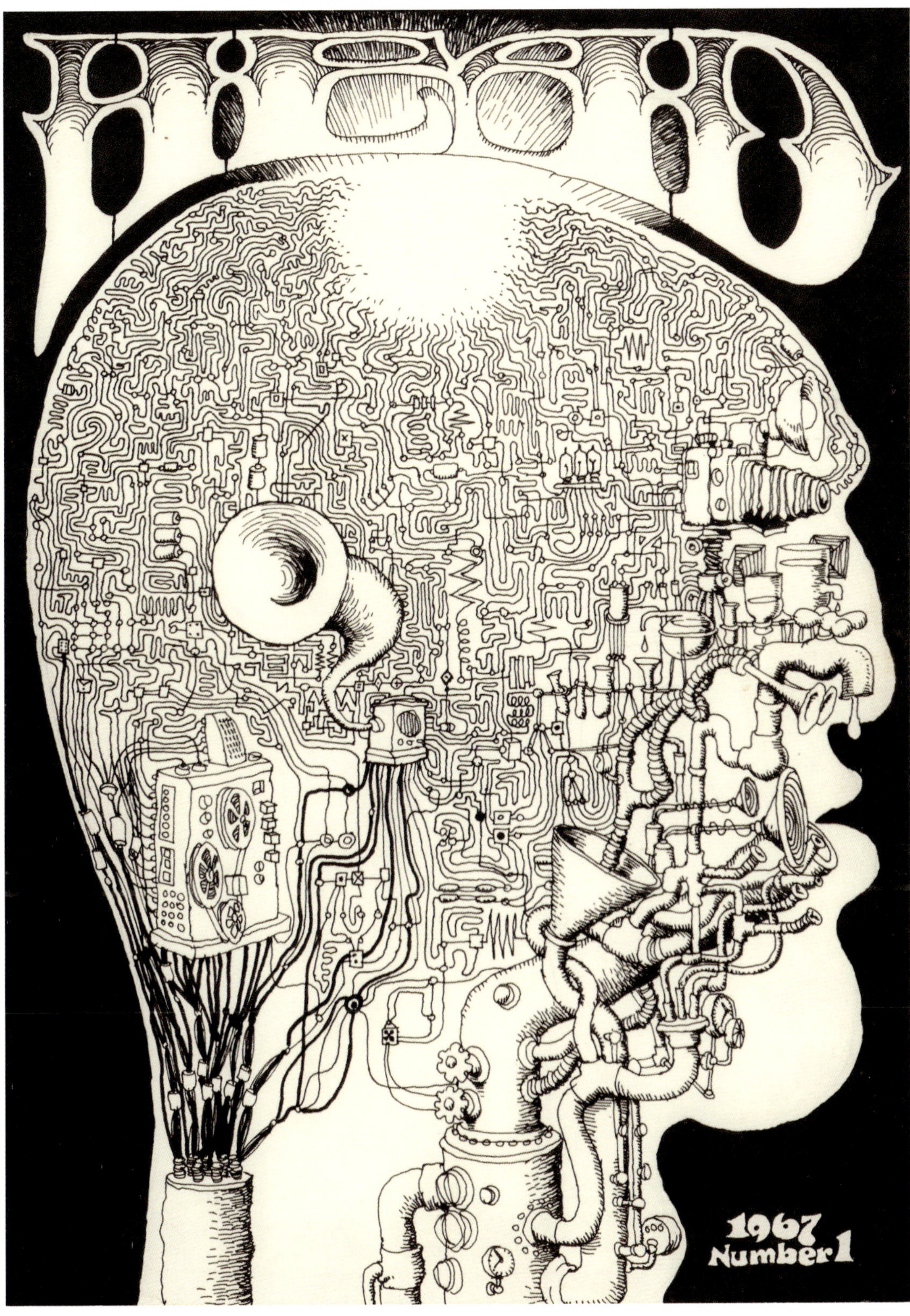

Robert Crumb, *Head #1*, 1967. Ink on paper, 10 × 7 in. (25.4 × 17.8 cm). Collection of Rubén Blades

1968

1968 • Inspired by discussions in a Black studies class at the University of California, Riverside, Ed Bereal establishes the Bodacious Buggerrilla, a political street-theater troupe. Other original members of the group include Larry Broussard, Bobby Farlice, DaShell Hart, Tendai Jordan, Barbara Lewis, and Alyce Smith-Cooper. The Bodacious Buggerrilla performs in the streets of Los Angeles, at arts festivals, and in state penitentiaries from 1968 through the late 1980s.

"Bodacious didn't come out of the whitewashed artist studios, the galleries or the museums of the art world, it was a creation of day laborers, students, janitors, and single-parent mothers," Bereal will later recount. "Bodacious came out of the back alleys, the jazz joints, and the rituals of the black church. . . . It was loud, raucous, raw, and irreverent. It was black guerrilla theater, performance, and radical farce. It was angry, compassionate, loving, and hopeful all rolled into one. . . . We are talking about The Bodacious Buggerrilla who used grotesque caricatures of 'Big Government,' 'Big Business,' 'Uncle Tom,' and the LAPD to examine, critique, and expose the political corruption and atrocities of our time."

January 30, 1968 • North Vietnamese and Communist Viet Cong forces launch a coordinated

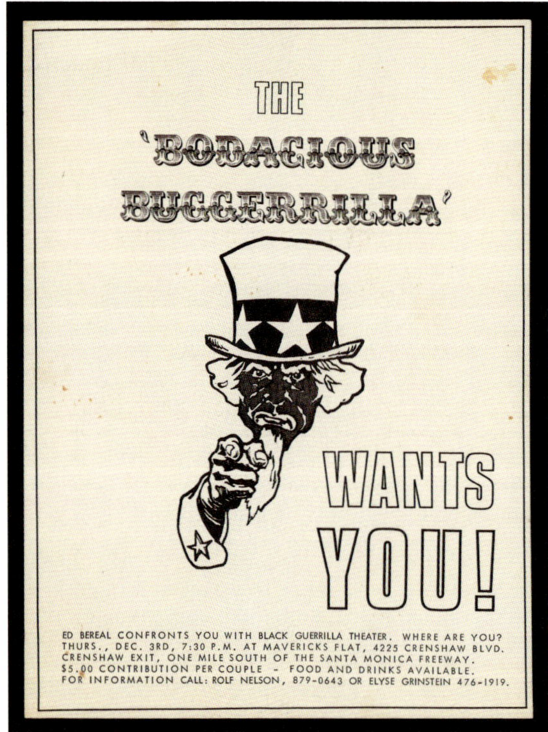

Poster for a performance by Ed Bereal's Bodacious Buggerrilla theater troupe, Los Angeles, 1970

attack against multiple targets during the lunar new year, or Tet holiday. The US and South Vietnamese militaries sustain heavy losses. The Tet Offensive, as it comes to be known, plays an important role in weakening American public support for the war in Vietnam and marks a turning point in the conflict.

February 25, 1968 • Robert Crumb (b. 1943) publishes *Zap* #1 in San Francisco, selling it by hand to bewildered hippies. The comic book takes the familiar mid-century format but strips it of its patriotic superheroes and funny animals, filling the pages instead with psychedelic and psychologically charged imagery. Crumb is the first to conceive of the comic book not simply as a genre but as a medium for any kind of expression. *Zap* includes stories that become instant calling cards: the satire about Crumb's parents and all other squares; "Whiteman," about an upright fellow trying to stay straight in a world on the brink of revolution; and the totemic visual poetry of "Keep On Truckin'."

Crumb is welcomed into the fraternity of hip artists and poets: he is mentioned alongside Wallace Berman as a fellow truth teller, and his art will be reviewed at length the following year by Öyvind Fahlström:

One of the few truly major American artists today is a barely thirty-year-old cartoonist. . . His drawing style is inspired by comics dating back to the thirties, such

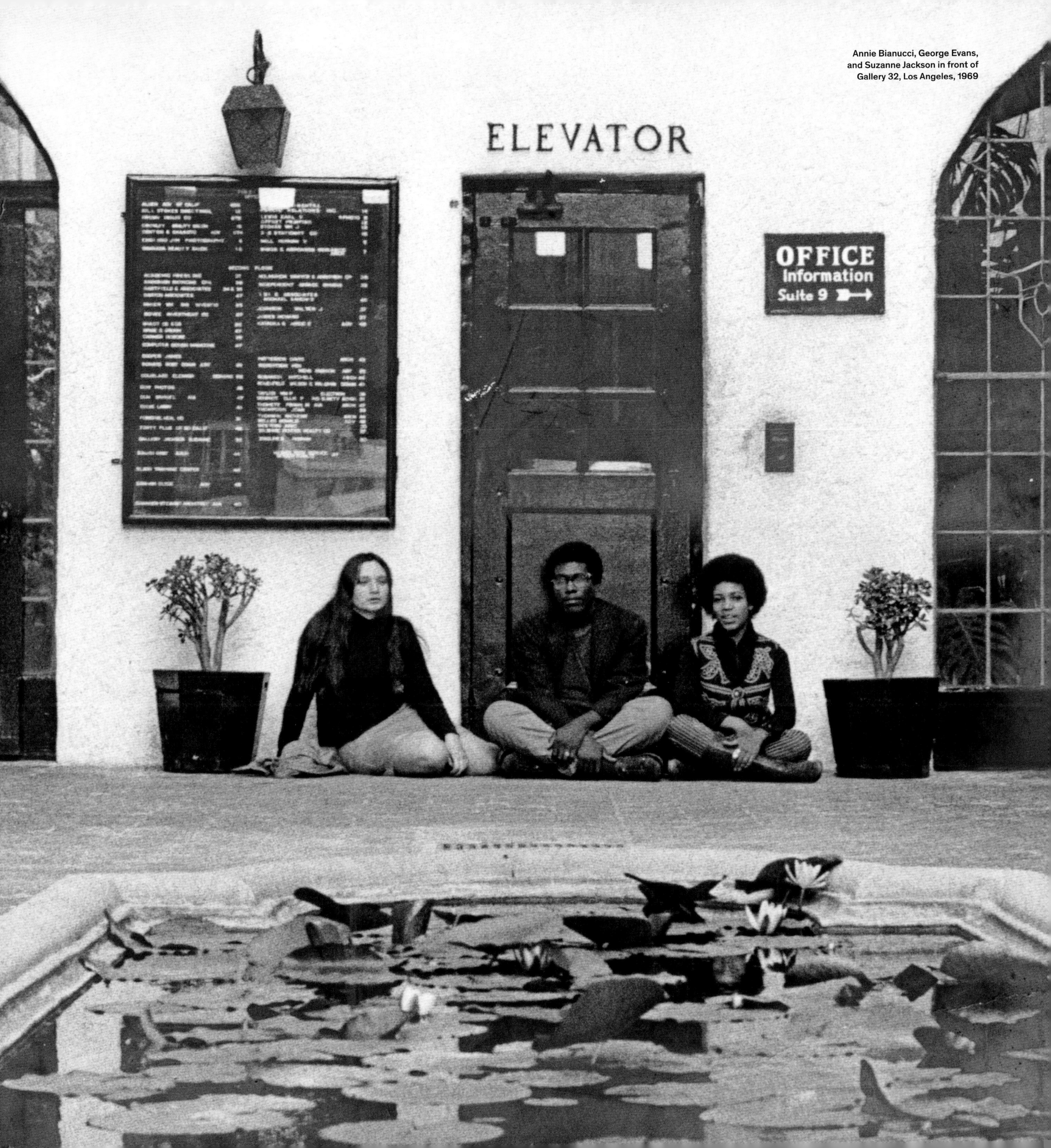

Annie Bianucci, George Evans, and Suzanne Jackson in front of Gallery 32, Los Angeles, 1969

as Popeye, The Katzenjammer Kids and Donald Duck. . . . At the same time, Robert Crumb stake[s] a claim in American underground culture, its values, lifestyle, jargon and myths. But he does not do so . . . in an ornamental, precious form, but rather in a raw and effective popular style. . . . [C]loser study of the drawings' chubby lines reveals a tight precision that cannot be separated from the devastating characterizations.

Crumb had grown up as one of five children in a peripatetic, irreligious household marked by trauma and abuse. His eldest sibling, Charles Jr., keeps the children together by staging elaborate plays and insisting that they produce comic books together. By Crumb's eighteenth birthday, he has written and drawn hundreds of pages of comics and absorbed a vast body of American vernacular culture culled from swap meets and trash bins: old newspapers, Walt Disney, Depression-era record graphics, the comic book *Little Lulu*, political cartoonist Thomas Nast, cosmetics packaging, artist Paul Cadmus, *Playboy*, and everything in between. He initially hopes to become a well-paid satirist like his heroes Jules Feiffer and *Mad* magazine creator Harvey Kurtzman. Instead, a spring 1966 LSD trip changes everything, and the work of his role models, no matter how critical, suddenly seems conventional, yoked too tightly to the very system they claim to be fighting. Crumb digs into his psyche, wipes away a traditional linear, story-based sensibility, and develops his distinctive mode of drawing.

March 5, 1968 • Shigeko Kubota photographs Marcel Duchamp onstage at *Reunion*, a concert in Toronto. Like many other neo-avant-garde artists, Kubota is deeply inspired by Duchamp's challenges to the limits of art itself and by his investigations into the nature of language and representation. At *Reunion*, Duchamp plays chess on a chessboard that activates electronic music; the event is part of a collaboration between Duchamp, S. N. Behrman, John Cage, Teeny Duchamp, Gordon Mumma, and David Tudor. Kubota later transfers her photographs of the event to videotape, incorporating the recording into an interactive video sculpture, *Video Chess* (1968–75), which features footage of Duchamp and Cage playing on an upturned television monitor that supports a transparent chessboard. In the 1970s Kubota will begin a series of video sculptures dedicated to Duchamp that she refers to as *Duchampiana*. These works include *Marcel Duchamp's Grave* (1972–75), *Nude Descending a Staircase* (1976), *Door* (1976–77), and *Meta-Marcel: Window (Snow)* (1976–77).

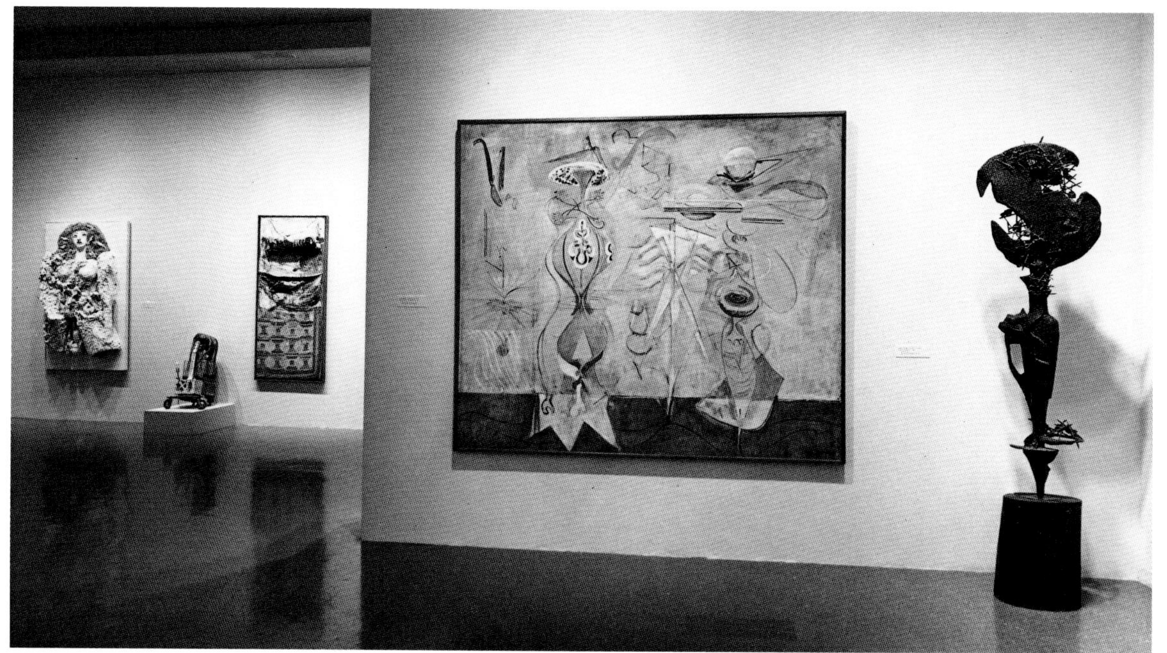

Dada, Surrealism and Their Heritage, The Museum of Modern Art, New York, 1968

March 17–April 21, 1968 • Franklin Williams's solo exhibition is on view at the Crocker Art Museum, Sacramento.

March 27–June 9, 1968 • After two years in development, and following a preview in the September 1966 issue of *Artforum*, the exhibition *Dada, Surrealism and Their Heritage* opens at the Museum of Modern Art, New York (MoMA), later traveling to the Los Angeles County Museum of Art (July 16–September 8) and the Art Institute of Chicago (October 19–December 8). With over three hundred artworks, the exhibition focuses on well-known early twentieth-century artists such as Jean Arp, André Breton, Salvador Dalí, Giorgio de Chirico, Max Ernst, René Magritte, and Yves Tanguy alongside artists considered their contemporary heirs by curator William Rubin, namely Robert Arneson, Jasper Johns, Edward Kienholz, Claes Oldenburg, Niki de Saint Phalle, and H. C. Westermann, among others.

The exhibition is met with jeers from Gene Swenson, who decries what he feels is the curatorial focus on formal tropes rather than the subversive, sexual appeal of Dada and Surrealism. He publishes unsigned advertisements in the *Village Voice* criticizing the show and inviting the public to "join Les Enfants du Parody" outside the "Mausoleum Of Modern Art" during the exhibition's private preview.

Swenson, spinning into his own paranoia, will go on to describe the moment in an October 1, 1968, column for the newspaper *Other Scenes*:

I devised a celebration to honor the Dada and Surrealist artists at the opening of their show on March 25. Although neither Dalí nor Duchamp appreciated my gesture, it had the most Dada effect of emptying the museum at 5:15 p.m. for a bomb search!!! And that evening hundreds and hundreds of police (the Tactical kind), a dozen paddy wagons lined up on fashionable Fifth Avenue, and a wholly Surrealistic atmosphere had been produced by my modest efforts. My group, about 14 strong, danced and sang our incantations to the living spirit of Dada and went home around 10:30, without incident.

Similarly critical, though in a more conventional mode, poet and critic John Ashbery declares in the May 1968 issue of *ARTnews* that the entire world is surreal, and as such, the movement itself is now irrelevant.

Revolutions happen only once. The Surrealist Revolution cannot happen again because it is no longer necessary. We all "grew up Surreal" without even being aware of it. . . . Only, Mr. Rubin ought to remember that not only is he a Surrealist but that Alfred Barr and the trustees of the Museum of Modern Art are too; that all artists now working in America . . . are Surrealists; that Thomas B. Hess, Clement Greenberg and Hilton Kramer are Surrealists; that President Johnson is a Surrealist, that Congress is 95 percent Surrealist and that the entire nation and the world including Vietnam are Surrealist places.

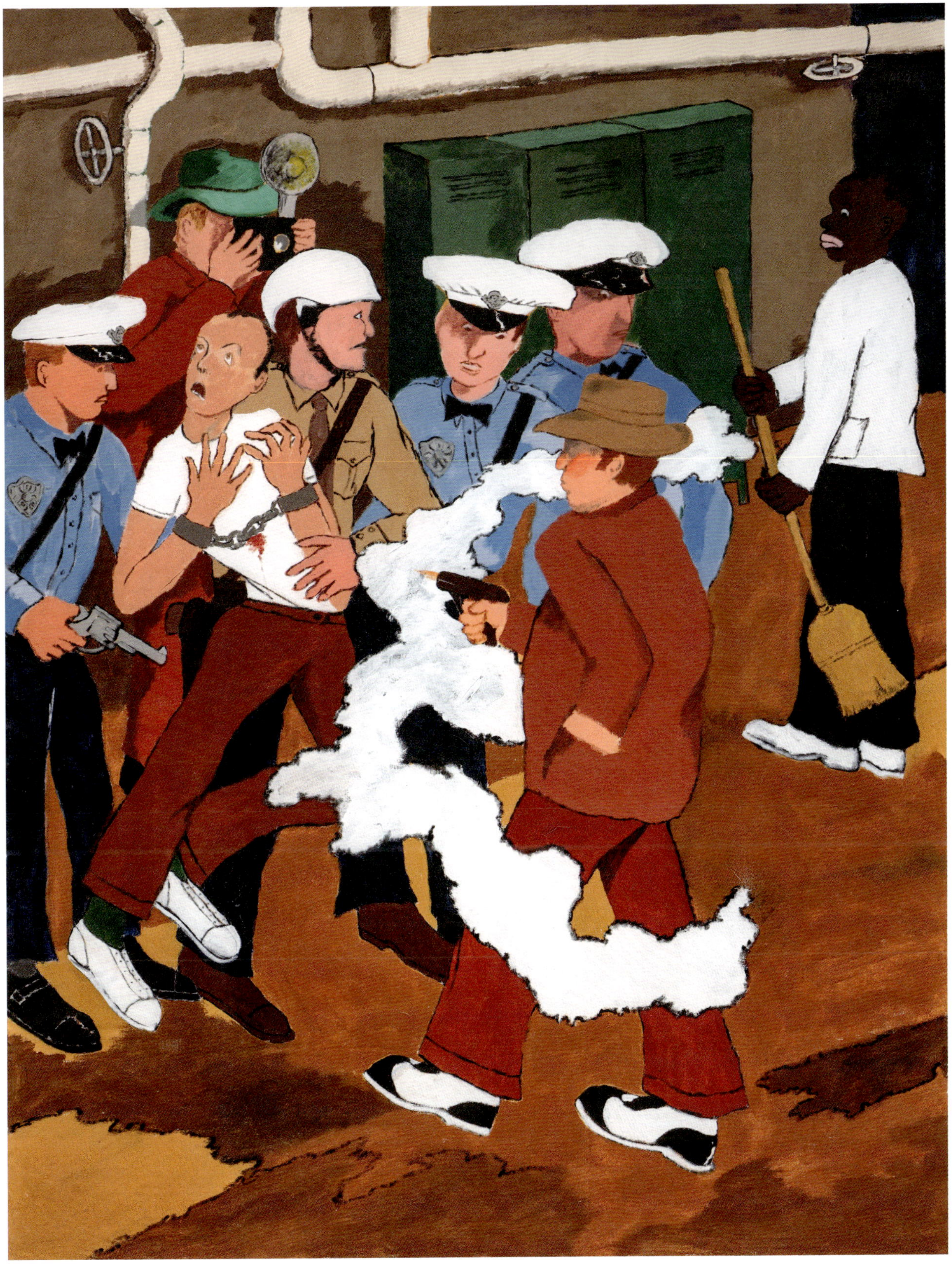

Robert Colescott, *Assassin Down*, 1968–70. Acrylic on linen, 78 ¼ × 58 ¾ in. (198.8 × 149.2 cm). Dallas Museum of Art; TWO x TWO for AIDS and Art Fund 2018.59

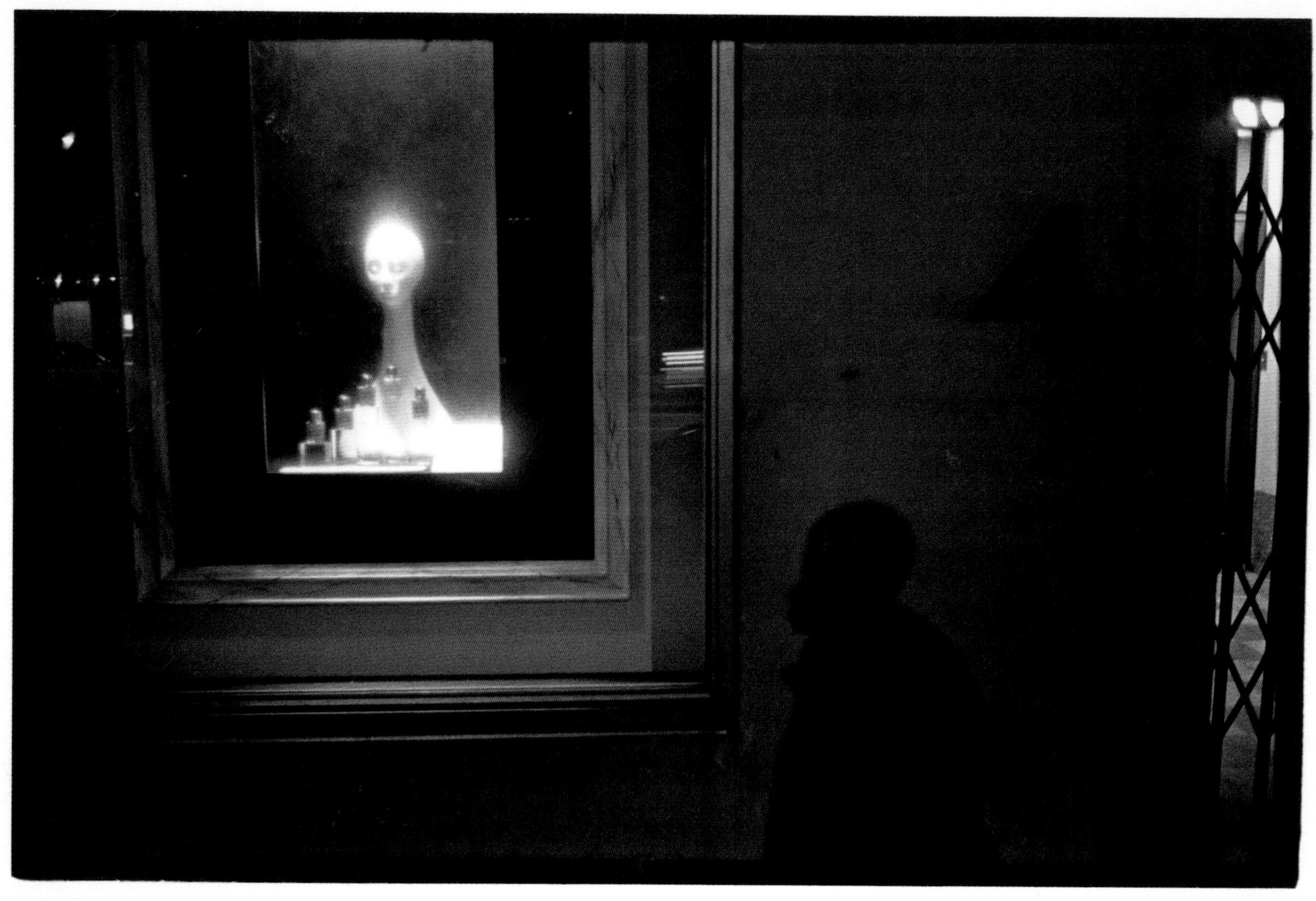

Shawn Walker, *Tiffany's Window on 57th Street, NYC*, c. 1968–72. Gelatin silver print, 4 ¾ × 7 ⅛ in. (12.1 × 17.9 cm). Virginia Museum of Fine Arts, Richmond; National Endowment for the Arts Fund for American Art

1968 • Shawn Walker accompanies Newsreel as a cameraman on a three-month trip to Cuba to film *Isle of Youth*, a documentary about the transformation of the prison Presidio Modelo into a school. Walker later describes the experience as one of the most important political things he has done: "I used to lock myself in my room and I used to read a book by Che Guevara and Mao's Little Red Book to get up to speed to the Cuban kids that would ask you political questions that I didn't know the answer to. . . . It was like taking a crash course in political science." Earlier this same year, Walker travels through the South as a cameraman for the groundbreaking Black public affairs television program *Black Journal*, but when he returns from Cuba, he finds that he has been blacklisted as a radical for his activities, and, unable to find work, he leaves for Guyana.

Walker will later recall the 1960s as the most active time of his artistic career: "The period 1962–1972 was the most intense time of shooting for me. It was a period where a lot of cultural, social and political change took place in Harlem and I found myself at the centre of a lot of it. I consider this time to be a monumental, historical period."

March 30–May 12, 1968 • Barbara Rossi is included in the seventy-first annual *Exhibition of Chicago and Vicinity* at the Art Institute of Chicago, and it is the first time she is associated with other artists referred to as Chicago Imagists. Rossi is awed by the experience. "My work was up next to Ray Yoshida and Suellen Rocca, and one person away from us was Gladys Nilsson," she will later recall. "And I looked at the work and I thought, 'Oh! I would like to know these people!'" Curator and artist Don Baum subsequently invites her to join Roger Brown, Ed Paschke, Christina Ramberg, and Rocca, among others, in the exhibitions *Marriage Chicago Style* and *Chicago Antigua*, both in 1970 at the Hyde Park Art Center.

April 4, 1968 • Martin Luther King Jr. is assassinated while standing on a balcony outside his second-floor room at the Lorraine Motel in Memphis, Tennessee, where he had traveled to join a march supporting striking sanitation workers. News of King's death provokes major outbreaks of protest and racial violence across the United States.

April 5–May 11, 1968 • *Now! Hairy Who Makes You Smell Good* is on view at the Hyde Park Art Center, Chicago, and includes wallpaper, display cases for collections of toys, ephemera, and

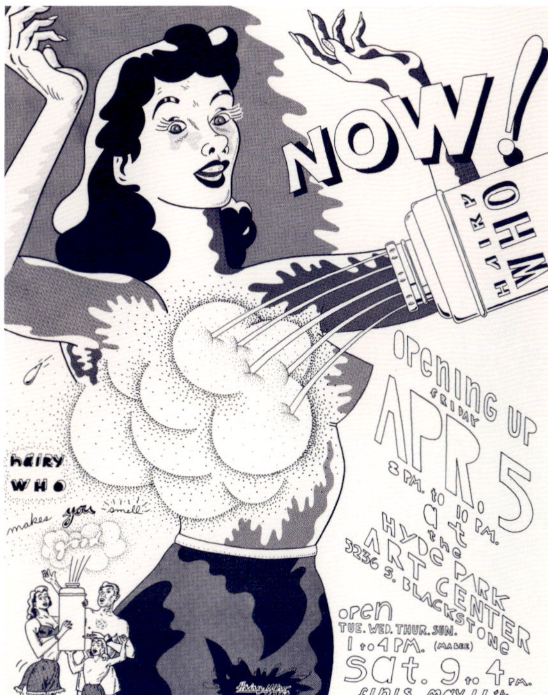

Poster for *Now! Hairy Who Makes You Smell Good*, Hyde Park Art Center, Chicago, 1968

novelties, labels made from found photographs, and other non-art elements. Another Hairy Who exhibition is on view at the San Francisco Art Institute (May 3–29). These two shows are accompanied by the group's third artists' book that is formatted, like the others, as a nonnarrative comic book. Soon after, Gladys Nilsson and Jim Nutt move to California to teach at Sacramento State College, and Karl Wirsum follows them in 1971. In Northern California, their work will influence a generation of mostly female painters who will find inspiration in their fantastical and explicit images.

April 30–June 2, 1968 • Curated by James Monte, the first of two separate Wallace Berman retrospectives is on view at the Los Angeles County Museum of Art. Later this year, Kynaston McShine curates the second exhibition, *Wallace Berman: Verifax Collages*, at the Jewish Museum, New York (September 17–November 17). These shows will be Berman's only museum presentations in his lifetime.

May 1968 • William T. Wiley's solo exhibition at Allan Frumkin Gallery, New York, opens and features for the first time watercolors and constructions the artist has made in New Jersey, where he is living with his family while on sabbatical from the University of California, Davis. The watercolor images are often sketches for sculptures or ideas for future development. One of the constructions in this exhibition is *Movement to Black Ball*

Violence (Homage to Martin Luther King) (1968), a tribute to the slain civil rights leader comprised of a ball of black tape with a halo around it. Wiley includes the following note next to the work:

> This is a piece in progress, those who wish to participate may do so by buying black friction tape and adding it to the ball. Those who wish to participate but feel they don't have the time could buy the tape and then hire people in need of some work to put the tape on for them. After you have added a minimum of 15 feet leave your name. I would like the process to continue for a year or until the anniversary of Mr. King's death. At this time the results of the piece will be donated to an appropriate person or place.

Moved by the work, H. C. Westermann sends Wiley a hollowed-out log as a container for additional rolls of tape, which the artist incorporates into future showings.

Writing in *ARTnews*, John Perreault notes that "Wiley's new work operates out of a sensibility that is completely aware of current esthetic concerns. His work is a reaction to and a denial of these concerns. His own approach, however, is

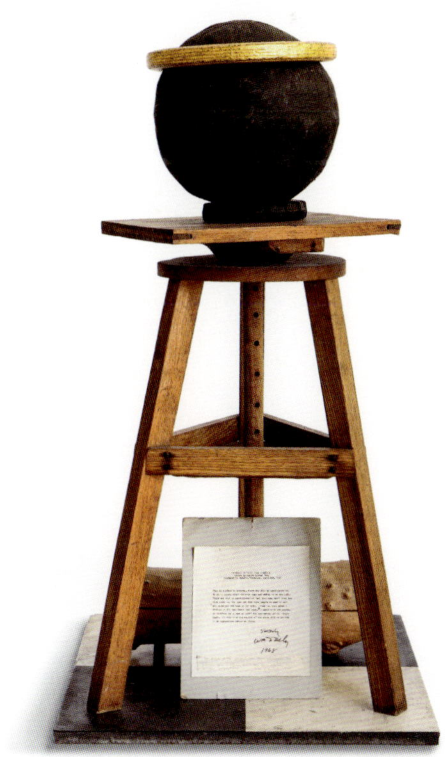

William T. Wiley, *Movement to Black Ball Violence (Homage to Martin Luther King)*, 1968. Black friction tape, wooden stool, gold leaf, rubber tricycle tires, carved wood log by H. C. Westermann, paper and tape on board and linoleum flooring, 50 × 24 × 24 in. (127 × 61 × 61 cm)

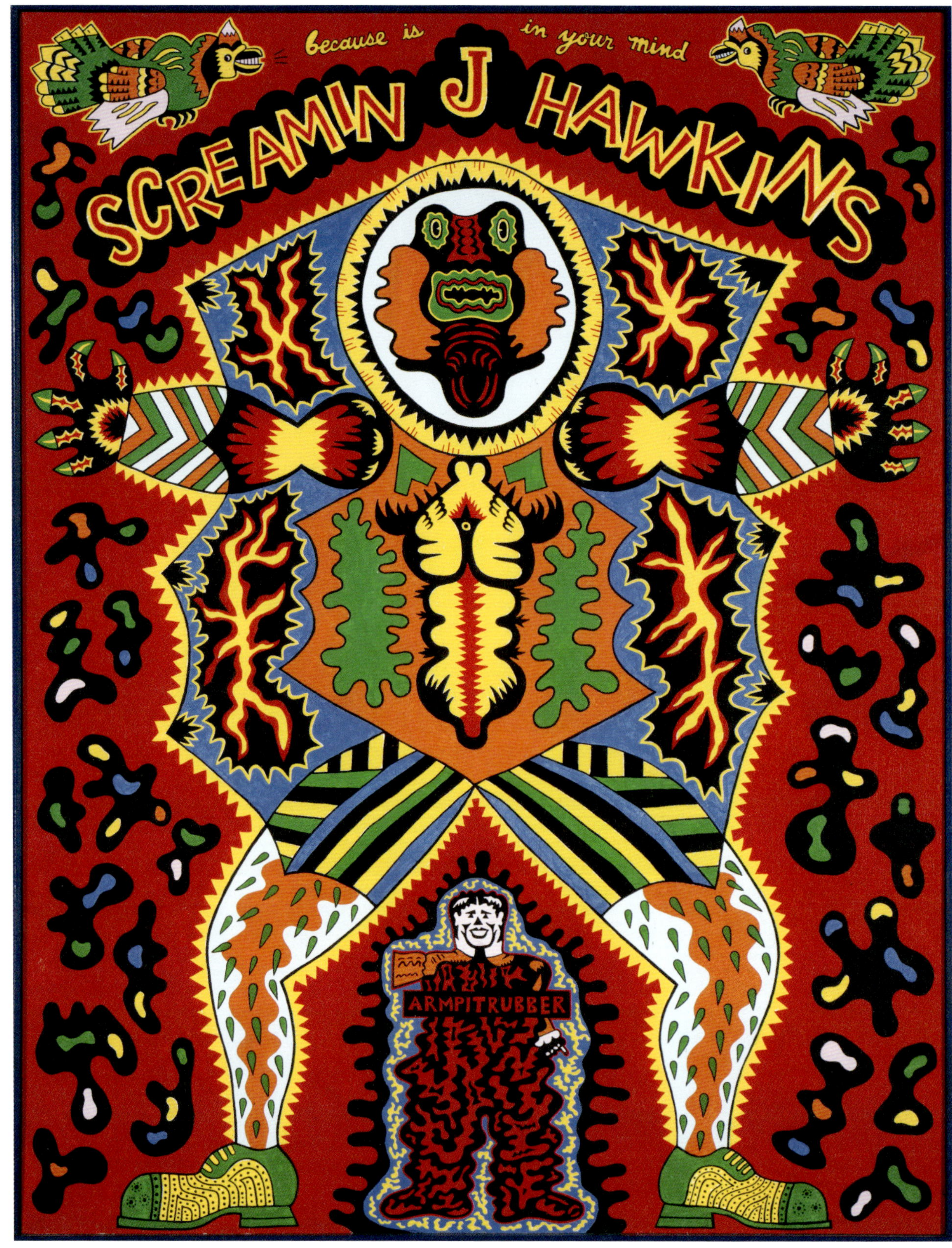

Karl Wirsum, *Screamin' Jay Hawkins*, 1968. Acrylic on canvas, 48 × 36 in. (121.9 × 91.4 cm). Art Institute of Chicago; Mr. and Mrs. Frank G. Logan Purchase Prize Fund 1969.248

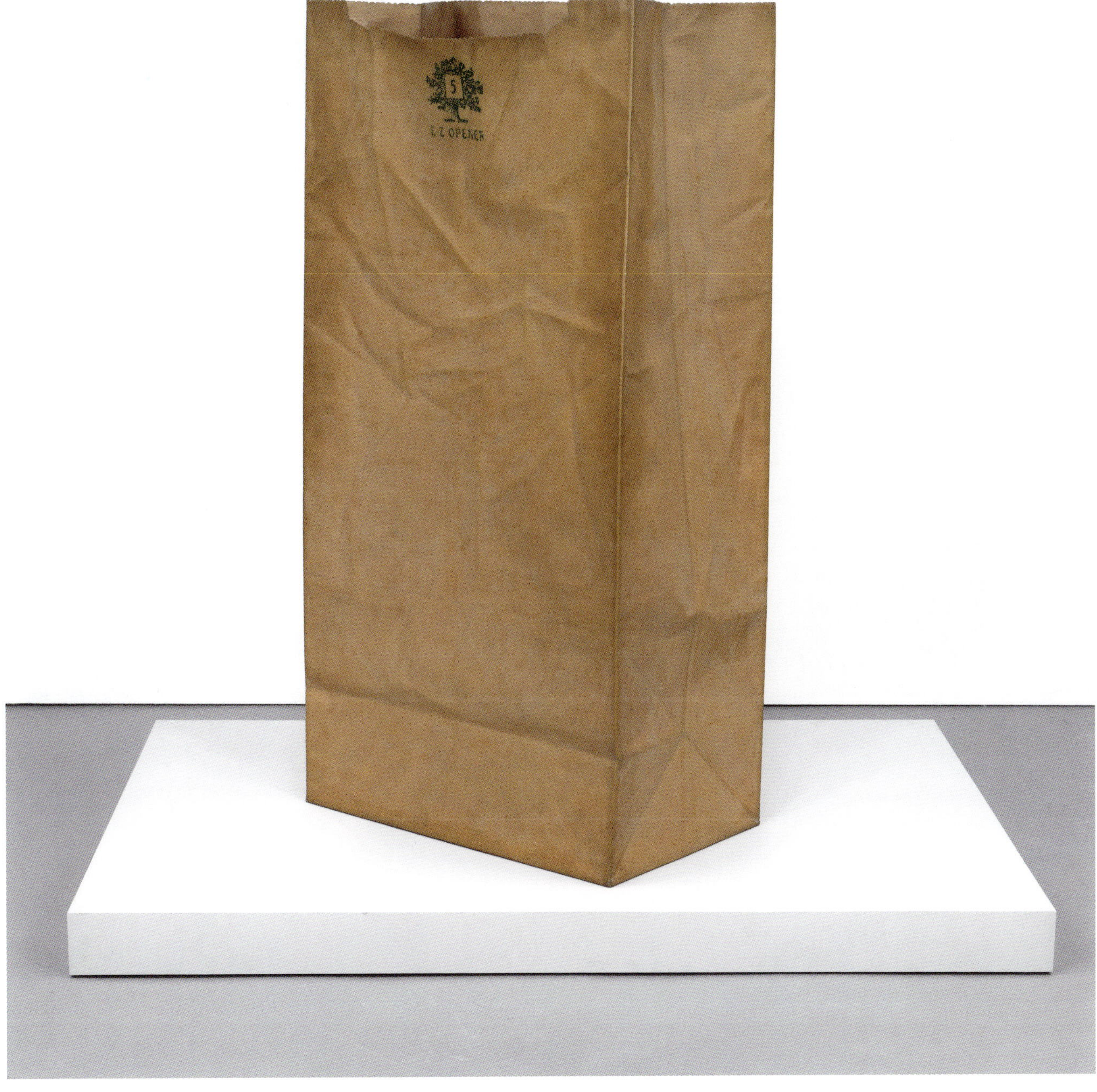

Alex Hay, *Paper Bag*, 1968. Fiberglass, epoxy, paint, and paper, 59 ¼ × 29 ¼ × 17 ¾ in. (150.5 × 74.3 × 45.1 cm). Whitney Museum of American Art, New York; purchase, with funds from the Friends of the Whitney Museum of American Art 69.9

not less sophisticated, but in many regards more sophisticated, more complex, more exciting on its own terms, as well as in its antithetical relationship to the Primary Structures, Minimal, or Stained Canvas, blank strangle-hold upon 'seriousness' and 'modernity.'"

1968 • Barbara Jones-Hogu becomes a founding member of the African Coalition of Black Revolutionary Artists, an artist collective that shares a belief in the importance of visualizing tenets of the Black Power movement, namely, self-determination, unity, and Black pride. The group will rename itself the African Commune of Bad Relevant Artists the following year, keeping the acronym AFRICOBRA. As Jeffrey Donaldson, another founding member, will write of the group, "We strive for images inspired by African people/ experience and images which African people can relate to directly without formal art training and/ or experience. Art for people and not for critics whose peopleness is questionable. We try to create images that appeal to the senses—not to the intellect." Other founding members include Jae and Wadsworth Jarrell and Gerald Williams.

May 31–June 30, 1968 • After two decades as an artist in San Francisco, Jess Collins (1923–2004), who uses the mononym Jess, opens his first museum solo exhibition, *Paste-Ups by Jess*, at the San Francisco Museum of Modern Art. Returning to his childhood love of collage, he calls his works "Paste-Ups," a self-effacing but historically accurate term for the commercial job of creating reproducible art for publication. He deems his own methods no more extravagant than that. For him, "collage was a way of coming to terms with getting a network of images, times, and space and freeze framing them a bit," making new meanings through disjunctions and dialectical tensions: "fusion versus anarchy, logic versus absurdity, layering versus flatness, erotic versus mechanical." Taking what he learns from abstract painters such as Edward Corbett and Clyfford Still, he produces works that defy the narrative tendency of Surrealist collage in favor of an immense field of ideas. In the early 1960s, he finds national recognition for his *Tricky Cad* series of collages made the previous decade, which precede and inspire Pop, queering the ultimate straight comic strip, *Dick Tracy*. As the decade continues, he makes ever more elaborate and metaphysical Paste-Ups, reimagining the tarot, for example, through a mix of source material from across the century, rendering the final image out of time and entirely his own.

A California native, Jess had grown up in Long Beach. In 1943, while still an undergraduate at the

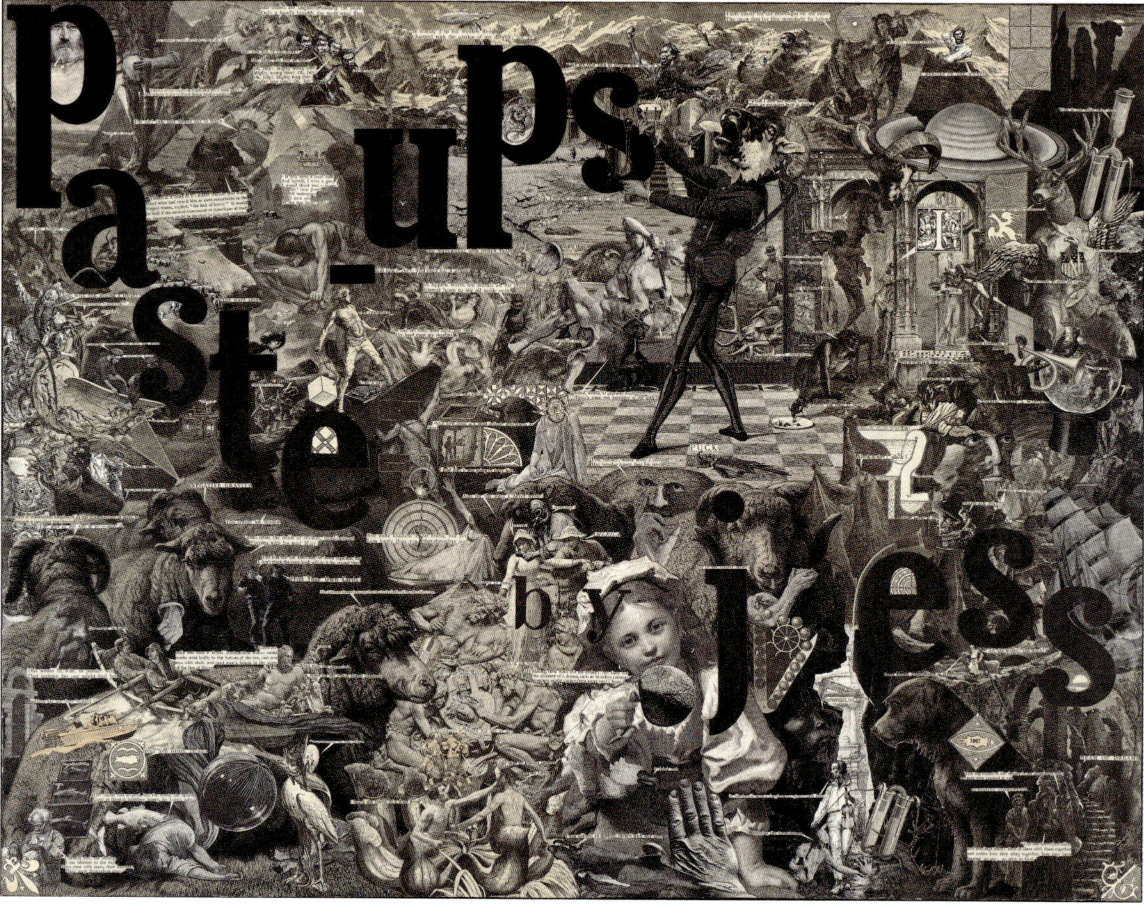

Jess, *Paste-Ups by Jess*, 1967. Collage on paper, 22 × 28 in. (55.9 × 71.1 cm)

California Institute of Technology, he is drafted into the Army Corps of Engineers and assigned to the Manhattan Project in Oak Ridge, Tennessee. The atomic bomb is dropped on Hiroshima, Japan, on August 6, 1945, his twenty-second birthday. After working in plutonium production in Richland, Washington, for a year, Jess leaves his job. Having developed a second life as a self-described "Sunday painter," he moves to the Bay Area to study art at the California School of Fine Arts and embarks on a quest-like exploration of the possibilities of paint, tilting toward fleshy handling and the complex poetics of his beloved James Joyce, whose *Finnegans Wake* he had discovered during his time on the Manhattan Project. In 1950 he meets the poet Robert Duncan, and the following year they move in together, establishing a home in which their lives and art comingle, as they offer a base to the thriving avant-garde culture of the area and cofound King Ubu Gallery with artist Harry Jacobus.

June 1968 • Ching Ho Cheng (1946–1989) graduates with a bachelor of fine arts from the Cooper Union School of Art in New York. Born in Havana, Cuba, Cheng had been raised primarily in Queens, New York, after his father, a Chinese

diplomat before the Communist Revolution of 1949, relocated the family to the United States. As a young artist, he nurtures a growing interest in painting and drawing by participating in local art competitions, and as a teenager spends his summers taking classes at the Art Students League. He enrolls at Cooper Union in 1964, where he studies under members of the abstractionist vanguard, including Op artists Nicholas Krushenick and Richard Anuskiewicz and expressionist painter Michael Goldberg. Living in the East Village, he also becomes enmeshed in the underground music and performance scene, whose many faces and figures—including Warhol superstar Tally Brown and dancer Vali Myers—will become his staunch supporters, collaborators, and, occasionally, lovers. Art school is a struggle for Cheng, however, as he will explain years later in an interview for the *Village Voice*:

> I had been painting since I was six and stopped after I went to art school. They made me feel that it was all pointless. So I stopped and didn't do anything for years. . . . It was a nice school, most of the professors were very hip. They would say to me 'Go home and paint. There is nothing we can teach you. You Continued on page 235

HOW SURREALISM BECAME BLACK

REBECCA ZORACH

In *The Cry of Jazz*, the 1959 film by musician and composer Ed Bland, documentary-style footage of Black life in Chicago alternates with scripted scenes of members of a jazz discussion club, both Black and white, debating the origins of jazz and its connection to Black experience in America. Celebrated today as a trailblazing example of Black avant-garde filmmaking, the film visually layers the constraints of economic hardship with creative lines of flight, in parallel with its Black characters' arguments about jazz form. Intercut throughout are snippets of musical performances by Sun Ra and his Arkestra, who also provide the film's soundtrack. The film's protagonist, Alex, explains that Sun Ra sees his music as "a portrayal of everything the Negro really was, is, and is going to be."[1] Although the idiosyncratic musical genius—who now stands as a key progenitor of Afrofuturism—left Chicago in 1961, he made abundant marks there. His demanding and prodigiously visionary approach to music infused the city's Black and progressive white artworlds with imaginative possibilities.

What happens if we view Sun Ra as the center and not the periphery of Chicago's sense of itself as a surrealist city? Many artists followed in his footsteps. Arkestra percussionist and artist Ayé Aton covered interior walls around Chicago's South Side with futuristic abstract murals. The Art Ensemble of Chicago followed Sun Ra's fantastical and futuristic lead by donning flamboyant costumes and face paint, intertwining their musical performances with poetry and theater, and weaving together past, present, and future to dissolve temporal boundaries. The street-corner speaker KeRa Upra preached cosmic mysteries, interspersing oratory with the sound of his modified kazoo, and painted surrealist allegories of Blackness. And beyond Sun Ra's direct influence, the inspiration offered by Black music unites many of Chicago's key artistic movements in the decades that followed *The Cry of Jazz* and offers critical insight into the broad and deep conjunction of surrealism and Blackness in the city.

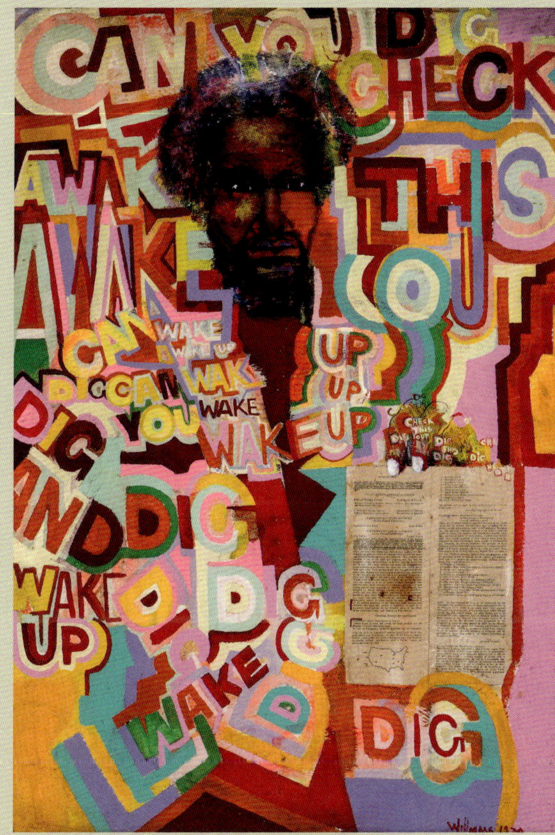

Fig. 1. Gerald Williams, *Wake Up*, 1970. Acrylic on canvas with applied paper, 42 × 28 in. (106.7 × 71.1 cm)

To ask what is "Black" about Chicago surrealism might also require asking what is surrealist about Chicago, or what is *Chicago* about the threads of surrealism woven into the art of the American 1960s. Many artists, both Black and white, who explored surrealist tendencies in their work of the period had a connection to the city, from H. C. Westermann to Benny Andrews to Claes Oldenburg to Nancy Spero to John Outterbridge. They came from Chicago, studied at the Art Institute of Chicago, or in some significant way spent time in the city. In 1987, Chicago gallerist, writer, and curator Katharine Kuh would characterize

the city's artistic styles as surrealist: "Because life is so difficult, in order to live in Chicago you turn to something that is unreal, like surrealism, which is, after all, unreal realism."[2] Artistic culture in the city also vibrated with the legacy of Jean Dubuffet's famous lecture "Anticultural Positions," given at Chicago's Arts Club in 1951. The French artist, promoting a sensibility strongly marked by Surrealism, assailed European "culture" and advanced an everyday aesthetic: "The culture of the Occident is a coat which doesn't fit . . . I think this culture is very much like a dead language, without anything in common with the language spoken in the street."[3]

Artists in Chicago set out to find the artistic language spoken in the street, and the inspiration they found was not limited to social documentary. The street was not just the gritty "real." It was fantastical too, weird and lush and inflected with the expansive genius of Black music. Blackness and the "street" were, of course, not identical, but street life had particular significance in Black Chicago. The intensely crowded housing situation of segregated Bronzeville, the city's historical Black neighborhood, pushed people to conduct their lives outside whenever possible. Art in the form of mural making took shape on the streets, in the company of a broad swath of community members. The artists of AFRICOBRA, a group born partly out of the experience of creating *The Wall of Respect*—a major 1967 mural and public event—also took cues from street life.[4] The "coolade colors" they chose to emphasize in their work came from the fashions they saw people wearing. Artists incorporated graffiti and posters and the remnants of social encounters into their work, as in Gerald Williams's 1970 painting *Wake Up* (fig. 1), into which the artist collaged a political broadside he was handed on the street.

The liveliness of the street resonates in Gwendolyn Brooks's comment that living as she did in Woodlawn, at 63rd and Champlain, if you wanted a poem "you only had to look out of a window. There was material always, walking or running, fighting or screaming or singing."[5] (In this she appears to echo Romare Bearden on living in Harlem: "As a Negro, I do not need to go looking for 'happenings,' the absurd, or the surreal, because I have seen things out of my studio window on 125th Street that neither Dalí nor Beckett nor Ionesco could have thought possible."[6]) Real and imaginary overlapped and overlaid one another. The primarily white artist groups loosely designated "Chicago Imagists," such as the Hairy Who, also worked the street into their freewheeling, pop culture–inspired compositions. Jane Allen and Derek Guthrie discerned an "urban nostalgia" in the Hairy Who artists' taste for "old dime stores, cigar stores, lingerie shops, B movie houses, and girlie shows"—that is, the vernacular culture of ethnic white neighborhoods.[7] Another of their haunts

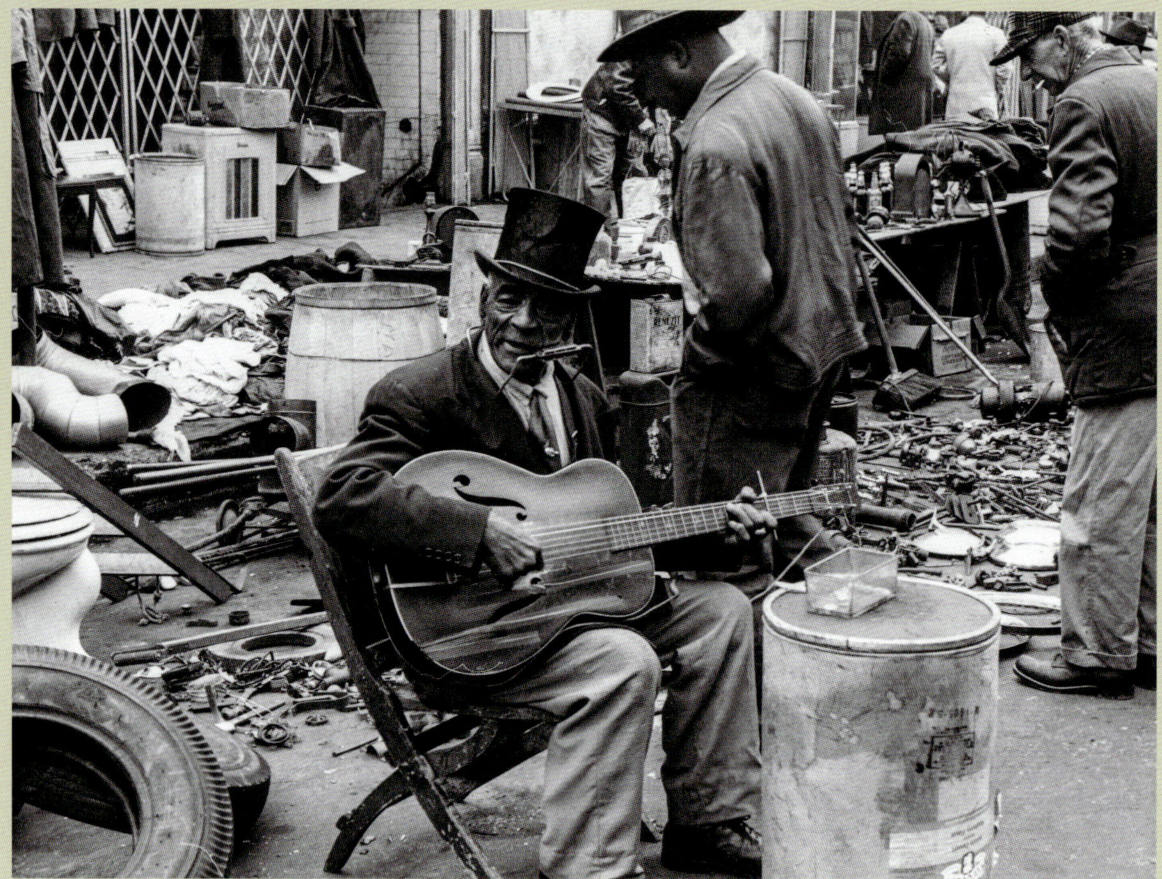

Fig. 2. Daddy Stovepipe performing on Maxwell Street, Chicago, 1959

was the legendary, multicultural Maxwell Street on the near South Side, where they found materials and ideas amid the jumble of discount bulk items and secondhand treasures that were sold informally from pushcarts and from tables on the street (fig. 2). A cultural melting pot since the early twentieth century for immigrant (largely Jewish) and Black communities, Maxwell Street was also the birthplace of the Chicago blues, whose musicians developed its distinctive electrified sound to play over the din of the bustling market. Among the Imagists, Karl Wirsum's devotion to Black music and theatrical expression comes alive in his intricately vibrant *Screamin' Jay Hawkins* (1968; p. 230).

For many artists who identified as surrealist, the influence of Black music extended beyond its singular ability to capture something essential about the modern urban experience: it embraced demands for revolution. Franklin Rosemont and Paul Garon, for example, wrote extensively on the blues and jazz as surrealist artistic modes, which, as members of the Chicago Surrealist Group (founded by Rosemont and others in 1966), they melded with radical politics.[8] Any mere repetition of conventional patterns and forms, a surrealism that could be defined and historicized, was for them the opposite of surrealism's transformative, liberatory, abolitionist energies. For these white artists and writers traversing the political moment of the late 1960s, the essential project

of making the real malleable and the surreal real not only inspired but *obliged* affinity with Black liberation movements, with the insurrection that was alive within Black politico-cultural forms. The first issue of *Surrealist Insurrection*, published by the Chicago Surrealist Group in January 1968, prominently requested donations for the campaign to free Black Panther Party chairman Huey P. Newton from prison.

For their part, Black artists in the 1960s did not necessarily embrace the term *surrealism*, and it wasn't for lack of access to its significance. Black Chicago had a cosmopolitan intellectual culture: *Ebony* and *Jet* magazines had an office in Paris, and Aimé Césaire's work was well known and frequently cited in the pages of their intellectual sibling, *Negro Digest*. Césaire thus offered a ready model for Black surrealism in the realm of poetry. And in an earlier generation of Surrealist-inspired Chicagoans, African American artists—in particular Eldzier Cortor and Frederick D. Jones—held a prominent place. Charles White, who later became famous for his politically engaged social realism, designed a mischievously machinic dancer for a 1937 Chicago Artists Union event poster under the heading "Surrealist Brawl." But by the 1960s there was resistance to any term or movement drawn from European or Euro-American art, a sentiment that is palpable in Romare Bearden's observation, quoted above, about his art as a record of street experience. Perhaps we should

speak not of the surreal, but of the "superreal." In his essay "10 in Search of a Nation," Jeff Donaldson argued that the "superreal" in AFRICOBRA's aesthetic represented "the superreality that is our every day all day thang."[9] The group created "superreal images for SUPERREAL people." Donaldson insisted on the richly layered realness of the superreal: It represented life as lived, not a purely fantastical surreal, but it was intense, vibrating with luminous color, repeated lines, and text layered upon images. It exceeded reality without substituting for it; as the musician James T. (Jimmy) Stewart wrote, Black art "moved with existence."[10] Stewart's suggestion came in an essay about the Black aesthetic in music, in which he argued that music forms "the ideal paradigm of our understanding of the creative process as a movement *with* existence," meaning "to accompany reality, to 'move with it' . . . and not against it, which all, yes *all,* the white cultural art forms do." Superreal art forms added dimensions to the real, intertwining with it, taking off from it into other realms—and returning to engage with it, politically and aesthetically.

With her poems walking down the street, Gwendolyn Brooks's gloss on Bearden's 125th Street almost implies a sense of modesty about her own poetic prowess. But her poetry, never simply "what was there," opens up luxuriant inner lives that stand in rich dissonance with the drab facts of existence, a doubleness that chimes with the "double consciousness" that W. E. B. Du Bois identified in the subjective experience of Black people in the United States. Through its origins in the dominant society's violent constructions of Black identity, double consciousness produces unwarranted pain, but DuBois also suggests that it brings with it the insights of a surreal sense of self: "The Negro is a kind of seventh son, born with a veil, and gifted with second sight in this American world."[11]

Artists fleshed out the notion of second sight with their own conceptions of the intensity of Black life. As in Bearden's work, the layering made possible by collage was one way to express the superreal. Ralph Arnold used collage techniques to accumulate news imagery and to comment on contemporary issues. In Donaldson's *J. D. McClain's Day in Court* (1970; p. 299), the artist collages a newspaper image of the Marin County Courthouse Rebellion of 1970 into a painting that symbolically enhances the events. Donaldson turns the judge in the case into a skeletal figure, adding the word "GLASS," which he used frequently to refer to white supremacy, and "1A" (bedecked with the Stars and Stripes) for the draft status meaning "available for military service," perhaps an allusion to the young age of the event's instigator, seventeen-year-old Jonathan Jackson.[12] In this case, the superreal adds dimension and interpretation to the documentary "real," moving alongside it—movement with existence. The layering of real and unreal in *The Cry of Jazz* serves as a precedent—and in its conclusion it, too, preached revolution.

The urgency of rebellion against the Vietnam War—against the US regime's draft of Black young men in particular—infused Barbara Jones-Hogu's stunning and complex *Mother of Man* (1968; p. 250). Jones-Hogu, a member of AFRICOBRA who trained as a printmaker, developed a figural vocabulary that critiqued US imperialism using skeletons and the American flag, its stripes abstracted into swastikas and its stars into Klan-like hooded white figures. The woodcut, made from a block measuring 24 × 15½ inches, presents a towering skeletal figure who wears a large, deep-black Afro and whose pelvic area contains an abstract coil of white-hot energy. In a contemporaneous description of the work, the artist made clear that she was thinking not only of Black mothers but of their sons, soldiers dying in the Vietnam War: "A black and white woodcut depicting the creator of man. The figure is to symbolize the Black mother's refusal to give up her [offspring] to die for America's racist government. The skeleton is the symbol of the death of many young men who have lost their lives."[13] In the same text, Jones-Hogu approvingly quoted Bearden's rejection of the "surreal."[14] But her work embodies revolutionary political arguments in ways that are symbolic and real, gritty and hallucinatory—a vision of the superreal that addresses the political facts of the late 1960s.

NOTES
1   Ed Bland (director), *The Cry of Jazz* (Chicago: KHTB Productions, 1959), 34 min., 23:25.
2   Katherine Kuh, quote in Avis Berman, "An Interview with Katharine Kuh," *Archives of American Art Journal* 27, no. 3 (1987): 2–36, 13.
3   Jean Dubuffet, "Anticultural Positions" [1951], in *Theories and Documents of Contemporary Art: A Sourcebook of Artists' Writings*, ed. Kristine Stiles and Peter Howard Selz (Berkeley: University of California Press, 1996), 192.
4   On *The Wall of Respect*, see Abdul Alkalimat, Romi Crawford, and Rebecca Zorach, *The Wall of Respect: Public Art and Black Liberation in 1960s Chicago* (Evanston, IL: Northwestern University Press, 2017).
5   Gwendolyn Brooks, *Report from Part One* (Detroit: Broadside Press, 1972), 69.
6   Romare Bearden, quoted in "Art: Uptown," *Time*, Oct. 23, 1964.
7   Jane Allen and Derek Guthrie, "The Tradition," in *The Essential New Art Examiner*, ed. Terri Griffith et al. (DeKalb: Northern Illinois University Press, 2011), 29.
8   Chicago Surrealist Group, *Surrealist Insurrection* 1 (January 1968). Available at Labadie Collection, University of Michigan Library, Ann Arbor, Michigan. Franklin Rosemont, "Black Music & the Surrealist Revolution," *Arsenal: Surrealist Subversion* 3 (1976): 17–27; Paul Garon, "Blues and the Poetry of Revolt," *Arsenal: Surrealist Subversion* 1 (1970): 24–30.
9   Jeff Donaldson, "10 in Search of a Nation," *Black World*, October 1970: 86.
10   Jimmy Stewart, "Introduction to Black Aesthetics in Music," *The Black Aesthetic*, ed. Addison Gayle Jr. (Garden City, NY: Doubleday, 1971), 77–91, 80.
11   W. E. B. Du Bois, *The Souls of Black Folk: Essays and Sketches* (Chicago: A. C. McClurg, 1903), 3.
12   See Rebecca Zorach, *Art for People's Sake: Artists and Community in Black Chicago* (Durham, NC: Duke University Press, 2019), 272. On the use of "GLASS" in Donaldson's work, see Barbara Jones-Hogu (Barbara J. Jones), "Black Imagery: The Black Experience" (master's thesis, Illinois Institute of Technology, June 1970), 19.
13   Jones-Hogu, "Black Imagery," 39–40.
14   Ibid., 13.

should have the freedom to paint whatever you wish. When you do something that makes you happy, bring it back and then we can talk about it.' As a result I spent a lot of time doing nothing.

More impactful than Cheng's formal art education is his reading of the *Tao Te Ching*, which will come to shape his lifelong spiritual practice, and his experimentation with psychedelic drugs; mescaline, in particular, allows him to "[feel] and [see] a great sense of order in everything," an experience he describes as "profoundly religious." In 1969 he begins a series of epic paintings on paper he calls *Psychedelics*: richly colored and highly detailed hallucinogenic meditations on form teeming with wriggling, cell-like shapes, inspired by Taoist philosophy and Cheng's study of Navajo and Hopi artifacts, as well as by Tibetan art and the surrealistic work of Dutch Renaissance painter Hieronymus Bosch. By 1973 these explosive imaginary works are superseded by the minimal, earthly *Gouaches*, which capture everyday objects—matches, lightbulbs, a showerhead—with careful regard for the effects of light and shadow. Across both series of works and regardless of subject matter, Cheng's penchant for looking deeply is made evident. As he will later describe, painting is not simply a means of recording but a "way of seeing. . . . It is a very personal view of the universe. . . . It's energy."

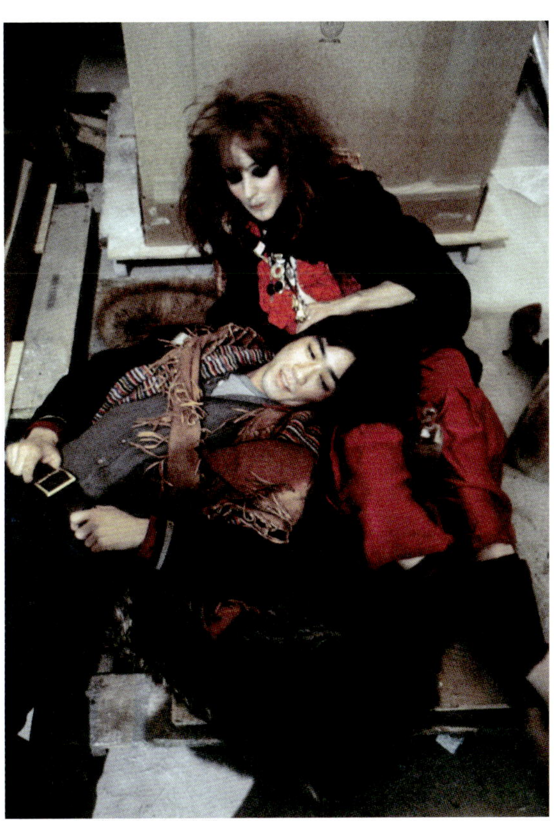
Ching Ho Cheng and Vali Myers, New York, c. 1970

Cheng will live and work between New York and various European locales throughout the mid-1970s, culminating in his first solo show, in early 1976 at Kunsthandel K276 in Amsterdam. That same year, he will return to New York and take up residence in the iconic Chelsea Hotel, thriving amid the vibrant art and club scene in the West Village. There he maintains both an apartment and studio space until his death from AIDS-related causes in 1989.

———

June 1, 1968 • The first solo screening in New York of Edward Owens's films is organized by Jonas Mekas at the Film-Makers' Cinematheque in SoHo. The program description reads, "First New York One Man Show: Films by Edward Owens: *J'Ai Aimé une Femme*; *Remembrance: A Portrait Study*; *Tomorrow's Promise*; *Avalon Lee and Patrick Sullivan*; Also New Film Work in Progress and Live Dance/Film Piece."

———

June 4, 1968 • Following his speech the night he wins the California Democratic presidential primary, Senator Robert F. Kennedy is assassinated shortly after midnight at the Ambassador Hotel in Los Angeles.

———

1968 • Martha Rosler moves to San Diego and begins participating in the vital feminist arts scene of Southern California, where Judy Chicago and Miriam Schapiro will soon establish the Feminist Arts Program at the California Institute of the Arts, Valencia. While earning her master of fine arts from the University of California, San Diego, Rosler initiates a series of feminist performances and, soon, videos. "If I had moved to California as a semilapsed painter but also a maker of photographs, photomontages, and a bit of sculpture, I soon became a performance artist on the understanding that performance could be taken to include a spectrum of actions, stretching from guerrilla hit-and-run activities to temporary or even long-term installation," she later writes.

———

Summer 1968 • Gene Youngblood interviews Jordan Belson for the book that will become *Expanded Cinema* (1970). Youngblood, a twenty-six-year-old film critic for the *Los Angeles Free Press*, finds Belson, forty-two, in his small North Beach studio. Youngblood describes a scene of monastic seclusion, a sparsely furnished apartment with a small, six-seat theater: "The little room was dark as a planetarium. I sat and waited. For a long time there was no movement, no sound. Then a projector started up and a beam streaked forward from

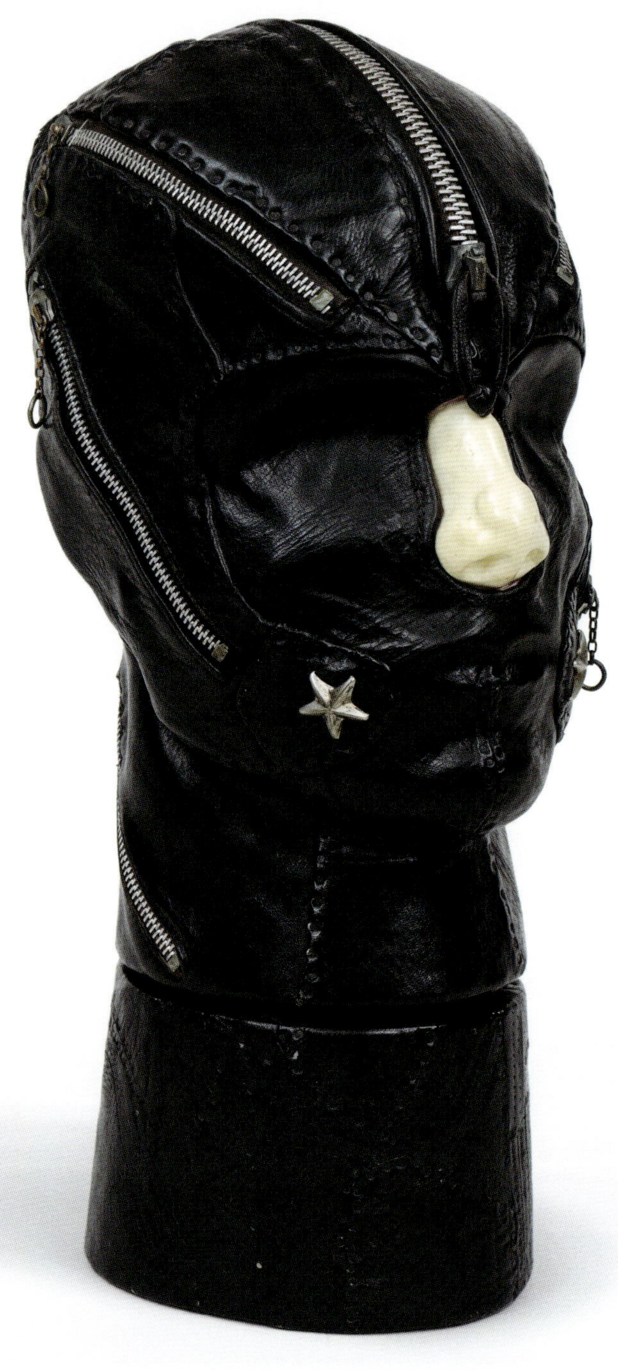

Nancy Grossman, *Head*, 1968. Wood, leather, metal zippers, paint, and metal nails, 16 ¼ × 6 ⅝ × 8 ¹⁵⁄₁₆ in. (41.3 × 16.8 × 22.7 cm) overall; sculpture, 12 × 7 ¾ × 8 ¾ in. (30.5 × 19.7 × 22.2 cm); base, 4 × 5 ¼ × 5 ¾ in. (10.2 × 13.3 × 14.6 cm). Whitney Museum of American Art, New York; purchase with funds from the Howard and Jean Lipman Foundation, Inc. 68.81a–b

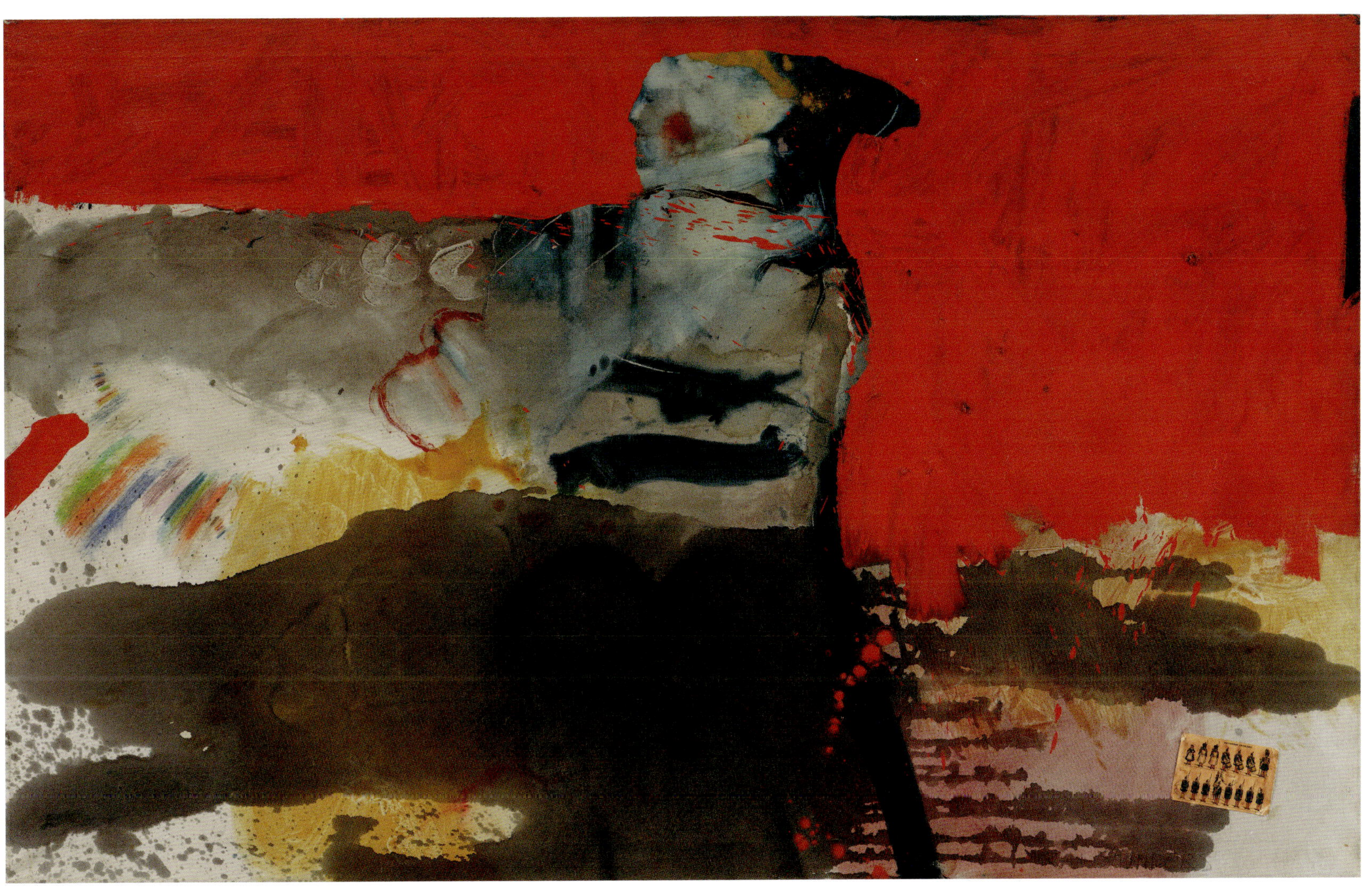

Raymond Saunders, *Untitled*, 1968. Oil on canvas with collage, 52 × 81 in. (132.1 × 205.7 cm). Andrew Kreps Gallery, New York

the back of my mind." The filmmaker Bruce Baillie will recall that Belson "maintained an aloof distance from the mid-sixties explosion of expanded cinema events, insisting that his films be showed separately in highly controlled situations and refusing to join the Canyon Co-Op or to participate in hippie rituals." This aloofness is consistent with the antisocial ideology of the earlier Beat counterculture and with the deeply private character of its vision of transcendence—a defeat of alienation not at the level of social relations or material conditions but in the consciousness of the individual. "The Cosmic Cinema of Jordan Belson" is the most widely reproduced chapter of Youngblood's wildly popular survey of 1960s multimedia art.

1968 • Following several years of protest against the war in Vietnam, Claes Oldenburg is commissioned by a group of students, faculty, and alumni to create an outdoor sculpture at Yale University. The next year he collaborates with students and realizes *Lipstick (Ascending) on Caterpillar Tracks*. It is a prodigiously phallic, inflatable, pulsating red tube rising from a military tank that has been rolled onto campus and situated near an existing World War I memorial. According to the writer David Shapiro, "*Lipstick* was constructed by a team of students . . . and raised like the flag of Iwo Jima: a tank-cum-lipstick."

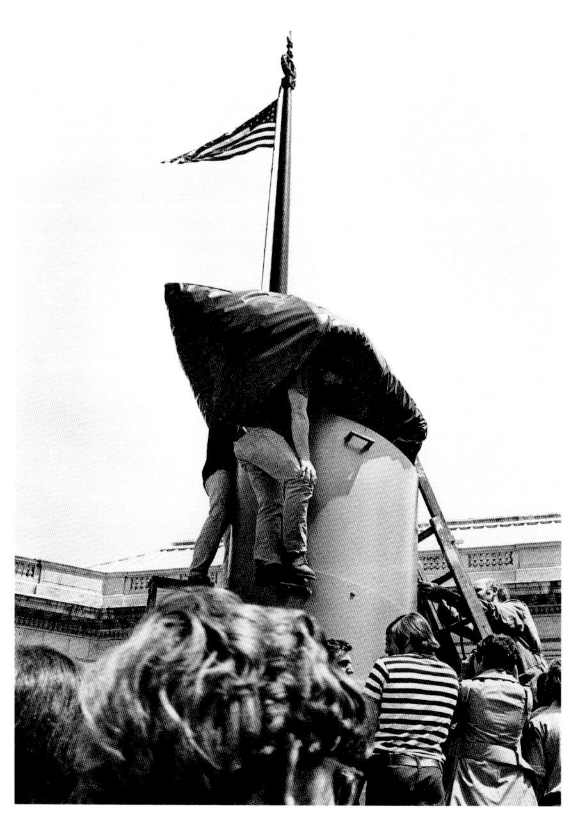

Students raising Claes Oldenburg's *Lipstick (Ascending) on Caterpillar Tracks* (1969) at Yale University, New Haven, CT, 1969

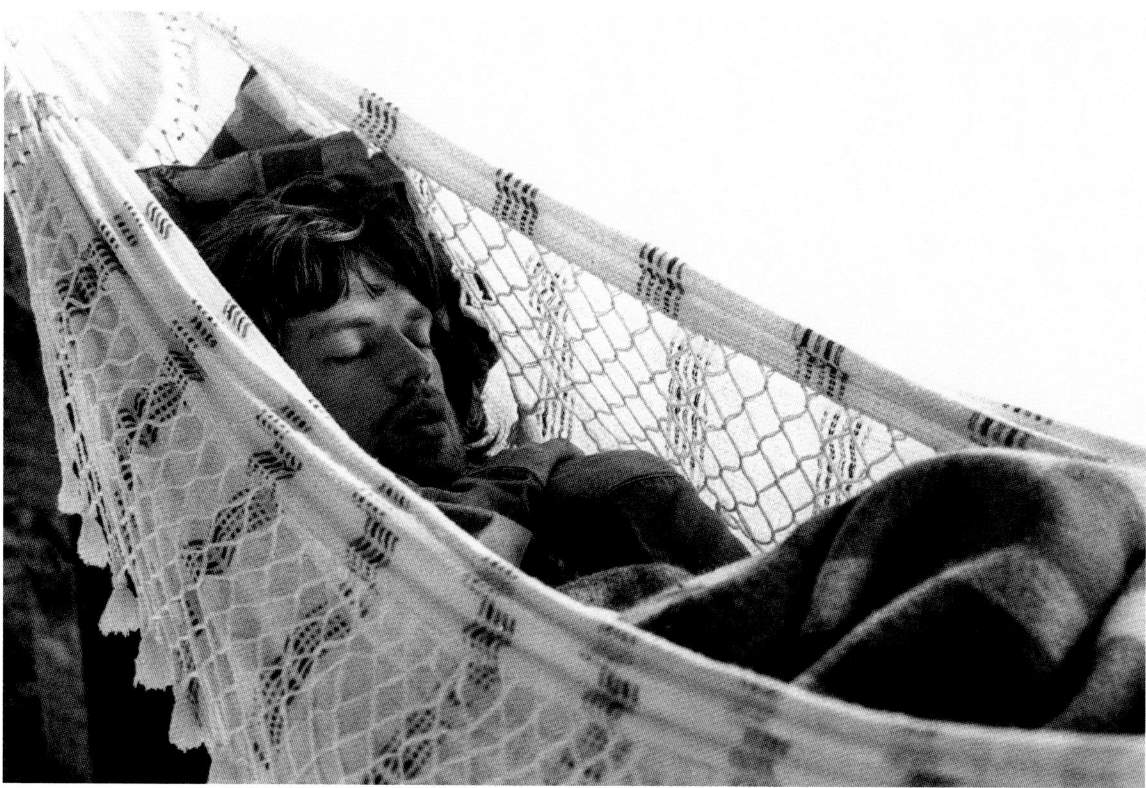

Adger Cowans, *Mick Jagger, Brazil*, 1968–69. Gelatin silver print, 8 × 11 ½ in. (20.3 × 29.2 cm)

Summer 1968 • Adger Cowans travels to Brazil and spends nearly a year in the country, calling the trip a "creative breakthrough." Cowans is initially sent to Brazil by *Esquire* to take photographs for a feature on the revolutionary vanguard of underground filmmakers, but, unfortunately, the project falls through. He decides to stay and befriends Mick Jagger, whom he meets by chance at a hotel in Rio de Janeiro. The pair travel to Salvador de Bahia, ultimately shooting over a dozen rolls of film. The apartment that Cowans rents on Afonso Celso Street in Salvador de Bahia becomes a gathering place for local musicians such as Caetano Veloso and Gilberto Gil. Cowans also befriends local visual artists, including the Afro-Brazilian artist Emanoel Araújo, who teaches him to etch. For Cowans, the culture "opened up a whole new thing for me because of the Afro-Brazilian thing." His practice expands as he increasingly thinks of himself as an "imagist" rather than strictly a photographer, using different techniques—photography, painting, printmaking—to create images. Already a founding member of the Kamoinge Workshop for photographers, Cowans will join the new Chicago-based movement AFRICOBRA (African Commune of Bad Relevant Artists), which provides an outlet for his non-photographic work.

July 1968 • The first issue of *NEWSPAPER* appears, a broadsheet publication that is eclectic and wordless and illustrates a group of artists networked together by Peter Hujar. Spanning fourteen issues between now and 1971, it will include the work of Diane Arbus, Yayoi Kusama, Joseph Raffaele, Lucas Samaras, William Schwedler, and William T. Wiley. It is produced by Hujar in collaboration with his then partner Steve Lawrence as well as Andrew Ullrick.

August 2–29, 1968 • In *Recent Paintings*, an exhibition curated by Phil Linhares at the San Francisco Art Institute, Peter Saul debuts his Vietnam paintings in the Bay Area.

August 26–29, 1968 • Violence and chaos break out in Chicago as the Democratic National Convention meets to select a candidate for president. Inside the convention center, there is infighting among Democrats and pointed animosity toward the press. Outside in the streets, antiwar activists and revolutionaries from diverse groups stage protests and often clash with the twenty thousand Chicago police officers and Illinois National Guardsmen that Mayor Richard Daley has assembled in a show of force. One particularly brutal melee in front of the Conrad Hotel, where many of the delegates are staying, is broadcast live, bringing the violent unrest into living rooms across the country.

Artists' reactions to this vision of a police state are swift and take many forms. Claes Oldenburg,

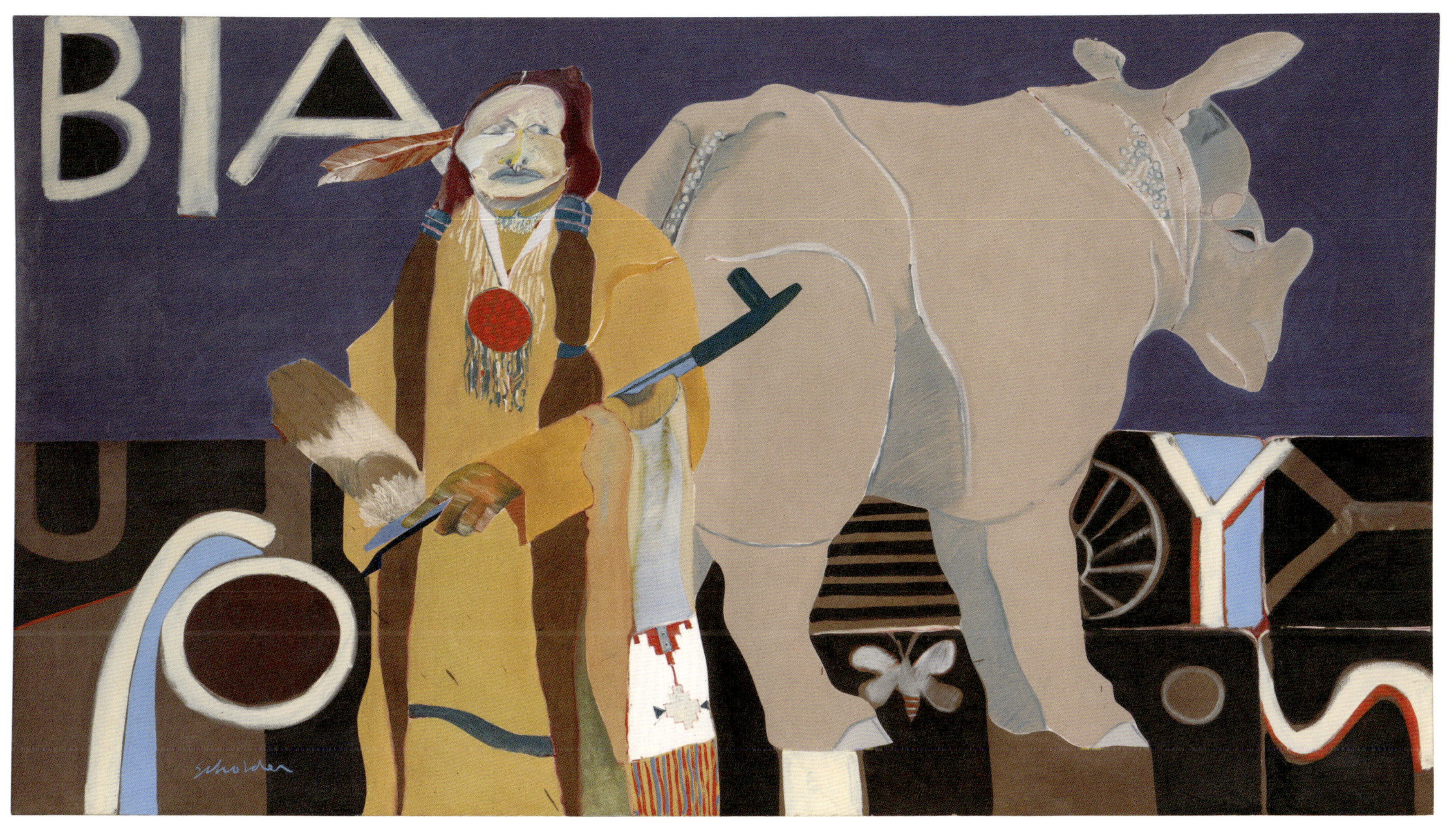

Fritz Scholder, *Indian and Rhinoceros*, 1968. Oil on canvas, 68 × 120 in. (172.7 × 304.8 cm). National Museum of the American Indian, Smithsonian Institution; purchase 26/8066

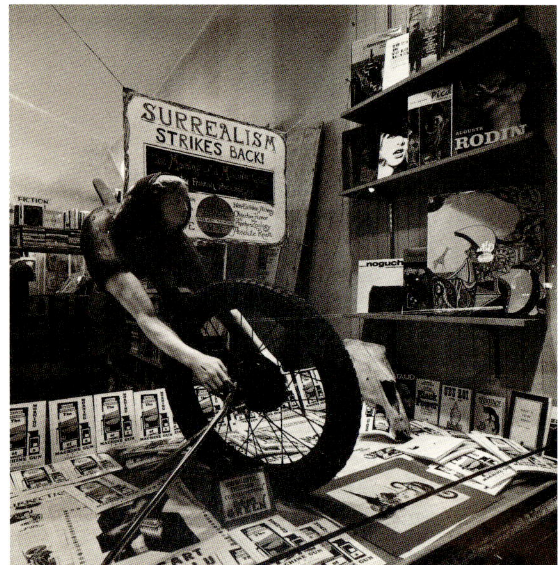

Window display featuring a found-object sculpture by Robert Green, Barbara's Bookstore, Chicago, 1968

who is assaulted by police during the protests, asks dealer Richard Feigen to cancel the artist's upcoming show; instead, Feigen and ten other Chicago gallerists organize exhibitions in protest of Mayor Daley. Over fifty artists from across the country also call for a two-year boycott of Chicago, to end at the conclusion of the mayor's term in 1970. "As painters and sculptors, we know that art cannot exist where repression and brutality are tolerated," the artists announce in their statement, parts of which are published in the *New York Times*. As a result, James Ernst, the son of Surrealist Max Ernst, cancels a show of paintings at the Arts Club of Chicago, Tony Smith terminates a commission for a sculpture on the University of Illinois's Chicago campus, and Barnett Newman asks for his work to be withdrawn from the Art Institute's presentation of *Dada, Surrealism, and Their Heritage.*

The presentation in Chicago of the Museum of Modern Art exhibition is also protested for other reasons. Franklin and Penelope Rosemont, founders of the Chicago Surrealist Group, organize a counter exhibition that opens October 27 and distribute flyers on the steps of the Art Institute to advertise the show. Works by members of the group—formed in 1966 after the Rosemonts had met with André Breton, Ted Joans, Man Ray, and other Surrealists—are hung at Gallery Bugs Bunny in the Old Town neighborhood, highlighting the collective's belief that Surrealism is a movement that can unite art and politics for revolutionary aims.

September 17–November 17, 1968 • Wallace Berman exhibits his Verifax collages at the Jewish Museum, New York.

October 1968 • The fifth edition of *S.M.S. (Shit Must Stop)* is published and includes contributions from William Copley, Bruce Nauman, Yoko Ono, Mel Ramos, William Schwedler, Lawrence Weiner, and others. The Fluxus-style artist-portfolio publication series is produced by Copley and Dimitri Petrov, both self-fashioned surrealists, who intend for the collaborative, proto-Conceptual project to be a direct challenge to the prevailing museum and gallery system, and a protest to the inability of artists to assign value to their own works. In this way, two thousand copies of each issue are produced, and they largely go out unsigned. Previous issues of the intermedia and intergenerational publication have featured such prominent figures as John Cage, Bruce Conner, Marcel Duchamp, Meret Oppenheim, Man Ray, and H. C. Westermann.

October 15–November 24, 1968 • *Assemblage in California: Works from the Late '50s and Early '60s* is on view at University of California, Irvine's art gallery and includes works by Wallace Berman, Bruce Conner, and Edward Kienholz. Curated by John Coplans, it is one of the first exhibitions to examine its titular phenomenon.

October 31–November 3, 1968 • The Museum of Modern Art, New York, hosts a fundraising exhibition for the Southern Christian Leadership Conference. *In Honor of Dr. Martin Luther King Jr.* is often characterized as the first large-scale showing of Black contemporary artists at the museum, and King's widow attends the opening. A

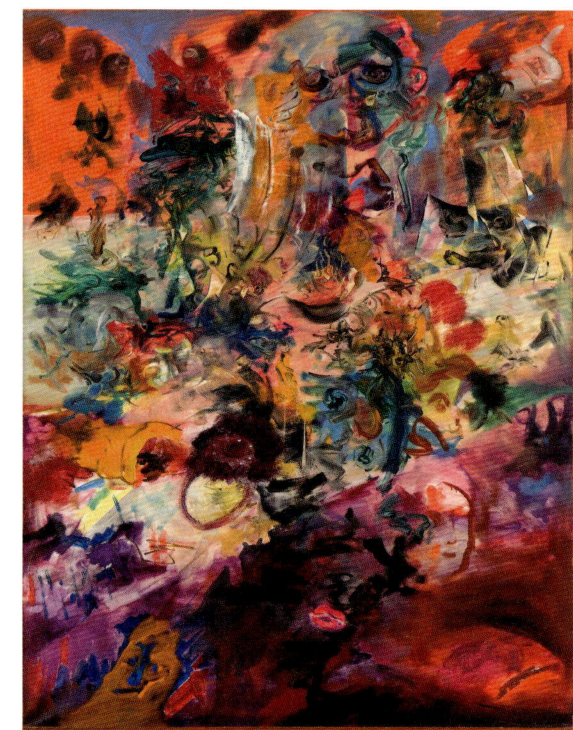

Jack Whitten, *King's Wish (Martin Luther's Dream)*, 1968. Oil on canvas, 67 ⅞ × 51 ⅛ in. (172.4 × 129.7 cm)

group of artists who call themselves Black and Puerto Rican Students and Artists for a Black Wing in Memory of Dr. Martin Luther King Jr. protest the placement of prominent Black artists in the "back room" of the exhibition.

Eighty-one artists participate in the show, including Benny Andrews, Romare Bearden, Daniel LaRue Johnson, Marisol, Claes Oldenburg, Faith Ringgold, Betye Saar, and Jack Whitten, whose *Painting for Martin Luther King, Jr.* (1968) is featured. Having met King during the bus boycotts

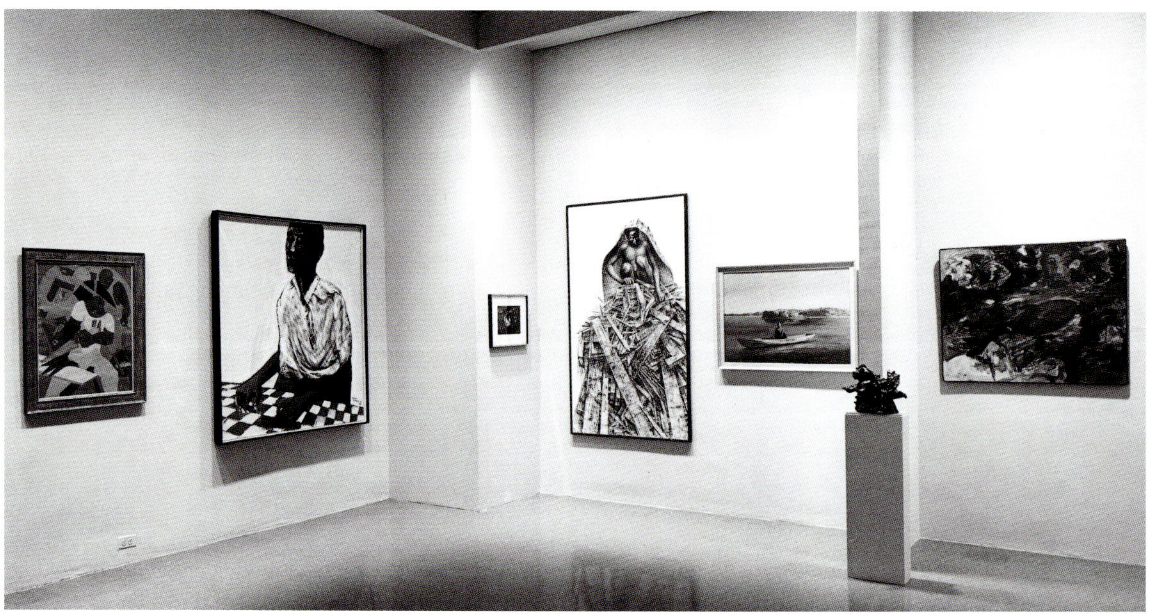

In Honor of Dr. Martin Luther King Jr., The Museum of Modern Art, New York, 1968

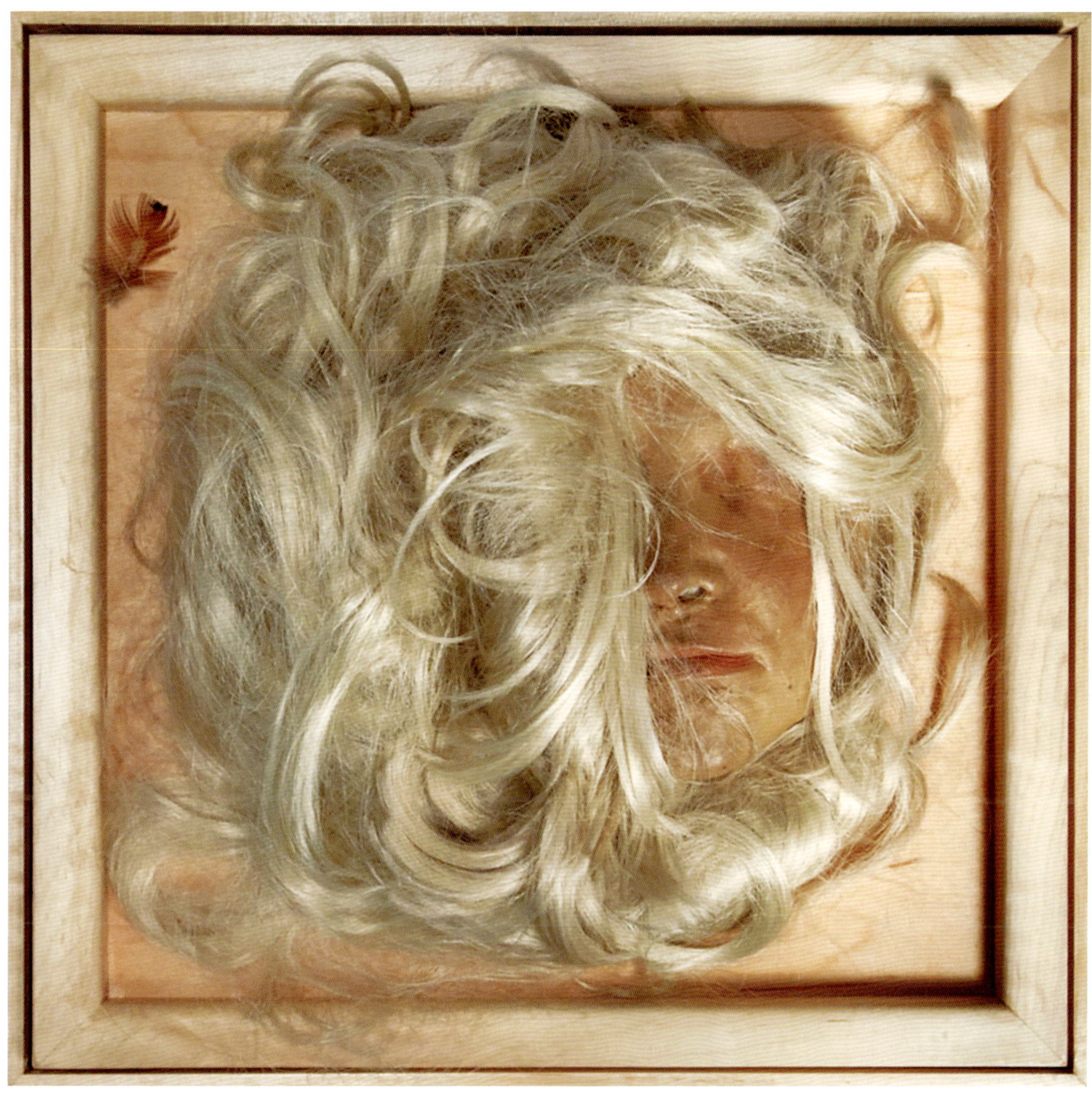

Lynn Hershman Leeson, *Giggling Machine, Self-Portrait as Blonde*, 1968. Wax, wig, feathers, Plexiglas, wood, sensor, and sound, 16 ½ × 16 ½ × 13 in. (41.9 × 41.9 × 33 cm). Collection of Scott Mueller; promised gift to the Cleveland Museum of Art

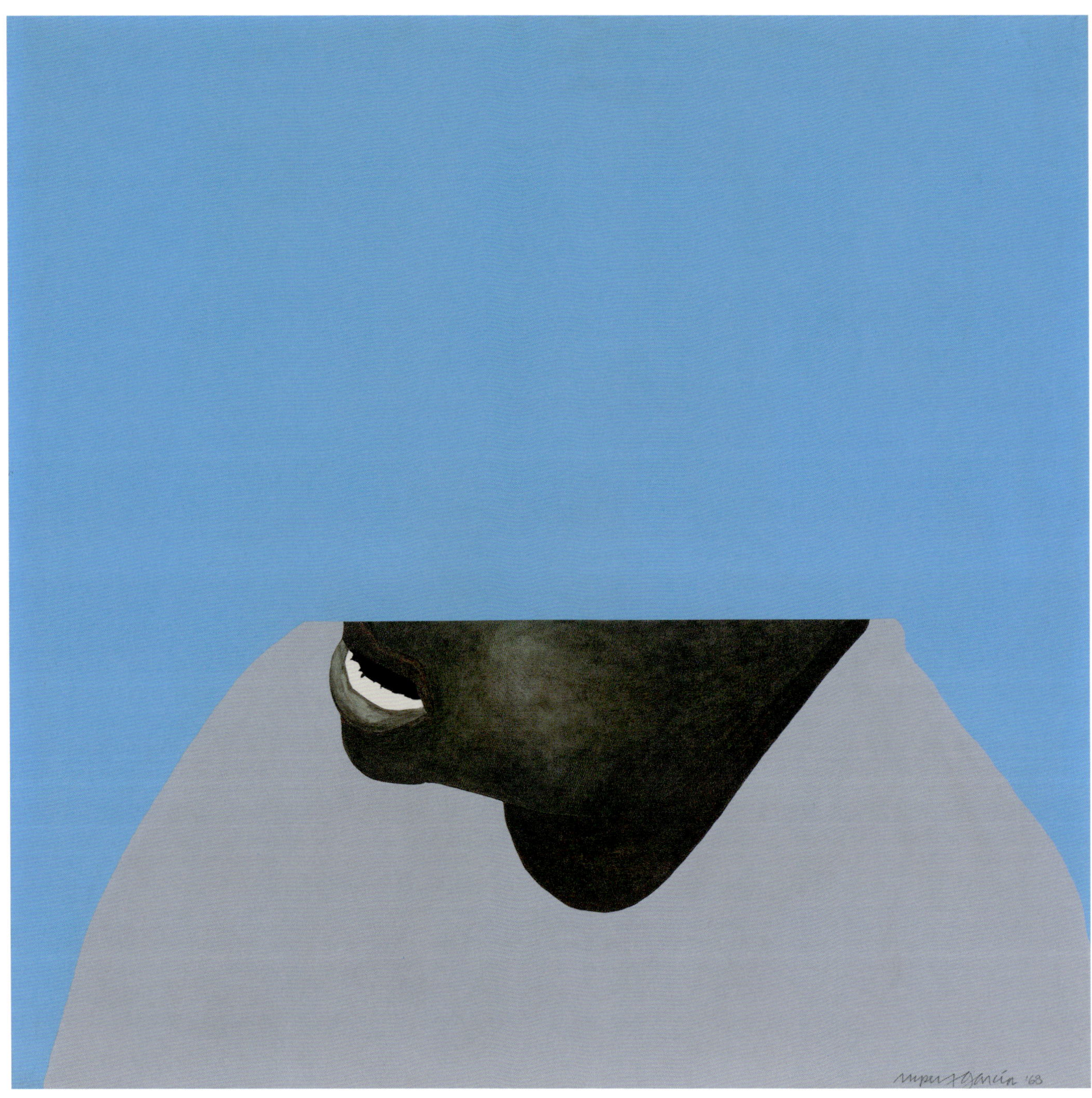

Rupert Garcia, *Unfinished Man*, 1968. Acrylic on canvas, 48 × 48 in. (121.9 × 121.9 cm). The Museum of Modern Art, New York; Painting and Sculpture Deaccession Funds 73.2024

in Montgomery, Alabama, in 1957, Whitten remains an active participant in the civil rights movement while living in Louisiana. King's assassination inspires him to complete *King's Wish (Martin Luther's Dream)* (1968) and *USA Oracle (Assassination of M. L. King)* (1968), which memorialize the civil rights leader. These paintings mark a conscious turn away from the social realism of many of his Black contemporaries, whom he characterizes as lacking the "risk" necessary for a "profound plastic language" that leans toward the abstract. Critics see the influence of Willem de Kooning in these colorful, surrealistic works. Whitten himself cites as his "first influence" Arshile Gorky, often deemed the last Surrealist and the first Abstract Expressionist. Writing to Henry Geldzahler in 1983, Whitten will summarize his work of the 1960s as "intense emotional images arrived at through self-psychoanalytical procedures, using techniques taken from Surrealism and Abstract Expressionism."

November 1968 • Barry and Josephine Plotkin, a white Jewish man from Baltimore and a Black woman from Chicago's South Side, open Lakeside Gallery near Hyde Park in Chicago. Cofounder of AFRICOBRA Jeff Donaldson will have his first show here; Wadsworth Jarrell and Barbara Jones-Hogu will also exhibit their work at the space. Lakeside Gallery is one of a number of galleries, cultural centers, and stores supporting the work of Black artists in the vicinity of Hyde Park, another being Jarrell's studio, WJ Studios, where he also hosts exhibitions and meetings.

November 5, 1968 • Republican Richard M. Nixon is elected president, defeating Democrat Hubert H. Humphrey. Nixon wins 43.4 percent of the vote whereas Humphrey earns 42.7 percent; American Independent and ardent segregationist George C. Wallace captures 13.5 percent.

November 6, 1968–March 21, 1969 • Rupert Garcia makes his first silkscreen posters, part of his involvement in the student strike at San Francisco State College. The walkout interrupts Garcia's studies and changes the course of his artistic career. Initially part of separate cultural organizations, the striking students come together as the Third World Liberation Front, a coalition that pressures the school to establish ethnic studies departments and to expand educational access to nonwhite students. The strike—the longest student-led walkout in the history of the United States—is energized by the civil rights activism, anti-imperialism, and antiwar sentiment taking

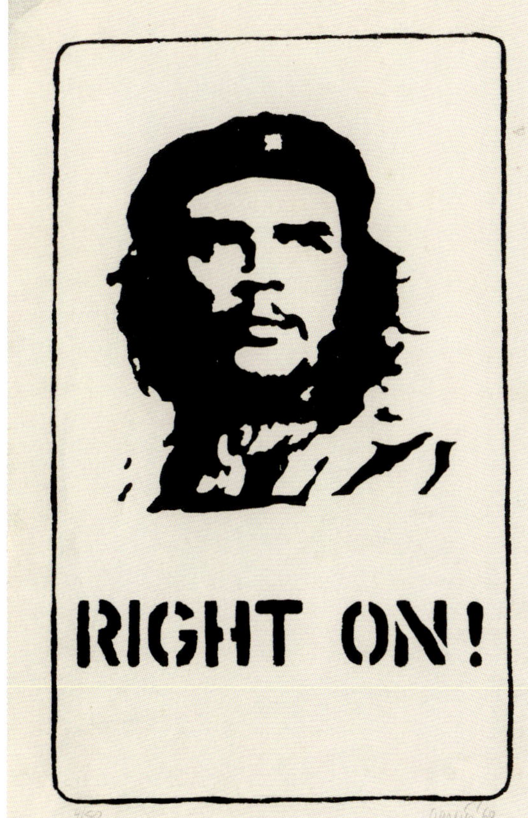

Rupert Garcia, *Right On!*, 1968. Screenprint on paper, 23 ½ × 14 ⅜ in. (59.7 × 36.5 cm)

hold of the nation and the world. As Garcia will recall, one of the school's faculty had recently returned to campus from France, where he had witnessed the demonstrations and civil unrest that had convulsed Paris in May 1968. He "mentioned to us what he saw some students doing there—which was to make posters. And so we—some faculty and students—organized a poster brigade." Professor Dennis Beall offers the brigade his studio and a crash course in silkscreening, and Garcia turns his attention from painting to printmaking, which will be his primary medium for the next decade. The artist considers his poster featuring the revolutionary icon Che Guevara to be one of his first mature works of art.

November 8, 1968–January 12, 1969 • Ralph Arnold (1928–2006) debuts *Unfinished Collage* (1968) in the exhibition *Violence! in Recent American Art* at the Museum of Contemporary Art Chicago. Other artists featured in the show include Ray Johnson, Edward Kienholz, Joseph Raffaele, Peter Saul, Andy Warhol, and William T. Wiley. Arnold's most visible artwork to date, *Unfinished Collage* hangs column-like in the exhibition, memorializing John F. Kennedy, Robert F. Kennedy, and Martin Luther King Jr., its blank

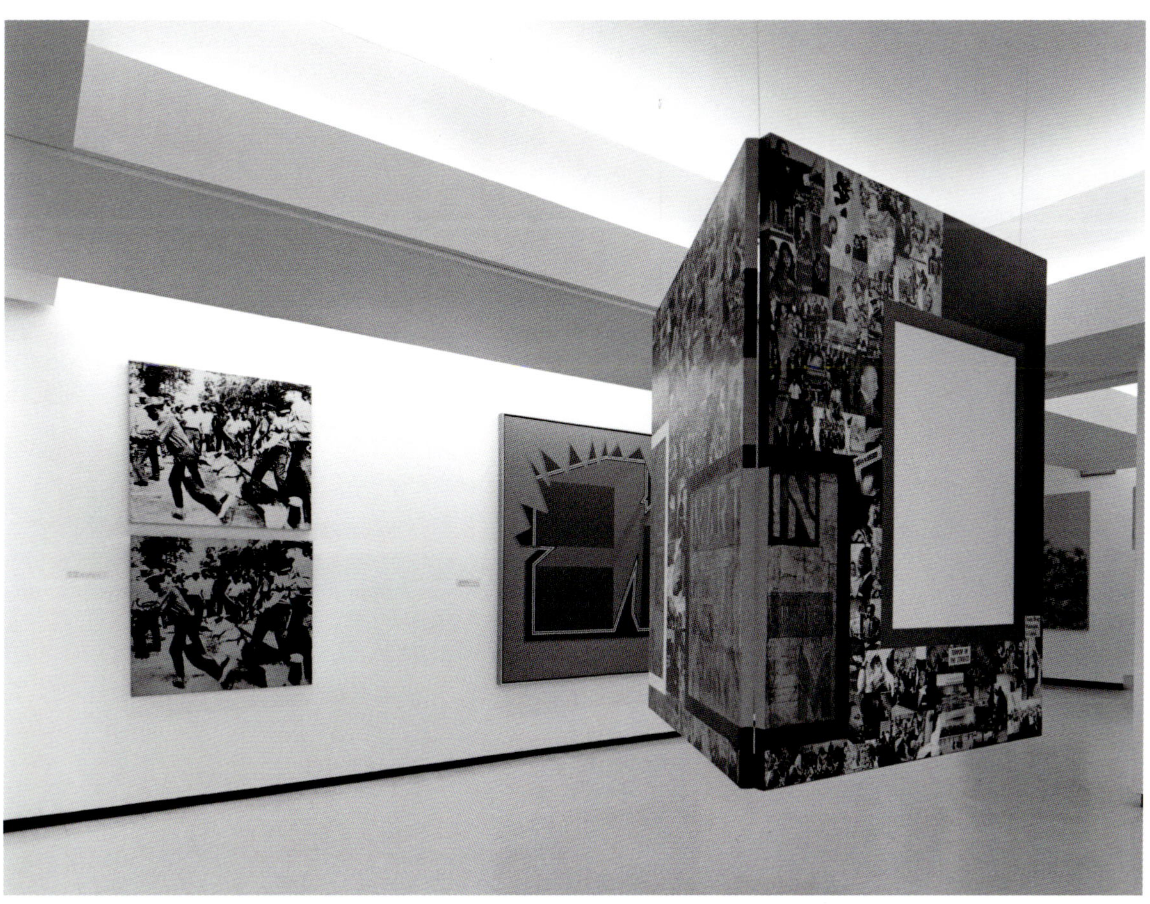

Violence! in Recent American Art, Museum of Contemporary Art Chicago, 1969, with Andy Warhol's *Race Riot* (1963), Stanley Edwards's *Smash-up at Tompkins Square Park* (1968), and Ralph Arnold's *Unfinished Collage* (1968)

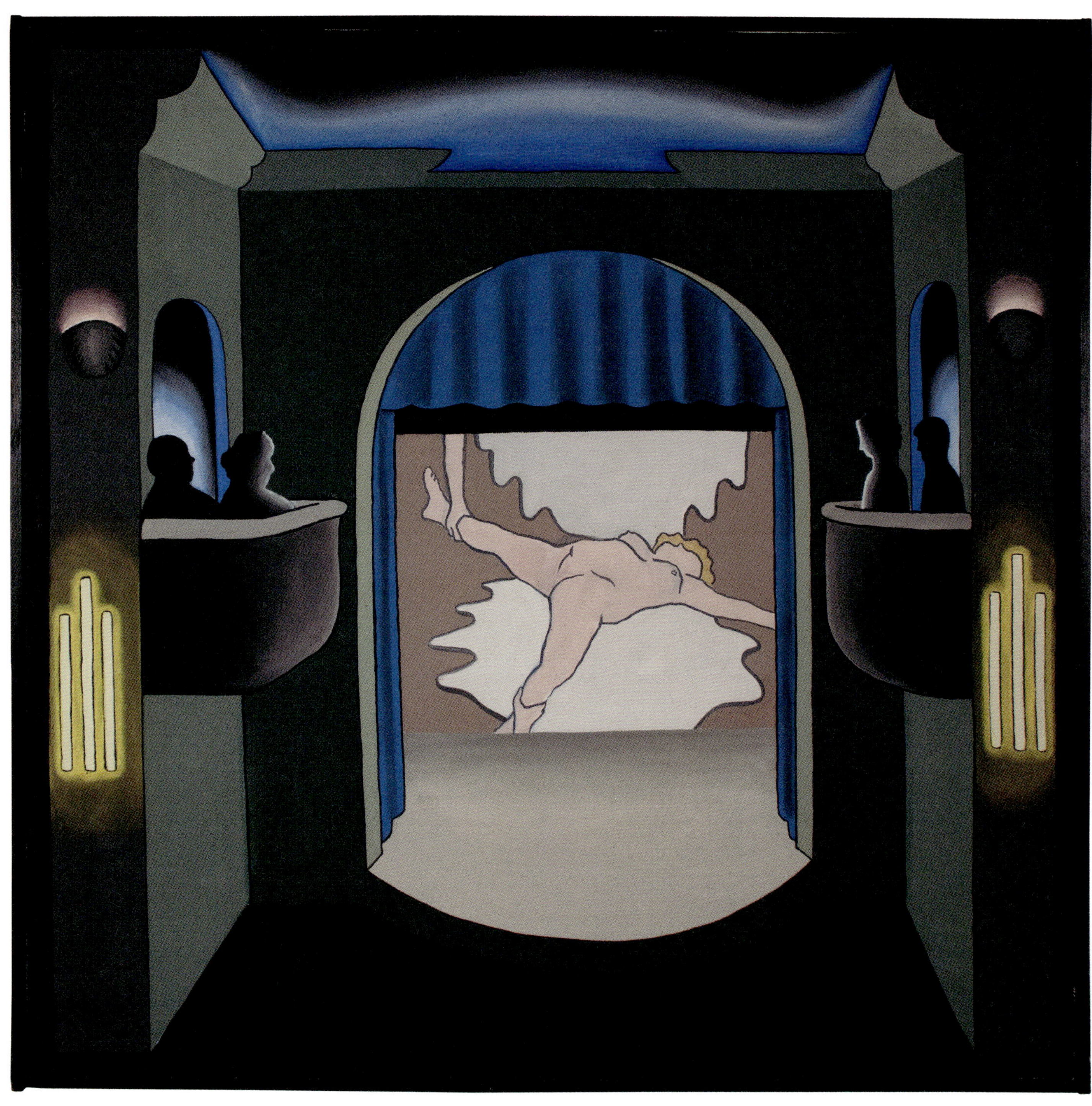

Roger Brown, *Untitled (Movie house with nude female)*, 1968. Oil on canvas, 24 ¾ × 24 ⅝ in. (62.9 × 62.5 cm). Collection of the John Michael Kohler Arts Center, Gift of the Kohler Foundation, Inc.

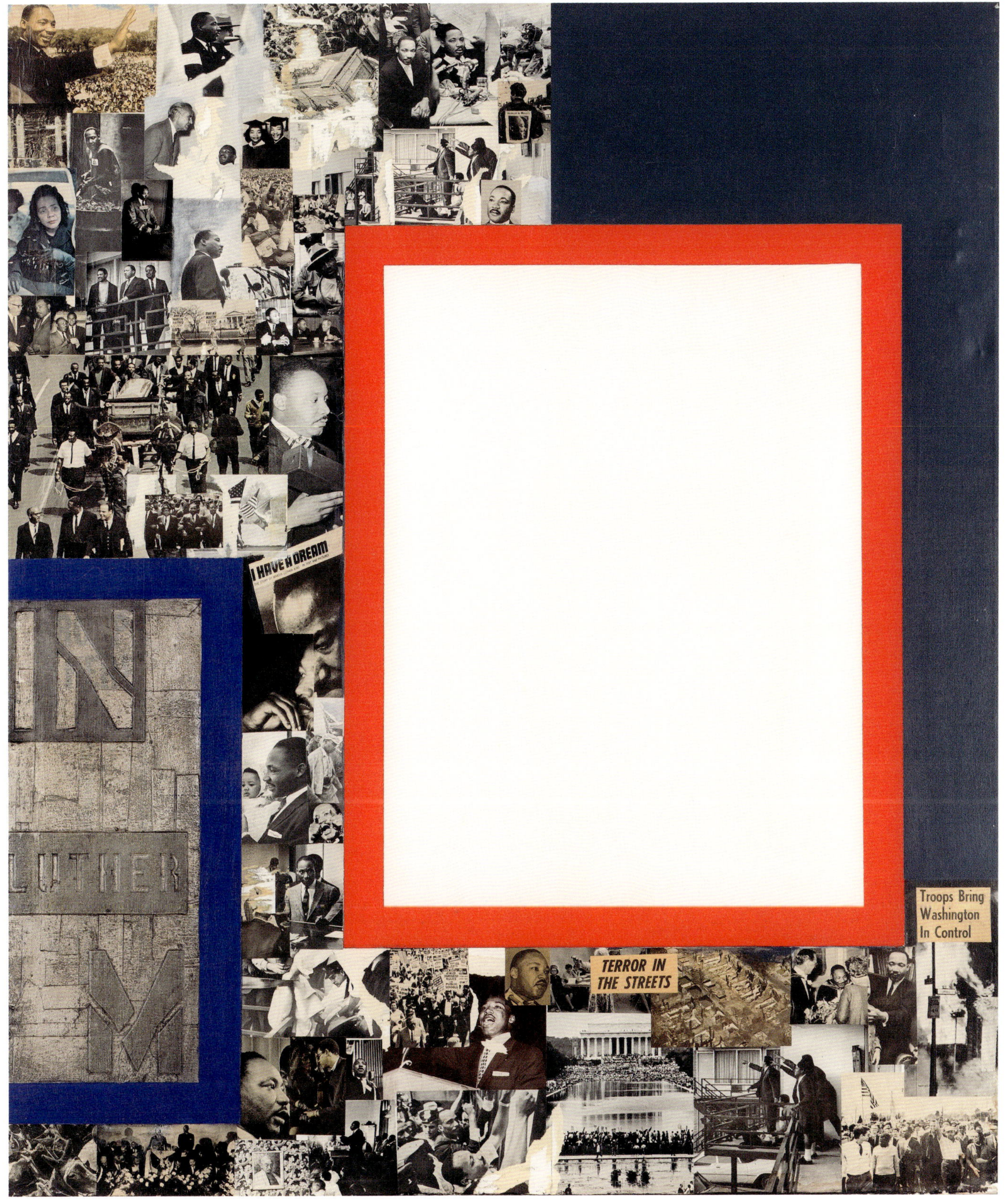

Ralph Arnold, *Unfinished Collage* (detail), 1968. Collage and acrylic on canvas: three panels, 60 ½ × 20 in. (153.7 × 50.8 cm) each; approximately 60 ½ × 60 in. (157.3 × 152.4 cm) overall. South Side Community Art Center, Chicago

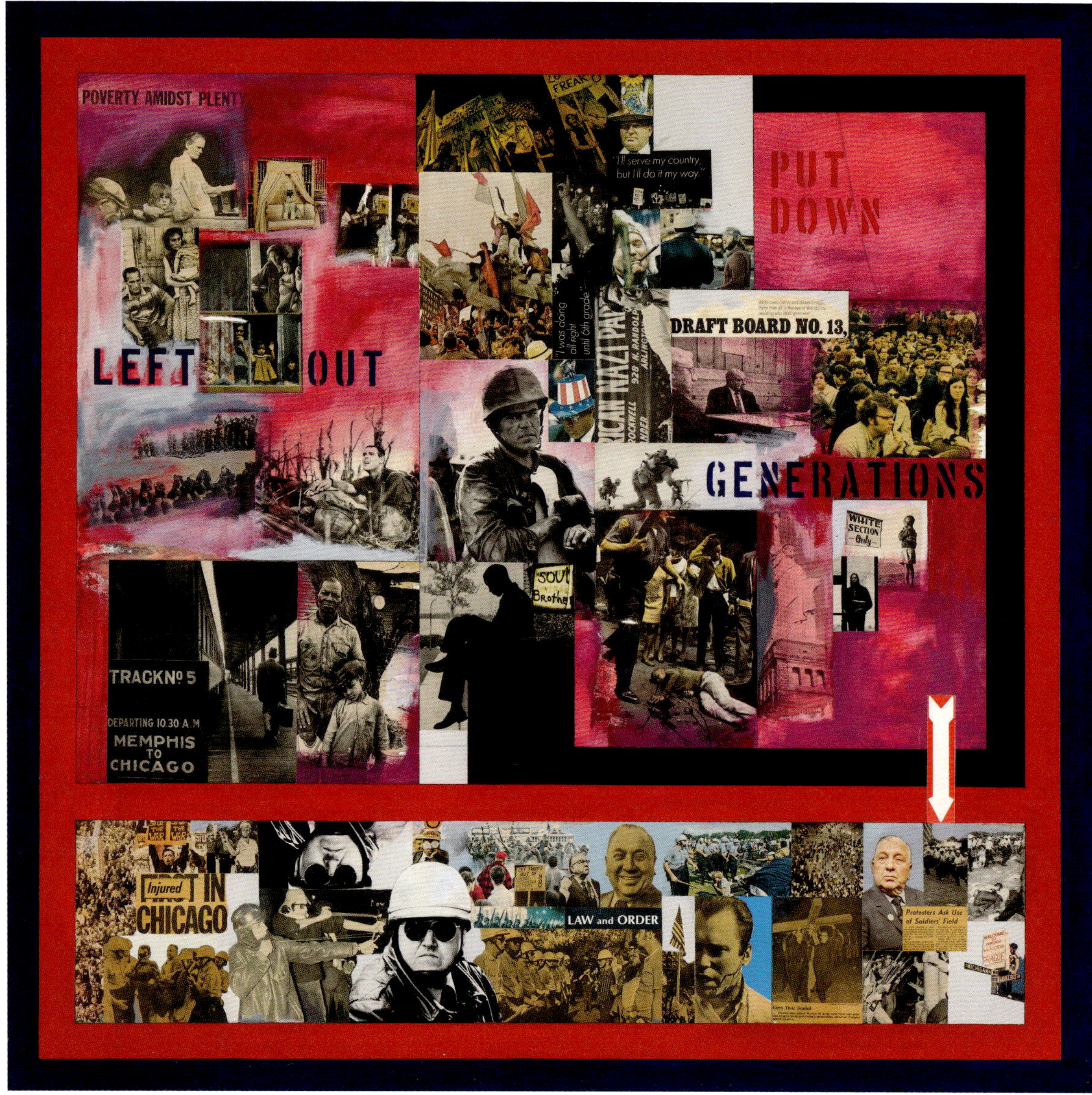

Ralph Arnold, *One Thing Leads to Another*, 1968. Collage and acrylic on canvas, 60 × 60 in. (152.4 × 152.4 cm)

panel begging the terrible question of who might be assassinated next.

Born and raised in Chicago, Arnold will later maintain that growing up Black and gay in a segregated city gave him confidence to move through any world he desires; there are too many strikes against him for him to care. He served in the Korean War in the early 1950s, returning to study at the University of Illinois Urbana-Champaign, Roosevelt University, and the School of the Art Institute of Chicago, from which he will receive a master of fine arts in 1977. Throughout the 1960s, Arnold shifts between the nascent gay liberation movement, antiwar protests, and the civil rights movement, maintaining a home and studio with his partner in the bohemian neighborhood of Old Town. For Arnold, the nation's social injustices are directly linked to the Vietnam War and the subsequent draft, which disproportionately impact people of color and low-income communities.

Arnold mounts solo exhibitions in Chicago galleries throughout the decade and participates in a few group shows at the Hyde Park Art Center. His collages—inspired by Romare Bearden (who becomes a friend), Jasper Johns, and Robert Rauschenberg—are his primary vehicle for encoding messages about the intersection between the self and the wider culture. Sometimes violent, sometimes erotic, Arnold's collages incorporate photographic material within a structure of bold color bands and stenciled communications, as in *One Thing Leads to Another* (1968), in which the artist connects Mayor Richard Daley's violent proposition of law and order in the supposedly liberal city of Chicago with the actuality of the social injustices of racism and poverty that its citizens experience.

Late 1968 • Inspired by her professor Charles White and his ideals of art as a vehicle for social change, Suzanne Jackson (b. 1944) opens Gallery 32 near MacArthur Park in Los Angeles. Jackson is a painter and dancer who, though born in St. Louis, Missouri, had spent much of her childhood in the Yukon, in rural, pre-statehood Alaska. She graduates from San Francisco State College in 1966 before moving to Los Angeles and taking classes from White at the Otis Art Institute. Jackson's paintings include dreamlike depictions of plants, human forms, and birds, often mirroring and overlapping in evocative compositions that speak to the artist's personal experience of nature and the freedom it allows—outside the expectations she sometimes feels as a Black woman and an artist. Looking for a place to work on her paintings, Jackson originally rents unit 32 of the Granada Buildings as a studio and living space but soon gives over much of her own studio for the presentation of work by fellow artists—many of whom are also White's students—and as a gathering place for conversation and activism. Named for its suite number, Gallery 32 offers "a space where people could express an independent voice in their work and not be labeled," as Jackson will later explain. "Gallery 32 was never a black gallery, a woman's gallery, or a man's gallery; it was a gallery about artists who came through with something to say."

While being a space in which Jackson's artist-friends such as David Hammons, Senga Nengudi, and Timothy Washington can show some of their earliest works, the gallery is also a place where direct political engagement and art can come together. Gallery 32 hosts fundraisers for organizations that reflect Jackson's activism, such as the Black Arts Council and Watts Towers Arts Center. In October 1969, the Black Panther Party of Los Angeles will present the work of Emory Douglas at the gallery in a show advertised as a "Revolutionary Art Exhibit" and a fundraiser for the organization's children's breakfast program. When the Panthers ask her to give over the gallery as a permanent exhibition space for the controversial organization, Jackson replies, "I can't do that, because as it is, the gallery [Gallery 32] gets to a lot of people who would not normally come to see this work. This Panther show is seen by a lot of working-class, middle-class, you know, all levels of people, white, black, green, purple, because they don't feel afraid to come into this space. They feel the space is theirs to come into. But if it was owned by the Panthers or taken over by the Panthers, then the connotation—they would not have this freedom to come and look at Emory's work."

November 14, 1968 • The experimental art center Art & Soul opens in the North Lawndale

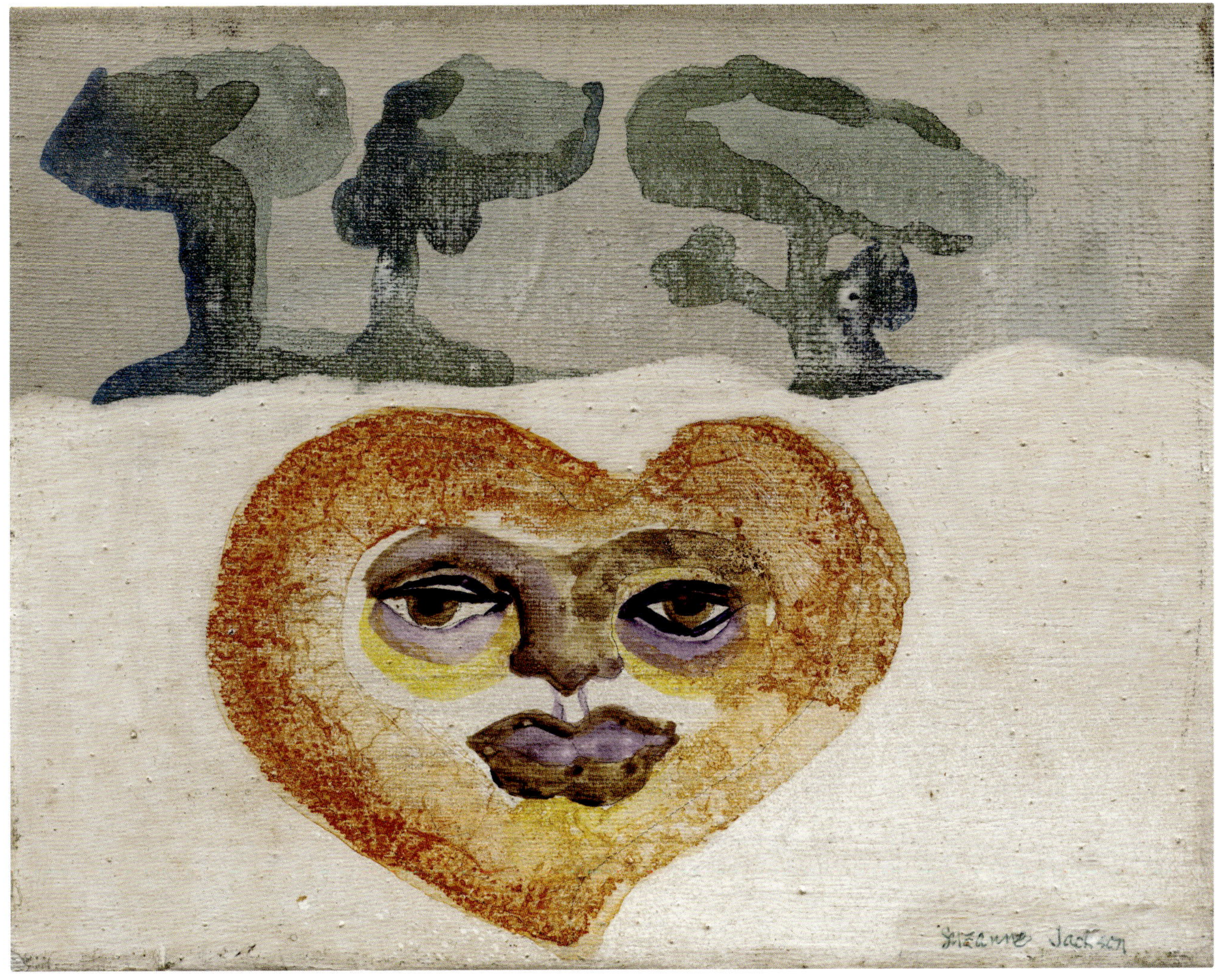

Suzanne Jackson, *We Were Waiting*, c. 1968–69. Acrylic on canvas, 8 × 10 ⅛ in. (20.3 × 25.7 cm). Collection of Larry and Tina Jones

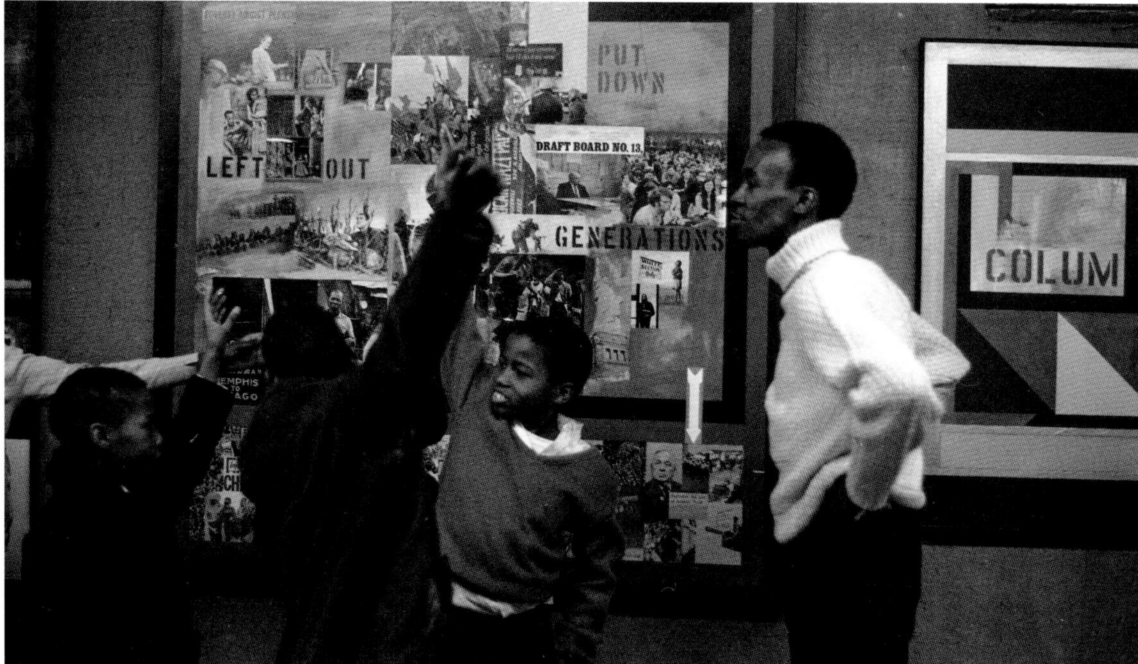

Daniel Hetherington talks with students about Ralph Arnold's *One Thing Leads to Another* (1968), Art & Soul, Chicago, c. 1968

neighborhood on the west side of Chicago. The center is a joint project between Conservative Vice Lords Inc.—a refashioning of the Vice Lords street gang and its emphasis on community organization and investment—and the relatively new Museum of Contemporary Art Chicago. Art & Soul operates as more than a place for presenting art, offering a studio for children's art classes, a library for books and art supplies, and an artist residency. Its first artist in residence, Ralph Arnold, displays his collage paintings in its space and teaches an art class. The center's assistant director, artist Daniel Hetherington, and others involved with establishing Art & Soul also help youth engage with Arnold's provocative works.

November 16–December 6, 1968 • *Eva Hesse: Chain Polymers*, the artist's first solo exhibition of sculpture, is on view at Fischbach Gallery, New York. Hesse had started her investigation of new materials after taking a class on polymers, casting, and molding that was part of a series of scientific lectures and demonstrations organized by the service organization Experiments in Art and Technology. She had first turned to latex, but by early 1968, her private notes indicate her desire that her sculptures be transparent, a quality she can achieve with fiberglass. She starts working with Aegis Reinforced Plastics, a Staten Island fabrication facility, and begins corresponding with West Coast sculptor Bruce Nauman, who is already working with fiberglass. That summer, Hesse realizes her first work of art at Aegis. She wants, as she often professes, to manifest

"absurdity," eroticism through "repetition," and "humor based on incongruity."

The first room of *Eva Hesse: Chain Polymers* contains several fiberglass sculptures: *Repetition Nineteen III*, *Accession II*, *Accretion*, and *Sans II* (all 1968). Critic Lucy Lippard describes the space as filled with light, a result of what Hesse explains is the inherent disposition of her materials: "If you use reinforced fiberglass clear and thin, the light is there by its nature and the light does beautiful things to it." Through her work, Hesse strives to achieve a complex liminal state, to embody conflict. "Bundles of eccentric contradictions, impossible to resolve," is how John Perreault characterizes her efforts in what will become an oft-cited review in the *Village Voice*. "It's the kind of show that makes one nervous: all that unfinished fiberglass. . . . It's surreal serialism." Widely

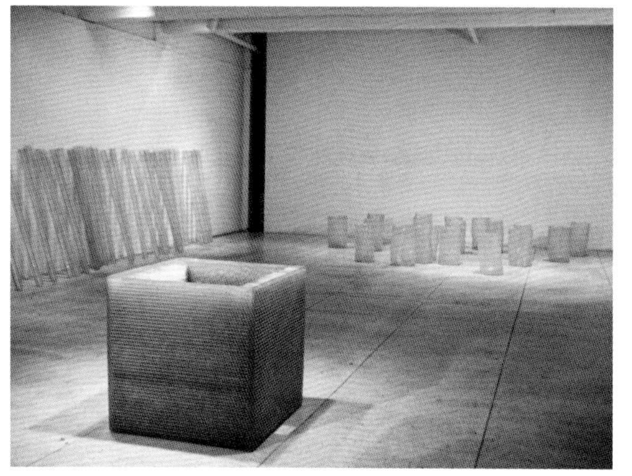

Eva Hesse: Chain Polymers, Fischbach Gallery, New York, 1968

reviewed, *Chain Polymers* contributes to the near-mythic status Hesse will achieve after her premature death in 1970.

November 17–December 21, 1968 • The Chicago artist group False Image have their first exhibition at the Hyde Park Art Center. The success of the Hairy Who exhibitions had prompted curator Don Baum to look for other young artists who might be shown together as a group with a distinct identity, and Jim Nutt and Ray Yoshida suggest the four recent School of the Art Institute of Chicago (SAIC) graduates who have dubbed themselves False Image: Roger Brown, Eleanor Dube, Philip Hanson, and Christina Ramberg. A second show will follow in November 1969.

The work of Roger Brown (1941–1997) in these years arrives from a diverse mix: Giorgio de Chirico, Marcel Duchamp, Edward Hopper, and the cars, parks, movie theaters, apartments, city squares, pastures, and roads of Brown's youth. Raised the son of a grocer in a small town about sixty miles north of Montgomery, Alabama, and aware he is gay from a young age, Brown had built a life as an observer of the codes of the conservative, religious world around him. He impulsively joins the Marines but is swiftly outed and discharged, the news of which makes him an outcast in his hometown. He moves to Chicago in 1962 and thrives there, enrolling at SAIC in 1964 and eventually receiving a master's degree.

Christina Ramberg (1946–1995) had been born into a military family and grown up between Germany, Japan, Virginia, and Illinois. Fascinated with paper dolls, she attends summer classes at SAIC as a child, before going on to earn a bachelor of arts in 1968; she will earn a master of fine arts in 1973. At the school, she solidifies her artistic methodologies thanks in part to Whitney Halstead and Ray Yoshida. Halstead is an art historian and artist who gives equal weight to the fine art at the Art Institute and the natural history collections at the Field Museum, while Yoshida, an artist not much older than Ramberg and already a friend and mentor to other Chicago painters, encourages collecting as both art and inspiration.

In these early days, Ramberg finds her subjects and mediums: hair, urns, corsets, and transmutable bodies rendered in acrylic on Masonite, a surface resistant enough for her careful brushwork and her desired ultraflat finish. She has already started working serially, beginning with the backs of heads and carefully posed hands before moving on to torsos and urns, often seemingly made of swatches of coiffed hair. "I have always recognized two parallel strains in my work," Ramberg will later explain. "One was the readable, recognizable-as-figure image, and the second was

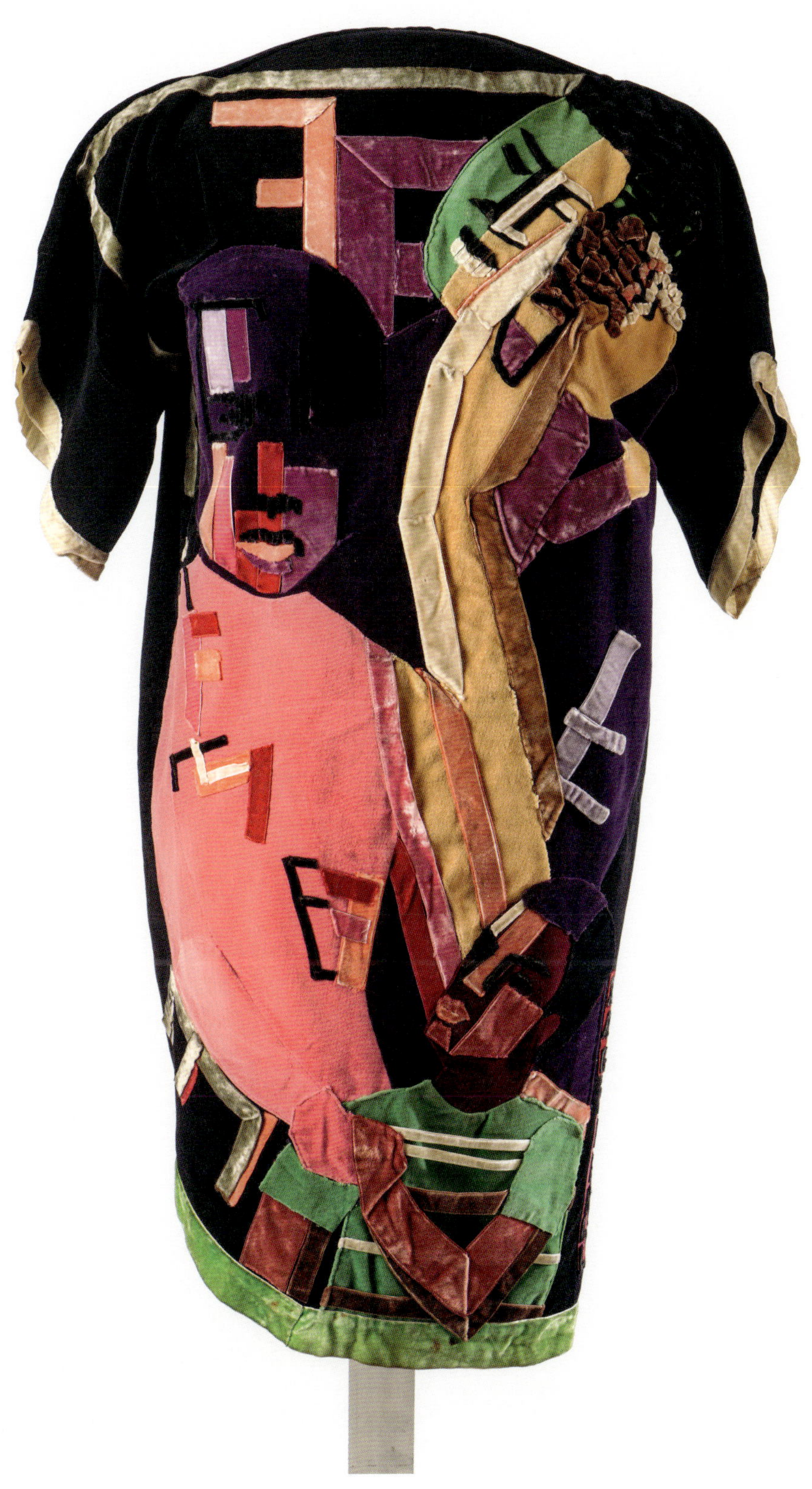

Jae Jarrell, *Ebony Family*, c. 1968. Velvet dress with velvet collage, 38 ½ × 38 × ½ in. (97.8 × 96.5 × 1.3 cm). Brooklyn Museum, New York; gift of R. M. Atwater, Anna Wolfrom Dove, Alice Fiebiger, Joseph Fiebiger, Belle Campbell Harriss, and Emma L. Hyde, by exchange, Designated Purchase Fund, Mary Smith Dorward Fund, Dick S. Ramsay Fund, and Carll H. de Silver Fund 2012.80.15

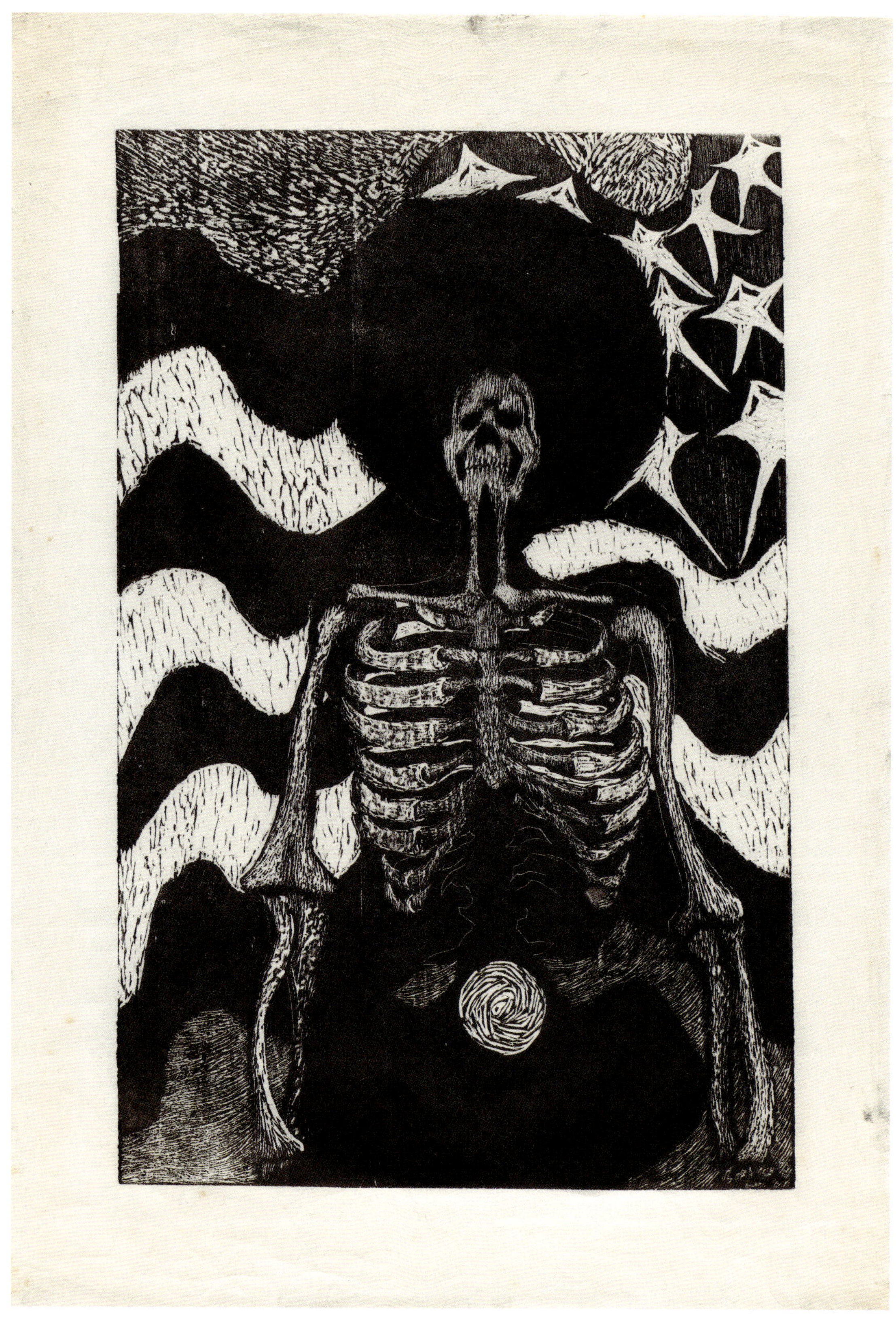

Barbara Jones-Hogu, *Mother of Man*, 1968. Woodblock print on paper, 30 ½ × 21 ½ in. (77.5 × 54.6 cm). The Museum of Modern Art, New York; The Deborah Wye Endowment Fund 738.2019

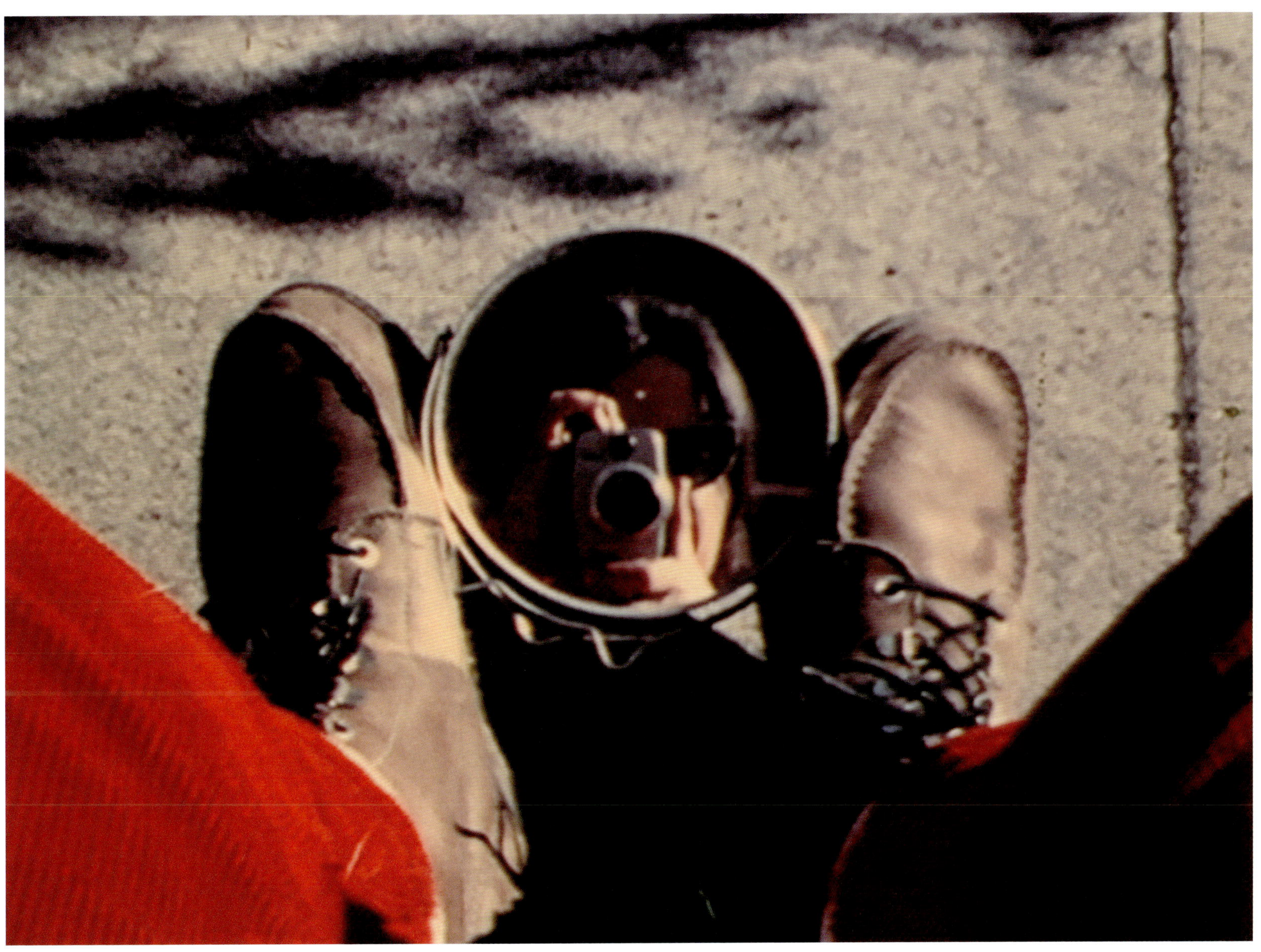

Barbara Hammer, *Schizy*, 1968. Super 8mm film transferred to video, color, silent; 3:59 min. Electronic Arts Intermix, New York

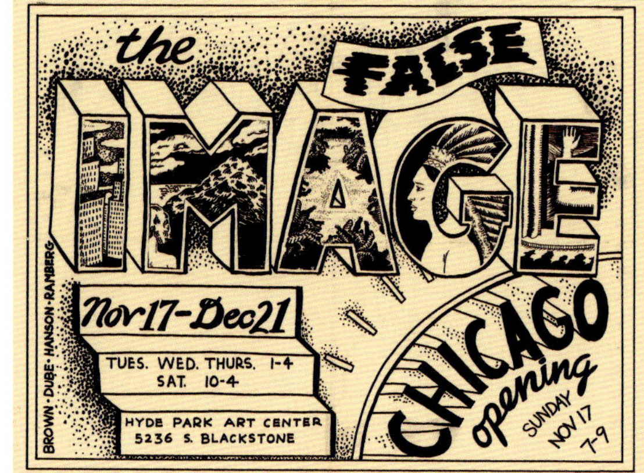

Poster for *The False Image*, Hyde Park Art Center, Chicago, 1968

a more abstract, metaphorical image often reading as torso/urn." Her analysis taps into the Surrealist idea of one form embodying dual meanings and objects, as the torso/urn can symbolize sex/death. This single-minded focus, compact forms, and disinterest in visual and verbal puns set her apart from even her fellow Chicagoans.

___

November 26, 1968–January 12, 1969 • The first museum retrospective of H. C. Westermann's work is on view at the Los Angeles County Museum of Art; an expanded version will travel to the Museum of Contemporary Art Chicago (January 25–March 2, 1969). The exhibition is organized by Maurice Tuchman and cocurated by James Monte and Jane Livingston. Westermann himself makes his entrance walking on his hands. The *Los Angeles Times* calls Westermann "the most important artist of his type since Joseph Cornell" and characterizes *Memorial to the Idea of Man If He Was an Idea* (1958) as deceptive: "This authoritarian monster, who appears to have the capability of laying down the abstract law, is a fraud. If we open the hinged cabinet that is his chest we find he is but the confused compound of personal experiences like the rest of us."

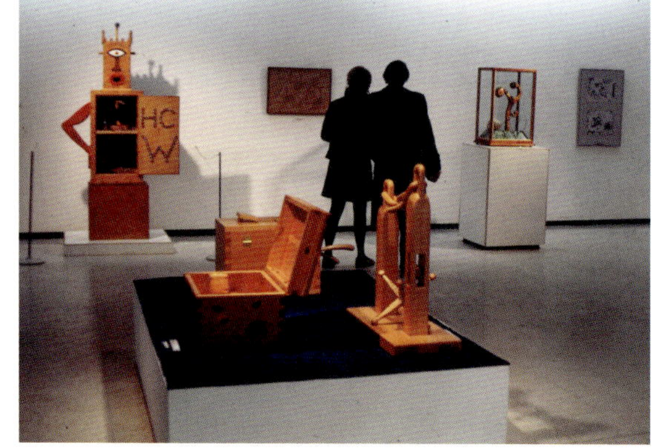

H. C. Westermann, Museum of Contemporary Art Chicago, 1969

December 17, 1968–February 9, 1969 • The Whitney Museum of American Art's *1968 Annual Exhibition: Contemporary American Sculpture* features artists Lee Bontecou, Louise Bourgeois, Nancy Grossman, Alex Hay, Eva Hesse, Daniel LaRue Johnson, Claes Oldenburg, Kenneth Price, Lucas Samaras, Robert Smithson, Michael Todd, H. C. Westermann, and Franklin Williams. The exhibition catalogue acknowledges the expanding geographic scope of these Whitney Annuals in recent years, in large part due to additional funding to allow curators to travel more broadly.

___

December 1968 • Barbara Hammer premieres her film *Schizy* (1968) at the Sonoma State Super 8 Film Festival and wins honorable mention. A few months later, she will leave her husband and move to Berkeley. Both the film and the move precipitate from an experience she has while driving her motorcycle to Sonoma State University to take her first filmmaking class. Hammer happens upon an abandoned dilapidated shack in Bodega, California, covered in red ivy and stops to explore. Inside, she becomes fascinated by the appearance of colorful leaves being filtered through the cobwebbed and dust-clouded windows and takes out her Super 8 camera to film them, placing a bifocal lens, sourced from her optometrist, in front of the camera lens. The result is an image that splits, doubles, and snaps in and out of focus as Hammer moves with the camera—according to the artist, a perfect encapsulation of the disjointed experience of being a woman in a patriarchal society. She will later recount:

> I ran outside on the sidewalk in the tiny town of Bodega filming my shadow until I saw a chair in the viewfinder. I slipped the bifocal in front of the camera lens and split the chair in two. I was filming the sidewalk again until I saw a man's shoes in the frame. I climbed on a raised platform behind the man and shot him from above his head as he sat in the chair. I asked him to put a mirror between his feet, zoomed into the mirror filming his face, then I cut to my own. I was literally a woman living in a man's world.

___

December 28, 1968 • A Black Culture Festival is held at the Los Angeles County Museum of Art (LACMA), coordinated by Sergeant William Knight and organized entirely by the museum's Black security officers in conjunction with the exhibition currently on view, *The Sculpture of Black Africa: The Paul Tishman*

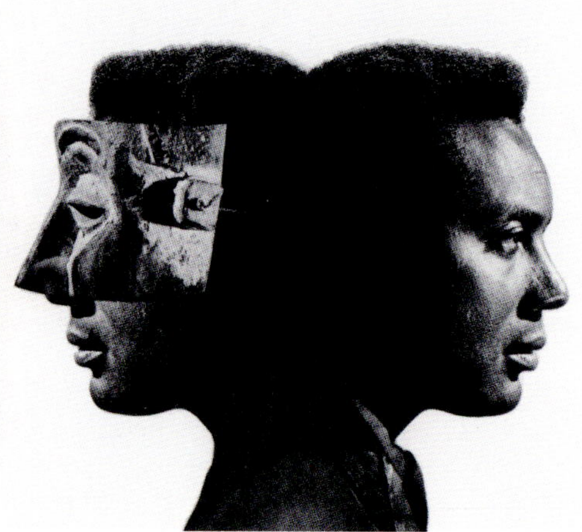

Invitation for A Black Culture Festival, Los Angeles County Museum of Art, December 28, 1968

Collection. The festival offers a full program of music, dance, fashion, and lectures as well as tours of the exhibition by the security officers. The event inspires LACMA employees Claude Booker and Cecil Fergerson to form the Black Arts Council (BAC), a network to support Black art and artists in Los Angeles and to make the museum more accessible and welcoming to Black Americans. BAC's earliest members include artists and gallerists Gloria Bohanon, Dan R. Concholar, Alonzo Davis, Marion Epting, David Hammons, Raymond Lark, Leon Leonard, John Outterbridge, John Riddle, Arenzo Smith Jr., Donald Stinson, John Stinson, Ruth Waddy, Timothy Washington, and Charles White.

This same year, the Black Arts Alliance (BAA) also forms in Los Angeles. Partially developing out of Alonzo and Dale Davis's Brockman Gallery, BAA is engaged with formal concerns and art-making practices.

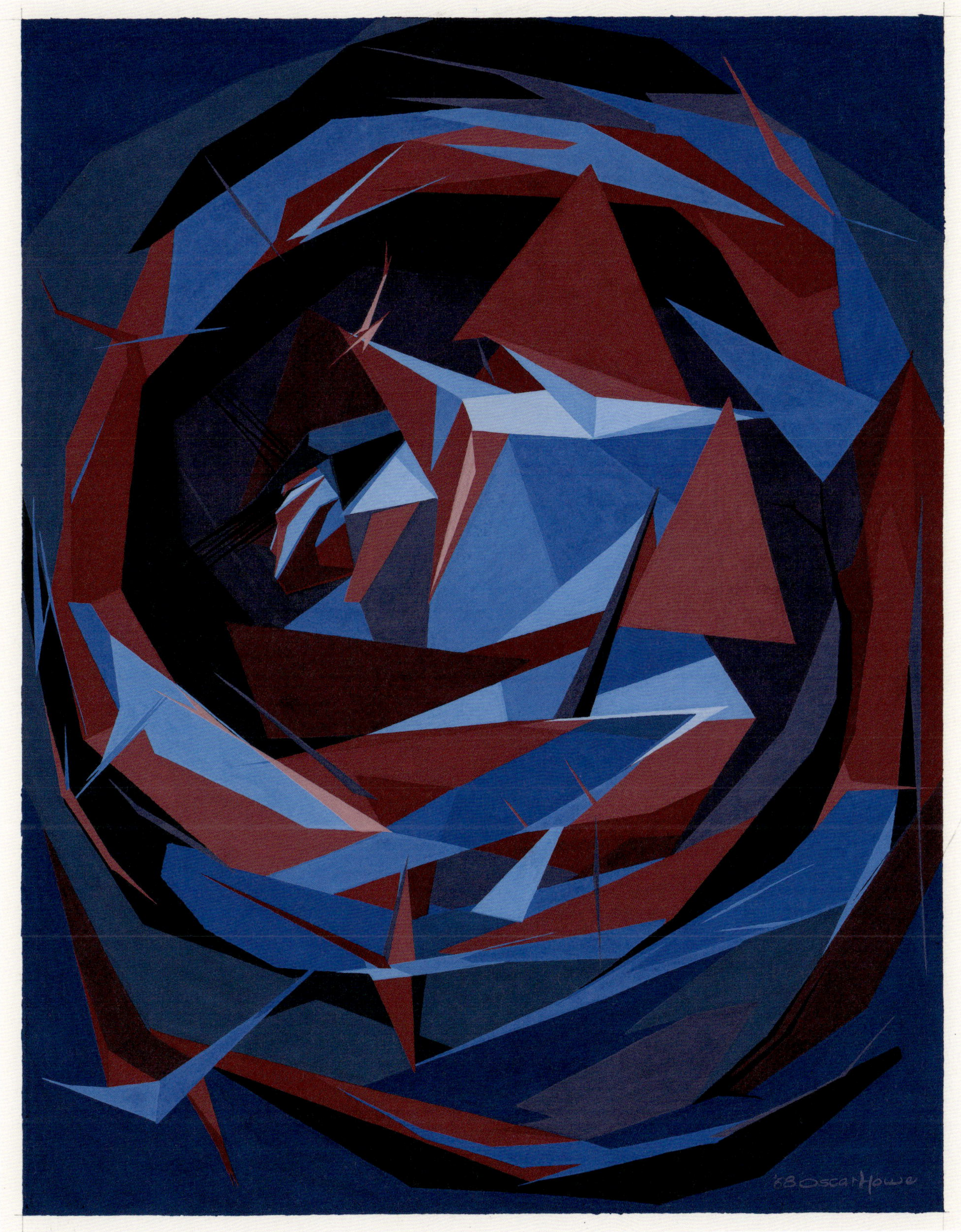

Oscar Howe, *Retreat*, 1968. Casein on paper, 24 × 18 ¼ in. (61 × 46.3 cm). Whitney Museum of American Art, New York; purchase, with funds from the Director's Discretionary Fund 2023.86

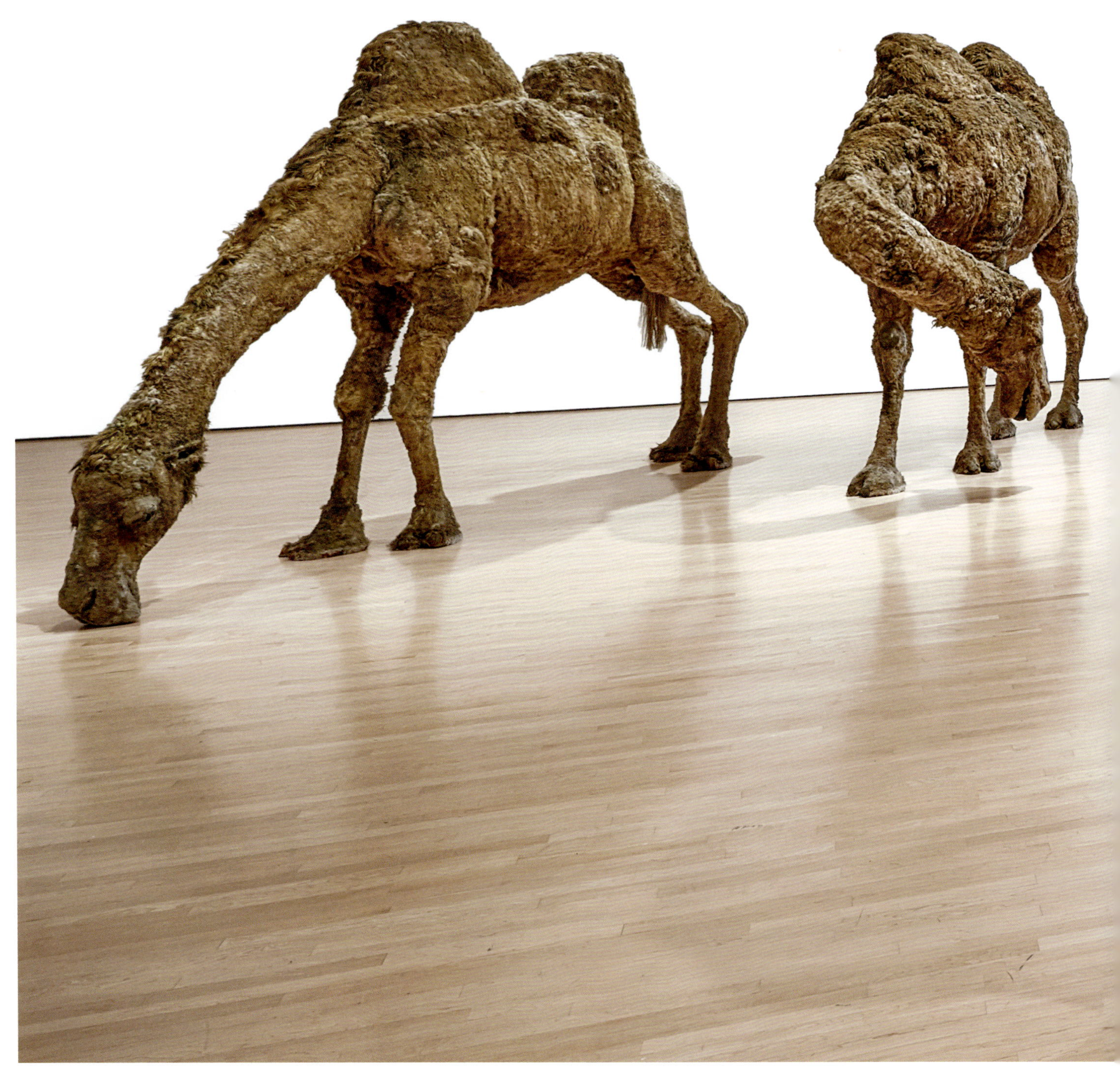

Nancy Graves, *Camel VI*, 1968–69. Wood, steel, burlap, polyurethane, animal skin, wax, and oil paint, approx. 90 × 144 × 47 ⅝ in. (228.6 × 365.8 × 121.9 cm). National Gallery of Canada, Ottawa; purchase, 1969
Nancy Graves, *Camel VII*, 1968–69. Wood, steel, burlap, polyurethane, animal skin, wax, and oil paint, approx. 96 × 108 × 47 ⅝ in. (243.8 × 274.3 × 121.9 cm). National Gallery of Canada, Ottawa; gift of Allan Bronfman, Montreal, 1969

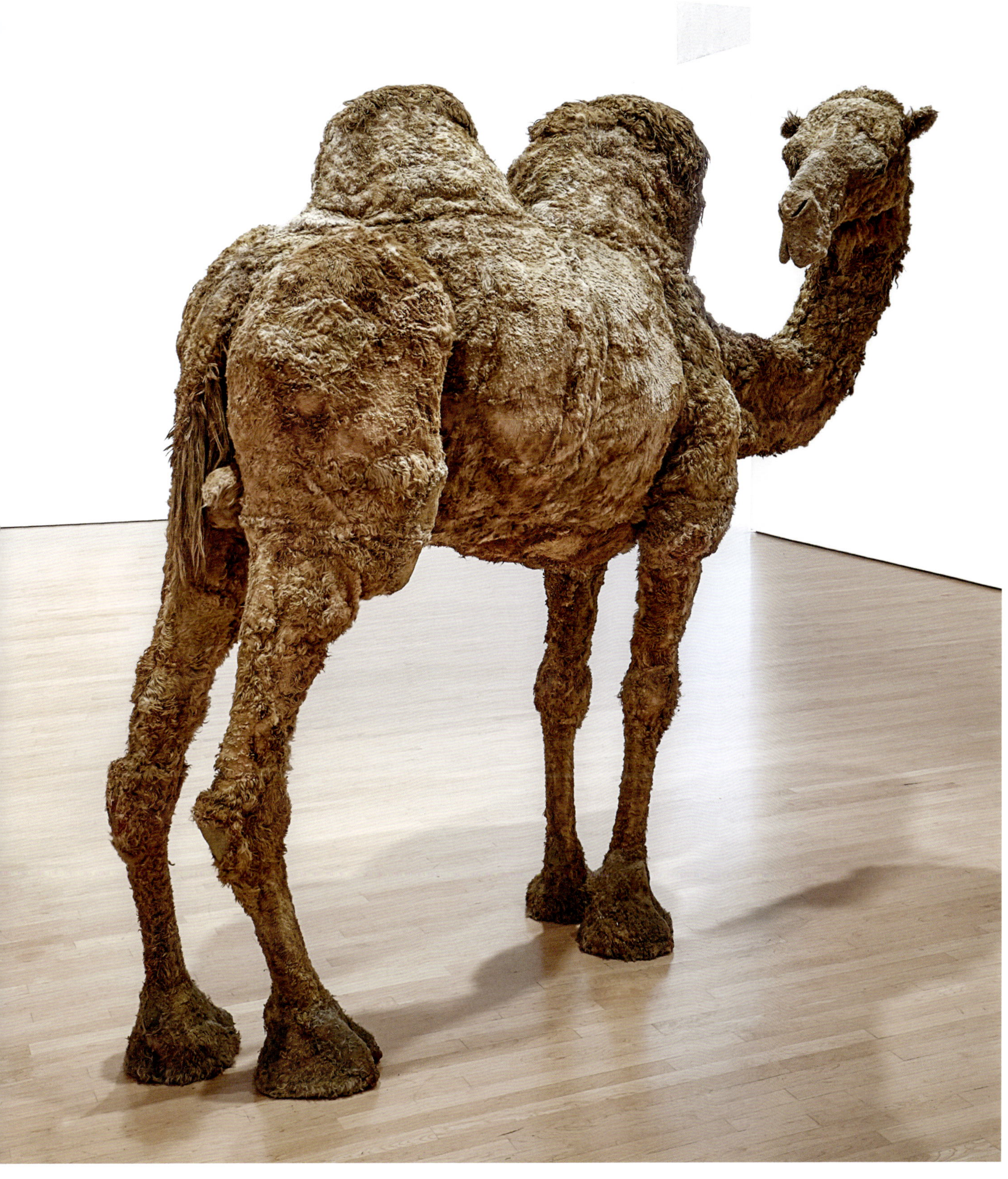

Nancy Graves, *Camel VIII*, 1968–69. Wood, steel, burlap, polyurethane, animal skin, wax, and oil paint, approx. 90 × 120 × 47 ⅝ in. (228.6 × 304.8 × 121.9 cm). National Gallery of Canada, Ottawa; gift of Allan Bronfman, Montreal, 1969

1969

1969 • Throughout his time at the University of Southern California (USC), while studying ceramics and getting his teaching certification, Dale Brockman Davis (b. 1945) grapples with his pacifist convictions and his strong feelings against the Vietnam War in particular, especially considering the looming change to his draft status: upon graduation, it will shift from II-S (deferred because of activity in study) to I-A (available for military service). Shortly before graduating, Davis begins the process of becoming a conscientious objector, as he will later recall:

> I had met someone at one of these tables who was a part of a draft resistance kind of movement, and I found a group of women called Women Strike for Peace. And that was comprised of probably some old school Jewish girls that were anti-war people, and I went and had an interview with them and got information on how to fill out forms, what the process would be for me to become a conscientious objector. . . . My next move is to go to the draft board . . . [and] you take that deep breath and sit before a military board and explain why I was a conscientious objector.

Davis's work *Viet Nam War Games* (1969) references the way that his life feels like it is part of a military game whose aims are in extreme conflict with the artist's own beliefs.

January 2, 1969 • James Monte and Marcia Tucker are announced as new curators at the Whitney Museum of American Art, New York. Tucker is noted as having been a former curator of the William N. Copley Collection, while Monte is coming from a brief stint at the Los Angeles County Museum of Art. Both bring with them an understanding of Surrealism and an appreciation for alternative modes of art making—Monte from his time as a Bay Area artist, critic, and curator, and Tucker from two years managing the Copley collection, which is rich in American and European Surrealist art and the work of emerging artists.

January 9, 1969 • During a meeting at Benny Andrews's Beekman Street loft, a group of artists and arts professionals form the Black Emergency Cultural Coalition (BECC) in response to dissatisfaction over the Metropolitan Museum of Art's soon-to-open exhibition *Harlem on My Mind: Cultural Capital of Black America, 1900–1968* (January 18–April 6, 1969). Among the group's founders are Romare Bearden, Vivian Browne, Reginald Gammon, Henri Ghent, Cliff Joseph, Norman Lewis, Mahler Ryder, Raymond Saunders, and Ed Taylor. Foremost among their critiques are the omission from the exhibition of artworks by any contemporary Black artists in Harlem (James Van Der Zee's photographs are indeed included but are unattributed and exhibited as mural-size blow-ups); the lack of Black curators and administrators at the museum; and the museum's failure to engage the Harlem community in any meaningful way. Three days later, the group gathers to protest the opening of the show, and a statement released by Andrews and co-chair Cliff Joseph describes the BECC as an "action-oriented and watchdog group to implement the legitimate rights and aspirations of individual artists and the total art community." The BECC focuses on institutional actions, and although it does not prescribe a particular definition of "Black art" and its artist members are stylistically varied, the group shows a preference for politically engaged, often surrealist-inflected representational art while criticizing the way in which museums instrumentalize Black abstraction to evade political commentary.

Shortly after its protests of *Harlem on My Mind*, the BECC applies its strategy of direct action to negotiations with the Whitney Museum of American Art, whose exhibition *The 1930s:*

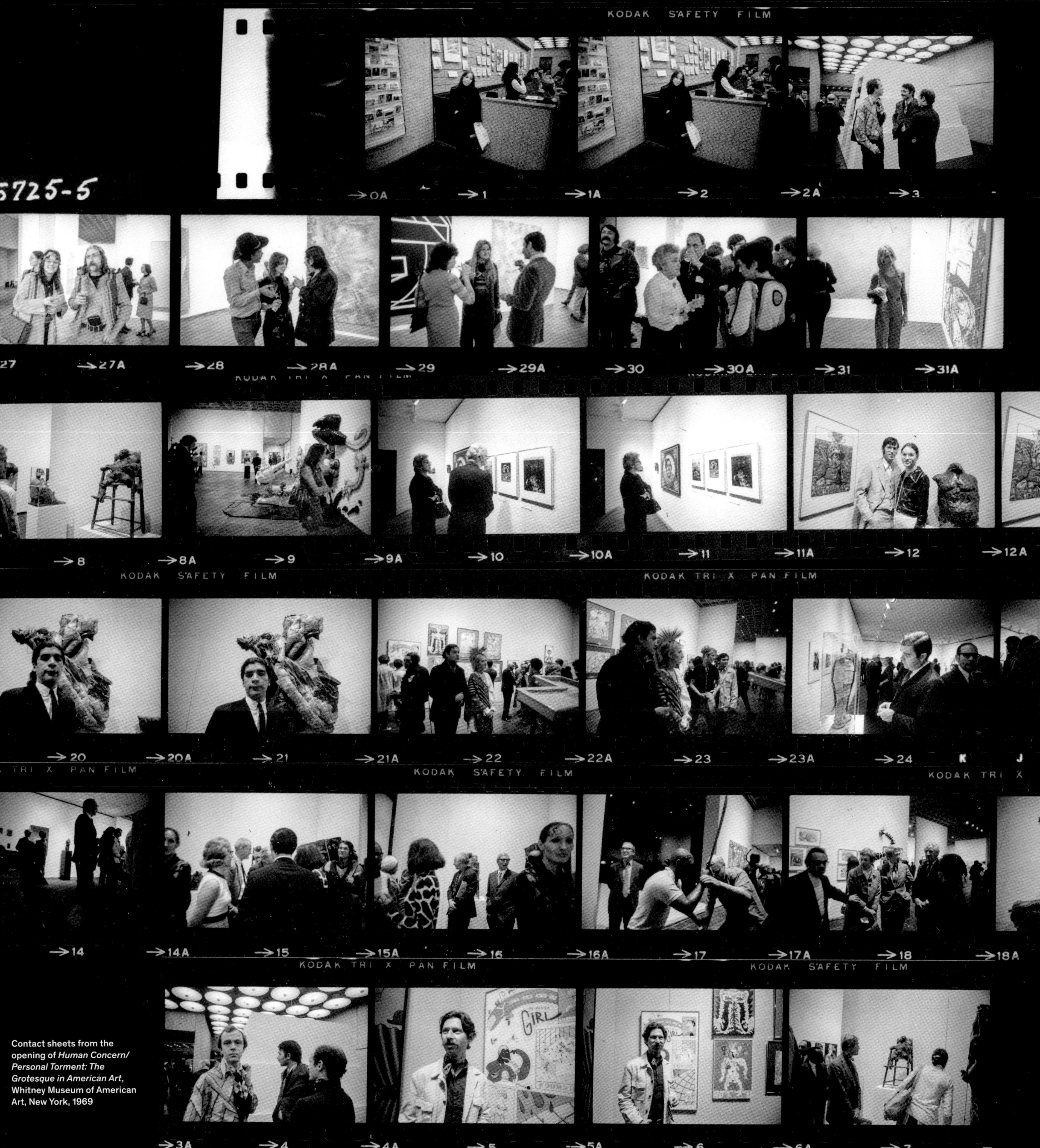

Contact sheets from the opening of *Human Concern/Personal Torment: The Grotesque in American Art*, Whitney Museum of American Art, New York, 1969

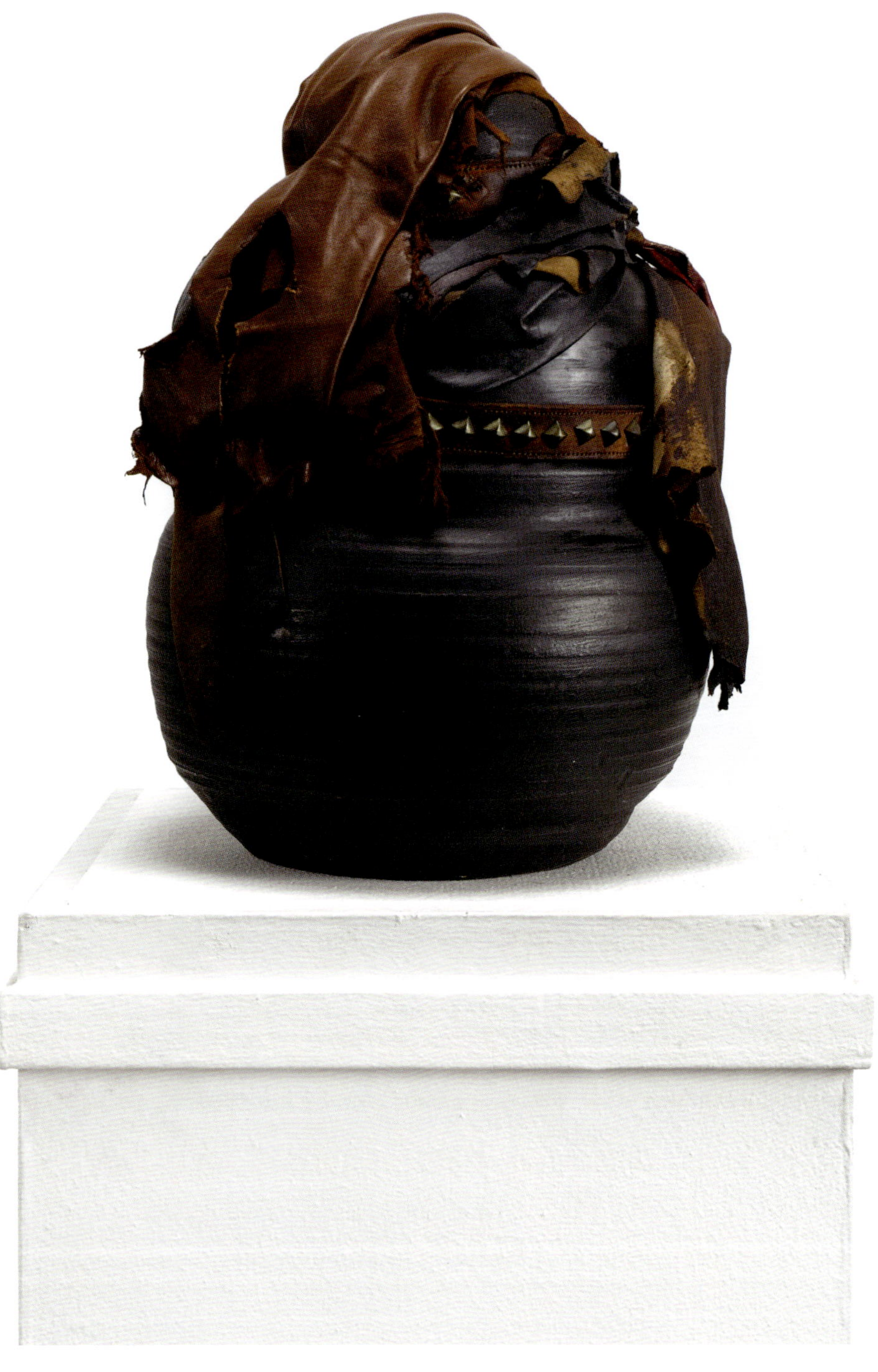

Dale Brockman Davis, *Arabian Nights, #2*, c. 1969–70. Clay, leather, and metal, 18 × 12 × 12 in. (45.7 × 30.5 × 30.5 cm). Collection of the artist

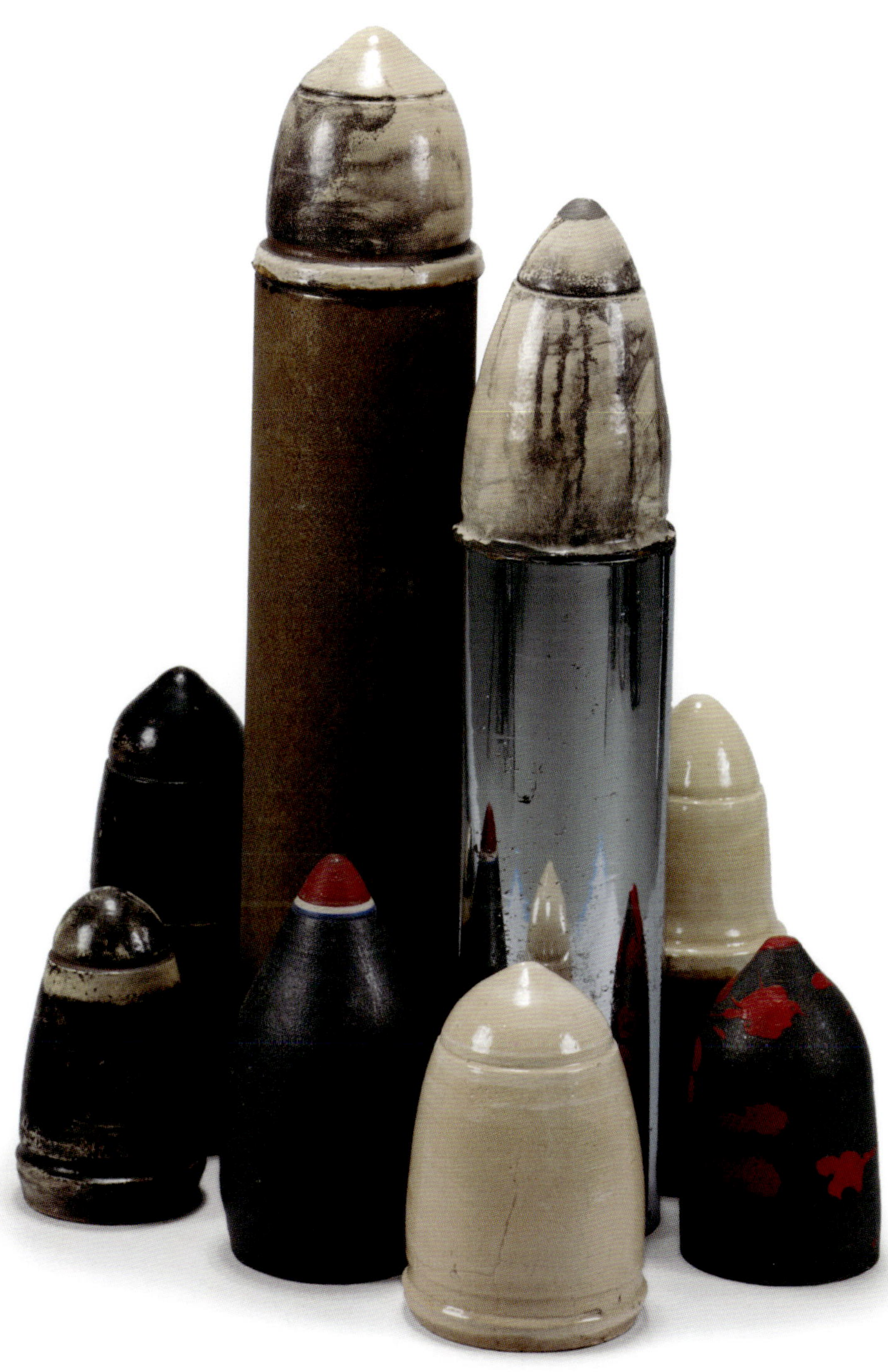

Dale Brockman Davis, *Viet Nam War Games*, 1969. Clay and metal, approximately 48 × 48 in. (121.9 × 121.9 cm). Los Angeles County Museum of Art; gift of the 2021 Decorative Arts and Design Acquisition Committee (DA²) M.2021.194.1–8

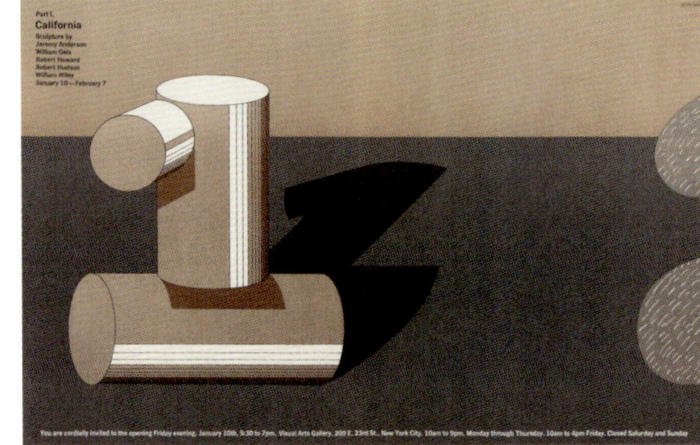

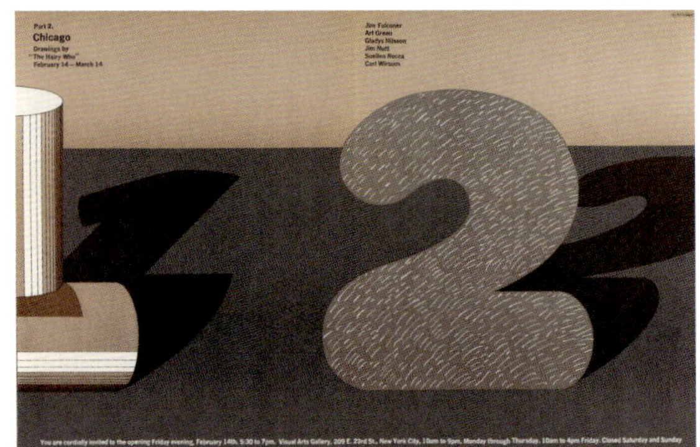

Posters by Milton Glaser, from top, *California Funk (Part 1, California)* and *California Funk (Part 2, Chicago)*, Visual Arts Gallery, New York, 1969

Painting and Sculpture in America the previous autumn had already stirred outrage for its total exclusion of Black artists. The BECC delivers a list of demands to the museum that includes organizing more solo shows for Black artists; creating a survey exhibition of contemporary Black artists' work; including Black artists in the Whitney Annual; acquiring work by Black artists; and recruiting Black curators and staff to work on these initiatives. The Whitney concedes on most points but does not hire a Black curator.

The BECC sees the importance of involving other Black arts organizers in their mission and reaches out to gallery owners, nonprofit leaders, artists, and activists across the country. To this end, Andrews and Joseph circulate their position paper to Alonzo Davis of Brockman Gallery in Los Angeles. "While you are removed from the immediate vicinity of our particular fight, it is a national battle that actually transcends Black artists," they write, arguing that the struggle is of significance to "every man and woman in the country." They encourage Davis to make copies of the BECC position available to Black artists in his area.

January 10–February 7, 1969 • The exhibition *California Funk* is on view at the Visual Arts Gallery, New York. Organized by Shirley Glaser at the School of Visual Arts, the show is the first of two that looks to trends outside of New York and features artists Jeremy Anderson and William T. Wiley, among others. The second exhibition (February 14–March 12) will consist of drawings by the Hairy Who.

1969 • Feeling alienated by New York's arts scene, Carlos Villa moves back to the Bay Area, where he teaches at the San Francisco Art Institute, Sacramento State College, and the Telegraph Hill Neighborhood Center. His relationship with the latter will shape future projects that revolve around cross-cultural arts education and community involvement. Villa's research into Filipino art history and his approach to arts education are also influenced by the demands against oppression in higher education and for self-determination in curriculum being raised by the Third World Liberation Front in the Bay Area at the time, particularly at Berkeley.

During this year and into 1970, Villa's own practice begins to shift as he looks to non-European artistic sources to help him "realize the truth" about his own Filipino background. His materials—bones, blood, feathers, mirrors, shells—reflect his interest in art from Melanesia, and he abandons his formal art-school training. As he will later recall:

> I went to Chinatown and bought some beef blood and then started painting with it in a room with windows that wouldn't open because they were painted shut. It was a hot day and I was gagging. And my stomach was churning and I knew it was right. It was because I was affected physically by what I was doing. And the directness was what I was striving for. In New York the thing that bothered me was that art was very conceptual . . . an extension of conversations of esthetics. . . . There was a lot of fantastic art I loved in New York—Ken Noland, Mark di Suvero, Carl Andre—but there was something about it that wasn't sensual, that didn't move me physically. So when I smelled the blood and began to get nauseated by it, I just said, "God, this is what art is supposed to do to you."

February 2, 1969 • Less than two weeks after the inauguration of President Richard M. Nixon, Jack Smith shows *No President* (1967–70) at the Elgin Theatre, New York. *No President* is a reassemblage of several other films and film fragments that Smith had shot with Bob Fleischner between 1959 and 1963, namely *Reefers of Technicolor Island*, *Scrub-Woman of Atlantis*, *Rat-Droppings of Uranus*, *Marshgas of Flatulandia*, *The Flake of Soot*, and *Overstimulated*. It also incorporates found newsreel footage of the 1940 Republican convention and nomination of Wendell Willkie, as well as fantastical narrative tableaux recycled from Smith's *The Kidnapping of Wendell Willkie by the Love Bandit*. The program evolves over multiple runnings under different titles and will continue to change, a testament to Smith's performative and improvisatory approach to film.

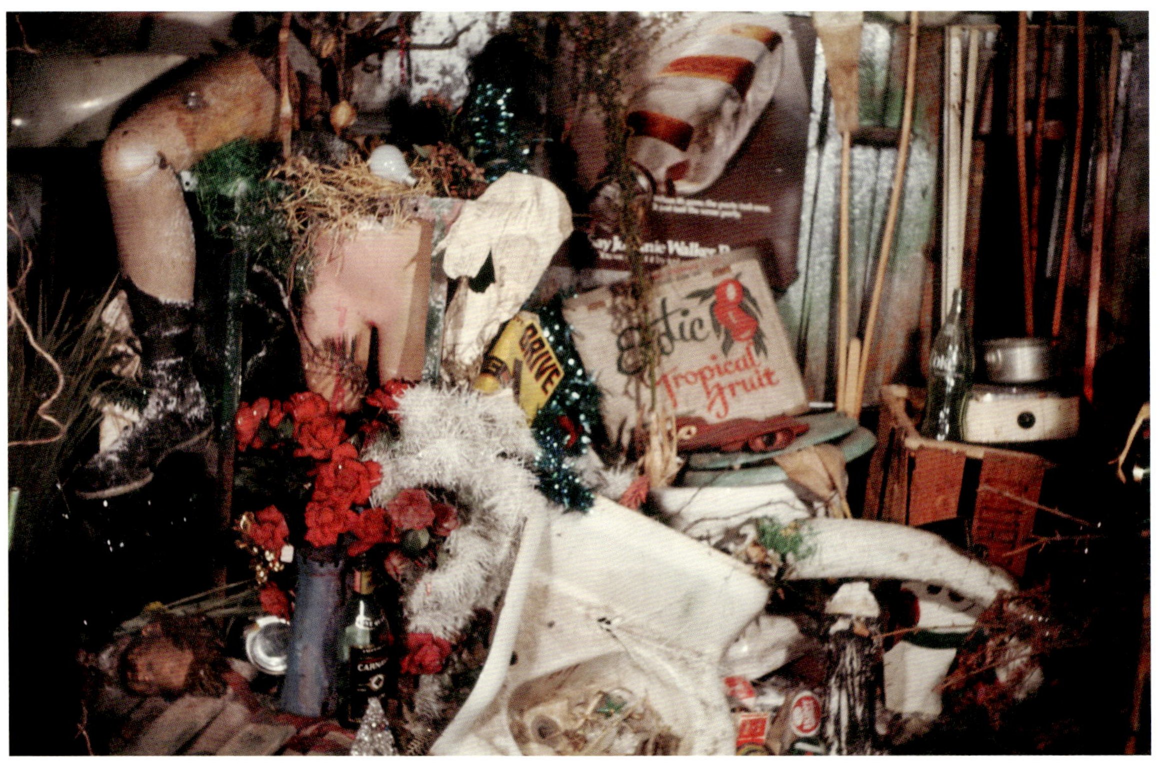

Jack Smith, *Untitled (Plaster Foundation of Atlantis)*, c. 1970. 35mm film slide

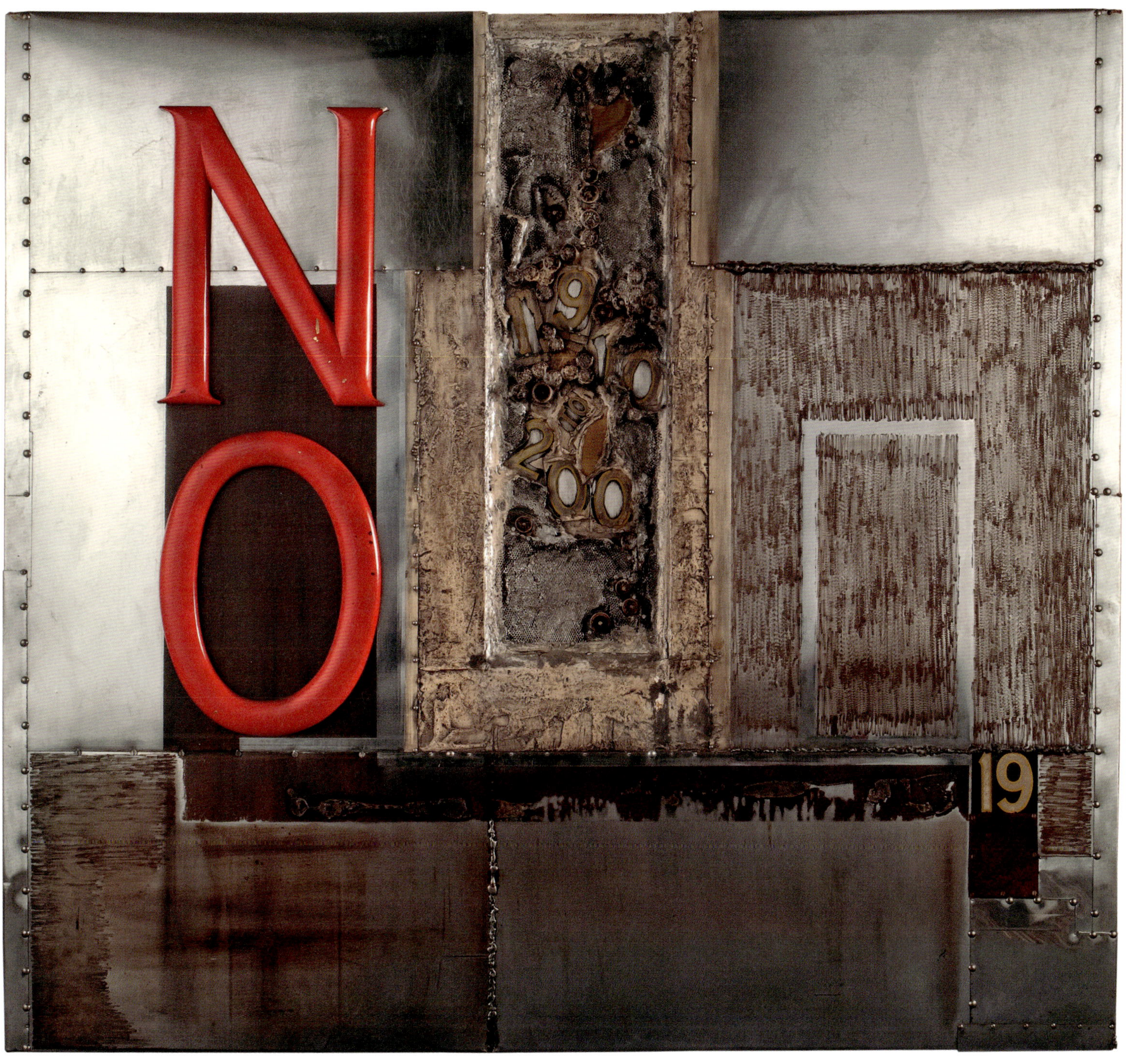

John Outterbridge, *No Time for Jivin'*, 1969, from the *Containment Series*. Mixed media, 56 × 60 in. (142.2 × 152.4 cm). Mills College Art Museum, Northeastern University, Oakland, CA; Museum Purchase, Susan L. Mills Fund 1971.31

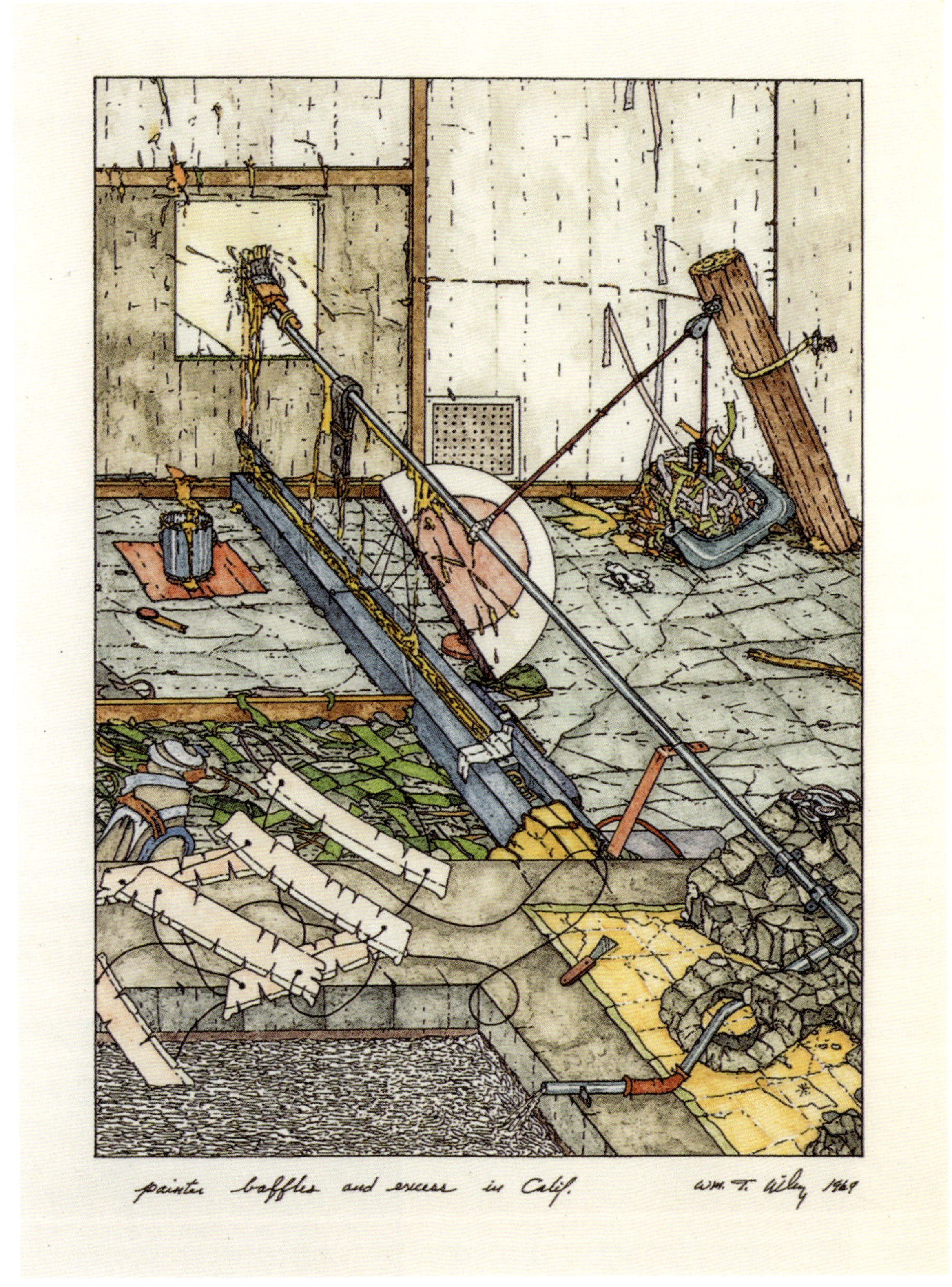

William T. Wiley, *Painter Baffles and Excess in California*, 1969. Ink, pencil, felt-tip pen, and watercolor on paper, 28 ¼ × 20 ¼ in. (71.8 × 51.4 cm). Collection of Susan W. Paine

Around this time, Smith moves to a new two-floor loft space in SoHo that he calls "The Plaster Foundation of Atlantis." The loft becomes a "free theater" where artists in the downtown arts scene congregate for free performances every Saturday at midnight. Deepening his shift toward emphasizing theater and performance, and away from finished products, Smith conceives the space as an always-live film set filled with trash and junk—the raw material, or "plaster," that Smith and others re-enliven through performance.

February 5–March 2, 1969 • David Hammons and Noah Purifoy have a two-person exhibition at Brockman Gallery, Los Angeles. Hammons shows some of his earliest body-print works, made by first coating his own body, clothes, and hair with a grease such as margarine and then pressing himself against board or paper before setting the grease with a dusting of pigment. Hammons had begun making these works the year before in a former dance hall on Slauson Avenue, having at least an offhand awareness of the performances of French artist Yves Klein: naked women, covered in International Klein Blue paint, imprint their bodies onto canvases against a backdrop of tuxedos and classical music. "I was using a Klein technique to achieve a Charles White feel," Hammons will explain. The artist's assertion of the Black body, both intimate and performative, also often includes symbols of politics and struggle, from American flags to prison bars to raised fists.

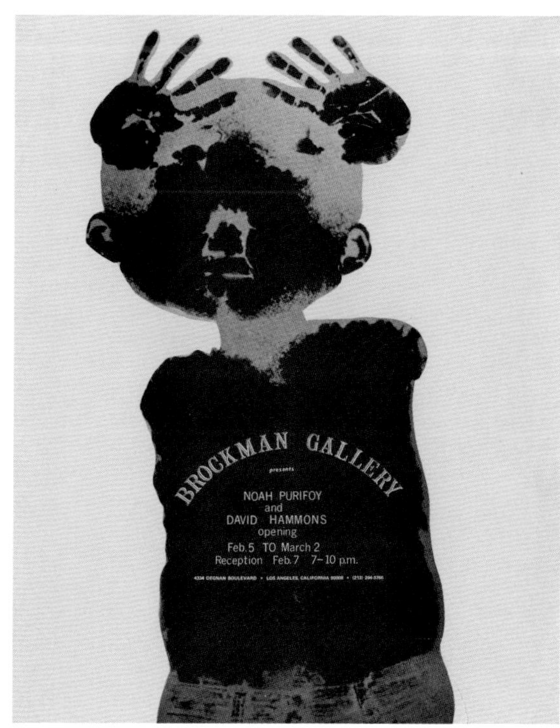

Poster for *Noah Purifoy and David Hammons*, Brockman Gallery, Los Angeles, 1969

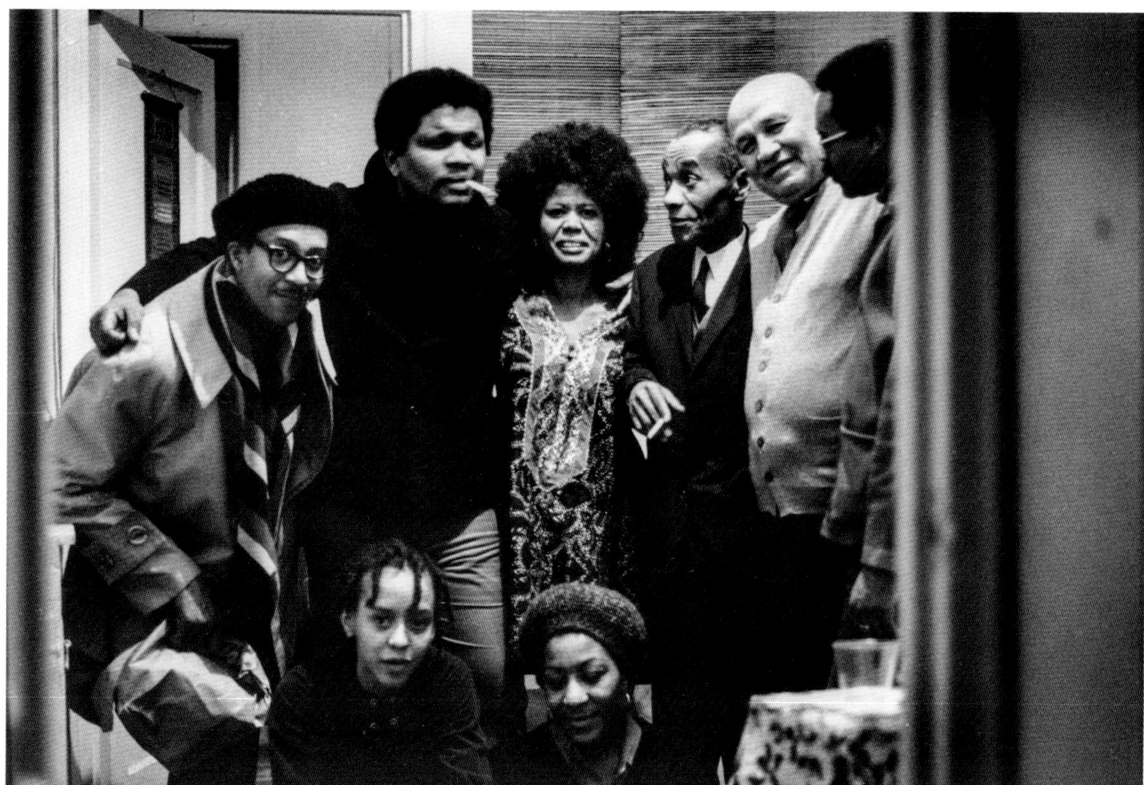

Bob Rogers, Nikki Giovanni, Ishmael Reed, Evelyn Neal, Jayne Cortez, Léon-Gontran Damas, Romare Bearden, and Larry Neal, New York, 1969

February 25–May 4, 1969 • Kay Sekimachi participates in *Wall Hangings*, an international survey of contemporary fiber art at the Museum of Modern Art, New York, organized by MoMA curator of design Mildred Constantine and textile designer Jack Lenor Larsen, a friend of Sekimachi's from the Haystack Mountain School of Crafts who had invited her to contribute to the show. *Wall Hangings* marks a watershed moment for fiber art: bringing together a selection of abstract, nonfunctional woven works, Larsen and Constantine identify a mode of artistic textile production whose beginnings they locate in the Wiener Werkstätte and the Bauhaus weaving workshop. "Decorative" is how Louise Bourgeois ultimately describes the works in the show, however, signaling unresolved debates over the proximity of art to craft as experiments in weaving and soft sculpture converge in the 1960s. Constantine and Larsen will further develop their ideas about contemporary fiber art in their book *Beyond Craft: The Art Fabric* (1973), in which they highlight Sekimachi's innovative multilayered weavings.

Spring 1969 • Melvin Edwards makes illustrations for *Pissstained Stairs and the Monkey Man's Wares*, the first book of poetry by activist and poet Jayne Cortez, which she publishes in summer. The two had become acquainted in Los Angeles through their mutual friend the designer Bob Rogers, and it is Rogers who suggests to both that Edwards illustrate Cortez's book. In June, Cortez attends the opening of the group show *X to the Fourth Power* at the Studio Museum in Harlem, where Edwards's work is on display. With his first marriage having ended in 1968, Edwards becomes close with Cortez, the pair eventually marrying in 1975 and continuing to collaborate artistically. Cortez's poems evoke surrealist imagery, but as historian Robin D. G. Kelley has suggested: "Surrealism was less a revelation than a recognition of what already existed in the black tradition. For Cortez surrealism is merely a tool to help create a strong revolutionary movement and a powerful, independent poetry." For Cortez and Edwards, who in the 1970s will increasingly derive meaning from unlikely sculptural juxtapositions, surrealism is a language, both written and visual, by which to articulate anti-imperialist sentiment.

In October of the same year, Edwards meets Léon-Gontran Damas, the French-Guianese poet and cofounder (along with Aimé Césaire and Léopold Sédar Senghor) of the midcentury anticolonist Négritude movement. Damas's poetry resonates deeply with Edwards, and he become a mentor to the artist, who drives him around whenever he visits New York. When Damas dies in January 1978, Edwards makes the sculpture *Homage to the Poet Leon Gontran Damas* (1978), basing it on

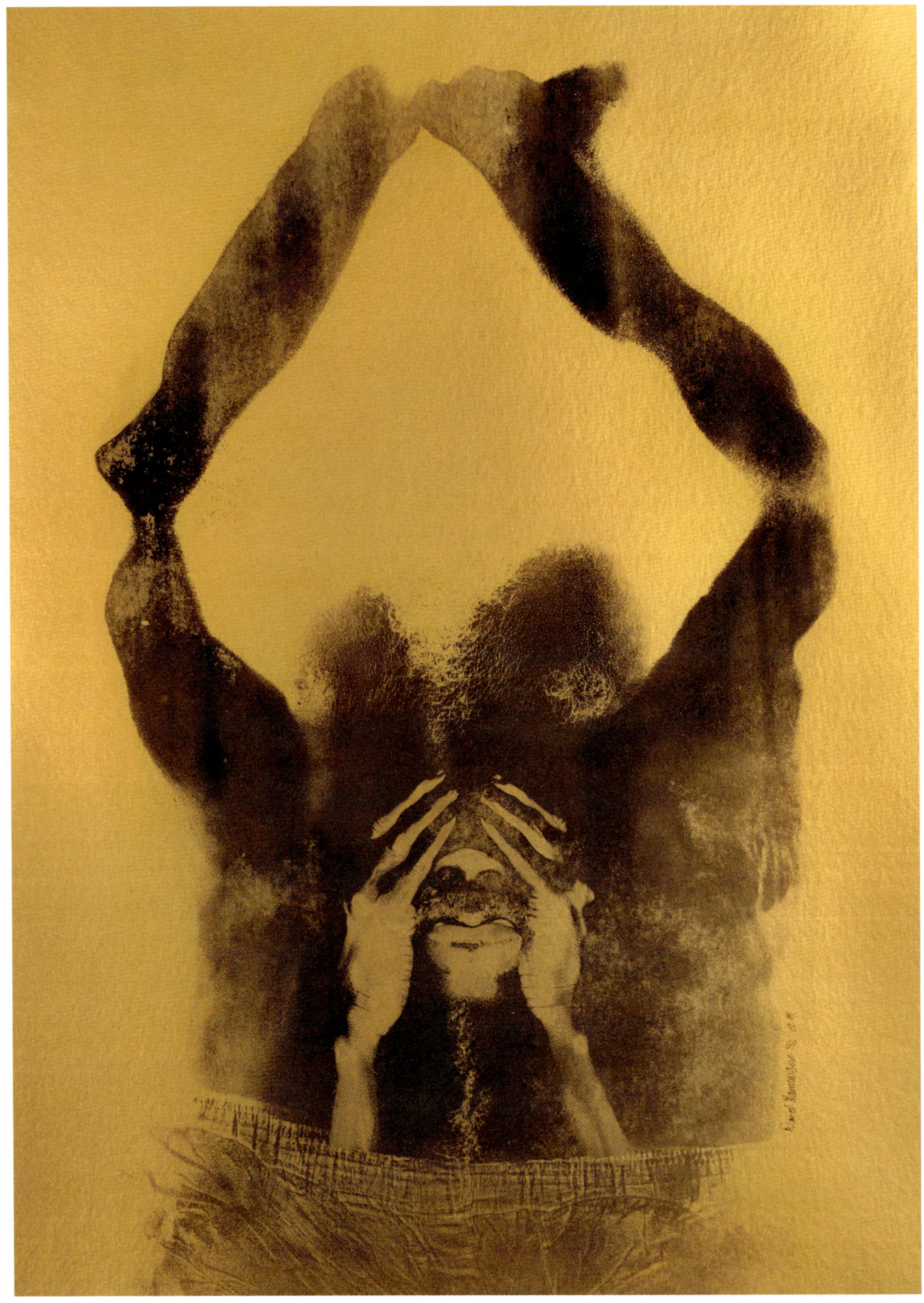

David Hammons, *Close Your Eyes and See Black*, 1969. Pigment on gold-coated paperboard, 35 ⅞ × 24 ¾ in. (91.1 × 62.9 cm). Solomon R. Guggenheim Museum, New York; purchased through prior gifts of Daimler-Benz in honor of Thomas M. Messer, the National Endowment for the Arts in Washington, DC, William C. Edwards Jr., in memory of Sibyl H. Edwards, the Estate of Karl Nierendorf, Mr. and Mrs. Morton L. Ostow, and Dr. Solomon W. Schaefer, 2018

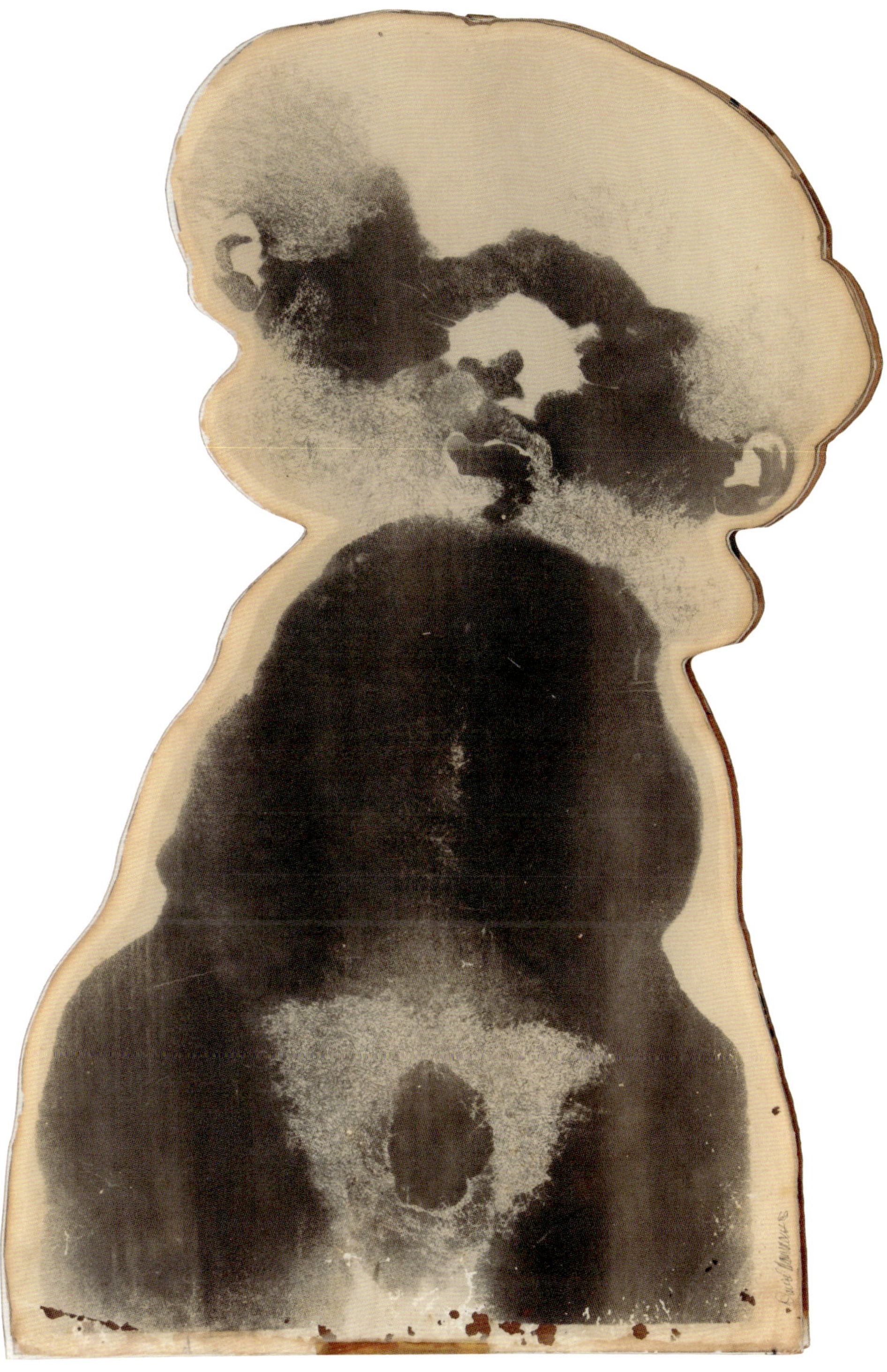

David Hammons, *Untitled*, 1969. Grease and pigment on paper in Plexiglas, 32 ⅜ × 19 ¼ × ¼ in. (82.2 × 48.9 × 0.6 cm). Tilton Gallery, New York

discussions they had surrounding a commission for the poet's house in his home country.

March 1–29, 1969 • Anita Steckel exhibits works from her series *Multiple Images* and debuts her series *Giant Women on New York* at Kozmopolitan Gallery, New York. The exhibition announcement consists of a succession of blurbs by various friends and admirers, among them artist Richard Lindner, who writes, "Don't let them change your work; don't let them get to you."

March 8–April 13, 1969 • The exhibition *Don Baum Says "Chicago Needs Famous Artists"* at the Museum of Contemporary Art Chicago is a roundup of Baum's vision of Chicago art of the moment and includes Roger Brown, Gladys Nilsson, Jim Nutt, Christina Ramberg, Barbara Rossi, H. C. Westermann, and Karl Wirsum. The installation riffs on the vernacular interiors of the city as well as the Hairy Who exhibitions at the Hyde Park Art Center, and it includes wallpaper printed with bricks or faux-wood paneling, patterned wallpaper, shelving, and cabinets—earnest evocations of the environments in which these artists lived and worked.

March 15–April 10, 1969 • Luis Jimenez's first solo show is on view, at Graham Gallery, a result of the artist's audacity and luck after three years in New York. Frustrated by the difficulty of using slides to garner gallery interest in his work, he had loaded his sculptures into the back of his truck a couple of months earlier and, finding the front of Castelli Gallery empty between exhibitions, brought a number of fiberglass sculptures into the space, set them up, and asked to speak to gallery director Ivan Karp. This despite the fact that, as Jimenez will later confess, "I knew that Castelli wasn't going to show my pieces. If you've been in New York for three years you know that every gallery has a certain thing they're going to show." Karp is taken aback by Jimenez's audacity but immediately takes two drawings and suggests that David Herbert, the new director at Graham Gallery, may be interested. Indeed, Jimenez's first solo show at Graham Gallery will be followed by another in 1970. These include two influential works: *American Dream*—originally made in 1967 but recast and sprayed in 1969—which depicts a car and a woman in a sexual embrace, demonstrating the artist's ongoing interest in human-machine hybridity; and *Sunbather* (1969), in which a heavyset man, sunburned, lies with a newspaper exclaiming "RIOT" over his face, a humorous

Continued on page 271

MEL CASAS AND LUIS JIMENEZ: TWO CHICANO TRAILBLAZERS FROM TEXAS

RUBEN C. CORDOVA

Mel Casas was a thirty-five-year-old art professor at San Antonio College and an artist working in an Abstract Expressionist vein when, on a nighttime drive in 1965, he glimpsed the screen of the San Pedro Outdoor Theater. The larger-than-life actress, instead of speaking, appeared to be "munching" on trees in the landscape, a visual experience Casas characterized as "surreal."[1] It inaugurated his cycle of 153 *Humanscape* paintings, a sustained critique of the psychological manipulations performed by media images that the artist would produce over the next twenty-four years, inspired as much by Marshall McLuhan's *The Mechanical Bride: Folklore of Industrial Man* (1951) as by his glimpse of the drive-in movie screen.[2]

Each *Humanscape* features a large "screen" image—the functional equivalent of the San Pedro drive-in screen—against which Casas juxtaposes objects and/or people in the foreground, often images from popular culture and the mass media that serve symbolic functions. The artist's turn to figuration coincided with the burgeoning Chicano movement, which had commenced the same year as Casas's drive-in revelation, when farm workers went on strike against grape growers in California. Though Texas state laws forbade picketing and other standard union practices, workers in Starr County nevertheless undertook a wildcat strike against melon growers.[3] As David Montejano notes, the melon strike and its brutal suppression "ignited a broad resentment among all classes of the Mexican American community" in Texas, radicalizing high school and college students, and "even the usually proper middle class."[4]

The nebulous spectators of Casas's early *Humanscape* paintings gradually evolved into fully fleshed beings, and in January 1968, with *Humanscape 40 (Game)*, he inaugurated the use of subtitles to multiply the verbal–visual puns

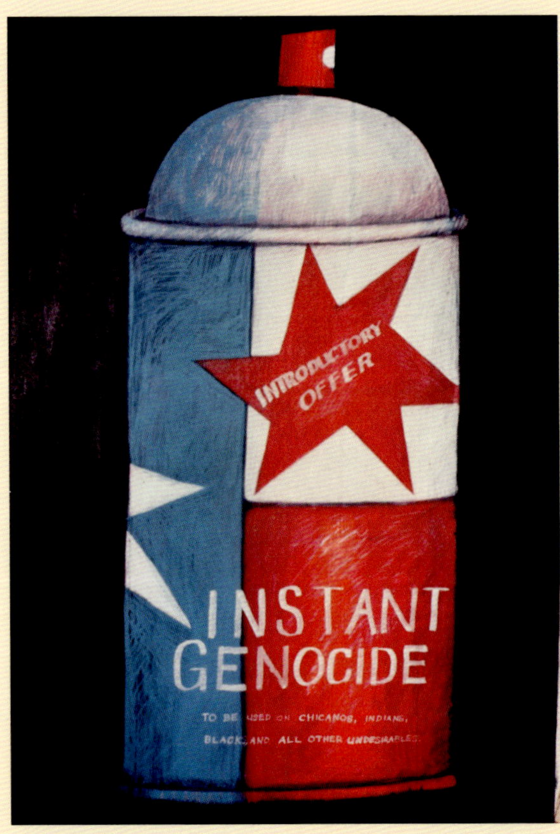

Fig. 1. Felipe Reyes, *Peace on Earth Good Will Towards Men aka Instant Genocide*, c. 1971. Acrylic on canvas, dimensions unknown

present in these painted ensembles.[5] The following month, in California, United Farm Workers leader César Chávez began a twenty-five-day hunger strike, which culminated in a Catholic mass attended by Senator Robert F. Kennedy, who would be killed in June, two months after Martin Luther King Jr. That year, Casas told a journalist that he wanted his screen images to be "more real than reality," a surreal description of their intended symbolic valence.[6] He abandoned oneiric cinemascapes for increasingly vivid political paintings and depictions of the sexual revolution, and at the same time emerged at the vanguard of artists situating the Chicano struggle for civil rights within a broader context of the country's social and political upheavals. An American flag–draped coffin dominates the foreground of *Humanscape #47 (Still-Life)* (1968); the letters "KKK" that are emblazoned on it refer to the assassinations of the Kennedy brothers and King as well as to the racism that fueled much of that era's political violence. *Humanscape #49 (Meta-Ethics)* (1968) features human-shaped shooting-range targets, with one of the white shooters taking direct aim at the viewer.[7]

"The concept of American beauty is not only physical beauty, it's also racial beauty," Casas once said.[8] He connected the American veneration of blondness to what he termed the "Barbie ideal," a point he dramatically made when he received 1968 artist-of-the-year honors from a San Antonio art group and proceeded to strip a Barbie doll while lecturing about white privilege, which resulted in the revocation of the prize.[9] The following year, Casas issued an arresting rejoinder in the form of *Humanscape #56 (San Antonio Circus)* (p. 274). It critiques Fiesta, the city's annual festival celebrating the defeat of the Mexican army in 1836 at the Battle of San Jacinto. This victory enabled the establishment of the Republic of Texas, the culmination of a "revolution" for independence that was, in fact, a land grab that also sought to perpetuate the enslavement of Black people.[10] Specifically, Casas addresses the crowning of a Fiesta queen and her court by the Order of the Alamo, an elite, racially exclusive group.[11] As such, these faux royals are traditionally drawn from a coterie of Anglo and German American families, chosen more for their wealth and Texas heritage than for their beauty, talent, or congeniality.

Although Casas sometimes represented blond women as malevolent symbols of hegemonic power in the screen images of his early *Humanscape* paintings, here his eight vacant Alamo queens appear both villainous and preposterous. Most dramatically, they are eyeless, their empty sockets instead occupied by elements from the ridiculous tiaras worn by their adjacent royals: crystal scrollwork, red orbs (a symbolic cherry?), yellow

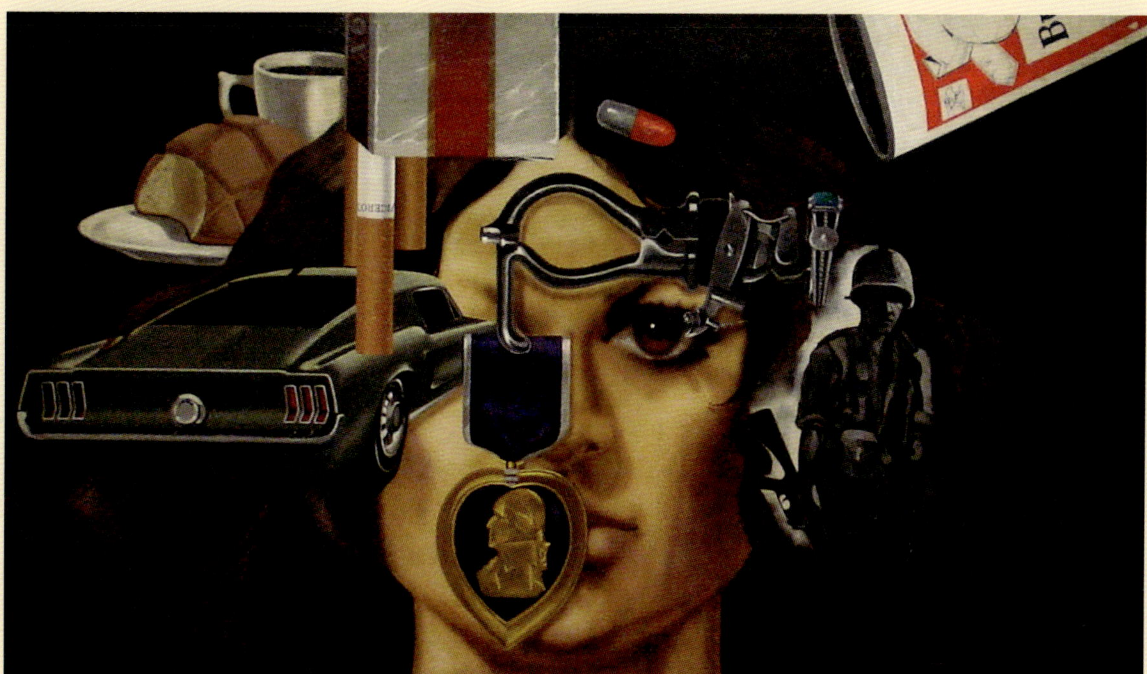

Fig. 2. Jesse Treviño, *Mi Vida*, 1971–72. Acrylic on gypsum board, 96 × 168 in. (243.9 × 426.7 cm)

stars, and dollar signs. Atop this social pyramid, the queen of queens surmounts a bell-capped fool. Her red eye and the horn-like aspect of her Lone Star crown make her appear demonic, yet her elongated neck seems to connect her to the giraffes that lean in for their photo op and to their unwittingly comic expressions.

If the not-quite-fully-formed figures of this royal court seem to hark back to the dreamlike, somnambulistic figures in earlier *Humanscapes*, the caged, growling tiger, by contrast, is startlingly realistic and vigorous. It represents the excluded people of color, their righteous anger as well as their nascent power, currently held at bay—but for how long? The year after Casas painted this *Humanscape*, the white establishment in Texas was dumbfounded when Chicanos swept elections in Crystal City and Zavala County, where they held large pluralities. Chicano activists who had launched a nationwide campaign against the Vietnam War were met with violence in Los Angeles, where police killed two youths and the journalist Rubén Salazar. The killing of a bystander at a demonstration against police brutality in Pharr, Texas, in 1971 led to the mobilization of Mexican American and Chicano residents, who would go on to win political offices in Pharr and other cities in the Rio Grande Valley.[12]

Felipe Reyes, the primary founder of the Chicano artist group Con Safo, which Casas subsequently joined and chaired, responded to the state-sponsored violence with *Instant Genocide* (fig. 1). Its label based on the Texas flag, this genocidal spray can bears the inscription: "To be used on Chicanos, Indians, Blacks, and all other

undesirables."[13] Objects of popular consumer culture are likewise connected to potentially lethal violence in *Mi Vida* (fig. 2), a mural Casas's student Jesse Treviño created on his bedroom wall. The haunting, phantasmatic painting was a response to the grave injuries the artist sustained in Vietnam, which resulted in the amputation of his painting hand.[14]

In *Humanscape #68 (Kitchen Spanish)* (fig. 3) Casas depicts furtive resistance. A cartoonish undocumented Mexican maid (taken from a handbook instructing housewives to boss their servants) appears to be all-obeisant: She says yes to everything. But *perra* ("dog") is also slang for "bitch."[15] Casas demonstrates that even the most powerless have the ability to resist. And, above all, Chicano history is the history of resistance.

Indeed, at the same moment Casas was confronting the legacy of Anglo supremacy in his *Humanscape #56 (San Antonio Circus)*, fellow El Paso native Luis Jimenez was also emerging as a critical figure giving visual expression to the Chicano movement's spirit of defiance. From a remarkable crucible filled with mythic, historical, artistic, personal, and popular sources *Man on Fire* (1969–70; p. 269) emerged, a work that Jimenez described as a "spiritual self-portrait."[16] Its fiberglass material and intense, reflective, colorful finish connect it to popular culture and commercial products, in particular the automobile, that quintessential symbol of postwar American prosperity and a fixation that figured prominently in the contemporaneous imagery of the artist, who grew up in El Paso working at his father's neon sign shop, where he also learned to work fiberglass auto bodies and custom spray-paint hot rods. In 1967, Jimenez had feverishly penned images of a Volkswagen and a woman in sexual union, inaugurating a human–machine theme rooted in Jungian myth that would prove fertile.[17] The artist intended his mating cars and humans as contemporary versions of ancient European and Mesoamerican myths, manifestations of archetypal content in the imagery and technology of the auto-industrial age, with motorcycles, Porsches, or a Jaguar-like *Cat Car* (1967) replacing Olympian or Mesoamerican gods. Jimenez also depicted the offspring of the carnal machine–human union in the drawing *Woman Giving Birth to Motorcycle Man* (1969) and the sculpture *Birth of the Machine Age Man* (1970). The latter features an auto–man hybrid blasting out of the womb, replete with a neon umbilical chord, a modern-day incarnation of the Aztec patron god Huitzilopochtli, who was born with full regalia and a lust for vengeance.[18]

If *Man on Fire* is a human torch that represents the ideal of liberty, it contrasts pointedly with Jimenez's take on that more conventional representation, the Statue of Liberty. In multiple works at this time, the artist satirized the American icon, whose promise he regarded as "racially exclusive," the works' titles alone indicative of his jaundiced view: *Fallen Statue of Liberty* (1963), *Statue of Liberty with Pack of Cigarettes* (1969), and *Statue of Liberty with Wine* (1969).[19] Jimenez monumentalized his depiction of a white, blond Lady Liberty—slattern, inebriated, decadent—in *The Barfly—Statue of Liberty* (fig. 4) the same year he produced *Man on Fire*. Like *Man on Fire*, his immoral Lady Liberties are expressions of the artist's opposition to the Vietnam War.

Jimenez's inspirations for *Man on Fire* suggest it as a far nobler representation of liberty, rooted in heroic struggle against oppression and injustice. A colored pencil study from 1969 depicts a man tossing a Molotov cocktail, inspired by Black and Puerto Rican protestors Jimenez witnessed in

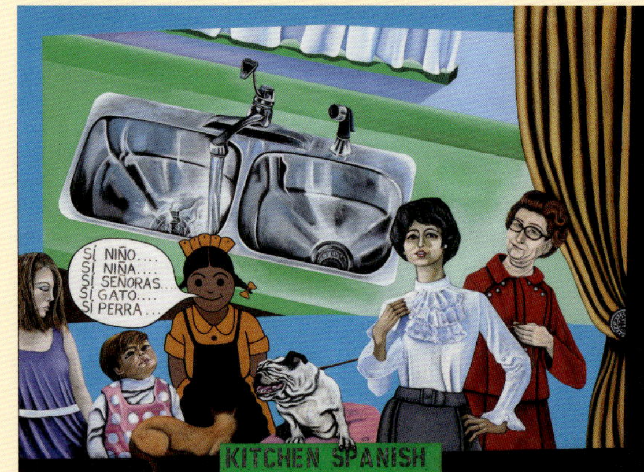

Fig. 3. Mel Casas, *Humanscape #68 (Kitchen Spanish)*, 1973. Acrylic on canvas, 72 × 96 in. (182.9 × 243.9 cm)

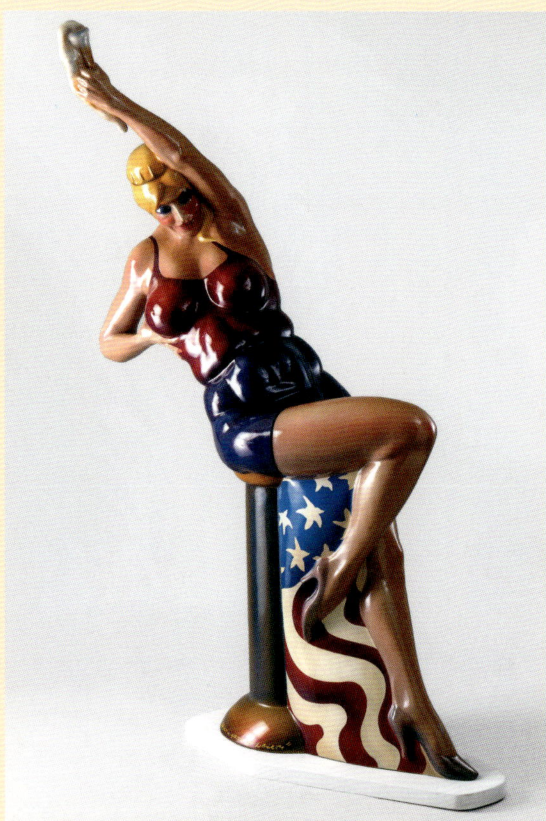

Fig. 4. Luis Jimenez, *The Barfly—Statue of Liberty*, 1969–74. Acrylic on fiberglass, 88 × 54 × 30 in. (223.5 × 137.2 × 76.2 cm)

New York, whom he viewed as mythic, fire-giving Promethean figures. The artist also drew Buddhist monks, whose self-immolations in protest of persecution at the hands of the South Vietnamese government and of the Vietnam War were widely televised. He likened their mute suffering to that of the last Aztec leader, Cuauhtémoc, who was tortured by fire and executed by the Spanish, and whom Jimenez regarded as a stoic superman.[20] Even as the visual association of the flaming head of *Man on Fire* to the hood ornaments on the Pontiac cars owned by Jimenez's father connects on one level to the artist's automotive–human hybrids, it also connects to another Indigenous leader who confronted European colonialist forces, the Odawa chief Pontiac, who fought the British in the mid-eighteenth century.[21]

While sacrifice—especially self-sacrifice—and defiance are significant aspects of the statue's meaning, the colored pencil study *Red Angel* (1969) confers another layer of meaning. The twin plumes that arise from the burning man in this sketch resemble wings; as the title implies, the man is something more than a torture victim or self-immolating protestor: he is a formidable, supernatural force, a revivified Cuauhtémoc/Pontiac/superman, a guardian of the just, perhaps even an avenger.

NOTES

1 Ruben C. Cordova, "The Cinematic Genesis of the Mel Casas Humanscape, 1965–1967," *Aztlán: A Journal of Chicano Studies* 36, no. 2 (Fall 2011): 51.

2 Ibid., 53–54, 60, 62–64, 68, 73.

3 Ruben C. Cordova, "Felipe Reyes, Part 2: The United Farm Workers and UFW Imagery, c. 1970–72," *Glasstire*, August 3, 2020, https://glasstire.com/2020/08/03/felipe-reyes-part-2-the-united-farm-workers-and-ufw-imagery-c-1970-72/.

4 David Montejano, *Anglos and Mexicans in the Making of Texas, 1836–1986* (Austin: University of Texas Press, 1987), 284.

5 Cordova, "Cinematic Genesis," 51–53, 55, 76–77.

6 Ibid., 63, 76–77.

7 Ruben C. Cordova, "Getting the Big Picture: Political Themes in the Humanscapes of Mel Casas, 1968–1977," in *Born of Resistance: Cara a Cara Encounters with Chicana/o Visual Culture*, ed. Victor A. Sorell and Scott L. Baugh (Tucson: University of Arizona Press, 2015), 175–76, 181–82.

8 Mel Casas, quoted in Jacinto Quirarte, *Mexican American Artists* (Austin: University of Texas Press, 1973), 133.

9 Cordova, "Cinematic Genesis," 58–60. See also, Ruben C. Cordova, "Is It Time for San Antonio's Fiesta to Secede from San Jacinto? A Modest Proposal," *Glasstire*, June 23, 2021 (updated April 17, 2023), https://glasstire.com/2021/06/23/is-it-time-for-san-antonios-fiesta-to-secede-from-san-jacinto-a-modest-proposal/.

10 In Texas mythology, the "sacrifice" of the Anglo American occupiers of the Alamo enabled the victory at San Jacinto. The Alamo became a potent anti-Mexican symbol and a central element in the rituals of elite Anglo groups that are enacted annually at Fiesta. See Ruben C. Cordova, *The Other Side of the Alamo: Art Against the Myth* (San Antonio: Guadalupe Cultural Arts Center and Blurb, 2018).

11 Cordova, "Getting the Big Picture," 176–77. For an expanded analysis of this painting, see Cordova, "Is It Time for San Antonio's Fiesta to Secede from San Jacinto?"

12 Ruben C. Cordova, "Felipe Reyes, Part 3: Struggles in Pharr and San Antonio; Race, Trump and the 2020 Election," *Glasstire*, October 26, 2020, https://glasstire.com/2020/10/26/felipe-reyes-part-3-struggles-in-pharr-and-san-antonio-race-trump-and-the-2020-election/.

13 Ruben C. Cordova, "Felipe Reyes, Part 1: 'Instant Genocide,' Rubén Salazar, and Black Lives Matter," *Glasstire*, July 20, 2020, https://glasstire.com/2020/07/20/felipe-reyes-part-i-instant-genocide-ruben-salazar-and-black-lives-matter/.

14 Ruben C. Cordova, "A Baptism of Fire: Jesse Treviño Paints *Mi Vida*," *Glasstire*, January 26, 2019, https://glasstire.com/2019/01/26/a-baptism-of-fire-jesse-trevino-paints-mi-vida/.

15 See Cordova, "Getting the Big Picture," 179–80; and Constance Cortez, "Aztlan in Tejas: Chicano/Chicana Art from the Third Coast," in Cheech Marin, *Chicano Visions: American Painters on the Verge* (Boston: Bullfinch Press, 2002), 37.

16 The statue includes a self-referential anatomical anomaly that the artist referred to as his "deformed" rib cage, the edge of which has a pronounced wishbone-like character. See Ruben C. Cordova, "Luis Jimenez's *Man on Fire*: From the Olmec Were-Jaguar and the Vietnam War to Spiritual Self-Portrait," *Glasstire*, March 16, 2022, https://glasstire.com/2022/03/16/luis-jimenezs-man-on-fire-from-the-olmec-were-jaguar-and-the-vietnam-war-to-spiritual-self-portrait/.

17 Jimenez valued Jungian psychology because he shared Jung's belief that universal archetypal forms reappeared repeatedly across time and space. See Cordova, "Jimenez's *Man on Fire*."

18 Ibid.

19 Ibid.

20 Ibid.

21 Like Cuauhtémoc, Pontiac led an anticolonial resistance movement, one that was more prolonged. Some Pontiac Indian hood ornaments morph into jet airplanes, which may have influenced Jimenez's machine–men hybrids. These hybrid hood ornaments likely inspired his works that treat the theme of progress (from the horse age to the jet age). See Cordova, "Jimenez's *Man on Fire*."

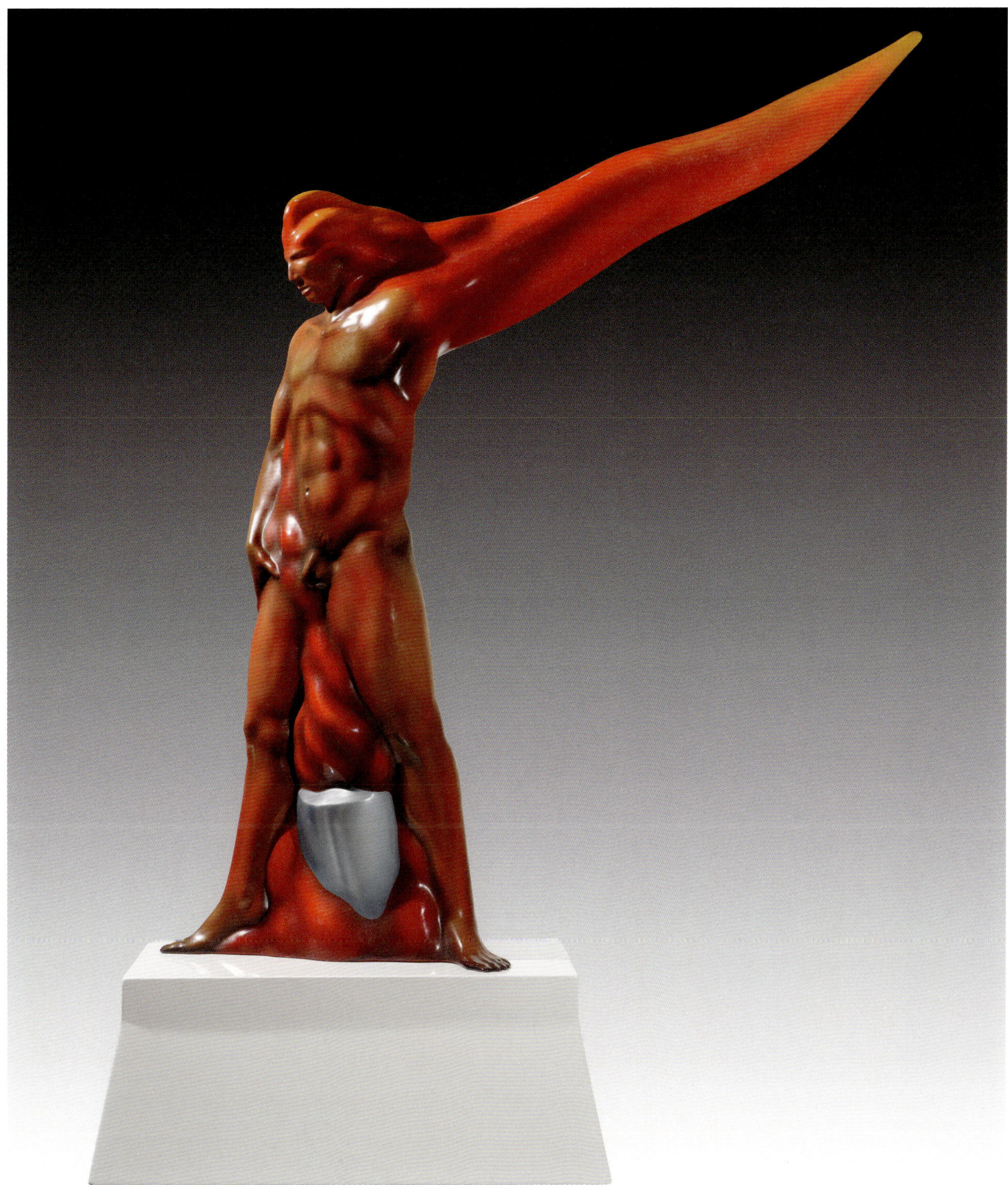

Luis Jimenez, *Man on Fire*, 1969–70. Fiberglass with urethane finish on painted fiberboard base, 89 × 60 × 19 in. (226.1 × 152.4 × 48.3 cm). The Museum of Fine Arts, Houston; Museum purchase funded by the Caroline Wiess Law Accessions Endowment Fund 2010.1760

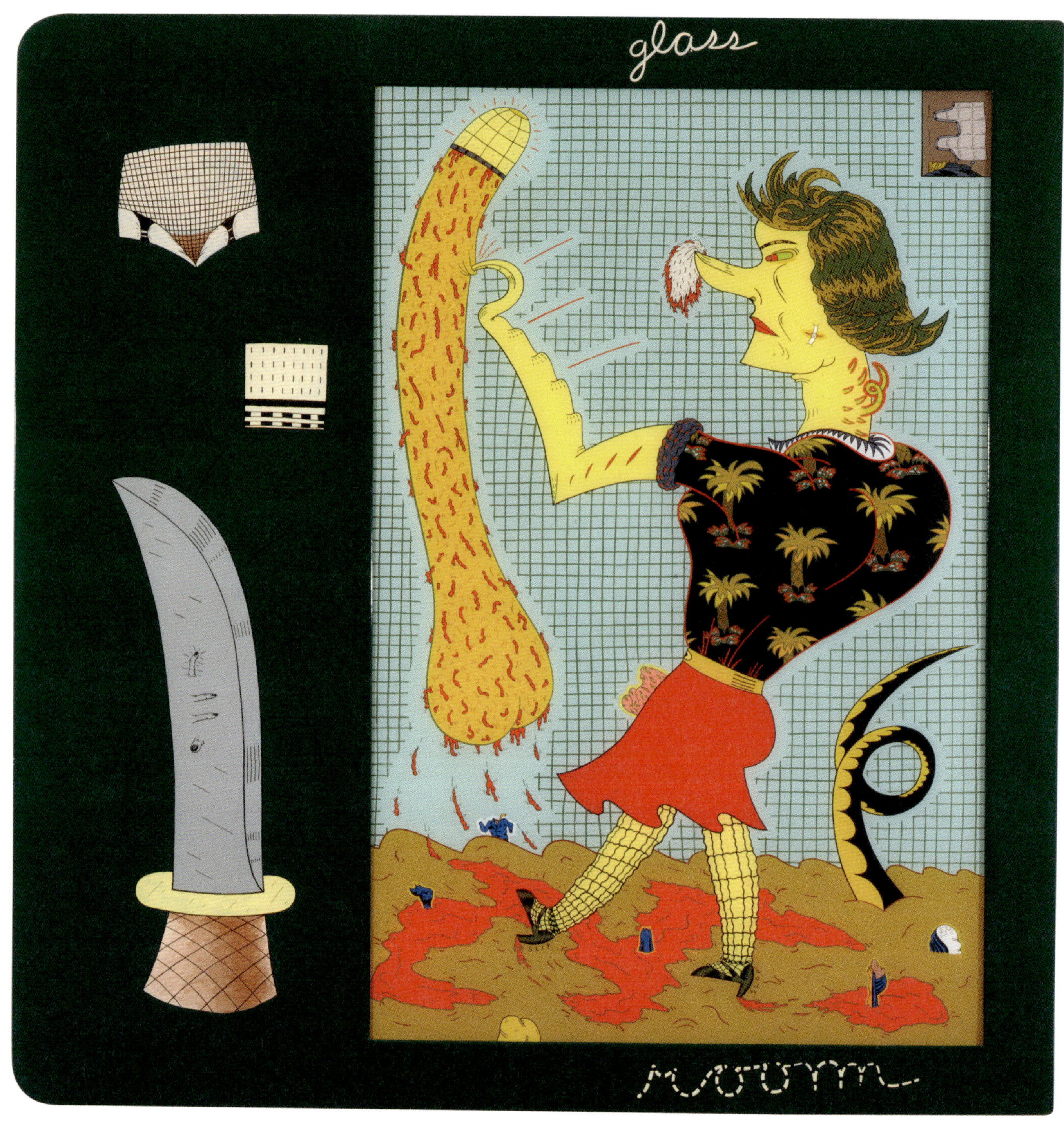

Jim Nutt, *Running Wild*, 1969–70. Acrylic on Plexiglas, enamel on wood frame, 46 × 43 ½ in. (116.8 × 110.5 cm). Collection of Lawrence and Evelyn Aronson

commentary on the apathy of the American public during a time of upheaval. Reviewing the second show, *New York Times* critic Hilton Kramer proclaims: "The imagery [is] almost ostentatiously vulgar, the general spirit of the enterprise open, robust, and unrestrained."

March 22–April 27, 1969 • *Live in Your Head: When Attitudes Become Form*, curated by Harald Szeemann, is on view at the Kusthalle Bern, Switzerland, and includes work by Eva Hesse, Edward Kienholz, Bruce Nauman, Claes Oldenburg, Robert Smithson, Paul Thek, and William T. Wiley, among others. The show highlights a symbiotic relationship between curator and artist and also process-oriented practices: many of the artists make and install their works in the exhibition space. Szeemann will return to Wiley when organizing 1972's documenta 5, *Questioning Reality—Pictorial Worlds Today*.

1969 • Dorothea Tanning (1910–2012) has an epiphany while attending a concert at the recently constructed headquarters of Paris Radio, one that will mark a momentous shift away from the artist's lifelong engagement with painting. It is during a performance of avant-garde composer Karlheinz Stockhausen's *Hymnen*, a piece which orchestrates a veritable wall of overlapping and fragmented electronic sound that can be paired with vocal soloists and/or symphonic accompaniment when played live, that Tanning first envisions the basis of what will become her "soft sculptures," a moment she will recall decades later in her memoirs: "Spinning among the unearthly sounds of *Hymnen* were the earthy, even organic shapes that I would make, had to make, out of cloth and wool; I saw them so clearly, living materials becoming living sculptures, their lifespan something like ours. Fugacious they would be, and fragile, to please me, their creator and survivor. I was suddenly content and powerful as I looked around. No one knew what was going on inside me . . . This, then, was the genesis of what became five years of sculpture activity." *Xmas*, one of Tanning's first soft sculptures from later this year, appears to capture the dynamism of this moment in its portrayal of a kneeling biomorphic figure whose torso attenuates upward in a rising, twisting expression of inner ecstasy and tumult.

Born and raised in Galesburg, Illinois, Tanning had immersed herself in the stacks at the local public library where she found her first love, literature, which nearly took her down the writer's path before she discovered painting. Largely self-taught as an artist, she studied to be a teacher for two years at Knox College in her hometown before moving to Chicago in 1930, where she briefly attended the Chicago Academy of Art. Upon relocating to New York City in 1935, Tanning works as a freelance illustrator and the following year attends the blockbuster exhibition *Fantastic Art, Dada, Surrealism* at the Museum of Modern Art, inspiring her turn to a surrealist style in her art. After a visit to her studio in 1942, Max Ernst includes her *Birthday* (1942) in an exhibition of women artists at Peggy Guggenheim's Art of This Century Gallery. Falling in with the circle of European Surrealists in wartime exile in New York, Tanning holds her first solo show, at Julien Levy Gallery in 1944, and marries Ernst two years later. By the 1960s, the couple are settled between Paris and Provence, and Tanning has shifted from her more painstaking renderings of elaborate domestic dreamscapes to fluid figural abstractions, a move that anticipates the soft sculptures.

March 24–April 30, 1969 • *Nancy Graves: Camels* is on view at the Whitney Museum of American Art, New York. At twenty-nine years old, Graves is the youngest woman artist to have a solo show at the museum. Upon her return to the United States in 1966, and after settling in New York, Graves had delved into intensive historical and taxonomic research on camels, supplementing her firsthand experience with the animals in Morocco by spending days studying them and other large mammals at libraries,

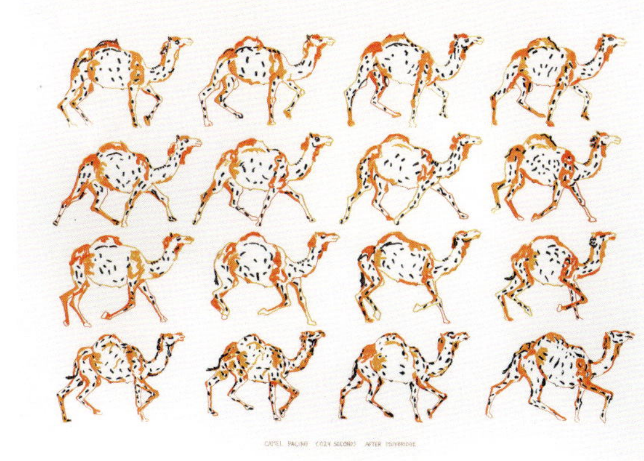

Nancy Graves, *Camel Pacing (.024 second) After Muybridge*, 1971. Gouache on paper, 22.5 × 30 in. (57.2 × 76.2 cm)

natural history museums, and slaughterhouses. In 1968, when she returns to the camel sculptures, she studies carpentry in order to fabricate the armature of the camel models herself. She pads the wooden skeletons with "muscle" and "fat" in the form of polyurethane and burlap before covering the structures with sheep- and goatskin to achieve realistic-looking camel skin. Between 1965 and 1969, she produces twenty-five camels, five of which remain extant. The Whitney exhibits three of the camels, confounding late-1960s visitors who have grown accustomed to encountering abstract and Minimalist sculpture in museum shows. Art historian Linda Nochlin has identified the subversiveness of the

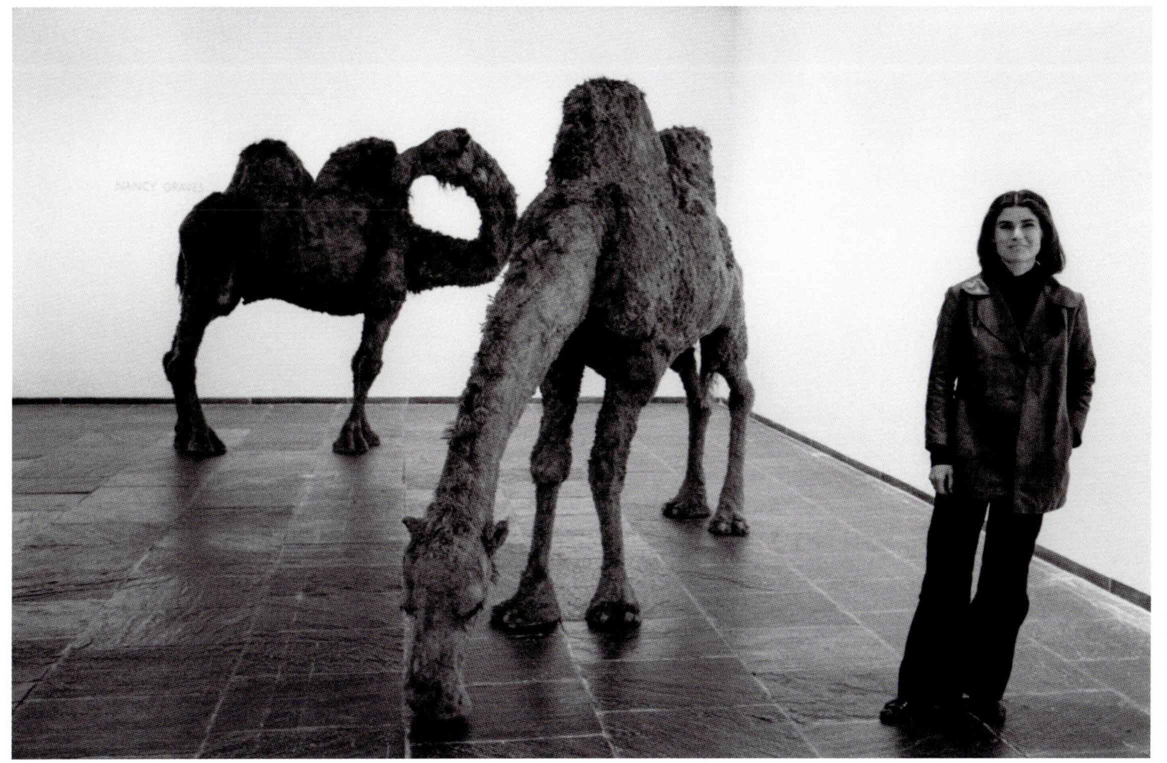

Nancy Graves with *Camel VII* and *Camel VI* (both 1968–69), Whitney Museum of American Art, New York, 1969

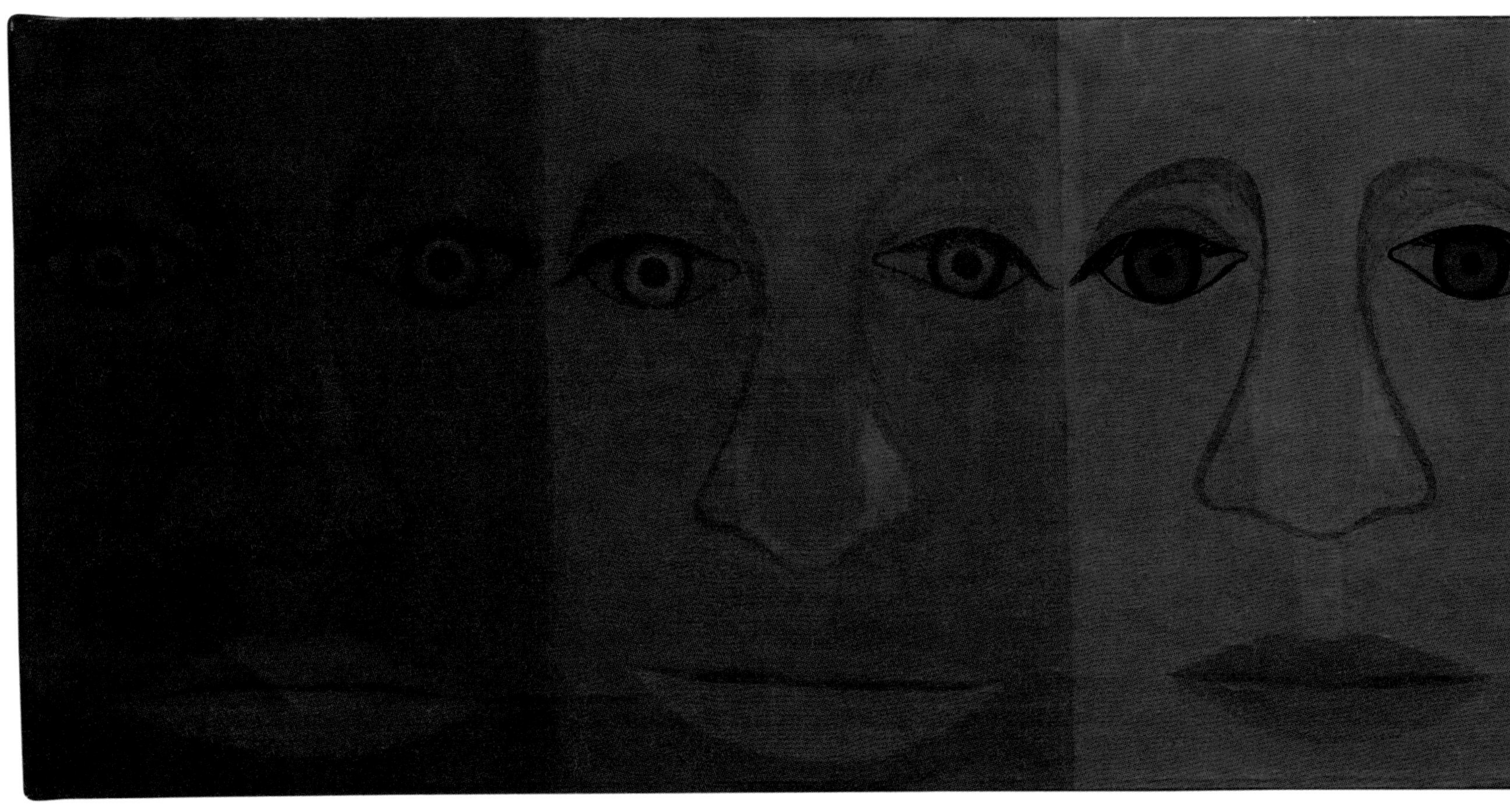

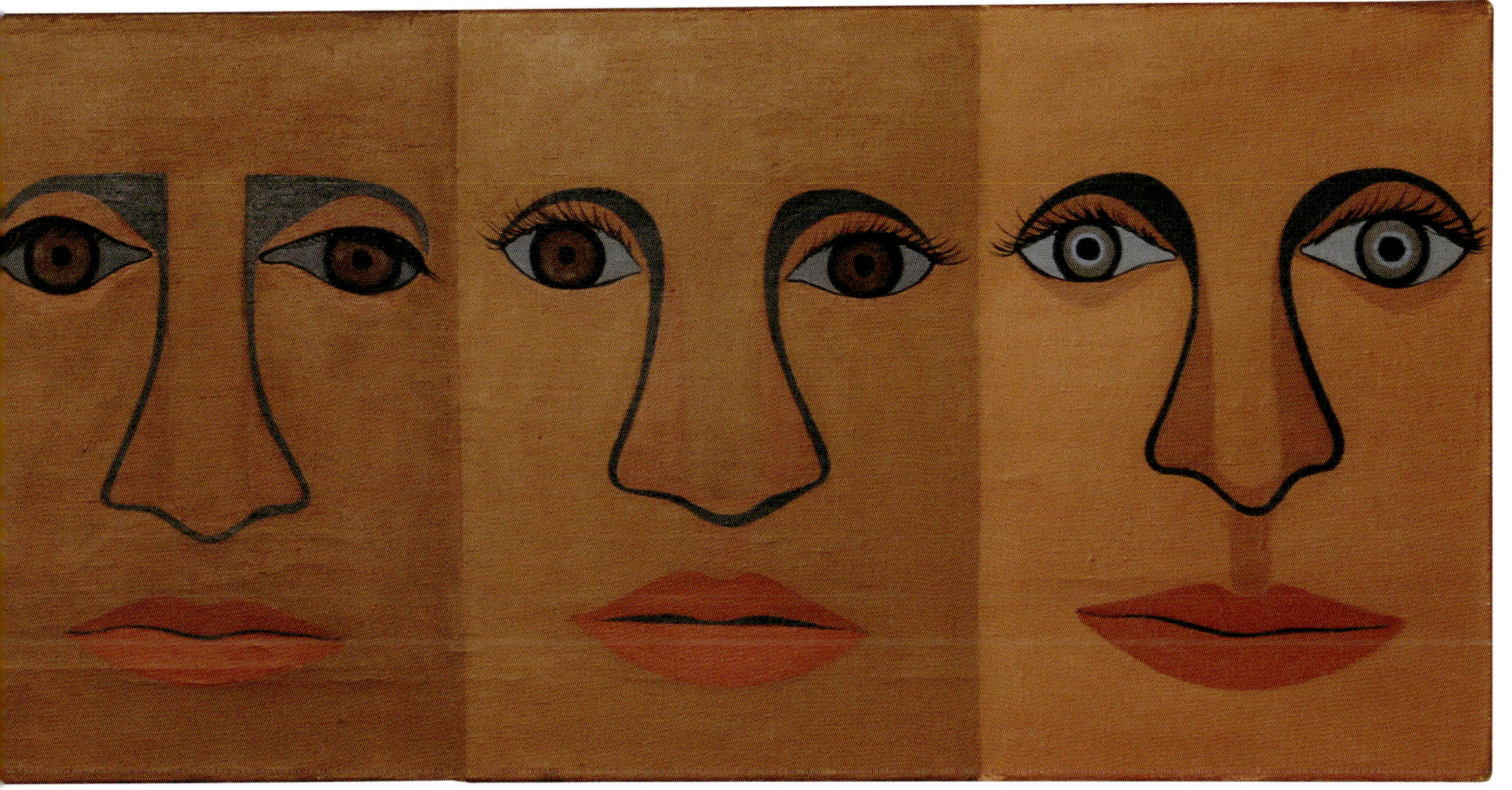

Faith Ringgold, *Black Light Series #9: The American Spectrum*, 1969. Oil on canvas, 18 × 72 in. (45.7 × 182.9 cm). The JP Morgan Chase Art Collection, New York

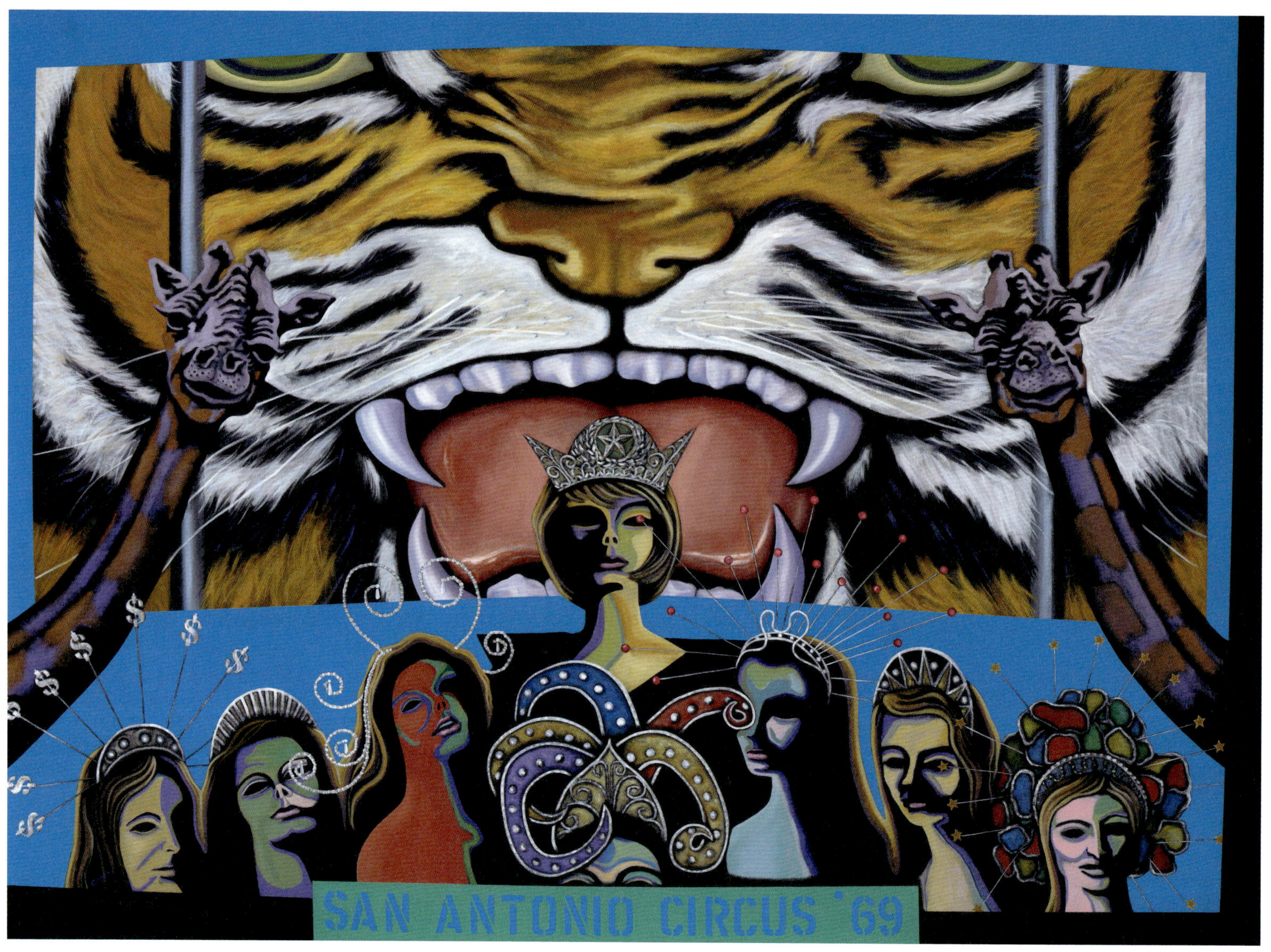

Mel Casas, *Humanscape #56 (San Antonio Circus)*, 1969. Acrylic on canvas, 72 × 96 in. (182.9 × 243.8 cm). Mel Casas Family Trust

Camels as lying "in the fact that their status can never be satisfactorily resolved: they can never be defined as clearly art or as non-art; or by assigning them unequivocally to the category of representation or that of abstraction. Their relationship to science or natural history is equally ambiguous: it is a relationship that is there but not there at the same time."

Having pored over the camel's external anatomy for five years, Graves becomes interested in exploring the animal's internal skeleton as she is working on the sculptures for the Whitney show. Between 1969 and 1970, Graves makes a series of fossil works, faithfully simulating camel bones from wax, marble dust, acrylic, and steel. She detaches the skeletal armature from the exterior of the camel, as if replicating her own anatomical research process. As Graves will later explain, "By going inside and using the bones as a point of departure or illusion, I was questioning a post-Brancusi, post-Andre, late '60s notion of armature."

———

April 10, 1969 • At an open meeting of the Art Workers' Coalition (AWC)—the activist group organized by Lucy Lippard and others that calls for increased representation of women and artists of color at museums and galleries, as well as more accessible museum admission policies—Lee Lozano reads the following statement:

> FOR ME THERE CAN BE NO ART REVOLUTION THAT IS SEPARATE FROM A SCIENCE REVOLUTION, A POLITICAL REVOLUTION, AN EDUCATION REVOLUTION, A DRUG REVOLUTION, A SEX REVOLUTION OR A PERSONAL REVOLUTION. I CANNOT CONSIDER A PROGRAM OF MUSEUM REFORMS WITHOUT EQUAL ATTENTION TO GALLERY REFORMS AND ART MAGAZINE REFORMS WHICH WOULD AIM TO ELIMINATE <u>STABLES</u> OF ARTISTS AND WRITERS. I WILL NOT CALL MYSELF AN ART WORKER BUT RATHER AN ART DREAMER AND I WILL PARTICIPATE ONLY IN A TOTAL REVOLUTION SIMULTANEOUSLY PERSONAL AND PUBLIC.

She refuses to participate in future AWC events, and the next day, she "officially" commences her *General Strike Piece*, in which she announces her gradual withdrawal from the art world and records her final visits to museums and galleries. The conceptual work—a form she first explores in the late 1960s with other "pieces" (her terminology) such as *Grass Piece*

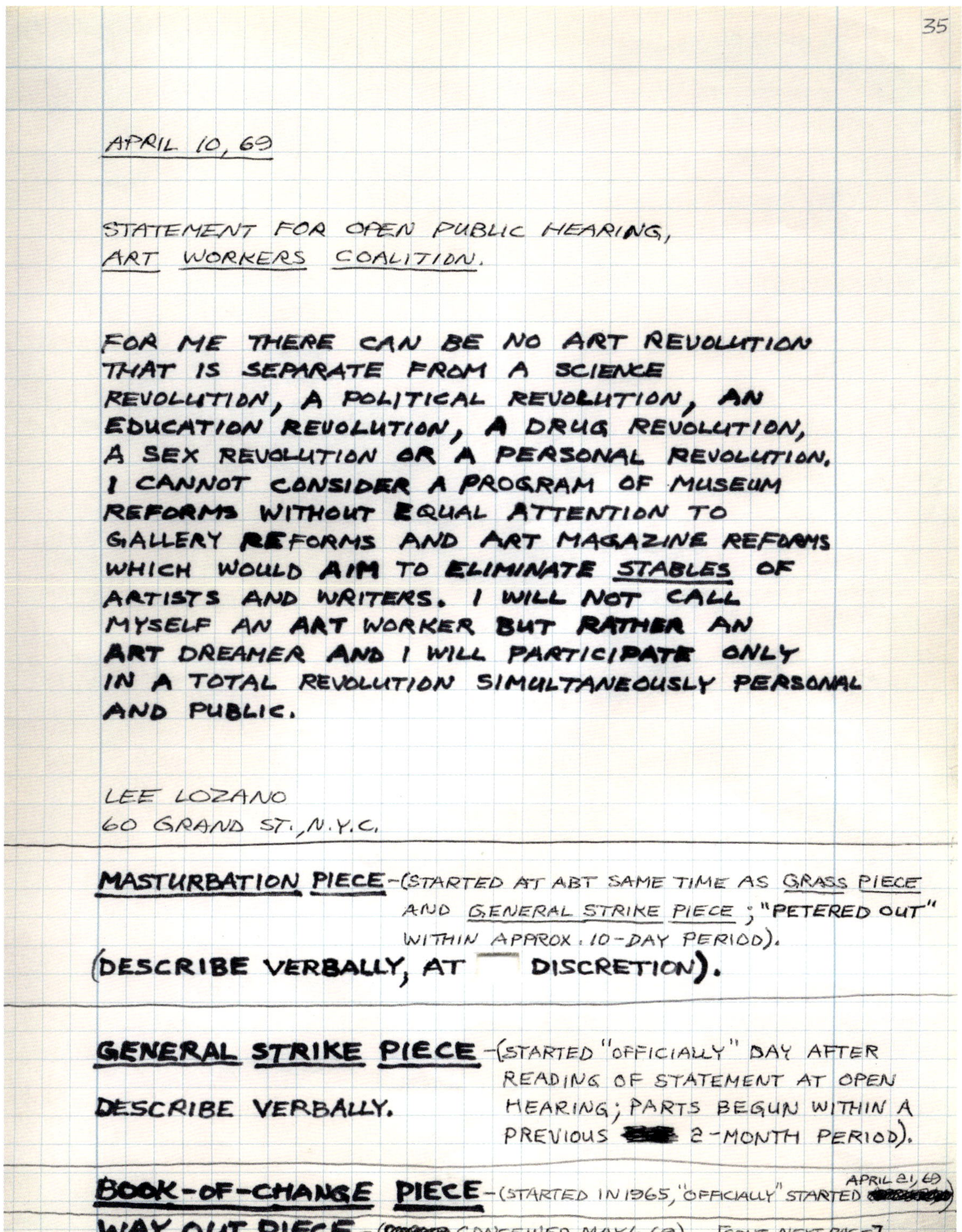

Lee Lozano, *Statement for Open Public Hearing, Art Workers Coalition, Masturbation Piece, General Strike Piece, Book of Change Piece, Way Out Piece*, 1969. Ink on paper, 8 ½ × 11 in. (21.6 × 27.9 cm)

and *No Grass Piece*, in which she experiments with maintaining a marijuana high and abstaining from marijuana—intensifies a year later with the self-explanatory action to "boycott women" and, finally, *Dropout Piece*. On April 5, 1970, she writes about the latter in her notebook:

IT WAS INEVITABLE, SINCE I WORK IN SETS OF COURSE, THAT I DO THE <u>DRO**POUT**</u> (NOTE THE PUN) <u>PIECE</u>. IT HAS BEEN CHURNING FOR A LONG TIME BUT I THINK IT'S ABT TO BLOW. <u>DROPOUT PIECE</u> IS THE <u>HARDEST WORK</u> I HAVE EVER DONE.

These two decisions culminate in Lozano abandoning the art world and New York City. She will travel throughout Europe for a time before settling in Texas, where her family lives. She no longer creates art and will be largely forgotten until the late 1980s and 1990s, when a few museums and galleries mount solo exhibitions of her work. For the rest of her life, she avoids and ignores women as much as she possibly can.

——

April 11, 1969 • The Museum of Modern Art, New York, screens Ken Jacobs's experimental film *Tom, Tom, the Piper's Son*, the first of multiple screenings at the museum of the film, which had premiered earlier in the year in a program put together by Jonas Mekas at New York's Huntington Hartford Gallery of Modern Art. In *Tom, Tom, the Piper's Son*, Jacobs takes a 1905 short film of the same title and deftly manipulates the footage by filming a screen projection; recontextualizing the footage, he puts on display the full range of filmmaker tools to speed up, slow down, zoom in on, crop, and reframe the moving image. The film receives rave reviews as a groundbreaking example of what is dubbed "structural film." Moreover, Jacobs realizes—in his own avant-garde fashion—a new potential for the use of found footage, a dynamic form of artistic appropriation he had been exposed to in the mid-1950s in the form of *Rose Hobart* (1936), a Joseph Cornell found-footage film collage. Jacobs will subsequently show Cornell's film to fellow filmmaker Jack Smith and, as critic Annette Michelson will note in 1973, "The consequences were particularly important for the development of the taste, the sensibility, and styles of both men, as for independent filmmaking as a whole." Michelson also refers to *Tom, Tom* as *Rose Hobart*'s "ultimate descendant."

——

April 15–May 17, 1969 • Hairy Who artwork is on view at the Corcoran Gallery of Art at Dupont Center, Washington, DC. Jim Nutt and Karl Wirsum install the exhibition, adding wallpaper, wall paintings, and painted chairs to the mix.

——

May 20–June 15, 1969 • Hosted by the Corcoran Gallery of Art at Dupont Center in Washington, DC, and organized by Walter Hopps in collaboration with Bhob Stewart, *Phonus Balonus Show of Some Real Heavy Stuff* is the first exhibition of underground comic-book art by a major American museum. Robert Crumb is one of the artists featured.

——

June 28, 1969 • The Stonewall uprising begins when New York City police raid the popular Greenwich Village gay bar the Stonewall Inn. Patrons and workers resist arrest, and fighting breaks out with law Continued on page 280

QUEER LIFE AND ITS AVOIDANCE IN THE ART OF THE 1960S

DAVID J. GETSY

When I teach the history of queer American art of the 1960s, I'm always struck by that most modernist of criteria—medium. Simply put, there is far less painting or sculpture that directly represented queer life of the 1960s than as can be found in film, literature, theater, photography, and performance. To be sure, there are plenty of lesbian, gay, bisexual, and otherwise nonheterosexual artists making work across all artistic practices during the decade. The art objects they created, however, were rarely direct, and they might only hint at aspects of queer experience.[1] That is, they employed abstraction or relied on codes, keeping at arm's length the queer cultures that were proliferating in American cities during the decade.[2] Abstraction has much queer potential, to be sure, but it also relies on a committed aniconism, critical dissemblance, and a tactical use of nonfiguration's capacities for metaphor.[3] Similarly, codes and private symbolisms can be pleasurable, life-saving, or fraternizing, but they do so with plausible deniability and by trafficking in the implicit. Neither abstract nor allusive modes are, or want to be, unambiguous or singular in their registration of queer themes. By contrast, in 1960s literature, film, and performance, there were an increasing number of explicit representations of queer life that, in turn, became central to the histories of those forms of cultural production.

Such a claim is schematic and generalizing, I know. Nevertheless, when I make a list of the most often discussed (but by no means only) artists through which the queer art history of the 1960s has been conventionally understood, this pattern emerges: those artists who made paintings or sculptures for display and consumption in galleries and museums generally avoided direct representations of queer life, sexuality, or nonnormative genders. Here, I'm thinking of the likes of Robert Rauschenberg, Jasper Johns, Beauford Delaney, Louise Nevelson, Ellsworth Kelly, Agnes Martin, and Lowell Nesbitt. Even David Hockney gets less direct after arriving in Los Angeles in the 1960s.[4] Of course, there is Andy Warhol, but his paintings, prints, and sculptures so successfully analogized their queer themes that the voluminous literature on him could go decades until it was called out for willful omissions.[5] The question of medium is telling in Warhol's case: It was Warhol *the filmmaker* who made work about queer life in the 1960s, and he did so with an explicitness unparalleled in his paintings, prints, and sculptures of the decade.[6] As Gavin Butt has argued, Warhol even suppressed (in partial emulation of Johns and Rauschenberg) his more sexual and clearly campy work of the 1950s as a means to be acceptable to the gallery world of the 1960s.[7]

So, what are we to make of the seeming contradiction between, on the one hand, the understanding that the 1960s were a particularly dynamic period in American art and, on the other, the relative lack of overt representations of the queer communities that swelled in American cities in the same decade?

There are a few ready answers, but none are fully satisfying. Some might reply that, in this decade, versions of abstraction and conceptual practices dominated the discourse in galleries and art magazines, and that any sort of representation or figuration was viewed with suspicion. (The present exhibition, however, contradicts that stereotype by, among other things, demonstrating how complex figuration and the image were in the 1960s.) As well, some might answer that this silence must be the result of a pervasive and unchecked oppression of nonheterosexual lives and cultures in the decade before the Stonewall uprising of 1969 sparked a national movement based on the politics of lesbian and gay visibility. Without a doubt, structural oppression, widespread homophobia and transphobia, and threats of violence were daily parts of queer life in the 1960s. However, it is both reductive and inaccurate to see the pre-Stonewall years merely as a wasteland of inopportunity and isolated suffering.[8]

Despite the pervasiveness of the repressive legal and social climate of the 1960s, the decade also saw the burgeoning of queer cultures and communities.[9] Cities became magnets for those seeking refuge and anonymity, and networks of gay men and lesbians proliferated in urban centers. Some people (especially those with privileges such as financial security and higher education that were overwhelmingly available to white men) could live in relative secrecy. Perhaps they moved through covert networks of like-minded people who would rarely express their same-gender desires and love outside of the two-person unit of the couple or the hookup. Nevertheless, they found each other in increasing numbers during the 1960s, establishing sex lives and relationships among the crowds of the city and the anonymity they afforded. (In his memoir *Great Demon Kings*, John Giorno gives a good example of how this non-identitarian network looked in the art world through his detailing of his sexual and social relationships with Rauschenberg, Johns, and their circle.)[10]

However, not everyone was able to operate in such networks. Those without the privilege of relative economic security nevertheless established their own communities and geographies at the margins of mainstream society.[11] Often characterized at the time as an underworld of bars, cruising zones, hustling, and street life, this geography became locatable and visible—both to its denizens and to wider publics—as the primary image of queer life in the decade.[12] Cautionary tales about these enclaves circulated in the mass media while simultaneously producing a discourse about homosexuality as an effect of its proscription.[13] As *Life* magazine declared in its 1964 story "Homosexuality in America": "A secret world grows open and bolder. Society is forced to look at it—and try to understand it."[14] Moralizing and sensationalizing exposés became regular in tabloids, newspapers, and national magazines. Pulp novels with often ill-fated queer characters and cheap paperbacks purporting to explain the homosexual "revolution" or "explosion" multiplied in the 1960s. In 1965, *Life* ran another feature, this time about crime in Times Square where, the magazine warned, "lesbians try to peddle each other" and "men dressed as women con Johns and romp in the streets." The story also made the case for how fights among Black trans and queer "germs" justified, in the magazine's view, police brutality.[15]

Throughout the 1960s, the accounts that increasingly circulated in mainstream media—such as CBS's disparaging prime-time documentary "The Homosexuals" (1967)—painted queer life as deviant, criminal, outcast, poor, and racially mixed in ways that found neither reflection nor sympathy in the mainstream ideals of America. Yet paradoxically, the circulation of these accounts also made queer neighborhoods, streets, bars, and their economies more recognizable, which in turn drew more and more of those people who sought out these zones in which queer *contact*—of many types—was imaginable and possible.[16]

This imagining was furthered by the first-person, often sympathetic accounts in literature and film that ran parallel to the moralizing and sensationalism of the mass media. Chief among these is John Rechy's *City of Night*, widely regarded as one of the first major novels about queer life to cross over into a more general readership.[17] Rechy's breathtaking book from 1963 describes his experiences of the urban street, the bar, the cruising site, and the acts of survival required of those outlawed for refusing to hide their queer desires.[18] The communities and cultures he documented were made up of people of color, trans people, overt queer folks, sex workers, middle-class homosexuals seeking connection, sympathetic straights, and others who found community or confraternity, for a time, in the bars, the parks, and on the streets—that is, in the vast and diverse subterranean "gay world."[19]

The effects of oppression and the precarity of survival are omnipresent in Rechy's novel, but it nevertheless describes how people found each other and made their lives outside of mainstream society's boundaries. Similarly, you see pictures of this queer underground culture and its many varieties in other novels of the 1960s, such as James Baldwin's *Another Country* (1963), Charles Wright's *The Messenger* (1963), Hubert Selby Jr.'s *Last Exit to Brooklyn* (1964), James Leo Herlihy's *Midnight Cowboy* (1965), and Rechy's *Numbers* (1967). It is also vividly documented in less lauded but widely read experimental and pulp novels and memoirs that also circulated in this decade, such as Kate (then writing as Kenneth) Marlowe's *Mr. Madam: Confessions of a Male Madam* (1964), Victor J. Banis's *The Why Not* (1966), or William Carney's *The Real Thing* (1968)—a leather-and-BDSM updating of the eighteenth-century epistolary novel *Les Liaisons dangereuses* by Pierre Choderlos de Laclos—as well as in the unflinching volume of poems by Paul Goodman, *Hawkweed*, published in 1967. These books are only sometimes about same-gender sex or desire or eroticism. They discuss sex as part of a larger examination of the experience of queer life. Identities such as gay or lesbian are part of these cultures, but they are by no means the only

(or central) players in this wider and more diverse constituency of queer life in the 1960s.

This visibility had no foothold in the galleries through which the dominant art history of the 1960s was made, even though—in addition to literature—it became prominent in the theater and films of the decade. For instance, in geographic proximity to the downtown galleries of New York, independent theater Off-Off-Broadway grew, with queer hubs such as the history-making Caffe Cino at its core.[20] Out of this milieu and its sometimes frank discussions of queer themes, playwrights such as Robert Heide, Ronald Tavel, Lanford Wilson, Charles Ludlam, and Doric Wilson emerged—or, to the side of this boys club and without the same acceptance, Valerie Solanas. Off-Broadway, Matthew Crowley's acidic *Boys in the Band* premiered in 1968 to much outrage and acclaim for its caricature of gay shame. During these years, critics warned of the homosexual presence on Broadway, casting playwrights such as Edward Albee, Tennessee Williams, and William Inge in undisguised homophobic terms.[21] I do not have space here detail here the expansion of queer themes in major motion pictures, but it's worth noting that explicit gay or queer texts such as Crowley's *Boys in the Band* and Herlihy's *Midnight Cowboy* were quickly made into mainstream films (in 1970 and 1969, respectively, with *Midnight Cowboy* being the first X-rated film to win an Oscar for best picture).[22] Even more direct was independent film, which exploded in the 1960s. Its history would be unthinkable without the explicit queer content that helped to define its terms and future.[23] The inimitable Jack Smith, Kenneth Anger, George Kuchar, Gregory Markopolous, Warhol, and Paul Morrissey featured queer and trans life, hustlers, sex, and desire with an uncompromising and often matter-of-fact directness.[24] Even the straight filmmaker Shirley Clarke (with her 1967 *Portrait of Jason*) contributed to the widespread fascination with the queer culture of hustling and street life.[25] One of the most widely read essays of the 1960s was Susan Sontag's "Notes on Camp" with its dissection of homosexual presence in culture.[26] Camp was central not just to the Theater of the Ridiculous but also to performance art being made by the Cockettes in San Francisco and, in Los Angeles, to the collaborations of Gronk and Robert Legorreta ("Cyclona") that shocked audiences.[27]

In short, despite broad oppression, queer life in the 1960s found significant representation in the cultural forms of literature, film, theater, performance, and mass media. Those images were not wholly sympathetic, of course. They could be stilted, were frequently moralizing, and remain problematic. In both mainstream media and more specialized audiences such as those of underground cinema, there was a fetishistic and exoticizing fascination with the economic and social precarity and daily threats of violence experienced by the diversity of queer people living on the margins of American life. Nevertheless, even those deleterious representations attest to the pre-Stonewall visibility of queer communities that were less white, less privileged, and more defiant than the images promoted by the post-Stonewall gay-and-lesbian rights movements built on the foundations established by the 1960s "underworld." Importantly, the increasing circulation of these representations in the media, in underground film, in literature, and in the theater *produced* a counterpublic, following Michael Warner's usage, that found via these media both an edifying community and a critical distance from the exclusionary norms of mainstream society.[28]

This brings me back to the nagging question of medium. Where are the representations of this diversity of queer life in the art world of the 1960s and, more particularly, in art objects such as paintings or sculptures? Whether as an object of revulsion or fascination, the visible queer underworld captivated viewers and readers in the 1960s, yet its direct registration was nowhere to be found on the walls of the white cube. Again, consider the case of Andy Warhol, who could be so much more direct in his films than in the objects shown at galleries.[29] There, one could see flowers, silver clouds, and celebrities rendered by Warhol, but at screenings and movie houses viewers could witness such films as *Blow Job* (1964), *My Hustler* (1965), and *Bike Boy* (1967)—as well others such as Morrissey's *Flesh* (1968) and *Trash* (1970) and John Waters's *Mondo Trasho* (1969) and *Multiple Maniacs* (1970).

What was it that made the network of art galleries (and collectors and museums) so different? The obvious answer—pervasive homophobia, transphobia, and racism—does not, to my mind at least, fully explain the divergence of 1960s gallery-based art from the fascination with queer life as seen in film, literature, theater, and mass media of the same decade. There was clearly something resistant, if not hostile, to queer artists wanting to make art objects explicitly about queer life in this era. The engine of American art of the postwar period was the gallery-collector-museum complex.[30] For this reason, we must ask how that complex sought to purge (or, at best, manage) difference—especially of those forms of intersectional difference such as queer-of-color life, street life, and trans experience that were barred from the spaces of privilege, wealth, and status. The inhospitable climate of the American art world's object-based institutions does not accord with the more diverse and varied representations of queer life in performance, literature, and film.

To be stark about what an attention to medium tells us: The forms of cultural production that were expensive (i.e., paintings, sculptures, and other gallery-based work) avoided direct and uncoded representation of queer life and themes, whereas those forms that had relatively inexpensive, and often ephemeral, means of access and distribution (i.e., novels, magazines, movies, street-based performance art, and Off-Off-Broadway theater admission) evidenced a fascination with images of a so-called queer underworld of the 1960s. In those forms of cultural production not reliant on the big sale, there was a greater interest in (even, one could say, a foregrounding of) images of queer life. The prevailing story of the art of the 1960s has been corralled by its medium-specific prudery, and that story has been ultimately told through luxury commodities that have ended up in museums and that reflect the willful avoidance (or tactful coding) of queer life.

The speculative and preliminary answer I offer is more descriptive than diagnostic. Such generalizations as I have made are bound to fail, and I have no doubt that some will object to this simplification or to such rhetorical moves as my division of Warhol into two facets. I expect others will have examples that buck these tendencies I've outlined, and I hope to learn of them. I have been speaking about the widely circulated stories of art in the 1960s, but I know there are more histories yet to be told and canons to be overturned. I will summarize a few exceptions and complications that are, I feel, important to signal here. For example, there are outliers such as Jess (most notably), Ray Johnson, Paul Thek, Ralph Arnold, Robert Indiana (in his sculpture, especially), Joe Brainard, and the photographs of Peter Hujar. All of these artists found different ways to make objects that at least partially represented queer themes and life. It's significant, however, that Johnson's queerest work often operated outside of the realm of the commodifiable object and the gallery.[31] Similarly, in the 1960s, photography such as Hujar's was not as frequently understood to be part of the same galleries and conversations that were being had around painting and sculpture. There are drawings and paintings that render nonheterosexual loves and lives directly, but they are often more private works (such as Sonja Sekula's 1963 *Lesbiennes* and other late works). Oddly, some of the most forthright works about queer life and themes are by predominately straight artists, including George Segal's *Girlfriends* (1969), the photographs of Diane Arbus (and, published later, Larry Clark), and Yayoi Kusama's *Homosexual Wedding* (1968). As well, there are artists associated with earlier decades (such as Paul Cadmus and Edward Melcarth) who were still making work in the 1960s but are rarely considered part of the picture of the decade. The artists directly engaging with images of homosexual desire—such as Tom of Finland (Touko Laaksonen), Etienne (Juan Esteban "Dom" Orejudos), and Chuck Arnett—did their work outside the artworld, with their images circulating through the distribution networks of magazines such as *Physique Pictorial* or being created as murals in bars.[32] There were painters of homoerotica, such as those who form the basis of the Leslie-Lohman Museum collection, but you will be hard pressed to find them in other museums or in art history.[33] Harold Stevenson's *The New Adam* (1962; pp. 76–77) perhaps got closest to being the artworld's most visible painting of homoeroticism of the 1960s. But this monumental painting was removed from the planning for the Guggenheim's *Six Artists and the Object* in 1963 and—despite its being shown in Los Angeles (along with a film by Warhol on Stevenson)—there is consequently "no mention of it in the major histories of art of the 1960s," as Jonathan Weinberg has noted.[34] These exceptions are all tentative and partial. They stand timidly next to other paintings of the 1960s that made representational politics more central: for example, the direct, political, and unambiguous imagery that was being deployed by artists in the Black Power movement or by heterosexual women artists demanding the right to use sexual imagery critically.[35] Queer artists in the white cube, by contrast, were as a group more demure, and diverse queer lives were absent from the gallery and museum walls that displayed what would be canonized as the art of the 1960s.

The received narratives of that art often leave little enough room for queer content as it is, and many of the artists I have just cited as exceptions have been tough to fit into the triumphal story of the 1960s. As the current exhibition attests, the story of the 1960s is messy, full of competing aims and desires. One way to understand what the dominant narratives have left out is to ask whether an explicitly queer art could have been sustained in the economic and social realities of a decade in which the commercial art gallery was the primary site for the establishment of contemporary artists—and contemporary art history. Even as ideas, rather than objects, became the commodities in the 1960s art world, queer didn't sell—or at least that is what was assumed. But it *was* selling (to expanded audiences) in theaters, lofts, bookstands, movie houses, and through mail order. A telling exception is the work of Nancy Grossman. When she first created and exhibited her leather-bound sculptures of heads in 1968 (p. 236), many assumed that they were direct representations of the sexual culture of leather and BDSM. (They were not.)[36] Because of this ascription of queer sexuality to the works, however, they appealed to privileged gay men, who collected them, effectively making Grossman one of the best-selling women artists of the 1960s. Her complex and moving artistic practice struck a chord (and achieved a regrettably short-lived acclaim) because of its departure from the rest of the sculpture of the decade.

By and large, however, gallery-based art (and the subsequent canonical histories based on it) failed to register one of the major cultural shifts of the 1960s—that of the proliferation and visibility of diverse queer life. Other arts and even popular culture saw this change (with horror or hope) and represented it. But the privileged arenas of the gallery, the art collection, and the museum kept themselves walled off from the places and people of queer life that surged and eventually revolted in the decade of social change that was the 1960s.

NOTES

1   I use the adjective *queer* in this essay to refer to the range of life experiences that are outside of presumptions of heterosexuality and binary gender and that have been the target of systemic discrimination, legalized harassment, and disenfranchisement. While the term has since been adopted as an activist stance or used as a convenient umbrella for nonnormative sexual identities, I use it as a historically available term for the range of outcast and outlaw life experiences that include (but are not limited to) those who identify as gay, lesbian, and bisexual. Nonnormative gender was interwoven with some of these experiences and identity positions in the 1960s (and beyond), and I will also use the contemporary term *trans* to signal the different positions, obstacles, and potentials of those life experiences of committed defiance to an imposed system of static, binary gender. For a longer discussion of my usage of queer experience over a language of identity, see the introduction to David J. Getsy, *Queer Behavior: Scott Burton and Performance Art* (Chicago: University of Chicago Press, 2022); and, for later histories of the term, David J. Getsy, ed., *Queer* (Cambridge, MA: MIT Press, 2016).
2   Silence was an important strategy in postwar art. See Jonathan D. Katz, "The Silent Camp: Queer Resistance and the Rise of Pop Art," in *Visions of a Future: Art and Art History in Changing Contexts*, ed. Kornelia Imesch and Hans-Jörg Heusser (Zurich: Swiss Institute for Art Research, 2004), 147–58.
3   I have outlined some reasons that queer artists have employed abstraction in David J. Getsy, "Ten Queer Theses on Abstraction," in Jared Ledesma, ed., *Queer Abstraction*, exh. cat. (Des Moines, IA: Des Moines Art Center, 2019), 65–75; and "Queer Possibilities: Lesbian Feminist Abstract Painting in the 1970s and After," in *Making Their Mark: Art by Women in the Shah Garg Collection*, ed. Katy Siegel and Mark Godfrey (New York: Gregory R. Miller & Co., 2023), 70–79.
4   For instance, the sexual content evident in works Hockney showed in London in the early 1960s, such as *We Two Boys Together Clinging* from 1961 or *Cleaning Teeth, Early Evening (10pm) W11* from 1962, is much more direct than the many paintings of Los Angeles pools later in the decade. Importantly, his homoerotic *Domestic Scene, Los Angeles* (1963) was inspired by the American magazine *Physique Pictorial* but painted before he moved to Los Angeles.
5   This was the situation that sparked the 1993 conference at Duke University that resulted in Jennifer Doyle, Jonathan Flatley, and José Esteban Muñoz, eds., *Pop Out: Queer Warhol* (Durham, NC: Duke University Press, 1996). See also the commentary on this historiographic situation in Douglas Crimp, "Getting the Warhol We Deserve," *Social Text* 59 (1999): 49–66. In the wake of Doyle, Flatley, and Muñoz's work (and of their own writings on the artist), there has been a wealth of complex writing on queer themes in Warhol's work—as well as authors who continue to avoid the topic altogether.
6   See discussion in Douglas Crimp, *"Our Kind of Movie: The Films of Andy Warhol* (Cambridge, MA: MIT Press, 2012); and "Tricks of the Trade: Pop Art and the Rhetoric of Prostitution," in Jennifer Doyle, *Sex Objects: Art and the Dialectics of Desire* (Minneapolis: University of Minnesota Press, 2006), 45–70.
7   Gavin Butt, *Between You and Me: Queer Disclosures in the New York Art World, 1948–1963* (Durham, NC: Duke University Press, 2005), 106–35. See also Caroline A. Jones, *Machine in the Studio: Constructing the Postwar American Artist* (Chicago: University of Chicago Press, 1996), 244; and discussions of Warhol's early work in Richard Meyer, *Outlaw Representation: Censorship and Homosexuality in Twentieth-Century American Art* (Boston: Beacon Press, 2002); and Jonathan Flatley, *Like Andy Warhol* (Chicago: University of Chicago Press, 2017).
8   Many others have also attempted to challenge this stereotype. Most pertinent to the art history of the 1960s is Jonathan D. Katz, "Naked Politics: The Art of Eros 1955–1975," in *Queer Difficulty in Art and Poetry: Rethinking the Sexed Body in Verse and Visual Culture*, ed. Jongwoo Jeremy Kim and Christopher Reed (New York: Routledge, 2017), 74–86. For a summary view of the growing visibility of transgender lives in the 1960s, see David J. Getsy, *Abstract Bodies: Sixties Sculpture in the Expanded Field of Gender* (New Haven, CT: Yale University Press, 2015), 26–34.
9   As has been well documented, this consolidation into neighborhoods and networks had a much longer history, especially in New York City. See, especially, George Chauncey, *Gay New York: Gender, Urban Culture, and the Making of the Gay Male World, 1890–1940* (New York: Basic Books, 1994); Barry Reay, *New York Hustlers: Masculinity and Sex in Modern America* (Manchester: Manchester University Press, 2010); and Hugh Ryan, *When Brooklyn Was Queer* (New York: St. Martin's Press, 2019).
10   John Giorno, *Great Demon Kings: A Memoir of Poetry, Sex, Art, Death, and Enlightenment* (New York: Farrar, Straus, and Giroux, 2020).
11   For a history of queer kinship networks of street life and its locations in American cities, see Joseph Plaster, *Kids on the Street: Queer Kinship and Religion in San Francisco's Tenderloin* (Durham, NC: Duke University Press, 2023).
12   A good example (published in a book meant to introduce the real New York City) is Leo Skir, "The Gay World," in *The New York Spy*, ed. Alan Rinzler (New York: David White Company, 1967), 372–93; or Antony James, *America's Homosexual Underground* (New York: Imperial Books, 1965). For a perceptive analysis of the changing idea of the "gay underground" from the 1950s to the 1970s, see Guy Davidson, "Hipsters and Homosexuals: Chandler Brossard's *Who Walk in Darkness* and the Midcentury Gay Underground," *Post45*, June 2, 2022: https://post45.org/2022/06/hipsters-and-homosexuals/.
13   See Anna Lvovsky, "The Popular Press and the Gay World," in *Vice Patrol: Cops, Courts, and the Struggle over Urban Gay Life Before Stonewall* (Chicago: University of Chicago Press, 2021), 220–56.
14   "Homosexuality in America," *Life*, June 26, 1964: 66–80.
15   James Mills, "The Detective," *Life*, December 3, 1965: 90D–123.
16   Here, I rely on the important discussion of network and contact in relationship to queer experiences of urban space in Samuel R. Delany, *Times Square Red, Times Square Blue* (New York: New York University Press, 1999).
17   Rechy's achievement was preceded, importantly, in the United States by such books as James Baldwin's *Giovanni's Room* in 1956 and the translations of Jean Genet, as well as Marijane Meaker's *Spring Fire* and Patricia Highsmith's *Price of Salt*—two 1952 novels that helped to establish the genre of the lesbian pulp novel through which queer ideas circulated widely in American culture in the 1950s. On the pulp novel, see Susan Stryker, *Queer Pulp: Perverted Passions from the Golden Age of the Paperback* (San Francisco: Chronicle Books, 2001); and Michael Bronski, *Pulp Friction: Uncovering the Golden Age of Gay Male Pulps* (New York: St. Martin's Griffin, 2003).
18   Some of those portrayed in Rechy's semiautobiographical novel have criticized his partial characterization of them, most notably Miss Destiny in "The Common Sense of Miss Destiny," *Drag* 1, no. 2 (1971): 12–16, 24, 33.
19   The term was used in the abovementioned *Life* magazine article of 1964, and the notion became popularized in one of the first sympathetic accounts of gay male culture published in the later 1960s: Martin Hoffman, *The Gay World: Male Homosexuality and the Social Creation of Evil* (New York: Basic Books, 1968).
20   For an account of the final years of the Caffe Cino as a queer site for theater, community, and sex, see Jimmy McDonough, *The Ghastly One: The 42nd Street Netherworld of Andy Milligan* (Surrey, UK: FAB Press, 2022). See also Stephen J. Bottoms, *Playing Underground: A Critical History of the 1960s Off-Off-Broadway Movement* (Ann Arbor: University of Michigan Press, 2006).
21   See Stephen J. Bottoms, "The Efficacy/Effeminacy Braid: Unpacking the Performance Studies/Theatre Studies Dichotomy," *Theatre Topics* 13, no. 2 (September 2003): 173–87.
22   See the now-classic studies by Vito Russo, *The Celluloid Closet: Homosexuality in the Movies* (New York: Harper and Row, 1981); and Thomas Waugh, *Hard to Imagine: Gay Male Eroticism in Photography and Film from Their Beginnings to Stonewall* (New York: Columbia University Press, 1996).
23   See the astute analysis in Richard Dyer, "Underground and After," in Dyer, *Now You See It: Studies on Lesbian and Gay Film* (New York: Routledge, 1990), 102–73.
24   For a useful discussion of the relationship of underground gay film to popular culture, see Juan A. Suárez, *Bike Boys, Drag Queens, & Superstars: Avant-Garde, Mass Culture, and Gay Identities in the 1960s Underground Cinema* (Bloomington: Indiana University Press, 1996).
25   That in the 1960s Clarke's *Portrait of Jason* was seen in relation to sex work and street life is attested to by the advertising of it at "L.A.'s First Homosexual Film Festival" in 1968 as *Portrait of Jason—Male Hustler!* It was programmed alongside films by Pat Rocco and Andy Milligan's groundbreaking bathhouse film *Vapors* (1965).
26   Susan Sontag, "Notes on Camp" [1964], in *Against Interpretation and Other Essays* (New York: Picador, 1966), 275–92. For an illuminating discussion of this essay—originally titled "Notes on Homosexuality"—see Benjamin Moser, *Sontag: Her Life and Work* (New York: Ecco, 2019).
27   See C. Ondine Chavoya and David Evans Frantz, eds., *Axis Mundo: Queer Networks in Chicano L.A.* (Munich: DelMonico Books–Prestel, 2017).
28   See Michael Warner, *Publics and Counterpublics* (New York: Zone Books, 2002). For detailed discussions of how this worked with underground film in the 1960s, see Janet Staiger, "Finding Community in the 1960s," in *Perverse Spectators: The Practices of Film Reception* (New York: New York University Press, 2000), 125–60; and Ryan Powell, *Coming Together: The Cinematic Elaboration of Gay Male Life, 1945–1979* (Chicago: University of Chicago Press, 2019).
29   As well, New York's attempts to check the growth of queer life on its streets and to "sanitize" the city in advance of the 1964 World's Fair informed the censorship of Warhol's queer-leaning but still coded *13 Most Wanted Men* (1964), as is argued in Meyer, *Outlaw Representation*, 95–156.
30   The history of the 1960s has often been told through the story of commercial galleries and artist-run spaces. For a lucid account of galleries and their financial strategies in the development of 1960s art, see Michael Maizels, *Collecting the Now: On the Financial Side of Postwar Art History* (Ann Arbor: University of Michigan Press, 2022). For a helpful account of how shifts in galleries' infrastructure and spaces made, in the later 1960s, new trends in contemporary art possible through the gentrification of formerly industrial spaces, see Aaron Shkuda, *The Lofts of SoHo: Gentrification, Art, and Industry in SoHo, 1950–1980* (Chicago: University of Chicago, 2016). For examples of how queer themes were managed in postwar galleries, see Ann Gibson, "Lesbian Identity and the Politics of Representation in Betty Parsons Gallery," in *Gay and Lesbian Studies in Art History*, ed. W. Davis (Binghamton, NY: Haworth Press, 1994), 245–70; and the discussion of Leo Castelli Gallery in Butt, *Between You and Me*, 136–62.
31   See Miriam Kienle, *Queer Networks: Ray Johnson's Correspondence Art* (Minneapolis: University of Minnesota Press, 2023).
32   With distribution in the hundreds of thousands, physique magazines established a vibrant gay male visual culture (albeit one that was overwhelmingly white and middle-class) and were foundational to the emergence of gay political and social movements, as David K. Johnson has argued in *Buying Gay: How Physique Entrepreneurs Sparked a Movement* (New York: Columbia University Press, 2021). See further Waugh, *Hard to Imagine*.
33   See Gonzalo Casals and Noam Parness, eds., *Queer Holdings: A Survey of the Leslie-Lohman Museum Collection* (Munich: Hirmer Publishers, 2019).
34   Jonathan Weinberg, *Male Desire: The Homoerotic in American Art* (New York: Harry N. Abrams, 2004), 133. The story is recounted in more detail in Carol Vogel, "Exposure for a Nude," *New York Times*, September 30, 2005. For more on the articulation and suppression of queer themes in the reception of Pop art in 1963, see Jennifer Sichel, "'Do You Think Pop Art's Queer?' Gene Swenson and Andy Warhol," *Oxford Art Journal* 41, no. 1 (2018): 59–83.
35   See, for instance, Mark Godfrey and Zoé Whitley, eds., *Soul of a Nation: Art in the Age of Black Power* (London: Tate Publishing, 2017); and Rachel Middleman, *Radical Eroticism: Women, Art, and Sex in the 1960s* (Berkeley: University of California Press, 2018). Such direct political commitments were also expressed in abstract or semi-abstract work of the 1960s, as is discussed in Roderick A. Ferguson, "Purifoy: The Shit, the World, and their Remaking," *SAQ: South Atlantic Quarterly* 119, no. 3 (July 2020): 447–60.
36   For a discussion of Grossman's complex identifications with and of these sculptures as well as a discussion of the ways in which they were received as BDSM icons, see Getsy, *Abstract Bodies*, 147–207.

enforcement as more gay, lesbian, trans, and queer people are drawn to the scene. Violent demonstrations flare over the next five days, and the rebellion goes on to catalyze the gay rights movement in the United States.

July 20, 1969 • After four days of space travel, Apollo 11 astronauts Neil Armstrong and Buzz Aldrin become the first humans to land and walk on the surface of the moon. An estimated 640 million people watch footage of the event on television. Over a million spectators, including Vice President Spiro Agnew and former president Lyndon Johnson, had attended the craft's liftoff from Cape Kennedy, Florida, on July 16. This mission fulfills President John F. Kennedy's 1961 call for human exploration of the moon.

Summer 1969 • In the summer following their November 1968 marriage, Jack Whitten and his second wife, Mary Staikos, travel to Crete. She is of Greek descent, but neither has been to Europe before. They live cheaply, and Whitten spends the trip carving a tree into a totem sculpture, a feat motivated by a dream he has just before departing for Greece. The tree, a dead one rooted in the ground, remains in place while he carves, and the process turns him into a local celebrity, as children come to watch him work all day. The trip, along with Whitten's continuing study of Greek, will also inspire his notable series *Greek Alphabet* (1975–78).

August 13, 1969 • Lucas Samaras's film *Self*, made with cinematographer Kim Levin, premieres at the Museum of Modern Art, New York. "For the past ten years or so I had been doing these sparkly touchable, crusty, seeable and only seldom moving things utilizing change, past art, geometry, pins, wool, mirrors, photographs and sex while secretly I wanted to become a movie actor," Samaras will later explain. "I wanted to speak only with my body." With Levin as his camerawoman and film editor, Samaras finally gets his chance. The film plays with the construction and destruction of the self, documenting Samaras spelling his name using the letters of his alphabet soup before eating them, or systematically destroying an intricate box he has spent months making. "The idea was not to photograph the fury of a destruction but its deliberate, logical, slow separation so that various parts and materials could be recorded as they became revealed by the knife," Samaras will reflect. "Ending one kind of art for another. Revealing the aggression hidden in all choices."

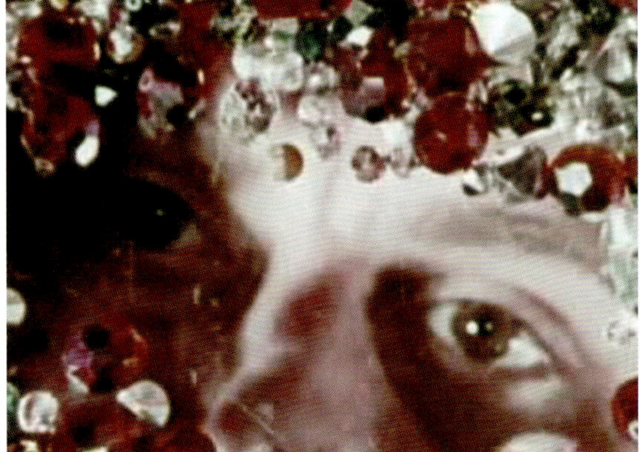

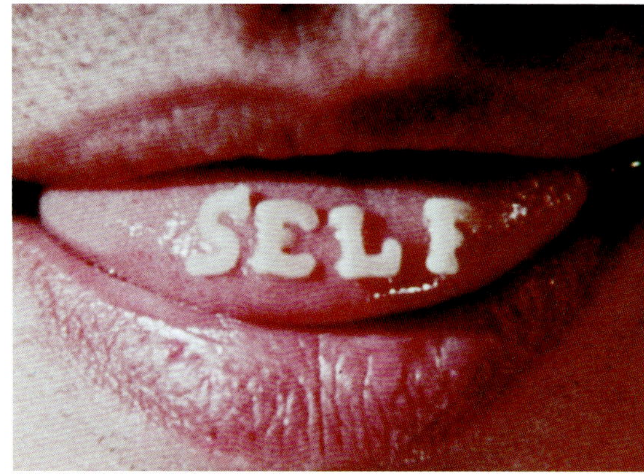

Lucas Samaras and Kim Levin, *Self*, 1969. 16mm film, color; 23 min.

This experience in front of the camera motivates the artist to begin a series of nude self-portraits that he takes between 1969 and 1971 using a Polaroid camera, thus subjecting himself to further and ever more intensive scrutiny. He later comments on his *AutoPolaroids*: "Other than being an autobiographic postulate of some of my present attitudes or a complicated gift to others, these photographs are a way of studying my pictured self as an abstraction or translation for esthetic speculation, psychological perspicacity, sensual subtlety and warm embarrassment. . . . I have wanted to photographically explore my body for years and was going to have a professional photographer do it. But I have never been able to work well with others, and I was not going to go to a photography school and learn photography. Polaroid came in handy."

August 13, 1969 • Thirty-five-year-old Gene Swenson and his mother, Josephine Swenson, are killed in a multivehicle crash south of Concordia, Kansas.

August 1969 • Based on his work at the Rice Media Center at Rice University, Roy Fridge is recruited by the University of Oklahoma to start a bachelor of fine arts and a master of fine arts program in film. He will return to Houston and his studio space with sculptor Jim Love in 1973.

October 1–November 9, 1969 • *The Spirit of the Comics*, curated by Stephen S. Prokopoff, is on view at the Institute of Contemporary Art at the University of Pennsylvania in Philadelphia. The exhibition brings together artists through their interest in either the iconography, sequential potential, or pictorial language found in comic books and comic strips. "From a formal point of view," art historian Joan Siegfried writes in the catalogue, "the emblematic character of much art of the sixties, has helped make the comics congenial to its creators. From the point of view of expression, the comics were an ally in the artists' stand against the constrictions of good taste, which on the artistic level meant the aesthetic preoccupations of the preceding Abstract Expressionists." Notably, the genre expands far beyond the appropriation of Pop art into the idea that seriality itself has formal potential in art—as in the works of Wallace Berman and Jess, for example. And

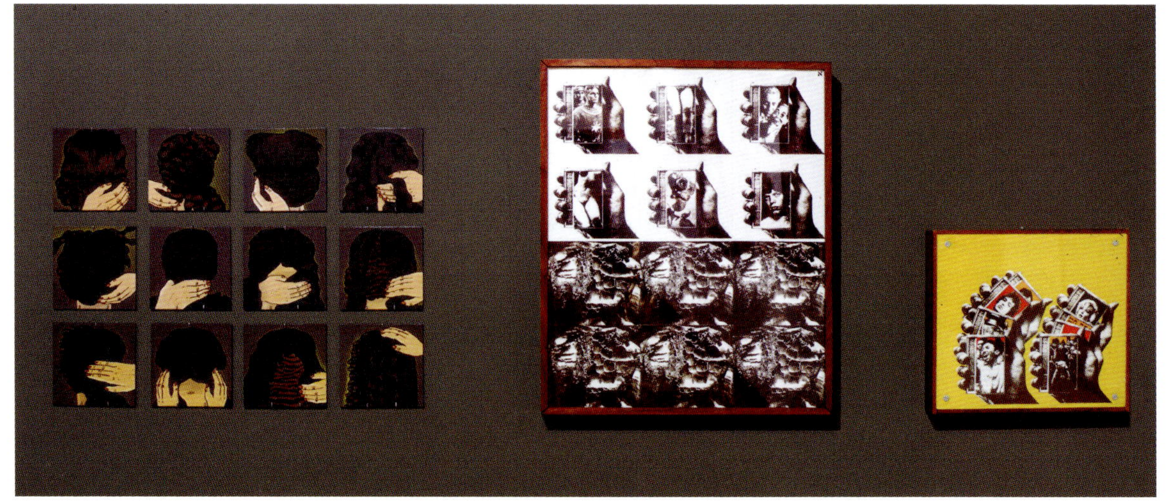

The Spirit of the Comics, Institute of Contemporary Art, Philadelphia, 1969

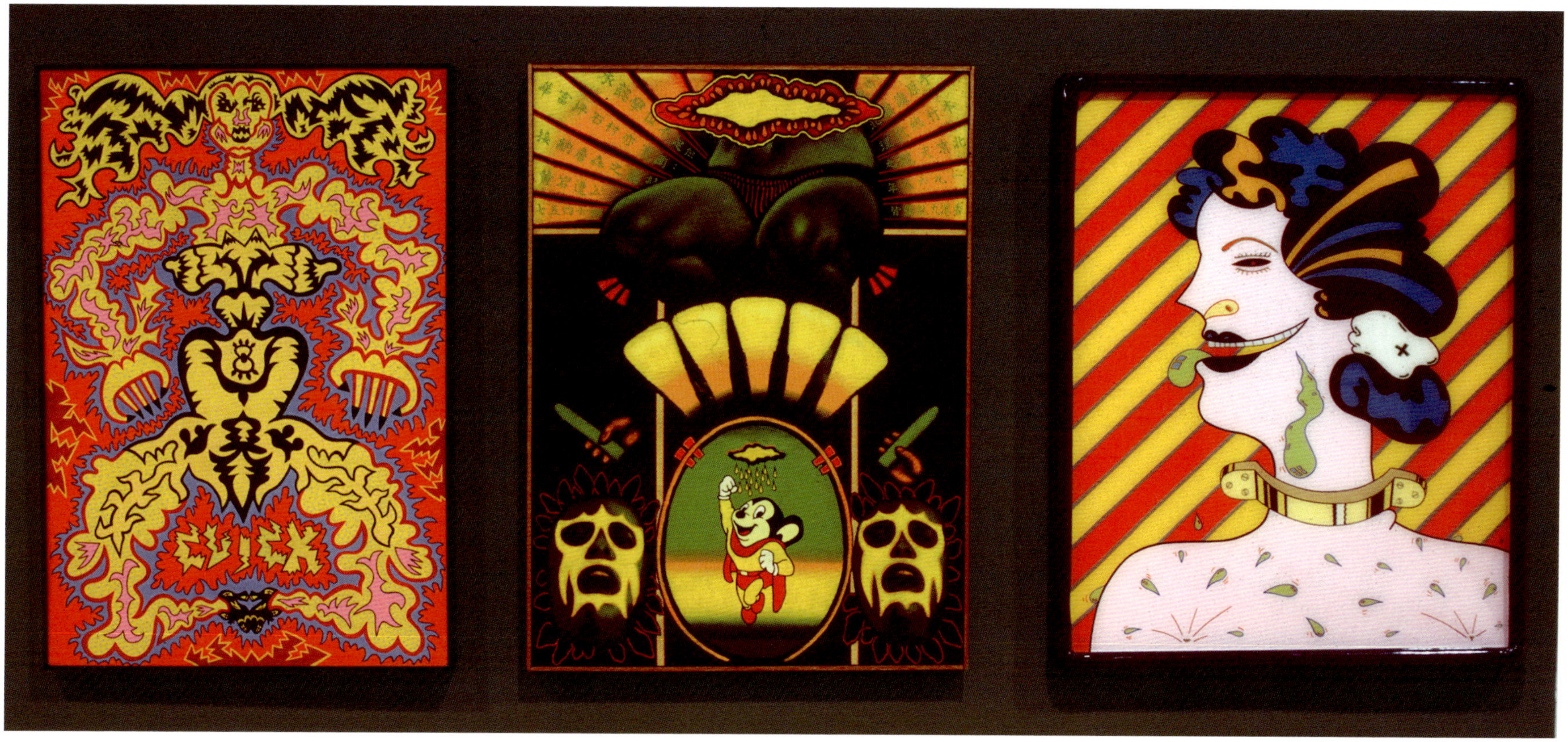

The Spirit of the Comics, Institute of Contemporary Art, Philadelphia, 1969

the pictorial language offers the possibility of spreading into inventive spaces, as in the cases of Gladys Nilsson's and Barbara Rossi's pieces. The exhibition locates this throughline in the artists but doesn't take it a step further to say something larger about the medium itself. The catalogue weaves comics into the histories of twentieth-century assemblage, painting, and sculpture. Among the other artists on view are Jeremy Anderson, Robert Arneson, Roger Brown, Roy De Forest, Jim Nutt, Claes Oldenburg, Christina Ramberg, Suellen Rocca, Peter Saul, H. C. Westermann, William T. Wiley, and Karl Wirsum.

1969 • Diane Arbus begins work on the iconic portfolio *A box of ten photographs* (1969–70). The completed project eventually includes *Identical twins, Roselle, N.J. 1966* (1966), which she has already exhibited in *New Documents* (1967) at the Museum of Modern Art. Another selection from the portfolio, *Xmas tree in a living room in Levittown, L.I. 1962* (1962), will appear in curator Robert Doty's *Human Concern/Personal Torment: The Grotesque in American Art* at the Whitney Museum of American Art in October.

October 14–November 30, 1969 • *Human Concern/Personal Torment: The Grotesque in American Art* is on view at the Whitney Museum of American Art, New York; the show will travel

to the art museum at the University of California, Berkeley in January. A rallying cry for explicitly figurative art in New York, the exhibition brings together a mishmash of twentieth-century drawing, painting, and sculpture with an emphasis on depictions of distress, horror, and outrage. Curator Robert Doty frames the show as an attempt to catalogue the responses to the turbulent 1960s while tracing such sensibilities decades back to, among others, George Grosz and Thomas Nast. In the exhibition catalogue, Doty describes the "grotesque" as an outgrowth of Surrealism, finding that it "threatens the foundations of existence through the subversion of order and the treacherous reversal of familiar and hostile. Its value and

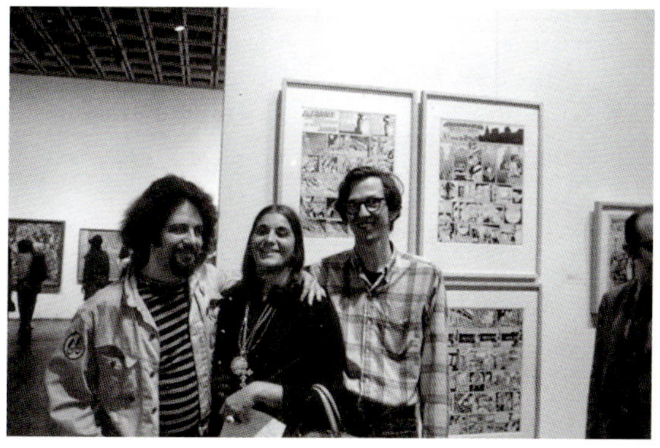

Spain Rodriguez, Janet Shapiro, and Robert Crumb at the opening of
Human Concern/Personal Torment: The Grotesque in American Art,
Whitney Museum of American Art, New York, 1969

vitality stem from the aberrations of human relationships and acts and therefore from man and his foibles, weakness and irresistible attractions. It is a direct and forceful means of exposing man to man, and man to himself."

The exhibition includes books and boxes by Lucas Samaras; Paul Thek's *Tomb* (here titled *Death of a Hippie*; 1967); drawings and paintings by Robert Crumb, Jim Nutt, and Peter Saul; installations by Edward Kienholz; assemblages by Daniel LaRue Johnson and David McManaway; photographs by Diane Arbus; and sculptures by Bruce Conner, Nancy Grossman, Luis Jimenez, and H. C. Westermann. By ranging broadly, Doty captures many artists who otherwise are beginning to fall out of history, as overt subject matter is increasingly frowned upon by a rising generation of academics and curators. This kind of pictorial approach, for all its inclusiveness, is seen as out of step with advanced art. The show receives mostly disappointing reviews, including a particularly scathing response from critic Robert Pincus-Whitten, who describes it as a "disaster" and an exploitation of the exhibited artists: "That Doty should contend, in his sophomoric catalog essay, that the kind of art shown at the present exhibition has cornered Humanity and Morality is a lie and a museological blunder."

October 16–November 8, 1969 • The exhibition *5+1* is on view at Stony Brook University,

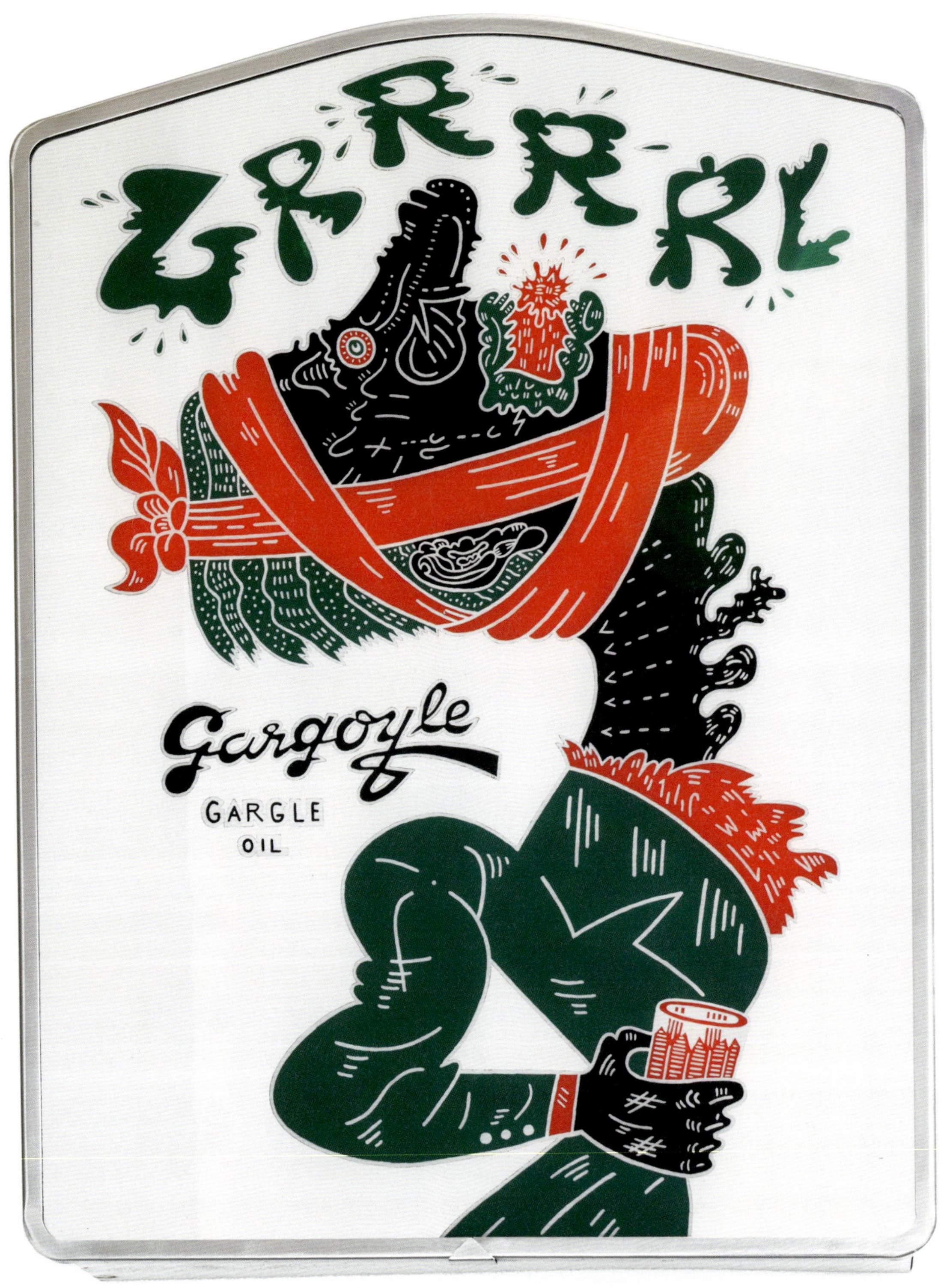

Karl Wirsum, *Gargoyle Gargle Oil*, c. 1969. Acrylic painted on mirror, 22 × 16 ⅜ × 5 in. (55.9 × 41.6 × 12.7 cm). KAWS Collection

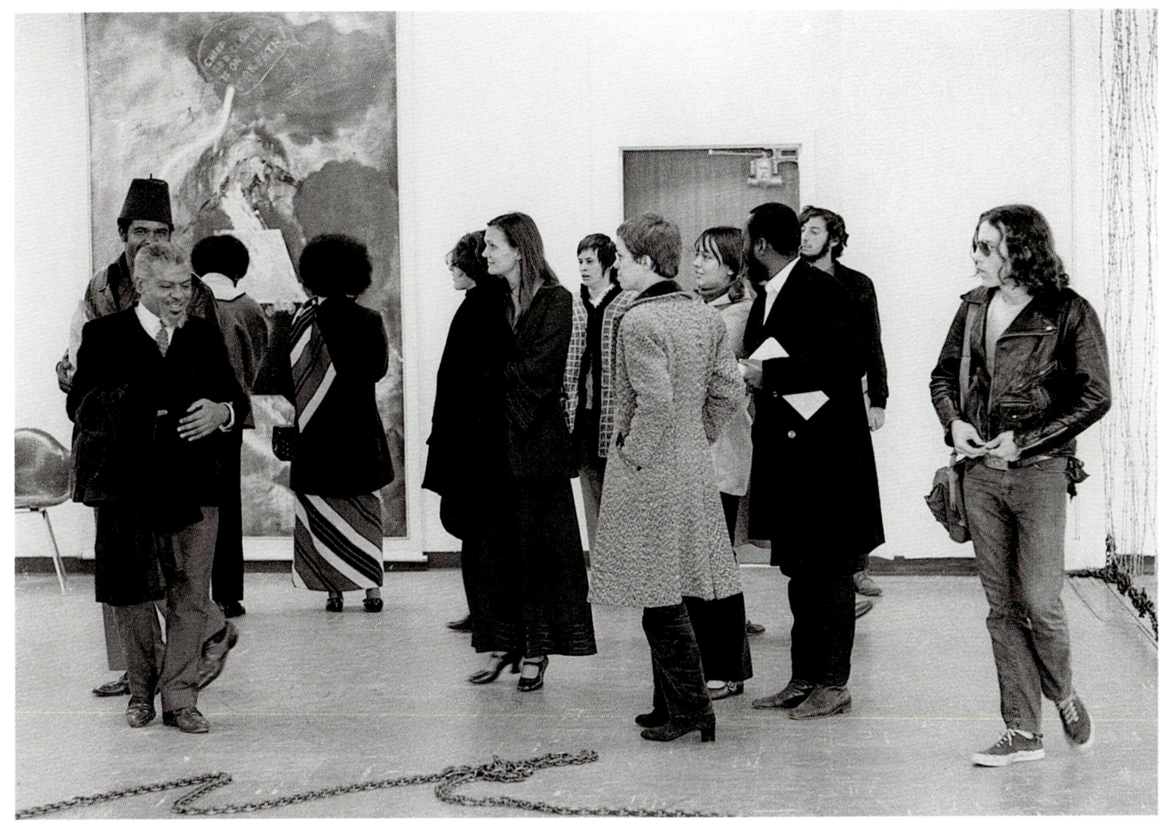

Melvin Edwards (far left), Jayne Cortez (fourth from left), Frank Bowling (third from right), and others at the opening of *5+1*, Stony Brook University, NY, 1969

New York, and includes work by the show's curator, Frank Bowling, as well as Melvin Edwards, Daniel LaRue Johnson, Alvin Loving, Jack Whitten, and William T. Williams. The show is a small but important installation of Black artists working abstractly that articulates a middle ground between the politics of representation associated with the Black Arts Movement and the presumption of abstraction as being apolitical. Critic Lawrence Alloway notes in the exhibition brochure that through the work of these artists, "the two themes of aesthetics and protest can be joined."

Johnson invites Adger Cowans to document the show photographically; the two had met in the late 1960s through their mutual friend Ornette Coleman. At this point, Cowans is living below Canal Street at 136 West Broadway, within a few blocks of the studios of Edwards, Johnson, Loving, Whitten, and Williams. The group frequently visit one another, and Cowans will remember that "everybody came by my studio because I was a photographer."

November 13, 1969 • Newspapers across the United States publish journalist Seymour Hersh's exposé on the massacre at My Lai, in which US Army soldiers killed hundreds of unarmed civilians, including women, children, and the elderly, in the South Vietnamese town. Although the massacre had taken place in March 1968, it had been covered up by the military. Details of the atrocities shock the public and increase antiwar sentiment.

November 20, 1969–June 11, 1971 • A group of Native Americans operating under the name Indians of All Tribes occupy Alcatraz Island in San Francisco Bay. The federal prison on Alcatraz has been closed for six years, and the nearly one hundred protestors demand land rights to the island, citing the 1868 Treaty of Fort Laramie, which they argue requires the return of unused federal land to Native Americans. In a proclamation to President Richard M. Nixon and "all his people," the occupiers offer to purchase the 16 acres of land for $24 in glass beads and red cloth—a proposal that more than equals the price Dutch settlers paid for Manhattan three hundred years before. On the island, Indians of All Tribes organizes a free school and healthcare, a food distribution system, and Radio Free Alcatraz.

December 16, 1969–February 1, 1970 • The Whitney Museum of American Art's *1969 Annual Exhibition: Contemporary American Painting* features artists Romare Bearden, Roy De Forest, James Rosenquist, Edward Ruscha, Jack Whitten, and William T. Wiley. In the catalogue's foreword, museum director John I. H. Bauer admits that, despite the Annuals' historical purpose, "an exhibition of this size can no longer even approximate a cross section of creative trends of the moment" and that the organizers in 1969 instead focused on "presenting those new directions which seem to us to be generating the most creative excitement."

1969 • Louise Bourgeois initiates her series *Femme Couteau* (*Knife Woman*). "There has always been sexual suggestiveness in my work. Sometimes I am totally concerned with female shapes—clusters of breasts like clouds—but often I merge the imagery—phallic breasts, male and female, active and passive," she will write, explaining that the recumbent pale-pink marble object "embodies the polarity of women, the destructive and the seductive." Throughout the 1970s, Bourgeois will participate in feminist exhibitions and activities, and her comments appear in a February 1974 issue of *New York* magazine, in the article "The Female View of Erotica." Her reflections complement statements by artists Anita Steckel and Hannah Wilke, as well as critic Barbara Rose, who adds that "by depicting female genitals, women artists attack a fundamental idea of male supremacy—that a penis is superior."

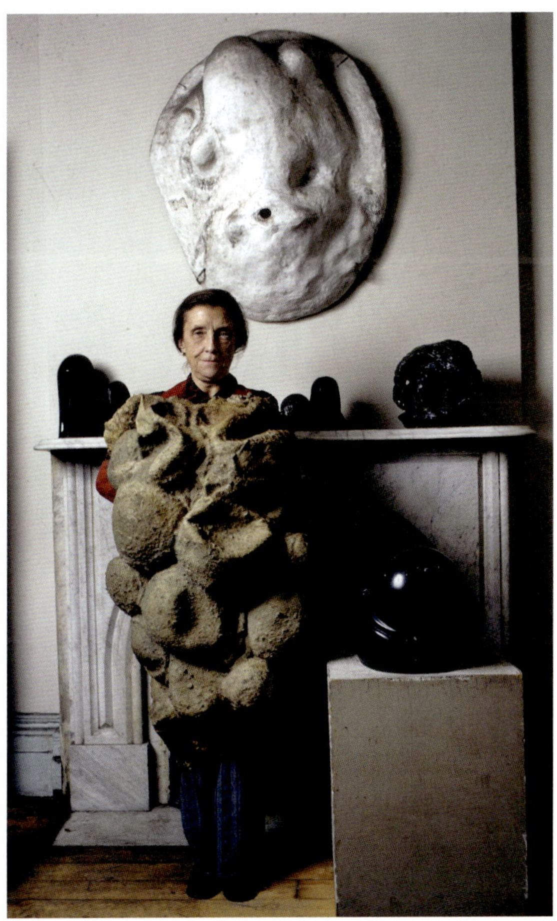

Louise Bourgeois in her home, surrounded by her sculptures and wearing a costume of her design, 1973

1970

January 27–February 10, 1970 • Nancy Graves spends two weeks in the Sahara Desert to shoot the film *Goulimine* (1970); she will return to shoot *Izy Boukir* (1971) during the month of June. Embracing the abilities of film to examine the intricate movement of the camel through the vastness of the desert landscape, Graves is inspired by the work of Eadweard Muybridge who, almost a century prior, had employed the camera to scrutinize the particularities of motion. The artist will go on to make *Aves* (1973), in which she similarly records the flight patterns of birds. For each of these films, Graves is interested not only in documenting the singular movement of herds or flocks but also in revealing "the irrational ways in which vision bounces back and forth across a surface, bringing motion to an initially static experience." *Goulimine* and *Izy Boukir* mark the conclusion of her work on the subject of the camel. Soon after, she becomes increasingly interested in topographical maps, lunar images, and satellite photographs.

1970 • Barbara Hammer comes out as a lesbian after auditing a sociology class focusing on women's liberation that is offered at Santa Rosa Junior College, where she has been teaching English classes to earn a living after leaving her husband. "When I made love with a woman for the first time," she will later recall, "my entire worldview shifted. I was touching a body much like my own which heightened all my senses. In addition to the sensual pleasures, my social network completely changed; I was swept up with the energies and dreams of a feminist revolution. We could make a new world where everyone was equal. We believed it, and we tried our best to live it." In a series of black-and-white photographs from this period, and through films such as *Marie and Me* (1970) and *Dyketactics* (1974), Hammer depicts women's bodies in idyllic natural settings, giving life and dimension to this flourishing social network.

March 3–29, 1970 • Melvin Edwards is the first Black sculptor to have a solo exhibition at the Whitney Museum of American Art, New York. *Melvin Edwards: Works* features pieces of the artist's new work as he shifts away from the welded metal of his series *Lynch Fragments* (1963–67). Upon his move to New York, Edwards had concluded the series both as part of a commitment to a new artistic chapter and because of the logistical difficulties of welding in Manhattan. In 1968 he had began to experiment with barbed wire, debuting large-scale geometrical installations the following year in two important group shows: *X to the Fourth Power*, curated by William T. Williams at the Studio Museum in Harlem, and *5+1*, organized by British-Guyanese painter Frank Bowling at Stony Brook University, New York. With these

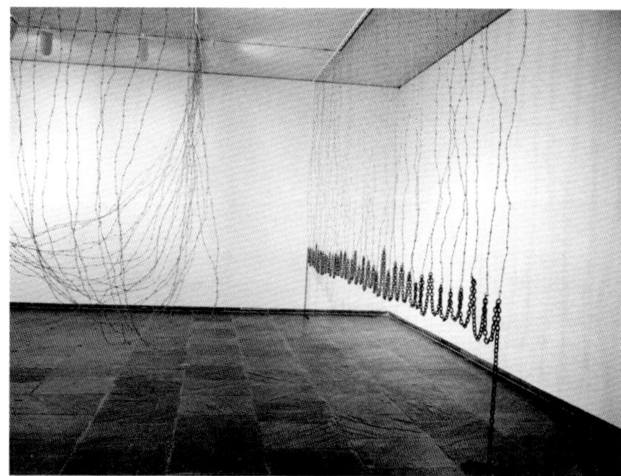

Melvin Edwards: Works, Whitney Museum of American Art, New York, 1970, with *"Look through minds mirror distance and measure time"—Jayne Cortez* (1970) and *Curtain for William and Peter* (1969)

site-specific works, Edwards employs the then dominant aesthetic of Minimalism, but in his use of highly charged materials, he injects social meaning into an otherwise apolitical visual language. When he is given the solo exhibition at the Whitney in 1970, he exhibits four barbed-wire installations that make a particular impression on David Hammons, who will later recall: "That was the first abstract piece of art that I saw that had cultural value in it for black people. I couldn't believe that piece when I saw it because I didn't think you could make abstract art with a message. I saw the symbols in Mel's work. . . . After that, I

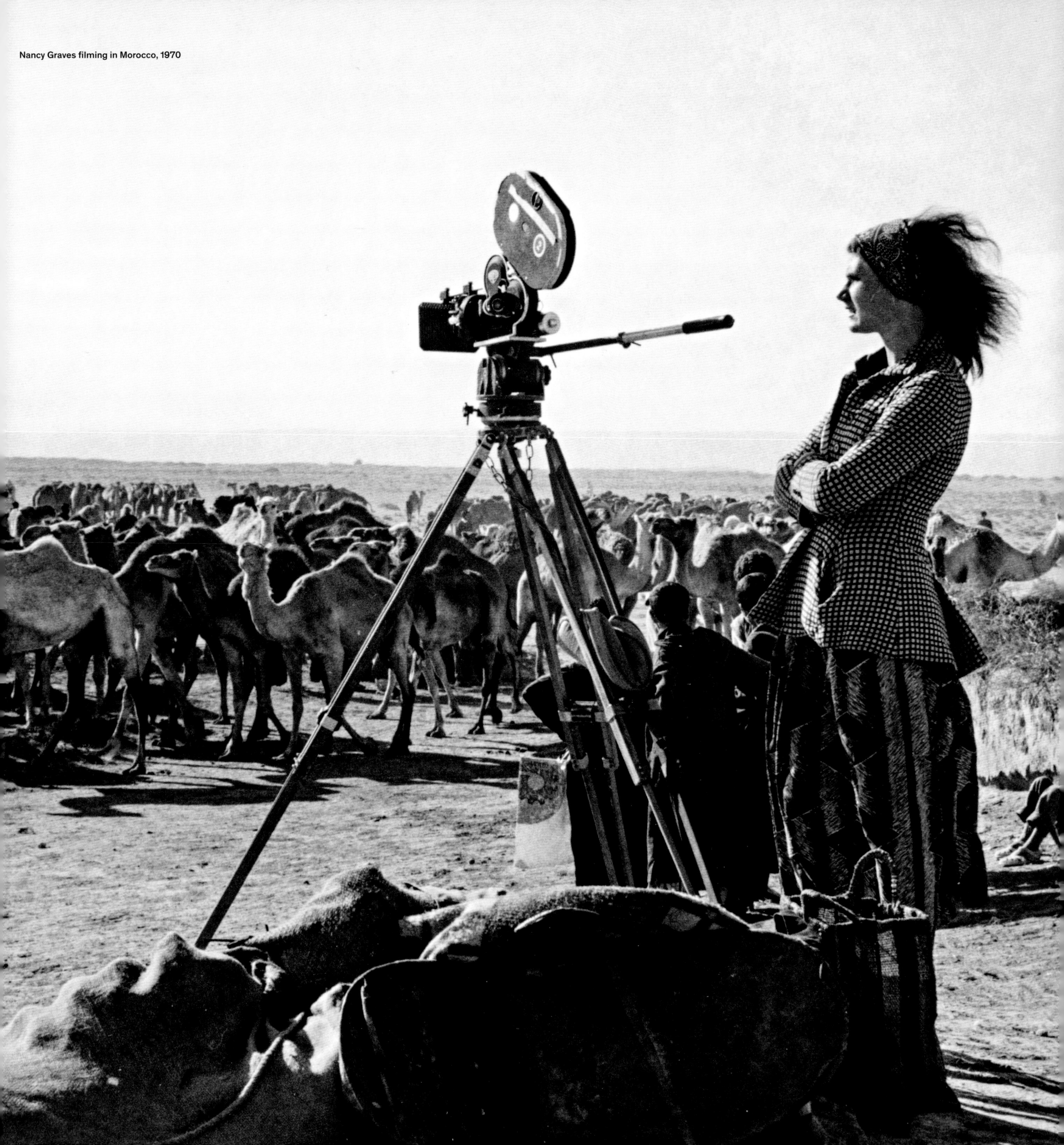

Nancy Graves filming in Morocco, 1970

PRESS RELEASE

Release Date: Immediate
Press Contact: Alonzo Davis
Photographs upon request

brockman gallery

DAVID HAMMONS will be featured in his first one man
exhibition at Brockman Gallery, April 8 through May
2, 1970. The gallery is located at 4334 Degnan
Blvd., L.A., Calif. and is open from 1:00 to 7:00
p.m. Wednesday through Sunday.

This exhibition will feature recent body prints from
the "Belly Series" which deal with social commentary
on Man's dilemma. Mr. Hammons' works deal with
reality, a true meaning of life as it really exist
with no restraints or distortion as seen through the
eyes of this artist.

The "body print" is a new media to the established
art world done by direct physical contact with the
canvas which gives an X ray - photo effect; mysterious yet very graphic. Mr. Hammons was recently
contacted by Time Magazine for an artical reguarding
this unusual technique.

Mr. Hammons is the recipient of the first place
award at the L.A. Annual Art Exhibition, 1969. His
work has been desplayed in many exhibitions throughout California including the La Jolla Museum of Art,
Gallery 32, Ankrum Gallery and the Laguna Beach Art
Ass. His work hangs in the permanent collection of
the Oakland Museum and San Jose State College.

Press release for *David Hammons*, Brockman Gallery, Los Angeles, 1970

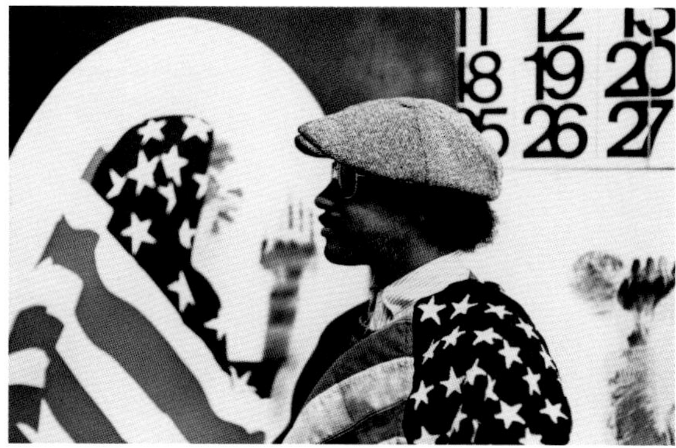

David Hammons in his studio, Los Angeles, 1970, with *Pray for America* (1969) and *The Wine Leading the Wine* (c. 1969)

beginning of the Women's Movement in New York." The show becomes known as the "Liberated Venice Biennale" and is open to all artists. After this experience, Ringgold and her daughter Michele Wallace establish the Women Students and Artists for Black Art Liberation (WSABAL) to counter the predominantly male Art Workers' Coalition.

April 8–May 2, 1970 • David Hammons's first solo show is on view at Brockman Gallery, Los Angeles, just a year after his two-person show with Noah Purifoy at the same gallery. Hammons presents body prints from what the gallery's press release calls his "Belly Series," continuing his experimentation with this artistic technique. The media statement also mentions *Time* magazine's interest in writing about Hammons's body-print method, though this doesn't transpire.

1970 • Screamin' Jay Hawkins's album *Because Is In Your Mind* is released and features Karl Wirsum's 1968 portrait of the musician on its cover, Wirsum's largest and most complex painting. As the artist will later recall:

Screamin' Jay hit a particular chord of connection for me with his bizarre surrealist lyrics such as "eating a wax feather sandwich in the middle of nineteen hundred and yesterday." His wild acoustic gymnastics of grunts and shouts, coupled with a marvelous, almost operatic Paul Robeson–esque voice, was a study in contrasts that I also appreciated. It was this rawness of style that I tried to convey in my portrait of him. I depicted a full figure with a splayed torso that was stretched like bat wings to the sides of his body and head to reveal the inner guts of the performer. I wanted to reveal the interior of his body to express his electric energy and vibrancy of his act. This also mimicked the cape he often wore onstage during his performances.

started using the symbol of the spade; that was before I did the greasy bags."

1970 • Faith Ringgold organizes a protest of an exhibition being planned at the School of Visual Arts in New York. The show, which is being organized by Robert Morris, develops out of the withdrawal of thirty-eight artists from the American Pavilion at the 1970 Venice Biennale in protest of US imperialism abroad and social injustice at home. "In the

1960s I had rationalized that we were all fighting for the same issues and why shouldn't the men be in charge," Ringgold will later recount. Yet a switch flipped "the day I decided to launch a protest against an exhibit, to be held at the School of Visual Arts in New York, protesting the US policy of war, repression, racism and sexism—an exhibit that itself was all male! I declared that if the organizers didn't include fifty percent women, there would be 'war.' Robert Morris, the organizer, agreed to open the show to women, and that was, so far as I'm concerned, the

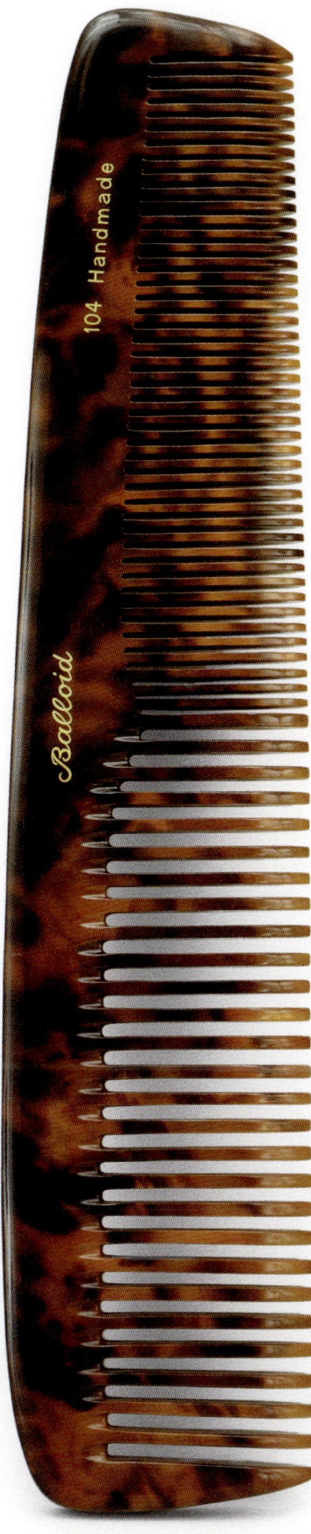

Vija Celmins, *Untitled (Comb)*, 1970. Enamel on wood, 75 × 14 ⅝ × 2 ⅜ in. (190.5 × 37.2 × 6 cm). Los Angeles County Museum of Art; purchase, Contemporary Art Council Fund M.72.26

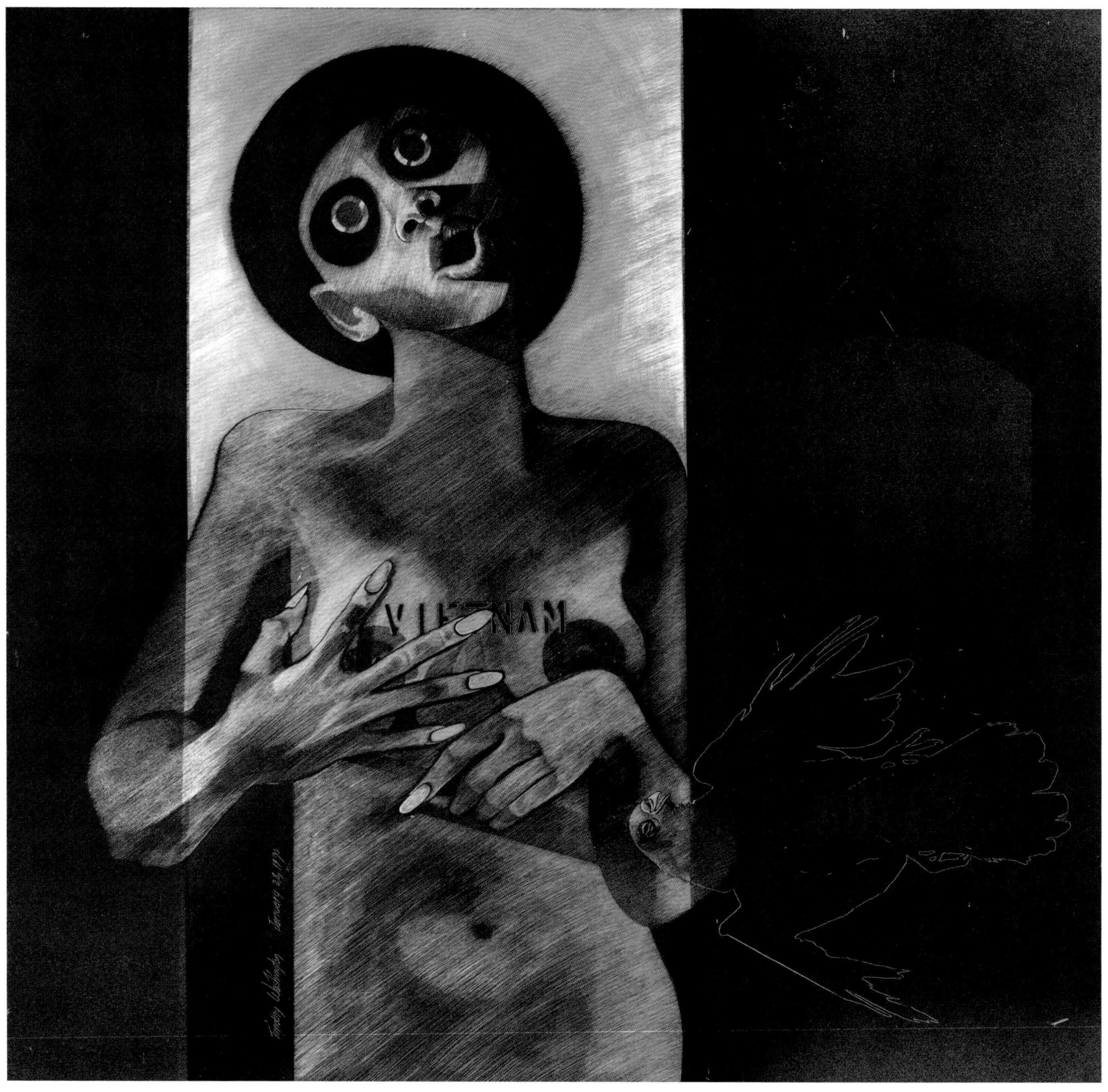

Timothy Washington, *Viet Nam*, 1970. Spray paint on aluminum, 36 ⅛ × 36 ⅛ in. (91.8 × 91.8 cm). Collection of Larry and Tina Jones

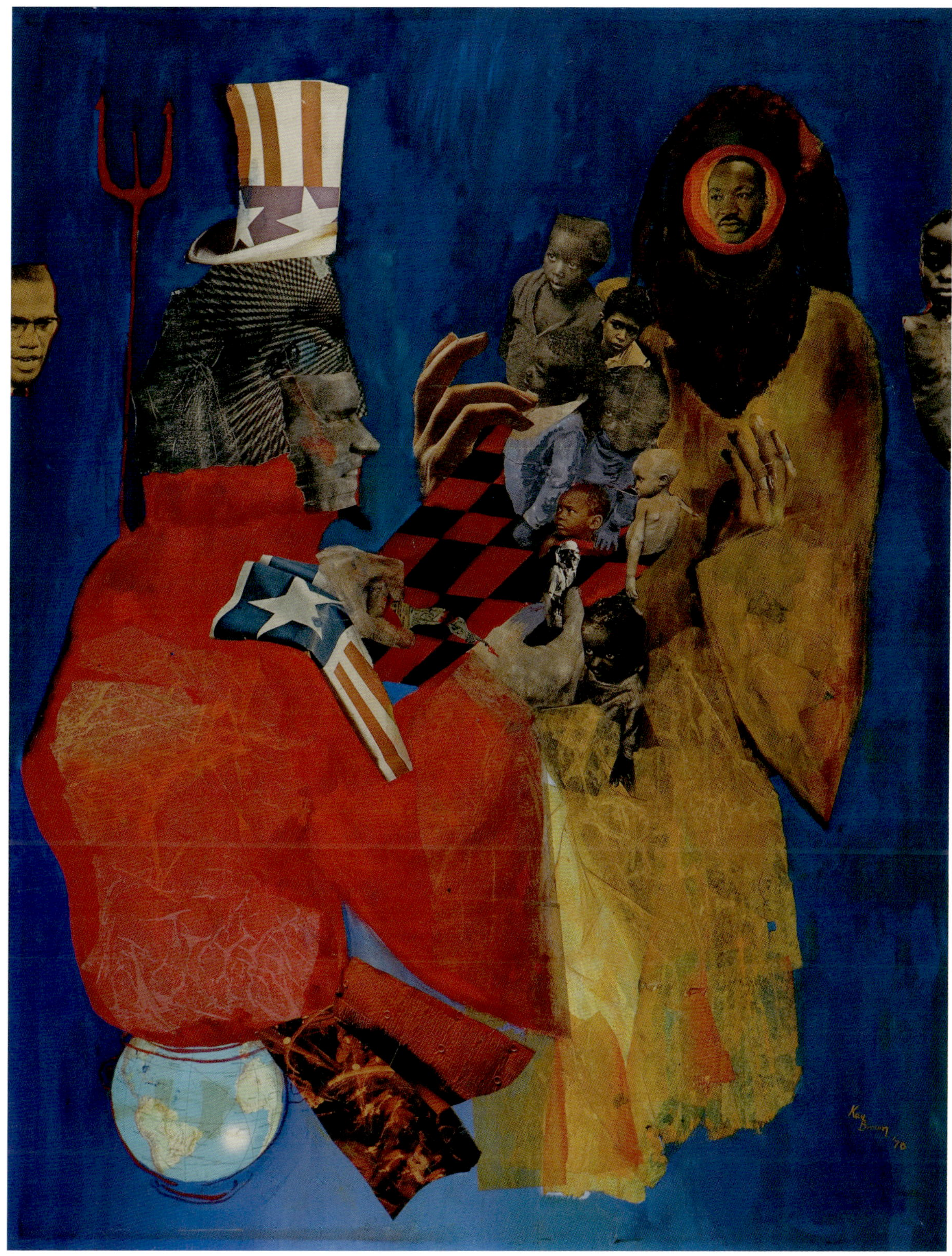

Kay Brown, *The Devil and His Game*, 1970. Collage of various papers and mixed media on canvas, 48 × 36 in. (121.9 × 91.4 cm). Collection of Larry and Tina Jones

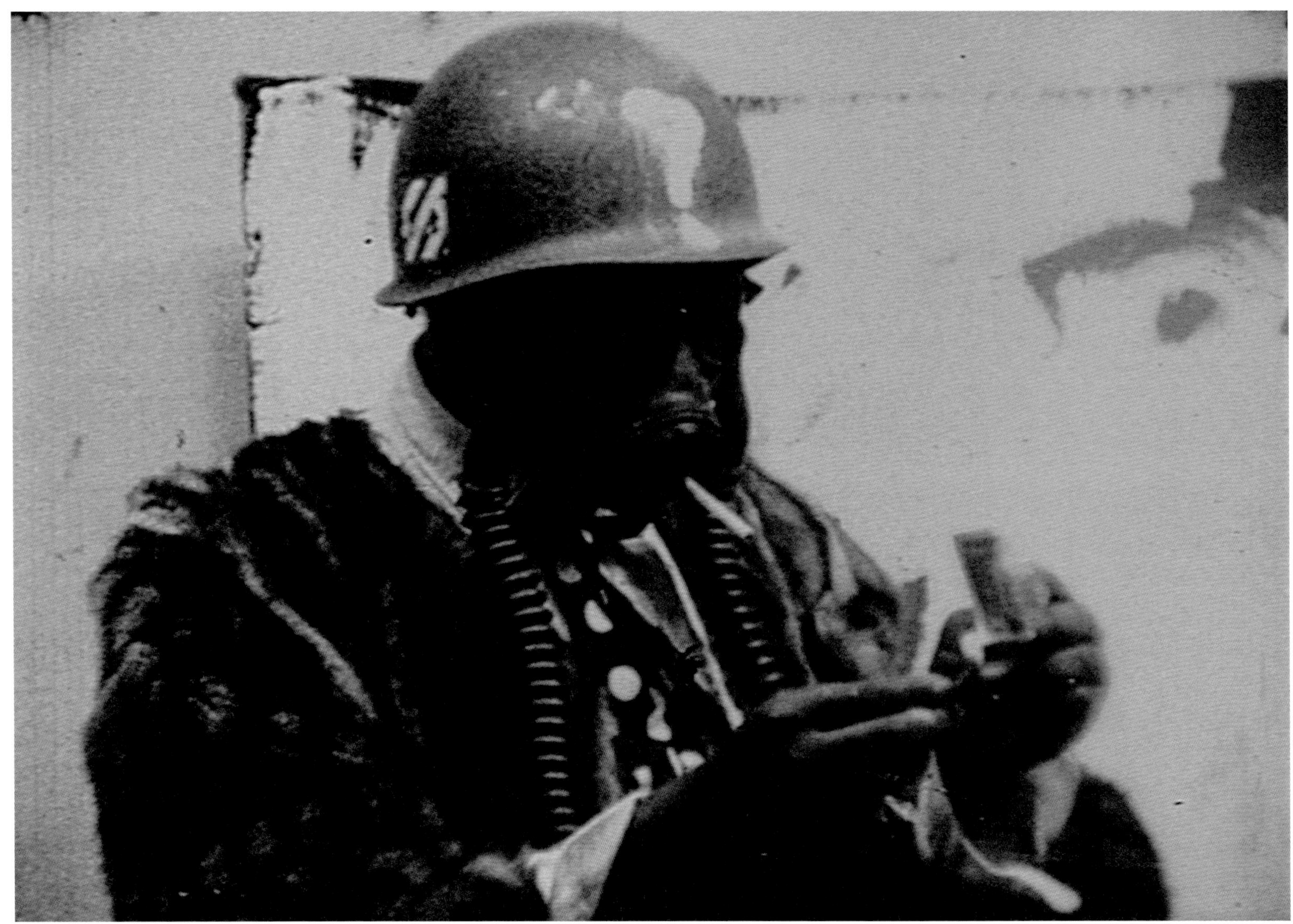

Mike Henderson, *Dufus*, 1970/73. 16mm film, black-and-white, sound, 8 min. Academy Film Archive, Los Angeles

April 16–May 16, 1970 • *Surplus Slop from the Windy City* is on view at the San Francisco Art Institute. The exhibition is organized by Jim Nutt and brings a slew of Chicago artists to the Bay Area, including Roger Brown, Gladys Nilsson, Christina Ramberg, Suellen Rocca, Barbara Rossi, and Karl Wirsum. *Famous Artists of Chicago*, an earlier iteration of the exhibition, had appeared at Sacramento State College in March.

June 1970 • Mike Henderson (b. 1943) receives his master of fine arts from the San Francisco Art Institute (SFAI), having earned his bachelor of fine arts the year before. The beginning of the decade will also see the debuts of his first films, *The Last Supper* (1970) and *Dufus* (1970/73). Henderson puts aside his *Protest Paintings*, a series of large-scale works completed between 1966 and 1968, and pursues his interest in film not only as a new outlet for his images but also as a medium with which he can contribute to the aims of the Black Panther Party. With a 16mm camera he buys from his filmic mentor Robert Nelson, he indeed shoots film for the group, but he also volunteers at their children's breakfast program, delivers appliances to families in need, and even sandbags leader Eldridge Cleaver's house to protect it against potential violence.

William Howard Henderson Jr.—nicknamed "Mike" as a child and "Hindu" as a teenager—had been born in Marshall, a small, predominantly white farming town in central Missouri. He had grown up without electricity or indoor plumbing in a three-room house on the eastern edge of the enforced "colored section of town." His father is physically and emotionally abusive, and Henderson always has his eye on an exit. He gradually works his way through school, takes out loans, and works double shifts to attend SFAI, the only art school he applies to that will accept a Black person.

Throughout Henderson's life there is a consistent push and pull between the liberatory possibilities of the arts and the repressive forces of race and capital, mitigated by both his talent and a generosity of spirit he tends to inspire in those around him. That generosity is not without its costs, and the masks he wears are fervently explored in his film masterpiece *Dufus*. But rather than attempt to reconcile these oppositions, he makes his own space to cohabit with them.

June 1970 • Linda Lomahaftewa (b. 1947) graduates from the San Francisco Art Institute (SFAI) with her bachelor of fine arts. Lomahaftewa is part of a small wave of Native American alumni of the Institute of American Indian Arts (IAIA) in Santa Fe who enrolled in SFAI in the mid-1960s,

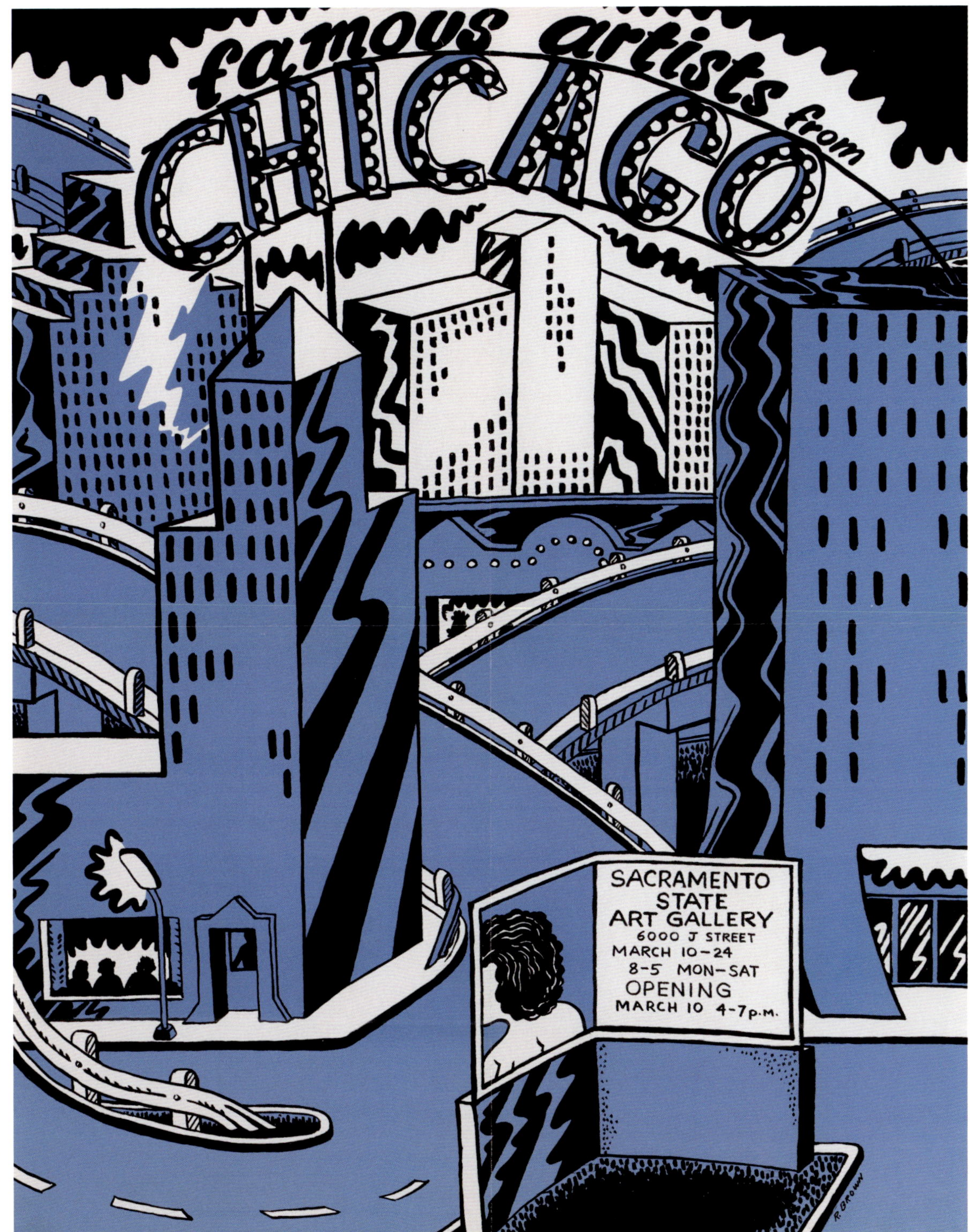

Poster by Roger Brown for *Famous Artists from Chicago*, Sacramento State Art Gallery, CA, 1970

including Kevin Red Star, Earl Biss, and T. C. Cannon. There, she had felt that she was starting over, and her works shifted away from the abstract landscapes she had been making. The live models that are prevalent in her studio classes become a starting point for her work *Untitled (Women's Faces)* (1965–71), an early example of the melding of representational forms with symbolism from Hopi culture and the Southwest landscape that she will continue to explore in her work. As she later recalls, "I got tired of painting the model the way I had been instructed. So one day I flipped my canvas around and started painting parts of the body and putting in my own color schemes. I began drawing all these Indian geometric designs. . . . After that, my teachers left me alone and didn't try to force me to paint in any particular way."

Lomahaftewa had been born in Phoenix, Arizona, to a Hopi father and Choctaw mother. During her childhood the family moved back and

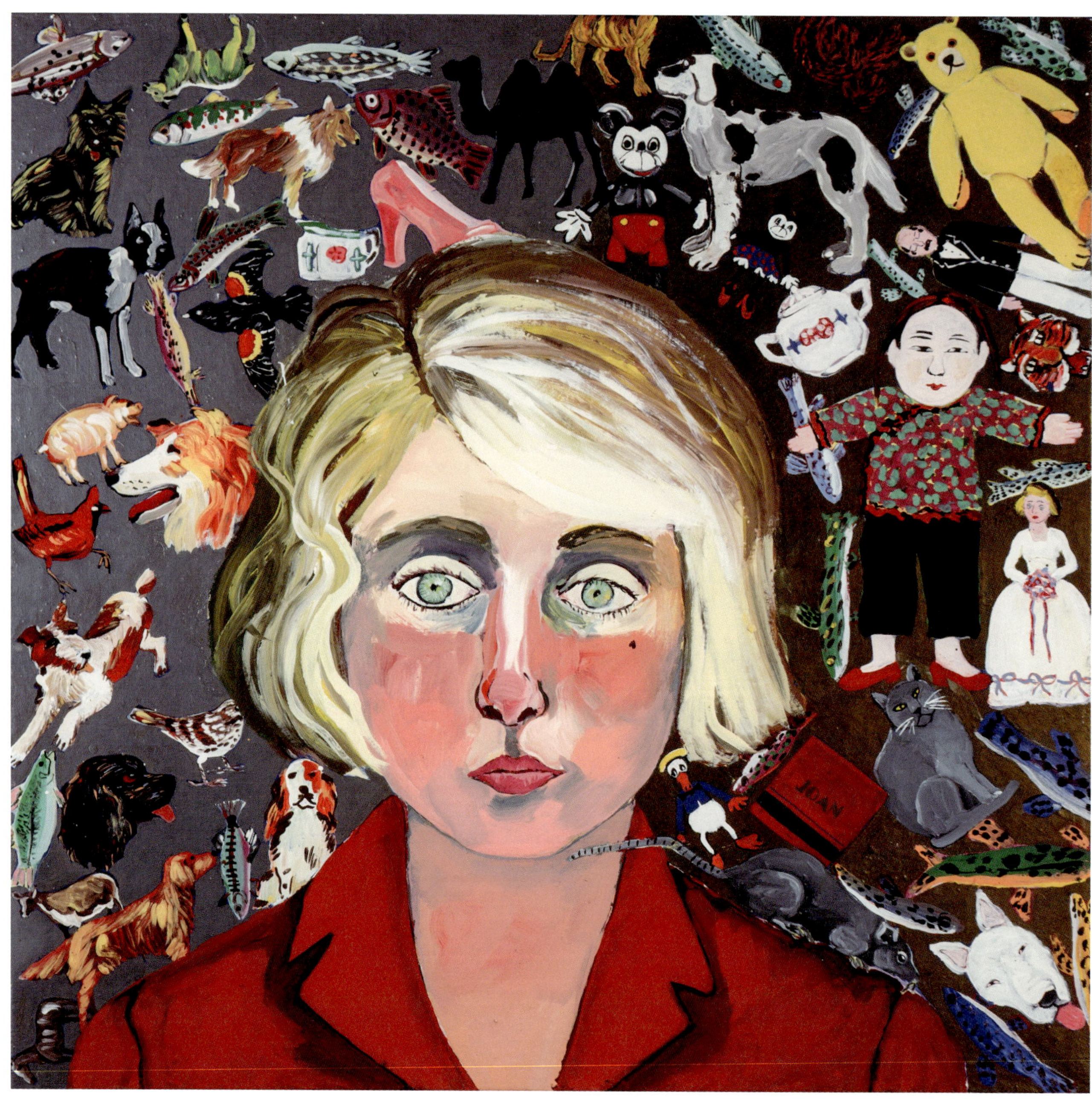

Joan Brown, *Self Portrait*, 1970. Oil and enamel on canvas, 26 × 26 in. (66 × 66 cm). Christine Buck, The Buck Collection

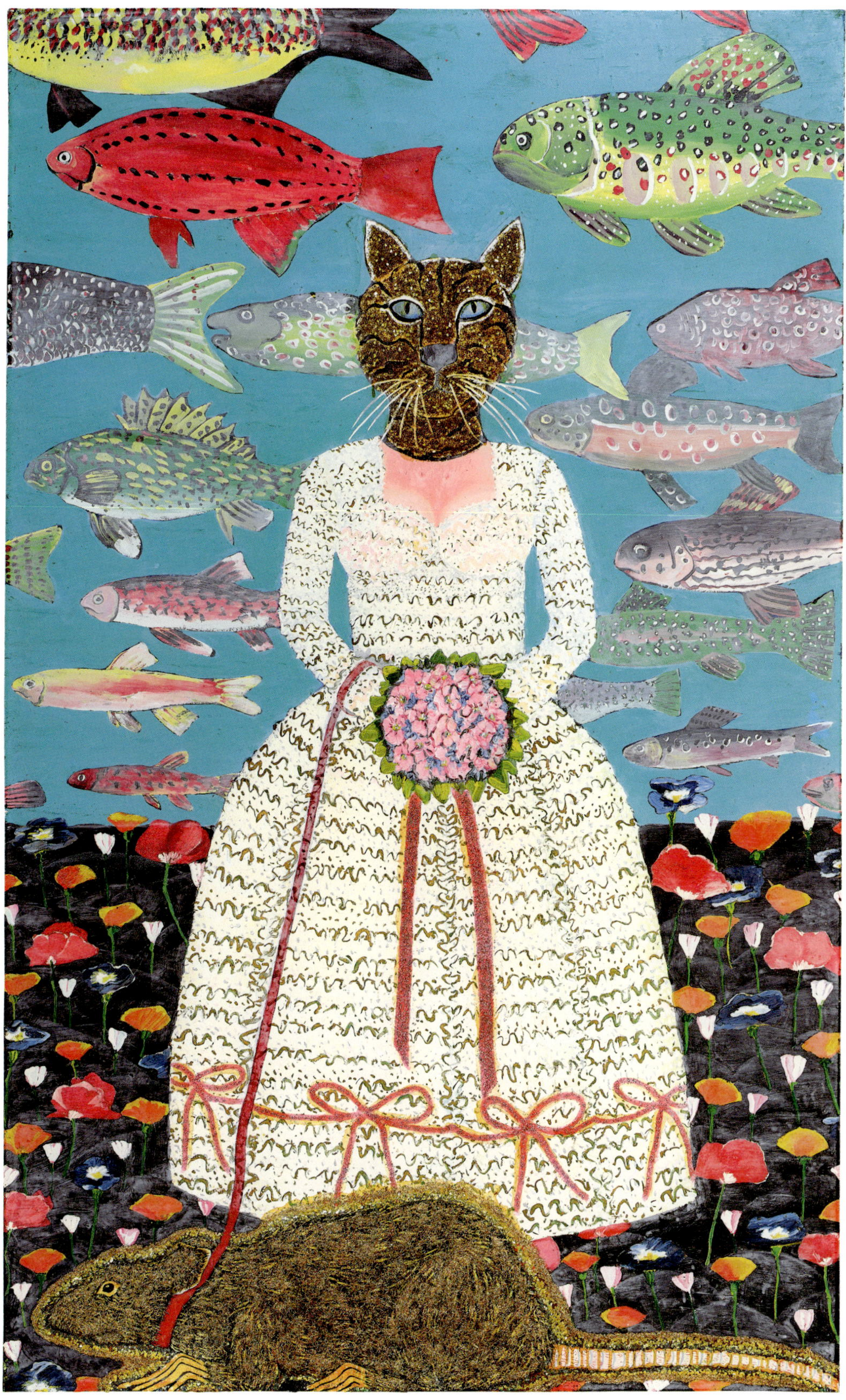

Joan Brown, *The Bride*, 1970. Oil, enamel, and glitter on canvas, 91 × 55 in. (231.1 × 139.7 cm). University of California, Berkeley Art Museum and Pacific Film Archive; bequest of Earl David Peugh III

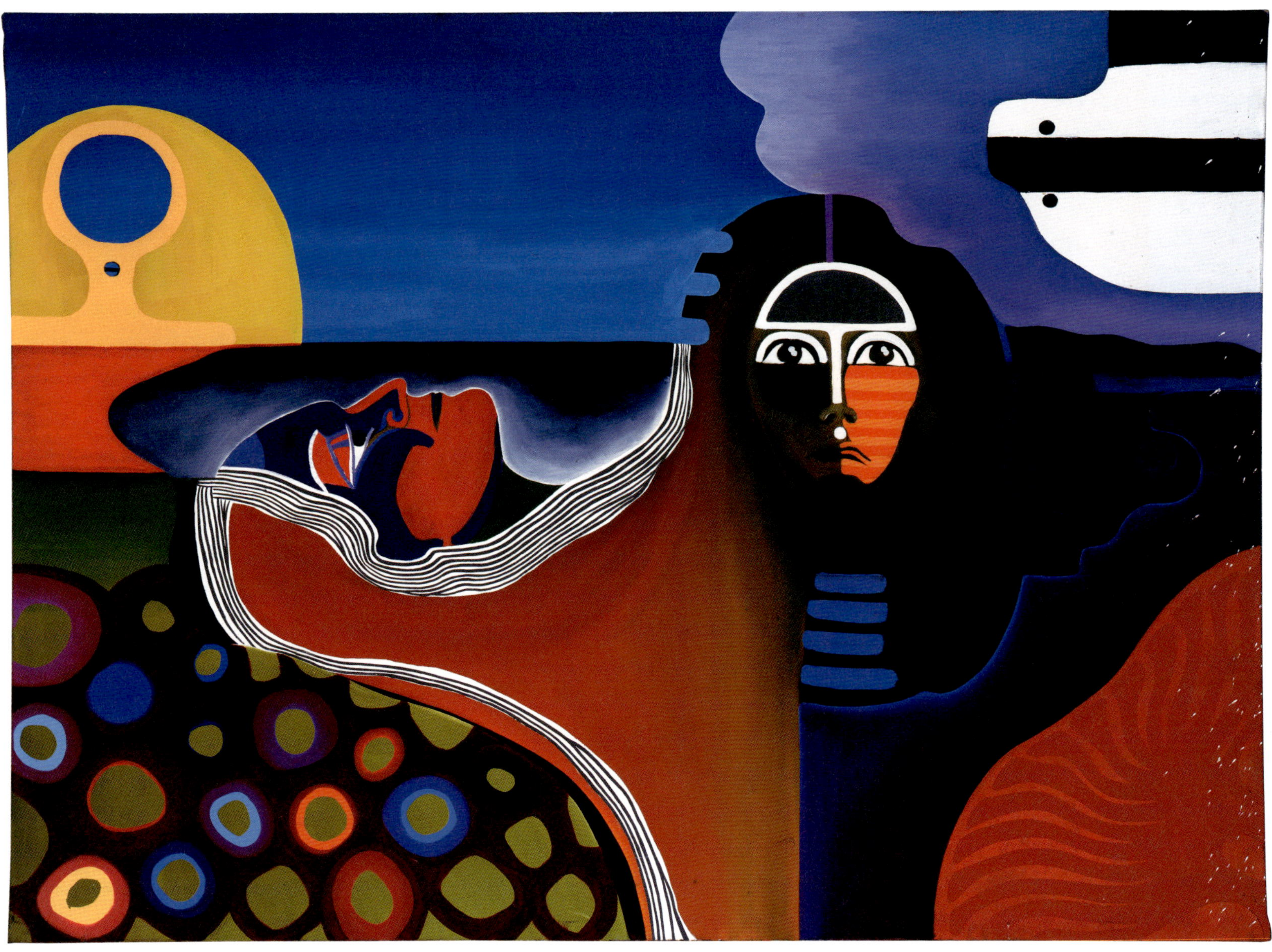

Linda Lomahaftewa, *Untitled (Women's Faces)*, 1965–71. Oil on canvas, 36 × 48 in. (91.4 × 121.9 cm). Heard Museum, Phoenix, AZ; Gift of the artist 4052-1

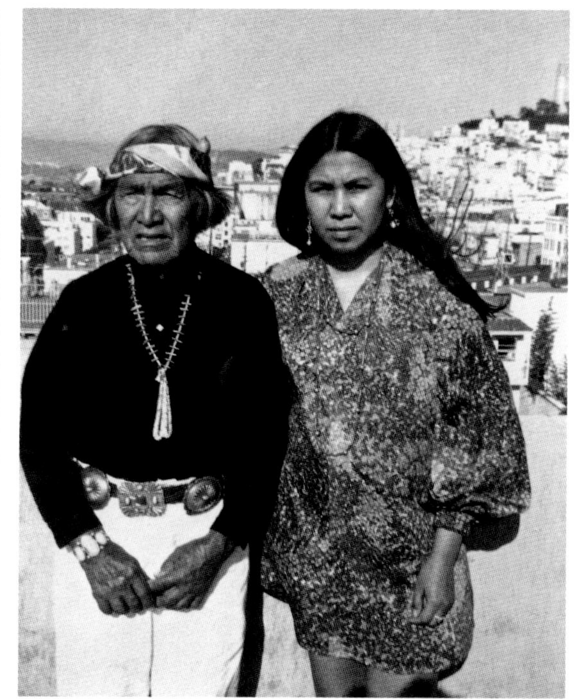

Linda Lomahaftewa with her grandfather Viets Lomahaftewa at her graduation from the San Francisco Art Institute, 1970

forth between Phoenix and Los Angeles, but in the summers she spent time in the Hopi village of Shungopavi on Second Mesa. After attending the strict Holbrook Indian School, run by the Seventh-day Adventist Church, and the Phoenix Indian High School, she finds the intensely collaborative arts-and-culture program at IAIA revelatory. Lomahaftewa thinks she will become a commercial artist, but she is encouraged in her final year to begin painting. She will receive her master of fine arts from SFAI in 1971 and teach at Sonoma State University and the University of California, Berkeley, before returning to IAIA to teach in 1976.

June 21–August 30, 1970 • *AFRICOBRA 1: Ten in Search of a Nation* is on view at the Studio Museum in Harlem, New York. Curated by the museum's director, Edward Spriggs, it is the group's first exhibition and features more than fifty artworks from AFRICOBRA's ten founding members across a wide range of media, including paintings, drawings, serigraphs, fashion designs, and weavings. The show will travel to Boston's Museum of the National Center of Afro-American Artists (September 13–October 11). In a review that is at times critical of the group's other artists, *New York* magazine critic John Gruen praises Jae Jarrell (b. 1935) as one of the "stars" of the group for her "arresting" series of mixed-media fashion designs. Gruen quotes the artist as saying, "I want to produce garments with patterns, textures and colors that duplicate the richness of the patterns, textures and colors of Blackness," and he goes on

to enthuse: "Miss Jarrell uses her cloth surfaces as picture planes. She paints or appliques images relevant to today's black urban American. One quite elegant dress features a suddenly shocking bullet-belt across the chest. The 'bullets' are actually many-colored pellets that shine ominously against the somber brown-gray of the fabric."

Born Elaine Janette Johnson and raised in the historic Glenville neighborhood of Cleveland, Ohio, Jae Jarrell had been inspired from a young age to pursue a life in fashion and clothing design. The granddaughter of a tailor and niece of a haberdasher, she was taught early on to appreciate the materials and craftsmanship of the trade on trips with her mother to vintage clothing stores. In the fall of 1958, Jarrell transferred from Bowling Green State University to the School of the Art Institute of Chicago, a move that would put her in the circle of her future husband, Wadsworth Jarrell, and fellow AFRICOBRA founder Jeff Donaldson. Taking on the name Jae (a reversal of her initials, E.A.J.), she opened her shop Jae of Hyde Park in 1964, where she gave custom fittings and developed her own fashion designs for women. By the end of the 1960s, she had become a central figure within the AFRICOBRA artist collective, exhibiting her fashion designs with the other nine members in major metropolitan hubs such as Chicago, New York, and Boston. During this period the artist began to incorporate mixed-media elements into her designs and to introduce graphic imagery, text, and uncanny elements such as the

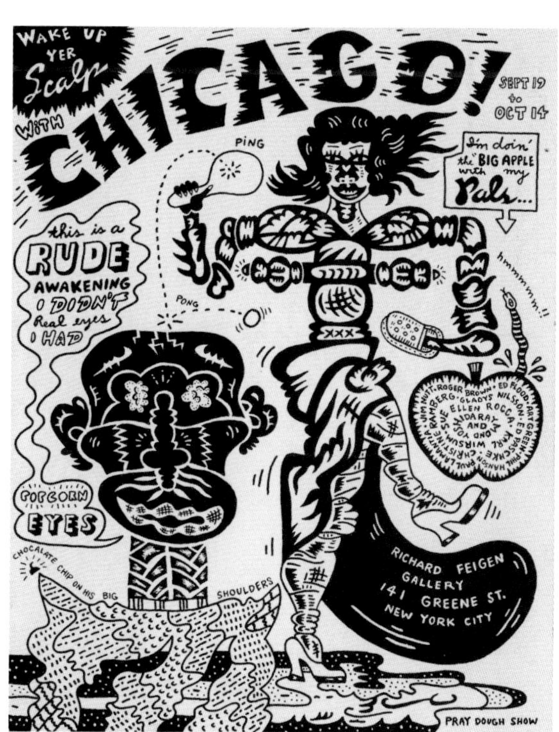

Poster by Karl Wirsum for *Wake Up Yer Scalp with Chicago*, Richard Feigen Gallery, New York, 1970

bandolier belt on *Revolutionary Dress*, reflecting the collective's aims in pursuit of a revolutionary Black aesthetic.

September 19–October 14, 1970 • A group show of Chicago artists, *Wake Up Yer Scalp with Chicago*, is on view at the Richard Feigen Gallery, New York. The show attempts to once again bring the Chicagoans en masse to the coasts. Artists include Roger Brown, Art Green, Jim Nutt, Christina Ramberg, Suellen Rocca, and Karl Wirsum. A similar show, *Transplant: Famous Heart-Tits from Chicago*, appears from August 30 to October 11 at the Madison Art Center, Madison, Wisconsin. The wordplay and inflated claims of these exhibition titles are the artists' way of not only acknowledging their own relative isolation—and thus the need for these shows—but also poking fun at the idea of fame and art having any relationship whatsoever. Making the art is a serious matter; what happens afterward is anyone's guess.

October 1970 • *Black World* magazine publishes the AFRICOBRA manifesto written by Jeff Donaldson (1932–2004), in which the founding member of the artist collective lays out the brief history of the group's formation, its central tenets for art making, and its ambitions, alongside a dozen illustrations documenting work that had been exhibited in *AFRICOBRA 1: Ten in Search of a Nation*. Donaldson provides a list of significant qualities that the group's artists seek to emphasize in their "image-making," which includes "the *expressive awesomeness* that one experiences in African Art and life in the U.S.A."; "*symmetry* that is *free*, repetition with change, based on African music and African movement"; and "images that mark the spot where the real and the overreal, the plus and the minus, the abstract and the concrete—the reet and the replete meet. *Mimesis*." Donaldson also discusses the importance of color, which "defines, identifies and directs. Superreal color for Superreal images . . . Coolade color for coolade images for the superreal people."

Donaldson had been raised in the college town of Pine Bluff, Arkansas, where he receives his bachelor of studio arts at the Black college there, what will ultimately become known as the University of Arkansas at Pine Bluff. The artist will recall being three years old and seeing his older brother drawing cartoons, which soon inspires him to create his own cartoons and comic strips. Donaldson is the first arts major at Pine Bluff, where he is steeped in teachings on the legacy of the Harlem Renaissance, and soon after graduation moves north to Chicago, receiving his master of art education and administration in 1963

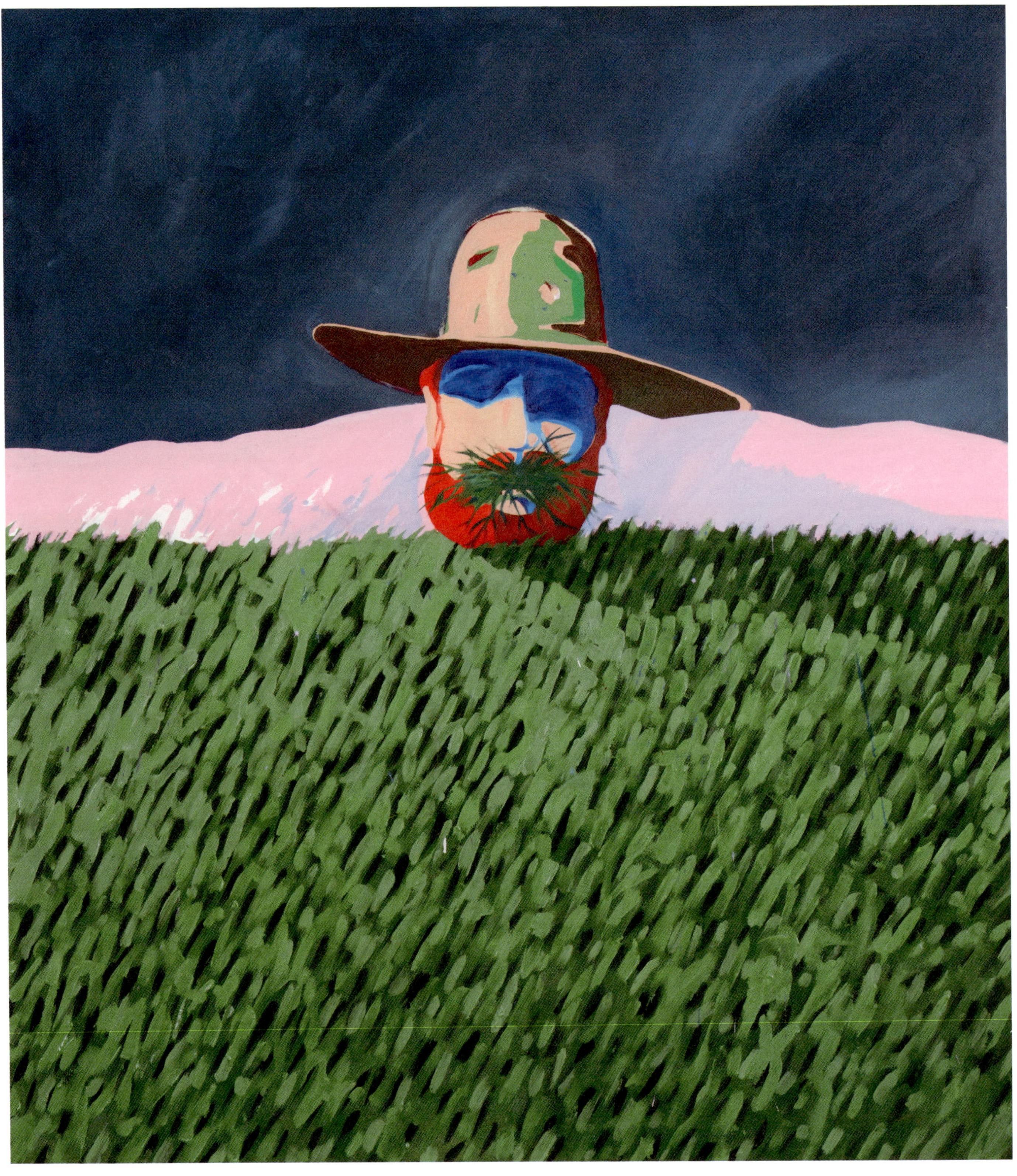

T. C. Cannon, *"Andrew Myrick–Let Em Eat Grass,"* 1970. Acrylic on canvas, 46 × 40 in. (116.8 × 101.6 cm). United States Department of the Interior, Indian Arts and Crafts Board, Southern Plains Indian Museum, Anadarko, OK

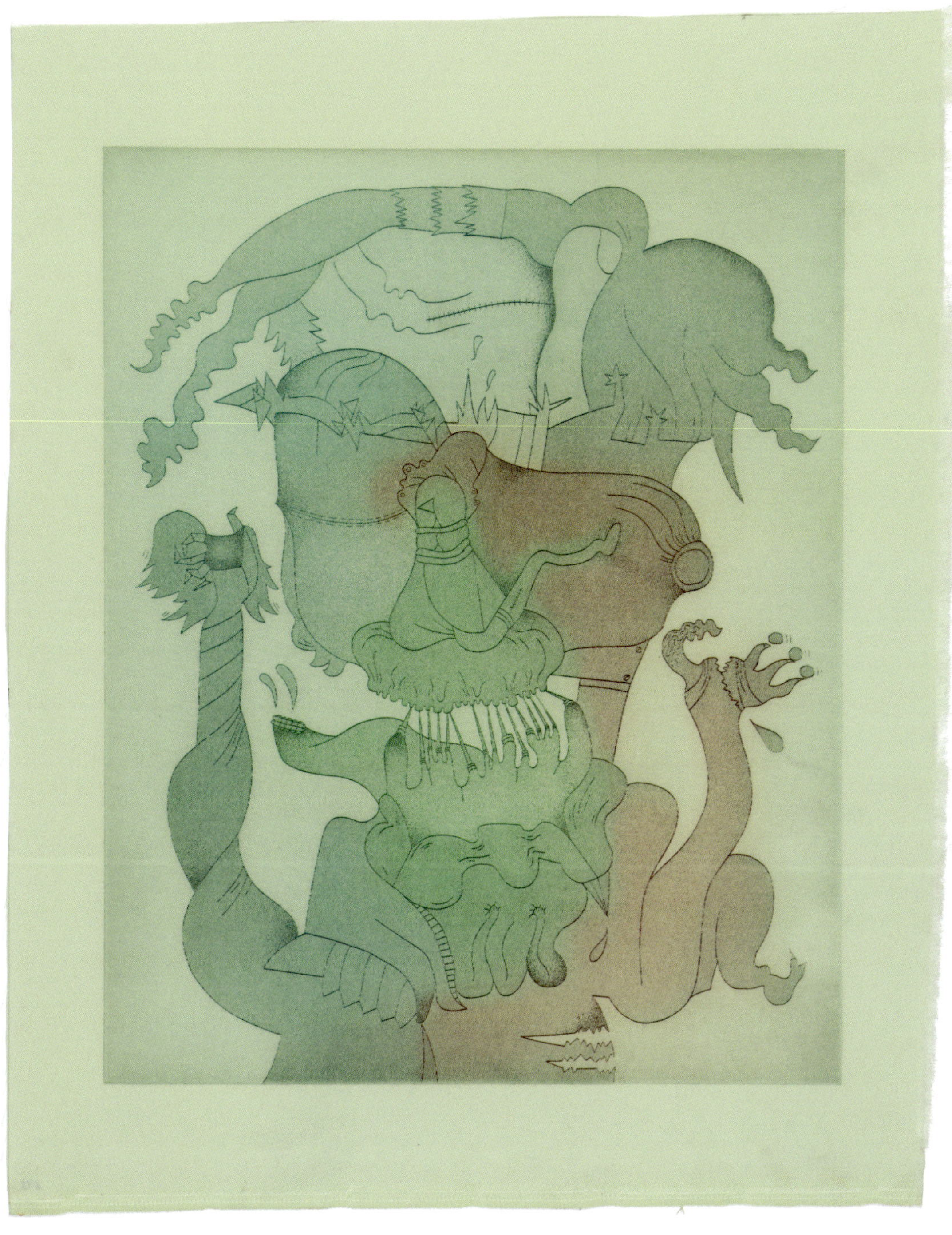

Barbara Rossi, *Male of Sorrows #5*, 1970. Print on satin: sheet, 19 × 13 ⅝ in. (48.3 × 34.6 cm); image, 15 × 11 ⅛ in. (38.1 × 28.3 cm). Whitney Museum of American Art, New York; gift of the Kohler Foundation, Inc. 2021.140

from the Institute of Design at the Illinois Institute of Technology. Inspired by the Black Power and civil rights movements, he helps to found the Organization of Black American Culture (OBAC) and organizes the group's visual arts workshop, which produces the *Wall of Respect* mural project in 1967. Donaldson brings together the AFRICOBRA group under the collective pursuit of pioneering a syncretic, revolutionary Black aesthetic that would draw simultaneously on African American and African diasporic visual culture, art, and sociopolitical lifeworlds. Subsequently, Donaldson pursues his PhD in art history from Northwestern University in the early 1970s.

1970 • Rupert Garcia cofounds Galería de la Raza in San Francisco's Mission District with a group of Chicano and Latino collaborators. The gallery evolves out of Artes Seis, an art center run by Mexican American artist Francisco Camplís and several of his fellow Latino artists. In 1969 Camplís had approached Garcia as he was hanging up posters in the student union at San Francisco State College, inviting him to join Artes Seis. There, Garcia participates in conversations about the Chicano movement and other activist causes in the Bay Area, and he holds silkscreening classes. As Artes Seis outgrows its original space, it develops into Galería de la Raza. *La Raza*, meaning "the community" in Spanish, is deliberately chosen to be as inclusive as possible, embracing both Latinos in the United States as

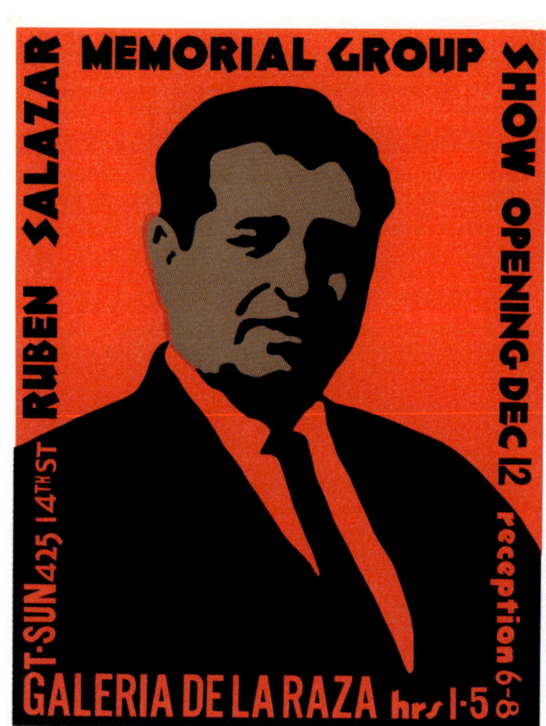

Poster by Rupert Garcia for *Ruben Salazar Memorial Group Show*, Galería de la Raza, San Francisco, 1970

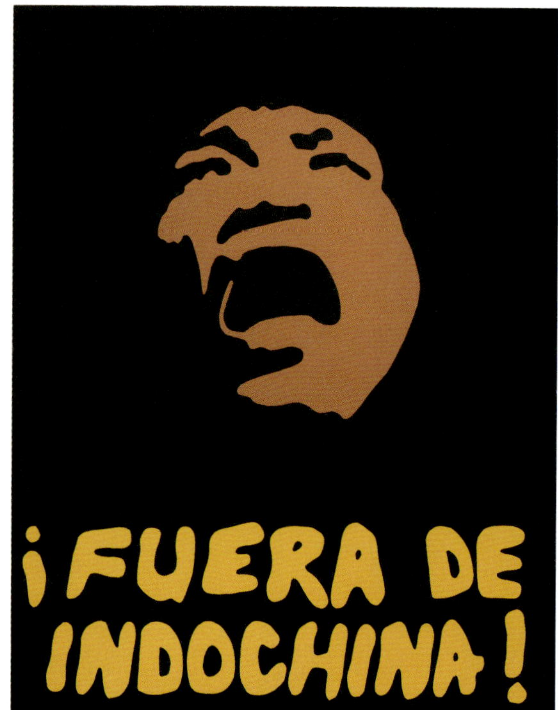

Rupert Garcia, *¡Fuera de Indochina!*, 1970. Screenprint on paper, 26 ⅛ in. × 20 in. (66.4 × 50.8 cm)

well as those struggling against American imperialism abroad—a point of contention with other artists' spaces in California dedicated solely to the Chicano cause.

October 1970 • Judy Gerowitz legally changes her name to Judy Chicago, running an advertisement in *Artforum* to announce not only the shift from the surname of her deceased first husband to the city of her birth but also to publicize her exhibition *Judy ~~Gerowitz~~ Chicago One ~~Man~~ Woman Show* at California State College at Fullerton (October 23–November 25). Hers is "an act of identifying myself as an independent woman," according to Chicago, and the ad proclaims: "Judy Gerowitz hereby divests herself of all names imposed upon her through male social dominance and freely chooses her own name." A second ad, in December, will feature an image of the artist posed in a boxing ring. "During this period my male artist buddies were all prone to very macho announcements and posters in relation to their own shows, something Jack [Glenn] suggested spoofing with a picture of me in a boxing ring, the very one in which Muhammad Ali trained," Chicago will later explain. "One result was that for many years, pugnacious male artists around the country asked me if I wished to 'fight.'"

Feminism progressively becomes a more explicit topic for Chicago, unconstrained by the externally enforced need to separate her feminist experience and philosophy from her artistic output.

October 8–24, 1970 • *Studio Equipment* at the San Francisco Art Institute features three tools made by Don Potts (1936–2011) to construct his car sculptures: a vacuum former, a metal worktable, and a pantograph. Early in his artistic life, Potts had become obsessed with the idea of the objects he makes having a use-value and thereby making them inextricable from his life. Born and raised in San Francisco, he had trained in commercial art at San Francisco State College before earning his bachelor of arts in painting at San José State College in 1963, where his graduate exhibition consists of objects he has built, such as a flamenco guitar, pencil sharpener, and deacon's bench, that he finds useful yet also insists upon them as artworks. For his 1965 master's thesis at San José State College, he organizes an exhibition of what he refers to as totems, which he explains as such: "The ancient Viking was most resourceful when he built his ships. . . . The form of this ship constantly reminded the Viking of his identity; a proud conqueror bound, by a heroic religion, to a warrior's death. He could not accomplish his raids and explorations in just any ship, for the voyages were too long and strenuous. He required a totem as a reminder of his task. . . . My purpose, then, is to construct objects which exist as totemic beings evocative of my feelings and attitudes about life."

A similar idea informs his ongoing work. From 1964 to 1966, he makes larger pieces, mostly in leather and wood, that catch the attention of others at the University of California, Berkeley—where he teaches—as well as curators. These works seem to have a human function but in fact only allude to a human presence. In 1966, just as he is gaining recognition for this art, Potts steps away from it. He decides that his forms are too arbitrary, too easily dismissed as weird, and he instead turns to a core shape that will exert its own demands on him: a car. The car will need to function, and not arbitrarily, and in the late 1960s, it will stand in for a human being.

Potts embarks on a six-year project with help from his brother, Bob Potts, building his own tools for the construction of cars. In 1969 he completes *The Master Chassis*, a radio-controlled four-cylinder sculpture with running gears, a clutch, and steering. He then builds "bodies" that can be integrated into the chassis, changing its form while maintaining its structure. Although each part can be seen separately, the entire work comprises the wood *Basic Chassis*; the motorized and radio-controlled *Master Chassis*; and two bodies, one of stainless steel and the other of fabric and steel.

Fall 1970 • Robert Colescott begins teaching at Stanislaus State College in Northern California, where he becomes friendly with the small circle

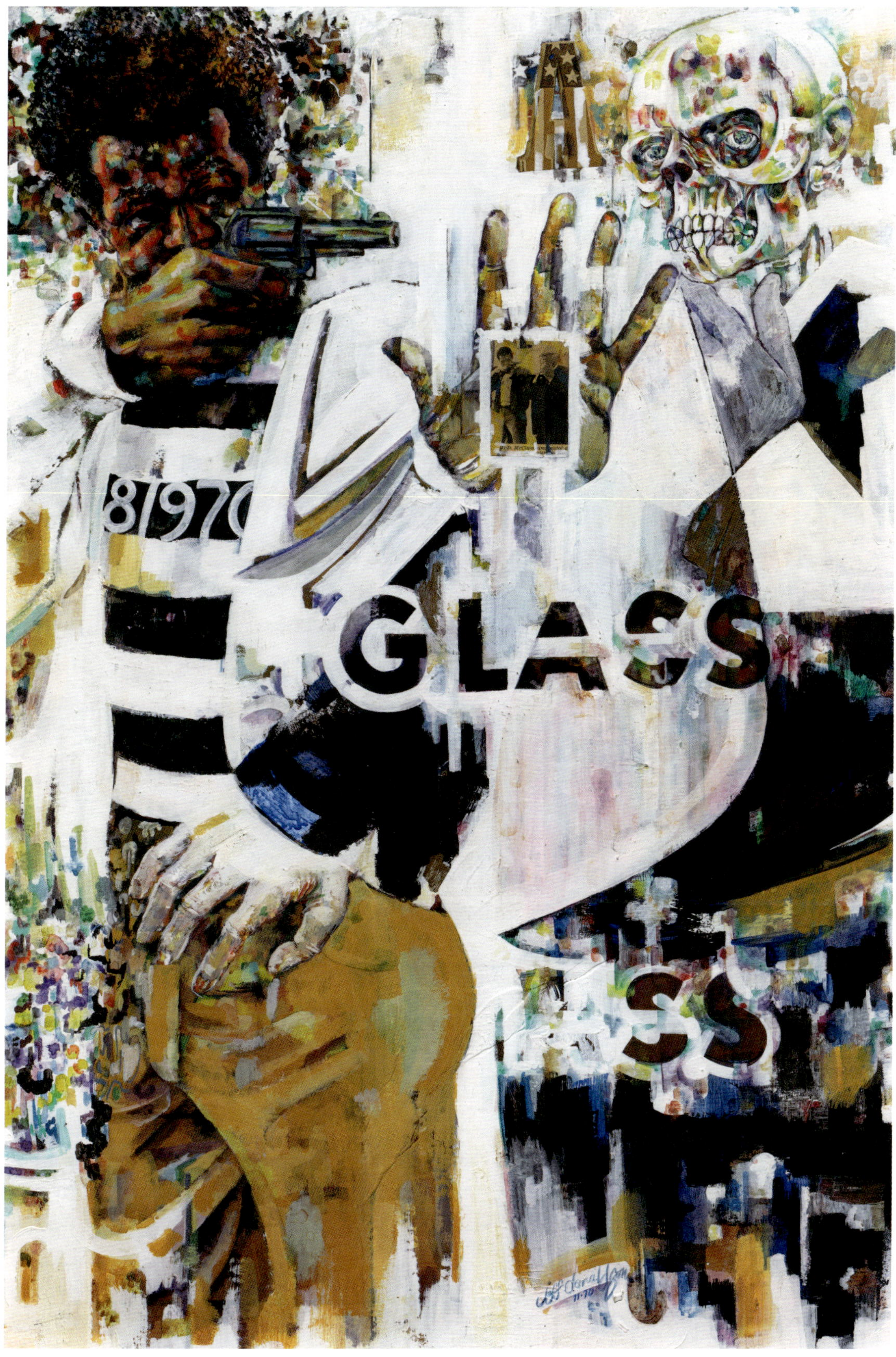

Jeff Donaldson, *J. D. McClain's Day in Court*, 1970. Paint on cardboard with ink on paper, 29 ⅛ × 19 ⁵⁄₁₆ in. (74 × 49 cm). Smithsonian National Museum of African American History and Culture, Washington, DC; 2017.33.2

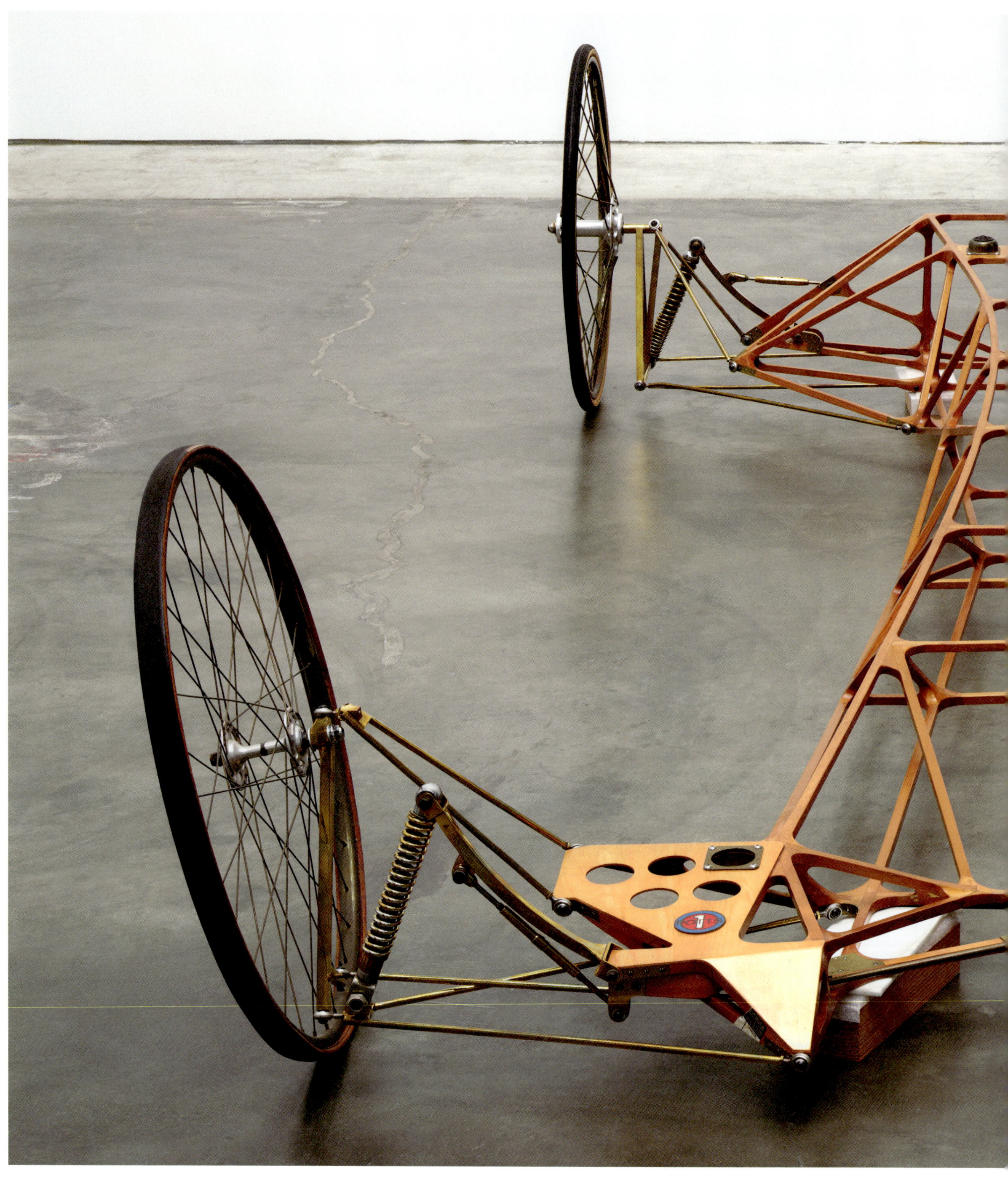

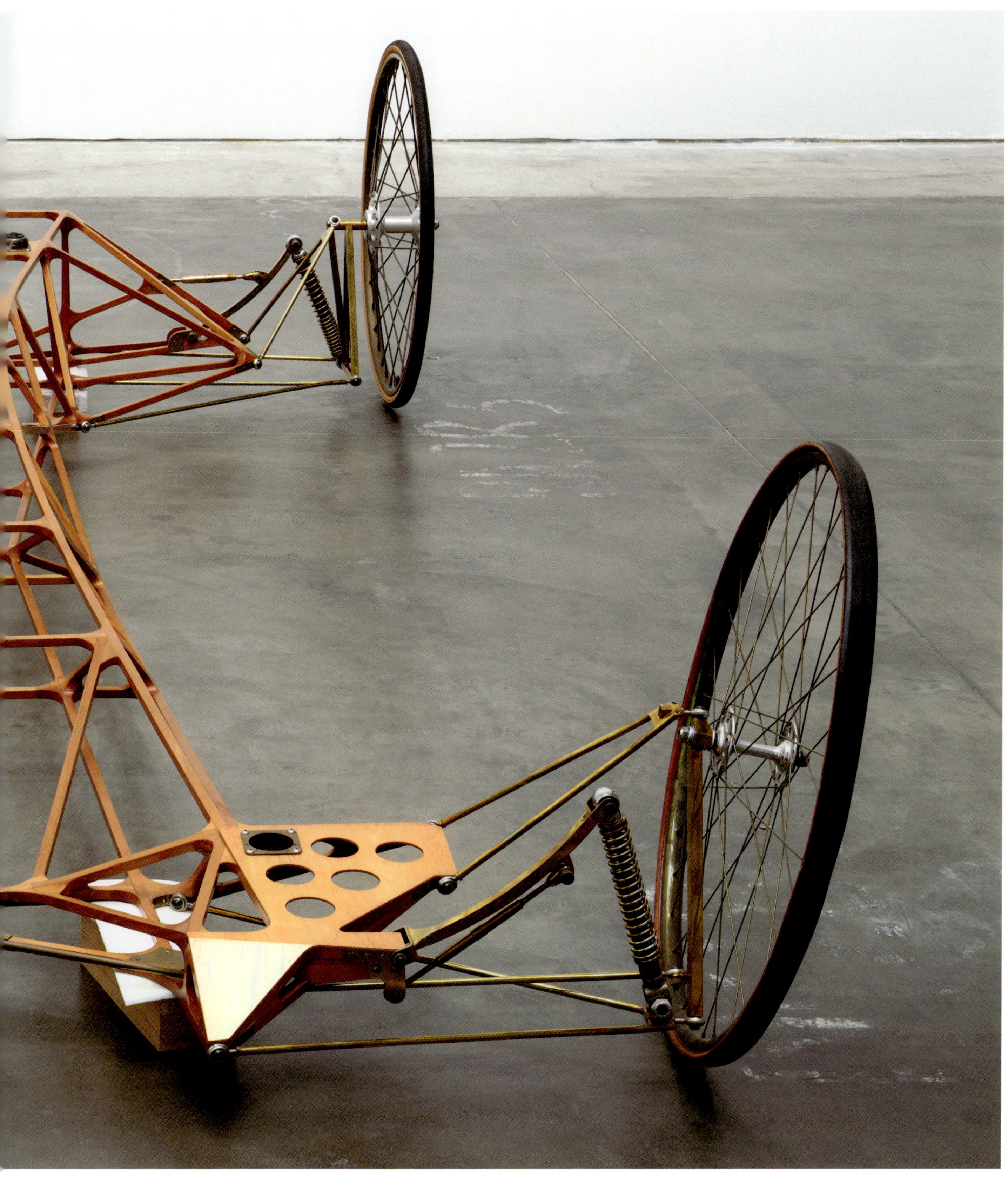

Don Potts, *My First Car: Basic Chassis*, 1970. Wood, metal, and rubber, 27 ½ × 74 × 141 in. (69.9 × 188 × 358.1 cm). San Francisco Museum of Modern Art; gift of James B. Gubelmann 2018.405

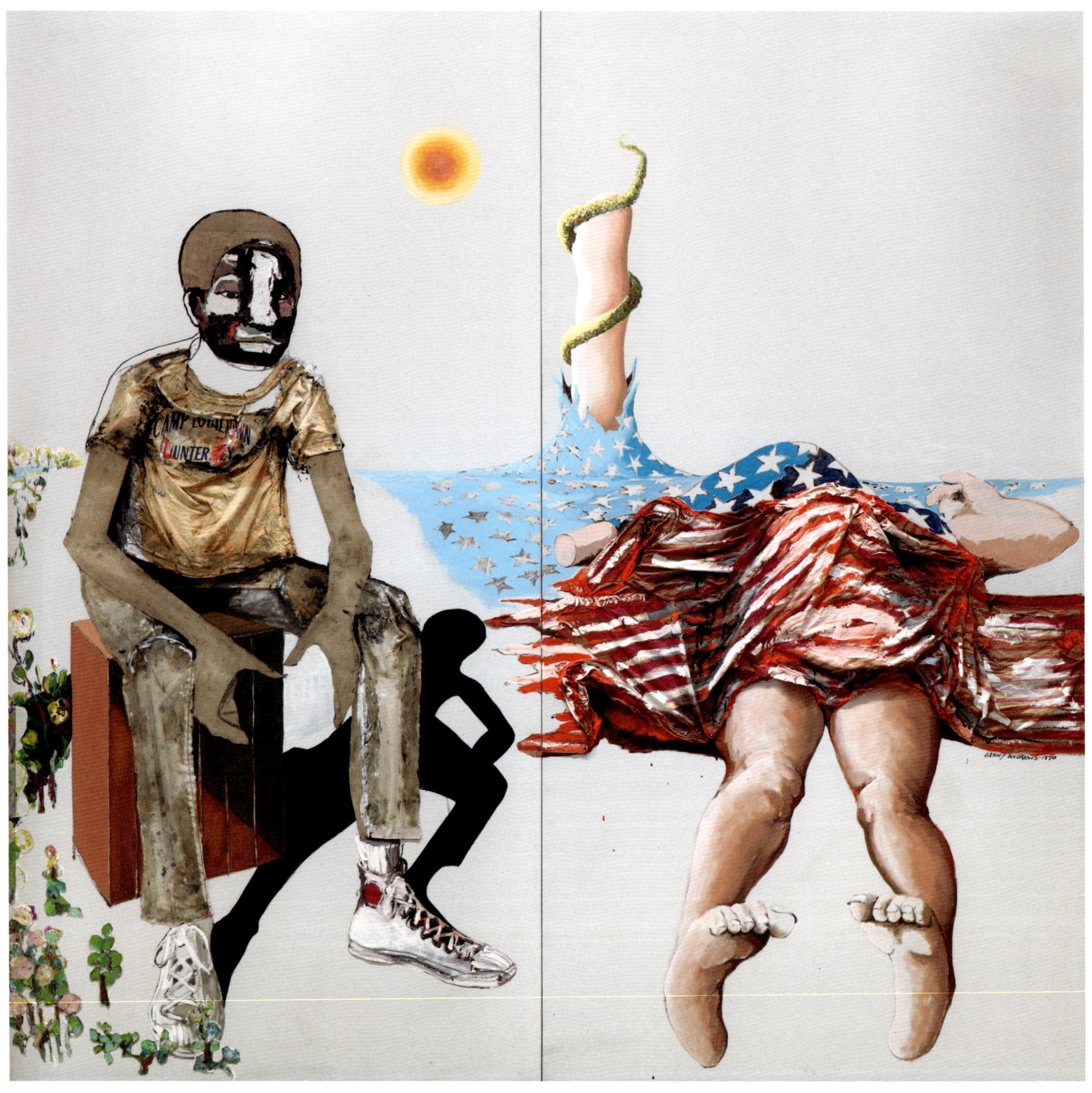

Benny Andrews, *No More Games*, 1970. Oil on canvas with cut-and-pasted primed and raw canvas, T-shirt, garment fragments, and partially painted printed fabrics: two panels, 100 ⅞ × 101 ¼ in. (256.2 × 257.2 cm) overall; panels, 100 ⅞ × 49 ⅞ in. (256.2 × 126.7 cm) and 100 ⅞ × 51 in. (256.2 × 129.3 cm). The Museum of Modern Art, New York; Blanchette Hooker Rockefeller Fund 35.1971.a–b

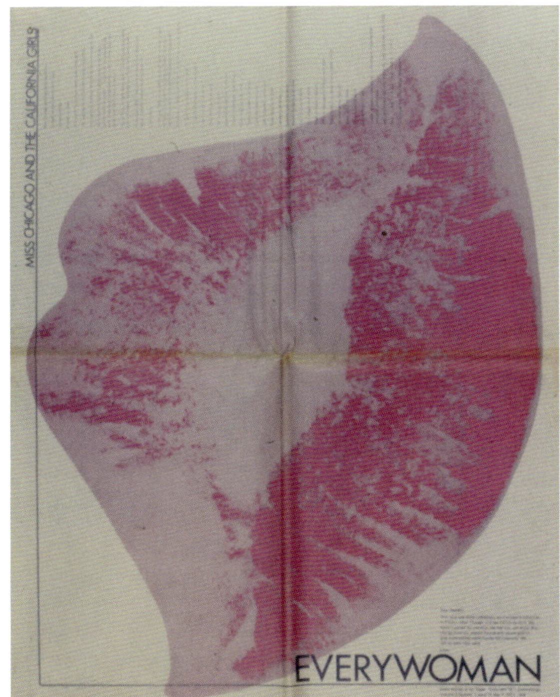

Spread from *Everywoman*, May 7, 1971, written and produced by the Fresno Feminist Art Program, with an essay by Judy Chicago

of forward-thinking artists in and around the Bay Area. Robert Arneson, Joan Brown, Roy De Forest, and Carlos Villa are among the group.

1970 • Judy Chicago establishes the Feminist Art Program at Fresno State College. Developed in conjunction with fifteen female art students, the program is the first in the United States to follow a pedagogy that foregrounds the female experience in the process of women's art-making. The project is such a success that the California Institute of the Arts asks Chicago to establish a similar program for its women student-artists the following year.

November 1–20, 1970 • T. C. Cannon's first solo gallery exhibition is on view at Larkins Gallery in Santa Fe, New Mexico. The show comes after the artist had returned to college to complete the degree he had abandoned when he enlisted in the Army, and its title, *American Before Columbus*, reflects the political direction in which his work is moving, in particular his interest in Native American activism. Despite his own propensity for quiet reflection and poetry, the artist explains that he wants his art to provoke "a heated exchange of ideas and rendezvous of facts and visions"—the American Indian Movement's bold protests and the Indians of All Tribes's occupation of Alcatraz Island the year before are obviously on his mind.

1970 • Luchita Hurtado and her husband, Lee Mullican, make plans to move to Taos, New Mexico, lured by the arid landscape and open sky they had experienced on earlier visits there. They commission architect Jean-Louis Bourgeois, Louise Bourgeois's son, to build their house. "He lived in Taos and we were friends," Hurtado will later recall. "I told him how much I admired his mother—I had never met her, but little did I know that, through this house, Louise Bourgeois would be a part of my life. It was magical."

In Taos, Hurtado will begin a new series of paintings by mid-decade titled *Sky Skins* in which the artist turns the perspective of the *I Am* self-portraits upward. Framed by clouds or by the craggy ridges of desert mountains, the blue skies of the *Sky Skins* series seem to both protrude and recede at the same time, oscillating between depth and flatness.

November 9–13, 1970 • Judith Bernstein shows *Union Jack Off Flag* (1967) in the antiwar exhibition *People's Flag Show* at Judson Memorial Church, New York. In addition to talks from Abbie Hoffman, Kate Millett, and Stephen Radich, more than 150 works appear in the show, which is organized by Jon Hendricks, Faith Ringgold, and Jean

Toche, who are later arrested and charged with public desecration of the national flag.

December 1970 • The show *South Texas Sweet Funk* appears at St. Edward's University, Austin, Texas, curated by Dave Hickey, who had previously owned the gallery A Clean, Well-Lighted Place in the city. Named after a short story by Ernest Hemingway, the gallery had quickly become an important space for contemporary art in Texas after it opened in 1967. *South Texas Sweet Funk* continues to press Hickey's case that there is a specific, idiosyncratic brand of Texas Funk—and that it is worth seeing. Artists in the show include Terry Allen, Barry Buxkamper, Mel Casas, Tom Cooney, George T. Green, Frank Hein, Luis Jimenez, Bobbie Moore, Jim Morris, June Robinson, Jim Roche, Robert Wade, Fred Whitehead, Glenn Whitehead, and underground comic-book artists Jim Franklin, Steve Gosnell, and Gilbert Shelton. Writing in *Artforum*, Martha Utterback comments:

> As usual, when considering a group, the concern is with a number of particulars, which here are extremely diversified, the stylistic differences being far more visibly apparent and esthetically significant than any similarities. But the genotype of funk

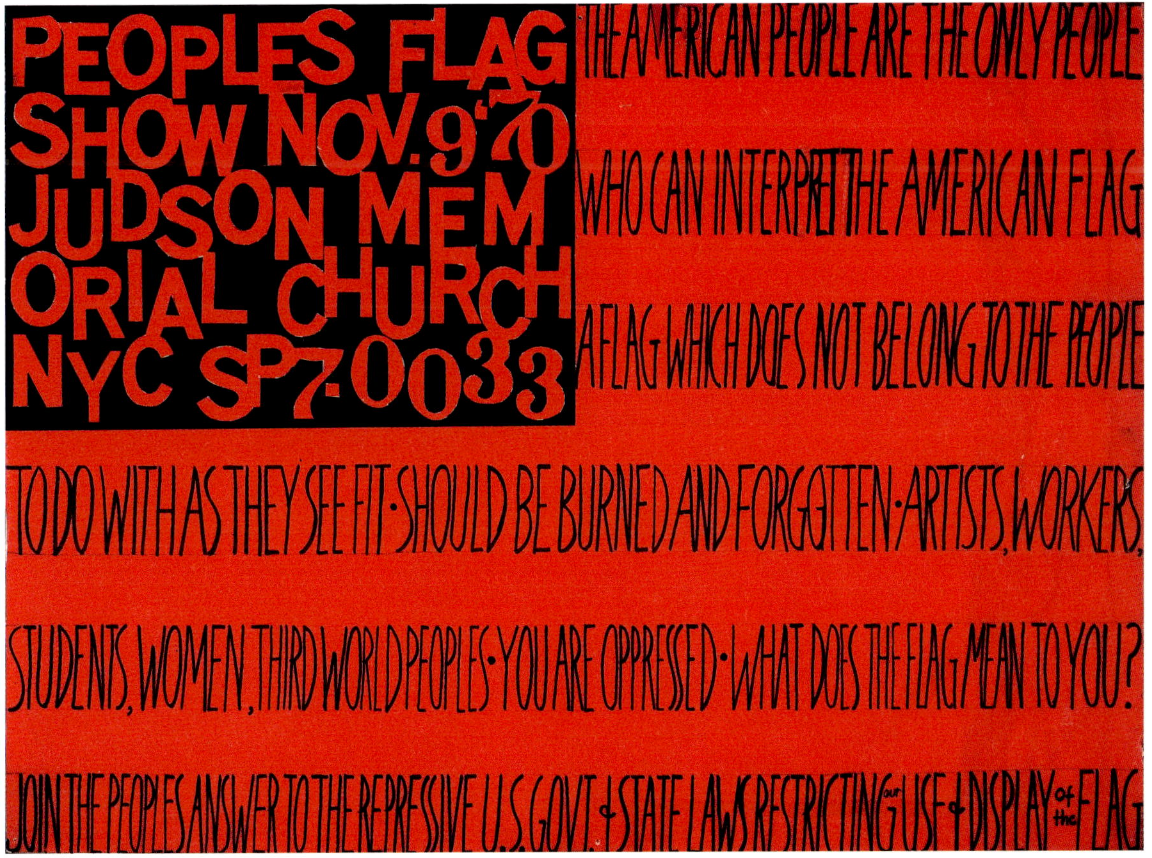

Poster by Faith Ringgold for *The People's Flag Show*, Judson Memorial Church, New York, 1970

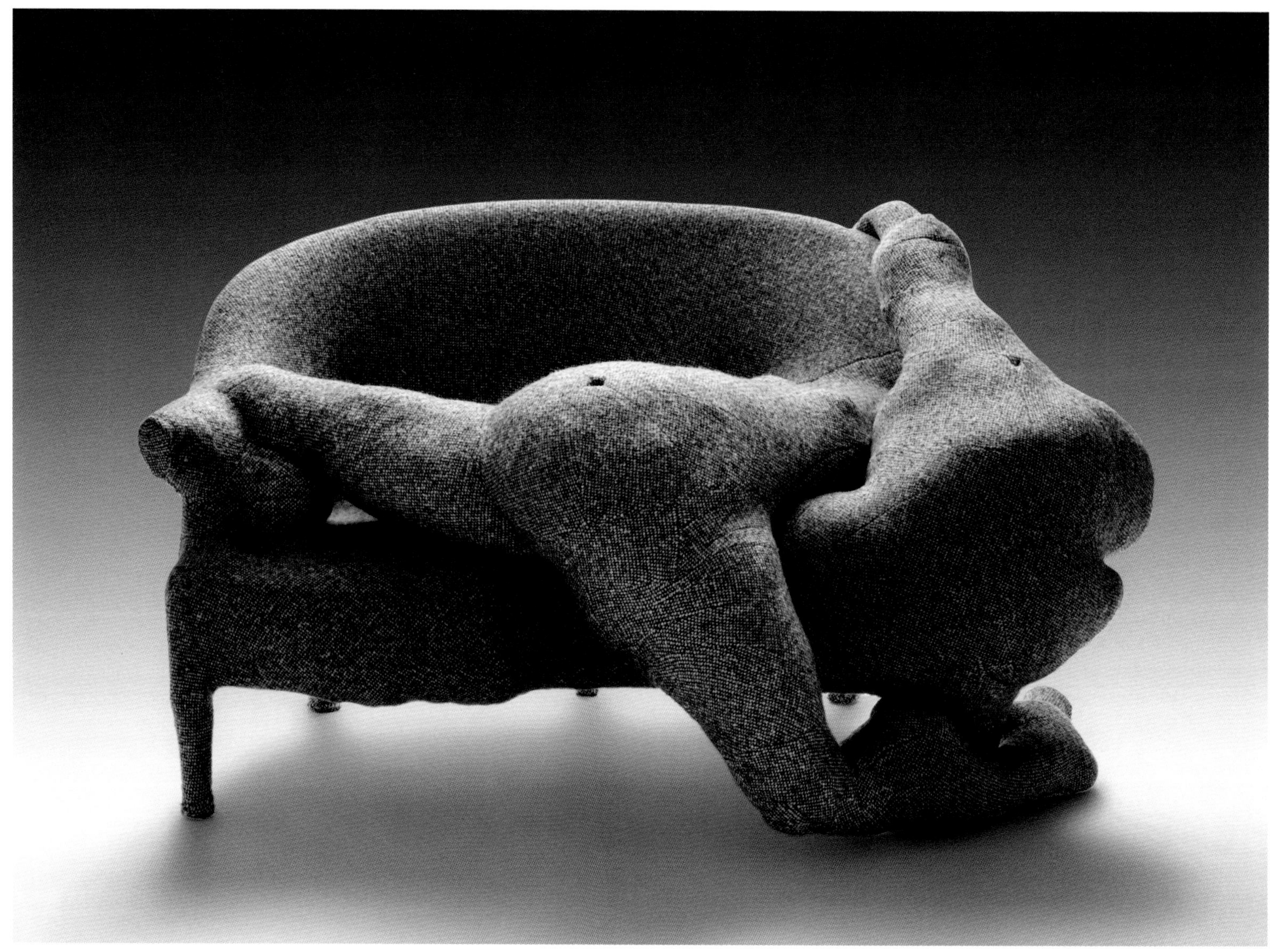

Dorothea Tanning, *Rainy Day Canapé*, 1970. Upholstered wood sofa with wool, polyester, and rayon plain-weave cover, wool batting, cardboard, and ping-pong balls, 31 ½ × 57 × 33 in. (80 × 144.8 × 83.8 cm). Philadelphia Museum of Art; 125th Anniversary Acquisition, gift of an anonymous donor, 2002 2002.86-1

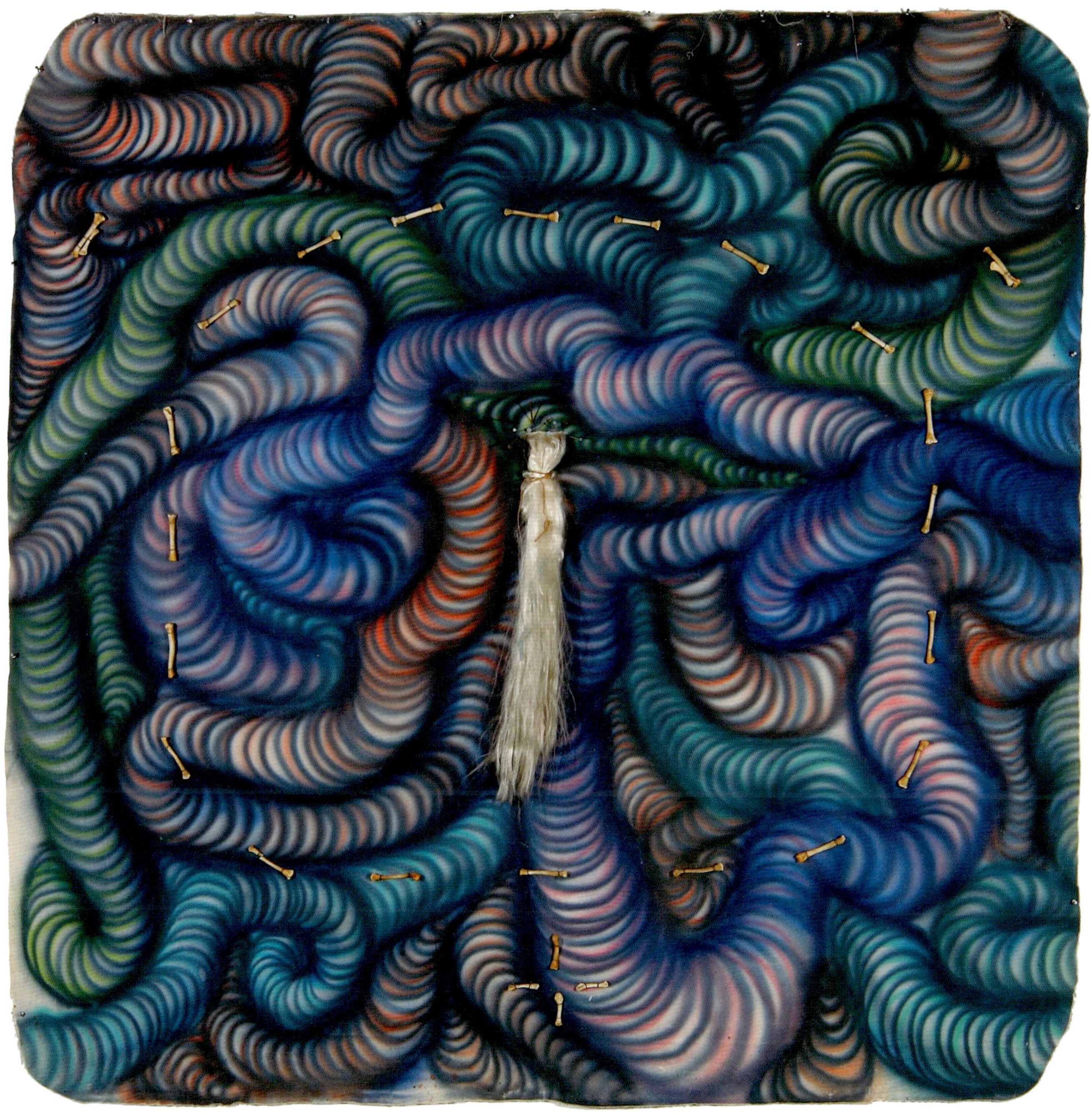

Carlos Villa, *Ritual*, 1970. Wig, chicken bones, and canvas, 101 × 95 in. (256.5 × 241.3 cm). Collection of Kim and Lito Camacho

NEWS RELEASE

St. *Edward's University*
NEWS BUREAU
Austin, Texas 78704

FOR RELEASE _______ Sunday, December 13, 1970

FUNK ART ON EXHIBIT

CONTACT: Rose Batson
444-2621 (248)
836-0746

South Texas Sweet Funk, a "blow-your-mind" look at a contemporary art style not generally conceded to Texas artists, is on display now through Jan. 1 in Moody Hall Atrium at St. Edward's University.

Jim Roche's buxom Mama Plants are there, right alongside Jim Franklin's omnipresent armadillos. Exotic 10-foot weiners float across canvas with exquisite grace, while an oversized toy airplane sculpture is perched for take-off.

There are plump, juicy kernels of corn fit for the Jolly Green Giant, squiggly noodles cavorting in a Swiss-cheese meadow, and San Antonio debutantes promenading surrealistically with tigers and giraffes.

The unique art exhibit, assembled by Austin curator Dave Hickey, is the first exhibition of funk art by Texas artists. Hickey, who owns the Clean, Well Lighted Place gallery, conceived the exhibit because he wanted to prove that "this kind of work is being done in Texas, that it is indigenous work, and that it is first-class work...."

He defines funk art as a "technical celebration of rather banal subject matter." It is also biting satire, although the Texas variety is sweetened a little compared to that of the West Coast where funk art first appeared.

- more -

Press release for *South Texas Sweet Funk*, St. Edward's University, Austin, TX, 1970

---

has never seemed so much a unilateral manner as multiple manifestations of an attitude—accommodatingly spacious and porous and also exceedingly persistent.

Jan Butterfield, in a review in the *Texas Observer*, considers the recent roots of the term *funk* to describe artists' proclivities in both Lucy Lippard's exhibition *Eccentric Abstraction* (1966) and Peter Selz's *Funk* (1967), while also noting its Texas-specific permutation: "There is a Funk thing growing here which has been coming along quietly for some time. In this vast art wasteland there are just enough people who are sufficiently isolated from all of the precious verbiage and critical nonsense that they can unselfconsciously thumb their noses with great gusto."

1970 • Eduardo Carrillo and the artists Sergio Hernandez, Ramses Noriega, and Saul Solache produce the epic nine-panel mural *Chicano History* (1970) for the Chicano Studies Center at the University of California, Los Angeles. Carrillo has quickly become a leader in the Chicano art movement in Los Angeles, and *Chicano History* is just one among a number of other large-scale paintings and murals he will create that build on a visual language of Indigenous California history and mythology.

December 12, 1970–February 7, 1971 • The Whitney Museum of American Art's *1970 Annual Exhibition: Contemporary American Sculpture* features artists Robert Arneson, Louise Bourgeois, Vija Celmins, Barbara Chase-Riboud, Melvin Edwards, Nancy Graves, Daniel LaRue Johnson, Bruce Nauman, Claes Oldenburg, Kenneth Price, Betye Saar, Lucas Samaras, Robert Smithson, Michael Todd, H. C. Westermann, and William T. Wiley. With the inclusion of Chase-Riboud's *Ultimate Ground* (c. 1969–70) and Saar's *Omen* (1967), the exhibition features Black women for the first time.

The milestone follows Chase-Riboud's first solo show in the United States, in which she exhibited her *Malcolm X* sculptures at the Massachusetts Institute of Technology's Hayden Gallery the prior spring. She will later adopt the word *steles* for works in this series: "The Egyptians had a tradition of these memorial funeral steles dedicated to a person. . . . As soon as I decided that they were going to be dedicated to him, not as portraits and not as gravestones but as memorials, they became themselves and they became an abstraction of what he stood for."

The exhibition's initial reviews are mixed. In the *New York Times*, Hilton Kramer criticizes the discrepancy between the works' provocative themes, which focus on the civil rights movement, and their French "high-fashion" formal elegance. His comments prompt a firestorm of debate in the pages of the *Times* and *Art in America* on the contradictory expectations imposed on Black artists at the time. Chase-Riboud will recall that "discussions, arguments, and counter-arguments erupted on the 'role' of visual artists of color and what they could and could not do. Or should and should not do." And her response is simple: "My position was that I was free to do what I pleased and that no political agenda, especially a racist one, was going to stop me."

1970 • Shigeko Kubota makes her first work of video art, *Self-Portrait* (c. 1970–71). The Sony Portapak, a handheld video system, had entered the market in 1965, and Kubota and others in her circle—most notably, Jonas Mekas and Nam June Paik—are among the very first artists to experiment with the formal and conceptual possibilities of the novel technology. "To me Portapak was like a new paintbrush," Kubota will later explain. "It was certainly in the same spirit as Fluxus, 'do it yourself.'" The democratic nature of the camera—its relative affordability and the ability of a single individual to operate it—appeals to Kubota's progressive ideals.

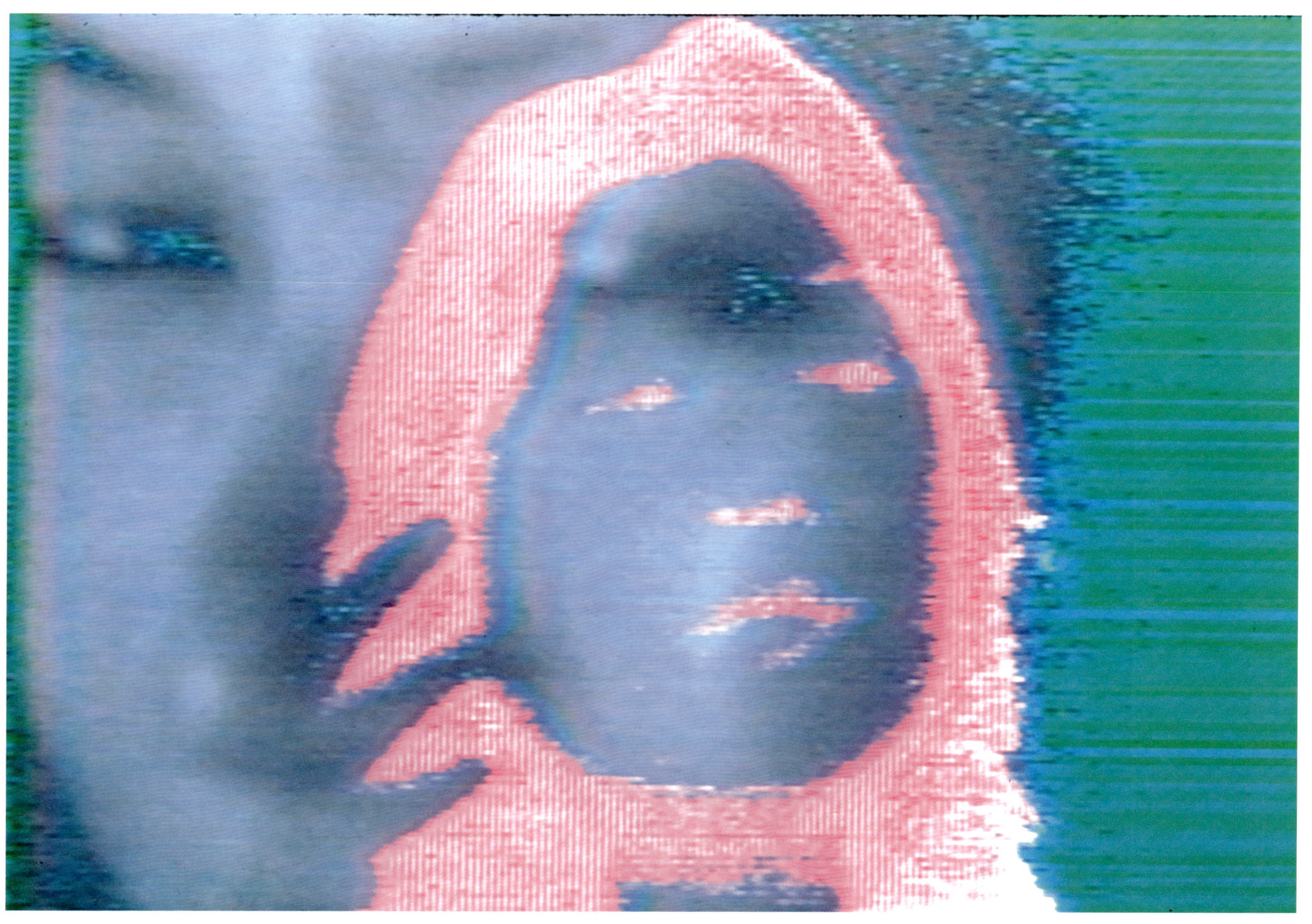

Shigeko Kubota, *Self-Portrait*, c. 1970–71. Standard-definition video, color, silent; 5:28 min. The Museum of Modern Art, New York; gift of the Shigeko Kubota Video Art Foundation 334.2021

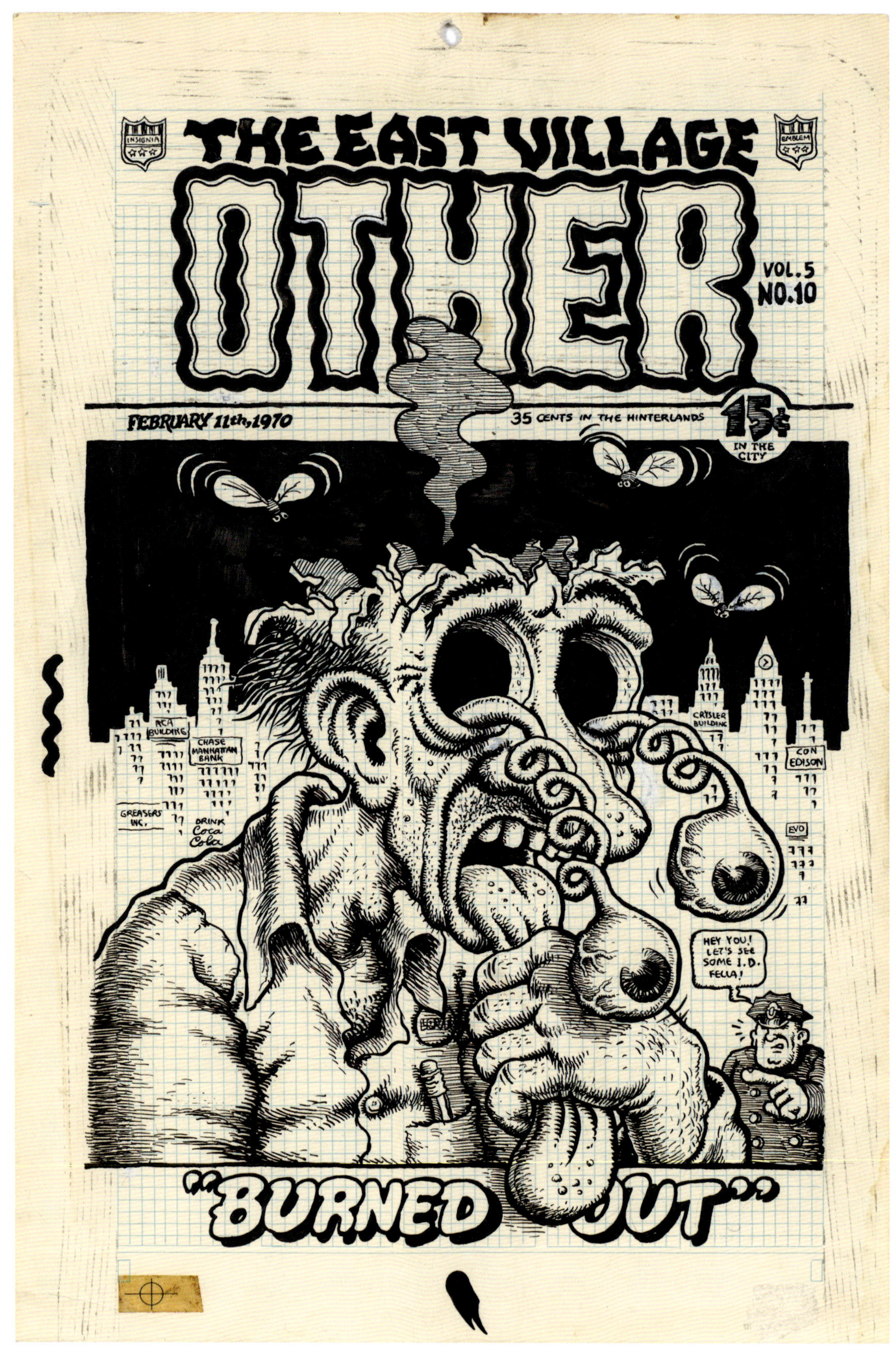

Robert Crumb, *Burned Out, cover of the "East Village Other" 5, no. 10*, 1970. Ink on paper, 16 × 10 in. (40.6 × 25.4 cm). Lucas Museum of Narrative Art, Los Angeles 2019.61.19

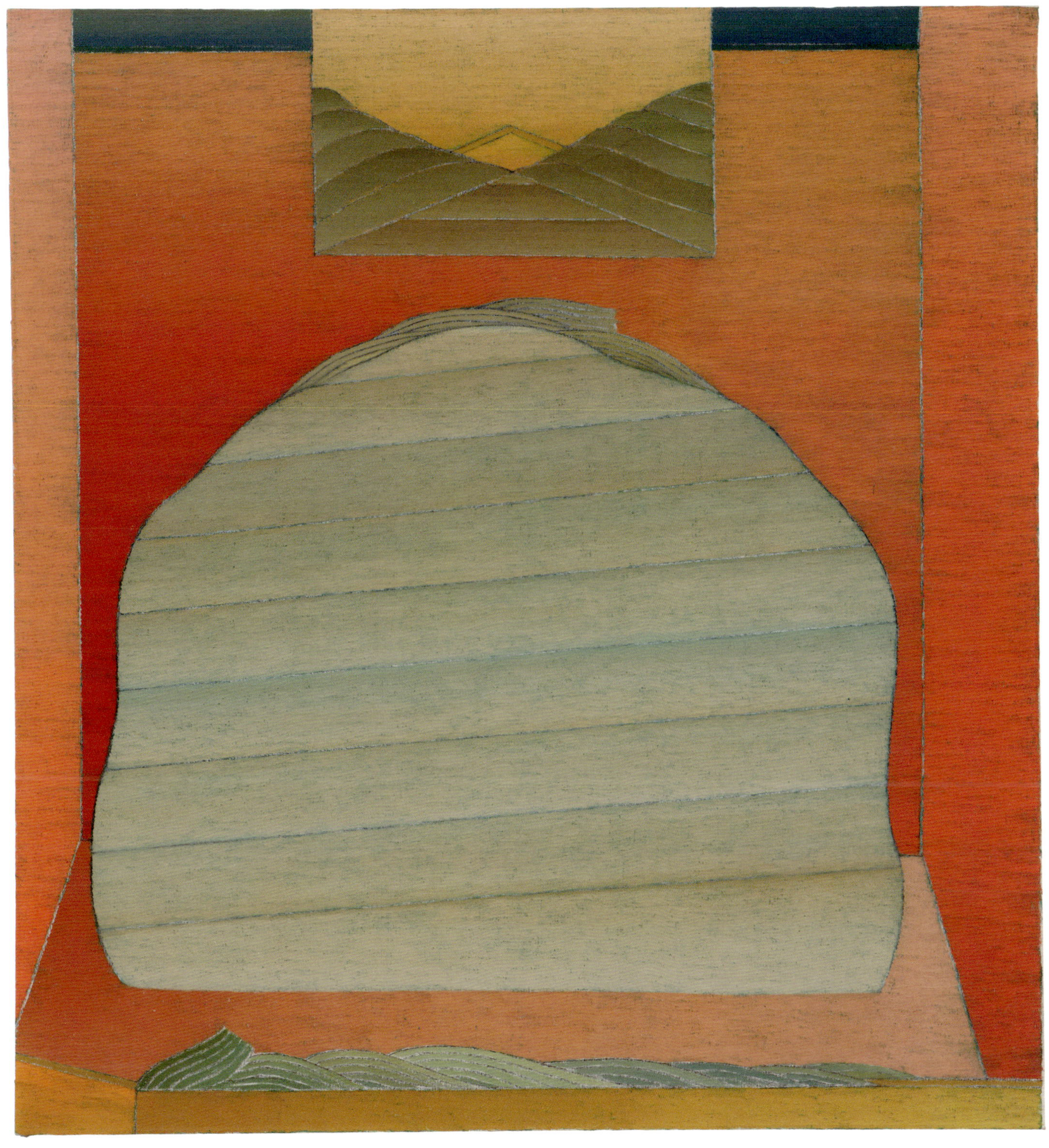

Miyoko Ito, *Untitled*, 1970. Oil on canvas, 46 × 42 in. (117 × 107 cm). Collection of Wade Guyton

1971

January 15–March 21, 1971 • *Continuing Surrealism* at La Jolla Museum of Art attempts to show the long reach of the movement in greater detail than William Rubin's Surrealism exhibition at the Museum of Modern Art two years prior. Artists include William Allen, Jeremy Anderson, Vija Celmins, Robert Hudson, Jasper Johns, Edward Kienholz, Claes Oldenburg, Edward Ruscha, Lucas Samaras, and others.

January 26, 1971 • The landmark exhibition *Three Graphic Artists* opens at the Los Angeles County Museum of Art (LACMA), featuring work exclusively by contemporary Black artists: Charles White, David Hammons, and Timothy Washington (b. 1946). The exhibit is one of three the museum develops in direct response to protest actions led by the Black Arts Council (BAC) in 1970, including "a letter-writing campaign, picketing, and other agitation techniques to pressure LACMA to showcase black artists." Featuring eleven of Washington's mixed-media works, including several of his aluminum engravings, the show spotlights the artist's dynamic and often jarring combination of surrealist/magical-realist juxtapositions, stylized figures, and content that blends the starkly political and deeply personal. In his provocatively titled *One Nation Under God* (1970),

Washington presents the psychically charged image of a nude Black male figure posed behind a bridled donkey with the American flag draped across its body. The figure places a protective arm across both donkey and flag, staring out at the viewer with two grotesquely enlarged, hollowed eye-sockets rimmed in white.

Born in the Watts neighborhood of Los Angeles, Washington will recall the participation of his third-grade class in a school-wide mural project at Virginia Road Elementary School as among his earliest exposure to the arts. The experience fired a passion in him, and he would go on to excel in fine arts courses throughout junior high and high school before winning a scholarship to Chouinard Art Institute in his senior year at Dorsey High School. In 1967, during his second year at Chouinard, Washington receives notice that his draft status has been reclassified to IA, an impactful event that shifts his concerns to the politics of antiwar protest and informs his choice of subject matter when he is assigned to create a series of artworks dealing with something intensely personal. In looking for a material that is "cold and hard" to match the intensity of his visual statements, Washington turns to aluminum, marking his first use of the material. After receiving his bachelor of fine arts in 1969, Washington found success exhibiting in the early 1970s at Brockman Gallery, Gallery 32, and LACMA, among other institutions

in Los Angeles, quickly gaining a national audience for his continually evolving multimedia work.

February 12–March 13, 1971 • Miyoko Ito (1918–1983) opens a one-person exhibition at the Hyde Park Art Center, Chicago, where she presents the work for which she will become known: thickly painted bands of color, undulating forms, jutting geometries, crosscurrent patterns, semicircles, and short, wavy lines that employ surrealism, minimal abstraction, and Synthetic Cubism to create meditative color spaces of intermingling forms that allude to landscapes,

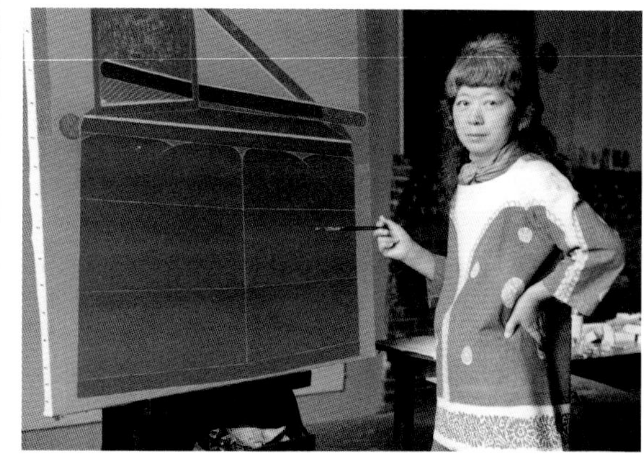

Miyoko Ito in the studio during her MacDowell residency, Peterborough, NH, 1970

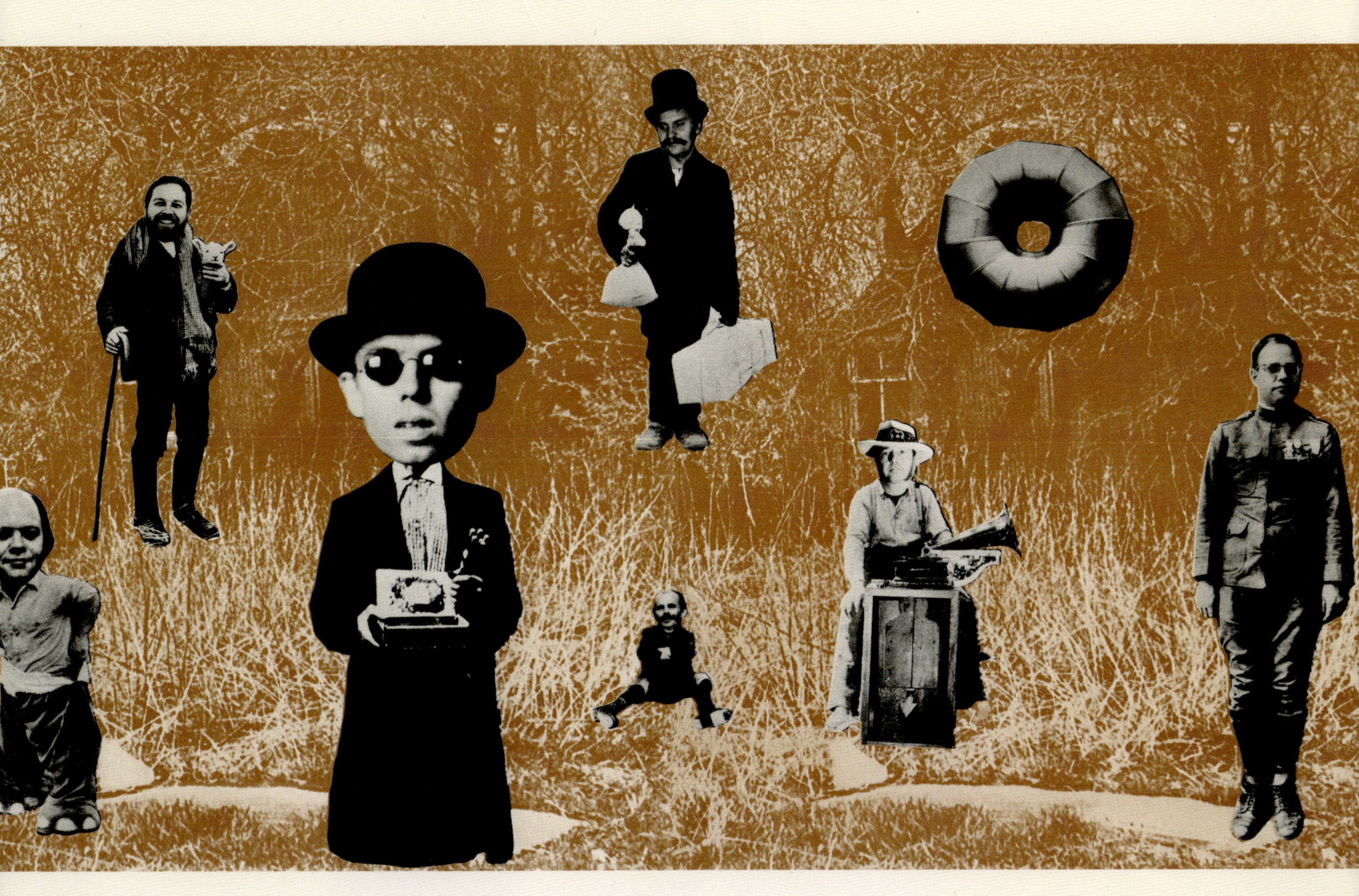
one i at a time

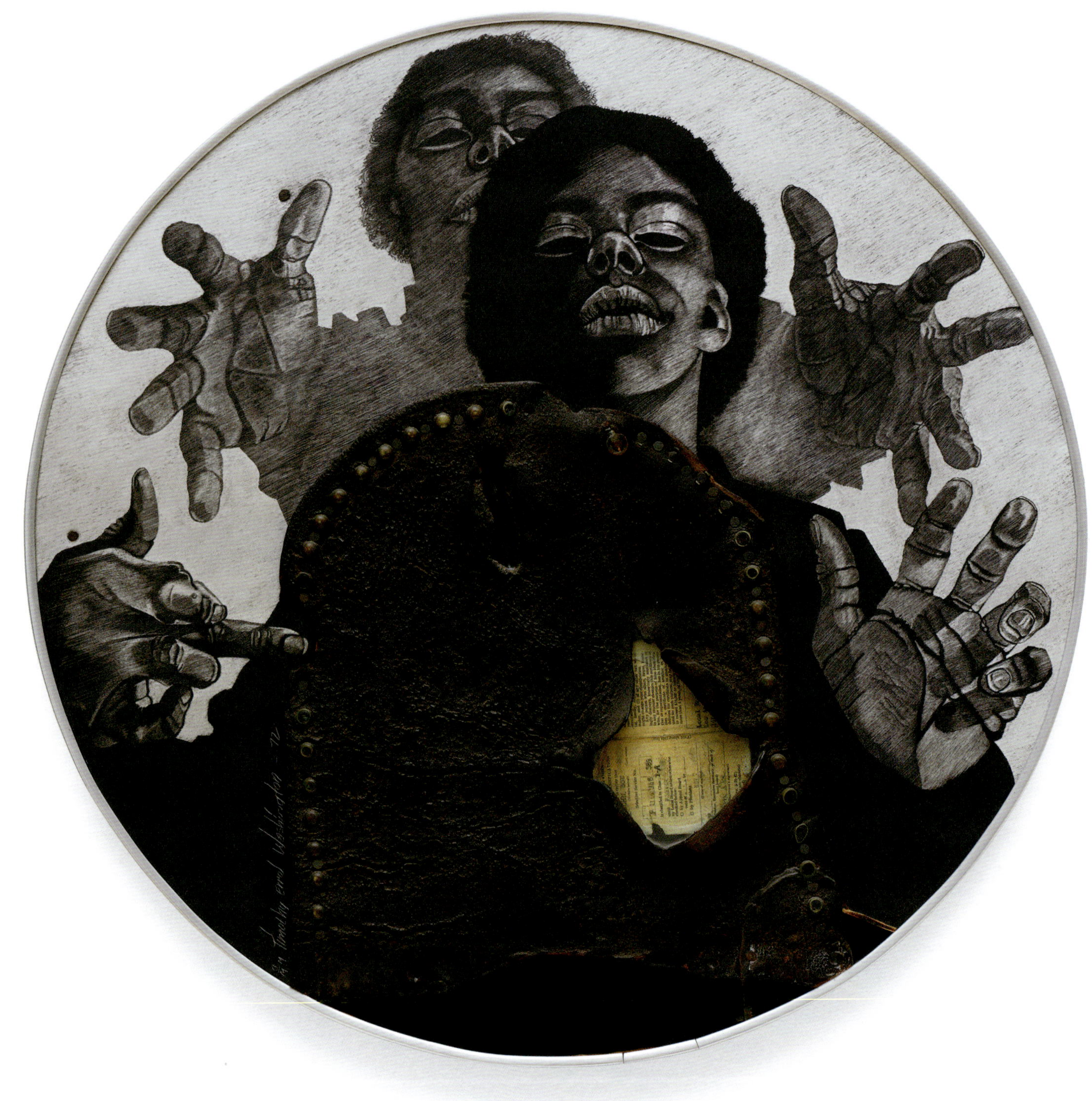

Timothy Washington, *1A*, 1971. Etched aluminum, leather, metal studs, nail, and draft card, 23 ½ × 23 ¼ in. (59.7 × 59.1 cm). San Francisco Museum of Modern Art; purchase, by exchange, through a gift of Peggy Guggenheim 2020.46

sexual organs, and urban architecture. Ito has been making art for nearly two decades by now, though working sporadically.

The eldest of two children, Ito had been born in Berkeley, California, to Japanese parents just after the end of World War I. Her time in California is spent in the Japanese community, which keeps itself separate as protection against the kind of persecution that is legislated two decades later. From 1923 to 1928, Ito lives with her mother, grandmother, and sister in Japan. She excels in school at reading, calligraphy, and watercolor painting, and although she doesn't consider it influential to her future work, her early education in achieving luminosity in color and fluidity in line seems crucial to her later paint application and attention to sinuous kanji-like marks.

After returning to the United States, she attends the University of California, Berkeley, where she feels at home in the art department, studying watercolor painting under now obscure Western landscape masters such as Erle Loran and Worth Ryder. Ito is set to graduate in May 1942, but in April she and her new husband are sent to Tanforan, a racetrack turned incarceration camp in San Bruno. She will speak little of her imprisonment. When she is released in 1943, she conducts a year of postgraduate work at Smith College and then another at the School of the Art Institute of Chicago. Her husband remains imprisoned until 1945, at which point he joins her in Chicago. But she faces fresh difficulties over the next few decades. She is a stay-at-home mother to her two children and endures breast cancer and a double mastectomy. She is able to turn to painting full-time only in the 1970s, encouraged and collected by a cohort of artists and admirers, namely Vera Berdich, Whitney Halstead, Tom Kapsalis, Evelyn Statsinger, and Ray Yoshida.

1971 • Months after graduating from California State University, Los Angeles with a master of fine art in sculpture, Senga Nengudi moves to New York City. She stays briefly with family in Queens before relocating with her significant other, artist René Pyatt, to a brownstone in Spanish Harlem, which serves as a hub of creativity for artists in the neighborhood as well as a crash pad for those visiting from the West Coast, including friend and future collaborator David Hammons.

Via a network of friends and colleagues Nengudi is quickly immersed in the Black arts scene of New York. Uptown, she makes frequent trips to the Studio Museum in Harlem and is introduced to the Weusi Artist Collective and their [Weusi] Nyumba Ya Sanaa Gallery; downtown, she connects with painter William T. Williams and takes classes at Robert

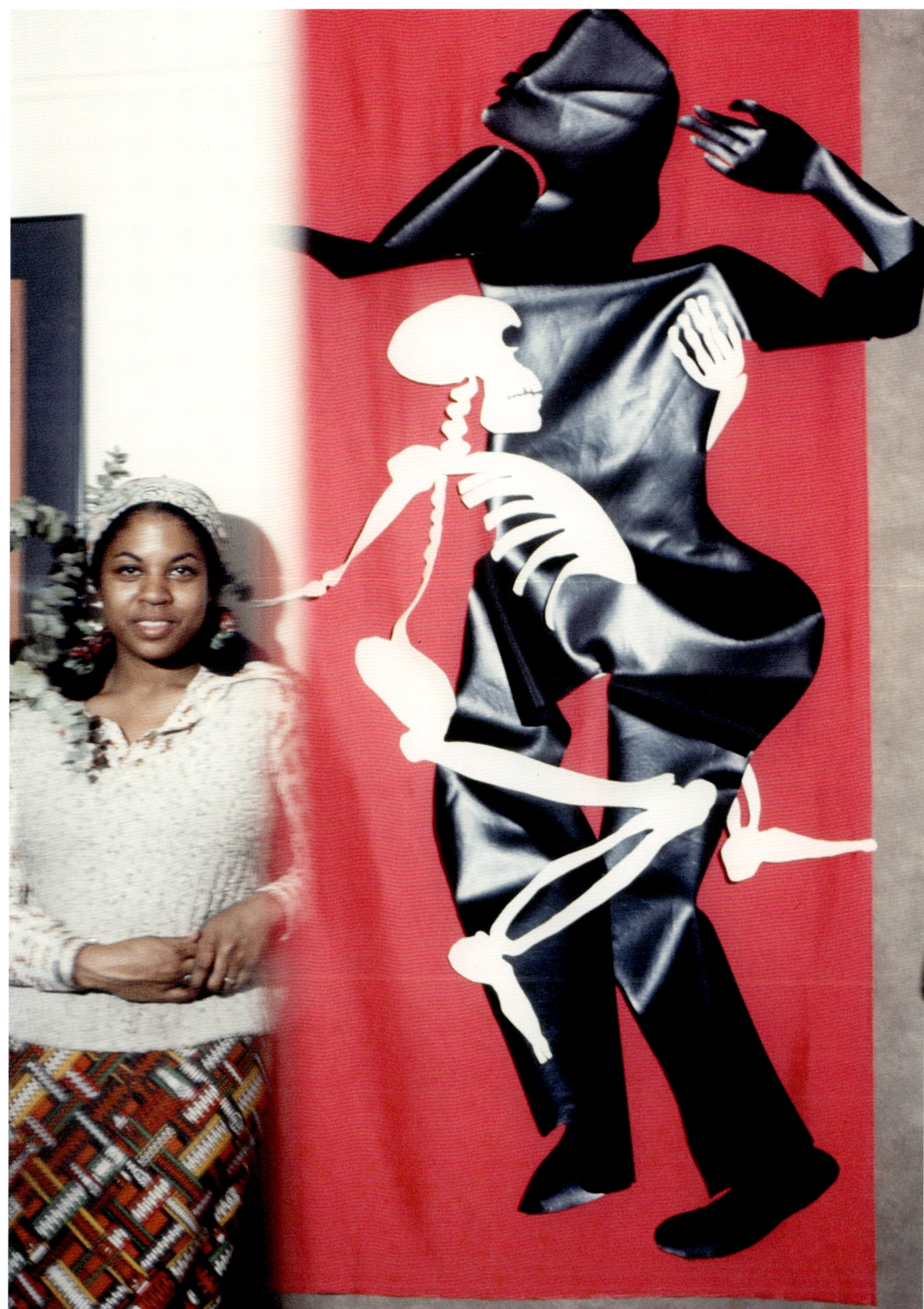

Senga Nengudi with *Death's Got a Hold on Me* (1972), 1972

Blackburn's printshop. She soon comes to feel that her predominantly abstract work is out of place, as she will later recall: "I guess I felt a little intimidated in New York—where so much work being done by black artists tended toward the figural—to do what I'd been doing in L.A."

The following year Nengudi will find something of a compromise in her series of *Spirit Flags*, large-scale, humanesque forms cut from durable nylon or vinyl and typically affixed to her apartment's fire escape. The works draw inspiration equally from African mythology, Yoruba art, and the drug-addled movements of some of her fellow Harlem denizens.

> When people were high, they would just kind of weave around and go like that and like this, but they would never fall. They would just be like swaying trees, to the point where on street corners it would be like almost like a forest of them. . . . And so there'd be this amazing movement, this amazing choreography, even, that would go on. . . . obviously it was a terrible thing. But that is what I got out of it: this grace, in a sense, that was happening.

Installed outdoors, the figures could bob and weave freely with the wind, capturing the same sort of bodily motion. Merging similarly quotidian or found elements and materials with the mythic or ritualistic will become a recurring theme in Nengudi's career, such as in her series *R.S.V.P.* (1975–77) and *Ceremony for Freeway Fets* (1978).

After traveling between New York and Los Angeles for several years, Nengudi will return to California in 1974 upon becoming pregnant with her first child. Once back in Los Angeles she will also change her name from Sue Irons to Senga Nengudi, a name given to her by a friend—"Senga" meaning "a woman of the village that people come to" for wisdom and advice, and "Nengudi" loosely referring to "a woman who comes to power as a traditional healer."

March 1, 1971 • On the invitation of her friend Joyce Kozloff, Luchita Hurtado attends the first meeting of what will become the Los Angeles Council of Women Artists. Her participation in the women's rights movement will grant her the confidence to step into the light as an artist, "to

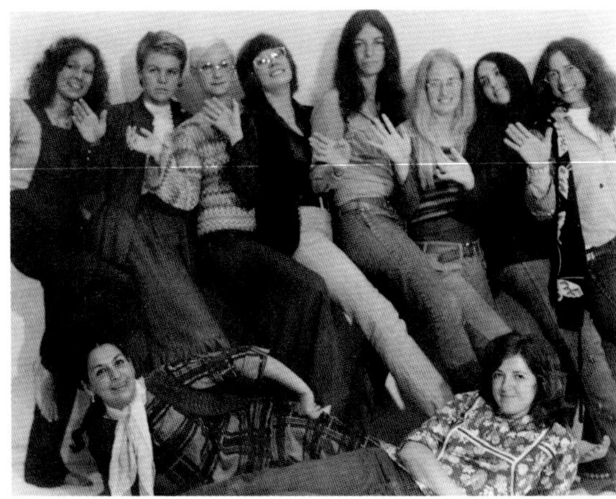

Members of the Los Angeles Council of Women Artists (clockwise from left): Alexis Smith, Ann McCoy, Barbara Haskell, Janice Brown, Avilda Moses, Barbara Munger, Lois Miller, Susan Titelman, Vija Celmins, and Luchita Hurtado, Los Angeles, c. 1971

show people my work and not turn my paintings toward the wall." As Hurtado will later recall of this early meeting: "It was a group of very strong-willed women, artists like Vija Celmins, Alexis Smith, Miriam Schapiro, Judy Chicago, June Wayne, and Mako Idemitsu. At the time I was going by Luchita Mullican, but when we went around the room to introduce ourselves, June encouraged me to say, 'Luchita Hurtado.' That was a very important moment in my life, remembering my name. When they discovered me again, I lived again." Hurtado organizes the group's next meeting at her home in Los Angeles, and in June the women issue a draft report on the status of women in the West Coast art world, focusing on the dire lack of representation in museum collections.

March 18, 1971 • Gunvor Nelson's *My Name Is Oona* (1969) and *Kirsa Nicholina* (1969) appear in the second program of the Whitney Museum of American Art's New American Filmmakers Series, "Steps Toward a New Consciousness," which is devoted to countercultural film. Joining work by Jordan Belson and Yayoi Kusama in the program, Nelson's films are the first for which she receives credit as an individual filmmaker. Writing in the *Village Voice*, prominent film curator Amos Vogel hails Nelson as the standout artist in the series and describes *My Name Is Oona* as capturing "in haunting, intensely lyrical images, fragments of the coming to consciousness of a child girl."

In this portrait of Nelson's daughter, the filmmaker turns from the dream images of *Fog Pumas* to the unreality of child's play. An eerie, looping soundtrack, made with help from composer Steve Reich, accompanies a similarly repetitive sequence of black-and-white shots of Oona in motion. The progression of images seems to be determined less by conscious logical processes than by the circular causal relations that cybernetic science calls "feedback loops." Indeed, in interviews Nelson will sometimes characterize her filmmaking process in terms of "feedback" between consciously sensed images and the involuntary responses these elicit from the unconscious: "Once a film gets direction & feeds back to me, the film takes over and I lose myself so that . . . the only question is what is the film's best interest." The film's visual and aural repetitions give way to its striking central images: shots of Oona riding on horseback, silhouetted against the sun, hair and robes trailing in the wind.

March 20–April 25, 1971 • The contemporary sensibility that Douglas MacAgy has cultivated as the director of the short-lived but influential Dallas Museum for Contemporary Arts

culminates in the exhibition *one i at a time*, now on view at the Meadows Museum at Southern Methodist University, Dallas. The artists MacAgy includes in the show—Roy Fridge, Bill Komodore, Jim Love, David McManaway, Hal Pauley, Herb Rogalla, Charles Williams, Roger Winter—represent an ad hoc, though often close-knit, group based in Dallas and Houston. MacAgy feels that the particular amalgamation of assemblage, humor, sculptural sophistication, and engagement with both Surrealism and Pop art evident in these artists' work could only have developed in Texas.

April 6–May 16, 1971 • *Contemporary Black Artists in America* is on view at the Whitney Museum of American Art, New York, following the withdrawal by twenty-four artists of their work. Included in the initial selection are Romare Bearden, Melvin Edwards, Mike Henderson, Daniel LaRue Johnson, Betye Saar, and Raymond Saunders. Five works by Saunders from a 1970 series that he calls "colorings" are in the show, small works in crayon, pencil, and collage on paper that oscillate between expressive abstraction and recognizable imagery, such as a lightbulb, hearts, or pallid profiles with crude pink lips and abstracted hair. Dense compositions of bright colors and pencil scrawls on white grounds, the works channel children's drawings, a reference made explicit by one title, *First Grade Reader, D. and J.* Another of Saunders's paintings, *Marie's Bill* (1970), is published as the frontispiece to the exhibition catalogue.

The controversy surrounding the exhibition stems from the approach of its curator, Robert Doty, as articulated in his catalogue essay, where he quotes Saunders's manifesto "Black Is a Color" and concludes that "for artists such as these, freedom of expression signifys [*sic*] freedom for the individual." Doty then declaims against the "extremist exhortations" of other artists. His dismissal of radical politics, along with what some charge as a preference for Black artists working abstractly, alienates many. The Black Emergency Cultural Coalition (BECC) announces a boycott of the exhibition, and two dozen artists, including Edwards and Johnson, withdraw their work.

April 6–May 10, 1971 • *Rebuttal to the Whitney Museum Exhibition: Black Artists in Rebuttal* is on view at Acts of Art Gallery, which had been established in Greenwich Village by Patricia Grey and Nigel Jackson in response to the Whitney Museum's refusal to hire a Black curator for its survey of contemporary Black artists now on view. The *Rebuttal* show, organized by Benny Andrews and Cliff Joseph of the BECC, targets the same Whitney exhibition and includes works

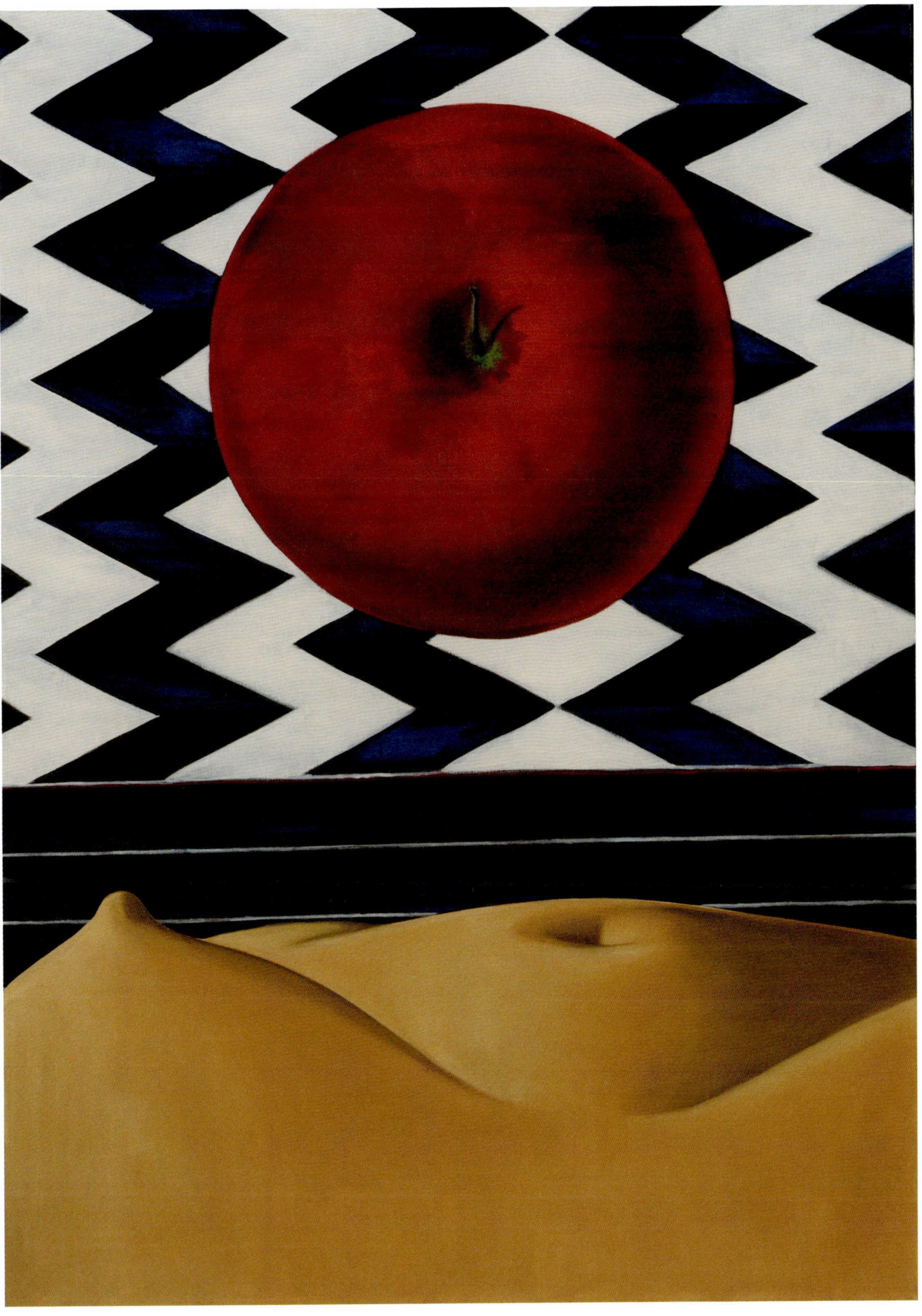

Luchita Hurtado, *Untitled*, 1971. Oil on canvas, 50 × 34 ⅞ inches (127 × 88.6 cm). The Estate of Luchita Hurtado and Hauser & Wirth

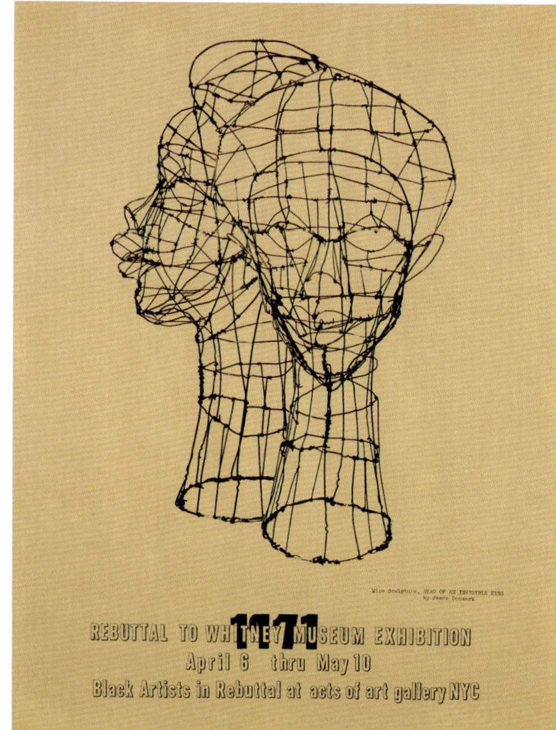

Poster for *Rebuttal to the Whitney Museum Exhibition: Black Artists in Rebuttal*, Acts of Art Gallery, New York, 1971, with James Denmark's *Head of an Invisible King* (c. 1971)

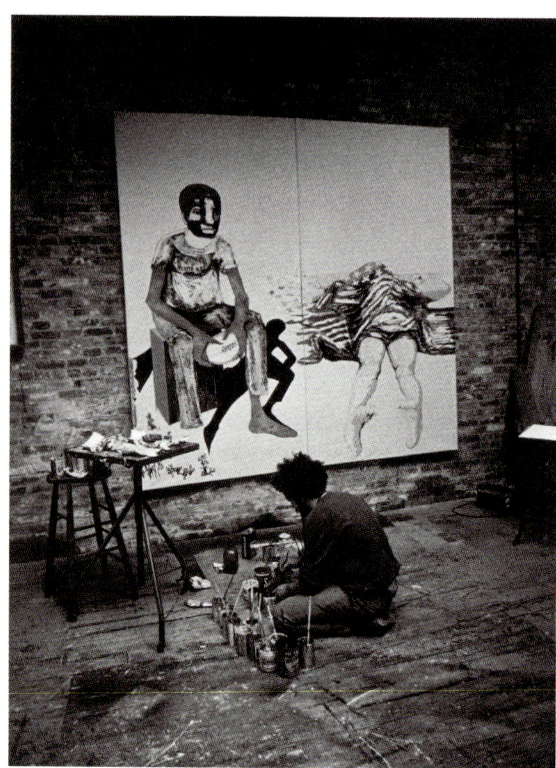

Benny Andrews in his studio, New York, 1970, with *No More Games* (1970)

THE BLACK EMERGENCY CULTURAL COALITION presents the following proposals demands to the Whitney Museum of Art:

1. An exhibition of contemporary black artists, with a black guest curator.

2. To give at least five (5) one man exhibitions to black artists in the contemporary gallery each year....

3. To increase the number of black artists in The Whitney Annual, and, to include a black curator on the Whitney Annual's selection committee.

4. To buy more black artists' work, for inclusion in the permanent collection of the Whitney Museum.

5. To have a black curatorial staff coordinate all such endeavors and projections in the future.

THE BLACK EMERGENCY CULTURAL COALITION

Co Chairmen: Benny Andrews
Henri Ghent

List of proposals made by the Black Emergency Cultural Coalition in response to the exhibition *Contemporary Black Artists in America* at the Whitney Museum of American Art and delivered to museum director John Bauer, 1971

by Andrews and Adger Cowans alongside forty-five other artists. Andrews's work of this period increasingly undertakes an absurdist satire of the nation's history and its ongoing social inequalities. For *Rebuttal*, Andrews exhibits *American Gothic* (1971), part of the *Bicentennial Series* that he started in 1970 and will continue working on for the next five years leading up to the nation's two hundredth birthday.

April 20–August 29, 1971 • The large mid-career survey *Alex Hay: Recorded and Performed Activities Since 1962* is on view at the New York Cultural Center, following the artist's three consecutive solo exhibitions at the Kornblee Gallery. The retrospective includes fifty works spanning Hay's wide breadth of multidisciplinary, intermedia practice: paintings, sculptures, conceptual works, and dance pieces that are exhibited using photographic documentation. Crucially, the survey demonstrates the evolution of Hay's work across a ten-year span, from his performance art and large, Pop and surreal-style facsimile blow-ups of everyday objects to the more process-based, proto-conceptual pieces created in California during his time with collectors Elyse and Stanley Grinstein.

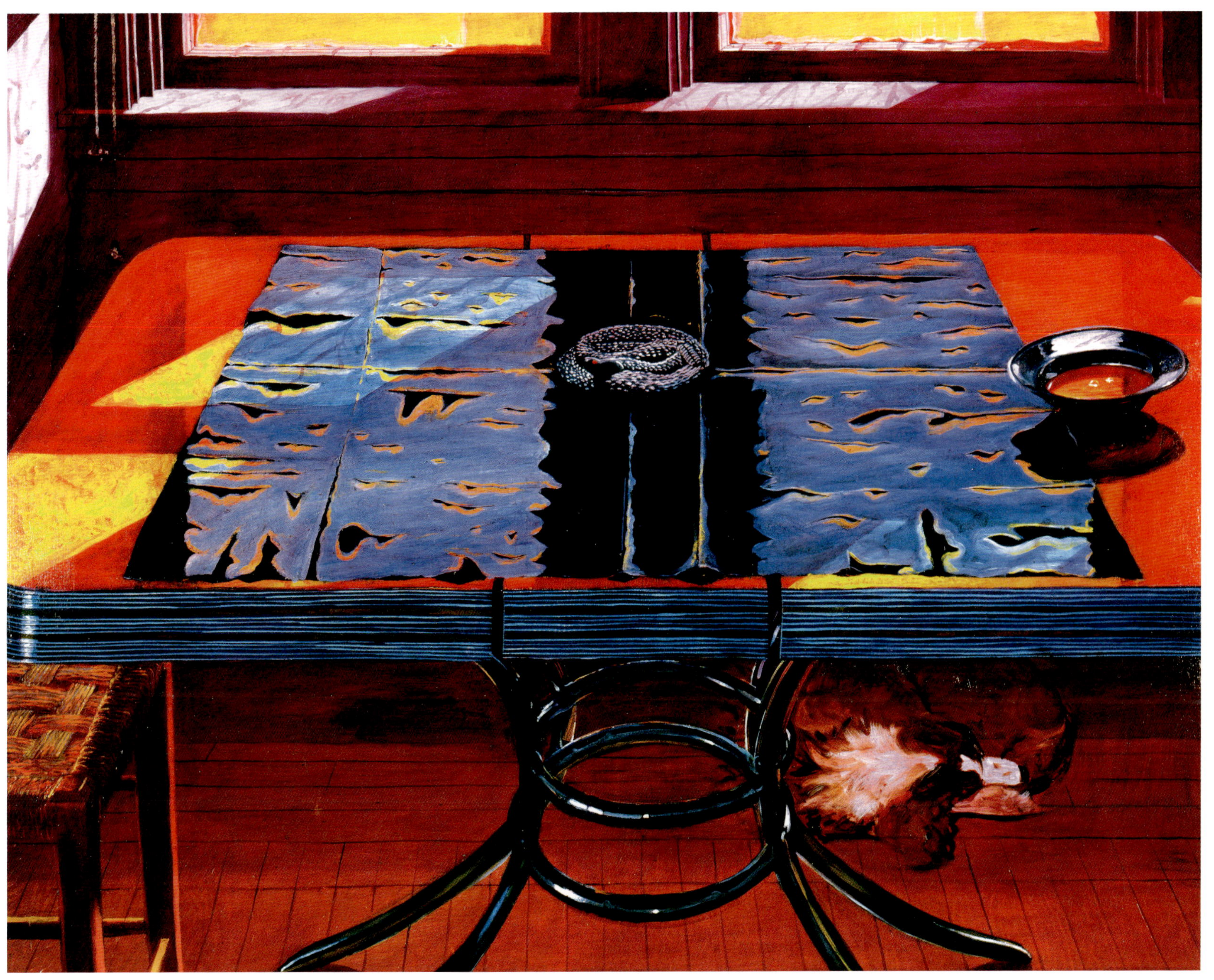

Eduardo Carrillo, *Testament of the Holy Spirit*, 1971. Oil on panel, 47 ¾ × 60 in. (121.3 × 152.4 cm). Crocker Art Museum, Sacramento, CA; purchase with funds from the Maude T. Pook Acquisition Fund 1972.24

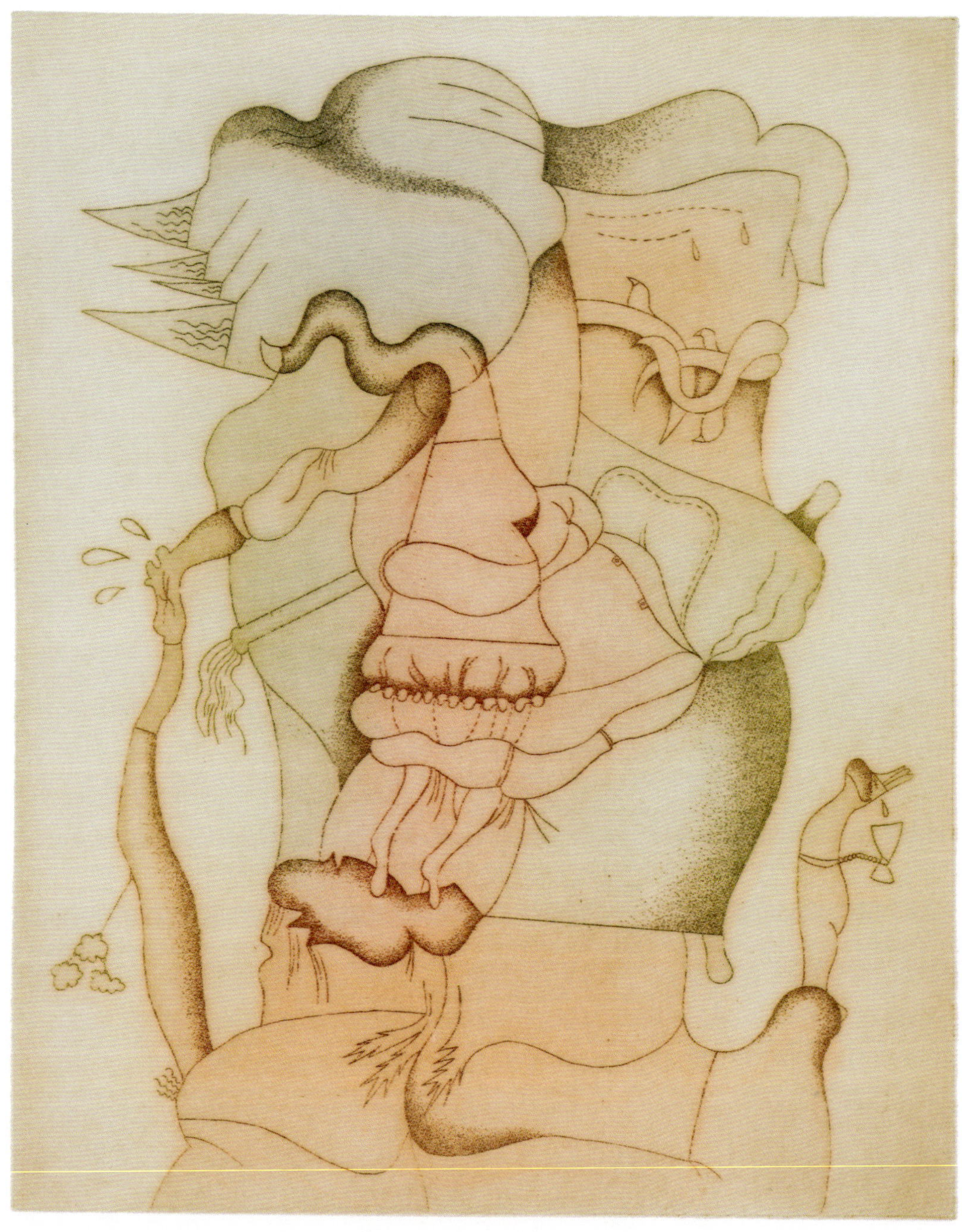

Barbara Rossi, *Male of Sorrows #4*, 1971. Print on satin: sheet, 19 × 15 ⅞ in. (48.3 × 40.3 cm); image, 14 × 11 in. (35.6 × 27.8 cm). Whitney Museum of American Art, New York; gift of the Kohler Foundation, Inc. 2021.142

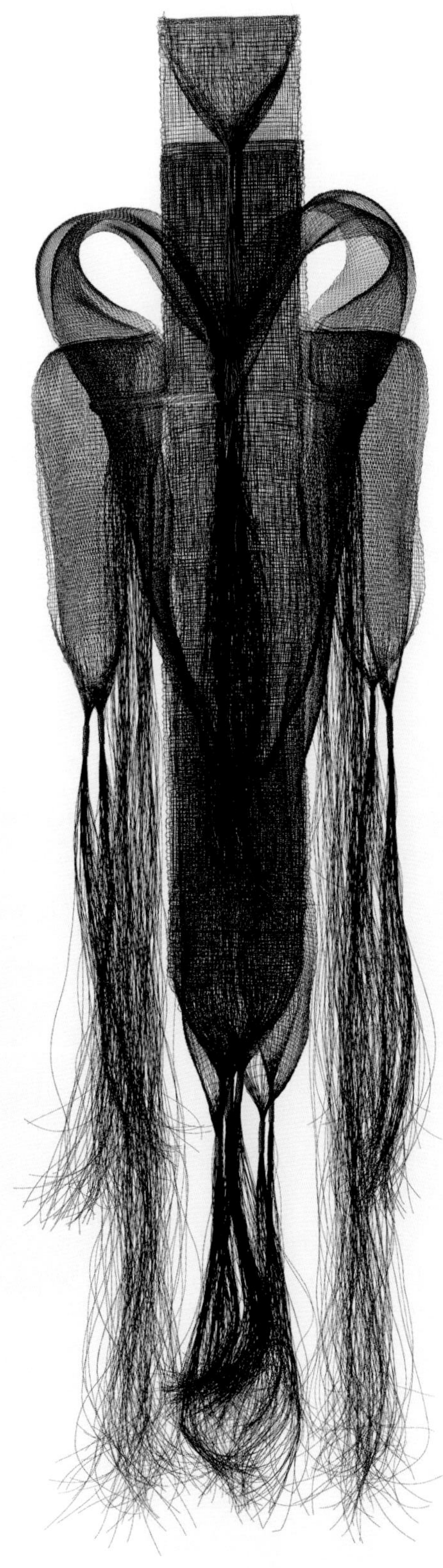

Kay Sekimachi, *Katsura*, 1971. Dyed nylon monofilament; 4-layer and tubular weaves on an 8-harness loom, 43 × 15 × 13 in. (109.2 × 38.1 × 33 cm).
Fine Arts Museums of San Francisco; Foundation purchase, George and Dorothy Saxe Endowment Fund 2016.7

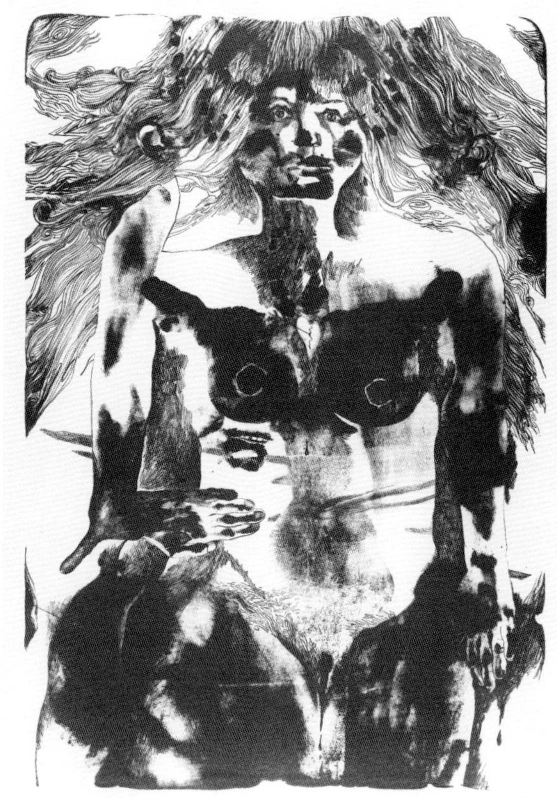

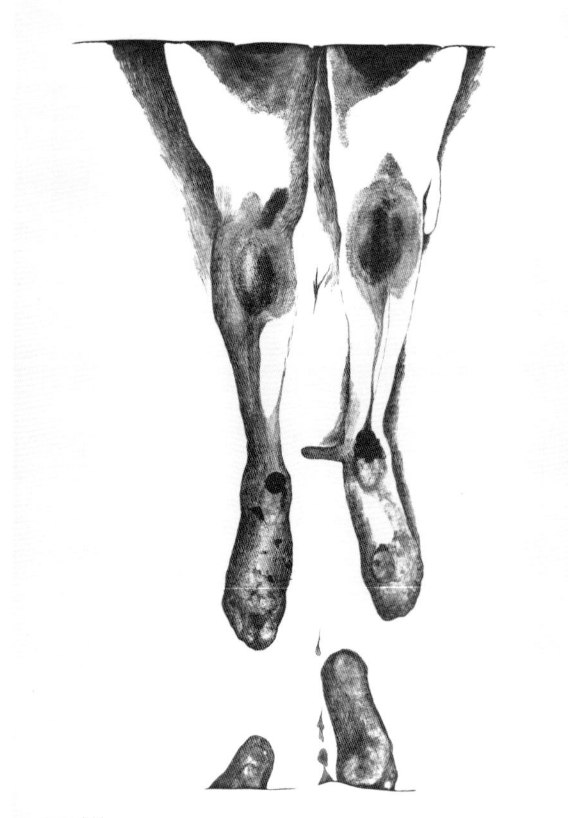

Marisol, *Diptych*, 1971. Lithograph in two colors: two sheets, 47 ¾ × 31 ⅞ in. (121.3 × 81 cm) each. Whitney Museum of American Art, New York; purchase, with funds from the Drawing and Print Committee 2024.363a–b

Critic Peter Schjeldahl dubs Hay the "Gentle Maverick" in his review of the retrospective for the *New York Times*, describing him as an artist working in Rauschenberg's proverbial gap between art and life.

But the main pleasure one takes in his work is not the frisson of its aesthetic savvy but, within the context of a nearly ascetic commitment to ideas, the exquisite taste and skill with which it is given form. Typically blown up in scale . . . Hay's object-based works communicate both the close-range elegance of their models . . . and the presence . . . of good, big abstraction. And their virtuoso marriage of handcraft and technological techniques . . . is simply dazzling. . . . No avoidable trace remains in their finished form of the elaborate pains that were taken to create them.

April 29–May 19, 1971 • Karl Wirsum's solo project *Dr. Chicago* is on view at the Wabash Transit Gallery at the School of the Art Institute of Chicago. This, the artist's first institutional exhibition, features new work, including life-size cardboard figures with limbs attached with grommets so that the artist can pose them as he wishes.

May 1971 • *Artforum* publishes six images from Diane Arbus's portfolio *A box of ten photographs*, the first time the magazine has included the work of any photographer. As Leider will later remark, "with Diane Arbus, one could find oneself interested in photography or not, but one could no longer . . . deny its status as art." An image from the portfolio, *Boy with a straw hat waiting to march in a pro-war parade, N.Y.C. 1967*, appears on the magazine's cover. A short text by Arbus inside concludes: "A photograph is a secret about a secret. The more it tells you the less you know." On July 26, Arbus commits suicide. Shortly thereafter, John Szarkowski begins work on the photographer's first major retrospective, *Diane Arbus*, which will open at the Museum of Modern Art, New York, in November 1972.

May 18–June 12, 1971 • Lee Bontecou has her fourth solo exhibition at Castelli Gallery, marking her last show in New York for three decades. Even as she had begun her experiments with vacuum-formed shapes four years prior, carving molds out of Styrofoam and using them to create plastic forms reminiscent of natural formations, flowers, and animals, this is the first formal showing of such work. The numerous translucent, freestanding sculptures on view at Castelli Gallery are a departure from her distinctive style and garner mixed reviews. Bontecou's new work seems "trapped between the claims of fantasy and realism, lacking the formal independence and authority . . . necessary to bring them off," writes James R. Mellow in the *New York Times*. The following March, the artist is honored with a retrospective at the Museum of Contemporary Art Chicago, after which she retreats from regular shows in galleries but continues an active life as a teacher.

June–July 1971 • Having receded from the arts scene in the mid-1960s after her early success, Joan Brown reemerges with a solo show at the San Francisco Museum of Modern Art. *Joan Brown: Paintings* features works in enamel on Masonite and showcases the artist as a powerfully expressive figurative painter who creates bright representational canvases that boast dream imagery and highlight her long-standing interest in Egyptian mythology.

June 22–July 30, 1971 • *"Where We At" Black Women Artists* is on view at Acts of Art Gallery in Greenwich Village, New York, which had been established by Nigel Jackson earlier in the year in response to the Whitney Museum of American Art's reluctance to hire a Black curator to organize its survey *Contemporary Black Artists in America*. The current show takes its name from the group founded by Faith Ringgold, Kay Brown (1932–2012), Dindga McCannon, and others to protest the lack of representation of Black women both in the feminist art movement and in male-dominated art spaces. The organization will also run workshops in schools, hospitals, and cultural centers and offers youth art classes in their communities.

A 1968 bachelor of fine arts graduate of the City College of New York, Brown had been one of only two women—McCannon being the other—to be a part of the Weusi Artist Collective, which formed in Harlem in 1965. The word *Weusi* translates as "blackness" in Swahili, and throughout the late 1960s and into the 1970s, the organization seeks to promote and disseminate the work of Black artists. Brown's sociopolitical prints, paintings, and collages explore various aspects of Black narratives, including commentary on the large number of Black men drafted into the Vietnam War as well as the complexities of motherhood.

July 1–September 27, 1971 • The sprawling exhibition *Artist as Adversary* is on view at the Museum of Modern Art, New York. The show, though limited to pieces currently in the museum's collection, presents the work of artists focused on issues of war and protest and includes Benny Andrews's *No More Games* (1970) and Daniel LaRue Johnson's *Freedom Now, Number 1* (1963–64).

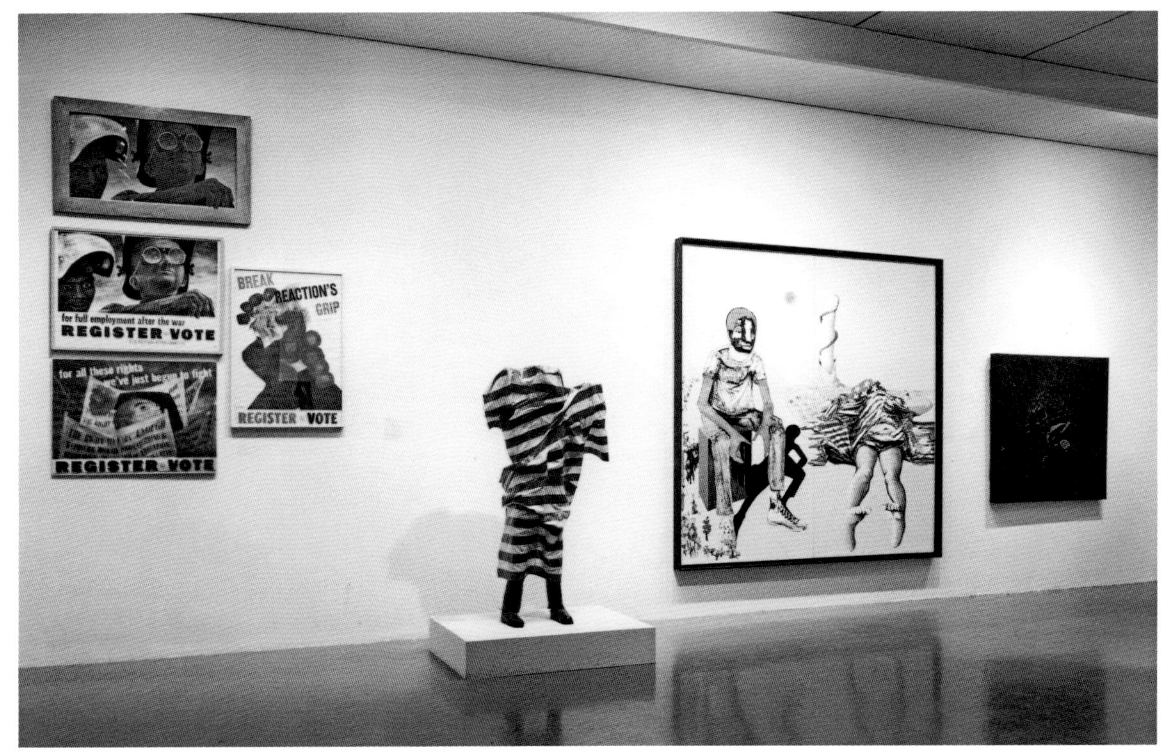

The Artist as Adversary, The Museum of Modern Art, New York, 1971, with Benny Andrews's *No More Games* (1970) and Daniel LaRue Johnson's *Freedom Now, Number 1* (1963–64)

Summer 1971 • Marisol prints *Diptych* (1971), a vertical lithographic self-portrait, with Universal Limited Art Editions (ULAE), a printshop that artist Tatyana Grosman had established on Long Island in the 1950s. Lee Bontecou, Claes Oldenburg, Edward Ruscha, and Saul Steinberg have all produced prints with the same shop. Marisol's ULAE residency marks her return to the studio.

In order to produce *Diptych*, Marisol oils her body and presses it against two large lithographic stones. After making the successive impressions, she adds hand-drawn elements: sinuous hair surrounds her head and covers her genitals, hatch marks delineate her nipples, and a small cracked heart pierced by an arrow appears like a tattoo at the center of her chest. Like her sculptures, *Diptych* subverts the conventions of spatial representation. Seemingly standing and reclining at once, Marisol presses her voluminous body into two dimensions, an awkward experience humorously conveyed to the viewer through the troubled expression on her face.

September 1971–February 1972 • Organized by Brenda Richardson, *Wizdumb: William T. Wiley*, Wiley's first museum retrospective, opens at the University Art Museum, Berkeley, and includes paintings, drawings, and sculptures from 1959 to 1971.

1971 • Struggling with depression and drug use, Edward Owens returns to Chicago. Although he does not complete any more known films, he does not stop working. Letters to his former lover Charles Boultenhouse, with whom he maintains a decades-long correspondence that ends only with Boultenhouse's death in 1994, recount his involvement with theater, his exploration of the new video technology of the early 1970s, the undertaking of a new film project in 1979, and ongoing work in collage. Owens's films, however, remain unscreened from the late 1960s until the early 2000s, when *Tomorrow's Promise* (1967) and *Private Imaginings and Narrative Facts* (1968–70) are included in the 2006 University of Chicago symposium Beyond Warhol, Smith, and Anger: Recovering the Significance of Postwar Queer Underground Cinema, 1950–1968. In 2009 film critic Ed Halter comes across *Private Imaginings and Narrative Facts* in the catalog of the Film-Makers' Cooperative and organizes the first solo screening of Owens's work since the 1960s, at Light Industry.

Fall 1971 • Joan Semmel (b.1932) enrolls in the master of fine art program at Pratt Institute, New

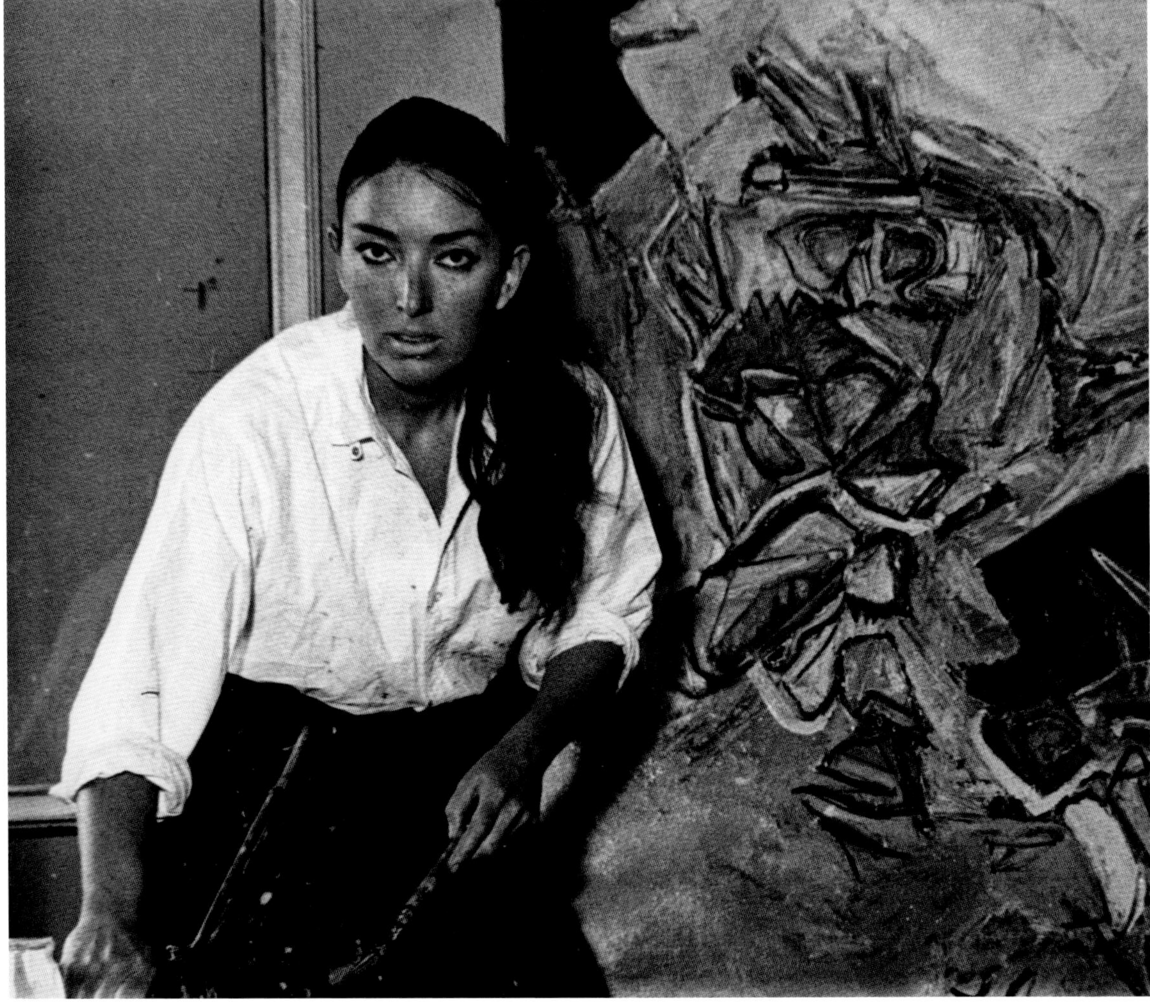

Joan Semmel in Spain, c. 1965

York, and continues her exploration of figurative imagery in her paintings. During a seven-year stay in Spain, the artist had moved from the style of action painting she had pursued during her undergraduate work to incorporate a European Surrealist influence in her paintings of the late 1960s. Formal elements from this period can be seen to carry over into the *Sex Painting* series, as the artist will later explain: "There was a kind of overlay of surrealism in [the abstract paintings], I would say, because of my European experience . . . the kind of forms that evolved had certain psychological overtones." The *Sex Painting* series is a critical response to the prevalent objectification of women in American popular visual culture of the 1960s and '70s. Introducing what the artists refers to as an "erotic theme" in her work is a way for her to express "the woman's point of view" in contrast to the male gaze dominant across popular media. Semi-abstract and pushed up against the extreme foreground of the picture plane, Semmel's erotic, expressionistically colored configurations of nude, copulating couples place the viewer directly in the position of the female subject. "The reason I wanted to use an erotic element had to do with what I was seeing on the newsstands," the artist will later recall. "When I came back to New York, the girlie magazines, the sexploitation all over was a shocker . . . I was seeing all this stuff that for me wasn't even sexual, it was just hard sell. And hard sell in a way I found demeaning of women. In the past, women's sexuality had always been used against them. I felt very strongly [that] the sexual issue was crucial in terms of real liberation."

Born in the Bronx, Semmel had pursued her education as an artist across many of the city's vested institutions, beginning at the High School of Music and Art in Manhattan. She completed a certificate program at the Cooper Union Art School in the early 1950s, studied briefly at the Art Students League, and earned a bachelor and master of fine art from Pratt Institute. She began exhibiting in New York in the early 1960s, and in 1963 moved to Spain, working and exhibiting her abstract paintings in Europe and South America. Upon her return to New York, Semmel becomes immersed in the ongoing women's art movement, participating in the Ad Hoc Committee of Women Artists co-founded by Lucy Lippard. In 1972, she will turn to a photorealistic idiom to capture the

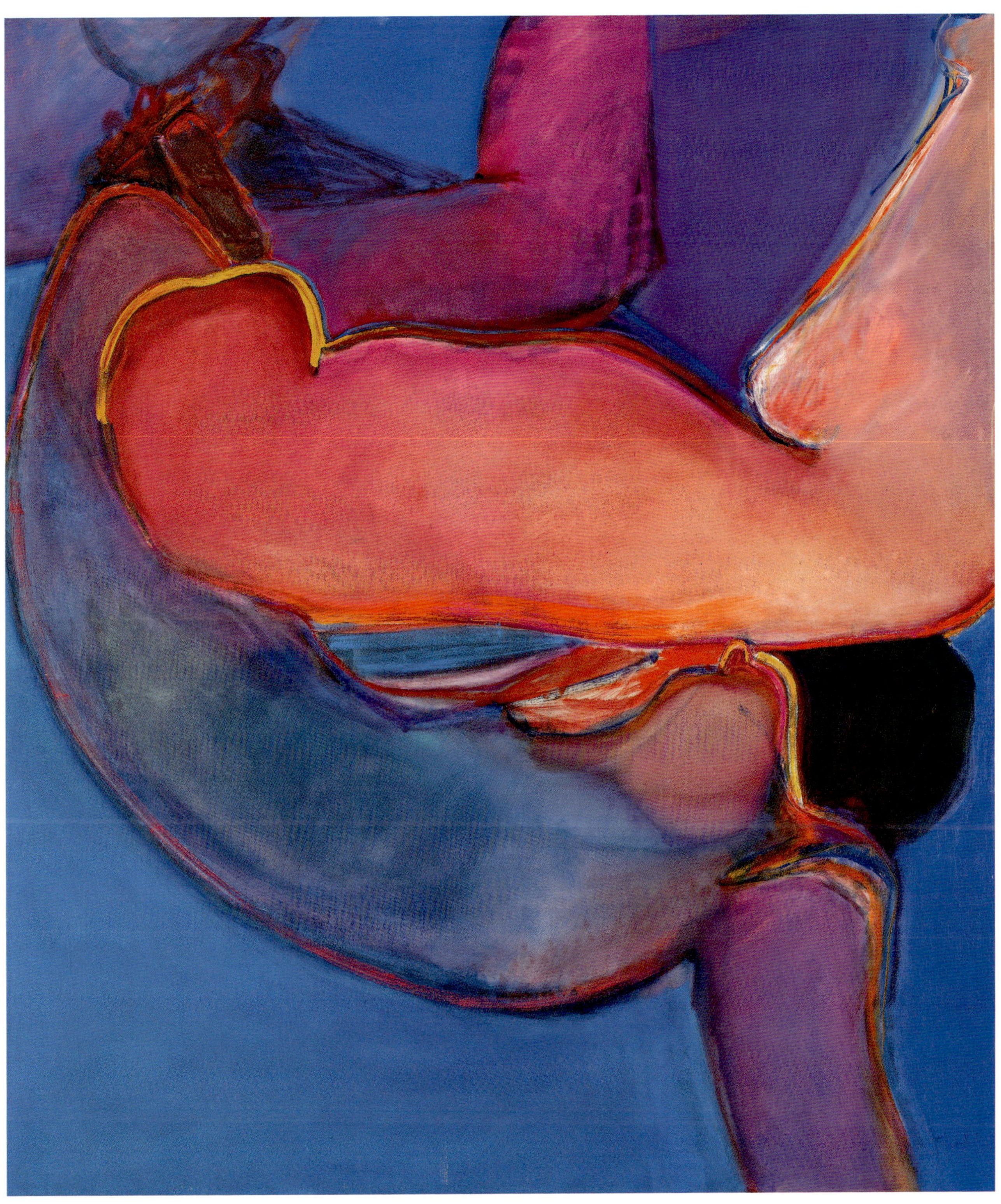

Joan Semmel, *Untitled*, 1971. Oil on canvas, 69 × 58 in. (175.3 × 147.3 cm). Green Family Art Foundation and Adam Green Art Advisory

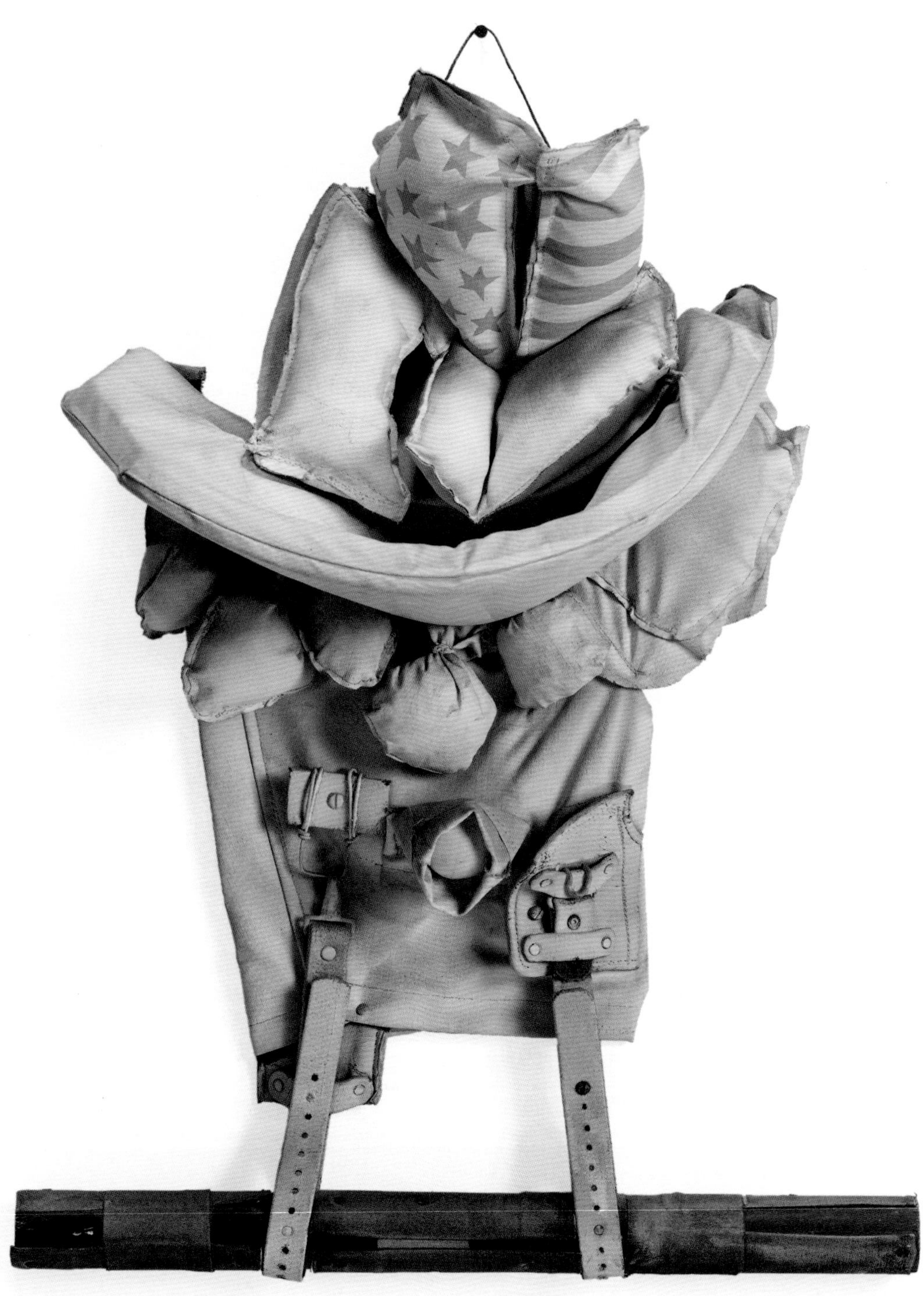

John Outterbridge, *Jive Ass Bird*, 1971. Mixed media, 22 ¼ × 31 × 12 ½ in. (56.5 × 78.7 × 31.8 cm). The Greg and Diane Pitts Family Collection

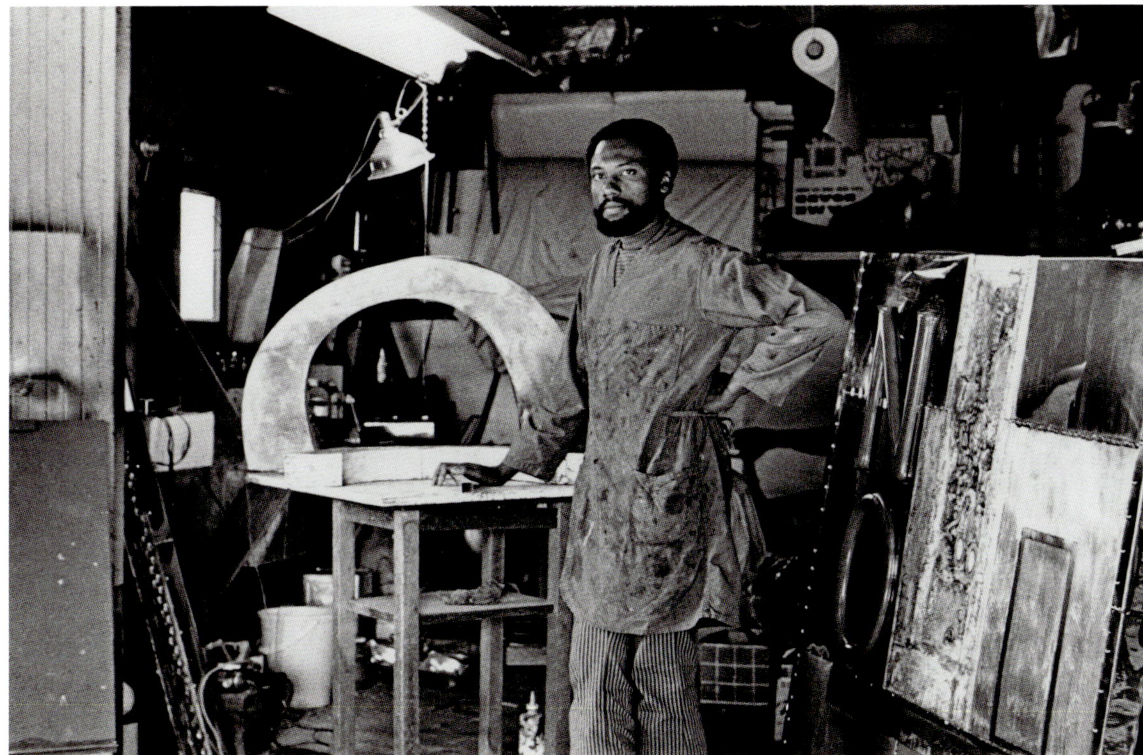

John Outterbridge in his studio, Los Angeles, 1970, with *No Time for Jivin'* (1969)

drawn and sculptural forms, which coalesce into a body and then, finally, a head, a form that she will explore in her work for decades. As Arlene Raven writes:

> Grossman integrates a knowledge of race and gender oppression, of the self in the world, and of the synergy of individual and global issues, in her portrayal of the human head. Grossman wanted to exemplify black beauty in her black-leather-heads, and based the shapes of the first group of head sculptures on the clenched fist of the black-power salute. Yet they were also conceived as self-portraits and looked substantially like the artist. Grossman claims never to have seen garments and toys associated with sadomasochistic practice when, in 1968, she began to use the trappings of restraint in her work. Rather, she traces the origin of her imagery to the equestrian tack-bridles, halters, lip straps, martingales she used as a young girl.

When Lindner sees her head sculptures for the first time, he immediately suggests she exhibit them at the gallery with which he had success, Cordier & Ekstrom; with its long history of involvement with Surrealism, it is a natural fit for these uncanny objects.

likenesses of her anonymous nude models in her *Erotic Paintings* series before turning the focus to her own body.

October 12–November 2, 1971 • John Outterbridge debuts works from his *Containment* series at a solo show at Brockman Gallery, Los Angeles. These sculptural assemblages are made from metal sheets and wood he salvaged from junkyards around the city, an activity that is a long-standing part of Outterbridge's process: "Early in my life I started to use materials to build things. . . . And I used to enjoy going to junkyards then. Even in high school I used to use my father's truck, my friends and I, and we collected metals and sold metals. Some things you'd save and salvage. So that's something that I kind of grew up being around. When it came to using it, I started to use metal primarily right here in California as a gesture of my thought process."

During a stint working at the Pasadena Arts Center, he gets to know Mark di Suvero, who is fascinated by Outterbridge's process. When di Suvero moves away, he gives Outterbridge some tools, including a pair of electric metal-cutting shears that allow Outterbridge's prolific production of *Containment* series works.

November 17–December 18, 1971 • Nancy Grossman (b. 1940) debuts her leather-covered heads in her first solo exhibition, which is on view at Cordier & Ekstrom Gallery, New York. Of these works, which she began constructing in 1968 and describes as self-portraits, she says: "It all begins with the head, the head has a mouth and we kill with words and we are wounded by words."

Grossman had arrived at this genre of sculpture after experimenting with assemblage wall reliefs made from tubes, zippers, and leather jackets, the latter material she finds in bulk at an old Bowery loft. She attempts to make unnamable forms that she feels express truths about her body, her mother's body, and the bodies of the women around her. Grossman comes to these transformations from an organic place, having worked with her parents drawing and manufacturing garments in Oneonta, New York; she is familiar with the textures and shapes of fabrics and zippers as well as with sewing techniques.

Grossman had earned her bachelor of fine arts from Pratt Institute, where she was greatly encouraged by the painter Richard Lindner, who she later remembers emphasized that ideas would find a form but that they needed to be developed to do so. His paintings of pneumatic humans in congress or conflict become influential for her own sense of the quiet violence beneath even the smoothest surfaces. After graduating in 1963, Grossman begins exhibiting her expressionist figurations and assemblages while also doing some illustration work to make ends meet.

In collaboration with her friend and fellow artist Anita Siegel, as well as the sculptor David Smith, Grossman develops her vocabulary of

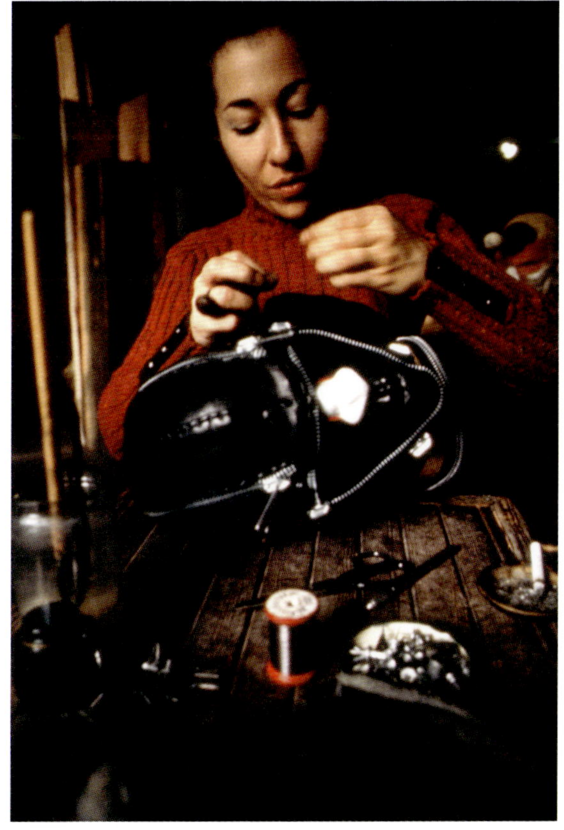

Nancy Grossman in her studio working on *A.F.F.* (1971), 1970

1972

January 1972 • Judy Chicago creates *Womanhouse* with Miriam "Mimi" Schapiro and their students at the California Institute of the Arts (CalArts), Los Angeles. Having already established the Feminist Art Program at Fresno State College in 1970, Chicago develops a similar program at CalArts with Shapiro's help; Chicago's second husband, Lloyd Hamrol, already teaches in the sculpture department there. *Womanhouse* is conceived as a temporary exhibition to inaugurate the arrival of the Feminist Arts Program, available only to female students on the recently opened CalArts campus. The show is a monumental, collaborative effort, embracing openly feminist subject matter such as housework and menstruation. As Chicago will later comment, "At the time of *Womanhouse*, art that clearly exposed women's authentic feelings was absolutely unknown, which probably helps explain both the audience and media response, which was quite intense."

January 25–March 19, 1972 • The Whitney Museum of American Art's *1972 Annual Exhibition: Contemporary American Painting* is on view. Curated by James Monte, the show includes works by Romare Bearden, Joan Brown, Nancy Graves, Christina Ramberg, Deborah Remington, Raymond Saunders, Carlos Villa, and Jack Whitten.

Saunders's painting *Jack Johnson* (1971) in the show is part of the series he makes from 1971 to 1972 of the first Black world heavyweight boxing champion, here silhouetted against a red ground and incorporating collage materials. Of the series, Richard J. Powell will later argue that "Saunders lifted blackness out of a purely political category and deposited it within his 'wider reality' of visual perception, racial illusion, and an improvisational space that put artistic risk-taking and process at the front."

February 1972 • Ed Emshwiller joins Shirley Clarke, Douglas Davis, and Nam June Paik as the first cohort of artists in residence at TV Lab, an initiative of New York–area public television station WNET. Studio access allows Emshwiller to continue exploring his interest in television, video, and computer animation. At WNET, lab director David Loxton helps Emshwiller plan a trip to the Dolphin Computer Image Corporation, where his experiments with the Scanimate analog computer animation system lead to the creation of *Thermogenesis* (1972) and *Scape-mates* (1972), the latter of which will air on PBS in March 1973. Set to an eerie synthesizer soundtrack, *Scape-mates* draws viewers into a series of virtual spaces: rooms and landscapes in vibrant glowing phosphor, some containing 3D forms, some evoking the sort of alien landscapes found on Emshwiller's book covers,

notably, a luminescent green mist under a blue sun-like orb. The presence of two animated dancers lend these spaces an uncanny pseudo-reality.

February 2–25, 1972 • Anita Steckel's solo exhibition *The Sexual Politics of Feminist Art* is on view at Rockland Community College, Suffern, New York. The show attracts charges of obscenity, eliciting local outrage and calls for its closure. In response, Steckel will form the group Fight Censorship the following year, along with fellow women artists Louise Bourgeois, Martha Edelheit, Eunice Golden, Joan Glueckman, Anne Sharp, Juanita McNeely, Joan Semmel, and Hannah Wilke. Steckel writes a simple manifesto: "If the erect penis is not wholesome enough to go into museums it should not be considered wholesome enough to go into women."

March 1972 • Peter Selz, now a professor of art history at the University of California, Berkeley (UC Berkeley), sees Barbara Chase-Riboud's sculpture *Why Did We Leave Zanzibar* (1971) in this month's issue of *ARTnews*. "I had become tired of what was considered the mainstream in sculpture, all these depersonalized fabricated cubes taking space in gallery floors," he will later recall. "Here was an authentic highly personal statement, sculpture

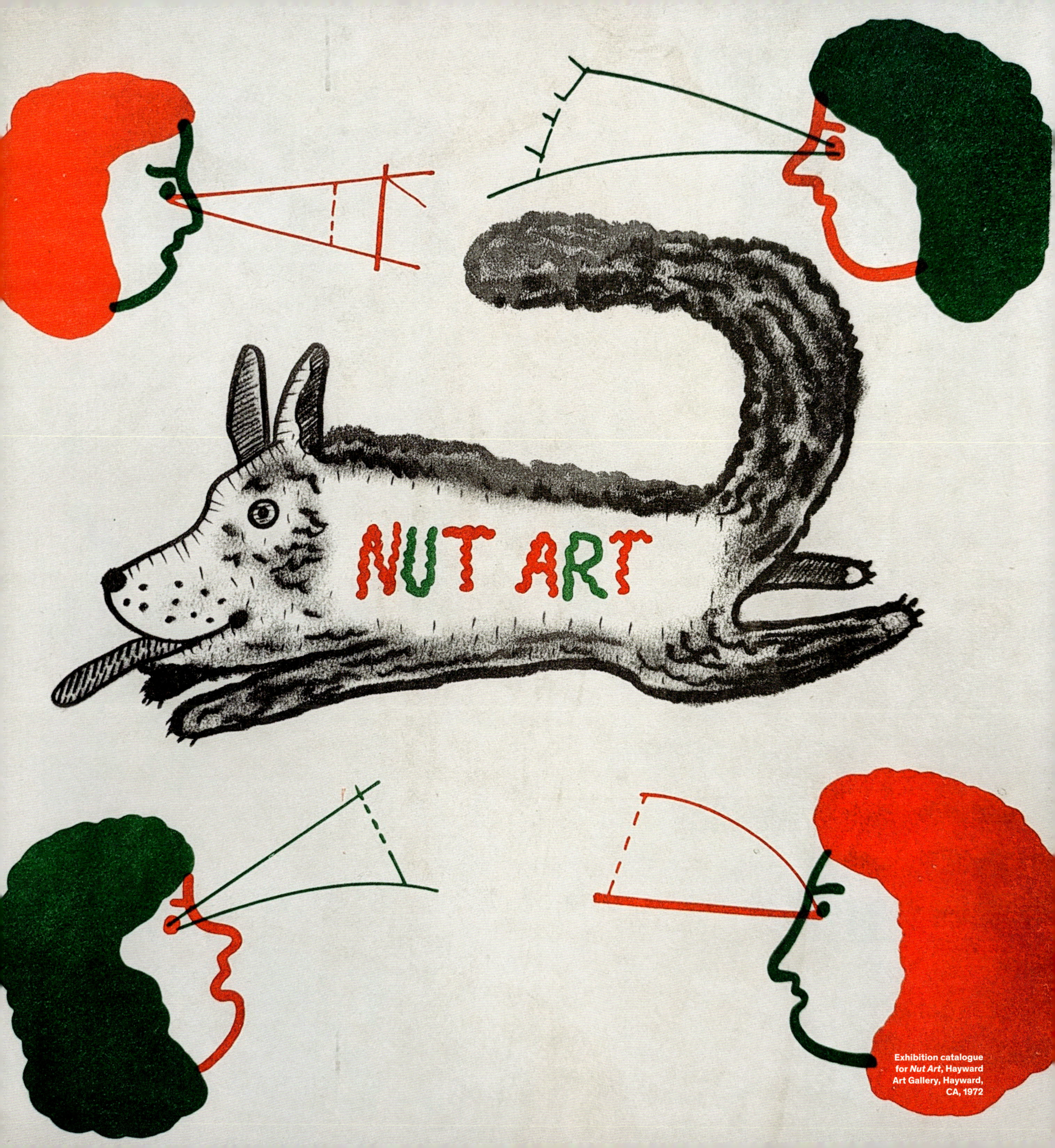

Exhibition catalogue for *Nut Art*, Hayward Art Gallery, Hayward, CA, 1972

of inherent mystery and beauty." He is moved to commission a new work for UC Berkeley's art museum, and the result, *Confessions for Myself* (1972), is Chase-Riboud's largest sculpture to date. Its monumental scale, serrated bronze, and thick wool set it apart from her Minimalist contemporaries; the bronze "suddenly took on a life of its own," as the artist will later relate. The sculpture will be featured in Chase-Riboud's first solo museum exhibition, at the University Art Museum, Berkeley, in January 1973, which, as the artist will note in her autobiography, makes her only the second American woman to have a solo show at a major American museum, more than a quarter century after Georgia O'Keeffe's 1946 solo exhibition at the Museum of Modern Art, New York.

April 7–May 29, 1972 • *Two American Painters: Fritz Scholder, T. C. Cannon* is on view at the National Collection of Fine Arts, Washington, DC. By this point, both Scholder and Cannon have been painting Native American subjects for years: Scholder's abstract male figures are often invented and aggressive depictions of the darker sides of contemporary Native American life, such as poverty and alcoholism, while Cannon's clarion approach appoints both male and female figures with details that gesture toward cultural and political histories and injustices, such as clothing specific to Native ceremonies or backdrops reminiscent of battlefields. Despite the different aspects of Indigenous life that these two painters choose to depict—and the implication of conflict in these differences—Scholder, ever the teacher and elder, asks Cannon to share this exhibition opportunity with him. In an interesting twist, a single collector—who goes on to support Cannon's career for years—purchases almost all of the artist's paintings from the show.

The show is organized as a partnership between the Smithsonian Institution and the US Information Agency (USIA), the federal agency charged with communicating American values Continued on page 333

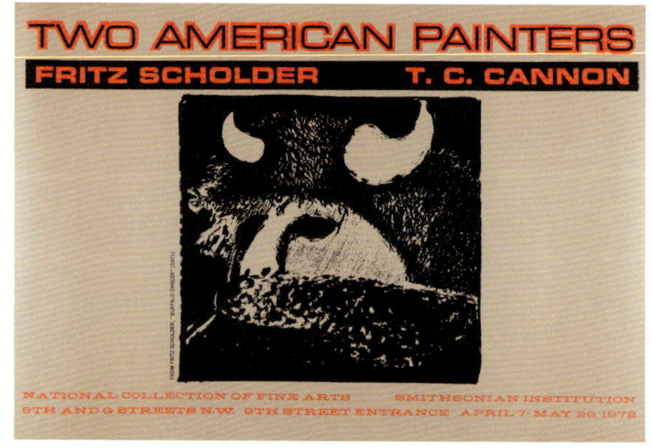

Poster for *Two American Painters: Fritz Scholder, T. C. Cannon*, National Collection of Fine Arts, Washington, DC, 1972

TO WALK THROUGH THE FRONT DOOR OF HISTORY: BARBARA CHASE-RIBOUD'S *CONFESSIONS FOR MYSELF*

RUJEKO HOCKLEY

No more than a sword point away from landing
In the attic of our dreams, Chloe and me
Ready to do battle with sons and lovers
In rustling fields and sand and gravel
Paths leading to the magic of poets.

— Barbara Chase-Riboud, "La Chenillère," 1973[1]

In 2023, the artist Radcliffe Bailey died of brain cancer, at the heartbreaking age of fifty-four. His was a practice of bricolage, incorporating photographs and other objects into paintings and sculptures that traversed American history and culture. His *New York Times* obituary ends with a thought the artist shared in an interview two years prior: "I . . . felt like I was dealing with two different worlds, one world of things that were tangible, and another world that was abstract and surreal. *I always thought the surreal was real to Black people*."[2]

The surreal as real, as something that *is* real, and especially to Black people. Why should that be?

Bailey is not the first or only Black artist to note this phenomenon. Jeff Donaldson expressed a similar sentiment five decades prior in his 1970 manifesto on the formation of the Black Arts Movement collective AFRICOBRA, or African Commune of Bad Relevant Artists. Explaining the qualities most important to the collective's work as Black image-makers focused explicitly on the physical, mental, and aesthetic liberation of Black people in the United States and abroad—"everywhere we are"—Donaldson references the "superreality that is our every day all day thang" and highlights the

need for "superreal images for SUPERREAL people."[3] For Donaldson and his peers, the superreal people who lived this unexceptional superreality were connected by shared history, lived experience, aesthetics, and beliefs.

Though the surreal is most often defined as something bizarre or dreamlike—i.e., distinct from reality, or even unreal—there is another, or additional, way to think of it. Literally, as per the prefix "sur," meaning over, above, beyond: over-real, above the real, beyond what is real. I am interested here in considering this expanded definition of the surreal, particularly as it pertains to Black women artists who came of age in the 1960s and '70s—a group whose relationship to reality (as defined by others, emphatically not themselves) had been historically strained, which is to say, they hadn't been thought to exist.

For a Black woman such as Barbara Chase-Riboud, born in 1939, her existence as an artist and as an individual has often been marked both by uniquely singular life experiences and by overcoming the doubt—if not outright dismissal—of others. Chase-Riboud is a fascinating and important figure for many reasons, chief among these her practice as a sculptor. But there is also the person, or the many versions of the person, herself. She is the youngest artist to have had work acquired by the Museum of Modern Art, a woodblock print when she was fifteen (fig. 2), and she was an extra in the Hollywood epic *Ben-Hur* (1959), playing, in her words, a "sexy slave girl in Technicolor."[4] She was the first Black woman to receive a master of fine arts from Yale University; the first American woman to be invited

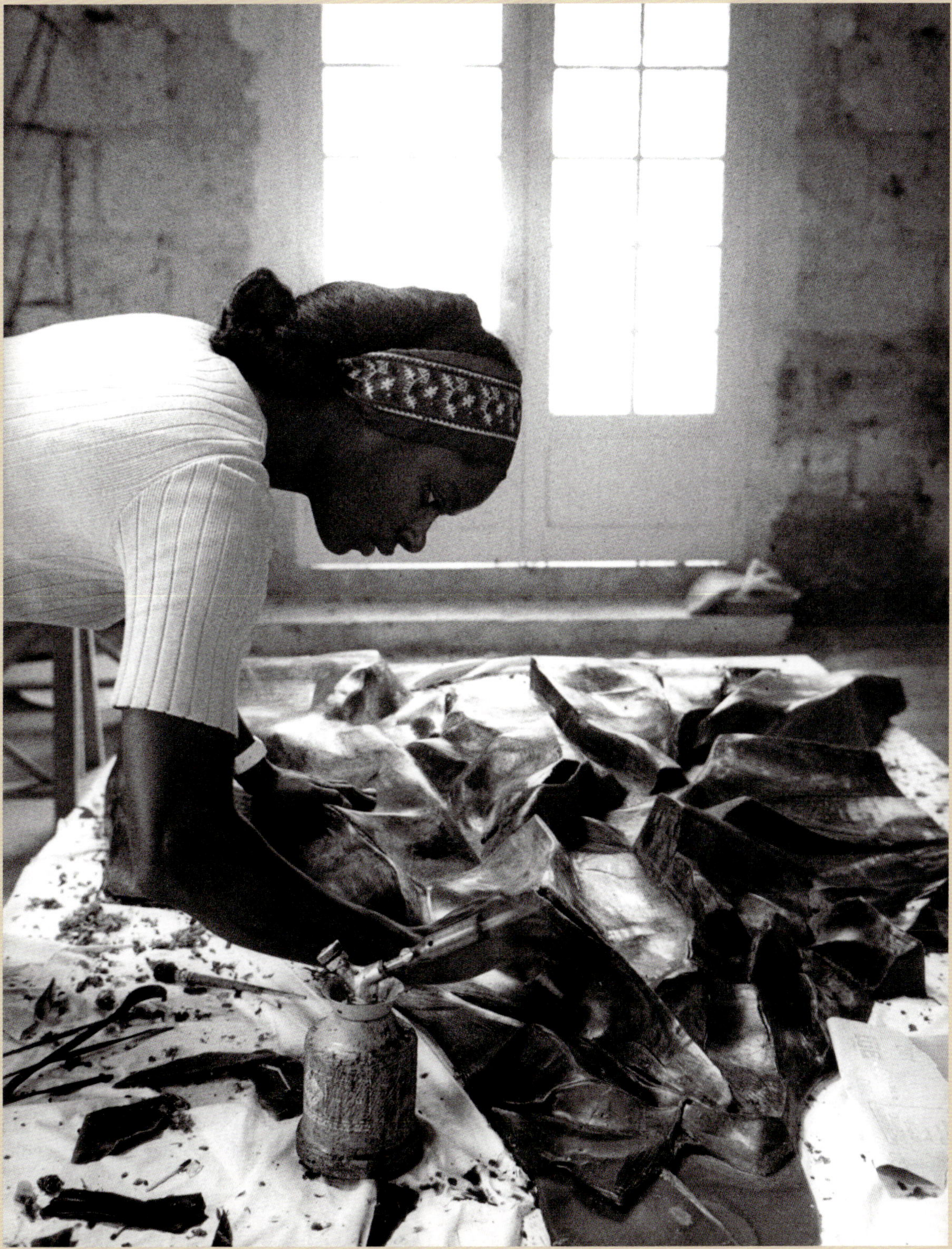

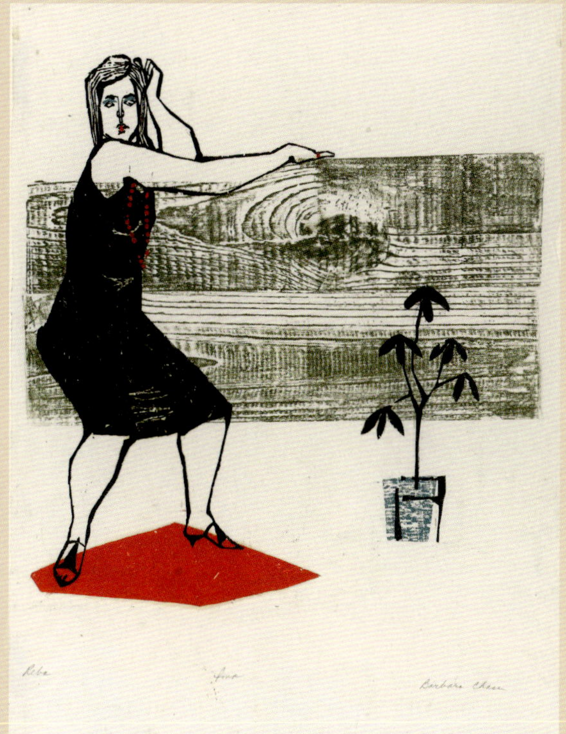

Fig. 2. Barbara Chase-Riboud, *Reba*, c. 1953–54. Woodcut, 23 7/16 × 17 3/8 in. (59.5 × 44.1 cm)

Fig. 1. Barbara Chase-Riboud in her studio, La Chenillère, France, 1969

to visit the People's Republic of China following the Cultural Revolution, traveling the breadth of the country alone in a train compartment, without a guide or interpreter, for seven days in 1965; and only the second American woman artist to have a one-person show at a major American museum (*Barbara Chase-Riboud*, Berkeley Art Museum, 1973).[5] Toni Morrison was her editor at Random House, which published her first book of poetry, *From Memphis & Peking*, in 1974, and it was at the encouragement of Morrison as well as Jacqueline Kennedy Onassis that she wrote the historical novel *Sally Hemings* (1979). At the time, the idea that Thomas Jefferson had taken an enslaved woman as his mistress and gone on to father at least six children with her over a period of nearly four decades was widely dismissed as preposterous—i.e., unreal—but today it has been accepted as historical fact, and the novel

has sold millions of copies worldwide in multiple languages.[6]

This abbreviated list of Chase-Riboud's accomplishments is just the tip of the iceberg, but it perhaps details exactly the sort of head-spinning, surreal—i.e., surpassing what was considered "real," or possible—life that the artist imagined for herself, a self-described "child prodigy and freak of nature, best-dressed, white-gloved, highly popular Black dream girl."[7] Born and raised in Philadelphia, Chase-Riboud was homeschooled for a period when she was eleven following a teacher's false allegation: she was accused of plagiarizing a poem that she herself had, in fact, written. Her mother and grandmother, explaining that they had seen her working on the poem at home, refused to allow her to apologize and insisted on an apology from the school instead. Of course, none was given, so they pulled her out of school.[8] Rather than see what is real and right in front of you—i.e., consider that, yes, this young Black girl might actually have written the poem—rather than listen to her family and admit fault and apologize, why not lean into fantasy instead, led by the illogic of racism? Surreal.

It seems as if every world-changing, paradigm-shifting Black woman artist has a story like this. Linda Goode Bryant, born in 1949 in Columbus, Ohio, was expelled in seventh grade for resisting a white principal who, every morning, greeted the students over the PA system by telling them that he worked in a "black boy's jungle" and that they, the (primarily Black) students, were all on welfare

329

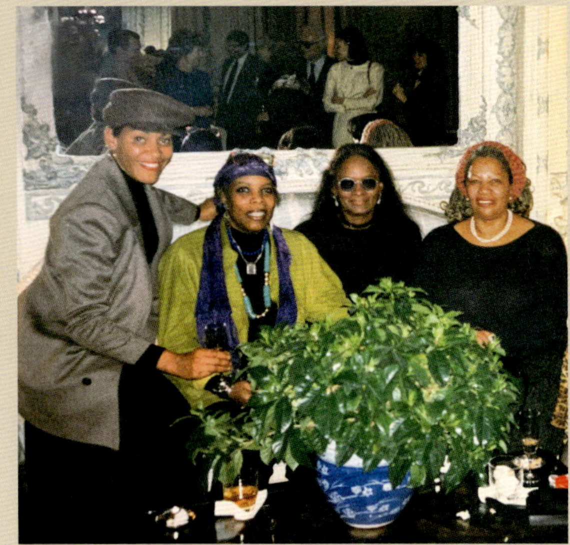

Fig. 3. Carrie Mae Weems, Mary Lovelace O'Neal, Barbara Chase-Riboud, and Toni Morrison, US Embassy, Paris, 1993

and would never amount to anything.[9] Bryant was put in detention daily for yelling back at the loudspeaker; this eventually culminated in her expulsion not just from her school but from all Columbus public schools. As with Chase-Riboud, her parents figured it out, taking out a mortgage on their home to pay for her tuition at a private school—one of precious few difficult options after their daughter was blacklisted from an entire city's public school system for having the temerity to refuse to listen to hate speech directed at children.[10]

What is the connection between these incidents, these refusals to engage with a system that will only allow you if you passively accept its version of so-called reality? Which is to say, for these particular Black girls and the artists they would become, to swallow the lies the system tells about Black people to you and to itself. On some

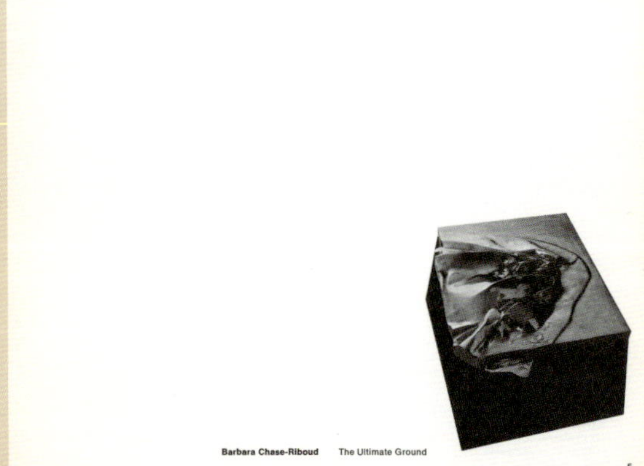

Fig. 4. Exhibition catalogue for the *1970 Annual Exhibition: Contemporary American Sculpture*, Whitney Museum of American Art, New York, 1970, with Barbara Chase-Riboud's *The Ultimate Ground* (c. 1969–70)

level, the only way to deal with an irrational belief system such as racism, a system rooted in both an over- and underestimation of what is real, is to behave irrationally yourself, to say and do unexpected things that may not make "sense" within the context of a world ordered by something as arbitrary and inherently meaningless as melanin. Understanding this, and acting accordingly, maybe that makes you "SUPERREAL." Perhaps this is part of what makes the surreal particularly *real* to Black people.

Having settled in Paris in the early 1960s, Chase-Riboud was physically removed from the protests and social unrest taking place in the United States at the time, in both the art world and American society at large. She did not attend 1963's March on Washington, as Linda Goode Bryant did at age thirteen. She was not part of the Black Arts Movement or organizations such as WAR (Women Artists in Revolution) or WSABAL (Women Students and Artists for Black Art Liberation, founded by Faith Ringgold and her daughter Michele Wallace), though she was a beneficiary of the groups' protests against institutional racism and the exclusion of Black women artists from museum exhibitions and collections.[11] She did, however, travel extensively throughout the non-Western, and nonwhite, world, visiting Egypt, Turkey, China, and India as political and social change swept through those nations, and everywhere. Her work of this period—large-scale sculptures made of metal and fiber—speaks both to the social issues of the moment and to deeper ideas of history and memory. *Confessions for Myself* (1972; p. 331), a monumental all-black sculpture made of bronze and wool, is among the works in which Chase-Riboud pushes most successfully beyond the natural and humanistic imagery that she had utilized prior into something she names "visually surrealistic."[12] However, describing this work, with its ropey, matte black, woolen "skirt" pooling below the sinews of gleaming bronze, painted black, she says: "There is an aura which remains. . . . These personages, even though they're abstract . . . you do have this feeling that [they] are spirits. You are looking at them, but they are looking at you."[13]

What is Chase-Riboud confessing? It isn't really for us to know: as the work's title makes pointedly clear, she is doing it for herself. The aura that she references is what we are left with. That, and the surreal feeling that the presumably unidirectional flow between observer and observed is being quietly destabilized, by the sculpture and, thus, by the artist. In a world in which Black people are both over- and under-seen, perceived as both too much and not enough—superreal—this work stands as a sentinel. It obscures what is not to be consumed, what is not for anyone but the self;

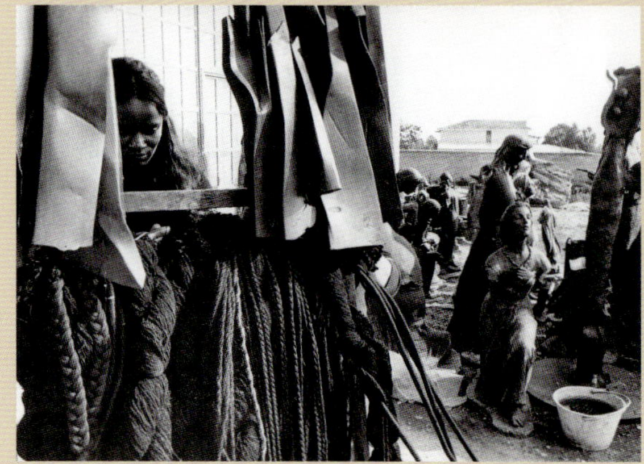

Fig. 5. Barbara Chase-Riboud, Fonderia Bonvicini, Verona, Italy, 1972, with *Confessions for Myself* (1972)

it protects that which would otherwise be trammeled. Photographed working on the sculpture at her foundry in Verona in 1972 (fig. 5), Chase-Riboud appears fully herself: self-possessed and intent, deeply absorbed in the task at hand. It feels as though nothing, and no one, could shake her focus. In the absence of a world where Black people's individuality, inherent worthiness, and interiority are assumed, she makes a place for herself and for those like her, who would also presume to walk through the front door of history.

NOTES

1   Barbara Chase-Riboud, "La Chenillère" [1973], as quoted in Chase-Riboud, *I Always Knew: A Memoir* (Princeton, NJ: Princeton University Press, 2022), 277. "Chloe" is Chloe Wofford, aka Toni Morrison. In August 1973, the two women and their children spent three weeks together at La Chenillère, Chase-Riboud's country home in the Loire Valley, editing the artist's first book of poetry, *From Memphis & Peking*. As the title for the current text, I have taken as inspiration a comment Chase-Riboud made about her motivation for writing a historical novel about Sally Hemings, explaining that she wanted to "walk Sally Hemings through the front door of history." Chase-Riboud, *I Always Knew*, 266.
2   Alex Williams, "Radcliffe Bailey, Artist Who Explored Black Migration, Dies at 54," *New York Times*, Nov. 20, 2023. Emphasis mine.
3   Jeff Donaldson, "10 in Search of a Nation," *Black World*, October 1970; reprinted in Catherine Morris and Rujeko Hockley, eds., *We Wanted a Revolution: Black Radical Women, 1965–85: A Sourcebook* (New York: Brooklyn Museum, 2018), 58.
4   Chase-Riboud, *I Always Knew*, 43.
5   On the artist's travels to China, see Barbara Chase-Riboud, oral history interview, June 7–11, 2019. Archives of American Art, Smithsonian Institution, Washington, DC. *Confessions for Myself* (1972) was commissioned for the Berkeley exhibition. See Chase-Riboud, *I Always Knew*, 265.
6   Chase-Riboud, oral history interview, June 7–11, 2019.
7   Chase-Riboud, *I Always Knew*, 2.
8   Chase-Riboud, oral history interview, June 7–11, 2019.
9   "An Oral History with Linda Goode Bryant by Rujeko Hockley," *BOMB*, April 11, 2019: https://bombmagazine.org/articles/2019/04/11/linda-goode-bryant/.
10   Ibid.
11   Such protests resulted in Chase-Riboud and Betye Saar becoming the first Black women artists to exhibit at the Whitney Museum of American Art; both were included in the museum's *1970 Annual Exhibition: Contemporary American Sculpture*. Chase-Riboud's sculpture *Ultimate Ground* (c. 1969–70) was among the first works illustrated in the exhibition catalogue.
12   "Barbara Chase-Riboud: The Malcolm X Steles," Feb. 28, 2014, Berkeley Art Museum and Pacific Film Archive, video, 02:38, https://www.youtube.com/watch?v=YiXTn1UfM9U.
13   Ibid., 04:27.

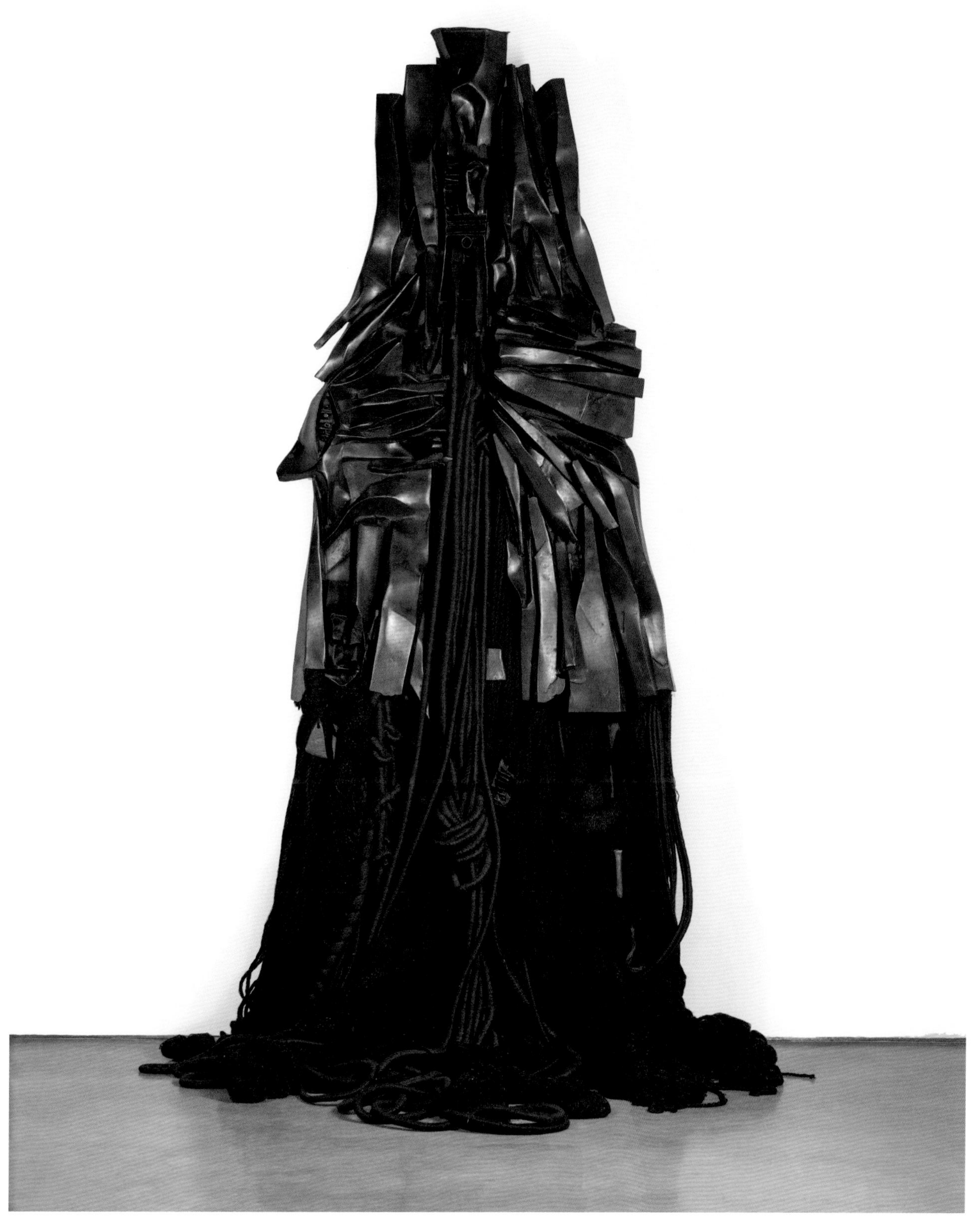

Barbara Chase-Riboud, *Confessions for Myself*, 1972. Bronze, paint, and wool, 120 × 40 × 12 in. (304.8 × 101.6 × 30.5 cm).
University of California, Berkeley Art Museum and Pacific Film Archive; purchased with funds from the H. W. Anderson Charitable Foundation

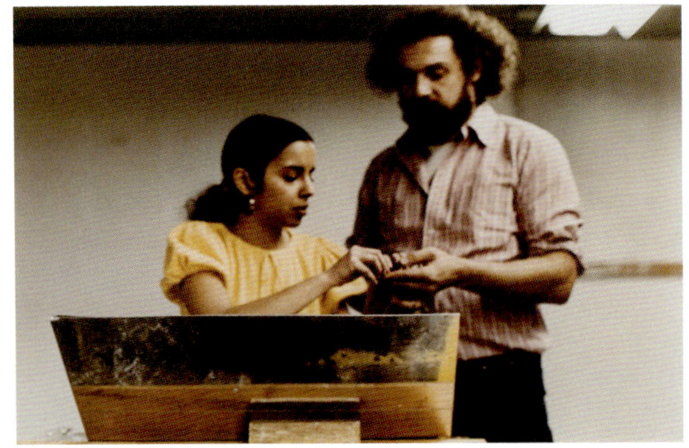
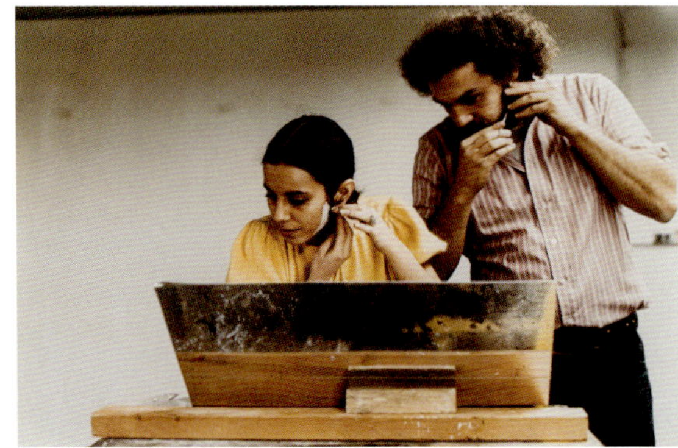
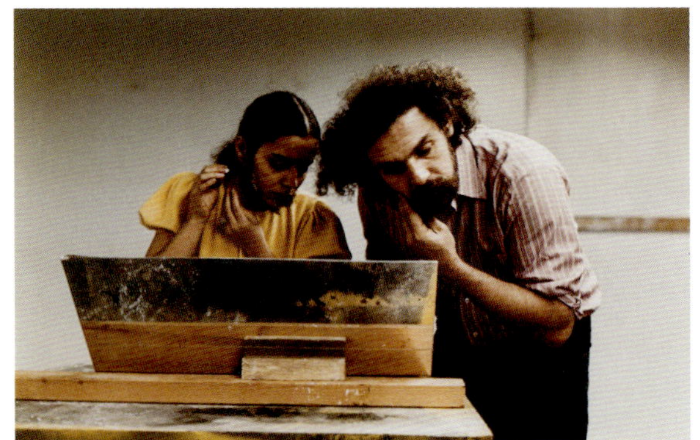
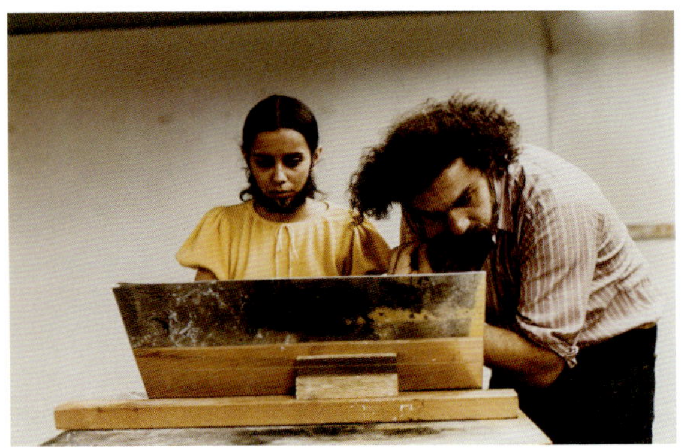
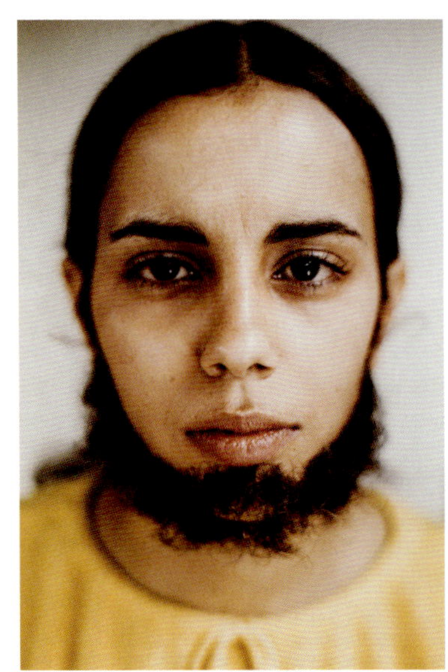
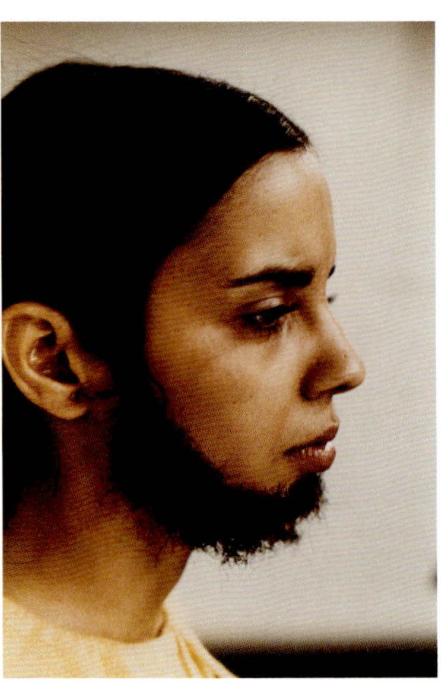
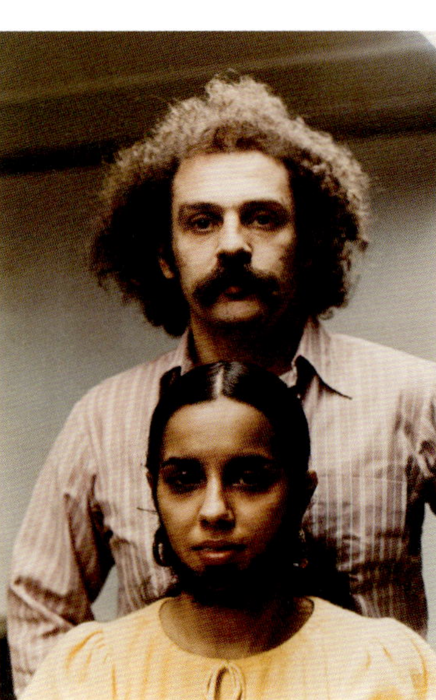

Ana Mendieta, *Untitled (Facial Hair Transplants)*, 1972. Set of seven color photographs, dimensions variable. The Estate of Ana Mendieta Collection, LLC

of democracy around the world, and it will travel to Romania, West Germany, England, Yugoslavia, and Turkey. Cannon's and Scholder's works are used by USIA in an attempt to acknowledge historical oppression of Native Americans and, more significantly, to highlight the government's progress in redressing those injustices. Scholder will recall not realizing the way that his own image and his art were being exploited until he arrived for the opening events in Bucharest, Romania, and saw images of himself and his students at the Institute of American Indian Arts in glossy coffee-table books at the ambassador's home.

———

April 25–May 12, 1972 • Curated by Clayton Bailey, the group exhibition *Nut Art* is on view at California State University's art gallery on the Hayward campus, featuring artists including Robert Arneson, Roy De Forest, Peter Saul, and Franklin Williams. The phrase *nut art* is the moniker adopted by a loose group of artists who prefer it over the more common term *funk*, the idea being that these artists are involved in creating what De Forest describes as "a miniature world into which the nut could retire with all his friends, animals, and paraphernalia. The little world becomes a 'completely fitted out' phantasmagoria."

———

May 1972 • Ana Mendieta submits her thesis for her first master of arts degree at the University of Iowa. The work consists of three photographs of herself titled *Self-Portraits*: one with a mustache, one with a beard, and one of her face unadorned. A related work, *Untitled (Facial Hair Transplants)*, sets up themes and strategies of ritual and transformation as well as performance and documentation that Mendieta will develop further over her career.

In her thesis statement, Mendieta provides a historical and cultural context for her work:

In 1919, Marcel Duchamp drew a mustache and a beard to a color reproduction of the Mona Lisa. He stated: "The curious thing about that moustache and goatee is that when you look at it the Mona Lisa becomes a man. It is not a woman disguised as a man. It is a real man, and that was my discovery, without realizing it at the time."

As an extension of Duchamp's piece, I asked my friend Morty Sklar to cut his beard off and give me the hairs. I attached the hairs on my face in the same place where he had cut them off his face. [. . .]

After looking at myself in a mirror, the beard became real. It did not look like a disguise. It

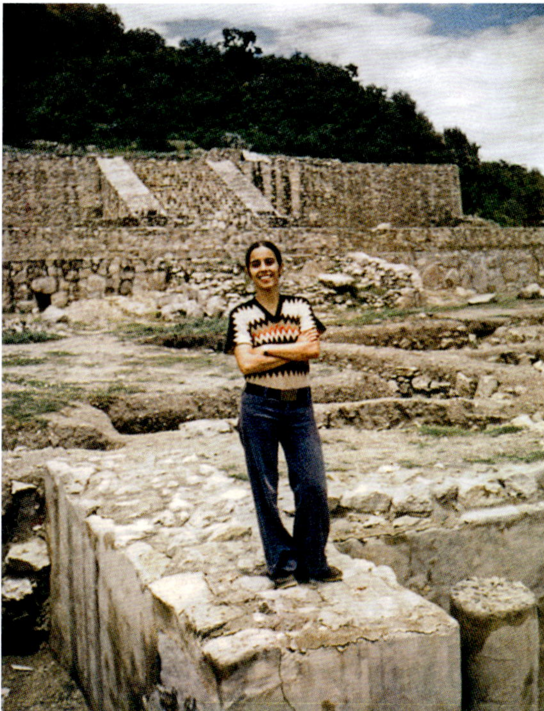

Ana Mendieta at Calixtlahuaca, Toluca, Mexico, 1971

became a part of myself and not at all unnatural to my appearance.

In a year the artist will later characterize as a turning point, Mendieta also begins making earth/body works. The turn to embedding her own figure in the landscape is inspired by a constellation of experiences: her first trip to Mexico, in summer 1971; her performance with Robert Wilson in 1970; a movement class with Elaine Summers; and her participation in the University of Iowa's Center

for the New Performing Arts, which had been co-founded by Hans Breder to host contemporary artists to discuss video, performance, body, and kinetic art. Mendieta will make six more summer trips to Mexico through the rest of the decade, where she will produce much of the art for which she will become best known.

———

May 13–June 26, 1972 • *Chicago Imagist Art* is on view at the Museum of Contemporary Art Chicago. It is the first of two exhibitions this year to codify the effluence of activity centered around the Hyde Park Art Center, the second being *What They're Up to in Chicago* at the National Gallery of Canada, Ottawa (December 1, 1972–November 16, 1973). These two shows survey the artists that Don Baum and Whitney Halstead have long championed, among them Roger Brown, Art Green, Jim Nutt, Christina Ramberg, Suellen Rocca, Barbara Rossi, and Karl Wirsum.

———

June 14–July 16, 1972 • The Whitney Museum of American Art hosts *Don Potts: My First Car*. For Potts, his car sculptures represent a melding of human consciousness with machine form, "not a public object," the exhibition catalogue states, "but a way to probe more deeply into himself, to stress his ego and capacities as a builder to the utmost, to seek a higher, more refined level of consciousness with a massive, almost endless project." In his own rare statement, Potts says:

When I do Art, I put my mind on the floor in whatever form it may be. With my senses

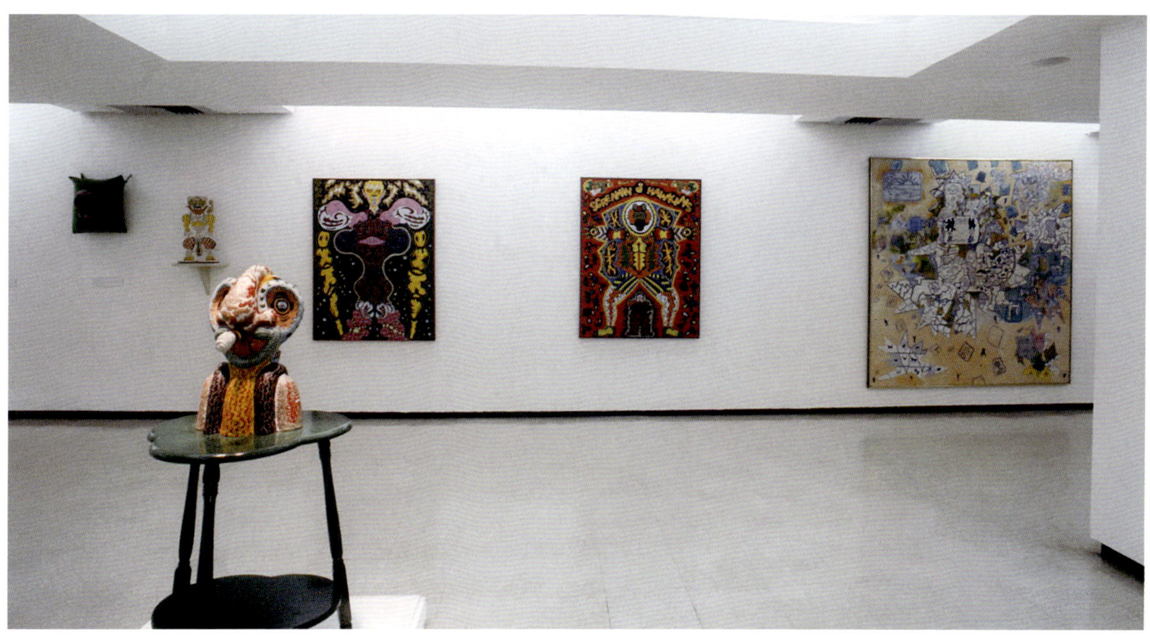

Chicago Imagist Art, Museum of Contemporary Art Chicago, 1972

I sort out this mind. When this is finished, the mind returns to the place in which it has never left. What is left lying on the floor is a byproduct of the evolution of my mind which could be called an expression of my evolution, or art. Art is the most beautiful of all man's products because it expresses the creative intelligence of man, which is the key to greater happiness and bliss. For the artist his art is his most beloved possession because it vibrates the essence of his montra [*sic*]. Only when the artist has evolved to a point where the whole cosmos becomes his montra [*sic*] will it be easy for him to give up his work.

———

September 12–October 17, 1972 • Hannah Wilke's first New York solo exhibition is on view at Ronald Feldman Fine Arts. Wilke presents her latex sculptures for the first time, returning to a material she had experimented with as an undergraduate and extending her investigation of female

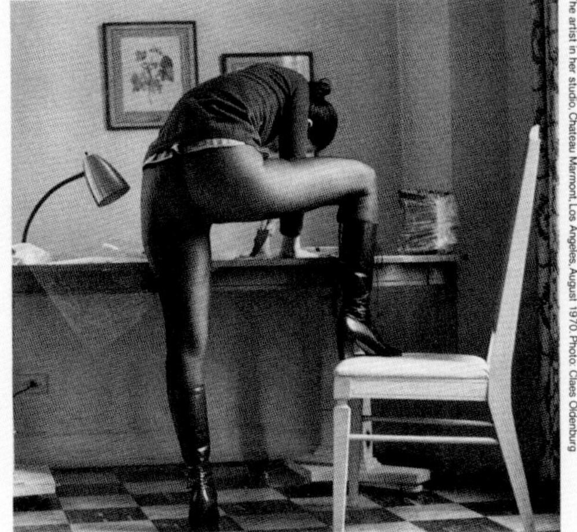

Advertisement by Hannah Wilke for *Hannah Wilke*, Ronald Feldman Fine Arts, New York, 1972, with *The Artist in Her Studio at the Chateau Marmont, Los Angeles* (1970)

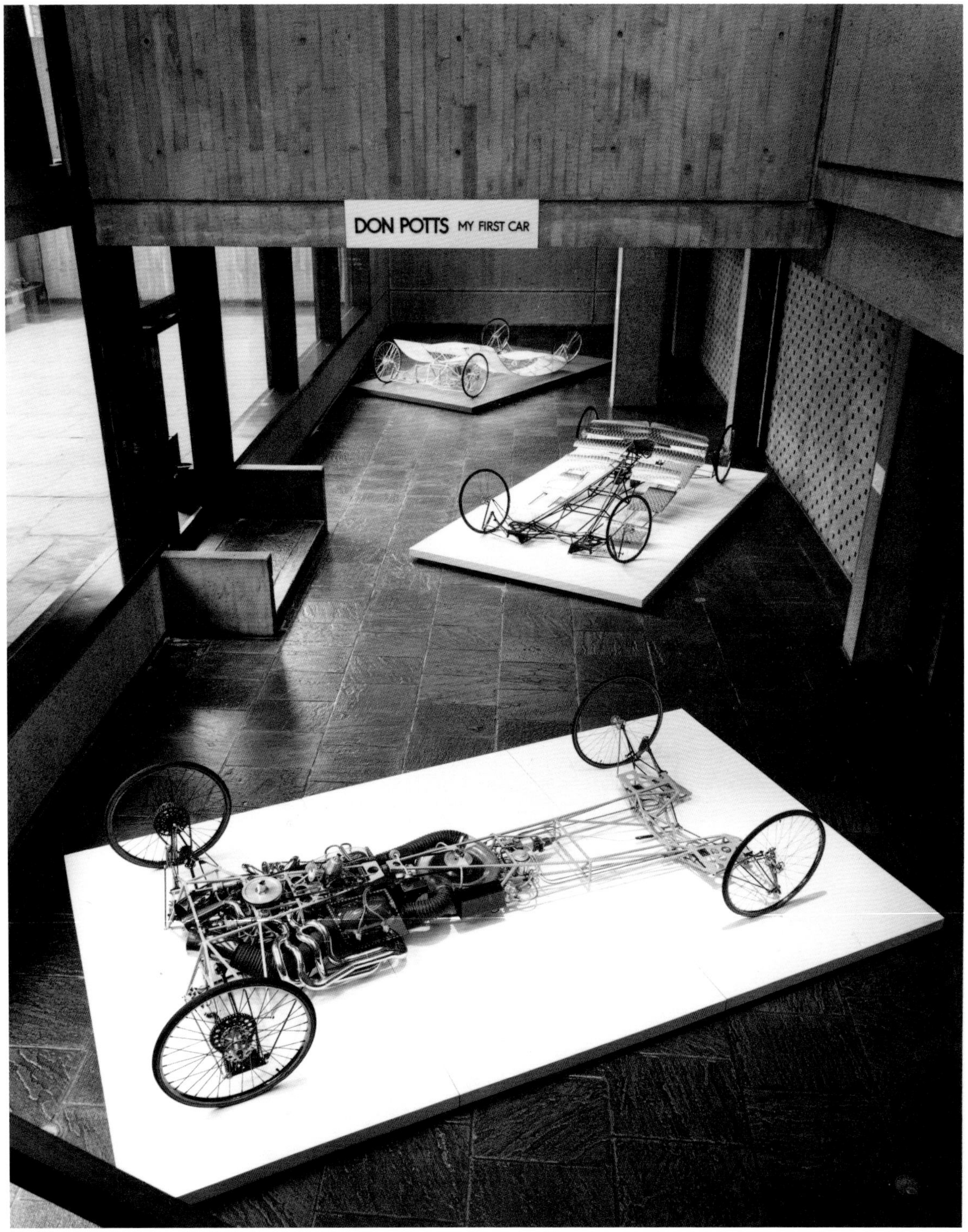

imagery. From dried but malleable pours of latex, the artist assembles layered structures, snapping the pieces together and hanging them on the wall, displaying them alongside her ceramic boxes and works on paper. Her show is well reviewed by critics in major art publications. In *Artforum*, April Kingsley emphasizes the erotic, "sensualist approach" the artist has taken to the sculptures: "The submissive sagging of Wilke's material, its natural liplike ruffling, and the unavoidability of vulvic connotations conjoin to create an almost mesmerizing state of sexual-visceral vulnerability. It is very honest work." This same year, Wilke begins teaching sculpture and ceramics at the School of Visual Arts, New York, where she will work for almost twenty years.

———

October 1–November 12, 1972 • After making photographs while traveling through Senegal, Ming Smith (b. 1947) shows her work for the first time in a Kamoinge Workshop group exhibition at the Studio Museum in Harlem. Adger Cowans and Shawn Walker also contribute work to the show. On the occasion of the exhibition, in a history of the workshop published in the December issue of the James Van Der Zee Institute of Photography's newsletter, Louis C. Draper writes: "It is our endeavor to produce significant visual images of our time. In the area of human relationships, political and social interactions and the spiritual world of pure imagery, the needs are basically the same: that being the establishment of contact with self is key, the source point from which all messages flow. We speak of our lives as only we can."

Born in Detroit, Michigan, and raised in Columbus, Ohio, Smith had come of age during

Don Potts: My First Car, Whitney Museum of American Art, New York, 1972

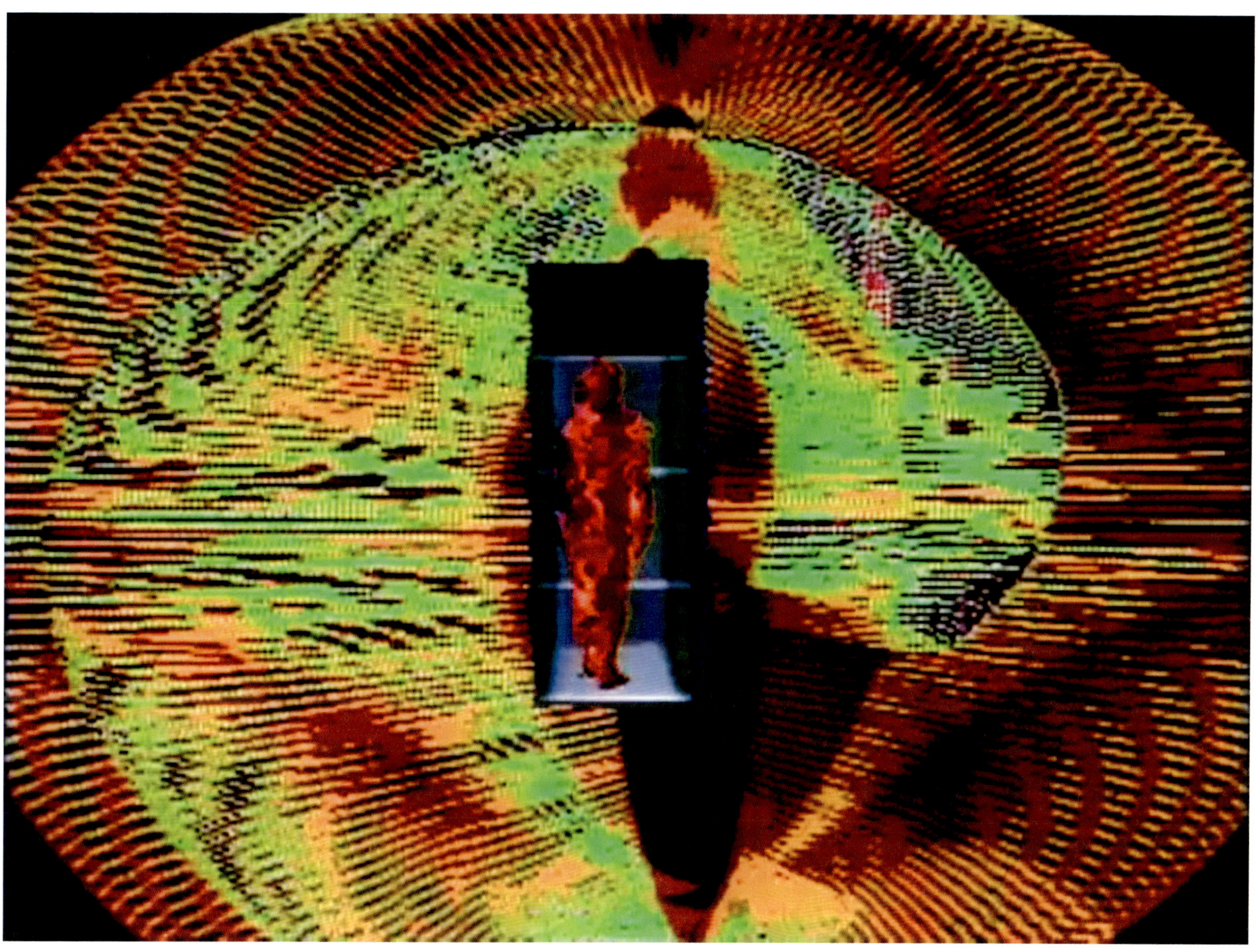

Ed Emshwiller, *Scape-mates*, 1972. Video, color, sound; 28:16 min. Electronic Arts Intermix, New York

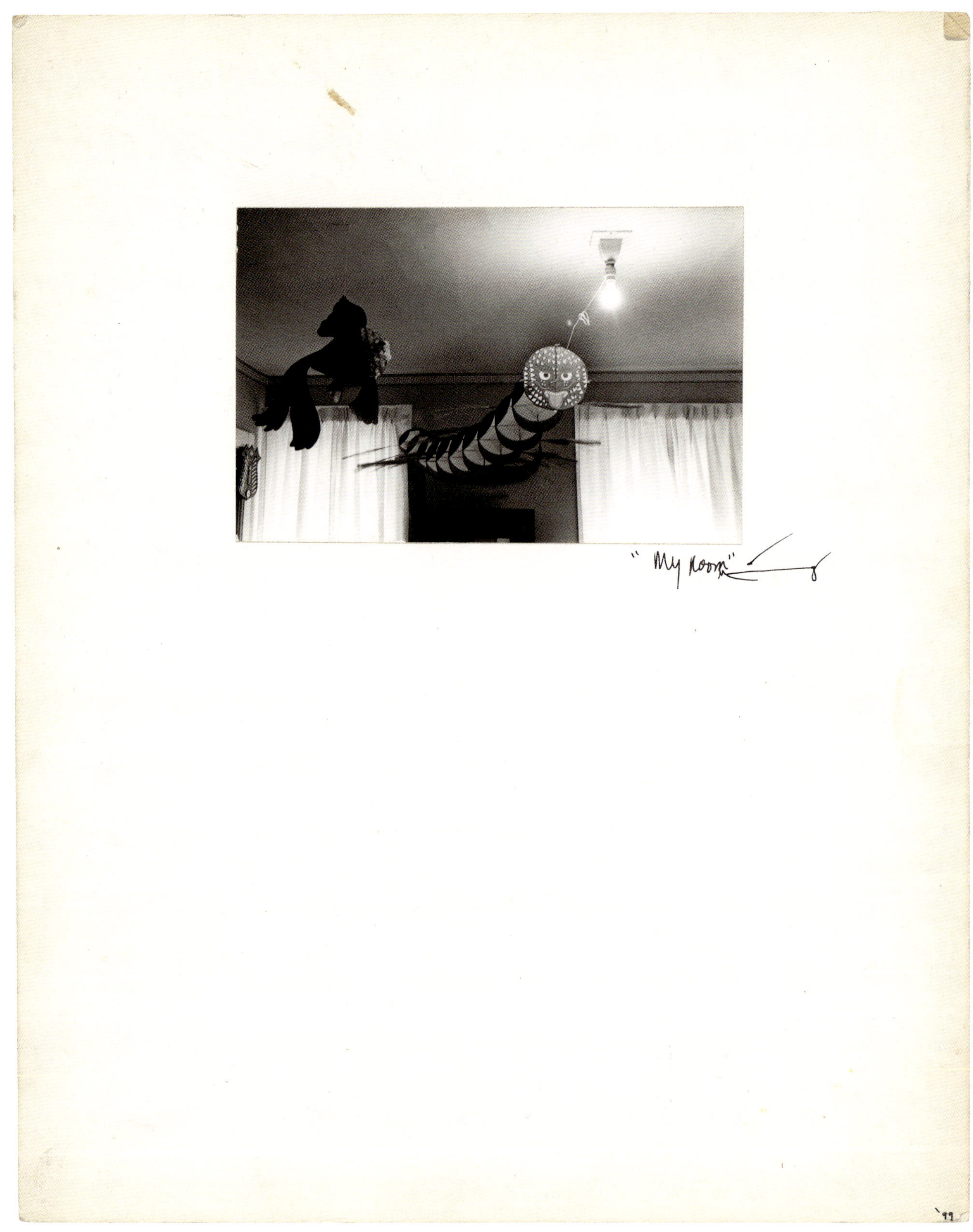

Ming Smith, *Kites Inside, Columbus, Ohio*, c. 1972. Gelatin silver print: mount, 14 × 11 in. (35.6 × 27.9 cm); image: 3 ⅞ × 5 ⅞ in. (9.8 × 14.8 cm). Whitney Museum of American Art, New York; purchase, with funds from the Anne Levy Fund 2017.194

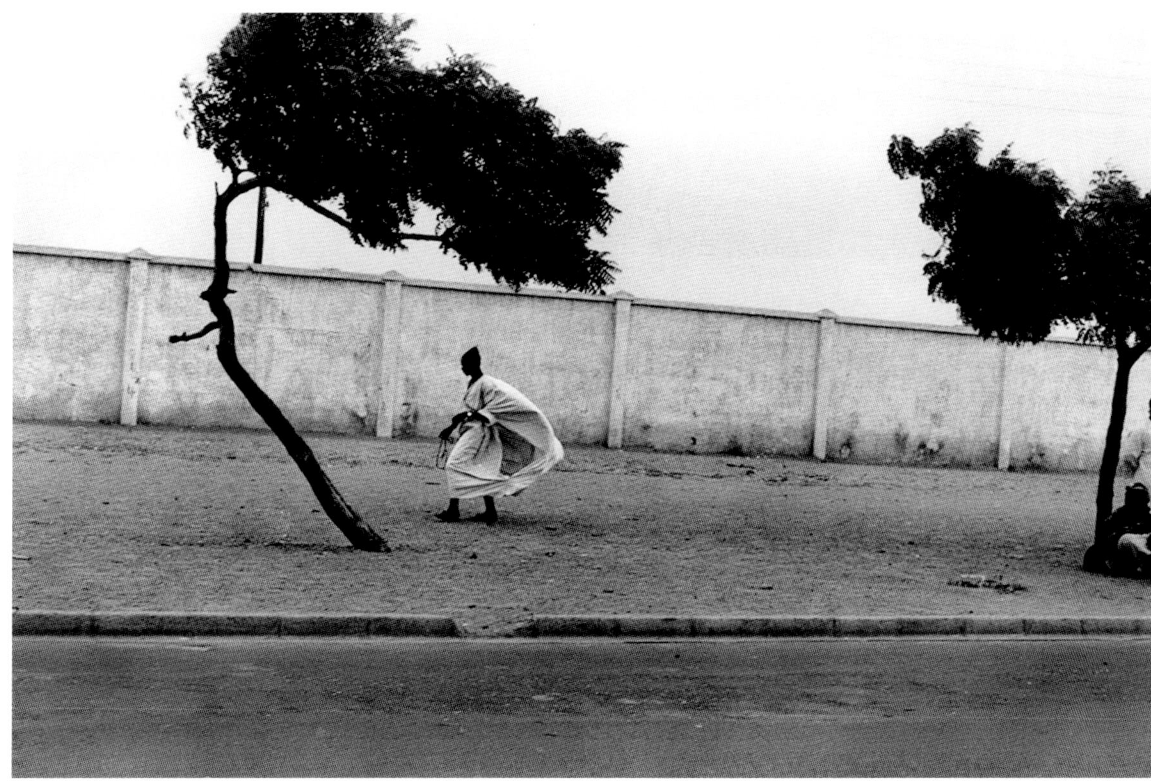

Ming Smith, *Dakar Roadside with Figures (Senegal)*, 1972. Archival pigment print, 24 ⁵⁄₁₆ × 36 in. (61.7 × 91.4 cm)

the civil rights era and the Black Power movement. She will graduate from Howard University with a degree in microbiology in 1973 and will go on to build a successful modeling career in New York, working alongside other prominent Black models of the moment, such as Grace Jones and Toukie Smith, to break down the industry's obstinate color barrier. At the same time, Smith will develop a photographic practice and artistic vision of her own, becoming the first woman to officially join the Kamoinge Workshop, in 1975, and the first Black woman photographer to have her work acquired by the Museum of Modern Art, New York (MoMA) after submitting her portfolio through an open call. *Christmas Constellation, Brussels, Belgium* (1978) and *David Murray in the Wings, Padova, Italy* (1978) enter the museum's collection in 1979; MoMA will later acquire more of Smith's photographs from the 1970s as well as works from the 1990s.

Smith's dreamlike photographs depict Black life at its most lyrical, abundant, and tender, frequently employing a range of in-camera effects and post-production techniques to achieve atmospheric blurs and a vaporous, otherworldly sense of dimensionality. She focuses on a range of subjects in moments of everyday life. Her photographs of literary and musical icons like James Baldwin, Nina Simone, and Sun Ra as well as of anonymous city dwellers express the dignity of both local and global Black communities and offer visions for its future.

November 8–26, 1972 • Lynn Hershman Leeson's exhibition *Completed Fragments* is on view at the art museum at the University of California,

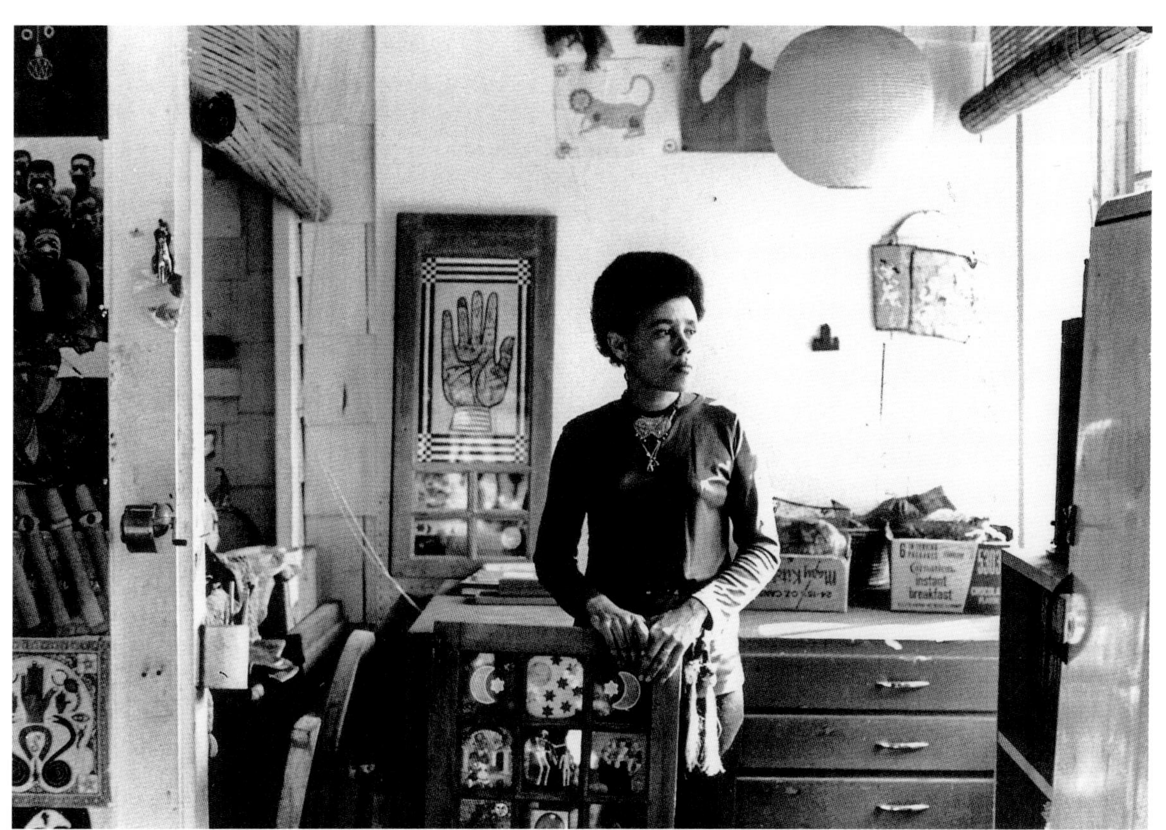

Betye Saar in her studio, Los Angeles, 1970, with *View from the Palmist Window* (1966) and *Black Girl's Window* (1969)

Berkeley, four months after *Lynn Lester Hershman: Mouths and Other Pieces* had opened at the de Saisset Museum at Santa Clara University. This same year she earns a master's degree from San Francisco State College, focusing on art criticism, a skill she will hone as she embarks on her exploration of identity with her fictional character Roberta Breitmore.

December 15, 1972–January 15, 1973 • Betye Saar's solo show *Black Girl's Window* is on view at Berkeley Art Center. The exhibition demonstrates her continued and growing interest in the assemblage of objects as a way of creating an iconography that alludes to her own biography and ancestry, as well as her fascination with astrology. Lending its title to the show, the pointedly autobiographical work *Black Girl's Window* (1969) is included.

1972 • Louise Bourgeois joins Lucy Lippard, Faith Ringgold, and Nancy Spero as a member of the Ad Hoc Committee of Women Artists, which had been founded in 1970 as a consortium of women's groups to protest the lack of representation of female artists in Whitney Annuals. In the spring, Judy Chicago discusses Bourgeois's "biomorphic" sculpture at Cornell University's Festival of Women in the Arts. The following year Bourgeois and Chicago will show their work alongside Judith

Bernstein, Kiki Kogelnik, and Anita Steckel in *Witticisms by Women* at the Erotic Art Gallery, New York. To the exhibition Bourgeois contributes *Cumul* (1969), part of a series praised by William Rubin in 1969, and *Trani Episode* (1971), a soft plaster-and-latex sculpture consisting of two interlocking, breast-like shapes. Maryse Holder covers the show in the feminist magazine *off our backs*, discussing not only Bourgeois's pieces but also the work of Diane Arbus, Martha Edelheit, and Niki de Saint Phalle, writing: "The sexualist work I saw (and some related 'organic' work) struck me as being art that women, as a group, were for the first time not copying from men. A record of female experience, it offered a completely different view of reality. And it was imaginative, often brilliant work about an area of human experience that had not been dealt with before, or even now, by men. 'Sexualism,' then, to use a more accurate term than 'Eroticism,' is exciting. It is new and it is a movement."

December 16, 1972 • Shigeko Kubota participates in the first of three "multimedia concerts" organized by the video-art collective Red, White, Yellow, and Black, which also includes Mary Lucier, Cecilia Sandoval, and Charlotte Warren-Huey. The collective's colorful name references each member's race and is also a winking allusion to the American flag. Taking place at The Kitchen in New York, a space that had hosted early

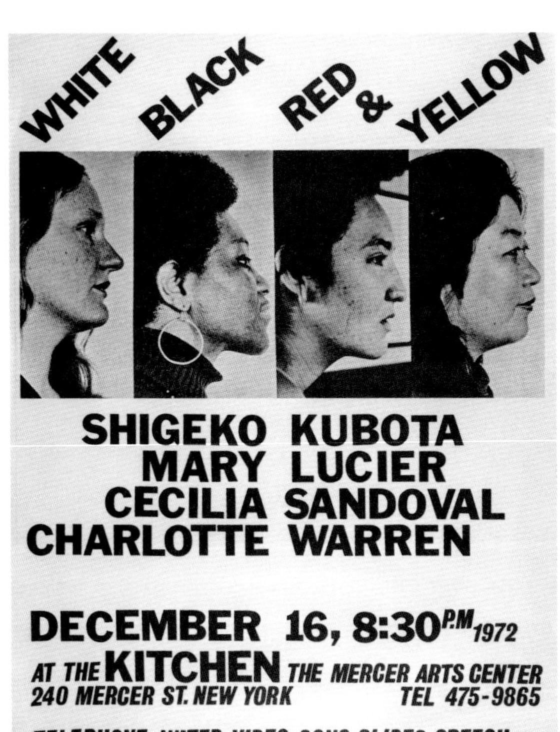

Poster for one of Red, White, Yellow, and Black's multimedia concerts, The Kitchen, New York, 1972

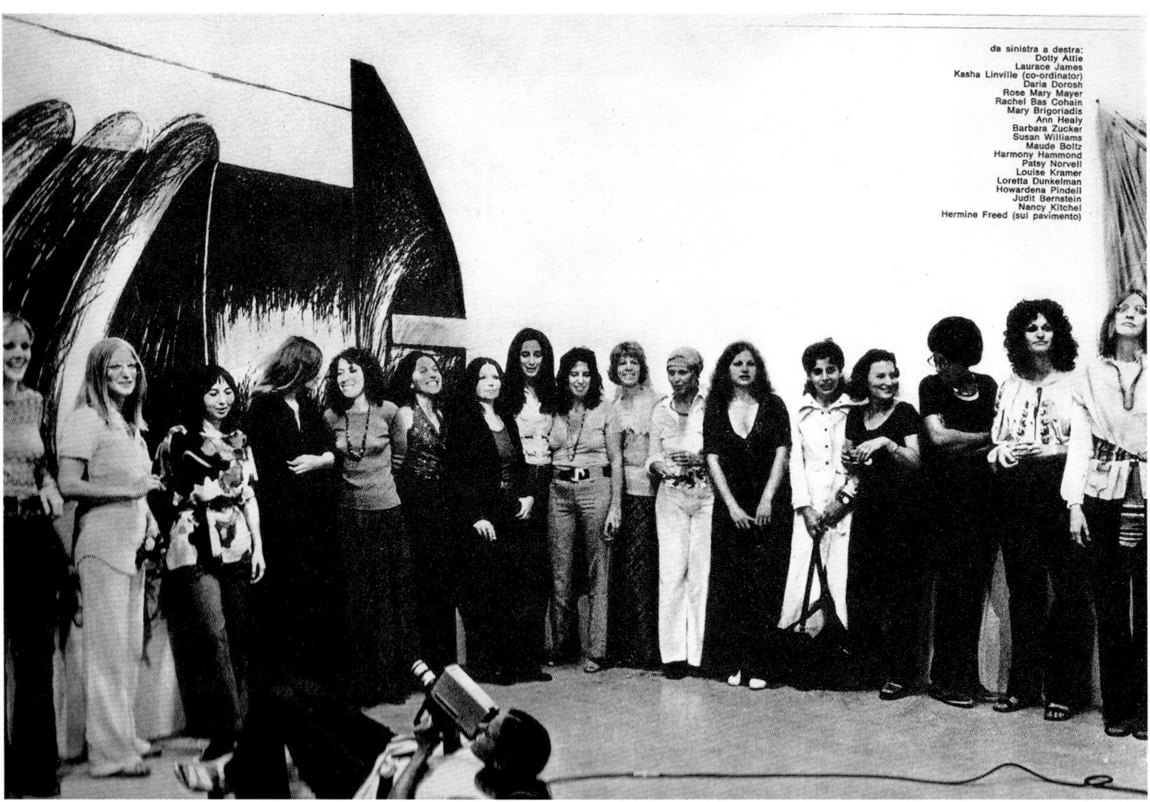

Seventeen of the founding artists of Artists in Residence, Inc. (A.I.R.) in front of Judith Bernstein's *Hardware* (1972), A.I.R. Gallery, New York, 1972

Women's Video Festivals that featured Kubota, each concert is designed to synchronize the women's individual artistic projects rather than synthesize them into a single collaborative identity. In this first concert, Kubota's pioneering multi-channel video installation *Riverrun—Video Water Poem* (1972) serves as a sort of set for presentations by Lucier and Warren-Huey, while Sandoval performs by telephone from the Navajo Nation. *Riverrun* is the first piece in which Kubota incorporates both footage of running water and actual liquid in a sculptural element, marking a debut of a motif that will persist throughout her oeuvre.

December 19, 1972–February 18, 1973 • Bruce Nauman's first museum retrospective, *Work from 1965 to 1972*, organized by the Los Angeles County Museum of Art (LACMA) and the Whitney Museum of American Art, New York, is on view at LACMA. It will travel to the Whitney Museum in March.

December 30, 1972–January 10, 1973 • *Open A.I.R.: A.I.R. Members Invite 20 Women Artists* is the first group exhibition by Artists in Residence, Inc. (A.I.R.) and is on view at A.I.R. Gallery in SoHo. Founded six months earlier by Susan Williams and Barbara Zucker with a committee of eighteen other women artists, including Judith Bernstein, Howardena Pindell, and Nancy Spero, A.I.R. is the first not-for-profit artist-led cooperative gallery for women artists in the United States. Bernstein shows her monumental charcoal drawing *Hardware* (1972), an early example of her series of large-scale drawings that includes graphic hybridizations that blur the penis with industrial and mechanical details. Other exhibiting members include Pindell, Spero, Williams, and Zucker as well as Agnes Denes, Harmony Hammond, and Rosemary Mayer.

The following March, Spero's *Codex Artaud* (1971–72) will be among A.I.R. Galley's first solo exhibitions. The thirty-four scrolls of gouache and collage are inspired by the work of Antonin Artaud and are a continuation of Spero's engagement with the Surrealist writer's work that began with a series of collages she made while living in Paris. As Spero will later explain, "I went to Artaud because I wanted a vehicle to show my anger, and he was the angriest poet there was." Her fixation on phallic tongues that allude to her experience of being silenced are echoed in Artaud's texts, most notably in lines such as "I cut off my tongue" or "the obscene phallic weight of a praying tongue." Like several of his peers in Surrealist circles, however, Artaud reveals his well-documented misogyny in other writings. Nevertheless, Spero finds in his unbridled rage an unlikely kindred spirit for the feminist art movement.

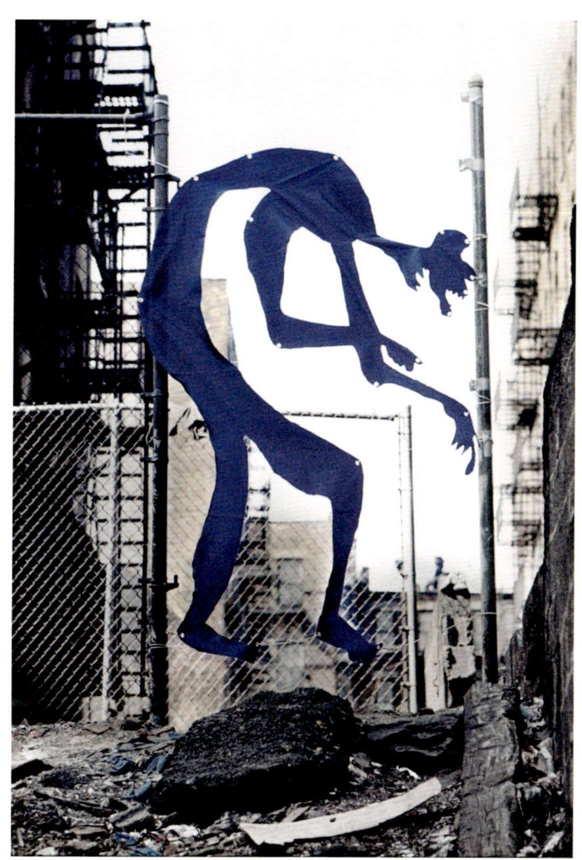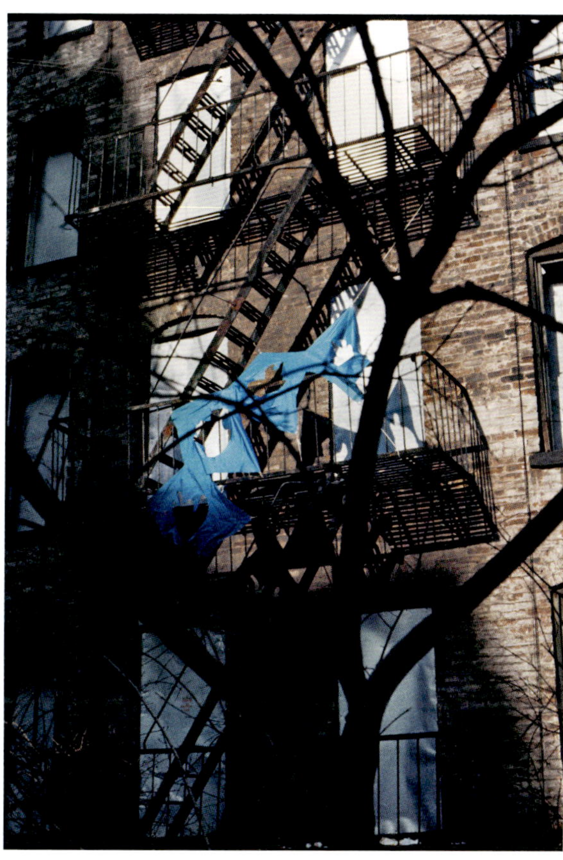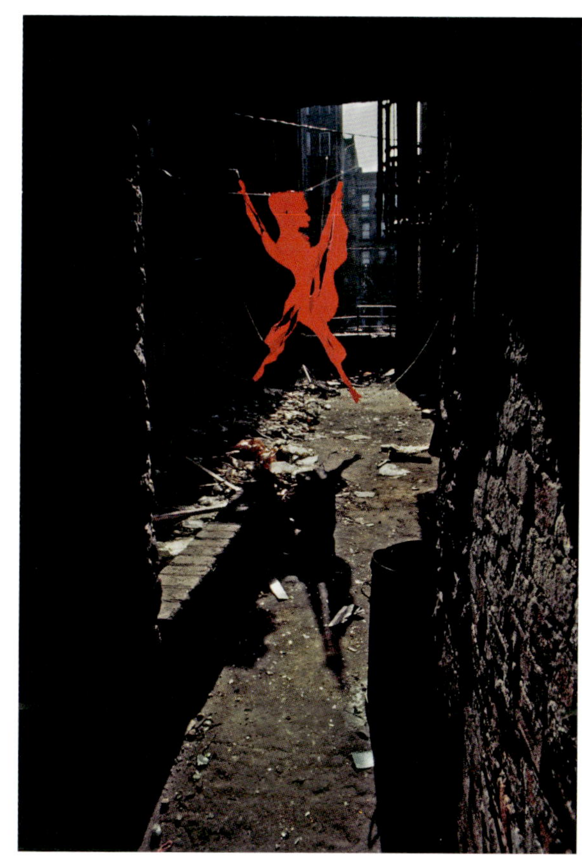

Senga Nengudi, *Down (Purple), Drifting Leaves, Red Devil (soul 2),* 1972. Three Cibachrome prints, 28 × 41 ½ in. (70.8 × 105.4 cm) overall. Amistad Research Center Collection, New Orleans, LA

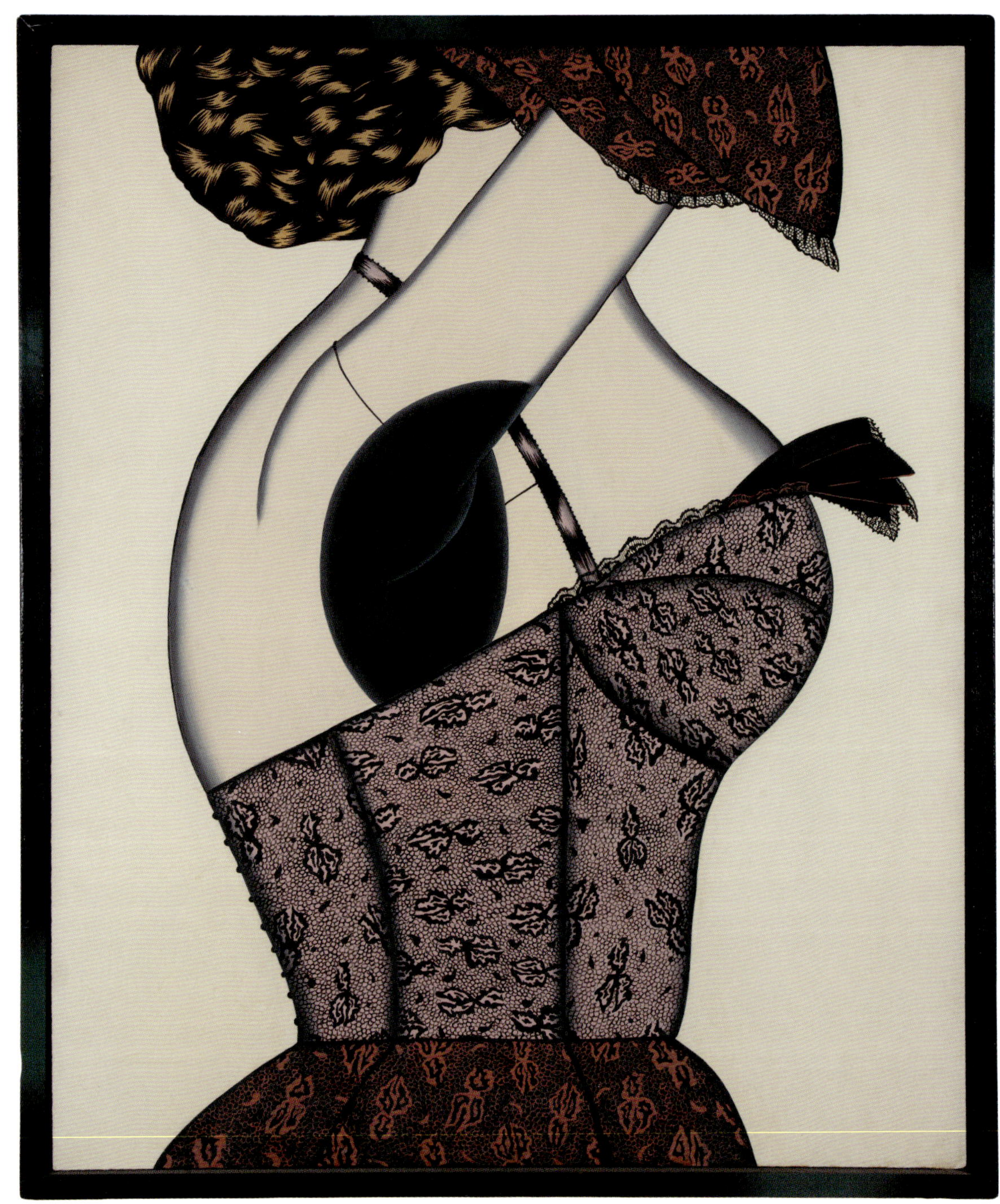

Christina Ramberg, *Shadow Panel*, 1972. Acrylic, wood, and glass, 23 × 19 in. (58.4 × 48.3 cm). Collection of Beth Rudin DeWoody

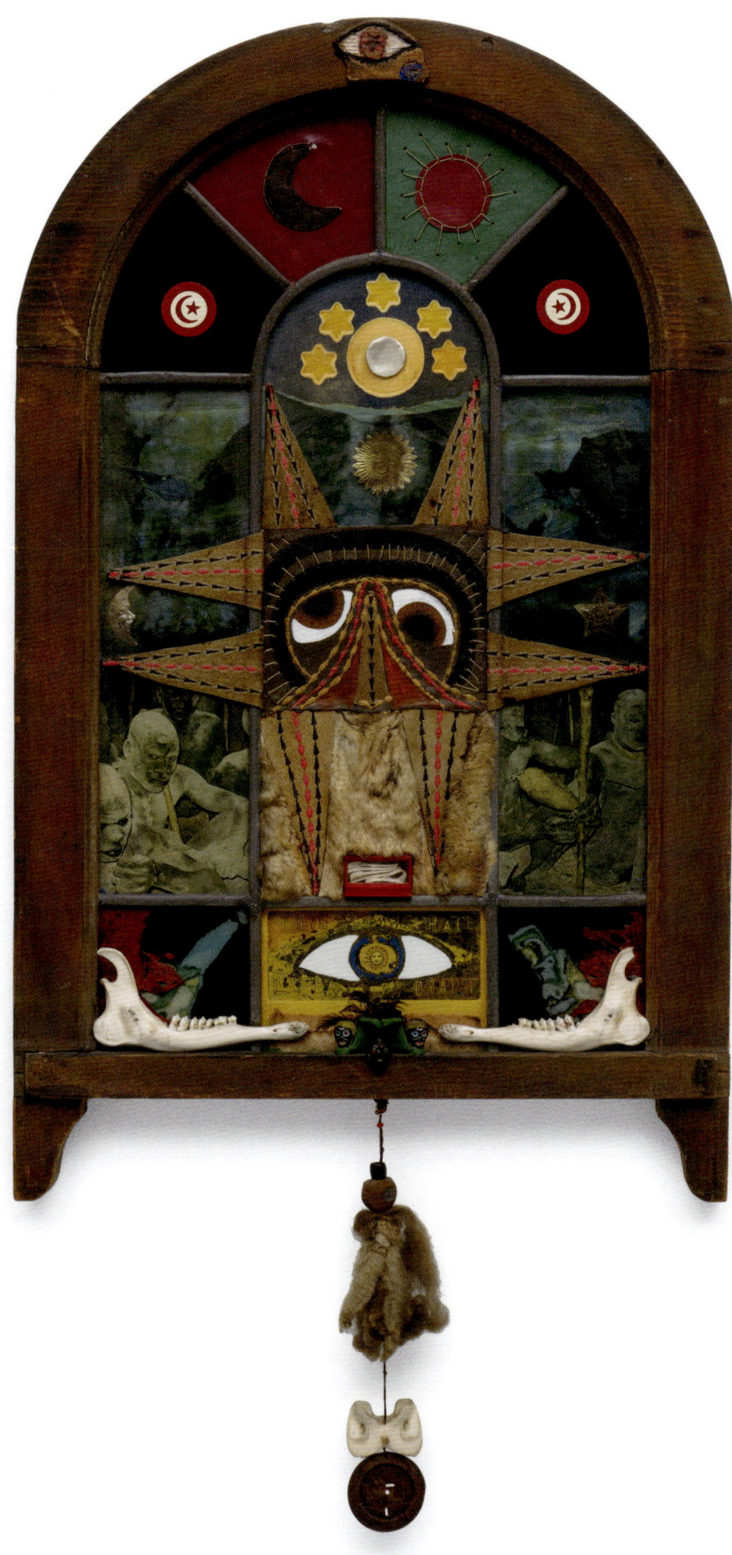

Betye Saar, *Ten Mojo Secrets*, 1972. Leather, fur, yarn, fabric, printed paper, photographs, acrylic paint, plastic bones, poker chips, and chutney-tin lid, 40 × 20 × 2 in. (101.6 × 50.8 × 5.1 cm). Collection of Kyle Kepcke

CITATIONS

p. 2 "honest, though somewhat uneven": Jules Langsner, "Art News from Los Angeles," *ARTnews*, March 1958.

p. 2 "a sudden esthetic": Michael McClure quoted in Constance Lewallen, "Mountain Climbing," in *Jay DeFeo: Selected Works, 1952–1989* (Philadelphia: Goldie Paley Gallery, Moore College of Art and Design, 1996), https://www.jaydefeofoundation.org/exhibitions/jay-defeo-selected-works-1952-1989/.

p. 2 "Nobody would have us": Deborah Remington, quoted in Anastasia Aukeman, *Welcome to Painterland: Bruce Conner and the Rat Bastard Protective Association* (Berkeley: University of California Press, 2016), 104.

p. 5 Brown initially planned: Anastasia Aukeman, "The Rat Bastard Protective Association: Bruce Conner and His San Francisco Cohort, 1958–1968" (PhD diss., Graduate Center, City University of New York, 2013), 200.

p. 5 "The only artist": Joan Brown, "Oral History Interview with Joan Brown," interview by Paul Karlstrom, July 1–September 9, 1975, Archives of American Art, Smithsonian Institution, Washington, DC, 28.

p. 5 This same summer: Aukeman, "Rat Bastard Protective Association," 200.

p. 5 "Elmer, although I'd": Brown, "Oral History Interview," 43.

p. 5 Brown and Neri: Aukeman, "Rat Bastard Protective Association," 260.

p. 9 "one could easily": Oscar Howe to Jeanne Snodgrass, April 18, 1958, reprinted in *Dakota Modern: The Art of Oscar Howe*, ed. Bill Anthes and Kathleen Ash-Milby (Washington, DC: National Museum of the American Indian, Smithsonian Institution, 2022), 26.

p. 10 "Surrealism provided fertile": Midori Yamamura, "Rising from Totalitarianism: Yayoi Kusama 1945–1955," in *Yayoi Kusama*, ed. Frances Morris (London: Tate, 2012), 174.

p. 10 "Dada and Surrealism": Lucy Lippard, "Oral History Interview with Lucy Lippard," interview by Sue Heinemann, March 15, 2011, Archives of American Art, Smithsonian Institution, Washington, DC, https://www.aaa.si.edu/collections/interviews/oral-history-interview-lucy-lippard-15936.

p. 10 "The only gallery": Bruce Conner, "Oral History Interview with Bruce Conner," interview by Paul Cummings, April 16, 1973, Archives of American Art, Smithsonian Institution, Washington, DC, https://www.aaa.si.edu/collections/interviews/oral-history-interview-bruce-conner-12017.

p. 12 "We always felt": J. Richard Gruber, *American Icons: From Madison to Manhattan, the Art of Benny Andrews, 1948–1997* (Augusta, GA: Morris Museum of Art, 1997), 116–18.

p. 15 "freer and more": Amy Chaloupka, ed., *Wanted: Ed Bereal for Disturbing the Peace* (Bellingham, WA: Whatcom Museum, 2019), 43n5.

p. 15 "There was always": Chaloupka, *Wanted*, 43n14.

p. 15 "I became very": Deborah Remington, "Oral History Interview with Deborah Remington," interview by Paul Cummings, May 18–July 19, 1973, Archives of American Art, Smithsonian Institution, Washington, DC, https://www.aaa.si.edu/collections/interviews/oral-history-interview-deborah-remington-13319.

p. 16 "People are always": Anne Livet, ed., *David McManaway: Works, Twenty Years* (Dallas: Southern Methodist University, 1980), n.p.

p. 16 "I like to deal": Ed Emshwiller, "Image Maker Meets Video, or, Psyche to Physics and Back," in *The New Television: A Public/Private Art*, ed. Douglas Davis and Allison Simmons (Cambridge, MA: MIT Press, 1977), 55.

p. 18 "Bruce and I were both": Jean Conner, "Interview with Jean Conner," unpublished interview by Robert Conway, 2015–17, Conner Family Trust, San Francisco.

p. 18 "a series of": Jordan Belson, quoted in Cindy Keefer, "Jordan Belson, Cosmic Cinema, and the San Francisco Museum of Art,"

Open Space (blog), San Francisco Museum of Modern Art, October 12, 2010, https://openspace.sfmoma.org/2010/10/jordan-belson.

p. 21 "both Chicago imagery": Peter Selz, "Surrealism and the Chicago Imagists of the 1950s: A Comparison and Contrast," *Art Journal* 45, no. 4 (Winter 1985): 306.

p. 21 After spending several: Lynn Zelevansky, "Life Is Just a Bowl of Cherries: The Life and Art of Paul Thek," in *Paul Thek: Diver, A Retrospective*, ed. Lynn Zelevansky and Elisabeth Sussman (New York: Whitney Museum of American Art, 2010), 11.

p. 21 Thek also befriends: Zelevansky, "Life Is Just a Bowl," 12.

p. 22 Born into what: Zelevansky, "Life Is Just a Bowl," 11.

p. 22 "agnostic": Paul Thek, "Beneath the Skin: Interview with Paul Thek," interview by Gene Swenson, *ARTnews*, April 1966, 35.

p. 22 In his final: Paisid Aramphongphan, "An Artist in the Secular World: Paul Thek's Relics," *American Art* 35, no. 1 (Spring 2021): 42.

p. 22 "I use traditional . . . In each": Yoshiko Uchida, "Kay Sekimachi," *Craft Horizons* 19, no. 3 (May 1, 1959): 22.

p. 26 While living in Paris: Matthew Israel, *Kill for Peace: American Artists against the Vietnam War* (Austin: University of Texas Press, 2013), 26.

p. 26 "I was in": Nancy Spero, "Interview: Word into Image," interview by Marjorie Welish, *BOMB*, Spring 1994, https://bombmagazine.org/articles/word-into-image/.

p. 27 "The art world": Mignon Nixon, "Spero's Curses," *October* 122, no. 3 (Fall 2007): 7.

p. 27 "a nice-looking . . . At that point": Lucy Lippard, quoted in *Gene Swenson: Retrospective for a Critic* (Lawrence: University of Kansas Museum of Art, 1971), n.p.

p. 28 "We looked at it": P. Adams Sitney, *Visionary Film: The American Avant-Garde, 1943–2000* (London: Oxford University Press, 2002), 331.

p. 28 "My desire was . . . Did infinite": Yayoi Kusama, "Taking My Stand with a Single Polka Dot," in *Infinity Net: The Autobiography of Yayoi Kusama*, trans. Ralph F. McCarthy (Chicago: University Press, 2011), 23.

p. 28 "archetypal imagistic . . . latent imagery": Robert Smithson, "Oral History Interview with Robert Smithson," interview by Paul Cummings, July 14–19, 1972, Archives of American Art, Smithsonian Institution, Washington, DC, https://www.aaa.si.edu/collections/interviews/oral-history-interview-robert-smithson-12013.

p. 28 "monsters, whelped": Irving Sandler, "Robert Smithson," *ARTnews*, October 1959, 18.

p. 28 "Eye staring without": Robert Smithson, "From the Walls of Dis," in *Robert Smithson: The Collected Writings*, ed. Jack Flam (Berkeley: University of California Press, 1996), 316.

p. 28 "Rough handling": Lawrence Alloway, *Samaras: Selected Works 1960–1966* (New York: Pace Gallery, 1966), 6.

p. 31 "crooked mirrors": Harold Rosenberg, "The Audience as Subject," in *Out of the Ordinary* (Houston: Contemporary Arts Association of Houston, 1959), n.p.

p. 31 "Would one of": Rosenberg, "Audience as Subject."

p. 31 "I'm a used car salesman": Wally Hedrick, "Di Rosa Artist Interview Series: Wally Hedrick," interview by Leslie Goldberg, August 16, 2002, Di Rosa Center for Contemporary Art, https://wallyhedrick.org/pdfs/di_rosa_artist_interview_series.pdf.

p. 31 "He was not a precursor": Fred Martin, "Wally Hedrick," in *Wally Hedrick, Sam Tchakalian* (Balboa, CA: Balboa Pavilion Gallery, 1967), n.p.

p. 32 "a black statement": Stan VanDerBeek, *Snapshots of the City*, 1961, film catalogue, Film-Makers' Co-op, 16mm, 5 min., accessed October 19, 2023, https://film-makerscoop.com/catalogue/stan-vanderbeek-snapshots-of-the-city.

p. 32 "The theme of": Irving Sandler, "Claes Oldenburg, Reuben Gallery," *ARTnews*, July 1960, 16.

p. 32 "can justly be": David Irwin, "Pop Art and Surrealism," *Studio International*, May 1966, 189.

p. 34 "My work has evolved": Stephanie Barron and Lauren Bergman, eds., *Ken Price Sculpture: A Retrospective* (Los Angeles: Los Angeles County Museum of Art; Munich: Prestel, 2013), 199.

p. 37 Barbara Chase-Riboud is: Barbara Chase-Riboud, "Oral History Interview with Barbara Chase-Riboud," interview by Erin Gilbert, June 7–11, 2019, Archives of American Art, Smithsonian Institution,

Washington, DC, https://www.aaa.si.edu/collections/interviews/oral-history-interview-barbara-chaseriboud-21702.

p. 37 "homesick for adults": Barbara Chase-Riboud, *I Always Knew: A Memoir* (Princeton, NJ: Princeton University Press, 2022), 55.

p. 37 "just gradually": Ed Ruscha, "Oral History Interview with Edward Ruscha," interview by Paul Karlstrom, October 29, 1980–October 2, 1981, Archives of American Art, Smithsonian Institution, Washington, DC, https://www.aaa.si.edu/collections/interviews/oral-history-interview-edward-ruscha-12887.

p. 39 "a thousand souvenirs": Diane Arbus, *Diane Arbus: Revelations* (San Francisco: San Francisco Museum of Modern Art, 2003), 177.

p. 39 "A photograph has": Frederick Gross, "Portraits, Pastiche, and Magazine Work," in *Diane Arbus's 1960s: Auguries of Experience* (Minneapolis: University of Minnesota Press, 2012), 67.

p. 42 "If Cooper Union": Jack Whitten in *Jack Whitten: Notes from the Woodshed*, ed. Katy Siegel (Zurich: Hauser & Wirth, 2018), 14.

p. 42 "I knew I had": Jack Whitten, quoted in *Jack Whitten: Jack's Jacks*, ed. Sven Beckstette and Udo Kittelmann (Munich: Prestel, 2019), 225.

p. 42 "antidote . . . poison of": Jack Whitten, "A Circle of Blood," *Walker Art Center Magazine*, December 2015, https://walkerart.org/magazine/jack-whitten-art-violence.

p. 42 "everybody's darling": Richard Cándida Smith, *Utopia and Dissent: Art, Poetry, and Politics in California* (Berkeley: University of California Press, 1995), 173.

p. 42 Brown enters: Aukeman, "Rat Bastard Protective Association," 204.

p. 42 The Whitney Museum: Aukeman, "Rat Bastard Protective Association," 222.

p. 43 "a new generation": John F. Kennedy, "The New Frontier," acceptance speech, Democratic National Convention, Memorial Coliseum, July 15, 1960, Los Angeles, transcript, https://www.jfklibrary.org/learn/about-jfk/historic-speeches/acceptance-of-democratic-nomination-for-president.

p. 43 "I finally got": Museum of Modern Art, New York (website), "Compass in Hand: Selections from The Judith Rothschild Foundation Contemporary Drawings Collection," accessed October 19, 2023, https://www.moma.org/audio/playlist/210/2767.

p. 43 "one of the": Donald Judd, "In the Galleries," *Arts Magazine*, January 1963, reprinted in *Donald Judd: Complete Writings, 1959–1975, Gallery Reviews, Book Reviews, Articles, Letters to the Editor, Reports, Statements, Complaints* (Halifax: Press of the Nova Scotia College of Art and Design, 1975), 65.

p. 43 "numerous and varied . . . from something": Judd, reprinted in *Donald Judd*, 65.

p. 44 "The new ideas": Dana Miller, "Leaving an Impression: The Art of Kiki Kogelnik," in *Kiki Kogelnik* (New York: Mitchell-Innes & Nash, 2019), 8.

p. 44 "art experience . . . No one": Raymond Saunders, "San Francisco Museum of Art Interviews Raymond Saunders," San Francisco Museum of Art, 1994, video, 98 min., https://archive.org/details/cocac_000011.

p. 44 "finds you; you find it": Hank Chase, "Raymond Saunders: Come Full Circle," *Black Renaissance* 7, no. 3 (Fall 2007): 51.

p. 46 "The major draw": Dan Nadel, ed., *Karl Wirsum* (New York: Derek Eller Gallery, 2013), 15.

p. 46 "In my teens": Nadel, *Karl Wirsum*, 14.

p. 46 "Kathleen Blackshear": Nadel, *Karl Wirsum*, 15.

p. 53 "It was an amazing": Niki de Saint Phalle, quoted in Molly Everett, "Chronology of Tirs Séances: Niki de Saint Phalle's Shooting Sessions, 1961–72," in *Niki de Saint Phalle in the 1960s*, ed. Jill Dawsey and Michelle White (Houston: Menil Collection, 2021), 15.

p. 53 "through painting": Niki de Saint Phalle, *Harry and Me, 1950–1960: The Family Years* (Zurich: Bentelli, 2006), 52.

p. 53 "artworks for and about": Catherine Dossin, "Niki de Saint Phalle and the Masquerade of Hyperfemininity," *Woman's Art Journal* 31, no. 2 (Fall/Winter 2010): 31.

p. 53 While Gunvor won't: Gunvor Nelson, "Excerpts from an Interview with Gunvor Nelson," *Canyon Cinemanews*, May/June 1974, n.p.

p. 55 For filmmakers such as: Patricia Rodden Zimmerman,

Reel Families: A Social History of Amateur Film (Bloomington: Indiana University Press, 1995), 129.

p. 55 "At the project": John P. Lukavic, Jessica L. Horton, Eric Berkemeyer, and Kent Logan, eds., *Super Indian: Fritz Scholder, 1967–1980* (Denver: Denver Art Museum, 2015), 23n6.

p. 55 "The paintings": Jennifer Roberts, "History in Smithson's Religious Paintings," in *Mirror-Travels: Robert Smithson and History* (New Haven, CT: Yale University Press, 2004), 13.

p. 57 "the fractured plane": Carolee Schneemann, "The Articulate Body: Schneemann in Conversation," interview by Robert Enright, *Border Crossings*, February 1998, https://bordercrossingsmag.com/article/the-articulate-body.

p. 57 "muse": Carolee Schneemann, "Double Knowledge," interview by Ron Hanson, *White Fungus* 16 (2019), https://www.whitefungus.com/carolee-schneemann-double-knowledge.

p. 58 "started on black": James Rosenquist, "James Rosenquist by Mary Ann Staniszewsk," interview by Mary Ann Staniszewsk, *BOMB*, October 1, 1987, https://bombmagazine.org/articles/james-rosenquist/.

p. 58 "duplicate the sensation": James Rosenquist and David Dalton, *Painting Below Zero: Notes on a Life in Art* (New York: Alfred A. Knopf, 2009), 102.

p. 58 "farm-boy who just": Sarah Bancroft and Walter Hopps, eds., *James Rosenquist: A Retrospective* (New York: Guggenheim Museum, 2003), 4.

p. 58 "some of the world's": James Rosenquist and David Dalton, *Painting Below Zero: Notes on a Life in Art* (New York: Alfred A. Knopf, 2009), 61.

p. 58 "Every work of art": William C. Seitz, introduction to *The Art of Assemblage* (New York: Museum of Modern Art, 1961), 9.

p. 58 "Assemblage has become": Seitz, "The Realism and Poetry of Assemblage," in *The Art of Assemblage*, 87.

p. 61 "A moment of . . . . When we": Rachel Federman, "Bruce Conner: Fifty Years in Show Business," in *Bruce Conner: It's All True*, ed. Rudolf Friedling and Gary Garrels (San Francisco: San Francisco Museum of Modern Art in association with University of California Press, 2016), 33.

p. 61 "align certain aspects:" Douglas MacAgy, acknowledgements to *The Art That Broke the Looking Glass* (Dallas: Dallas Museum for Contemporary Arts, 1961), n.p.

p. 62 "I had my razor": Bill Landis, *Anger: The Unauthorized Biography of Kenneth Anger* (New York: Harper Collins, 1995), 40.

p. 62 "awkward and harsh": L. C., "Benny Andrews," *ARTnews*, February 1962, quoted in Elsa Honig Fine, *The Afro-American Artist: A Search for Identity* (New York: Holt, Rinehart, and Winston, 1973), 252.

p. 64 "they temporarily had": Gene Swenson, "Genius and James Rosenquist," *Gene Swenson: Retrospective for a Critic, the Register of the Museum of Art, University of Kansas* 4, nos. 6–7 (October 24–December 5, 1971): 57.

p. 64 "the viewer's experience": Gene Swenson, "Exhibition at Green Gallery," *ARTnews*, February 1962, 20.

p. 64 "soft, close-up . . . of being": Alexi Worth, "First Break: James Rosenquist," *Artforum*, March 2002, https://www.artforum.com/print/200203/james-rosenquist-2448.

p. 64 "like all artists": Gene Swenson, "The New American 'Sign Painters,'" *ARTnews*, September 1962, 45.

p. 64 "Sorbonne": Shawn Walker, "Artist Interview: Shawn Walker," Virginia Museum of Fine Arts, 2020, video, 5 min., https://vmfa.museum/wp-subsite/videos/artist-interview-shawn-walker/.

p. 64 "We decided that": Shawn Walker, "Preserving Our History: The Kamoinge Workshop and Beyond," *Ten.8* 24 (1987): 25.

p. 64 "been taken by": Maurice Berger, "A Photographer's Search for Magic in Everyday Life," *New York Times*, January 9, 2018, https://archive.nytimes.com/lens.blogs.nytimes.com/2018/01/09/a-photographers-search-for-the-magic-in-everyday-life/.

p. 64 "I lived in the": Deborah Willis, *Reflections in Black: A History of Black Photographers, 1840 to the Present* (New York: W. W. Norton, 2000), 173.

p. 64 "Rarely has the": Irving Sandler, "In the Art Galleries," *New York Post*, May 20, 1962, 10.

p. 67 "ranges from the": Henry Seldis, "In the Galleries," *Los Angeles Times*, August 10, 1964, 19.

p. 70 "carefully wrought": Susan B. Larsen, "Ceeje Revisited: A Warm Spot in the Cool Sixties," in *Ceeje Revisited* (Los Angeles: Municipal Art Gallery, 1984).

p. 70 Judith F. Rodenbeck will suggest: Judith F. Rodenbeck, "Yayoi Kusama: Surface, Stitch, Skin," in *Inside the Visible: An Elliptical Traverse of 20th Century Art in, of, and from the Feminine*, ed. M. Catherine de Zegher (Cambridge, MA: MIT Press, 1996), 149–55.

p. 75 "He hung out": Lloyd Wise, "Alex Hay," *Artforum*, September 2021, https://www.artforum.com/events/alex-hay-2-248757/.

p. 75 "I tried to bypass": Vija Celmins, "Oral History Interview with Vija Celmins," interview by Julie Brown, February 11–October 15, 2009, Archives of American Art, Smithsonian Institution, Washington, DC, https://www.aaa.si.edu/collections/interviews/oral-history-interview-vija-celmins-15807.

p. 75 "vulgarized": Sonya Rudikoff, "New Realists in New York," *Art International*, January 1963, 40.

p. 75 "unnecessarily gross": Sidney Tillim, "Month in Review," *Arts Magazine*, February 1962, 37.

p. 75 "debauched": Sonya Rudikoff, "New Realists in New York," *Art International*, January 1963, 40.

p. 75 "Oldenburg's food": Rudikoff, "New Realists," 40.

p. 75 "influenced by . . . surreal": David Irwin, "Pop and Surrealism," *Studio International*, May 1966, 188.

p. 75 "major prototype": Lucy Lippard, "Eccentric Abstraction," *Art International*, November 1966, 36.

p. 78 "Neither philosophical newness": John Coplans, "The New Paintings of Common Objects," *Artforum*, November 1962, https://www.artforum.com/features/the-new-paintings-of-common-objects-212213/.

p. 78 "Ruscha's art reminds us": Coplans, "The New Paintings."

p. 78 "As I work": Jon Bird, Jo Anna Isaak, and Sylvère Lotringer, *Nancy Spero* (London: Phaidon, 1996), 122.

p. 78 "isolated, surrounded": Brian O'Doherty, "Art: Avant-Garde Revolt: 'New Realists' Mock U.S. Mass Culture Exhibition at Sidney Janis Gallery," *New York Times*, October 31, 1962, 59.

p. 78 *The Eye of Lightning Billy* (1962), a painting that: In discussing his model Lightning Billy (Lloyd L. Billy), Stevenson notes that Billy was "what I had always kind of imagined the ideal youth to be, that is in the classic sense, in the romantic sense, this culmination of ideas gleaned from ancient history, ideas gleaned from Southern history, ideas from the conquering of the West, all of which were very dear to me. So in a sense the heroic ideal was established in my mind but was in need of a model . . . this boy Lloyd L. Billy epitomized that. By some strange coincidence he had all of the kind of magic of both personality and physical appearance." Harold Stevenson, "Oral History Interview with Harold Stevenson," interview by Paul Cummings, March 17–29, 1973, Archives of American Art, Smithsonian Institution, Washington, DC, https://www.aaa.si.edu/collections/interviews/oral-history-interview-harold-stevenson-11898.

p. 80 January 8–February 2, 1963: Lynn Zelevansky, *Love Forever: Yayoi Kusama, 1958–1968* (Los Angeles: Los Angeles County Museum of Art, 1998), 174.

p. 80 "I was using . . . I think": Kim Levin, *Lucas Samaras* (New York: H. N. Abrams, 1975), 26.

p. 80 "intimate but quite": Thomas McEvilley, Donald Kuspit, and Roberta Smith, *Lucas Samaras: Subjects and Objects, 1969–1986* (New York: Abbeville Press, 1988), 16.

p. 80 "I got very fascinated . . . I wanted": Kay Sekimachi, "Oral History Interview with Kay Sekimachi [Stocksdale]," interview by Suzanne Baizerman, July 26–August 6, 2001, Archives of American Art, Smithsonian Institution, Washington, DC, https://www.aaa.si.edu/collections/interviews/oral-history-interview-kay-sekimachi-stocksdale-11768.

p. 82 "everybody in the": Stevenson, "Oral History Interview."

p. 82 "very well-proportioned": Stevenson, "Oral History Interview."

p. 82 "the message of art": Stevenson, "Oral History Interview."

p. 82 "the only thing": Stevenson, "Oral History Interview."

p. 82 "Since people had stopped": Stevenson, "Oral History Interview."

p. 82 "could always draw": Lucy Lippard, *Eva Hesse* (New York: New York University Press, 1976), 15.

p. 82 "among the most": Lippard, *Eva Hesse*, 15.

p. 85 "Oldenburg: As eroticism": *Eva Hesse: Diaries*, ed. Barry Rosen (Zurich: Hauser & Wirth, 2020), 853.

p. 85 "Marisol . . . will try": *Eva Hesse: Diaries*, 575.

p. 85 "It was just . . . We felt": Adger Cowans, "Adger Cowans by Carrie Mae Weems," interview by Carrie Mae Weems, *BOMB*, July 30, 2014, https://bombmagazine.org/articles/adger-cowans-carrie-mae-weems/.

p. 85 "a group of": Sarah Eckhardt, ed., *Working Together: Louis Draper and the Kamoinge Workshop* (Richmond: Virginia Museum of Fine Arts, 2020), 33.

p. 85 "were very loyal": Lawrence Jordan, "The Venue Vanguard: Artists as Exhibitors," in *Radical Light: Alternative Film & Video in the San Francisco Bay Area, 1945–2000*, ed. Steve Anker, Kathy Geritz, and Steve Seid (Berkeley: University of California Press, 2010), 83.

p. 87 "an oneiric vision": Kenneth Anger, prospectus for *Kustom Kar Kommandos*, reprinted in P. Adams Sitney, *Visionary Film: The American Avant-Garde, 1943–2000* (London: Oxford University Press, 2002), 110–13.

p. 87 "American rites": Diane Arbus, *Diane Arbus: Revelations* (San Francisco: San Francisco Museum of Modern Art, 2003), 166.

p. 87 "the stuff of": Arbus, *Diane Arbus: Revelations*, 163.

p. 87 "a place where": Jack Smith, "The Perfect Filmic Appositeness of Maria Montez," *Film Culture*, Winter 1962, reprinted in *Wait for Me at the Bottom of the Pool: The Writings of Jack Smith*, ed. J. Hoberman and Edward Leffingwell (New York: Serpent's Tail, 1997), 30.

p. 89 "These movies are": Jonas Mekas, "On the Baudelairean Cinema," *Village Voice*, May 2, 1963, reprinted in *Movie Journal: The Rise of the New American Cinema, 1959–1971*, 2nd ed., ed. Gregory Smulewicz-Zucker (New York: Columbia University Press, 2016), 91.

p. 89 "conspiracy of homosexuality": Jonas Mekas, "The Experimental Film in America," *Film Culture*, May/June 1955, reprinted in *Film Culture Reader*, ed. P. Adams Sitney (New York: Cooper Square Press, 2000), 22.

p. 89 "an erratic narrative": Electronic Arts Intermix, "Ken Jacobs: *Blonde Cobra*," accessed September 21, 2023, https://www.eai.org/titles/blonde-cobra.

p. 89 "No matter how": Anita Steckel, quoted in Rachel Middleman, *Radical Eroticism: Women, Art, and Sex in the 1960s* (Oakland: University of California Press, 2018), 156.

p. 90 "I was doing them": Michael Todd, unpublished interview by Dan Nadel, February 2020.

p. 94 "8,000 corpses": Paul Thek, "Beneath the Skin: Interview with Paul Thek," interview by Gene Swenson, *ARTnews*, April 1966, 35.

p. 94 "You could say . . . our works": Carolee Schneemann, "Body of Influence: Six Views on Paul Thek," *Artforum*, January 2011, https://www.artforum.com/features/body-of-influence-six-views-on-paul-thek-215949/.

p. 94 "We, as Negroes": Artists' statement from *First Group Showing: Works in Black and White*, quoted in Shira Wolfe, "The Life and Legacy of the Spiral Group," *Artland Magazine*, accessed June 18, 2024, https://magazine.artland.com/the-life-and-legacy-of-the-spiral-group/.

p. 99 "a comprehensive civil rights": "Goals of Rights March," *New York Times*, August 29, 1963, 16.

p. 99 "I think that I . . . I did": John W. Outterbridge, "African-American Artists of Los Angeles: John W. Outterbridge," interview by Richard Candida Smith, 1993, Department of Special Collections, University of California, Los Angeles Library, https://oac.cdlib.org/ark:/13030/hb229006xm/?brand=oac4, 195.

p. 100 "a middle-classic": Robert Smithson, "The Iconography of Desolation," in *Robert Smithson: The Collected Writings*, ed. Jack Flam (Berkeley: University of California Press, 1996), 324.

p. 100 "With less knowledge": Judd, "In the Galleries," 99.

p. 100 "is no editor . . . In *Scorpio*": Ken Kelman, "Thanatos in Chrome," *Film Culture*, Winter 1963–64, 6.

p. 100 "very American motion picture": Gregory Markopoulos, "*Scorpio Rising*," in *Film as Film: The Collected Writings of Gregory J. Markopoulos*, ed. Mark Webber (London: Visible Press, 2014), 135–36.

p. 100 "These images subsume": Carolee Schneemann, "Kenneth Anger's *Scorpio Rising*," *Film Culture*, Spring 1964, 278.

p. 105 "What do you say": Jennifer Sichel, "'Do you think Pop Art's queer?' Gene Swenson and Andy Warhol," *Oxford Art Journal* 41, no. 1 (2018): 59.

p. 105 "In 1962 I": Carolee Schneemann, "Eye Body," in *More Than Meat Joy: Performance Works and Selected Writings*, ed. Bruce R. McPherson (Kingston, NY: McPherson, 1997), 52.

p. 105 "genuine, obscurely poetic": Brian O'Doherty, "Christmas Exhibitions Playing a Wide Field: International Selection of Painting and Sculpture in Local Galleries," *New York Times*, December 29, 1963, 67.

p. 105 "We were both": Yayoi Kusama, "People I've Known, People I've Loved," in *Infinity Net*, 180.

p. 106 "failed to capture": Scott MacDonald, "Carolee Schneemann," in *A Critical Cinema: Interviews with Independent Filmmakers* (Berkeley: University of California Press, 1979), 142.

p. 106 "the sense of": Carolee Schneemann, "Film and Performance: An Interview with Carolee Schneemann," interview by Scott MacDonald, *Millennium Film Journal* 7–9 (Fall 1980/81): 98.

p. 106 "they all share": Daniel Robbins, "Sculpture by Louise Bourgeois," *Art International*, October 20, 1964, 30.

p. 106 "Like living flesh": Robbins, "Sculpture by Louise Bourgeois," 30.

p. 106 "a socialist": Marie-Laure Bernadac and Hans Ulrich Obrist, eds., *Louise Bourgeois: Destruction of the Father/Reconstruction of the Father, Writings and Interviews, 1923–1997* (Cambridge, MA: MIT Press, 1998), 112.

p. 106 "fantastic reality": Deborah Wye, "Louise Bourgeois: *One and Others*," in *Louise Bourgeois* (New York: Museum of Modern Art, 1982), 18.

p. 106 "Louise Bourgeois' flexible": Lucy Lippard, announcement for *Eccentric Abstraction* at Fischbach Gallery, New York, September 20–October 8, 1966.

p. 108 The house is: John Vick, "Chronology," in *Barbara Chase-Riboud: The Malcolm X Steles*, ed. David Updike and Sarah Noreika (Philadelphia: Philadelphia Museum of Art, 2013), 111–12.

p. 108 "tyranny": Barbara Chase-Riboud, *I Always Knew: A Memoir* (Princeton, NJ: Princeton University Press, 2022), 244.

p. 111 "grew up in": Dan Nadel, "The Repeating Beauty of Suellen Rocca," in *Suellen Rocca* (New York: Matthew Marks Gallery, 2016), 9.

p. 111 "I wasn't an artist": Noah Purifoy, "African American Artists of Los Angeles: Noah Purifoy," interview by Karen Anne Mason, September 8–9 and 22–23, 1990, University of California, Los Angeles, Oral History Program, https://oralhistory.library.ucla.edu/catalog/21198-zz0008zm4z.

p. 111 "For what you're doing": Luis Jimenez, "Oral History Interview with Luis Jimenez," interview by Peter Bermingham, December 15–17, 1985, Archives of American Art, Smithsonian Institution, Washington, DC, https://www.aaa.si.edu/collections/interviews/oral-history-interview-luis-jimenez-13554.

p. 114 "When I got down": Jimenez, "Oral History Interview."

p. 114 "It could mean": Lee Bontecou quoted in "Art on the Wing: Jet-Age Sculpture at Lincoln Center," *Life*, April 10, 1964, 46.

p. 114 "to glimpse some": Lee Bontecou, quoted in *Americans 1963*, ed. Dorothy C. Miller (New York: Museum of Modern Art, 1963), 12.

p. 114 "The bellicose detail": Judd, "Local History," in *New York: The Art World*, Arts Yearbook 7, ed. James R. Mellow (New York: Art Digest, 1964), reprinted in *Donald Judd: Complete Writings*, 152.

p. 114 "The complexity of": *Eva Hesse: Diaries*, 510.

p. 114 "from going over": Jack Whitten in *Jack Whitten: Notes from the Woodshed*, ed. Katy Siegel (Zurich: Hauser & Wirth, 2018), 20.

p. 114 "The image is": Richard Shiff, *Jack Whitten: Cosmic Soul* (Zurich: Hauser & Wirth, 2022), 37.

p. 117 "I was doing very": Aukeman, "Rat Bastard Protective Association," 225.

p. 117 "I did a lot": Joan Brown, "Joan Brown," San Francisco Museum of Modern Art, 1979, video, 5 min., https://www.sfmoma.org/watch/joan-brown/.

p. 117 "the great artist": Smith, *Utopia and Dissent*, 214.

p. 117 "I would watch . . . I would do": Carlos Villa, quoted in *Carlos Villa: Worlds in Collision*, ed. Mark Dean Johnson, Trisha Lagaso Goldberg, and Sherwin Rio (Oakland: University of California Press, 2021), 110.

p. 117 "doesn't have to come": Colin Gardner, "The Influence of Wallace Berman on the Visual Arts," in *Support the Revolution: Wallace Berman*, ed. Tosh Berman, Colin Gardner, and Walter Hopps (Amsterdam: Institute of Contemporary Art, 1992), 83.

p. 118 "intolerable invasions": Lucas Samaras, *Lucas Samaras: Selected Works, 1960–1966* (New York: Pace Gallery, 1966), 39.

p. 118 "the Indian had": John P. Lukavic, "Re-Figuring Scholder: His Indian Series, 1967–1980," in *Super Indian: Fritz Scholder, 1967–1980*, ed. John P. Lukavic, Jessica L. Horton, Eric Berkemeyer, and Kent Logan (Denver: Denver Art Museum, 2015), 27nn12–13.

p. 121 "As a Negro": Romare Bearden quoted in "Art: Uptown," *Time*, October 23, 1964, https://time.com/archive/6832299/art-uptown-oct-23-1964/.

p. 123 "Reality plus . . . Perfectly done": Lil Picard, "The New School of New York," *Das Kunstwerk*, December 1964, quoted in *Paul Thek: The Wonderful World That Almost Was*, ed. Roland Groenenboom (Rotterdam: Witte de With Center for Contemporary Art, 1995), 186.

p. 123 "The ultimate ceramic": Jonathan Fineberg, *A Troublesome Subject: The Art of Robert Arneson* (Berkeley: University of California Press, 2013), 52.

p. 125 "Simone De B[eauvoir]": *Eva Hesse: Diaries*, 409.

p. 125 "breast and penis": *Eva Hesse: Diaries*, 460.

p. 125 "The idea of Vietnam": Peter Saul in *Peter Saul: Professional Artist Correspondence*, ed. Dan Nadel (Los Angeles: Bad Dimension Press, 2020), 134.

p. 126 "This is a landscape": Luchita Hurtado, "Oral History Interview with Luchita Hurtado," interview by Paul Karlstrom, April 3, 1995, Archives of American Art, Smithsonian Institution, Washington, DC, https://www.aaa.si.edu/collections/interviews/oral-history-interview-luchita-hurtado-13583.

p. 126 "surrealist undercurrent": Hurtado, "Oral History Interview."

p. 128 "familiar-form . . . can also": Catherine Craft, *Melvin Edwards: Five Decades* (Dallas: Nasher Sculpture Center, 2015), 14.

p. 128 "[A chain is a] steel rope": Melvin Edwards, "Melvin Edwards in Conversation with Manthia Diawara and Lydie Diakhaté," interview by Manthia Diawara and Lydie Diakhaté, *Nka* 30 (Spring 2012): 129.

p. 128 "proposed colossal monuments": Maartje Oldenburg, "Chronology," in *Claes Oldenburg: The Sixties*, ed. Achim Hochdörfer (New York: Prestel, 2012), 290.

p. 128 "magnified and set": Claes Oldenburg, "Studio Notes by C.O.," in *New Work by Oldenburg* (New York: Sidney Janis Gallery, 1966), n.p.

p. 128 "a square slab": Lucy Lippard, "Homage to the Square," *Art in America*, July 1967, 50.

p. 128 Oldenburg starts exhibiting: *Recent Work by Arman, Dine, Fahlstrom, Marisol, Oldenburg, Segal* (New York: Sidney Janis Gallery, 1965), n.p.

p. 128 "HUMAN SCAPES": *Mel Casas: Humanscapes* (Houston: Contemporary Arts Museum, 1976), n.p.

p. 133 "We are truly": Jacinto Quirante, "Mexican, Mexican American, Chicano Art: Two Views," in *Mexican American Artists* (Austin: University of Texas Press, 1973), 134.

p. 133 "I had virtually": Roger Brown, "Why Was Hairy Who?????," in *What Nerve! Alternative Figures in American Art, 1960 to the Present*, ed. Dan Nadel (Providence: Museum of Art, Rhode Island School of Design; New York: D.A.P./Distributed Art Publishers, 2014), 52.

p. 133 "Dear Sir, I am not": David McCarthy, "When William T. Wiley and Bruce Nauman Wrote to H. C. Westermann," *Art Inquiries* 18, no. 1 (2020), Gale Academic OneFile, accessed December 5, 2023, https://link.gale.com/apps/doc/A641160366/AONE?u=nysl_oweb&sid=googleScholar&xid=e794749d.

p. 137 Graves constructs: Michael Edwards Shapiro, "Inside-Out/Outside-In: The Anatomy of Nancy Graves's Sculpture," in *The Sculpture of Nancy Graves: A Catalogue Raisonné with Essays*, ed. E. A. Carmean (New York: Hudson Hills Press, 1987), 25.

p. 137 action painters: Kristine Stiles, "Between Water and Stone," in *In the Spirit of Fluxus*, ed. Elizabeth Armstrong and Joan Rothfuss (Minneapolis: Walker Art Center, 1993), 82.

p. 137 "I opened my front door": Ed Bereal, "Oral History Interview with Ed Bereal," interview by Hunter Drohojowska-Philp, February 13, 2016, Archives of American Art, Smithsonian Institution, Washington, DC, https://www.aaa.si.edu/collections/interviews/oral-history-interview-ed-bereal-16308.

p. 138 "a vehicle for": Jill Dawsey, "The First Free Women: Niki de Saint Phalle's *Nanas*," in *Niki de Saint Phalle in the 1960s*, ed. Jill Dawsey and Michelle White (Houston: Menil Collection, 2021), 99.

p. 138 "the symbol of": Niki de Saint Phalle, *Niki de Saint Phalle: My Art, My Dreams*, ed. Carla Schulz-Hoffmann (Munich: Prestel, 2003), quoted in Dawsey, "The First Free Women," 99.

p. 138 "was not whether . . . Saint Phalle's personal": Catherine Dossin, "Niki de Saint Phalle and the Masquerade of Hyperfemininity," *Women's Art Journal* 31, no. 2 (Fall/Winter 2010): 36.

p. 138 Although the *Nanas*: Dossin notes that while Saint Phalle insisted her art was concerned with women and women's issues, she was never active in the women's movement and refused to participate in women-centric exhibitions. Later in the essay, she describes how Uta Grosenick devised a similar sentiment, writing in her book *Women Artists in the 20th and 21st Century* that Saint Phalle "refused to be part of numerous exhibitions and publications devoted exclusively to women artists, and also did not make any pictures available for this book." Uta Grosenick, ed., *Women Artists in the 20th and 21st Century* (Cologne: Taschen, 2005), quoted in Dossin, "Niki de Saint Phalle," 37n19.

p. 144 "made future feminist": Amelia Jones, "Wild Maid, Wild Soul, a Wild, Wild Weed: Niki de Saint Phalle's Fierce Femininities in the 1960s," in *Niki de Saint Phalle: 1930–2002*, ed. Camille Morineau (Madrid: La Fábrica, 2015), quoted in Jill Dawsey, "The First Free Women: Niki de Saint Phalle's *Nanas*," in *Niki de Saint Phalle in the 1960s*, ed. Jill Dawsey and Michelle White (Houston: Menil Collection, 2021), 100.

p. 144 "neither intimidated nor": Gloria Emerson, "Jean Shrimpton Beware! 'Nanas' of Paris Are After You: Female Statues Are Exultant and Active," *New York Times*, October 25, 1965, 39.

p. 144 "trembling on the": Alfred Frankenstein, "Dilexi Gallery Honored," *San Francisco Chronicle*, October 4, 1965, 45.

p. 144 "must be the . . . gag . . . so perfectly . . . trademarks . . . But there": John Canaday, "Art Shows Worth Seeing: Picasso, Pop, Peru, Modern Sculpture and Synchronism Bolster Gallery Fare," *New York Times*, October 16, 1965, 22.

p. 144 "style as her medium": Peter Eleey, "Dangerous Concealment: The Art of Sturtevant," in *Sturtevant: Double Trouble* (New York: Museum of Modern Art, 2014), 50.

p. 151 "Wandering into": Yayoi Kusama, "To New York: My Debut as an Avant-garde Artist," in *Infinity Net*, 51.

p. 151 "Stylistically, Miss Kusama": Jay Jacobs, "In the Galleries," *Arts Magazine*, January 1966, 16.

p. 151 Jo Applin will: Jo Applin, "I'm Here but Nothing: Yayoi Kusama's Environments," in *Yayoi Kusama*, ed. Frances Morris (London: Tate, 2012), 189.

p. 151 "the uses of": Program for New Cinema Festival I, Filmmakers' Cinematheque, New York, November 1–9, 1965.

p. 151 "digging into psychological . . . these little": Roy Fridge, Roy Fridge Journals, June 1959–August 1997, Menil Archives, The Menil Collection, Houston.

p. 151 "unrelated material": Ed Emshwiller, "Ed Emshwiller," interview by James Mullins, *Film Culture*, Summer 1966, 109.

p. 151 "another world": P. Adams Sitney, *Visionary Film: The American Avant-Garde, 1943–2000* (London: Oxford University Press, 2002), 20.

p. 154 "funky, irreverent stance": Tomás Ybarra-Frausto, quoted in Shifra M. Goldman, "Luis Jiménez: Recycling the Ordinary into the Extraordinary," in *Man on Fire: Luis Jiménez, El Hombre en Llamas* (Albuquerque, NM: Albuquerque Museum, 1994), 8.

p. 154 "An area couldn't": Luis Jimenez, quoted in Lucy Lippard, "Dancing with History: Culture, Class, and Communication," in *Man on Fire*, 25.

p. 154 "nonformal . . . intellectual . . . neglected": Gene Swenson, *The Other Tradition* (Philadelphia: Institute of Contemporary Art, 1966), vii–viii.

p. 154 "The paintings of . . . They are": Swenson, *Other Tradition*, 28.

p. 154 "It is as if": Swenson, *Other Tradition*, 25.

p. 154 "post-Freudian": Swenson, *Other Tradition*, 35.

p. 154 "leaves me cold": Lucy Lippard, "An Impure Situation (New York and Philadelphia Letter)," *Art International*, May 1966, 62.

p. 159 "eccentric abstraction": Lippard, "Impure Situation," 63.

p. 159 "radical theater/antitheater": Martha Rosler, "Exit through the Thrift Shop," in *Martha Rosler: Irrespective* (New York: Jewish Museum, 2018), 18.

p. 159 "fueled by a": Martha Rosler, "Lookers, Buyers, Dealers, and Makers: Thoughts on Audience," *Exposure* 17, no. 1 (Spring 1979): 20.

p. 159 "There were very few": Jim Nutt, quoted in Roger Brown, "Why Was Hairy Who?????," in Nadel, *What Nerve!*, 52.

p. 159 "it was hard . . . Jim Falconer": Nutt, quoted in Brown, "Why Was Hairy Who?????," 52–53.

p. 166 "The only thing": Suellen Rocca, quoted in quoted in Dan Nadel, "Hairy Who's History of the Hairy Who," *Ganzfeld*, no. 3 (2003): 138.

p. 166 "We never talked": Art Green, quoted in Nadel, "Hairy Who's History," 133–34.

p. 166 Constructed in an: Francis Frascina, *Art, Politics and Dissent: Aspects of the Art Left in Sixties America* (Manchester, UK: Manchester University Press, 1999), 66.

p. 166 Around the tower's: Frascina, *Art, Politics and Dissent*, 66.

p. 166 "a personal attempt": Jon Bird, Jo Anna Isaak, and Sylvère Lotringer, *Nancy Spero* (London: Phaidon, 1996), 122.

p. 166 "The *Bombs* are": Bird, Isaak, and Lotringer, *Nancy Spero*, 122.

p. 166 "in the studio": Vija Celmins, quoted in *Vija Celmins* (London: Phaidon, 2004), 15.

p. 169 "this young artist's": Peter Plagens, "Judy Gerowitz: Rolf Nelson Gallery," *Artforum*, April 1966, 14.

p. 169 Born Judy Cohen: Gail Levin, *Becoming Judy Chicago: A Biography of the Artist* (Berkeley: University of California Press, 2018), 120.

p. 169 "Surrealism may have": Lippard, "Impure Situation," 63.

p. 169 "There is a": Lippard, "Impure Situation," 64.

p. 170 "Imagine a California": Audrey Sabol, quoted in Marina Pacini, "Who But the Arts Council," *Archives of American Art Journal* 27, no. 4 (1987): 16.

p. 170 "dreamy, mystical people": Susan Landauer, ed., "A Room of His Own," in *Eye Fruit: The Art of Franklin Williams* (Santa Rosa, CA: Museums of Sonoma County), 1.

p. 170 "One day I was": Gunvor Nelson and Dorothy Wiley, "Women, Wives, Film-Makers: An Interview with Gunvor Nelson and Dorothy Wiley," interview by Brenda Richardson, *Film Quarterly* 25, no. 1 (1971): 34.

p. 172 "Since 1960 I have": Hannah Wilke, artist's statement for Guggenheim Memorial Foundation Grant, 1976, reprinted in *Hannah Wilke: A Retrospective*, ed. Thomas H. Kochheiser (Columbia: University of Missouri Press, 1989), 139.

p. 172 "How would you describe": Paul Thek, "Beneath the Skin: Interview with Paul Thek," interview by Gene Swenson, *ARTnews*, April 1966, reprinted in *Paul Thek: Artist's Artist*, ed. Harald Falckenberg and Peter Weibel (Cambridge, MA: MIT Press, 2008), 347.

p. 175 "Martha Edelheit's interest": Press release, Martha Edelheit at Byron Gallery, April 12–May 7, 1966, reprinted in Rachel Middleman, *Radical Eroticism: Women, Art, and Sex in the 1960s* (Oakland: University of California Press, 2018), 80.

p. 175 "The gaiety and": Lawrence Campbell, "Marisol," *ARTnews*, June 1966, 13.

p. 175 "the women's movement . . . trying to": Cindy Nemser, quoted in "Marisol: Interview with Cindy Nemser (1973)," interview by Cindy Nemser, in *Modern Sculpture: Artists in Their Own Words*, ed. Douglas Dreishpoon (Oakland: University of California Press, 2022), 179.

p. 175 "Yes. There comes": Marisol, quoted in Nemser, "Marisol: Interview," 179.

p. 175 "the master of": Lynn Hershman Leeson, "The Human Spirit Is What Makes It Work: Lynn Hershman Leeson in Conversation with Margot Norton," in *Lynn Hershman Leeson: Twisted*, ed. Margot Norton (New York: New Museum, 2021), 27.

p. 177 "The cyborg drawings": Leeson, "The Human Spirit," 14.

p. 177 "strongest influence": Connie M. Lewallen, "A Rose Has No Teeth," in *A Rose Has No Teeth: Bruce Nauman in the 1960s* (Berkeley: University of California Press, 2007), 13.

p. 177 "I was always": Betye Saar, "Influences: Betye Saar," *Frieze*,

September 27, 2016, https://www.frieze.com/article/influences-betye-saar.

p. 178 "As a child": Betye Saar, "A TEI Project: Interview of Betye Saar," interview by Karen Anne Mason, June 4 and 27, 1990, August 15, 1990, September 12, 1990, and June 19, 1991, University of California, Los Angeles, https://static.library.ucla.edu/oralhistory/pdf/masters/21198-zz0008zpzb-8-master.pdf.

p. 178 NOW's purpose: Betty Friedan, statement of purpose, National Organization for Women, October 29, 1966, https://now.org/about/history/statement-of-purpose/.

p. 180 "an all too isolated": John Fitz Gibbon, ed., "E is for Eduardo Carrillo," in *California A–Z and Return* (Youngstown, OH: The Butler Institute of American Art, 1990), https://museoeduardo-carrillo.org/e-is-for-eduardo-carrillo/.

p. 180 "*Metronomic Irregularity [II]*": Lucy Lippard, *Eva Hesse* (New York: New York University Press, 1976), 83.

p. 180 "fetishistic aspects": Lippard, *Eva Hesse*, 67.

p. 180 "sculpts the mediocrities . . . He also": Geri Trotta and Diane Arbus, "Not to Be Missed: The American Art Scene," *Harper's Bazaar*, July 1966, 84.

p. 183 "a third kind": Lucy Lippard, "Kenneth Price," in *Robert Irwin/Kenneth Price* (Los Angeles: Los Angeles County Museum of Art, 1966), reprinted in *Ken Price Sculpture: A Retrospective*, ed. Stephanie Barron (Los Angeles: Los Angeles County Museum of Art; Munich: Prestel, 2012), 265.

p. 183 "Judson and I": Noah Purifoy and Ted Michel, *Junk Art: 66 Signs of Neon* (Los Angeles: 66 Signs of Neon, 1966), n.p.

p. 183 "exists on several": Purifoy and Michel, *Junk Art*.

p. 187 "embraced by something": Senga Nengudi, "Senga Nengudi: Black Avant Garde Visual and Performance Artist," interview by Bridget Cooks and Amanda Tewes, 2020, Oral History Center, The Bancroft Library, University of California, Berkeley, https://www.getty.edu/research/special_collections/oral_histories/pdfs/nengudi_senga_2022.pdf, 14.

p. 187 "There was this": Nengudi, "Senga Nengudi," 36.

p. 187 "I don't think": Philip Leider, quoted in *Challenging Art: "Artforum," 1962–1974*, ed. Amy Newman (New York: Soho Press, 2000), 153.

p. 187 "terrible": Philip Leider, quoted in Sandra Zalman, "Secret Agency: Magritte at MoMA in the 1960s," *Art Journal* 71 (Summer 2012): 102.

p. 187 "My art is . . . In using": Rupert García, unpublished master's thesis, 1970, reprinted in *The Art of Rupert García*, ed. Ramón Favela (San Francisco: Chronicle Books; Mexican Museum, 1986), 19.

p. 188 "When the slant-steppers": Grace Glueck, "The Slant Step," *New York Times*, June 2, 1968, D22.

p. 188 "wholly sensuous": Lucy Lippard, "Eccentric Abstraction," *Art International*, November 1966, 28.

p. 188 "to caress . . . takes longer": Lucy Lippard, *Eccentric Abstraction* (New York: Fischbach Gallery, 1966), n.p.

p. 188 "Funky art or . . . typical of": Lippard, "Eccentric Abstraction," 38.

p. 188 "The distinction made": Lippard, "Eccentric Abstraction," 39.

p. 188 "Bay Area Funk": Lucy Lippard, "Oral History Interview with Lucy Lippard," interview by Susan Heinemann, March 15, 2011, Archives of American Art, Smithsonian Institution, Washington, DC, https://www.aaa.si.edu/collections/interviews/oral-history-interview-lucy-lippard-15936.

p. 188 "the works are": Lil Picard, "Erotic, Eccentric, Electric," *East Village Other*, October 1–15, 1966, 10.

p. 191 "I'm exploring the conscious": Gene Swenson, "Paint, Flesh, Vesuvius," *Arts Magazine*, November 1966, 33–34.

p. 191 "I was impressed": Joseph Raffaele, unpublished correspondence with Dan Nadel, 2017.

p. 193 "Brown rubbered circle": Joseph Raffaele, note to Eva Hesse, undated (c. 1966), Eva Hesse, papers, 1914–70, Allen Memorial Art Museum, Oberlin College, Oberlin, OH.

p. 193 "Distant attachments to": Elizabeth Baker and Joseph Raffaele, "The Way-Out West: Interviews with Four San Francisco Artists," *ARTnews*, Summer 1967, 39.

p. 193 "Two years in": Robert Colescott, *Robert Colescott "Recent Paintings"* (Roswell, NM: Roswell Museum and Art Center, 1987), reprinted in *Art and Race Matters: The Career of Robert Colescott*,

ed. Raphaela Platow and Lowery Stokes Sims (New York: Rizzoli, 2019), 224.

p. 194 "Mr. Janis, I am": John Canaday, "This Way to the Big Erotic Art Show," *New York Times*, October 9, 1966, 467.

p. 194 "Your work is": Michael Todd, "Mike Todd: An Interview," interview by Gene Swenson, *Art and Artists*, November 1966, 25.

p. 194 "Often a slight shift": Jeremy Anderson, "A Few Thoughts on Sculpture and Related Subjects," in *Jeremy Anderson: The Critical Link, A Quiet Revolution*, ed. Jo Farb Hernandez (Monterey, CA: Monterey Peninsula Museum of Art, 1995), 73–74.

p. 196 "tableaus in stasis . . . in a more": Martha Rosler, "*House Beautiful (Bringing the War Home)*, 1967–72," Museum of Modern Art, 2019, video, 7 min., https://www.youtube.com/watch?v=hJbR4jXsrXU.

p. 196 "I saw the": Rosler, "*House Beautiful*."

p. 199 "SNOWS: to concretize": Carolee Schneemann, "SNOWS," in *More Than Meat Joy: Performances and Selected Writings*, ed. Bruce R. McPherson (Kingston, NY: McPherson, 1997), 129.

p. 199 "wanted to use": Schneemann, "SNOWS," 129.

p. 199 "happenings, poetry readings": Matthew Israel, *Kill for Peace: American Artists against the Vietnam War* (Austin: University of Texas Press, 2013), 70.

p. 199 The *Collage of Indignation*: Israel, *Kill for Peace*, 76.

p. 201 "One winter evening": John P. Lukavic, "Re-Figuring Scholder: His Indian Series, 1967–1980," in *Super Indian: Fritz Scholder, 1967–1980*, ed. John P. Lukavic, Jessica L. Horton, Eric Berkemeyer, and Kent Logan (Denver: Denver Art Museum, 2015), 27.

p. 201 "the Indian the way": Fritz Scholder quoted in Lukavic, "Re-Figuring Scholder: His Indian Series, 1967–1980," 28.

p. 201 "mixture of the": Stan VanDerBeek to John Szarkowski, May 17, 1966, Museum of Modern Art Archives, Museum of Modern Art, New York.

p. 201 "Thanks very much": John Szarkowski to Stan VanDerBeek, May 25, 1966, Museum of Modern Art Archives, Museum of Modern Art, New York.

p. 201 "like the real world": John Szarkowski, wall text for *New Documents*, reprinted in *Arbus, Friedlander, Winogrand: "New Documents," 1967*, ed. Sarah Hermanson Meister (New York: Museum of Modern Art, 2017), n.p.

p. 201 "[I]n the San Francisco": James Monte, "The Grotesque Image," in *Six Touring Exhibitions 1967/68 from the San Francisco Art Institute* (San Francisco: San Francisco Art Institute, 1967), 5.

p. 202 "Wouldn't it be": Alonzo Davis, "TEI Project: Interview of Alonzo Davis," interview by Karen Mason, October 26–28, 1990, December 1, 1990, and April 20–24, 1991, University of California, Los Angeles Center for Oral History, https://static.library.ucla.edu/oralhistory/text/masters/21198-zz0008zngm-4-master.html.

p. 202 "gallery displays, which": Brochure, "Brockman Gallery Presents the Leimert Park Festival of the Arts, July 22, 23," 1969.

p. 202 "After a couple years": Peter Saul, *Peter Saul: Professional Artist Correspondence, 1945–1976*, ed. Dan Nadel (Los Angeles: Bad Dimension Press, 2020), 150.

p. 205 "The casual, irreverent": Harold Paris, "The Sweet Land of Funk," *Art in America*, March 1967, quoted in *Funk*, ed. Peter Selz (Berkeley: University Art Museum, University of California, Berkeley, 1967), 6.

p. 205 "In the current": Peter Selz, "Notes on Funk," in *Funk* (Berkeley: University Art Museum, University of California, Berkeley, 1967), 3.

p. 205 "The older artists": Joan Brown, quoted in James Monte, "'Making It' with Funk," *Artforum*, July 1967, https://www.artforum.com/features/making-it-with-funk-211338/.

p. 205 "[A] great deal": Monte, "'Making It' with Funk."

p. 208 "Westermann's multi-directional": James Monte, "Bagless Funk," in *American Sculpture of the Sixties*, ed. Maurice Tuchman (Los Angeles: Los Angeles County Museum of Art, 1967), 35.

p. 208 "concentrated on formal . . . running": Thomas Micchelli, "The Transcendence of Rage," in *Judith Bernstein: Rising* (Stavanger, Norway: Kunsthall Stavanger, 2016), 27.

p. 211 "frivolous": Sarah Eckhardt, ed., *Working Together: Louis Draper and the Kamoinge Workshop* (Richmond: Virginia Museum of Fine Arts, 2020), 60.

p. 211 "the only Black": Shawn Walker, "Artist Interview: Shawn Walker," Virginia Museum of Fine Arts, 2020, video, 5 min., https://vmfa.museum/wp-subsite/videos/artist-interview-shawn-walker/.

p. 211 "Burn Wall Street": Yayoi Kusama, press release for *Naked Protest at Wall Street*, 1968.

p. 212 "He gave me": Barbara Jones-Hogu, "Barbara Jones-Hogu," interview by Rebecca Zorach and Skyla Hearn, July 2013, Never the Same: Conversations about Art Transforming Politics & Community in Chicago & Beyond, https://never-the-same.org /interviews/barbara-jones-hogu/.

p. 212 "blew my mind . . . I stretched": Barbara Hammer, *Hammer! Making Movies Out of Sex and Life* (New York: Feminist Press at the City University of New York, 2010), 12–13.

p. 212 "black is bound": Raymond Saunders, "Black Is a Color," in *The "Soul of a Nation" Reader: Writings by and about Black American Artists, 1960–1980*, ed. Mark Godfrey and Allie Biswas (New York: Gregory R. Miller, 2021), 71.

p. 212 "the cramped boundaries": Saunders, "Black Is a Color," 71.

p. 212 "Welcome: You are": Falckenberg and Weibel, *Paul Thek: Artist's Artist*, 591.

p. 217 "The marvelous is": André Breton, "Manifesto of Surrealism" (1924), in *Manifestoes of Surrealism*, trans. Richard Seaver and Helen R. Lane (Ann Arbor: University of Michigan Press, 1969), 16.

p. 217 Disaffected young people: Bill Van Niekerken, "'Death of the Hippies': Haight-Ashbury's 1967 Funeral for Counterculture," *San Francisco Chronicle*, October 3, 2017, https://www.sfchronicle .com/thetake/article/Death-of-the-Hippies-Haight-Ashbury-s -12245473.php#photo-14060811.

p. 217 Despite the recognition: Margrit Brehm, "'Keep trying to get IN not OUT': Paul Thek in the Context of American Art, 1964–1970," in Falckenberg and Weibel, *Paul Thek: Artist's Artist*, 88.

p. 217 "wanted me to": Faith Ringgold, *We Flew Over the Bridge: The Memoirs of Faith Ringgold* (Boston: Little, Brown, 1995), 156.

p. 220 "Race prejudice has": *Report of the National Advisory Commission on Civil Disorders* (Washington, DC: U.S. Government Printing Office, 1968), 5.

p. 220 Edward Owens's film: Although this fact had previously not been verified, the film is indeed listed on the festival program, published in "List of Films Shown at Knokke-le-Zoute, 1967," *Film Culture*, Autumn 1967, 10.

p. 220 "a film about": Ed Halter, "Edward Owens: Private Imaginings and Narrative Facts," Light Industry, 2015, http:// www.lightindustry.org/owens.

p. 220 "a style so": Halter, "Edward Owens."

p. 224 "Bodacious didn't come": Ed Bereal, quoted in announcement for "Pacific Standard Time Performance and Public Art Festival, The Bodacious Buggerrilla: A Reprise Performance and Conversation," 2012, https://www.getty.edu/research/exhibitions _events/events/bodacious_buggerrilla/index.html.

p. 224 "One of the": Öyvind Fahlström, "Invasion of the Underground Comics," 1969, reprinted in Öyvind *Fahlström: Another Space for Painting*, ed. Manuel J. Borja-Villel (Barcelona: Museu D'Art Contemporani De Barcelona; North Adams: Massachusetts Museum of Contemporary Art, 2001), 237.

p. 226 "I devised a": Gene Swenson, "News of MoMA and Miami," *Other Scenes*, October 1, 1968, n.p.

p. 226 "Revolutions happen only": John Ashbery, "Growing Up Surreal," *ARTnews*, May 1968, 41.

p. 229 "I used to lock": Shawn Walker, "Artist Interview: Shawn Walker," Virginia Museum of Fine Arts, 2020, video, 5 min., https:// vmfa.museum/wp-subsite/videos/artist-interview-shawn -walker/.

p. 229 "The period 1962–1972": Shawn Walker, "Preserving Our History: The Kamoinge Workshop and Beyond," *Ten.8* 24 (1987): 25.

p. 229 "My work was . . . And I looked": Barbara Rossi, "Marriage Chicago Style," Smart Museum of Art, University of Chicago, undated (c. 2013), video, 3 min., https://vimeo.com/76023234.

p. 229 "Wiley's new work": John Perreault, "Metaphysical Funk Monk," *ARTnews*, May 1968, 52.

p. 232 "We strive for images": Jeff Donaldson, AFRICOBRA manifesto for *AFRICOBRA 1: Ten in Search of a Nation* exhibition, *Black World*, October 1970, reprinted in *Nka: Journal of Contemporary African Art* 30 (Spring 2012): 80.

p. 232 "collage was a way": Michael Auping, ed., *Jess: A Grand Collage, 1951–1993* (Buffalo: Albright-Knox Art Gallery, 1993), 47.

p. 232 "fusion versus anarchy": Auping, *Jess*, 47.

p. 232 "I had been painting": Ching Ho Cheng, "Ching Ho Cheng: A Conversation," interview by Jaakov Kohn, *Village Voice*, January 27, 1977, 27.

p. 235 "[feel] and [see] . . . profoundly religious": Cheng, "Ching Ho Cheng," 27.

p. 235 "way of seeing": Cheng, "Ching Ho Cheng," 27.

p. 235 "If I had moved": Rosler, "Exit through the Thrift Shop," 19.

p. 235 "The little room": Gene Youngblood, "In Memoriam: Jordan Belson (1926–2011)," *Millennium Film Journal*, no. 55 (Spring 2012): 85.

p. 238 "maintained an aloof": Scott MacDonald, *Canyon Cinema: The Life and Times of an Independent Film Distributor* (Berkeley: University of California Press, 2008), 132.

p. 238 "*Lipstick* was constructed": David Shapiro, "Sculpture as Experience: The Monument That Suffered," *Art in America*, May–June 1974, 57.

p. 238 "creative breakthrough": Adger Cowans, *Art in the Moment: Life and Times of Adger Cowans* (Beverly Hills, CA: Noah's Ark, 2019), 79.

p. 238 "opened up a": Adger Cowans, "One on One: Adger Cowans and Hank Willis Thomas," interview by Hank Willis Thomas, *Cultured*, October 24, 2019, https://www.culturedmag.com/article/2019 /10/24/adger-cowans-and-hank-willis-thomas.

p. 238 "imagist": Cowans, *Art in the Moment: Life and Times of Adger Cowans*, 81.

p. 240 "As painters and sculptors": Dan Sullivan, "Artists Agree on Boycott of Chicago Showings," *New York Times*, September 5, 1968, 41.

p. 240 *In Honor of Dr. Martin Luther King Jr.* is: John Canaday, "Art: Modern Museum Honors Dr. King," *New York Times*, October 31, 1968, 53.

p. 240 A group of artists: Susan E. Cahan, *Mounting Frustration: The Art Museum in the Age of Black Power* (Durham, NC: Duke University Press, 2016), 275n122.

p. 240 Eighty-one artists: Museum of Modern Art, Exhibition checklist for *In Honor of Dr. Martin Luther King Jr.*, organized by and presented at the Museum of Modern Art, New York, October 31– November 3, 1968, accessed September 20, 2023, https://www .moma.org/momaorg/shared/pdfs/docs/press_archives/4123 /releases/MOMA_1968_July-December_0055_98a.pdf.

p. 243 "risk . . . profound plastic": Jack Whitten, *Jack Whitten: Notes from the Woodshed*, ed. Katy Siegel (New York: Hauser & Wirth, 2018), 112.

p. 243 Critics see the: Saul Ostrow, "From the Archives: Process, Image, and Elegy," ARTnews.com, April 1, 2008, https://www .artnews.com/art-in-america/features/archives-process-image -elegy-63405/.

p. 243 "first influence": Jack Whitten, "Jack Whitten: An Artist's Life," Art21 Extended Play, March 21, 2018, video, 9 min., https:// www.youtube.com/watch?v=GFVsd450nCU.

p. 243 "intense emotional images": Whitten, *Notes from the Woodshed*, 166.

p. 243 "mentioned to us": Rupert García, "Oral History Interview with Rupert García," interview by Paul Karlstrom, September 7, 1995– June 24, 1996, Archives of American Art, Smithsonian Institution, Washington, DC, https://www.aaa.si.edu/collections/interviews /oral-history-interview-rupert-garcia-13572.

p. 246 "a space where . . . Gallery 32": Suzanne Jackson, quoted in Carolyn Peter, *Gallery 32 and Its Circle* (Los Angeles: Laband Art Gallery, 2009), 2.

p. 246 "I can't do that": Suzanne Jackson, "TEI Project: Interview of Suzanne Jackson," interview by Karen Mason, August 12–16, 1992, University of California, Los Angeles Center for Oral History, https://static.library.ucla.edu/oralhistory/pdf/masters/21198 -zz0008zszs-4-master.pdf.

p. 248 "absurdity . . . humor": *Eva Hesse: Diaries*, 854.

p. 248 "If you use": Eva Hesse, "A Conversation with Eva Hesse," interview by Cindy Nemser, in *Eva Hesse*, ed. Mignon Nixon (Cambridge, MA: MIT Press, 2002), 15.

p. 248 "Bundles of eccentric": John Perreault, "The Materiality of Matter," *Village Voice*, November 28, 1968, 19.

p. 248 "It's the kind": Perreault, "Materiality of Matter," 19.

p. 248 "I have always . . . One was": Christina Ramberg, quoted in Dan Nadel, "How Would a Comb That Cannot Untangle Hair Look?: On the Art of Christina Ramberg," *Artforum*, February 2018, https:// www.artforum.com/features/dan-nadel-on-the-art-of-christina -ramberg-237540/.

p. 252 "the most important . . . This authoritarian": "Works of Westermann at the County Museum," *Los Angeles Times*, December 8, 1968, 664.

p. 252 "I ran outside": Hammer, *Hammer! Making Movies Out of Sex and Life*, 13–14.

p. 256 "I had met someone": Dale Brockman Davis, "Dale Brockman Davis: Artist, Educator, and Gallerist," interview by Bridget Cooks and Amanda Tewes, 2021, Oral History Center, The Bancroft Library, University of California, Berkeley, https://digitalassets .lib.berkeley.edu/roho/ucb/text/davis_dale_2021.pdf.

p. 256 "action-oriented and": Benny Andrews and Cliff Joseph, "Untitled Statement, Early 1969," reprinted in Godfrey and Biswas, *"Soul of a Nation" Reader*, 135.

p. 260 The BECC delivers: See Susan E. Cahan, *Mounting Frustration: The Art Museum in the Age of Black Power* (Durham, NC: Duke University Press, 2016), 134.

p. 260 "While you are": Benny Andrews and Cliff Joseph to Alonzo Davis, January 5, 1971, Brockman Gallery Archives, Los Angeles Public Library.

p. 260 "realize the truth": Carlos Villa quoted in *Carlos Villa: Selected Work, 1961–1984* (Davis: Memorial Union Art Gallery, University of California, Davis, 1985), n.p.

p. 260 "I went to Chinatown": Villa, quoted in *Carlos Villa: Selected Work*, n.p.

p. 263 "I was using": Elena Filipovic, *David Hammons: Bliz-aard Ball Sale* (London: Afterall Books, 2017), 38.

p. 263 "Decorative" is how: Louise Bourgeois, "The Fabric of Construction," *Craft Horizons*, no. 29 (March 1969): 34.

p. 263 Constantine and Larsen: Mildred Constantine and Jack Lenor Larsen, *Beyond Craft: The Art Fabric* (New York: Van Nostrand Reinhold, 1973), 258–59.

p. 263 "Surrealism was less": Robin D. G. Kelley, "Keepin' It (Sur) real: Dreams of the Marvelous," in *Freedom Dreams: The Black Radical Imagination* (Boston: Beacon Press, 2002), 187.

p. 263 Damas's poetry resonates: Rebecca Wolff, "Assembling Pan-Africanism in Melvin Edward's *Homage to the Poet Léon Gontran Damas*," *Nka: Journal of Contemporary African Art* 50 (2022): 109.

p. 263 When Damas dies: Wolff, "Assembling Pan-Africanism," 109.

p. 266 "Don't let them": Richard Lindner, quoted in "Scenes," *Village Voice*, February 27, 1969, 12.

p. 266 "I knew that": Luis Jimenez, "Oral History Interview with Luis Jimenez," interview by Peter Bermingham, December 15–17, 1985, Archives of American Art, Smithsonian Institution, Washington, DC, https://www.aaa.si.edu/collections/interviews /oral-history-interview-luis-jimenez-13554.

p. 271 "The imagery [is]": Hilton Kramer, "Art: Sculpture Emphasizing Poetry," *New York Times*, May 2, 1970, 29.

p. 271 "Spinning among the": Dorothea Tanning, *Between Lives: An Artist and Her World* (New York: W. W. Norton, 2001), 281–82.

p. 275 "in the fact": Linda Nochlin, "Nancy Graves: The Subversiveness of Sculpture," in *Nancy Graves: Painting, Sculpture, Drawing, 1980– 1985*, ed. Debra Bricker Balken (Poughkeepsie, NY: Vassar College Art Gallery, 1986), 16.

p. 275 "By going inside": Linda Cathcart, *Nancy Graves: A Survey 1969/1980* (Buffalo: Albright-Knox Art Gallery, 1980), 14.

p. 275 "IT WAS INEVITABLE": Lee Lozano, page from Private Notebook 8, April 5, 1970, reprinted in Jo Applin, "Hard Work: Lee Lozano's Dropouts," *October* 156 (Spring 2016): 76.

p. 276 "The consequences were": Annette Michelson, "Rose Hobart and Monsieur Phot: Early Films from Utopia Parkway," *Artforum*, Summer 1973, 54.

p. 280 August 13, 1969: Marla Prather, *Unrepentant Ego: The Self-Portraits of Lucas Samaras* (New York: Whitney Museum of American Art, 2003), 28.

p. 280 "For the past . . . I wanted": Lucas Samaras, *Lucas Samaras* (New York: Whitney Museum of American Art, 1972), n.p.

p. 280 "The idea was . . . Ending one": Samaras, *Lucas Samaras*.

p. 280 "Other than being": Samaras, *Lucas Samaras*.

p. 280 "From a formal": Joan Siegfried, "Art from Comics," in *The*

346

Spirit of the Comics, ed. Stephen S. Prokopoff (Philadelphia: University of Pennsylvania, 1969), n.p.

p. 281 "threatens the foundations": Robert Doty, *Human Concern/ Personal Torment: The Grotesque in American Art* (New York: Whitney Museum of American Art, 1969), n.p.

p. 281 "That Doty should": Robert Pincus-Witten, "Human Concern, Personal Torment," *Artforum*, December 1969, 69.

p. 283 "the two themes": Lawrence Alloway, brochure for the exhibition *5+1* at the Stony Brook University Art Gallery, New York, October 8–November 16, 1969.

p. 283 "everybody came": Elise Armani, Amy Khang, and Gabriella Shypula, eds., *Revisiting "5+1"* (Stony Brook, NY: Paul W. Zuccaire Gallery, 2022), 26.

p. 281 "an exhibition of . . . presenting those": John I. H. Bauer, foreword to *1969 Annual Exhibition: Contemporary American Painting* (New York: Whitney Museum of American Art, 1969), n.p.

p. 281 "There has always . . . embodies the": Louise Bourgeois, quoted in Dorothy Seiberling, "The Female View of Erotica," *New York*, February 11, 1974, 56.

p. 281 "by depicting female": Barbara Rose, "Vaginal Iconology," *New York*, February 11, 1974, 59.

p. 281 "The irrational ways": Lucy Lippard, *Nancy Graves: "Aves," Forms in Flight* (New York: Knoedler & Company, 2002), 8.

p. 281 "When I made": Hammer, *Hammer! Making Movies Out of Sex and Life*, 26.

p. 281 "That was the first": David Hammons, "Interview with David Hammons (1986)," interview by Kellie Jones, in *EyeMinded: Living and Writing Contemporary Art*, ed. Kellie Jones (Durham, NC: Duke University Press, 2011), 249.

p. 286 "In the 1960s . . . the day I": Faith Ringgold, "Faith Ringgold," interview by Eleanor Munro, in *Originals: American Women Artists*, ed. Eleanor Munro (New York: Simon and Schuster, 1979), 412.

p. 286 "Screamin' Jay hit": Karl Wirsum, quoted in *Karl Wirsum*, ed. Dan Nadel (New York: Derek Eller Gallery, 2013), 13–14.

p. 291 "I got tired": Linda Lomahaftewa, quoted in Dottie Indyke, "Linda Lomahaftewa: A Well Known Artist and Teacher Discusses Her Long Career," *Southwest Art Magazine*, March 2003, https:// www.southwestart.com/native-american-arts/linda_lomahaftewa _phoenix_hopi_native_american_art_teacher_and_artist_kachina _shapes_hopi_culture_choctaw_sf_art_institute_santa_fes_indian _market_art_of_hopi_gallery_sedona_az.

p. 295 "stars . . . arresting": John Gruen, "The Big Bad Relevance," *New York Magazine*, July 13, 1970, 57.

p. 295 "I want to produce": Jae Jarrell, quoted in Gruen, "Big Bad Relevance," 57.

p. 295 "Miss Jarrell": Gruen, "Big Bad Relevance," 57.

p. 295 "the *expressive awesomeness* . . . defines": Jeff Donaldson, AFRICOBRA manifesto for *AFRICOBRA 1: Ten in Search of a Nation* exhibition, *Black World*, October 1970, reprinted in *Nka: Journal of Contemporary African Art* 30 (Spring 2012): 81.

p. 298 "an act of identifying": Levin, *Becoming Judy Chicago*, 139.

p. 298 "During this period . . . One result": Judy Chicago, *Beyond the Flower: The Autobiography of a Feminist Artist* (New York: Viking, 1996), 20.

p. 298 "The ancient Viking": Thomas Garver, introduction to *Don Potts: "My First Car"* (Newport Beach, CA: Newport Harbor Art Museum, 1972), n.p.

p. 303 "a heated exchange": Trevor Fairbrother, "T. C. Cannon and the Times of Change," in *T. C. Cannon: At the Edge of America*, ed. Karen Kramer (Salem, MA: Peabody Essex Museum, 2018), 113.

p. 303 "He lived in . . . I told him": Luchita Hurtado and Hans Ulrich Obrist, *Luchita Hurtado*, ed. Karen Marta (Zurich: Hauser & Wirth, 2020), 206.

p. 303 "As usual, when": Martha Utterback, "South Texas Sweet Funk," *Artforum*, May 1971, https://www.artforum.com/events/south -texas-sweet-funk-233636/.

p. 306 "There is a Funk": Jan Butterfield, "South Texas Funk: A Review," *Texas Observer*, January 8, 1971, 18.

p. 306 "The Egyptians had": Stephanie Weissberg, ed., *Barbara Chase-Riboud Monumentale: The Bronzes* (Princeton, NJ: Princeton University Press, 2023), 22.

p. 306 "high-fashion": Hilton Kramer, "Black Experience and Modernist Art," *New York Times*, February 14, 1970, https://www.nytimes .com/1970/02/14/archives/black-experience-and-modernist-art -romare-bearden-uses-photos-in.html.

p. 306 "discussions, arguments . . . My position": Chase-Riboud, *I Always Knew*, 244.

p. 306 "To me Portapak . . . It was": Mary Jane Jacobs, ed., *Shigeko Kubota: Video Sculpture* (Astoria, NY: American Museum of the Moving Image, 1991), 16.

p. 310 "a letter-writing campaign": Paul Von Blum, "Before and After Watts: Black Art in Los Angeles," in *Black Los Angeles: American Dreams and Racial Realities*, ed. Darnell M. Hunt and Ana-Christina Ramón (New York: New York University Press, 2010), 255.

p. 310 "cold and hard": Timothy Washington, quoted in *Three Graphic Artists: Charles White, David Hammons, Timothy Washington* (Los Angeles: Los Angeles County Museum of Art, 1971), n.p.

p. 313 "I guess I felt": Senga Nengudi, quoted in Linda Goode Bryant, "Making Doors: Linda Goode Bryant in Conversation with Senga Nengudi," interview by Randy Kennedy and Senga Nengudi, in *Ursula* no. 1 (December 1, 2018), https://www.hauserwirth.com /ursula/23020-making-doors-linda-goode-bryant-conversation -senga-nengudi/.

p. 314 "When people were": Senga Nengudi, "Senga Nengudi: Black Avant Garde Visual and Performance Artist," interview by Bridget Cooks and Amanda Tewes, 2020, Oral History Center, The Bancroft Library, University of California, Berkeley, https://www.getty .edu/research/special_collections/oral_histories/pdfs/nengudi _senga_2022.pdf, 72.

p. 314 "a woman of . . . a woman that": Senga Nengudi, "Oral History Interview with Senga Nengudi," interview by Elissa Auther, July 9–11, 2013, Archives of American Art, Smithsonian Institution, Washington, DC, https://www.aaa.si.edu/download_pdf_transcript /ajax?record_id=edanmdm-AAADCD_oh_363699.

p. 314 "to show people": Hurtado and Obrist, *Luchita Hurtado*, 227–28.

p. 314 "It was a group": Hurtado and Obrist, *Luchita Hurtado*, 227.

p. 314 "in haunting, intensely": Amos Vogel, "Sweet Fireworks," *Village Voice*, March 18, 1971, 71.

p. 314 "Once a film": Nelson, "Excerpts from an Interview with Gunvor Nelson."

p. 314 "for artists such": Robert Doty, *Contemporary Black Artists in America* (New York: Whitney Museum of American Art, 1971), 11.

p. 314 "extremist exhortations": Robert Doty, quoted in Susan E. Cahan, *Mounting Frustration: The Art Museum in the Age of Black Power* (Durham, NC: Duke University Press, 2016), 160.

p. 321 "Gentle Maverick": Peter Schjeldahl, "Finding Alex Hay: 'Gentle Maverick,'" *New York Times*, May 2, 1971, 21.

p. 321 "But the main": Schjeldahl, "Finding Alex Hay," 21.

p. 321 "With Diane Arbus": *Photographs*, sale cat., Sotheby's, New York, October 16, 2004, 150.

p. 321 "A photograph is": Diane Arbus, "Five Photographs by Diane Arbus," *Artforum*, May 1971, 64.

p. 321 "trapped between": James R. Mellow, "Bontecou's Well-Fed Fish and Malevolent Flowers," *New York Times*, June 6, 1971, D19.

p. 322 "There was a kind": Joan Semmel, "Joan Semmel Interview," interview by Ellen Lubell, *Womanart*, Winter 1977–78, 14.

p. 322 "erotic theme . . . the woman's": Semmel, "Joan Semmel Interview," 15.

p. 322 "The reason . . . When I came": Semmel, "Joan Semmel Interview," 15.

p. 325 "Early in my life": John W. Outterbridge, "African-American Artists of Los Angeles: John W. Outterbridge," interview by Richard Candida Smith, 1993, Department of Special Collections, University of California, Los Angeles Library, https://oac.cdlib.org /ark:/13030/hb229006xm/?brand=oac4, 197.

p. 325 "It all begins": Corinne Robbins, "Man Is Anonymous: The Art of Nancy Grossman," *Art Spectrum* 1, no. 2 (February 1975): 37.

p. 325 "Grossman integrates": Arlene Raven, "Notes on Nancy Grossman," reprinted in *Nancy Grossman: Tough Life Diary*, ed. Ian Berry (Saratoga Springs, NY: Frances Young Tang Teaching Museum and Art Gallery; Munich: Prestel, 2012), 214.

p. 326 The show is: Judy Chicago, *Beyond the Flower: The Autobiography of a Feminist Artist* (New York: Viking, 1996), 33.

p. 326 "At the time of": Chicago, *Beyond the Flower*, 33.

p. 326 "Saunders lifted blackness": Richard J. Powell, *Black Art and Culture in the 20th Century* (London: Thames & Hudson, 1997), 126.

p. 326 "If the erect": Richard Meyer and Rachel Middleman, eds., introduction to *Anita Steckel: The Feminist Art of Sexual Politics* (Stanford, CA: Stanford Art Gallery, 2022), 2.

p. 326 "I had become . . . Here was": Peter Selz, "Retrospective: Reflections on Barbara Chase-Riboud (2008)," *Callaloo* 32, no. 3 (2009): 879.

p. 326 "suddenly took on": Barbara Chase-Riboud, "Memory Is Everything: Barbara Chase-Riboud in Conversation with Hans Ulrich Obrist," interview by Hans Ulrich Obrist, *Mousse*, October 4, 2017, https://moussemagazine.it/magazine/barbara -chase-riboud-hans-ulrich-obrist-2017.

p. 326 The sculpture will: Chase-Riboud, *I Always Knew*, 253.

p. 333 "a miniature world": Roy DeForest, "Nut Art," in *Nut Art* (Hayward: California State University, Hayward Art Gallery, 1972), n.p.

p. 333 "In 1919, Marcel Duchamp": Ana Mendieta, "Self-Portraits" (master's thesis, University of Iowa, [May] 1972).

p. 333 "not a public": Thomas Garver, introduction to *Don Potts: "My First Car"* (Newport Beach, CA: Newport Harbor Art Museum, 1972), n.p.

p. 333 "When I do Art": Garver, introduction to *Don Potts*, n.p., n2.

p. 334 "sensualist approach . . . The submissive": April Kingsley, "Hannah Wilke, Ronald Feldman Gallery," *Artforum*, December 1972, 84.

p. 334 Adger Cowans and: Sarah Eckhardt, ed., *Working Together: Louis Draper and the Kamoinge Workshop* (Richmond: Virginia Museum of Fine Arts, 2020), 2.

p. 334 "It is our endeavor": Eckhardt, *Working Together*, 7.

p. 337 At the same time: Lovia Gyarkye, "The Ecstatic, Elusive Art of Ming Smith," *New York Times*, February 3, 2023, https://www .nytimes.com/2023/02/03/t-magazine/ming-smith-moma.html.

p. 338 "The sexualist work": Maryse Holder, "Another Cuntree: At Last, a Mainstream Female Art Movement," *Off Our Backs* 3, no. 10 (1973): 17.

p. 338 "I went to Artaud": Lucy Bradnock, *No More Masterpieces: Modern Art after Artaud* (New Haven, CT: Yale University Press, 2021), 185.

p. 338 Her fixation on: Roel Arkesteijn, ed., *Codex Spero: Nancy Spero, Selected Writings and Interviews, 1950–2008* (Amsterdam: Roma Publications, 2008), 11.

p. 338 Nevertheless, Spero finds: Bradnock, *No More Masterpieces*, 161.

Note to the Reader:
Throughout, the term *Surrealism* and its variants are capitalized in direct reference to the movement that emerged in Europe following World War I; all other uses, including those connected to the surrealist tendencies of the 1960s, are lowercase.

When possible, artworks prominent in installation views of exhibitions are identified in the caption by artist, title, and date.

The original spelling of the name Joseph Raffaele has been retained throughout for consistency. The artist changed the spelling to Raffael in 1967.

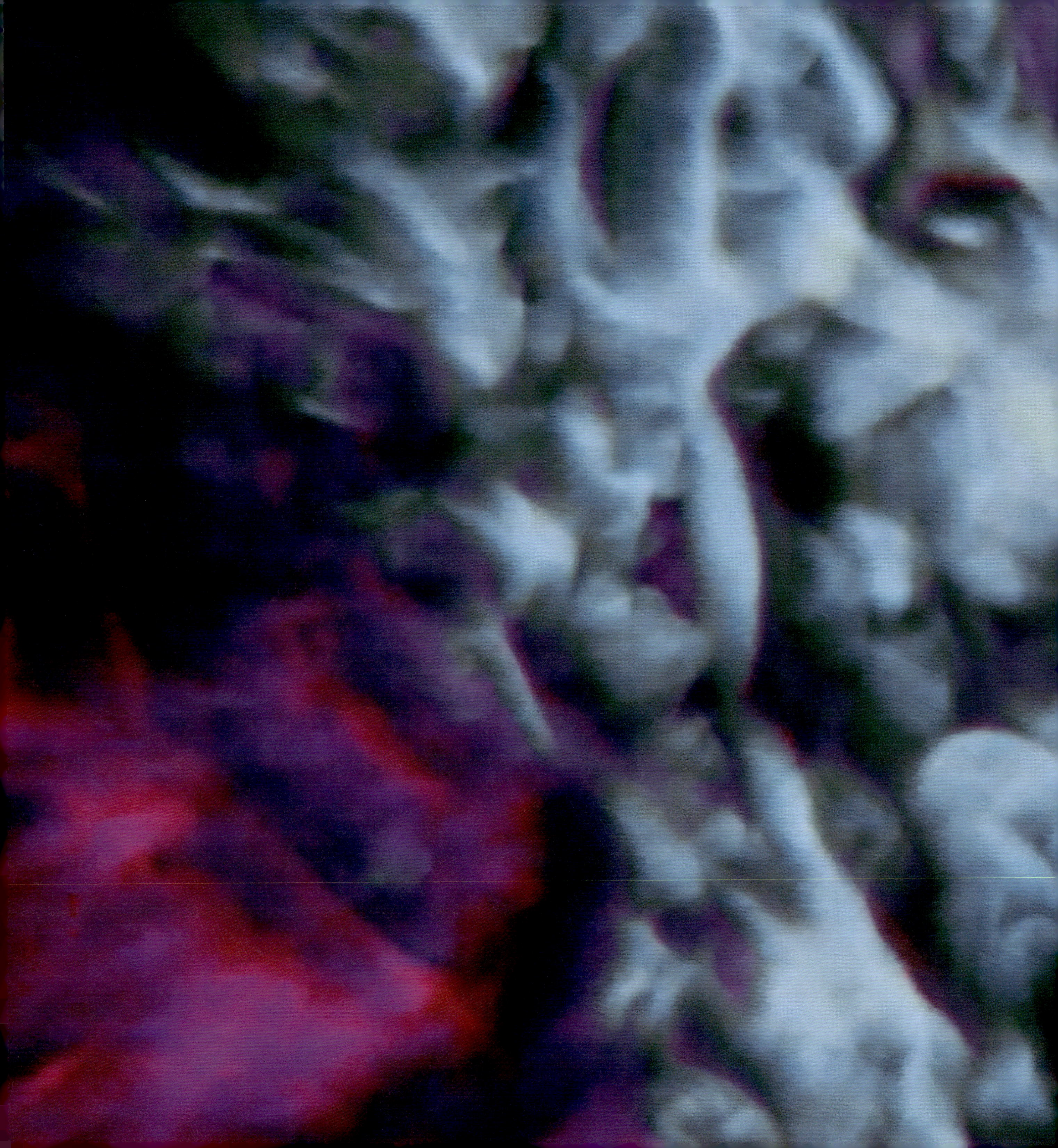

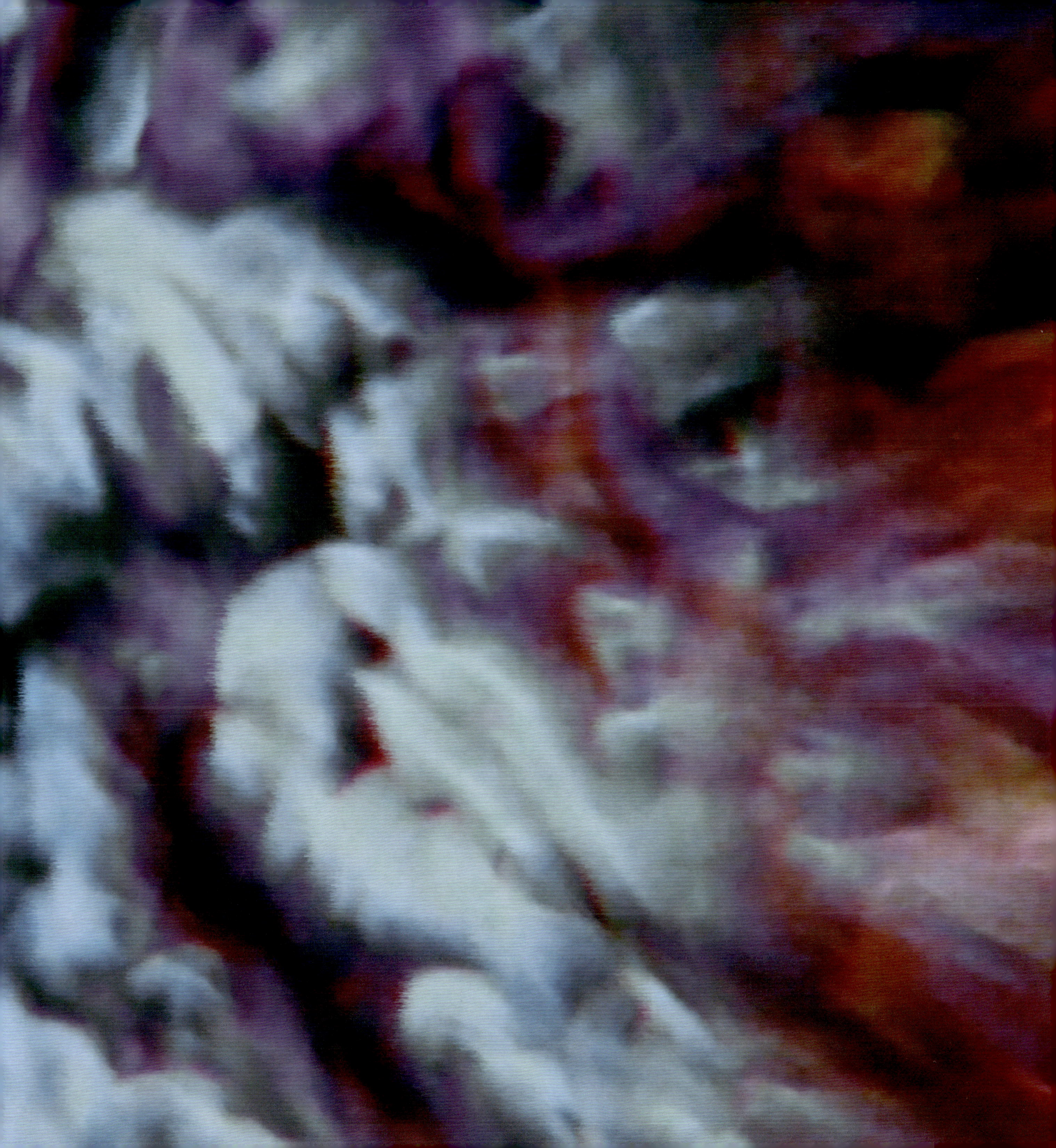

CHECKLIST OF THE EXHIBITION

As of February 3, 2025

Jeremy Anderson

Riverrun, 1965. Redwood, pine, and enamel, 57 × 81⅜ × 16½ in. (144.8 × 206.7 × 41.9 cm). University of California, Berkeley Art Museum and Pacific Film Archive; gift of the University Art Museum Council **p. 145**

Benny Andrews

No More Games, 1970. Oil on canvas with cut-and-pasted primed and raw canvas, T-shirt, garment fragments, and partially painted printed fabrics: two panels, 100⅞ × 101¼ in. (256.2 × 257.2 cm) overall; panels, 100⅞ × 49⅞ in. (256.2 × 126.7 cm) and 100⅞ × 51 in. (256.2 × 129.3 cm). The Museum of Modern Art, New York; Blanchette Hooker Rockefeller Fund 35.1971.a–b **p. 302**

Diane Arbus

Bela Lugosi as Dracula on television 1958, 1958. Gelatin silver print: sheet, 11 × 14 in. (27.9 × 35.6 cm); image, 6½ × 9¾ in. (16.5 × 24.8 cm). Fraenkel Gallery, San Francisco **p. 8**

Clouds on-screen at a drive-in movie, N.J. 1961, 1961. Gelatin silver print: sheet, 16 × 20 in. (40.6 × 50.8 cm); image, 12¼ × 18¼ in. (31.1 × 46.4 cm). The Metropolitan Museum of Art, New York; gift of Neil Selkirk, 2012 2012.552.60 **p. 48**

Five members of The Monster Fan Club, N.Y.C. 1961, 1961. Gelatin silver print, 10 ⅜ × 6 ½ in. (26.4 × 16.5 cm). Collection of Steve Lockshin and Allison Schaengold Lockshin **p. 47**

Robert Arneson

Call Me Lover, 1965. Glazed ceramic and mixed media, 8 × 11 × 9 in. (20.3 × 27.9 × 22.9 cm). Private collection **p. 134**

Klick, 1965. Glazed ceramic, 5¼ × 5½ × 7¼ in. (13.3 × 14 × 18.4 cm). Collection of Beth Rudin DeWoody **p. 135**

Ralph Arnold

Unfinished Collage, 1968. Collage and acrylic on canvas: three panels, 60½ × 20 in. (153.7 × 50.8 cm) each; approximately 60½ × 60 in. (153.7 × 152.4 cm) overall. South Side Community Art Center, Chicago **p. 245**

Romare Bearden

Pittsburg Memory ⅖, 1964. Gelatin silver print (Photostat) mounted on fiberboard: mount, 27¼ × 35½ in. (69.2 × 90.2 cm). Collection of Beth Rudin DeWoody

Jordan Belson

Samadhi, 1967. 16mm film transferred to video, color, sound; 6 min. The Estate of Jordan Belson and Matthew Marks Gallery, New York **p. 216**

Ed Bereal

Focke-Wulf FW 190, 1960. Mixed-media assemblage, 21¼ × 12 × 6 in. (54 × 30.5 × 15.2 cm). The Buck Collection at the UCI Institute and Museum of California Art **p. 38**

Wallace Berman

Papa's got a brand new bag, 1964. Mixed-media collage, 44½ × 32¼ in. (113 × 81.9 cm). Collection of David Yorkin and Alix Madigan **p. 115**

Judith Bernstein

Vietnam Garden, 1967. Charcoal, oil stick, and steel wool on paper: sheet, 26 × 40 in. (66 × 101.6 cm); image (irregular), 26⅜ × 41¼ in. (67 × 104.8 cm). Whitney Museum of American Art, New York; purchase, with funds from the Drawing Committee 2010.80 **p. 209**

Lee Bontecou

Untitled, 1961. Steel, canvas, wire, and rope, 72½ × 66 × 24¾ in. (184.2 × 167.6 × 62.9 cm). Whitney Museum of American Art, New York; purchase 61.41 **p. 60**

Louise Bourgeois

Fée Couturière, 1963. Plaster, 39½ × 22 ½ × 22½ in. (100.3 × 57.2 × 57.2 cm). Collection of the Easton Foundation **p. 96**

Joan Brown

The Bride, 1970. Oil, enamel, and glitter on canvas, 91 × 55 in. (231.1 × 139.7 cm). University of California, Berkeley Art Museum and Pacific Film Archive; bequest of Earl David Peugh III **p. 293**

Kay Brown

The Devil and His Game, 1970. Collage of various papers and mixed media on canvas, 48 × 36 in. (121.9 × 91.4 cm). Collection of Larry and Tina Jones **p. 289**

Roger Brown

Untitled (Movie house with nude female), 1968. Oil on canvas, 24¾ × 24⅝ in. (62.9 × 62.5 cm). Collection of the John Michael Kohler Arts Center, Gift of the Kohler Foundation, Inc. **p. 244**

T. C. Cannon

"Andrew Myrick – Let 'Em Eat Grass," 1970. Acrylic on canvas, 46 × 40 in. (116.8 × 101.6 cm). United States Department of the Interior, Indian Arts and Crafts Board, Southern Plains Indian Museum, Anadarko, OK **p. 296**

Eduardo Carrillo

Testament of the Holy Spirit, 1971. Oil on panel, 47¾ × 60 in. (121.3 × 152.4 cm). Crocker Art Museum, Sacramento, CA; purchase with funds from the Maude T. Pook Acquisition Fund 1972.24 **p. 317**

Mel Casas

Humanscape #56 (San Antonio Circus), 1969. Acrylic on canvas, 72 × 96 in. (182.9 × 243.8 cm). Mel Casas Family Trust **p. 274**

Vija Celmins

House #1, 1965. Oil on wood, metal, fur, and plastic: house, 7½ × 6½ × 10 in. (19.1 × 16.5 × 25.4 cm); roof, 2¼ × 7⅜ × 10½ in. (5.7 × 18.7 × 26.7 cm). The Museum of Modern Art, New York; Gift of Edward R. Broida 670.2005.a–b **p. 150**

Barbara Chase-Riboud

Confessions for Myself, 1972. Bronze, paint, and wool, 120 × 40 × 12 in. (304.8 × 101.6 × 30.5 cm). University of California, Berkeley Art Museum and Pacific Film Archive; purchased with funds from the H. W. Anderson Charitable Foundation **p. 331**

Ching Ho Cheng

Sun Drawing, 1967. Fiber-tipped pen on paper mounted on found paper on board: sheet, 20 × 20 in. (50.8 × 50.8 cm); mount (board), 21¹⁵⁄₁₆ × 20¼ × ⅛ in. (55.7 × 51.4 × 0.3 cm). Whitney Museum of American Art, New York; gift of the Ching Ho Cheng Estate 2010.46 **p. 210**

Judith Bernstein

Judy Chicago

In My Mother's House, c. 1962–64. Acrylic on stoneware, 24 × 18 × 6 in. (61 × 45.8 × 15.2 cm). Monterey Museum of Art, CA; purchase by exchange: Gift of Mr. and Mrs. Gerald Bates, Mrs. J. B. Heywood, Elizabeth George Lawlor in memory of Dorothy George Meakin, William and Renee Peterson, Mr. and Mrs. John Shephard, Mr. and Mrs. E. V. Stuade, Carolyn Lewis Nielson, Albert Denney, Nancy Stillwell Easterbrook, Margaret Wentworth Owings, Naedra B. Robinson, Elizabeth Tompkins, and an anonymous donor 2019.002 **p. 71**

Bruce Conner

RAT PURSE, 1959. Nylon, wax, gold leaf, tin can, fur, sequins, string, and cardboard box, 37 × 6 × 7 in. (94 × 15.2 × 17.8 cm). Los Angeles County Museum of Art; purchase, with funds provided by the Modern and Contemporary Art Council and the Modern and Contemporary Art Council Acquisitions Endowment and Gift of the Tomeo Family and Michael Kohn Gallery **p. 19**

Jean Conner

Are You a Springmaid?, 1960. Collage, 10⅛ × 8⅛ in. (25.7 × 20.6 cm). Whitney Museum of American Art, New York; purchase, with funds from Sheree and Jerry Friedman 2018.203 **p. 40**

Are You a Springmaid? II, 1960. Collage, 11⅞ × 9 ¾ in. (30.2 × 24.8 cm). Whitney Museum of American Art, New York; purchase, with funds from Sheree and Jerry Friedman 2018.204 **p. 41**

Adger Cowans

Shadows, 1966. Gelatin silver print: sheet, 11 × 14 in. (27.8 × 35.6 cm); image, 7⅝ × 11¼ in. (19.2 × 28.6 cm). Virginia Museum of Fine Arts, Richmond; Aldine S. Hartman Endowment Fund 2018.315 **p. 179**

Robert Crumb

Burned Out, cover of the *"East Village Other"* 5, no. 10, 1970. Ink on paper, 16 × 10 in. (40.6 × 25.4 cm). Lucas Museum of Narrative Art, Los Angeles 2019.61.19 **p. 308**

Head #1, 1967. Ink on paper, 10 × 7 in. (25.4 × 17.8 cm). Collection of Rubén Blades **p. 223**

Dale Brockman Davis

Arabian Nights, #2, c. 1969–70. Clay, leather, and metal, 18 × 12 × 12 in. (45.7 × 30.5 × 30.5 cm). Collection of the artist **p. 258**

Jay DeFeo

The Eyes, 1958. Graphite pencil on paper, 42 × 84 ¾ in. (106.7 × 215.3 cm). Whitney Museum of American Art, New York; gift of the Lannan Foundation 96.242.3 **p. 4**

Roy De Forest

Drifting Down the Mississippi, 1959. Acrylic, enamel, string, and wood on wood, 55½ × 37 ½ × 5 in. (141 × 95.3 × 12.7 cm). San Francisco Museum of Modern Art; gift of Kathan Brown 84.1465 **p. 30**

Niki de Saint Phalle

Vivian, 1965. Yarn, fabric, paper, and epoxy, 42 × 47 × 40 in. (106.7 × 119.4 × 101.6 cm). Museum of Contemporary Art Chicago; gift of Joseph and Jory Shapiro

Martha Edelheit

Flesh Wall–Female, 1965. Oil on canvas: three panels, 80 × 195 in. (203.2 × 495.3 cm) overall. Minneapolis Institute of Art; The Mary Ingebrand-Pohlad Endowment for Twentieth-Century Paintings and the William Hood Dunwoody Fund 2019.24a–c **pp. 152–53**

Melvin Edwards

Cotton Hangup, 1966. Steel, 32 × 30 × 30 in. (81.3 × 76.2 × 76.2 cm). Studio Museum in Harlem; gift of Mr. and Mrs. Hans Burkhardt 1991.21 **p. 167**

Roy Fridge

The Great Spinning Arrow Consolating Console, c. 1966. Wood and metal, 72 × 24½ × 14¼ in. (182.9 × 62.2 × 36.2 cm); stool, 17⅞ × 18⅛ × 11⅜ in. (45.4 × 46 × 28.9 cm). The Menil Collection, Houston **p. 168**

Lee Friedlander

Florida, 1963. Gelatin silver print, 8¾ × 13⅛ in. (22 × 33.1 cm). The Museum of Modern Art, New York, purchase 695.2000 **p. 102**

Galax, Virginia, 1962. Gelatin silver print, 5⅞ × 8⅞ in. (14.9 × 22.5 cm). The Museum of Modern Art, New York; acquired through the generosity of Celeste Bartos 56.1975 **p. 72**

Nashville, 1963. Gelatin silver print, 9¼ × 6⅛ in. (23.5 × 15.5 cm). The Metropolitan Museum of Art, New York; purchase, The Horace W. Goldsmith Foundation Gift, through Joyce and Robert Menschel, 1995 1995.168.2 **p. 103**

Rupert Garcia

Unfinished Man, 1968. Acrylic on canvas, 48 × 48 in. (121.9 × 121.9 cm). The Museum of Modern Art, New York; Painting and Sculpture Deaccession Funds 73.2024 **p. 242**

Nancy Graves

Camel VI, 1968–69. Wood, steel, burlap, polyurethane, animal skin, wax, and oil paint, approximately 90 × 144 × 47⅝ in. (228.6 × 365.8 × 121.9 cm). National Gallery of Canada, Ottawa; purchase, 1969 **p. 254**

Camel VII, 1968–69. Wood, steel, burlap, polyurethane, animal skin, wax, and oil paint, approximately 96 × 108 × 47⅝ in. (243.8 × 274.3 × 121.9 cm). National Gallery of Canada, Ottawa; gift of Allan Bronfman, Montreal, 1969 **p. 254**

Camel VIII, 1968–69. Wood, steel, burlap, polyurethane, animal skin, wax, and oil paint, approximately 90 × 120 × 47⅝ in. (228.6 × 304.8 × 121.9 cm). National Gallery of Canada, Ottawa; gift of Allan Bronfman, Montreal, 1969 **p. 255**

Nancy Grossman

Head, 1968. Wood, leather, metal zippers, paint, and metal nails, 16¼ × 6⅝ × 8¹⁵⁄₁₆ in. (41.3 × 16.8 × 22.7 cm) overall; sculpture, 12 × 7¾ × 8¾ in. (30.5 × 19.7 × 22.2 cm); base, 4 × 5¼ × 5¾ in. (10.2 × 13.3 × 14.6 cm). Whitney Museum of American Art, New York; purchase, with funds from the Howard and Jean Lipman Foundation, Inc. 68.81a–b **p. 236**

Barbara Hammer

Schizy, 1968. Super 8mm film transferred to video, color, silent; 3:59 min. Electronic Arts Intermix, New York **p. 251**

Tee Corinne #7, 1972. Gelatin silver print on RC paper: image, 8¼ × 11¼ in. (21 × 28.6 cm). Estate of Barbara Hammer

Tee Corinne Sleeping, 1972. Gelatin silver print: image, 6¾ × 8½ in. (17.1 × 21.6 cm). Estate of Barbara Hammer

David Hammons

Close Your Eyes and See Black, 1969. Pigment on gold-coated paperboard, 35⅞ × 24¾ in. (91.1 × 62.9 cm). Solomon R. Guggenheim Museum, New York; purchased through prior gifts of Daimler-Benz in honor of Thomas M. Messer, the National Endowment for the Arts in Washington, DC, William C. Edwards Jr., in memory of Sibyl H. Edwards, the Estate of Karl Nierendorf, Mr. and Mrs. Morton L. Ostow, and Dr. Solomon W. Schaefer, 2018 **p. 264**

Untitled, 1969. Grease and pigment on paper in Plexiglas, 32⅜ × 19¼ × ¼ in. (82.2 × 48.9 × 0.6 cm). Tilton Gallery, New York **p. 265**

Alex Hay

Paper Bag, 1968. Fiberglass, epoxy, paint, and paper, 59¼ × 29¼ × 17¾ in. (150.5 × 74.3 × 45.1 cm). Whitney Museum of American Art, New York; purchase, with funds from the Friends of the Whitney Museum of American Art 69.9 **p. 231**

Wally Hedrick

HERMETIC IMAGE, 1961. Oil on canvas, 84 × 60 in. (213.3 × 152.4 cm). Mills College Art Museum, Northeastern University, Oakland, CA; Museum Purchase 1984.21 **p. 59**

Mike Henderson

Dufus, 1970/73. 16mm film, black-and-white, sound, 8 min. Academy Film Archive, Los Angeles **p. 290**

Lynn Hershman Leeson

Giggling Machine, Self Portrait as Blonde, 1968. Wax, wig, feathers, Plexiglas, wood, sensor, and sound, 16½ × 16½ × 13 in. (41.9 × 41.9 × 33 cm). Collection of Scott Mueller; promised gift to the Cleveland Museum of Art **p. 241**

Eva Hesse

C-Clamp Blues, 1965. Paint, metal, found objects, unknown modeling compound, particleboard, and wood, 25⅝ × 21⅝ × 1½ in. (65.1 × 54.9 × 3.8 cm). Collection of Tony and Gail Ganz **p. 146**

Oscar Howe

Retreat, 1968. Casein on paper, 24 × 18¼ in. (61 × 46.3 cm). Whitney Museum of American Art, New York; purchase, with funds from the Director's Discretionary Fund 2023.86 **p. 253**

Luchita Hurtado

Untitled, 1971. Oil on canvas, 50 × 34⅞ inches (127 × 88.6 cm). The Estate of Luchita Hurtado and Hauser & Wirth **p. 315**

Miyoko Ito

Untitled, 1970. Oil on canvas, 46 × 42 in. (117 × 107 cm). Collection of Wade Guyton **p. 309**

Suzanne Jackson

We Were Waiting, c. 1968–69. Acrylic on canvas, 8 × 10⅛ in. (20.3 × 25.7 cm). Collection of Larry and Tina Jones **p. 247**

Jae Jarrell

Ebony Family, c. 1968. Velvet dress with velvet collage, 38 ½ × 38 × ½ in. (97.8 × 96.5 × 1.3 cm). Brooklyn Museum, New York; gift of R. M. Atwater, Anna Wolfrom Dove, Alice Fiebiger, Joseph Fiebiger, Belle Campbell Harriss, and Emma L. Hyde, by exchange, Designated Purchase Fund, Mary Smith Dorward Fund, Dick S. Ramsay Fund, and Carll H. de Silver Fund 2012.80.15 **p. 249**

Jess

If All the World Were Paper and All the Water Sink, 1962. Oil on canvas, 38 × 56 in. (96.5 × 142.2 cm). Fine Arts Museums of San Francisco; Museum purchase, Roscoe and Margaret Oakes Income Fund, Museum Society Auxiliary, Mr. and Mrs. John N. Rosekrans, Jr., Walter H. and Phyllis J. Shorenstein Foundation Fund, Mrs. Paul L. Wattis Fund, Bobbie and Michael Wilsey, Mr. and Mrs. Steven McGregor Read, Mr. and Mrs. Gorham B. Knowles, Mrs. Edward T. Harrison, Mrs. Nan Tucker McEvoy, Harry and Ellen Parker in honor of Steven Nash, Katherine Doyle Spann, Mr. and Mrs. William E. Steen, Mr. and Mrs. Leonard E. Kingsley, George Hopper Fitch,

Princess Rainieri di San Faustino, Mr. and Mrs. Richard Madden 1994.31 **p. 74**

Luis Jimenez

Blonde TV Image, 1967. Fiberglass with polychrome, 27 × 19 × 30 in. (68.6 × 48.3 × 76.2 cm). Whitney Museum of American Art, New York; Josephine N. Hopper Bequest, by 2024.352 **p. 215**

Man on Fire, 1969–70. Fiberglass with urethane finish on painted fiberboard base, 89 × 60 × 19 in. (226.1 × 152.4 × 48.3 cm). The Museum of Fine Arts, Houston; Museum purchase funded by the Caroline Wiess Law Accessions Endowment Fund 2010.1760 **p. 269**

Daniel LaRue Johnson

Freedom Now, Number 1, August 13, 1963–January 14, 1964. Pitch on canvas with "Freedom Now" button, broken doll, hacksaw, mousetrap, flexible tube, and wood, 53⅞ × 55⅜ × 7½ in. (136.6 × 140.5 × 18.9 cm). The Museum of Modern Art, New York; given anonymously 4.1965 **p. 110**

Barbara Jones-Hogu

Mother of Man, 1968. Woodblock print on paper, 30½ × 21½ in. (77.5 × 54.6 cm). The Museum of Modern Art, New York; The Deborah Wye Endowment Fund 738.2019 **p. 250**

Edward Kienholz

John Doe, 1959. Oil, metallic paint, resin, plaster, and graphite on mannequin parts with wood, metal, plastic, paper, rubber, and stroller, 39 ½ × 19 × 31¼ in. (100.3 × 48.3 × 79.4 cm). The Menil Collection, Houston **p. 20**

Kiki Kogelnik

Gee Baby – I'm Sorry, 1965. Oil and acrylic on canvas, 50⅛ × 39⅞ in. (127.4 × 101.4 cm). Kiki Kogelnik Foundation, New York **p. 136**

Shigeko Kubota

Self-Portrait, c. 1970–71. Standard-definition video, color, silent; 5:28 min. The Museum of Modern Art, New York; gift of the Shigeko Kubota Video Art Foundation 334.2021 **p. 307**

Yayoi Kusama

Accumulation, c. 1963. Sewn and stuffed fabric, wood chair frame, and paint, 34⅜ × 38⅜ × 36⅜ in. (87.2 × 98.9 × 92.2 cm). Whitney Museum of American Art, New York; purchase 2001.342 **p. 84**

Linda Lomahaftewa

Untitled (Women's Faces), 1965–71. Oil on canvas, 36 × 48 in. (91.4 × 121.9 cm). Heard Museum, Phoenix, AZ; gift of the artist 4052-1 **p. 294**

Lee Lozano

No title, 1964. Oil on canvas, 65¾ × 118¾ in. (167 × 301.5 cm). The Estate of Lee Lozano **p. 109**

Marisol

Women and Dog, 1963–64. Wood, plaster, synthetic polymer, and taxidermied dog head, 73⁹⁄₁₆ × 76⅝ × 26 ¾ in. (186.8 × 194.6 × 67.9 cm) overall. Whitney Museum of American Art, New York; purchase, with funds from the Friends of the Whitney Museum of American Art 64.17a–i

David McManaway

Poseidon's Icon, 1965. Mixed media on wood, 23 × 12 ½ × 2 ¾ in. (58.4 × 31.8 × 7 cm). Collection of Peter and Carol York **p. 143**

(21.9 × 18.4 cm). Whitney Museum of American Art, New York; gift of Sascha S. Bauer and Kristen Dickey 2013.102 **p. 176**

Paul Thek

Untitled, 1963, from the series *Television Analyzations*. Oil on canvas, 39 ½ × 39 ¾ in. (100.3 × 101 cm). Collection of Beth Rudin DeWoody **p. 95**

Untitled, 1966, from the series *Technological Reliquaries*. Wax, paint, polymer resin, nylon monofilament, wire, plaster, plywood, melamine laminate, rhodium-plated bronze, and acrylic, 14 × 15 ¹⁄₁₆ × 7 ½ in. (35.6 × 38.3 × 19.1 cm). Whitney Museum of American Art, New York; purchase, with funds from the Painting and Sculpture Committee 93.14 **p. 173**

Michael Todd

Fetish 2, 1963. Wood and metal, 12 ½ × 7 × 6 in. (31.7 × 17.8 × 15.2 cm). Collection of Mia Doi Todd **p. 92**

Fetish 3, 1963. Wood and metal, 12 ½ × 6 ½ × 7 in. (31.7 × 16.5 × 17.8 cm). Collection of Mia Doi Todd **p. 93**

Carlos Villa

Ritual, 1970. Wig, chicken bones, and canvas, 101 × 95 in. (256.5 × 241.3 cm). Collection of Kim and Lito Camacho **p. 305**

Shawn Walker

Man with Bubble, Central Park (Near Bandshell), c. 1960–79, printed 1989. Gelatin silver print: sheet, 8 × 10 in. (20.3 × 25.4 cm); image, 7 ⅜ × 9 ⅜ in. (18.7 × 23.9 cm). Whitney Museum of American Art, New York; purchase, with funds from the Photography Committee 2020.62 **p. 36**

Tiffany's Window on 57th Street, NYC, c. 1968–72. Gelatin silver print: 4 ¾ × 7 ⅛ in. (12.1 × 17.9 cm). Virginia Museum of Fine Arts, Richmond; National Endowment for the Arts Fund for American Art **p. 228**

Timothy Washington

Viet Nam, 1970. Spray paint on aluminum, 36 ⅛ × 36 ⅛ in. (91.8 × 91.8 cm). Collection of Larry and Tina Jones **p. 288**

H. C. Westermann

The Big Change, 1963. Douglas-fir marine plywood, Masonite, and ink, 75 ⅜ × 20 ¼ × 20 ¼ in. (191.5 × 51.4 × 51.4 cm). The Art Institute of Chicago; gift of the Estate of Alan and Dorothy Press in acknowledgment of their family 2023.2906 **p. 101**

Memorial to the Idea of Man If He Was an Idea, 1958. Pine, bottle caps, cast-tin toys, glass, metal, brass, ebony, and enamel, 56 ½ × 38 × 14 ¼ in. (143.5 × 96.5 × 36.2 cm). Museum of Contemporary Art Chicago; Susan and Lewis Manilow Collection of Chicago Artists 1993.34 **p. 13**

The Plush, 1963–64. Cotton-pile shag carpet with latex backing, cast iron, paint, wood, and metal casters, 59 × 29 × 21 in. (149.8 × 73.7 × 53.3 cm) overall. National Gallery of Art, Washington, DC; Corcoran Collection (gift of Samuel J. Wagstaff Jr.) 2014.136.287 **p. 83**

Jack Whitten

Christ, 1964. Acrylic on canvas, 15 × 16 in. (38.1 × 40.6 cm). The Jack Whitten Estate **p. 112**

William T. Wiley

Modern Art Teacher, 1966. Acrylic on canvas, 66 × 86 in. (167.6 × 218.4 cm). Wiley Family Collection **p. 192**

Hannah Wilke

Teasel Cushion, 1967. Terra-cotta, acrylic, and plastic, 12 × 12 × 4 in. (30.5 × 30.5 × 10.2 cm). Walker Art Center, Minneapolis; T. B. Walker Acquisition Fund 2002.69.1–.2 **p. 213**

Franklin Williams

Untitled, 1966. Acrylic, crochet thread, and yarn on canvas stuffed with cotton batting, over wooden support, 20 × 20 × 9 in. (50.8 × 50.8 × 22.9 cm). Collection of the artist **p. 185**

Untitled, 1967. Acrylic, crochet thread, and cotton on canvas, 24 × 31 ¾ in. (61 × 80.6 cm). Collection of the artist **p. 204**

Karl Wirsum

Gargoyle Gargle Oil, c. 1969. Acrylic painted on mirror, 22 × 16 ⅜ × 5 in. (55.9 × 41.6 × 12.7 cm). KAWS Collection **p. 282**

Screamin' Jay Hawkins, 1968. Acrylic on canvas, 48 × 36 in. (121.9 × 91.4 cm). Art Institute of Chicago; Mr. and Mrs. Frank G. Logan Purchase Prize Fund 1969.248 **p. 230**

ADDITIONAL ILLUSTRATED WORKS

Kenneth Anger

Scorpio Rising, 1963. 16mm film, color, sound; 28 min. UCLA Film & Television Archive **p. 104**

Romare Bearden

Conjur Woman, 1964. Photo projection on paper, 64 × 50 in. (162.6 × 127 cm). The Studio Museum in Harlem, New York; gift of the artist 1972.5 **p. 120**

Wallace Berman

Untitled (Jack Ruby), 1964. Positive Verifax with poem, 28 ½ × 29 in. (72.4 × 73.7 cm). The Estate of Wallace Berman **p. 116**

Lee Bontecou

Untitled, 1966. Painted iron, fiberglass, and fabric, 41 × 29 × 8 in. (104.1 × 73.7 × 20.3 cm). Akron Art Museum; gift of Leo Castelli, Castelli Galleries 1974.122 **p. 181**

Louise Bourgeois

Portrait, 1963. Latex over plaster, 15 ⅜ × 12 ⅜ × 4 ⅛ in. (39 × 31.5 × 10.5 cm). The Museum of Modern Art, New York; gift of Arthur Drexler 385.1986 **p. 97**

Joan Brown

Self Portrait, 1970. Oil and enamel on canvas, 26 × 26 in. (66 × 66 cm). Christine Buck, The Buck Collection **p. 292**

Vija Celmins

Untitled (Comb), 1970. Enamel on wood, 75 × 14 ⅝ × 2 ⅜ in. (190.5 × 37.2 × 6 cm). Los Angeles County Museum of Art; purchase Contemporary Art Council Fund M.72.26 **p. 287**

Judy Chicago

Bigamy, 1964. Acrylic on stoneware, 24 × 18 × 6 in. (61 × 45.7 × 15.2 cm). Private collection **p. 119**

Robert Colescott

Assassin Down, 1968–70. Acrylic on linen, 78 ¼ × 58 ¾ in. (198.8 × 149.2 cm). Dallas Museum of Art; TWO x TWO for AIDS and Art Fund 2018.59 **p. 227**

Dale Brockman Davis

Viet Nam War Games, 1969. Clay and metal, approximately 48 × 48 in. (121.9 × 121.9 cm). Los Angeles County Museum of Art; gift of the 2021 Decorative Arts and Design Acquisition Committee (DA²) M.2021.194.1–.8 **p. 259**

Jay DeFeo

Doctor Jazz, 1958. Ink, acrylic, graphite, synthetic polymer, and tinsel on paper, 125 ½ × 42 ½ × 3 ½ in. (318.8 × 108 × 8.9 cm). Nora Eccles Harrison Museum of Art, Logan, UT; gift of the Marie Eccles Caine Foundation 2001.11 **p. 14**

Niki de Saint Phalle

Annette, 1964. Paper, fabric, pencil, colored pencil, ink, ink stamp, photomechanical reproduction, gouache, watercolor, pastel, and enamel on canvas, 67 ¾ × 59 ⅛ in. (172.1 × 150 cm). Hirshhorn Museum and Sculpture Garden, Smithsonian Institution, Washington, DC; gift of Joseph H. Hirshhorn, 1966 66.4436 **p. 113**

Jeff Donaldson

J. D. McClain's Day in Court, 1970. Paint on cardboard with ink on paper, 29 ⅛ × 19 ⁵⁄₁₆ in. (74 × 49 cm). Smithsonian National Museum of African American History and Culture, Washington, DC; 2017.33.2 **p. 299**

Martha Edelheit

Leg, c. 1966. Mixed media, 33 ¼ × 33 × 12 ¾ in. (84.5 × 83.8 × 32.4 cm). Collection of the artist **p. 174**

Ed Emshwiller

Scape-mates, 1972. Video, color, sound; 28:16 min. Electronic Arts Intermix, New York **p. 335**

Lee Friedlander

Washington, D.C., 1962. Gelatin silver print, 8 ⅛ × 5 ½ in. (20.6 × 13.8 cm). The Museum of Modern Art, New York; purchase 8.2006 **p. 73**

Nancy Grossman

The Bride, 1965. Leather, metal, fur, and fabric on canvas mounted on wood, 22 ⅝ × 22 ¾ × 5 ⅛ in. (57.5 × 57.8 × 13 cm). Collection of halley k harrisburg and Michael Rosenfeld **p. 147**

Lynn Hershman Leeson

Butterfly Woman Sleeping, 1967, from the series *Breathing Machines*. Wax, wig, paint, butterflies, feathers, sensors, sound, wood base, and acrylic, 16 ½ × 16 ½ × 13 in. (41.9 × 41.9 × 33 cm). Collection of Marguerite Steed Hoffman **p. 214**

Ken Jacobs

Blonde Cobra, 1963. 16mm film transferred to video, color and black-and-white, sound; 33 min. Electronic Arts Intermix, New York **p. 86**

Lee Lozano

No Title, c. 1962–63. Oil on wood, 14 ¾ × 13 ⅛ × ¾ in. (37.5 × 33.5 × 2 cm). Pinault Collection, Paris **p. 68**

No title (Grinning Face with Ear/Crank), 1962. Graphite pencil on paper: sheet, 9 ¼ × 8 ⅝ in. (23.5 x 21.9 cm). Whitney Museum of American Art, New York; gift of Susan Lorence 2008.247 **p. 69**

Marisol

Diptych, 1971. Lithograph in two colors: two sheets, 47 ¾ × 31 ⅞ in. (121.3 × 81 cm) each. Whitney Museum of American Art, New

York; Purchase, with funds from the Drawing and Print Committee 2024.363a–b **p. 320**

Ana Mendieta

Untitled (Facial Hair Transplants), 1972. Set of seven color photographs: dimensions variable. The Estate of Ana Mendieta Collection, LLC **p. 332**

Claes Oldenburg

Giant Fagends, 1967. Canvas, urethane foam, wire, wood, latex, and melamine laminate, 52 × 96 × 96 in. (132.1 × 243.8 × 243.8 cm) overall (with base, irregular). Whitney Museum of American Art, New York; purchase, with funds from the Friends of the Whitney Museum of American Art 70.44a–o **p. 206**

Soft Drainpipe—Red (Hot) Version, 1967. Vinyl filled with expanded polystyrene chips, on painted metal: drainpipe, 120 × 60 × 45 in. (304.8 × 152.4 × 114.3 cm); stand, 96 in. (243.9 cm) high. National Gallery of Art, Washington, DC; Robert and Jane Meyerhoff Collection, gift in honor of the 50th anniversary of the National Gallery of Art 1990.75.1 **p. 207**

John Outterbridge

Jive Ass Bird, 1971. Mixed media, 22¼ × 31 × 12½ in. (56.5 × 78.7 × 31.8 cm). The Greg and Diane Pitts Family Collection **p. 324**

Kenneth Price

Red, 1965. Ceramic, paint, and wood, 14⅞ × 17 × 16¼ in. (37.8 × 43.2 × 41.3 cm). Rhode Island School of Design Art Museum, Providence; Museum purchase with the aid of the National Endowment for the Arts 71.062 **p. 131**

Joseph Raffaele

Lipsticks, Braces, 1965. Oil on canvas, 55 ¾ × 45 ¾ in. (141.6 × 116.2 cm). The Estate of Joseph Raffael and Nancy Hoffman Gallery, New York **p. 148**

Betye Saar

Omen, 1967. Mixed-media assemblage, 12 × 9 ¼ × 3 ⅛ in. (32.5 × 23.5 × 8 cm). Collection of Candace Weir **p. 200**

Carolee Schneemann

Viet-Flakes, 1962–67. 16mm film transferred to HD video, black-and-white, sound; 8:31 min. Electronic Arts Intermix, New York **p. 65**

Nancy Spero

Male Bomb II, 1966. Gouache and ink on paper, 34 × 27¼ in. (86.4 × 69.2 cm). The Morgan Library and Museum, New York; Gift of the Modern and Contemporary Collectors' Committee 2014.22 **p. 165**

Dorothea Tanning

Rainy Day Canapé, 1970. Upholstered wood sofa with wool, polyester, and rayon plain-weave cover, wool batting, cardboard, and ping-pong balls, 31 ½ × 57 × 33 in. (80 × 144.8 × 83.8 cm). Philadelphia Museum of Art; 125th Anniversary Acquisition, gift of an anonymous donor, 2002 2002.86-1 **p. 304**

Paul Thek

Meat Piece with Warhol Brillo Box, 1965. Beeswax, painted wood, and Plexiglas, 14 × 17 × 17 in. (35.6 × 43.2 × 43.2 cm). Philadelphia Museum of Art; purchased with funds contributed by the Daniel W. Dietrich Foundation, 1990 1990-111-1 **p. 130**

Timothy Washington

1A, 1971. Etched aluminum, leather, metal studs, nail, and draft card,

23½ × 23¼ in. (59.7 × 59.1 cm). San Francisco Museum of Modern Art; purchase, by exchange, through a gift of Peggy Guggenheim 2020.46 **p. 312**

William T. Wiley

Painter Baffles and Excess in California, 1969. Ink, pencil, felt-tip pen, and watercolor on paper, 28 ¼ × 20 ¼ in. (71.8 × 51.4 cm). Collection of Susan W. Paine **p. 262**

Karl Wirsum

Doggerel II, 1966. Acrylic on linen, 33 × 25 in. (83.8 × 63.5 cm). Whitney Museum of American Art, New York; purchase with funds from the Larry Aldrich Foundation Fund 67.38 **p. 162**

APPENDIX

This appendix is intended to offer another point of access to the information within the Chronology, specifically by providing a concise list of the schools, collectives, galleries, and museums that had particular significance in the lives and careers of the artists of *Sixties Surreal*. Further detail is provided in the case of schools and museums, where past and present names are listed when applicable, and for galleries, where active dates and founders are included when possible.

Schools

Academy André L'Hote
Academy of Applied Arts Vienna (now University of Applied Arts Vienna)
Academy of Fine Arts Vienna
Alabama State Teachers College (now Alabama State University)
Alfred University
American Academy of Art College
American University
The ArtCenter School (now ArtCenter College of Design)
Art Students League of New York
Atlanta University
Bard College
Barnes Foundation
Baylor University
Berkeley Adult School
Binghamton University
Bowling Green State University
Bradford Junior College
Briar Cliff University
Brooklyn Museum Art School
California College of Arts and Crafts (now California College of the Arts)
California Institute of Technology
California School of Fine Arts (now San Francisco Art Institute)
California State College at Fullerton (now California State University, Fullerton)
California State University, Los Angeles
Carnegie Museum of Natural History
Case Western Reserve University
Chicago Academy of Art
Chouinard Art Institute (now California Institute of the Arts, or CalArts)
City College of New York
Ciudad Universitaria, Mexico City
Columbia High School, Richland, WA
Columbia University
Communicative Arts Academy
The Cooper Union School of Art
Dorsey High School, Los Angeles
École des Beaux-Arts

Florida State University
Fort Valley State College (now Fort Valley State University)
Free University of New York
Fresno State College (now California State University, Fresno)
Haystack Mountain School of Crafts
Hans Hofmann School of Fine Arts
High School of Music & Art, New York (now LaGuardia High School)
Holbrook Indian School
Howard University
Humboldt State University
Institute of American Indian Arts (IAIA)
Institute of Design (ID) at Illinois Tech
The Institute of Fine Arts, New York University
Jepson Art Institute
Knox College
Los Angeles City College
Los Angeles Trade-Technical College
Mills College (now Mills College at Northeastern University)
The New School for Social Research (now The New School)
New York University (NYU)
North Carolina Agricultural and Technical State University
Northwestern University
Ohio University
Otis Art Institute (now Otis College of Art and Design)
Pasadena City College
Pennsylvania Academy of Fine Arts (PAFA)
The Pennsylvania State University
Pepperdine University
Phoenix Indian High School
Pierre Indian School
Pratt Institute
Regis High School, Cedar Rapids, IA
Rice University
Rockland Community College
Rutgers University
Sacramento State College (now California State University, Sacramento)
Saint Xavier College (now Saint Xavier University)
San Antonio College
San Francisco Art Institute (SFAI)
San Francisco State College (now San Francisco State University)
San José State College (now San José State University)
Santa Fe Indian School
Santa Monica City College (now Santa Monica College)
Santa Rosa Junior College
School of the Art Institute of Chicago (SAIC)
School of Visual Arts
Shawnigan Lake School
Smith College
Sonoma State University
Southern University, Baton Rouge (now Southern University and A&M College)
Stanislaus State College (now California State University Stanislaus)
Temple University
Texas Western College (now the University of Texas at El Paso)
Tokyo University of Education
Tuskegee Institute (now Tuskegee University)
The University of Arizona
University of Arkansas
University of Arkansas at Pine Bluff
University of California, Berkeley (UC Berkeley)
University of California, Davis (UC Davis)
University of California, Irvine
University of California, Riverside
University of California, San Diego
The University of Chicago
University of Colorado Boulder
University of Illinois Urbana-Champaign
University of Iowa
University of Kansas
University of Michigan
University of Minnesota
University of Notre Dame
The University of Oklahoma
University of Pennsylvania
University of Southern California (USC)

The University of Texas at Austin

University of the Americas in Mexico City (now Universidad de las Américas Ciudad de México)

University of Wisconsin, Madison (now University of Wisconsin–Madison)

Vassar College

Waseda University

Washington University, St. Louis (now Washington University in St. Louis)

Yale University

Art Nonprofits, Collectives, Community Centers, and Programs

Ad Hoc Committee of Women Artists

African Commune of Bad Relevant Artists (AFRICOBRA)

Agricultural Workers Organizing Committee (merged with National Farm Workers Association; now United Farm Workers [UFW])

Art & Soul

Artes Seis

Art Workers' Coalition (AWC)

Black Arts Alliance (BAA)

Black Arts Council (BAC)

Black Arts Movement

Bodacious Buggerrilla

Black and Puerto Rican Students and Artists for a Black Wing in Memory of Dr. Martin Luther King Jr.

Black Emergency Cultural Coalition (BECC)

Black Panther Party for Self-Defense

Camera Obscura Film Society

Canyon Cinema

Collective for Living Cinema

Conservative Vice Lords Inc.

Experimental Cinema Group

Experiments in Art and Technology (E.A.T.)

False Image

Fight Censorship

Filmmakers' Cinematheque

Galería de la Raza

Group 35

The Hairy Who

Indians of All Tribes

Judson Dance Theater

Kamoinge Workshop

The Kitchen, New York

La MaMa

The Living Theater

Los Angeles Council of Women Artists

Martinique Theater

Millennium Film Workshop

Newsreel (now Third World Newsreel)

National Farm Workers Association (merged with Agricultural Workers Organizing Committee; now United Farm Workers [UFW])

The National Organization for Women (NOW)

The New York State Theater (now the David H. Koch Theater)

Nouveau Réalisme

Organization of Black American Culture (OBAC)

Painterland, San Francisco

"The Plaster Foundation of Atlantis"

Progressive Art Workers

Rat Bastard Protective Association (RBPA)

South Side Community Art Center

Southwest Indian Art Program (SWIAP)

Student Nonviolent Coordinating Committee (SNCC)

Telegraph Hill Neighborhood Center

Third World Liberation Front

TV Lab

Watts Towers Arts Center

Weusi Artist Collective

Where We At Black Women Artists, Inc. (WWA)

Women Students and Artists for Black Art Liberation (WSABAL)

Young Men and Young Women's Hebrew Association (now the Gershman Y)

Galleries

A Clean, Well-Lighted Place, Austin (active 1967–1971, founded by Dave Hickey)

Acts of Art Gallery, New York (active 1969–1975, founded by Patricia Grey and Nigel Jackson)

A.I.R. Gallery, New York (founded 1972 by 20 A.I.R. artists)

Alexander Iolas Gallery, New York (active 1954–1987, founded by Alexander Iolas)

Allan Frumkin Gallery, Chicago and New York (active 1952–1979, founded by Allan Frumkin)

Allan Stone Gallery, New York (now Allan Stone Projects, founded 1960 by Allan Stone)

An American Place, New York (active 1929–1946, founded by Alfred Stieglitz)

Ankrum Gallery, Los Angeles (active 1966–1990, founded by Joan Akrum)

Art of This Century Gallery, New York (active 1942–1947, founded by Peggy Guggenheim)

Berkeley Gallery, San Francisco (active 1965–1972, founded by Marian Parmenter)

Bianchini Gallery, New York (active 1958–1967, founded by Paul Bianchini)

Brata Gallery, New York (active 1957–1962, founded by Al Held and John and Nicholas Kruschenick)

Brockman Gallery, Los Angeles (active 1967–1990, founded by Alonzo and Dale Davis)

Bykert Gallery, New York (active 1966–1975, founded by Klaus Kertess)

Byron Gallery, New York (active 1961–1971, founded by Charles Byron)

Castagno Gallery, New York (active c. 1964–1966)

Castellane Gallery, New York (active 1962–1967, founded by Richard Castellane)

Castelli Gallery, New York (founded 1957 by Leo Castelli)

Ceeje Gallery, Los Angeles (active 1962–1970, founded by Cecil Hedrick and Jerry Jerome)

Cordier & Ekstrom Gallery, New York (active 1959–1990, founded by Daniel Cordier and Arne Ekstrom)

David Stuart Galleries, Los Angeles (active 1910–1984, founded by David Stuart)

Dell Gallery, Chicago (active c. 1966–1968, founded by Marjorie Dell)

Dilexi Gallery, San Francisco (active 1958–1969, founded by Bob Alexander and Jim Newman)

Dwan Gallery, Los Angeles and New York (active 1959–1971, founded by Virginia Dwan)

East & West Gallery, San Francisco (active 1955–1958, founded by Ethel Gechtoff)

Erotic Art Gallery, New York (active c. 1973–1974)

Feigen Gallery, Chicago (founded 1957 by Richard L. Feigen)

Ferus Gallery, Los Angeles (active 1957–1966, founded by Walter Hopps, Shirley Hopps, and Edward Kienholz)

Fischbach Gallery, New York (founded 1960 by Marilyn Cole Fischbach)

Forum Gallery, New York (founded 1961 by Bella Fishko)

Galerie Alexandre Iolas, Paris (active c. 1964–early 1970s, founded by Alexandre Iolas)

Galerie Breteau, Paris (active 1937–1987, founded by René Breteau)

Galerie Iris Clert, Paris (active 1956–1971, founded by Iris Clert)

Galerie J, Paris (active 1961–1966, founded by Jeannine Restany [de Goldschmidt] and Pierre Restany)

Galerie St. Stephan, Vienna (as of 1964, Galerie nächst St. Stephan, now Galerie nächst St. Stephan Rosemarie Schwarzwälder, founded 1954 by Otto Mauer)

Galleria George Lester, Rome (active 1961–1964, founded by George Lester)

Gallery 32, Los Angeles (active 1968–1970, founded by Suzanne Jackson)

Gallery Bugs Bunny, Chicago (active c. 1968–1969, founded by Robert Green and Franklin and Penelope Rosemont)

Gallery Gertrude Stein, New York (active c. 1962–2006, founded by Gertrude Stein)

Graham Gallery, New York (now Taylor | Graham, founded 1857 by Samuel Graham)

Green Gallery, New York (active 1960–1965, founded by Richard Bellamy)

Hacker Gallery, New York (active c. 1948–1963, founded by Seymour Hacker)

Howard Wise Gallery, Cleveland and New York (active 1957–1971, founded by Howard Wise)

Huysman Gallery, Los Angeles (active 1960–1961, founded by Henry Hopkins)

Judson Gallery, New York (active 1959–1962, founded by Jim Dine, Claes Oldenburg, Marc Ratliff, Bud Scott, and Tom Wesselmann)

Julien Levy Gallery, New York (active 1931–1949, founded by Julien Levy)

King Ubu Gallery, San Francisco (active 1952–1953, founded by Robert Duncan, Jess, and Harry Jacobus)

Kornblee Gallery, New York (active 1961–1986, founded by Jill Kornblee)

Kozmopolitan Gallery, New York (active 1968–1970, founded by Barbara Koz Paley)

Lakeside Gallery, Chicago (active c. 1968–1971, founded by Barry and Josephine Plotkin)

Larkins Gallery, Sante Fe (active c. 1970–1971, founded by Dennis Larkins)

Motion Gallery, San Jose (founded by Joseph Hawley)

New York City Arts Theater Association Gallery, New York

New York Cultural Center, New York (active 1964–1975, founded by Huntington Hartford)

Nicholas Wilder Gallery, Los Angeles (active 1965–1979, founded by Nicholas Wilder)

Nyumba Ya Sanaa Gallery, New York (active c. 1967–1978, founded by the Weusi Artist Collective)

OK Harris Works of Art, New York (active 1969–2014, founded by Ivan C. Karp)

Pace Gallery, Boston and New York (founded 1960 by Arne Glimcher)

Reuben Gallery, New York (active 1959–1961, founded by Anita Reuben)

Richard L. Feigen & Co., Chicago and New York (founded 1957 by Richard L. Feigen)

Rolf Nelson Gallery, Los Angeles (1953–1973, founded by Rolf Nelson)

Ronald Feldman Fine Arts, New York (now Ronald Feldman Gallery, founded 1971 by Ronald and Frayda Feldman)

Sidney Janis Gallery, New York (active 1948–1999, founded by Sidney Janis)

Six Gallery, San Francisco (active 1954–1957, founded by Wally Hedrick, Hayward King, Deborah Remington, John Ryan, Jack Spicer, and David Simpson)

Spatsa Gallery, San Francisco (active 1957–1961, founded by Dimitri Grachis)

Spectrum Gallery, New York (active c. 1966–1975, founded by Robert Newman)

Stable Gallery, New York (active 1953–1970, founded by Eleanor Ward)

Staempfli Gallery, New York (active 1959–1992, founded by George Staempfli)

Tibor de Nagy Gallery, New York (founded 1950 by Tibor de Nagy)

Van Bovenkamp Gallerie, New York (active 1963–1965, founded by Hans and Gerrit Van De Bovenkamp)

Zoë Dusanne Gallery, Seattle (active 1950–1964, founded by Zoë Dusanne)

Museums

Albright-Knox Art Gallery (now Buffalo AKG Art Museum)

Berkeley Art Center

Brooklyn Museum

Contemporary Arts Association of Houston (now Contemporary Arts Museum Houston)

Corcoran Gallery of Art (now The Corcoran Collection at the National Gallery of Art)

Crocker Art Museum, Sacramento

Dallas Museum for Contemporary Arts

Dallas Museum of Fine Arts

de Saisset Museum at Santa Clara University

de Young Museum

George Eastman House (now Eastman Museum)

Hyde Park Art Center (HPAC)

Jewish Museum, New York

Kunsthalle Bern, Switzerland

La Jolla Museum of Art (now Museum of Contemporary Art San Diego)

Little Gallery at San Bernardino Valley College

Massachusetts Institute of Technology's Hayden Gallery (now List Visual Arts Center)

Meadows Museum at Southern Methodist University, Dallas

The Metropolitan Museum of Art

Museum of Contemporary Art Chicago

The Museum of Modern Art, New York

Museum of the National Center of Afro-American Artists, Boston

National Collection of Fine Arts (now Smithsonian American Art Museum)

Oakland Museum (now Oakland Museum of California)

Pasadena Art Museum (now Norton Simon Museum)

Paul W. Zuccaire Gallery at Stony Brook University (formerly Fine Arts Center Art Gallery; University Art Gallery)

Philadelphia Museum of Art

Philbrook Museum of Art in Tulsa, Oklahoma

San Francisco Art Institute

San Francisco Museum of Art (now San Francisco Museum of Modern Art)

Santa Barbara Museum of Art

The Solomon R. Guggenheim Museum

Studio Museum in Harlem

University Art Museum, Berkeley (now Berkeley Art Museum and Pacific Film Archive)

Whitney Museum of American Art

SELECTED BIBLIOGRAPHY

1969 Annual Exhibition: Contemporary American Painting. New York: Whitney Museum of American Art, 1969. Published in conjunction with an exhibition of the same title, organized by and presented at the Whitney Museum of American Art, New York, December 16, 1969–February 1, 1970.

1972 Annual Exhibition: Contemporary American Painting. New York: Whitney Museum of American Art, 1972. Published in conjunction with an exhibition of the same title, organized by and presented at the Whitney Museum of American Art, New York, January 25–March 19, 1972.

Ades, Dawn, and Simon Baker, eds. *Undercover Surrealism: Georges Bataille and "DOCUMENTS."* Cambridge, MA: MIT Press, 2006.

Adrian, Dennis. "The Art of H. C. Westermann." *Artforum*, September 1967.

———. "Barbara Rossi." In *Barbara Rossi: Selected Works, 1967–1990*, 3–16. Chicago: Renaissance Society at the University of Chicago, 1991. Published in conjunction with an exhibition of the same title, organized by and presented at the Renaissance Society, Chicago, January 13–February 24, 1991.

———. *Sight Out of Mind: Essays and Criticism on Art.* Ann Arbor, MI: UMI Research Press, 1985.

Albright, Thomas. *Art in the San Francisco Bay Area, 1945–1980: An Illustrated History.* Berkeley: University of California Press, 1985.

Aldrich, Larry. "New Talent USA." *Art in America*, July–August 1966.

Alexander, M. Darsie, and Bartholomew Ryan, eds. *International Pop.* Minneapolis: Walker Art Center, 2015. Published in conjunction with an exhibition of the same title, organized by and presented at the Walker Art Center, Minneapolis, April 11–August 29, 2015, and at the Dallas Museum of Art, October 11, 2015–January 17, 2016, and the Philadelphia Museum of Art, February 24–May 15, 2016.

Alkalimat, Abdul, Rebecca Zorach, and Romi Crawford, eds. *The Wall of Respect: Public Art and Black Liberation in 1960s Chicago.* Chicago: Northwestern University Press, 2017.

Alloway, Lawrence. *Samaras: Selected Works, 1960–1966.* New York: Pace Gallery, 1966. Published in conjunction with an exhibition of the same title, organized by and presented at Pace Gallery, New York, October 8–November 5, 1966.

Andrews, Benny, and Cliff Joseph. "Untitled Statement, Early 1969." Reprinted in *The "Soul of a Nation" Reader: Writings by and about Black American Artists, 1960–1980*, edited by Mark Godfrey and Allie Biswas, 134–35. New York: Gregory R. Miller, 2021.

Anker, Steve, Kathy Geritz, and Steve Seid, eds. *Radical Light: Alternative Film & Video in the San Francisco Bay Area, 1945–2000.* Berkeley: University of California Press, 2010.

Annual Exhibition 1962. New York: Whitney Museum of American Art, 1962. Published in conjunction with an exhibition of the same title, organized by and presented at the Whitney Museum of American Art, New York, December 12, 1962–February 3, 1963.

Anthes, Bill, and Kathleen Ash-Milby, eds. *Dakota Modern: The Art of Oscar Howe.* Washington, DC: National Museum of the American Indian, Smithsonian Institution, 2022. Published in conjunction with an exhibition of the same title, organized by and presented at the Smithsonian's National Museum of the American Indian, New York, March 11–September 11, 2022, and at the Portland Museum of Art, Portland, OR, October 29, 2022–May 14, 2023, and the South Dakota Art Museum, South Dakota State University, Brookings, June 10–September 17, 2023.

Antin, David. "Another Category: 'Eccentric Abstraction.'" *Artforum*, November 1966.

Applin, Jo. *Eccentric Objects: Rethinking Sculpture in 1960s America.* New Haven, CT: Yale University Press, 2012.

———. "Hannah Wilke's Agreeable Objects." In *Eva Hesse, Hannah Wilke: Erotic Abstraction*, edited by Eleanor Nairne, 78–93. New York: Rizzoli, 2020.

———. "'Strange Encounters': Claes Oldenburg's 'Proposed Colossal Monuments' for New York and London." *Art History* 34, no. 4 (September 1, 2011): 839–57.

Aramphongphan, Paisid. "An Artist in the Secular World: Paul Thek's Relics." *American Art* 35, no. 1 (Spring 2021): 40–61.

Arbus, Diane. "Five Photographs by Diane Arbus." *Artforum*, May 1971.

———. "The Full Circle." *Harper's Bazaar*, November 1961.

———. "The Vertical Journey: Six Movements of a Moment within the Heart of the City." *Esquire*, July 1, 1960.

Arkansas Museum of Fine Arts. "Linda Lomahaftewa, *The Quiet Land, the Warm Land*." Accessed March 25, 2024. https://guide.arkmfa.org/audio-guides/guides/410.

Arkesteijn, Roel, ed. *Codex Spero: Nancy Spero, Selected Writings and Interviews, 1950–2008.* Amsterdam: Roma Publications, 2008.

Armani, Elise, Amy Khang, and Gabriella Shypula, eds. *Revisiting "5+1."* Stony Brook, NY: Paul W. Zuccaire Gallery, 2022. Published in conjunction with an exhibition of the same title, organized by and presented at the Paul W. Zuccaire Gallery, Stony Brook University, Stony Brook, NY, November 10, 2022–March 31, 2023.

Art '65: Lesser Known and Unknown Painters/Young American Sculpture, East to West. New York: Star Press, 1965. Published in conjunction with an exhibition of the same title, held at the American Express Pavilion at the 1964–65 New York World's Fair, April 22–October 18, 1964, and April 21–October 17, 1965.

Arthur, Paul. "'A Panorama Compounded of Great Human Suffering and Ecstatic Filmic Representation': Texts on Ken Jacobs." In *Optic Antics: The Cinema of Ken Jacobs*, edited by Michele Pierson, David E. James, and Paul Arthur, 25–37. Oxford: Oxford University Press, 2011.

"Art on the Wing: Jet-Age Sculpture at Lincoln Center." *Life*, April 10, 1964.

"Art: Uptown." *Time*, October 23, 1964.

Ashbery, John. "Growing Up Surreal." *ARTnews*, May 1968.

Ashton, Dore. *Richard Lindner.* New York: Harry N. Abrams, 1969.

———. "Romare Bearden: Projections." *Quadrum* 17 (1964): 99–110.

"Assemblage at the Frontier." *Time*, October 15, 1965.

Aukeman, Anastasia. "The Rat Bastard Protective Association: Bruce Conner and His San Francisco Cohort, 1958–1968." PhD diss., Graduate Center, City University of New York, 2013.

———. *Welcome to Painterland: Bruce Conner and the Rat Bastard Protective Association.* Berkeley: University of California Press, 2016.

Auping, Michael. Conversation with Dan Nadel, Laura Phipps, Elisabeth Sussman, and Kelly Long. June 23, 2020.

———, ed. *Jess: A Grand Collage, 1951–1993.* Buffalo: Albright-Knox Art Gallery, 1993. Published in conjunction with an exhibition of the same title, organized by and presented at the Albright-Knox Art Gallery, Buffalo, September 12–October 31, 1993.

Auther, Elissa. "Fiber Art and the Hierarchy of Art and Craft, 1960–1980." *Journal of Modern Craft* 1, no. 1 (2008): 13–33.

Bancroft, Sarah, and Walter Hopps, eds. *James Rosenquist: A Retrospective.* New York: Guggenheim Museum, 2003. Published in conjunction with an exhibition of the same title, organized by the Solomon R. Guggenheim Museum, New York, and presented at the Menil Collection, Houston, and the Museum of Fine Arts, Houston, May 17–August 17, 2003; the Solomon R. Guggenheim Museum, New York, October 17, 2003–February 4, 2004; and the Guggenheim Museum Bilbao, May 13–October 17, 2004.

Baker, Elizabeth, and Joseph Raffaele. "The Way-Out West: Interviews with Four San Francisco Artists." *ARTnews*, Summer 1967.

Baltrip-Balagás, Ayana. "The Art of Self-Defense." *Print*, March/April 2005.

Baraka, Amiri. "Henry Dumas: Afro-Surreal Expressionist." *Black American Literature Forum* 22, no. 2 (Summer 1988): 164–66.

Barron, Stephanie, and Lauren Bergman, eds. *Ken Price Sculpture: A Retrospective.* Los Angeles: Los Angeles County Museum of Art; Munich: Prestel, 2013. Published in conjunction with an exhibition of the same title, organized by and presented at the Los Angeles County Museum of Art, September 16, 2012–January 6, 2013, and at the Nasher Sculpture Center, Dallas, February 9–May 12, 2013, and the Metropolitan Museum of Art, New York, June 18–September 22, 2013.

Beck, Jessica, Michelle Piranio, and Matthew Newton, eds. *Marisol and Warhol Take New York.* Pittsburgh: Andy Warhol Museum, 2021. Published in conjunction with an exhibition of the same title, organized by and presented at the Andy Warhol Foundation, Pittsburgh, October 14, 2021–February 14, 2022, and at the Pérez Art Museum Miami, April 15–September 5, 2022.

Beckstette, Sven, and Udo Kittelmann, eds. *Jack Whitten: Jack's Jacks.* Munich: Prestel, 2019. Published in conjunction with an exhibition of the same title, organized by and presented at the Hamburger Bahnhof – Nationalgalerie der Gegenwart, Berlin, March 29–September 1, 2019.

Bell, Larry, Ron Miyashiro, Joe Goode, and Jerry McMillan. "Oral History Interview with Larry Bell, Ron Miyashiro, Joe Goode, and Jerry McMillan, 2010." By the Getty Research Institute. June 5, 2010. The Getty Research Institute, Institutional Archives, Modern Art in Los Angeles Recordings, 2003–2011.

Benny Andrews: The Bicentennial Series. Atlanta: High Museum of Art, 1975. Published in conjunction with an exhibition of the same title, organized by and presented at the High Museum of Art, Atlanta, January 18–February 23, 1975.

Bereal, Ed. "Oral History Interview with Ed Bereal." By Hunter Drohojowska-Philp. February 13, 2016. Archives of American Art, Smithsonian Institute, Washington, DC. https://www.aaa.si.edu/collections/interviews/oral-history-interview-ed-bereal-16308.

Berger, Maurice. "A Photographer's Search for Magic in Everyday Life." *New York Times*, January 9, 2018.

Berman, Tosh, Colin Gardner, and Walter Hopps. *Support the Revolution: Wallace Berman*. Amsterdam: Institute of Contemporary Art, 1992. Published in conjunction with an exhibition of the same title, organized by and presented at the Institute of Contemporary Art, Amsterdam, December 13, 1992–February 7, 1993.

Bernadac, Marie-Laure, and Hans-Ulrich Obrist, eds. *Louise Bourgeois: Destruction of the Father/Reconstruction of the Father, Writings and Interviews, 1923–1997*. Cambridge, MA: MIT Press, 1998.

Bernstein, Judith. *Dicks of Death: Judith Bernstein*. Zurich: Edition Patrick Frey, 2016.

———. "Sinister Pop: Judith Bernstein." Whitney Museum of American Art, April 16, 2013. Video, 2 min. https://whitney.org/media/392.

Bird, Jon, Jo Anna Isaak, and Sylvère Lotringer. *Nancy Spero*. London: Phaidon, 1996.

Bishop, Joan, and Nancy Lim, eds. *Joan Brown*. Berkeley: University of California Press, 2022. Published in conjunction with an exhibition of the same title, organized by and presented at the San Francisco Museum of Modern Art, November 19, 2022–March 12, 2023.

Blauvelt, Andrew, ed. *Hippie Modernism: The Struggle for Utopia*. Minneapolis: Walker Art Center, 2015. Published in conjunction with an exhibition of the same title, organized by and presented at the Walker Art Center, Minneapolis, October 24, 2015–February 28, 2016, and at the Cranbrook Art Museum, Bloomfield Hills, MI, June 19–October 9, 2016, and the Berkeley Art Museum and Pacific Film Archive, Berkeley, CA, February 8–May 21, 2017.

Bogzaran, Fariba, ed. *Gordon Onslow Ford: A Man on a Green Island*. Inverness, CA: Lucid Art Foundation, 2019.

Borja-Villel, Manuel J., ed. *Öyvind Fahlström: Another Space for Painting*. Barcelona: Museu D'Art Contemporani De Barcelona; North Adams: Massachusetts Museum of Contemporary Art, 2001. Published in conjunction with the exhibition *Öyvind Fahlström*, organized by and presented at the Barcelona Museum of Contemporary Art, October 18, 2000–January 8, 2001, and at the Centro Studi sull'arte Fondazione Ragghianti, Lucca, Italy, March 17–May 15, 2001; the Massachusetts Museum of Contemporary Art, North Adams, June 15–October 22, 2001; the Institute d'Art Contemporain Villeurbanne, Villeurbanne, France, February 15–May 26, 2002; and Baltic Centre for Contemporary Art, Newcastle, UK, September 29–November 24, 2002.

Boultenhouse, Charles, and Parker Tyler. Papers. Manuscripts and Archives Division, The New York Public Library.

Bourgeois, Louise. "The Fabric of Construction." *Craft Horizons*, no. 29 (March 1969): 31–35.

Bradnock, Lucy. *No More Masterpieces: Modern Art after Artaud*. New Haven, CT: Yale University Press, 2021.

Bradnock, Lucy, and Rani Singh. "PAPA'S GOT A BRAND NEW BAG: Crafting an Art Scene." In *Pacific Standard Time: Los Angeles Art, 1945–1980*, edited by Rebecca Peabody, 67–123. Los Angeles: Getty Research Institute and J. Paul Getty Museum, 2011. Published in conjunction with the exhibition *Pacific Standard Time: Crosscurrents in L.A. Painting and Sculpture, 1950–1970*, organized by and presented at the J. Paul Getty Museum, Los Angeles, October 1, 2011–February 5, 2012.

Braun, Christiaan, ed. *Eye Infection*. Düsseldorf: Richter, 2001. Published in conjunction with an exhibition of the same title, organized by and presented at the Stedelijk Museum, Amsterdam, November 3, 2001–January 20, 2002.

Breitweiser, Sabine, ed. *Carolee Schneemann: Kinetic Painting*. Munich: Prestel, 2015. Published in conjunction with an exhibition of the same title, organized by and presented at the Museum der Moderne Salzburg, May 31–September 24, 2017, and at MoMA PS1, New York, October 22, 2017–March 11, 2018.

Breton, André. "Manifesto of Surrealism" (1924). In *Manifestoes of Surrealism*, translated by Richard Seaver and Helen R. Lane, 3–47. Ann Arbor: University of Michigan Press, 1969.

Brockman Davis, Dale. Brockman Gallery Archives, Los Angeles Public Library.

———. "Dale Brockman Davis: Artist, Educator, and Gallerist." By Bridget Cooks and Amanda Tewes. 2021. Oral History Center, The Bancroft Library, University of California, Berkeley. https://digital assets.lib.berkeley.edu/roho/ucb/text/davis_dale_2021.pdf.

Brooks, Kalia. "Ron Miyashiro." Hammer Museum. Accessed October 31, 2023. https://hammer.ucla.edu/now-dig-this/artists/ron-miyashiro.

Brooks, LeRonn, Huey Copeland, and Jacob Stewart-Halevy. Conversation with Dan Nadel, Laura Phipps, Elisabeth Sussman, and Kelly Long. December 9, 2019. Whitney Museum of American Art, New York.

Brown, Joan. "Joan Brown." San Francisco Museum of Modern Art, 1979. Video, 5 min. https://www.sfmoma.org/watch/joan-brown/.

———. "Oral History Interview with Joan Brown." By Paul Karlstrom. July 1–September 9, 1975. Archives of American Art, Smithsonian Institution, Washington, DC.

Brown, Roger. "Why Was Hairy Who?????" In *What Nerve! Alternative Figures in American Art, 1960 to the Present*, edited by Dan Nadel, 52–57. Providence: Museum of Art, Rhode Island School of Design; New York: D.A.P./Distributed Art Publishers, 2014. Published in conjunction with an exhibition of the same title, organized by and presented at the Museum of Art, Rhode Island School of Design, Providence, September 19, 2014–January 4, 2015.

Bryant, Linda Goode. "Making Doors: Linda Goode Bryant in Conversation with Senga Nengudi." By Randy Kennedy and Senga Nengudi. In *Ursula*, no. 1 (December 1, 2018). https://www.hauser wirth.com/ursula/23020-making-doors-linda-goode-bryant-conversation-senga-nengudi/.

Bryan-Wilson, Julia. *Art Workers: Radical Practice in the Vietnam War Era*. Berkeley: University of California Press, 2009.

Butler, Cornelia. *From Conceptualism to Feminism: Lucy Lippard's Number Shows, 1969–74*. London: Afterall Books, 2012.

Butterfield, Jan. "South Texas Funk: A Review." *Texas Observer*, January 8, 1971.

Cagle, R. L. *"Scorpio Rising": A Queer Film Classic*. Vancouver: Arsenal Pulp Press, 2019.

Cahan, Susan E. *Mounting Frustration: The Art Museum in the Age of Black Power*. Durham, NC: Duke University Press, 2016.

Calas, Nicolas. "Surrealism Hits Back." *Arts Magazine*, May 1968.

———. "Surrealist Heritage?: Focus on Super-Reality at the Museum of Modern Art." *Arts Magazine*, March 1968.

———. "Unsupportable Support." *Arts Magazine*, April 1967.

Camfield, William A. "Two Museums and Two Universities: Toward the Menil Collection." In *Art and Activism: Projects of John and Dominique de Menil*, edited by Josef Helfenstein and Laureen Schipsi, 49–71. Houston: Menil Collection, 2010.

Campbell, Lawrence. "Marisol." *ARTnews*, June 1966.

Canaday, John. "Art: Modern Museum Honors Dr. King." *New York Times*, October 31, 1968.

———. "Art Shows Worth Seeing: Picasso, Pop, Peru, Modern Sculpture and Synchronism Bolster Gallery Fare." *New York Times*, October 16, 1965.

———. "This Way to the Big Erotic Art Show." *New York Times*, October 9, 1966.

Carlos Villa: Selected Work, 1961–1984. Davis: Memorial Union Art Gallery, University of California, Davis, 1985. Published in conjunction with an exhibition of the same title, organized by and presented at the C. N. Gorman Museum and Memorial Union Art Gallery, University of California, Davis, January 14–February 22, 1985.

Carrillo, Eduardo. *"Four x Four* Artist Statement." Museo Eduardo Carrillo. August 3, 1993. https://museoeduardocarrillo.org/in-his-own-words-artist-statement/.

Casas, Mel. "Oral History Interview with Mel Casas." By Paul Karlstrom. August 14 and 16, 1996. Archives of American Art, Smithsonian Institution, Washington, DC. https://www.aaa.si.edu/collections/interviews/oral-history-interview-mel-casas-5449.

Cathcart, Linda. *Nancy Graves: A Survey 1969/1980*. Buffalo: Albright-Knox Art Gallery, 1980. Published in conjunction with an exhibition of the same title, organized by and presented at the Albright-Knox Art Gallery, Buffalo, May 3–June 15, 1980, and at the Akron Art Institute, Akron, OH, July 5–August 31, 1980; Contemporary Arts Museum Houston, September 20–October 26, 1980; the Brooks Memorial Art Gallery, Memphis, November 15, 1980–January 6, 1981; the Neuberger Museum of Art, Purchase, NY, January 25–March 15, 1981; the Des Moines Art Center, March 30–May 3, 1981; and the Walker Art Center, Minneapolis, May 30–June 12, 1981.

Celmins, Vija. "Oral History Interview with Vija Celmins." By Julie Brown. February 11–October 15, 2009. Archives of American Art, Smithsonian Institution, Washington, DC. https://www.aaa.si.edu/collections/interviews/oral-history-interview-vija-celmins-15807.

Celmins, Vija, Briony Fer, Robert Gober, and Lane Relyea. *Vija Celmins*. London: Phaidon, 2004.

Césaire, Suzanne. *The Great Camouflage: Writings of Dissent (1941–1945)*. Edited by Daniel Maximin. Translated by Keith L. Walker. Middletown, CT: Wesleyan University Press, 2012.

Chadwick, Whitney. "Narrative Imagism and the Figurative Tradition in Northern California Painting." *Art Journal* 45, no. 4 (Winter 1985): 309–14.

Chaloupka, Amy, ed. *Wanted: Ed Bereal for Disturbing the Peace*. Bellingham, WA: Whatcom Museum, 2019. Published in conjunction with an exhibition of the same title, organized and presented at the Whatcom Museum, Bellingham, WA, September 7, 2019–January 5, 2020.

Chase, Hank. "Raymond Saunders: Come Full Circle." *Black Renaissance* 7, no. 3 (Fall 2007): 51.

Chase-Riboud, Barbara. *I Always Knew: A Memoir*. Princeton, NJ: Princeton University Press, 2022.

———. "Memory Is Everything: Barbara Chase-Riboud in Conversation with Hans Ulrich Obrist." By Hans Ulrich Obrist. *Mousse*, October 4, 2017. https://www.moussemagazine.it/magazine/barbara-chase-riboud-hans-ulrich-obrist-2017.

———. "Oral History Interview with Barbara Chase-Riboud." By Erin Gilbert. June 7–11, 2019. Archives of American Art, Smithsonian Institution, Washington, DC. https://www.aaa.si.edu/collections/interviews/oral-history-interview-barbara-chaseriboud-21702.

Cheng, Ching Ho. "Ching Ho Cheng: A Conversation." By Jaakov Kohn. *Village Voice*, January 27, 1977.

Cheng-Wilson, Sybao. "Ching Ho Cheng: Sybao Cheng-Wilson with Simon Wu." By Simon Wu. *PUBLIC* 33, no. 65 (Summer 2022): 105–19.

Chicago Film Society. "The Films of Edward Owens." Accessed November 2, 2023. https://www.chicagofilmsociety.org/preservation/the-films-of-edward-owens/.

Chicago, Judy. *Beyond the Flower: The Autobiography of a Feminist Artist*. New York: Viking, 1996.

Clifford, James. "On Ethnographic Surrealism." *Comparative Studies in Society and History* 23, no. 4 (October 1981): 539–64.

Clothier, Peter, and Jim Edwards, eds. *The Poetic Object*. San Antonio: San Antonio Museum of Art, 1988. Published in conjunction with an exhibition of the same title, organized by and presented at the San Antonio Museum of Art, September 9–October 30, 1988; and at the Boise Art Museum, December 1, 1988–January 29, 1989; the Art Museum of South Texas, Corpus Christi, February 17–April 9, 1989; and the Amarillo Art Center, Amarillo, TX, May 13–June 25, 1989.

Cohen, Jennifer Rose. "Surrealism and the Art of Consumption." PhD diss., University of Chicago, 2017.

Conner, Bruce. "Oral History Interview with Bruce Conner." By Paul Cummings. April 16, 1973. Archives of American Art, Smithsonian Institution, Washington, DC. https://www.aaa.si.edu/collections/interviews/oral-history-interview-bruce-conner-12017.

Conner, Jean. Unpublished interview. By Robert Conway. 2015–17. Conner Family Trust, San Francisco.

Constable, Joseph, and Rebecca Lewin, eds. *Luchita Hurtado: I Live, I Die, I Will Be Reborn*. London: Serpentine Galleries, 2019. Published in conjunction with an exhibition of the same title, organized by and presented at Serpentine North Gallery, London, May 23–October 20, 2019, and at the Los Angeles County Museum of Art, February 16–November 20, 2020.

Constantine, Mildred, and Jack Lenor Larsen. *Beyond Craft: The Art Fabric*. New York: Van Nostrand Reinhold, 1973.

Cooper, Helen A., ed. *Eva Hesse: A Retrospective*. New Haven, CT: Yale University Press, 1992. Published in conjunction with an exhibition of the same title, organized by and presented at the Yale University Art Gallery, New Haven, CT, April 15–July 31, 1992.

Coplans, John. "The New Paintings of Common Objects." *Artforum*, November 1962. https://www.artforum.com/features/the-new-paintings-of-common-objects-212213/.

———. "Reviews, San Francisco: Angel-Hipsterism, Beat and Zen Versus New Materials." *Artforum*, September 1962.

———. "Sculpture in California." *Artforum*, August 1963.

Cowans, Adger. "Adger Cowans by Carrie Mae Weems." By Carrie Mae Weems. *BOMB*, July 30, 2014. https://bombmagazine.org/articles/adger-cowans-carrie-mae-weems/.

———. *Art in the Moment: Life and Times of Adger Cowans*. Beverly Hills, CA: Noah's Ark, 2019.

———. "One on One: Adger Cowans and Hank Willis Thomas." By Hank Willis Thomas. *Cultured*, October 24, 2019. https://www.culturedmag.com/article/2019/10/24/adger-cowans-and-hank-willis-thomas.

Cozzolino, Robert. *Art in Chicago: Resisting Regionalism, Transforming Modernism*. Philadelphia: Pennsylvania Academy of the Fine Arts, 2007.

Craft, Catherine. *Melvin Edwards: Five Decades*. Dallas: Nasher Sculpture Center, 2015. Published in conjunction with an exhibition of the same title, organized by and presented at the Nasher Sculpture Center, Dallas, January 31–May 10, 2015.

Crow, Thomas. "Eyes on California: Oldenburg, Warhol, Hockney, and Ruscha Take the Trip." In *The Long March of Pop: Art, Music, and Design, 1930–1995*, 233–69. New Haven, CT: Yale University Press, 2014.

———. *The Rise of the Sixties: American and European Art in the Era of Dissent*. New Haven, CT: Yale University Press, 1996.

Curlee, Kendall. "Clean, Well-Lighted Place." *Handbook of Texas Online*. December 1, 1994. http://www.tshaonline.org/handbook/online/articles/kjclt.

Dalí, Salvador. "How an Elvis Presley Becomes a Roy Lichtenstein." *Arts Magazine*, April 1967.

Dallas Museum of Art. *DallasSITES: A Developing Art Scene, Postwar to Present*. Dallas: Dallas Museum of Art, 2013. https://publications.dma.org/publication/dallas-sites. Published in conjunction with the exhibition *DallasSITES: Charting Contemporary Art, 1963 to Present*, organized by and presented at the Dallas Museum of Art, May 26–September 15, 2013.

Davis, Alonzo. "A TEI Project: Interview of Alonzo Davis." By Karen Mason. October 26–28, 1990, December 1, 1990, and April 20–24, 1991. University of California, Los Angeles Center for Oral History. https://static.library.ucla.edu/oralhistory/text/masters/21198-zz0008zngm-4-master.html.

Dawsey, Jill, and Michelle White, eds. *Niki de Saint Phalle in the 1960s*. Houston: Menil Collection, 2021. Published in conjunction with an exhibition of the same title, co-organized by the Menil Collection, Houston, and the Museum of Contemporary Art, San Diego, and presented at the Menil Collection, Houston, September 10, 2021–January 23, 2022, and the Museum of Contemporary Art, San Diego, April 9–July 17, 2022.

Deaton, Judy. Unpublished interview by Laura Phipps. April 10, 2020.

Dervaux, Isabelle. *Surrealism USA*. New York: National Academy Museum; Ostfildern-Ruit, Germany: Hatje Cantz, 2005. Published in conjunction with an exhibition of the same title, organized by and presented at the National Academy Museum, New York, February 17–May 8, 2005.

Diane Arbus: An Aperture Monograph. Millerton, NY: Aperture, 1972.

Diane Arbus: in the beginning. New York: Metropolitan Museum of Art, 2016. Published in conjunction with an exhibition of the same title, organized by and presented at the Metropolitan Museum of Art, New York, July 12–November 27, 2016, and at the San Francisco Museum of Modern Art, January 21–April 30, 2017, and the Fundación Malba, Buenos Aires, July 14–October 9, 2017.

Diane Arbus: Magazine Work. Millerton, NY: Aperture, 1984.

Diane Arbus: Revelations. New York: Random House, 2003. Published in conjunction with an exhibition of the same title, organized by and presented at the San Francisco Museum of Modern Art, October 25, 2003–October 8, 2006, and the Los Angeles County Museum of Art, February 29–May 30, 2004; and at the Museum of Fine Arts, Houston, June 27–August 29, 2004; the Metropolitan Museum of Art, New York, February 28–May 29, 2005; Museum Folkwang, Essen, Germany, June 17–September 18, 2005; the Victoria and Albert Museum, London, October 13, 2005–January 15, 2006; Fundació la Caixa, Barcelona, February 14–March 15, 2006; and the Walker Art Center, Minneapolis, July 9–October 8, 2006.

Diane Arbus: Revelations. New York: Aperture, 2022.

Donaldson, Jeff. AFRICOBRA manifesto for *AFRICOBRA 1: Ten in Search of a Nation* exhibition. *Black World*, October 1970. Reprinted in *Nka: Journal of Contemporary African Art* 30 (Spring 2012): 76–83.

———. Papers, 1918–2005. Archives of American Art, Smithsonian Institution, Washington, DC.

Don Potts: "My First Car." Newport Beach, CA: Newport Harbor Art Museum, 1972. Published in conjunction with an exhibition of the same title, organized by and presented at the Newport Harbor Art Museum, Newport Beach, CA, April 26–May 28, 1972, and at the Whitney Museum of American Art, New York, June 14–July 16, 1972; the Walker Art Center, Minneapolis, August 5–September 17, 1972; the Hayden Gallery, Massachusetts Institute of Technology, Cambridge, October 1–November 5, 1972; the Utah Museum of Fine Arts, University of Utah, Salt Lake City, January 7–February 18, 1973; the Vancouver Art Gallery, March 15–April 30, 1973; the Museum of Contemporary Art Chicago, May 15–June 30, 1973; and the University Art Museum, University of California, Berkeley, September 25–October 28, 1973.

Dossin, Catherine. "Niki de Saint Phalle and the Masquerade of Hyperfemininity." *Woman's Art Journal* 31, no. 2 (Fall/Winter 2010): 29–38.

Doty, Robert. *Contemporary Black Artists in America*. New York: Whitney Museum of American Art, 1971. Published in conjunction with an exhibition of the same title, organized by and presented at the Whitney Museum of American Art, New York, April 6–May 16, 1971.

———. *Extraordinary Realities*. New York: Whitney Museum of American Art, 1973. Published in conjunction with an exhibition of the same title, organized by and presented at the Whitney Museum of American Art, New York, October 16–December 2, 1973.

———. *Human Concern/Personal Torment: The Grotesque in American Art*. New York: Whitney Museum of American Art, 1969. Published in conjunction with an exhibition of the same title, organized by and presented at the Whitney Museum of American Art, New York, October 14–November 30, 1969.

Douglas, Emory. "Art in Service for the People." *Black Scholar*, November 1977.

Duncan, Michael, and Christopher Wagstaff. *An Opening of the Field: Jess, Robert Duncan, and Their Circle*. Portland, OR: Pomegranate Communications, 2013. Published in conjunction with an exhibition of the same title, organized by and presented at the Crocker Art Museum, Sacramento, June 9–September 1, 2013, and at the Grey Art Gallery, New York University, January 14–March 29, 2014.

Dyson, Frances. "9 Evenings: Alex Hay." In *And then it was now*. Montreal: Daniel Langlois Foundation for Art, Science, and Technology, 2006. https://www.fondation-langlois.org/html/e/page.php?NumPage=2151.

Eckhardt, Sarah, ed. *Working Together: Louis Draper and the Kamoinge Workshop*. Richmond: Virginia Museum of Fine Arts, 2020. Published in conjunction with an exhibition of the same title, organized by and presented at the Virginia Museum of Fine Arts, Richmond, February 1–October 18, 2020, and at the Whitney Museum of American Art, New York, July 17–October 25, 2020; the J. Paul Getty Museum, Los Angeles, June 29–September 26, 2021; and the Cincinnati Art Museum, February 25–May 15, 2022.

Edwards, Brent Hayes. "The Ethnics of Surrealism." *Transition*, no. 78 (1998): 84–135.

Edwards, Melvin. "Melvin Edwards in Conversation with Manthia Diawara and Lydie Diakhaté." By Manthia Diawara and Lydie Diakhaté. *Nka* 30 (Spring 2012): 114–29.

Ehrlich, Susan, ed. *Pacific Dreams: Currents of Surrealism and Fantasy in California Art, 1934–1957*. Los Angeles: UCLA at the Armand Hammer Museum of Art and Cultural Center, 1995. Published in conjunction with an exhibition of the same title, organized by and presented at the Hammer Museum, Los Angeles, July 11–September 17, 1995, and at the Oakland Museum of California, February 25–June 11, 1995, and the Nora Eccles Harrison Museum of Art, Utah State University, Logan, October 10–December 11, 1995.

Electronic Arts Intermix. "Ken Jacobs: *Blonde Cobra*." Accessed September 21, 2023. https://www.eai.org/titles/blonde-cobra.

Eleey, Peter. "Dangerous Concealment: The Art of Sturtevant." In *Sturtevant: Double Trouble*, 47–78. New York: Museum of Modern Art, 2014. Published in conjunction with an exhibition of the same title, organized by and presented at the Museum of Modern Art, New York, November 9, 2014–February 22, 2015, and at the Museum of Contemporary Art, Los Angeles, March 15–July 27, 2015.

Emerson, Gloria. "Jean Shrimpton Beware! 'Nanas' of Paris Are After You: Female Statues Are Exultant and Active." *New York Times*, October 25, 1965.

Emshwiller, Ed. "Ed Emshwiller." By James Mullins. *Film Culture*, Summer 1966.

———. "Image Maker Meets Video, or, Psyche to Physics and Back." In *The New Television: A Public/Private Art*, edited by Douglas Davis and Allison Simmons, 53–57. Cambridge, MA: MIT Press, 1977.

Engelbach, Barbara, Friederike Wappler, and Hans Winkler, eds. *Looking for Mushrooms: Beat Poets, Hippies, Funk, Minimal Art, San Francisco 1955–68*. Cologne: Walther König, 2008. Published in conjunction with an exhibition of the same title, organized by and presented at Museum Ludwig, Cologne, November 8, 2008–March 1, 2009.

English, Darby. *1971: A Year in the Life of Color*. Chicago: University of Chicago Press, 2016.

Ennis, Michael. "Got My Jomo Workin'." *Texas Monthly*, July 1980.

Exhibition Momentum 1956. Chicago: Momentum, 1956. Published in conjunction with an exhibition of the same title, organized by and presented at 72 East 11th Street, Chicago, May 23–June 20, 1956.

Exile on Main Street. Cologne: Walther König, 2009. Published in conjunction with an exhibition of the same title, organized by and presented at the Bonnefantenmuseum, Maastricht, Netherlands, February 17–August 16, 2009.

Falckenberg, Harald, and Peter Weibel, eds. *Paul Thek: Artist's Artist*. Cambridge, MA: MIT Press, 2008.

Favela, Ramón. *The Art of Rupert García*. San Francisco: Chronicle Books; Mexican Museum, 1986. Published in conjunction with an exhibition of the same title, organized by and presented at the Mexican Museum, San Francisco, August 20–October 19, 1986.

The Feminist Institute. "A.I.R. Gallery: Chapter 1, the First Year." Google Arts and Culture. Accessed November 8, 2023. https://artsandculture.google.com/story/zwWRX0hZNpbILQ.

Filipovic, Elena. *David Hammons: Bliz-aard Ball Sale*. London: Afterall Books, 2017.

Fine, Elsa Honig. *The Afro-American Artist: A Search for Identity*. New York: Holt, Rinehart, and Winston, 1973.

Fineberg, Jonathan. *Art Since 1940: Strategies of Being*. New York: H. N. Abrams, 1995.

———. *A Troublesome Subject: The Art of Robert Arneson*. Berkeley: University of California Press, 2013.

Fitz Gibbon, John, ed. "E Is for Eduardo Carrillo." In *California A–Z and Return*. Youngstown, OH: Butler Institute of American Art, 1990. https://museoeduardocarrillo.org/e-is-for-eduardo-carrillo/. Published in conjunction with an exhibition of the same title, organized by and presented at the Butler Institute of American Art, Youngstown, OH, June 23–August 19, 1990.

Forty Years of California Assemblage. Los Angeles: Wight Art Gallery, University of California, Los Angeles, 1989. Published in conjunction with an exhibition of the same title, organized by and presented at the Wight Art Gallery, University of California, Los Angeles, April 4–May 21, 1989.

Foster-Rice, Greg, ed. *The Many Hats of Ralph Arnold: Art, Identity & Politics*. Chicago: Museum of Contemporary Photography, Columbia College Chicago, 2018. Published in conjunction with an exhibition of the same title, organized by and presented at the Museum of Contemporary Photography, Columbia College Chicago, October 11–December 21, 2018.

Fox, John. "Ed in Spain 1960–61." Museo Eduardo Carrillo. Accessed September 20, 2023. https://museoeduardocarrillo.org/ed-in-spain-1960-61/.

Francis, Terri. "Introduction: The No-Theory Chant of Afrosurrealism." *Black Camera* 5, no. 1 (Fall 2013): 95–111.

Frankenstein, Alfred. "Dilexi Gallery Honored." *San Francisco Chronicle*, October 4, 1965.

Franzen, Bridget, and Annette Lagler, eds. *Nancy Graves Project & Special Guests*. Ostfildern, Germany: Hatje Cantz, 2013. Published in conjunction with an exhibition of the same title, organized by and presented at the Ludwig Forum for International Art, Aachen, Germany, October 13, 2013–February 16, 2014.

Frascina, Francis. *Art, Politics and Dissent: Aspects of the Art Left in Sixties America*. Manchester, UK: Manchester University Press, 1999.

Fridge, Roy. Roy Fridge Journals, June 1959–August 1997. Menil Archives, The Menil Collection, Houston.

Friedan, Betty. Statement of Purpose. National Organization for Women. October 29, 1966. https://now.org/about/history/statement-of-purpose/.

Friedling, Rudolf, and Gary Garrels, eds. *Bruce Conner: It's All True*. San Francisco: San Francisco Museum of Modern Art in association with University of California Press, 2016. Published in conjunction with an exhibition of the same title, organized by and presented at the San Francisco Museum of Modern Art, October 19, 2016–January 22, 2017, and at the Museum of Modern Art, New York, July 3–October 2, 2016.

Friendly, Alfred. "Design Unveiled for Ellis Island." *New York Times*, February 25, 1966.

Fuller, Mary. "You're Looking for Bruce Conner, the Artist, or 'What Is This Crap You're Trying to Put Over Here?'" *Currant Art Magazine*, May–July 1976.

García, Rupert. "Oral History Interview with Rupert García." By Paul Karlstrom. September 7, 1995–June 24, 1996. Archives of American Art, Smithsonian Institution, Washington, DC. https://www.aaa.si.edu/collections/interviews/oral-history-interview-rupert-garcia-13572.

Gene Swenson: Retrospective for a Critic. Lawrence: University of Kansas Museum of Art, 1971. Published in conjunction with an exhibition of the same title, organized by and presented at the University of Kansas Museum of Art, Lawrence, October 24–December 5, 1971.

Gershon, Pete. *Collision: The Contemporary Art Scene in Houston, 1972–1985*. College Station: Texas A&M University Press, 2018.

Getsy, David, Sandra Zalman, and Rebecca Zorach. Conversation with Dan Nadel, Laura Phipps, Elisabeth Sussman, and Kelly Long. December 2, 2019. Whitney Museum of American Art, New York.

Getty Research Institute. Announcement for "Pacific Standard Time Performance and Public Art Festival, The Bodacious Buggerrilla: A Reprise Performance and Conversation." 2012. https://www.getty.edu/research/exhibitions_events/events/bodacious_buggerrilla/index.html.

Gibson, Gregory. *Hubert's Freaks: The Rare-Book Dealer, the Times Square Talker, and the Lost Photos of Diane Arbus*. Orlando: Harcourt, 2008.

Glazer, Lee Stephens. "Signifying Identity: Art and Race in Romare Bearden's *Projections*." *Art Bulletin* 76, no. 3 (September 1994): 411–26.

Glueck, Grace. "ABC to Erotic." *Art in America*, September–October 1966.

———. "It's Not Pop, It's Not Op—It's Marisol." *New York Times*, March 7, 1965.

———. "The Slant Step." *New York Times*, June 2, 1968.

———. "A Strange Assortment of Flags Is Displayed at 'People's Show.'" *New York Times*, November 10, 1970.

Godfrey, Mark, and Allie Biswas, eds. *The "Soul of a Nation" Reader: Writings by and about Black American Artists, 1960–1980*. New York: Gregory R. Miller, 2021.

Godfrey, Mark, and Zoé Whitley, eds. *Soul of a Nation: Art in the Age of Black Power*. London: Tate, 2017. Published in conjunction with an exhibition of the same title, organized by and presented at Tate Modern, London, July 12–October 22, 2017, and at the Crystal Bridges Museum of Art, Bentonville, AR, February 3–April 23, 2018; the Brooklyn Museum, September 14, 2018–February 3, 2019; the Broad Museum, Los Angeles, March 23–September 1, 2019; the de Young Museum, San Francisco, November 9, 2019–March 15, 2020; and the Museum of Fine Arts, Houston, June 27–August 30, 2020.

Goldberg, Aron. "Ed Carrillo—Ceeje Alumnus." *Artweek*, April 12, 1975.

Goldman, Shifra M. "A Public Voice: Fifteen Years of Chicano Posters." *Art Journal* 44, no. 1 (Spring 1984): 50–57.

"Gosta Oldenburg." *New York Times*, April 1, 1992.

Graham, Dan. "Oldenburg's Monuments." *Artforum*, January 1968.

Greene, Alison de Lima, ed. *Texas: 150 Works from the Museum of Fine Arts, Houston*. Houston: Museum of Fine Arts, Houston, 2000.

Grosenick, Uta, ed. *Women Artists in the 20th and 21st Century*. Cologne: Taschen, 2005.

Gross, Frederick. "Portraits, Pastiche, and Magazine Work." In *Diane Arbus's 1960s: Auguries of Experience*. Minneapolis: University of Minnesota Press, 2012.

Gruber, J. Richard. *American Icons: From Madison to Manhattan, the Art of Benny Andrews, 1948–1997*. Augusta, GA: Morris Museum of Art, 1997. Published in conjunction with an exhibition of the same title, organized by and presented at the Morris Museum of Art, Augusta, GA, September 4–November 2, 1997.

Gruen, John. "The Big Bad Relevance." *New York*, July 13, 1970.

Gyarkye, Lovia. "The Ecstatic, Elusive Art of Ming Smith." *New York Times*, February 3, 2023. https://www.nytimes.com/2023/02/03/t-magazine/ming-smith-moma.html.

Halstead, Whitney. "Chicago." *Artforum*, March 1966.

———. "Chicago." *Artforum*, July 1966.

Halter, Ed. "Edward Owens: Private Imaginings and Narrative Facts." Light Industry. 2015. http://www.lightindustry.org/owens.

Halter, Ed. Conversation with Dan Nadel, Laura Phipps, Elisabeth Sussman, and Kelly Long. November 20, 2019. Whitney Museum of American Art, New York.

Hammen, Scott. "Ed Emshwiller: An Interview." *Afterimage* 2, no. 3 (September 1974): 2–5.

Hammer, Barbara. *Hammer! Making Movies out of Sex and Life*. New York: Feminist Press at the City University of New York, 2010.

Hammons, David. "Interview with David Hammons (1986)." By Kellie Jones. In *EyeMinded: Living and Writing Contemporary Art*, edited by Kellie Jones, 247–59. Durham, NC: Duke University Press, 2011.

Haskell, Barbara. *H. C. Westermann*. New York: Whitney Museum of American Art, 1978. Published in conjunction with an exhibition of the same title, organized by and presented at the Whitney Museum of American Art, New York, May 17–July 16, 1978.

Hay, Alex. Curriculum Vitae. Peter Freeman, Inc. Accessed September 20, 2023. https://www.peterfreemaninc.com/artists/alex-hay/biography.

———. *Grass Field*. 1966. Excerpt of performance presented as part of 9 Evenings: Theatre & Engineering. The 69th Regiment Armory, New York, October 13–22, 1966. Footage by Alfons Schilling. 16mm, 55 sec. https://www.fondation-langlois.org/html/e/media.php?NumObjet=62800.

———. "Robert Rauschenberg Oral History Project: The Reminiscences of Alex Hay." By Alessandra Nicifero. December 8, 2014. Columbia Center for Oral History Research, Columbia University, New York. https://www.rauschenbergfoundation.org/artist/oral-history/alex-hay.

Haywood, Robert E. "Heretical Alliance: Claes Oldenburg and the Judson Memorial Church in the 1960s." *Art History* 18, no. 2 (June 1995): 185–212.

Hedrick, Wally. "Di Rosa Artist Interview Series: Wally Hedrick." By Leslie Goldberg. August 16, 2002. Di Rosa Center for Contemporary Art. https://wallyhedrick.org/pdfs/di_rosa_artist_interview_series.pdf.

Henderson, Mike. Unpublished interview by Dan Nadel. August 2019.

Hernandez, Jo Farb, ed. *Jeremy Anderson: The Critical Link, A Quiet Revolution*. Monterey, CA: Monterey Peninsula Museum of Art, 1995. Published in conjunction with an exhibition of the same title, organized by and presented at the Monterey Peninsula Museum of Art, Monterey, CA, September 22–November 26, 1995, and at the Oakland Museum of California, February 24–June 30, 1996.

Hesse, Eva. "A Conversation with Eva Hesse." By Cindy Nemser. In *Eva Hesse*, edited by Mignon Nixon, 1–24. Cambridge, MA: MIT Press, 2002.

———. *Eva Hesse: Diaries*. Edited by Barry Rosen. Zurich: Hauser & Wirth, 2020.

———. "An Interview with Eva Hesse." By Cindy Nemser. *Artforum*, May 1970.

———. Papers, 1914–70. Allen Memorial Art Museum, Oberlin College, Oberlin, OH.

Hobbs, Robert. "Chronology." In *Robert Smithson: Sculpture*, 231–43. Ithaca, NY: Cornell University Press, 1980. Published in conjunction with an exhibition of the same title, organized by and presented at the Herbert F. Johnson Museum of Art, Cornell University, Ithaca, NY, November 14–December 21, 1980, and at the Walker Art Center, Minneapolis, February 8–March 22, 1981; the Museum of Contemporary Art Chicago, April 10–June 14, 1981; La Jolla Museum of Contemporary Art, San Diego, August 14–September 25, 1981; the Laguna Gloria Art Museum, Austin, November 13, 1981–January 10, 1982; and the Whitney Museum of American Art, New York, February 16–April 18, 1982.

Hoberman, J. *On Jack Smith's 'Flaming Creatures' (and Other Secret-Flix of Cinemaroc)*. New York: Granary Books, 2001.

Hoberman, J., and Edward Leffingwell, eds. *Wait for Me at the Bottom of the Pool: The Writings of Jack Smith*. New York: Serpent's Tail, 1997.

Hochdörfer, Achim, ed. *Claes Oldenburg: The Sixties*. New York: Prestel, 2012. Published in conjunction with an exhibition of the same title, organized by and presented at the Museum moderner Kunst Stiftung Ludwig Wien, Vienna, February 4–May 28, 2012, and at the Museum Ludwig, Cologne, June 22–September 30, 2012; the Guggenheim Museum Bilbao, October 30, 2012–February 17, 2013; the Museum of Modern Art, New York, April 14–August 5, 2013; and the Walker Art Center, Minneapolis, September 14, 2013–January 12, 2014.

Holder, Maryse. "Another Cuntree: At Last, a Mainstream Female Art Movement." *Off Our Backs* 3, no. 10 (1973): 11–17.

Hopper, Dennis. "Reviews: The West Coast." *Art and Artists*, May 1966.

Hough, Katherine Plake, and Michael Zakian. *Michael Todd: 25 Year Survey*. Palm Springs, CA: Palm Springs Desert Museum, 1989. Published in conjunction with an exhibition of the same title, organized by and presented at the Palm Springs Desert Museum, Palm Springs, CA, February 3–April 23, 1989.

Hujar, Peter, and Susan Sontag. *Portraits in Life and Death*. New York: Da Capo Press, 1976.

Hunt, Darnell M., and Ana-Christina Ramón, eds. *Black Los Angeles: American Dreams and Racial Realities*. New York: New York University Press, 2010.

Hurtado, Luchita. "Oral History Interview with Luchita Hurtado." By Paul Karlstrom. April 3, 1995. Archives of American Art, Smithsonian Institution, Washington, DC. https://www.aaa.si.edu/collections/interviews/oral-history-interview-luchita-hurtado-13583.

Hurtado, Luchita, and Hans Ulrich Obrist. *Luchita Hurtado*. Edited by Karen Marta. Zurich: Hauser & Wirth, 2020.

Indyke, Dottie. "Linda Lomahaftewa: A Well Known Artist and Teacher Discusses Her Long Career." *Southwest Art Magazine*, March 2003. https://www.southwestart.com/native-american-arts/linda-lomahaftewa_phoenix_hopi_native_american_art_teacher_and_artist_kachina_shapes_hopi_culture_choctaw_sf_art_institute_santa_fes_indian_market_art_of_hopi_gallery_sedona_az.

Irwin, David. "Pop Art and Surrealism." *Studio International*, May 1966.

Israel, Matthew. *Kill for Peace: American Artists against the Vietnam War*. Austin: University of Texas Press, 2013.

Ito, Miyoko. "Miyoko Ito: An Interview." By Kate Horsfield. *Profile* 4, no. 1 (January 1984): 19.

Jackson, Suzanne. "TEI Project: Interview of Suzanne Jackson." By Karen Mason. August 12–16, 1992. University of California, Los Angeles Center for Oral History. https://static.library.ucla.edu/oralhistory/pdf/masters/21198-zz0008zszs-4-master.pdf.

Jacobs, Jay. "In the Galleries." *Arts Magazine*, January 1966.

Jacobs, Mary Jane, ed. *Shigeko Kubota: Video Sculpture*. Astoria, NY: American Museum of the Moving Image, 1991. Published in conjunction with an exhibition of the same title, organized by and presented at the American Museum of the Moving Image, New York, April 26–September 15, 1991.

Jimenez, Luis. "Luis Jimenez." By Marcia Tucker. In *Early Work: Lynda Benglis, Joan Brown, Luis Jimenez, Gary Stephan, Lawrence Weiner*, 23–31. New York: New Museum, 1982. Published in conjunction with an exhibition of the same title, organized by and presented at the New Museum of Contemporary Art, New York, April 3–June 3, 1982.

———. "Luis Jiménez." By Susie Kalil. *Art Lies*, no. 24 (Fall 1999): 55–58.

———. "Oral History Interview with Luis Jimenez." By Peter Bermingham. December 15–17, 1985. Archives of American Art, Smithsonian Institution, Washington, DC. https://www.aaa.si.edu/collections/interviews/oral-history-interview-luis-jimenez-13554.

Jim Nutt. Milwaukee: Milwaukee Art Museum, 1994. Published in conjunction with an exhibition of the same title, organized by and presented at the Milwaukee Art Museum, June 17–August 28, 1994.

"Joan Brown: Frieze New York." George Adams Gallery. May 5, 2019. https://www.georgeadamsgallery.com/exhibitions/joan-brown4/selected-works?view=thumbnails.

Johnson, Mark Dean, Trisha Lagaso Goldberg, and Sherwin Rio, eds. *Carlos Villa: Worlds in Collision*. Oakland: University of California Press, 2021. Published in conjunction with an exhibition of the same title, co-organized by the San Francisco Art Institute and the Asian Art Museum, San Francisco, and presented at the Asian Art Museum, San Francisco, June 17–October 24, 2022, and at the Newark Museum of Art, Newark, NJ, February 17–May 8, 2022.

Johnston, Jill. "Dance Journal: Like a Boy in a Boat," *Village Voice*, September 11, 1969.

Jones, Kellie. "It's Not Enough to Say 'Black is Beautiful'": Abstraction at the Whitney, 1969–1974." In *Discrepant Abstraction*, edited by Kobena Mercer, 154–80. Cambridge, MA: MIT Press; London: Institute of International Visual Arts, 2006.

———, ed. *Now Dig This! Art and Black Los Angeles, 1960–1980*. Los Angeles: Hammer Museum, 2011. Published in conjunction with an exhibition of the same title, organized by and presented at the Hammer Museum, Los Angeles, October 2, 2011–January 8, 2012.

———. *South of Pico: African American Artists in Los Angeles in the 1960s and 1970s*. Durham, NC: Duke University Press, 2017.

Jones-Hogu, Barbara. "Barbara Jones-Hogu." By Rebecca Zorach and Skyla Hearn. July 2013. Never the Same: Conversations about Art Transforming Politics & Community in Chicago & Beyond. https://never-the-same.org/interviews/barbara-jones-hogu/.

Jordan, Dian. *Art in Community: The Harold Stevenson Collection*. Idabel, OK: Museum of the Red River, 2020. Published in conjunction with an exhibition of the same title, organized by and presented at the Museum of the Red River, Idabel, OK, March 7–August 23, 2020.

Judd, Donald. *Donald Judd: Complete Writings, 1959–1975, Gallery Reviews, Book Reviews, Articles, Letters to the Editor, Reports, Statements, Complaints*. Halifax: Press of the Nova Scotia College of Art and Design, 1975.

———. "In the Galleries: Don Berry, Eva Hesse, Harold Jacobs." *Arts Magazine*, April 1961.

———. "Lee Bontecou." *Arts Magazine*, December 1960.

———. "Lee Bontecou." *Arts Magazine*, January 1963.

———. "Lee Bontecou." *Arts Magazine*, April 1965.

Judd Foundation. "Donald Judd and Yayoi Kusama." Local History. Accessed October 31, 2023. https://juddfoundation.org/research/local-history/local-history-donald-judd-yayoi-kusama/.

Judith Bernstein: Rising. Stavanger, Norway: Kunsthall Stavanger, 2016. Published in conjunction with an exhibition of the same title, organized by and presented at the Kunsthall Stavanger, Stavanger, Norway, February 4–May 15, 2016.

K. L. "Arman, Dine, Marisol, Oldenburg, and Segal." *ARTnews*, April 1965.

Kalil, Susie. "Trash Men." *Houston Press*, May 5, 1994.

Katz, Anna C. "Hybrid Species: Lee Bontecou's Sculpture and Drawing, 1958–1971." PhD diss., Princeton University, 2013.

Kee, Joan. "Corroborators in Arms: The Early Works of Melvin Edwards and Ron Miyashiro." *Oxford Art Journal* 43, no. 1 (March 2020): 49–74.

Keefer, Cindy. "Jordan Belson, Cosmic Cinema, and the San Francisco Museum of Art." *Open Space* (blog). San Francisco Museum of Modern Art, October 12, 2010. https://openspace.sfmoma.org/2010/10/jordan-belson.

———. "Raumlichtmusik: Early 20th Century Abstract Cinema Immersive Environments." *Leonardo Electronic Almanac* 16, nos. 6–7 (October 2009): 1–5. https://leonardo.info/LEA/CreativeData/CD_Keefer.pdf.

Kelley, Robin D. G. "Keepin' It (Sur)real: Dreams of the Marvelous." In *Freedom Dreams: The Black Radical Imagination*, 157–94. Boston: Beacon Press, 2002.

———. Zoom conversation with Dan Nadel, Laura Phipps, Elisabeth Sussman, and Kelly Long. January 21, 2021.

Kelly, Madeline, and Joan Banach. "A Drawing Chronology, 1931–2014." In *Lee Bontecou: Drawn Worlds*, edited by Michelle White, 133–39. Houston: Menil Collection, 2014. Published in conjunction with an exhibition of the same title, organized by and presented at the Menil Collection, Houston, January 31–May 11, 2014, and at the Princeton University Art Museum, Princeton, NJ, June 28–September 21, 2014.

Kelman, Ken. "Thanatos in Chrome." *Film Culture*, Winter 1963–64.

Kiki Kogelnik. New York: Mitchell-Innes & Nash, 2019. Published in conjunction with an exhibition of the same title, organized by and presented at Mitchell-Innes & Nash, New York, May 23–June 29, 2019.

King, Elliott H., and Abigail Susik, eds. *Radical Dreams: Surrealism, Counterculture, Resistance*. University Park: Pennsylvania State University Press, 2022.

Kingsley, April. "Hannah Wilke, Ronald Feldman Gallery." *Artforum*, December 1972.

Kiplinger, Suzanne. "Art." *Village Voice*, December 20, 1962.

Kirshner, Judith Russi, ed. *Surfaces: Two Decades of Painting in Chicago, Seventies and Eighties*. Chicago: Terra Museum of American Art, 1987. Published in conjunction with an exhibition of the same title, organized by and presented at the Terra Museum of American Art, Chicago, September 12–November 15, 1987.

Kochheiser, Thomas H., ed. *Hannah Wilke: A Retrospective*. Columbia: University of Missouri Press, 1989. Published in conjunction with an exhibition of the same title, organized by and presented at Gallery 210, University of Missouri–St. Louis, April 3–28, 1989.

Kozloff, Max. "Inwardness: Chicago Art Since 1945." *Artforum*, October 1972.

Kramer, Hilton. "Art: Sculpture Emphasizing Poetry." *New York Times*, May 2, 1970. https://www.nytimes.com/1970/05/02/archives/art-sculpture-emphasizing-poetry-15-heads-by-baizerman-shown-at.html.

———. "Black Experience and Modernist Art." *New York Times*, February 14, 1970. https://www.nytimes.com/1970/02/14/archives/black-experience-and-modernist-art-romare-bearden-uses-photos-in.html.

———, ed. *T. C. Cannon: At the Edge of America*. Salem, MA: Peabody Essex Museum, 2018. Published in conjunction with an exhibition of the same title, organized by and presented at the Peabody Essex Museum, Salem, MA, March 3–June 10, 2018, and at the Gilcrease Museum, Tulsa, OK, July 14–October 7, 2018, and the Smithsonian Museum of the American Indian, New York, March 16–September 16, 2019.

Kubitza, Anette. "Fluxus, Flirt, Feminist? Carolee Schneemann, Sexual Liberation and the Avant-Garde of the 1960s." *n.paradoxa*, no. 15 (July/September 2001): 15–29.

Kusama, Yayoi. *Infinity Net: The Autobiography of Yayoi Kusama*. Translated by Ralph F. McCarthy. Chicago: University Press, 2011.

———. Press release for *Naked Protest at Wall Street*. 1968.

Landauer, Susan, ed. *Eye Fruit: The Art of Franklin Williams*. Santa Rosa, CA: Museums of Sonoma County. Published in conjunction with an exhibition of the same title, organized by and presented at Museums of Sonoma County, Santa Rosa, CA, May 13–August 27, 2017.

———. *The Not-So-Still-Life: A Century of California Painting and Sculpture*. Berkeley: University of California Press, 2003. Published in conjunction with an exhibition of the same title, organized by and presented at the San Jose Museum of Art, San Jose, CA, November 22, 2003–February 15, 2004, and at the Pasadena Museum of California Art, March 6–June 27, 2004.

Landi, Ann. "Lost and Found." *ARTnews*, September 2003.

Landis, Bill. *Anger: The Unauthorized Biography of Kenneth Anger*. New York: Harper Collins, 1995.

Langsner, Jules. "Art News from Los Angeles." *ARTnews*, March 1958.

Larsen, Susan B. "Ceeje Revisited: A Warm Spot in the Cool Sixties." In *Ceeje Revisited*, Los Angeles: Municipal Art Gallery, 1984. https://museoeduardocarrillo.org/ceeje-revisited-a-warm-spot-in-the-cool-sixties/. Published in conjunction with an exhibition of the same title, organized by and presented at the Los Angeles Municipal Art Gallery, April 10–May 13, 1984.

Lebovici, Elizabeth. "Is She? Or Isn't She?" In *Louise Bourgeois*, edited by Frances Morris, 131–37. New York: Rizzoli, 2008.

Leffingwell, Edward G., ed. *Flaming Creature: Jack Smith, His Amazing Life and Times*. London: Serpent's Tail, 1997.

Levin, Gail. *Becoming Judy Chicago: A Biography of the Artist*. Berkeley: University of California Press, 2018.

Levin, Kim. *Lucas Samaras*. New York: H. N. Abrams, 1975.

Lewallen, Constance. "Mountain Climbing." In *Jay DeFeo: Selected Works, 1952–1989*. Philadelphia: Goldie Paley Gallery, 1996. https://www.jaydefeofoundation.org/exhibitions/jay-defeo-selected-works-1952-1989/.

———. *A Rose Has No Teeth: Bruce Nauman in the 1960s*. Berkeley: University of California Press, 2007. Published in conjunction with an exhibition of the same title, organized by and presented at the Berkeley Art Museum and Pacific Film Archive, Berkeley, CA, January 17–April 15, 2007, and at the Castello di Rivoli Museo d'Arte Contemporanea, Turin, Italy, May 23–September 9, 2007, and the Menil Collection, Houston, October 12, 2007–January 13, 2008.

Lewis, Charles A., and Cynthia Yao, eds. *Chicago: The City and Its Artists, 1945–1978*. Ann Arbor: University of Michigan Museum of Art, 1978. Published in conjunction with an exhibition of the same title, organized by and presented at the University of Michigan Museum of Art, Ann Arbor, March 17–April 23, 1978.

Linder, Mark. "'Towards a New Type of Building': Robert Smithson's Architectural Criticism." In *Robert Smithson*, edited by Eugenie Tsai and Cornelia Butler, 188–99. Los Angeles: Museum of Contemporary Art, 2004. Published in conjunction with an exhibition of the same title, organized by and presented at the Museum of Contemporary Art, Los Angeles, September 12–December 13, 2004, and at the Dallas Museum of Art, January 14–April 3, 2005, and the Whitney Museum of American Art, New York, June 23–October 16, 2005.

Lippard, Lucy. *Eccentric Abstraction*. New York: Fischbach Gallery, 1966. Published in conjunction with an exhibition of the same title, organized by and presented at Fischbach Gallery, New York, September 20–October 3, 1966.

———. "Eccentric Abstraction." *Art International*, November 1966.

———. *Eva Hesse*. New York: New York University Press, 1976.

———. "Homage to the Square." *Art in America*, July 1967.

———. "An Impure Situation (New York and Philadelphia Letter)." *Art International*, May 1966.

———. "Kenneth Price." In *Ken Price Sculpture: A Retrospective*, edited by Stephanie Barron, 263–65. Los Angeles: Los Angeles County Museum of Art; Munich: Prestel, 2012. Published in conjunction with an exhibition of the same title, organized by and presented at the Los Angeles County Museum of Art, September 16, 2012–January 6, 2013, and at the Nasher Sculpture Center, Dallas, February 9–May 12, 2013, and the Metropolitan Museum of Art, New York, June 18–September 22, 2013.

———. *Mixed Blessings: New Art in a Multicultural America*. New York: Pantheon Books, 1990.

———. *Nancy Graves: "Aves," Forms in Flight*. New York: Knoedler & Company, 2002. Published in conjunction with an exhibition of the same title, organized by and presented at Knoedler & Company, New York, March 7–April 27, 2002.

———. "Oral History Interview with Lucy Lippard." By Sue Heinemann. March 15, 2011. Archives of American Art, Smithsonian Institution, Washington, DC. https://www.aaa.si.edu/collections/interviews/oral-history-interview-lucy-lippard-15936.

"List of Films Shown at Knokke-le-Zoute, 1967." *Film Culture*, Autumn 1967.

Livet, Anne, ed. *David McManaway: Works, Twenty Years*. Dallas: Southern Methodist University, 1980. Published in conjunction with an exhibition of the same title, organized by and presented at University Gallery, Meadows School of the Arts, Southern Methodist University, Dallas, November 18, 1979–January 6, 1980.

Lodhie, Lindsey, and Michael Maizels. "S.M.S. Digital Survey Statement." Accessed September 20, 2023. http://sms.sensate journal.com/.

Lomahaftewa, Linda, and Lara M. Evans. "Gallery Talk with Linda Lomahaftewa (Hopi/Choctaw) and Dr. Lara M. Evans (Cherokee)." IAIA Museum of Contemporary Native Arts, March 4, 2021. Video, 55 min. https://youtu.be/nkZFu_GLpjU?si=F3gpxk4E0IDVZqcV.

Lukavic, John P., Jessica L. Horton, Eric Berkemeyer, and Kent Logan, eds. *Super Indian: Fritz Scholder, 1967–1980.* Denver: Denver Art Museum, 2015. Published in conjunction with an exhibition of the same title, organized by and presented at the Denver Museum of Art, October 4, 2015–January 17, 2016.

MacAgy, Douglas. *The Art That Broke the Looking Glass.* Dallas: Dallas Museum for Contemporary Arts, 1961. Published in conjunction with an exhibition of the same title, organized by and presented at the Dallas Museum for Contemporary Arts, November 15 –December 31, 1961.

———. *one i at a time.* Dallas: Southern Methodist University Press, 1971. Published in conjunction with an exhibition of the same title, organized by and presented at the Pollock Galleries, Meadows School of the Arts, Southern Methodist University, Dallas, March 20–April 25, 1971.

MacDonald, Scott. *Canyon Cinema: The Life and Times of an Independent Film Distributor.* Berkeley: University of California Press, 2008.

———, ed. *Cinema 16: Documents Toward History of Film Society.* Philadelphia: Temple University Press, 2010.

Made in Chicago. Washington, DC: Smithsonian Institution Press, 1974. Published in conjunction with an exhibition of the same title, organized by and presented at the National Collection of Fine Arts, Smithsonian Institution, Washington, DC, November 1–December 29, 1974, and at the Museum of Contemporary Art, Chicago, January 11 –March 2, 1975.

Man on Fire: Luis Jiménez, El Hombre en Llamas. Albuquerque, NM: Albuquerque Museum, 1994. Published in conjunction with an exhibition of the same title, organized by and presented at the Albuquerque Museum, Albuquerque, NM, February 20, 1994–May 15, 1994.

Marisol. "Marisol: Interview with Cindy Nemser (1973)." By Cindy Nemser. In *Modern Sculpture: Artists in Their Own Words*, edited by Douglas Dreishpoon, 179–82. Oakland: University of California Press, 2022.

Markopoulos, Gregory. "*Scorpio Rising.*" In *Film as Film: The Collected Writings of Gregory J. Markopoulos*, edited by Mark Webber, 135–36. London: Visible Press, 2014.

Martha Rosler: Irrespective. New York: Jewish Museum, 2018. Published in conjunction with an exhibition of the same title, organized by and presented at the Jewish Museum, New York, November 2, 2018–March 3, 2019.

Martin, Fred. "Wally Hedrick." In *Wally Hedrick, Sam Tchakalian*, unpaginated. Balboa, CA: Balboa Pavilion Gallery, 1967. Published in conjunction with an exhibition of the same title, organized by and presented at the Balboa Pavilion Gallery, Newport Harbor, CA, May 3–June 11, 1967.

Mauer, Otto, ed. *Kiki*. Vienna: Galerie St. Stephan, 1961. Published in conjunction with the exhibition *Kiki Kogelnik*, organized by and presented at Galerie St. Stephan, Vienna, October 9–November 3, 1961.

McCarthy, David. "Of *Plush* and *Imitation Knotty Pine*: H. C. Westermann and American Sculpture of the 1960s." *American Art* 33, no. 3 (Fall 2019): 32–55.

———. "An Open-Ended Question: H. C. Westermann's *Untitled*, 1962." *Source: Notes in the History of Art* 39, no. 3 (Spring 2020): 194–202.

———. "A Thank-You Note from H. C. Westermann." *Archives of American Art Journal* 58, no. 1 (Spring 2019): 28–47.

———. "When William T. Wiley and Bruce Nauman Wrote to H. C. Westermann." *Art Inquiries* 18, no. 1 (2020): 46–59.

McEvilley, Thomas, Donald Kuspit, and Roberta Smith. *Lucas Samaras: Objects and Subjects, 1969–1986.* New York: Abbeville Press, 1988. Published in conjunction with an exhibition of the same title, organized by and presented at the Denver Art Museum, May 7–July 10, 1988.

McNally, Brendan. "The Oak Cliff 4 (or 5): When Funky Art Ruled Dallas—and Beyond." *Art&Seek*, May 31, 2013. https://artandseek .org/2013/05/31/the-oak-cliff-four-or-five-when-funky-art-ruled -dallas-and-beyond/.

Meister, Sarah Hermanson, ed. *Arbus, Friedlander, Winogrand: "New Documents," 1967.* New York: Museum of Modern Art, 2017.

Mekas, Jonas. *Movie Journal: The Rise of the New American Cinema, 1959–1971.* 2nd ed. Edited by Gregory Smulewicz-Zucker. New York: Columbia University Press, 2016.

Mel Casas: Humanscapes. Houston: Contemporary Arts Museum, 1976. Published in conjunction with an exhibition of the same title, organized by and presented at the Contemporary Arts Museum, Houston, October 22–November 23, 1976.

Mellow, James R. "Bontecou's Well-Fed Fish and Malevolent Flowers." *New York Times*, June 6, 1971.

Mendelson, Jordana. "Paintings Based on Collages, 1933." In *Joan Miró: Painting and Anti-Painting, 1927–1937*, edited by Anne Umland, 119–39. New York: Museum of Modern Art, 2008.

Mendieta, Ana. "Self-Portraits." Master's thesis, University of Iowa, 1972. The Estate of Ana Mendieta Collection Archives, Galerie Lelong & Co., New York.

Meyer, Richard, and Rachel Middleman, eds. *Anita Steckel: The Feminist Art of Sexual Politics.* Stanford, CA: Stanford Art Gallery, 2022. Published in conjunction with an exhibition of the same title, organized by and presented at the Stanford University Art Gallery, Stanford, CA, February 3–March 11, 2022.

Michelson, Annette. "Rose Hobart and Monsieur Phot: Early Films from Utopia Parkway." *Artforum*, Summer 1973.

Middleman, Rachel. *Radical Eroticism: Women, Art, and Sex in the 1960s.* Oakland: University of California Press, 2018.

Miller, D. Scot. "Afrosurreal Manifesto: Black Is the New Black—A 21st-Century Manifesto." *Black Camera* 5, no. 1 (Fall 2013): 113–17.

Miller, Dorothy C., ed. *Americans 1963.* New York: Museum of Modern Art, 1963. Published in conjunction with an exhibition of the same title, organized by and presented at the Museum of Modern Art, New York, May 22–August 18, 1963.

Monte, James. "'Making It' with Funk." *Artforum*, July 1967. https:// www.artforum.com/features/making-it-with-funk-211338/.

Morris, Frances, ed. *Louise Bourgeois.* New York: Rizzoli, 2008. Published in conjunction with an exhibition of the same title, co-organized by the Solomon R. Guggenheim Foundation, Tate Modern, London, and Centre Pompidou, Paris, and presented at Tate Modern, London, October 10, 2007–January 20, 2008; Centre Pompidou, Paris, March 5–June 2, 2008; the Solomon R. Guggenheim Museum, New York, June 27–September 28, 2008; and at the Museum of Contemporary Art, Los Angeles, October 26, 2008–January 26, 2009; and the Hirshhorn Museum and Sculpture Garden, Washington, DC, February 28–June 7, 2009.

———, ed. *Yayoi Kusama.* London: Tate, 2012. Published in conjunction with an exhibition of the same title, organized by and presented at Tate Modern, London, February 9–June 5, 2012.

Morrison, C. L. "Chicago Dialectic." *Artforum*, February 1978.

Moser, Joann, ed. *What's It All Mean: William T. Wiley in Retrospect.* Washington, DC: Smithsonian American Art Museum; Berkeley: University of California Press, 2009. Published in conjunction with an exhibition of the same title, organized by and presented at the Smithsonian American Art Museum, Washington, DC, October 1, 2009 –January 24, 2010, and at the Berkeley Museum and Pacific Film Archive, Berkeley, CA, March 17–July 18, 2010.

Museum of Modern Art, New York. "Compass in Hand: Selections from The Judith Rothschild Foundation Contemporary Drawings Collection." Accessed October 19, 2023. https://www.moma.org /audio/playlist/210/2767.

———. Exhibition checklist for *In Honor of Dr. Martin Luther King Jr.*, organized by and presented at the Museum of Modern Art, New York, October 31–November 3, 1968. Accessed September 20, 2023. https://www.moma.org/momaorg/shared/pdfs/docs /press_archives/4123/releases/MOMA_1968_July-December _0055_98a.pdf.

Nadel, Dan. "Hairy Who's History of the Hairy Who." *Ganzfeld*, no. 3 (2003): 110–45.

———. "How Would a Comb That Cannot Untangle Hair Look?: On the Art of Christina Ramberg." *Artforum*, February 2018. https://www.artforum.com/features/dan-nadel-on-the-art-of -christina-ramberg-237540/.

———. "Humanly Possible: Dan Nadel on the Art of William T. Wiley." *Artforum*, April 2019.

———, ed. *Karl Wirsum.* New York: Derek Eller Gallery, 2013. Published in conjunction with an exhibition of the same title, organized by and presented at Derek Eller Gallery, New York, October 12–November 16, 2013.

———. "The Repeating Beauty of Suellen Rocca." In *Suellen Rocca*, 6–19. New York: Matthew Marks Gallery, 2016. Published in conjunction with the exhibition *Suellen Rocca: Bare Shouldered Beauty, Works from 1965 to 1969*, organized by and presented at Matthew Marks Gallery, New York, September 9–October 22, 2016.

National Gallery of Art. "Symbolism and Place: Linda Lomahaftewa." Accessed March 25, 2024. https://www.nga.gov/learn/teachers /lessons-activities/symbolism-place-linda-lomahaftewa.html.

Nauman, Bruce. "Oral History Interview with Bruce Nauman." By Michele De Angelus. May 27–30, 1980. Archives of American Art, Smithsonian Institution, Washington, DC. https://www. aaa.si.edu/collections/interviews/oral-history-interview-bruce -nauman-12538.

Nelson, Gunvor. "Excerpts from an Interview with Gunvor Nelson." *Canyon Cinemanews*, May/June 1974.

Nelson, Gunvor, and Dorothy Wiley. "Women, Wives, Film-Makers: An Interview with Gunvor Nelson and Dorothy Wiley." By Brenda Richardson. *Film Quarterly* 25, no. 1 (1971): 34–40.

Nengudi, Senga. "Oral History Interview with Senga Nengudi." By Elissa Auther. July 9–11, 2013. Archives of American Art, Smithsonian Institution, Washington, DC. https://www.aaa.si.edu /download_pdf_transcript/ajax?record_id=edanmdm-AAADCD _oh_363699.

———. "Senga Nengudi: Black Avant Garde Visual and Performance Artist." By Bridget Cooks and Amanda Tewes. 2020. Oral History Center, The Bancroft Library, University of California, Berkeley. https:// www.getty.edu/research/special_collections/oral_histories /pdfs/nengudi_senga_2022.pdf.

Newman, Amy, ed. *Challenging Art: "Artforum," 1962–1974.* New York: Soho Press, 2000.

New Work by Oldenburg. New York: Sidney Janis Gallery, 1966. Published in conjunction with an exhibition of the same title, organized by and presented at Sidney Janis Gallery, New York, March 9–April 2, 1966.

Nixon, Mignon. "Spero's Curses." *October* 122, no. 3 (Fall 2007): 3–30.

Nochlin, Linda. "Nancy Graves: The Subversiveness of Sculpture." In *Nancy Graves: Painting, Sculpture, Drawing, 1980–1985*, edited by Debra Bricker Balken, 13–21. Poughkeepsie, NY: Vassar College Art Gallery, 1986. Published in conjunction with an exhibition of the same title, organized by and presented at Vassar College Art Gallery, Poughkeepsie, NY, April 17–June 11, 1986.

Norton, Margot, ed. *Lynn Hershman Leeson: Twisted.* New York: New Museum, 2021. Published in conjunction with an exhibition of the same title, organized by and presented at the New Museum of Contemporary Art, New York, June 30–October 3, 2021.

Nut Art. Hayward: California State University, Hayward Art Gallery, 1972. Published in conjunction with an exhibition of the same title, organized by and presented at California State University, Hayward Art Gallery, Hayward, April 25–May 12, 1972.

O'Doherty, Brian. "Art: Avant-Garde Revolt: 'New Realists' Mock U.S. Mass Culture Exhibition at Sidney Janis Gallery." *New York Times*, October 31, 1962.

———. "Christmas Exhibitions Playing a Wide Field: International Selections of Painting and Sculpture in Local Galleries." *New York Times*, December 29, 1963.

———. "Six Surrealist Painters." *New York Times*, January 18, 1946.

Oldenburg, Claes. *Claes Oldenburg: Writing on the Side, 1956–1969.* Edited by Achim Hochdörfer, Maartje Oldenburg, and Barbara Schröder. New York: Museum of Modern Art, 2013. Published in conjunction with the exhibition *Claes Oldenburg: "The Street" and "The Store"/"Mouse Museum" and "Ray Gun Wing,"* co-organized by the Museum moderner Kunst Stiftung Ludwig Wien, Vienna, and the Museum of Modern Art, New York, and presented at the Museum of Modern Art, New York, April 14–August 5, 2013.

Ortiz, Luis. *Emshwiller: Infinity x Two.* New York: Nonstop Press, 2007.

Ortiz, María Elena, ed. *Surrealism and Us: Caribbean and African Diasporic Artists since 1940.* Fort Worth, TX: Modern Art Museum of Fort Worth, 2024. Published in conjunction with an exhibition of the same title, organized by and presented at the Modern Art Museum of Fort Worth, Fort Worth, TX, March 10–July 28, 2024.

Ostrow, Saul. "From the Archives: Process, Image, and Elegy." ARTnews.com, April 1, 2008. https://www.artnews.com/art-in-america/features/archives-process-image-elegy-63405/.

Out of the Ordinary. Houston: Contemporary Arts Association of Houston, 1959. Published in conjunction with an exhibition of the same title, organized by and presented at the Contemporary Arts Association of Houston, November 26–December 27, 1959.

Outterbridge, John W. "African-American Artists of Los Angeles: John W. Outterbridge." By Richard Candida Smith. 1993. Department of Special Collections, University of California, Los Angeles Library. https://oac.cdlib.org/ark:/13030/hb229006xm/?brand=oac4.

Pacini, Marina, ed. "Marisol: A Biographical Sketch." In *Marisol: Sculptures and Works on Paper*, 11–70. Memphis: Memphis Brooks Museum of Art; New Haven, CT: Yale University Press, 2014. Published in conjunction with an exhibition of the same title, organized by and presented at the Memphis Brooks Museum of Art, June 14–September 7, 2014, and at El Museo del Barrio, New York, October 9, 2014–January 10, 2015.

———. "Who But the Arts Council." *Archives of American Art Journal* 27, no. 4 (1987): 9–23.

Packard, Cassie. "Red, White, Yellow, and Black: 1972–73." *Brooklyn Rail*, April 2023. https://brooklynrail.org/2023/04/artseen/Red-White-Yellow-and-Black-197273.

Padon, Thomas. *Nancy Graves: Excavations in Print, A Catalogue Raisonné.* New York: Harry N. Abrams, 1996. Published in conjunction with the exhibition *Nancy Graves: Excavations in Print*, organized by the American Federation of the Arts, New York, and presented at the Nelson-Atkins Museum of Art, Kansas City, MO, January 26–April 7, 1996; and at the Frances Lehman Loeb Art Center, Vassar College, Poughkeepsie, NY, May 3–July 14, 1996; the Butler Institute of American Art, Youngstown, OH, August 9–October 20, 1996; the Cornell Fine Arts Museum, Rollins College, Winter Park, FL, November 9, 1996–January 12, 1997; the Mitchell Art Gallery, St. Johns College, Annapolis, MD, September 5–November 16, 1997; the Middlebury College Museum of Art, Middlebury, VT, January 6–February 22, 1998; the Thorne-Sagendorph Art Gallery, Keene, NH, March 28–May 2, 1998; the Memphis Brooks Museum of Art, June 26–September 7, 1998; and the Bermuda National Gallery, Hamilton, September 26, 1998–January 9, 1999.

Papernik-Shimizu, Erica, ed. *Shigeko Kubota: Liquid Reality.* New York: Museum of Modern Art, 2021. Published in conjunction with an exhibition of the same title, organized by and presented at the Museum of Modern Art, New York, August 21, 2021–February 13, 2022.

Perkins, Constance M. "Los Angeles: The Way You Look at It." *Art in America*, March–April 1966.

Perreault, John. "The Materiality of Matter." *Village Voice*, November 28, 1968.

———. "Metaphysical Funk Monk." *ARTnews*, May 1968.

Peter, Carolyn. *Gallery 32 and Its Circle.* Los Angeles: Laband Art Gallery, 2009. Published in conjunction with an exhibition of the same title, organized by and presented at Laband Art Gallery, Loyola Marymount University, Los Angeles, January 24–March 22, 2009.

Peter Freeman, Inc. Press release for *Alex Hay: Circumstance/Art*. Organized by and presented at Peter Freeman Inc., New York, January 7–February 20, 2016. https://www.peterfreemaninc.com/exhibitions/alex-hay3/press-release.

Photographs. Sale cat. Sotheby's, New York, October 16, 2004.

Picard, Lil. "Erotic, Eccentric, Electric." *East Village Other*, October 1–15, 1966.

———. "The New School of New York." *Das Kunstwerk*, December 1964. Quoted in *Paul Thek: The Wonderful World That Almost Was*, edited by Roland Groenenboom, 186. Rotterdam: Witte de With Center for Contemporary Art, 1995. Published in conjunction with an exhibition of the same title, organized by and presented at the Witte de With Center for Contemporary Art, Rotterdam, June 3–October 8, 1995; and at Neue Nationalgalerie, Berlin, December 7, 1995–February 18, 1996; Fundació Antoni Tàpies, Barcelona, June 21–September 2, 1996; and MAC, Galeries Contemporaines des Musées de Marseille, Marseille, France, January 15–May 11, 1997.

Pigott, Michael. *Joseph Cornell Versus Cinema.* London: Bloomsbury, 2015.

Pincus-Witten, Robert. "Human Concern, Personal Torment." *Artforum*, December 1969.

———. "New York: Joe Raffaele, Stable Gallery." *Artforum*, December 1965.

Pires, Jesse, ed. *Dreamdance: The Art of Ed Emshwiller.* New York: Anthology Editions Lightbox Film Center, 2019. Published in conjunction with an exhibition of the same title, organized by and presented at the Lightbox Film Center and Rosenwald-Wolf Gallery at University of the Arts, Philadelphia, October 18–December 7, 2019.

Plagens, Peter. "Judy Gerowitz: Rolf Nelson Gallery." *Artforum*, April 1966.

———. *Sunshine Muse: Art on the West Coast, 1945–1970.* Berkeley: University of California Press, 1999.

Platow, Raphaela, and Lowery Stokes Sims, eds. *Art and Race Matters: The Career of Robert Colescott.* New York: Rizzoli, 2019. Published in conjunction with an exhibition of the same title, organized by and presented at Contemporary Arts Center, Cincinnati, OH, September 20, 2019–January 12, 2020, and at the Portland Art Museum, Portland, OR, February 15–May 17, 2020; the Chicago Cultural Center, June 20–September 27, 2020; the Akron Art Museum, Akron, OH, October 25, 2020–January 31, 2021; the Sarasota Art Museum, Sarasota, FL, May 29–October 31, 2021; and the New Museum of Contemporary Art, New York, June 30–October 9, 2022.

Polley, E. M. "San Francisco: East Bay." *Artforum*, December 1965.

Powell, Richard J. *Black Art and Culture in the 20th Century.* London: Thames & Hudson, 1997.

Prather, Marla. *Unrepentant Ego: The Self-Portraits of Lucas Samaras.* New York: Whitney Museum of American Art, 2003. Published in conjunction with an exhibition of the same title, organized by and presented at the Whitney Museum of American Art, New York, November 12, 2003–February 7, 2004.

"Prints and Portfolios Published." *Print Collector's Newsletter* 2, no. 3 (July/August 1971): 56–58.

Program for New Cinema Festival I. Film-makers' Cinematheque, New York. November 1–9, 1965.

Prokopoff, Stephen S., ed. *The Spirit of the Comics.* Philadelphia: University of Pennsylvania, 1969. Published in conjunction with an exhibition of the same title, organized by and presented at the Institute of Contemporary Art, University of Pennsylvania, Philadelphia, October 1–November 9, 1969.

Purifoy, Noah. "African-American Artists of Los Angeles: Noah Purifoy." By Karen Anne Mason. September 8–9 and 22–23, 1990. University of California, Los Angeles, Oral History Program. https://oralhistory.library.ucla.edu/catalog/21198-zz0008zm4z.

Purifoy, Noah, and Ted Michel. *Junk Art: 66 Signs of Neon.* Los Angeles: 66 Signs of Neon, 1966. Published in conjunction with an exhibition of the same title, organized by and presented at the Simon Rodia Renaissance of the Arts Festival, Jordan Markham High, Watts, CA, April 3–9, 1966.

Purvis, Rye. "SFAI and IAIA." Orbits of Known and Unknown Objects: SFAI Histories/Matrix 277. Accessed July 11, 2024. https://matrix277.org/Object-61.

Quirarte, Jacinto. "Mexican, Mexican American, Chicano Art: Two Views." In *Mexican American Artists*, 132–36. Austin: University of Texas Press, 1973.

Raffaele, Joseph. "Allusive Structure: A Conversation with Joe Raffaele." By Robert Pincus-Witten. *Artforum*, December 1966.

———. "An Interview with Joseph Raffael." By Mary Fuller. *Currant Art Magazine*, August–October 1976.

———. Unpublished correspondence with Dan Nadel. 2017.

Ragin, Robin. Unpublished interview by Laura Phipps. April 17, 2020.

Ratcliff, Carter. *Lee Bontecou.* Chicago: Museum of Contemporary

Art, 1972. Published in conjunction with an exhibition of the same title, organized by and presented at the Museum of Contemporary Art Chicago, March 24–May 7, 1972.

Raven, Arlene. "Notes on Nancy Grossman." Reprinted in *Nancy Grossman: Tough Life Diary*, edited by Ian Berry, 211–15. Saratoga Springs, NY: Frances Young Tang Teaching Museum and Art Gallery; Munich: Prestel, 2012. Published in conjunction with an exhibition of the same title, organized by and presented at the Frances Young Tang Teaching Museum and Art Gallery, Saratoga Springs, NY, February 18–May 20, 2012.

Recent Work by Arman, Dine, Fahlstrom, Marisol, Oldenburg, Segal. New York: Sidney Janis Gallery, 1965. Published in conjunction with an exhibition of the same title, organized by and presented at Sidney Janis Gallery, New York, May 5–31, 1965.

Reed, Anthony. "After the End of the World: Sun Ra and the Grammar of Utopia." *Black Camera* 5, no. 1 (Fall 2013): 118–39.

Reed, Ishmael. "The Black Artist: Calling a Spade a Spade." *Arts Magazine*, May 1967. Reprinted in *The "Soul of a Nation" Reader: Writings by and about Black American Artists, 1960–1980*, edited by Mark Godfrey and Allie Biswas, 64–67. New York: Gregory R. Miller, 2021.

Reif, Rita. "Auctions." *New York Times*, March 23, 1979. https://www .nytimes.com/1979/03/23/archives/auctions-wealth-of-deco -and-nouveau.html.

Remington, Deborah. "Oral History Interview with Deborah Remington." By Paul Cummings. May 18–July 19, 1973. Archives of American Art, Smithsonian Institution, Washington, DC. https:// www.aaa.si.edu/collections/interviews/oral-history-interview -deborah-remington-13319.

Ringgold, Faith. "Faith Ringgold." By Eleanor Munro. In *Originals: American Women Artists*, edited by Eleanor Munro, 409–16. New York: Simon and Schuster, 1979.

———. *We Flew over the Bridge: The Memoirs of Faith Ringgold*. Boston: Little, Brown, 1995.

Robbins, Corinne. "Man Is Anonymous: The Art of Nancy Grossman." *Art Spectrum* 1, no. 2 (February 1975): 33–37.

Robbins, Daniel. "Sculpture by Louise Bourgeois." *Art International*, October 20, 1964.

Robert Irwin/Kenneth Price. Los Angeles: Los Angeles County Museum of Art, 1966. Published in conjunction with an exhibition of the same title, organized by and presented at the Los Angeles County Museum of Art, July 7–September 4, 1966.

Roberts, Jennifer. "History in Smithson's Religious Paintings." In *Mirror-Travels: Robert Smithson and History*, 13–35. New Haven, CT: Yale University Press, 2004.

Robinson, Julia, ed. *New Realisms, 1957–1962: Object Strategies Between Readymade and Spectacle*. Cambridge, MA: MIT Press, 2010. Published in conjunction with an exhibition of the same title, organized by and presented at the Museo Nacional Centro de Arte Reina Sofía, Madrid, June 16–October 4, 2010.

Robinson, Lia, and Lumi Tan. "Red, White, Yellow, and Black: 1972–73." By Wyatt Allgeier. *Gagosian Quarterly*, Spring 2023. https:// gagosian.com/quarterly/2023/02/10/interview-red-white-yellow -and-black-1972-73/.

Rodenbeck, Judith F. "Yayoi Kusama: Surface, Stitch, Skin." In *Inside the Visible: An Elliptical Traverse of 20th Century Art in, of, and from the Feminine*, edited by M. Catherine de Zegher, 149–55. Cambridge, MA: MIT Press, 1996. Published in conjunction with an exhibition of the same title, co-organized by the Kanaal Art Foundation, Kortrijk, Belgium, and the Institute of Contemporary Art, Boston, and presented at the Béguinage of Saint-Elizabeth,

Kortrijk, Belgium, April 16, 1994–May 28, 1995; and at the Institute of Contemporary Art, Boston, January 30–May 12, 1996; the National Museum of Women in the Arts, Washington, DC, June 15–September 15, 1996; Whitechapel Art Gallery, London, October 11–December 8, 1996; and the Art Gallery of Western Australia, Perth, February 13–April 6, 1997.

Romare Bearden: The Prevalence of Ritual. New York: Museum of Modern Art, 1971. Published in conjunction with an exhibition of the same title, organized by and presented at the Museum of Modern Art, New York, March 25–June 7, 1971, and at the National Collection of Fine Arts, Washington, DC, July 16–September 12, 1971; the University Art Museum, University of California, Berkeley, October 25–December 5, 1971; the Pasadena Art Museum, Pasadena, CA, December 21, 1971–January 30, 1972; and the High Museum of Art, Atlanta, February 27–April 9, 1972.

Rooks, Michael, and Lynne Warren, eds. *H. C. Westermann: Exhibition Catalogue and Catalogue Raisonné of Objects*. Chicago: Museum of Contemporary Art, 2001. Published in conjunction with the exhibition *H. C. Westermann*, organized by and presented at the Museum of Contemporary Art Chicago, June 30–September 23, 2001.

Rose, Barbara. "Los Angeles: The Second City." *Art in America*, January–February 1966.

———. "Portrait of the Artist." In *Claes Oldenburg*, 19–27. New York: Museum of Modern Art, 1970. Published in conjunction with an exhibition of the same title, organized by and presented at the Museum of Modern Art, New York, September 25–November 23, 1969.

———. "Vaginal Iconology." *New York*, February 11, 1974.

Rosemont, Franklin, and Robin D. G. Kelley, eds. *Black, Brown, & Beige: Surrealist Writings from Africa and the Diaspora*. Austin: University of Texas Press, 2009.

Rosen, Barry, ed. *Eva Hesse: Diaries*. Zurich: Hauser & Wirth, 2020.

Rosenquist, James. "James Rosenquist by Mary Ann Staniszewsk." By Mary Ann Staniszewsk. *BOMB*, October 1, 1987. https://bomb magazine.org/articles/james-rosenquist/.

Rosenquist, James, and David Dalton. *Painting Below Zero: Notes on a Life in Art*. New York: Alfred A. Knopf, 2009.

Rosler, Martha. "*House Beautiful (Bringing the War Home)*, 1967–72." Museum of Modern Art, 2019. Video, 7 min. https://www.youtube .com/watch?v=hJbR4jXsrXU.

———. "Lookers, Buyers, Dealers, and Makers: Thoughts on Audience." *Exposure* 17, no. 1 (Spring 1979): 10–25.

Rossi, Barbara. "Marriage Chicago Style." Smart Museum of Art, University of Chicago, undated (c. 2013). Video, 3 min. https:// vimeo.com/76023234.

Rothkopf, Scott. "Banned and Determined." *Artforum*, Summer 2002. https://www.artforum.com/print/200206/banned-and-determined -gene-swenson-2917.

Roy Fridge: Heroes, Hermits, Shamans and Boats, Selected Works 1959–1984. Corpus Christi: Art Museum of South Texas, 1985. Published in conjunction with an exhibition of the same title, organized by and presented at the Art Museum of South Texas, Corpus Christi, April 12–June 9, 1985.

Roznoy, Cynthia. *Chicago Loop: Imagist Art, 1949–1979*. New York: Whitney Museum of American Art, 2000. Published in conjunction with an exhibition of the same title, organized by and presented at the Whitney Museum of American Art, Fairfield County, Stamford, CT, September 15–December 6, 2000.

Rubin, William S. "Some Reflections Prompted by the Recent Work of Louise Bourgeois." *Art International*, April 1969.

Rudikoff, Sonya. "New Realists in New York." *Art International*, January 1963.

Ruscha, Ed. "Oral History Interview with Edward Ruscha." By Paul Karlstrom. October 29, 1980–October 2, 1981. Archives of American Art, Smithsonian Institution, Washington, DC. https://www.aaa .si.edu/collections/interviews/oral-history-interview-edward -ruscha-12887.

Saar, Betye. "Influences: Betye Saar." *Frieze*, September 27, 2016. https://www.frieze.com/article/influences-betye-saar.

———. "A TEI Project: Interview of Betye Saar." By Karen Anne Mason. June 4 and 27, 1990; August 15, 1990; September 12, 1990; and June 19, 1991. University of California, Los Angeles. https:// static.library.ucla.edu/oralhistory/pdf/masters/21198-zz0008zpzb -8-master.pdf.

Saint Phalle, Niki de. *Niki de Saint Phalle: My Art, My Dreams*. Edited by Carla Schulz-Hoffmann. Munich: Prestel, 2003.

Samaras, Lucas. *Lucas Samaras*. New York: Whitney Museum of American Art, 1972. Published in conjunction with an exhibition of the same title, organized by and presented at the Whitney Museum of American Art, New York, November 18, 1972–January 7, 1973.

———. *Lucas Samaras: Selected Works, 1960–1966*. New York: Pace Gallery, 1966. Published in conjunction with an exhibition of the same title, organized by and presented at Pace Gallery, New York, October 8–November 5, 1966.

Sandler, Irving. "Claes Oldenburg, Reuben Gallery." *ARTnews*, July 1960.

———. "In the Art Galleries." *New York Post*, May 20, 1962.

———. "Robert Smithson." *ARTnews*, October 1959.

Saul, Peter. *Peter Saul: Professional Artist Correspondence, 1945–1976*. Edited by Dan Nadel. Los Angeles: Bad Dimension Press, 2020.

Saunders, Raymond. "Black Is a Color." In *The "Soul of a Nation" Reader: Writings by and about Black American Artists, 1960–1980*, edited by Mark Godfrey and Allie Biswas, 68–71. New York: Gregory R. Miller, 2021.

———. "San Francisco Museum of Art Interviews Raymond Saunders." San Francisco Museum of Art, 1994. Video, 98 min. https://archive.org/details/cocac_000011.

Sawin, Martica. *Surrealism in Exile and the Beginning of the New York School*. Cambridge, MA: MIT Press, 1997.

"Scenes." *Village Voice*, February 27, 1969.

Schjeldahl, Peter. "Finding Alex Hay: 'Gentle Maverick.'" *New York Times*, May 2, 1971.

Schneemann, Carolee. "The Articulate Body: Schneemann in Conversation." By Robert Enright. *Border Crossings*, February 1998. https://bordercrossingsmag.com/article/the-articulate-body.

———. "Body of Influence: Six Views on Paul Thek." *Artforum*, January 2011. https://www.artforum.com/features/body-of-influence-six -views-on-paul-thek-215949/.

———. "Carolee Schneemann." By Scott MacDonald. In vol. 1 of *A Critical Cinema: Interviews with Independent Filmmakers*, edited by Scott MacDonald, 134–51. Berkeley: University of California Press, 1988.

———. "Double Knowledge: In Conversation with Carolee Schneemann." By Ron Hanson. *White Fungus* 16 (2019). https://www .whitefungus.com/carolee-schneemann-double-knowledge.

———. "Film and Performance: An Interview with Carolee Schneemann." By Scott MacDonald. *Millennium Film Journal* 7–9 (Fall 1980/81): 95–114.

———. "Kenneth Anger's *Scorpio Rising*." *Film Culture*, Spring 1964.

———. *More Than Meat Joy: Performances and Selected Writings*. Edited by Bruce R. McPherson. Kingston, NY: McPherson, 1997.

Schulze, Franz. *Chicago Imagist Art*. Chicago: Museum of Contemporary Art, 1972. Published in conjunction with an exhibition of the same title, organized by and presented at the Museum of Contemporary Art Chicago, May 13–June 25, 1972.

———. "Chicago Popcycle." *Art in America*, November–December 1966.

———. *Fantastic Images: Chicago Art since 1945*. Chicago: Follett, 1972.

Seckler, Dorothy Gees. "The Artist in America: The Audience Is His Medium!" *Art in America*, April 1963.

Seiberling, Dorothy. "The Female View of Erotica." *New York*, February 11, 1974.

Seitz, William C. *The Art of Assemblage*. New York: Museum of Modern Art, 1961. Published in conjunction with an exhibition of the same title, co-organized by the Museum of Modern Art, New York, the Dallas Museum for Contemporary Arts, and the San Francisco Museum of Art, and presented at the Museum of Modern Art, New York, October 2–November 12, 1961, and at the Dallas Museum for Contemporary Arts, January 9–February 11, 1962, and the San Francisco Museum of Art, March 5–April 15, 1962.

Sekimachi, Kay. "Memories of Japan." In *The Weaver's Weaver: Explorations in Multiple Layers and Three-Dimensional Fiber Art*, 40–47. Berkeley: Regional Oral History Office, the Bancroft Library, University of California, Berkeley, 1996.

———. "Oral History Interview with Kay Sekimachi [Stocksdale]." By Suzanne Baizerman. July 26–August 6, 2001. Archives of American Art, Smithsonian Institution, Washington, DC. https://www.aaa.si.edu/collections/interviews/oral-history-interview-kay-sekimachi-stocksdale-11768.

Seldis, Henry. "Four Painters at Ceeje." *Los Angeles Times*, July 20, 1962.

Selz, Peter, ed. *Funk*. Berkeley: University Art Museum, University of California, Berkeley, 1967. Published in conjunction with an exhibition of the same title, organized by and presented at the University Art Museum, University of California, Berkeley, April 18–May 29, 1967.

———. "Funk Art." *Art in America*, March–April 1967.

———. "Retrospective: Reflections on Barbara Chase-Riboud (2008)." *Callaloo* 32, no. 3 (2009): 879–81.

———. "Surrealism and the Chicago Imagists of the 1950s: A Comparison and Contrast." *Art Journal* 45, no. 4 (Winter 1985): 303–6.

Semmel, Joan. "Joan Semmel Interview." By Ellen Lubell. *Womanart*, Winter 1977–78.

Serra, M. M. "Eye/Body: The Cinematic Paintings of Carolee Schneemann." In *Women's Experimental Cinema: Critical Frameworks*, edited by Robin Blaetz, 103–26. Durham, NC: Duke University Press, 2007.

Shaman, Sanford Sivitz. *Contemporary Chicago Painters*. Cedar Falls: University of Northern Iowa, 1978. Published in conjunction with an exhibition of the same title, organized by and presented at the Gallery of the Department of Art, University of Northern Iowa, Cedar Falls, April 2–30, 1978.

Shapiro, David. "Sculpture as Experience: The Monument That Suffered." *Art in America*, May–June 1974.

Shapiro, Michael Edwards. "Inside-Out/Outside-In: The Anatomy of Nancy Graves's Sculpture." In *The Sculpture of Nancy Graves: A Catalogue Raisonné with Essays*, edited by E. A. Carmean, 25–35. New York: Hudson Hills Press, 1987. Published in conjunction with the exhibition *Nancy Graves: A Sculpture Retrospective*, organized by the Fort Worth Art Museum, Fort Worth, TX, and presented at the Hirshhorn Museum and Sculpture Garden, Washington, DC, February 19–April 26, 1987; and at the Fort Worth Art Museum, Fort Worth, TX, May 17–July 12, 1987; the Santa Barbara Museum of Art, Santa Barbara, CA, August 29–October 25, 1987; and the Brooklyn Museum, December 11, 1987–February 29, 1988.

Shaw, Goldene, ed. *History of the Hyde Park Art Center, 1939–1976*. Chicago: Hyde Park Art Center, 1976.

Shiff, Richard. *Jack Whitten: Cosmic Soul*. Zurich: Hauser & Wirth, 2022. Published in conjunction with an exhibition of the same title, organized by and presented at Hauser & Wirth, Zurich, June 10–July 29, 2022.

Sichel, Jennifer. "'Do you think Pop Art's queer?' Gene Swenson and Andy Warhol." *Oxford Art Journal* 41, no. 1 (2018): 59–83.

Singerman, Howard, and Sarah Watson, eds. *Acts of Art and Rebuttal in 1971*. New York: Hunter College Art Galleries, 2018. Published in conjunction with an exhibition of the same title, organized by and presented at the Bertha and Karl Leubsdorf Gallery, Hunter College, New York, October 4–November 25, 2018.

Sitney, P. Adams, ed. *Film Culture Reader*. New York: Cooper Square Press, 2000.

———. *Visionary Film: The American Avant-Garde, 1943–2000*. 3rd ed. London: Oxford University Press, 2002.

Six Touring Exhibitions 1967/68 from the San Francisco Art Institute. San Francisco: San Francisco Art Institute, 1967.

Slifkin, Robert. *The New Monuments and the End of Man: U.S. Sculpture between War and Peace, 1945–1975*. Princeton, NJ: Princeton University Press, 2019.

Smith, Elizabeth A. T. "Abstract Sinister." *Art in America*, September 1993.

———, ed. *Lee Bontecou: A Retrospective*. Los Angeles: Hammer Museum; Chicago: Museum of Contemporary Art, 2004. Published in conjunction with an exhibition of the same title, co-organized by the Museum of Contemporary Art Chicago, and the Hammer Museum, Los Angeles, and presented at the Hammer Museum, Los Angeles, October 5, 2003–January 11, 2004, and at the Museum of Contemporary Art Chicago, February 14–May 31, 2004, and the Museum of Modern Art, New York, July 28–September 27, 2004.

Smith, Jack. "Rehearsal for the Destruction of Atlantis: A Dream Weapon Ritual by Jack Smith Dedicated to Irving Rosenthal." In *Wait for Me at the Bottom of the Pool: The Writings of Jack Smith*, edited by J. Hoberman and Edward Leffingwell, 90–95. New York: High Risk Books, 1997.

Smith, Richard Cándida. *Utopia and Dissent: Art, Poetry, and Politics in California*. Berkeley: University of California Press, 1995.

Smithson, Robert. "Interview with Robert Smithson for the Archives of American Art/Smithsonian Institution, July 14–19, 1972." By Paul Cummings. In *Robert Smithson: The Collected Writings*, edited by Jack Flam, 270–96. Berkeley: University of California Press, 1996.

———. "Oral History Interview with Robert Smithson." By Paul Cummings. July 14–19, 1972. Archives of American Art, Smithsonian Institution, Washington, DC. https://www.aaa.si.edu/collections/interviews/oral-history-interview-robert-smithson-12013.

———. "Quasi-Infinities and the Waning of Space." *Arts Magazine*, November 1966.

———. Robert Smithson and Nancy Holt Papers, 1905–87. Archives of American Art, Smithsonian Institution, Washington, DC.

———. *Robert Smithson: The Collected Writings*. Edited by Jack Flam. Berkeley: University of California Press, 1996.

Sontag, Susan. *Against Interpretation and Other Essays*. New York: Picador, 2001.

Spero, Nancy. "Interview: Word into Image." By Marjorie Welish. *BOMB*, Spring 1994. https://bombmagazine.org/articles/word-into-image/.

Stable Gallery Records, 1916–99, bulk 1953–70. Archives of American Art, Smithsonian Institution, Washington, DC.

Starr, Sandra Leonard. *Lost and Found in California: Four Decades of Assemblage Art*. Santa Monica, CA: James Corcoran Gallery, 1988. Published in conjunction with an exhibition of the same title, organized by James Corcoran Gallery, Santa Monica, CA, and presented at James Corcoran Gallery, Santa Monica, CA, Shoshana Wayne Gallery, Santa Monica, CA, and Pence Gallery, Santa Monica, CA, July 16–September 7, 1988.

Stevenson, Harold. "Oral History Interview with Harold Stevenson." By Paul Cummings. March 17–29, 1973. Archives of American Art, Smithsonian Institution, Washington, DC. https://www.aaa.si.edu/collections/interviews/oral-history-interview-harold-stevenson-11898.

Stewart-Halevy, Jacob. *Slant Steps: On the Art World's Semi-Periphery*. Oakland: University of California Press, 2020.

Stiles, Knute. "Don Potts' Game of Car." *Artforum*, October 1970. https://www.artforum.com/features/don-potts-game-of-car-210518/.

Stiles, Kristine. "Between Water and Stone." In *In the Spirit of Fluxus*, edited by Elizabeth Armstrong and Joan Rothfuss, 62–99. Minneapolis: Walker Art Center, 1993. Published in conjunction with an exhibition of the same title, organized by and presented at the Walker Art Center, Minneapolis, February 14–June 6, 1993, and at the Whitney Museum of American Art, New York, July 8–October 10, 1993; the Museum of Contemporary Art Chicago, November 13, 1993–January 16, 1994; the Wexner Center for the Visual Arts, Columbus, OH, February 18–April 17, 1994; the San Francisco Museum of Modern Art, May 12–July 24, 1994; and the Fundació Antoni Tàpies, Barcelona, November 17, 1994–January 21, 1995.

Strain, Christopher B. *The Long Sixties: America, 1955–1973*. Chichester, UK: Wiley Blackwell, 2017.

Sturhahn, Larry, and Jordan Belson. "Experimental Filmmaking: The Film Art of Jordan Belson." *Filmmakers Newsletter* 8, no. 7 (May 1975): 22–26.

Sullivan, Dan. "Artists Agree on Boycott of Chicago Showings." *New York Times*, September 5, 1968.

Swenson, Gene. "Exhibition at Green Gallery." *ARTnews*, February 1962.

———. "Genius and James Rosenquist." *Gene Swenson: Retrospective for a Critic, the Register of the Museum of Art, University of Kansas* 4, nos. 6–7 (October 24–December 5, 1971): 57–73.

———. "The New American 'Sign Painters.'" *ARTnews*, September 1962.

———. "News of MoMA and Miami." *Other Scenes*, October 1, 1968.

———. *The* Other *Tradition*. Philadelphia: Institute of Contemporary Art, 1966. Published in conjunction with an exhibition of the same title, organized by and presented at the Institute of Contemporary Art, Philadelphia, January 27–March 7, 1966.

———. "Paint, Flesh, Vesuvius." *Arts Magazine*, November 1966.

Szarkowski, John, ed. *From the Picture Press*. New York: Museum of Modern Art, 1973. Published in conjunction with an exhibition of the same title, organized by and presented at the Museum of Modern Art, New York, January 30–April 29, 1973.

Taft, Maggie, Robert Cozzolino, Judith Russi Kirshner, and Erin Hogan, eds. *Art in Chicago: A History from the Fire to Now*. Chicago: University of Chicago Press, 2018.

Tanning, Dorothea. *Between Lives: An Artist and Her World*. New York: W. W. Norton, 2001.

———. *Birthday*. Santa Monica, CA: Lapis Press, 1986.

Tepper, Allie. "Individual Collective: A Conversation with Senga Nengudi." In *Side by Side: Collaborative Artistic Practices in the United States, 1960s–1980s*, vol. 3 of *Living Collections*, edited by Gwyneth Shanks and Allie Tepper. Minneapolis: Walker Art Center, 2020. https://walkerart.org/collections/publications/side-by-side/individual-collective-a-conversation-with-senga-nengudi.

Thek, Paul. "Beneath the Skin: Interview with Paul Thek." By Gene Swenson. *ARTnews,* April 1966.

Thill, Vanessa. "At the Borderline of Uncontrollability: Six Lessons from Eva Hesse." *Art in America*, August 8, 2017.

Three Graphic Artists: Charles White, David Hammons, Timothy Washington. Los Angeles: Los Angeles County Museum of Art, 1971. Published in conjunction with an exhibition of the same title, organized by and presented at the Los Angeles County Museum of Art, January 26–March 7, 1971, and at the Santa Barbara Museum of Art, March 20–April 18, 1971.

Tilton, Connie Rogers, and Lindsay Charlwood, eds. *L.A. Object & David Hammons Body Prints*. New York: Tilton Gallery, 2011. Published in conjunction with an exhibition of the same title, organized by and presented at Tilton Gallery, New York, October 20–November 25, 2006, and at Roberts & Tilton, Los Angeles, June 30–July 28, 2007.

Todd, Michael. "Mike Todd: An Interview." By Gene Swenson. *Art and Artists*, November 1966.

———. Unpublished interview by Dan Nadel. February 2020.

Trachtman, Paul. "Lee Bontecou's Brave New World." *Smithsonian Magazine*, September 2004.

Trotta, Geri, and Diane Arbus. "Not to Be Missed: The American Art Scene." *Harper's Bazaar*, July 1966.

Tsai, Eugenie. "Early Smithson." In *Robert Smithson Unearthed: Drawings, Collages, Writings*, 3–24. New York: Columbia University Press, 1991.

———. "Robert Smithson: Plotting a Line from Passaic, New Jersey, to Amarillo, Texas." In *Robert Smithson*, 10–31. Berkeley: University of California Press, 2004. Published in conjunction with an exhibition of the same title, organized by and presented at the Museum of Contemporary Art, Los Angeles, September 12–December 13, 2004, and at the Dallas Museum of Art, January 14–April 3, 2005, and the Whitney Museum of American Art, New York, June 23–October 16, 2005.

Tuchman, Maurice, ed. *American Sculpture of the Sixties*. Los Angeles: Los Angeles County Museum of Art, 1967. Published in conjunction with an exhibition of the same title, organized by and presented at the Los Angeles County Museum of Art, April 28–

June 25, 1967, and at the Philadelphia Museum of Art, September 15–October 29, 1967.

Turner, Christopher. "Analyzing Louise Bourgeois: Art, Therapy, and Freud." *Guardian*, April 6, 2012.

Tyler, Parker. *Underground Film: A Critical History*. New York: Grove Press, 1969.

Uchida, Yoshiko. "Kay Sekimachi." *Craft Horizons* 19, no. 3 (May 1, 1959): 22–25.

Updike, David, and Sarah Noreika, eds. *Barbara Chase-Riboud: The Malcolm X Steles*. Philadelphia: Philadelphia Museum of Art, 2013. Published in conjunction with an exhibition of the same title, organized by and presented at the Philadelphia Museum of Art, September 14, 2013–January 20, 2014, and at the Berkeley Art Museum and Pacific Film Archive, Berkeley, CA, February 12–April 27, 2014.

Utterback, Martha. "South Texas Sweet Funk." *Artforum*, May 1971. https://www.artforum.com/events/south-texas-sweet-funk-233636/.

VanDerBeek, Stan. *Snapshots of the City*. 1961. Film Catalogue. Film-Makers' Co-op. 16mm, 5 min. Accessed October 19, 2023. https://film-makerscoop.com/catalogue/stan-vanderbeek-snapshots-of-the-city.

Van Niekerken, Bill. "'Death of the Hippies': Haight-Ashbury's 1967 Funeral for Counterculture." *San Francisco Chronicle*, October 3, 2017. https://www.sfchronicle.com/thetake/article/Death-of-the-Hippies-Haight-Ashbury-s-12245473.php#photo-14060811.

Viso, Olga, ed. *Ana Mendieta: Earth Body, Sculpture and Performance, 1972–1985*. Washington, DC: Hirshhorn Museum and Sculpture Garden, Smithsonian Institution; Ostfildern-Ruit, Germany: Hatje Cantz, 2004. Published in conjunction with an exhibition of the same title, organized by the Hirshhorn Museum and Sculpture Garden, Washington, DC, and presented at the Whitney Museum of American Art, New York, July 1–September 19, 2004; and at the Hirshhorn Museum and Sculpture Garden, Washington, DC, October 14, 2004–January 2, 2005; the Des Moines Art Center, February 25–May 22, 2005; and the Miami Art Museum, October 7, 2005–January 15, 2006. .

Vogel, Amos. "Brakhage, Brecht, Berlin, Eden West & East." *Village Voice*, December 23, 1965.

———. "Sweet Fireworks." *Village Voice*, March 18, 1971.

Vogel, Carol. "Exposure for a Nude." *New York Times*, September 30, 2005. https://www.nytimes.com/2005/09/30/arts/design/exposure-for-a-nude.html.

Walker, Shawn. "Artist Interview: Shawn Walker." Virginia Museum of Fine Arts, 2020. Video, 5 min. https://vmfa.museum/wp-subsite/videos/artist-interview-shawn-walker/.

———. "Preserving Our History: The Kamoinge Workshop and Beyond." *Ten.8* 24 (1987): 20–25.

Ward, Tom, dir. *Don Potts: "My First Car."* 1971. 16mm, 9 min. 30 sec. https://www.youtube.com/watch?v=sGtg3uKL1Rk&t=0s.

Weissberg, Stephanie, ed. *Barbara Chase-Riboud Monumentale: The Bronzes*. Princeton, NJ: Princeton University Press, 2023.

Wenger, Lesley. "William T. Wiley: Fall Fashions." *Currant Art Magazine*, September/October 1975.

What They're Up to in Chicago. Ottawa: National Gallery of Canada, 1972. Published in conjunction with an exhibition of the same title, organized by the Extension Services of the National Gallery of Canada, Ottawa, and presented at Rodman Hall Arts Centre, St. Catharines, ON, December 1–31, 1972; and at Owens

Art Gallery, Mount Allison University, Sackville, NB, January 15–February 15, 1973; Musée d'art contemporain de Montréal, March 1–31, 1973; Beaverbrook Art Gallery, Fredericton, NB, April 15–May 15, 1973; University of Guelph, Guelph, ON, June 1–30, 1973; Dalhousie Art Gallery, Halifax, NS, July 15–August 15, 1973; Burnaby Art Gallery, Burnaby, BC, September 1–30, 1973; and the London Public Library and Art Museum, London, ON, October 15–November 15, 1973.

Whitcomb, Laura. *Dilexi: A Gallery and Beyond*. Los Angeles: Label Curatorial, 2021.

Whitten, Jack. "A Circle of Blood." *Walker Art Center Magazine*, December 2015. https://walkerart.org/magazine/jack-whitten-art-violence.

———. "Jack Whitten: An Artist's Life." Art21 Extended Play, March 21, 2018. Video, 9 min. https://www.youtube.com/watch?v=GFVsd450nCU.

———. *Jack Whitten: Notes from the Woodshed*. Edited by Katy Siegel. Zurich: Hauser & Wirth, 2018.

Williamson, Beth. "Robert Smithson and Robert Morris: The Hidden Order of Process Art." In *Between Art Practice and Psychoanalysis Mid-Twentieth Century: Anton Ehrenzweig in Context*, 151–76. New York: Routledge, 2020.

Willis, Deborah. *Reflections in Black: A History of Black Photographers, 1840 to the Present*. New York: W. W. Norton, 2000.

Wirsum, Karl. "Transfigured: An Interview with Karl Wirsum." By Nicole Rudick. *Hyperallergic*, October 10, 2015. https://hyperallergic.com/242785/transfigured-an-interview-with-karl-wirsum/.

Wise, Lloyd. "Alex Hay." *Artforum*, September 2021. https://www.artforum.com/events/alex-hay-2-248757/.

Wolfe, Shira. "The Life and Legacy of the Spiral Group." *Artland Magazine*. Accessed June 18, 2024. https://magazine.artland.com/the-life-and-legacy-of-the-spiral-group/.

Wolff, Rebecca. "Assembling Pan-Africanism in Melvin Edward's *Homage to the Poet Léon Gontran Damas*." *Nka: Journal of Contemporary African Art* 50 (May 2022): 107–15.

"Works of Westermann at the County Museum." *Los Angeles Times*, December 8, 1968.

Worth, Alexi. "First Break: James Rosenquist." *Artforum*, March 2002. https://www.artforum.com/print/200203/james-rosenquist-2448.

Wye, Deborah. *Louise Bourgeois*. New York: Museum of Modern Art, 1982. Published in conjunction with an exhibition of the same title, organized by and presented at the Museum of Modern Art, New York, November 3, 1982–February 8, 1983.

Young, Cynthia Ann. *Soul Power: Culture, Radicalism, and the Making of a U.S. Third World Left*. Durham, NC: Duke University Press, 2006.

Youngblood, Gene. "In Memoriam: Jordan Belson (1926–2011)." *Millennium Film Journal*, no. 55 (Spring 2012): 85.

Zalman, Sandra. *Consuming Surrealism in American Culture: Dissident Modernism*. London: Routledge, 2018.

———. "Secret Agency: Magritte at MoMA in the 1960s." *Art Journal* 71 (Summer 2012): 100–113.

Zegher, M. Catherine de, ed. *Eva Hesse Drawing*. New York: Drawing Center, 2006. Published in conjunction with an exhibition of the same title, co-organized by the Drawing Center, New York, and the Menil Collection, Houston, and presented at the Menil Collection, Houston, February 3–April 23, 2006; and at the Drawing Center, New York, May 6–July 15, 2006; the Los Angeles Museum of

Contemporary Art, August 6–October 28, 2006; and the Walker Art Center, Minneapolis, November 12, 2006–February 18, 2007.

Zelevansky, Lynn. "Life Is Just a Bowl of Cherries: The Life and Art of Paul Thek." In *Paul Thek: Diver, A Retrospective*, edited by Lynn Zelevansky and Elisabeth Sussman, 10–27. New York: Whitney Museum of American Art, 2010. Published in conjunction with an exhibition of the same title, co-organized by the Whitney Museum of American Art, New York, and the Carnegie Museum of Art, Pittsburgh, and presented at the Whitney Museum of American Art, New York, October 21, 2010–January 9, 2011, and at the Carnegie Museum of Art, Pittsburgh, February 5–May 1, 2011, and the Hammer Museum, Los Angeles, May 22–September 4, 2011.

———. *Love Forever: Yayoi Kusama, 1958–1968*. Los Angeles: Los Angeles County Museum of Art, 1998. Published in conjunction with an exhibition of the same title, co-organized by the Los Angeles County Museum of Art, the Japan Foundation, and the Museum of Modern Art, New York, and presented at the Los Angeles County Museum of Art, March 8–June 8, 1998; and at the Museum of Modern Art, New York, July 9–September 22, 1998; the Walker Art Center, Minneapolis, December 13–March 7, 1999; and the Museum of Contemporary Art, Tokyo, April 29–July 4, 1999.

Zimmermann, Patricia Rodden. *Reel Families: A Social History of Amateur Film*. Bloomington: Indiana University Press, 1995.

Zorach, Rebecca. *Art for People's Sake: Artists and Community in Black Chicago, 1965–1975*. Durham, NC: Duke University Press, 2019.

CONTRIBUTORS

Jo Applin is the Walter H. Annenberg Professor in the History of Art at the Courtauld Institute of Art, London.

Sampada Aranke writes and teaches about Black American art as an associate professor of art history and comparative studies at the Ohio State University.

Lucy Bradnock is dean for research and reader in modern and contemporary art history at the Courtauld Institute of Art, London, and editor of the journal *Art History*.

Jennifer Buonocore-Nedrelow specializes in interdisciplinary art since 1960. She holds a PhD in art history from the Institute of Fine Arts, New York University.

Claire Carcara is a PhD student in the Department of Art History at the University of Southern California, where she is a provost fellow.

Elise Y. Chagas is an art historian specializing in modern and contemporary art of the Americas. She is a PhD candidate at Princeton University, where she is writing a dissertation on representations of indigeneity in Peruvian art of the 1920s.

Ruben C. Cordova (BA Brown University, PhD University of California, Berkeley) has curated or co-curated thirty-four exhibitions, written or contributed to twenty-two catalogues and books, and published more than eighty articles and reviews.

Rowan Diaz-Toth is a curatorial project assistant at the Whitney Museum of American Art.

Isabel Elson-Enriquez is an art historian specializing in US art of the Cold War era. She is working on a dissertation on the emergence of plastic as an artistic medium.

Philomena Epps is a writer. She is currently a PhD candidate in the History of Art Department at University College London, working on issues of fetishism and sexual difference.

Alexandra Germer is a PhD student in the Department of Art & Archaeology at Princeton University, focusing on twentieth-century art and its provenance.

David J. Getsy is the Eleanor Shea Professor of Art History at the University of Virginia. His books include *Queer Behavior: Scott Burton and Performance Art* and *Abstract Bodies: Sixties Sculpture in the Expanded Field of Gender*.

Kirsten Gill is an art historian specializing in the moving image. She is a PhD candidate at the Graduate Center, CUNY, where she is completing a dissertation on the influence of Black freedom struggles on postwar experimental cinema in the United States.

Ed Halter is founder and director of Light Industry, Brooklyn, and critic in residence at Bard College.

Rujeko Hockley is the Arnhold Associate Curator at the Whitney Museum of American Art.

Jonathan Judd is a PhD student in the Department of Comparative Humanities at the University of Louisville. He has written on the art and visual culture of the interwar period and is researching the role of art criticism and aesthetics in postwar American art.

Finn Le Maitre is a PhD candidate in English at Princeton University, where he works on twentieth-century American literature and culture. His dissertation is about sleeping spectatorship and American underground film.

Kelly Long is a senior curatorial assistant at the Whitney Museum of American Art.

Hannah Maier-Katkin is a PhD student at the Graduate Center, CUNY, an instructor at Brooklyn College, and an alumna of the Whitney Independent Study Program. She studies the histories of film and photography.

Rachel Middleman is a professor of art history at California State University, Chico. She is the author of *Radical Eroticism: Women, Art, and Sex in the 1960s*.

Jennifer Sichel is assistant professor of contemporary art and theory at the University of Louisville. She holds a PhD in art history from the University of Chicago.

Jacob Stewart-Halevy is an associate professor of art history at Tufts University.

Lauren Young is a former senior curatorial assistant at the Whitney Museum of American Art and currently a director at Ortuzar.

Rebecca Zorach teaches art history at Northwestern University. She is the author most recently of *Temporary Monuments: Art, Land, and America's Racial Enterprise*.

LENDERS TO THE EXHIBITION

Academy Film Archive
Amistad Research Center Collection
Andrew Kreps Gallery
Larry and Evelyn Aronson
The Art Institute of Chicago
Rubén Blades
Joe Bradley
Brooklyn Museum
The Buck Collection at the UC Irvine Jack and Shanaz Langson
   Institute and Museum of California Art
Kim and Lito Camacho
Crocker Art Museum
Dale Brockman Davis
Beth Rudin DeWoody
de Young Museum
The Easton Foundation
Electronic Arts Intermix
Estate of Barbara Hammer
Estate of Jordan Belson
Estate of Joseph Raffael, courtesy Nancy Hoffman Gallery
The Estate of Lee Lozano, courtesy Hauser & Wirth
The Estate of Luchita Hurtado, courtesy Hauser & Wirth
Filmform
Fine Arts Museums of San Francisco
Fraenkel Gallery
Tony and Gail Ganz
Robert Gober
Green Family Art Foundation, courtesy Adam Green Art Advisory
Wade Guyton
Heard Museum
Hirshhorn Museum and Sculpture Garden, Smithsonian Institution
John Michael Kohler Arts Center
Tina and Larry Jones
JPMorgan Chase Art Collection
KAWS
Kyle Kepcke
Kiki Kogelnik Foundation
Steve Lockshin and Allison Schaengold Lockshin
Los Angeles County Museum of Art
Lucas Museum of Narrative Art
Madison Museum of Contemporary Art
Mel Casas Family Trust
The Menil Collection
The Metropolitan Museum of Art
Mills College Art Museum
Minneapolis Institute of Art
Monterey Museum of Art
The Morgan Library and Museum
Scott Mueller
The Museum of Contemporary Art Chicago
The Museum of Fine Arts, Houston
The Museum of Modern Art, New York
National Gallery of Canada
National Museum of the American Indian
The New School University Art Collection
Nora Eccles Harrison Museum of Art
Christine Ogata and John Baker
Martha Rosler, courtesy Mitchell-Innes & Nash
San Francisco Museum of Art
Shigeko Kubota Video Art Foundation
Solomon R. Guggenheim Museum
South Side Community Art Center
The Studio Museum in Harlem
Tilton Gallery
Mia Doi Todd
United States Department of the Interior, Indian Arts and Crafts
   Board, Southern Plains Museum
University of California, Berkeley Art Museum and Pacific Film
   Archive
Virginia Museum of Fine Arts
Walker Art Center
Whitney Museum of American Art
Whitten Family Collection
Wiley Family Collection
Franklin Williams, courtesy Parker Gallery
Peter and Carol York
David Yorkin and Alix Madigan

Brenna Cothran
Heather Cox
Mary Creed
David Critides
Haley Cummings
Anton Davis
Scott Davis
Monica Adame Davis
Lawrence DeBlasio
Monserrate DeLeon
Margo Delidow
Ophelia Deng
Marcia Diaz Claudio
Rowan Diaz-Toth
Yolanda Dixon
Angela Dizon
sage donahue
Marisa Donovan
Sarika Doppalapudi
Isaac Dunne
John Dyer
Kasim Earl
Adrienne Edwards
Sarah Ehtisham
Shanique Emelife
Joanna Epstein
David Ertel
Gabriel Esparza
Natalia Sofia Espinoza
Nakai Falcon
Thursday Farrar
Ezra Feldman
Joel Fennell
Desiree Fermin
Meghan Ferrucci
Judine Fiddler
Dalaeja Foreman
Sarah Fortini
Angel Fosuhene
Ryan Fox
Emilie Foy
Debora Francis
William Francis
Samuel Franks
Denis Frederick
Annie French
Melinda Freudenberger
Eve Frohm
Emma Gabel
Kendall Galant
Behrang Garakani
Steven Garcia
Viridiana Garcia Choy
Karina Garcia Labrana
Donald Garlington
John Gasper
John Gaudio
Jesse Gelaznik
Ronnie George
Alana Giarrano
Michael Gibbons
Gabrielle Giles
Bonnie Glover
Brian Glover
Reina Gochez
Claire Golder
Jennie Goldstein
Nora Gomez-Strauss
Amber Gonzalez
Lucas Gonzalez
Jonathan Gorman
Caitlin Green
Hilary L. Greenbaum
Olivia Gregory

Steven Grimaldi
Kaylee Grippando
Jennifer Groch
Nicole Grullon
Marcela Guerrero
Peter Guss
Abigail Hack
Rita Hall
Alec Harris
Tara Hart
Barbara Haskell
Andrew Hawkes
Maura Heffner
William Hempel
Araya Henry
Elizabeth Henschen
Lawrence Hernandez
Megan Heuer
Jonathan Heutmaker
Rebecca Hickey
Rujeko Hockley
Nicholas S. Holmes
Michael Honigsberg
Aya Horikoshi
Charlotte Houngbedji
Andreas Huang
Ronald Hudson
Ashley Hudson
Jared Huggins
Felicia Huguley
Beth Huseman
Scout Hutchinson
Chrissie Iles
Gina Im
Junichiro Ishida
Luccas Israel
Carlos Jacobo
Emily Jacoby
Armando Jaramillo Garcia
Jesse Jenkins
Nic Jerabek
Jennifer Jhagroo
Julia McKenzie Johnson
Alyssa Johnson
Caitlin Jones
Charles Joseph
Joel Kaplan
Alexandra Karpovich
Faith Kaufman
William Kennedy
Tim Kerins
Christopher Ketchie
Thomas Killie
Leslie King
Daniel Kingery
Tom Koehler
Ashley Kok
Thomas Kotik
Tim Kovolenko
Joanna Kozak
Timothy Kuffner
Hayley Kuhlmann
Josephine Kunkle-Schoen
Courtney Kupferschmidt
Denise Kupferschmidt
Caroline LaCava
Midrene Lamy
Sandy LaPorte
Annalisa LaPuma
Martha LaRose
Joe Laureiro
Dixie Law
Meredith Lawhead
Eunice Lee

Deanna Lee
Heeae Lee
Sang Lee
Emma LeHocky
Doyle Lewis
Paul Li
David Liburd
Benjamin Lipnick
David Lisbon
Brian Lloyd
Robert Lomblad
Kelly Long
Joel Lopez
Iris Loughran
Eleanor Lovinsky
Brianna Lowndes
Angie Lu
Joshua Lubin-Levy
Kiersten Lukason
Jonita Luti
Jason Lutz
Douglas Madill
Drew Madland
Kenneth Madore
Damien Marchese
Alexis Markopoulos
Keyahna Marks
Wilmer Martinez
Genevieve Martinez
John Martins
Kyla Mathis-Angress
Noel McCarthy
James McKnight
Molly McLaughlin
Emma McMillan
Elissa Medina Mejia
Lourdes Mejia
Chanell Melendez
Bridget Mendoza
Marek Milde
Graham Miles
Zack Millicent
Atticus Moorman
David Morales
Robert Morales
Michael Morrissey
Victor Moscoso
Majida Mugharbel
Lane Muniz
Meer Musa
Micah Musheno
Sara Nadal-Melsio
Jared Nangle
Daniel Nascimento
David Neary
Will Neer
Malaika Newsome
Alice Nguyen
Giulia Nicita
William Norton
James Nunez
Jaison O'Blenis
Megan O'Brien
Colin O'Con
Bradon O'Connell
Bridget O'Keefe
Arden Orth
Nelson Ortiz
Justin Antonio Ortiz
Vada Ortiz
Ahmed Osman
Julian Osti
Nicky Ozir
Angela Rose Paccione

Luis Padilla
Kimie Page
Alexander Page
Debbie Page
Rose Pallone
Jacqueline Panama
Noam Parness
Max Parry-McDonell
Christiane Paul
Andrew Pazmino
Sasha Peck
Chelsey Pellot
Natasha Pereira
Roberto Perez
Hubert Peterson
Daniel Peterson
Jason Phillips
Laura Phipps
Timothy Pickerill
Angelo Pikoulas
Laura Pitt
Anna Piwowar
Carla Posner
Eliza Proctor
Laura Protzel
Joe Quartararo
Emma Quaytman
Georgina Quintana
Will Raines
Ashley Reese
Robert Reese
Julie N. Rega
Andryck Requena
Gregory Reynolds
Gene Riftin
Belen Rincon
Felix Rivera
Nina Roberts
Melissa Robles
Salvatore Roccaforte
Clare Roche
Anibal Rodriguez
Mario Rodriguez
Victor Ignacio Rodriguez
Clara Rojas-Sebesta
Antonio Rosa
Joshua Rosenblatt
Nicole Rosengurt
Amy Roth
Scott Rothkopf
Angela Rubin
CJ Salapare
Laura Salomon
Leonel Sanchez
Kevin Sanchez
Awa Sanogo
Vincent Santiago
Cythali Sapuis
Bermet Sargazakova
Lynnette Sauer
Lisa Saunders
Drew Sawyer
Lynn E. Schatz
Laura Schwarz
Elizabeth Schweitzer
Cristina Scorza
Peter A. Scott
Shawnace Seegars
Monica Sekaquaptewa
David Selimoski
Jason Senquiz
Leslie Sheridan
Irene Shifman
Dyeemah Simmons

David Simpson
Elizabeth Skalka
Elisabeth Skjaervold
Matthew Skopek
James Skuldt
Roxanne Smith
Daniel Smith
Nathan Smith
Madeline Smith
Michele Snyder
Mary-Jean Sobiesiak
Elizabeth Soland
Cree Solomon
Barbi Spieler
Susan Steinfield
Minerva Stella
Natalia Sterling
Emily Stoller-Patterson
Emilie Sullivan
Charley Summers
Rabinda Surujnath
Denis Suspitsyn
Elisabeth Sussman
Jo Tam
Adin Tannin
Alonso Tapia-Benitez
Andres Tawil
Melanie Taylor
Joseph Teliha
Eva Tenby
Ellen Tepfer
Darlene Thevenin
Alex Tonetta
Matthew Torres
Ana Torres-Hurtado
Julius Treadway
Aislinn Tucker
David Tufino
Tiaalea Tupuola
Beth Turk
Jorge Ulrich
Khaleiah Vasquez
Matthew Vega
Yuyu Vega
Eric Vermilion
Andrew Viola-Lopez
Christopher Voegels
Cynthia Vogt
Eva Von Schweinitz
Farris Wahbeh
David Walker
Patrick Walsh
Rowan Walter
Audrey Wang
Sunny Wang
Vivian Wang
Audrey Warne
Caroline Webb
Rachael Wehrle
Maggie Wei
Erika Wentworth
Joshua Wertheimer
Jason Wimbish
Henry Witherow-Culpepper
Marcia Witter
Michael Woodward
Elliot Degrassi Yokum
Christine Zheng
Andrea Zlotowitz
Connie Zuo
Alex Zylka

As of June 28, 2024

p. 123 (left/fig. 3): Courtesy Howard University Gallery of Art, Washington, DC / Licensed by Art Resource, NY; © 2025 Romare Bearden Foundation / Licensed by VAGA at Artists Rights Society (ARS), NY

p. 123 (right): Collection of San José Museum of Art, gift of the Lipman Family Foundation 2006.20; courtesy San José Museum of Art; photograph by Douglas Sandberg; © 2025 Estate of Robert Arneson / Licensed by VAGA at Artists Rights Society (ARS), NY

p. 124: Courtesy Hannah Hoffman Gallery, Los Angeles, and Ortuzar Projects, New York; photograph by Timothy Doyen; © Estate of Anita Steckel

p. 125 (right): David & Zeynap Siegel Collection; courtesy the artist and Venus Over Manhattan, New York; photograph by Zachary Fischman; © 2025 Peter Saul / Artists Rights Society (ARS), NY

p. 128 (left): Courtesy Alexander Gray Associates, New York, and Stephen Friedman Gallery, London; © 2025 Melvin Edwards

p. 128 (right): © Mel Casas

p. 129: Courtesy Filmform, Stockholm; © Gunvor Nelson and Dorothy Wiley

pp. 130, 173: © Estate of Paul Thek

p. 131: Courtesy the RISD Museum, Providence, RI; © Estate of Ken Price

pp. 132, 144 (bottom left): © Deborah Remington Charitable Trust for the Visual Arts / Licensed by VAGA at Artists Rights Society (ARS), NY

p. 133 (left): Photograph by Lester Beall; © 2025 Dumbarton Arts, LLC / Licensed by VAGA at Artists Rights Society (ARS), NY

pp. 133 (top right), 133 (bottom right): The David and Alfred Smart Museum of Art, The University of Chicago, The H. C. Westermann Study Collection, gift of Joanna Beall TR1715/1.1084; courtesy the David and Alfred Smart Museum of Art, The University of Chicago

p. 134: Courtesy David Zwirner, New York; © 2025 Estate of Robert Arneson / Licensed by VAGA at Artists Rights Society (ARS), NY

p. 135: Photograph by Capehart Photography; © 2025 Estate of Robert Arneson / Licensed by VAGA at Artists Rights Society (ARS), NY

pp. 136, 211 (right): Courtesy Kiki Kogelnik Foundation; © Kiki Kogelnik

p. 137: The Museum of Modern Art, New York, the Gilbert and Lila Silverman Fluxus Collection Gift 2308.2008.x1–x4; photograph by George Maciunas; © The Museum of Modern Art / Licensed by SCALA / Art Resource, NY; © 2025 Estate of Shigeko Kubota / Licensed by VAGA at Artists Rights Society (ARS), NY

pp. 138 (left), 138 (right): Collection of the artist; courtesy Alexander Gray Associates, New York, and Stephen Friedman Gallery, London; © 2025 Melvin Edwards / Artists Rights Society (ARS), NY

p. 140 (left/fig. 1): Photographs by Dennis Hopper; © Hopper Art Trust

p. 142 (left/fig. 4): Noah Purifoy Papers, 1935–98, bulk 1971–98, Archives of American Art, Smithsonian Institution, Washington, DC

p. 143: Courtesy Heritage Auctions / HA.com; © Estate of David McManaway

p. 144 (top left): Photograph by André Morain; © André Morain

p. 144 (right): Courtesy Semiotext(e); © Sturtevant Estate

p. 145: © Estate of Jeremy Anderson

pp. 146, 248 (bottom): Courtesy Hauser & Wirth; © The Estate of Eva Hesse

p. 147: Courtesy Michael Rosenfeld Gallery, New York; © Nancy Grossman

pp. 148, 188 (bottom): Courtesy Nancy Hoffman Gallery; © Estate of Joseph Raffael

pp. 149 (left top), 149 (left bottom): Courtesy the Conner Family Trust; © Conner Family Trust, San Francisco

p. 149 (right): Courtesy YAYOI KUSAMA, Inc.; photograph by Peter Moore; © Northwestern University; © YAYOI KUSAMA

p. 150: © The Museum of Modern Art / Licensed by SCALA / Art Resource, NY; © Vija Celmins

p. 151: Courtesy the Menil Archives, the Menil Collection, Houston; photograph by Caroline Philippone

pp. 152–53: Courtesy the Minneapolis Institute of Art; © 2025 Martha Edelheit / Artists Rights Society (ARS), NY

p. 154: Photograph by Will Brown

pp. 155, 183: Courtesy Noah Purifoy Foundation; photographs by Harry Drinkwater; © 2025

pp. 156, 157: Courtesy the artist and Mitchell-Innes & Nash, New York; © Martha Rosler

p. 158: Courtesy the Madison Museum of Contemporary Art; © The Estate of Suellen Rocca

p. 161 (top/fig. 3): © Estate of Ann Wilson

p. 162: © Estate of Karl Wirsum

p. 163 (bottom left): The Art Institute of Chicago, gift of Gladys Nilsson and Jim Nutt 2018.26; courtesy The Art Institute of Chicago / Art Resource, NY; © James Falconer, Art Green, Gladys Nilsson, Jim Nutt, Suellen Rocca, and Karl Wirsum

p. 164: Courtesy The New School Art Collection; © 2025 The Nancy Spero and Leon Golub Foundation for the Arts / Licensed by VAGA at Artists Rights Society (ARS), NY

p. 165: Photograph by The Morgan Library & Museum, New York; © 2025 The Nancy Spero and Leon Golub Foundation for the Arts / Licensed by VAGA at Artists Rights Society (ARS), NY

p. 166: Getty Research Institute, Los Angeles (JT484FACS); photograph by Annette Del Zoppo; © Annette Del Zoppo and Susan Sontag

p. 167: Photograph by Tom Little; © 2025 Melvin Edwards / Artists Rights Society (ARS), NY

p. 168: Photograph by Caroline Philippone; © Estate of Roy Fridge

p. 169 (left): Courtesy the Menil Archives, the Menil Collection, Houston

p. 170: Courtesy Parker Gallery, Los Angeles; photograph by Carol Williams

p. 171: Photograph by Jason Mandella; © Estate of Claes Oldenburg

p. 172 (artist statement): Hannah Wilke Collection & Archive, Los Angeles; © 2025 Marsie, Emanuelle, Damon, and Andrew Scharlatt, Hannah Wilke Collection & Archive, Los Angeles / Artists Rights Society (ARS), NY

p. 172 (left): Hannah Wilke Collection & Archive, Los Angeles; © 2025 Marsie, Emanuelle, Damon, and Andrew Scharlatt, Hannah Wilke Collection & Archive, Los Angeles / Artists Rights Society (ARS), NY

p. 172 (right): *Herald Examiner* Collection / Los Angeles Public Library

p. 174: Courtesy Eric Firestone Gallery, New York; © 2025 Martha Edelheit / Artists Rights Society (ARS), NY

p. 175 (left): Byron Gallery Records, c. 1950s–91, Archives of American Art, Smithsonian Institution, Washington, DC

p. 176: © Sturtevant Estate

p. 177 (left): © Hearst Communications, Inc.

p. 177 (right): Courtesy the artist and Roberts Projects, Los Angeles; photograph by Richard Saar

p. 178 (left): Julius Shulman Photography Archive, Getty Research Institute, Los Angeles (2004.R.10); photograph by Julius Schulman; © J. Paul Getty Trust

pp. 179, 238 (right): © Adger Cowans

p. 180 (left): Eduardo Carrillo Papers, c. 1953–99, Archives of American Art, Smithsonian Institution, Washington, DC

pp. 180 (right), 208 (top), 208 (bottom left), 208 (bottom center), 208 (bottom right): © Museum Associates / LACMA

p. 181: © Field Studio; © Estate of Lee Bontecou

p. 182: Courtesy Noah Purifoy Foundation; photograph by Swann Auction Galleries; © 2025

p. 184: © Ed Ruscha

pp. 185, 204: Courtesy Parker Gallery, Los Angeles; © Franklin Williams

p. 186: Photograph by Nathan Keay; © MCA Chicago; © 2025 Bruce Nauman / Artists Rights Society (ARS), NY

p. 187 (top): Courtesy the artist and Gagosian; photograph by Paul Ruscha; © Ed Ruscha

pp. 188 (top), 190 (right/fig. 4): Fischbach Gallery Records, 1937–2015, Archives of American Art, Smithsonian Institution, Washington, DC

p. 189 (top/fig. 1): Courtesy BPK Bildagentur / Art Resource, NY; photograph by Dietmar Katz

p. 189 (bottom/fig. 2): Collection of the artist; © 2025 Keith Sonnier / Artists Rights Society (ARS), NY

p. 190 (left/fig. 3): Daros Collection, Switzerland; courtesy Hauser & Wirth; photograph by Abby Robinson, New York; © The Estate of Eva Hesse

p. 192: Courtesy Parker Gallery, Los Angeles; © Estate of William T. Wiley

p. 193: Private Collection, New York; photograph by Adam Reich; © 2025 The Robert H. Colescott Separate Property Trust / Artists Rights Society (ARS), NY

p. 194: Peter Moore Photography Archive, Charles Deering McCormick Library of Special Collections, Northwestern University Libraries; photograph by Peter Moore; © Northwestern University

p. 195: © New American Cinema Group, Inc. / The Film-Makers' Cooperative

p. 196: The Museum of Modern Art, New York, committee on Photography and The Modern Women's Fund 933.2011.x1–x2; © The Museum of Modern Art / Licensed by SCALA / Art Resource, NY; © Martha Rosler

p. 199 (left): The Norton Simon Museum Archives, Pasadena; photograph by Frank J. Thomas; © Frank J. Thomas Photography

p. 199 (right): George Washington University, Corcoran School of Arts and Design, Visual Resources Collection; photograph by E. Tulchin; © E. Tulchin

p. 200: Courtesy the artist and Roberts Projects, Los Angeles; photograph by Robert Wedemeyer; © Betye Saar

p. 201 (top): The Museum of Modern Art, New York, Photographic Archive, The Museum of Modern Art Archives; photograph by Rolf Petersen; © The Museum of Modern Art / Licensed by SCALA / Art Resource, NY

p. 201 (bottom): IAIA Archives, Santa Fe, NM (RG03.01.05.0051.03); courtesy IAIA Archives

pp. 202 (left), 202 (right), 263 (left), 286 (left): Brockman Gallery Archive, Los Angeles Public Library Special Collections; courtesy Brockman Gallery Archive

p. 203: © 2025 Peter Saul / Artists Rights Society (ARS), NY

pp. 206, 207: © Estate of Claes Oldenburg

p. 209: © Judith Bernstein

p. 210: © 2025 Estate of Ching Ho Cheng / Artists Rights Society (ARS), NY

p. 212: Photograph by Robert Abbott Sengstacke / Getty Images

p. 213: © 2025 Marsie, Emanuelle, Damon, and Andrew Scharlatt, Hannah Wilke Collection & Archive, Los Angeles / Artists Rights Society (ARS), NY

p. 214: Courtesy Bridget Donahue, New York, and Altman Siegel, San Francisco; © Lynn Hershman Leeson

p. 215: © 2025 Luis A. Jimenez, Jr. Copyright Trust / Artists Rights Society (ARS), NY

p. 216: Courtesy Matthew Marks Gallery, New York; © Estate of Jordan Belson

p. 217: Photograph by Peter Breinig / *The San Francisco Chronicle*; © 2025 Hearst Newspapers

p. 218: Courtesy The Art Institute of Chicago / Art Resource, NY; © Jim Nutt

pp. 219, 270: © Jim Nutt

p. 220 (bottom/fig. 1): Philadelphia Museum of Art, purchased with funds contributed by Donor's Trust, 2015 2015-66-8

p. 223: Courtesy Heritage Auctions / HA.com; © Robert Crumb, 1967

p. 224: Stanley and Elyse Grinstein Papers, c. 1937–20, Archives of American Art, Smithsonian Institution, Washington, DC

p. 225: Photograph by Gregory Edwards

pp. 226, 240 (bottom): Photograph by James Matthews; © The Museum of Modern Art / Licensed by SCALA / Art Resource, NY

p. 227: Courtesy Dallas Museum of Art; © 2025 The Robert H. Colescott Separate Property Trust / Artists Rights Society (ARS), NY

p. 229 (left): The Art Institute of Chicago, gift of Gladys Nilsson and Jim Nutt 2018.40; courtesy David Nolan Gallery; © Jim Nutt

p. 229 (right): Quenza Collection; courtesy Parker Gallery, Los Angeles; © Estate of William T. Wiley

p. 230: Courtesy The Art Institute of Chicago / Art Resource, NY; © Estate of Karl Wirsum

p. 231: © Alex Hay

p. 232: Collection SFMOMA, purchase in memory of Edith Bransten; photograph by Don Ross; © The Jess Collins Trust

p. 233 (top/fig. 1): The David and Alfred Smart Museum of Art, The University of Chicago, purchase, The Paul and Miriam Kirkley Fund for Acquisitions 2017.7; courtesy The David and Alfred Smart Museum of Art, The University of Chicago

p. 234 (top/fig. 2): Chicago History Museum ICHi-012834; photograph by Clarence W. Hines; © Chicago Historical Society

p. 235: Courtesy Ching Ho Cheng Estate

p. 236: © Nancy Grossman

p. 237: Courtesy the artist and Andrew Kreps Gallery, New York; photograph by Thomas Barratt; © Raymond Saunders

p. 238 (left): Getty Research Institute, Los Angeles (2014.R.20), gift of the Roy Lichtenstein Foundation in memory of Harry Shunk and Janos Kender; photograph by Shunk-Kender; © J. Paul Getty Trust; © Estate of Claes Oldenburg

p. 239: Courtesy the National Museum of the American Indian, Smithsonian Institution; photograph by NMAI Photo Services; © Estate of Fritz Scholder

p. 240 (top left): University of Michigan Library, Special Collections Research Center

p. 241: Courtesy Bridget Donahue, New York, and Altman Siegel, San Francisco; © Lynn Hershman Leeson

p. 242: Courtesy Rena Bransten Gallery, San Francisco; photograph by John Janca; © Rupert García

p. 243 (top): Smithsonian American Art Museum, museum purchase through the Luisita L. and Franz H. Denghausen Endowment 2020.42.3; © Rupert García

pp. 243 (bottom), 333 (bottom): Museum of Contemporary Art Chicago; © MCA Chicago

p. 244: Courtesy the Roger Brown Study Collection of the School of the Art Institute of Chicago; © Estate of Roger Brown

p. 245: Courtesy the Museum of Contemporary Photography at Columbia College Chicago; © Estate of Ralph Arnold

p. 246: The Art Institute of Chicago, photography and Media Purchase Fund 2011.131; courtesy The Art Institute of Chicago / Art Resource, NY; © Estate of Ralph Arnold

p. 247: Photograph by Jason Mandella; © Suzanne Jackson

p. 248 (top): Photograph by Ann E. Zelle / Getty Images

p. 249: © Jae Jarrell

p. 250: © The Museum of Modern Art / Licensed by SCALA / Art Resource, NY; © The Estate of Barbara Jones-Hogu

p. 251: Courtesy the Estate of Barbara Hammer and Electronic Arts Intermix (EAI), New York; © Estate of Barbara Hammer

p. 252 (bottom left): Museum of Contemporary Art Chicago; photograph by David Van Riper; © MCA Chicago

p. 253: Oscar Howe Family

pp. 254–55: © Nancy Graves Foundation Inc / Licensed by VAGA at Artists Rights Society (ARS), NY

pp. 257, 281 (bottom): Box 2, folder 25, Historical Photographs Collection, Series I: Education and Special Events Photographs, 1961–2006, Frances Mulhall Achilles Library and Archives, Whitney Museum of American Art, New York; photographs by Steve Balkin

pp. 258, 259: Courtesy the Hammer Museum, Los Angeles; © Dale Brockman Davis

p. 260 (top and bottom left): The Art Institute of Chicago, gift of Gladys Nilsson and Jim Nutt 2018.31, 2018.30; © Milton Glaser / Permission of the Estate of Milton Glaser

p. 261: © Estate of John Outterbridge

p. 262: Courtesy *Artforum* and the Estate of William T. Wiley; © Estate of William T. Wiley

p. 263 (right): Photograph by Melvin Edwards; © 2025 Melvin Edwards / Artists Rights Society (ARS), NY

p. 264: Courtesy the Solomon R. Guggenheim Foundation / Art Resource, NY; © 2025 David Hammons / Artists Rights Society (ARS), NY

p. 265: Courtesy Tilton Gallery, New York; © 2025 David Hammons / Artists Rights Society (ARS), NY

p. 266 (bottom/fig. 1): Tomás Ybarra-Frausto Research Material on Chicano Art, 1965–2004, Archives of American Art, Smithsonian Institution, Washington, DC; photograph by Cesar Martinez

p. 267 (top/fig. 2): Collection of Inez Cindy Gabriel; courtesy the Jesse Treviño Art Conservancy; photograph by Gabriel Quintero Velasquez; © The Estate of Jesse Treviño

p. 268 (right/fig. 4): El Paso Museum of Art, Gift of Warren and Suellen Haber 1992.1; © 2025 Luis Jimenez, Jr. Copyright Trust / Artists Rights Society (ARS), NY

p. 269: Photograph by Thomas R. DuBrock; © The Museum of Fine Arts, Houston; © 2025 Luis A. Jimenez, Jr. Copyright Trust / Artists Rights Society (ARS), NY

p. 271 (top): Courtesy the Nancy Graves Foundation; photograph by Adam Reich; © Nancy Graves Foundation Inc / Licensed by ARS, NY

p. 271 (bottom): Photograph by David Gahr / Getty Images; © Nancy Graves Foundation, Inc. / Licensed by ARS, New York, NY

pp. 272–73: © 2025 Faith Ringgold Estate / Artists Rights Society (ARS), NY

p. 274: Courtesy the Mel Casas Family Trust; photograph by Ansen Seale; © The Mel Casas Family Trust

p. 275: Collection of Bob Nickas, New York; courtesy Hauser & Wirth; © The Estate of Lee Lozano

p. 280 (top): Whitney Museum of American Art, New York, gift of the artist 2004.10; courtesy Pace; © Lucas Samaras

pp. 280 (bottom), 281 (top): Institute of Contemporary Art, University of Pennsylvania, Philadelphia

p. 282: Courtesy Derek Eller Gallery, New York; photograph by Adam Reich; © Estate of Karl Wirsum

p. 283 (left): Courtesy Bruce Silverstein Gallery, New York; photograph by Adger Cowans; © Adger Cowans

p. 283 (right): Photograph by Henry Groskinsky; © 2025 The Easton Foundation / Licensed by VAGA at Artists Rights Society (ARS), NY

p. 285: © David Anderson

p. 286 (right): Photograph by Robert A. Nakamura

p. 287: © Museum Associates / LACMA; © Vija Celmins

p. 288: Photograph by Jason Mandella; © Timothy Washington

p. 289: Courtesy Swann Auction Galleries; © Estate of Kay Brown

p. 290: Courtesy Film-Makers' Cooperative; © Mike Henderson

p. 291: National Gallery of Art, Washington, DC, purchased as the Gift of Stephen Dull 2015.157.19

p. 292: © Estate of Joan Brown

p. 293: Photograph by Johnna Arnold / Impart Photography; © Estate of Joan Brown

p. 294: © Linda Lomahaftewa

p. 295 (left): Courtesy Linda Lomahaftewa

p. 295 (right): The Art Institute of Chicago, gift of Gladys Nilsson and Jim Nutt 2018.50; courtesy The Art Institute of Chicago / Art Resource, NY; © Estate of Karl Wirsum

p. 296: Courtesy the US Department of the Interior, Indian Arts and Crafts Board, Southern Plains Indian Museum; © US Department of the Interior, Indian Arts and Crafts Board

pp. 297, 318: © Barbara Rossi

p. 298 (left): Fine Arts Museums of San Francisco, gift of Mr. and Mrs. Robert Marcus 1990.1.86; © Rupert García

p. 298 (right): Fine Arts Museums of San Francisco, gift of Mr. and Mrs. Robert Marcus 1990.1.83; courtesy Rena Bransten Gallery; © Rupert García

p. 299: Courtesy Jameela K. Donaldson; © Jeff Donaldson

pp. 300–301: Photograph by Katherine Du Tiel; © Estate of Don Potts

p. 302: © The Museum of Modern Art / Licensed by SCALA / Art Resource, NY; © 2025 Estate of Benny Andrews / Licensed by VAGA at Artists Rights Society (ARS), NY

p. 303 (left): Pennsylvania State University, Special Collections Library, Judy Chicago Art Education Collection; © 2025 Judy Chicago / Artists Rights Society (ARS), NY

p. 303 (right): Courtesy ACA Galleries, New York; © 2025 Faith Ringgold Estate / Artists Rights Society (ARS), NY

p. 304: © 2025 Artists Rights Society (ARS), NY / ADAGP, Paris

p. 305: Courtesy Asian Art Museum, San Francisco; photograph by Jay Jones; © Carlos Villa Art Estate

p. 306: St. Edward's University Archives, Austin, TX

p. 307: Courtesy Shigeko Kubota Video Art Foundation; © 2025 Estate of Shigeko Kubota / Licensed by VAGA at Artists Rights Society (ARS), NY

p. 308: © Robert Crumb, 1970

p. 309: Courtesy Matthew Marks Gallery, New York; © Estate of Miyoko Ito

p. 310: Photograph by Bernice B. Perry / Milford NH Historical Society; © Karen Lennox Gallery / Estate of Miyoko Ito

p. 312: Photograph by Katherine Du Tiel; © Timothy Washington

p. 313: Senga Nengudi Papers, Amistad Research Center, New Orleans, LA; courtesy the artist, Amistad Research Center, Sprüth Magers, and Thomas Erben Gallery; © Senga Nengudi

p. 315: Courtesy The Estate of Luchita Hurtado and Hauser & Wirth; photograph by Jeff McLane; © The Estate of Luchita Hurtado

p. 316 (top left): Courtesy Swann Auction Galleries

p. 316 (bottom left): Courtesy the Benny Andrews Estate and Michael Rosenfeld Gallery, New York; photograph by Rudolph Robinson; © 2025 Estate of Benny Andrews / Licensed by VAGA at Artists Rights Society (ARS), NY

p. 317: © Estate of Eduardo Carrillo

p. 319: Courtesy the Fine Arts Museums of San Francisco; photograph by Randy Dodson; © 2025 Kay Sekimachi / Artists Rights Society (ARS), NY

p. 320: Photograph by Brenda Bieger, Buffalo AKG Art Museum; © 2025 Estate of Marisol / Artists Rights Society (ARS), NY

p. 321: Photograph by James Mathews; © The Museum of Modern Art / Licensed by SCALA / Art Resource, NY

p. 322: Joan Semmel Papers, 1949–2013, Archives of American Art, Smithsonian Institution, Washington, DC

p. 323: Courtesy Alexander Gray Associates; © 2025 Joan Semmel / Artists Rights Society (ARS), NY

p. 324: Courtesy the Hammer Museum, Los Angeles; photograph by Ed Glendinning; © Estate of John Outterbridge

p. 325 (left): Courtesy the estate of the artist and Tilton Gallery, New York; photograph by Bob Nakamura

p. 325 (right): Courtesy the artist and Michael Rosenfeld Gallery, New York; photograph by Guido Mangold

p. 327: Courtesy California State University East Bay

p. 328: Image #SIA2024-009415, Record Unit 452, Smithsonian Institution Archives, Washington, DC; courtesy Mitch Toda

p. 329 (left/fig. 1): Courtesy the artist and Hauser & Wirth; photograph by Marc Riboud; © Marc Riboud / Fonds Marc Riboud au MNAAG / Magnum Photos; © Barbara Chase-Riboud

p. 329 (right/fig. 2): The Museum of Modern Art, New York 209.1955; courtesy the artist and Hauser & Wirth; © The Museum of Modern Art / Licensed by SCALA / Art Resource, NY; © Barbara Chase-Riboud

p. 330 (top left/fig. 3): Courtesy the artist, Hauser & Wirth, and Carrie Mae Weems

pp. 330 (bottom left/fig. 4), 331: © Barbara Chase-Riboud

p. 330 (top right/fig. 5): Courtesy Michael Rosenfeld Gallery, New York; photograph by Massimo Vitali; © Massimo Vitali; © Barbara Chase-Riboud

p. 332: Courtesy Galerie Lelong & Co.; © 2025 The Estate of Ana Mendieta Collection, LLC / Licensed by Artists Rights Society (ARS), NY

p. 333 (top): Courtesy Galerie Lelong & Co.; © 2025 The Estate of Ana Mendieta Collection, LLC

p. 334 (right): Hannah Wilke Collection & Archive, Los Angeles; Performalist Self-Portrait with Claes Oldenburg; © 2025 Marsie, Emanuelle, Damon, and Andrew Scharlatt, Hannah Wilke Collection & Archive, Los Angeles / Artists Rights Society (ARS), NY

p. 335: Courtesy Electronic Arts Intermix (EAI), New York; © Estate of Ed Emshwiller

p. 336: © 2025 Ming Smith / Artists Rights Society (ARS), NY

p. 337 (top): Courtesy the artist and Nicola Vassell Gallery; © 2025 Ming Smith / Artists Rights Society (ARS), NY

p. 337 (bottom): Courtesy the artist and Roberts Projects, Los Angeles; photograph by Bob Nakamura

p. 338 (left): Courtesy Shigeko Kubota Video Art Foundation; photograph by Mary Lucier; © 2025 Estate of Shigeko Kubota / Licensed by VAGA at Artists Rights Society (ARS), NY

p. 338 (right): Courtesy Judith Bernstein and Kasmin, New York

p. 339: Courtesy the artist, Sprüth Magers, and Thomas Erben Gallery; © Senga Nengudi

p. 340: Courtesy The Art Institute of Chicago; © Estate of Christina Ramberg

p. 341: Courtesy the artist and Roberts Projects, Los Angeles; photograph by Robert Wedemeyer; © Betye Saar

INDEX

Page numbers in **boldface** indicate illustrations.

This book was published on the occasion of the exhibition *Sixties Surreal* organized by Dan Nadel, independent curator; Laura Phipps, Associate Curator, Whitney Museum of American Art; Scott Rothkopf, Alice Pratt Brown Director, Whitney Museum of American Art; and Elisabeth Sussman, Curator, Whitney Museum of American Art; with Kelly Long, Senior Curatorial Assistant, and Rowan Diaz-Toth, Curatorial Project Assistant, Whitney Museum of American Art.

Whitney Museum of American Art, New York
September 24, 2025–January 29, 2026

Major support for *Sixties Surreal* is provided by the Barbara Haskell American Fellows Legacy Fund; The KHR McNeely Family Foundation | Kevin, Rosemary, and Hannah Rose McNeely; and the Whitney's National Committee.

Generous support is provided by the Keith Haring Foundation Exhibition Fund and the Robert Lehman Foundation.

Additional support is provided by George Freeman.

Support for the catalogue is provided by the Wyeth Foundation for American Art.

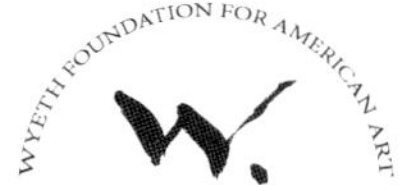

Whitney Museum of American Art
99 Gansevoort Street
New York, NY 10014
whitney.org

Distributed by
Yale University Press
302 Temple Street
P.O. Box 209040
New Haven, CT 06520-9040
yalebooks.com/art

This publication was produced by the Publications Department at the Whitney Museum of American Art, New York: Beth Huseman, Director of Publications; Beth Turk, Editor; Monica Adame Davis, Editor; and Audrey Warne, Editorial Coordinator.

Project manager: Elizabeth Levy
Editor: Jason Best with Jane Takac Panza
Designer: Joseph Logan with Anamaria Morris
Production: Nerissa Dominguez Vales and Sue Medlicott, The Production Department
Editorial coordinator: Audrey Warne
Proofreader: Polly Watson
Indexer: David Luljak
Separations: Gray Balance Studio, Shenzhen
Printing and binding: Artron

Typeset in Century Old Style and Theinhardt

Printed and bound in China
10 9 8 7 6 5 4 3 2 1

Authorized representative in the EU: Easy Access System Europe, Mustamäe tee 50, 10621 Tallinn, Estonia, gpsr.requests@easproject.com

Cataloging-in-publication data is on file with the Library of Congress.
ISBN 978-0-300-28450-8

Cover: Shigeko Kubota, *Self-Portrait*, c. 1970–71 (detail, p. 307); front, inset: H. C. Westermann, *The Big Change*, 1963 (p. 101); back, inset: Nancy Graves, *Camel VIII*, 1968–69 (p. 255); p. xii: Martha Edelheit, *Flesh Wall–Female*, 1965 (detail, pp. 152–53); pp. xx–xxi and 348–49: stills from Jordan Belson, *Samadhi*, 1967 (p. 216)